International Marketing

International Marketing

Fourth edition

Pervez N. Ghauri

Philip Cateora

London Boston Burr Ridge, IL Dubuque, IA Madison, WI New York San Francisco
St. Louis Bangkok Bogotá Caracas Kuala Lumpur Lisbon Madrid Mexico City Milan Montreal
New Delhi Santiago Seoul Singapore Sydney Taipei Toronto

International Marketing, Fourth edition
Pervez N. Ghauri and Philip Cateora

ISBN-13 9780077148157
ISBN-10 0077148150

Published by McGraw-Hill Education
Shoppenhangers Road
Maidenhead
Berkshire
SL6 2QL
Telephone: 44 (0) 1628 502 500
Fax: 44 (0) 1628 770 224
Website: www.mcgraw-hill.co.uk

British Library Cataloging in Publication Data
A catalogue record for this book is available from the British Library

Library of Congress Cataloging in Publication Data
The Library of Congress data for this book has been applied for from the Library of Congress

Acquisitions Editor: Peter Hooper
Production Editor: Alison Davis
Marketing Manager: Geeta Kumar

Cover design by Doodle

ISBN-13 9780077148157
ISBN-10 0077148150
© 2014. Exclusive rights by McGraw-Hill Education for manufacture and export. This book cannot be re-exported from the country to which it is sold by McGraw-Hill Education.

10 09 08 07 06 05 04 03 02 01
20 15 14 13
CTP MPM

Printed in Singapore

Dedication

For Saad P. Ghauri

Brief Contents

Detailed Table of Contents

Preface

During the last decade the international marketing field has developed enormously and the marketing function has now taken the central position in most companies. Increasing interdependence of the world economies has created new markets but also has led to increased competition and new challenges in the marketplace. The globalisation of the marketplace is now a reality, but it has led us into certain misunderstandings. The concept of the global market, or global marketing, thus needs clarification. It generally views the world as one market and is based on identifying and targeting cross-cultural similarities. In our opinion, the global marketing concept should be based on the premise of cultural differences and be guided by the belief that each foreign market requires its own culturally adapted marketing strategies. Although consumers dining at McDonald's in New Delhi, Moscow and Beijing is a reality, the idea of marketing a standardised product with a uniform marketing plan remains 'purely theoretical'.

The global marketing strategy is, therefore, different from the globalisation of the market. One has to do with efficiency of operations, competitiveness and orientation, the other with homogeneity of demand across cultures. In this book we consider it important to make this distinction and to see how it affects international marketing strategies.

In Europe, where home markets are smaller, companies like Philips, Unilever, Ericsson, IKEA, HSBC, Akzo Nobel and Nestlé are deriving up to 80 per cent of their revenues from abroad. The companies that succeed in the twenty-first century are those capable of adapting to constant change and responding to new challenges.

The economic, political and social changes that have occurred over the last decade have dramatically altered the landscape of global business. Consider the present and future impact of:

- China as a full player in the international market
- the persistent economic crisis in the Western economies
- emerging markets in Eastern Europe, Asia and Latin America where, in spite of economic and political crises, more than 75 per cent of the growth in world trade over the next 20 years is expected to occur
- the job shift in services from Western to emerging markets
- the rapid move away from traditional distribution structures in Europe, the USA and many emerging markets
- the growth of middle-income households the world over
- an increasingly (in)effective World Trade Organization (WTO) and increasing/decreasing restrictions on trade
- the transformation of the Internet from a toy for 'cybernerds' to a major international business tool for research, advertising, communications, exporting and marketing
- the increased awareness of ethical issues and social responsibility by companies.

As global economic growth occurs, understanding marketing in all cultures is increasingly important. Whether a company wants to involve itself directly in international marketing or not, it cannot escape increasing competition from international firms. This book addresses global issues and describes concepts relevant to all international marketers, regardless of the extent of their international involvement. Emphasis is on the strategic implications of competition in the markets of different countries. An environmental/cultural approach to international marketing permits a truly global orientation. The reader's horizons are not limited to any specification or to the particular ways of doing business in a single country. Instead, we provide an approach and framework for identifying and analysing the important cultural and environmental uniqueness of any country or global region.

The text is designed to stimulate curiosity about the management practices of companies, large and small, seeking market opportunities outside their home country and to raise the reader's consciousness about the importance of viewing international marketing management strategies from a global perspective.

Although this revised edition is infused throughout with an international orientation, export marketing and operations of smaller companies are not overlooked. Issues specific to exporting are discussed where strategies applicable to exporting arise and examples of marketing practices of smaller companies are examined throughout the chapters.

New and expanded features in this edition

As a result of extensive review work with the publishers and comments from many reviewers, we evaluated the contents of this book and for this new edition have reorganised them to better reflect the way topics are taught on most international marketing courses. In particular the chapter on ethics and social responsibility has been brought forward in Part 4, emphasising its importance for international marketing strategies.

New content

As segmentation and positioning are the bases for marketing strategy in any market, we have gathered these important issues together in a new chapter on international segmentation and positioning. This chapter explains and provides guidelines for segmentation and targeting the right customers in international markets. It also explains how companies can position their products and company image in customers' minds in different markets.

The new and expanded topics in this edition reflect issues in competition, changing marketing structures, the importance of cultural issues, ethics and social responsibility, and negotiations. The global market is swiftly changing from a seller's market to a buyer's market. This is a period of profound social, economic and political change. To remain competitive globally, companies must be aware of all aspects of the emerging global economic order.

Additionally, the evolution of information technology and global communications and their impact on how international business is conducted cannot be ignored. In the third millennium, people in the 'global village' will grow closer than ever, and will hear and see each other as a matter of course. An executive in the UK will be able to routinely pick up his or her video-phone to hear and see his or her counterpart in an Australian company or anywhere else in the world. In many respects, distance is becoming irrelevant.

Information – and, in its wake, the flow of goods – is moving around the globe at lightning speed. Increasingly powerful networks spanning the globe enable the delivery of services that reach far beyond national and continental boundaries, fuelling and fostering international trade. The connections of global communications bring people all around the world together in new and better forms of dialogue and understanding.

The dynamic nature of the international marketplace is reflected in the number of new and expanded topics in this edition, including:

- brand new dedicated chapter on international segmentation and positioning
- the importance of ethics and social responsibility at home as well as in international markets
- the impact of the persistent economic crisis
- the European Union of 27 countries and the impact of the euro
- the Internet and its expanding role in international marketing
- big emerging markets, particularly Brazil, Russia, India and China (BRICs) and others
- evolving global middle-income households
- the importance of marketing research for marketing decision making

- enhanced emphasis on cultural issues relevant for international marketing
- the emergence of a new breed of market driving companies such as IKEA, Apple and Starbucks.

New features

More than 80 per cent of the boxed **Going International** examples are brand new to this edition. These examples are carefully chosen to illustrate the points made in the text. For the fourth edition, most of these examples now act as provocative mini-cases that can be used as discussion points, featuring questions aimed at initiating exercises and discussion in the classroom. Relevant Exhibits and real-life pictures have been added to enhance the visual understanding and bases for discussion.

The **key terms feature**, which we introduced in the previous edition, has been kept and expanded following the reviewers' comments. All key terms are emboldened in the text the first time they are used, and definitions provided in the margin for quick reference. A full **glossary** of key terms is provided at the back of the book and on the Online Learning Centre (OLC).

At the end of each chapter, you'll find an improved **Further Reading** feature, where we present a selection of publications that reflect the classic, most influential and most recent studies in the area covered by the chapter. This feature has been updated throughout to include the most interesting and provocative new research to not only encourage students to go deeper into different topics, but also to help teachers in preparing interesting and enriched lectures.

Structure of the text

The text is divided into six parts. In **Part 1**, 'An Overview', the two chapters introduce the reader to international marketing and to three international marketing management concepts: the domestic market expansion concept, the multidomestic market concept and the global marketing concept. As companies restructure for the global competitive rigours of the twenty-first century, so too must tomorrow's managers. The successful manager must be globally aware and have a frame of reference that goes beyond a country, or even a region, and encompasses the world. What global awareness means and how it is acquired is discussed early in the text; it is the foundation of global marketing.

Chapter 2 focuses on the dynamic environment of international trade and the competitive challenges and opportunities confronting today's international marketer. The importance of the creation of the World Trade Organization (WTO), as the successor to GATT, is fully explored. The chapter is totally updated with new facts and realities.

The three chapters in **Part 2** deal with the impact of culture and the political environment on international marketing. A global orientation requires the recognition of cultural and institutional differences and the critical decision of whether or not it is necessary to accommodate them. These three chapters are totally re-written and streamlined. As a result, this edition has two chapters on culture instead of the three in the previous edition.

Geography and history (**Chapter 3**) are included as important dimensions in understanding cultural and market differences between countries. Not to be overlooked is concern for the deterioration of the global ecological environment and the multinational company's critical responsibility to protect it.

Chapter 4 presents a broad review of culture and its impact on human behaviour as it relates to international marketing. Specific attention is paid to Geert Hofstede's study of cultural value and behaviour. Knowledge of the business culture, management attitudes and business methods existing in a country and a willingness to accommodate the differences are important to success in an international market. This new integrated chapter provides several examples to deal with these different business practices and customs.

The political climate in a country is a critical concern for the international marketer. In **Chapter 5**, we take a closer look at the political environment. We discuss the stability of government policies, the political risks confronting a company, and the assessment and reduction of political vulnerability of products. Increasingly, interaction between business and politics is becoming important and cannot be ignored. Legal problems common to most international marketing transactions are also discussed in this chapter.

In **Part 3**, **Chapters 6**, **7** and **8** are concerned with assessing global marketing opportunities. As markets expand, segments grow within markets, and as market segments across country markets evolve, marketers are forced to understand market behaviour within and across different cultural contexts. Multicultural research and qualitative and quantitative research are discussed in **Chapter 6**.

Chapters 7 and **8** explore the impact of the three important trends in global marketing: (1) the growth and expansion of the world's big emerging markets; (2) the rapid growth of middle-income market segments; (3) the steady creation of regional market groups that include the European Union (EU), the North American Free Trade Agreement (NAFTA), the Southern Cone Free Trade Area (Mercosur), the ASEAN Free Trade Area (AFTA) and the Asia–Pacific Economic Cooperation (APEC).

The strategic implications of the shift from socialist-based to market-based economies in Eastern Europe and the returning impact of China on international commerce are examined. Attention is also given to the efforts of the governments of India and many Latin American countries to reduce or eliminate barriers to trade, open their countries to foreign investment and privatise state-owned enterprises.

In **Part 4**, 'Developing International Marketing Strategies', planning and organising for international marketing are discussed in **Chapter 9**. Many multinational companies realise that to capitalise fully on the opportunities offered by global markets, they must have strengths that often exceed their capabilities. **Chapter 10** has been dedicated to entry strategies. Here we provide a model that can be followed to analyse different markets while making decisions on market selection.

Chapter 11 is the brand new chapter on international segmentation and positioning. Once a company has decided on an overall strategy and has decided which market to enter, it has to quickly analyse whether there is a customer segment in that particular market that is relevant and can be targeted for its product/service. A company must understand the target group so that it can position its product/service in the minds of that target group, in a way that is consistent with its overall objectives and strategy.

Chapter 12 is the chapter on international branding strategies that we introduced in the previous edition. It examines the different issues surrounding branding, in recognition of its growing importance to international marketing. This chapter has been further improved and updated. In **Chapter 13**, the special issues involved in moving a product from one country market to another, and the accompanying mechanics of exporting, are addressed. The exporting mechanisms and documentation are explained.

Chapter 14 deals with an expanded discussion on ethical issues in marketing. This chapter has been brought forward to emphasise the strategic nature of these issues. It is imperative that before a company decides on marketing strategies, it is fully aware of ethical and social issues in general and for the particular market it is entering/operating in.

Part 5 looks at developing international marketing strategies and **Chapters 15** and **16** focus on product management, reflecting the differences in strategies between consumer and industrial products and the growing importance in world markets for business services. Additionally, the discussion on the development of global products stresses the importance of approaching the adaptation issue from the viewpoint of building a standardised product platform that can be adapted to reflect cultural differences. The competitive importance in today's global market of quality, innovation and technology as the keys to marketing success is explored.

Chapter 17 takes the reader through the distribution process, from home country to the consumer in the target country market. The structural impediments to market entry imposed by a country's distribution system are examined within the framework of a detailed presentation of the American and European distribution structure. In addition, the rapid changes in channel structure that are occurring in emerging and in other countries, and the emergence of e-commerce as a distribution channel, are presented.

The challenges faced by international marketers in foreign markets are discussed and presented in **Chapter 18**. Price escalations and ways in which these can be lessened; countertrade practices and pricing strategies under varying currency conditions are also discussed in this chapter. The factors influencing pricing decisions in different markets are thoroughly discussed.

Chapter 19 covers advertising and addresses the promotional element of the international marketing mix. Included in the discussion of global market segmentation are recognition of the rapid growth of market segments across country markets and the importance of market segmentation as a strategic competitive tool in creating an effective promotional message.

Chapter 20 discusses personal selling and sales management, and the critical nature of training, evaluating and controlling sales representatives. Here we also pay attention to negotiating with customers, partners and other actors in our networks. We discuss the factors influencing business negotiations, and varying negotiation styles.

Finally, in **Part 6**, the **Country Notebook** presents an excellent framework for assignments and for marketing research exercises. This focuses on the new realities of international marketing and factors that may influence entry and competitive strategies in different markets are presented. Also in **Part 6**, building on the success of the case section from the previous edition, we have included a substantial section of excellent case-study material that can be used by students and lecturers to aid learning. You'll find 20 cases in total, half of which are brand new to this edition. The cases reflect all regions and by working through them you will encounter all kinds of marketing scenarios in all kinds of companies in all geographical territories. From supermarket chains in Germany to footballers in China; from Fiat 500 to Abercrombie & Fitch's global success as a brand – each case study is lively, contemporary, thought-provoking and expertly designed to bring out the real issues in international marketing. The shorter cases focus on a single problem, serving as the basis for discussion of a specific concept or issue. The longer, more integrated cases are broader in scope and focus on more than one international marketing problem. Information is provided in a way that enables the cases to be studied as complete works in themselves but, importantly, they also lend themselves to more in-depth analysis that requires students to engage in additional research and data collection.

Pedagogical features of the text

The text portion of the book provides a thorough coverage of its subject, with specific emphasis on the planning and strategic problems confronting companies that market across cultural boundaries. The pedagogy we have developed for this textbook is designed to complement the rest of the book perfectly, and has been constructed with the very real needs of students and lecturers in mind.

Current, pithy, sometimes humorous and always relevant examples are used throughout each chapter to stimulate interest and increase understanding of the ideas, concepts and strategies presented, emphasising the importance of understanding the cultural uniqueness and relevant business practices and strategies.

The **Going International** boxes, an innovative feature since the first edition of *International Marketing*, have always been popular with students. This edition includes over 50 new boxes, now with questions and all providing up-to-date and insightful examples of cultural differences and international marketing at work, as well as illustrating concepts presented in the text with illustrations and pictures. They reflect contemporary issues in international marketing and real-life marketing scenarios, and can be used as a basis for solo study and as mini-case studies for lectures, as well as to stimulate class discussion. They are unique to this text, lively to read, and will stimulate all who use this book.

'**The Country Notebook: a Guide for Developing a Marketing Plan**', found in **Part 6**, is a detailed outline that provides both a format for a complete cultural and economic analysis of a country and guidelines for a marketing plan. This can be readily used by students and teachers for extended assignments.

Online supplements

In addition to the resources in this textbook, you'll find more supplements in the **Online Learning Centre (OLC)**, which can be found at: **www.mcgraw-hill.co.uk/textbooks/ghauri**.

A full list of features can be found on page xxvi

Acknowledgements

Publisher's acknowledgements

Our thanks go to the following reviewers for their comments at various stages in the text's development:

Christine Sorensen, University of Northumbria

Caroline Burr, Bournemouth University

Paul Ankers, Portsmouth University

Keith Burton, University of the West of England

Natasha Evers, National University of Ireland, Galway

Al Halborg, Coventry University

Mat Robson, University of Leeds

Jyoti Navare, Middlesex University

Patrick L'Espoir Decosta, Stockholm University

We would also like to thank the following who have contributed case studies to the new edition:

Aisha Kandil, The American University in Cairo

Anna Jonsson, School of Economics and Management, Lund University

Antonio Majocchi, University of Pavia, Italy

Birgit Hagen, University of Pavia, Italy

Claire Roederer, École de Management Strasbourg, University of Strasbourg

Dina El Alaily

Dr Marina Apaydin, The American University of Beirut

Farida El Zomor

Farida Hossam, The American University in Cairo

Federico Marinelli, Colegio Universitario de Estudios Financieros (CUNEF)

Hadiya Faheem, ICMR Center for Management Research

Heini Vanninen, Lappeenranta University of Technology

Hend Mostafa, The American University in Cairo

Indu P., ICMR Center for Management Research

Joaquín López Pascual, Colegio Universitario de Estudios Financieros (CUNEF)

Jocelyn Probert, CEIBS

Mayamin El Saady, The American University in Cairo

Nadia Gamal El Din

Olli Kuivalainen, Lappeenranta University of Technology

Rudolf R. Sinkovics, University of Manchester, Manchester Business School

Salma Shafie, The American University in Cairo

Sherine Kabesh, The American University in Cairo

Stefan Schmid, ESCP Europe

Sumelika Bhattacharyya, CEIBS

Syeda Maseeha Qumer, ICMR Center for Management Research

Sylvie Hertrich, École de Management Strasbourg, University of Strasbourg

Thomas Kotulla, ESCP Europe

Tobias Dauth, ESCP Europe

Ulf Elg, School of Economics and Management, Lund University

Ulrike Mayrhofer, IAE Lyon, Jean Moulin Lyon 3 University

V. Sarvani, ICMR Center for Management Research

Veronika Tarnovskaya, School of Economics and Management, Lund University

Vivek Gupta, ICMR Center for Management Research

Authors' acknowledgements

We also would like to thank a team of colleagues who helped us in typing, editing and preparing the manuscript. Our special thanks in this regard to Ibne Hassan, Ayse Akcal and Saad Ghauri.

We appreciate the help of all the many students and professors who have shared their opinions of past editions, and we welcome their comments and suggestions on this and future editions of *International Marketing*.

A very special thank you to Peter Hooper at McGraw-Hill, Maidenhead, who helped us in more than one way to finish this edition on time.

Pervez Ghauri and Philip Cateora

Every effort has been made to trace and acknowledge ownership of copyright and to clear permission for material reproduced in this book. The publishers will be pleased to make suitable arrangements to clear permission with any copyright holders whom it has not been possible to contact.

Guided Tour

Chapter Learning Objectives

What you should learn from Chapter 1
- What is meant by international marketing
- To understand the scope of the international marketing task
- To comprehend the meaning and the importance of the self-reference criterion (SRC) in international marketing
- To identify and manage the factors influencing the internationalisation of companies
- To evaluate the progression of becoming an international marketer
- To see how international marketing concepts influence international marketers
- To appreciate the increasing importance of global awareness and marketing opportunities

Learning Objectives
Each chapter opens with a set of learning objectives, summarising what you will learn from each chapter.

Marshall Plan

a plan designed to assist in the rebuilding of Europe after the Second World War

After the Second World War, as a means to dampen the USA set out to infuse the ideal of capitalism throughout as sible. The **Marshall Plan** to assist in rebuilding Europe, fin opment assistance to rebuild Japan and funds channelle International Development and other groups designed to fos underdeveloped world were used to help create a strong tion of colonial powers created scores of new countries in striving of these countries to gain economic independence offered by the Western countries, most of the developing new markets were created.

Key Terms
These are highlighted throughout the chapter and definitions are provided in the margins for quick and easy reference.

EXHIBIT 1.4: Most spoken languages in 2012

Most spoken languages in 2012	Number of people (millions)
1 Chinese (Mandarin)	1,213
2 Spanish	329
3 English	328
4 Arabic	221
5 Hindi	182
6 Bengali	181
7 Portuguese	178
8 Russian	144
9 Japanese	122
10 German	90

Source: Ethnologue, 16th edn (2013).

Exhibits
Each chapter provides a number of figures and tables to illustrate and summarise important information.

Going International 1.2

EVOLUTION OF A MULTINATIONAL COMPANY

1964	Phil Knight, an accountant at Price Waterhouse, and college track coach Bill Bowerman put in $500 each to start Blue Ribbon Sports.
1970	Bowerman, inspired by the waffle iron, dreams up new shoe treads, which evolve to become the best-selling US training shoe.
1971	Blue Ribbon changes its name to Nike and adopts the swoosh as its logo, designed by a college student for $35. She later gets an undisclosed number of stocks.

Going International boxes
This book is full of these relevant and contemporary examples of international marketing, which bring the topic to life. Many of them include discussion questions designed to prompt class debates.

SUMMARY

The first section of *International Marketing* offers an overview of international marketing, and a discussion of the global business, political and legal environments confronting the marketer. International marketing is defined as the performance of business activities beyond national borders. The task of the international marketer is explained. Key obstacles to international marketing are not just foreign environments but also our own self-reference criteria (SRC) and ethnocentrism. This section deals exclusively with the uncontrollable elements of the environment and their assessment. The next section offers chapters on assessing international market opportunities. Then, management issues in developing global marketing strategies are discussed. In each chapter the impact of the environment and culture on the marketing process is illustrated. Space prohibits an encyclopaedic approach to all the issues; nevertheless, we have tried to present sufficient detail so readers appreciate the real need to make a thorough analysis whenever the challenge arises. The next chapter provides a framework for this task.

Summary

These summaries briefly review and reinforce the main topics covered in each chapter to ensure you have acquired a solid understanding of the topics.

QUESTIONS

1 lsquo;The marketer's task is the same whether applied in Amsterdam, London or Kuala Lumpur'. Discuss.
2 How can the increased interest in international marketing on the part of European firms be explained?
3 Discuss the four phases of international marketing involvement.
4 Discuss the conditions that have led to the development of global markets.
5 Differentiate between a global company and a multinational company.
6 Differentiate among the three international marketing orientations.
7 Relate the three international marketing orientations to the EPRG schema.

Questions

These questions help you test the knowledge you have acquired from the chapter.

FURTHER READING

• Theodore Levitt, 'The Globalization of Markets', *Harvard Business Review*, 1983, May–June, pp 92–102.
• Peter Buckley and Pervez Ghauri, 'Globalization, Economic Geography and Multinational Enterprises', *Journal of International Business Studies*, 2004, 35(2), pp 81–98.
• Esther Tippmann, Pamela Sharkey Scott and Vincent Mangematin, 'Problem Solving in MNCs: How Local and Global Solutions are (and are not) Created', *Journal of International Business Studies*, 2012, 43(8), pp 746–71.

Further Reading

The further reading for each chapter guides you towards the best secondary sources available.

Preliminary marketing plan

Information gathered in the previous sets of guidelines serves as the basis for developing a marketing plan for your product/brand in a target market. How the problems and opportunities that surfaced in the preceding steps are overcome and/or exploited to produce maximum sales/profits are presented here. The action plan reflects, in your judgement, the most effective means of marketing your product in a country market. Budgets, expected profits and/or losses, and additional resources necessary to implement the proposed plan are also presented.

Guidelines

I The marketing plan.
  A Marketing objectives.
    1 Target market(s) (specific description of the market segment).
    2 Expected sales 20–.
    3 Profit expectations 20–.
    4 Market penetration and coverage.
  B Product adaptation, or modification – using the product component model as your guide,

    a Marking
    b Containe
  4 Documentati
  5 Insurance cl
  6 Freight forw
If your company tion or traffic m consider using a distinct advantag ing one.

E Channels of distr
This section pres types of distribu
  1 Retailers.
    a Type and
    b Retail m type of r
    c Methods (cash/cre
    d Scale o (small/la
  2 Wholesale m
    a Type a

Country Notebook

This feature provides a format for undertaking both a complete cultural and economic analysis of a country, as well as guidelines for a marketing plan.

Cases Outline

Case 1.1 Strategy Formulation at Audi
Case 1.2 Starbucks: Going Global Fast
Case 1.3 Walmart in Africa

Case Studies

The book includes an extensive case study section, featuring in-depth studies of a variety of companies from around the world.

Case 1.1

Strategy Formulation at Audi

Audi: the success of cars 'Made in Germany'

The German company Audi, part of the Volkswagen Group, is enjoying unprecedented levels of success, particularly in the international marketplace. In 2012,

Audi: a brand of the Volkswagen Group

Audi is part of the German Vol is one of the world's leading aut ers and the largest carmaker

Glossary

act of God – An extraordinary natural event not reasonably anticipated by either party to a contract, ie earthquakes, floods, etc.

activist groups – See *Green activist*. Refers to these groups, eg Greenpeace.

adaptation – Making changes to fit a particular culture/ environment/conditions, eg when we produce special/ modified products for different markets.

administered pricing Relates to attempts to establish prices for an entire market.

advertising campaign – Designing and implementing particular advertising for a particular product/purpose over a fixed period.

by refusing to allow impor currency for the seller's cu

Boston Consulting Grou strategy and general mana specific models to tackle

boycott – A coordinated r services of a certain comp

brand loyalty – When cus brand.

branding – Developing an brand name.

broker – A catchall term f performing low-cost agent

Glossary

The comprehensive glossary at the end of the text provides a quick reference tool for learning.

Online Learning Centre

www.mcgraw-hill.co.uk/textbooks/ghauri

Students – Helping you to Connect, Learn and Succeed

We understand that studying for your module is not just about reading this textbook. It's also about researching online, revising key terms, preparing for assignments, and passing the exam. The website above provides you with a number of **FREE** resources to help you succeed on your module, including:

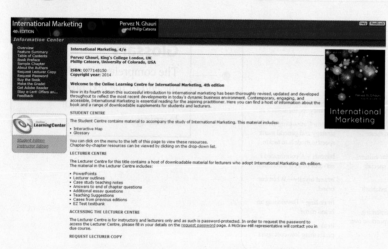

- **Self-test questions** to prepare you for mid-term tests and exams
- **Glossary** of key terms to revise core concepts
- **Web links** to online sources of information to help you prepare for class

Lecturer support – Helping you to help your students

The Online Learning Centre also provides lecturers adopting this book with a range of resources designed to offer:

- **Faster course preparation** – time-saving support for your module
- **High-calibre content to support your students** – resources written by your academic peers, who understand your need for rigorous and reliable content
- **Flexibility** – edit, adapt or repurpose; test in EZ Test or your department's Course Management System. The choice is yours.

The materials created specifically for lecturers adopting this textbook include:

- *Lecturer's Manual to support your module preparation, with case notes, guide answers, teaching tips and more*
- *PowerPoint presentations to use in lecture presentations*
- *Image library of artwork from the textbook*
- *Solutions manual providing accuracy-tested answers to the problems in the textbook*
- *Case Notes with guide answers to case questions, written to help support your students in understanding and analysing the cases in the textbook*

- *Cases from previous editions*
- *Answers to end of chapter questions*
- *Additional essay questions*
- *Teaching suggestions*

To request your password to access these resources, contact your McGraw-Hill Education representative or visit www.mcgraw-hill.co.uk/textbooks/ghauri

Test Bank available in McGraw-Hill EZ Test Online

A test bank of hundreds of questions is available to lecturers adopting this book for their module through the EZ Test online website. For each chapter you will find:

- A range of multiple choice, true or false, or essay questions
- Questions identified by type to help you to select questions that best suit your needs

McGraw-Hill EZ Test Online is:

- **Accessible** anywhere with an Internet connection – your unique login provides you access to all your tests and material in any location
- **Simple** to set up and easy to use
- **Flexible**, offering a choice from question banks associated with your adopted textbook or allowing you to create your own questions
- **Comprehensive**, with access to hundreds of banks and thousands of questions created for other McGraw-Hill titles
- **Compatible** with Blackboard and other course management systems
- **Time-saving** – students' tests can be immediately marked and results and feedback delivered directly to your students to help them to monitor their progress.

To register for this FREE resource, visit www.eztestonline.com

Let us help make our **content** your **solution**

At McGraw-Hill Education our aim is to help lecturers to find the most suitable content for their needs, delivered to their students in the most appropriate way. Our **custom publishing solutions** offer the ideal combination of content delivered in the way which best suits lecturer and students.

Our custom publishing programme offers lecturers the opportunity to select just the chapters or sections of material they wish to deliver to their students from a database called CREATE™ at

www.mcgrawhillcreate.co.uk

CREATE™ contains over two million pages of content from:

- textbooks
- professional books
- case books – Harvard Articles, Insead, Ivey, Darden, Thunderbird and BusinessWeek
- Taking Sides – debate materials

Across the following imprints:

- McGraw-Hill Education
- Open University Press
- Harvard Business Publishing
- US and European material

There is also the option to include additional material authored by lecturers in the custom product – this does not necessarily have to be in English.

We will take care of everything from start to finish in the process of developing and delivering a custom product to ensure that lecturers and students receive exactly the material needed in the most suitable way.

With a Custom Publishing Solution, students enjoy the best selection of material deemed to be the most suitable for learning everything they need for their courses – something of real value to support their learning. Teachers are able to use exactly the material they want, in the way they want, to support their teaching on the course.

Please contact your local McGraw-Hill Education representative with any questions or alternatively contact Warren Eels **e: warren_eels@mcgraw-hill.com**.

PART 1

An Overview

Chapter 1

The Scope and Challenge of International Marketing

Chapter Learning Objectives

What you should learn from Chapter 1

- What is meant by international marketing
- The scope of the international marketing task
- The meaning and the importance of the self-reference criterion (SRC) in international marketing
- How to identify and manage the factors influencing the internationalisation of companies
- How to evaluate the progression of becoming an international marketer
- How international marketing concepts influence international marketers
- The increasing importance of global awareness and marketing opportunities

The modern world is organised on the basis that each nation state is sovereign and independent from other countries. In reality, however, no country can completely isolate its internal affairs from external forces. Even the most inward-looking regimes have realised the limitations of their own resources as well as the benefits of opening up their borders. This major change in the orientation of most regimes has led to an enormous amount of activity in the international marketplace.

The global economic boom of the 1990s has been one of the drivers for efficiency, productivity and open, unregulated markets that has swept the world.[1] Never before in world history have businesses been so deeply involved in and affected by international global developments. The first decade of the twenty-first century, on the other hand, brought political turmoil and economic crisis that swept throughout the world and affected almost every country. Powerful economic, technological, industrial, political and demographic forces are converging to form the foundation of a new global economic order on which the structure of a world economic and market system will be built.[2]

Whether or not a company wants to participate directly in international business, it cannot escape the effect of the ever-increasing number of domestic firms exporting, importing and/or manufacturing abroad; the number of foreign-based firms operating in most markets; the growth of regional trade areas; the rapid growth of world markets; and the increasing number of competitors for global markets. Of all the trends affecting global business today, five stand out as the most dynamic and as the ones that are influencing the shape of international business:

1 the interdependence of the world economies and globalisation of production and consumption[2]

2 the rapid growth of regional **free-trade areas** such as the EU, NAFTA, **ASEAN** and **APEC**

3 the increase in wealth and growth in most parts of the world, causing enhanced purchasing power as well as volatility in financial markets throughout the world

4 the evolution of large emerging markets such as Brazil, China, India, Russia, Indonesia, Turkey and Pakistan

5 availability of advanced methods of communication and transportation due to developments in information technology.

free-trade area

where products can move freely, without tariffs and restrictions

ASEAN

the fourth-biggest trade area of the world comprising 10 Southeast Asian countries

APEC

Asia–Pacific cooperation among 21 member states. APEC promotes free trade and economic cooperation between members

economic change

change in economic conditions, eg growth or recession

These forces affecting international business have led to a dramatic growth in international trade and have contributed to a perception that the world has become a smaller and more interdependent place.[3] If we look at the Swiss multinational company Nestlé, 'The Food Company of the World', it claims its products are sold in every country in the world. It has factories in more than 80 countries and has many brands that are recognised all over the world.[4] Toyota and its subsidiaries sell their cars in more than 170 countries, giving it a presence in more countries than any other auto manufacturer.[5]

Every business must be prepared to compete in an increasingly interdependent global economic environment, and all business people must be aware of the effects of these trends when managing a multinational conglomerate or a domestic company that exports. As one international expert noted, 'every company is international, at least to the extent that its business performance is conditioned in part by events that occur abroad'.[6] Even companies that do not operate in the international arena are affected to some degree by the **economic changes** taking place in China and India as well as the recent economic crisis. The interdependence among nations and markets has, however, not been affected. Companies have become even more aggressive to capture new markets in order to compensate for recessions at home or economic slow down in their traditional markets.

As competition for world markets intensifies, the number of companies operating solely in domestic markets is decreasing. Or, to put it another way, it is increasingly true that the business of any business is international business. The challenge of international marketing is to develop strategic plans that are competitive in the intensifying global markets. These and other issues affecting the world economy, trade, markets and competition will be discussed throughout this text.

The internationalisation of business

With the increasing globalisation of markets, companies find they are unavoidably enmeshed with foreign customers, competitors and suppliers, even within their own borders. They face competition on all fronts – from domestic firms and from foreign firms. A significant portion of all televisions, mobile phones, clothes and tableware sold in Western Europe is foreign made. Sony, Panasonic, Samsung, Nokia, LG, Toyota and Nissan are familiar brands all over the world and for Western industry, they are formidable opponents in a competitive struggle for world markets.

Many familiar domestic companies are now foreign controlled. When you shop for groceries at Aldi or Lidl supermarkets, or buy a SEAT car, you are buying indirectly from a German company. Some well-known brands no longer owned by Western companies are Carnation (Swiss), Brooks Brothers clothing (Canada), Land Rover and Jaguar that are now owned by TATA, an Indian conglomerate, and the Godiva chocolate brand, which is now owned by a Turkish company. There is hardly any country that is not involved in international trade and investment (Exhibit 1.1 shows the top 30 trading countries). In fact, both inward and outward foreign investment in most countries is quite common. This is illustrated by Exhibit 1.2.

EXHIBIT 1.1: Top 30 countries for trade and expansion

Rank	2011	Country GDP (purchasing power parity) (billion $)	Population (millions)	Export (billion $)	Import (billion $)
1	USA	15,290	313	1,497	2,236
2	China	11,440	1343	1,904	1,743
3	India	4,515	1205	299.4	461.4
4	Japan	4,497	127	788	808.4
5	Germany	3,139	81	1,408	1,198
6	Russia	2,414	142	520.9	322.5
7	Brazil	2,324	199	256	219.6
8	UK	2,290	63	479.7	639.5
9	France	2,246	65	587.1	688.5
10	Italy	1,871	61	523.9	556.4
11	Mexico	1,683	114	349.7	350.8
12	Korea, South	1,574	48	556.5	524.4
13	Spain	1,432	47	303.6	363.1
14	Canada	1,414	34	462.4	461
15	Indonesia	1,139	248	201.5	166.1
16	Turkey	1,087	79	143.5	232.9
17	Iran	1,003	78	131.8	76.1
18	Australia	926.2	22	272.1	243.4
19	Taiwan	887.3	23	307.1	279.4
20	Poland	781.5	38	193.9	208
21	Argentina	725.6	42	84.27	70.73
22	Netherlands	713.1	16	551.8	493.1
23	Saudi Arabia	691.5	26	359.9	117.4
24	Thailand	609.8	67	221.6	196.3
25	South Africa	562.2	48	104.5	102.6
26	Egypt	525.6	83	27.91	53.97
27	Pakistan	494.8	190	25.35	35.82
28	Colombia	478	45	56.22	54.7
29	Malaysia	453	29	225.6	177.1
30	Nigeria	418.7	170	103.9	69.49

Source: *CIA World Factbook* (1 January 2012).

EXHIBIT 1.2: Direct foreign investment flows in selected countries, 2011

Countries	Inflow (million $)	Outflow (million $)	Net outflow (million $)
USA	226,937	396,656	−169,719
Canada	40,932	49,569	−8,637
Belgium	89,142	70,706	18,436
UK	53,949	107,086	−53,137
France	40,945	90,146	−49,201
Italy	29,059	47,210	−18,151
Poland	15,139	5,860	9,279
Switzerland	(196)	69,612	
Spain	29,476	37,256	−7,780
Sweden	12,091	26,850	−14,759
The Netherlands	17,129	31,867	−14,738
Germany	40,402	54,368	−13,966
Japan	(1,758)	114,353	

Source: *World Investment Report 2012*, p 203.

Companies with existing foreign operations realise they must be more competitive to succeed against other foreign and domestic multinationals in every market. They have found it necessary to spend more money and time improving their marketing positions abroad because competition for these growing markets is intensifying. For the firm venturing into international marketing for the first time, and for those already experienced (for example, MNC versus SME), the requirement is generally the same – a thorough and complete commitment to foreign markets and, for many, new ways of operating to handle the uncertainties of foreign markets.

Going International 1.1

APPLE'S JOURNEY TOWARDS TOP POSITION

Apple: The beginning	1976	Apple Computer is founded. **Apple I** is introduced
	1979	Jobs and team of engineers visit Xerox PARC, where they see a demo of mouse and graphical user interface
	1980	Apple **goes public in biggest IPO** since Ford Motor in 1956. Jobs' 15 per cent stake is worth more than $200m
	1983	The **Apple Lisa** is released, inspired by Xerox's user interface
	1984	The **Macintosh** is introduced. The '1984' commercial airs during the Super Bowl
Out of a Job. What's next ?	1985	Jobs is ousted from Apple. Launches **Next**, pays Paul Rand $100,000 to design logo
	1986	Jobs buys **Pixar** from George Lucas for $10m
	1988	The **Next Cube** is released. Price: $6,500
	1993	After years of sluggish sales, Jobs lays off half the employees of Next and repositions it as a software company
	1995	Pixar releases ***Toy Story***, the first full-length computer animated film, to rave reviews. + Pixar goes public one week later; Jobs' 80 per cent stake is worth $585m
	1996	Apple announces acquisition of Next for $430m; posts $816m loss for the year

▶

	1997	Jobs becomes interim CEO of Apple, replaces board, launches **'Think Different' campaign**
Jobs' return to Apple	1998	Apple returns to profitability. The **iMac** debuts, becomes the fastest-selling Macintosh ever. Pixar releases *A Bug's Life*
	2000	Jobs becomes permanent CEO of Apple. + Board gives Jobs a **Gulfstream V jet** and 40 million options
iTunes and beyond	2001	Big year for introductions: first Apple stores, the **iPod**, **iTunes** and the OS X operating system. Apple grants Jobs another 15 million options. + Pixar releases ***Monsters Inc***
	2003	Jobs swaps underwater options for restricted shares. + Jobs is diagnosed with pancreatic cancer; board decides not to disclose it. + Pixar releases ***Finding Nemo*** to record box office
	2004	Jobs undergoes cancer surgery, discloses both cancer and 'cure' the next day. + ***The Incredibles*** is released
	2005	**iPod Nano** is released. Huge hit
Apple ascendant	2006	**Pixar** is sold to Disney, making Jobs its largest shareholder, with a stake now worth $4.6bn + ***Cars*** is released. + Apple board announces backdating investigation, informs SEC. + board confirms backdating, but clears Jobs and management. Company announces $105m restatement. + Disney launches internal investigation of backdating at Pixar
	2007	**iPhone** is introduced. + Apple stock hits a record $199.83 a share. + SEC files suit against Fred Anderson and Nancy Heinen. SEC clears company. **Anderson settles with SEC**, issues statement challenging Jobs' account. + Disney board acknowledges backdating but clears Pixar management
	2008	Apple stock **drops 40 per cent** in two months in a down market
	2009	Apple introduces the next generation of iPhone and launches iPod Nano with video camera
	2010	Apple awards Cook a bonus valued at $22m for leading the company during Jobs' six-month leave, during which its shares soared about 70 per cent. Apple begins selling the **iPad** in April 2010, a 10-inch touchscreen tablet, and has an 84 per cent share of the tablet market by year's end. Researcher iSuppli estimates 12.9 million iPads were shipped as of 10 December. The Beatles' 13 albums become available on iTunes, ending years of talks between Jobs, Beatles' management company Apple Corps and Beatles label **EMI Group**
	2011	Jobs announces that he will take another medical leave. Verizon Wireless, a venture of **Verizon Communications Inc** and **Vodafone Group Plc**, starts selling the iPhone in stores and puts an end to AT&T's exclusive contract for the phone in the USA. Apple launches a long-awaited subscription service for magazines, newspapers, videos and music – a move that could hurt streaming services Netflix and Hulu. Apple launches the **iPad 2**, a sleeker, lighter version of its tablet with a new dual-core processor, two cameras and, for the first time, it comes in either white or black

Source: *Fortune*, 17 March 2008, pp 56–62. http://www.reuters.com/article/2011/03/02/us-apple-timeline-idUSTRE72170T20110302.

The world that has lost its kings echoes the reality of today's technology industry, where the battle lines between the four large companies seen as dominating the customer Internet (Google, Apple, Facebook and Amazon) are in furious flux. The death of Steve Jobs, Apple's monarch, robbed the technology world of the nearest thing that it had to royalty. But even before Jobs' passing, tension was growing between the great powers of the web generation as the onset of mobile computing upset the previous balance of power.

The tech industry has a history of bitter rivalries: IBM and Apple in the 1980s; Microsoft and Netscape in the 1990s. But the rivalries shaping the market today are even richer and more complicated, not least because they have a personal edge. Three of the big four are still run by men who made their billions as founder, or co-founder, of their empires: Amazon's Jeff Bezos, Google's Larry Page and Facebook's Mark Zuckerberg. And although Jobs no longer rules Apple, he groomed Tim Cook, his successor as chief executive. 'In the modern history of technology we have never seen such a highly engaged group of chief executives and founders,' says Mary Meeker, a partner at Kleiner Perkins Caufield & Byers, a venture-capital company.

This has allowed the companies to pile cash into their war chests (Exhibit 1.3). They will need them. All four grew up when computing was basically something done at a desk or on a laptop with the programs you had to hand. Now, as in Mr Martin's realm of Westeros, where the reader is always being apocalyptically assured that 'winter is coming', their world is undergoing great change.

EXHIBIT 1.3: Coins and the realms

	Year founded	Employees	Market value	Revenue ($bn)	Profit/loss ($bn)	Cash ($bn)
Apple	1976	76,100	548.2	156.5	41.7	121.3
Amazon	1994	81,400	110.7	57.3	Nil	5.2
Google	1998	53,546	222.8	47.5	10.6	46.8
Facebook	2004	4,331	56.9	4.6	−0.1	10.5

Apple now finds itself competing with rivals that have radically different ways of making money. Amazon is flogging its Kindle e-readers and tablet computers, which use a modified version of Android, at pretty much what it costs to produce and sell them. Where Apple used iTunes to sell iPods, Amazon uses its tablets to sell everything else in the world.

Apple has been lobbing lawsuits around in the smartphone arena as if armed with a trebuchet. Google snapped up Motorola Mobility in large part to get its hands on the firm's thousands of patents issued and pending, thus bulking up its own defences and accumulating ammunition to fling at the fortresses of the competition.

No one looks likely to win quickly. 'There will be a lot of trench warfare,' predicts Roelof Botha of Sequoia Capital, a venture investor. And that looks likely to be great news for consumers, who will be able to choose from an ever wider range of innovative and cheap (or free) technologies.

- Can Apple win this battle?

Source: *Bloomberg* and *The Economist*, 1 December 2012, p 27.

International marketing defined

International marketing is the performance of business activities that direct the flow of a company's goods and services to consumers or users in more than one nation for a profit. The only difference in the definitions of domestic marketing and international marketing is that the marketing activities take place in more than one country. This difference accounts for the complexity and diversity found in international marketing operations. Marketing concepts, processes, and principles are to a great extent universally applicable, and the marketer's task is the same whether doing business in Amsterdam, London or Jakarta. The goal of a business is to make a profit by promoting, pricing and distributing products for which there is a market. If this is the case, what is the difference between domestic and international marketing?

The answer lies not with different concepts of marketing, but with the environment within which marketing plans must be implemented. The uniqueness of foreign marketing comes from the range of unfamiliar problems and the variety of strategies necessary to cope with the different levels of uncertainty encountered in foreign markets.

Competition, legal constraints, government controls, weather, consumer behaviour and any number of other uncontrollable elements can, and frequently do, affect the profitable outcome of good, sound marketing plans. Generally speaking, the marketer cannot control or influence these uncontrollable elements, but instead must adjust or adapt to them in a manner consistent with a successful outcome. What makes marketing interesting is the challenge of moulding the controllable elements of marketing decisions (positioning, product, price, promotion and distribution) within the framework of the uncontrollable elements of the marketplace (competition, politics, laws, consumer behaviour, level of technology and so forth) in such a way that marketing objectives are achieved. Even though marketing principles and concepts are universally applicable, the environment within which the marketer must implement marketing plans can change dramatically from country to country. The difficulties created by different environments and cultures and adjusting membership strategies accordingly are the international marketer's primary concern.

The international marketing task

The international marketer's task is more complicated than that of the domestic marketer because the international marketer must deal with at least two levels of uncontrollable uncertainty instead of one. Uncertainty is created by the uncontrollable elements of all business environments, but each foreign country in which a company operates adds its own unique set of uncontrollables. Exhibit 1.4 illustrates the total environment of an international marketer. The inner circle depicts the controllable elements that constitute a marketer's decision area, the second circle encompasses those environmental elements at home that have some effect on foreign-operation decisions, and the outer circles represent the elements of the foreign environment for each foreign market within which the marketer operates. As the

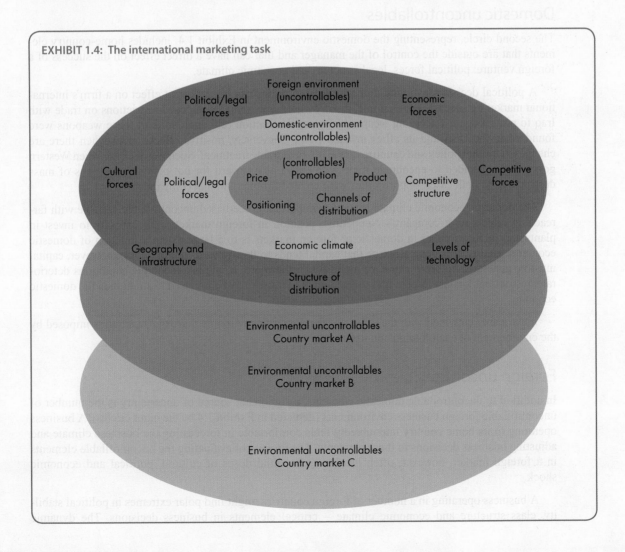

EXHIBIT 1.4: The international marketing task

outer circles illustrate, each foreign market in which the company does business presents separate problems involving some or all of the uncontrollable elements. Thus, the greater the number of foreign markets in which a company operates, the greater the possible variety of foreign environmental uncontrollables with which to contend. Frequently, a solution to a problem in country market A is not applicable to a problem in country market B.

Marketing controllables

The successful manager constructs a marketing programme designed for optimal adjustment to the uncertainty of the business climate. The inner circle in Exhibit 1.4 represents the area under the control of the marketing manager. Assuming the necessary overall corporate resources, the marketing manager blends price, product, promotion and channels-of-distribution activities to capitalise on anticipated demand. The controllable elements can be altered in the long run and, usually, in the short run, to adjust to changing market conditions or corporate objectives.

The outer circles surrounding the market controllables represent the levels of uncertainty that are created by the domestic and foreign environments. Although the marketer can blend a marketing mix from the controllable elements, the uncontrollables are precisely that and there must be active adaptation. These are the elements that are outside the control of the managers but need to be handled. That effort, the adaptation of the marketing mix to the uncontrollables, determines the ultimate outcome of the marketing enterprise.

Domestic uncontrollables

The second circle, representing the domestic environment in Exhibit 1.4, includes home-country elements that are outside the control of the manager and that can have a direct effect on the success of a foreign venture: political forces, legal structure and economic climate.

A political decision involving domestic foreign policy can have a direct effect on a firm's international marketing success. For example, most Western governments imposed restrictions on trade with Iraq to protest against accruing weapons of mass-destruction (although none of these weapons were found when the USA and its allies invaded Iraq). Conversely, positive effects occur when there are changes in foreign policy and countries are given favourable treatment. Such was the case when Western governments decided to encourage trade with Libya as a reward for not pursuing weapons of mass destruction. In both cases, opportunities were created for international companies.

The domestic economic climate is another important home-based uncontrollable variable with far-reaching effects on a company's competitive position in foreign markets. The capacity to invest in plants and facilities either in domestic or foreign markets is to a large extent a function of domestic economic vitality. It is generally true that capital tends to flow towards optimum use; however, capital must be generated before it can have mobility. Furthermore, if internal economic conditions deteriorate, restrictions against foreign investment and purchasing may be imposed to strengthen the domestic economy.

Inextricably entwined with the effects of the domestic environment are the constraints imposed by the environment of each foreign country.

Foreign uncontrollables

In addition to uncontrollable domestic elements, a significant source of uncertainty is the number of uncontrollable foreign business environments (depicted in Exhibit 1.4 by the outer circles). A business operating in its home country undoubtedly feels comfortable in forecasting the business climate and adjusting business decisions to these elements. The process of evaluating the uncontrollable elements in a foreign market, however, often involves substantial doses of cultural, political and economic shock.

A business operating in a number of foreign countries might find polar extremes in political stability, class structure and economic climate – critical elements in business decisions. The dynamic upheavals in some countries further illustrate the problems of dramatic change in cultural, political and economic climates over relatively short periods of time.

The more significant elements in the uncontrollable foreign environment include: (1) political/legal forces; (2) economic forces; (3) competitive forces; (4) level of technology; (5) structure of distribution; (6) geography and infrastructure; and (7) cultural forces. They constitute the principal elements of uncertainty that an international marketer must cope with in designing a marketing programme. Each is discussed in some detail in subsequent chapters.

Also, a problem for some marketers attuned to one environment is the inability to recognise easily the potential impact of certain uncontrollable elements within another environment, one to which they have not been culturally acclimatised. Warning signs of danger and indicators of potential in a foreign market may not always be read or interpreted accurately. The level of technology is an uncontrollable element that can often be misread because of the vast differences that may exist between home and foreign countries. For example, a marketer cannot assume that the understanding of the concept of preventive maintenance for machinery and equipment is the same in other countries as it is in the home country.

The problem of foreign uncertainty is further complicated by a frequently imposed 'alien status' that increases the difficulty of properly assessing and forecasting the dynamic international business climate. There are two dimensions to the alien status of a foreign business: alien in that the business is controlled by foreigners; and alien in that the culture of the host country is alien to the foreign company. The alien status of a business results in greater emphasis being placed on many of the uncontrollable elements than would be found in relation to those same elements in the domestic market.

The political environment offers the best example of the alien status. Domestic marketers must consider the political ramifications of their decisions, although the consequences of this environmental element are generally minor. The political and legal environment can be extremely critical, and shifts in governments often mean sudden changes in attitudes that can result in expropriation, expulsion or major restrictions on operations.

The uncertainty of different foreign business environments creates the need for a close study of the operating environment within each new country relevant for your industry/product. Different solutions to fundamentally identical marketing tasks are often in order and are generally the result of changes in the environment of the market. Thus, a strategy successful in one country can be rendered ineffective in another by differences in political climate, stages of economic development, level of technology or other cultural variation.

(Going International 1.2

EVOLUTION OF A MULTINATIONAL COMPANY

1964	Phil Knight, an accountant at Price Waterhouse, and college track coach Bill Bowerman put in $500 each to start Blue Ribbon Sports.
1970	Bowerman, inspired by the waffle iron, dreams up new shoe treads, which evolve to become the best-selling US training shoe.
1971	Blue Ribbon changes its name to Nike and adopts the swoosh as its logo, designed by a college student for $35. She later gets an undisclosed number of stocks.

© Istockphoto.com/tupungato

▶

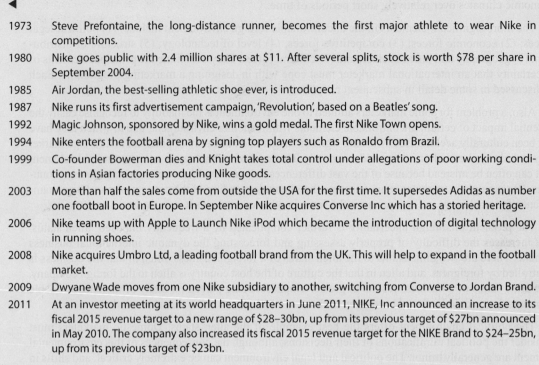

◄

1973	Steve Prefontaine, the long-distance runner, becomes the first major athlete to wear Nike in competitions.
1980	Nike goes public with 2.4 million shares at $11. After several splits, stock is worth $78 per share in September 2004.
1985	Air Jordan, the best-selling athletic shoe ever, is introduced.
1987	Nike runs its first advertisement campaign, 'Revolution', based on a Beatles' song.
1992	Magic Johnson, sponsored by Nike, wins a gold medal. The first Nike Town opens.
1994	Nike enters the football arena by signing top players such as Ronaldo from Brazil.
1999	Co-founder Bowerman dies and Knight takes total control under allegations of poor working conditions in Asian factories producing Nike goods.
2003	More than half the sales come from outside the USA for the first time. It supersedes Adidas as number one football boot in Europe. In September Nike acquires Converse Inc which has a storied heritage.
2006	Nike teams up with Apple to Launch Nike iPod which became the introduction of digital technology in running shoes.
2008	Nike acquires Umbro Ltd, a leading football brand from the UK. This will help to expand in the football market.
2009	Dwyane Wade moves from one Nike subsidiary to another, switching from Converse to Jordan Brand.
2011	At an investor meeting at its world headquarters in June 2011, NIKE, Inc announced an increase to its fiscal 2015 revenue target to a new range of $28–30bn, up from its previous target of $27bn announced in May 2010. The company also increased its fiscal 2015 revenue target for the NIKE Brand to $24–25bn, up from its previous target of $23bn.

With revenues over $12bn (2004), the company has come a long way from its early years when Phil Knight used to sell sneakers out of his car trunk at tracks. As for advertising, Nike spent $8m in 1986 and $48m in 1987. It has improved its gross margin from 39.9 per cent in 1998 to 42.9 per cent in 2004. It makes only 3 per cent of shoes without a firm order from a retailer (30 per cent in 1998).

As for production, Nike does not own any manufacturing facility. However, factories such as Yue Yuen in an industrial estate in Dongguan, China, are geared towards Nike standards and reflect Nike needs. A particular Nike shoe is made up of 52 different components, coming from five different countries, excluding non-material inputs such as design, transportation and marketing. It will be touched by at least 120 pairs of hands during production. The new production system is a network of logistics; not only do all the materials have to come together, but they also have to come together at the right time.

Nike is an American firm and, though our statesmen and trade negotiators haggle over local content, how would they classify Nike from the Dongguan factory? The leather comes from South Korea; those putting it together are mainland Chinese; the factory is owned by a Taiwanese; some components come from Japan and Indonesia; and the design and marketing come from America. And if this is the case for a simple pair of shoes, imagine what it must be for a computer or a car.

● Is Nike an American product?

Sources: abstracted from *Far Eastern Economic Review*, 29 August 1996, p 5; and Stanley Holmes, 'The New Nike', Cover Story, *Business Week*, 20 September 2004, pp 54–64, and www.nikein.com, 2012.

Environmental adaptations

To adjust and adapt a marketing programme to foreign markets, marketers must be able to interpret effectively the influence and impact of each of the uncontrollable environmental elements on the marketing plan for each foreign market in which they hope to do business. In a broad sense, the uncontrollable elements include the culture; the difficulty facing the marketer in adjusting to the culture (ie uncontrollable elements of the marketplace) lies in recognising their impact. In a domestic market, the reaction to much of the uncontrollables' (cultural) impact on the marketer's activities is automatic;

the various cultural influences that fill our lives are simply a part of our history. We react in a manner acceptable to our society without thinking about it because we are culturally responsive to our environment. The experiences we have gained throughout life have become second nature and serve as the basis for our behaviour.

When a marketer operates in other cultures, marketing attempts may fail because of unconscious responses based on frames of reference acceptable in one's own culture but unacceptable in different environments. Unless special efforts are made to determine local cultural meanings for every market, the marketer is likely to overlook the significance of certain behaviours or activities and proceed with plans that result in a negative or unwanted response.

For example, a Westerner must learn that white is a symbol of mourning in parts of Asia, quite different from Western culture's white for bridal gowns. Also, time-conscious Westerners are not culturally prepared to understand the meaning of time to Latin Americans or Arabs. These differences must be learned in order to avoid misunderstandings that can lead to marketing failures.

To avoid such errors, the foreign marketer should be aware of the principle of *marketing relativism*: that is, marketing strategies and judgements are based on experience, and experience is interpreted by each marketer in terms of his or her own culture and experience. We take into the marketplace, at home or in a foreign country, frames of reference developed from past experiences that determine or modify our reactions to the situations we face.

Cultural conditioning is like an iceberg – we are not aware of nine-tenths of it. In any study of the market systems of different people, their political and economic structures, religions and other elements of culture, foreign marketers must constantly guard against measuring and assessing the markets against the fixed values and assumptions of their own cultures. They must take specific steps to make themselves aware of the home cultural reference in their analyses and decision making.

Self-reference criterion: an obstacle

The key to successful international marketing is adaptation to the environmental differences from one market to another. Adaptation is a conscious effort on the part of the international marketer to anticipate the influences of both the foreign and domestic uncontrollable environments on a marketing mix, and then to adjust the marketing mix to minimise the effects.

The primary obstacle to success in international marketing is a person's **self-reference criterion (SRC)** in making decisions; that is, an unconscious reference to one's own cultural values, experiences and knowledge as a basis for decisions. The SRC impedes the ability to assess a foreign market in its true light.

> **self-reference criterion (SRC)**
>
> considering our own conditions, values and norms while evaluating others

When confronted with a set of facts, we react spontaneously on the basis of knowledge assimilated over a lifetime: knowledge that is a product of the history of our culture. Quite often we do not know ourselves why we behave in a certain way in a certain situation, because we do so unconsciously. We seldom stop to think about a reaction; we react. Thus, when faced with a problem in another culture, the tendency is to react instinctively, referring only to our SRC for a solution.

Your SRC can prevent you from being aware that there are cultural differences or from recognising the importance of those differences. Thus, you fail to recognise the need to take action, discount the cultural differences that exist among countries or react to a situation in a way that is offensive to your hosts. A common mistake made by Westerners is to refuse food or drink when offered it. In Europe, a polite refusal is certainly acceptable, but in many countries in Asia and the Middle East, a host is offended if you refuse hospitality.

If we evaluate every situation through our SRC, then we are ethnocentric. Ethnocentrism and the SRC can influence an evaluation of the appropriateness of a domestically designed marketing mix for a foreign market. If Western marketers are not aware, they may evaluate a marketing mix on Western experiences (ie their SRC) without fully appreciating the cultural differences requiring adaptation. One example is 'Pet' in Pet Milk. The name has been used for decades; yet in France, the word *pet* means, among other things, flatulence – again, not the desired image for canned milk. In international marketing, relying on one's SRC can produce an inadequately adapted marketing programme that ends in failure.

The most effective way to control the influence of the SRC is to recognise its existence in our behaviour. Although it is almost impossible for someone to appreciate every culture in depth and to be aware of every important difference, an awareness of the need to be sensitive to differences and to ask questions when doing business in another culture can avoid many of the mistakes possible in international marketing. Asking the appropriate question helped the Vicks Company avoid making a mistake in Germany. It discovered that, in German, 'Vicks' sounds like the crudest slang equivalent of intercourse, so it changed the name to 'Wicks' before introducing the product.[7]

Also be aware that not every activity within a marketing programme is different from one country to another: there are probably more similarities than differences. Such similarities may lull the marketer into a false sense of apparent sameness. This apparent sameness, coupled with our SRC and ethnocentrism, is often the cause of international marketing problems. Undetected similarities do not cause problems; however, the one difference that goes undetected can create a marketing failure.[8]

Different marketing orientations

Although not articulated as such in current literature, it appears that the differences in the international orientation and approach to international markets that guide the international business activities of companies can be described by one of three orientations to international marketing management:

1 domestic market extension orientation

2 multi-domestic market orientation

3 global marketing orientation.

It is to be expected that differences in the complexity and sophistication of a company's marketing activity depend on which of these orientations guides its operations. The ideas expressed in each concept reflect the philosophical orientation that also can be associated with successive stages in the evolution of the international operations in a company.

> **EPRG schema**
>
> classifies firms by their orientation: ethnocentric, polycentric, regiocentric or geocentric

Among the approaches describing the different orientations that evolve in a company as it moves through different phases of international marketing involvement – from casual exporting to global marketing – is the often-quoted **EPRG schema**. The authors of this schema suggest that firms can be classified as having an **E**thnocentric, **P**olycentric, **R**egiocentric or **G**eocentric orientation (EPRG) depending on the international commitment of the firm. Further, the authors state that 'a key assumption underlying the EPRG framework is that the degree of internationalisation to which management is committed or willing to move towards affects the specific international strategies and decision rules of the firm'.[9] The EPRG schema is incorporated into the discussion of the three concepts that follows in that the philosophical orientations described by the EPRG schema help explain management's view when guided by one of the orientations.

Domestic market extension orientation

This orientation to international marketing is illustrated by the domestic company seeking sales extension of its domestic products into foreign markets. It views its international operations as secondary to and an extension of its domestic operations. Domestic business is its priority and foreign sales are seen as a profitable extension of domestic operations. Even though foreign markets may be vigorously pursued, the firm's orientation remains basically domestic. Its attitude towards international sales is typified by the belief that, if it sells in London, it will sell anywhere else in the world.

Minimal, if any, efforts are made to adapt the marketing mix to foreign markets; the firm's orientation is to market to foreign customers in the same manner as the company markets to domestic customers. It seeks markets where demand is similar to the home market and its domestic product will be acceptable. This domestic market extension strategy can be very profitable; large and small exporting companies approach international marketing from this perspective. Sporadic export of cheese to Germany and Belgium by some Dutch dairy producers is an example of this concept. Firms with this marketing approach are classified as *ethnocentric* in the EPRG schema.

Multi-domestic market orientation

Once a company recognises the importance of differences in overseas markets and the importance of offshore business to the organisation, its orientation towards international business may shift to a multi-domestic market strategy. A company guided by this concept has a strong sense that country markets are vastly different (and they may be, depending on the product) and that market success requires an almost independent programme for each country. Firms with this orientation market on a country-by-country basis, with separate marketing strategies for each country.

Subsidiaries operate independently of one another in establishing marketing objectives and plans, and the domestic market and each of the country markets have separate marketing mixes with little interaction among them. Products are adapted for each market with minimal coordination with other country markets; advertising campaigns are localised, as are the pricing and distribution decisions.

A company with this concept does not look for similarity among elements of the marketing mix that might respond to standardisation; rather, it aims for adaptation to local country markets. Control is typically decentralised to reflect the belief that the uniqueness of each market requires local marketing input and control. Production and sale of detergents and soaps by Unilever, all over the world, is a typical example of this concept. Firms with this orientation would be classified in the EPRG schema as *polycentric*.

Going International 1.3

STRIKING A BALANCE BETWEEN GLOBAL AND LOCAL

Multinational companies are often either 'hopelessly local' or 'mindlessly global' in their approach. Unilever tends to be the former, where far away subsidiaries used to work independently with minimal supervision. More recently, however, a new strategy, 'path to growth', has been introduced to correct this. It will ensure that the biggest brands will be managed more centrally.

The best-performing Unilever brands now tend to be those that have undergone this process of globalisation, such as deodorants. But Unilever's €24bn-a-year food business is lagging behind the toiletries. The difference lies in the

With thanks to Unilever Ice Cream and Frozen Food.

need to accommodate local tastes. The food division has priority brands ranging from Lipton tea to Bertolli olive oil. In spite of best efforts, a local nuance to sales strategies has been missing. The newly installed marketing president for the food division says tomato soup has to taste different in the UK, the Netherlands and Germany.

One opinion is that Unilever managers are too focused on abstract problems, while they should be aspiring for customer management. As one analyst says, 'They have pretty good brands. It just seems like they have not produced things that the consumer wants.' To overcome this, Unilever has increasingly been poaching staff from rivals to diversify its gene pool. The path to growth strategy, launched in 1999/2000, is designed to conquer a perennial problem of big companies – how to make scale an asset rather than an encumbrance.

▶

One reason that Unilever's performance is questioned is its comparison with Procter & Gamble, its old rival, which has shown vibrant growth after its own restructuring. One analyst believes that breaking up the company into food, and home and personal care would help it to focus on its markets and adapt to local needs, while others say that the group enjoys distribution and purchasing benefits from combining the two businesses worldwide. The management's opinion is, 'The business has been in transformational changes for a number of years. I have no doubt there will be other changes in the future. Nobody can take refuge in saying we haven't quite got the structure right, or we haven't got the brands right, or we haven't got the people right, or we haven't quite got the margins or the cost structure right. All this has been put into place and now we have to build on it.'

- Do you think Unilever is on the right track for growth? Discuss its path to growth strategy.

Facts on Unilever

- Products are sold in more than 190 countries, generating sales of €51bn in 2012.
- Emerging markets now account for 55 per cent of its business.
- It has 14 brands with sales of more than €1bn a year.
- More than 173,000 people work for Unilever.
- Number 1 fast-moving consumer goods employer of choice among graduates in 20 countries.
- Winner of the prestigious 2013 Catalyst Award, which honours exceptional business initiatives for women in the workplace.
- Almost 80,000 entrepreneurs, including 48,000 women, in over 135,000 villages across India have now joined its rural selling operation.
- It has reached 127 million with its Lifebuoy handwashing programmes since 2010, and 49 million people through its Brush Day and Night oral care campaign during 2010–2012.
- 100 per cent of its palm oil purchases in 2012 were from sustainable sources.
- 39 per cent of all its tea sourced comes from farms certified by Rainforest Alliance.
- The greenhouse gas footprint of the use of its products has reduced by around 6 per cent since 2010.
- Over half of its 252 manufacturing sites across the world send no non-hazardous waste to landfill.

Sources: compiled from Adam Jones, 'No Nimble Giant: The Stumbling Blocks Unilever Faces on its Path to Growth', *Financial Times*, 23 August 2004, p 15, and company information at http://www.unilever.com/aboutus/introductiontounilever/unileverataglance/, 2013.

Global marketing orientation

A company guided by this orientation or philosophy is generally referred to as a *global company* – its marketing activity is global and its market coverage is the world. A company employing a global marketing strategy strives for efficiencies of scale by developing a product, to be sold at a reasonable price to a global market, that is somewhat the same as in the home market. Important to the global marketing concept is the premise that world markets are being 'driven towards a converging commonality',[10] seeking in much the same ways to satisfy their needs and desires. Thus, they constitute significant market segments with similar demands for the same basic product the world over. With this orientation a company attempts to standardise as much of the company effort as is practical on a worldwide basis.

Some decisions are viewed as applicable worldwide, while others require consideration of local influences. The world as a whole is viewed as the market and the firm develops a global marketing strategy, although pricing, advertising or distribution channels may differ in different markets. The development and marketing of the iPad or PlayStation are good examples of a global marketing orientation. The global marketing company would fit the *regiocentric* or *geocentric* classifications of the EPRG schema.

The global marketing concept views an entire set of country markets (whether the home market and only one other, or the home market and 100 other countries) as a unit, identifying groups of prospective buyers with similar needs as a global market segment, and developing a marketing plan that strives for some level of standardisation wherever it is culturally and cost effective. This might mean a company's global marketing plan has a standardised product but country-specific advertising, or has a standardised theme in all countries with country- or cultural-specific appeals to a unique market characteristic, a standardised brand or image but adapted products to meet specific country needs, and so on. In other words, the marketing planning and marketing mix are approached from a global perspective and, where feasible in the marketing mix, efficiencies of standardisation are sought. Wherever cultural uniqueness dictates the need for adaptation of the product, its image and so on, it is accommodated.

As the competitive environment facing today's businesses becomes more internationalised, the most effective orientation for all firms involved in marketing into another country will be a multi-domestic or a global orientation. This means operating as if all the country markets in a company's scope of operations (including the domestic market) are approachable by standardising the overall marketing strategy and adapting the marketing mix as much as possible according to cultural and other uncontrollable factors. Here companies such as IKEA and Nike are good examples.

Globalisation of markets

Theodore Levitt's article 'The Globalization of Markets' has spawned a host of new references to marketing activities: global marketing, global business, global advertising and global brands, as well as serious discussions of the processes of international marketing.[11] Professor Levitt's premise is that world markets are being driven 'towards a converging commonality'. He sees substantial market segments with common needs; that is, a high-quality, reasonably priced, standardised product.

The 'global corporation sells the same thing in the same way everywhere'. Professor Levitt argues that segmenting international markets on political boundaries, and customising products and marketing strategies for country markets or on national or regional preferences are not cost effective. The company of the future, according to Levitt, will be a global company that views the world as one market to which it sells a global product.[12]

As with all new ideas, interpretations abound, and discussions and debates flow. Professor Levitt's article provoked many companies and marketing scholars to re-examine a fundamental idea that has prevailed for decades; that is, products and strategies must be adapted to the cultural needs of each country when marketing internationally. This approach is contrasted with a global orientation suggesting a commonality in marketing needs and thus a standardised product for the whole world. While the need for cultural adaptation exists in most markets and for most products, the influence of mass communications in the world today and its influence on consumer wants and needs cannot be denied.[13]

Certainly, the homogenising effect of mass communications in the EU has eliminated many of the regional differences that once existed. Based on these experiences, it seems reasonable to believe that to some extent people in other cultures exposed to the same influences will react similarly and that there is a converging commonality of the world's needs and desires. For example, over the last century there has been a significant decrease in number of languages spoken in the world.

According to studies in linguistics, in 1900 a population of 1.5 billion people spoke around 6,000 languages. By the end of the century, a population of 6 billion people spoke fewer than 4,000 languages and many of these are just spoken languages. It is suggested that, by 2025, half of these languages will disappear. Also, about half of the world population speaks only the top 10 languages and Chinese is the most commonly spoken language (see Exhibit 1.5).

Does this mean markets are now global? The answer is yes, to some extent; there are market segments in most countries with similar demands for the same product. Levi Strauss, Revlon, Toyota, Apple, Philips, Starbuck, McDonald's and Coca-Cola are companies that sell a relatively standardised product throughout the world to market segments seeking the same products. Does this mean there is no need to be concerned with cultural differences when marketing in different countries? The answer is no: for some products adaptation is not necessary, but for other products adaptation is still necessary. The issue of adaptation versus standardisation of marketing effort is, however, more complicated.

EXHIBIT 1.5: Most spoken languages in 2012

Most spoken languages in 2012	Number of people (millions)
1 Chinese (Mandarin)	1,213
2 Spanish	329
3 English	328
4 Arabic	221
5 Hindi	182
6 Bengali	181
7 Portuguese	178
8 Russian	144
9 Japanese	122
10 German	90

Source: *Ethnologue*, 16th edn (2013).

Even an apparently standardised product such as McDonald's hamburgers needs a different marketing effort and mix. For example, for a McDonald's restaurant in Manhattan, New York, the target customers are working people coming for breakfast or lunch. In Maastricht (the Netherlands) the target customers are families with children; here the restaurant has a big playground with swings and slides attached to it. The restaurant is thus almost empty during the evenings. In Jakarta the target market is more well-to-do youngsters and yuppies. In this case, the restaurant is placed beside the Hard Rock Café, is open 24 hours a day and, in fact, does more business in the night than during the day.

The astute marketer always strives to present products that fulfil the perceived needs and wants of the consumer. An apparently standardised product is also modified according to the tastes and wants of the customers in different markets. McDonald's, for example, has restaurants in India, but it serves non-beef 'beef-burgers'. In Thailand, it sells pork burgers and, in the Philippines, chicken and rice is one of the best-selling meals.

Marketing internationally should entail looking for market segments with similar demands that can be satisfied with the same product, standardising the components of the marketing mix that can be standardised and, where there are significant cultural differences that require parts of the marketing mix to be culturally adapted, adapting. Throughout the text, the question of adaptation versus standardisation of products and marketing effort will be discussed. International marketing is not a concern of multinational or global firms only. Today all (small and large) firms are involved in or influenced by international marketing activities.

Developing a global awareness

Opportunities in global business abound for those prepared to confront the myriad obstacles with optimism and a willingness to continue learning new ways. The successful business person in the twenty-first century will be globally aware and have a frame of reference that goes beyond a region, or even a country, and encompasses the world. To be globally aware is to have:

- objectivity
- tolerance towards cultural differences[14]
- knowledge of
   cultures
   history
   world market potential
   global economic, social and political trends.

To be globally aware is to be *objective*. Objectivity is important in assessing opportunities, evaluating potential and responding to problems. Millions of dollars were lost by companies that blindly entered the Chinese market in the belief that there were untold opportunities, when, in reality, opportunities were in very select areas and generally for those with the resources to sustain a long-term commitment. Many were caught up in the euphoria of envisioning 1 billion consumers; they made uninformed and not very objective decisions.

To be globally aware is to have *tolerance and respect towards cultural differences*. Tolerance is understanding cultural differences, and accepting and working with others whose behaviour may be different from yours. No culture is right or wrong or better or worse. You do not have to accept the cultural ways of another but you must allow others to be different and equal. The fact that punctuality is less important in some cultures does not make them less productive, only different. The tolerant person understands the differences that may exist between cultures and uses that knowledge to relate effectively.

A globally aware person is *knowledgeable* about cultures, history, world market potentials and global economic and social trends. Knowledge of cultures is important in understanding behaviour in the marketplace or in the boardroom. Knowledge of history is important because the way people think and act is influenced by their history.

Over the next few decades there will be enormous changes in market potential in almost every region of the world. A globally aware person will continuously monitor the markets of the world. Finally, a globally aware person will keep abreast of social and economic trends because a country's prospects can change as social and economic trends shift direction or accelerate. The knowledgeable marketer will identify opportunity long before it becomes evident to others. It is our goal in this text to guide the reader towards acquiring a global awareness.

Going International 1.4

GLOBALISATION: GOOD OR BAD?

The book by Robert Gilpin, Emeritus Professor of Public and International Affairs at Princeton University, *The Challenge of Global Capitalism*, provides a cooler outlook on the results of globalisation and what can be done to improve the present system.

Professor Gilpin suggests that to view globalisation as all bad is ridiculous, as such a view ignores the massive increase in income and wealth that results from globalisation and means it is here to stay whether we like it or not, so our task now is to consider ways of maximising the gains from globalisation while minimising the losses. One of the challenges that should be addressed by policy-makers now is the weakening of the political elements that supported the open economy in the post-war era, and that were based on strong relations between the Western capitalist powers.

© Istockphoto.com/godrick

On the trading front, the greatest challenge is posed by the increased exposure of national economies to the forces of global competition. The result is increased pressure for protection and more trade disputes, both

▶

◀

of which threaten to reverse the gains reaped from trade liberalisation. On the monetary front, removal of restrictions on capital flows left many countries more vulnerable to sudden changes in the mood of investors and conditions on the world financial markets, as the financial crisis of 2007/08 amply demonstrated. Emergence of new trading techniques and greater availability of information means that a crisis occurring in one country is likely to spread quickly to others. The challenge for global policy-makers is to devise institutional forums for anticipating such crises, preventing them when possible and providing the countries that are the victims with assistance.

The rise of multinational corporations and the growing concentration of power in the hands of a comparatively small number of giant firms have left consumers and workers feeling overwhelmed by forces outside their control. Exposing firms to more competition and tougher national anti-trust laws combined with international agreements imposing strict codes of conduct on multinationals is likely to be the most effective way of ensuring protection for the interests of consumers and workers.

A danger also exists that the increasingly more pronounced regional groupings such as Europe, North America and Asia will become more closed and inward looking, distorting patterns of global trade and leading to more protectionism, thus damaging the smaller, weaker nations. The solution here would be to build up and strengthen global economic institutions in order to make them more effective in meeting the challenges posed by globalisation – a move completely opposite to the desires of the anti-globalisation protesters.

- Is government intervention in regenerating multinationals good or bad? Discuss.

Source: N. Grimwade, 'Riders of Capitalism's Storms', 19 January 2001, *http://www.timeshighereducation.co.uk/books/riders-of-capitalisms-storms/156647.article.*

A number of authors do accept that most people live and behave within their culture and milieu; there are, however, some values that characterise people as converging towards a relatively more globalised culture. The members of a global culture normally possess the following characteristics.[15]

Educated More and more education, particularly higher education, is converging, with universities and schools using the same textbooks and concepts. This is particularly true for business education.

Connected These people are using the most advanced communications, from mobile phones and the Internet to frequent travelling.

Pragmatic This new group is more concerned with getting things done as compared to sticking with their principles and old traditions.

Unintimidated by national boundaries and cultures National cultures or boundaries are not considered obstacles by these people. Instead they are quite keen to explore the world beyond their national boundaries.

Flexible and open These people demonstrate an ability to adapt to changes and unexpected circumstances. They may even seek these situations for gaining novel experiences or having new adventures.

Begin from a position of trust These people are able to maintain relationships as they often begin from a position of trust when starting new relationships. This makes them tolerant and more approving of others.

International marketing orientation

Most problems encountered by the foreign marketer result from the unfamiliar environment within which marketing programmes must be implemented. Success hinges, in part, on the ability to assess and adjust properly to the impact of new environments. In light of all the variables involved, with what should a text in international marketing be concerned? In our opinion, a study of foreign marketing environments and cultures, and their influences on the total marketing process is of primary concern and is the most effective approach to a meaningful presentation.

Consequently, the orientation of this text can best be described as an environmental and cultural approach to international strategic marketing. By no means is it intended to present principles of marketing; rather it is intended to demonstrate the unique problems of international marketing. It attempts to relate the foreign environment to the marketing process and to illustrate the many ways in which the environment can influence the marketing task. Although marketing principles are universally applicable, the environment and culture within which the marketer must implement marketing plans can change dramatically from country to country. It is with the difficulties created by different environments and cultural differences that this text is primarily concerned.

Further, the text is concerned with any company marketing in or into any other country or groups of countries, however slight the involvement or the method of involvement. Hence, this discussion of international marketing ranges from the marketing and business practices of small exporters, such as a Groningen-based company that generates more than 50 per cent of its $40,000 (€36,000) annual sales of fish-egg sorters in Canada, Germany and Australia, to the practices of global companies, such as Philips, British Airways, Nokia, ABB and IKEA, which generate more than 70 per cent of their annual profits from the sale of multiple products to multiple country-market segments all over the world.[16]

SUMMARY

The first section of *International Marketing* offers an overview of international marketing, and a discussion of the global business, political and legal environments confronting the marketer. International marketing is defined as the performance of business activities beyond national borders. The task of the international marketer is explained. Key obstacles to international marketing are not just foreign environments but also our own self-reference criteria (SRC) and ethnocentrism. This section deals exclusively with the uncontrollable elements of the environment and their assessment. The next section offers chapters on assessing international marketing opportunities. Then, management issues in developing global marketing strategies are discussed. In each chapter the impact of the environment and culture on the marketing process is illustrated. Space prohibits an encyclopaedic approach to all the issues; nevertheless, we have tried to present sufficient detail so readers appreciate the real need to make a thorough analysis whenever the challenge arises. The next chapter provides a framework for this task.

QUESTIONS

1 'The marketer's task is the same whether applied in Amsterdam, London or Kuala Lumpur.' Discuss.
2 How can the increased interest in international marketing on the part of European firms be explained?
3 Discuss the four phases of international marketing involvement.
4 Discuss the conditions that have led to the development of global markets.
5 Differentiate between a global company and a multinational company.
6 Differentiate among the three international marketing orientations.
7 Relate the three international marketing orientations to the EPRG schema.

8 Discuss the factors necessary to achieve global awareness.

9 What is meant by global markets? How does this influence the adaptation of products and marketing strategies?

10 Define and explain the following:
- controllable elements in the international marketer's task
- uncontrollable elements in the international marketer's task
- self-reference criterion (SRC)
- international marketing orientation
- global awareness.

FURTHER READING

- Theodore Levitt, 'The Globalization of Markets', *Harvard Business Review*, 1983, May–June, pp 92–102.
- Peter Buckley and Pervez Ghauri, 'Globalization, Economic Geography and Multinational Enterprises', *Journal of International Business Studies*, 2004, 35(2), pp 81–98.
- Esther Tippmann, Pamela Sharkey Scott and Vincent Mangematin, 'Problem Solving in MNCs: How Local and Global Solutions are (and are not) Created', *Journal of International Business Studies*, 2012, 43(8), pp 746–71.

NOTES

1 S. Tamer Cavusgil, Pervez Ghauri and Ayse Akcal, *Doing Business in Emerging Markets* (London: Sage, 2013).

2 Peter Buckley and Pervez Ghauri, 'Globalization, Economic Geography and International Business', *Journal of International Business Studies*, 2004, 35(2), 81–98.

3 S. Tamer Cavusgil, et al. (2013), and T. Clark and L.L. Mathur, 'Global Myopia: Globalisation Theory in International Business', *Journal of International Management*, 2003, 9, 361–72.

4 Nestlé: http://www.nestle.com, 2012.

5 Toyota: http://www.toyota.co.jp, 2012.

6 'Borderless Management: Companies Strive to Become Truly Stateless', *Business Week*, 23 May 1994, pp 24–26.

7 David A. Ricks, *Blunders in International Business* (Cambridge, MA: Blackwell Publishers, 1993), p 43.

8 For a report on research that examines the internationalisation of a firm, see Peter Buckley and Pervez Ghauri (eds), *The Internationalization of the Firm: A Reader*, 2nd edn (London: Dryden Press, 1999).

9 Yoram Wind, Susan P. Douglas and Howard V. Perlmutter, 'Guidelines for Developing International Marketing Strategy', *Journal of Marketing*, April 1973, pp 14–23.

10 Theodore Levitt, 'The Globalization of Markets', *Harvard Business Review*, May–June 1983, pp 92–102.

11 Levitt, 'Globalization', p 92.

12 Jan-Erik Vahlne, Inge Ivarsson and Jan Johanson, ' The Tortuous Road to Globalization for Volvo's Heavy Truck Business: Extending the Scope of the Uppsala Model,' *International Business Review,* 2011, 20(1), 1–14.

13 Punkaj Ghemawat, 'Semiglobalisation and International Business Strategy', *Journal of International Business Studies*, 2003, 34(1), 139–52.

14 *Webster's* unabridged dictionary defines tolerance as a fair and objective attitude towards those whose opinions, practices, race, religion, nationality, etc differ from one's own: freedom from bigotry. It is with this meaning that the authors are using tolerance.

15 Esther Tippmann, Pamela Sharkey Scott and Vincent Mangematin, 'Problem Solving in MNCs: How Local and Global Solutions are (and are not) Created,' *Journal of International* Business Studies, 2012, 43(8), 746–71.

16 Here, and in the rest of the book, the euro (€) to dollar ($) exchange rate is that of €1 = US$0.71 and US$1 = €1.40.

Chapter 2

The Dynamics of International Markets

Chapter Outline

Chapter Learning Objectives

What you should learn from Chapter 2

- The basis for the re-establishment of world trade following the Second World War
- The emergence of MNCs and their impact on international marketing
- The effects of protectionism on world trade
- The seven types of trade barrier
- The importance of GATT and the emergence of the World Trade Organization
- The role of the International Monetary Fund and the World Bank

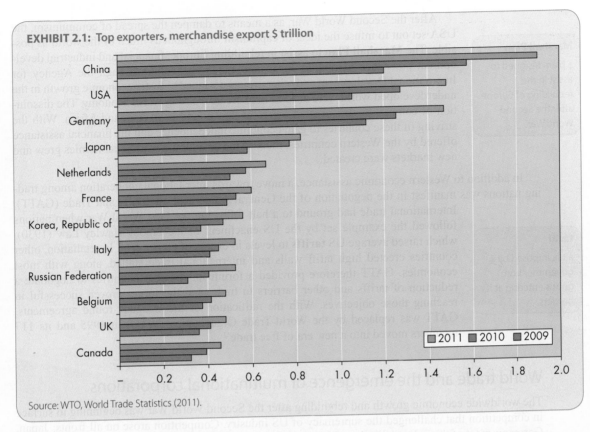

EXHIBIT 2.1: Top exporters, merchandise export $ trillion

Source: WTO, World Trade Statistics (2011).

Yesterday's competitive market battles were fought in Western Europe, Japan and the USA; tomorrow's competitive battles will extend to Russia, China, Asia, Latin America and Africa as these emerging markets become more actively involved in international business. More of the world's people, from the richest to the poorest, now participate in the world's wealth through global trade. The emerging global economy in which we live brings us into worldwide competition with significant advantages for both marketers and consumers, and for both the First World and the Third World.[1] Marketers benefit from new markets opening and smaller markets growing large enough to offer viable business opportunities. Consumers benefit by being able to select the lowest-priced and widest range of goods produced anywhere in the world. Bound together by satellite communications and global companies, consumers in every corner of the world are demanding an ever-expanding variety of goods.

As Exhibit 2.1 illustrates, world trade is an important economic activity. Because of this importance, the inclination is for countries to control international trade to their own advantage. As competition intensifies, the tendency towards protectionism gains momentum. If the benefits of the social, political and economic changes now taking place are to be fully realised, free trade must prevail throughout the global marketplace.

The twentieth century

At no time in modern economic history have countries been more economically interdependent, have greater opportunities for international trade existed or has the potential for increased demand existed than during the last decade of the twentieth century. In the preceding 90 years, world economic development has been erratic.

The first half of the century was marred by a major worldwide economic depression that occurred between the two world wars and that all but destroyed most of the industrialised world. The last half of the century, while free of a world war, was marred by struggles between countries espousing the **Marxist-socialist approach** and those following a capitalist approach to economic development. As a result of this ideological split, traditional trade patterns were disrupted.

> **Marxist-socialist approach**
>
> where a communist or socialist economic system is followed

After the Second World War, as a means to dampen the spread of communism, the USA set out to infuse the ideal of capitalism throughout as much of the world as possible. The **Marshall Plan** to assist in rebuilding Europe, financial and industrial development assistance to rebuild Japan and funds channelled through the Agency for International Development and other groups designed to foster economic growth in the underdeveloped world were used to help create a strong world economy. The dissolution of colonial powers created scores of new countries in Asia and Africa. With the striving of these countries to gain economic independence and the financial assistance offered by the Western countries, most of the developing world's economies grew and new markets were created.

> **Marshall Plan**
>
> a plan designed to assist in the rebuilding of Europe after the Second World War

In addition to Western economic assistance, a move towards international cooperation among trading nations was manifest in the negotiation of the General Agreement on Tariffs and Trade (GATT). International trade had ground to a halt following the First World War when nations followed the example set by the US enactment of the Smoot–Hawley Law (1930), which raised average US **tariffs** to levels in excess of 60 per cent. In retaliation, other countries erected high tariff walls and international trade stalled, along with most economies. GATT therefore provided a forum for member countries to negotiate a reduction of tariffs and other barriers to trade, and the forum proved successful in reaching those objectives. With the ratification of the Uruguay round agreements, GATT was replaced by the World Trade Organization (WTO) in 1995 and its 117 members moved into a new era of free trade.[2]

> **tariff**
>
> a tax imposed by a government on goods entering at its borders

World trade and the emergence of multinational corporations

The worldwide economic growth and rebuilding after the Second World War was beginning to surface in competition that challenged the supremacy of US industry. Competition arose on all fronts: Japan, Germany, most of the industrialised world and many developing countries were competing for demand in their own countries and were looking for world markets as well. Countries once classified as less developed were reclassified as newly industrialised countries (NICs). The NICs, such as South Korea, Taiwan, Singapore and Hong Kong, experienced rapid industrialisation in selected industries and became aggressive world competitors in steel, shipbuilding, consumer electronics, automobiles, light aircraft, shoes, textiles, clothing and so forth. In addition to the NICs, a number of developing countries have been reclassified as emerging markets, including China, India, Indonesia, Turkey, Thailand, Malaysia, Brazil, Mexico, Pakistan and Vietnam. A number of countries from the former Eastern Bloc, such as Russia, Poland, Hungary and the Czech Republic, are also included in the list. The four biggest emerging markets, with greatest growth potential, are now often referred to as **BRIC** (Brazil, Russia, India and China) **countries**. The volume of trade has grown much faster than the world GDP (see Exhibit 2.2).

> **BRIC countries**
>
> Brazil, Russia, India and China

In short, economic power and potential became more evenly distributed among countries than was the case when Servan-Schreiber warned Europe about US multinational domination.[3] Instead, the US position in world trade is now shared with multinational corporations (MNCs) from other countries. Exhibit 2.3 shows the dramatic change between 1963 and 2004. In 1963 the USA had 67 of the world's largest industrial corporations. By 2004 that number had dropped to 36, while Japan moved from having three of the largest to having 14, South Korea from zero to two and China from zero to three. The European Union (EU) has 40 companies among the 100 largest in the world.

Although European markets are quite diverse and constantly changing, Europe, and more so the EU, presents a highly interdependent group of economies in which consumer segments can show a great deal of similarity as well as dissimilarity. Careful thought and analysis is required to plan marketing strategies in Europe. Different industrial sectors, such as capital goods manufacturers, financial services, telecommunications, retail chains and branded goods, show different trends and structures. The restructuring of most industries at European level is posing new challenges for companies within as well as outside Europe.

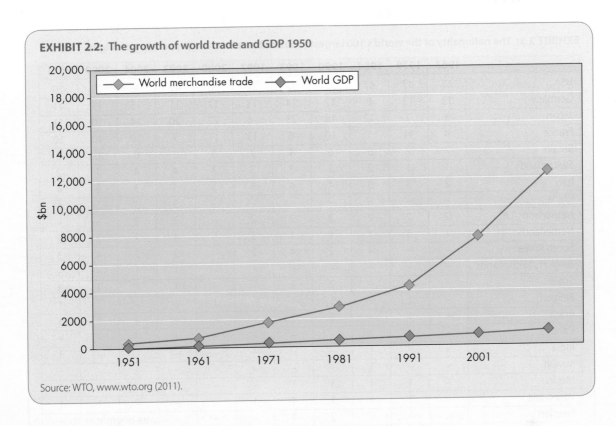

EXHIBIT 2.2: The growth of world trade and GDP 1950

Source: WTO, www.wto.org (2011).

The twenty-first century and beyond

Trends already under way in the last decade of the previous century are destined to change the patterns of trade for decades to come. The economies of the industrialised world have begun to mature and rates of growth will be more modest in the future than they have been for the past 20 years. Conversely, the economies of the developing world will grow at unprecedented rates. As a consequence, there will be a definite shift in economic power and influence away from industrialised countries – Japan, the USA and the EU – to countries in Asia, Latin America, Eastern Europe and Africa. According to recent calculations, a number of Asian countries will join Western economies as being among the world's largest. This is illustrated in Exhibit 2.4.

Demand in Asia for motor vehicles is expected to more than triple, from 16 to 58 million in less than a decade. China is a good example of what is happening in Asia that will make such a prediction reality. The Chinese government has announced a consolidation of its motor vehicle production into a few large manufacturing plants to produce an affordable compact sedan for the masses.[4] Production is expected to double to 3 million units over the next couple of years.[5] Tata, the Indian conglomerate, has introduced a people's car that costs around £2,000 in emerging markets.[6] Such increases in consumer demand are not limited to motor vehicles; the shopping lists of the hundreds of millions of households that will enter or approach the middle class over the next decade will include washing machines, televisions and all the other trappings of affluence.

This does not mean that markets in Europe, Japan and the USA will cease to be important; those economies will continue to produce large, lucrative markets and the companies established in those markets will benefit. It does mean that for a company to be a major player in the next century, now is the time to begin laying the groundwork.

How will these changes that are taking place in the global marketplace impact on international marketing? For one thing, the level and intensity of competition will change as companies focus on gaining entry into or maintaining their position in emerging markets, regional trade areas and the established markets in Europe, Japan and the USA.

EXHIBIT 2.3: The nationality of the world's 100 largest industrial corporations (by country of origin)

	1963	1979	1984	1990	1993	1997	2000	2003	2004	2009	2011
USA	67	47	47	33	32	32	36	42	36	29	29
Germany	13	13	8	12	14	13	12	11	15	15	11
Japan	3	7	12	18	23	26	22	20	14	10	11
France	4	11	5	10	6	13	11	7	10	10	10
Britain	7	7	5	6	4	2	5	3	6	6	8
Switzerland	1	1	2	3	3	3	3	4	4	1	2
Italy	2	3	3	4	4	3	3	3	3	5	4
China	–	–	–	–	–	–	2	3	3	5	6
Netherlands/UK	2	2	2	2	2	2	–	2	2	–	–
Netherlands	1	3	1	1	1	3	5	4	2	2	2
South Korea	–	–	4	2	4	2	–	2	2	4	3
Belgium/Netherlands	–	–	–	–	–	–	–	1	1	–	–
Spain	–	–	–	2	2	–	–	1	1	3	3
Belgium	–	1	1	1	–	–	1	–	–	1	1
Brazil	–	1	–	1	1	–	–	–	–	1	1
Canada	–	2	3	–	–	–	–	–	–	–	–
India	–	–	1	–	–	–	–	–	–	–	1
Kuwait	–	–	1	–	–	–	–	–	–	–	–
Mexico	–	1	1	1	1	–	–	–	–	1	1
Venezuela	–	1	1	1	1	1	–	–	–	1	1
Sweden	–	–	1	2	1	–	–	–	–	–	–
South Africa	–	–	1	1	–	–	–	–	–	–	–
Turkey	–	–	–	–	1	–	–	3	–	–	–
Luxemburg	–	–	–	–	–	–	–	–	–	1	1
Malaysia	–	–	–	–	–	–	–	–	–	1	1
Mexico	–	–	–	–	–	–	–	–	–	1	1
Norway	–	–	–	–	–	–	–	–	–	1	1
Russia	–	–	–	–	–	–	–	–	–	2	2

Sources: adapted from 'The Fortune 500 Archive', www.fortune.com (2004) and CNNMoney.com (2009, 2011).

EXHIBIT 2.4: The top 10 economies, GDP at PPP(Purchasing-Power Parity), 2007 and 2011, $ trillion

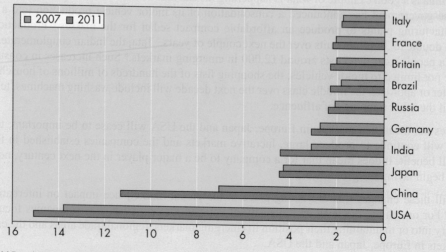

Sources: World Development Indicators database (World Bank, 2007) and CIA, *The World Factbook, 2011* https://www.cia.gov/library/publications/the-world-factbook/rankorder/2001rank.html.

Going International 2.1

A RISE IN PROTECTION WOULD WORSEN THE ALREADY GRIM OUTLOOK FOR WORLD TRADE

It is not just that China's export juggernaut has stalled. Caroline Freund, an economist at the bank [the World Bank], says that most countries for which data are available have reported double-digit declines in exports in the year to November. Exports from Chile, South Korea and Taiwan dropped by about 20 per cent. November's figures may have exaggerated the gloom because of a precautionary run-down of inventories and a shortage of trade finance, both of which may be short lived. But there is little dispute that a serious slowdown in trade is under way.

Overlaying the worsening economic outlook is the lingering threat of protectionism, which could drive trade volumes even lower next year. It is always tempting for politicians to throw up new trade barriers when jobs and wages are at risk, even if such a response, though individually appealing, is collectively futile.

Tariff increases may be the protectionist's barrier of choice, despite limits agreed by members of the WTO. This is because in the past decade many countries have unilaterally cut tariffs to well below those limits. They have plenty of room to raise them without breaking any rules.

If all countries were to raise tariffs to the maximum allowed, the average global rate of duty would be doubled, according to Antoine Bouet and David Laborde of the International Food Policy Research Institute in Washington, DC. The effect could shrink global trade by 7.7 per cent.

There are other, more subtle, means of protection available. Marc Busch, a professor of trade policy at Georgetown University in Washington, DC, worries that health and safety standards and technical barriers to trade, such as licensing and certification requirements, will be used aggressively to shield domestic industries as the global downturn drags on.

Five years on from the start of the financial crisis, the global economy is enduring a feeble convalescence. The euro zone's debt crisis became less acute in 2012, thanks largely to the promise by Mario Draghi, the European Central Bank's president, to do 'whatever it takes' to save the single currency. In such lifeless company America's economy looked almost vibrant [see adjacent graph].

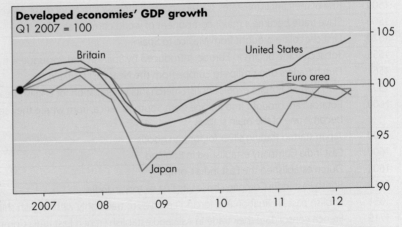

Developed economies' GDP growth
Q1 2007 = 100

Its housing market turned a corner in 2012 [see graph], and its unemployment rate fell steadily. But the recovery is still very weak. The numbers of long-term jobless stayed high; export markets drooped.

- Is protectionism on the rise? Is it good for national economies? Is it good for global economies?

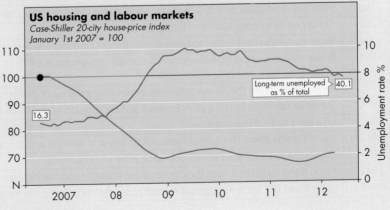

US housing and labour markets
Case-Shiller 20-city house-price index
January 1st 2007 = 100

Long-term unemployed as % of total   40.1

16.3

Unemployment rate %

Sources: 'Finance and Economics', *The Economist*, 20 December 2008; 'The long Road to Recovery', *The Economist* 22 December 2012.

Companies are looking for ways to become more efficient, improve productivity and expand their global reach while maintaining an ability to respond quickly to deliver a product the market demands. For example, large multinational companies, such as Matsushita of Japan and Samsung of Korea, continue to expand their global reach.[7] Nestlé is consolidating its dominance in global consumer markets by acquiring and vigorously marketing local-country major brands.[8] These are a few examples of changes that are sweeping multinational companies as they gear up for the future. Exhibit 2.5 shows the state of the world during the last millennium.

EXHIBIT 2.5: A review of the last millennium

1054	Italy and Egypt signed contract for commercial relationship
1081	Venice and Byzantium signed a commercial treaty
1100	China invents marine compass and becomes a trading power
1189	German merchants signed treaty with Novgorod in Russia
1206	Genghis Khan conquers much of Asia including northern China and promotes trade, reviving ancient silk road
1229	German merchants signed trade treaty with Prince of Smolensk in Russia
1358	German Hanseatic League officially formed by Hansa companies for trade and mutual protection. It eventually included 70 cities and lasted for 300 years
1392	England forbids foreigners from trading goods in the country
1404	Chinese forbid private trading in foreign countries, but foreigners could trade in China
1415	Chinese begin trading with Africa through government agencies. Some believe they also sailed to North America in 1421
1479	Venice agreed to pay tribute to the Ottoman Empire in exchange for trading rights; Treaty of Constantinople (now Istanbul)
1500	Rise of mercantilism. States started accumulating wealth to increase power
1500	Slave trade became a major component of world commerce
1520	First chocolate brought from Mexico to Spain
1555	Tobacco trade begins in Europe, introduced by Spanish and Portuguese traders
1561	Dutch traders bring tulips to Europe from the Near East (Turkey)
1597	Holy Roman Empire expels English merchants in retaliation for English treatment of Hanseatic League
1600	Potatoes are brought into Europe from South America, from where they spread all over the world and become one of the main staples
1600	Japan started trading silver for foreign goods
1600	East India Company established in England
1602	Dutch established the East India Company
1612	British East India Company builds its first factory in India
1651	English pass Navigation Act, forcing colonies to trade only with English ships
1719	French consolidate their trade in Asia and establish French East India Company
1750	Industrial Revolution begins with steam engines and increased hardship for workers
1760	China begins strict regulation of foreign trade
1764	Victories in India help Britain to take control of most Eastern trade and trade routes
1764	British started numbering houses to make postal delivery more efficient, opening doors for direct mail merchants
1776	Adam Smith wrote *The Wealth of Nations*, presenting a theory of modern capitalism and free trade
1804	Steam locomotives introduced in England and become dominant force in international trade
1807	USA bans trade with Europe
1817	David Ricardo wrote *Principles of Political Economy and Taxation* and proposed a modern trade theory
1821	Britain first to adopt gold standard to back value of its currency
1842	Hong Kong ceded to Britain, the city becomes financial and trading centre for Asia
1848	John Stuart Mill wrote *Principles of Political Economy*, completing the modern theory of trade

▶

1851	First International World Trade Fair held in London
1856	Declaration of Paris recognises principle of free movement of trade even in wartime
1857	Russia and France sign trade treaty
1860	Cobden Treaty to create free trade between Britain and France
1860	First passport issued in the USA to regulate foreign travel
1869	Suez Canal completed, cutting travel between Europe and Asia by 4,000 miles
1873	USA adopts the gold standard to back the value of dollar
1913	Assembly line introduced by Henry Ford, revolutionising manufacturing
1914	First World War begins
1919	First non-stop flight over Atlantic, paving the way for air cargo around the world
1920	League of Nations established to boost international cooperation and peace
1929	Great Depression starts with crash of US stock market
1939	Second World War begins
1943	First programmable computer (Colossus I) created in England
1944	Bretton Woods Conference creates basis for economic cooperation in 44 countries. IMF founded to help stabilise exchange rates
1947	General Agreement on Tariffs and Trade (GATT) signed by 23 countries
1957	European Economic Community (EEC) established by six European countries (a forerunner of EU)
1961	Berlin Wall erected to create Eastern and Western Europe
1971	USA abandons gold standard, allowing international exchange rate to base on perceived values instead of fixed value
1989	Berlin Wall falls, opening Eastern Europe for trade and commerce
1991	Soviet Union breaks and formally abandons communism
1991	Maastricht Treaty signed among 12 European countries to establish EU
1993	North American Free Trade Area (NAFTA) formed between the USA, Canada and Mexico
1995	World Trade Organization (WTO) to take over GATT, by 2004 more than 140 members accounting for more than 90 per cent of world trade
1999	Seattle round of WTO puts USA vs EU and causes protests against globalisation
2000	Euro as new currency for EU countries introduced in 12 countries
2004	Ten new countries, mainly from Eastern Europe, join EU, making it a union of 25 countries with almost 454 million people, the biggest market in the Western world
2008	Major financial and economic crisis in the world markets starting from the USA and the UK, perhaps as a consequence of wars in Afghanistan and Iraq
2009	The European sovereign-debt crisis sends Europe's economy into decline, having a major effect on European politics
2010	Many American auto brands have been phased out, such as Saturn by General Motors in 2010 and Mercury by Ford in 2010
2012–2013	Several countries in Europe, such as Cyprus, Greece, Ireland and Spain, in deep financial crisis

Balance of payments

When countries trade, financial transactions among businesses or consumers of different nations occur and money moves from one country to another. Products and services are exported and imported, monetary gifts are exchanged, investments are made, cash payments are made and cash receipts received, and vacation and foreign travel occurs. In short, over a period of time, there is a constant flow of money into and out of a country. The system of accounts that records a nation's international financial transactions is called its **balance of payments**.

balance of payments

system of accounts that records a nation's international financial transactions

A nation's balance-of-payments statement records all financial transactions between its residents and those of the rest of the world during a given period of time – usually one year. Because the balance-of-payments record is maintained on a double-entry bookkeeping system, it must always be in balance. As on an individual's financial statement, the assets and liabilities or the credits and debits must offset each other. And, like an individual's statement, the fact that they balance does not mean a nation is in particularly good or poor financial condition. A balance of payments is a record of condition, not a determinant of condition. Each of the nation's financial transactions with other countries is reflected in its balance of payments.

> **current account**
>
> record of all merchandise exports, imports and services plus unilateral transfers of funds
>
> **capital account**
>
> record of direct investment portfolio activities, and short-term capital movements to and from countries
>
> **reserves account**
>
> a record of exports and imports of gold, foreign exchange and liabilities to foreign banks

A nation's balance of payments presents an overall view of its international economic position and is an important economic measure used by treasuries, central banks and other government agencies whose responsibility it is to maintain external and internal economic stability. A balance of payments represents the difference between receipts from foreign countries on one side and payments to them on the other. On the plus side are export sales, money spent by foreign tourists, payments to the country for insurance, transportation and similar services, payments of dividends and interest on investments abroad, return on capital invested abroad, new foreign investments in the country and foreign government payments to the country.

A balance-of-payments statement includes three accounts: the **current account** – a record of all merchandise exports, imports and services plus unilateral transfers of funds; the **capital account** – a record of direct investment portfolio transactions, and short-term capital movements to and from countries; and the official **reserves account** – a record of exports and imports of gold, increases or decreases in foreign exchange, and increases or decreases in liabilities to foreign central banks. Of the three, the current account is of primary interest to international business.

Protectionism

International business must face the reality that this is a world of tariffs, quotas and non-tariff barriers designed to protect a country's markets from intrusion by foreign companies. Although the General Agreement on Tariffs and Trade (GATT) and the WTO have been effective in reducing tariffs, countries still resort to protectionist measures. Countries utilise legal barriers, exchange barriers and psychological barriers to restrain entry of unwanted goods. Businesses work together to establish private market barriers, while the market structure itself may provide formidable barriers to imported goods. The complex distribution system in Japan is a good example of a market structure creating a barrier to trade. However, as effective as it is in keeping some products out of the market, in a legal sense it cannot be viewed as a trade barrier.

Protection logic and illogic

Countless reasons are espoused by protectionists to maintain government restrictions on trade, but essentially all arguments can be classified as follows:

1 protection of an infant industry
2 protection of the home market
3 need to keep money at home
4 encouragement of capital accumulation
5 maintenance of the standard of living and real wages
6 conservation of natural resources
7 industrialisation of a low-wage nation
8 maintenance of employment and reduction of unemployment
9 national defence
10 increase of business size
11 retaliation and bargaining.

Economists in general recognise as valid only the arguments for infant industry, national defence and the industrialisation of developing countries. The resource conservation argument becomes increasingly valid in an era of environmental consciousness and worldwide shortages of raw materials and agricultural commodities.

Most protectionists argue the need for tariffs on one of the three premises recognised by economists whether or not they are relevant to their products. Proponents are also likely to call on the maintenance of employment argument because it has substantial political appeal. When arguing for protection, the basic economic advantages of international trade are ignored. The fact that the consumer ultimately bears the cost of tariffs and other protective measures is conveniently overlooked. Agriculture and textiles are good examples of protected industries in the USA and European countries, where not only are high tariffs imposed on imports but also the sectors are heavily subsidised, which cannot be justified by any of the three arguments. In 2008 these subsidies represented about 45 per cent of the European Commission's budget. Local prices are artificially held higher than world prices for no sound economic reason (see Exhibit 2.6)

EXHIBIT 2.6: The price of protectionism

Protected industry	Jobs saved	Total cost (in $m)	Annual cost per job saved ($)
Benzenoid chemicals	216	297	1,376,435
Luggage	226	290	1,285,078
Softwood lumber	605	632	1,044,271
Sugar	2,261	1,868	826,104
Polyethylene resins	298	242	812,928
Dairy products	2,378	1,630	685,323
Frozen concentrated orange juice	609	387	635,103
Ball bearings	146	88	603,368
Maritime services	4,411	2,522	571,668
Ceramic tiles	347	191	551,367
Machine tools	1,556	746	479,452
Ceramic articles	418	140	335,876
Women's handbags	773	204	263,535
Canned tuna	390	100	257,640
Glassware	1,477	366	247,889
Apparel and textiles	168,786	33,629	199,241
Peanuts	397	74	187,223
Rubber footwear	1,701	286	168,312
Women's non-athletic footwear	3,702	518	139,800
Costume jewellery	1,067	142	132,870
Total	191,764	44,352	

Sources: 2002 Annual Report – Federal Reserve Bank of Dallas; Oxelhiem and Ghauri (2003).

Going International 2.2

PROTECTIONISM WILL PROLONG THE ECONOMIC CRISIS

Are we already seeing the beginning of the kind of downward spiral in trade and cross-border investment that turned the 1930s into an economic and political catastrophe?

▶

◄

'Woolworth's closing down' © Ian Britton, freefotouk. CC BY 2.0 UK.

The extent of the integration of most of the world's economies means twenty-first-century protectionism takes many forms, and we are starting to see a number of them. The US House of Representatives attached 'Buy America' provisions to the government stimulus package. The British government has persuaded oil company Total to give jobs to British workers in order to end wildcat strikes over the employment of Italians. Malaysia's government has instructed its firms to lay off foreign nationals first. Brazil's government has edged up tariffs on manufactured goods. Some commentators in the UK have welcomed devaluation as a useful tool in the policy armoury.

It is all too easy to disguise protectionist measures and all too tempting to engage in them, given the political pressures from voters to safeguard their jobs and living standards. Many politicians continue to pay lip service to the importance of trade and open economies while advocating measures that will actually undermine the openness which is the only possible engine for restoring growth in the future.

I am not sure that the lessons of the 1930s have been absorbed by our political leaders. They have poured taxpayers' money into bank bail-outs, increased spending programs and encouraged central banks to slash interest rates and 'print money'. But there is no sign that they understand that all the nations of the world economy sink or swim together, and that history's verdict on their management of this crisis will depend on looking outward for our lifeboats.

As worries rise about an economic slowdown, major nations around the world are ramping up measures to protect their economies from trade threats.

Global Trade Alert, an independent monitoring group, says in a new report today that at least 110 new protectionist measures were implemented around the world since the Group of 20 advanced and developing economies met in France last November. Of those 110, 89 were by G-20 members, who meet again next week in Mexico.

Protectionist measures such as export restrictions and higher tariffs spiked after the 2008 financial crisis but didn't subside afterward. Since then, nations have been pursuing stealthier measures – 'murky protectionism' – to circumvent international trade rules, the group says.

The latest updated tally names the 27-member EU as the leading culprit since November 2008, with 302 discriminatory measures, followed by Russia and Argentina with about half that number each. China ranked at the top of a list of 'number of trading partners affected' with 193, or nearly all of them, followed by the EU at 187.

The G-20's promises to fight protectionism 'are a debacle,' said Simon Evenett, a professor of international trade at the University of St. Gallen in Switzerland who coordinates the tracking effort. 'The G-20 has shown just how little priority it gives to keep the world trading system open.'

- Is the present economic crisis leading towards protectionism? Are countries justified in protecting their economies? Discuss.

Sources: Editorials & Opinion, *Wall Street Journal*, 10 February 2009, p 13.

Trade barriers

To encourage the development of domestic industry and protect existing industry, governments may establish such barriers to trade as tariffs, quotas, boycotts, **monetary barriers**, non-tariff barriers and **market barriers**. Barriers are imposed against imports and against foreign businesses. While the inspiration for such barriers may be economic or political, they are encouraged by local industry. Whether or not the barriers are economically logical, the fact is that they exist.

Tariffs

A tariff, simply defined, is a tax imposed by a government on goods entering at its borders. Tariffs may be used as a revenue-generating tax or to discourage the importation of goods, or for both reasons. In general, tariffs:

- *increase*

  inflationary pressures

  special-interest privileges

  government control and political considerations in economic matters

  the number of tariffs (they beget other tariffs)

- *weaken*

  balance-of-payments positions

  supply-and-demand patterns

  international understanding (they can start trade wars)

- *restrict*

  manufacturers' supply sources

  choices available to consumers

  competition.

> **monetary barriers**
>
> putting monetary restrictions on trade, eg availability of foreign exchange for imports
>
> **market barriers**
>
> barriers to trade imposed in an attempt to promote domestic industry

---

Going International 2.3

THE NOBEL LAUREATE SPEAKS ON THE CRISIS IN THE ECONOMY AND IN ECONOMICS

Paul Krugman returned to the LSE on 8 June to give the annual Lionel Robbins memorial lectures. Mr Krugman, who gave the Robbins lectures 21 years ago, tried to answer two big questions in the course of his three talks. Why did economists not foresee calamity? And how will the world economy climb out of recession?

The immediate cause of the crisis, 'the mother of all global housing bubbles', was spotted by many economists. That house prices had risen too far was obvious, even if policymakers had seemed less sure. The surprise was that the bursting of the bubble would be so damaging. 'I had no idea it would end so badly,' said Mr Krugman.

One big blind spot was the financial system. The mistake was to think 'a bank had to look like something Jimmy Stewart could run', with rows of tellers taking deposits in a marble-fronted building. In fact, a bank is anything that uses short-term borrowing to finance long-term assets that are hard to sell at a push. The shadow banking system was as important to the economy as the ordinary kind, but was far more vulnerable. Its collapse was the modern re-run of the bank failures of the 1930s, said Mr Krugman.

The excess borrowing that did for shadow banks threatens consumers, too. They are scrambling to save more as house prices plunge. Their mortgage debts loom larger because of vanishing inflation. This urge to shore up wealth is self-defeating in aggregate, as it curbs spending and incomes. It also renders conventional monetary policy impotent, as the interest rate that prevents too much saving is below zero.

If zero interest rates cannot get consumers to spend, then governments must spend instead. That remedy comes from economics, so the discipline is not without merit. The trouble is, 'the analysis we're using is decades old'. It dates back to Keynes, one of the few economists whose reputation has been burnished by the crisis. Most

▶

work in macroeconomics in the past 30 years has been useless at best and harmful at worst, said Mr Krugman. As for the economy, the road back to health will be long and painful. The big lesson from past bubbles is that recovery is export-led, which is not helpful 'unless we can find another planet to export to'. Otherwise, recovery will have to wait for savings to be rebuilt, and that will not happen quickly. Higher inflation than before the crisis might help, he said.

- Do you agree with Krugman? Have economic theories been useful?

Source: *The Economist*, Finance and Economics, 13 June 2009, p 81.

In addition, tariffs are arbitrary, discriminatory and require constant administration and supervision. They are often used as reprisals against protectionist moves of trading partners. In March 2002 the US government imposed 30 per cent tariffs on a range of imported steel products. The tariff was imposed due to findings by the US International Trade Commission that an unexpected surge of imported steel had swamped US markets and damaged US steelmakers. The nine steel-producing countries complained to the WTO with success. The US government disagrees with the ruling but has not indicated whether it will comply with it. In case the USA does not comply with the ruling of the WTO, the countries whose steel imports have been reduced by the US tariffs are entitled to impose retaliatory tariffs equal to the amount of damage the illegal US tariffs caused to their industries.

Non-tariff barriers

Imports are restricted in a variety of ways other than tariffs. These non-tariff barriers include quality standards on imported products, sanitary and health standards, quotas, embargoes and **boycotts**. Exhibit 2.7 provides a list of non-tariff barriers.

Quotas

A quota is a specific unit or dollar limit applied to a particular type of good. There is a limit on imported television sets in the UK, and there are German quotas on Japanese ball bearings, Italian restrictions on Japanese cars and motorcycles, and US quotas on sugar, textiles and peanuts. **Quotas** put an absolute restriction on the quantity of a specific item that can be imported. Like tariffs, quotas tend to increase prices. In Europe, quotas on textiles are estimated to add 50 to 100 per cent to the wholesale price of clothing.

Voluntary export restraints

Similar to quotas are voluntary export restraints (**VERs**). Common in textiles, clothing, steel, agriculture and motor vehicles, the VER is an agreement between the importing country and the exporting country for a restriction on the volume of exports. Japan has a VER on vehicles to France, Italy and the USA; that is, Japan has agreed to export a fixed number of these annually. A VER is called 'voluntary' in that the exporting country sets the limits; however, it is generally imposed under the threat of stiffer quotas and tariffs being set by the importing country if a VER is not established.

Boycott

A government boycott is an absolute restriction against the purchase and importation of certain goods from other countries. A public boycott can be either formal or informal and may be government sponsored or sponsored by an industry. It is not unusual for the citizens of a country to boycott goods of other countries at the urging of their government or civic groups. Nestlé products were boycotted by a citizens' group that considered that the way Nestlé promoted baby milk formula to Third World mothers was misleading and harmful to their babies.[9]

boycotts

a coordinated refusal to buy or use products or services of a certain company/country

quotas

limitations on the quantity of certain goods imported during a specific period

VER

an agreement between the importing country and the exporting country for a restriction on the volume of exports

EXHIBIT 2.7: Types of non-tariff barrier

Specific limitations on trade

Quotas
Import licensing requirements
Proportion restrictions of foreign to domestic goods (local content requirements)
Minimum import price limits
Embargoes

Customs and administrative entry procedures

Valuation systems
Anti-dumping practices
Tariff classifications
Documentation requirements
Fees

Standards

Standards disparities
Intergovernmental acceptances of testing methods and standards
Packaging, labelling, marking standards

Governmental participation in trade

Government procurement policies
Export subsidies
Countervailing duties
Domestic assistance programmes

Charges on imports

Prior import deposit requirements
Administrative fees
Special supplementary duties
Import credit discriminations
Variable levies
Border taxes

Others

Voluntary export restraints
Orderly marketing agreements

Monetary barriers

A government can effectively regulate its international trade position by various forms of **exchange-control** restrictions. A government may enact such restrictions to preserve its balance-of-payments position or specifically for the advantage or encouragement of particular industries. There are three barriers to consider: blocked currency, differential exchange rates and government approval requirements for securing foreign exchange.

> **exchange control**
> when rate of exchange (eg for money) is controlled or fixed by the authority

---

Going International 2.4

ARE HIGHER TARIFFS JUSTIFIED?

According to the development group Oxfam, US tariffs on imports from developing countries are as much as 20 times higher than those charged on imports from other rich nations. The average rate of tariffs on imports

▶

◄

from Bangladesh in 2002 was 14 per cent, and duties amounted to $301m, although the country supplied only 0.1 per cent of total US imports. That value was only slightly smaller than the duties paid on imports from France, which bore an average tariff of 1 per cent and accounted for 2.4 per cent of US imports. Tariffs on imports from India were four times higher than on those from the UK.

The EU was also said to be discriminating heavily against developing countries. Its duties on imports from India were about four times higher than on those from the US, and more than eight times higher in the case of Sri Lanka and Uruguay. In 2008 Vietnam's footwear makers claimed that an EU plan to increase tariffs would cost them over $100m and harm their workers.

Oxfam said, 'The overall effect of discriminatory tariff systems is to lower demand for goods produced by the poor, and to exclude them from a stake in global prosperity . . . northern tariff structures are designed to undermine developing country exports in precisely those areas where they have a comparative advantage', such as textiles and clothing. Rich countries also charge escalating tariffs on products at each stage of processing: the EU tariff on yarn imports was less than 4 per cent, but 14 per cent on garments. The USA and EU charged no tariffs on imports of raw cocoa beans, but as much as 14 per cent on items such as paste and chocolate. As a result, developing countries produced more than 90 per cent of all cocoa beans, but less than 5 per cent of world chocolate output. Also developing countries are competing with each other. For example, Chinese manufactures are competing hard against Brazilian clothing and footwear products. Chinese products are usually a lot cheaper. Because of this trend, Brazilian manufacturers suffered from the Chinese ability to enter foreign markets, both in terms of their competitiveness in export markets as well as their position in Brazil. Brazilian associations and unions pressured the government to take action to protect their products and some legal measures were achieved.

- Do you think developed countries are justified in putting high tariffs on technology products? Discuss.

Sources: adapted from Guy de Janquières, 'Oxfam Report: US and EU Tariffs Higher for Third World', *Financial Times*, 2 September 2003, p 13; *EU Business*, 17 June 2008.

---

blocked currency

cuts off all importing or all importing above a certain level; accomplished by refusing to allow importers to exchange national currency for the seller's currency

differential exchange rate

requires the importer to pay varying amounts of domestic currency for foreign exchange with which to purchase products

exchange permits

give permission to exchange money

Blocked currency is used as a political weapon or as a response to difficult balance-of-payments situations. In effect, blockage cuts off all importing or all importing above a certain level. Blockage is accomplished by refusing to allow importers to exchange national currency for the seller's currency.

The **differential exchange rate** encourages the importation of goods the government deems desirable, and discourages importation of goods the government does not want. The essential mechanism requires the importer to pay varying amounts of domestic currency for foreign exchange with which to purchase products in different categories. For example, the exchange rate for a desirable category of goods might be one unit of domestic money for one unit of a specific foreign currency. For a less desirable product, the rate might be two domestic currency units for one foreign unit. For an undesirable product, the rate might be three domestic units for one foreign unit.

Government approval to secure foreign exchange is often used by countries experiencing severe shortages of foreign exchange. At one time or another, most Latin American and Eastern European, and some Asian countries have required all foreign exchange transactions to be approved by a central ministry or bank. Thus, importers who want to buy a foreign good must apply for an **exchange permit**: that is, permission to exchange an amount of local currency for foreign currency.

Standards

Non-tariff barriers of this category include standards to protect health, safety and product quality. The standards are sometimes used in an unduly stringent or discriminating way to restrict trade, but the sheer volume of regulations in this category is a problem in itself. For example, fruit content regulations for jam vary so much from country to country that one agricultural specialist says, 'A jam exporter needs a computer to avoid one or another country's regulations.'

The USA and EU require some products (motor vehicles in particular) to contain a percentage of 'local content' in order to gain admission to their markets. The North American Free Trade Agreement (NAFTA) stipulates that all vehicles coming from member countries must have at least 62.5 per cent North American content to deter foreign manufacturers from using one member nation as the back door to another.[10]

Going International 2.5

A BRIEF HISTORY OF PROTECTIONISM

Protectionism has an illustrious history. Founding fathers Alexander Hamilton and George Washington used a tariff on foreign imports to nurture US industries. Britain, too, favoured high tariffs during its early economic development, and France under Napoleon banned almost all manufactured imports – a regime which stayed in force until the mid-nineteenth century.

In Britain the controversial Corn Laws, tariffs on imported grain, imposed in 1815, looked after British land-owners at the expense of the poor, who saw the price of bread increase rapidly. After a militant campaign by the Manchester-based Anti-Corn Law league, Prime Minister Robert Peel eventually accepted that the tariffs had to be repealed – and split the Conservative Party down the middle. The 'Peelites' – the most notable of whom was William Gladstone, went on to form one wing of the Liberal Party.

Protectionism reared its head on the global stage after the Wall Street Crash of 1929, when US President Herbert Hoover used the notorious 'Smoot–Hawley' tariff to ramp up the cost of agricultural imports – later extending the tariffs to many other areas, and sparking what became known as the beggar-thy-neighbour policies which caused global trade to decline by two-thirds in just five years, and are widely seen as having exacerbated the Great Depression.

The 1930s proved to be the high watermark of protectionism, and the prevailing wisdom since then has generally been that free trade is a win–win proposition.

When Japan's prime minister announced on 15 March 2013 that he would lead his country into free-trade negotiations with 11 countries, including America, to forge the so-called Trans-Pacific Partnership (TPP), he deployed two tools to make his case. One was rhetorical, the other subliminal.

- Is free trade a win–win proposition? Is free trade working?

Sources: *Guardian*, 5 March 2006, p 4; 'Free Trade Across the Atlantic: Come On, TTIP, *The Economist*, 16 February 2013; 'Japan and Free Trade: Better Late than Never', *The Economist*, 23 March 2013.

Easing trade restrictions

As the global marketplace evolves, trading countries have focused attention on ways of eliminating tariffs, quotas and other barriers to trade. Two ongoing activities to make international trade easier are: (1) the WTO; and (2) the International Monetary Fund (IMF).

General Agreement on Tariffs and Trade (GATT)

Historically, trade treaties were negotiated on a bilateral (between two nations) basis, with little attention given to relationships with other countries. Further, there was a tendency to raise barriers rather than extend markets and restore world trade. In total, 23 countries signed the General Agreement on Tariffs and Trade (GATT) shortly after the Second World War. Although not all countries participated, this agreement paved the way for the first effective worldwide tariff agreement. The original agreement provided a process to reduce tariffs and created an agency to serve as watchdog over world trade. GATT's agency director and staff offered countries a forum for negotiating trade and related issues.

Member countries (117 in 1994) sought to resolve their trade disputes bilaterally; if that failed, special GATT panels were set up to recommend action. The panels were only advisory and had no enforcement powers.

While the Tokyo round addressed **non-tariff barriers**, there were some areas not covered that continued to impede free trade. In addition to market access, there were issues of trade in services, agriculture and textiles, intellectual property rights and investment and capital flows. Based on these concerns, the eighth set of negotiations (the Uruguay round) was begun in 1986 at a GATT trade ministers' meeting in Punta del Este, Uruguay, and finally concluded in 1994. By 1995, 80 GATT members including the USA, the EU (and its member states), Japan, a number of Asian countries and Canada had accepted the agreement.[11]

The final outcome went well beyond the initial Uruguay-round goal of a one-third reduction in tariffs. Instead, virtually all tariffs in 10 vital industrial sectors[12] with key trading partners were eliminated.[13] This resulted in deep cuts (ranging from 50 to 100 per cent) on electronic items and scientific equipment, and the harmonisation of tariffs in the chemical sector at very low rates (5.5–0 per cent).[14]

Equally significant were the results of negotiations in the investment sector. **Trade-Related Investment Measures (TRIMs)** established the basic principle that investment restrictions can be major trade barriers and were therefore included, for the first time, under GATT procedures.[15] An initial set of prohibited practices included local content requirements specifying that some amount of the value of the investor's production must be purchased from local sources or produced locally; trade balancing requirements specifying that an investor must export an amount equivalent to some proportion of imports or condition the amount of imports permitted on export levels; and foreign exchange balancing requirements limiting the importation of products used in local production by restricting its access to foreign exchange to an amount related to its exchange inflow.

> **non-tariff barriers**
>
> hurdles or restrictions on trade that are other than tariff rates, eg quotas
>
> **Trade-Related Investment Measures (TRIMS)**
>
> established the basic principle that investment restrictions can be major trade barriers
>
> **intellectual property**
>
> a non-material asset that can be bought, sold, licensed, exchanged or gradually given away like any other form of property

Going International 2.6

ROUND AND ROUND: A GATT/WTO CHRONOLOGY

1947	Birth of GATT, signed by 23 countries on 30 October at the Palais des Nations in Geneva
1948	GATT comes into force. First meeting of its members in Havana, Cuba
1949	Second round of talks in Annecy, France. Some 5,000 tariff cuts agreed; 10 new countries admitted
1950–51	Third round in Torquay, England. Members exchange 8,700 trade concessions and welcome four new countries
1956	Fourth round in Geneva. Tariff cuts worth $1.3 trillion (€1.17 trillion) at today's prices
1960–62	The Dillon round, named after US Under-Secretary of State Douglas Dillon, who proposed the talks. A further 4,400 tariff cuts
1964–67	The Kennedy round. Many industrial tariffs halved. Signed by 50 countries. Code on dumping agreed to separately
1973–79	The Tokyo round, involving 99 countries. First serious discussion of non-tariff trade barriers, such as subsidies and licensing requirements. Average tariff on manufactured goods in the nine biggest markets cut from 7 to 4.7 per cent
1986–93	The Uruguay round. Further cuts in industrial tariffs, export subsidies, licensing and customs valuation. First agreements on trade in services and **intellectual property**
1995	Formation of WTO with power to settle disputes between members
1997	Agreements concluded on telecommunication services, information technology and financial services

▶

1998	The WTO has 132 members. More than 30 others are waiting to join
2001	The Doha agenda. A new round of negotiations, which includes tariffs, agriculture, services and anti-dumping. China becomes the 143rd member of the WTO
2004	The WTO has 148 members
2007	A deadlock in Doha found, as developing countries demand that the USA and EU should cut their state subsidies to agricultural sector
2008	After eight years of negotiating, an agreement on the Doha Development Agenda is expected in 2009. The 153 members have to make a decision by consensus
2009	WTO says that global trade flows are set to shrink by 9 per cent during 2009. Hardest hit will be developed nations, where trade is set to fall by 10 per cent. Poorer countries will see exports fall by 2–3 per cent
2010	The WTO rules that the EU paid illegal subsidies to aircraft giant Airbus after the USA lodged a complaint in a long-running dispute between the EU and USA. G-20 meeting of major economic powers in Seoul sees 2011 'window of opportunity' for the conclusion of the WTO Doha round. The EU expresses support for Russia's bid to join the WTO after Moscow agreed to cut timber export tariffs and rail freight fees. Russia is the only major economy outside the WTO. China says it plans to appeal against a WTO ruling that the USA was entitled to impose extra duties on Chinese tyre imports
2011	Former WTO Director-General Peter Sutherland joins British Prime Minister David Cameron and German Chancellor Angela Merkel in demanding the conclusion of the Doha talks by the end of 2011. Both the USA and the EU claim victory after the WTO partly overturned an earlier ruling that Airbus received billions of euros in illegal subsidies. WTO upholds complaints by the USA, EU and Mexico that China had broken global free-trade rules by imposing quotas and taxes on exports of certain key materials, including minerals like bauxite, magnesium and zinc. China complains. WTO rules that a tax levied in the Philippines on imports of alcohol breaks global rules on free trade on the grounds that it grants domestic producers who use local cane and palm sugar an unfair advantage. The USA has previously urged the Philippines to open its market to foreign alcoholic drinks. Russia finally joins the WTO after 18 years negotiating its membership. Switzerland brokered a deal to persuade Georgia to lift its veto, which it had imposed after the 2008 Russo–Georgian war
2012	The WTO rejects China's appeal against a ruling that it broke free-trade rules by imposing quotas and taxes on exports of key materials

Sources: WTO, www.wto.org and BBC News, 'Timeline: World Trade Organization', 15 February 2012, http://news.bbc.co.uk/2/hi/europe/country_profiles/2430089.stm.

Another objective of the EU for the Uruguay round was achieved by an agreement on **Trade-Related Aspects of Intellectual Property Rights (TRIPs)**. The TRIPs agreement establishes substantially higher standards of protection for a full range of intellectual property rights (patents, copyrights, trademarks, trade secrets, industrial designs and semiconductor chip mask works) than are embodied in current international agreements, and it provides for the effective enforcement of those standards both internally and at the border.[16]

World Trade Organization (WTO)

The WTO is an institution, not an agreement as was GATT. It sets the rules governing trade between its members, provides a panel of experts to hear and rule on trade disputes between members, and, unlike GATT, issues binding decisions. It requires, for the first time, the full participation of all members in all aspects of the current GATT and the Uruguay round agreements, and, through its enhanced stature and scope, provides a permanent, comprehensive forum to address the trade issues of the twenty-first-century global market.

Former American president Bush and his trade representative have brought a complaint about Airbus' subsidies to the WTO. The European trade commissioner is bent

Trade-Related Aspects Of Intellectual Property Rights (TRIPs) establishes substantially higher standards of protection for a full range of intellectual property rights than are embodied in current international agreements, and provides for the effective enforcement of those standards

on confrontation, his office announced. It is high time to put an end to massive illegal US subsidies to Boeing. Boeing claims Airbus received launch aid to market its new plane, the A380. Airbus claims that Boeing gets tax breaks from the US government and support in the shape of government orders. Moreover, Washington State gave it billions of dollars to develop its new plane, the 7E7, in the state. There are allegations and counter-allegations.

Going International 2.7

THE DOHA DILEMMA – DOES FREER FARM TRADE HELP POOR PEOPLE?

For years reformers have advocated freer trade on the grounds that market distortions, particularly the rich world's subsidies, depress prices, and hurt rural areas in poor countries, where three-quarters of the world's indigents live. The Doha round of trade talks is dubbed the 'development round' in large part because of its focus on farms. But now high food prices are being blamed for hurting the poor (the topic of a big United Nations summit in Rome starting on 3 June).

The links between trade, food prices and poverty reduction are more subtle. Different types of reform have diverse effects on prices. When countries cut their tariffs on farm goods, their consumers pay lower prices. In contrast, when farm subsidies are slashed, world food prices rise. The lavishness of farm subsidies means that the net effect of fully freeing trade would be to raise prices, by an average of 5.5 per cent for primary farm products and 1.3 per cent for processed goods, according to the World Bank.

The World Bank has often argued that the balance of all these factors is likely to be positive. Although freer farm trade – and higher prices – may raise poverty rates in some countries, it will reduce them in more. One much-cited piece of evidence is a study by Thomas Hertel, Roman Keeney, Maros Ivanic and Alan Winters. This analysis simulated the effect of getting rid of all subsidies and barriers on global prices and trade volumes. It then mapped these results on to detailed household statistics in 15 countries, which between them covered 1 billion people. Fully free trade in farm goods would reduce poverty in 13 countries while raising it in two.

A question of numbers

But lately the bank seems to be taking a different line. Robert Zoellick, the bank's president, claims that the food-price crisis will throw 100 million people below the poverty line, undoing seven years of progress. His figure comes from extrapolating the results of a different study by Mr Ivanic and Will Martin, another World Bank economist. This study analyses the effects of more expensive staple foods on poverty by examining household surveys in nine countries. In seven cases, higher food prices meant more poverty. (Dani Rodrik, a blogging Harvard economist, was one of the first to highlight the tension between these studies.)

- Are the USA and EU justified in subsidising their agricultural sector so heavily?

Source: *The Economist*, 31 May 2008, p 98.

---

customs union

creation of a common external tariff that applies for non-members, the establishment of a common trade policy and the elimination of rules

The membership of GATT/WTO rose from 92 in 1986 to 153 in 2008 (see Exhibit 2.8). World trade has also been booming: it grew by 8 per cent in 1995, four times the rate of growth of world GDP. Foreign direct investment (FDI), another measure of international economy integration, also soared: in 1995 cross-border investment flows rose by 40 per cent. Finally, the spread of regional trading agreements, from the EU and NAFTA to APEC, is gaining ground. Almost every member of the WTO is also a member of such a group. According to WTO records, there have been 76 free trade areas or **customs unions** set up since 1948. Of these, more than 50 per cent have come in the 1990s.[17]

All member countries have equal representation in the WTO's ministerial conference, which meets at least every two years to vote for a director-general who then appoints other officials. Trade disputes are heard by a panel of experts selected by the WTO from a list

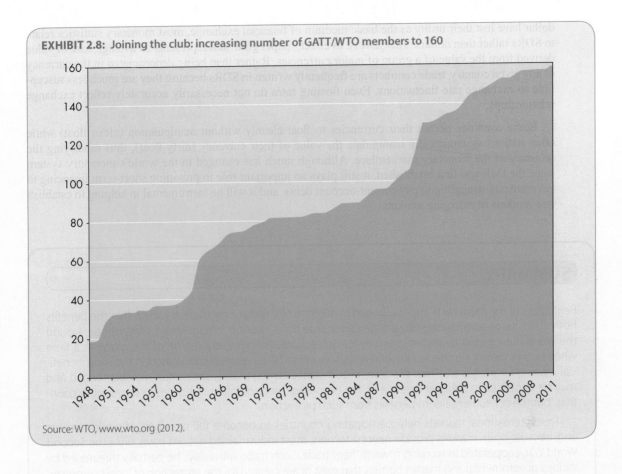

EXHIBIT 2.8: Joining the club: increasing number of GATT/WTO members to 160

Source: WTO, www.wto.org (2012).

of trade experts provided by member countries. The panel hears both sides and issues a decision; the winning side is authorised to retaliate with **trade sanctions** if the losing country does not change its practices. While the WTO has no actual means of enforcement, international pressure to comply with WTO decisions from other member countries is expected to force compliance.

The WTO ensures that member countries agree to the obligations of all the agreements, not just those they like. For the first time, member countries, including developing countries (the fastest-growing markets of the world), will undertake obligations to open their markets and to be bound by the rules of the multilateral trading system. As the number of members is increasing, the trade disputes among countries and regions is also increasing.

International Monetary Fund (IMF)

Inadequate monetary reserves and unstable currencies are particularly vexing problems in world trade. So long as these conditions exist, world markets cannot develop and function as effectively as they should. To overcome these particular market barriers, which plagued international trading before the Second World War, the **International Monetary Fund (IMF)** was formed. Among its objectives were the stabilisation of foreign exchange rates and the establishment of freely convertible currencies. Later, the European Payments Union was formed to facilitate multinational payments. While the IMF has some severe critics, most agree that it has performed a valuable service and at least partially achieved many of its objectives.

To cope with universally floating exchange rates, the IMF developed **special drawing rights (SDRs)**, one of its more useful inventions. Because both gold and the US

---

trade sanctions

stringent penalties imposed on a country by means of import tariffs or other trade barriers

International Monetary Fund (IMF)

formed to overcome market barriers such as inadequate monetary reserves and unstable currency

special drawing rights (SDRs)

developed by the IMF to overcome universally floating exchange rates

dollar have lost their utility as the basic medium of financial exchange, most monetary statistics relate to SDRs rather than dollars. The SDR is, in effect, 'paper gold' and represents an average base of value derived from the value of a group of major currencies. Rather than being denominated in the currency of any given country, trade contracts are frequently written in SDRs because they are much less susceptible to exchange rate fluctuations. Even floating rates do not necessarily accurately reflect exchange relationships.

Some countries permit their currencies to float cleanly without manipulation (clean float) while other nations systematically manipulate the value of their currency (dirty float), thus modifying the accuracy of the monetary marketplace. Although much has changed in the world's monetary system since the IMF was first established, it still plays an important role in providing short-term financing to governments struggling to pay current-account debts, and it will be instrumental in helping to establish free markets in emerging markets.

SUMMARY

Regardless of the theoretical approach used in defence of international trade, it is clear that the benefits from absolute or comparative advantage can accrue to any country. Heightened competition around the world has created increased pressure for protectionism from every region of the globe at a time when open markets are needed if world resources are to be developed and utilised in the most beneficial manner for all. It is true that there are circumstances when market protection may be needed and may be beneficial to national defence or the encouragement of infant industries in developing countries, but the consumer seldom benefits from such protection.

Free international markets help participating countries to become full members of world markets and, because open markets provide new customers, most industrialised nations have, since the Second World War, cooperated in working towards freer trade. Such trade will always be partially threatened by various governmental and market barriers that exist or are created for the protection of local businesses. However, the trend has been towards freer trade. The changing economic and political realities are producing unique business structures that continue to protect certain major industries. The emergence of the WTO has played a positive role in easing international trade among different countries and regions. The WTO works on open global markets with controlled and equitable reduction of trade barriers.

QUESTIONS

1 Is protectionism good or bad for world trade?
2 Differentiate between the current account, balance of trade and balance of payments.
3 'Theoretically, the market is an automatic, competitive, self-regulating mechanism that provides for the maximum consumer welfare and that best regulates the use of the factors of production.' Explain.
4 Why does the balance of payments always balance even though the balance of trade does not?
5 Enumerate the ways in which a country can overcome an unfavourable balance of trade.
6 France exports about 18 per cent of its gross domestic product, while neighbouring Belgium exports 46 per cent. What areas of economic policy are likely to be affected by such variations in exports?
7 Does widespread unemployment change the economic logic of protectionism?

8 Discuss the evolution of world trade that has led to the formation of the WTO.

9 What are the major differences between GATT and the WTO?

10 Why do countries use trade barriers? What types of trade barrier are used in what countries?

FURTHER READING

- A.K. Bhattacharya and D.C. Michael, 'How Local Companies Keep Multinationals at Bay', *Harvard Business Review*, 2011, pp 65–9.
- Gary Hamel and C.K. Prahalad, 'Do you Really Have a Global Strategy?', *Harvard Business Review*, 1985, 63(4), pp 139–48.
- Brigitte Lévy, 'The Interface between Globalization, Trade and Development: Theoretical Issues for International Business Studies', *International Business Review*, 2007, 16(5), 594–612.

NOTES

1 Paul Krugman, 'Does Third World Growth Hurt First World Prosperity?', *Harvard Business Review*, July 1994, pp 113–21.

2 Michael Hunt, 'Free Trade, Free World: The Advent of GATT', *Business History Review*, 2000, 74(2), 350–52.

3 J.J. Servan-Schreiber, *The American Challenge* (New York: Athenaeum, 1968).

4 'Behind the Mask: A Survey of Business in China', *The Economist*, www.economist.com/surveys, September 2004.

5 James Kynge, 'Nissan may Sue Chinese Rivals over Design', *Financial Times*, 28 November 2003, p 21.

6 'Corporate India Rushes to Defence of Tata', *Financial Times*, 30 August 2008, p 9.

7 Charles Hill, *International Business: Competing in the Global Business Today* (New York: McGraw-Hill, 2011).

8 N. Gupta, 'Globalization Does Lead to Change in Consumer Behavior: An Empirical Evidence of the Impact of Globalization on Changing Materialistic Values in Indian Consumers and its After Effects', *Asia Pacific Journal of Marketing and Logistics,* 2011, 23(3), 251–69.

9 For a comprehensive review, see Thomas V. Greer, 'International Infant Formula Marketing: The Debate Continues', *Advances in International Marketing*, 1990, 4, 207–25.

10 Anne M. Driscoll, 'Embracing Change, Enhancing Competitiveness: NAFTA's Key Provisions', *Business America*, 18 October 1993, pp 14–25.

11 Jim Sanford, 'World Trade Organization Opens Global Markets, Protects US Rights', *Business America*, January 1995, p 4.

12 Construction, agriculture, medical equipment, steel, beer, brown distilled spirits, pharmaceuticals, paper, pulp and printed matter, furniture and toys.

13 EU, Japan, Austria, Switzerland, Sweden, Finland, Norway, New Zealand, Korea, Hong Kong and Singapore.

14 K.C. Hagel, *International Management* (Munich: Grin Verlag, 2010).

15 For a complete review of the Uruguay round of GATT, see Louis J. Murphy, 'Successful Uruguay Round Launches Revitalized World Trading System', *Business America*, January 1994, pp 4–27; and George Pitcher, 'Trade War Looms as West Faces Third World Uprising', *Marketing Week*, 3 April 2003, p 29.

16 P.M. Rao and P.N. Ghauri, 'Intellectual Property, Multinational Enterprises and the Developing World', paper presented at the Academy of International Business (AIB) Annual Conference, in Stockholm, Sweden, July 2004.

17 'All Free Traders Now?', *The Economist*, 7 December 1996, pp 23–25.

PART 2

The Impact of Culture and Political Systems on International Marketing

Chapter 3

Geography and History: The Foundations of Cultural Understanding

Chapter Learning Objectives

What you should learn from Chapter 3

- How geography and history influence the understanding of international markets
- How effects of topography and climate impact on products, population centres, transportation and international trade
- How to evaluate the importance of non-renewable resources for international trade and marketing
- The effects on the world economy of population increases and shifts, and of the level of employment
- The importance and impact of the history of each culture in understanding its response to international marketing

Knowledge of a country's geography and history is essential if a marketer is to interpret a society's behaviour and fundamental attitudes. Culture can be defined as a society's programme for survival, the accepted basis for responding to external and internal events. Without understanding the geographical characteristics to which a culture has had to adapt and to which it must continuously respond, it cannot be completely understood. Nor can one fully appreciate the fundamental attitudes or behaviour of a society without knowledge of the historical events that have shaped its cultural evolution.[1]

Geography and international markets

> **Geography**
>
> the study of the earth's surface, climate, continents, countries, peoples, industries and resources

Geography, the study of the earth's surface, climate, continents, countries, peoples, industries and resources, is an element of the uncontrollable environment that confronts every marketer but that receives inadequate attention. There is a tendency to study climate, topography and available resources as isolated entities rather than as important causal agents in the marketing environment. The physical character of a nation is perhaps the principal and broadest determinant of both the characteristics of a society and the means by which that society undertakes to supply its needs.

The purpose of this section is to provide a greater awareness of the world, its complexities and its diversities; an awareness that can mean the difference between success and failure in marketing ventures. Climate and topography are examined as facets of the broader and more important elements of geography. A brief look at the earth's resources and population – the building blocks of world markets – and world trade routes completes the presentation on geography and global markets.

Climate and topography

As elements of geography, the physical terrain and climate of a country are important environmental considerations when appraising a market. The effect of these geographical features on marketing ranges from the obvious influences on product adaptation to more profound influences on the development of marketing systems.

Altitude, humidity and temperature extremes are climatic features that affect the uses and functions of products and equipment. Products that perform well in temperate zones may deteriorate rapidly or require special cooling or lubrication to function adequately in tropical zones. Manufacturers have found that construction equipment used in northern Europe requires extensive modification to cope with the intense heat and dust of the Sahara Desert. Within even a single national market, climate can be sufficiently diverse to require major adjustments. In Ghana, a product adaptable to the entire market must operate effectively in extreme desert heat and low humidity and in tropical rainforests with consistently high humidity.

South America represents an extreme but well-defined example of the importance of geography in marketing considerations. The economic and social systems there can be explained, in part, in terms of the geographical characteristics of the area. It is a continent 7,242 km (4,500 miles) long and 4,800 km (3,000 miles) wide at its broadest point. Two-thirds of it is comparable to Africa in its climate, 48 per cent of its total area is made up of forest and jungle, and only 5 per cent is arable. Mountain ranges cover South America's west coast for 7,242 km (4,500 miles), with an average height of 4,000 m (13,000 ft) and a width of 480–650 km (300–400 miles). This is a natural, formidable barrier that has precluded the establishment of commercial routes between the Pacific and Atlantic coasts.

Once the Andes are surmounted, the Amazon basin of 2.5m square km (2m square miles) lies ahead. It is the world's greatest rainforest, almost uninhabitable and impenetrable. Through it runs the Amazon, the world's second-longest river, which, with its tributaries, has almost 65,000 km (40,000 miles) of navigable water. On the east coast is another mountain range covering almost the entire coast of Brazil, with an average height of 1,200 m (4,000 ft).

There are many other regions of the world that also have extreme topographic and climatic variations. China, the former Soviet Union, India, Pakistan and Canada each have formidable physical and/or climatic conditions within their trading regions.

Rolls-Royce found that fully armour-plated cars from England require extensive bodywork and renovations after a short time in Canada. It was not the cold that damaged the cars but the salted sand spread to keep the streets passable throughout the four or five months of virtually continuous snow. The bumpers and side panels corroded and rusted and the oil system leaked. This problem illustrates the harshness of a climate and why it needs to be considered in all facets of product development.

The effect of natural barriers on market development is also important. Because of the ease of distribution, coastal cities or cities situated on navigable waterways are more likely to be trading centres than are landlocked cities. Cities not near natural physical transportation routes are generally isolated from one another, even within the same country. Consequently, natural barriers rather than actual distance may dictate distribution points.

In discussing distribution in Africa, one marketer pointed out that a shipment from Mombassa on the Kenya east coast to Freetown on the bulge of West Africa could require more time than a shipment from New York or London to Kenya over established freight routes.

Road conditions in Ecuador are such that it is almost impossible to drive a car from the port of Guayaquil to the capital of Quito only 320 km (200 miles) away. Contrast this with more economically advanced countries where formidable mountain barriers have been overcome. A case in point is the 11.6 km (7.2-mile) tunnel that cuts through the base of Mont Blanc in the Alps. This highway tunnel brings Rome and Paris 200 km (125 miles) closer and provides a year-round route between Geneva and Turin of only 270 km (170 miles). Before the tunnel opened, it meant a trip of nearly 800 km (500 miles) when snow closed the highway over the Alps.

Some countries have preserved physical barriers as protection and have viewed them as political as well as economic statements. Increasing globalisation, however, has brought about changes in attitudes. The tunnel beneath the English Channel to connect England and France, and the bridge between Denmark and Sweden are good examples. The bridge to connect Denmark and Sweden over the Baltic strait has connected the Nordic countries with the rest of Europe. The project has made it possible to drive from Lapland in northernmost Scandinavia to Calabria in southern Italy. It has ended millennia of geographic isolation for these Nordic nations. Politically the bridge is seen as a powerful, tangible symbol that they are ending their political isolation from the rest of Europe and are linking themselves economically to the continent's future and to membership in the EU.

After more than 200 years of speculation, a tunnel under the English Channel between Britain and France was officially opened in 1994.[2] Historically, the British have resisted a tunnel; they did not trust the French or any other European country and saw the English Channel as protection. When they became members of the EC, economic reality meant that a tunnel had to be built. The Chunnel, as it is sometimes known, carried more than 17m tonnes of freight and over 30 million people during the first year it was open.[3]

Going International 3.1

WHERE DO EUROPEANS GO ON HOLIDAY?

Each large circle represents a member of the EU and is sized according to the number of trips abroad its citizens made in 2006. The smaller, inner circles represent the top three destinations for citizens of that state. Within the EU, the most popular destination was Spain, which hosted more than 350 million European visitors. But for every five Europeans arriving for a holiday in Spain, only one Spaniard leaves. Germans, meanwhile, took 750 million trips abroad, but only played host to 72 million visits from fellow Europeans. The only non-EU country to make it into those top-three lists was the USA. Cost does not seem to dictate travel destination. France and Spain were popular among citizens of poorer EU countries. And Latvians, who took an average of three trips abroad, tended to head to Germany and Britain.

▶

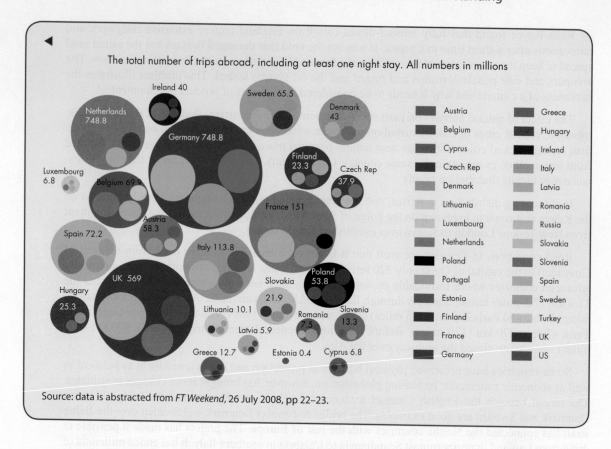

The total number of trips abroad, including at least one night stay. All numbers in millions

Source: data is abstracted from *FT Weekend*, 26 July 2008, pp 22–23.

Geography, nature and international trade

As countries prosper and expand their economies, natural barriers are overcome. Tunnels are dug, bridges and dams built, and sound environmental practices implemented to control or adapt to climate, topography and the recurring extremes of nature. Man has been reasonably successful in overcoming or minimising the effects of geographical barriers and natural disasters except in the developing countries

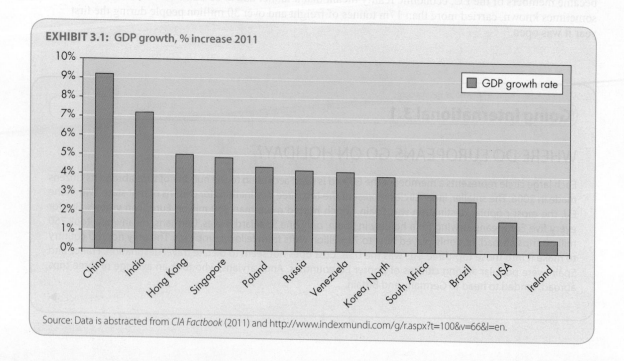

EXHIBIT 3.1: GDP growth, % increase 2011

Source: Data is abstracted from *CIA Factbook* (2011) and http://www.indexmundi.com/g/r.aspx?t=100&v=66&l=en.

of the world. Most rich countries have constant economic growth (see Exhibit 3.1), while growth in emerging countries can be much higher.

Always on the slim margin between subsistence and disaster, some developing countries suffer disproportionately from natural and human-assisted catastrophes. Climate and topography coupled with civil wars, poor environmental policies and natural disasters push these countries further into economic ruin. Without irrigation and water management, they are afflicted by droughts, floods, soil erosion and creeping deserts, which reduce the long-term fertility of the land. Population increases, deforestation and overgrazing intensify the impact of drought and lead to malnutrition and ill-health, further undermining the countries' ability to solve their problems.

Experts expect mass famine to have killed between 20 million and 30 million Africans in the 1990s. Cyclones cannot be prevented nor inadequate rainfall, but there are means to control their effects. Unfortunately, each disaster seems to push these countries further away from effective solutions. Countries that suffer the most from major calamities are among the poorest in the world. Many have neither the capital nor the technical ability to minimise the effects of natural phenomena; they are at the mercy of nature.[4]

Social responsibility and environmental management

The twenty-first century has been called the **century of the environment**, in that nations, companies and people are reaching a consensus: environmental protection is not an optional extra, 'it is an essential part of the complex process of doing business'.[5] The self-styled **Green activists**, and governments, media and businesses are focusing on ways to stem the tide of pollution and to clean up their decades of neglect. Many view the problem as a global issue rather than a national one, and one that poses common threats to humankind and thus cannot be addressed by nations in isolation.[6]

Companies looking to build manufacturing plants in countries with more liberal pollution regulations than they have at home are finding that regulations everywhere are becoming stricter. Many Asian governments are drafting new regulations and strictly enforcing existing ones. A strong motivator for Asia and the rest of the world is the realisation that pollution is on the verge of getting completely out of control. Russia, the EU and a number of other countries have now signed the **Kyoto agreement** to decrease pollution in the coming years. However, the USA has decided not to sign or comply with the Kyoto agreement.

Neither Western Europe nor the rest of the industrialised world are free of environmental damage. Rivers are polluted and the atmosphere in many major urban areas is far from clean (eg Athens, Los Angeles, Rome and Mexico City, to mention a few). The very process of controlling industrial waste leads to another and perhaps equally critical issue: the disposal of hazardous waste, a by-product of pollution control. Estimates of hazardous waste collected annually exceed 300m tonnes; the critical question concerns disposal that does not move the problem elsewhere.

The export of hazardous waste by developed countries to developing nations has ethical implications and environmental consequences. Countries finding it more difficult to dispose of such waste at home are seeking countries willing to assume the burden of disposal. Some waste disposal in developing countries is illegal and some is perfectly legal because of governments that are directly involved in the business of hazardous waste. Illegal dumping is the most reprehensible act since it is done clandestinely and often without proper protection for those who unknowingly come into contact with the poisons.

Governments, organisations and businesses are becoming increasingly concerned with the social responsibility and ethical issues surrounding the problem of generating and disposing of waste. The Organisation for Economic Co-operation and Development (OECD), the United Nations, the EU and international activist groups are undertaking programmes to strengthen environmental policies. Their influence and leadership are reflected in a broader awareness of pollution problems by businesses and people in general. Responsibility for cleaning up the environment does not rest solely with governments, businesses or **activist groups**; each citizen has a social

century of the environment

in the early 2000s the environment was considered the most important issue

Green activists

organisations or individuals who actively want to protect the environment

Kyoto agreement

agreement signed by the EU, Russia and a number of countries, determining the decrease required in pollution over the coming years

activist groups

people or organisations acting to bring about social, political, economic or environmental change, eg Greenpeace

Going International 3.2

WATER IS NEEDED TO PRODUCE EVERYDAY BEVERAGES AND GOODS

We all know that water is a very valuable commodity, as any farmer in drought-besieged parts of China, America or Kenya knows only too well. Consumers may already be aware of the environmental impact of producing goods in terms of energy or pollution, but they might be surprised to learn how much water is needed to create some daily goods. For example, a single cup of coffee needs a great deal more water than that poured into the pot. According to a new book on the subject, 1,120 litres of water go into producing a single litre of the beverage, once growing the beans, packaging and so on are measured. Only 120 litres go into making the same amount of tea. As many as four litres of water are used to make a litre of the bottled stuff. Household items need even more water and thus we can say they are thirstier. Thousands of litres are needed to make shoes, hamburgers, microchips and litres cotton textiles.

- How can we save water? Discuss.

Source: abstracted from *The Economist*, 29 February 2009.

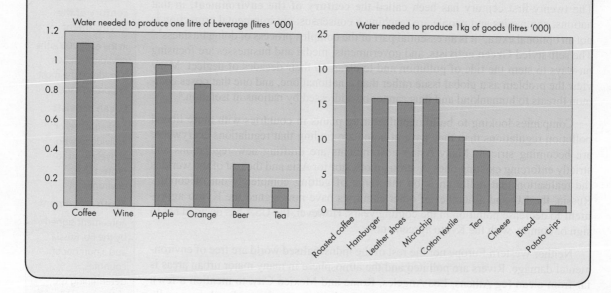

and moral responsibility to include environmental protection among his or her highest goals. The main issue is whether international trade and economic development can co-exist with protection of the environment. There is thus a lot of discussion on sustainable development; striking a long-lasting balance between trade, the environment, technological development and society is necessary. More and more companies are realising that sustainable development is of mutual importance to companies and societies.[7]

Resources

The availability of minerals and the ability to generate energy are the foundations of modern technology. The location of the earth's resources, as well as the available sources of energy, are geographical accidents, and the world's nations are not equally endowed; nor does a nation's demand for a particular mineral or energy source necessarily coincide with domestic supply (see Exhibit 3.2).

Energy is necessary to power the machinery of modern production, and to extract and process the resources necessary to produce the goods reflecting economic prosperity. In much of the underdeveloped world, human labour provides the preponderance of energy. The principal supplements to human energy

EXHIBIT 3.2: Energy consumption per capita versus GDP per capita, 2012

	Countries	GDP (per capita)	Kw/ capita		Countries	Kw/h	GDP (per capita)	Kw/ capita
1	Iceland	19,800	53	16	France	7,022.63	20,600	7
2	Norway	54,200	25	17	Japan	6,749.73	19,800	7
3	Kuwait	42,200	16	18	Netherlands	6,724.19	42,700	7
4	Canada	41,100	16	19	Germany	6,696.93	20,600	7
5	United Arab Emirates	48,800	13	20	Hong Kong	6,030.60	15,000	6
6	Luxembourg	81,100	13	21	Russia	6,017.50	17,000	6
7	USA	49,000	12	22	Spain	5,686.29	31,000	6
8	Australia	5,500	10	23	Greece	5,528.51	20,600	6
9	Qatar	104,300	10	24	Ireland	5,527.29	19,800	6
10	Korea, South	6,000	9	25	UK	5,467.34	36,600	5
11	New Zealand	28,000	9	26	Italy	5,058.66	19,800	5
12	Belgium	23,700	8	27	China	3,493.79	43,800	3
13	Austria	5,500	8	28	Malaysia	3,214.54	15,800	3
14	Singapore	60,500	8	29	Argentina	2,481.48	17,700	2
15	Switzerland	43,900	7					

Sources: Data abstracted from *CIA Factbook,* 1 January 2012, and http://www.indexmundi.com/g/r.aspx?t=0&v=81000&l=en.

are animals, wood, fossil fuel, nuclear power, and, to a lesser and more experimental extent, the ocean's tides, geothermal power and the sun. Of all the energy sources, petroleum usage is increasing most rapidly because of its versatility and the ease with which it can be stored and transported.

As an environmental consideration in world marketing, the location, quality and availability of resources will affect the pattern of world economic development and trade for at least the remainder of the century. This factor must be weighed carefully by astute international marketers in making worldwide international investment decisions. In addition to the raw materials of industrialisation, there must be an available and economically feasible energy supply to successfully transform resources into usable products.

Because of the great disparity in the location of the earth's resources, there is world trade between those who do not have all they need and those who have more than they need and are willing to sell. Importers of most of the resources are industrial nations with insufficient domestic supplies. Oil is a good example: the Middle East accounts for over 65 per cent of the world's reserves, while Western countries consume most of it. Exhibit 3.3 shows the oil reserves in the world.

Aside from the geographical unevenness in which most resources occur, there is no immediate cause for concern about the availability of supply of most resources. These estimates of reserves are based on current rates of consumption and will change as new reserves are discovered, as greater proportions are obtained by recycling, as substitutes are introduced, and as rates of consumption increase or abate. Substitutions are already being used to replace many of the minerals. The replacement of steel with fibreglass and plastic in automobile manufacturing is but one example.

World population trends

While not the only determinant, the existence of sheer numbers of people is significant in appraising potential consumer demand. Current population, rates of growth, age levels and rural–urban population distribution are closely related to today's demand for various categories of goods. Changes in the composition and distribution of population among the world's countries during the next 40 years will profoundly affect future demand.

EXHIBIT 3.3: World's oil reserves

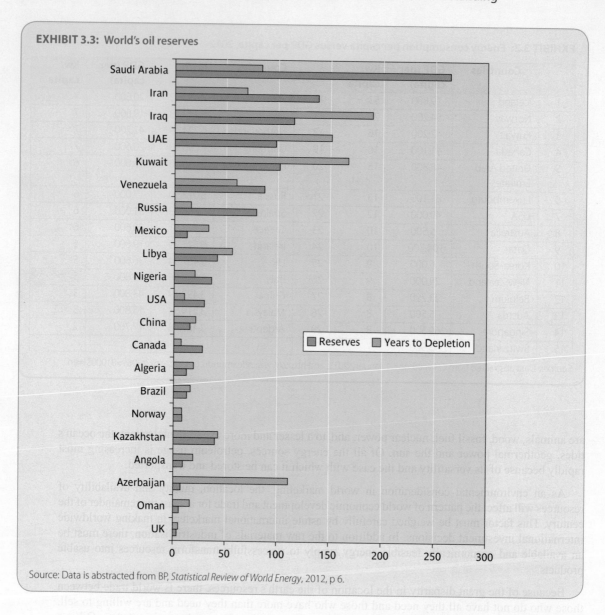

Source: Data is abstracted from BP, *Statistical Review of World Energy*, 2012, p 6.

Recent estimates claim there are over 6.2 billion people in the world. Exhibit 3.4 presents the population by major areas and the change expected between 2020 and 2150.[8] The majority of the people will reside in less-developed countries least able to support such population increases. By the year 2025, the World Bank predicts that over four-fifths of the world's population will be concentrated in developing countries. Most governments are trying to control the explosive birth rates by encouraging birth control. China has the strictest policy: only one child is allowed per couple except in rural areas where, if the first child is female, a second child is permitted.

The United Nations projected that humankind will enter the twenty-first century with a global population of 6.2 billion people (see Exhibit 2.5). Its projections for world population for the next 150 years are shown in Exhibit 3.4. The rapid growth rate will continue for some time and by the year 2025, the world population is projected to be around 8.3–8.5 billion people. It is projected that the growth rate will slow down after 2025, and even more so after the year 2075, so that the global population in the year 2100 should be around 11.2 billion and in 2150 perhaps 11.5 billion people.[9]

EXHIBIT 3.4: World population projections by major areas, based on a medium-fertility scenario,* 1950–2150

	1950 (millions)	1995 (millions)	2050 (millions)	2100 (millions)	2150 (millions)
World	2,524	5,687	9,364	10,414	10,806
Africa	224	719	2,046	2,646	2,770
Asia (including China and India)	1,402	3,438	5,443	5,851	6,059
China	555	1,220	1,517	1,535	1,596
India	358	929	1,533	1,617	1,669
Europe	547	728	638	579	595
Latin America	166	477	810	889	916
North America	172	297	384	401	414
Oceania	13	28	46	49	51

*The medium-fertility scenario assumes that the total fertility rates will ultimately stabilise by the year 2055 at replacement levels, which are slightly above two children per woman. If fertility rates stay constant at 1990–1995 levels, the world population projection is 14,941 million in 2050, 57,182 million in 2100 and 296,333 million in 2150.

Source: based on *World Population Projections to 2150* (New York: United Nations, Department of Economic and Social Affairs, Population Division, 1998).

EXHIBIT 3.5: Estimates and projections of the world population between 1950 and 2150, based on medium-fertility projection

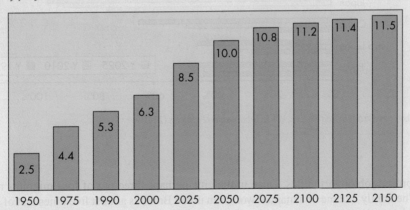

Source: data abstracted from http://www.gfmer.ch/Books/bookmp/11.htm.

Rural/urban shifts

A relatively recent phenomenon is a pronounced shift of the world's population from rural to urban areas. In the early 1800s, less than 3.5 per cent of the world's people were living in cities of 20,000 or more and less than 2 per cent in cities of 100,000 or more. Today, more than 40 per cent of the world's people are urbanites and this trend is accelerating (see Exhibit 3.6).

By 2020 it is estimated that more than 60 per cent of the world's population will live in urban areas, and at least 26 cities will have populations of 10 million or more; most of these will be in the developing world.[10] Tokyo has already overtaken Mexico City as the largest city on earth, with a population of 35 million,[11] a jump of almost 9 million since 1975 (see Going International 3.5).[12] Migration from rural to urban areas is largely a result of a desire for greater access to sources of education, health care

EXHIBIT 3.6: Urban population

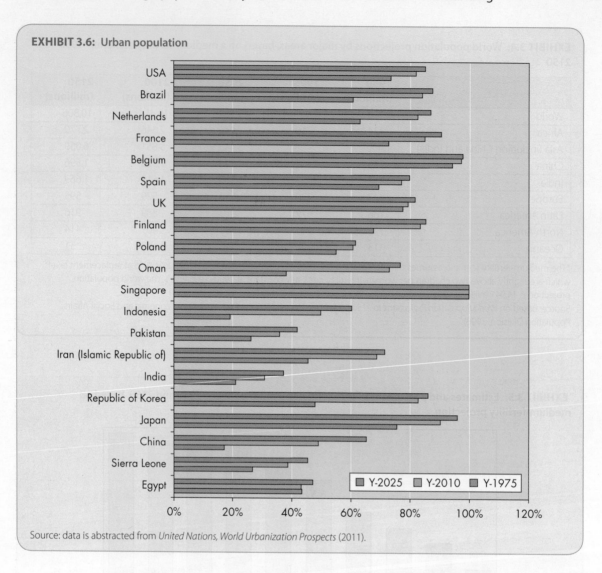

Source: data is abstracted from *United Nations, World Urbanization Prospects* (2011).

and improved job opportunities. Once in the city, perhaps three out of four migrants make economic gains. The family income of a manual worker in urban Brazil is almost five times that of a farm labourer in a rural area.

urban growth

growth of urban areas or cities

At some point, the disadvantages of unregulated **urban growth** begin to outweigh the advantages for all concerned.

Although migrants experience some relative improvement in their living standards, intense urban growth without commensurate investment in services eventually leads to profound problems. Slums populated with unskilled workers living hand to mouth put excessive pressure on sanitation systems, water supplies and other social services.

Many fear that, as we approach the year 2020, the bulging cities will become hotbeds of social unrest unless conditions in urban areas are improved. Prospects for improvement are not encouraging because most of the growth will take place in developing countries already economically strained. Further, there is little progress in controlling birth rates in most populous countries.

Increasing unemployment

Rapid population increases without commensurate economic development create other difficulties. Among the most pressing are the number of new jobs needed to accommodate the flood of people

Going International 3.3

According to the United Nations the world will soon become predominantly urban. By 2020 at least 23 cities will have passed the 10 million mark. Many parts of the Asia-Pacific region are facing 'hyper-urbanisation'; while London took 130 years to grow from 1 million to 8 million, Bangkok took 45 years, Dhaka 37 years and Seoul only 25 years. The table below shows the Top 10 Largest Urban Agglomerations in 1975, 2000 and 2025.

As the population increases, more people will live in large cities. Many people will live in the growing number of cities with over 10 million inhabitants, known as megacities. In 1975, just three cities had populations of 10 million or more, only one of them in a less-developed country. Mega-cities numbered 16 in 2000. By 2025, 27 mega-cities will exist, 21 in less-developed countries.

London, Oxford Street's famously busy crossing.
© Pervez Ghauri

Population in millions								
1975			**2000**			**2025**		
1 Tokyo, Japan		26.6	1 Tokyo, Japan		34.5	1 Tokyo, Japan		36.4
2 New York, USA		15.9	2 Mexico City, Mexico		18	2 Bombay, India		26.4
3 Mexico City, Mexico		10.7	3 New York, USA		17.9	3 Delhi, India		22.5
4 Osaka, Japan		9.8	4 São Paulo, Brazil		17.1	4 Dhaka, Bangladesh		22
5 São Paulo, Brazil		9.6	5 Bombay, India		16.1	5 São Paulo, Brazil		21.4
6 Los Angeles, USA		8.9	6 Shanghai, China		13.2	6 Mexico City, Mexico		21
7 Buenos Aires, Argentina		8.8	7 Calcutta, India		13.1	7 New York, USA		20.6
8 Paris, France		8.6	8 Delhi, India		12.4	8 Calcutta, India		20.6
9 Calcutta, India		7.9	9 Buenos Aires, Argentina		11.9	9 Shanghai, China		19.4
10 Moscow, Russian Federation		7.6	10 Los Angeles, USA		11.8	10 Karachi, Pakistan		19.1

Although some people believe that this urbanisation will bring prosperity and will thus lift many out of poverty, the United Nations believes it will in fact cause growing poverty and deepening inequalities. As the table shows, most of the growth is taking place not in the Western world but in the Third World. It will be increasingly difficult to provide clean water, jobs and infrastructure. Take Lagos, for example, with ever-increasing fumes, smoke, unsanitary water and overcrowded communities. Battered yellow minibuses are the nearest the city has to public transport, with the biblical message of hope decorated all over them: 'No condition is permanent.'

- What can be done to stop these growing cities?

Sources: Venessa Houlder, '60 per cent of the World will Live in Cities by 2030', *Financial Times*, 10 September 2004, p 9; John Reader, 'No City Limits, Our World in 2020', *Guardian*, 11 September 2004, pp 2–9; and United Nations, *World Urbanization Prospects*, The 2007 Revision, http://www.prb.org/Educators/TeachersGuides/HumanPopulation/Urbanization.aspx.

entering the labour pool. During the period 1970 to 2000, one billion people entered the labour market in the Third World; by the year 2020, an additional 1.5 billion will be of working age. The International Labour Organization (ILO) estimates that 1 billion jobs must be created worldwide by the year 2015.[13]

The mismatch between population growth and economic growth is another major problem to be faced in the next century. While it is true that cheap labour costs, brought on in part by vast labour pools in less-developed countries, attract labour-intensive manufacturers from higher-cost industrialised countries, the number of new jobs created will not be sufficient to absorb the projected population growth. The ability to create enough jobs to keep pace with population growth is one problem of uncontrolled growth; another is providing enough to eat.

World food production

Having enough food to eat depends on a country's ability to produce sufficient quantities, the ability to buy food from other sources when not self-sufficient, and the physical ability to distribute food when the need arises. The world produces enough food to provide adequate diets for all its estimated 6.2 billion people, yet famine exists, most notably in Africa. Long-term drought, economic weakness, inefficient distribution and civil unrest have created conditions that have led to tens of thousands of people starving.

Going International 3.4

WHERE HAVE ALL THE WOMEN GONE?

© Istockphoto.com/bo1982.

Three converging issues in China have the potential to cause a serious gender imbalance: issue 1 – China, the world's most populous country, has a strict one-child policy to curb population growth; issue 2 – traditional values dictate male superiority and a definite parental preference for boys; and issue 3 – prenatal scanning allows women to discover the sex of their foetuses and thereby abort unwanted female children.

As a consequence, Chinese statisticians have begun to forecast a big marriage gap for the generation born in the late 1980s and early 1990s. In 1990 China recorded 113.8 male births for every 100 female births, far higher than the natural ratio of 106 to 100. In rural areas, where parental preference for boys is especially strong, newborn boys outnumber girls by an average of 144.6 to 100. In one rural township, the ratio was reported to be 163.8 to 100.

Not only is there a gender mismatch on the horizon, but there may also be a social mismatch because most of the men will be peasants with little education, while most of the women will live in cities and more likely have high-school qualifications or college degrees. In China, men who do physical labour are least attractive as mates, while women who labour with their minds are least popular.

Thanks to technological advancements (prenatal scanning), India is facing the same problem. Families that are able to pay Rs10,000 ($217, €177, £121) can identify and abort female foetuses. Traditionally, boys are preferred in Indian culture. According to the latest census report, proportions of Indian girls to boys among children up to six years fell from 945 girls to 1,000 boys (1991) to 927 girls in 2001. The trend is most pronounced in richer states (as people can pay for the test). For example, Punjab has 798 girls and Gujarat 883 to every 1,000 boys. This disparity can have worrying implications especially when, unlike China, India has not been able to impose any family planning.

● Is a one-child policy a good one for China? Should other countries such as India also follow this policy?

Sources: adapted from 'Sex Determination before Birth', *Reuters News Service*, 3 May 1994; 'Seven Times as Many Men', *AP News Service*, 31 March 1994; and Edward Luc, 'Indian Fears Over Falling Female Birth Ratio', *Financial Times*, 15 September 2004, p 12.

Controlling population growth

Faced with the ominous consequences of the population explosion, it would seem logical for countries to take appropriate steps to reduce growth to manageable rates, but procreation is one of the most culturally sensitive uncontrollables.

The prerequisites for population control are adequate incomes, higher literacy levels, education for women, better hygiene, universal access to health care, improved nutrition and, perhaps most important, a change in basic cultural beliefs about the importance of large families. Unfortunately, progress in providing improved conditions and changing beliefs is hampered by the increasingly heavy demand placed on institutions responsible for change and improvement.

Developed world population decline

While the developing world faces a rapidly growing population, it is estimated that the industrialised world's population will decline. Birth rates in Western Europe and Japan have been decreasing since the early or mid-1960s; more women are choosing careers instead of children, and many working couples are electing to remain childless. As a result of these and other contemporary factors, population growth in many countries has dropped below the rate necessary to maintain present levels. The populations of France, Sweden, Italy, Switzerland and Belgium are all expected to drop within a few years. Austria, Denmark, Germany, Japan and several other nations are now at about zero population growth and will probably slip to the minus side in another decade. Exhibit 3.7 reveals the old-age dependency in the Europe of the future. All this will have a profound impact on companies, their segmentation and marketing strategies.

The economic fallout of a declining population has many ramifications. Businesses find their domestic market shrinking for items such as maternity and infant goods, school equipment and selected durables. This leads to reduced production and worker layoffs that affect living standards. Europe, Japan and the USA have special problems because of the increasing percentage of elderly people who must be supported by shrinking numbers of active workers. The elderly require higher government outlays for health care and hospitals, special housing and nursing homes, and pension and welfare assistance, but the workforce that supports these costs is dwindling. In addition, a shortage of skilled workers is anticipated in these countries because of the decreasing population.

The trends of increasing population in the developing world, with substantial shifts from rural to urban areas and declining birth rates in the industrialised world, will have profound effects on the state of world business and world economic conditions well beyond 2020.

EXHIBIT 3.7: Europe's old-age dependency

Country	Population		Dependency ratio[†]	
	2005	**2050**	**2005**	**2050**
	Millions		**Millions**	
Spain	41.2	37.3	28	72
Italy	57.5	48.1	31	66
Poland	38.5	33.0	20	55
EU	445.2*	431.2*	29**	52**
Germany	83.0	76.0	30	52
France	60.3	62.2	28	50
USA	295.5	419.9	21	39

Notes: [†] Age 65+ as % of those 20–65; * EU 25; ** EU 15.
Sources: Eurostat, UN population Division, US Census Bureau and *The Economist*, 2 October 2004, p 36.

World trade routes

Major world trade routes have developed among the most industrialised countries of the world: Europe, North America and Japan. It may be said that trade routes bind the world together, minimising distance, natural barriers, lack of resources, and the fundamental differences between peoples and economies. Early trade routes were, of course, overland; later came sea routes and, finally, air routes to connect countries. Trade routes represent the attempts of countries to overcome economic and social imbalances created in part by the influence of geography.

triad trade

the process of trade undertaken between the EU, North America and Canada, Japan and China

A careful comparison among the world population figures in Exhibit 3.4, the **triad trade** figures in Exhibit 3.8 and the world trade figures in Exhibit 3.9 illustrates how small a percentage of the world's land mass and population accounts for the majority of trade. It is no surprise that the major sea lanes and the most developed highway and rail systems link these major trade areas. The more economically developed a country, the better developed the surface transportation infrastructure is to support trade.

Although air routes are the heaviest between points in the major industrial centres, they are also heavy to points in less-developed countries. The obvious reason is that, for areas not located on navigable waters or where the investment in railways and effective roads is not yet feasible, air service is often the best answer.

Historical perspective in international trade

To understand, explain and appreciate a people's image of itself and the fundamental attitudes and unconscious fears that are often reflected in its view of foreign cultures, it is necessary to study the culture as it is now as well as to understand the culture as it was; that is, a country's history. An awareness of the history of a country is particularly effective for understanding attitudes about the role of government and business, the relations between managers and the managed, the sources of management authority, and attitudes towards foreign multinational corporations. History helps define a nation's 'mission', how it perceives its neighbours, and how it sees its place in the world.

EXHIBIT 3.8: The triad: merchandise trade between the USA and Canada, the EU, Japan and China, 2007 ($b)

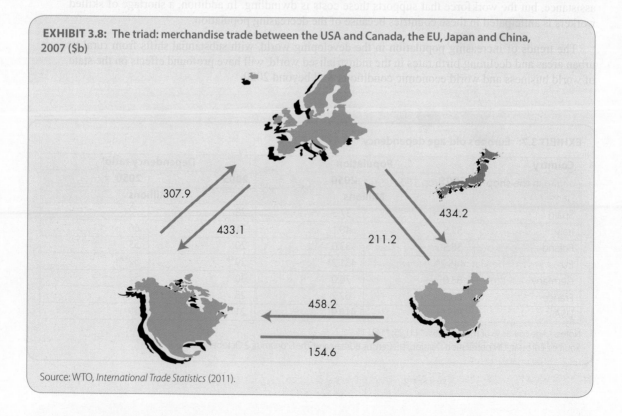

307.9
433.1
434.2
211.2
458.2
154.6

Source: WTO, *International Trade Statistics* (2011).

EXHIBIT 3.9: Leading exporters and importers in world merchandise trade, 2011 ($bn)

Country	Exports	Imports
China	1,904	1,743
USA	1,497	2,236
Germany	1,408	1,198
Japan	788	808.4
France	587.1	688.5
Korea, South	556.5	524.4
Netherlands	551.8	493.1
Italy	523.9	556.4
Russia	520.9	322.5
UK	479.7	639.5
Canada	462.4	461
Hong Kong	427.9	482.6
Singapore	414.8	366.3
Saudi Arabia	359.9	117.4
Mexico	349.7	350.8

Source: *CIA World Factbook* (2011).

History and contemporary behaviour

Unless you have a historical sense of the many changes that have buffeted Japan, the isolation before the coming of Admiral Perry in 1853, the threat of domination by colonial powers, the rise of new social classes, Western influences, the humiliation of the Second World War and involvement in the international community, it is difficult to fully understand its contemporary behaviour. Why do the Japanese have such strong loyalty towards their companies? Why is the loyalty found among participants in the Japanese distribution systems so difficult for an outsider to develop? Why are decisions made by consensus? Answers to such questions can be explained in part by some sense of Japanese history.[14]

Going International 3.5

VICTORIAN VALUES

Christmas as a festival of consumerism? It all began in the shop-till-you-drop 1800s, says Judith Flanders.

What we are dreaming about is a traditional Victorian Christmas, as seen on Christmas cards. But the mythical Christmas turns out to be just that: a myth. The Victorians invented Christmas as we know it, and it was a consumer bonanza from the beginning. Materialism is nothing new, and the nineteenth-century merchants knew that bigger festivals meant bigger sales.

When Charles Dickens first described a typical Christmas – in 1837, the year Queen Victoria came

© Istockphoto.com/dynasoar

▶

◄

to the throne – some of the trappings of the modern festival were in place: family parties, mistletoe and holly, church-going, charity, turkey, plum pudding and mince pies. But there were no trees, no carols, no cards, no Father Christmas and, perhaps most surprising of all, no presents.

The holiday had been in hibernation since the seventeenth century, when the Puritans condemned it as a 'pagan' festival. It swiftly died in popular memory, replaced by the riot of Twelfth Night, which was a continuation of the old, rowdy winter-solstice celebrations.

The railways also brought turkeys to the mass-market. Traditionally, families had eaten goose for the celebration meal, although in the early nineteenth century turkey was also gaining popularity as a larger alternative, better suited to the extended Victorian family.

The ritual of gift-giving to family and the needy started to be associated with Father Christmas towards the end of the century. After the Reformation, St Nicholas, whose Saint's Day was on 6 December, vanished, and was replaced by Sir Christmas, representing the spirit of the season. Illustrations in the late 1840s show a thin old man, bearded and a bit droopy, rather like Old Father Time. In the 1840s Christmas presents were still mainly given to children, not adults.

By the end of the century, shopping and Christmas were so firmly linked that companies that produced non-Christmas items refused to be left behind. Many ran seasonal advertisements for the most non-seasonal of goods: Pears' Soap advertisements showed a small child hiding under an overturned bathtub, with the caption, 'Oh! Here's a Merry Christmas'.

● Is the ritual of gift giving good? Is it important for creating harmony in society?

Source: *FT* magazine, 9 December 2006, pp 22–3.

History is subjective

History is important in understanding why people in a country behave as they do, but history from whose viewpoint? Historical events are always viewed from one's own perspective, and thus what is recorded by one historian may not be what another records, especially if the historians are from different cultures. Historians are traditionally objective, but few can help filtering events through their own self-reference criteria. Not only is history sometimes subjective, but there are other subtle influences on our perspective. Maps of the world sold in the USA generally show the USA as the centre, as maps in Britain show Britain at the centre, while maps in Australia look totally different, with Australia being the centre of the world and the rest lying east, west or north of the centre.

SUMMARY

One British authority admonishes foreign marketers to study the world until 'the mere mention of a town, country or river enables it to be picked out immediately on the map'. Although it may not be necessary for the student of international marketing to memorise the world map to that extent, a prospective international marketer should be reasonably familiar with the world, its climate and topographic differences. Otherwise, the important marketing characteristics of geography could be completely overlooked when marketing in another country. The need for geographical and historical knowledge goes deeper than being able to locate continents and their countries. For someone who has never been in a tropical rainforest with an annual rainfall of at least 1.5 m and sometimes more than 5 m, it is difficult to anticipate the need for protection against high humidity, or to anticipate the difficult problems caused by dehydration in constant 38°C or more heat in the Sahara region. Without a historical understanding of a culture, the attitudes within the marketplace may not be understood. An understanding of world population and its expected growth in regions and countries can have a profound impact on a company's international marketing strategies. The same goes for the geographic locations of resources and other raw materials.

Aside from the simpler and more obvious ramifications of climate and topography, there are complex geographical and historical influences on the development of the general economy and society of a country. In this case, the need for studying geography and history is to provide the marketer with an understanding of why a country has developed as it has rather than as a guide for adapting marketing plans. Geography and history are two of the environments of foreign marketing that should be understood and that must be included in foreign marketing plans to a degree commensurate with their influence on marketing effort.

QUESTIONS

1 Study the data in Exhibit 3.1 and briefly discuss the long-term prospects for industrialisation of an underdeveloped country with high population growth and minimum resources.

2 Why study geography in international marketing?

3 Pick a country and show how employment and topography affect marketing within that country.

4 Discuss the bases of world trade. Give examples illustrating the different bases.

5 The marketer 'should also examine the more complex effect of geography on general market characteristics, distribution systems and the state of the economy.' Comment.

6 The world population pattern is shifting from rural to urban areas. Discuss the marketing ramifications.

7 Select a country with a stable population and one with a rapidly growing population. Contrast the marketing implications of these two situations.

8 'The basis of world trade can be simply stated as the result of equalising an imbalance in the needs and wants of society on one hand and its supply of goods on the other.' Explain.

9 How do differences in people constitute a basis for trade?

10 'World trade routes bind the world together.' Discuss.

11 Why are the 1990s called the 'Decade of the Environment'? Explain.

12 Some say the global environment is a global issue rather than a national one. What does this mean? Discuss.

FURTHER READING

- Peter J. Buckley and Pervez N. Ghauri, 'Globalisation, Economic Geography and the Strategy of Multinational Enterprises', *Journal of International Business Studies*, 2004, 35(2), 81–98.

- A.J. Scott, 'Economic Geography: The Great Half Century', in G.L. Clark, M.P. Feldman and M.S. Gertler (eds), *The Oxford Handbook of Economic Geography* (Oxford: Oxford University Press, 2000), pp 483–504.

- T. M. Hout and P. Ghemawat, *China vs the World* (Boston, MA: Harvard Business School Press, 2011).

NOTES

1   For an interesting book on the effects of geography, technology and capitalism on an economy, see Dean M. Hanik, *The International Economy: A Geographical Perspective* (New York: Wiley, 1994).

2   'Chunnel Vision', *Europe*, May 1994, p 43.

3   *Euromonitor International*, httpp://www.Euromonitor.com.

4   World Bank, *World Development Indicators*, CD-ROM, 2012.

5   'A Survey on Development and the Environment', *The Economist*, 21 March 1998.

6   Yoshihide Soeya, 'Balance and Growth', *Look Japan*, January 1994, p 19.

7   Visit the OECD's website to find out more about sustainable development: www.oecd.org.

8   United Nations, *World Population Projections to 2150*, Department of Economic and Social Affairs, Population Division (New York: United Nations, 1998).

9   United Nations Department for Economic and Social Information and Policy Analysis, Population Division. World Population Prospects: The 1994 Revision. Document ST/ESA/SER/A/145 (New York: United Nations, 1995).

10 'Our World in 2020', Special Survey, *Guardian*, 11 September 2004.

11 This figure represents Tokyo's core suburbs and exurbs.

12 United Nations, *World Urbanization Prospects* (New York: United Nations, 2003).

13 United Nations, *World Population Projections to 2150* (New York: United Nations, Department of Economic and Social Affairs, Population Division, 1998).

14 Tamer Cavusgil, Pervez Ghauri and Ayse Akcal, *Doing Business in Emerging Markets* (London: Sage, 2013).

Chapter 4
Cultural Dynamics and International Marketing

Chapter Outline

Chapter Learning Objectives

What you should learn from Chapter 4

- How important the culture is to an international marketer and how one can handle cultural differences
- The effects of self-reference criterion (SRC) on marketing objectives
- How to identify the elements of culture and understand how these are related to international marketing
- How the local customs and traditions of doing business influence international marketing
- The effect of high-context, low-context cultures on people's behaviour and on business practices
- How to handle communication in cross-cultural deals and marketing efforts

economic needs

eg minimum food, drink, shelter and clothing

economic wants

arise from desire for satisfaction and, due to their non-essential quality, are limitless

culture

a set of values and norms followed by a group of people

collective programming

when groups of people are taught/ indoctrinated with certain values

Humans are born creatures of need; as they mature, want is added to need. **Economic needs** are spontaneous and, in their crudest sense, limited. Humans, like all living things, need a minimum level of nourishment and, like a few other living things, they need shelter. Unlike any other being, they also need essential clothing. **Economic wants**, however, are for non-essentials and, hence, are limitless. Unlike basic needs, wants are not spontaneous and not characteristic of the lower animals. They arise not from an inner desire for preservation of self or species, but from a desire for satisfaction above absolute necessity. To satisfy their material needs and wants, humans consume.

The manner in which people consume, the priority of needs and the wants they attempt to satisfy, and the manner in which they satisfy them, are functions of their culture that temper, mould and dictate their style of living. **Culture** is the human-made part of the human environment – the sum total of knowledge, beliefs, art, morals, laws, customs and any other capabilities and habits acquired by humans as members of society. Culture is 'everything that people have, think and do as members of their society'.[1]

Culture is often defined as 'ethical habit', consisting of values and ideas. Ethical systems create moral communities because their shared languages of good and evil give their members a common moral life.[2]

According to Hofstede,[3] culture is always a collective phenomenon, because it is at least partially shared with people who live or lived within the same environment, which is where it was learned. It is the **collective programming** of the mind that distinguishes the members of one group or category of people from another.

Culture's essence is captured in the above definitions. In sum, the concept is representative when:[4]

- the members of a group share a set of ideas and values
- these are transmitted by symbols from one generation to another
- culture is an outcome of past actions of a group or its members
- culture is learned
- culture shapes behaviour and our perception of the world
- it is reinforced by components such as language, behaviour and 'nation'.

Hofstede's seminal work on culture contains more than 11,600 questionnaires in more than 50 countries. He derived four main conceptual dimensions on which national cultures exhibit significant differences. The dimensions are named *individualism/collectivism*, *power distance*, *masculinity/femininity* and *uncertainty avoidance*. For example, in collective countries there is a close-knit social structure, while in individualistic countries people are basically supposed to care for themselves. Power distance refers to the extent to which a society and its individuals tolerate an unequal distribution of power. A society is masculine when it favours assertiveness, earning money, showing off possessions and caring little for others, while feminine societies are the opposite. Uncertainty avoidance refers to the degree to which a society feels threatened by uncertain, ambiguous or undefined situations. In a high uncertainty avoidance society people look for stable careers and follow rules and procedures. Exhibit 4.1 shows the values of these dimensions for 53 different countries/regions.[5] Exhibit 4.2 shows the grouping of countries according to these differences.

EXHIBIT 4.1: Values of Hofstede's cultural dimensions for 53 countries or regions

Country/region	Dimensions				
	Power distance	Uncertainty avoidance	Individualism	Masculinity	Long- or short-term orientation
Arabic countries (ARA)	80	68	38	53	–
Argentina (ARG)	49	86	46	56	–
Australia (AUL)	36	51	90	61	31

▶

Austria (AUS)	11	70	55	79	31
Belgium (BEL)	65	94	75	54	38
Brazil (BRA)	69	76	38	49	65
Canada (CAN)	39	48	80	52	23
Chile (CHI)	63	86	23	28	–
Colombia (COL)	67	80	13	64	–
Costa Rica (COS)	35	86	15	21	–
Denmark (DEN)	18	23	74	16	46
East African region (EA)	64	52	27	41	25
Ecuador (ECUA)	78	67	8	63	–
Finland (FIN)	33	59	63	26	41
France (FRA)	68	86	71	43	39
Great Britain (GB)	35	35	89	66	25
Greece (GRE)	60	112	35	57	–
Guatemala (GUA)	96	101	6	37	–
Hong Kong (HON)	68	29	25	57	96
India (IND)	77	40	48	56	61
Indonesia (INDO)	78	48	14	46	–
Iran (IRA)	58	59	41	43	–
Ireland (IRE)	28	35	70	68	43
Israel (ISR)	13	81	54	47	–
Italy (ITA)	50	75	76	70	34
Jamaica (JAM)	45	13	39	68	–
Japan (JAP)	54	92	46	95	80
Malaysia (MAL)	104	36	26	50	–
Mexico (MEX)	81	82	30	69	–
Netherlands (NETH)	38	53	80	14	44
New Zealand (NZ)	22	49	79	58	30
Norway (NOR)	31	50	69	8	44
Pakistan (PAK)	55	70	14	50	–
Panama (PAN)	95	86	11	44	–
Peru (PER)	64	87	16	42	–
Philippines (PHI)	94	44	32	64	19
Portugal (POR)	63	104	27	31	30
Salvador (SAL)	66	94	19	40	–
Singapore (SIN)	74	8	20	48	48
South Africa (SA)	49	49	65	63	–
South Korea (KOR)	60	85	18	39	75
Spain (SPA)	57	86	51	42	19
Sweden (SWE)	31	29	71	5	33
Switzerland (SWI)	34	58	68	70	40
Taiwan (TAI)	58	69	17	45	87
Thailand (THA)	64	64	20	34	56
Turkey (TUR)	66	85	37	45	–
United States (USA)	40	46	91	62	29
Uruguay (URU)	61	100	36	38	–
Venezuela (VEN)	81	76	12	73	–
West African region (WA)	77	54	20	46	16
West Germany (WG)	35	65	67	66	31
Yugoslavia	76	88	27	21	–
Overall mean	*57*	*65*	*43*	*49*	*39*
Standard deviation	*22*	*24*	*25*	*18*	*22*

Source: cited in J.-C. Usunier, *Marketing Across Cultures*, 6th edn (Harlow: Prentice Hall, 2012).

EXHIBIT 4.2: The positions of 50 countries and three regions on the power distance and uncertainty avoidance dimensions (for country name abbreviations, see Exhibit 4.1)

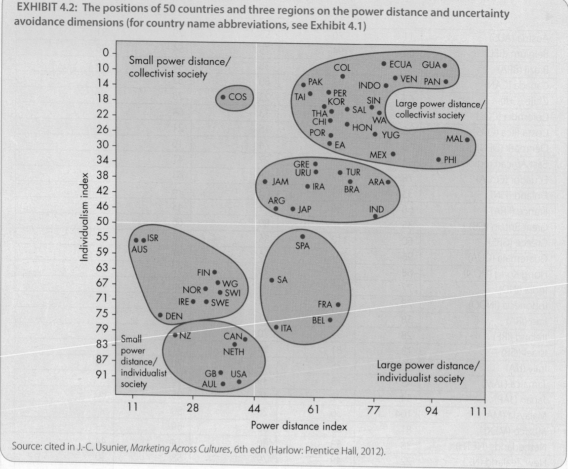

Source: cited in J.-C. Usunier, *Marketing Across Cultures*, 6th edn (Harlow: Prentice Hall, 2012).

The results of Hofstede's study have been discussed and questioned. It is valid to ask whether the data collected in the late 1970s from employers of one single company (IBM) and the behaviour of people in many countries is still applicable following radical changes in the world during the last 30 years. The results provided by Hofstede's study are thus questionable and should be used with care. However, the study was the first one to study systematically culture relevant to business and management and has thus taken this concept beyond anecdotal references.

Because culture deals with a group's design for living, it is pertinent to the study of marketing, especially international marketing. If you consider for a moment the scope of the marketing concept – the satisfaction of consumer needs and wants at a profit – it becomes apparent that the successful marketer must be a student of culture. What a marketer is constantly dealing with is the culture of the people (the market). When a promotional message is written, symbols recognisable and meaningful to the market (the culture) must be used. When designing a product, the style, uses and other related marketing activities must be made culturally acceptable (ie acceptable to the present society) if they are to be operative and meaningful. In fact, culture is pervasive in all marketing activities – in pricing, promotion, channels of distribution, product, packaging and styling – and the marketer's efforts actually become a part of the fabric of culture. The marketer's efforts are judged in a cultural context for acceptance, resistance or rejection. How such efforts interact with a culture determines the degree of success or failure of the marketing effort.

The marketer's **frame of reference** must be that markets do not occur or exist naturally – they become, they evolve; they are not static but change, expand and contract in

frame of reference

structure of concepts, views, customs, etc through which an individual interprets the world

response to marketing effort, economic conditions and other cultural influences. Markets and market behaviour are part of a country's culture. One cannot truly understand how markets evolve or how they react to a marketer's effort without appreciating that markets are a result of culture. Markets are dynamic living phenomena, expanding and contracting not only in response to economic change, but also in response to changes in other aspects of the culture. Marketers are constantly adjusting their efforts to the cultural demands of the market, but they are also acting as agents of change whenever the product or idea being marketed is innovative. Whatever the degree of acceptance in whatever level of culture, the use of something new is the beginning of **cultural change** and the marketer becomes a change agent.

> **cultural change**
> change in cultural conditions, eg Americanisation

Cultural knowledge

There are two kinds of knowledge about cultures. One is **factual knowledge** about a culture; it is usually obvious and must be learned. Different meanings of colour, different tastes and other traits indigenous to a culture are facts that a marketer can anticipate, study and absorb. The other is **interpretive knowledge**: an ability to understand and to appreciate fully the nuances of different cultural traits and patterns. For example, the meaning of time, attitudes towards other people and certain objects, the understanding of one's role in society, and the meanings of life can differ considerably from one culture to another and may require more than factual knowledge to be fully appreciated.

> **factual knowledge**
> something that is usually obvious but that must be learnt, ie different meaning of colours
>
> **interpretive knowledge**
> ability to understand and appreciate fully the nuances of different cultural traits and patterns

Factual knowledge

Frequently, factual knowledge has meaning as a straightforward fact about a culture, but assumes additional significance when interpreted within the context of the culture. For example, that Mexico is 98 per cent Roman Catholic is an important bit of factual knowledge. But equally important is what it means to be Catholic within Mexican culture versus being Catholic in Spain or Italy. Each culture practises Catholicism in slightly different ways. For example, All Souls' Day is an important celebration among some Catholic countries; in Mexico, however, the celebration receives special emphasis. The Mexican observance is a unique combination of pagan (mostly Indian influence) and Catholic tradition. On the Day of the Dead, as All Souls' Day is called by many in Mexico, it is believed that the dead return to feast. Hence, many Mexicans visit the graves of their departed, taking the dead's favourite foods to place on the graves for them to enjoy. Prior to All Souls' Day, bakeries pile their shelves with bread shaped like bones and coffins, and sweet shops sell sugar skulls and other special treats to commemorate the day. As the souls feast on the food, so do the living celebrants. Although the prayers, candles and the idea of the soul are Catholic, the idea of the dead feasting is very pre-Christian Mexican. Thus, a Catholic in Mexico observes All Souls' Day quite differently from a Catholic in Spain. This interpretive, as well as factual, knowledge about a religion in Mexico is necessary to understand Mexican culture fully.[6]

Going International 4.1

MORE EQUAL THAN OTHERS

In a peaceful revolution – the last revolution in Swedish history – the nobles of Sweden in 1809 deposed King Gustav IV, whom they considered incompetent, and surprisingly invited Jean Baptiste Bernadotte, a French general who served under their enemy Napoleon, to become King of Sweden. Bernadotte accepted and he became King Charles XIV; his descendants occupy the Swedish throne to this day. When the new king was installed he addressed the Swedish parliament in their language. His broken Swedish amused the Swedes and

▶

they roared with laughter. The Frenchman who had become king was so upset that he never tried to speak Swedish again. In this incident Bernadotte was a victim of culture shock: never in his French upbringing and military career had he experienced subordinates who laughed at the mistakes of their superior. Historians tell us he had more problems adapting to the egalitarian Swedish and Norwegian mentality (he later became King of Norway as well) and to his subordinates' constitutional rights. He was a good learner, however (except for language!), and he ruled the country as a highly respected constitutional monarch until 1844.

The Nobel Prize award ceremony, 2010.
© Istockphoto.com/ EdStock

One of the aspects in which Sweden differs from France is the way its society handles *inequality*. There is inequality in every society. Even in the most simple hunter-gatherer band, some people are bigger, stronger or smarter than others. The next thing is that some people have more power than others: they are more able to determine the behaviour of others than vice versa. Some people are given more status and respect than others.

● Is inequality in society good or bad?

Source: Geert Hofstede, *Cultures and Organizations: Software of the Mind* (London: McGraw-Hill, 1991), p 23.

Interpretive knowledge

Interpretive knowledge requires a degree of insight that may best be described as a feeling. It is the kind of knowledge most dependent on past experience for interpretation and most frequently prone to misinterpretation if relying on one's **self-reference criterion (SRC)**.

Ideally, the foreign marketer should possess both kinds of knowledge about a market. Most facts about a particular culture can be learned by researching published material about that culture. This effort can also transmit a small degree of empathy, but to appreciate the culture fully, it is necessary to live with the people for some time. Because this ideal solution is not practical for a marketer, other solutions are sought. Consultation and cooperation with bilingual nationals with marketing backgrounds is the most effective answer to the problem. This has the further advantage of helping the marketer acquire an increasing degree of empathy through association with the people who understand the culture best: the locals.

> **self-reference criterion (SRC)**
>
> considering our own conditions, values and norms while evaluating others
>
> **cultural sensitivity**
>
> being attuned to the nuances of culture, which thus can be viewed objectively, evaluated and appreciated

Cultural sensitivity and tolerance

Successful foreign marketing begins with **cultural sensitivity** – being attuned to the nuances of culture so that a new culture can be viewed objectively, evaluated and appreciated. Cultural empathy must be cultivated carefully. Perhaps the most important step is the recognition that cultures are not right or wrong, better or worse; they are simply different. For every amusing, annoying, peculiar or repulsive cultural trait we find in a country, there is a similarly amusing, annoying or repulsive trait others see in our culture. We find it peculiar that the Chinese eat dogs, while they find it peculiar that we eat lambs, rabbits and most other animals but not dogs and cats.

Just because a culture is different does not make it wrong. Marketers must understand how their own culture influences their assumptions about another culture. The more exotic the situation, the more sensitive, tolerant and flexible one needs to be. Being more culturally sensitive will reduce conflict, improve communications and thereby increase success in collaborative relationships.

It is necessary for a marketer to investigate the assumptions on which judgements are based, especially when the frames of reference are strictly from his or her own culture.

Culture and its elements

The student of international marketing should approach an understanding of culture from the viewpoint of the anthropologist. Every group of people or society has a culture because culture is the entire social heritage of the human race: 'the totality of the knowledge and practices, both intellectual and material of society … [it] embraces everything from food to dress, from household techniques to industrial techniques, from forms of politeness to mass media, from work rhythms to the learning of familiar rules'.[7] Culture exists in New York, London and Moscow just as it does among the Gypsies, the South Sea Islanders or the Aborigines of Australia.

Elements of culture

The anthropologist studying culture as a science must investigate every aspect of a culture if an accurate, total picture is to emerge. To implement this goal, there has evolved a cultural scheme that defines the parts of culture. For the marketer, the same thoroughness is necessary if the marketing consequences of cultural differences within a foreign market are to be accurately assessed.

Culture includes every part of life. The scope of the term 'culture' to the anthropologist is illustrated by the elements included within the meaning of the term. These are:

1 material culture
   technology
   economics
2 social institutions
   social organisation
   political structures
3 education
   literacy rate
   role and levels
4 belief systems
   religion
   superstitions
   power structure
5 aesthetics
   graphic and arts
   folklore
   music, drama and dance
6 language[8]
   usage of foreign languages
   spoken versus written language.

In the study of humanity's way of life, the anthropologist finds these six dimensions useful because they encompass all the activities of social heritage that constitute culture (Exhibit 4.3). Foreign marketers

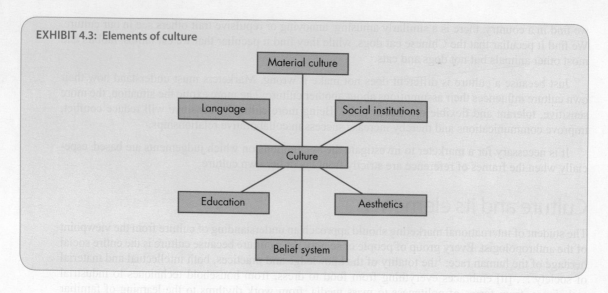

EXHIBIT 4.3: Elements of culture

may find such a cultural scheme a useful framework in evaluating a marketing plan or in studying the potential of foreign markets. All the elements are instrumental to some extent in the success or failure of a marketing effort because they constitute the environment within which the marketer operates. Furthermore, because we react automatically to many of these factors in our native culture, we must purposely learn them in another. Finally, these are the elements with which marketing efforts interact and so are critical to understanding the character of the marketing system of any society.

Material culture

Material culture is divided into two parts: technology and economics. Technology includes the techniques used in the creation of material goods; it is the technical know-how possessed by the people of a society. A culture's level of technology is manifest in many ways. Such concepts as preventive maintenance are foreign in many low-technology cultures. In Germany, the USA, Japan or other countries with high levels of technology, the general population has a broad level of technical understanding that allows them to adapt and learn new technology more easily than populations with lower levels of technology. Simple repairs, preventive maintenance and a general understanding of how things work all constitute a high level of technology. In China, one of the burdens of that country's economic growth is providing the general working population with a modest level of mechanical skill; that is, a level of technology.

Economics is the manner in which people employ their capabilities and the resulting benefits. Included in the subject of economics are the production of goods and services, their distribution, consumption, means of exchange and the income derived from the creation of utilities.

Material culture affects the level of demand, the quality and types of products demanded and their functional features, as well as the means of production of these goods and their distribution. The marketing implications of the material culture of a country are many: electric can-openers and electric juicers are acceptable in the USA, but, in less affluent countries and even some European countries, not only are they unattainable and probably unwanted, they would be a spectacular waste because **disposable income** could be spent more meaningfully on better houses, clothing or food.

> **disposable income**
>
> that proportion of your income that is not already accounted for – for example, by mortgages, loans, bills and so on

Social institutions

Social organisation and political structures are concerned with the ways in which people relate to one another, organise their activities to live in harmony with one another and govern themselves. The positions of men and women in society, the family, social classes, group behaviour and age groups are

EXHIBIT 4.4:   Concepts of self and others

Basic problem/cultural orientations	Contrasts across cultures
How should we treat unknown people? (a) Is human nature basically good or bad?	Unknown people are considered favourably and treated with confidence or, conversely, they are treated with suspicion when met for the first time

Appraising others
(b) When appraising others, emphasis
    placed on
    (i) age
    (ii) social class
	Who are the persons to be considered trustworthy and reliable, with whom it is possible to do business?
	(i) Older (younger) people are seen more favourably
	(ii) Social class plays a significant role (or not) in concepts of the self and others

Appraising oneself
(c) Emphasis placed on the self-concept
perceived as culturally appropriate:
    (i) self-esteem – low/high
    (ii) perceived potency – low/high
    (iii) level of activity – low/high
	(i) Shyly and modestly vs extrovert or even arrogant
	(ii) Power should be shown vs hidden
	(iii) Busy people are the good ones vs unoccupied/idle people are well thought of

Relating to the group (d) Individualism vs collectivism	The individual is seen as the basic resource and therefore individual-related values are strongly emphasised (personal freedom, human rights, equality between men and women); vs the group is seen as the basic resource and therefore group values favoured (loyalty, sense of belonging, sense of personal sacrifice for the community, etc.)

Source: J.-C. Usunier, *Marketing Across Cultures*, 2nd edn (Hemel Hempstead: Prentice Hall, 1996), p 66.

interpreted differently within every culture (see Exhibit 4.4). Each institution has an effect on marketing because each influences behaviour, values and the overall patterns of life.

In cultures where social organisation results in close-knit family units, for example, it is more effective to aim a promotional campaign at the family unit than at individual family members. Travel advertising in culturally divided Canada pictures a wife alone for the English audience, but a man and wife together for the French segments of the population because the French are traditionally more closely bound by family ties. The roles and status positions found within a society are influenced by the dictates of social organisation.

To illustrate the impact of the Self-Reference Criterion (SRC), consider misunderstandings that can occur about personal space between people of different cultures. In the West unrelated individuals keep a certain physical distance between themselves and others when talking to each other or in groups. We do not consciously think about that distance; we just know what feels right without thinking. When someone is too close or too far away, we feel uncomfortable and either move further away or get closer to correct the distance – we are relying on our SRC (see Exhibit 4.5).

In some cultures the acceptable distance between individuals is substantially less than that comfortable to Westerners. When Westerners, unaware of another culture's acceptable distance, are approached too closely by someone from another culture, they unconsciously react by backing away to restore the proper distance (ie proper by their own standards) and confusion results for both parties. Westerners assume 'foreigners' are pushy, while foreigners assume Westerners are unfriendly and standoffish. Both react to the values of their own SRCs, making them all victims of a cultural misunderstanding.

Education

In each society, we teach our generation what is acceptable or not acceptable, right or wrong, and other ways of behaviour. The literacy rate in each society is an important aspect and influences the behaviour of people. For a marketer it is important to know the role and level of education in a particular market. It will influence the marketing strategy and techniques used. Which type of advertising and communication is used depends highly on the level of education.

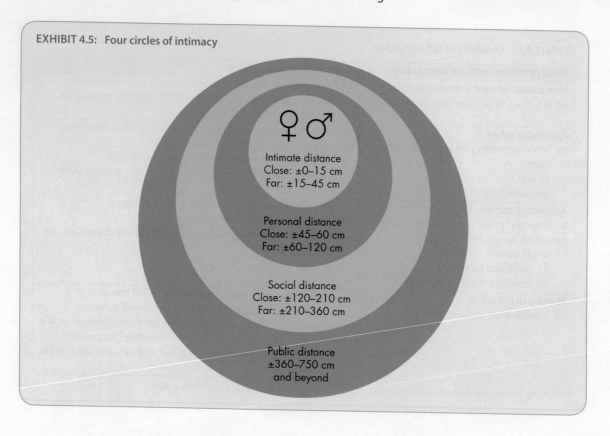

EXHIBIT 4.5:   Four circles of intimacy

Intimate distance
Close: ±0–15 cm
Far: ±15–45 cm

Personal distance
Close: ±45–60 cm
Far: ±60–120 cm

Social distance
Close: ±120–210 cm
Far: ±210–360 cm

Public distance
±360–750 cm
and beyond

Belief system

Within this category are religion, superstitions and their related power structures. The impact of religion on the value systems of a society and the effect of **value systems** on marketing must not be underestimated. Religion has an impact upon people's habits, their outlook on life, the products they buy, the way they buy them, even the newspapers they read. Acceptance of certain types of food, clothing and behaviour are frequently affected by religion, and such influence can extend to the acceptance or rejection of promotional messages as well. In some countries, too much attention to bodily functions or personal hygiene featured in advertisements would be judged immoral or improper and the products would be rejected.

> **value systems**
>
> values that are followed unconsciously

Going International 4.2

RELIGIOUS RITUALS

Life is filled with little rituals that we do every day or week, and there are some rituals we do only once in our lifetime. Every Muslim is enjoined to make the *hajj*, or pilgrimage, to Mecca once in his or her lifetime if physically and financially able. Here, some 2 million faithful from all over the world gather annually to participate in what is the largest ritual meeting on earth. Catholics have a ritual such as a pilgrimage to Rome, Lourdes, Czestochowa or Santiago de Compostela. Pilgrimages are made to the places where the gods or prophets were born, worked or died. In some cultures people visit shrines or temples and expect miracles and wonders.

▶

In some countries Catholics are supposed to make a pilgrimage on foot to one of these places, and it can take months before they arrive at the holy place.

Hard numbers are often scant in questions of faith. But a new report from the Pew Research Center, a self-described 'fact tank' in Washington, DC, on the state of religious belief in 2010 provides some welcome light. It estimates that 5.8 billion adults and children (around 84 per cent of the world population in 2010) have some kind of religious affiliation.

The largest ritual meeting on earth © AFP/CORBIS.

The world religious make-up

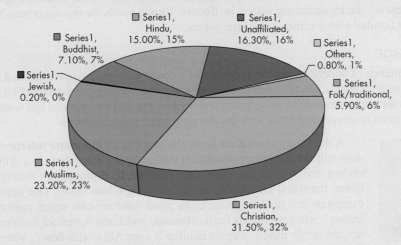

- Series1, Buddhist, 7.10%, 7%
- Series1, Jewish, 0.20%, 0%
- Series1, Hindu, 15.00%, 15%
- Series1, Unaffiliated, 16.30%, 16%
- Series1, Others, 0.80%, 1%
- Series1, Folk/traditional, 5.90%, 6%
- Series1, Muslims, 23.20%, 23%
- Series1, Christian, 31.50%, 32%

Of the 1.1 billion unaffiliated, many profess some belief in a higher power. Asia has by far the largest number of people who claim to have no religion; China's official atheism explains much of that. But 44 per cent of Chinese say they have worshipped at a graveside or tomb in the past year. And China has the world's seventh-largest Christian population, estimated at 68 million.

The report also contains data on believers who do not adhere to any of the Abrahamic religions, to Hinduism or to Buddhism. These include 405 million followers of folk religions, which are hard to measure. Other beliefs that often elude census-takers are Shintoism, Jainism, the Bahai faith, Sikhism, Wicca and Zoroastrianism. Their adherents are among the quarter of the world's believers who live as religious minorities: a category that also includes most Jews and Buddhists.[9]

Religion is one of the most sensitive elements of a culture. When the marketer has little or no understanding of a religion, it is easy to offend, albeit unintentionally. Like all cultural elements, one's own religion is often not a reliable guide of another's beliefs. Many do not understand religions other than their own, and what is 'known' about other religions is often incorrect. The Islamic religion is a good example of the need for a basic understanding. There are more than 1 billion people in the world who embrace Islam.

Superstition plays a much larger role in a society's belief system in some parts of the world than it does in Western culture. What Westerners might consider as mere superstition can be a critical aspect of a belief system in another culture. For example, in some countries, ghosts, fortune-telling, palmistry, head-bump reading, phases of the moon, demons and soothsayers are all integral parts of certain cultures. Astrologers are routinely called on in India, China and Thailand to determine the best location for a structure. The Thais insist that all wood in a new building must come from the same forest to prevent the boards from quarrelling with each other. Houses should have an odd number of rooms for luck, and they should be one storey because it is unlucky to have another's foot over your head.

It can be an expensive mistake to make light of superstitions in other cultures when doing business there. To make a fuss about being born in the right year under the right phase of the moon and to rely heavily on handwriting and palm-reading experts, as in Japan, can be worrisome to a Westerner who seldom sees a thirteenth floor in a building, refuses to walk under a ladder or worries about the next seven years after breaking a mirror.[10]

Aesthetics

Closely interwoven with the effect of people and the universe on a culture are its aesthetics; that is, the arts, folklore, music, drama and dance. Aesthetics are of particular interest to the marketer because of their role in interpreting the symbolic meanings of various methods of artistic expression, colour and standards of beauty in each culture. The uniqueness of a culture can be spotted quickly in symbols having distinct meanings.

Without a culturally correct interpretation of a country's aesthetic values, a whole host of marketing problems can arise. Product styling must be aesthetically pleasing to be successful, as must advertisements and package designs. Insensitivity to aesthetic values can offend, create a negative impression and, in general, render marketing efforts ineffective. Strong symbolic meanings may be overlooked if one is not familiar with a culture's aesthetic values.

Language

The importance of understanding the language of a country cannot be overestimated. The successful marketer must achieve expert communication; this requires a thorough understanding of the language as well as the ability to speak it. Advertising copywriters should be concerned less with obvious differences between languages and more with the idiomatic meanings expressed.

idiomatic interpretation

interpretation according to the characteristics of a particular language

A dictionary translation is not the same as an **idiomatic interpretation**, and seldom will the dictionary translation suffice. Quite often there is a difference between spoken and written language. One national food-processor's familiar 'Jolly Green Giant' translated into Arabic as 'Intimidating Green Ogre'. One airline's advertising campaign designed to promote its plush leather seats urged customers to 'fly on leather'; when translated for its Hispanic and Latin American customers, it told passengers to 'fly naked'. Pepsi's familiar 'Come Alive with Pepsi', when translated into German, conveyed the idea of coming alive from the grave. Schweppes was not pleased with its tonic water translation into Italian: 'Il Water' idiomatically means the bathroom. Electrolux's advertisement for its vacuum cleaner with the slogan 'Nothing Sucks Better than Electrolux' was not particularly appreciated in Ireland.

Many believe that to appreciate the true meaning of a language it is necessary to live with that language for years. Whether or not this is the case, foreign marketers should never take it for granted that they are communicating effectively in another language. Until a marketer can master the vernacular, the aid of a national within the foreign country should be enlisted; even then, the problem of effective communications may still exist. For example, in French-speaking countries, the trademark toothpaste brand name 'Cue' was a crude slang expression for *derrière*. The intent of a major fountain pen company advertising in Latin America suffered in translation when the new pen was promoted to 'help prevent unwanted pregnancies'.

Analysis of elements

Each cultural element must be evaluated in light of how it could affect a proposed marketing programme; some may have only indirect impact, others may be totally involved. Generally, it could be said that the more complete the marketing involvement or the more unique the product, the greater the need for thorough study of each cultural element. If a company is simply marketing an existing product in an already developed market, studying the total culture is certainly less crucial than for the marketer involved in total marketing – from product development, through promotion, to the final selling.

While analysis of each cultural element *vis-à-vis* a marketing programme could ensure that each facet of a culture is included, it should not be forgotten that culture is a total picture, not a group of unrelated elements. Culture cannot be separated into parts and be fully understood.

Going International 4.3

IT'S NOT THE GIFT THAT COUNTS, BUT HOW YOU PRESENT IT

Giving a gift in another country requires careful attention if it is to be done properly. Here are a few suggestions.

© Istockphoto.com/gmast3r

Japan

Do not open a gift in front of a Japanese counterpart unless asked and do not expect the Japanese to open your gift.

Avoid ribbons and bows as part of gift wrapping. Bows as we know them are considered unattractive, and ribbon colours can have different meanings.

Do not offer a gift depicting a fox or badger. The fox is the symbol of fertility, the badger, cunning.

Europe

Avoid red roses and white flowers, even numbers and the number 13. Unwrap flowers before presenting.

Do not risk the impression of bribery by spending too much on a gift.

Arab world

Do not give a gift when you first meet someone. It may be interpreted as a bribe.

Do not let it appear that you contrived to present the gift when the recipient is alone. It looks bad unless you know the person well. Give the gift in front of others in less personal relationships.

Latin America

Do not give a gift until after a somewhat personal relationship has developed unless it is given to express appreciation for hospitality.

Gifts should be given during social encounters, not in the course of business.

Avoid the colours black and purple; both are associated with the Catholic Lenten season.

China

Never make an issue of a gift presentation – publicly or privately.

Gifts should be presented privately, with the exception of collective ceremonial gifts at banquets.

Source: adapted from *International Business Gift-Giving Customs*, available from The Parker Pen Company.

Cultural change

Culture is dynamic in nature; culture is not static but a living process. That change is constant seems paradoxical in that another important attribute of culture is that it is conservative and resists change. The dynamic character of culture is significant in assessing new markets even though changes occur in the face of resistance. In fact, any change in the currently accepted way of life meets with more initial resistance than acceptance.[11]

There are a variety of ways in which a society solves the problems created by its existence. Accident has provided solutions to some of them; invention has solved many others. More commonly, however, societies have found answers by looking to other cultures from which they can borrow ideas. Cultural borrowing is common to all cultures.[12]

Cultural borrowing

Cultural borrowing is a responsible effort to borrow those cultural ways seen as helpful in the quest for better solutions to a society's particular problems. If what it does adopt is adapted to local needs, once the adaptation becomes commonplace, it is passed on as cultural heritage. Thus, cultures unique in their own right are the result, in part, of borrowing from others.[13]

Regardless of how or where solutions are found, once a particular pattern of action is judged acceptable by society, it becomes the approved way and is passed on and taught as part of the group's cultural heritage. Cultural heritage is one of the fundamental differences between humans and other animals. Culture is learned; societies pass on to succeeding generations solutions to problems, constantly building on and expanding the culture so that a wide range of behaviours is possible. The point is, of course, that although much behaviour is borrowed from other cultures, it is combined in a unique manner, which becomes typical for a particular society. To the foreign marketer, this similar-but-different feature of cultures has important meaning in gaining cultural empathy.

Going International 4.4

WHY DON'T MONKEYS GO BANANAS?

© P. N. Ghauri.

A number of behavioural scientists concluded an experiment where 10 monkeys were held in a room. A ladder was standing in the middle of the room and on top of the ladder some bananas were placed. It did not take long before one of the monkeys discovered the bananas and tried to reach them. As soon as the monkey climbed the ladder the whole group of monkeys was hosed down with pressured water by the scientists.

The drill was repeated until not one of the monkeys dared to reach for the bananas. Now one monkey was replaced by a new monkey. Of course the new monkey discovered the bananas. On his attempt to reach the bananas, the other monkeys attacked him because they knew what was going to happen to them if this new monkey tried to reach the bananas.

The scientists kept replacing the monkeys that had experienced the hosing until all of them were replaced by new monkeys. Eventually none of the monkeys in the community had experienced the hosing, yet as soon as a new monkey tried to reach for the bananas the other monkeys would pull it down from the ladder and attack it. The monkeys thus declined to get the bananas.

- Do we know why we behave in a certain manner in a given situation?

Source: translated from T. Pauka and R. Zunderdorp, *De Banaan Wordt Bespreekbaar. Cultuurverande ring in Ambtelijk en Politiek Groningn* (Amsterdam: Nijgh and van Ditmar, 1988).

Similarities: an illusion

For the inexperienced marketer, the similar-but-different aspect of culture creates illusions of similarity that usually do not exist. Several nationalities can speak the same language or have similar race and heritage, but it does not follow that similarities exist in other respects – that a product acceptable to one culture will be readily acceptable to the other, or that a promotional message that succeeds in one country will succeed in the other. A common language does not guarantee a similar interpretation of even a word or phrase. Both the British and the Americans speak English, but their cultures are sufficiently different that a single phrase has different meanings to each and can even be completely misunderstood. In England, one asks to be directed to a lift instead of an elevator, and an American, when speaking of a bathroom, generally refers to a toilet, while in England a bathroom is a place to take a bath. Also, the English 'hoover' a carpet whereas Americans vacuum clean it.

There is also the tendency to speak of the 'European consumer' as a result of growing integration in Europe. A marketer anxious to enter the market must not jump to the conclusion that a unified Europe means a common set of consumer wants and needs. Cultural differences among the members of the EU are the products of centuries of history that will take further centuries to erase.

Even the USA has many subcultures that today, with mass communications and rapid travel, defy complete homogenisation. It would be folly to suggest that the South is in all respects culturally the same as the Northeastern or Midwestern parts of the USA.[14]

India is another example: people from the south speak different languages and do not even understand Hindi or other languages of the north, west or east. There are more than 100 languages spoken in India, 25 of which are official languages. In fact, the only language that unites India is English.

Resistance to change

A characteristic of human culture is that change occurs. That people's habits, tastes, styles, behaviour and values are not constant but are continually changing can be verified by reading 20-year-old magazines. This gradual cultural growth does not occur without some resistance. New methods, ideas and products are held to be suspect before they are accepted, if ever, as right.

Most cultures tend to be **ethnocentric**, that is, they have intense identification with the known and the familiar of their culture and tend to devalue the foreign and unknown of other cultures. **Ethnocentrism** complicates the process of cultural assimilation by producing feelings of superiority about one's own culture and, in varying degrees, generates attitudes that other cultures are inferior, barbaric or at least peculiar.

> **ethnocentric**
>
> intense identification with the known and the familiar of a particular culture and a tendency to devalue the foreign and unknown of other cultures
>
> **ethnocentrism**
>
> when we behave in an ethnocentric way, there is an exaggerated tendency to believe our own values/norms/culture are superior to those of others

Planned cultural change

Marketers have two options when introducing an innovation to a culture: they can wait or they can cause change. The former requires hopeful waiting for eventual cultural changes that prove their innovations of value to the culture; the latter involves introducing an idea or product and deliberately setting about overcoming resistance and causing change that accelerates the rate of acceptance.

An innovation that has advantages, but requires a culture to learn new ways to benefit from these advantages, establishes the basis for eventual cultural change. Both a strategy of unplanned change and a strategy of planned change produce cultural change. The fundamental difference is that unplanned change proceeds at its own pace, whereas in planned change the process of change is accelerated by the change agent. When culturally congruent strategy, strategy of unplanned change and strategy of planned change are not clearly articulated in international marketing literature, the third situation occurs. The marketer's efforts become part of the fabric of culture, planned or unplanned.

Required adaptation

Adaptation is a key concept in international marketing and willingness to adapt is a crucial attitude. **Adaptation**, or at least accommodation, is required on small matters as well as large ones. In fact, the small, seemingly insignificant situations are often the

> **adaptation**
>
> making changes to fit a particular culture/environment/conditions

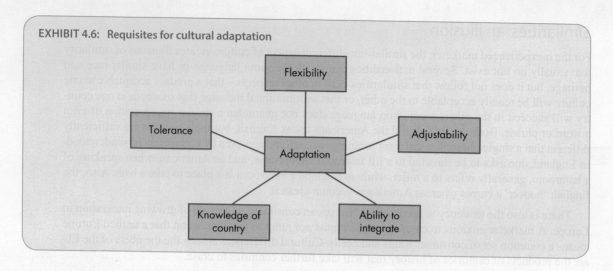

EXHIBIT 4.6: Requisites for cultural adaptation

most crucial. There is a need for affirmative acceptance; that is, open tolerance of the concept 'different but equal'. Through such affirmative acceptance, adaptation becomes easier because empathy for another's point of view naturally leads to ideas for meeting cultural differences.

As a guide to adaptation, there are five basic requisites that all who wish to deal with individuals, firms or authorities in foreign countries should be able to meet. These are given in Exhibit 4.6.

1 tolerance
2 flexibility
3 adjustability to varying tempos
4 knowledge of the country
5 ability to integrate oneself into the environment

In short, add the quality of adaptability to the qualities of a good executive for a composite of the perfect international marketer (see Exhibit 4.6).

Degree of adaptation

Adaptation does not require business executives to forsake their ways and change to conform with local customs; rather, executives must be aware of local customs and be willing to accommodate those differences that can cause misunderstanding. Essential to effective adaptation is awareness of one's own culture and the recognition that differences in others can cause anxiety, frustration and misunderstanding of the host's intentions.

The key to adaptation is to remain yourself but to develop an understanding of and willingness to accommodate differences that exist. A successful marketer knows that in Asia it is important to make points without winning arguments; criticism, even if asked for, can cause a host to 'lose face'. In Germany and the Netherlands it is considered discourteous to use first names unless specifically invited to do so: always address a person as Herr, Frau or Fräulein, and Meneer or Mevrouw with the last name.

A Chinese, Indian or Brazilian person does not expect you to act like one of them. After all, you are not Chinese, Indian or Brazilian but a Westerner, and it would be foolish for a Westerner to give up the ways that have contributed so notably to Western success. It would be equally foolish for others to give up their ways. When different cultures meet, open tolerance and a willingness to accommodate each other's differences are necessary.

Imperatives, adiaphora and exclusives

Although you are not obliged to adhere to the maxim 'while in Rome, do as Romans do', you need to be aware of the culture of the market that you are entering, or are planning to enter. This will allow you to be culturally sensitive so that you will not, at least, annoy people/locals with your behaviour. There are certain characteristics of a culture you must know and certain that you need to follow. Business customs can be grouped into imperatives (customs that must be recognised and accommodated), adiaphora (customs to which adaptation is optional) and exclusives (customs in which an outsider must not participate). An international marketer must appreciate the nuances of cultural imperative, cultural adiaphora and cultural exclusives.

Cultural imperative refers to the business customs and expectations that must be met and conformed to if relationships are to be successful. Successful business people know the Chinese word **guan-xi**, the Japanese **ningen kankei** and the Latin American **compadre**. All refer to friendship, human relations or attaining a level of trust. They also know there is no substitute for establishing friendship in some cultures before effective business relationships can begin.

Informal discussions, entertaining, mutual friends, contacts and just spending time with others are ways *guan-xi*, *ningen kankei*, *compadre* and other trusting relationships are developed. In those cultures where friendships are a key to success, the business person should not skimp on the time required for their development. Friendship motivates local agents to make more sales and friendship helps establish the right relationship with end users, leading to more sales over a longer period.[15]

Cultural adiaphora relates to areas of behaviour or to customs that cultural aliens may wish to conform to or participate in but that are not required. It is not particularly important, but it is permissible to follow the custom in question; the majority of customs fit into this category. One need not adhere to local dress, greet another man with a kiss (a custom in some countries) or eat foods that disagree with the digestive system (so long as the refusal is gracious). On the other hand, a symbolic attempt to participate in adiaphora is not only acceptable, but may also help to establish rapport. It demonstrates that the marketer has studied the culture.

Most jokes, even though well intended, don't translate well. Sometimes a translator can help you out. One speaker, in describing his experience, said, 'I began my speech with a joke that took me about two minutes to tell. Then my interpreter translated my story. About 30 seconds later the Japanese audience laughed loudly. I continued with my talk, which seemed well received but at the end, just to make sure, I asked the interpreter, "How did you translate my joke so quickly?" The interpreter replied, "Oh I didn't translate your story at all. I didn't understand it. I simply said our foreign speaker has just told a joke so would you all please laugh."'

cultural imperative
business customs and expectations that must be met and conformed to if relationships are to be successful

guan-xi
relationship building/friendship according to Chinese culture

ningen kankei
human relationships according to Japanese culture

compadre
friendship according to Latin American culture

cultural adiaphora
areas of behaviour or customs that cultural aliens may wish to conform to or participate in

Going International 4.5

COLOURS, THINGS, NUMBERS AND EVEN SMELLS HAVE SYMBOLIC MEANINGS … OFTEN NOT THE ONES YOU THINK!

Green, America's favourite colour for suggesting freshness and good health, is often associated with disease in countries with dense green jungles; it is a favourite colour among Arabs but forbidden in portions of Indonesia. In Japan green is a good high-tech colour, but Americans would shy away from green electronic equipment. Black is not universal for mourning: in many Asian countries white is worn; in Brazil purple, yellow in Mexico and dark red in the Ivory Coast. Americans think of blue as the most masculine colour, but red is manlier in the UK or France. While pink is the most feminine colour in America, yellow is more feminine in most of the world. Red suggests good fortune in China but death in Turkey. In America a sweet wrapped in blue or green is probably a mint; in Africa the same sweet would be wrapped in red. In every culture, things, numbers and even

▶

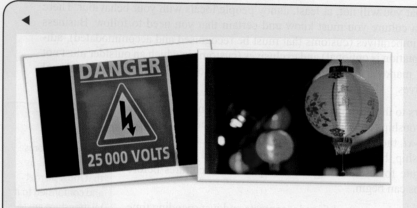

In some cultures the colour red is used to convey danger, whilst in others, it is considered lucky.
© Istockphoto.com/justinecottonphotography; tiposoy

smells have meanings. Lemon scent in the USA suggests freshness; in the Philippines lemon scent is associated with illness. In Japan the number 4 is like our 13; and 7 is unlucky in Ghana, Kenya and Singapore. The owl in India means bad luck, like our black cat. In Japan a fox is associated with witches. In China a green hat is like a dunce's cap; specifically it marks a man with an unfaithful wife. The stork symbolises maternal death in Singapore, not the kind of message you want to send to a new mother.

Cultural exclusives

customs or behaviour patterns reserved exclusively for the local people, from which the foreigner is excluded

Cultural exclusives are those customs or behaviour patterns reserved exclusively for the local people and from which the foreigner is excluded. For example, a foreigner criticising a country's politics, mores and peculiarities (that is, peculiar to the foreigner) is offensive even though locals may, among themselves, criticise such issues. There is truth in the old adage, 'I'll curse my brother, but if you curse him, you'll have a fight.' There are few cultural traits reserved exclusively for locals, but a foreigner must refrain from participating in those that are reserved. Religion, politics, treatment of women and minorities are some examples of such traits.

Communications emphasis

Probably no language readily translates into another because the meanings of words differ widely among languages. Even though it is the basic communication tool of marketers trading in foreign lands, managers, particularly from the USA and the UK, often fail to develop even a basic understanding of a foreign language, much less master the linguistic nuances that reveal unspoken attitudes and information. One writer comments that 'even a good interpreter doesn't solve the language problem'.[4]

The translation and interpretation of clearly worded statements and common usage is difficult enough, but when slang is added, the task is almost impossible. In an exchange between an American and a Chinese official, the American answered affirmatively to a Chinese proposal with, 'It's a great idea, Mr Li, but who's going to put wheels on it?' The interpreter, not wanting to lose face but not understanding, turned to the Chinese official and said, 'And now the American has made a proposal regarding the automobile industry'; the entire conversation was disrupted by the misunderstanding of a slang expression.

Linguistic communication, no matter how imprecise, is explicit, but much business communication depends on implicit messages that are not verbalised. E.T. Hall, Professor of Anthropology and for decades consultant to business and government on intercultural relations, says, 'In some cultures, messages are explicit; the words carry most of the information. In other cultures . . . less information is contained in the verbal part of the message since more is in the context.' Hall divides cultures into high-context and low-context cultures. Communication in a high-context culture depends heavily on the context or non-verbal

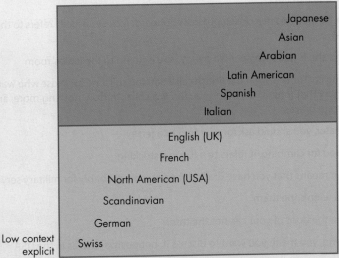

EXHIBIT 4.7: Contextual background of various countries

High context
implicit

Japanese
Asian
Arabian
Latin American
Spanish
Italian

English (UK)
French
North American (USA)
Scandinavian
German
Swiss

Low context
explicit

Source: patterned after E.T. Hall and M. Hall, 2001.

aspects of communication, whereas the low-context culture depends more on explicit, verbally expressed communications (see Exhibit 4.7). Managers in general probably function best at a low-context level because they are accustomed to reports, contracts and other written communications.

In a **low-context culture**, one gets down to business quickly. In a **high-context culture** it takes considerably longer to conduct business because of the need to know more about a business person before a relationship develops. They simply do not know how to handle a low-context relationship with other people. Hall suggests that 'in the Middle East, if you aren't willing to take the time to sit down and have coffee with people, you have a problem. You must learn to wait and not be too eager to talk business. You can ask about the family or ask, "how are you feeling?" but avoid too many personal questions about wives because people are apt to get suspicious. Learn to make what we call chit-chat. If you don't, you can't go to the next step. It's a little bit like a courtship' – the preliminaries establish a firm foundation for a relationship.

Even in low-context cultures, our communication is heavily dependent on our cultural context. Most of us are not aware of how dependent we are on the context and, as Hall suggests, 'since much of our culture operates outside our awareness, frequently we don't even know what we know'.

> **low-context culture**
>
> cultures that demand explicit communication
>
> **high-context culture**
>
> cultures that demand implicit communication

Going International 4.6

YOU SAY YOU SPEAK ENGLISH?

The English speak English and the North Americans speak English, but can the two communicate? It is difficult for a North American unless they understand that in England:

- newspapers are sold at newsagents
- the ground floor is the main floor, while the first floor is what Americans call the second, and so on up the building

▶

◀

- an apartment house is a block of flats

- in England you put your clothes, not in a closet, but in a cupboard; A closet usually refers to the WC or water closet, which is the toilet

- when a British friend says she is going to 'spend a penny', she is going to the ladies' room

- a bathing dress or bathing costume is what the British call a bathing suit, and for those who want to go shopping, it is essential to know that a tunic is a blouse; a stud is a collar button, nothing more; and garters are suspenders; suspenders are braces

- if you want to buy a sweater, you should ask for a jumper or a jersey

- a ladder is not always used for climbing, it refers to a run in a stocking

- if someone is called up, it means that you have drafted the person – probably for military service

- to ring someone up is to telephone them

- you put your packages in the boot of your car, not the trunk

- when you table something, you mean you want to discuss it, not postpone it, as in the USA

- any reference to an MD will probably not bring a doctor; the term means managing director in Britain

- when the receptionist asks what time you want to be knocked up in the morning, he is only referring to your wake-up call.

Marketers who expect maximum success have to deal with foreign executives in ways that are acceptable to the foreigner. Latin Americans depend greatly on friendships but establish these friendships only in the South American way: slowly, over a considerable period of time. A typical Latin American is highly formal until a genuine relationship of respect and friendship is established.

Going International 4.7

TIME: A MANY CULTURED THING

© Istockphoto.com/dsafanda

Time is cultural, subjective and variable. One of the most serious causes of frustration and friction in cross-cultural business dealings occurs when counterparts are out of sync with each other.

Differences often appear with respect to the pace of time, its perceived nature and its function. Insights into a culture's view of time may be found in their sayings and proverbs.

For example:

'Time is money' (USA).

'Those who rush arrive first at the grave' (Spain).

'The clock did not invent man' (Nigeria).

'If you wait long enough, even an egg will walk' (Ethiopia).

'Before the time, it is not yet the time; after the time, it's too late' (France).

Source: adapted from Edward T. Hall and Mildred Reed Hall, *Understanding Cultural Differences* (Yarmouth, ME: Intercultural Press, 1990), p 196; and Gart M. Wederspahn, 'On Trade and Cultures', *Trade and Culture*, Winter 1993–94, pp 4–6.

EXHIBIT 4.8: Monochronic (M-time) and polychronic (P-time) behaviour

Monochronic	Polychronic
Do one thing at a time	Do many things at a time
Task oriented	People oriented
Focused and concentrated	Easily distracted and subject to interceptions
Take deadlines seriously	Deadlines are flexible and are followed if possible
Follow schedules and procedures	Schedules and procedures are considered flexible
Make and follow plans	Make plans that can easily be changed and updated
Individualist	Collectivist
Seldom borrow or lend	Borrow and lend often
Exercise promptness	Base promptness on the matter and relationship
Accustomed to short-term relationships	Accustomed to lifelong relationships
Treat time as tangible	Treat time as intangible
Value privacy	Like to be surrounded by people (family and friends)

Source: compiled from Edward Hall, 'Monochronic and Polychronic Time', in Larry Samovar and Richard Porter, *International Communication: A Reader* (Belmont, CA: Thompson, 2003), pp 262–68.

The Westerner's desire to get straight to the point, to get down to business and other indications of directness are all manifestations of M-time cultures. The P-time system gives rise to looser time schedules, deeper involvement with individuals and a wait-and-see-what-develops attitude. For example, two Latins conversing would probably opt to be late for their next appointments rather than abruptly terminate the conversation before it came to a natural conclusion.

P-time is characterised by a much looser notion of on time or late. Interruptions are routine; delays to be expected. It is not so much putting things off until *mañana*, but the concept that human activities are not expected to proceed like clockwork (see Exhibit 4.8).

Most cultures offer a mix of P-time and M-time behaviour, but have a tendency to be either more P-time or M-time in regard to the role time plays. Some are similar to Japan where appointments are adhered to with the greatest M-time precision, but P-time is followed once a meeting begins. The Japanese see Western business people as too time-bound, and driven by schedules and deadlines that thwart the easy development of friendships. The differences between M-time and P-time are reflected in a variety of ways throughout a culture.

When business people from M-time and P-time meet, adjustments need to be made for a harmonious relationship. Often clarity can be gained by specifying tactfully, for example, whether a meeting is to be on Middle Eastern time or Western time. A Westerner who has been working successfully with the Saudis for many years says he has learned to take plenty of things to do when he travels. Others schedule appointments in their offices so they can work until their P-time friend arrives.

SUMMARY

A complete and thorough appreciation of the dimensions of culture may well be the single most important gain to a foreign marketer in the preparation of marketing plans and strategies. Marketers can control the product offered to a market – its promotion, price and eventual distribution methods – but they have only limited control over the cultural environment within which these plans must be implemented. Because they cannot control all the influences on their marketing plans, they must attempt to anticipate the eventual effect of the uncontrollable elements and plan in such a way that these elements do not preclude the achievement of marketing objectives. For these reasons, special effort and study are needed to absorb enough understanding of the foreign culture to cope with the uncontrollable features. Perhaps it is safe to generalise that of all the tools the foreign marketer must have, those that help generate empathy for another culture are the most valuable. Business customs and practices in different world markets vary so much that it is difficult to make valid generalisations about them; it is even difficult to classify the different kinds of business behaviour that are encountered from country to country. The only safe generalisations are that business people working in another country must be sensitive to the business environment and must be willing to adapt when necessary. Unfortunately, it is not always easy to know when such adaptation is necessary; in some instances adaptation is optional and, in others, it is actually undesirable. Understanding the culture you are entering is the only sound basis for planning.

Varying motivational patterns inevitably affect methods of doing business in different countries. Marketers in some countries thrive on competition, while in others they do everything possible to eliminate it. International variation characterises contact level, ethical orientation, negotiation outlook, and nearly every part of doing business. The foreign marketer can take no phase of business behaviour for granted.

The new breed of international business person that has emerged in recent years appears to have a heightened sensitivity to cultural variations. Sensitivity, however, is not enough; the international trader must constantly be alert and prepared to adapt when necessary. One must always realise that, no matter how long the outsider is in a country, that person is not a native; in many countries he or she may always be treated as an outsider. Finally, one must avoid the critical mistake of assuming that knowledge of one culture will provide acceptance in another.

QUESTIONS

1 Which role does the marketer play as a change agent?

2 Discuss the three cultural change strategies a foreign marketer can pursue.

3 'Culture is pervasive in all marketing activities.' Discuss.

4 Why should a foreign marketer be concerned with the study of culture?

5 What is the popular definition of culture? What is the viewpoint of cultural anthropologists? What is the importance of the difference?

6 It is stated that members of a society borrow from other cultures to solve problems, which they face in common. What does this mean? What is the significance to marketing?

7 'For the inexperienced marketer, the "similar-but-different" aspect of culture creates an illusion of similarity that usually does not exist.' Discuss and give examples.

8 Outline the elements of culture as seen by an anthropologist. How can a marketer use this 'cultural scheme'?

9 What is material culture? What are its implications for marketing? Give examples.

10 What are some particularly troublesome problems caused by language in foreign marketing? Discuss.

11 Cultures are dynamic. How do they change? Are there cases where changes are not resisted but actually preferred? Explain. What is the relevance to marketing?

12 How can resistance to cultural change influence product introduction? Are there any similarities in domestic marketing? Explain, giving examples.

13 Defend the proposition that a multinational corporation has no responsibility for the consequences of an innovation beyond the direct effects of the innovation such as the product's safety, performance and so forth.

14 Find a product whose introduction into a foreign culture may cause dysfunctional consequences. Describe how the consequences might be eliminated and the product still profitably introduced.

15 What are the requisites for cultural adaptation? Discuss.

16 What is meant by cultural imperatives, adiaphora and exclusives? Explain with examples.

FURTHER READING

- Kendall Roth, Tatiana Kostova and Mourad Dakhli, ' Exploring Cultural Misfit: Causes and Consequences', *International Business Review*, 2011, 20(1), pp 15-26.
- C. Barmeyer and U. Mayrhofer, 'The Contribution of Intercultural Management to the Success of International Mergers and Acquisitions: An Analysis of the EADS Group', *International Business Review*, 2008, 17(1), pp 28–38.
- A. Zueva-Owens, M. Fotaki and P. N. Ghauri, 'Cultural Evaluation and Subjectivity in Mergers and Acquisitions', *British Journal of Management,* 2012, 23 February: 272-90.

NOTES

1   J.-C. Usunier, *Marketing Across Cultures*, 6th edn (Harlow: Prentice Hall, 2012).

2   Francis Fukuyama, *Trust: The Social Virtues and the Creation of Prosperity* (London: Penguin, 1996).

3   Geert Hofstede, *Cultures and Organizations: Software of the Mind* (London: McGraw-Hill, 1991), p 5; see also other publications by Hofstede, eg *Culture's Consequences: Comparing Values, Behaviours, Institutions and Organisations Across Nations* (Thousand Oaks, CA: Sage, 2001).

4   Kendall Roth, Tatiana Kostova and Mourad Dakhli, ' Exploring Cultural Misfit: Causes and Consequences', *International Business Review,* 2011, 20(1), 15–26.

5   Cited in J.-C. Usunier, *Marketing Across Cultures*.

6   Lawrence Rout, 'To Understand Life in Mexico, Consider the Day of the Dead', *Wall Street Journal*, 4 November 1981, p 1.

7   T.M. Magstadt, *Understanding Politics: Ideas Institutions and Issues* (Stamford, CT: Wadsworth, 2010).

8   Melvin Herskovits, *Man and His Works* (New York: Knopf, 1952), p 634.

9   *The Economist*, 22 December, 2012, p 92.

10 See, for example, R.W. Scribner, 'Magic, Witchcraft and Superstition', *The Historical Journal*, March 1994, p 219.

11 Elizabeth K. Briody, 'On Trade and Cultures', *Trade and Culture*, March–April 1995, pp 5–6.

12 For an interesting article on cultural change, see Norihiko Shimizu, 'Today's Taboos May Be Gone Tomorrow', *Tokyo Business Today*, January 1995, pp 29–51.

13 R. Linton, *The Study of Man* (New York: Appleton-Century-Crofts, 1936), p 327.

14 See, for example, Denise M. Johnson and Scott D. Johnson, 'One Germany ... But is There a Common German Consumer? East–West Differences for Marketers to Consider', *The International Executive*, May–June 1993, pp 221–28.

15 P. Dimitratos, I. Voudouris, E. Plakoyiannaki and G. Nakos, ' International Entrepreneurial Culture – Towards Comprehensive Opportunity-based Operationalization of International Entrepreneurship', *International Business Review*, 2012, 21(4), 708–21.

Chapter 5

The International Political and Legal Environment

Chapter Outline

Chapter Learning Objectives

What you should learn from Chapter 5

- How political environment and stability influence international marketing
- What is meant by political risk
- How to evaluate risks and controls associated with investments in foreign markets
- How political vulnerability can be assessed and reduced
- The bases for today's legal systems
- How to protect intellectual property rights

Political environments

Every country has the recognised right to grant or withhold permission to do business within its political boundaries and to control where its citizens conduct business. A government controls and restricts a company's activities by encouraging and offering support or by discouraging and banning its activities – depending on the objectives of the government. A country's overall goals for its economic, political and social systems form the base for the political environment. Thus, the political climate in a country is a critical concern for the international marketer.[1]

National environments differ widely. Some countries are economically developed, some underdeveloped; some countries have an abundance of resources, others few or none; some countries are content with the status quo, others seek drastic changes to improve their relative positions in the world community.[2]

The ideal **political climate** for a foreign firm is a stable and friendly government. Unfortunately, governments are not always friendly and stable, nor do friendly, stable governments always remain so; changes in attitudes and goals can cause a stable and friendly situation to become risky. Changes are brought about by any number of events: a radical shift in the government when a political party with a philosophy different from the one it replaces ascends to power, government response to pressure from nationalist and self-interest groups, weakened economic conditions that cause a government to recant trade commitments, or an increasing bias against foreign investment. Since foreign businesses are judged by standards as variable as there are countries, the friendliness and stability of the government in each one must be assessed as an ongoing business practice. In so doing, a manager is better able to anticipate and plan for change and to know the boundaries within which the company can operate successfully.

> **political climate**
> political environment/ conditions

Stability of government policies

At the top of the list of political conditions that concern foreign businesses is the stability or instability of prevailing government policies. Governments might change or new political parties might be elected, but the concern of the foreign firm is the continuity of the set of rules or code of behaviour – regardless of which government is in power. In Italy, for example, there have been more than 55 different governments formed since the end of the Second World War.[3]

Conversely, radical changes in policies towards foreign business can occur in the most stable governments. If there is potential for profit and if permitted to operate within a country, companies can function under any type of government as long as there is some long-run predictability and stability. PepsiCo operated profitably in the Soviet Union under one of the most extreme political systems. It established a very profitable business with the USSR by exchanging Pepsi syrup for Russian vodka.[4] Socioeconomic and political environments invariably change; these changes are often brought about or reflected in changes in political philosophy and/or a surge in feelings of nationalistic pride.

Nationalism

Economic nationalism, which exists to some degree within all countries, is another factor leading to an unfavourable business climate. **Nationalism** can best be described as an intense feeling of national pride and unity, an awakening of a nation's people to pride in their country. Public opinion often tends to become anti-foreign business, and many minor harassments and controls of foreign investment are supported, if not applauded. **Economic nationalism** has as one of its central aims the preservation of national economic autonomy in that residents identify their interests with the preservation of the sovereignty of the state in which they reside. In other words, national interest and security are more important than international consideration.

These feelings of nationalism can be manifest in a variety of ways including 'buy our country's products only', restrictions on imports, restrictive tariffs and other

> **nationalism**
> an intense feeling of national pride and unity
> **economic nationalism**
> the preservation of national economic autonomy

barriers to trade. They may also lead to control over foreign investment, which is often regarded with suspicion and may be the object of intense scrutiny and control.[5] Generally speaking, the more a country feels threatened by some outside force, the more nationalistic it becomes in protecting itself against the intrusion. The American government's behaviour towards foreign trade and the refusal to sign the International Criminal Court (ICC) and Kyoto agreements, is a good example.[6]

expropriation

taking companies away from their owners and into state ownership (in this case)

During the period after the Second World War, when many new countries were founded and many others were seeking economic independence, manifestations of militant nationalism were rampant. **Expropriation** of foreign companies, restrictive investment policies and nationalisation of industries were common practices in some parts of the world. This was the period when India imposed such restrictive practices on foreign investments that companies such as Coca-Cola, IBM and many others chose to leave rather than face the uncertainty of a hostile economic climate.[7] Nationalism comes and goes as conditions and attitudes change, and foreign companies welcome today may be harassed tomorrow, and vice versa.[8]

While militant economic nationalism has subsided, nationalistic feelings can be found even in the most economically prosperous countries. Nationalism became an issue when Norwegian people said no to membership of the EU in a referendum. The UK has been reluctant to adopt the single European currency (the euro) for the same reasons.

It is important to appreciate that attitudes towards foreign companies and investments have totally changed in the last two decades. Today, most countries welcome foreign companies and in fact compete with each other to attract foreign firms by offering different types of benefit such as direct subsidies and tax relief.[9]

import restrictions

when it is not permitted to import into a country

confiscation

seizing a company's assets without payment

domestication

taking steps to transfer foreign investments to national control and ownership through a series of government decrees

joint venture

when two companies together open/start a third company

local content

portion of the local cost of a product that has to be produced locally

Political risks

The kinds of political risk confronting a company range from exchange controls, **import restrictions** and price controls. The most severe political risk is **confiscation** – seizing a company's assets without payment. Another type of risk is **domestication**, when host countries take steps to transfer foreign investments to national control and ownership through a series of government decrees. Governments seek to domesticate foreign-held assets by mandating:

- a transfer of ownership, in part or totally, to nationals
- the promotion of a large number of nationals to higher levels of management
- greater decision-making powers resting with nationals; for example, a number of countries demand that foreign companies can enter their market only through minority **joint ventures**
- a greater number of component products locally produced; for example, a number of countries (also EU and NAFTA) demand that at least 60 per cent of a product's content must be produced in the country (**local content**) to be classified as a local product and to avoid taxes or quotas.

A combination of all of these mandates is issued over a period of time and eventually control is shifted to nationals. The ultimate goal of domestication is to force foreign investors to share more of the ownership and management with nationals than was the case before domestication.

Political risk is still an important issue despite a more positive attitude towards MNCs and foreign investment. The transformation of China, the Commonwealth of Independent States (CIS), and Eastern Europe from Marxist-socialist economies to free market economies is a reality. Companies can reduce the political risk through efficient handling of a number of factors (see Exhibit 5.1).

EXHIBIT 5.1: Factors influencing the risk-reduction process in international marketing

Home-country factors	International legal factors	Host-country factors
• Reciprocal agreements • Legal restrictions • Sanctions/disputes	• WTO • Sanctions	• Political stability • Legal restrictions • Infrastructure • Sanctions/disputes

Political risk analysis
- Economic risk
- Local content regulation
- Assessing political vulnerability
- Import/export regulations
- Encouraging/discouraging foreign investments

Reducing political vulnerability
- Good corporate citizenship
- Strategies to lessen political risk
- Managing external affairs and PR

Going International 5.1

EU BATTLE OVER GM IMPORTS: NEW RULES, NEW NEGOTIATIONS

In 1999, the European Union established a moratorium on imports of new, genetically modified foods. In October 2002, it seemed that the European Union would remain closed to **GM foods** for the foreseeable future, despite the tough regulations on authorising the growing and importation of new GM crops passed on 17 October. The directive set stringent conditions for the use of new GM crops, and was designed to ease fears in some EU states about potential risks of GM foods. However, several EU governments, including those of France and Italy, called for extra rules allowing GM products to be traced and labelled through the food chain before the lifting of the moratorium.

© Istockphoto.com/
EduardHarkonen

The lack of progress angered the USA, where the use of GM crops is widespread. US exporters have been unable to ship to Europe commodities worth millions of dollars. However, after the initial reaction of threatening the EU with litigation through the World Trade Organization, the USA decided to try to influence the EU debate on the traceability and labelling legislation, which could potentially permanently block US farmers from selling GM crops in the EU.

The USA will certainly face difficulties in the negotiations with the EU over GM crops. Margot Wallstrom, EU environment commissioner said: 'In some member states, they are very much against GMOs. They will probably take every chance to move the goalposts and find another obstacle. Others are more constructive.' Negotiations are further complicated by the internal divisions within the EU itself. Washington wants the EU to drop its insistence on labelling processed food derived from GM crops where no traces of GM material remain, a

▶

position supported by the UK but few other EU governments. The EU is also divided on the level of accidental GM content that should be allowed in a conventional product or shipment before labelling rules would kick in. In addition, some states are calling for meat and eggs from animals fed on GM feed to be labelled.

In 2008 Japan gave the green light on the sale of cloned meat, however it seems that this will not happen in Europe. Despite many reports from Canada and the USA, claiming that meat and dairy produce from cloned meat is OK, the EU see things differently. The European Food Safety Authority would not give the milk and meat from cloned animals a clean bill of health.

The EU findings contrast with those of the US Food and Drug Administration, which concluded that regarding cloned meat products were safe. The European approach is similar to the approach they adopted regarding GM food.

- Do you think Europe should allow GM foods to be imported and sold in European countries?

Sources: adapted from M. Mann and E. Alden, 'EU Ban Stays on New GM Crops', *Financial Times*, 18 October 2002, p 7; *Farming UK*, 12 January 2009.

GM foods
genetically modified foods

Economic risks

Even though expropriation and confiscation are waning in importance, international companies are still confronted with a variety of economic risks. Restraints on business activity may be imposed under the banner of national security, to protect an infant industry, to conserve scarce foreign exchange, to raise revenue, to retaliate against unfair trade practices and a score of other real or imagined reasons.

Exchange controls

Exchange controls stem from shortages of foreign exchange held by a country. When a nation faces shortages of foreign exchange, controls may be levied over all movements of capital to conserve the supply of foreign exchange for the most essential uses.

Local content laws

In addition to restricting imports of essential supplies to force local purchase, a country often requires a portion of any product sold within that country to have local content; that is, to contain locally made parts. This is often imposed on foreign companies that assemble products from foreign-made components. The EU and NAFTA have had a local-content requirement as high as 65 per cent for some products.

Import restrictions

Selective restrictions on the import of raw materials, machines and spare parts are fairly common strategies to force foreign industry to purchase more supplies within the host country and thereby create markets for local industry. Although this is done in an attempt to support the development of domestic industry, the result is often to hamstring and sometimes interrupt the operations of established industries.

Tax controls

Taxes must be classified as a political risk when used as a means of controlling foreign investments. In such cases they are raised without warning and in violation of formal agreements. A squeeze on profits results from taxes being raised significantly as a business becomes established. In those countries where the economy is constantly threatened with a shortage of funds, unreasonable taxation of successful foreign investments appeals to some governments as the quickest means of finding operating funds.

Price controls

Essential products that command considerable public interest, such as pharmaceuticals, food, petrol and cars, are often subjected to price controls. Such controls applied during inflationary periods can be

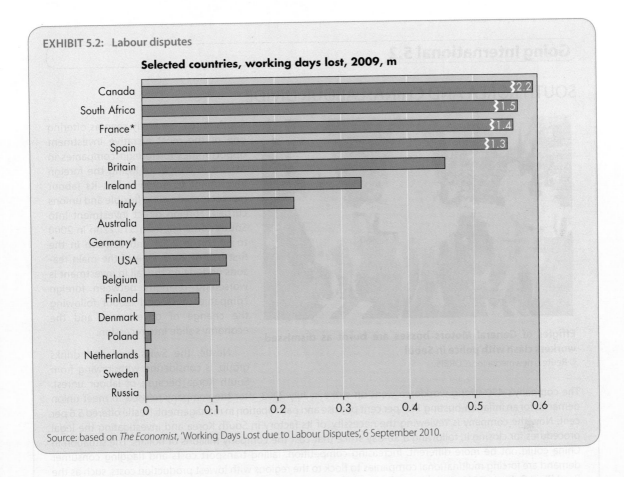

EXHIBIT 5.2: Labour disputes

Selected countries, working days lost, 2009, m

Canada	2.2
South Africa	1.5
France*	1.4
Spain	1.3
Britain	
Ireland	
Italy	
Australia	
Germany*	
USA	
Belgium	
Finland	
Denmark	
Poland	
Netherlands	
Sweden	
Russia	

Source: based on *The Economist*, 'Working Days Lost due to Labour Disputes', 6 September 2010.

used by a government to control the cost of living. They may also be used to force foreign companies to sell equity to local interests.

Labour problems

In many countries, labour unions have strong government support which they use effectively in obtaining special concessions from business. Layoffs may be forbidden, profits may have to be shared and an extraordinary number of services may have to be provided. In fact, in many countries, foreign firms are considered fair game for the demands of the domestic labour supply. Labour issues are not only a problem in developing countries; they are equally crucial in developed countries (see Exhibit 5.2).

Encouraging foreign investment

Governments also encourage foreign investment. In fact, within the same country, some foreign businesses fall prey to politically induced harassment while others may be placed under a government umbrella of protection and preferential treatment. The difference lies in the evaluation of a company's contribution to the national interest.

The most important reason to encourage foreign investment is to accelerate the development of an economy. An increasing number of countries are encouraging foreign investment with specific guidelines aimed at economic goals. Multinational corporations may be expected to create local employment, transfer technology, generate export sales, stimulate growth and development of local industry, and/or conserve foreign exchange as a requirement for market concessions.[10] Recent investments in China, India and countries in Eastern Europe include provisions stipulating specific contributions to economic goals of the country that must be made by foreign investors.[7]

Going International 5.2

SOUTH KOREA AND CHINA: LABOUR DIVIDE

Effigies of General Motors bosses are burnt as dismissed workers clash with police in Seoul
© Reuters newmedia Inc./CORBIS.

South Korea, generally seen as offering one of the most lucrative investment opportunities for foreign companies in Asia, is in danger of losing the foreign investment to China unless its labour market is made more flexible and unions curbed. Foreign direct investment into South Korea fell from $15.22bn in 2000 to $9.1bn in 2001 and $2.66bn in the first half of 2002. One of the main reasons underlying the fall in investment is worsening relations between foreign companies and local labour following the change of government and the economy's slide into recession.

Nestlé, the Swiss food and drinks group, is considering withdrawing from South Korea because of labour unrest. The company's 450-strong workforce went on strike in July 2003 after the company refused to meet union demands for an inflation-busting 11.7 per cent pay rise and participation in management. Nestlé offered 5.6 per cent. Now the company is 'reviewing the necessity' of its factory in South Korea and investigating the legal procedures for closing it, following a 50-day strike that cost the company millions of dollars. The situation in China could not be more different. Increasing competition, falling transport costs and flagging consumer demand are forcing multinational companies to flock to the regions with lowest production costs, such as the Pearl River Delta. In 2002 more goods were exported from China's Guangdong province, which encompasses the Pearl River Delta, than during the entire 13-year period from 1978 to 1990. Total Chinese exports grew 21 per cent in 2002 to $322bn and have doubled in just over five years. In contrast, it took Germany 10 years to double exports in the 1960s and seven for Japan in the 1970s. China's inexhaustable supply of land, labour and government encouragement has kept costs down and exported price deflation around the world. Dr Martens, one of many companies driven to China by fierce price competition from firms already manufacturing in China, used small groups of workers assembling complete shoes in its Northampton factory, paid them about $490 a week and has built a stadium for its local football club. Pou Chen, a manufacturer that Dr Martens contracted upon moving its operations to China from the UK, pays about $100 a month, or 36 cents an hour, for up to 69 hours a week and provides dormitories for migrant workers, who must obey strict curfews.

The relentless competition among local suppliers also keeps the profit margins almost invisible. Pou Chen has to worry about more than 800 other shoemakers in the Pearl River Delta. However, companies are avoiding labour shortages and rising wages by moving inland where labour is more plentiful. In the words of Mitsuhiko Ikuno, a Japanese managing director, 'There are high levels of engineers and college graduates and plenty of girls with good eyes and strong hands. If we run out of people, we just go deeper into China.'

● Are labour unions to be blamed for falling FDI in South Korea? Are labour unions good?

Sources: adapted from Andrew Ward, 'Nestlé Threat to Pull Out of South Korea', *Financial Times*, 4 September 2003, p 31; and Dan Roberts and James Kynge, 'How Cheap Labour, Foreign Investment and Rapid Industrialisation are Creating a New Workshop of the World', *Financial Times*, 4 February 2003, p 21.

When Pepsi re-entered India in early 1992, it was restricted to a minority position (40 per cent) in a joint venture. In addition, it was required to develop an agricultural research centre to produce high-yielding seed varieties, construct and operate a snack-food processing plant and a vegetable processing plant, and, among other foreign exchange requirements, guarantee that export revenues would be five times greater than money spent on imports. Pepsi agreed to these conditions and by 1994 had captured 26 per cent of the Indian soft drinks market. In contrast, when Coke re-entered the Indian market a few years later, requirements for entry were minimal. Unlike Pepsi, Coca-Cola was able to have 100 per cent ownership of its subsidiary.[11]

Along with direct encouragement from a host country, a company may receive assistance from its home government. The intent is to encourage investment by helping to minimise and shift some of the risks encountered in some foreign markets. A number of other facilities are often also available such as **export credit guarantee**.

> **export credit guarantee**
>
> when a government/ organisation ensures to give a loan to an exporter
>
> **high-priority industries**
>
> when some industries are given extra benefits by the authorities because they are considered important

Assessing political vulnerability

Some products appear to be more politically vulnerable than others, in that they receive special government attention. This special attention may result in positive actions towards the company or in negative attention, depending on the desirability of the product. It is not unusual for countries seeking investments in **high-priority industries** to excuse companies from taxes, customs duties, quotas, exchange controls and other impediments to investment.

Politically sensitive products

There are at least as many reasons for a product's political vulnerability as there are political philosophies, economic variations and cultural differences. Unfortunately, there are no absolute guidelines a marketer can follow to determine whether or not a product will be subject to political attention. Fast-food companies have been subject to protests in India. As McDonald's admitted that it used beef flavours to lace its French fries, a lawsuit was filed against the company for secretly misleading the customers. Beef is forbidden according to Hindu religion. The EU is quite sensitive about genetically modified (GM) food. Recently Unilever announced that it will stop using GM ingredients in its food products in Britain. Additionally, 11 leading fast-food restaurants, such as McDonald's, Burger King and Pizza Hut, have eliminated GM ingredients in their European branches.

Forecasting political risk

In addition to qualitative measures of political vulnerability, a number of firms are employing systematic methods of measuring political risk.[12] **Political risk assessment** is an attempt to forecast political instability to help management identify and evaluate political events and their potential influence on current and future international marketing decisions. Political risk assessment can:

> **political risk assessment**
>
> an attempt to forecast political instability to help management identify and evaluate political events and their potential influence on current and future business decisions

- help managers decide if risk insurance is necessary
- devise an intelligence network and an early warning system
- help managers develop contingency plans for unfavourable future political events
- build a database of past political events for use by corporate management
- interpret the data gathered by its intelligence network to advise and forewarn corporate decision makers about political and economic situations.

These days there are a number of political rankings available (see Exhibit 5.3).

For a marketer doing business in a foreign country, a necessary part of any market analysis is an assessment of the probable political consequences of a marketing plan; some marketing activities are more susceptible to political considerations than others. Basically, it boils down to evaluating the essential nature of the immediate activity. The following section explores ways businesses can reduce political vulnerability.

EXHIBIT 5.3: Country risk ratings

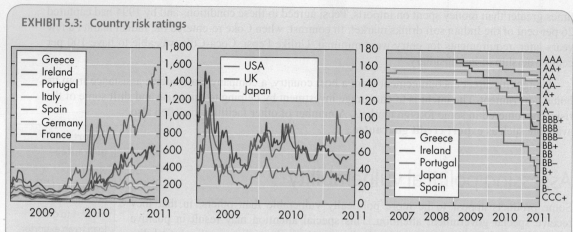

Five-year on-the-run CDS spreads, in basis points and Average of Fitch, Moody's and Standard & Poor's foreign currency long-term sovereign ratings.

Grades	Investment rating	Grades	Investment rating
AAA	Prime	BB+	Non-investment grade
AA+	High grade	BB	Speculative
AA		BB–	
AA–		B+	Highly speculative
A+	Upper medium grade	B	
A		B–	
A–		CCC	Substantial risks
BBB+	Lower medium grade		Extremely speculative
BBB			Default imminent with little prospect for recovery
BBB–			

Sources: Bloomberg; Markit.

Reducing political vulnerability

Even though a company cannot directly control or alter the political environment of the country within which it operates, there are measures that can lessen the degree of susceptibility of a specific business venture to politically induced risks. Foreign investors are frequently accused of exploiting a country's wealth at the expense of the national population and for the sole benefit of the foreign investor.

Good corporate citizenship

There is certainly much to be said for attempting to become more closely identified with the ideals and desires of the host country. To do so might render a marketer's activities and products less politically vulnerable; and, although it would not eliminate all the risks of the political environment, it might reduce the likelihood and frequency of some politically motivated risks. In addition to being good citizens, responsive to various publics, there are other approaches that help minimise the effects of hostile political environments.[13]

Strategies to lessen political risk

In addition to corporate activities focused on the social and economic goals of the host country and good corporate citizenship, MNCs can use other strategies to minimise political vulnerability and risk.

Joint ventures

Typically less susceptible to political harassment, joint ventures can be with either locals or other third-country multinational companies; in both cases, a company's financial exposure is limited. A joint venture with locals helps minimise anti-MNC feeling, and a joint venture with another MNC adds the additional bargaining power of a third country. It is also a preferred entry strategy in countries with relatively higher political risk.

Going International 5.3

INDIAN COURT ORDERS TESTS ON COCA-COLA AND PEPSI'S SOFT DRINKS

A New Delhi court ordered independent testing of Pepsi soft drinks following allegations that they and those of Coca-Cola's Indian subsidiary were polluted with pesticides. The ruling, which follows a decision of the Indian Parliament to ban the two brands from its premises, was welcomed by PepsiCo.

The Centre for Science and Environment (CSE), the pressure group that made the allegations, said it also welcomed the ruling since it believed it would corroborate its own tests, which it says were conducted under US government protocols. The CSE alleged that 12 soft drinks owned by the two companies contained traces of deadly pesticide, including DDT, from the groundwater that is used in the drinks.

The pressure group said the threat to public health extended far beyond the quality of soft drinks, since it was the broader contamination of water that was at issue. Indian law does not define clean water. However, the campaign to boycott Pepsi and Coke appears to be gaining momentum in parts of India. The youth wing of the Hindu nationalists organised demonstrations where bottles of Coke and Pepsi were smashed. The Indian arms of Coca-Cola and PepsiCo hinted strongly that they were planning legal action against the CSE, a non-government body.

Locals protest against Pepsi
© Sharad Saxena/India Today

Four of the 30 state governments said they would test Pepsi and Coca-Cola for toxins. The two companies placed advertisements in the largest-circulation Indian newspapers seeking to counter the CSE's allegations. But many of the newspapers also carried editorials accusing the two of double standards. 'This is trial by media,' said Rajeev Bakshi, chairman of Pepsi India. 'We are also concerned that there are other players [parliament and government] getting in on the act.' Pepsi said that its regular in-house tests showed that the quality of its products did conform to European Union norms. But India's standards left room for confusion. 'Our aim must surely be to get the Indian government to establish transparent standards and procedures so that campaigns like this do not happen in this way again,' said the chairman of Pepsi India.

- How should Pepsi and Coca-Cola handle this situation?

Sources: Edward Luce, 'Coca-Cola and Pepsi May Take Legal Action Over "Pesticide" Claim', *Financial Times*, 8 August 2003, p 10; and Edward Luce, 'Indian Court Orders Further Tests on Pepsi's Soft Drinks', *Financial Times*, 12 August 2003, p 8.

Expanding the investment base

Including several investors and banks in financing an investment in the host country is another strategy. This has the advantage of engaging the power of the banks whenever any kind of government takeover or harassment is threatened. This strategy becomes especially powerful if the banks have made loans to the host country; if the government threatens expropriation or other types of takeover, the financing bank has substantial power with the government.

Marketing and distribution

Controlling distribution in world markets can be used effectively if an investment should be expropriated; the expropriating country would lose access to world markets. This has proved especially useful for MNCs in the extractive industries where world markets for iron ore, copper and so forth are crucial to the success of the investment. Peru found that, when Marcona Mining Company was expropriated, the country lost access to iron ore markets around the world and ultimately had to deal with Marcona on a much more favourable basis.

Licensing

A strategy that some firms find eliminates almost all risks is to license technology for a fee. It can be effective in situations where the technology is unique and the risk is high. Of course, there is some risk assumed because the licensee can refuse to pay the required fees while continuing to use the technology.

Legal environments

Laws governing business activities within and between countries are an integral part of the legal environment of international marketing. A Chinese company doing business with France has to contend with two jurisdictions (China and France), two tax systems, two legal systems and a third supranational set of EU laws and regulations that may override French commercial law. Because no single, uniform international commercial law governing foreign business transactions exists, the international marketer must pay particular attention to the legal environment of each country within which it operates.

Going International 5.4

MARKET-DRIVEN POLITICAL REFORMS

There have long been two official perceptions of China in the USA: those who welcome economic engagement with the country and those who, by limiting contracts, would restrain its ascending power. Those committed to containment, represented mainly by the Republican Party's right wing, insist that economic engagement does not foster changes to China's repressive political system. The engagement school, on the other hand, holds that as the Chinese become wealthier, so their demands for political representation increase.

Important changes now under way in China support the case for engagement: cities in coastal China, motivated by foreign investors, are embarking on experiments to introduce checks and balances to single-party rule. Yu Youjun, mayor of Shenzhen, says that foreign companies, especially those establishing high-technology factories, are mindful of the need to protect intellectual property: 'Every multinational company and investor is influenced by the investment climate created by governments.' The 'hard environment' of roads, railways, ports and telecommunications was important, but more crucial was the 'soft environment', meaning a government that is 'democratic' and transparent.

The crux of the current reform is a strict separation of the roles of the Communist Party, the executive government and the local legislature. The party would be responsible for setting the broad direction of policy, but would be prevented from interfering in its execution. The local legislature would be charged

▶

with reviewing and supervising the government's work. In addition, seizing on the trend for greater accountability, many cities last year opened themselves to criticism from local and foreign companies. This practice, known as *wan ren ping zhengfu*, or '10 000 people criticise the government', has become something of a phenomenon. The Chaoyang district of Beijing sent questionnaires to companies – 40 per cent of them foreign – asking participants to rate the performance of the local government departments. The top-rated departments will receive a bonus; the bottom ones will have their bonuses reduced. China has decreed that local governments will have to survive purely from tax income, cutting them off from the dividends they used to collect from local state-owned enterprises. This means their income will be decided by how many companies invest in their locality.

- Do you think the world should force China to adopt a Western-style democracy?

Source: adapted from 'To Woo Investors, Cities Experiment with Political Reform', *Financial Times*, 4 February 2003, p 21.

www.adrianbradshaw.com.

Bases for legal systems

Two common heritages form the bases for the majority of the legal systems of the world:

1 common law, derived from English law and found in England, Australia, the USA, Canada[14] and other countries once under English influence

2 civil or code law, derived from Roman law and found in Germany, Japan, France and a number of other countries

3 Islamic law, derived from the interpretation of the Koran and found in Iran, Saudi Arabia and some other Islamic states

4 socialist law, derived from the Marxist-socialist system and found in some of the Newly Independent States (NIS) of the former Soviet Union, and in China and other socialist states.

The differences among these systems are of more than theoretical importance because due process of law may vary considerably among and within these legal systems. Even though a country's laws may be based on one of these legal systems, its individual interpretation may vary significantly.

Common and code law

The basis for **common law** is tradition, past practices and legal precedents set by the courts through interpretations of statutes, legal legislation and past rulings. Common law seeks 'interpretation through the past decisions of higher courts, which interpret the same statutes or apply established and customary principles of law to a similar set of facts'.

Code law is based on an all-inclusive system of written rules (codes) of law. Under code law, the legal system is generally divided into three separate codes: commercial, civil and criminal. Common law is recognised as not being all inclusive, while code law is considered complete as a result of catch-all provisions found in most code-law systems. For example, under the commercial code in a code-law country, the law governing contracts is made inclusive with the statement that 'a

common law

tradition, past practices and legal precedents set by the courts through interpretations of statutes, legal legislation and past rulings

code law

law based on written (coded) rules

person performing a contract shall do so in conformity with good faith as determined by custom and good morals'. Although code law is considered all-inclusive, it is apparent from the foregoing statement that some broad interpretations are possible in order to include everything under the existing code.

intellectual property rights

laws governing the ownership of intellectual property

As we discuss later, in the section on protection of **intellectual property rights**, laws governing intellectual property offer the most striking differences between common-law and code-law systems.[15] Under common law, ownership is established by use; under code law, ownership is determined by registration. Although every country has elements of both common and code law, the differences in interpretation between common- and code-law systems regarding contracts, sales agreements and other legal issues are significant enough that an international marketer familiar with only one system must enlist the aid of legal counsel for the most basic legal questions.

An illustration of where fundamental differences in the two systems can cause difficulty is in the performance of a contract. Under common law in the USA, it is fairly clear that impossibility of performance does not necessarily excuse compliance with the provisions of a contract unless it is impossible to comply for reasons of an **act of God**, such as some extraordinary happening of nature not reasonably anticipated by either party to a contract. Hence, floods, lightning, earthquakes and similar occurrences are generally considered acts of God. Under code law, acts of God are not limited solely to acts of nature but are extended to include 'unavoidable interferences with performance, whether resulting from forces of nature or unforeseeable human acts', including such things as labour strikes and riots.

act of God

an extraordinary happening of nature not reasonably anticipated by either party to a contract, ie earthquakes, floods, etc

Shari'ah

Islamic law

Islamic and socialist law

The basis for the **Shari'ah** (Islamic law) is the interpretation of the Koran. It encompasses religious duties and obligations as well as the secular aspect of law regulating human acts. Broadly speaking, Islamic law defines a complete system that prescribes specific patterns of social and economic behaviour for all individuals. It includes issues such as property rights, economic decision making and types of economic freedom. The overriding objective of the Islamic system is social justice.

riba

the unlawful advantage by way of excess of deferment; that is, excessive interest or usury

Among the unique aspects of Islamic law is the prohibition of the payment of excessive interest. The Islamic law of contracts states that any given transaction should be devoid of **riba**, defined as unlawful advantage by way of excess of deferment; that is, excessive interest or usury. This impacts on banking practices severely; however, a method for payment for the use of money has been developed by Islamic banks through an ingenious compromise.[16] Instead of an interest-bearing loan, banks finance trade by buying some of the borrower's stock, which it then sells back to the company at a higher price. The size of the mark-up is determined by the amount and maturity of the loan and the creditworthiness of the borrower – all traditional yardsticks for determining interest rates. This is practised and is an example of the way Islamic law can be reconciled with the laws of non-Islamic legal systems.[17]

socialist laws

cluster around the core concept of economic, political and social policies of the state; socialist countries are, or were, those whose laws derived from the Roman or code-law system

Socialist laws, based on the fundamental tenets of the Marxist-socialist state, cluster around the core concept of economic, political and social policies of the state. Socialist countries are, or were, generally those that formerly had laws derived from the Roman or code-law system. Some of the characteristics of Roman law have been preserved within their legal systems. Although much of the terminology and other similarities of code law have been retained in socialist law, the basic premise on which socialist law is based is that 'law, according to socialist tenets, is strictly subordinate to prevailing economic conditions'.[18] Thus, the words property, contract and arbitration denote different realities because of the collectivisation of the means of production and state planning.

As socialist countries become more liberal, laws governing ownership, contracts and other business realities have been developed to reconcile the differences between socialist law and the common or code law that prevails in most of the industrialised world.

China, for example, has had to pass laws covering the protection of intellectual property rights, clarifying ownership rights in joint ventures, and other pieces of commercial legislation necessary for international business.

The international marketer must be concerned with the differences among systems when operating between countries because the rights of the principals of a contract or some other legal document under one law may be significantly different from the rights under the other. It should be kept in mind that there can also be differences between the laws of two countries whose laws are based on the same legal system. Thus, the problem of the marketer is one of anticipating the different laws regulating business, regardless of the legal system of the country.

Going International 5.5

WAL-MART ARM SETTLES OVER FAKES

Sam's Club, a division of the US retailer Wal-Mart, has admitted selling fake Fendi bags and wallets and has agreed to pay an unspecified amount of money in order to make amends to the Italian fashion house's owner, LVMH. The settlement is the latest example of how luxury-brand owners are becoming more publicly assertive in protecting themselves from counterfeiting.

Sam's Club operates on a membership system and promises customers 'name brands at warehouse savings'. Fendi was founded in Rome in 1925 and has become an important brand for LVMH, whose fashion and leather goods division is dominated by Louis Vuitton. Fendi sued Sam's Club last year. As part of the settlement announced yesterday afternoon, it will abandon this litigation. LVMH also sued

© P. N. Ghauri.

eBay last year, alleging that the products sold on the auction site bearing the Louis Vuitton name were fakes in the vast majority of cases.

Doug McMillon, president and chief executive of Sam's Club, said in the same statement: 'We have programmes in place to protect the intellectual property rights of others. However, during this litigation, Fendi provided us with information that the 12 types of bags and wallets specifically listed in its complaint were not genuine. We accept this information.' He added: 'We recognise the importance of enforcing intellectual property rights. We expect our suppliers to respect these rights as well, and we will not tolerate deviation from that high standard.' Sam's Club members will be allowed to return any fake Fendi products that they might have bought from its stores and receive a full refund.

Source: *Financial Times*, 7 June 2008, p 25.

Determining whose legal system has **jurisdiction** when a commercial dispute arises is another problem of international marketing. A frequent error is to assume that disputes between citizens of different nations are adjudicated under some supranational system of laws. Unfortunately, no judicial body exists to deal with

> **jurisdiction**
> overall legal authority

legal commercial problems arising between citizens of different countries. Confusion probably stems from the existence of international courts, such as the World Court in The Hague and the International Court of Justice, the principal judicial organ of the United Nations. These courts are operative in international disputes between sovereign nations of the world rather than between private citizens.

Legal recourse in resolving international disputes

Should the settlement of a dispute on a private basis become impossible, the foreign marketer must resort to more resolute action. Such action can take the form of conciliation, arbitration or, as a last resort, litigation. Most international business people prefer a settlement through arbitration rather than by suing a foreign company.

Conciliation

conciliation

a non-binding agreement between parties to resolve disputes by asking a third party to mediate

Although arbitration is recommended as the best means of settling international disputes, conciliation can be an important first step for resolving commercial disputes. **Conciliation** is a non-binding agreement between parties to resolve disputes by asking a third party to mediate the differences.

Conciliation is considered to be especially effective when resolving disputes with Chinese business partners because they are less threatened by conciliation than arbitration. The Chinese believe that, when a dispute occurs, friendly negotiation should be used first to solve the problem; if that fails, conciliation should be tried. In fact, some Chinese companies may avoid doing business with companies that resort first to arbitration.

Conciliation can be either formal or informal. Informal conciliation can be established by both sides agreeing on a third party to mediate. Formal conciliation is conducted under the auspices of the Beijing Conciliation Centre, which assigns one or two conciliators to mediate. If agreement is reached, a conciliation statement based on the signed agreement is recorded. Although conciliation may be the friendly route to resolving disputes in China, it is not legally binding, so an arbitration clause should be included in all conciliation agreements.

Arbitration

arbitration

mediation done by a third party in case of a commercial dispute

International commercial disputes are often resolved by **arbitration** rather than litigation. The usual arbitration procedure is for the parties involved to select a disinterested and informed party or parties as referee(s) to determine the merits of the case and make a judgement that both parties agree to honour.

Tribunals for arbitration

Although the preceding informal method of arbitration is workable, most arbitration is conducted under the auspices of one of the more formal domestic and international arbitration groups organised specifically to facilitate the mediation of commercial disputes. These groups have experienced arbitrators available and formal rules for the process of arbitration. In most countries, decisions reached in formal mediation are enforceable under the law.

Among the formal arbitration organisations are:

1 the International Chamber of Commerce (ICC)
2 the London Court of Arbitration; decisions are enforceable under English law and in English courts
3 the American Arbitration Association

The history of ICC effectiveness in arbitration has been spectacular. An example of a case that involved arbitration by the ICC concerned a contract between an English business and a Japanese manufacturer. The English business agreed to buy 100,000 plastic dolls for 80 cents each. On the strength of the contract, the English business sold the entire lot at $1.40 per doll. Before the dolls were delivered, the Japanese manufacturer had a strike; the settlement of the strike increased costs and the English business was informed that the delivery price of the dolls had increased from 80 cents to $1.50 each. The English business maintained that the Japanese firm had committed to make delivery at 80 cents and should deliver at that price. Each side was convinced that it was right. The Japanese, accustomed to code law, felt that the strike was beyond control, was an act of God, and thus compliance with the original provisions of the contract was excused. The English, accustomed to common law, did not accept the Japanese reasons for not complying because they considered a strike the normal course of doing business and not an act of God. The dispute could not be settled except through arbitration or litigation. They chose arbitration; the ICC appointed an arbitrator who heard both sides and ruled that the two parties would share proportionately in the loss. Both parties were satisfied with the arbitration decision and costly litigation was avoided. Most arbitration is successful, but success depends on the willingness of both parties to accept the arbitrator's rulings.

Litigation

Lawsuits in public courts are avoided for many reasons. Most observers of **litigation** between citizens of different countries believe that almost all victories are spurious because the cost, frustrating delays and extended aggravation that these cases produce are more oppressive by far than any matter of comparable size. The best advice is to seek a settlement, if possible, rather than sue.

> **litigation**
> taking the other party to court

One authority suggests that the settlement of every dispute should follow three steps: first, try to placate the injured party; if this does not work, conciliate, arbitrate; and, finally, litigate. The final step is typically taken only when all other methods fail.

Protection of intellectual property rights: a special problem

Companies spend millions of dollars establishing brand names or trademarks to symbolise quality and a host of other product features designed to entice customers to buy their brands to the exclusion of all others. Such intellectual or industrial properties are among the more valuable assets a company may possess. Names such as Philips, Sony, Swatch, Kodak, Coca-Cola and Gucci, and rights to processes such as xerography and computer software are invaluable.

Estimates are that more than 10 million fake Swiss watches carrying famous brand names such as Cartier and Rolex are sold every year, netting illegal profits of at least €550m ($600m). Although difficult to pinpoint, lost sales from the unauthorised use of patents, **trademarks** and copyrights amount to more than €90bn ($100bn) annually. That translates into more than a million lost jobs. Software is an especially attractive target for pirates because it is costly to develop but cheap to reproduce. Unauthorised software that sells for €450 ($500) in the USA and UK can be purchased for less than €9 ($10) in the Far East.

> **trademarks**
> registered 'mark' or 'logo' for a company or business
>
> **patent**
> any product or formula/technology registered with the relevant office that establishes who possesses the right of ownership

The failure to protect intellectual or industrial property rights adequately in the world marketplace can lead to the legal loss of these rights in potentially profitable markets. Because **patents**, processes, trademarks and copyrights are valuable in all countries, some companies have found their assets appropriated and profitably exploited in foreign countries without a licence or reimbursement. Further, they often learn that not only are other firms producing and selling their products or using their trademarks, but also that the foreign companies are the rightful owners in the countries where they are operating.

Going International 5.6

CHINESE COURT HANDS VICTORY TO NIKE IN TRADEMARK CASE

© Istockphoto.com/TonyV3112

Nike, the US sports clothing company, has won a controversial court order in China to prevent a Spanish company from manufacturing and exporting clothing from the mainland using the 'Nike' name. The Spanish company, Cidesport, owns the right to use the Nike name in Spain and had been planning to sell the goods made in China solely in its home country, according to evidence before the court. However, the court ruled that the sample of the goods in China had breached Nike's China registered trademark.

The protection of the brand [in China] covers not only final consumption, but also the manufacturing of it,' said Tao Xinliang of Shanghai University.

Despite the unusual circumstances, the decision reflects the growing propensity of Chinese courts to uphold the intellectual property rights of foreign brands.

Cidesport had confirmed its right to use the name Nike on apparel in Spain in 1999 after a lengthy court battle with the much larger US company. But the court decision, announced on Chinese websites, will restrict the Spanish company's commercial options by preventing it from manu-facturing in China, the global hub of the clothing industry.

The Spanish company argued that, as its products were not sold in China, it did not infringe Nike's China registered trademark. Cidesport had commissioned a factory in eastern China to manufacture a male ski jacket, affixed with the Nike label and Nike packaging. A lawyer advising Nike, Zhou Bin of the Hongqiao law firm in Shanghai, said the US company had found about 300 shipments ready for export in China which it considered were using the trademark illegally. Those shipments will be impounded by Chinese customs, and possibly destroyed, if the Spanish company loses a planned appeal. 'This is a very controversial issue internationally; in Holland, there was an identical case, which Nike lost,' said Mr Zhou.

Source: Richard McGregor, 'Chinese Court Hands Victory to Nike in Trademark Case', *Financial Times*, 21 February 2003, p 9.

There have been many cases where companies have legally lost the rights to trademarks and have had to buy back these rights or pay royalties for their use. Such was the case with McDonald's in Japan. Its 'Golden Arches' trademark was registered by an enterprising Japanese company. Only after a lengthy and costly legal action with a trip to the Japanese Supreme Court was McDonald's able to regain the exclusive right to use the trademark in Japan. After having to 'buy' its trademark for an undisclosed amount, McDonald's maintains a very active programme to protect its trademarks.

Prior use versus registration

In many code-law countries, ownership is established by registration rather than by prior use – the first to register a trademark or other property right is considered the rightful owner. In the USA, a common-law country, ownership of intellectual property rights is established by prior use – whoever can establish first use is typically considered the rightful owner. In Jordan a trademark belongs to whoever registers it first in that country. Thus, you can find a 'McDonald's' restaurant, 'Microsoft' software and 'Safeway' groceries all legally belonging to a Jordanian.[19] A company that believes it can always establish ownership in another country by proving it used the trademark or brand name first is wrong and risks the loss of these assets. It is best to protect intellectual property rights through registration. Several international conventions provide for simultaneous registration in member countries.

International conventions

Many countries participate in international conventions designed for mutual recognition and protection of intellectual property rights. There are three major international conventions.

1 The **Paris Convention** for the Protection of Industrial Property, commonly referred to as the Paris Convention, is a group of 100 nations that have agreed to recognise the rights of all members in the protection of trademarks, patents and other property rights. Registration in one of the member countries ensures the same protection afforded by the home country in all the member countries.

2 The **Madrid Arrangement** established the Bureau for International Registration of Trademarks. There are some 26 member countries in Europe that have agreed to automatic trademark protection for all members. Even though the USA is not a participant of the Madrid Arrangement, if a subsidiary of a US company is located in one of the member countries, the subsidiary could file through the membership of its host country and thereby provide protection in all 26 countries for the US company.

3 The **Inter-American Convention** includes most of the Latin American nations and the USA. It provides protection similar to that afforded by the Paris Convention.

With these multi-countries, arrangements have streamlined patent procedures in Europe. The Patent Cooperation Treaty (PCT) facilitates the application of patents among its member countries. The European Patent Convention (EPC) establishes a regional patent system allowing any nationality to file a single international application for a European patent. Once the patent is approved, it has the same effect as a national patent in each individual country designated on the application.

In addition, the EU has approved its Trademark Regulation, which will provide intellectual property protection throughout all member states. Companies have a choice between relying on national systems, when they want to protect a trademark in just a few member countries, or the European system, when protection is sought throughout the EU. Trademark protection is valid for 10 years and is renewable. However, if the mark is not used for five years, protection is forfeited.[20]

> **Paris Convention**
> a group of 100 nations that have agreed to recognise the rights of all members in the protection of trademarks, patents and other property rights
>
> **Madrid Arrangement**
> some 26 member countries in Europe that have agreed to automatic trademark protection for all members
>
> **Inter-American Convention**
> provides protection similar to that afforded by the Paris Convention

Commercial law within countries

All countries have laws regulating marketing activities in promotion, product development, labelling, pricing and channels of distribution. In some, there may be only a few laws, with lax enforcement; in others, there may be detailed, complicated rules to follow that are stringently enforced. There often are vast differences in enforcement and interpretation among countries having laws covering the same activities. Laws governing sales promotions in the EU offer good examples of such diversity.

In Austria, **premium offers** to consumers come under the discount law that prohibits any cash reductions that give preferential treatment to different groups of customers. Because most premium offers would result in discriminatory treatment of buyers, they normally are not allowed. Premium offers in Finland are allowed with considerable scope as long as the word 'free' is not used and consumers are not coerced into buying products. France also regulates premium offers, which are, for all practical purposes, illegal because it is illegal to sell for less than cost price or to offer a customer a gift or premium conditional on the purchase of another product. Furthermore, a manufacturer or retailer cannot offer products different from the kind regularly offered (ie a detergent manufacturer cannot offer clothing or kitchen utensils). German law

> **premium offers**
> special offers or high-priced offers

covering promotion in general is about as stringent as can be found. Building on an 80-year-old statute against 'unfair competition', the German courts currently prevent businesses from offering all sorts of incentives to lure customers. Most incentives that target particular groups of customers are illegal, as are most offers of gifts.[21]

Legal environment of the EU

The concept of free competition is a fundamental element in the Rome Treaty, which embodies the premise that any restriction on free competition is intrinsically reprehensible. There are in practice some exceptions, but the principle itself is that of positive general condemnation of any limits on competition. Article 85 deals with agreements, between two or more parties, that constitute restrictive practices. Article 86 is concerned with the abuse by individual organisations of a dominant trading position enjoyed in the EU; that is to say, monopolies.

The decision-making process

One practice that has developed has been that of giving publicity to any Commission decision in an attempt to influence and educate the market as a whole. To the annoyance of a number of firms, commissioners responsible for the competition rules have often called press conferences to inform the public of decisions actually made, the state of investigations in progress and, indeed, those about to begin.

Mergers

merger

when two companies decide to join together

We have seen a wave of **mergers** in the EU since the early 1990s. However, such mergers could threaten the existence of competition in important markets by giving the newly merged company a dominant position. It was clear that national legislation was inadequate for the control of many of the new mergers, because they were often transfrontier, whereas national legislation was confined to the territory of the individual member state.

Companies considering merging were obliged to give the Commission prior notification, after which the Commission was to operate under strict time limits. It had one month after notification in which to decide whether to initiate proceedings, so that where it saw no objection, the parties would receive the green light to go ahead promptly. If an investigation into the proposed merger was mounted, the Commission had four months in which either to approve or block the merger. During the investigation period companies concerned could propose changes in the merger arrangements that would make the merger more acceptable to the Commission.

Competition policy

common market

a free-trade area with a common external tariff, international labour mobility and common economic policies among member states

Competition policy has three established objectives. As the Commission has stated, it aims to keep the **Common Market** 'open and unified', ie to create a single market for the benefit of industry and consumers. Second, it must 'ensure that at all stages of the Common Market's development, there exists the right amount of competition'. By ensuring some degree of commercial rivalry, the EU can help European industry to be competitive in world markets, as the competition will encourage firms to rationalise and change. The third objective is to ensure that competition is subject to 'the principles of fairness in the market place', by which the Commission means 'equality of opportunity for all operators in the Common Market'. In practice, this means preventing companies from setting up restrictive agreements and cartels or from abusing a dominant position.

The capacity of the Commission to fine heavily was amply demonstrated in the Tetra-Pak case. In July 1991, this Swedish/Swiss-based packaging company was fined €75m for abusing its dominant position in breach of Article 86. Following a complaint from Elepak, one of Tetra-Pak's main competitors, the Commission concluded that Tetra-Pak had carried out a deliberate policy of eliminating actual or potential competitors in the aseptic and non-aseptic markets in machinery and cartons. Tetra-Pak's restrictive use of contracts enabled it to segment the European market and therefore charge prices that differed between state members by up to about 300 per cent for machines and up to about 50 per cent for cartons. Evidence gathered during the Commission's inquiry also showed that, at least in Italy and the UK, Tetra-Pak sold its 'Rex' non-aseptic products at a loss for a long time in order to eliminate competitors.[22]

SUMMARY

Vital to every marketer's assessment of a foreign market is an appreciation of the political environment of the country within which he or she plans to operate. Government involvement in business activities, especially foreign-controlled business, is generally much greater than business is accustomed to in the West. The foreign firm must strive to make its activities politically acceptable or it may be subjected to a variety of politically condoned harassment.

In addition to the harassment that can be imposed by a government, the foreign marketer frequently faces the problem of uncertainty of continuity in government policy. As governments change political philosophies, a marketing firm accepted under one administration may find its activities completely undesirable under another. An unfamiliar or hostile political environment does not necessarily preclude success for a foreign marketer if the marketer's plans are such that the company becomes a local economic asset.

Business faces a multitude of problems in its efforts to develop a successful marketing programme. Not the least of these problems are the varying legal systems of the world and their effect on business transactions. A primary marketing task is to develop a plan that will be enhanced, or at least not adversely affected, by these and other environmental elements. The myriad questions created by different laws and different legal systems indicate that the prudent path to follow at all stages of foreign marketing operations is one leading to competent counsel well versed in the intricacies of the international legal environment.

QUESTIONS

1. Why would a country rather domesticate than expropriate?
2. How can government-initiated domestication be the same as confiscation?
3. What are the main factors to consider in assessing the dominant political climate within a country?
4. Why is a working knowledge of political party philosophy so important in a political assessment of a market? Discuss.
5. What are the most frequently encountered political risks in foreign business? Discuss.
6. What are the factors that influence the risk-reduction process in international marketing?
7. Discuss measures a company might take to lessen its political vulnerability.
8. Select a country and analyse it politically from a marketing viewpoint.
9. How does the international marketer determine which legal system will have jurisdiction when legal disputes arise?
10. Discuss some of the reasons why it is probably best to seek an out-of-court settlement in international commercial legal disputes rather than to sue.

11 Illustrate the procedure generally followed in international commercial disputes when settled under the auspices of a formal arbitration tribunal.

12 What are intellectual property rights? Why should a company in international marketing take special steps to protect them?

FURTHER READING

- A. L. Hadjikhani and P. N. Ghauri, 'Network View of MNCs' Socio-political Behaviour', *Journal of Business Research*, 2008, 61, pp 912–24.

- L.S. Amine, 'Country-of-origin, Animosity and Consumer Response: Marketing Implications of Anti-Americanism and Francophobia', *International Business Review*, 2008, 17(4), pp 402–22.

- P.-X. Meschi and L. Riccio, 'Country Risk, National Cultural Differences between Partners and Survival of International Joint Ventures in Brazil', *International Business Review*, 2008, 17(3), pp 250–66.

- A. L. Hadjikhani and P. N. Ghauri, 'The Behaviour of International Firms in Socio-political Environments in the European Union', *Journal of Business Research*, 2001, 52(3), pp 263–75.

NOTES

1 For an account of political change and potential effect on economic growth, see 'China: Is Prosperity Creating a Freer Society?', *Business Week*, 6 June 1994, pp 94–99.

2 Jean J. Boddewyn and Thomas L. Brewer, 'International-business Political Behavior: New Theoretical Directions', *Academy of Management Review*, 1994, 19(1), 119–43.

3 Niccolo d'Aguino, 'Italy's Political Future', *Europe*, June 1994, pp 4–8.

4 Visit Pepsi's Russian website for the history of Pepsi in Russia: www.pepsi.ru.

5 Kent Granzin and John Painter, 'Motivational Influences on "Buy Domestic" Purchasing: Marketing Management Implications from a Study of Two Nations', *Journal of International Marketing*, 2001, 9(2), 73–96.

6 Richard Whalen, 'The New Nationalism', *Across the Board*, January/February, 2002; and Harold James, *The End of Globalization: Lessons from the Great Depression* (Boston, MA: Harvard University Press, 2001).

7 Amitaz Ghosh, 'The Mask of Nationalism', *Business India*, 1993 Anniversary Issue, pp 47–50.

8 Peter J. Buckley and Pervez N. Ghauri (eds), *The Global Challenge for Multinational Enterprises* (Amsterdam: Elsevier, 1999).

9 Lars Oxelheim and Pervez Ghauri (eds), *European Union and the Race for Foreign Direct Investment in Europe* (Oxford: Elsevier, 2004).

10 Lars Oxelheim (ed), *The Global Race for Foreign Direct Investment: Prospects for the Future* (Berlin: Springer-Verlag, 1993).

11 Sandeep Tyagi, 'The Giant Awakens: An Interview with Professor Jagdish Bhagwatti on Economic Reform in India', *Columbia Journal of World Business*, Spring 1994, pp 14–23.

12 Rahul Jacob, 'Coke Adds Fizz to India', *Fortune*, 10 January 1994, pp 14–15.

13 For a comprehensive review of political risk analysis, see Frederick Stapenhurst, 'Political Risk Analysis in North American Multinationals: An Empirical Review and Assessment', *The International Executive*, March–April 1995, pp 127–45.

14 Goran Therborn, 'The World's Trader, the World's Lawyer: Europe and Global Processes', *European Journal of Social Theory*, November 2002, pp 403–17.

15 Industrial property rights and intellectual property rights are used interchangeably. The more common term used today is intellectual property rights to refer to patents, copyrights, trademarks and so forth.

16 See, for example, Mokhtar M. Metwally, 'Interest Free (Islamic) Banking: A New Concept in Finance', *Journal of Banking and Finance Law and Practice*, June 1994, pp 119–28.

17 An interesting report on doing business in Islamic countries can be found in 'Fundamental Facts', *Business Traveller*, February 1994, pp 8–10.

18 Rene David and John E.C. Brierley, *Major Legal Systems in the World Today* (London: Free Press, 1968), p 18.

19 'If It's Fake, This Must Be Jordan', *Reuters News Service*, 27 February 1994.

20 'EU Trademark Regulation', *Business Europe*, 10–16 January 1994, p 6.

21 'Consumer Protection Swaddled', *The Economist*, 24 July 1993, p 67.

22 Keith Perry, *Business and the European Community* (Oxford: Made Simple, Butterworth-Heinemann, 1994), pp 82–97.

PART 3

Assessing International Market Opportunities

Chapter 6
Researching International Markets

Chapter Learning Objectives

What you should learn from Chapter 6

- The importance of marketing research in international marketing decisions
- How to handle the problems of availability and use of secondary data
- How to manage the international marketing research process
- Multicultural sampling and its problems in less-developed countries
- How to estimate market demand and sales forecast
- The function of multinational marketing information systems

Information is the key component in developing successful marketing strategies. Information needs range from the general data required to assess market opportunities to specific market information for decisions about product, promotion, distribution and price. A study of international marketing blunders leads to one conclusion – the majority of mistakes cited could have been avoided if the decision-maker had better knowledge of the market.[1] The quality of information available varies from uninformed opinion, ie the marketer's self-reference criterion (SRC), to thoroughly researched fact. As an enterprise broadens its scope of operations to include international markets, the need for current, accurate information is magnified. A marketer must find the most accurate and reliable data possible within the limits imposed by time, cost and the present state of the art.[2]

> **Marketing research**
>
> the systematic gathering, recording and analysing of data to provide information useful in marketing decision making

Marketing research is the systematic gathering, recording and analysing of data to provide information useful in marketing decision making. When operating in foreign markets, the need for thorough information as a substitute for uninformed opinion is even more important than it is in domestic marketing.

Generally, the tools and techniques for research remain the same for foreign and domestic marketing, but the environments within which they are applied are different. Rather than acquire new and exotic methods of research, the international marketing researcher must develop the ability for imaginative and deft application of tried and tested techniques in sometimes totally strange milieu. The mechanical problems of implementing foreign marketing research might vary from country to country, but the overall objectives for foreign and domestic marketing research are basically the same. Within a foreign environment, the frequently differing emphasis on the kinds of information needed, the often limited variety of appropriate tools and techniques available, and the difficulty of implementing the research process constitute the challenges facing most international marketing management researchers.[3]

Breadth and scope of international marketing research

A basic difference between domestic and international marketing research is the broader scope needed for foreign research. Research can be divided into three types based on information needs:

1 general information about the country, area and/or market
2 information necessary to forecast future marketing requirements by anticipating social, economic and consumer trends within specific markets or countries
3 specific market information used to make product, promotion, distribution and price decisions and to develop marketing plans.

In domestic operations, most emphasis is placed on the third type (gathering specific market information) because the other data are often available from secondary sources.

A country's political stability, cultural attributes and geographical characteristics are some of the kinds of information not ordinarily gathered by domestic company marketing research departments but which are required for a sound assessment of a foreign country market. This broader scope of international marketing research entails collecting and assessing information that includes the following:

1 *Economic*: general data on growth of the economy, inflation, business cycle trends and the like, profitability analysis for the company's products, specific industry economic studies, analysis of overseas economies and key economic indicators for the home country and major foreign countries.

2 *Sociological and political climate*: a general non-economic review of conditions affecting the company's business. In addition to the more obvious subjects such as cultural differences, it also covers ecology, safety, leisure time and their potential impact on the company's business.

3 *Overview of market conditions*: a detailed analysis of market conditions the division faces, by market segment, including international.

4 *Summary of the technological environment*: a summary of the state-of-the-art technology as it relates to the company's business, carefully broken down by product segments.

5 *Competitors*: a review of competitors' market shares, methods of market segmentation, products and apparent strategies on an international scale.[4]

For the domestic marketer, most information such as this has been acquired after years of experience with a single market; but in foreign markets this information must be gathered for each new market.

There is a basic difference between information ideally needed and that which is collectible and/or usable. Many firms engaged in foreign marketing do not make decisions with the benefit of the information listed. Some have neither the appreciation for information nor adequate time or money for the implementation of research. As a firm becomes more committed to international marketing and the cost of possible failure increases, greater emphasis is placed on research. Consequently, a global firm is, or should be, engaged in the most sophisticated and exhaustive kinds of research activities. Exhibit 6.1 illustrates the recent growth of foreign agencies in marketing research and Exhibit 6.2 illustrates global market research turnover.

EXHIBIT 6.1: Top 10 global research agencies

Rank (2011)	Company	Parent country	Revenue ($m)	Growth (%)
1	Nielsen	USA	5,353.00	4.8
2	Kantar	UK	3,331.80	0.8
3	Ipsos	France	2,495.00	2.9
4	GfK	Germany	1,914.00	5.8
5	SymphonyIRI	USA	764.2	3.2
6	IMS Health	USA	750	4.5
7	Westat	USA	506.5	11.2
8	Intage	Japan	459.9	− 0.2
9	Arbitron	USA	422.3	6.4
10	The NPD Group	USA	265.3	9.9

Source: adapted from Research, http://www.research-live.com/news/financial/global-top-25-grow-41-to-$187bn-says-honomichl/4008168.article.

EXHIBIT 6.2: Global Market Research Turnover 2011, $33,540m

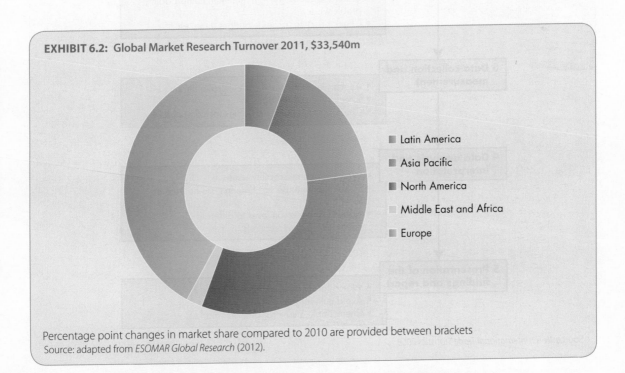

- Latin America
- Asia Pacific
- North America
- Middle East and Africa
- Europe

Percentage point changes in market share compared to 2010 are provided between brackets
Source: adapted from *ESOMAR Global Research* (2012).

The marketing research process

A marketing research study is always a compromise dictated by limits of time, cost and the present state of the art. The researcher must strive for the most accurate and reliable information within existing constraints. Key to successful research is a systematic and orderly approach to the collection and analysis of data. Whether a research programme is conducted in London or Jakarta, the research process should follow these steps:

1   define the research problem and establish research objectives
2   develop a research plan; how you are going to do the research
3   gather the relevant data from secondary and/or primary sources
4   analyse and interpret the collected data
5   draw findings and present the results.

Although the steps in a research programme are similar for all countries, variations and problems in implementation occur because of differences in cultural and economic conditions. While the problems of research in England or the Netherlands may be similar to those in the USA, research in Germany, South Africa or China may offer a multitude of very different and difficult distinctions. These distinctions become apparent with the first step in the research process – formulation of the problem. Exhibit 6.3 illustrates the marketing research process and its international dimensions.

EXHIBIT 6.3: The marketing research process and the international dimension

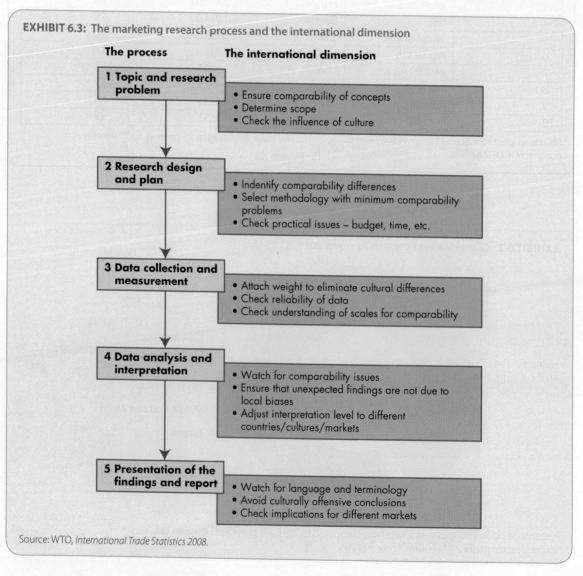

The process	The international dimension
1 Topic and research problem	• Ensure comparability of concepts • Determine scope • Check the influence of culture
2 Research design and plan	• Indentify comparability differences • Select methodology with minimum comparability problems • Check practical issues – budget, time, etc.
3 Data collection and measurement	• Attach weight to eliminate cultural differences • Check reliability of data • Check understanding of scales for comparability
4 Data analysis and interpretation	• Watch for comparability issues • Ensure that unexpected findings are not due to local biases • Adjust interpretation level to different countries/cultures/markets
5 Presentation of the findings and report	• Watch for language and terminology • Avoid culturally offensive conclusions • Check implications for different markets

Source: WTO, *International Trade Statistics 2008.*

MARKETING RESEARCH: TO ERR IS HUMAN (AND MARKETER-LIKE)

False consensus

People tend to think that their own attitudes are more common than they really are. When people estimate what others like and do, their own attitudes sway their responses. In one study US managers were asked to estimate various attributes of markets, including the percentage of beer sold in US supermarkets that was imported and the percentage of US households that purchased canned chilli. At the time of the study, only about 2 per cent of the beer sold in US supermarkets was imported. The executives, who tended to like and buy imported beer, gave an average estimate of 20 per cent. Canned chilli, on the other hand, was largely disliked and rarely purchased by US executives. While 40 per cent of US households buy it in a given year, the executives' average estimate was only 28 per cent. One explanation for this phenomenon is that it is easy for people to think of what they like and dislike and that they give these preferences extra weight. Another is that when they think of other people, they think of people they know well, who tend to be similar to them. A curious fact is that the false consensus effect occurs even when people are explicitly warned about it. The only way to overcome this effect is to use marketing research and observe the real data.

Overconfidence

The second error lies in failing to identify what we do not know. When executives in the study were asked to indicate how certain they were of their estimates, they were typically overconfident. Along with the estimates, executives provided 90 per cent confidence intervals (or upper and lower bounds for their estimates), representing their belief that the true value would fall, on average, nine out of ten times within these bounds. Overconfidence is not universal, but it is common. The best way to guard against it is to make explicit statements about how confident you are and to check how things turn out. You may start out being just as overconfident as the executives in the survey, but at least you have a chance to learn from your mistakes.

- According to your estimate, how many of your classmates drink coffee and how many drink tea? Write down your answers and then ask the class. Was there a false consensus in your estimate?

Source: adapted from Andrew Gershoff and Eric Johnson, 'Avoid the Trap of Thinking Everyone is Just Like You', *Financial Times Summer School*, 29 August 2003, p 11.

Defining the problem and establishing research objectives

The research process should begin with a definition of the research problem and the establishment of specific research objectives. The major difficulty here is converting a series of business problems into tightly drawn and achievable research objectives.[5] In this initial stage, researchers often embark on the research process with only a vague grasp of the total problem.

This first step in research is more critical in foreign markets since an **unfamiliar environment** tends to cloud problem definition. Researchers either fail to anticipate the influence of the local culture on the problem or fail to identify the SRC and so treat the **problem definition** as if it were in the researcher's home environment. In assessing some foreign business failures it is apparent that research was conducted, but the questions asked were more appropriate for the home market than for the foreign one. For example, Unilever introduced a super-concentrated detergent to the Japanese market only to find out that a premeasured package on which it was trying to differentiate its product was unacceptable to the market because it didn't dissolve in the wash, the product was not designed to work in a new, popular low-agitation washing machine and the 'fresh smell' positioning of the detergent was not relevant in Japan since most consumers hang their washing outside to dry in the fresh air.[6] Did the company conduct research? Yes. Were appropriate questions asked? No.

unfamiliar environment

environment with which a company is not familiar, especially when it is a foreign market

problem definition

explaining and understanding the research problem

Other difficulties in foreign research stem from a failure to establish problem limits broad enough to include all relevant variables. Information on a far greater range of factors is necessary to offset the unfamiliar cultural background of the foreign market. Consider proposed research about **consumption patterns** and attitudes towards hot milk-based drinks. In the UK hot milk-based drinks are considered to have sleep-inducing, restful and relaxing properties, and are traditionally consumed prior to bedtime. People in Thailand, however, drink the same hot milk-based drinks in the morning on the way to work and see them as being invigorating, energy-giving and stimulating. If one's only experience is in the USA, the picture is further clouded since hot milk-based drinks are frequently associated with cold weather, either in the morning or the evening, and for different reasons at each time of day. The market researcher must be certain the problem definition is sufficiently defined to cover the relevant range of response possibilities and not be clouded by his or her SRC.

> **consumption patterns**
>
> how consumers buy and consume a particular product

Developing a research plan

Once a research problem is clear and its objectives have been defined, it is important to plan the research process. This should be done irrespective of whether the company will undertake the work with its own resources or use outside agencies. The tasks to be undertaken should be specified and alternative methodologies should be evaluated. In this process an appropriate **methodology** should be selected. For example, which type of research, quantitative or qualitative, should be done. The theories/models we can use to find answers to research questions are also to be identified here. While selecting these methodologies, the comparability of research findings and their usefulness must be kept in mind.

> **methodology**
>
> way of collecting and analysing data/ information

Quantitative and qualitative research

Marketing research methods can be grouped into two basic types, quantitative and qualitative research. In both methods, the marketer is interested in gaining knowledge about the market.

> **quantitative research**
>
> structured questioning, producing answers that can easily be converted to numerical data

In **quantitative research**, the respondent is asked to reply either verbally or in writing to structured questions using a specific response format such as 'yes' or 'no', or to select a response from a set of choices. Questions are designed to get a specific response to aspects of the respondent's behaviour, intentions, attitudes, motives and demographic characteristics. This type of quantitative or survey-based research provides the marketer with responses that can be presented with precise estimations. The structured responses received in a survey can be summarised in percentages, averages or other statistics. For example, 76 per cent of the respondents prefer product A over product B, and so on.

Survey research is generally associated with quantitative research, and the typical instrument used is the questionnaire administered by personal interview, mail or telephone.

> **Qualitative research**
>
> open-ended and in-depth, seeking unstructured responses. Expresses the respondent's thoughts and feelings

Qualitative research, on the other hand, is open-ended, in-depth and seeks unstructured responses that reflect the person's thoughts and feelings on the subject. Qualitative research interprets what the 'people in the sample are like, their outlooks, their feelings, the dynamic interplay of their feelings and ideas, their attitudes and opinions, and their resulting actions'.[7] The most often used forms of qualitative questioning are the focus group, interviews and case studies.

Qualitative research is also used in international marketing research to formulate and define a problem more clearly and to determine relevant questions to be examined in subsequent research. It is used where interest is centred on gaining an understanding of a market, rather than quantifying relevant aspects.

When a British children's wear company was planning to enter the Spanish market, there was concern about the differences in attitudes and buying patterns of the Spanish from those in the UK, and about market differences that might possibly exist among Spain's five major trading areas of Barcelona, Madrid, Seville, Bilbao and Valencia. Because the types of retail outlet in Spain were substantially different from those in the UK, 'accompanied shopping' interviews[8] were used to explore shoppers' attitudes about different types of store. In the **interviews**, respondents were accompanied on visits to different outlets selling children's wear. During the visit to each shop, the respondent talked the interviewer through what she was seeing and feeling. This enabled the interviewer to see the outlet through the eyes of the shopper, and to determine the criteria with which she evaluated the shopping environment and the products available. Information gathered in these studies and other focus group studies helped the company develop a successful entry strategy into Spain.

> **interviews**
>
> when we talk to people to get information on specific matters

Qualitative research is also helpful in revealing the impact of sociocultural factors on behaviour patterns and to develop **research hypotheses** that can be tested in subsequent studies designed to quantify the concepts and relevant relationships uncovered in qualitative data collection. Research conducted by Procter & Gamble in Egypt offers an example of how qualitative research leads to specific points that can later be measured by using survey or quantitative research.

> **research hypothesis**
>
> a theory that can be proved or rejected via research

For years Procter & Gamble had marketed Ariel Low Suds brand laundry detergent to the 5 per cent of homes in the Egyptian market that had automatic washing machines. It planned to expand its presence in the Egyptian market and commissioned a study to: (1) identify the most lucrative opportunities in the Egyptian laundry market; and (2) develop the right concept, product, price, brand name, package and advertising copy once the decision was made to pursue a segment of the laundry market.

The 'Habits and Practices' study (P&G's name for this phase) consisted of home visits and discussion groups (qualitative research) to understand how the Egyptian housewife did her laundry. They wanted to know her likes, dislikes and habits (the company's knowledge of laundry practices in Egypt had been limited to automatic washing machines). Among the 95 per cent of homes that washed in a non-automatic washing machine or by hand, the process consisted of soaking, boiling, bleaching and washing each load several times. Several products were used in the process; bar soaps or flakes were added to the main wash, along with liquid bleach and blueing to enhance the cleaning performance of the poor-quality locally produced powders. These findings highlighted the potential for a high-performing detergent that would accomplish everything that currently required several products.

The company went back to **focus groups** to assess reactions to different brand names (they were considering Ariel, already in the market as a low-suds detergent for automatic washers, and Tide, which had been marketed in Egypt in the 1960s and 1980s) to get ideas about the appeal and relevant wording for promotions, and to test various price ranges, package design and size. Information derived from focus-group encounters helped the company eliminate ideas with low consumer appeal and focus on those that triggered the most interest. Further, the groups helped refine advertising and promotion wording to ensure clarity of communication through the use of everyday consumer language.

> **focus groups**
>
> a group of people who are considered relevant for our product and can provide us with useful information

The company proceeded to the next step, a research programme to validate the relative appeal of the concepts generated from focus groups with a survey (quantitative research) of a large sample from the target market. Additionally, brand name, price, size and the product's intended benefits were tested in large sample surveys. Information gathered in the final **surveys** provided the company with the specific information used to develop a marketing programme that led to a successful product introduction and brand recognition for Ariel throughout Egypt.[9]

> **surveys**
>
> when we collect information through a list of questions from a large number of respondents

In another case, Cadbury's, a UK firm, was looking for a way to give its chocolate cream liqueur a unique flavour. One idea was to add a hint of hazelnut flavouring. Yet when the company suggested verbally that the liqueur should be changed in this way, consumers reacted negatively because they were unfamiliar with the mix of the two flavours. However, when taste tests were done without revealing what the extra flavours were, consumers loved the result.[10]

Gathering secondary data

The breadth of many foreign marketing research studies and the marketer's lack of familiarity with a country's basic socioeconomic and cultural data result in considerable demand for information generally available from secondary sources in the Western countries. Unfortunately, such data are not as available in foreign markets. Most Western governments provide comprehensive statistics for their home markets: periodic censuses of population, housing, business and agriculture are conducted and, in some cases, have been taken for over 100 years. Commercial sources, trade associations, management groups, and state and local governments also provide the researcher with additional sources of detailed market information.

While data collection has only recently begun in many countries, it is improving substantially through the efforts of organisations such as the United Nations and the Organisation for Economic Cooperation and Development (OECD). As a country becomes more important as a market, a greater interest in basic data and better collection methods develop. The problems of availability, reliability, comparability of data and validating **secondary data** are described below.

> **secondary data**
>
> information that somebody else has collected, but that we can use for our purpose
>
> **database**
>
> a bank/storage of information on a particular issue

With the emergence of Eastern European countries as potentially viable markets, a number of private and public groups are funding the collection of information to offset a lack of comprehensive market data. As market activity continues in Eastern Europe and elsewhere, market information will improve in quantity and quality. To build a **database** on Russian consumers, one Western firm used a novel approach to conduct a survey. It ran a questionnaire in Moscow's *Komsomolskaya Pravda* newspaper asking for replies to be sent to the company. The 350,000 replies received (3,000 by registered mail) attested to the willingness of Russian consumers to respond to market enquiries.

Availability of data

A critical shortcoming of secondary data on foreign markets is the paucity of detailed data for many market areas. Much of the secondary data a Western marketer is accustomed to having about Western markets is just not available for many countries. Detailed data on the numbers of wholesalers, retailers, manufacturers and facilitating services, for example, are unavailable for many parts of the world; the same applies to data on population and income. Most countries simply do not have governmental agencies that collect, on a regular basis, the kinds of secondary data readily available in, say, the USA, the Netherlands, Germany and the Scandinavian countries. If such information is important, the marketer must initiate the research or rely on private sources of data.

Reliability of data

Available data may not have the level of reliability necessary for confident decision making for many reasons. Official statistics are sometimes too optimistic, reflecting national pride rather than practical reality, while tax structures and fear of the tax collector often adversely affect data.[11]

Seeking advantages or hiding failures, local officials, factory managers, rural enterprises and others filed fake numbers on everything from production levels to birth rates. For example, a petrochemical plant reported one year's output to be $20m (€18m), 50 per cent higher than its actual output of $13.4m (€12.1m).[12] An American survey team verified that 60 million frozen chickens had been imported into Saudi Arabia in one year, even though official figures reported only 10 million.

The EU tax policies can affect the accuracy of reported data also. Production statistics are frequently inaccurate because the countries in the EU collect taxes on domestic sales. Thus, some companies shave their production statistics a bit to match the sales reported to tax authorities. Conversely, foreign trade statistics may be blown up slightly because many countries in the EU grant some form of export subsidy. Knowledge of such 'adjusted reporting' is critical for a marketer who relies on secondary data for forecasting or estimating market demand.

Comparability of data

Comparability and currency of available data is the third shortcoming faced by international marketers. In most Western countries current sources of reliable and valid estimates of socioeconomic factors and business indicators are readily available. In other countries, especially those less developed, data can be many years out of date as well as having been collected on an infrequent and unpredictable schedule. Further, even though many countries are now gathering reliable data, there are generally no historical series with which to compare the current information.

A related problem is the manner in which data are collected and reported. Too frequently, data are reported in different categories or in categories much too broad to be of specific value. The term 'supermarket', for example, has a variety of meanings around the world. In Japan a supermarket is quite different from its German counterpart. Japanese supermarkets usually occupy two- or three-storey structures; they sell foodstuffs, daily necessities and clothing on respective floors. Some even sell furniture, electrical home appliances, stationery and sporting goods, and have a restaurant. General merchandise stores, shopping centres and department stores are different from stores of the same name in the UK or Germany. Furthermore, data from different countries are often not comparable. One report on the problems of comparing European cross-border retail store audit data states: 'Some define the market one way, others another; some define price categories one way, and others another. Even within the same research agency, auditing periods are defined differently in different countries.'[13] As a result, audit data are largely impossible to compare.

Validating secondary data

The shortcomings discussed here should be considered when using any source of information. Many countries have the same high standards of collection and preparation of data, but secondary data from any source, including Western countries, must be checked and interpreted carefully. As a practical matter, the following questions should be asked to judge the **reliability** of data sources effectively.

> **reliability**
> whether information/results of a study are trustworthy

1 Who collected the data? Would there be any reason for purposely misrepresenting the facts?

2 For what purpose were the data collected?

3 How were the data collected (methodology)?

4 Are the data internally consistent and logical in light of known data sources or market factors?

Checking the consistency of one set of secondary data with other data of known validity is an effective and often used way of judging **validity**. For example, check the validity of the sale of baby products with the number of women of childbearing age and with birth rates, or the number of patient beds in hospitals with the sale of related hospital equipment. Such correlations can also be useful in estimating demand and forecasting sales. In general, the availability and accuracy of recorded secondary data increase as the level of economic development increases.

> **validity**
> whether the measures used are reasonable to measure what it is supposed to measure

---

Going International 6.2

INTERNATIONAL DATA: *CAVEAT EMPTOR*

The statistics used are subject to more than the usual number of caveats and qualifications concerning comparability that are usually attached to economic data. Statistics on income and consumption were drawn from national-accounts data published regularly by the United Nations (UN) and the Organisation for Economic Cooperation and Development (OECD). These data, designed to provide a 'comprehensive statistical statement about the economic activity of a country', are compiled from surveys sent to each of the participating countries (118 nations were surveyed by the UN). However, despite efforts by the UN and the OECD to present the data on a comparable basis, differences among countries concerning definitions, accounting practices and

▶

◀

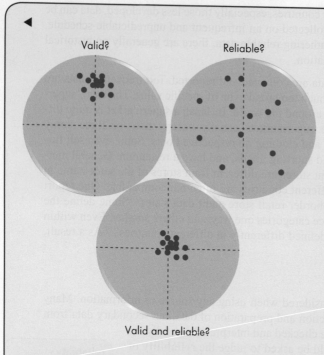

Valid?

Reliable?

Valid and reliable?

recording methods persist. In Germany, for instance, consumer expenditures are estimated largely on the basis of the turnover tax, while in the UK tax-receipt data are frequently supplemented by household surveys and production data.

Even if data-gathering techniques in each country were standardised, definitional differences would remain. These differences are relatively minor except in a few cases; for example, Germany classifies the purchase of a television set as an expenditure for 'recreation and entertainment', while the same expenditure falls into the 'furniture, furnishings and household equipment' classification in the USA.

While income and consumption expenditures consist primarily of cash transactions, there are several important exceptions. Both income and expenditures include the monetary value of food, clothing and shelter received in lieu of wages. Also included are imputed rents on owner-occupied dwellings, in addition to actual rents paid by tenants. Wages and salaries, which make up the largest share of consumer income, include employer contributions to social security systems, private pension plans, life and casualty insurance plans and family allowance programmes. Consumer expenditures include medical services, even though the recipient may make only partial payment; if, however, the same services are subsidised wholly by public funds, the transaction is listed as a government rather than a consumer expenditure.

Expenditures, as defined by both the UN (http://www.un.org) and the OECD (http://www.oecd.org), include consumption outlays by households (including individuals living alone) and private non-profit organisations.

Source: David Bauer, 'The Dimensions of Consumer Markets Abroad', *The Conference Board Record*, reprinted with permission.

Gathering primary data

If, after seeking all reasonable secondary data sources, research questions can still not be adequately answered, the market researcher must collect **primary data**. The researcher may question the firm's sales force, distributors, middlemen and/or customers to get appropriate market information. In most primary data collection, the researcher questions respondents to determine what they think about some topic or how they might behave under certain conditions.

> **primary data**
> data that has been collected for the research at hand

The problems of collecting primary data in foreign countries are different only in degree from those encountered at home. Assuming the research problems are well defined and objectives are properly formulated, the success of primary research hinges on the ability of the researcher to get correct and truthful information that addresses the research objectives. Most problems in collecting primary data in international marketing research stem from cultural differences among countries, and range from the inability of respondents to communicate their opinions to inadequacies in questionnaire translation (see Exhibit 6.4).

Ability to communicate opinions

The ability to express attitudes and opinions about a product or concept depends on the respondent's ability to recognise the usefulness and value of such a product or concept. It is difficult for a person to

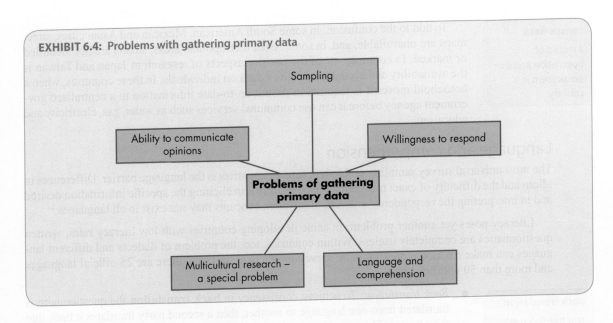

EXHIBIT 6.4: Problems with gathering primary data

formulate needs, attitudes and opinions about goods whose use may not be understood, that are not in common use within the community or that have never been available. For example, it may be impossible for someone who has never seen an iPad to provide any reasonable information about purchase intentions, or likes and dislikes concerning that product. The more complex the concept, the more difficult it is to design research that will help the respondent communicate meaningful opinions and reactions. Under these circumstances, the creative capabilities of the foreign marketing researcher are challenged.

Willingness to respond

Cultural differences offer the best explanation for the unwillingness or the inability of many to respond to research surveys. The role of the male, the suitability of personal gender-based enquiries, and other gender-related issues can affect willingness to respond. In some countries, the wife dictates exactly how the money be spent. Because the wife controls the spending, it is she, not the husband, who should be questioned to determine preferences and demand for many consumer goods. A French Canadian woman does not like to be questioned and is likely to be reticent in her responses.

Anyone asking questions about any topic from which tax assessment could be inferred is immediately suspected of being a tax agent. Citizens of many Western countries do not feel the same legal and moral obligations to pay their taxes. So, tax evasion is an accepted practice for many and a source of pride for the more adept. One of the problems revealed by the government of India in a recent population census was the underreporting of tenants by landlords trying to hide the actual number of people living in houses and flats. The landlords or tenants had been subletting properties illegally and were concealing their activities from the tax department.

Sampling in field surveys

The greatest problem of **sampling** stems from the lack of adequate **demographic data** and available lists from which to draw meaningful samples. If current reliable lists are not available, sampling becomes more complex and generally less reliable. In many countries, telephone directories, cross-index street directories, census tract and block data, and detailed social and economic characteristics of the population being studied are not available on a current basis, if at all.

sampling
selection of potential respondents

demographic data
information on characteristics (such as age, education, etc) of the population in a country/city/area

census data

a record of population and its breakdown in a country

To add to the confusion, in some South American, Mexican and Asian cities, street maps are unavailable, and, in some Asian metropolitan areas, streets are not identified or marked. In contrast, one of the positive aspects of research in Japan and Taiwan is the availability and accuracy of **census data** on individuals. In these countries, when a household moves it is required to submit up-to-date information to a centralised government agency before it can use communal services such as water, gas, electricity and education.

Language and comprehension

The most universal survey sampling problem in foreign countries is the language barrier. Differences in idiom and the difficulty of exact translation create problems in eliciting the specific information desired and in interpreting the respondents' answers. Equivalent concepts may not exist in all languages.[14]

Literacy poses yet another problem; in some developing countries with low literacy rates, written questionnaires are completely useless. Within countries, too, the problem of dialects and different languages can make a national questionnaire survey impractical. In India, there are 25 official languages and more than 50 unofficial ones.

back translation

text translated into another language, then translated back to the original language by another party. Helps to pinpoint misinterpretation and misunderstandings

parallel translation

when more than two translators are used for a back translation, and a comparison of the results is undertaken

decentring

a successive iteration process of translation and retranslation of a questionnaire, each time by a different translator

- *Back translation*: To achieve consistency in **back translation** the questionnaire is translated from one language to another, then a second party translates it back into the original. This pinpoints misinterpretations and misunderstandings before they reach the public. A softdrink company wanted to use a very successful Australian advertising theme, 'Baby, it's cold inside', in Hong Kong. It had the theme translated from English into Cantonese by one translator and then retranslated by another from Cantonese into English, where the statement came out as, 'Small mosquito, on the inside it is very cold'. Although 'small mosquito' is the colloquial expression for small child in Hong Kong, the intended meaning was lost in translation.

- *Parallel translation*: Back translations may not always ensure an accurate translation because of commonly used idioms in both languages. **Parallel translation** is used to overcome this problem. In this process, more than two translators are used for the back translation; the results are compared, differences discussed and the most appropriate translation selected.

- *Decentring*: **Decentring** refers to a successive iteration process of translation and retranslation of a questionnaire, each time by a different translator. The process is as follows: an English version is translated into French and then translated back to English by a different translator. The two English versions are compared and, where there are differences, the original English version is modified and the process is repeated. If there are differences between the two English versions, the original English version of the second iteration is modified and the process of translation and back translation is repeated.

The process continues to be repeated until an English version can be translated into French and back translated, by a different translator, into the same English. In this process, the wording of the original instrument undergoes a change and the version that is finally used and its translation have equally comprehensive and equivalent terminologies in both languages.

Because of cultural and national differences, confusion can just as well be the problem of the researcher as of the respondent. The question itself may not be properly worded in the English version. One classic misunderstanding, which occurred in a *Reader's Digest* study of consumer behaviour in Western Europe, resulted in a report that France and Germany consumed more spaghetti than did Italy. This rather curious and erroneous finding resulted from questions that asked about purchases of 'packaged and branded spaghetti'. Italians buy their spaghetti in bulk; the French and Germans buy branded and packaged spaghetti. Because the Italians buy little branded or packaged spaghetti, the results underreported spaghetti purchases by Italians. However, the real question is what the researcher wanted to find out. Had the goal of the research been to determine how much branded and packaged spaghetti was purchased, the results would have been correct. However, because the goal was to know about total spaghetti consumption, the question and the results were incorrect.

> ### Going International 6.3
>
> ## BRINGING PRODUCT DEVELOPMENT CLOSER TO MARKETING RESEARCH
>
> Philips, a huge multinational with a net income of €1,172m in the third quarter of 2004, is definitely one of the leaders of European industry and research. Philips posted 2012 sales of €24.8bn and employs approximately 118,000 employees with sales and services in more than 100 countries. In 2012, Philips invested €1.810bn in research and development. Philips' IP portfolio currently consists of around 59,000 patent rights, 35,000 trademarks, 81,000 design rights and 4,200 domain name registrations. Philips filed approximately 1,500 patents in 2012, with a strong focus on the growth areas in health and well-being. Philips Design is widely recognised as a leader in people-centric design. In 2012, it won over 120 key design awards in the areas of product, communication and innovation design.
>
> However, despite these impressive resources and achievements, the company has a poor record of turning scientific brilliance into profits, and many of the electronics and electrical goods the company helped to invent are being commercialised by US venture capitalists. To combat the problem and to build up a market-oriented research effort, it developed the following strategies:
>
> 1 linking scientists more closely to the product development divisions: the product divisions pay for directed marketing research, covering two-thirds of the research costs with the funds generated from the contracts that they have instituted
>
> 2 chief technology officers, who work in each product division, scout for new technologies, devised either in Philips or outside, that could help the company's commercial efforts. These people have extensive business experience, which provides them with a different perspective from the scientists. They set targets for the ideas being pursued by the laboratories and timetables for potential commercialisation
>
>
> **Research at Philips, Eindhoven**
> Photo: Philips.
>
> 3 business development officers form a potential conduit between Philips research staff and other businesses with which Philips might want to form a partnership to commercialise particular ideas. Such partnerships are regarded as beneficial for Philips as sometimes other companies are in a better position to take on its scientific ideas than Philips itself
>
> 4 quantifying output of research employees: this approach is a controversial one because it is difficult to say what constitutes success. However, many think that this effort is worthwhile as part of the interest in getting away from valuing research solely in terms of how much is being spent. Additional factors that are being taken into account are licensing income, patent registrations, publications of scientific papers and revenue coming from scientific ideas.
>
> ● Do you think these changes in Philips' strategy would enable it to capitalise better on its research activities?
>
> Source: adapted from N. Buckley, 'The Need to Harvest Homegrown Creativity', *Financial Times*, 22 March 2001, p 9; and http://www.philips.com/about/company/companyprofile.page.

Multicultural research: a special problem

As companies become international marketers and seek to standardise various parts of the marketing mix across several countries, multicultural studies become more important. A company needs to determine whether standardisation or adaptation of the marketing mix is appropriate. Thus, market

multicultural studies

studies that are performed in different cultures

comparability and equivalence

information that is comparable and is understood in the same way as intended

characteristics across diverse cultures must be compared for similarities and differences before a company proceeds with a marketing strategy. The research difficulties discussed thus far have addressed problems of conducting research within a culture. When engaging in **multicultural studies**, many of these same problems further complicate the difficulty of cross-cultural comparisons.

When designing multicultural studies, it is essential that the differences be taken into account. An important point to keep in mind when designing research to be applied across cultures is to ensure **comparability and equivalence** of results. Such differences may mean that different research methods should be applied in individual countries. For example, a mail survey may have a high level of reliability in country A but not in country B, whereas a personal interview in country B will have an equivalent level of reliability as the mail survey in country A. Thus, a mail survey should be used in country A and a personal interview in country B. In collecting data from different countries, it is more important to use techniques with equivalent levels of reliability than to use the same techniques.[15]

Analysing and interpreting research information

Once data have been collected, the final steps are the analysis and interpretation of findings in light of the stated marketing problem. Both secondary and primary data collected by the market researcher are subject to the many limitations just discussed. In any final analysis, the researcher must take into consideration these factors and, despite their limitations, produce meaningful guides for management decisions.[16]

Accepting information at face value in foreign markets is imprudent. The meanings of words, the consumer's attitude towards a product, the interviewer's attitude or the interview situation can distort research findings. Just as culture and tradition influence the willingness to give information, they also influence the information given. Newspaper circulation figures, readership and listenership studies, retail outlet figures and sales volume can all be distorted through local business practice. To cope with such disparities, the foreign market researcher must possess three talents to generate meaningful marketing information.

First, the researcher must possess a high degree of cultural understanding of the market in which research is being conducted. In order to analyse research findings, the social customs, semantics, current attitudes and business customs of a society or a subsegment of a society must be clearly understood.

Second, a creative talent for adapting research findings is necessary. Ingenuity, a sense of humour and a willingness to be guided by original research findings even when they conflict with popular opinion or prior assumptions are all considered prime assets in foreign marketing research.

Third, a sceptical attitude in handling both primary and secondary data is helpful. It might be necessary to check a newspaper press run over a period of time to get accurate circulation figures, or deflate or inflate reported consumer income in some areas by 25 to 50 per cent on the basis of observable socioeconomic characteristics.

Presenting the findings and results

Presentation of findings and results in a summarised and easy-to-understand manner is crucial to the success of research. Before writing the final report of the project, it is necessary to consider the purpose of the report and to whom it is addressed. The researcher has to convince the reader that he or she has done the job in a systematic and logical manner, and that the findings are reliable. This is particularly important in international marketing research, as the results and findings are to be understood and executed by international marketers and managers.

Culturally biased and offensive conclusions need to be avoided, especially in respect of local sensitivities. The report to managers must be concise and convincing. It should include a very short, maximum two pages, executive summary explaining the major issues, some interpretations of collected data, results and managerial implications.

How to organise marketing research

A company in need of foreign market research can rely on an outside foreign-based agency or on a domestic company with a branch within the country in question. It can conduct research using its own facilities or employ a combination of its own research force with the assistance of an outside agency.

The ideal approach is to have local researchers in each country, with close coordination between the client company and the local research companies. This cooperation is important at all stages of the research project from **research design**, through data collection, to final analysis. Furthermore, two stages of analysis are necessary. At the individual country level, all issues involved in each country must be identified, and at the multicountry level, the information must be distilled into a format that addresses the objectives. Such recommendations are supported on the grounds that two heads are better than one and that multicultural input is essential to any understanding of multicultural data.

> **research design**
>
> overall plan for relating a research problem to practical empirical research

If a company wants to use a professional marketing research firm, many are available. Most major advertising agencies and many research firms have established branch offices worldwide. There has also been a healthy growth in foreign-based research and consulting firms. An interesting aside on data collection agencies involves the changing role of the Central Intelligence Agency (CIA). Members of the US Congress have suggested that the CIA should be active in protecting America's economic commercial interests worldwide and in gathering international trade data to improve the information base for US businesses.

Estimating market demand

In assessing current product demand and forecasting future demand, reliable **historical data** are required. As previously noted, the quality and availability of secondary data are frequently inadequate. Despite limitations, there are approaches to demand estimation usable with minimum information. The success of these approaches relies on the ability of the researcher to find meaningful substitutes or approximations for the needed economic and demographic relationships.

> **historical data**
>
> information over a period of time

Going International 6.4

FRANCE HAS STOLEN A MARCH ON THE USA IN ECONOMIC INTELLIGENCE

In a report to the US Congress, the CIA named the French services, along with those of the Israelis, as the most active in launching operations against American interests, both inside and outside the USA. Recently, the DGSE, the French secret service, has stepped up operations in areas such as Bosnia, Algeria and Russia.

The emphasis has continued to shift towards economic intelligence. The ability to intercept secret offers made by US armament firms to Middle Eastern countries has allowed French firms to propose better deals. In 1997 they broke into the lucrative Saudi defence market for the first time by signing a contract for the sale of 12 helicopters built by Eurocopter. The recent CIA report accused the French specifically of launching intelligence operations against US military contractors and high-technology firms. In the report, national security specialist David E. Cooper described the intelligence-gathering of a particular country, clearly identifiable as France, which 'recruited agents at the European offices of three US computer and electronic firms'.

© iStockphoto.com/ SteveStone.

▶

◀

According to sources, IBM in Brussels and Texas Instruments were two of those targets. Clearly, France is not the only country to seek such information. Former DGSE director Admiral Pierce Lacoste told *The European*:

'It is part of an indirect strategy by the US. They want all the trumps. Initially their target was Japan. But now it is France, for two main reasons. First, France is seen as one of the most vocal and active countries over the strengthening of the European Union and a single currency; and second, because this country is organizing a new economic intelligence system.'

While continuing with traditional intelligence, the French president set up a special economic and technological intelligence coordination body. The Comité pour la Competitivité et la Securité Économique (CCSE) is led by seven 'wise men'.

'This is essentially the start of a cultural shift on the part of French industrial and commercial intelligence. But this process will take some time to come to fruition,' said Lacoste. 'Obviously, the French and future European intelligence would play some role in this. They could not allow the CIA to be the only secret service operating in that field.'

- Do you think companies should have economic intelligence departments, to forecast demand more efficiently?

Source: *The European*, 29 August–4 September 1996.

When the desired statistics are not available, a close approximation can be made using local production figures plus imports, with adjustments for exports and current inventory levels. These data are more readily available because they are commonly reported by the United Nations and other international agencies. Once approximations for sales trends are established, historical series can be used as the basis for projections of growth. In any straight extrapolation, however, the estimator assumes that the trends of the immediate past will continue into the future. For example, if there has been 10 per cent growth per year, on average, in the last five years, we can expect that that market will grow by 10 per cent also next year.

Going International 6.5

MARKETING TOOL: THE SEMANTIC DIFFERENTIAL

An important tool in attitudinal research, image studies and positioning decisions is the *semantic differential*. It was originally developed to measure the meaning that a concept – perhaps a political issue, a person, a work of art or, in marketing, a brand, product or company – might have for people in terms of various dimensions. As first presented, the instrument consisted of pairs of polar adjectives with a seven-interval scale separating the opposite members of each pair. For example:

Extremely good   – – – – – – –   Extremely bad

This instrument has been refined to obtain greater sensitivity through the use of descriptive phrases. Examples of such bipolar phrases for determining the image of a particular brand of beer are:

Something special   – – – – – – –   Just another drink
Local flavour   – – – – – – –   Foreign flavour
Really peps you up   – – – – – – –   Somehow doesn't pep you up

The number of word pairs varies considerably but may be as many as 50 or more. Flexibility and appropriateness to a particular study are achieved by constructing tailor-made word and phrase lists.

▶

Semantic differential scales have been used in marketing to compare images of particular products, brands, firms and stores against competing ones. The answers of all respondents can be averaged and then plotted to provide a 'profile', as shown in the illustration for three competing beers on four scales (actually, a firm would probably use more scales in such a study).

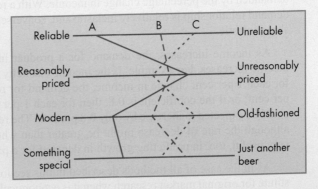

In this profile, brand A shows the dominant image over its competing brands in three of the four categories; however, the negative reaction to its price should alert the company to review pricing practices. Brand C shows a negative image, especially regarding the reliability of its product. The profile indicates that brand C is perceived as being distinctive from the other two brands. Probably the weakest image of all is that of brand B; respondents viewed this brand as having no distinctive image, neither good nor bad.

Simple, easy to administer and analyse, the semantic differential is useful not only in identifying segments and positions where there might be opportunities because these are currently not well covered by competitors, but it is also useful to a well-established firm – such as Coca-Cola – to determine the strength and the various dimensions of attitudes towards its product. Semantic differential scales are also useful in evaluating the effectiveness of a changed marketing strategy, such as a change in advertising theme. Here the semantic differential could be administered before the campaign and again after the campaign, and any changes in perception pinpointed.

- Develop eight semantic differential scales for soft drinks, and then profile Coke and Pepsi. What differences do you perceive in the two brands? Are they important? Do you see any untapped soft drink opportunities?

Source: Robert Hartley, *Marketing Mistakes*, 6th edn (New York: Wiley, 1995), pp 139–40

Analogy

Another technique is to estimate by **analogy**. This assumes that demand for a product develops in much the same way in all countries as comparable economic development occurs in each country. First, a relationship must be established between the item to be estimated and a measurable variable in a country that is to serve as the basis for the analogy. Once a known relationship is established, the estimator then attempts to draw an analogy between the known situation and the country in question.

> **analogy**
> reasoning from parallel/similar cases/examples

For example, suppose a company wanted to estimate the market growth potential for a beverage in country X, for which it had inadequate sales figures, but the company had excellent beverage data for neighbouring country Y. In country Y it is known that per capita consumption increases at a predictable ratio as per capita gross domestic product (GDP) increases. If per capita GDP is known for country X, per capita consumption for the beverage can be estimated using the relationships established in country Y.

Caution must be used with analogy because the method assumes that factors other than the variable used (in this example, GDP) are similar in both countries, such as the similar culture, tastes, taxes, prices, selling methods, availability of products, consumption patterns and so forth. Despite the apparent drawbacks to analogy, it is useful where data are limited. For example, developments at the Dow Jones Stock Exchange in the USA are often used to predict stock development in the UK.

> **income elasticity**
> when higher or lower income would influence demand for a product

Income elasticity

Measuring the changes in the relationship between personal or family income and demand for a product can be used in forecasting market demand. In **income-elasticity** ratios, the sensitivity of demand for a product to income changes is measured. The elasticity coefficient is determined by dividing the percentage change in the quantity of a product demanded by the percentage change in income. With a result of less than one, it is said that the income–demand relationship is relatively inelastic and, conversely, if the result is greater than one, the relationship is elastic.

As income increases, the demand for a product increases at a rate proportionately higher than income increases. For example, if the income elasticity coefficient for recreation is 1.2, it implies that for each 1 per cent change in income, the demand for recreation could be expected to increase by 1.2 per cent; or if the coefficient is 0.8, then for each 1 per cent change in income, demand for recreation could be expected to increase by only 0.8 per cent. The relationship also occurs when income decreases, although the rate of decrease might be greater than when income increases. Income elasticity can be very useful, too, in predicting growth in demand for a particular product or product group.

As in the case of all methods described in this section, income elasticity measurements are no substitute for original market research when it is economically feasible and time permits. As more adequate data sources become available, more technically advanced techniques such as multiple regression analysis or input–output analysis can be used.

Multinational marketing information systems

As firms become established, and their information needs shift from those necessary to make initial market investment decisions to those necessary for continuous operation, there is a growing demand for continuous sources of information both at the country operational level and at the worldwide corporate level. However, as the abundance of information increases, it reaches a point of 'information overload' and requires some systematic method of storing, interpreting and analysing data.

multinational marketing information system (MMIS)

a system designed to generate an orderly flow of relevant information and to bring all the flows of recorded information into a unified whole for decision making

In short, companies have a need for a **multinational marketing information system (MMIS)**.

Conceptually, an MMIS embodies the same principle as any information system; that is, an interacting system of people, machines and procedures designed to generate an orderly flow of relevant information and to bring all the flows of recorded information into a unified whole for decision making. The only differences from a domestic marketing information system are: (1) scope – an MMIS covers more than one country; and (2) levels of information – an MMIS operates at each country level, with perhaps substantial differences among country systems, and at a worldwide level encompassing an entire international operation. The system (see Exhibit 6.5) includes a subsystem for each country designed for operational decision making – a country-level marketing information system. Each country system also provides information to an MMIS designed to provide for corporate control and strategic long-range planning decisions.

EXHIBIT 6.5: Multinational marketing information system (MMIS)

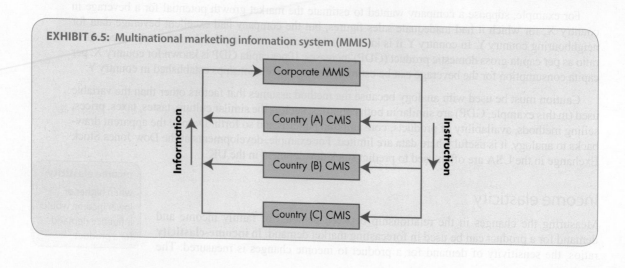

In developing an MMIS, it is necessary to design an adequate *country marketing information system (CMIS)* for each country/market. Because of the vast differences among a company's various markets, each CMIS will probably have different data requirements. Once a CMIS is set for each country/market, then an overall MMIS for the worldwide operation is designed. Each level of management has substantially different data needs because country/market systems are designed to provide information for day-to-day operations, while the MMIS is concerned with broader issues of control and long-range strategic planning. Some of the most challenging tasks facing the developer of the MMIS are determining the kinds of data and the depth of detail necessary, and analysing how it should be processed. This implies that models for decision making have been thought through and are sufficiently specific to be functional.

An MMIS can be designed as a basic system that provides only a source of information or as a highly sophisticated system that includes specific decision models. Experience has shown that success is greater when a company begins with a basic system and continues perfecting it to the desired level of sophistication.

SUMMARY

The basic objective of the market research function is providing management with information for more accurate decision making. This objective is the same for domestic and international marketing. In international marketing research, however, achieving that objective presents some challenges not encountered on the domestic front.

Consumer attitudes about providing information to a researcher are culturally conditioned. Foreign market information surveys must be carefully designed to elicit the desired data and at the same time not offend the respondent's sense of privacy. The concepts and ideas might have different meanings in different cultures. It is therefore particularly important in cases where research data or results from different markets are compared with each other. Besides the cultural and managerial constraints involved in gathering information for primary data, many foreign markets have inadequate and/or unreliable bases of secondary information.

Three generalisations can be made about the direction and rate of growth of marketing research in foreign marketing. First, both home-based and foreign management are increasingly aware of and accept the importance of marketing research's role in decision making. Second, there is a current trend towards the decentralisation of the research function to put control closer to the area being studied. Third, the most sophisticated tools and techniques are being adapted to foreign information gathering with increasing success. They are so successful, in fact, that it has become necessary to develop structured information systems to appreciate and utilise effectively the mass of information available.

Appendix: sources of secondary data

For almost any marketing research project, an analysis of available secondary information is a useful and inexpensive first step. The principal agencies that collect and publish information useful in international marketing are presented here, with some notations of selected publications.

International organisations

A number of international organisations provide information and statistics on international markets. The *Statistical Yearbook*, an annual publication of the United Nations, provides comprehensive social and economic data for more than 250 countries around the world. Many regional organisations, such as the Organisation for Economic Cooperation and Development (OECD), the Pan American Union and the EU, publish

> **Statistical Yearbook**
>
> an annual publication of the United Nations, which provides comprehensive social and economic data for more than 250 countries around the world

information, statistics and market studies relating to their respective regions. The United Nations *Investment Report* and *Development Report* present a lot of information every year. The EU gathers information on all aspects of European trade issues that are public (see, for example, www.euromonitor.org).

Chambers of commerce

In addition to government and organisational publications, many foreign countries maintain chamber of commerce offices in the EU, functioning as permanent trade missions. These foreign chambers of commerce generally have research libraries available and are knowledgeable regarding further sources of information on specific products or marketing problems.

Trade, business and service organisations

Foreign trade associations are particularly good sources of information on specific products or product lines. Many associations perform special studies or continuing services in collecting comprehensive statistical data for a specific product group or industry. Although some information is proprietary in nature and available only to members of an association, non-members frequently have access to it under certain conditions.

Foreign service industries also supply valuable sources of information useful in international business. Service companies – such as commercial and investment banks, international advertising agencies, foreign-based research firms, economic research institutes, foreign carriers, shipping agencies and freight forwarders – generally regard the furnishing of current, reliable information as part of their service function.

US government

In the process of keeping US businesses informed of foreign opportunities, the US government generates a considerable amount of general and specific market data for use by international market analysts. The principal source of information from the US government is the Department of Commerce; it works closely with trade associations, chambers of commerce and other interested associations in providing information, consultation and assistance in developing international commerce.

1 **International Economic Indicators**: quarterly reports providing basic data on the economy of the USA and seven other principal industrial countries. This report measures changes in key competitive indicators and highlights economic prospects and recent trends in the eight countries.

2 **Business Information Service for the Newly Independent States (BISNIS)**: this is a one-stop source for firms interested in obtaining assistance on selling in the markets of the Newly Independent States of the former Soviet Union. BISNIS provides information on trade regulations and legislation, defence conversion opportunities, commercial opportunities, market data, sources of financing and government and industry contacts.

3 **National Trade Data Bank (NTDB)**: the Commerce Department provides a number of the data sources mentioned above and others in its computerised information system in the *National Trade Data Bank* (NTDB). This source can be accessed via the Internet (http://www.statusa.gov/). The NTDB contains:

- the latest census data on US imports and exports by commodity and country
- the complete *CIA World Factbook*
- current market research reports compiled by the US and Foreign Commercial Service
- the complete *Foreign Traders Index*, which contains over 55,000 names and addresses of individuals and firms abroad that are interested in importing US products
- State Department country reports on economic policy and trade practices
- the publications *Export Yellow Pages*, *A Basic Guide to Exporting* and the *National Trade Estimates Report on Foreign Trade Barriers*

- the *Export Promotion Calendar*
- many other data series.

Other sources: abstracts, bibliographies and indexes

The Economist Intelligence Unit (London). Covers Economist Intelligence publications.

F&S Index International and *F&S Europe* (Cleveland). Predicasts. Monthly with quarterly and annual compilations. Indexes foreign companies, and product and industry information with emphasis on sources, giving data or statistics.

Business International. Worldwide Economic Indicators (New York). Annual. Economic, demographic, trade and other statistics.

Consumer Europe (London Euromonitor Publications). Annual. Marketing indicators and trends for various markets.

European Marketing Data and Statistics (London: Euromonitor Publications). Annual.

International Marketing Data and Statistics (London: Euromonitor Publications). Annual. Covers the Americas, Asia, Africa and Australia. Includes data on retail and wholesale sales, living standards and general consumer marketing data.

The Markets of Asia/Pacific: Thailand, Taiwan, People's Republic of China, Hong Kong, South Korea, the Philippines, Indonesia, Singapore and Malaysia (London: Asia Pacific Centre Ltd).

Facts on File, various years. An excellent source for data on prices, retail sales, consumer purchases and other country information.

Internet sources

1 http://globaledge.msu.edu/ibrd/ibrd.asp.
2 http://web.idirect.com/~tiger/supersite.htm.
3 http://www.europa.eu.int.
4 http://www.exportusa.com.
5 http://www.odci.gov/cia/publications/factbook.
6 http://www.webofculture.com.
7 http://www.oecd.org.
8 http://www.worldbank.org.
9 http://www.census.gov.
10 http://www.iser.essex.ac.uk/bhps.
11 http://www.euromonitor.com.

QUESTIONS

1 Discuss how the shift from making 'market entry' decisions to 'continuous operations' decisions creates a need for different types of information and data. What assistance does an MMIS provide?

2 Using a hypothetical situation, illustrate how an MMIS might be established and how it would be used at different levels.

3 Discuss the breadth and scope of international marketing research. Why is international marketing research generally broader in scope than domestic marketing research?

4 What is the task of the international market researcher? How is it complicated by the foreign environment?

5 Discuss the stages of the research process in relation to the problems encountered due to the international dimension. Give examples.

6 Why is the formulation of the research problem difficult in foreign market research?

7 Discuss the problems of gathering secondary data in foreign markets.

8 What are some of the problems created by language and the ability to comprehend in collecting primary data? How can an international market researcher overcome these difficulties?

9 Discuss how 'decentring' is used to get an accurate translation of a questionnaire.

10 Discuss when qualitative research may be more effective than quantitative research.

11 Select a country. From secondary sources compile the following information for at least a 10-year period prior to the present:

- principal imports
- principal exports
- gross national product
- chief of state
- major cities and population
- principal agricultural crop.

FURTHER READING

- P. N. Ghauri and K. Grønhaug, *Research Methods in Business Studies: A Practical Guide*, 4th edn (London: FT Pearson), 2010.
- Samuel Craig and Susan Douglas, 'Conducting International Marketing Research in the Twenty-first Century', *International Marketing Review*, 2001, 18(1), pp 80–90.
- P. N. Ghauri, 'Designing and Conducting Case Studies in International Business Research', in Rebecca Marchan-Piekkeri and Cathrine Welch (eds), *Handbook of Qualitative Research Methods for International Business* (Cheltenham: Edward Elgar, 2004), pp 109–24.

NOTES

1 Tamer Cavusgil, Pervez Ghauri and Ayse Akcal, *Doing Business in Emerging Markets*, 2nd edn (London: Sage, 2013).

2 For a complete discussion of marketing research in foreign environments, see Susan P. Douglas and C. Samuel Craig, *International Marketing Research* (Chichester/New York: Wiley, 2000).

3 John Cantwell, 'The Methodological Problems Raised by the Collection of Foreign Direct Investment Data', *Scandinavian International Business Review*, 1992, 1(1), 86–103.

4 Susan Douglas and Samuel Craig, 'The Changing Dynamic of Consumer Behavior: Implications for Cross-cultural Research', *International Journal of Research in Marketing*, 1997, 14(4), pp 373–95.

5 Pervez Ghauri and Kjell Grønhaug, *Research Methods in Business Studies: A Practical Guide*, 3rd edn (Hemel Hempstead: Prentice Hall, 2005).

6   David Kilburn, 'Unilever Struggles with Surf in Japan', *Advertising Age*, 6 May 1991, p 22.

7   'Analyzing Textual Data in International Marketing Research', *Qualitative Market Research: An International Journal* (with Rudolf Sinkovics and Elfriede Penz), 2005, 8(1), 9–38.

8   N.K. Malhotra, J. Agarwal and F.M. Ulgado, 'Internationalization and Entry Modes: A Multitheoretical Framework and Research Propositions', *Journal of International Marketing*, 2004, 11(4), 1–31.

9   Adapted from Mahmoud Aboul-Fath and Loula Zaklama, 'Ariel High Suds Detergent in Egypt – A Case Study', *Marketing and Research Today*, May 1992, pp 130–34.

10 R. Sinkovics, P.N. Ghauri and E. Penz, 'Measuring International New Product Development Projects: An Evaluation Process', *Journal of Business and Industrial Marketing* (with Helen Rogers and Kul Pawar), 2005, 20(2), pp 79–87.

11 R. Sinkovics, E. Penz and P.N. Ghauri, 'Enhancing the Trustworthiness of Interview Based Qualitative Research', *Management International Review* (with Rudolf Sinkovics and Elfriede Penz), 2008, 48(6), 689–714.

12 'Call for an End to Misreported Statistics', *New York Times*, 18 August 1994, p C17.

13 N.L. Reynold, A.C. Simintiras, and A. Diamantopoulos, 'Theoretical Justification for Sampling Choices in International Marketing Research: Key Issues and Guidelines for Researchers', *Journal of International Business Studies*, 2003, 34(1), pp 80–89.

14 R.R. Sinkovics, E. Penz and P.N. Ghauri, 'Enhancing the Trustworthiness of Qualitative Research in International Business', *Management International Review*, 2008, 48(6), 689–714.

15 Susan P. Douglas, and Samuel Craig, 'Researching Global Markets', in Sidney J. Levy *et al.* (eds), *The Dartnell Marketing Manager's Handbook* (Chicago, IL: The Dartnell Corporation, 1994), pp 1278–98.

16 B. Lee, S. Saklani and D. Tatterson, 'Top Prospects: State of the Marketing Research Industry in China', *Marketing News*, 10 June 2002, pp 12–13.

Chapter 7
Emerging Markets and Market Behaviour

Chapter Outline

Chapter Learning Objectives

What you should learn from Chapter 7

- The nature and the importance of emerging markets
- The connection between the economic level of a country and the marketing task
- New developments in market behaviour in these new markets
- The differences between emerging markets and developed markets
- How to evaluate the growth of developing markets and their importance to regional trade
- The marketing implications of growing homogeneous market segments

Major developments in communication and information technologies as well as transportation have accelerated globalisation and decreased geographic distances. Advancements in terms of liberalisation and economic integration have also contributed to the expansion of the international business environment. In this environment, the role of emerging markets has rapidly grown thereby leading to increased focus on analysing the potential of such markets. In developed markets, growth options are becoming relatively saturated. Meanwhile, opportunities offered by emerging markets are huge; analysing international marketing in the emerging market context is thus imperative in today's business environment.

What are emerging markets?

In general, emerging markets are countries which are transitioning from developing to developed markets due to rapid growth and industrialisation. The definition of emerging markets may sometimes be confusing as authors and institutions focus on a diverse range of factors in defining them. Still, only countries which have engaged in major reforms, increased their participation in global business and achieved steady growth can be referred to as emerging markets.

Most emerging markets are also in the process of moving towards a market-based economy from relatively closed economies. Continuous efforts to catch up with industrialised nations as depicted in their commitment to sustained growth, increased participation in world trade, ongoing improvements in the business environment and improvements in living standards differentiate emerging markets from less-developed markets.

In analysing emerging markets, BRICs are often singled out. The acronym BRIC stands for Brazil, Russia, India and China, which were selected as the markets which have a potential to surpass major economic powers by 2050. BRICs are the largest emerging markets, which are bound to be exceedingly influential due to their size and continuous growth.[1]

Going International 7.1

WHAT ARE THE FIRST, SECOND AND THIRD WORLDS?

The World Bank defined Third World countries as those with less than $7,300 annual GNP per capita. These included most of the countries of Asia (excluding Japan), Africa, the Middle East, the Caribbean, Central America and South America.

Industrialised countries, including North America and Western Europe, were often referred to as First World countries, while the Eastern Bloc was referred to as the Second World.

With the breakdown of the communist economies, the term Second the World has become redundant, and now the terms developed and developing or emerging nations are popularly used.

In classification, countries are divided in the following income groups by the World Bank, July 2012, on the basis of 2011 GNI per capita:

Low income: $1,025 or less.

Lower middle income: $1,026 to $4,035.

Upper middle income: $4,036 to $12,475.

High income: $12,476 or more.

© iStockphoto.com/janrysavy.

Low-income and middle-income economies are sometimes referred to as developing economies. The use of the term is convenient; it is not intended to imply that all economies in the group are experiencing similar development or that other economies have reached a preferred or final stage of development.

Source: *World Bank Report*, 2012

Growth of emerging markets

Traditionally, developing markets were characterised by protected domestic firms, significant trade and investment barriers, political instability, and volatility. As such, opportunities for foreign investors were limited and such markets were considered as being too risky for business. In the twentieth century many developing countries faced severe economic crises. A major factor leading to these crises was the maintenance of protectionist policies which led to limited development in the private sector.

As export income of such countries was low, governments often subsidised their economies by borrowing, which increased their dependence on foreign capital and generated significant debt burdens.[2] As a response to economic crisis, emerging markets undertook structural and economic reforms to increase stability and instigate growth. Such reforms often prioritised implementing aggressive industrialisation policies, increasing foreign income through trade liberalisation and focus on exports, and boosting market development through attracting foreign investments.

Today, foreign investors are seen as vital partners in economic development. In many emerging markets, experience with state-owned businesses proved to be a disappointment to most governments. Instead of being engines for accelerated economic growth, **state-owned enterprises (SOEs)** were often mismanaged, and created inefficient drains on state treasuries. Further, the rapid industrialisation of many emerging markets pointed towards private-sector investment as the most effective means of economic growth.

> **state-owned enterprises (SOEs)**
> companies owned by the government

New leaders have turned away from the traditional closed policies of the past to implement positive market-oriented reforms and seek ways for economic cooperation. **Privatisation** of SOEs and other economic, monetary and trade policy reforms show a broad shift away from inward-looking policies of import substitution (that is, manufacture products at home rather than import them) and protectionism that were so prevalent earlier. In a positive response to these reforms, investors are spending billions of dollars to buy airlines, banks, public works and telecommunications systems.

> **privatisation**
> when a government company is sold to private investors

As a result, in the past decade, production in emerging markets increased rapidly. In line with the growth of such economies, their markets have also grown significantly and consumption has shifted to such markets.[3] As seen in Exhibit 7.1, emerging and developing countries have been growing at higher rates when compared to developed markets. In fact aggregate GDP of emerging and developed countries is expected to surpass that of developed countries in the near future. This difference is more distinct when the figures are considered in terms of purchasing power parity (PPP).

At the same time, trade institutions such as the WTO and the credit providing agencies such as the IMF supported the growth of emerging markets and boosted their participation in global trade and

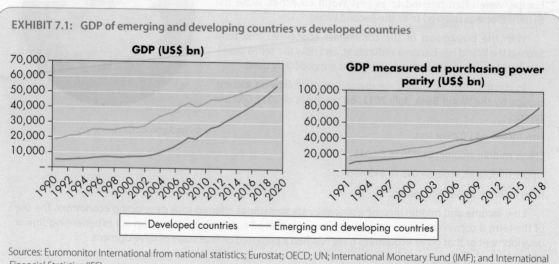

EXHIBIT 7.1: GDP of emerging and developing countries vs developed countries

Sources: Euromonitor International from national statistics; Eurostat; OECD; UN; International Monetary Fund (IMF); and International Financial Statistics (IFS).

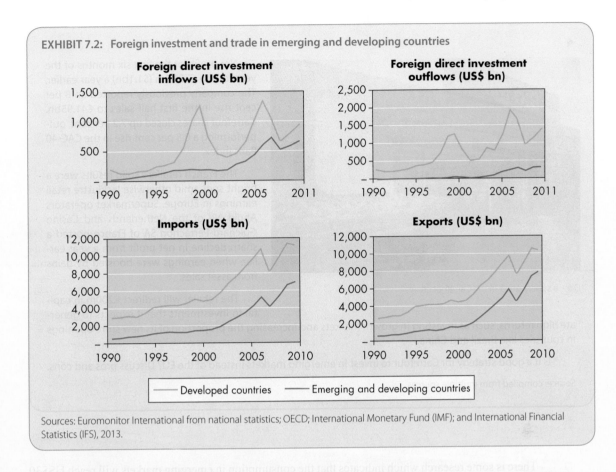

EXHIBIT 7.2:   Foreign investment and trade in emerging and developing countries

Sources: Euromonitor International from national statistics; OECD; International Monetary Fund (IMF); and International Financial Statistics (IFS), 2013.

investment by providing assistance in their trade and foreign investment policy reforms. As seen in Exhibit 7.2, foreign investment in emerging markets has increased significantly in the past decade. Import and export levels of emerging and developing countries have also been growing gradually, indicating their increased contribution to global trade.

Demand and consumption in emerging markets

The BRICs (Brazil, Russia, India and China) are some of the countries undergoing impressive changes in their economies and emerging as vast markets. In these and other countries, there is an ever-expanding and changing demand for goods and services. Markets are dynamic, developing entities reflecting the changing lifestyles of a culture. As economies grow, markets become different, larger and more demanding.

When economies grow and markets evolve beyond subsistence levels, the range of tastes, preferences and variations of products sought by the consumer increases; they demand more, better and/or different products. As countries prosper and their people are exposed to new ideas and behaviour patterns via global communications networks, old stereotypes, traditions and habits are cast aside or tempered and new patterns of consumer behaviour emerge.

Going International 7.2

CARREFOUR PROFIT RISES ON EMERGING MARKETS

Carrefour SA, the world's second-largest retailer after Wal-Mart Stores Inc, posted a 3.1 per cent rise in first-half net profit as strong growth in emerging markets helped the French company offset weakness at home.

Dia – a supermarket in the Carrefour chain.

Net profit for the first six months of the year rose to €751.1m ($1.1bn) a year earlier. The company previously reported an 8 per cent rise in the first half sales to €41.95bn. Carrefour shares closed up 7.2 per cent, outperforming a 0.5 per cent rise in the CAC-40 Paris index.

The French retailer's solid results were a bright spot amid otherwise lacklustre retail earnings in Europe. Supermarket operators Ahold NV of the Netherlands and Casino Guichard-Perrachon SA of France posted a sharp decline in net profit from a year earlier, when earnings were boosted by gains from asset sales.

The retailer will redirect €200m in capital to investments that it expects to generate high returns, such as investing in growth markets and increasing the proportion of its new store openings in countries like Brazil and China.

* Is it a good strategy for Carrefour to invest in emerging markets instead of the EU? Discuss pros and cons.

Source: compiled from multiple sources.

There is some research which indicates that the consumption in emerging markets will reach US$30 trillion by 2025 from US$ 12 trillion in 2010. Growth and industrialisation in emerging markets has led to urbanisation and rising incomes, which indicates a sharp increase in consumption.[4] Economic growth in emerging markets leads to higher income levels, which in turn implicate increased consumption and a growing middle class. For instance, the middle class population with income between US$30,0000 and US$50,000 is expected to increase to 26 million people from 1.5 million people in China.[5] In emerging markets urbanisation rates are also growing rapidly. As people move into the cities, they are able to join the formal workforce and raise their income levels.

At higher income levels, the consumption patterns are bound to change from stable goods to consumption goods, which highlights major opportunities for foreign companies. Moreover, urbanisation and growth of the cities also highlight the need for investment into the growth of such cities, which creates further opportunities. Exhibit 7.3 shows the breakdown of consumption expenditure in selected developed and emerging markets as of 2012. The charts in the exhibit indicate that consumption expenditure in emerging markets is growing rapidly and this growth is expected to accelerate in the near future.

Markets evolve from a three-way interaction of the economy, the culture and the marketing efforts of companies. Markets are not static but are constantly changing as they affect and are affected by changes in incomes, awareness of different lifestyles, exposure to new products and exposure to new ideas. Changing incomes raise expectations and the ability to buy more and different goods. The accessibility of global communications, TV, radio and print media means that people in one part of the world are aware of lifestyles in another. Global companies span the globe with new ideas on consumer behavior and new products to try. Exhibit 7.4 provides data related to the BRIC's changing consumption patterns in selected goods.

Middle income classes in emerging markets are growing rapidly and income levels are increasing significantly. However, in emerging markets, international marketers have to consider the distribution of income and the income level of different segments.

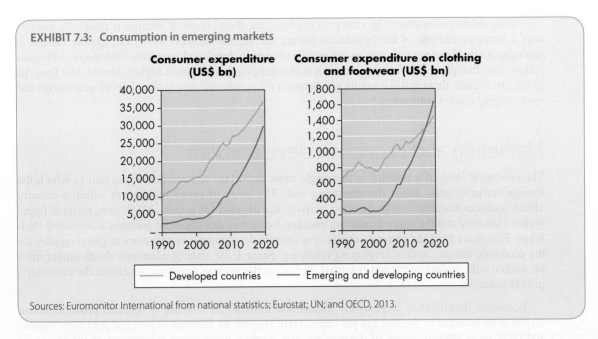

EXHIBIT 7.3: Consumption in emerging markets

Consumer expenditure (US$ bn)

Consumer expenditure on clothing and footwear (US$ bn)

— Developed countries   — Emerging and developing countries

Sources: Euromonitor International from national statistics; Eurostat; UN; and OECD, 2013.

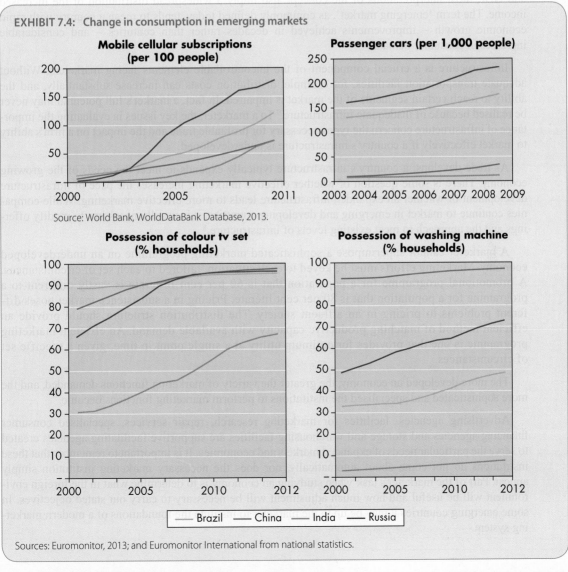

EXHIBIT 7.4: Change in consumption in emerging markets

Mobile cellular subscriptions (per 100 people)

Source: World Bank, WorldDataBank Database, 2013.

Passenger cars (per 1,000 people)

Possession of colour tv set (% households)

Possession of washing machine (% households)

— Brazil   — China   — India   — Russia

Sources: Euromonitor, 2013; and Euromonitor International from national statistics.

Unlike developed markets, in emerging markets, the distribution of income is relatively uneven, with a small percentage of the population having the highest income. Moreover, middle classes in emerging markets are not the same as the middle classes in developed countries. One major difference is that, even though middle-income consumers in emerging markets have higher income than they did in the past decade, there is still a wealth gap between the middle-income levels of developed market and the emerging market consumers.[5]

Marketing and economic development

The economic level of a country is the single most important environmental element to which the foreign marketer must adjust the marketing task. The stage of economic growth within a country affects attitudes towards foreign business activity, the demand for goods, distribution systems found within a country and the entire marketing process. Economic development presents a two-sided challenge. First, a study of the general aspects of economic development is necessary to gain empathy for the economic climate within developing countries. Second, the state of economic development must be studied with respect to market potential, including the present economic level and the economy's growth potential.

Economic development is generally understood to mean an increase in national production that results in an increase in the average per capita GDP. Besides an increase in average per capita income and GDP, most interpretations of the concept also imply a widespread distribution of the increased income. The term 'emerging market', as commonly defined today, tends to mean a country with rapid economic growth – improvements achieved in decades rather than centuries – and considerable increases in consumer demand.

Infrastructure is a crucial component of the uncontrollable elements facing marketers. Without adequate transportation facilities, for example, distribution costs can increase substantially, and the ability to reach certain segments of the market is impaired. In fact, a market's full potential may never be realised because of inadequate infrastructure.[7] To a marketer, the key issues in evaluating the importance of infrastructure concern the types necessary for profitable trade and the impact on a firm's ability to market effectively if a country's infrastructure is underdeveloped.

As trade develops, a country's infrastructure typically expands to meet the needs of the growing economy. There is some question of whether effective marketing increases the pace of infrastructure development or whether an expanded infrastructure leads to more effective marketing. While companies continue to market in emerging and developing countries, it is usually necessary to modify offerings and the approach to meet existing levels of infrastructure.[8]

A marketer cannot superimpose a sophisticated marketing programme on an underdeveloped economy. Marketing efforts must be keyed to each situation, tailored to each set of circumstances. A promotional programme for a population that is 60 per cent illiterate is vastly different to a programme for a population that is 80 per cent literate. Pricing in a subsistence market poses different problems to pricing in an affluent society. The distribution structure should provide an efficient method of matching productive capacity with available demand. An efficient marketing programme is one that provides for optimum utility at a single point in time, given a specific set of circumstances.

The more developed an economy, the greater the variety of marketing functions demanded, and the more sophisticated and specialised the institutions to perform marketing functions become.

Advertising agencies, facilities for marketing research, repair services, specialised consumer financing agencies and storage and warehousing facilities are supportive facilitating agencies created to serve the particular needs of expanded markets and economies. It is important to remember that these institutions do not come about automatically, nor does the necessary marketing institution simply appear. Part of the marketer's task when studying an economy is to determine what in the foreign environment will be useful and how much adjustment will be necessary to carry out stated objectives. In some emerging countries it may be up to the marketer to institute the foundations of a modern marketing system.

Marketing in emerging markets

Emerging markets offer tremendous opportunities for business. The attractiveness of such markets for firms from developed markets is also increasing given the relatively saturated structure of developed markets. Still, in order to be able to take advantage of the opportunities in emerging markets, firms from developed markets have to realise that such markets are different in terms of the economic landscape, infrastructure and consumer characteristics and formulate their strategies accordingly.

In analysing emerging markets, institutional voids – inefficiencies in capital, product and labour markets – are often emphasised. Institutions provide information, resources and services which assist market functions. For instance institutions can provide access to capital. They can also provide valuable information regarding the players within a value chain, firms' credibility, consumer characteristics and supply information. In addition, regulatory institutions governing the legal system ensure efficiency in business transactions and help resolve disputes.[9]

In developed markets, specialised intermediaries such as distributors, and logistics companies help distribute a firm's products. Information agencies, headhunters, and market research firms provide information regarding the consumers, competition and the potential employees. Financial intermediaries can help obtain funds for growth and also assist consumers with their purchases. On the other hand, in emerging markets, such intermediaries either do not exist or are inefficient. Such shortcomings in emerging markets increase the costs for the multinationals from developed markets.

On the other hand, emerging market environments are changing rapidly and the business environments in such markets are improving continually. Increased global participation and the need to attract further foreign investment lead to increased efforts in improving the business environments in emerging markets. For instance, Exhibit 7.5 shows the doing business rankings for selected countries for 2006 and for 2012. Doing business rankings are prepared by the World Bank and measure the ease of doing business in a given country in terms of the regulatory structure. As seen in the exhibit, most emerging markets have improved dramatically in terms of their overall ease of doing business scores.

The physical infrastructure of a country refers to the country's facilities which enable its economy to function and determine living conditions. In a given country, infrastructure can be analysed by considering factors such as the quality and efficiency of transportation and communication systems.

EXHIBIT 7.5: Doing business rankings

	2006	2012
UK	5	7
USA	3	4
Japan	12	24
Germany	21	20
Malaysia	25	12
Chile	24	37
South Africa	28	39
Mexico	62	48
Peru	124	43
Pakistan	130	107
Columbia	143	45
Turkey	157	71
China	147	91
Russia	166	112
Brazil	170	130

Source: The World Bank, 'Doing Business', http://www.doingbusiness.org/rankings.

A major difference between developed and emerging markets is that, in emerging markets, infrastructure may be inadequate or inefficient. For international marketers, infrastructural weaknesses especially highlight potential difficulties in distribution, logistics, and difficulties in communicating with potential consumers.

In Exhibit 7.6 data regarding selected variables reflecting life styles and infrastructure in selected developed and emerging markets is presented. As seen in the table, the infrastructure and the consumption is significantly lower in emerging markets when compared to developed markets.

In analysing the competitiveness of different countries, World Economic Forum researchers focus on factors which influence the productivity in a given country. In doing so, quality and availability of infrastructure is assessed on a country basis. Exhibit 7.7 shows the infrastructure quality scores of selected developed and emerging markets for 2006 and for 2013. In the exhibit, countries' ranks within the overall sample are provided. The quality values shown in the exhibit are values within 1 and 7, with 7 representing the highest possible quality. This exhibit also shows that the infrastructure quality in emerging markets is not at par with the quality in developed markets. On the other hand, a closer examination of the scores indicates that the quality of infrastructure in many emerging markets has improved significantly.

Unique characteristics of emerging markets influence the marketing process. For instance, limited information availability or the dispersed nature of the market population can create obstacles in segmenting and targeting consumers. Disparities among income levels also indicate the presence of multiple segments which are vastly different to each other. Moreover, emerging markets are often undergoing rapid changes and such changes may result in changes in segments.

In marketing to emerging markets, product features often need to be adjusted. Low incomes can indicate the need to focus on affordability and durability. Moreover, consumer needs as well as tastes in

---

EXHIBIT 7.6:   Infrastructure and living standards in selected developed and emerging markets

	Fixed broadband Internet subscribers (per 100 people) – 2011	Telephone lines (per 100 people) – 2011	Mobile cellular subscriptions (per 100 people) – 2011	Internet users (per 100 people) – 2011	Passenger cars (per 1,000 people) – 2010	Motor vehicles (per 1,000 people) – 2020
France	36	56	105	77	481	580
Germany	32	63	132	83	517	572
Japan	27	51	103	79	453	591
UK	33	53	131	82	457	519
USA	29	48	106	78	627	797
Argentina	11	25	135	48		
Brazil	9	22	123	45		
China	12	21	73	38	44	58
Egypt	2	11	101	36		
India	1	3	72	10		
Indonesia	1	16	98	18	37	
Malaysia	7	15	127	61	325	361
Pakistan	0	3	62	9	13	18
Russia	12	31	179	49		
South Africa	2	8	127	21	112	165
Thailand	5	10	113	24	67	157
Turkey	10	21	89	42	104	155

Source: World Bank, World Database, 2013.

EXHIBIT 7.7: Infrastructure quality scores

Entity	Rank – 2006	Value – 2006	Rank – 2013	Value – 2013
Germany	1	6.58	3	6.36
UK	12	5.71	6	6.22
Japan	6	6.16	11	5.92
USA	7	6.14	14	5.81
Malaysia	20	5.34	32	5.09
Chile	31	4.54	45	4.62
Thailand	29	4.68	46	4.62
Russia	66	3.27	47	4.52
China	52	3.73	48	4.46
Turkey	61	3.42	51	4.38
South Africa	32	4.45	63	4.13
Mexico	57	3.55	68	4.03
Brazil	68	3.15	70	4.00
Indonesia	78	2.81	78	3.75
Egypt	59	3.54	83	3.61
India	62	3.39	84	3.60
Argentina	63	3.35	86	3.58
Peru	92	2.55	89	3.51
Colombia	76	2.88	93	3.44
Philippines	88	2.64	98	3.19
Pakistan	69	3.15	116	2.73

Source: World Economic Forum, 2013, http://www.weforum.org/content/global-agenda-council-infrastructure-2012–2013.

emerging markets are considerably different when compared to developed markets. Hence, marketers need to adapt their products to fulfill the specific needs of the emerging market consumers and appeal to their tastes. In many cases limited infrastructure within emerging markets can also result in a higher emphasis on the products' durability and the availability of after-sales services.

In pricing, firms from developed markets may often be challenged by the pressure to lower their prices. Local firms in such markets may often excel in their ability to produce at lower costs and offer products which suit the needs of the emerging market consumers due to their knowledge of the business environment and culture. Faced with similar issues, many developed market firms have chosen to concentrate on targeting the high income segments within emerging markets. However, considering that the majority of emerging market populations are middle and lower income, such strategies may lead to limited growth opportunities.

In emerging markets, even the middle-income segments have relatively limited budgets which are lower than those of developed market consumers. In parallel, firms may not be successful in attracting middle-income consumers in emerging markets when they enter such markets with products and marketing strategies designed for the developed markets.

Limited infrastructure, limited availability of efficient distribution chains and the dispersed structure of rural populations may create challenges in distribution for international marketers. Moreover, the characteristics and the availability of promotion channels such as media and Internet are bound to influence marketing in emerging markets.

Many companies enter emerging markets with the belief that their products accepted in other countries will be welcomed by emerging market customers. However, such is not often the case due to cultural differences, different needs and wants. In emerging markets, marketers also need to consider cultural factors in designing marketing strategies. Such differences often necessitate adjustments in firms' marketing strategies. For instance, many emerging markets are associated with collective cultural characteristics which embrace social harmony and value relationships. In parallel, marketing strategies which emphasise building relations with the consumer are bound to be more effective in such markets.

International marketers also need to consider the culture's approach to new products and change in planning their marketing strategy and developing the marketing mix in emerging markets. For instance, if a culture is resistant to change or especially cautious, then it is imperative to emphasise product attributes, such as reliability, in marketing.

Going International 7.3

COKE TO SQUEEZE MORE FROM CHINA

Fruit juice drink growth in China

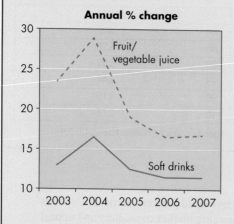

Annual % change

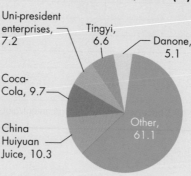

Market share, 2007 (%)

Coca-Cola's 47 products in China range from its trademark Coke to Ice Dew bottled water, and nearly everything in between. The company is now trying to fill it by making a $2.4bn offer for China Huiyuan Juice Group, the country's biggest juice-maker. The acquisition would more than double Coke's market share in China's fruit juices market to about 20 per cent, far ahead of its next closest rival, according to market research firm Euromonitor International.

China's non-alcoholic drinks market has grown by 82 per cent in the past five years, to $32.7bn, but of that, fruit juice sales have grown by 160 per cent over the same period. Two years ago Coke agreed to acquire its third major Chinese bottler, Kerry Beverages, from Robert Kuok, the Chinese-Malaysian tycoon. The deal would also be the first major test of China's new anti-competition policy, enacted last month. An online poll conducted by Internet portal sina.com showed 82 per cent of 52,000 respondents opposed the deal, saying it would be an example of foreign capital destroying a 'cultural pillar'.

- Is this a good strategy for Coke in China? Discuss.

Sources: *Financial Times*, 4 September 2008, p 20; and Euromonitor, 2012.

Emerging market groups

What is occurring in the emerging markets is analogous to the situation after the Second World War when tremendous demand was created during the reconstruction of Europe. As Europe rebuilt its infrastructure and industrial base, demand for capital goods exploded and, as more money was infused into its economies, consumer demand also increased rapidly. During that period, the USA was the principal supplier because most of the rest of the world was rebuilding or had underdeveloped economies. Now the USA, Japan, Europe and the BRICs will become fierce rivals in emerging markets.

Eastern Europe and the Baltic States

Eastern Europe and the Baltic states, satellite nations of the former USSR, have established free-market systems (see Exhibit 7.8). New business opportunities are emerging almost daily and the region is described as anywhere from chaotic with big risks to an exciting place with untold opportunities. Both descriptions fit, as countries adjust to the political, social and economic realities of changing from the restrictions of a Marxist-socialist system to some version of free markets and capitalism.

For the entrepreneur, freedom from communism has provided the opportunity to blossom. Nowhere is this more evident than in Poland. Reforms, coupled with the fact that Poland had a relatively large private sector under communism, have led to an explosion of private entrepreneurial activity. For example, 20 per cent of all retail sales in 1989 were private, and by 1991 the private-sale share rose to 80 per cent. The extent and size of emerging markets in Eastern Europe is illustrated in Exhibit 7.9.

A report of a Polish trader who started a business in a warehouse to outfit retail stores typifies the entrepreneurial spirit found in many of the countries. The business, Inter-commerce, has scales from Korea, cash registers from Japan, and stack upon stack of German shelves, racks, baskets, hangers, supermarket carts, barcode readers, price-tag tape and checkout counters. When a customer wants furnishings for a new store, the owner of Inter-commerce prepares a layout for the store, makes a list of what is needed, and then trucks it all to the new store. 'It takes about an hour,' he says. The company's sales were €9,000 ($10,000) a month in 1990 and €540,000 ($600,000) per month a year later.[11]

Asia

Asia is the fastest-growing market in the world and its share of global output was projected to account for almost one-half of the increase in global output through the next decade.[12] Both as sources of new products and technology and as vast consumer markets, the Pacific Rim and Asia are just beginning to get into their stride (see Exhibits 7.10 and 7.11).

South Korea is the centre of trade links with north China and the Asian republics of the former Soviet Union. Although North and South Korea do not officially recognise one another, trade between the two, mostly through Hong Kong, is in excess of €112m ($124m) annually.

EXHIBIT 7.8: EU member states

Member states of the EU	Year of entry	Member states of the EU	Year of entry
Belgium	1952	Sweden	1995
France	1952	Cyprus	2004
Germany	1952	Czech Republic	2004
Italy	1952	Estonia	2004
Luxembourg	1952	Hungary	2004
Netherlands	1952	Latvia	2004
Denmark	1973	Lithuania	2004
Ireland	1973	Malta	2004
UK	1973	Poland	2004
Greece	1981	Slovakia	2004
Portugal	1986	Slovenia	2004
Spain	1986	Bulgaria	2007
Austria	1995	Romania	2007
Finland	1995		

Source: http://europa.eu/about-eu/countries/index_en.htm, 2012.

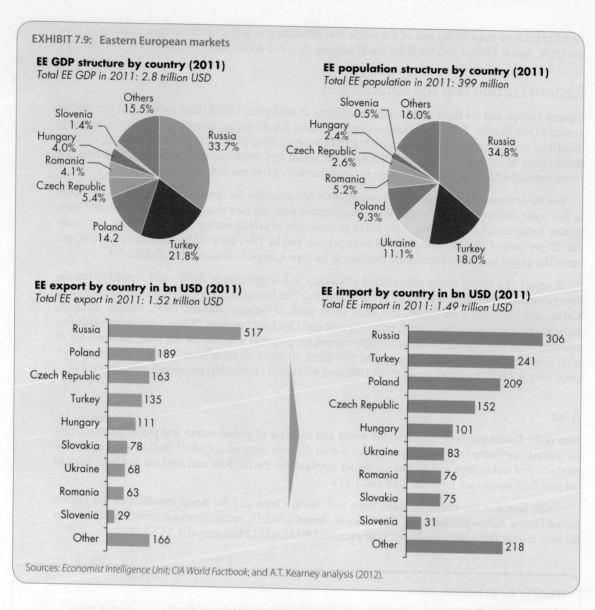

EXHIBIT 7.9:   Eastern European markets

EE GDP structure by country (2011)
Total EE GDP in 2011: 2.8 trillion USD

- Others 15.5%
- Slovenia 1.4%
- Hungary 4.0%
- Romania 4.1%
- Czech Republic 5.4%
- Poland 14.2
- Turkey 21.8%
- Russia 33.7%

EE population structure by country (2011)
Total EE population in 2011: 399 million

- Slovenia 0.5%
- Others 16.0%
- Hungary 2.4%
- Czech Republic 2.6%
- Romania 5.2%
- Poland 9.3%
- Ukraine 11.1%
- Turkey 18.0%
- Russia 34.8%

EE export by country in bn USD (2011)
Total EE export in 2011: 1.52 trillion USD

Country	Export
Russia	517
Poland	189
Czech Republic	163
Turkey	135
Hungary	111
Slovakia	78
Ukraine	68
Romania	63
Slovenia	29
Other	166

EE import by country in bn USD (2011)
Total EE import in 2011: 1.49 trillion USD

Russia	306
Turkey	241
Poland	209
Czech Republic	152
Hungary	101
Ukraine	83
Romania	76
Slovakia	75
Slovenia	31
Other	218

Sources: *Economist Intelligence Unit; CIA World Factbook*; and A.T. Kearney analysis (2012).

EXHIBIT 7.10:   Asian emerging markets: selected countries

	Population (in millions)	GDP ($bn)	GDP ($ per capita)	Export ($bn)	Imports ($bn)
China	1,343	11,480	8,500	1,899	1,740
Hong Kong	7	357.2	50,200	438	494
India	1,205	4,492	3,900	305	490
Indonesia	249	1,143	5,000	201.5	166.1
Japan	127	4,516	36,200	787	807.6
South Korea	49	1,579	32,400	552.8	521.6
Taiwan	23	890.2	38,500	307	279.2
Pakistan	190	230.5	2,900	24.66	40.82
Malaysia	29	307.2	16,900	239.8	197.2

Source: *CIA World Factbook*, 2012.

EXHIBIT 7.11: Asia

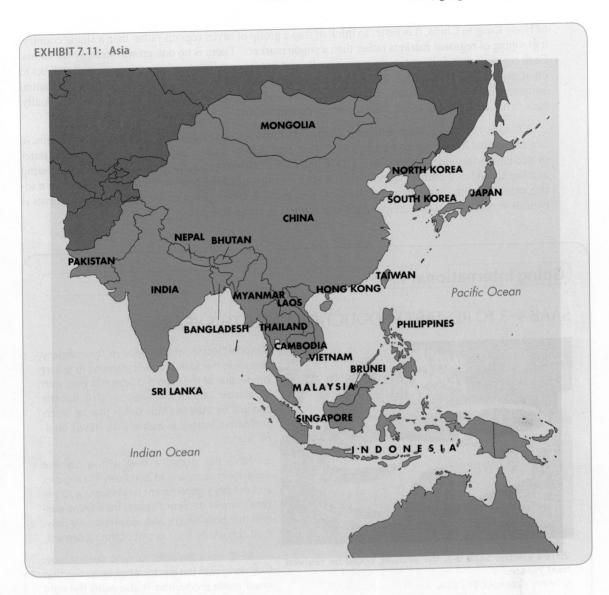

Japan's role in the Asian Pacific Rim is perhaps the most important in the area. While not part of a common market or any other economic cooperative alliance, Japan's influence is nevertheless increasingly dominant. Sales to Japan account for as much as 12 per cent of GDP in Malaysia and about 7 per cent of GDP in Indonesia, Thailand and South Korea.[8] That these economies influence each other was clearly seen in the 1997–98 Asian crisis.

As these Asian countries continue to develop, in spite of the major 1997–98 crisis, Chinese capital, technology and direction will be paramount. With Chinese leadership, the region is rapidly becoming a major economic power in global trade.[13] China's role among the Asian Pacific Rim countries may have the same economic trade impact for developing countries in that region as the EU provides for Eastern Europe and the USA provides for South America.

China

The economic and social changes occurring in China since it began actively seeking economic ties with the industrialised world have been dramatic.[14] China's dual economic system, embracing socialism along with many tenets of capitalism, produced an economic boom with expanded opportunity for foreign investment.

Anyone doing business in China must keep in mind a few fundamentals that have been overshadowed by Western euphoria. First, because of China's size, diversity, political organisation and the return of Hong Kong to China, it is better to think of it as a group of seven regions rather than a single country: a grouping of regional markets rather than a single market.[15] There is no one growth strategy for China. Each region is at a different stage economically and has its own link to other regions as well as links to other parts of the world. Each has its own investment patterns, is taxed differently and has substantial autonomy in how it is governed. But while each region is separate enough to be considered individually, each is linked at the top to the central government in Beijing.

China is not only a huge emerging market, but also an investor. There are thousands of Chinese companies that have invested heavily in the West, particularly Europe and the USA. A number of state-owned enterprises such as Sinochem, CITIC and COFCO have been active in real estate, manufacturing and finance. Also, a number of provincial and city companies have now set up their own Western trading, manufacturing, investment and finance companies. Another group active in foreign investments is hybrids working through wholly-owned subsidiaries in Hong Kong.[16]

Going International 7.4

SAAB 9–3 TO RESTART PRODUCTION LATER THIS YEAR

2010's electric Saab 9-3, the ePower, could be revived next year.
© Dmitry Valberg. CC BY 2.0 UK.

National Electric Vehicles Sweden, the company that owns the Saab brand, is planning to restart production of the Saab 9–3 later this year, with an electric version following in 2014. But the cars will be built in China rather than at Saab's Trollhattan factory, in a change to NEVS's original plan.

NEVS has signed a deal with a Chinese investment company to build cars in Qingdao, and the city's government has bought a 22 per cent share in the firm. Reports from China suggest that both electric and conventionally-powered cars will be built as part of the agreement.

NEVS owns the right to build the last Saab 9–3, along with the electric ePower version that never made production. It also owns the right to use the Saab name. Originally NEVS said it would only produce Saabs at Trollhattan.

China's government wants to get half a million electric vehicles on the country's roads within two years, so the market potential for electric Saabs is high. However, the 9–3 is elderly and the only model NVS has – it may not be enough to keep the firm afloat.

Despite the government's intentions, China has little infrastructure to support large numbers of electric cars, while new deals between local investors and foreign companies require lengthy and complex state approval that could take up to 18 months. This alone could make it impossible to start production this year.

- Do you think the time is ripe for electric cars and SAAB will be able to tap into this market in China? Discuss.

Source: Haymarket Consumer Media, 2013.

India

The wave of change that has been washing away restricted trade, controlled economies, closed markets and hostility to foreign investment in most developing countries finally reached India in the early 1990s. Since its independence, one of the world's largest markets had set a poor example as a model for economic growth for other developing countries and was among the last of the economically important developing nations to throw off traditional insular policies.

Times have changed and India has embarked on the most profound transformation since it won political independence from Britain in 1947. In 1992 the new direction promised to adjust the philosophy of self-sufficiency that had been taken to extremes and to open India to world markets. India had the look and feel of the next China.

Yet India is a mixed bag; while it did overthrow the restrictions of earlier governments, it did not move towards reforms and open markets with the same degree of vigour found in other emerging markets. Resistance to change comes from politicians, bureaucrats, union members and farmers, as well as from some industrialists who have lived comfortably behind protective tariff walls that excluded competition. Bureaucracy and rigid labour laws remain a drag on business, as does corruption. One foreign oil-company executive reports having to pay off the phone repairman: 'I complained to his company, but they just laughed. The police said they would arrest him – but only for a fee.'[15] India's present problems are not economic but a mix of political, psychological and cultural attitudes.

As a result India is becoming the favourite destination for outsourcing of services by Western companies. With a population of more than 1 billion, India is second in size only to China, and both contain enormous low-cost labour pools. India has a middle class numbering some 350 million, closer to the population of the EU and bigger than the USA. Among its middle class are large numbers of college graduates, 40 per cent of whom have degrees in science and engineering. India has a diverse industrial base and is developing as a centre for computer software.

The Americas

The North American Free Trade Agreement (NAFTA) marks the high point of a silent political and economic revolution that has been taking place in the Americas (see Exhibit 7.12) over the past decade. Most of the countries have moved from military dictatorships to democratically elected governments, while sweeping economic and trade liberalisation is replacing the economic model most Latin American countries followed for decades. Today many of them are at roughly the same stage of liberalisation that launched the dynamic growth in Asia during the last two decades.[17]

Argentina, Brazil, Chile and Mexico are among the countries that have quickly instituted reforms. Mexico has been the leader in privatisation and in lowering tariffs even before entering NAFTA. Over 750 businesses, including the telephone company, steel mills, airlines and banks, have been sold. Pemex, the national oil company, is the only major industry Mexico is not privatising, although restrictions on joint projects between Pemex and foreign companies have been liberalised.

In addition to privatisation and lowering tariffs, most Latin American countries are working at creating an environment to attract capital. Chile, Mexico and Bolivia were the first to make deep cuts in tariffs from a high of 100 per cent or more down to a maximum of 10 to 20 per cent. Taxes that act as non-tariff trade barriers are being eliminated, as are restrictions on the repatriation of profits. These and other changes have energised governments, people and foreign investors.[2]

The population of nearly 460 million is one-half greater than that of the USA. Almost 60 per cent of all the merchandise traded in Latin America is transacted with countries in the Western hemisphere. The USA alone provides more than 40 per cent of Latin America's imports and buys a similar share of its exports. Economic and trade policy reforms occurring in Latin American countries signify a tremendous potential for trade and investment.[18]

A study by the Institute for International Economics reported that Argentina, Brazil, Bolivia, Chile, Colombia, Paraguay, Uruguay and several Caribbean nations ranked higher on a scale of 'readiness criteria' – price stability, budget discipline, market-oriented policies and a functioning democracy – than did Mexico at the start of the NAFTA talks. Thus, they are viable candidates for a Western Hemisphere Free Trade Agreement (WHFTA) to replace NAFTA. Such an agreement would strengthen trade ties within the region, pre-empt a plethora of smaller trade agreements, increase trade and make economic sense for the region, the USA and Canada.

EXHIBIT 7.12: The Americas

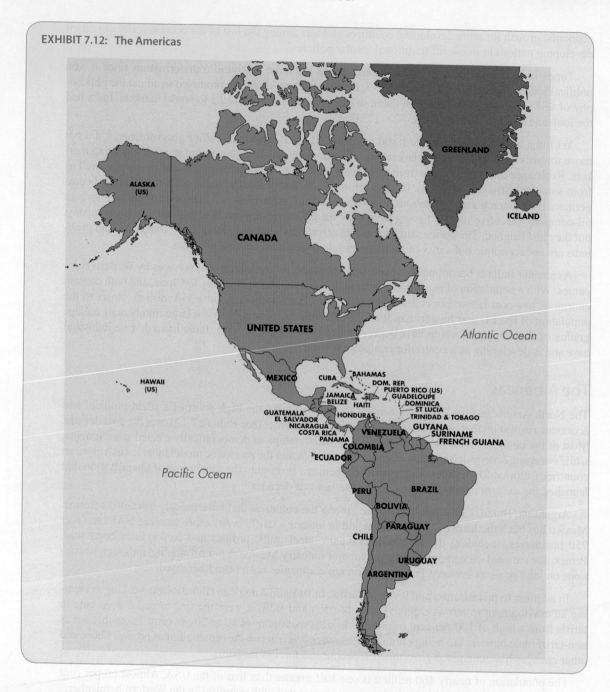

GREENLAND

ALASKA
(US)

ICELAND

CANADA

UNITED STATES

Atlantic Ocean

HAWAII
(US)

MEXICO   CUBA   BAHAMAS
DOM. REP.
PUERTO RICO (US)
JAMAICA   GUADELOUPE
BELIZE   DOMINICA
HAITI   ST LUCIA
GUATEMALA   TRINIDAD & TOBAGO
EL SALVADOR   HONDURAS   GUYANA
NICARAGUA   SURINAME
COSTA RICA   VENEZUELA   FRENCH GUIANA
PANAMA   COLOMBIA

ECUADOR

Pacific Ocean

PERU   BRAZIL

BOLIVIA

PARAGUAY

CHILE

URUGUAY

ARGENTINA

SUMMARY

The increasing scope and level of technical and economic growth have enabled many countries to advance their standards of living by as much as two centuries in a matter of decades. As countries develop their productive capacity, all segments of their economies will feel the pressure to improve. The impact of these social and economic trends will continue to be felt throughout the world, causing significant changes in marketing practices. Marketers must focus on devising marketing plans designed to respond fully to each level of economic development. China and the former Soviet Union continue to undergo rapid political and economic changes that have resulted in opening most communist-bloc countries to foreign direct investment and international trade. And although emerging markets present special problems, they are promising markets for a broad range of products.

This ever-expanding involvement of more and more of the world's people with varying needs and wants will test old trading patterns and alliances. The foreign marketer of today and tomorrow must be able to react to market changes rapidly and to anticipate new trends within constantly evolving market segments that may not have existed as recently as last year. Many of today's market facts will probably be tomorrow's historical myths.

QUESTIONS

1   Is it possible for an economy to experience economic growth as measured by total GNP without a commensurate rise in the standard of living? Discuss fully.

2   Discuss each of the stages of evolution in the marketing process. Illustrate each stage with the example of a particular country.

3   Discuss the impact of IT on the emerging markets. How can it influence company strategies?

4   Considering the developments in the two biggest markets (India and China), discuss the opportunities and threats in these two markets from a foreign company's perspective.

5   The infrastructure is important to the economic growth of an economy. Comment.

6   What is marketing's role in economic development? Discuss marketing's contributions to economic development.

7   Discuss the economic and trade importance of the big emerging markets.

8   What are the traits of those countries considered to be big emerging markets? Discuss.

9   The importance of China as a market and as a competitor to Western companies is widely discussed. You are required to analyse China's emergence as a competitor to the Western companies; will it be able to surpass the USA and/or the EU in terms of trade and GDP in the near future? Discuss with arguments and examples.

10   What are global market segments? Why are they important to global companies? Discuss.

FURTHER READING

- S.T. Cavusgil, P. N. Ghauri and A. Akcal, *Doing Business in Emerging Markets,* 2nd edn (Thousand Oaks, CA: Sage, 2013), Chs 1 and 2.
- T. Schuster and D. Holtbrugge, 'Market Entry of Multinational Companies in Markets at the Bottom of the Pyramid: A Learning Perspective,' *International Business Review,* 2012, 21(5), 817–30.
- A. Sahaym and D. Nam, 'International Diversification of the Emerging-market Enterprises: A Multi-level Examination,' *International Business Review,* 2013, 22(2), 421–36.

NOTES

1 'The Big Emerging Markets', *Business America*, March 1994, pp 4–6.

2 S. Tamer Cavusgil, P.N. Ghauri and A.A. Akcal, *Doing Business in Emerging Markets,* 2nd edn (Thousand Oaks, CA: Sage, 2012).

3 Gross domestic product (GDP) and gross national product (GNP) are two measures of a country's economic activity. GDP is a measure of the market value of all goods and services produced within the boundaries of a nation, regardless of asset ownership. Unlike GNP, GDP excludes receipts from that nation's business operations in foreign countries, as well as the share of reinvested earnings in foreign affiliates of domestic corporations.

4 Walt W. Rostow, *The Stages of Economic Growth*, 2nd edn (London: Cambridge University Press, 1971), p 10. For an interesting discussion, see Peter Buckley and Pervez Ghauri, *The Global Challenge for Multinational Enterprises* (Oxford: Pergamon Press, 1999).

5 'The Battle for Brazil', *Fortune*, 20 July 1998, pp 48–53.

6 For a description of how competitive South Korea has become, see David P. Hamilton and Steve Glain, 'Silicon Duel: Koreans Move to Grab Memory-chip Market from the Japanese', *Wall Street Journal*, 14 March 1995, p A–1.

7 For a discussion of the billions of dollars being invested in infrastructure, see Dave Savona, 'Remaking the Globe', *International Business*, March 1995, pp 30–36.

8 Goitom Tesfom, Clemens Lutz and Pervez Ghauri, 'Comparing Export Marketing Channels: Developed versus Developing Countries', *International Marketing Review*, 2004, 21(4/5), 409–22.

9 For a comprehensive review of one country's move towards a more open economy, see 'Argentina Survey', *The Economist*, 26 November 1994, 18 pages unnumbered beginning on p 62.

10 'India: How a Thirst for Energy Lead to a Thaw', *Business Week*, 15 November 2004, p 63.

11 When the US government lifted the trade embargo against Vietnam, many US companies found that their competitors had already made inroads in that market. See Marita Van Oldenborgy, 'Catch-up Ball', *International Business*, March 1994, pp 92–94.

12 'Big Emerging Markets' Share of World Exports Continues to Rise', *Business America*, March 1994, p 28.

13 John Naisbitt, *Megatrends Asia: Eight Asian Megatrends that are Reshaping Our World* (New York: Simon & Schuster, 1996).

14 *The Economist*, 20 June 1998, pp 17–18; and 'Three Futures for Japan', *The Economist*, 21 March 1998, pp 29–30.

15 'The China Connection', *Business Week*, 5 August 1996, pp 32–5; and 'China's WTO Accession', *Far Eastern Economic Review*, 2 July 1998, p 38.

16 China is divided into 23 provinces (including Taiwan) and five autonomous border regions. The provinces and autonomous regions are usually grouped into six large administrative regions: Northeastern Region, Northern Region (includes Beijing), Eastern Region (includes Shanghai), South Central Region, Southwestern Region, and the Northwestern Region. After Hong Kong's reversion to China, it is considered the seventh autonomous region.

17 Matt Moffett, 'Seeds of Reform: Key Finance Ministers in Latin America are Old Harvard-MIT Pals', *Wall Street Journal*, 1 August 1994, p 1.

18 Paul Magnusson, 'With Latin America Thriving, NAFTA Might Keep Marching South', *Business Week*, 24 July 1994, p 20.

Chapter 8

Regional Market Groups and Marketing Implications

Chapter Learning Objectives

What you should learn from Chapter 8

- The need for economic union and how current events are affecting that need
- The impact of the Triad power on the future of international trade
- How to differentiate between patterns of multinational cooperation
- How the European Community (EC) evolved to become the European Union (EU)
- How to evaluate the evolving patterns of trade in Eastern Europe
- The trade linkage of NAFTA and South America and its effect on other Latin American major trade areas
- The importance of the Asian Pacific Rim

During the past three decades an interest in regional integration in Europe, Asia and the Americas has increased. The emergence of the World Trade Organization (WTO) and the proliferation of regional arrangements have led to renewed interest in regional integration.[1]

Among the important global trends today is the evolution of the multinational market region – those groups of countries that seek mutual economic benefit from reducing intra-regional trade and tariff barriers. Organisational form varies widely among market regions, but the universal orientation of such multinational cooperation is economic benefit for the participants. Political and social benefits sometimes accrue, but the dominant motive for affiliation is economic.

Regional economic cooperative agreements have been around since the end of the Second World War. The most successful has been the EU; the world's largest multinational market region with 27 member countries is the foremost example of economic cooperation.

Multinational market groups form large markets that provide potentially significant market opportunities for international business. When it became apparent that the EU was to achieve its long-term goal of a single European market, a renewed interest in economic cooperation was sparked. The European Economic Area (EEA), a 29-country alliance between the EU and remaining members of the European Free Trade Association (EFTA), became the world's largest single unified market.

Canada, the USA and Mexico entered into a free-trade agreement to form the North America Free Trade Agreement (NAFTA).[2] Many countries in Latin America, Asia, Eastern Europe and elsewhere are either planning some form of economic cooperation or have entered into agreements (see Exhibit 8.1).

With the dissolution of the USSR (Soviet Union), linkages among the independent states and republics in Eastern Europe are also forming. The Commonwealth of Independent States (CIS) is an initial attempt at realignment into an economic union of some of the Newly Independent States (NIS) – former republics of the USSR.[3] The growing trend of economic cooperation is increasing concerns about the effect of such cooperation on global competition. Governments and businesses are concerned that the EEA, NAFTA and other cooperative regional groups have become regional trading blocs without trade restrictions internally but with borders protected from outsiders.[4]

In Kenichi Ohmae's book, *Triad Power*, he points out that the global companies that will be Triad powers must have significant market positions in each of the Triad regions.[5] At the economic centre of each Triad region there are one or two economic industrial powers: in the European Triad it is Germany; in the American Triad it is the USA; in the Asian Triad it is China. The Triad regions are the centres of economic activity that provide global companies with a concentration of sophisticated consumer- and capital-goods markets. Much of the economic growth and development that will occur in these regions and make them such important markets will result from single countries being forged into thriving free-trade areas.

EXHIBIT 8.1: Free trade agreements under negotiations, selected (2011 or latest)

	Value of bilateral trade in goods ($ bn)	Date launched	Status
Trans-Pacific Partnership	1492.2	Jun 2005	16th round Mar 2013
EU–India	110.8	2007	Concluding
EU–Canada	72.9	May 2009	Concluding
China–Switzerland	30.9	Sep 2010	4th round Feb 2012
Canada–India	5.2	Nov 2010	7th round Feb 2013
COMESA-EAC-SADC	29.8	Jun 2011	Concluding
Canada–Japan	19.7	Mar 2012	1st round Nov 2012
Regional Comprehensive Economic Partnership	1412.6	Nov 2012	Just launched
Transatlantic Trade and Investment Partnership	618.5	Feb 2013	Announced, not formally launched

Source: *The Economist*, 16 March 2013, p 74.

The focus of this chapter is on the various patterns of multinational cooperation and the strategic marketing implications of economic cooperation.

Why economic union?

Successful economic union requires favourable economic, political, cultural and geographic factors as a basis for success. Major flaws in any one factor can destroy a union unless the other factors provide sufficient strength to overcome the weaknesses. In general, the advantages of economic union must be clear-cut and significant, and the benefits must greatly outweigh the disadvantages before nations forgo any part of their sovereignty.

A strong threat to the economic or political security of a nation is often needed to provide the impetus for cooperation. The cooperative agreements among European countries that preceded the European Community (EC) certainly had their roots in the need for economic redevelopment after the Second World War. Many felt that if Europe was to survive there had to be economic unity; the agreements made then formed the groundwork for the EC.

Economic factors

Every type of economic union shares the development and enlargement of market opportunities as a basic orientation; usually markets are enlarged through preferential tariff treatment for participating members and/or common tariff barriers against outsiders. Enlarged, protected markets stimulate internal economic development by providing assured outlets and preferential treatment for goods produced within the customs union, and consumers benefit from lower internal tariff barriers among the participating countries.

The EU includes countries with diverse economies, distinctive monetary systems, developed agricultural bases and different natural resources. In the early days of the EU, agricultural disputes were common. The British attempted to keep French poultry out of the British market, France banned Italian wine, and the Irish banned eggs and poultry from other member countries. At one point, the EU, not any one country, banned British beef because of the effects of BSE (also called 'mad cow disease') on British animals and its linkages with the human affliction Creutzfeldt-Jakob disease (CJD). In all cases, the reason given was health and safety, but the probable motive, at least in some cases, was the continuation of the age-old policy of market protection.

Political factors

Political amenability among countries is another basic requisite for development of a supranational market arrangement. Participating countries must have comparable aspirations and general compatibility before surrendering any part of their national sovereignty. State sovereignty is one of the most cherished possessions of any nation and is relinquished only for a promise of significant improvement of the national position through cooperation.

The uniting of the original EC countries was partially a response to American dominance and threat of Russia's great political power; the countries of Western Europe were willing to settle their family squabbles to present a unified front. The communist threat no longer exists, but the importance of political unity to fully achieve all the benefits of economic integration has driven the EC countries to form the EU.[6]

Geographic proximity

Although it is not absolutely imperative that cooperating members of a customs union have geographic proximity, such closeness facilitates the functioning of a common market. Transportation networks basic to any marketing system are likely to be interrelated and well developed when countries are close together. One of the first major strengths of the EC was its transportation network: the opening of the Channel tunnel between England and France, and the bridge between Denmark and Sweden further bound this common market.

Cultural factors

Cultural similarity eases the shock of economic cooperation with other countries. The more similar the cultures, the more likely a market is to succeed because members understand the outlook and viewpoints of their colleagues. Although there is great cultural diversity in the EU, key members share a long-established Christian heritage and are commonly aware of being European.

Language, as a part of culture, has not created as much of a barrier for EU countries as was expected. Initially there were seven major languages, but such linguistic diversity did not impede trade because European businesses historically have been multilingual. Now even countries such as France, Germany and Italy are switching over to English as a language of trade and science.

Patterns of regional cooperation

Multinational market groups take several forms, varying significantly in the degree of cooperation, dependence and interrelationship among participating nations. There are five fundamental groupings for regional economic integration, ranging from regional cooperation for development, which requires the least amount of integration, to the ultimate of integration, political union. Exhibit 8.2 illustrates different levels of cooperation.

Regional cooperation groups

The most basic economic integration and cooperation is the regional cooperation for development (RCD). In the RCD arrangement, governments agree to participate jointly to develop basic industries beneficial to each economy. Each country makes an advance commitment to participate in the financing of a new joint venture and to purchase a specified share of the output of the venture. An example is

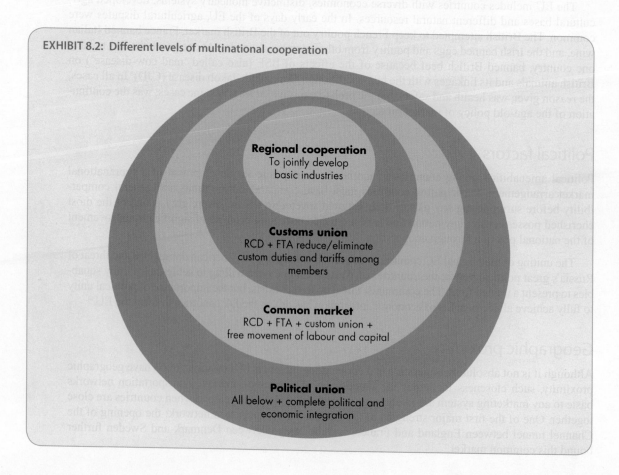

EXHIBIT 8.2: Different levels of multinational cooperation

Regional cooperation
To jointly develop basic industries

Customs union
RCD + FTA reduce/eliminate custom duties and tariffs among members

Common market
RCD + FTA + custom union + free movement of labour and capital

Political union
All below + complete political and economic integration

the project between Colombia and Venezuela to build a hydro-electric generating plant on the Orinoco river. They shared jointly in construction costs and they share the electricity produced.

Free-trade area

A free-trade area (FTA) requires more cooperation and integration than the RCD. It is an agreement among two or more countries to reduce or eliminate customs duties and non-tariff trade barriers among partner countries while members maintain individual tariff schedules for external countries. Essentially, an FTA provides its members with a mass market without barriers that impede the flow of goods and services. The USA has free-trade agreements with Canada, South Korea and Mexico (NAFTA) and separately with Israel. The seven-nation European Free Trade Association (EFTA), among the better-known free-trade areas, still exists although three of its members also belong to the EU and five to the EEA.

Going International 8.1

MERKEL PONDERS ATLANTIC FREE-TRADE ZONE

Spurred by concern about China's growing economic might, Germany is considering a plan for a free-trade zone between Europe and the USA. A senior aide to Angela Merkel said the chancellor was 'interested' in promoting the idea as long as such a zone did not create 'a fortress' but rather 'a tool' to encourage free trade globally, 'which she is persuaded is a condition of Germany's future prosperity'.

The USA, Canada and the EU complained to the WTO about China's tariffs on car parts, raising the prospect of Beijing facing its first WTO dispute. The three said they had lost patience with Beijing's refusal to open the $19bn (€15bn, £10bn)-a-year market.

© Istockphoto.com/axelbueckert

News that the free-trade zone, last pursued by Sir Leon Brittan, when European trade commissioner in 1998, is being debated in the German chancellery testifies to the rapprochement between Washington and Berlin since Ms Merkel's election last November.

This convergence of views was underlined this week when Wen Jiabao, Chinese premier, was politely chided by Ms Merkel for China's poor human rights record and recent restrictions on foreign news agencies, during an official visit to Berlin.

As German perceptions of China have grown more American, Washington's approach has also shifted. Speaking before his first trip to Beijing, Hank Paulson, US Treasury Secretary, outlined a more balanced policy, mixing traditional US criticism with praise for China's reforms.

● Do you think that an FTA between the EU and the USA is a good idea? Why/why not?

Source: *Financial Times*, 16 September 2008.

Customs union

A customs union represents the next stage in economic cooperation. It enjoys the free-trade area's reduced or eliminated internal tariffs and adds a common external tariff on products imported from countries outside the union. The customs union is a logical stage of cooperation in the transition from an

FTA to a common market. The EC was a customs union before becoming a common market. Customs unions exist between France and Monaco, Italy and San Marino, and Switzerland and Liechtenstein.

Common market

A common market agreement eliminates all tariffs and other restrictions on internal trade, adopts a set of common external tariffs, and removes all restriction on the free flow of capital and labour among member nations. Thus a common market is a common marketplace for goods as well as for services (including labour) and for capital. It is a unified economy and lacks only political unity to become a political union.

Going International 8.2

HOW SUBWAY OVERTOOK MCDONALD'S

Source: http://www.subway.co.uk/media/imagelibrary/stores.asp.

It is one of the UK's fastest-growing major fast-food chains and has just sneaked past McDonald's to hold the largest number of outlets in the UK and Ireland, yet Subway remains an underground success.

Now by far the UK's biggest seller of sandwiches, not including hamburgers, Subway has twice the market share of closest rival Tesco. The privately owned US company, which operates through dozens of franchisees around the country, has seen exponential growth in the past three years, opening 800 stores to reach 2,000 outlets in the UK and Ireland.

Although it is a sandwich shop, Subway's locations, customer profile and operating style, such as late opening hours, give it more in common with fast-food chains such as McDonald's and Kentucky Fried Chicken than Prêt à Manger. Subway, which sees 15–25 year olds as its core customers, is now trendier among teenagers than McDonald's in certain sectors of the country. Popular specials include its hefty Meatball Marinara, which has no less than 12 specific Facebook fanclubs, but also faces criticism from health food experts, who say it contains as much salt as 18 packets of ready-salted crisps.

Despite the downturn on the high street, the brand is likely to see continued rapid growth this year as it ramps up advertising and marketing spend by two-thirds. Having covered most towns and cities in the UK, it now wants to move into new locations like universities, football stadiums and even hospitals.

Subway may have just squeezed past McDonald's, but the private company does not report its profits and turnover in the UK and Northern Ireland. However, with an estimated turnover of £500m at present, it is less than half McDonald's £1bn-plus British sales. Still, the UK is an important model for Subway's spread into Europe, as the largest and fastest-growing market outside North America.

- Would Subway be equally successful in other European countries? Discuss.

Source: compiled from several sources.

Political union

Political union is the most fully-integrated form of regional cooperation. It involves complete political and economic integration; it may be voluntary or enforced.

The Commonwealth of Nations is a voluntary organisation providing for the loosest possible relationship that can be classified as economic integration. The British Commonwealth comprises Britain and countries formerly part of the British Empire. Its member states had received preferential tariffs when trading with Great Britain but, when Britain joined the EC, all preferential tariffs were abandoned. Heads of state meet every three years to discuss trade and political issues they face jointly, and compliance with any decisions or directives issued is voluntary.

Global markets and regional market groups

This section presents basic information and data on markets and market groups in Europe, the Americas, Africa, Asia and the Middle East. Existing economic cooperation agreements within each of these regions will be reviewed. The reader must appreciate that the status of cooperative agreements and alliances among nations has been extremely fluid in some parts of the world. Many are fragile and may cease to exist or may restructure into a totally different form. It will probably take the better part of a decade for many of the new trading alliances that are now forming to stabilise into semi-permanent groups.

Europe

The EU is the focus of the European region of the first Triad. Within Europe, every type of multinational market grouping exists. The EU, EC, European Economic Area (EEA), the European Free Trade Association (EFTA) and the Central European Free Trade Agreement (CEFTA) are the best-established cooperative groups (see Exhibit 8.3).

The EU

The idea of a united Europe is centuries old; from the Roman Empire to the empire of Charlemagne in the early ninth century, or even to the idea of a Catholic Europe with a pope at its head, all aimed at an integrated Europe. At the third Universal Peace Congress in 1849, Victor Hugo officially presented the idea of the United States of Europe.

The First World War, with all its senseless bloodshed, brought about a review of the idea of a united Europe. During this period, Count Coudenhove-Kalergi, who was of Greek and Dutch descent but was an Austro-Hungarian diplomat, started a Pan-European Union. He received support from a number of prominent political figures such as Aristide Briand, the French foreign minister, who presented a scheme to the League of Nations in the 1920s for a European Union.

The Second World War finally stimulated the idea of European integration. A group of European politicians worked on the idea with Jean Monet, who is often called the 'Father of Europe', at its head. In addition to being a French diplomat, Monet had been the deputy secretary general of the League of Nations in the interwar years.[7]

Exhibit 8.4 illustrates the evolution of the EU from its beginnings. In 1951 six European states (France, West Germany, Italy, the Netherlands, Belgium and Luxembourg) signed the Treaty of Paris to establish the European Coal and Steel Community (ECSC). It was the forerunner of the European Community.

In 1955, delegates from ECSC states met at Messina in Italy and agreed to form the European Economic Community (EEC), and in March 1957 the Treaty of Rome, formally setting up the EEC, was signed. The purpose was to achieve a customs union of the six countries and by 1969 abolish all tariffs on their mutual trade. The Treaty of Rome had three major political objectives: political unity,

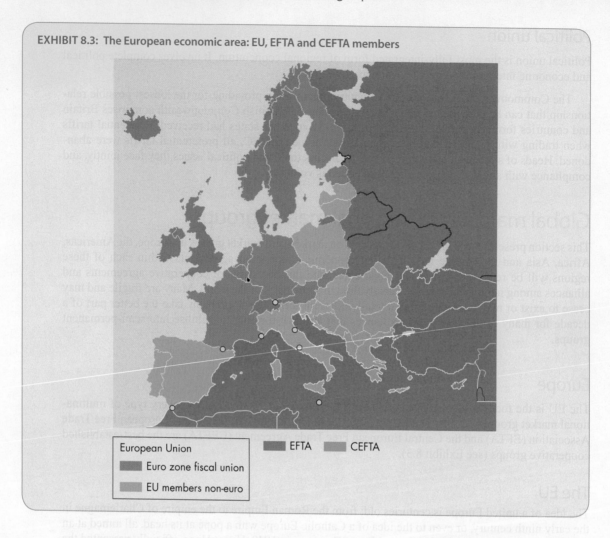

EXHIBIT 8.3: The European economic area: EU, EFTA and CEFTA members

European Union
- Euro zone fiscal union
- EU members non-euro

EFTA   CEFTA

peace and democracy. Other objectives included integration, improvement of living standards and encouragement of trade with other countries.[8]

The EU was created when the 12 nations of the European Community ratified the Maastricht Treaty. The members committed themselves to economic and political integration. The treaty allows for the free movement of goods, persons, services and capital throughout the member states, a common currency, common foreign and security policies, including defence, a common justice system and cooperation between police and other authorities on crime, terrorism and immigration issues. However, not all the provisions of the treaty have been universally accepted. The dismantling of border controls to permit passport-free movement between countries according to the Schengen Agreement, signed in Schengen (Luxembourg) in 1995, for example, has been accepted by most of the members except the UK and the new members from Eastern Europe.

Of all the multinational market groups, none is more secure in its cooperation or more important economically than the EU. From its beginning, it has successfully made progress towards achieving the goal of complete economic integration and, ultimately, political union. For a list of EU member countries and related economic data, see Exhibit 8.5.

The Single European Act

Europe without borders, 'Fortress Europe' and EC 92 refer to the Single European Act: the agreement designed to finally remove all barriers to trade and make the EC a single internal market. The ultimate goal of the Treaty of Rome, the agreement that founded the EC, was economic and political union, a United States of Europe. The Single European Act moved the EC one step closer to the goal of economic integration.

EXHIBIT 8.4: From European Coal and Steel Community to European Union

1951	Treaty of Paris	European Coal and Steel Community (ECSC) (founding members are Belgium, France, Germany, Italy, Luxembourg and the Netherlands)
1957	Treaty of Rome	Blueprint for European Economic Community (EEC)
1958	European Economic Community	Ratified by ECSC founding members. Common Market is established
1960	European Free Trade Area	Established by Austria, Denmark, Norway, Portugal, Sweden, Switzerland and UK
1973	Expansion	Denmark, Ireland and UK join EEC
1979	European Monetary System	The European Currency Unit (ECU) is created. All members except the UK agree to maintain their exchange rates within specific margins
1981	Expansion	Greece joins EEC
1985	1992 Single Market Programme	Introduced to European Parliament 'White Paper' for Action
1986	Expansion	Spain and Portugal join EEC
1987	Single European Act	Ratified with full implementation by 1992
1992	Treaty on European Union	Also known as Maastricht Treaty. Blueprint for Economic and Monetary Union (EMU)
1993	Europe 1992	Single European Act in force (1 January 1993)
1993	European Union	Treaty on European Union (Maastricht Treaty) in force with monetary union by 1999
1994	European Economic Area	The EEA was formed with EU members and Norway and Iceland
1995	Expansion	Austria, Finland and Sweden join EU
1997	Treaty of Amsterdam	Established procedures for expansion to Central and Eastern Europe
1999	Monetary union	Introduction of the single currency on the foreign exchange markets and for electronic payments
2002	Monetary union	Euro replaces all national banknotes and coins of EMU members
2004	Expansion	Ten new members join the EU. EC agrees that Turkey can be invited for membership negotiations
2007	Expansion	Bulgaria and Romania joined the EU in 2007
2008	Treaty of Lisbon	French and Dutch voters rejected the new European constitution.
2009	Treaty of Lisbon	Lisbon Treaty enters into force after ratification by remaining members: Poland, the Czech Republic and Ireland (after second referendum). Herman Van Rompuy is chosen as President of the European Council. Catherine Ashton is chosen as High Representative of the Union for Foreign Affairs and Security Policy. Slovakia joins euro zone.
2010	EU, IMF and World Bank	EU, IMF and the World Bank agree on bailouts for Greece (May), followed by Ireland (November) and Portugal (November).
2011		At summit meeting, most EU states (including all 17 in euro zone) agree to plan for closer fiscal union, which would safeguard euro by tighter collective controls on budgets and punishment for excessive deficits. Croatia signs accession treaty on track to EU membership in 2013 as the twenty-eighth member-state. At summit in Brussels, euro zone leaders agree to write off 50 per cent of Greece's debt, increase EFSF package to € 1m and install EU monitoring missions of government budgets in Athens and Rome.

Source: 'Timeline of the European Union', http://www.europeaninstitute.org/EU-Facts/timeline-of-the-european-union.html.

EXHIBIT 8.5: European market regions

Association	Country	Population (millions)	GDP($bn)	GDP per capita (current US$)	Imports of goods and services ($bn)	Exports of goods and services ($bn)
European Union (EU)	Belgium	11	513.66	46,663	438	430
	Denmark	6	333.62	59,852	159	177
	Greece	11	289.63	25,622	85	68
	Germany	82	3,600.83	44,060	1,629	1,812
	Spain	46	1,476.88	31,943	459	452
	France	65	2,773.03	42,377	883	815
	Ireland	4	217.27	48,423	183	231
	Italy	61	2,193.97	36,103	663	631
	Luxembourg	1	59.20	114,508	68	90
	Netherlands	17	836.07	50,076	579	656
	Austria	8	417.66	49,609	226	234
	Portugal	11	237.37	22,316	94	86
	Finland	5	263.01	48,823	107	106
	Sweden	9	539.68	57,091	230	263
	UK	63	2,445.41	39,038	821	773
	Czech Republic	11	217.03	20,579	153	162
	Estonia	1	22.15	16,533	21	22
	Cyprus	1	24.69	30,670	12	11
	Latvia	2	28.25	12,726	18	16
	Lithuania	3	42.73	13,339	34	33
	Hungary	10	140.03	14,044	117	126
	Poland	38	514.50	13,463	241	233
	Slovenia	2	49.54	24,142	36	36
	Slovak Republic	5	95.99	17,646	82	85
	Bulgaria	7	53.51	7,158	35	36
	Romania	21	179.79	8,405	83	73
	Malta	0.5	11.20 bn	27,022	na	na
European Free Trade Area (EFTA)	Iceland	0	14.03	43,969	7	8
	Liechtenstein	0	–	–	–	–
	Norway	5	485.80	98,102	137	203
	Switzerland	8	659.31	83,383	372	420

Source: World Bank, 2012.

In addition, the Single European Act proposed a wide range of new commercial policies, including single European standards, one of the more difficult and time-consuming goals to achieve. Technical standards for electrical products offer a good example of how overwhelming is the task of achieving universal standards. There are 29 types of electrical outlet, 10 types of plug and 12 types of flex used by EU member countries. The estimated cost for all EU countries to change wiring systems and electrical standards to a single European standard is €80bn, or about US$98bn.

The European Court of Justice's (ECJ) interpretation of Article 30, which establishes the principle of mutual recognition, is that a product put on sale legally in one member state should be available for sale in the same way in all others. The ECJ's landmark decision involved Germany's ban on the sale of Cassis de Dijon, a French liqueur. Germany claimed that selling the low-alcohol drink would encourage alcohol consumption, considered by authorities to be unhealthy. The Court of Justice rejected the argument, ruling that the restriction represented a non-tariff barrier outlawed by Article 30. In other words, once Cassis de Dijon was legally sold in France, Germany was obligated, under mutual recognition, to allow its sale in Germany.[9]

In March 1996, the EC decided that only goat's-milk or ewe's-milk cheese produced in Greece was entitled to be called feta. The ruling brought storms of protest from Danes, who now have five years to rename their cow's-milk feta. Greeks have a solid claim of name, backed by a thousand years of history.[10]

Some of the first and most welcome reforms were the single customs document that replaced the 70 forms originally required for transborder shipments to member countries, the elimination of sabotage rules (which kept a trucker from returning with a loaded truck after delivery), and EU-wide transport licensing. These changes alone were estimated to have reduced distribution costs by 50 per cent for companies doing cross-border business in the EU.

Going International 8.3

The population of the EU is projected to reach 517 million in 2060. Nearly one-third of the citizens will then be aged 65 or over.

The age profile of the EU is expected to change dramatically in the coming decades, according to the EU's latest Ageing report.

The population of the EU will be slightly higher in 2060 (517 million, up from 502 million in 2010). At the same time it will be much older. While longer lives are a major achievement of European societies, the ageing of the population also poses significant challenges for their economies and welfare systems.

© Istockphoto.com/vividpixels

Notably, the share of those aged 15–64 is projected to decline from 67 per cent to 56 per cent by 2060. The share of those aged 65 and over is projected to rise from 17 per cent to 30 per cent. As a consequence, the EU would move from having four people of working-age to each person aged over 65 years to about two people of working-age.

The total number of workers is projected to decline by 15.7 million over the forecast horizon to 195.6 million in 2060. The decline in the workforce will act as a drag on growth and per capita income, with a consequent trend decline in potential growth. The latter is estimated to converge to below 1.5 per cent in real terms in the long-term in the EU.

Moreover, the demographic changes are expected to have substantial consequences for public finances in the EU. On the basis of current policies, age-related public expenditures (pensions, healthcare and long-term care) are projected to increase by 4.1 percentage points to around 29 per cent of GDP between 2010 and 2060. Public pension expenditure alone is projected to rise by 1.5 percentage points to nearly 13 per cent of GDP by 2060.

All in all, further progress towards sustainable public finances remains a major challenge. The results of the report prepared by the European Commission services (Directorate-General for Economic and Financial Affairs) and the Ageing Working Group (AWG) of the EU Economic Policy Committee reveal that in some countries, there is a need to take due account of future increases in government expenditure, including through modernisation of social expenditure systems. In several countries, policy actions have been taken, significantly limiting the future increase in government expenditure.

In general, the extent and speed of ageing depend on future life expectancy, fertility and migration. Life expectancy at birth is projected to increase from 76.7 years in 2010 to 84.6 in 2060 for males and from 82.5 to 89.1 for females. The fertility rate in the EU is projected to climb modestly from 1.59 births per woman in 2010 to 1.71 in 2060. Cumulated net migration to the EU is projected to be about 60 million until 2060.

Source: 'Ageing Report: Europe Needs to Prepare for Growing Older', 15 May 2012, http://ec.europa.eu/economy_finance/articles/structural_reforms/2012-05-15_ageing_report_en.htm.

EU structure

The EU was created as a result of three treaties that established the European Coal and Steel Community, the European Economic Community and the European Atomic Energy Community. These three treaties are incorporated within the EU and serve as the community's constitution. They provide a policy framework and empower the commission and the Council of Ministers to pass laws to carry out EU policy. The union uses three legal instruments:

1 Regulations binding the member states directly and having the same strength as national laws
2 Directives also binding the member states but allowing them to choose the means of execution
3 Decisions addressed to a government, an enterprise or an individual binding the parties named.

Going International 8.4

TIME TO DEMOLISH THE MYTHS ABOUT EU ENLARGEMENT

© Istockphoto.com/invictus999

Enlargement is not as some claim the cause of Europe's ills, but has instead brought with it many advantages. Michael Leigh explains how the carrot of enlargement offers the EU the way out of the political impasse, economic stalemate and identity crisis it now faces.

When its major 2004 enlargement was in the offing, the EU embraced a narrative based on false assumptions that turned out to be enormously costly in terms of political capital and democratic legitimacy. This narrative was that the EU could not function at 27 members unless there was a 'deepening' of the integration process. This meant a significant step towards political union and a streamlining of the decision-making process.

In reality EU institutions functioned perfectly normally from May 2004, when 10 new members joined the EU, to December 2009 when the Lisbon treaty came into force. And the Lisbon treaty's main innovations – the creation of the European External Action Service and a stronger legislative role for the European Parliament – did little to bring the EU closer to political union, streamline decision making or overcome the 'democratic deficit'.

Against this background, the economic and financial crisis that began in 2008 and gave rise to the sovereign debt and euro crises, has further dampened the public mood on enlargement. There are fears that the kind of economic problems posed by the peripheral countries in the present EU could be replicated if fragile Balkan states were to be admitted.

But despite the benefits of enlargement, it is not exactly the flavour of the month in crisis-ridden Europe. This will not necessarily be an obstacle in the future given the likely timing of further accessions. Croatia will join the EU in July 2013 and Iceland possibly a year or two later. After that, no country will be ready to join until around 2020. That leaves time for aspirant countries to sort themselves out, for the EU to shake off its current malaise and for the European public to grasp the advantages of a wider and more differentiated EU. If it is to maintain its leverage for reform, the EU will need to devise new incentives to keep people in future member states engaged during these long years.

European integration is becoming increasingly differentiated, with 'coalitions of the willing' forming in different policy areas. These coalitions should remain open to participation by all. A multi-track EU will be better placed to receive new members once they have met the conditions, than an EU based on the fiction that one size fits all. During the decade before a new wave of countries is ready to join the EU, greater efforts must be made to stimulate an informed public debate in the EU about enlargement and to make the prospect of EU membership more credible and tangible in aspirant countries. This will demand strong leadership and ingenuity from those involved in piloting this historic process.

● What do you think is the future of the EU? Should the EU enlarge further? Discuss both pros and cons.

Source: adapted from 'Europe's World written by *Michael Leigh*, Summer 2012', http://www.europesworld.org/NewEnglish/Home_old/Article/tabid/191/ArticleType/ArticleView/ArticleID/22005/language/en-US/Default.aspx.

EU authority

Over the years the EU has gained an increasing amount of authority over its member states. The Union's institutions (the European Commission, the Council of Ministers, the European Parliament and the European Court of Justice) and their decision-making processes have legal status and extensive powers in fields covered by common policies. They form a federal pattern with executive, parliamentary and judicial branches. A number of private consultant companies specialise in lobbying the different EU institutions (see Exhibit 8.6).

- The European Commission is a group that initiates policy and supervises its observance by member states. It proposes and supervises the execution of laws and policies. The Commission has a president and four vice presidents; each of its members is appointed for a four-year term by mutual agreement of EU governments.

- The Council of Ministers, one from each member country, passes laws based on commission proposals. Because the council is the decision-making body of the EU, it is its responsibility to debate and decide which proposals of the Single European Act to accept as binding on EU members. In concert with the commission's White Paper, the Single European Act included the first and only amendment of the original Treaty of Rome (1957), which streamlined decision making. Under provisions in the Act, the council can enact into law many of the proposals in the White Paper by majority vote instead of the unanimity formerly required. However, proposals for changes in tax rates on products and services still require a unanimous vote.

- The European Parliament has 736 members elected every five years by universal suffrage (see Exhibit 8.7 for a breakdown per country). It is mainly a consultative body, which passes on most community legislation with limited but gradually increasing budgetary powers. The Single European Act gave Parliament greater powers.[11] Parliament can now influence legislation but it does not have the power to initiate legislation.

- The European Court of Justice (ECJ) consists of 13 judges and is the Union's Supreme Court. Its first responsibility is challenging any measures incompatible with the Treaty of Rome when they are adopted by the Commission, Council or national governments. Its second responsibility is passing

EXHIBIT 8.6: Top five lobbying consultancies in Europe

Consultancy	McKinsey & Company	The Boston Consulting Group, Inc. Stats	Bain & Company	Booz & Company	Deloitte Consulting LLP
Created	1926	1963	1973	1914	1845
Staff	17,500	5,000	5,400	3,300	193,000
Headquarters	New York City, USA	Boston, Massachusetts, USA	Boston, Massachusetts, USA	New York, USA	New York, USA
No. of offices	100	77 in 42 countries	49	60	
Consultancy	Pricewaterhouse Coopers LLP (consulting practice)	Ernst & Young LLP (consulting practice)	Accenture	Monitor Group	Oliver Wyman
Created	1998	1989	1989	1983	2007
Staff	39,951	23,304	236,000	1,200	3,500
Headquarters	New York, USA	New York, USA	New York, USA	Cambridge, Massachusetts, USA	New York, USA
No. of offices	154	695	200	27 offices in 17 countries	58

Source: based on 'Consulting Firm Rankings 2013: The Best Consulting Firms: Prestige', http://www.vault.com/wps/portal/usa/rankings/individual?rankingId1=77&rankingId2=-1&rankings=1&regionId=0&rankingYear=2013.

EXHIBIT 8.7: Members of EU Parliament from each country

Country	Total seats	Country	Total seats	Country	Total seats
Germany	99	Greece	22	Lithuania	12
France	72	Hungary	22	Latvia	8
Italy	72	Portugal	22	Slovenia	7
Britain	72	Sweden	18	Estonia	6
Spain	50	Bulgaria	17	Cyprus	6
Poland	50	Austria	17	Luxembourg	6
Romania	33	Denmark	13	Malta	5
Netherlands	25	Slovakia	13	**Total EU**	**736**
Belgium	22	Finland	13		
Czech Rep.	22	Ireland	12		

Source: based on *Euromonitor* and *The Economist*, January 2013.

judgement, at the request of a national court, on interpretation or validity of points of EU law. The court's decisions are final and cannot be appealed in national courts.

Court decisions are binding on EU members; through its judgements and interpretations, the court is helping to create a body of truly EU law that will apply to all EU institutions, member states, national courts and private citizens. Judgements of the court, in the field of EU law, overrule those of national courts. For example, the court overruled Germany's consumer protection rules, which had served as a major trade barrier.

Historically, German law has frowned on, if not prohibited, any product advertising that implies medicinal benefits. Estée Lauder Cosmetics was prevented, by German courts, from selling one of its products under the name 'Clinique'. Germany claimed the name would mislead German consumers, causing them to associate the product with medical treatment.

The European Court of Justice (ECJ) pointed out that the product is sold in other member states under the 'Clinique' name without confusing the consumer. Further, if the German court ruling against Estée Lauder was left to stand, it would make it difficult for companies to market their products across borders in an identical manner and thus increase the cost of advertising and packaging for the company and, ultimately, for the consumer.[12]

Going International 8.5

© Istockphoto.com/spaceport9

PROS AND CONS OF EURO ENTRY

In 2003 the *Financial Times* conducted a survey of 40 UK foreign-owned manufacturers to see how the UK's decision to join or not join the euro might be affecting their plans to invest in the UK. Nineteen of the companies stated that they would be less likely to invest if the UK did not join the euro. Twelve respondents expressed neutral attitudes, and nine declined to comment, either because the question was too difficult or because they preferred to keep their views private.

Manufacturers who expressed negative attitudes towards the decision not to join the euro tended to be companies with large exports to continental Europe.

▶

◄

The poll underlined the fact that many large exporters believed entry into the single currency would increase their expansion opportunities by reducing currency risks. Although these companies may have most of their customers in the UK, and so are not directly affected by the exchange rates, they feel that the health of their businesses will be improved if Britain becomes part of the euro zone.

Neutral responses came mostly from companies whose factories sold mainly in the UK (or sold UK-specific products such as boilers and ovens) and were in less competitive industries. Neutral responses were also provided by big exporters from the UK but who sold a considerable amount outside the euro zone. These businesses said that the euro decision would not make a huge difference to their investment calculations. Possibly the most interesting responses came from companies that might have been expected to say euro entry would help their investment opportunities, but that turned out to be neutral.

- Do you think the UK's entry into the euro zone would influence UK companies' competitive position in Europe or the UK economy in general?

Source: adapted from Peter Marsh, 'Industry Highlights Pros and Cons of Euro Entry', *Financial Times*, 18 February 2003.

The Maastricht Treaty and European union

The final step in the European Community's march to union was ratification of the Maastricht Treaty. The treaty provided for the Economic and Monetary Union (EMU) and European Union (EU). Under the EMU agreement, in 1998 the EU created a European Central Bank and introduced fixed exchange rates and a single currency.[13]

Denmark and the UK were the last to ratify the treaty. Despite some last-minute hesitation, Denmark approved the treaty on a second vote and, later, with the UK's approval, the EU became a reality. Within months of the ratification of the treaty, the EU was expanded when Austria, Finland and Sweden, members of the EEA, became members of the EU in 1995. Norway voted not to join the EU but will remain a member of the European Economic Area.[14]

European Economic Area (EEA)

Because of the success of the EC and concern that they might be left out of the massive European market, five members of the European Free Trade Association (EFTA) elected to join the 12 members of the EC in 1994 to form the European Economic Area (EEA), a single market with free movement of goods, services and capital.[15] The five EFTA countries joining the EEA adopted most of the EC's competition rules and agreed to implement EC rules on company law; however, they maintain their domestic farm policies. The EEA is governed by a special Council of Ministers composed of representatives from EEA member nations.

With nearly 500 million consumers and a gross national product of €13 trillion ($18 trillion), the EEA is the world's largest consumer market, eclipsing the USA even after the formation of the North American Free Trade Agreement (NAFTA). The EEA is a middle ground for those countries that want to be part of the EU's single internal market but do not want to go directly into the EU as full members or do not meet the requirements for full membership. Of the five founding EFTA members of the EEA, three joined the EU in 1995. Iceland and Norway chose not to become EU members with the other EFTA countries but will remain members of the EEA. Of the other EFTA members, Switzerland voted against joining the EEA but has formally requested membership of the EU, and Liechtenstein has not joined the EEA or requested admission to join the EU.

European Free Trade Association (EFTA)

The European Free Trade Association was conceived by the UK as a counterpart to the EC before it became a member of the EC. The original members of EFTA were Austria, Denmark, Norway, Portugal, Sweden, Switzerland and the UK. Iceland became a member in 1970, Finland in 1986 and Liechtenstein in 1991. As discussed earlier, several EFTA countries joined EC countries to form the

European Economic Area, and of the original members six went on to join the EU: the UK and Denmark in 1972, Portugal in 1986, and Austria, Finland and Sweden in 1995. The present members of EFTA are: Iceland, Liechtenstein, Norway and Switzerland. EFTA will most probably dissolve as its members either join the EEA or the EU.

The Commonwealth of Independent States (CIS)

The series of events after the aborted coup against Mikhail Gorbachev led to the complete dissolution of the USSR. The first to declare independence were the Baltic states, which quickly gained recognition by several Western nations. The remaining 12 republics of the former USSR,[16] collectively known as the Newly Independent States (NIS), regrouped into the Commonwealth of Independent States (CIS).

The 12 members of the CIS share a common history of central planning, and their close cooperation could make the change to a market economy less painful, but differences over economic policy, currency reform and control of the military may break them apart. How the CIS will be organised and its ultimate importance is anyone's guess.

The Americas

The Americas, the second Triad region, has as its centre the USA. Within the Americas, the USA, Canada, Central America and South America have been natural if sometimes contentious trading partners. As in Europe, the Americas are engaged in all sorts of economic cooperative agreements.

United States–Canada Free Trade Agreement (CFTA)

Historically, the USA and Canada have had the world's largest bilateral trade: each is the other's largest trading partner. Despite this unique commercial relationship, tariffs and other trade barriers hindered even greater commercial activity. To further support trade activity, the two countries established the United States–Canada Free Trade Area (CFTA), designed to eliminate all trade barriers between the two countries. CFTA was, however, to be short-lived.

North American Free Trade Agreement (NAFTA)

Mexico and the USA have been strong trading partners for decades but Mexico had never officially expressed an interest in a free-trade agreement until the president of Mexico, Carlos Salinas de Gortari, announced that Mexico would seek such an agreement with the USA. Because earlier overtures to Mexico from the USA had been rebuffed, Salinas' announcement was a surprise to Americans and Mexicans alike.

Even though Mexico has an abundance of oil and a rapidly growing population, the number of new workers is increasing faster than its economy can create new jobs. The USA needs resources (especially oil) and, of course, markets. The three need each other to compete more effectively in world markets, and they need mutual assurances that their already dominant trading positions in each other's markets are safe from protectionist pressures. When the NAFTA agreement was ratified and became effective in 1994, a single market of 360 million people with a €5.4 trillion ($6 trillion) GNP emerged.

NAFTA requires the three countries to remove all tariffs and barriers to trade, but each will have its own tariff arrangements with non-member countries.

In addition to the elimination of tariffs, countries will eliminate non-tariff barriers and other trade-distorting restrictions. NAFTA also eliminates a host of other Mexican barriers such as local content, local production and export performance requirements that have limited US exports.[17]

In the first six months after NAFTA's inception, US exports to Mexico rose to $24.5bn, an increase of 16 per cent over the previous 12 months. Mexican exports to the USA rose 21 per cent in those first six months to €20.2bn ($23.4bn). Equally impressive is the increase in trade between Mexico and Canada during the same period: exports from Canada to Mexico increased 33 per cent and Mexican exports to Canada increased by 31 per cent.[18]

Latin American Economic Cooperation

Prior to 1990, most Latin American market groups (see Exhibit 8.8) had varying degrees of success. The first and most ambitious, the Latin American Free Trade Association (LAFTA) gave way to the LAIA (Latin American Integration Association).

In addition to new trade agreements, many of the trade accords that have been in existence for decades, such as the Latin American Integration Association and the Andean Pact, have moved from a moribund to an active state, all of which makes the idea of a common market from Argentina to the Arctic Circle – a Western Hemisphere Free Trade Area (WHFTA) – not as unlikely as it might first appear.

An accord reached by Colombia, Mexico and Venezuela, the Group of Three (G-3), typifies the desire for establishing new free-trade areas in Latin America. By 2005, G-3 is scheduled to become a tariff-free zone. When approved, the accord will create a free market of 145 million people with a combined GDP of €337bn ($373bn).[19] G-3 has already sparked the possibility of expansion to include Ecuador and Chile; both currently have free-trade agreements with the G-3 nations.

Latin American Integration Association (LAIA)

The long-term goal of the LAIA is the establishment, in a gradual and progressive manner, of a Latin American common market. One of the more important aspects of LAIA is the differential treatment of member countries according to their level of economic development.

The Andean Common Market (ANCOM)

The Andean Pact, as it is generally referred to, has served its member nations with a framework to establish rules for foreign investment, common tariffs for non-member countries, and the reduction or elimination of internal tariffs. The Andean Pact members agreed to go beyond a free-trade agreement and implement a customs union in 1996. This revived interest in economic integration by Andean Pact members has resulted in an evaluation of alternatives for member countries to join NAFTA and the possibility of the integration of the Andean Pact and Mercosur (see below) to form a South American Free Trade Area (SAFTA).[20]

Southern Cone Common Market (Mercosur)

Mercosur is the newest common market agreement in Latin America. A successful bilateral trade pact between Argentina and Brazil led to the creation of Mercosur in 1991. Argentina, Brazil, Paraguay and Uruguay are members of Mercosur and seek to achieve free circulation of goods and services, establish a regional common external tariff (targeted at 20 per cent) for third-country imports, and implement harmonised macroeconomic trade and exchange-rate policies among the four partners by 1995. Unfortunately, they were unable to meet the 1995 deadline because the leaders failed to agree on a common external tariff. The most they were able to accomplish was a customs union comprising a free-trade zone with a reduction of internal tariffs.

Asia

What is happening in Asia is by far the most important development in the world today. Following this development a new commonwealth of nations based on economic symbiosis is emerging in the Far East. The Asian continent, from Pakistan to Japan and China down to Indonesia, now accounts for more than half of the world population.[21] Countries in Asia constitute the third Triad region. Japan and China are at the centre of this Triad region.

After decades of dependence on the USA and Europe for technology and markets, countries in Asia are preparing for the next economic leap, driven by trade, investment and technology aided by others in the region. Though few in number, trade agreements among some of the Asian emerging countries are seen as movement towards a regionwide intra-Asian trade area. This drive was strengthened after the 1996–97 economic crisis in a number of Asian countries.

At present, there is one multinational trade group, the Association of Southeast Asian Nations (ASEAN),[22] which has evolved into the ASEAN Free Trade Area (AFTA), and one forum, Asia-Pacific

EXHIBIT 8.8: Latin American market groups

Association	Member	Population (millions)	GDP ($bn)	GDP per capita ($)	Imports ($bn)
Andean Common Market (ANCOM)	Bolivia	10.1	23.95	2,374	7.65
	Colombia	46.9	333.37	7,104	54.67
	Ecuador	14.7	65.95	4,496	24.29
	Peru	29.4	176.93	6,018	38.01
	Argentina (Associate)	40.8	446.04	10,942	73.92
	Brazil (Associate)	196.7	2,476.65	12,594	236.87
	Paraguay (Associate)	6.6	23.84	3,629	12.32
	Uruguay (Associate)	3.4	46.71	13,866	10.73
	Chile (Associate)	17.3	248.59	14,394	74.20
Central American Common Market (CACM)	Belize	0.4	1.45	4,059	0.90
	Costa Rica	4.7	40.87	8,647	16.22
	El Salvador	6.2	23.05	3,702	10.12
	Guatemala	14.8	46.90	3,178	16.61
	Honduras	7.8	17.43	2,247	10.14
	Nicaragua	5.9	9.32	1,587	5.21
	Panama	3.6	26.78	7,498	21.60
	Dominican Republic (Associate)	10.1	55.61	5,530	17.60
	Haiti (Associate)	10.1	7.35	726	2.90
Caribbean Community and Common Market (CARICOM)	Antigua and Barbuda	0.1	1.12	12,480	0.75
	Bahamas	0.3	7.79	22,431	2.85
	Barbados	0.3	3.69	13,453	1.84
	Belize	0.4	1.45	4,059	0.90
	Dominica	0.1	0.48	7,154	0.23
	Grenada	0.1	0.82	7,780	0.32
	Guyana	0.8	2.58	3,408	1.82
	Haiti	10.1	7.35	726	2.90
	Jamaica	2.7	14.44	5,330	6.30
	Montserrat				
	St Kitts & Nevis	0.1	0.70	13,144	0.27
	Saint Lucia	0.2	1.26	7,154	0.66
	St Vincent & Grenadines	0.1	0.69	6,291	0.39
	Suriname	0.5	–		1.65
	Trinidad and Tobago	1.3	22.48	16,699	8.70
	Anguilla				
	Bermuda	0.1	–		0.93
	British Virgin Islands				
	Cayman Islands	0.1	–		–
	Turks & Caicos Islands	0.0	–		–
Latin American Integration Association (LAIA)	Argentina	40.8	446.04	10,942	73.92
	Bolivia	10.1	23.95	2,374	7.65
	Brazil	196.7	2,476.65	12,594	236.87
	Chile	17.3	248.59	14,394	74.20
	Colombia	46.9	333.37	7,104	54.67
	Cuba	11.3	–		14.30
	Ecuador	14.7	65.95	4,496	24.29
	Mexico	114.8	1,153.34	10,047	361.07
	Nicaragua	5.9	9.32	1,587	5.21
	Panama	3.6	26.78	7,498	21.60
	Paraguay	6.6	23.84	3,629	12.32
	Peru	29.4	76.93	6,018	38.01
	Uruguay	3.4	46.71	13,866	10.73
	Venezuela	29.3	16.48	10,810	47.60

Source: World Bank, 2012, http://databank.worldbank.org/ddp/home.do?

Economic Cooperation (APEC), which meets annually to discuss regional economic development and cooperation.[23]

ASEAN

The Association of Southeast Asian Nations (ASEAN) is the primary multinational trade group in Asia. The goals of the group are economic integration and cooperation through complementary industry programmes, preferential trading including reduced tariff and non-tariff barriers, guaranteed member access to markets throughout the region, and harmonised investment incentives. Like all multinational market groups, ASEAN has experienced problems and false starts in attempting to unify its combined economies.

As their economies became more diversified, they signed a framework agreement to create the ASEAN Free Trade Area (AFTA) in 2006. Since 2007, the ASEAN countries have gradually lowered their import duties among them and targeted will be zero for most of the import duties by 2015. Tariffs on all manufactured goods were to be reduced to 5 per cent or less by 2003.[24] The new free trade area consists of 10 countries: Brunei, Cambodia, Indonesia, Malaysia, the Philippines, Singapore, Thailand, Vietnam, Myanmar and Laos. It has a population of 601 million and a GDP of more than €900bn ($737bn) (see Exhibit 8.9).

APEC

Asia-Pacific Economic Cooperation (APEC) is the other important trade group in the Asian Pacific Rim. It provides a formal structure for the major governments of the region, including the USA and Canada, to discuss their mutual interests in open trade and economic collaboration. APEC is a unique forum that has evolved into the primary regional vehicle for promoting trade liberalisation and economic cooperation. The 21-member APEC,[25] which accounts for approximately 40 per cent of the world's population, approximately 54 per cent of world gross domestic product (GDP) and about 44 per cent of world trade also includes the most powerful regional economies in the world (see Exhibit 8.10).

EXHIBIT 8.9: GDP per capita in ASEAN countries

Members	Population 2004 (million)	GDP per capita 2004 ($)
Indonesia	242.33	3,495
Vietnam	87.84	1,407
Philippines	94.85	2,370
Thailand	69.52	4,972
Malaysia	28.86	9,977
Singapore	5.18	46,241
Brunei	0.41	40,301
Myanmar	48.34	1,393
Laos	6.50	3,004
Cambodia	14.31	897

Source: World Bank, 2012, http://databank.worldbank.org/ddp/home.do?Step=3&id=4.

EXHIBIT 8.10: Comparison of intra-trade among members of APEC and the EU

	Population 2011 (millions)	Exports 1980 ($bn)	Exports 2003 ($bn)	Exports 2011 ($bn)	GDP 2011 ($bn)
APEC	12,387	297	2,951	36,125	133,304
North America	542	129	945	2,397	18,972
Asia	4,286	150	1,650	6,920	34,055
Oceania	35	18	79	319	1,080
EU 27	675	1,466	1,330	18,467	6,465

Sources: APEC, World Bank, *World Development Indicators* (2011); World Trade Organization, *Time Series on International Trade* (2011); and *CIA World Factbook* (2011).

Africa

Africa's multinational market development activities can be characterised by a great deal of activity, but little progress. Including bilateral agreements, an estimated 200 economic arrangements exist between African countries (see Exhibit 8.11). Despite the large number and assortment of 'paper' organisations, there has been little actual economic integration. This is generally due to the political instability that has characterised Africa in the last decades and the unstable economic base on which it has had to build.[26]

The Economic Community of West African States (ECOWAS) is the most senior of the African regional cooperative groups and the most successful.[27] A 16-nation group, ECOWAS has an aggregate gross domestic product (GDP) of more than €60bn ($50bn) and is striving to achieve full economic integration. Some experts suggest that economic domination by Nigeria (45 per cent of all the market's exports) may create internal strains that cannot be overcome.

One of the groups becoming strong is the South African Development Community (SADC), with its 14 members. The members are Angola, Congo, Malawi, Tanzania, Zambia, Mozambique, Namibia, Botswana, Zimbabwe, Swaziland, Lesotho, Mauritius, Seychelles and South Africa. The group has a total population of 167.2 million, with a GDP of €263.8bn ($215.6bn).

Middle East

The Middle East has been less aggressive in the formation of successfully functioning multinational market groups (see Exhibit 8.12). Countries that belong to the Arab Common Market have set goals for free internal trade but have not achieved them.

Future regional market groups

A conjectural free-trade agreement that has emerged is one between the USA and the EU. Europe fears it will be isolated by free-trade agreements that the USA is trying to form with Latin American and Asian countries; the USA is concerned by the fact that Mexico is trying to negotiate its own free-trade accord with Europe and that Europe is seeking to establish free-trade ties with the countries of Mercosur.

Another more speculative trade group centres around the political and economic unification of China, Taiwan and Hong Kong. Although currently at odds politically, economic integration between Hong Kong, Taiwan and the coastal provinces of southern China, often unofficially referred to as the Chinese Economic Area (CEA), has advanced rapidly in recent years.

The current expansion of the triangular economic relationship can be attributed to a steady transfer of labour-intensive manufacturing operations from Taiwan and Hong Kong to the Chinese mainland. China provides a supply of cheap, abundant labour, and Taiwan and Hong Kong provide capital, technology and management expertise. Hong Kong, now formally part of China, also plays an important role as the financier, investor, supplier and provider of technology, and as a port of entry for China as a whole.[28]

As an economic region, the CEA's economic importance should not be undervalued. Combined exports of the CEA were valued at €254.1bn ($281.5bn), accounting for 7.6 per cent of the world's exports and ranking fourth worldwide, behind the USA, Germany and Japan. Their combined imports totalled €240bn ($266bn), accounting for 6.9 per cent of the world's imports and ranking third, behind the USA and Germany.[29]

Strategic implications for marketing

The complexion of the entire world marketplace has been changed significantly by the coalition of nations into multinational market groups. To international business firms, multinational groups spell opportunity writ large through access to greatly enlarged markets with reduced or abolished country-by-country tariff barriers and restrictions.

EXHIBIT 8.11: African market groups

Association	Member	Population (millions)	GDP ($bn)	GDP per capita (US$)	Imports of goods and services ($bn)	Exports of goods and services ($bn)
Arfo Malagasy Economic Union	Benin	8.8	7	741	2.29	1.7
	Burkina Faso	16.5	9	536	0.00	–
	Cameroon	19.6	22	1,144	6.41	5.6
	Central African Republic	4.4	2	451	0.00	–
	Chad	11.2	9	761	0.00	–
	Congo, Rep	4.0	12	2,970	0.00	–
	Congo, Dem Rep	66.0	13	199	0.00	–
	Cote d'Ivoire	19.7	23	1,161	10.78	12.6
	Gabon	1.5	13	8,768	0.00	–
	Mali	15.4	9	613	3.75	2.4
	Mauritania	3.5	4	1,045	0.00	–
	Niger	15.5	5	349	0.00	–
	Senegal	12.4	13	1,034	5.20	3.2
	Togo	6.0	3	530	1.83	1.3
East African Customs Union	Ethiopia	82.9	27	320	9.91	4.6
	Kenya	40.5	32	795	13.53	9.0
	Sudan	33.6	65	1,488	11.16	11.7
	Tanzania	44.8	23	527	9.02	6.4
	Uganda	33.4	17	515	6.42	3.5
	Zambia	12.9	16	1,252	5.65	7.7
Union of Arab Maghreb	Algeria	35.5	162	4,567	50.79	60.7
	Libya	6.4	–		30.69	49.3
	Tunisia	10.5	44	4,194	24.35	22.2
	Morocco	32.0	91	2,795	40.08	30.1
	Mauritania	3.5	4	1,045	2.29	1.7
Economic Community of West African States	Benin	8.8	7	741	0.00	–
	Burkina Faso	16.5	9	536	1.12	0.6
	Cape Verde	0.5	2	3,345	10.78	12.6
	Cote d'Ivoire	19.7	23	1,161	0.32	0.3
	Gambia, The	1.7	1	551	13.93	9.4
	Ghana	24.4	32	1,319	1.80	1.5
	Guinea	10.0	5	474	0.30	0.2
	Guinea-Bissau	1.5	1	551	1.80	0.4
	Liberia	4.0	1	324	3.75	2.4
	Mali	15.4	9	613	0.00	–
	Mauritania	3.5	4	1,045	0.00	–
	Niger	15.5	5	349	67.79	79.8
	Nigeria	158.4	229	1,443	5.20	3.2
	Senegal	12.4	13	1,034	1.04	0.4
	Sierra Leone	5.9	2	325	1.83	1.3
	Togo	6.0	3	530	35.42	51.5
Southern African Development Community	Angola	19.1	81	4,237	5.72	5.0
	Botswana	2.0	15	7,427	0.00	–
	Congo, Rep	4.0	12	2,970	0.00	–
	Congo, Dem Rep	66.0	13	199	2.44	0.9

▶

EXHIBIT 8.11: African market groups

Association	Member	Population (millions)	GDP ($bn)	GDP per capita (US$)	Imports of goods and services ($bn)	Exports of goods and services ($bn)
	Lesotho	2.2	2	1,004	5.62	4.9
	Namibia	2.3	11	4,876	2.50	1.2
	Malawi	14.9	5	362	6.14	5.0
	Mauritius	1.3	10	7,577	4.83	2.9
	Mozambique	23.4	9	394	1.16	1.0
	Seychelles	0.1	1	11,130	9.02	6.4
	Tanzania	44.8	23	527	5.65	7.7
	Zambia	12.9	16	1,252	0.00	–
	Zimbabwe	12.6	7	591	0.00	–

Source: World Bank, 2011.

EXHIBIT 8.12: Middle East market groups

Association	Countries	Population (millions)	GDP ($bn)	GDP ($ per capita)	Imports ($bn)
Arab Common Market	Egypt	83.6	527.4	6,600	55.1
	Yemen	24.7	59.9	2,300	8.2
	Mauritania	3.3	7.2	2,000	2.9
	Iraq	31.1	141.0	4,300	47.8
	Libya	5.6	39.6	6,100	10.1
	Syria	22.5	110.1	5,100	17.6
	Jordan	6.5	37.5	6,000	16.3
Economic Cooperation Organization (ECO)	Afghanistan	30.4	30.2	1,000	5.2
	Azerbaijan	9.4	94.6	10,400	10.2
	Iran	78.8	1,007.0	13,400	74.4
	Kazakhstan	17.5	220.3	13,200	41.2
	Kyrgyzstan	5.4	13.3	2,400	4.0
	Pakistan	190.0	463.3	2,900	38.9
	Tajikistan	7.7	16.5	2,100	3.5
	Turkey	79.7	1,093.0	15,000	232.9
	Turkmenistan	5.0	44.0	8,000	9.6
	Uzbekistan	28.0	96.8	3,300	8.5
Gulf Cooperation Council (GCC)	Bahrain	1.2	31.8	28,200	12.1
	Kuwait	2.6	156.0	42,400	22.0
	Qatar	1.9	177.8	100,600	26.9
	Saudi Arabia	26.5	698.8	24,800	120.0
	Oman	3.0	86.4	28,000	21.4
	United Arab Emirates	5.3	260.7	48,500	202.1

Source: *CIA World Factbook*, www.cia.gov/cia/publications/factbook, 2010.

As goals of the EEA and NAFTA are reached, new marketing opportunities are created; so are new problems. World competition will intensify as businesses become stronger and more experienced in dealing with large market groups. International managers will still be confronted by individual national markets with the same problems of language, customs and instability, even though they are packaged under the umbrella of a common market.

Opportunities

Economic integration creates large mass markets for the marketer. Many national markets, too small to bother with individually, take on new dimensions and significance when combined with markets from cooperating countries. Large markets are particularly important to businesses accustomed to mass production and mass distribution because of the economies of scale and marketing efficiencies that can be achieved. In highly competitive markets, the benefits derived from enhanced efficiencies are often passed along as lower prices, which lead to increased purchasing power.

Another major saving will result from the billions of dollars wasted in developing different versions of products to meet a hotchpotch of national standards. Philips and other European companies invested a total of €18bn ($20bn) to develop a common switching system for Europe's 10 different telephone networks. This compares with €2.7bn ($3bn) spent in the USA for a common system and €1.35bn ($1.5bn) in Japan for a single system.

Market barriers

The initial aim of a multinational market is to protect businesses that operate within its borders. An expressed goal is to give an advantage to the companies within the market in their dealings with other countries of the market group. Analysis of the intra-regional and international trade patterns of the market groups indicates that such goals have been achieved. Trade does increase among member nations and decrease with non-member nations.

Local preferences certainly spell trouble for the exporter located outside the market. Companies willing to invest in production facilities in multinational markets may benefit from such protection as they become a part of the market. Exporters, however, are in a considerably weaker position. This prospect confronts many US exporters faced with the possible need to invest in Europe to protect their export markets in the EU. Recent heavy investments by Japanese (Toyota, Honda and Nissan), American (MCI, GM and Procter & Gamble) and Korean (Lucky Goldstar and Samsung) companies are good examples of such investments.

Ensuring EU market entry

There are four levels of involvement that a firm may have *vis-à-vis* the EU: (1) firms based in Europe with well-established manufacturing and distribution operations in several European countries; (2) firms with operations in a single EU country; (3) firms that export manufactured goods to the EU from an offshore location; and (4) firms that have not actively exported to EU countries. The strategies for effective competitiveness in the EU are different for each type of firm.

The first type of firm, fully established in several EU countries with local manufacturing, is the best positioned. Marketers will have to exploit the opportunities of greater efficiencies of production and distribution that result from lowering the barriers. They will also have to deal with increased competition from European firms as well as other MNCs that will be aggressively establishing market positions.

European retailers and wholesalers as well as industrial customers are merging, expanding and taking steps to assure their success in this larger market. Nestlé has bought Rowntree, a UK confectionery company, and Britone, the Italian food conglomerate, to strengthen its ties to EU market firms. European banking is also going through a stage of restructuring.

A second type of firm – with operations in one European country – is vulnerable when barriers come down and competitors enter the company's market. The firm's biggest problem in this situation is not being large enough to withstand the competition from outside the country. The answer is to become larger, or withdraw. There are several choices for this firm: expand through acquisition or merger; enter a strategic alliance with a second company; or expand the company beyond being a local single-country firm to being a pan-European competitor.

Marketing mix implications

Companies are adjusting their marketing mix strategies to reflect anticipated market differences in a single European market. In the past, companies often charged different prices in different European markets. Non-tariff barriers between member states supported price differentials and kept lower-priced products from entering those markets where higher prices were charged. Colgate-Palmolive has adapted its Colgate toothpaste into a single formula for sale across Europe at one price. Before changing its pricing practices, Colgate sold its toothpaste at different prices in different markets. Badedas Shower Gel, for example, is priced in the middle of the market in Germany and as a high-priced product in the UK.

As long as products from lower-priced markets could not move to higher-priced markets, such differential price schemes worked. Now, however, under the EU rules, companies cannot prevent the free movement of goods, and parallel imports from lower-priced markets to higher-priced markets are more apt to occur. Some price standardisation among country markets will be one of the necessary changes to avoid the problem of parallel imports.

In addition to initiating uniform pricing policies, companies are reducing the number of brands they produce to focus advertising and promotion efforts. For example, Nestlé's current three brands of yoghurt in the EU will be reduced to a single brand.

A major benefit deriving from an integrated Europe is competition at the retail level. Europe lacks an integrated and competitive distribution system that would support small and midsize outlets. The elimination of borders could result in increased competition among retailers and the creation of Europe-wide distribution channels. Retail giants such as France's Carrefour, Germany's Aldi group and Holland's Ahold are planning huge hypermarkets with big advertising budgets.

SUMMARY

The experience of the multinational market groups developed since the Second World War reveals both the possible successes and the hazards such groups encounter. The various attempts at economic cooperation represent varying degrees of success and failure but, almost without regard to their degree of success, the economic market groups have created great excitement among marketers.

Economic benefits possible through cooperation relate to more efficient marketing and production: marketing efficiency is effected through the development of mass markets, encouragement of competition, the improvement of personal income and various psychological market factors. Production efficiency derives from specialisation, mass production for mass markets and the free movement of the factors of production. Economic integration also tends to foster political harmony among the countries involved; such harmony leads to stability, which is beneficial to the marketer.

The marketing implications of multinational market groups may be studied from the standpoint of firms located inside the market or of firms located outside that wish to sell to the markets. For each viewpoint the problems and opportunities are somewhat different; but regardless of the location of the marketer, multinational market groups provide a great opportunity for the creative marketer who wishes to expand volume. Market groupings make it economically feasible to enter new markets and to employ new marketing strategies that could not be applied to the smaller markets represented by individual countries.

The success of the EU, the creation of NAFTA, the expansion of ASEAN to the ASEAN Free Trade Area (AFTA) and the new Mercosur suggest the growing importance of economic cooperation and integration. Such developments will continue to challenge the international marketer by providing continually growing market opportunities.

QUESTIONS

1 Elaborate on the problems and benefits for international marketers deriving from multinational market groups.

2 Explain the political role of multinational market groups. Identify the factors on which one may judge the potential success or failure of a multinational market group.

3 Explain the marketing implications of the factors contributing to the successful development of a multinational market group.

4 Differentiate between a free-trade area and a common market. Explain the marketing implications of the differences.

5 Select any three countries that might have some logical basis for establishing a multinational market organisation. Identify the various problems that would be encountered in forming multinational market groups of such countries.

6 US exports to the EU are expected to decline in future years. What marketing actions may a US company take to counteract such changes?

7 'Because they are dynamic and because they have great growth possibilities, the multinational markets are likely to be especially rough and tumble for external business.' Discuss.

8 Why have African nations had such difficulty in forming effective economic unions?

9 Discuss the implications of the EU for marketing strategy in Europe.

10 Discuss the United States–Canada Free Trade Agreement and compare it with the EU.

11 What are some of the possibilities for other multinational marketing groups that are forming? Discuss the implications to global marketing if these groups should develop.

12 Using the factors that serve as the basis for success of an economic union (political, economic, social and geographic), evaluate the potential success of the EU, NAFTA, ASEAN, AFTA and Mercosur.

FURTHER READING

- B. Lévy, 'The Interface between Globalization, Trade and Development: Theoretical Issues for International Business Studies', *International Business Review*, 2007, 16(5), pp 594–612.

- P. Gabrielsson, M. Gabrielsson and H. Gabrielsson, 'International Advertising Campaigns in Fast-moving Consumer Goods Companies Originating from a SMOPEC Country', *International Business Review*, 2008, 17(6), pp 714–28.

- Andrew Delios, 'The Race for Japanese FDI in the European Union', in Lars Oxelheim and Pervez Ghauri (eds), *European Union and the Race for Foreign Direct Investment in Europe* (Oxford: Elsevier, 2004), pp 185–208.

NOTES

1 World Bank, *Doing Business in 2012: Doing Business in more Transparent Worlds* (Washington, DC: World Bank Publications, 2011).

2 Jay L. Camillo, 'Mexico: NAFTA Opens Door to US Business', *Business America*, March 1994, pp 14–21.

3   US Commerce, *Doing Business in Russia: Country Commercial Guide for US Companies* (Washington, DC: US Commercial Service, 2011).

4   The following website provides information on a number of trade blocs: www.mac.doc.org.

5   Kenichi Ohmae, *Triad Power* (New York: Free Press, 1985), p 220.

6   The EC still exists as a legal entity within the broader framework of the EU.

7   John Perry, *Business and the European Community* (Oxford: Butterworth-Heinemann, 1994).

8   James Mehring, 'High Hurdles for New EU Members to Clear', *Business Week*, 5 May 2003, p 26.

9   T. Buck and R. Waters, 'Commission Talk Tough over Microsoft "Abuses"', *Financial Times*, 7 August 2003, p 25.

10 'All Aboard the EuroTrain', *The Economist*, 5 April, 2003, p 50.

11 F. Guerrera and B. de Jonquieres, 'Something is Rotten Within our System: Europe's Mighty Competition Authorities are Cut Down to Size', *Financial Times*, 28 October 2002, p 25.

12 Euromonitor, *Euromonitor International,* httpp//:www.euromonitor.com/2012.

13 I. Bremmer, 'The End of the Free Market: Who Wins the War between State and Corporations? *European View*, 2010, 1–4.

14 *Financial Times* , 'A Year of Planes, Jeans and Price-fixing Deals', 20 March 2002, p 23.

15 EFTA countries joining the EEA were Austria, Finland, Iceland, Norway and Sweden.

16 The 12 republics of the former USSR, collectively referred to as the Newly Independent States (NIS), are: Russia, Ukraine, Belarus (formerly Byelorussia), Armenia, Moldova (formerly Moldavia), Azerbaijan, Uzbekistan, Turkmenistan, Tajikistan, Kazakhstan, Kyrgystan (formerly Kirghiziya) and Georgia. These same countries, the NIS, are also members of the CIS.

17 For more information on NAFTA, see the following website: www.mac.doc.gov.

18 C.J. Chippello, 'NAFTA's Benefits to Firms in Canada May Top Those for Mexico', *Wall Street Journal*, 23 February 2003, p A2.

19 V. Govindarajan and R. Ramamurti, ' Reverse Innovation, Emerging Markets and Global Strategy, *Global Strategy Journal*, 2011, 1(3–4), 191–205.

20 Richard Lapper, 'South American Unity Still a Distant Dream', *Financial Times*, 12 December 2004, p 8.

21 John Naisbitt, *Mega Trends in Asia* (New York: Simon & Schuster, 1996).

22 ASEAN countries are: Brunei, Indonesia, Malaysia, the Philippines, Singapore and Thailand. Vietnam entered ASEAN in 1996.

23 'A Great Slide Backward in Southeast Asia', *Business Week*, 5 August 1996, p 23.

24 For details, see: www.aseansec.org.

25 APEC members are: Australia, Brunei, Canada, Chile, China, Hong Kong, Indonesia, Japan, South Korea, Malaysia, Mexico, New Zealand, Papua New Guinea, Peru, Philippines, Russia, Singapore, Taiwan, Thailand, the United States and Vietnam.

26 'Opening South Africa: It Should Act Now to Rid Itself and the Region of Apartheid's Economic Remnants', *The Economist*, 8 March 1997, p 17.

27 'ECOWAS: Last Month ECOWAS Celebrated its 19th Anniversary', *West Africa*, 18 July 1994, pp 1258–63.

28 For more on China and the Pacific Rim, see www.apec.org.

29 Kenichi Ohmae, 'The New World Order: The Rise of the Region-State', *The Wall Street Journal*, 8 August 1994, p A–12.

PART 4

Developing International Marketing Strategies

Chapter 9

International Marketing Strategies

Chapter Learning Objectives

What you should learn from Chapter 9

- How international marketing management differs from global marketing
- Why adaptation is necessary
- How and when we can use standardised marketing
- The differences between market-driving versus market-driven strategies
- The importance of collaborative relationships in international marketing efforts
- The increasing importance of strategic international alliances
- The factors that influence strategy formulation
- Why there is a need for strategic planning in order to achieve company goals
- The importance of product life cycles for marketing strategy

Confronted with increasing global competition for expanding markets, multinational companies are changing their marketing strategies. Their goals are to enhance their competitiveness and to assure presence in many markets in order to capitalise on opportunities in the global marketplace.

A recent study of North American and European corporations indicated that nearly 75 per cent of the companies are revamping their business processes, that most have formalised **strategic planning** programmes and that the need to stay cost competitive was considered to be the most important external issue affecting their marketing strategies.[1] Change is not limited to the giant multinationals but includes small and medium-sized firms as well.[2] In fact, the flexibility of a smaller company may enable it to reflect the demands of international markets and redefine its programmes quicker than larger multinationals. Acquiring a global perspective is easy, but the execution requires planning, organisation and a willingness to try new approaches, from engaging in collaborative relationships to redefining the scope of company operations.[3]

> **strategic planning**
>
> a systematised way of relating to the future

This chapter discusses global marketing management, competition in the global marketplace, strategic planning and strategies.

International marketing management

> **domestic market extension concept**
>
> foreign markets are extensions of the domestic market; the domestic marketing mix is offered, as is, to foreign markets
>
> **multidomestic market concept**
>
> each country is viewed as being culturally unique; an adapted marketing mix for each country market is developed
>
> **global market concept**
>
> wherever cost- and culturally effective, an overall standardised marketing strategy is developed for entire sets of country markets; marketing mix elements are adapted where necessary
>
> **global marketing**
>
> using global (standardised) market concepts in marketing decisions

Determining a firm's overall international strategy to achieve goals and objectives is the central task of international marketing management that defines the level of international integration of the company. Companies must deal with a multitude of strategic issues including the extent of the internationalisation of operations.

As discussed in Chapter 1, a company's international orientation can be characterised as one of three operating concepts:

1. under the **domestic market extension concept**, foreign markets are extensions of the domestic market and the domestic marketing mix is offered, as is, to foreign markets
2. with the **multidomestic market concept**, each country is viewed as being culturally unique and an adapted marketing mix for each country market is developed
3. with the **global market concept**, the world is the market and, wherever cost- and culturally effective, an overall standardised marketing strategy is developed for entire sets of country markets, while only marketing mix elements are adapted wherever necessary.

Global versus international marketing management

The primary distinction between global marketing management and international marketing management is orientation (see Exhibit 9.1).[4] **Global marketing** management is guided by the global marketing concept, which views the world as one market and is based on identifying and targeting cross-cultural similarities.

International marketing management is based on the premise of cross-cultural differences and is guided by the belief that each foreign market requires its own culturally adapted marketing strategy. Although consumers in New Delhi dining at McDonald's and Western teens plugged into their iPads are a reality, the idea of marketing a standardised product with a uniform marketing plan around the world remains 'purely theoretical'.[5]

As discussed earlier, there is still debate about the extent of global markets today. A reasonable question concerns whether a global marketing strategy is possible and whether a completely standardised marketing mix can be achieved. Keep in mind that *global marketing* strategy, as used in this text, and the *globalisation of markets* are two separate, although interrelated, ideas. One has to do with efficiency of operations,

EXHIBIT 9.1: A comparison of assumptions about global and multinational companies

	Multinational companies	Global companies
Product life cycle	Products are in different stages of the product life cycle in each nation	Global product life cycles; all consumers want the most advanced products
Design	Adjustments to products initially designed for domestic markets	International performance criteria considered during design stage
Adaptation	Product adaptation is necessary in markets characterised by national differences	Products are adapted to global wants and needs; restrained concern for product suitability
Market segmentation	Segments reflect differences. Customised products for each segment. Many customised markets. Acceptance of regional/national differences	Segments reflect group similarities Group similar segments together Fewer standardised markets Expansion of segments into worldwide proportions
Competition	Domestic/national competitive relationships	Ability to compete in national markets is affected by a firm's global position
Production	Standardisation limited by requirements to adapt products to national tastes	Globally standardised production Adaptations are handled through modular designs
The consumer	Preferences reflect national differences	Global convergence of consumer wants and needs
Product	Products differentiated on the basis of design, features, functions, style and image	Emphasis on value-enhancing distinction
Price	Consumers willing to pay more for a customised product	Consumers prefer a globally standardised product
Promotion	National product image, sensitive to national needs	Global product image, sensitive to national differences and global needs
Place	National distribution channels	Global standardisation of distribution

competitiveness and orientation, the other with the homogeneity of demand across cultures. There are at least three points that help define a global approach to international marketing:

1 the world is viewed as the market (that is, sets of country markets)

2 homogeneous market segments are sought across country market sets

3 standardisation of the marketing mix is sought wherever possible but adapted whenever culturally necessary.

Standardisation versus adaptation

Why globalise? Several benefits are derived from globalisation and standardisation of the marketing mix. *Economies of scale in production and marketing* are the most frequently cited benefits. Black & Decker (electrical hand tools, appliances and other consumer products) realised significant production cost savings when it adopted a global strategy. It was able to reduce not only the number of motor sizes for the European market from 260 to eight, but also 15 different models to eight.

The savings in the standardisation of advertising can be substantial. Colgate-Palmolive introduced its Colgate tartar-control toothpaste in over 40 countries, each of which could choose one of two ads. The company estimates that for every country where the standardised commercial runs, it saves €0.9–€1.8m ($1–2m) in production costs. However, it soon realised that the standardised ads were not suitable for many countries and were not working. It had to change its strategy and went back to more versions/adaptations of the ads.

Transfer of experience and know-how across countries through improved coordination and integration of marketing activities is also cited as a benefit of globalisation. Unilever, NV, successfully introduced two global brands originally developed by two subsidiaries. Its South African subsidiary developed Impulse body spray and a European branch developed a detergent that cleaned effectively in European hard water. These are examples of how coordination and transfer of know-how from a local market to a world market can be achieved.

The most important benefit derived from globalisation is a *uniform international image*. Global recognition of brands accelerates new product introductions and increases the efficiency and effectiveness of advertising. Uniform global images are increasingly important as satellite communications spread throughout the world. Brands such as Samsung, Volvo, Shell, IBM and Ericsson are good examples. Philips International, an electronics manufacturer, had enormous impact with a global product image when it sponsored the soccer World Cup; the same advertisement was seen in 44 countries with voice-over translations in six languages. Another example is Microsoft's Windows Vista, which was launched simultaneously all over the world, from Chicago to Singapore.

Without doubt, market differences seldom permit complete standardisation. Government and trade restrictions, differences in the availability of media, differences in customer interests and response patterns, and the whole host of cultural differences presented in earlier chapters preclude complete standardisation of a global marketing mix.

Market-driven versus market-driving strategies

For a long time the market-driven approach and *market orientation* has been the dominant market strategy.[6] The market-orientation approach advocates that firms should continuously collect market information about customers and competitors, and disseminate it within the firm. This will help the firm to develop a more responsive strategy, ie responsive to the respective market demands and customer needs.[7] In this manner a firm can better serve existing customer preferences and gauge customer trends so as to be able to adapt to and prepare for these trends.

More recently, however, a *market-driving* approach has been put forward. According to this strategy, firms do not respond passively to current customer demands via adaptation. On the contrary, a market-driving firm has an ability to develop a unique value proposition for customers. It does not adapt its strategies to each and every customer group, but instead takes action to change the behaviours of different market actors, including customers and others in the value chain.[8] In this process it reconfigures the roles and relationships of different actors in its value chain. A market-driving firm claims to educate its customers towards better incentives and value propositions.

A market-driving firm thus introduces innovative channel management and customer relationships in order to acquire their loyalty.[9] A number of firms have demonstrated such a market-driving strategy approach. Firms such as CNN, IKEA, Apple, Starbucks and the Body Shop are good examples. These companies have changed customer behaviour in their respective markets. CNN provided the proposition that you can watch the news whenever you want, at your own leisure. IKEA provided the proposition that you can see and buy furniture instantly instead of waiting for weeks. Starbucks has gone to markets where coffee was never drunk and has thus changed consumer behaviour in most markets.

Market-driven companies perform exhaustive market research to understand fully an existing customer need. They perform multiple validation cycles, with heavy documentation of requirements and written detailed specifications of features and benefits. A serially laborious process is then followed through multiple cycles of develop-and-test until a differentiated product or service is identified. For some, static well-defined market segments, perhaps this approach can still work. Procter and Gamble, for many products, provides a good example of being driven by these segments.

Market-driving companies focus on a vision for the future, unhampered by traditional thinking and industry norms for product development. Market-driving companies are poised to make discontinuous leaps in innovation in terms of customer value (not just incremental capability and technology). These companies also have a mission to build unique value networks and engage in a bigger business ecosystem through technology and business model innovation. Apple's iPod with iTunes is a good example of a value network in a business ecosystem.

Consider Apple versus Microsoft. Apple is a market-driving company anticipating trends and taking risks to amaze and surprise customers consistently with delivered value. Microsoft is a market-driven company missing trends and failing to take risks, which forces it to react after dramatic market shifts have already occurred. Invariably, one can predict the fate of Zune versus iTunes, or understand the relative adoption of Windows mobile versus the iPhone. It's not hard to see which approach is also more cost-effective.[10]

At present, more research is being undertaken in order to understand how some companies refuse to adapt their strategies in local markets and instead change the behaviour of customers and other relevant actors in their industry.

Competition in the global marketplace

Global competition is placing new emphasis on some basic tenets of business. It is reducing time frames and focusing on the importance of quality, competitive prices and innovative products. Time is becoming a precious commodity for business, and expanding technology is shortening product life cycles and creating greater opportunities for innovative products. A company can no longer introduce a new product with the expectation of dominating the market for years while the idea spreads slowly through world markets.

Consider the effect on Hewlett-Packard's strategies and plans when, in any given year, two-thirds of its revenue comes from products introduced in the prior three years. Shorter product life cycles mean that a company must maximise sales rapidly to recover development costs and generate a profit by offering its products globally. However, companies need to understand the dynamic nature of the global marketplace as well as the culture and environment that cause this dynamism.

A failure to understand this results in failure in foreign markets. Wal-Mart's failure in Germany, McDonald's problems in Japan, Nike's problems in late 1980, when its sales fell drastically due to allegations that it exploits labour in its foreign markets, and Marks & Spencer's failure in European markets (France, Netherlands, Sweden, Belgium) are good examples. On the other hand, the German Müller yoghurt in the UK, Toyota's Lexus car in the USA, Tesco's internationalisation into Eastern Europe and McDonald's revival in France are good examples of understanding these forces and adapting marketing strategies to gain success.

Going International 9.1

BOEING QUESTIONS AIRBUS USA PLANS

Boeing Co has started attacking plans by rival European planemaker Airbus to begin building jets in the USA.

The move by Airbus onto Boeing's home turf could transform the domestic aerospace industry in the same way Toyota Motor Corp changed the auto industry when it and other 'transplants' started building cars in volume on US soil during the 1980s.

Chicago-based Boeing weighed in on Friday with a tersely worded statement that said any job creation in the USA won't offset the alleged damage caused by 'illegal subsidies' at Airbus, a unit of European Aeronautic Space and Defence Co.

'While it is interesting once again to see Airbus promising to move jobs from Europe to the United States, no matter how many are created, the numbers pale in comparison to the thousands of US jobs destroyed by illegal subsidies,' Boeing said.

The World Trade Organization over recent years has ruled that Toulouse, (France)-based Airbus received illegal subsidies. EU trade officials in December said they had fulfilled terms of a ruling against the EU on Airbus subsidies, but Boeing and the US government said the EU's remediation was insufficient.

▶

A separate EU case against Boeing and the US government is moving though appeals at the World Trade Organization, which has ruled that Boeing also received illegal subsidies.

No formal incentives for Airbus have been proposed or approved by the Albama State Legislature. But people familiar with the negotiations say the State is using the package outlined for the protracted US Air Force refuelling tanker contract, won by Boeing last year, as a framework for attracting Airbus to expand into the state.

Local media reports have indicated the package of incentives could run above $100m, with the intent of creating more than 1,000 jobs.

© Airbus S.A.S 2013, Photo by eˣm company/ A Doumenjou

Airbus already spends $12bn each year in the USA sourcing parts for its jets. 'We want to double that in the next 12 to 15 years,' Allan McArtor, chairman of the company's North America unit, said in June.

- Why does Airbus want to open an assembly plant in the USA? Is it good for Airbus? Is it good for America?

Source: based on several sources.

Quality and competitive marketing

As global competition increases for most businesses, many industry and government leaders have warned that a renewed emphasis on quality is a necessity for doing business in growing global markets. In most global markets the cost and quality of a product are among the most important criteria by which purchases are made. Further, the market has gradually shifted from a seller's market to a buyer's market. All over the world, customers have more power because they have more choices as more companies compete for their attention.

Quality is an important criterion for success, but what does quality mean? For many companies, quality is defined internally from the firm's point of view and is measured in terms of compliance with predetermined product specifications or standards and with minimum defects. The concept that quality is measured in terms of conformance to product specifications works if the specifications meet the needs of the market and if the product is delivered to the customer in a manner that fills the customer's needs.

total quality management (TQM)

method that permits continuous improvement of the production of goods and services

corporate strategy

strategy of the company as a whole

Total quality management (TQM) is a **corporate strategy** that focuses total company effort on manufacturing superior products that satisfy customer needs with continuous technological improvement and zero defects. Defining quality as customer satisfaction means the marketer must continually monitor the customer's changing requirements as well as competitive offerings and adjust product offerings as needed, because the customer evaluates a company's product relative to competing products. Your product may be the 'best engineered' in the market with zero defects, but if it does not fulfil your customer's expectations, the competition wins.[11]

Going International 9.2

SAMSUNG'S ROAD TO MOBILE DOMINATION

During the launch of Apple's iPhone 5, Samsung sold a record-breaking number of its own signature smartphone, the Galaxy S III.

© P.N. Ghauri

In recent years, the South Korean company has taken the mobile market – the USA included – by storm. Last year it overtook longtime leader Nokia to become the number one player in cellphones, with 29 per cent market share worldwide. In smartphones, those highend devices with advanced computing power, Samsung is also number one globally and in a dead heat with Apple in the USA. ABI Research says Samsung's share of smartphone shipments topped 33 per cent, compared with Apple's 30 per cent. (To be sure, Apple sells one device, the iPhone, while Samsung offers 25 unique smartphones in the USA.)

Although Samsung wasn't the first to develop a phone that runs on Google's Android operating system, it quickly moved ahead of the pack by introducing one with a strikingly thin, bright and large screen, and by rapidly rolling out cutting-edge features like the ability to 'beam' photos by pressing together the backs of two phones. Thanks to tight control over an extensive supply chain (Samsung makes everything from screens to memory chips), it's been able to move quickly to meet the rising demand for its mobile devices, churning out more than 215 million smartphones globally last year. And phone companies are so eager to stock Samsung devices that they've abandoned their practice of demanding exclusive deals on new phones.

While Samsung has done a phenomenal job of building itself into a cool brand in a short time, it doesn't wield much control over the wireless ecosystem – the mobile operating system, application store and other software services that have helped make smartphones so popular.

Samsung, which means 'three stars' in Korean, started out as a small supplier of dried fish and noodles in the city of Daegu back in 1938. Eventually the company's ambitious founder, Byung Chull Lee, moved the company headquarters to the country's capital, Seoul, and expanded into new businesses.

In the late 1960s Samsung officially entered the electronics business. In the early years the company was known for cheap televisions and air conditioners. That all changed in 1995, when its chairman (and the elder Lee's son), Kun Hee Lee, paid a momentous visit to the company's plant in Gumi. Legend has it that the younger Lee had sent out the company's newest mobile phones as New Year's presents and was horrified when word came back that they didn't work. Later, at Gumi, he made a giant heap of the factory's entire inventory and had it set on fire.

Spending on R&D increased, and Samsung started churning out top-notch products, like the world's first MP3 phone, the highest-megapixel camera phones, and other high-end devices that could run on South Korea's superfast cellular networks. But much of the world, especially the USA, didn't associate the Samsung brand with mobiles.

By 2010, some three years after the launch of the iPhone, Samsung decided that its low-key approach wasn't working.

▶

◄

By June 2011, Samsung had already launched its second-generation Galaxy smartphone, the S II. The $4\frac{1}{3}$-inch device came with built-in near-field communication capabilities and a cool function that mutes incoming calls when the phone is placed face down.

Samsung spent $349m on marketing in the USA in the first three quarters of 2012, compared with $191m a year earlier, according to Kantar Media, a research firm. Samsung spent $8.7bn on R&D efforts in 2011. One in four of the company's 220,000 employees works in R&D. Much of the phone technology is developed and produced by groups in Asia, then tweaked and packaged locally. Researchers are currently experimenting with innovations like bendable screens and new memory technologies.

In fact, the operating system is freely available to all other phone-makers, including up-and-coming Chinese manufacturers that are developing cheaper phones. Then there's the fact that Android's parent, Google, now owns Motorola Mobility. It remains to be seen if Samsung will enjoy the same friendly partnership with Android if Google decides it wants Motorola to grab market share.

Samsung is working hard to build up its own content and services on top of Android, like its Music Hub offering, which allows users to purchase and download songs or store them in the cloud for streaming.

Samsung's executives won't say if they intend to develop their own operating system. Industry observers say that without full control over all the pieces – hardware and software – Samsung could be missing out on a huge opportunity: getting all its consumer-electronics products to work together seamlessly. With a proprietary operating system, Samsung could enable its TVs to talk to Samsung-made phones and even washing machines. Applications and content could easily be shared among the different devices, making Samsung's entire line of consumer electronics much, much stickier with consumers.

If Samsung doesn't keep involving and creating experiences that customers love, it may find itself on the way out – and maybe even the subject of a cheeky ad campaign.

- Can Samsung beat Apple and stay at the top for a long time? Discuss.

Source: based on *Fortune*, 4 February 2013.

Cost containment and international sourcing

global sourcing

buying components and materials from all over the world

outsourcing

letting other companies take over part of your production process

As global competition intensifies, profit margins are squeezed. To stay profitable, companies seek ways to keep costs within a range that permits competitive pricing. **Global sourcing**, a major driving force behind companies producing goods around the world, is used to minimise costs and risks. It is rapidly becoming a prerequisite to competing in today's marketplace.

Lower costs are not the only advantage to global sourcing; flexibility and dependability are also important benefits. Worldwide sources strengthen the reliability of quality and supply. Companies can achieve technical supremacy by securing access to innovative technology from offshore sources and perhaps prevent competitors from obtaining the technology as well. The uniqueness of a company's needs and their availability lead a company to source globally. To establish a foothold in markets that might otherwise be closed, companies may source some goods to comply with a country's local-content requirements.

India and China have emerged as prime locations for **outsourcing** all types of jobs. Hundreds of thousands of jobs from the EU and the USA have already moved to these locations. The jobs for which a monthly salary of €3,000 is normal in Europe are going for €500 in India or China. For more qualified jobs in computers and software where the average salary in the USA or Europe is around €6,000–7,000 a month, companies can hire qualified people for €1,000 in India and China.

In addition to these two locations, the new entrants to the EU, such as Poland, Hungary, the Czech Republic and Slovakia, have also joined the race to attract outsourced jobs from the USA and

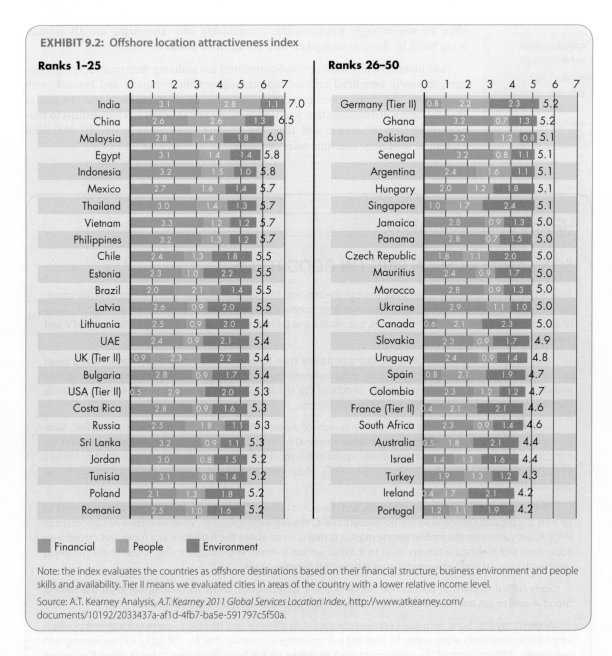

EXHIBIT 9.2: Offshore location attractiveness index

Ranks 1–25	Financial	People	Environment	Total
India	3.1	2.8	1.1	7.0
China	2.6	2.6	1.3	6.5
Malaysia	2.8	1.4	1.8	6.0
Egypt	3.1	1.4	1.4	5.8
Indonesia	3.2	1.5	1.0	5.8
Mexico	2.7	1.6	1.4	5.7
Thailand	3.0	1.4	1.3	5.7
Vietnam	3.3	1.2	1.2	5.7
Philippines	3.2	1.3	1.2	5.7
Chile	2.4	1.3	1.8	5.5
Estonia	2.3	1.0	2.2	5.5
Brazil	2.0	2.1	1.4	5.5
Latvia	2.6	0.9	2.0	5.5
Lithuania	2.5	0.9	2.0	5.4
UAE	2.4	0.9	2.1	5.4
UK (Tier II)	0.9	2.3	2.2	5.4
Bulgaria	2.8	0.9	1.7	5.4
USA (Tier II)	0.5	2.9	2.0	5.3
Costa Rica	2.8	0.9	1.6	5.3
Russia	2.5	1.8	1.1	5.3
Sri Lanka	3.2	0.9	1.1	5.3
Jordan	3.0	0.8	1.5	5.2
Tunisia	3.1	0.8	1.4	5.2
Poland	2.1	1.3	1.8	5.2
Romania	2.5	1.0	1.6	5.2

Ranks 26–50	Financial	People	Environment	Total
Germany (Tier II)	0.8	2.2	2.3	5.2
Ghana	3.2	0.7	1.3	5.2
Pakistan	3.2	1.2	0.8	5.1
Senegal	3.2	0.8	1.1	5.1
Argentina	2.4	1.6	1.1	5.1
Hungary	2.0	1.2	1.8	5.1
Singapore	1.0	1.7	2.4	5.1
Jamaica	2.8	0.9	1.3	5.0
Panama	2.8	0.7	1.5	5.0
Czech Republic	1.8	1.1	2.0	5.0
Mauritius	2.4	0.9	1.7	5.0
Morocco	2.8	0.9	1.3	5.0
Ukraine	2.9	1.1	1.0	5.0
Canada	0.6	2.1	2.3	5.0
Slovakia	2.3	0.9	1.7	4.9
Uruguay	2.4	0.9	1.4	4.8
Spain	0.8	2.1	1.9	4.7
Colombia	2.3	1.2	1.2	4.7
France (Tier II)	0.4	2.1	2.1	4.6
South Africa	2.3	0.9	1.4	4.6
Australia	0.5	1.8	2.1	4.4
Israel	1.4	1.3	1.6	4.4
Turkey	1.9	1.3	1.2	4.3
Ireland	0.4	1.7	2.1	4.2
Portugal	1.2	1.1	1.9	4.2

■ Financial   ■ People   ■ Environment

Note: the index evaluates the countries as offshore destinations based on their financial structure, business environment and people skills and availability. Tier II means we evaluated cities in areas of the country with a lower relative income level.

Source: A.T. Kearney Analysis, *A.T. Kearney 2011 Global Services Location Index*, http://www.atkearney.com/documents/10192/2033437a-af1d-4fb7-ba5e-591797c5f50a.

the EU. Exhibit 9.2 presents countries that are attracting outsourcing jobs, with an index of attractiveness.

Collaborative relationships

The accelerating rate of technological progress, market demand created by global industrialisation, and the creation of new middle classes will result in tremendous potential in global markets. But along with this surge in global demand comes an increase in competition as technology and management capabilities spread beyond global companies to new competitors from Asia, Europe and Latin America.[12]

Although global markets offer tremendous potential, companies seeking to function effectively in a fragmented global market of 5 billion people are being forced to stretch production, design and marketing resources and capabilities because of the intensity of competition and the pace of technology. Improving quality and staying on the cutting edge of technology are critical and basic for survival but

collaborative relationships

relationships between companies cooperating with each other for mutual benefit

often are not enough. Restructuring, reorganising and downsizing are all avenues being taken by firms to strengthen their competitive positions.

Additionally, many multinational companies are realising they must develop long-term, mutually beneficial relationships throughout the company and beyond: with competitors, suppliers, governments and customers. In short, multinational companies are developing orientations that focus on building **collaborative relationships** to promote long-term alliances, and they are seeking continuous, mutually beneficial exchanges instead of one-time sales or events.

Going International 9.3

SONY AND ERICSSON PART ON GOOD TERMS

Sony is buying out Ericsson's 50 per cent share in the business for €1.05bn ($1.5bn), and will integrate the smartphones created by the business into its broader 'four screen' strategy of reaching consumers through an array of network-connected computers, phones, televisions and tablets, all with access to Sony's music, film, TV and games content.

An alliance of 10 years between the two companies' then faltering mobile-phone divisions made a great deal of sense. Although Sony Ericsson never quite achieved its aim of beating Nokia to the number one spot in mobile phones, it had great success in the middle of the last decade with a number of mid-market handsets that incorporated Sony's Walkman and Cybershot brands.

Since the joint venture was formed, the launch of Apple's iPhones has transformed the market. Sony Ericsson's high-end, Xperia handsets have done reasonably well, taking about 11 per cent of the market for handsets using Google's Android operating system in the most recent quarter. But the competition continues to get tougher, with Nokia, Apple, Samsung and HTC all bringing out new Internet-connected handsets in the past month.

'They had some success in smartphones, but it was not enough. They were a niche player and they need to be a lot bigger,' said Francisco Jeronimo, analyst at IDC, the research company. 'What everyone has understood since Apple came into the mobile phone market is that it is not about the hardware any more, but creating an ecosystem and making customers loyal to it. What we see is Apple and Google trying to dominate the living room with connections between different devices,' Mr Jeronimo said.

Sony ruffled feathers at Ericsson by bringing out a tablet device under its own, rather than the shared, brand. A deal to get the PlayStation brand name on to a phone never quite materialised.

Analysts say that Sony, with huge content libraries at its disposal, will be able to carve out a strong position among the competing ecosystems. Sir Howard acknowledges, however, that he still faces some challenges in getting the different parts of the company to work together. He has been struggling to break down the various 'silos' inside Sony, even before integrating the handsets business.

Sony will have to get its strategy aligned fast, as analysts predict that the clash between competing, monolithic platforms will only intensify. With its alliance with Nokia, and its Xbox games console, Microsoft can already cover much of the same territory as Sony, while Apple is pushing into the living room with initiatives like Apple TV.

● Do you think it is a good move from Sony/Ericsson's point of view and future position?

Source: based on *Financial Times*, 27 October 2011.

These collaborative relationships are a mindset characterising an approach to management that can be described as relational exchanges. Relational exchanges occur: (1) internally among functional departments, business units, subsidiaries and employees; and (2) externally among customers (both intermediary and final), suppliers of goods and services, competitors, government agencies and related businesses where a mutually beneficial goal is sought.[13]

Collaborative relationships[14] can be grouped into two broad categories: relationship marketing – those relationships that focus on the marketing process; and strategic business enterprise.[9]

A study of CEOs of multinational companies on strategies for 2000 and beyond revealed that most felt that just satisfying the customer will not be enough. The focus will have to be more on the customer, who will be the strongest influence on the corporation.[15] Companies must rid themselves of the one-time-sale orientation, and focus instead on servicing the consumer's needs over time.

Relationship marketing

Relationship marketing is the category of collaborative relationships that focuses on the marketing process. Like all relational collaborations, relationship marketing has as its focus the creation, development and support of successful relational exchanges throughout the marketing process. The ultimate goal is to achieve a competitive advantage by establishing long-term, mutually beneficial associations with loyal, satisfied customers.[16]

To build a sustainable relationship with customers, businesses are changing their attitudes towards internal relationships and between themselves and traditional competitors, suppliers, distributors and retailers. It becomes a matter of working with customers and all others involved to produce goods that best serve the customer's needs.

Why relationship marketing? It helps cement customer loyalty, which means repeat sales and referrals and, thus, market share and revenue growth. A consulting company study estimates that a decrease in customer defection rate of 5 per cent can boost profits by 25 to 95 per cent. The adage that 20 per cent of your customers account for 50 to 80 per cent of your profits has some merit. It has always been good business to focus company resources on the best customers rather than those who are strictly price shoppers.[17] Relationship marketing strengthens that focus.

Formulating international marketing strategy

Strategic planning means designing ways to achieve growth of the firm, which often means going to new markets and/or developing new products. It may stem from a saturated home market or development of a competitive product/service that can be tried in new markets. However, knowledge of the foreign market is necessary to take the firm abroad. It is also restricted by resources and management perceptions/goals.

Considering the above, a company needs to adopt a **generic strategy** for the company as a whole. It is called 'generic' because it can be applied as an overall strategy across markets and products. Specific marketing strategies for each market/product are used as sub-strategies. Having a generic strategy does not mean having a standardised strategy for all markets and products. In fact, companies often use different marketing strategies for different markets for the same product or business unit. These strategies are influenced by the overall corporate strategy, the particular customer segment, positioning, product life cycle and market environment in the particular market. This is illustrated in Exhibit 9.3.

Companies normally use one of the two generic strategies: **differentiation strategy** or **focus strategy**. Differentiation strategy is one in which the marketer is trying to convince the market/customers that his or her product is different from that of his or her competitors. The company tries to give the message that its product offers

generic strategy
core strategy for the company as a whole

differentiation strategy
when the marketer tries to convince the market that his or her product is different from that of other competitors

focus strategy
when a company decides to focus on a particular market segment or part of the product line

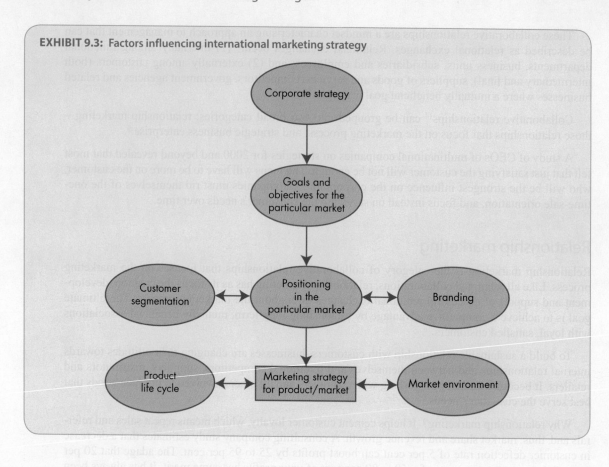

EXHIBIT 9.3: Factors influencing international marketing strategy

more value. In some cases it is done as offering premium quality and premier prices, while in other cases it is done as a low-cost advantage. For example, BMW is using differentiation strategy by conveying to the market that its cars have better quality and other features offering prestige and status. It can thus charge higher prices than its competitors: Audi, Volvo, Honda Accord and Toyota Camry.

Aldi, Lidl and Wal-Mart, on the other hand, are also using differentiation strategies and trying to convince the market/customers that they can provide more value for the money they spend by selling groceries at lowest prices. These companies thus claim to have a low-cost strategy. Companies such as easyJet and Ryanair are also good examples. This differentiation offers value to the customer, which has to be visible/verifiable.

Many companies make the mistake of promising to provide value to the customer which is not visible or valued by the customer to justify the premier price or the claims of low cost. Some companies try to offer other features as 'differentiation' such as convenience to order or delivery at home. Amazon is a good example of this type of company.

The key issue is, however, that a company has to develop a differentiation from the customer's perspective. In the 'quality and premier pricing' differentiation, the customer has to be convinced that the product is of superior quality as compared to competitors' to justify the premier price. When used properly, it provides **sustainable competitive advantage (SCA)**. In both cases, low-cost or quality differentiation strategies, the company can achieve SCA by being consistent.

Focus strategy is applied when a company decides to focus on a particular market segment or part of the product line. The company using this strategy does not want to compete across the whole market. This may be due to lack of resources, which means that the company cannot support multiple brands. Another reason might be that the

sustainable competitive advantage (SCA)

advantages over other competitors, enjoyed over a long period in the future company wants to provide a better match between its offer and customer needs/wants, thus creating SCA for itself. Companies such as Apple, Porsche and Harley-Davidson are good examples of companies using this strategy.

Having decided the overall strategy, a company needs to deal with positioning and branding that is consistent with the strategy chosen. These two aspects become crucial in formulation and then implementation of the strategy.

Going International 9.4

BMW, AUDI AND MERCEDES' DUAL STRATEGY TO PRODUCE MORE LOCALLY AND IMPORT HIGHER-END MODELS

Germany's luxury carmakers BMW, Audi and Mercedes-Benz are embarking on a two-pronged game plan to boost sales: produce more cars locally, thereby making them more price-competitive, and, at the same time, import new models – at least a dozen between the three of them – to keep the allure of their brands going.

© Istockphoto.com/vesilvio

BMW will assemble its flagship 7 Series sedan at the Chennai plant from next year and later roll out the all-new compact hatchback 1 Series from the same plant. BMW plans to launch three new products next year to maintain its leadership over Audi and Mercedes-Benz.

BMW is currently struggling to hit the previous fiscal year's level of sales. It has sold 12 per cent fewer cars in the April to October period even as arch-rival Audi's sales jumped 53 per cent in this period, resulting in both carmakers running neck and neck with sales of a little over 5,000 sedans and SUVs.

Philipp von Sahr, BMW Group India's newly-appointed president, remains confident of achieving the previous year's target. 'We are not chasing volumes, but are surely looking at some improvement in sales helped by the new product launches. We faced a slack period due to the model change of the high-volume 3 Series sedan, but will gain incremental numbers with the recently launched X-6 and other models.'

BMW launched the new X6 Sports Activity Coupe at a Delhi ex-showroom price of Rs79 lakh for the diesel variant and Rs93.4 lakh for petrol. It also plans to almost double its dealerships in India to 50 by 2014. Meantime, Audi will start assembling its compact SUV, the Q3, next year and will bring out the new version of its hugely popular Q5 SUV.

The all-new R8 PI coupe is also expected and the company is contemplating bringing the Audi S6 sedan to the Indian market. It has already launched the S4 sports sedan, the Q3 SUV and the iconic TT coupe to increase its portfolio, and would double its dealerships across India to 25 by the end of the 2012 calendar year. Mercedes-Benz has been lagging behind with sales of 3,651 cars in the first seven months of the fiscal year, a 10 per cent decline in relation to a year ago.

'We would start assembling the new GL Class SUV at our Pune plant next year. Besides, the all-new S Class, B Class CDI and the all-new A Class in both diesel and petrol variants are also a part of the launch plan of 2013,' a senior Mercedes-Benz executive added. From just 3,000 cars five years back, more than 25,000 cars are being sold every year, and demand is expected to exceed 100,000 by 2020.

Source: based on *The Economic Times*, 23 November 2012.

Positioning

> **positioning**
> creating an image of your product and its quality in customers' minds

Positioning is not what you do with the product, but what you do to the customer's mind. The better you understand the mind, the better you understand how positioning works. This means that companies are battling to capture the mind of the customer. This task has become more difficult due to an overload of information and communication by companies and other organisations such as Greenpeace and the World Trade Organization. The market is no longer responsive to old strategies because there are simply too many companies, too many products and too much communication/information in the market.

The most effective way of positioning a company/product is to know your customer segment and concentrate on understanding this target group, and create an image that matches with their needs/wants. Advertising is only one way to communicate with customers; companies communicate with their markets in many ways. Positioning is thus considered a systematic way to find a window into the customer's mind. It has to be done at the right time and under the right circumstances. Moreover, it has to be done constantly and consistently. Companies such as Apple and Gillette try to position themselves as most innovative and leaders in their industries, and they have consistently tried to do that through communication.

Going International 9.5

APPLE'S RUN TO THE TOP

The iPod nano.
© Apple. Http://www.apple.com/pr/products/

In the 15 years between 1996 and 2011, Apple has gone from a quirky, small PC competitor near bankruptcy to the world's most valuable company.[18] This remarkable change of fortunes required daring strategies, intuitive innovation and well-executed commercialisation but also for the established players to miss new market opportunities and the changes in demand in their markets. Apple's competition is not alone in these mistakes: the Australian car industry missing the shift of demand towards small cars, Australian retail ignoring online shopping, Prodigy ignoring AOL and Blockbuster ignoring Netflix at the dawn of the Internet era, or Kodak missing the digital photography revolution completely[19] are just some examples where the combination of inattentiveness to the customer and the desire to keep playing on old strengths can bring the demise of once powerful competitors.

Microsoft, in direct competition with Apple and the dominant IT player in the 1990s, was regularly a laggard in game-changing technologies such as the Internet. In addition, Microsoft, concentrating on its large corporate clients, missed the change in demand as the consumer market moved to the mass market phase and the early majority began to demand easy access to digital content and more user-friendly consumer devices 'that just work'. At the same time the music industry was wary of new, purely digital distribution channels, and Sony was reluctant to develop a competent digital version of its Walkman, leaving a perfect opening for the iPod.

▶

◄

Apple was able to leverage its business assets (such as its supply chain in digital goods and software capabilities) to develop the iPod and iPhone. The physical product would have been imitable, but the brilliance of the strategy was that the plethora of third-party application providers and media content owners connected through a single marketplace (iTunes).[20] Apple has repeated the successful formula of filling unoccupied differentiated product spaces by innovating, the results being the iPhone and its killer app, mobile Internet,[21] iTab, and now the latest rumoured venture, the iTV.[22] Each innovation was able to uncover a large market whose needs have not been previously met, and through the combination of being an early mover and skilful marketing/commercialisation, realise high prices and above-average profitability. Ironically Microsoft, by not protecting the consumer markets, has allowed Apple to grow strong and now, through young employees exerting pressure on IT departments, Apple is able to make inroads into Microsoft's heartland, the corporate market, as well.[23]

● Can Apple maintain its leadership?

Source: based on aubartus.com, 'Strategic Positioning of Apple in the Post-PC Markets', 2012, http://aubartus.com/blog/strategic-positioning-of-apple-in-the-post-pc-markets/.

Every now and then companies need to reposition themselves as a result of changes in the marketplace or changes in customer tastes. There are several such examples: McDonald's has been trying to reposition itself from a company perceived to be selling 'fast food' or 'junk food' or 'unhealthy food' towards a company selling healthy food; digital photography has forced Kodak to reposition itself as more and more customers have moved from film cameras to digital cameras; Toyota had to reposition itself, or create a new positioning, when it wanted to cover the luxury car market, initially in the USA, by introducing the Lexus.

Due to constant changes in technology, consumer tastes and competition, companies are increasingly in danger of losing their positioning. If companies are not proactive in analysing their positioning and repositioning, whenever needed, they lose their markets. The American automobile industry, Sega and Nintendo game consoles, WordPerfect and Lotus spreadsheet software are good examples of companies that lost their positioning; while Apple, IBM and Samsung are good examples of successfully repositioning companies and products.

Product life cycle and international marketing strategy

Most products go through the different stages of a life cycle; each stage demands different marketing strategies due to different market conditions. There is no fixed-length **product life cycle (PLC)**. It represents the sales history of a particular product following an S-shaped curve, which is divided into four **PLC stages**: introduction, growth, maturity and decline (see Exhibit 9.4). However, all products do not necessarily follow the S-shape through all four stages. Some products die after the first stage (introduction), while others mature very quickly.

Different stages of the PLC have different characteristics and the marketing objectives in each stage are different. Due to these differences, a marketer has to apply different marketing strategies in different stages. The intensity of competition increases with the stages and finally reaches a point where the market starts declining. At this point, companies can revive the PLC by introducing new features to the product. This is done successfully by automobile companies, by introducing new models every four or five years. Gillette razors are good examples of this strategy when the company keeps introducing the next generation of shaving razors, from Gillette Sensor to Mach 3 to Mach 3 Turbo and Mach 3 Power to six-blade Fusion and Fusion Proglide.

product life cycle (PLC)

different stages in a product's life, from introduction to death

PLC stages

stages in the product life cycle: introduction, growth, maturity and decline

EXHIBIT 9.4: Perspectives of the product life cycle

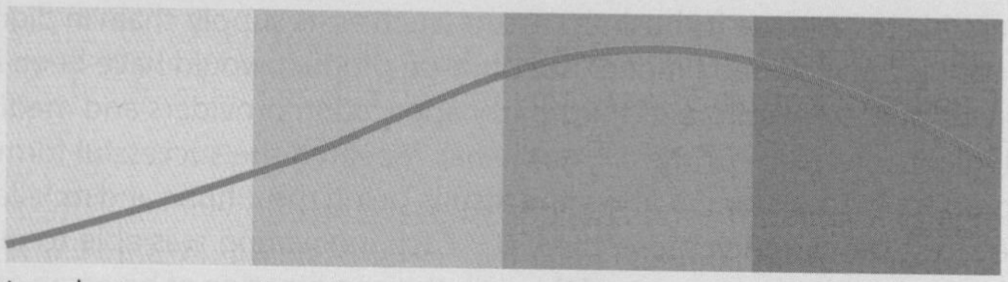

	Introduction	Growth	Maturity	Decline
Marketing objectives	Create product awareness and trial	Maximise market share	Maximise profit while defending market share	Reduce expenditure and milk the brand
Marketing strategies				
Product	Offer a basic product	Offer product extensions, service, warranty	Diversify brands and models	Phase out weak items
Price	Use cost-plus	Price to penetrate market	Price to match or beat competitors	Cut price
Distribution	Build selective distribution	Build intensive distribution	Build more intensive distribution	Go selective: phase out unprofitable outlets
Advertising	Build product awareness among early adopters and dealers	Build awareness and interest in the mass market	Stress brand differences and benefits	Reduce to level needed to retain hardcore loyals
Sales promotion	Use heavy sales promotion to entice trial	Reduce to take advantage of heavy consumer demand	Increase to encourage brand switching	Reduce to minimal level

Source: based on Philip Kotler, *Marketing Management: Analysis, Planning, Implementation and Control* (New Delhi: Prentice Hall of India, 2007).

Strategic planning

strategic planning

a systematised way of relating to the future

Strategic planning is a systematised way of relating to the future. It is an attempt to manage the effects of external, uncontrollable factors on the firm's strengths, weaknesses, objectives and goals to attain a desired end. Further, it is a commitment of resources to a country market to achieve specific goals. In other words, planning is the job of making things happen that may not otherwise occur. There is a lot of discussion on the goals of a company, and scholars often agree that the growth of the firm is the ultimate goal. All the big companies started off as smaller companies and, with clear goals for their growth, they have reached the desired status (see Exhibit 9.5). Companies of today have emerged out of several strategic decisions.

EXHIBIT 9.5: Mergers and cooperation in the auto industry

The auto industry has been consolidating since the 1960s when there were 42 companies. The number of companies decreased to 10–12 in 2012 and the consolidation is still going on. In 2004 the following groups were present.

1	GM	General Motors, Fiat, Alfa Romeo, Ferrari, Subaru, Suzuki, Daewoo, Kia, Lotus, Opel, Cadillac, Chevrolet, Pontiac, Buick, Saturn, Vauxhall and Isuzu
2	Ford	Ford, Mazda, Aston Martin and Lancia
3	VW	VW, Porsche, SEAT, Audi, Skoda and Bentley
4	Toyota	Toyota, Lexus and Daihatsu
5	Daimler-Chrysler	Mercedes, Chrysler, Mitsubishi, Hyundai and Smart
6	BMW	BMW, Rolls-Royce and Mini
7	Peugeot	Peugeot and Citroën
8	Renault	Renault, Nissan and Samsung
9	Tata	TATA Jaguar and Land Rover
10	Honda	Honda
11–12	A couple of Chinese companies	

Sources: compiled from M. Geutz, 'Turning Wheels between Europe, America and Asia: Mergers, Acquisition and Cooperation', paper presented at Carnegie Bosch Institute, Berlin, October 2001; and *Auto Intelligence*, 2002.

Going International 9.6

BATTLE OF THE GIANTS

From 1999 to 2000 Gillette was steadily losing market share to Schick. Traditionally, Gillette owned the razor and blade category in the market, and Jim Kilts, the company CEO, even laid out a strategy to lengthen the amount of time between major new product launches: with little competition in the market, it made sense to slow down spending on R&D. However, the purchase of Schick by Energiser created a serious rival for Gillette. Gillette has already seen its market share in women's blades eroding, and now its share in the male blade market, controlled by its top-selling three-blade razor Mach 3, is being threatened by the introduction of Schick's Quattro four-blade razor.

However, Gillette may have a chance to not only recover market share, but also lay successful claim to Schick's Quattro-generated revenues: Gillette launched a lawsuit seeking to ban Quattro from the market on the basis of patent infringement. The patent suit against Schick centres on the position of Quattro's blades. In developing Mach 3 in the 1990s, Gillette hit upon a way to achieve a closer shave without irritating the skin: the razor aligned blades progressively closer to the skin so that each one cut closer than the last.

Mach 3 is covered by over 50 patents describing the position of the blades in excruciating detail. Gillette claims

▶

◀

that the technology applies whether one uses three blades, four or five. If Gillette wins the case, the damages awarded will be more than substantial considering the tremendous sales generated by top-selling razors (in 2002, Mach 3 produced $2bn in revenues). However, even if Gillette wins, the company must face the fact that it is for the first time dealing with a serious rival. In 2004, Gillette introduced M3 Power, a battery-driven razor. Now, we have to see how Schick is going to counter that move.

● Do you think Gillette is justified in taking Schick to court for its Quattro?

Source: adapted from Victoria Griffith, 'Schick and Gillette Take Fight to the Edge', *Financial Times*, 16 September 2003, p 31.

Is there a difference between strategic planning for a domestic company and for an international company? The principles of planning are not in themselves different, but the intricacies of the operating environments of the multinational corporation (host country, home and corporate environments), its organisational structure and the task of controlling a multi-country operation create differences in the complexity and process of international planning.

Strategic planning allows for rapid growth of the international function, changing markets, increasing competition and the ever-varying challenges of different national markets. The plan must blend the changing parameters of external country environments with corporate objectives and capabilities to develop a sound, workable marketing programme. A strategic plan commits corporate resources to products and markets to increase competitiveness and profits.

Planning relates to the formulation of goals and methods of accomplishing them, so it is both a process and a philosophy. Structurally, planning may be viewed as corporate, strategic and/or tactical. International planning at the corporate level is essentially long term, incorporating generalised goals for the enterprise as a whole.

tactical planning

a systematic way of handling the issues and problems of today

market planning

a systematic way of producing and selling a product on a long-term basis

Strategic planning is conducted at the highest levels of management, and deals with products, capital and research, and the long- and short-term goals of the company. **Tactical planning** or **market planning** pertains to specific actions and to the allocation of resources used to implement strategic planning goals in specific markets. Tactical plans are made at the local level and address marketing and advertising questions.

A major advantage to a company involved in strategic planning is the discipline imposed by the process. An international marketer who has gone through the planning process has a framework for analysing marketing problems and opportunities, and a basis for coordinating information from different country markets. The process of planning may be as important as the plan itself because it forces decision-makers to examine all factors that affect the success of a marketing programme and involves those who will be responsible for its implementation.

Company objectives and resources

Evaluation of a company's objectives and resources is crucial in all stages of planning for international operations. Each new market entered can require a complete evaluation, including existing commitments, relative to the parent company's objectives and resources. As markets grow increasingly competitive, as companies find new opportunities, and as the cost of entering foreign markets increases, companies need such planning.

Foreign market opportunities do not always parallel corporate objectives; it may be necessary to change the objectives, alter the scale of international plans or abandon them. One market may offer immediate profit but have a poor long-run outlook, while another may offer the reverse. Only when corporate objectives are clear can such differences be reconciled effectively.

International commitment

The strategic planning approach taken by an international firm affects the degree of internationalisation to which management is philosophically committed. Such commitment affects the specific international strategies and decisions of the firm. After company objectives have been identified, management needs to determine whether it is prepared to make the level of commitment required for successful international operations – commitment in terms of resources to be invested, personnel for managing the international organisation and determination to stay in the market long enough to realise a return on these investments.

The planning process

Whether a company is marketing in several countries or entering a foreign market for the first time, planning is a major factor of success. The first-time foreign marketer must decide what products to develop, in which markets, and with what level of resource commitment. For the company already committed, the key decisions involve allocating effort and resources among countries and products, deciding on new markets to develop or old ones to withdraw from, and which products to develop or drop. Guidelines and systematic procedures are essential for evaluating international opportunities and risks and for developing strategic plans to take advantage of such opportunities. The process illustrated in Exhibit 9.6 offers a systematic guide to planning for the multinational firm operating in several countries.

Phase 1: preliminary analysis and screening – matching company/country needs

Whether a company is new to international marketing or already heavily involved, an evaluation of potential markets is the first step in the planning process. A critical first question in the international planning process is deciding in which existing country market to make a market investment. A company's strengths and weaknesses, products, philosophies and objectives must be matched with a country's constraining factors as well as limitations and potential. In the first part of the planning process, countries are analysed and screened to eliminate those that do not offer sufficient potential for further consideration.

The next step is to establish screening criteria against which prospective countries can be evaluated. These criteria are ascertained by an analysis of company objectives, resources and other corporate capabilities and limitations. It is important to determine the reasons for entering a foreign market and the returns expected from such an investment.

A company's commitment to international business and objectives for going international are important in establishing evaluation criteria. Minimum market potential, minimum profit, return on investment, acceptable competitive levels, standards of political stability, acceptable legal requirements and other measures appropriate for the company's products are examples of the evaluation criteria to be established.

Once evaluation criteria are set, a complete analysis of the environment within which a company plans to operate is made. The environment consists of the uncontrollable elements discussed earlier and includes both home-country and host-country restraints, marketing objectives and any other company limitations or strengths that exist at the beginning of each planning period.

Although an understanding of uncontrollable environments is important in domestic market planning, the task is more complex in foreign marketing because each country under consideration presents the foreign marketer with a different set of unfamiliar environmental constraints. It is this stage in the planning process that more than anything else distinguishes international from domestic marketing planning. The results of phase 1 provide the marketer with the basic information necessary to:

1 evaluate the potential of a proposed country market

2 identify problems that would eliminate the country from further consideration

3 identify environmental elements that need further analysis

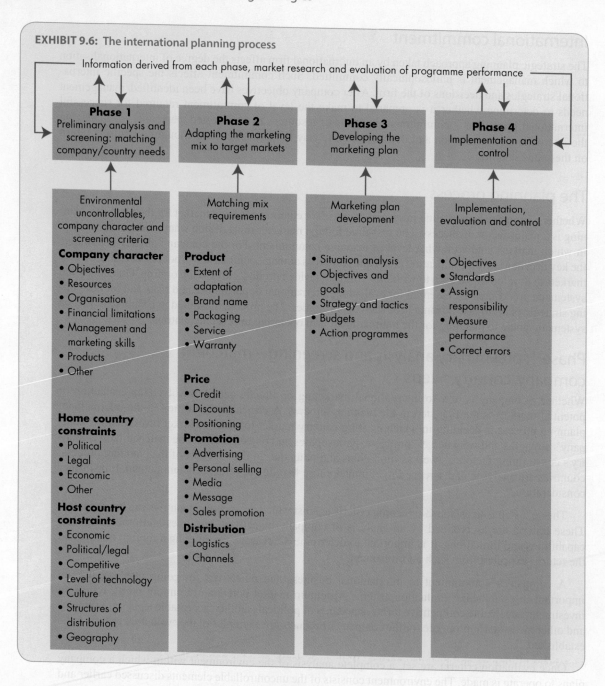

EXHIBIT 9.6: The international planning process

Information derived from each phase, market research and evaluation of programme performance

Phase 1
Preliminary analysis and screening: matching company/country needs

Phase 2
Adapting the marketing mix to target markets

Phase 3
Developing the marketing plan

Phase 4
Implementation and control

Environmental uncontrollables, company character and screening criteria

Company character
• Objectives
• Resources
• Organisation
• Financial limitations
• Management and marketing skills
• Products
• Other

Home country constraints
• Political
• Legal
• Economic
• Other

Host country constraints
• Economic
• Political/legal
• Competitive
• Level of technology
• Culture
• Structures of distribution
• Geography

Matching mix requirements

Product
• Extent of adaptation
• Brand name
• Packaging
• Service
• Warranty

Price
• Credit
• Discounts
• Positioning

Promotion
• Advertising
• Personal selling
• Media
• Message
• Sales promotion

Distribution
• Logistics
• Channels

Marketing plan development

• Situation analysis
• Objectives and goals
• Strategy and tactics
• Budgets
• Action programmes

Implementation, evaluation and control

• Objectives
• Standards
• Assign responsibility
• Measure performance
• Correct errors

4 determine which part of the marketing mix must be adapted to meet local market needs

5 develop and implement a marketing action plan.

Information generated in phase 1 helps a company avoid the mistakes that plagued Radio Shack Corporation, a leading merchandiser of consumer electronic equipment in the USA, when it first went international. Radio Shack's early attempts at international marketing in Western Europe resulted in a series of costly mistakes that could have been avoided had it properly analysed the uncontrollable elements of the countries targeted for the first attempt at multinational marketing. The company scheduled its first Christmas promotion for 25 December in the Netherlands, unaware that the Dutch celebrate St. Nicholas Day and gift-giving on 5 December.

Legal problems in various countries interfered with some of its plans; it was unaware that most European countries have laws prohibiting the sale of citizen-band radios, one of the company's most lucrative US products and one it expected to sell in Europe. A free flashlight promotion in German stores was promptly stopped by German courts because giveaways violate German sales laws. In Belgium, the company overlooked a law requiring a government tax stamp on all window signs, and poorly selected store sites resulted in many of the new stores closing shortly after opening.

Phase 2: adapting the marketing mix to target markets

A more detailed examination of the components of the **marketing mix** is the purpose of phase 2. When target markets are selected, the market mix must be evaluated in light of the data generated in phase 1. In which ways can the product, promotion, price and distribution be standardised and in which ways must they be adapted to meet target market requirements?

> **marketing mix**
>
> optimal combination of product, price, place (distribution) and promotion

Incorrect decisions at this point lead to costly mistakes through efficiency loss from lack of standardisation, products inappropriate for the intended market and/or costly mistakes in improper pricing, advertising and promotional blunders. The primary goal of phase 2 is to decide on a marketing mix adjusted to the cultural constraints imposed by the uncontrollable elements of the environment, which effectively achieves corporate objectives and goals.

An example of the type of analysis done in phase 2 is the process used by Nestlé. Each product manager has a country factbook that includes much of the information suggested in phase 1. The country factbook analyses in detail a variety of culturally related questions. In Germany, the product manager for coffee must furnish answers to a number of questions. How does a German rank coffee in the hierarchy of consumer products? Is Germany a high or a low per capita consumption market? (These facts alone can be of enormous consequence.)

In Sweden the annual per capita consumption of coffee is 18 pounds, while in Japan it is half a gram!) How is coffee used – in bean form, ground or powdered? If it is ground, how is it brewed? Which coffee is preferred – Brazilian Santos blended with Colombian coffee or robusta from the Cote d'Ivoire? Is it roasted? Do the people prefer dark roasted or blonde coffee? (The colour of Nestlé's soluble coffee must resemble as closely as possible the colour of the coffee consumed in the country.) As a result of the answers to these and other questions, Nestlé produces 200 types of instant coffee (Nescafé), from the dark robust espresso preferred in Latin countries to the lighter blends popular in the USA.

Almost €45m ($50m) a year is spent in four research laboratories around the world experimenting with new shadings in colour, aroma and flavour. Do the Germans drink coffee after lunch or with their breakfast? Do they take it black or with cream or milk? Do they drink coffee in the evening? Do they sweeten it? (In France, the answer is clear: in the morning, coffee with milk; at noon, black coffee – ie two totally different coffees.)

At what age do people begin drinking coffee? Is it a traditional beverage as in France? Is it a form of rebellion among the young as in England where coffee drinking has been taken up in defiance of tea-drinking parents? Or is it a gift, as in Japan? There is a coffee boom in tea-drinking Japan where Nescafé is considered a luxury gift item; instead of chocolates and flowers, Nescafé is toted in fancy containers to dinners and birthday parties. With such depth of information, the product manager can evaluate the marketing mix in terms of the information in the country factbook.

Phase 2 also permits the marketer to determine possibilities for standardisation. By grouping all countries together and looking at similarities, market characteristics that can be standardised become evident.

Frequently, the results of the analysis in phase 2 indicate that the marketing mix would require such drastic adaptation that a decision not to enter a particular market is made. For example, a product may have to be reduced in physical size to fit the needs of the market, but the additional manufacturing cost of a smaller size may be too high to justify market entry. Also, the price required to show a profit might be too high for a majority of the market to afford. If there is no way to reduce the price, sales potential at the higher price may be too low to justify entry.

On the other hand, additional research in this phase may provide information that can suggest ways to standardise marketing programmes among two or more country markets. This was the case for Nestlé when research revealed that young coffee drinkers in England and Japan had identical motivations. As a result, Nestlé now uses principally the same message in both markets.

The answers to three major questions are generated in phase 2:

1 Which elements of the marketing mix can be standardised and where is standardisation not culturally possible?

2 Which cultural/environmental adaptations are necessary for successful acceptance of the marketing mix?

3 Will adaptation costs allow profitable market entry?

Based on the results in phase 2, a second screening of countries may take place, with some countries dropped from further consideration. The next phase in the planning process is development of a marketing plan.

Phase 3: developing the marketing plan

At this stage of the planning process, a marketing plan is developed for the target market – whether a single country or a global market set. It begins with a situation analysis and culminates in a specific action programme for the market. The specific plan establishes what is to be done, by whom, how it is to be done and when. Included are budgets and sales and profit expectations. Just as in phase 2, a decision not to enter a specific market may be made if it is determined that company marketing objectives and goals cannot be met.

Phase 4: implementation and control

A 'go' decision in phase 3 triggers implementation of specific plans and anticipation of successful marketing. However, the planning process does not end at this point. All marketing plans require coordination and control (phase 4) during the period of implementation. Many businesses do not control marketing plans as thoroughly as they could, even though continuous monitoring and control could increase their success. An evaluation and control system requires performance objective action; that is, to bring the plan back on track should standards of performance fall short. A global orientation facilitates the difficult but extremely important management tasks of coordinating and controlling the complexities of international marketing.

While the model is presented as a series of sequential phases, the planning process is a dynamic, continuous set of interacting variables with information continuously building among phases. The phases outline a crucial path to be followed for effective, systematic planning. Furthermore, it provides the basis for viewing all country markets and their interrelationships as an integrated global unit.[24] By following the guidelines presented in Part 6, 'The Country Notebook – A Guide for Developing a Marketing Plan', the international marketer can put the strategic planning process into operation.[25]

SUMMARY

Expanding markets around the world have increased competition for all levels of international marketing. To keep abreast of the competition and maintain a viable position for increasingly competitive markets, a global perspective is necessary. Global competition also requires quality products designed to meet ever-changing customer needs and rapidly advancing technology. Cost containment, customer satisfaction and a greater number of players mean that every opportunity to refine international business practices must be examined in the light of company goals. Collaborative relationships, strategic international alliances and strategic planning are important avenues to global marketing that must be implemented in the planning of global marketing management.

Companies normally follow generic strategies as overall corporate strategies. These strategies are differentiation strategy or focus strategy. The choice of these strategies leads to sub-strategies for each and every product and market. These sub-strategies are influenced by a number of factors, such as branding, positioning and customer segments, the life cycle of the particular product and the market environment. This is achieved through a systematic marketing planning process.

QUESTIONS

1 Define strategic planning. How does strategic planning for international marketing differ from domestic marketing?

2 Discuss the benefits to an MNC of accepting the global market concept.

3 Define the concept of quality. How do the concept of quality and TQM relate?

4 Cost containment and technological improvement are said to be the basis for competition. Why? Discuss.

5 What is meant by positioning? Explain.

6 Explain the three points that define a global approach to international marketing.

7 Branding is considered a part of strategy – discuss how valuable branding is for a consumer products company. Give examples.

8 What is the importance of collaborative relationships to competition?

9 Discuss what is meant by relationship marketing and how it differs from traditional marketing.

10 In phases 1 and 2 of the international planning process, countries may be dropped from further consideration as potential markets. Discuss some of the conditions in each phase that may exist in a country that would lead a marketer to exclude it.

11 Assume that you are the director of international marketing for a company producing refrigerators. Select one country in Asia and one in Europe and develop screening criteria to use in evaluating the two countries. Make any additional assumptions that are necessary about your company.

FURTHER READING

- P.J.Buckley and P.N. Ghauri, 'Globalisation, Economic Geography and the Strategy of Multinational Enterprises', *Journal of International Business Studies*, 2004, 35(2), pp 81–98.

- P.N. Ghauri, U. Elg, V. Tarnovskaya and F. Wang, 'Developing a Market Driving Strategy for Foreign Markets: Internal Capabilities and External Activities', *Schmalenbach Business Review*, 2011, 11(3), 1–23.

- S. Schmid and T. Kotulla, ' 50 years of Research on International Standardization and Adaptation – from a Systematic Literature Analysis to a Theoretical Framework', *International Business Review*, 2011, 20(5), 491–507.

NOTES

1 John Dunning, *Making Globalization Good: The Moral Challenges of Global Capitalism* (Oxford: Oxford University Press, 2003).

2 X. Martin, 'Solving Theoretical and Empirical Conundrums in International Strategy Research: Linking Foreign Entry Modes and Performance', *Journal of International Business Studies,* 2013, 44(1), 28–41.

3 R. Aggarwal, J. Berrill, E. Hutson and C. Kearney, ' What is a Multinational Corporation: Classifying a Degree of Firm-level Multinationality', *International Business Review,* 2011, 20(5), 557–77.

4 Cyndee Miller, 'Chasing the Global Dream', *Marketing News*, 2 December 1996, pp 1–2.

5 Peter Buckley, *Multinational Firms, Cooperation and Competition in the World Economy* (Basingstoke: Macmillan, 1992).

6   A.K. Kohli and B.J. Jaworski, 'Market Orientation: The Construct, Research Proposition and Management Implications', *Journal of Marketing*, 1990, 54(2), 1–18.

7   B.J. Jaworski, A.K. Kohli and A. Sahay, 'Market Driven versus Market Driving Firms', *Journal of the Academy of Marketing Science*, 2000, 28(1), pp 45–54.

8   P.N. Ghauri, V. Tarnovskaya and U. Elg, 'Market Driving Multinationals and their Global Sourcing Network', *International Marketing Review*, 2008, 25(5), 504–19.

9   U. Elg, P.N. Ghauri and V. Tarnovskaya, 'The Role of Networks and Matching in Market Entry to Emerging Retail Markets', *International Marketing Review*, 2008, 25(6), 674–99.

10 James B. Shein, *Reversing the Slide: A Strategic Guide to Turnarounds and Corporate Renewal*, (San Francisco, CA: Jossey-Bass, 2011).

11 M.-J. Oesterle, H.N. Richta and J.H. Fisch, ' The Influence of Ownership Structure on Internationalization', *International Business Review*, 2013, 22(1), 187–201.

12 This section draws on Robert M. Morgan and Shelby D. Hunt, 'The Commitment–trust Theory of Relationship Marketing', *Journal of Marketing*, July 1994, pp 20–38.

13 U. Elg, S. Deligonul, E. Cavusgil and P.N. Ghauri, 'Developing Strategic Supplier Networks: An Institutional Perspective', *Journal of Business Research*, 2013, 66(4), 506–15.

14 The authors prefer to use the term *collaborative relationship* to refer to all forms of collaborative effort between a company and its customers, markets, suppliers, manufacturing partners, research and development partners, government agencies and all other types of alliance. Consumer orientation, *Keiretsu* and strategic alliances can all be grouped under the broad rubric of collaborative relationships. All seek similar universal 'truths': participant satisfaction, long-term ties, loyalty and mutually beneficial exchanges, yet there are some fundamental differences among them.

15 Saeed Smiee and Peter Walters, 'Relationship Marketing in an International Context', *International Business Review*, 2003, 12(2), 193–214.

16 For a complete discussion of the logic of SIAs, see Kenichi Ohmae, *The Borderless World* (New York: Harper Business, 1990), Ch 8, 'The Global Logic of Strategic Alliances', pp 114–36; and Kenichi Ohmae, 'Putting Global Logic First', *Harvard Business Review*, 1995, 73(1), 119–25.

17 This section draws on Michael Porter, *Competitive Advantage: Creating and Sustaining Superior Performance* (New York: Free Press, 1985); and Harold Chee and Rod Haris, *Global Marketing Strategy* (London: FT Management, 1998).

18 J. Menn and E. Crooks, 'Apple Touches Top Spot by Capitalisation', *Financial Times*, 10 August 2011, http://www.ft.com/cms/s/0/516e690e-c2d8-11e0-8cc7-00144feabdc0.html#axzz1kFiUiW72.

19 'How Kodak Squandered Every Single Digital Opportunity It Had', *The Age*, 23 January 2012, http://www.theage.com.au/digital-life/cameras/how-kodak-squandered-every-single-digital-opportunity-it-had-20120123-1qcui.html.

20 M. Kenney and B. Pon, 'Structuring the Smartphone Industry: Is the Mobile Internet OS Platform the Key?', *Journal of Industry, Competition and Trade*, 2011, 11(3), 239–61.

21 J. West and M. Mace, 'Browsing as the Killer App: Explaining the Rapid Success of Apple's iPhone,' *Telecommunications Policy*, 2010, 34(5–6), 270–86.

22 R. Blackden, 'Living Room Plan is Apple's to the Core', *The Age*, 23 January 2010, http://www.theage.com.au/business/world-business/living-room-plan-is-apples-to-the-core-20120122-1qc4f.html.

23 U. Elg, S. Delgonul, W. Denis and P.N. Ghauri, 'Market-driving Strategy Implementation through Global Supplier Relationships', *Industrial Marketing Management* 2012, 41, 919–28.

24 B.I. Park and P.N. Ghauri, 'Key Factors Affecting Acquisition of Technological Capabilities from Foreign Acquiring Firms by Small and Medium Sized Local Firms', *Journal of World Business*, 2011, 46(1), 116–25.

25 C.K. Prahalad and K. Lieberthal, 'The End of Corporate Imperialism', *Harvard Business Review*, 1998, 81(8), 109–17.

Chapter 10

International Market Entry Strategies

Chapter Outline

Chapter Learning Objectives

What you should learn from Chapter 10

- Why companies seek foreign markets
- How to assess market opportunities abroad
- How to screen countries to evaluate their suitability for the company
- How to evaluate the benefits of strategic alliances
- How to analyse those factors that will influence the mode of entry into a foreign market

Becoming international

Once a company has decided to go international, it has to decide how it will enter a foreign market, and the degree of marketing involvement and commitment it is prepared to make. These decisions should reflect considerable study and analysis of market potential and company capabilities, a process not always followed. Many companies appear to grow into international marketing through a series of phased developments. They gradually change strategy and tactics as they become more involved. Others enter international marketing after much research, with long-range plans fully developed.[1]

Phases of international marketing involvement

Regardless of the means employed to gain entry into a foreign market, a company may, from a marketing viewpoint, make no market investment; that is, its marketing involvement may be limited to selling a product with little or no thought given to development of market control. Or a company may become totally involved and invest large sums of money and effort to capture and maintain a permanent, specific share of the market. In general, a business can be placed in at least one of five distinct but overlapping phases of international marketing involvement, as outlined below.

No direct foreign marketing

In this phase, there is no active cultivation of customers outside national boundaries; however, a company's products may reach foreign markets. Sales may be made to trading companies and other foreign customers who come directly to the firm. Or products reach foreign markets via domestic wholesalers or distributors who sell abroad on their own without explicit encouragement or even knowledge of the producer. An unsolicited order from a foreign buyer is often what piques the interest of a company to seek additional international sales.

Infrequent foreign marketing

Temporary surpluses caused by variations in production levels or demand may result in infrequent marketing overseas. The surpluses are characterised by their temporary nature; therefore, sales to foreign markets are made as goods are available, with little or no intention of maintaining continuous market representation. As domestic demand increases and absorbs surpluses, foreign sales activity is withdrawn. In this phase, there is little or no change in company organisation or product lines.

Regular foreign marketing

At this level, the firm has permanent productive capacity devoted to the production of goods to be marketed on a continuing basis in foreign markets. A firm may employ foreign or domestic overseas middlemen or it may have its own sales force or sales subsidiaries in important foreign markets. The primary focus for products currently being produced is to meet domestic market needs. Investments in marketing and management effort and in overseas manufacturing and/or assembly are generally begun in this phase. Further, some products may become more specialised to meet the needs of individual foreign markets, pricing and profit policies tend to become equal with domestic business, and the company begins to be dependent on foreign profits.

International marketing

Companies in this phase are fully committed and involved in international marketing activities. Such companies seek markets throughout the world and sell products that are a result of planned production for markets in various countries. This generally entails not only the marketing but also the production of goods throughout the world. At this point a company becomes an international or multinational marketing firm dependent on foreign revenues.

Global marketing

At the global marketing level, companies treat the world, including their home market, as their market. This is one step further than the multinational or international company that views the world as a series of country markets (including their home market) with unique sets of market characteristics for which products and marketing strategies must be developed. A global company develops an overall strategy and image to reflect the existing commonalities of market needs among many countries to maximise returns through some global standardisation of its business activities – as it is culturally possible to achieve such efficiencies.

Changes in international orientation

Experience shows that a significant change in the international orientation of a firm occurs when that company relies on foreign markets to absorb permanent production surpluses and comes to depend on foreign profits. Businesses usually move through the phases of international marketing involvement one at a time, but it is not unusual for a company to skip one or more phases. As a firm moves from one phase to another, the complexity and sophistication of international marketing activity tends to increase and the degree of internationalisation to which management is philosophically committed tends to change. Such commitment affects the specific international strategies and decisions of the firm.

International operations of businesses reflect the changing competitiveness brought about by the globalisation of markets, interdependence of the world's economies, and the growing number of competing firms from developed and developing countries vying for the world's markets. *Global companies and global marketing* are terms frequently used to describe the scope of operations and marketing management orientation of these companies. Global markets are evolving for some products but do not yet exist for most products. In many countries there are still consumers for many products, reflecting the differences in needs and wants, and there are different ways of satisfying these needs and wants based on cultural influences.

Market entry objectives

Company resources and **psychic distance** are not the only reasons why a company enters a particular market. A particular market can attract foreign companies and a particular mode of entry. In other words, how a particular market will be served, by domestic or foreign firms or a certain combination of the two, depends on company objectives and market characteristics.

Research reveals that companies have three main objectives when entering a foreign market:[2]

1 market seeking
2 efficiency seeing
3 resource seeking.

A **market-seeking** strategy means that the company is looking for a considerable market for its products/offers. This can be due to a saturated market at home, or because the company believes that it has a strong product/brand that can penetrate into new markets. The firm thus wants to enter large or rapidly growing markets, for example China and India.

Efficiency seeking means that firms want to enter countries/markets where they can achieve efficiency in different ways, eg R&D and other infrastructural effects. Efficiencies can also be achieved because a certain industry has gathered at a place, creating a beneficial infrastructure, such as Silicon Valley. Philips and other consumer electronic product companies invested in Singapore and Malaysia, for example.

Resource-seeking firms try to enter into countries to get access to raw materials or other crucial inputs that can provide cost reduction and lower operation costs; for example, investment by most oil companies in the Middle East or textiles and garment companies in India and Pakistan.

In some markets companies may achieve more than one of these strategies. They will, however, influence the location decisions of companies. Moreover, depending on the knowledge and the need for control, the companies will like to increase resource

---

psychic distance

when a market is considered distant due to psychological barriers

market seeking

companies that venture into new countries/become international because they are looking for new markets, actively seeking customers worldwide

efficiency seeking

firms want to enter countries/markets where they can achieve efficiency in different ways

resource seeking

firms try to enter countries to get access to raw materials or other crucial inputs for cost reduction/lower operation costs

EXHIBIT 10.1: Important factors in country selection for Japanese entry into Europe

Aspect	UK	Germany	France	Netherlands
Labour availability	8	7	7	7
Wage level	9	6	8	6
Labour unions	8	8	8	8
Supporting industries	9	8	6	7
Support of development agency	10	7	4	7
Investment incentives	6	9	8	8
Language	10	7	4	8
Feelings against Japanese	8	7	7	7
Presence of other Japanese manufacturers	8	7	4	4
Total score	76	66	52	62

Sources: N. Hood and T. Truijens, 'European Location Decisions of Japanese Manufacturers', *International Business Review*, 1993, 2(1), pp 39–63; P.N. Ghauri, U. Elg and R.R. Sinkovics, 'Foreign Direct Investment – Location Attractiveness for Retailing Firms in the European Union', in L. Oxelheim and P. Ghauri (eds), *European Union and the Race for Foreign Direct Investment in Europe* (Oxford: Elsevier, 2004), pp 407–28.

commitment and would or would not want to own their operations in a particular foreign market. Here, benefits/incentives provided by host governments also play a major role. Several governments provide tax benefits; for example, foreign companies are exempt from any tax for the first few years, free land or other benefits.

A number of studies have looked into the location decision-making process of firms. Most conclude that the selection for market entry, particularly foreign direct investment, depends on factors such as the availability of infrastructure, language and supportive attitude of the home market (see the example in Exhibit 10.1).[3]

Depending upon the main objective of the company wanting to enter a particular market, different factors become more or less important. For market entry, the marketer needs to carry out a competition analysis to establish whether it will be possible to achieve desired market share or not. For resource-seeking firms we have to look at suppliers of those resources and their existing relationships and networks, and whether it will be possible for the company to penetrate into these networks or not. For efficiency-seeking firms the marketer has to look at efficiencies that can be achieved and sustained for a long period.

While making entry decisions, a company also has to see whether it is the first foreign company in the particular product group or not. To be the first in the market entails first-mover advantages: if the product is accepted by the market, it can gain a major share of the market. This was the case for Pepsi Cola, which entered Russia and India as the first mover. Coca-Cola entered these markets after a few years and had to struggle harder to gain respectable market share. Moreover, the first mover gains valuable experience/knowledge of the market, enabling it to lessen uncertainties and gain cost advantage. However, the first mover can also face certain disadvantages, such as convincing and educating the market that the new product is useful.

The first mover thus takes the initial costs and if the market reacts positively, other companies can come in and reap the benefits. For example, Royal Crown was the pioneer company to market diet colas, which were mainly sold to diabetics. When Coca-Cola and Pepsi Cola realised the market opportunity, they came with big advertising budgets and pushed Royal Crown out of the market. It took only one year for Coca-Cola to become the market leader.

First-mover advantage is also important when a market first opens for foreign companies. When the Soviet Union broke up and China opened its market, a number of companies wanted to be first to enter these countries in order to gain market recognition and share. Many companies, such as Philips and IKEA, entered these markets knowing that they would not make any profits in the first few years.

Going International 10.1

LOTTE AMBITION: A SOUTH KOREAN RETAILER PLANS A BOLD MOVE INTO CHINA

South Korean department stores provide some of the best service in the world. With a smile and a bow, sales assistants scurry after customers, attending to their whims while calming their tearful children. Lotte, South Korea's biggest department-store chain, thinks its experience at home makes it ideally suited to serving the new rich in other fast-developing economies. In July it plans to open a huge department store in China, in the Wangfujing shopping district in Beijing. It has set an annual sales target for the store of $150m. The wealthiest customers will be granted special parking spots and will be guided around the store by personal attendants. (Appealing to the very rich works well for Lotte at home: its richest 1 per cent of customers accounted for 17 per cent of its $5.8bn in sales last year.

'Lotte Department Store in Hanti', © Jonathan Tommy, JCT(Loves) Streisand* CC BY 2.0 UK.

It has asked consultants to analyse the Chinese market and help it choose a combination of foreign and local brands to appeal to Chinese shoppers. Lotte plans to sell South Korean cosmetics and clothes, banking on the appeal of Korean pop culture, which is popular throughout Asia. Lotte's Beijing staff have been sent to Seoul to learn about its procedures, marketing and service.

But Lotte's experience in Russia, where it opened its first foreign store last September, suggests that expanding abroad may prove harder than it thinks. It has had to spend a lot on advertising, has found it difficult to attract experienced staff for its Moscow store, and has cut its annual sales target from $140m to $120m. It hopes China will not prove such a tough nut to crack, since the cultural differences with South Korea will be less pronounced.

- Do you think Lotte will be more successful in China than in Russia? Why/why not?

Source: *The Economist*, 16 June 2008.

Market opportunity assessment

The main purpose of market opportunity assessment is to answer questions such as: should we enter a particular country or not? Is there a potential in that market for the particular industry and for a new competitor? Is there market/sales potential for the particular product?

The first question helps the company to screen the market in relation to the company's objectives, overall strategy, and the economic, cultural and legal environment of the country. The second question helps the company to assess whether the market is economically attractive or not. If it is a market where there is already fierce competition and overcapacity, it will be difficult to gain any market share from the existing competitors. The third question helps the company to make an advanced in-depth analysis of market opportunity for its particular product.[4]

Moreover, if the objective of the company is to seek efficiency when going into a particular market, it needs to do a different type of analysis. What type of efficiencies is it looking for, R&D or agglomeration? Most top companies in a particular sector gravitate to a certain market/area and create an efficient infrastructure for that particular industry, such as Silicon Valley in the USA and Bangalore in India for software, and Singapore/Malaysia for consumer electronics. If a company is moving to a market to achieve cost advantages, the analysis has to deal with the cost factors that are important for the particular product, such as cheap labour, cheap raw materials, taxation rules, and so on.[5]

proactive market selection

actively and systematically selecting a market

reactive market selection

selecting a market at random or without a systematic analysis

Market opportunity assessment and country selection for an entry also depend upon the proactive versus reactive approaches of the company. In a **proactive market selection**, a company is involved in a systematic approach. The marketer in this case proactively makes visits and does marketing research to assess the potential of a market. A number of companies with marketing research departments continuously collect information on different markets to detect a potential market at an early stage.

In a **reactive market selection**, the company is not actively collecting information or analysing any market to assess its potential. Companies following this approach often wait for an unsolicited order or an initiative taken by importers from a potential market. Often these companies wait for other companies (their competitors) to enter the market first. Such companies believe that the first movers will have to pave the way and handle initial problems, and then they can enter the market. This approach, however, is not always a wise choice as it is very difficult to snatch market share from existing foreign and domestic companies. Moreover, a company has to do its own assessment according to its objective, product and positioning.

Market/country selection

Boston Consulting Group (BCG)

an international strategy and general management consulting firm, it uses specific models to tackle management problems

Several methods are available for analysing countries prior to making investment decisions. The **Boston Consulting Group (BCG)** provides one such method. Basically, it is used to decide on the best mix of businesses or products in order to maximise the long-term profit and growth of the firm. It helps managers to analyse each and every business or product of the company and thus supports the designing of each business/product strategy. The main benefit is that it relates company products to the competition instead of analysing each product in isolation.

In international marketing, this model is used successfully to analyse each market/country (instead of business or product), which is then put into the context of competition and the company's own capabilities. It analyses two determining factors:

1 country attractiveness
2 competitive strength of the company.

Here the BCG portfolio analysis has been modified to include the above two factors: instead of products and relative market shares, we use country attractiveness and company strength to achieve market share in the new market. In spite of the limitations of using standardised models for different problems, this analysis can provide useful information when selecting a country/market in a marketing entry context.[6]

The factors that would influence the attractiveness of the country might include market size, market growth, competitive conditions and uncontrollable elements (eg the cultural, legal and political environments; see Exhibit 10.2).

competitive strength

strength of a product/company as compared to competitors

Assessing **competitive strength** means looking at whether the company has the resources and potential to achieve its goals in the particular market or not. For instance, is it possible to gain some market share? Do we have the marketing ability and resources? Is there a fit between the product and its positioning, and the market? There has to be some weighting of these factors to find the match between the market and the company. Exhibit 10.3 presents a nine-cell matrix depicting relative market investment opportunities for different types of match.[7]

The matrix reveals that, depending on the careful use of this analysis, a company may have several choices when making an entry decision.

EXHIBIT 10.2: Dimensions of country attractiveness and competitive strength

Country attractiveness	Competitive strength of the company
• Market size (total and segments) • Market growth (total and segments) • Competitive conditions • Market uncontrollables (cultural, legal and political environments)	• Market share (achievable) • Marketing ability and capacity • Product and positioning fit • Quality of distribution services

EXHIBIT 10.3: Market portfolio analysis: country attractiveness/competitive strength

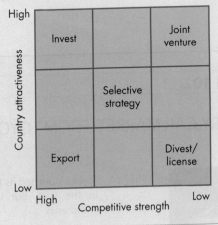

Invest

This represents a country that is very attractive due to the size of the market and its potential for growth. Moreover, this is a market where the company can attain the competitive strength to achieve its objectives. The analysis thus suggests that this country is suitable for entry and major investment.

Divest/license

This represents a market where the company should not invest. Moreover, if the company is already there, it should divest and get out. This is a market where the company will have problems or need to make heavy investments to gain some market share. It is therefore suggested that, if the company wants to enter this market, it is better to do it through 'licensing', the mode of entry that is least demanding of resources.

Joint venture

This refers to a market that is quite attractive but difficult. It demands huge investments/resources to gain considerable/acceptable market share. It is therefore suggested that if you cannot dominate the market (have major market share), then it is better not to enter or to enter through a joint venture, ie share the costs and local difficulties with a local partner.

Export

In a situation where a company realises that its product can achieve quick market share and that there is a very good match between its product and the market demand, but the market is not attractive due to its size or segment growth, it is better not to make heavy investments and sell the product through exports.

Selective strategy

This is a category of markets where there is fierce competition and it is therefore difficult to maintain a stable market share. However, if the company has other strengths, such as product/positioning fit with the market or a powerful brand, it can decide to invest. As is clear from Exhibit 10.3, the market is moderately attractive.

It is clear that the use of BCG portfolio analysis, as applied above for entry strategies, is useful as it provides some helpful insights into company/country match and compatibility. Together with other models/methods given in this chapter, this can be a useful tool in international-entry strategy decision making. Although each company might give different ratings or weights to each of the factors in country attractiveness and competitive strength, it can provide useful analysis for each entry decision. Its major strength is that a company can compare different markets, thus revealing which one is most suitable, and it helps the company to look at its capabilities in the context of international competition in each market.

Going International 10.2

ENTERING THE LUXURY CAR MARKET: FROM TOYOTA CROWN TO LEXUS

© Toyota, http://pressroom.toyota.com/lexus/photos/

1958	Toyota launched its first luxury sedan, named Crown in the USA. But it was a flop and was soon withdrawn.
1983	In a secret board meeting Toyota decided to create a top luxury car, code name 'F1'.
1985	Toyota sends a number of its designers to California to understand American luxury car customers and to develop the car.
1988	Lexus brand and logo made public, which was challenged for trademark infringement by computer company Lexis.
1989	First Lexus sedan introduced.
1990	Lexus select 121 special dealers for the car. J.D. Power ranks Lexus number one in quality survey.
1991	Lexus sells 71,206 cars, becoming America's top-selling luxury imported car.
1995	US government threatens to impose 100 per cent duty on Japanese import brand. Customers complain of uninspiring models. Mercedes takes over as number one luxury import.
1996	Lexus launches LX450 SUV and passes Range Rover in sales within two months of introduction.
1998	RX300 launched and became a big success, boosting total sales by 60 per cent.
2001	Lexus ranked number one by J.D. Power on customer satisfaction for the tenth time in 11 years.
2002	Lexus slides to number three in J.D. Power ranking, overtaken by Nissan's Infinity and Honda's Saturn. BMW close to becoming number one luxury import.
2003	Toyota starts selling Lexus brand in Japan.

The above chronology presents the planned market entry by Toyota into the US luxury car market segment. Now Toyota is about to announce yet another super-luxury car. At present it is nicknamed 'Mount

▶

◀

Everest' and will have a V10 engine (derived from its V12 Formula One race car) and, with a price tag of €150,000 ($183,510), it will compete with the Aston Martin DB7 (€141,800/$173,478) and the Mercedes-Benz SL55 (€113,250/$138,550).

Toyota is, however, facing a big problem: with the price as high as Mount Everest, it is planning to introduce the car as a Lexus model. The average buyer of Lexus is, however, 52 years old (which is four years older than an average Mercedes-Benz buyer and nine years older than a BMW buyer).

Existing Lexus models go for between €30,000/$36,702 (IS300) and €60,000/$73,404 (SC430). It is wondered whether the sporty 'Mount Everest' Lexus would attract the wealthy younger buyer. Normal impressions in the USA are that 'Grandpa drives a Lexus' and 'It look likes a grown-up's car'.

One idea at Toyota is to introduce the Mount Everest as the 1960s popular sports model Toyota 2000GT. Others say, 'We are creating something beyond the ordinary, not another Toyota!'

2005	Lexus completed an organisational separation from parent company Toyota, with dedicated design, engineering, training, and manufacturing centres working exclusively for the division.
2006	Lexus began sales of the GS 450h, a V6 hybrid performance sedan, and launched the fourth-generation flagship LS line, comprising both standard- and long-wheelbase V8 (LS 460 and LS 460 L) and hybrid (LS 600 h and LS 600 h L) versions.
2007	Lexus entered the Specialty Equipment Market Association show in the USA for the first time with the IS F, and announced its F-Sport performance trim level and factory-sanctioned accessory line.
2008	Amidst the late-2000s recession and a weakened world car market, global sales fell 16 per cent to 435,000, with declines in markets such as the USA and Europe, where deliveries fell by 21 per cent and 27.5 per cent, respectively.
2009	The marque launched the HS 250h, a dedicated hybrid sedan for North America and Japan, the RX 450h, the second-generation hybrid SUV replacing the earlier RX 400h, and later that year debuted the US$375,000 production LFA exotic coupe. In late 2009, citing higher sales of hybrid models over their petrol counterparts, Lexus announced plans to become a hybrid-only marque in Europe.
2010	Lexus underwent a gradual sales recovery in North America and Asia as the marque focused on adding hybrids and new model derivatives.
2011	Lexus began sales of the CT 200h, a compact four-door hybrid hatchback designed for Europe, in multiple markets.
2012	The marque began sales of the fourth-generation GS line, including GS 350 and GS 450h variants, as well as a lower-displacement GS 250 model for select markets. In April 2012, the sixth-generation ES line, including the ES 350 and ES 300h variants, debuted at the New York International Auto Show.

- Can you help Toyota in deciding which is the most suitable market (segment) to enter with this new model? How should it be named and positioned? Consult the Toyota/Lexus website and analyse its strategies.

Sources: *Business Week*, Special Report, 'Lexus's Big Test: Can it Keep its Cachet?', 24 March 2004, pp 48–51; and Wikipedia, http://en.wikipedia.org/wiki/Lexus#2000 s:_Global_reorganization, 2012.

Market entry strategies

When a company makes the commitment to go international, it must choose an entry strategy. This decision should reflect an analysis of market potential, company capabilities, and the degree of marketing involvement and commitment management is prepared to make. A company's approach to foreign marketing can require minimal investment and be limited to infrequent exporting with little thought given to market development. Or a company can make large investments of capital and management effort to capture and maintain a permanent, specific share of world markets. Both approaches can be profitable.

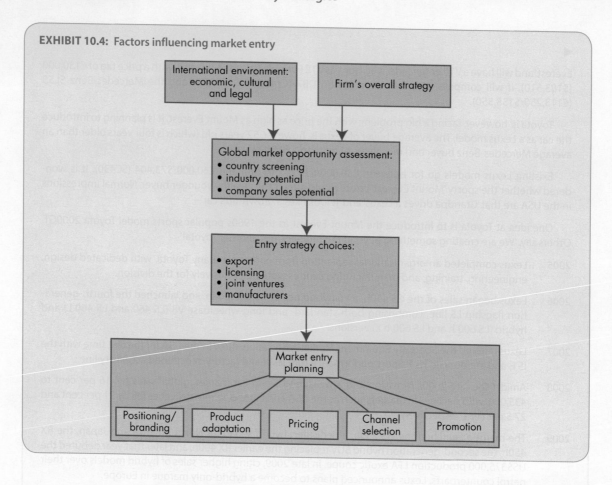

EXHIBIT 10.4: Factors influencing market entry

There is a variety of foreign market entry strategies from which to choose. Each has particular advantages and shortcomings, depending on company strengths and weaknesses, the degree of commitment the company is willing or able to make and market characteristics, as depicted in Exhibit 10.4.

Exporting

A company might decide to enter the international arena by exporting from the home country. This means of foreign-market development is the easiest and most common approach employed by companies taking their first international step because the risk of financial loss can be minimised. Exporting is a common approach for the mature international company as well. Several companies engage in exporting as their major market entry method. Generally, early motives are to skim the cream from the market or gain business to absorb overheads. Even though such motives might appear opportunistic, exporting is a sound and permanent form of operating in international marketing. The mechanics of exporting and the different middlemen available to facilitate the exporting process are discussed in detail in the next chapters.

Piggybacking

piggybacking

when a company sells its products abroad using another company's distribution facilities

Piggybacking occurs when a company (supplier) sells its product abroad using another company's (carrier) distribution facilities. This is quite common in industrial products, but all types of product are sold using this method. Normally, piggybacking is used when the companies involved have complementary but non-competitive products.

There has to be some benefit for the exporting (carrier) company. Some companies, such as General Electric or big retailers such as Wal-Mart or Tesco, use this as a way of broadening the product lines that they can offer to their foreign customers.

These companies believe that offering a broader range of products will help them in boosting the sales of their own products.

Some companies use this strategy to share transportation costs and some companies do it purely for the profits, as they can make profit on other companies' (suppliers') products. This is done either through increasing their margins or by getting commission from the suppliers. Some governments or regional development agencies also encourage their companies to use this method to support weaker or smaller companies. This can also be used as a first step towards a company's own international activities to test the market. This is particularly advantageous for smaller firms, as they often lack the necessary resources. Once they realise the market potential, they can start their own exporting.

Licensing

One means of establishing a foothold in foreign markets without large capital outlays is **licensing**. **Patent rights**, trademark rights and the rights to use technological processes are granted in foreign licensing. It is a favourite strategy for small and medium-sized companies, although by no means limited to such companies. Not many confine their foreign operations to licensing alone; it is generally viewed as a supplement to exporting or manufacturing, rather than the only means of entry into foreign markets.

The advantages of licensing are most apparent when capital is scarce, when import restrictions forbid other means of entry, when a country is sensitive to foreign ownership, or when it is necessary to protect patents and trademarks against cancellation for non-use. Although this may be the least profitable way of entering a market, the risks and headaches are less than for direct investments; it is a legitimate means of capitalising on intellectual property in a foreign market.

Licensing takes several forms. Licences may be granted for production processes, for the use of a trade name or for the distribution of imported products. Licences may be closely controlled or be autonomous, and they permit expansion without great capital or personnel commitment if licensees have the requisite capabilities. Not all licensing experiences are successful because of the burden of finding, supervising and inspiring licensees.[8]

> **licensing**
>
> to let a local company use a firm's trademark/ patent for a fee
>
> **patent rights**
>
> only the owner of these rights is authorised/can use the particular product technology

---

Going International 10.3

VUITTON IS BAGGING NEW MARKETS

Flip through *Vogue*, *Vanity Fair* or *Elle* and you'll find pages and pages of half-naked models, legs splayed, dangling handbags from Vuitton and rivals Gucci, Prada and Hermès. In the glam department Vuitton is great but not alone. You have to peek behind the glittery façade to see what makes Vuitton unique – what makes it, in fact, the most profitable luxury brand on the planet.

There's the relentless focus on quality. (That robot makes sure Vuitton rarely has to make good on its lifetime repair guarantee.) There's the rigidly controlled distribution network. (No Vuitton bag is ever marked down, ever.) Above

© P.N. Ghauri.

▶

◄

all, there's the efficiency of a finely tuned machine, fuelled by ever-increasing productivity in design and manufacturing – and, as Vuitton grows ever bigger, the ability to step up advertising and global expansion without denting the bottom line.

The Vuitton machine is running mighty smoothly right now. With $3.8bn in annual sales, it's about twice the size of runners-up Prada and Gucci Group's Gucci division. Vuitton has maintained double-digit sales growth and the industry's fattest operating margins as rivals have staggered through a global downturn during the past two years. That power was underscored anew when parent LVMH Moët Hennessy Louis Vuitton reported a 30 per cent earnings increase for 2003, fuelled by a record high 45 per cent operating margin at Vuitton. The average margin in the luxury accessories business is 25 per cent.

Does Vuitton – which started as a maker of steamer trunks during the reign of Napoleon III – have its best days ahead of it? It still needs to wean itself from Japanese customers, who account for an estimated 55 per cent of sales. Vuitton must build sales in the USA while tapping into rising affluence in China and India. It also needs to fight increasingly sophisticated global counterfeiting rings. Most of all, because Vuitton markets itself as an arbiter of style, it needs to keep convincing customers that they're members of an exclusive club. Vuitton has some serious strengths. One is the loyalty of its clients, shoppers who think one Vuitton bag in the closet just looks too lonely.

Another threat would be the departure of key personnel. For Vuitton, the biggest challenge may be to keep this powerful machine under control. The company opened 18 stores last year, about twice the rate of store openings a decade ago. Arnault, CEO LVMH, promises that Vuitton will never lose its discipline or its focus on quality. 'That's what differentiates Louis Vuitton,' he says. The message seems to be getting across. Just ask Ariella Cohen, a 24-year-old Manhattan legal assistant who already owns a Vuitton messenger bag and several Vuitton accessories, and now covets high-heeled Vuitton sandals – even though she'll have to put her name on a waiting list. 'Louis Vuitton never goes out of style,' she says, as she leaves its Fifth Avenue store.

● Will the Louis Vuitton machine ever run out of steam?

Source: *Business Week*, 'Money Machine', 22 March 2004.

Franchising

Franchising is a rapidly growing form of licensing in which the franchiser provides a standard package of products, systems and management services, and the franchisee provides market knowledge, capital and personal involvement in management. The combination of skills permits flexibility in dealing with local market conditions and yet provides the parent firm with a reasonable degree of control.

The franchiser can follow through on marketing of the products to the point of final sale. It is an important form of vertical market integration. Potentially, the franchise system provides an effective blending of skill centralisation and operational decentralisation, and has become an increasingly important form of international marketing. In some cases, franchising is having a profound effect on traditional businesses. In England, for example, it is estimated that annual franchised sales of fast foods total nearly €1.8bn ($2bn), which accounts for 30 per cent of all foods eaten outside the home.

By the 1990s more than 30,000 franchises of US firms were located in countries throughout the world. Franchises include soft drinks, motels, retailing, fast foods, car rentals, automotive services, recreational services and a variety of business services from print shops to sign shops. Franchising is the fastest-growing market entry strategy. It is often among the first types of foreign retail business to open in the emerging market economies of Eastern Europe, the former republics of Russia and China. McDonald's is in Moscow (its first store seats 700 inside and has 27 cash registers), and Kentucky Fried Chicken is in China (the Beijing KFC store has the highest sales volume of any KFC store in the world).

There are three types of franchise agreement used by franchising firms – master franchise, joint venture and licensing – any one of which can have a country's government as one partner. The master franchise is the most inclusive agreement and the method used in more than half of the international franchises. The master franchise gives the franchisee the rights to a specific area (many are for an entire country) with the authority to sell or establish subfranchises. The McDonald's franchise in Moscow is a master agreement owned by a Canadian firm and its partner, the Moscow City Council Department of Food Services.

Strategic international alliances

Strategic international alliances (SIAs) are sought as a way to shore up weaknesses and increase competitive strengths. Opportunities for rapid expansion into new markets, access to new technology, more efficient production and marketing costs, and additional sources of capital are all motives for engaging in strategic international alliances.

An SIA is a business relationship established by two or more companies to cooperate out of mutual need and to share risk in achieving a common objective. A strategic international alliance implies: (1) that there is a common objective; (2) that one partner's weakness is offset by the other's strength; (3) that reaching the objective alone would be too costly, take too much time or be too risky; and (4) that together their respective strengths make possible what otherwise would be unattainable. In short, an SIA is a synergistic relationship established to achieve a common goal where both parties benefit.

Opportunities abound the world over but, to benefit, firms must be current in new technology, have the ability to keep abreast of technological change, have distribution systems to capitalise on global demand, have cost-effective manufacturing and have capital to build new systems as necessary.[9]

The scope of what a company needs to do and what it can do is at a point where even the largest firms engage in alliances to maintain their competitiveness.

A company enters a **strategic alliance** to acquire the skills necessary to achieve its objectives more effectively, and at a lower cost or with less risk than if it acted alone.[10] For example, a company strong in research and development skills and weak in the ability or capital to successfully market a product will seek an alliance to offset its weakness – one partner to provide marketing skills and capital and the other to provide technology and a product. The majority of alliances today are designed to exploit markets and/or technology.

> **strategic alliance**
> when two companies cooperate for a certain purpose

Going International 10.4

RENAULT ENTERS INDIA WITH A JOINT VENTURE

Renault, the French auto-maker, is partnering with Mahindra and Mahindra, the Indian tractor and SUV maker, to launch its 'Logan'. It has developed the Logan especially for emerging markets. The four-door saloon car is already sold in Romania and is a low-cost car suitable for emerging market purchasing power.

Logan will enter India's mid-market and will compete head to head with Tata, Ford and Hyundai. The mid-market segment represents 20 per cent of the total auto market, which reached 1 million cars in 2004.

Renault's partnership with Mahindra and Mahindra will force the latter to dispose of its

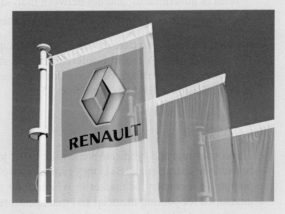
© Istockphoto.com/© xyno

▶

◀

small stake in the Indian Ford subsidiary. Renault, together with Nissan (now 44 per cent owned by Renault), is focusing on growing auto markets in emerging countries.

Source: K. Merchant, 'Renault/Mahindra to Launch Logan in India', *Financial Times*, 23 November 2004, p 28.

Joint ventures

Joint ventures (JVs), one of the more important types of collaborative relationship, have accelerated sharply during the past 20 years. Besides serving as a means of lessening political and economic risks by the amount of the partner's contribution to the venture, JVs provide a less risky way to enter markets that pose legal and cultural barriers than would be the case in the acquisition of an existing company.

Local partners can often lead the way through legal mazes and provide the outsider with help in understanding cultural nuances. A JV can be attractive to an international marketer:

1 when it enables a company to utilise the specialised skills of a local partner
2 when it allows the marketer to gain access to a partner's local distribution system
3 when a company seeks to enter a market where wholly-owned activities are prohibited
4 when it provides access to markets protected by tariffs or quotas
5 when the firm lacks the capital or personnel capabilities to expand its international activities.

In China, a country considered to be among the riskiest in Asia, there have been 49,400 JVs established in the first 15 years since they were first allowed. Among the many reasons JVs are so popular is that they offer a way of getting around high Chinese tariffs, allowing a company to gain a competitive price advantage over imports. By manufacturing locally with a Chinese partner rather than importing, China's high tariffs (the tariff on motor vehicles is 200 per cent, 150 per cent on cosmetics and the average on miscellaneous products is 75 per cent) are bypassed and additional savings are achieved by using low-cost Chinese labour.[11]

A JV is differentiated from other types of strategic alliance or collaborative relationship in that it is a partnership of two or more participating companies that have joined forces to create a separate legal entity. JVs should also be differentiated from minority holdings by an MNC in a local firm. Four factors are associated with joint ventures:

1 JVs are established, separate, legal entities
2 they acknowledge intent by the partners to share in the management of the JV
3 they are partnerships between legally incorporated entities, such as companies, chartered organisations or governments, and not between individuals
4 equity positions are held by each of the partners.

Nearly all companies active in world trade participate in at least one JV somewhere; many number their JVs in the dozens. A recent Conference Board study indicated that more than 50 per cent of *Fortune* 500 companies were engaged in one or more international JVs. In Japan alone, Royal Dutch Shell has more than 30 JVs; IBM has more than 35.

Consortia

The consortium and syndicate are similar to the joint venture and could be classified as such except for two unique characteristics: (1) they typically involve a large number of participants; (2) they frequently operate in a country or market in which none of the participants is currently active. Consortia are developed for pooling financial and managerial resources and to lessen risks. Often, huge construction projects are built under a consortium arrangement in which major contractors with different specialities form a separate company specifically to negotiate for and produce one job. One firm usually acts as the lead firm or the newly formed corporation may exist quite independently of its originators.

Manufacturing

Another means of foreign market development and entry is manufacturing, also called a wholly-owned subsidiary within a foreign country. A company may manufacture locally to capitalise on low-cost labour, to avoid high import taxes, to reduce the high costs of transportation to market, to gain access to raw materials, and/or as a means of gaining market entry. Seeking lower labour costs offshore is no longer an unusual strategy. A hallmark of global companies today is the establishment of manufacturing operations throughout the world. This is a trend that will increase as barriers to free trade are eliminated and companies can locate manufacturing wherever it is most cost-effective.

There are three types of manufacturing investment by firms in foreign countries: (1) market seeking; (2) resource seeking; and (3) efficiency seeking. Investments in China, for example, are often of the first kind, where companies are attracted by the size of the market. Investment in India, especially by a number of fashion garment producers such as Mexx and Marc O'Polo, are of the second type, while investments in Malaysia and Singapore by electronics manufacturers such as Intel and Motorola are of the third type.

Going International 10.5

PRIMARK GOES GLOBAL

Primark opened its first German store three years ago in an attempt to capitalise on German shoppers' nose for a bargain – a long-standing phenomenon to which the country's many 'hard discount' grocery chains bear witness.

'Germany is a very discount-oriented market,' says Clive Black, an analyst at Shore Capital. 'Primark has come along with good sites, fabulous merchandising and good customer service at attractive prices. It is a very good fit for the market.'

Primark has only nine stores in the country so far, four of which opened in the past financial year, but the retailer has given an indication of its long-term expansion plans by opening a distribution warehouse in western Germany, from where observers expect it to push into the Benelux countries and France.

Istockphoto.com/© SoopySue

Primark has already told analysts it sees potential for 150 German stores.

Primark's revenues rose 15 per cent in its past financial year to €3.5bn as it added 19 stores, but only three of these were in the UK or Ireland.

Primark's largest overseas market remains the Iberian Peninsula. Last year, it added 11 stores and 45 per cent more sales space in Spain and Portugal, despite the economic crisis there.

Nevertheless, Germany remains a difficult market for foreign retailers. Wal-Mart, for example, failed in its German hypermarkets venture.

▶

◄

Isabel Cavill, a senior retail analyst at Planet Retail, says Primark's emergence in Germany could become a threat to retailers such as KiK, a discount fashion chain with 2,600 German branches and sales in 2011 of €1.7bn, and Takko, another 'value' fashion retailer that Apax Partners, the private equity group, bought in a €1.3bn deal two years ago. 'What Germany really missed was a big low-cost fashion brand,' Ms Cavill says.

C&A, the European clothing retailer, is another that will be worried, she says.

- Should German retailers be worried from Primark's success?

Source: compiled from several sources.

Countertrade

Countertrade deals are now on the increase and represent a significant proportion of world trade. Countertrade ties the export and other foreign sales to an undertaking from the seller to purchase products from the buyer or a third party in the buyer's country. There are several reasons behind the demand for countertrade, such as promotion of local exports, saving scarce foreign exchange, balancing trade flows and/or ensuring guaranteed supplies.

The terms and conditions for countertrade are not standardised and may be different from market to market. Other terms used for countertrade include counter-purchase, buyback, compensation and offset, and barter. In the 1960s, Eastern European countries started demanding countertrade to achieve a balance in foreign trade. Nowadays, however, it is common practice in developing as well as in developed markets, and there are a number of companies that specialise in advising on countertrade and a number of trading houses that act as clearing houses for countertrade products.[12]

When to choose which strategy

Internationalisation of the firm – why and how firms go to foreign markets – has been the most important issue in international business and international marketing research. As we argued earlier, growth of the firm is the main driver of internationalisation. Do firms go international through a gradual, incremental process? Is this 'stage of internationalisation model' valid for smaller as well as bigger firms?

Can multinational companies, having earlier experience, leapfrog these stages or should they go step by step, first to closer markets and then to far-away markets? And how can companies analyse the suitability of a market for their product? These are some of the questions that interest all companies that are active or are planning to be active in cross-border markets.

> **establishment chain model**
>
> stepwise internationalisation to foreign markets

A number of studies have already addressed these questions. The **establishment chain model**, one of the earlier studies, presented gradual internationalisation, from no regular export to manufacturing subsidiaries. It states that companies gradually develop their operations abroad.[11] The firm first grows in the domestic market and then expands into close-by foreign markets. The obstacles to internationalisation include a lack of knowledge of foreign markets and resources. The psychic distance, that some markets are perceived far away and difficult due to different culture and environments, is considered another obstacle. Psychic distance is sometimes correlated with geographic distance but not always. For example, Britain and Australia are geographically far away but have very little psychic distance. France and Britain are, however, in an opposite situation. This psychic distance is not constant and changes as the result of communication and experience. The establishment chain model suggests five different stages of going abroad:

1 no regular export
2 export via representatives (eg agent)

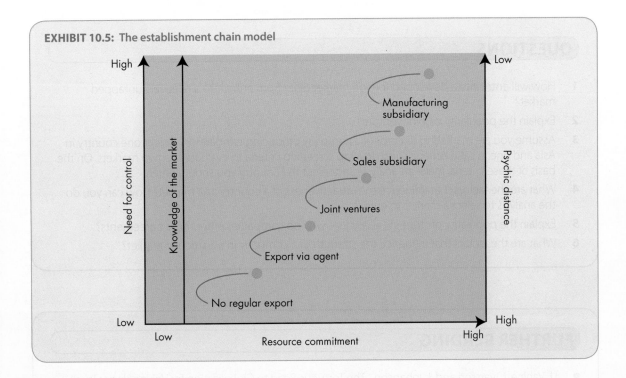

EXHIBIT 10.5: The establishment chain model

3 joint ventures

4 sales subsidiary

5 production/manufacturing subsidiary.

This means the more experience a firm gets in a market, the more knowledge (of the market) it acquires and the more resources it is willing to commit. In stage 1 the firm has not committed any resources, while resource commitment increases with every stage. Whether a firm will proceed from stage 1 to 5 depends on the psychic distance and the size of the market as well as the need for control. With some industries/products it is crucial for the company to have control of its activities; for example, to ensure consistent positioning or brand image. This is illustrated in Exhibit 10.5.

The other main obstacle to going abroad is the psychic distance that a company can perceive in a particular market when it is thought to be psychologically far away. If this is the case, then the company would not like to commit a large amount of resources in that market. It would prefer to choose a successive involvement and follow an establishment chain model (see Exhibit 10.5). In such a market it might even like to use a licensee as an entry strategy.

SUMMARY

Expanding markets around the world have increased competition for all levels of international marketing. To keep abreast of the competition and maintain a viable position for increasingly competitive markets, a global perspective is necessary. Global competition also requires quality products designed to meet ever-changing customer needs and rapidly advancing technology. Cost containment, customer satisfaction and a greater number of players mean that every opportunity to refine international business practices must be examined in the light of company goals. Collaborative relationships, strategic international alliances, strategic planning and alternative market entry strategies are important avenues to global marketing that must be implemented in the planning of global marketing management.

QUESTIONS

1 How will entry into a developed foreign market differ from entry into a relatively untapped market?

2 Explain the popularity of joint ventures.

3 Assume you are marketing director of a company producing refrigerators. Select one country in Asia and one in Latin America and develop screening criteria to evaluate the two markets. On the basis of these criteria, make an analysis and select the country you should enter.

4 What are the factors that influence the attractiveness of a country as a market? How can you do the analysis to select a market to enter?

5 Explain the popularity of strategic alliances – why do companies enter these agreements?

6 What are the factors that influence the strength of a company in a particular market?

FURTHER READING

- J.E Vahlne, I. Ivarsson and J. Johanson, 'The Tortuous Road to Globalization for Volvo's Heavy Truck Business: Extending the Scope of the Uppsala Model, *International Business Review*, 2011, 20(1), 1–14.

- A.Y. Lewin and H.W. Volbreda, 'Co-evolution of Global Sourcing: The Need to Understand the Underlying Mechanisms of Firm-decisions to Offshore', *International Business Review*, 2011, 20(3), 241–51.

- F.R. Root, *Entry Strategies for International Markets* (Lexington, MA: Lexington Books, 1994).

NOTES

1 J. Johanson and J.E. Vahlne, 'The Internationalisation Process of the Firm: A Model of Knowledge Development and Increasing Foreign Market Commitments', *Journal of International Business Studies*, 1977, 8(1), 23–32.

2 This section draws on Pervez Ghauri and Peter Buckley, 'Globalization and the End of Competition', in V. Havila, M. Forsgren and H. Håkansson (eds), *Critical Perspectives on Internationalisation* (Oxford: Elsevier, 2002), pp 7–28.

3 Lars Oxelheim and Pervez Ghauri (eds), *European Union and the Race for Foreign Direct Investment in Europe* (Oxford: Elsevier, 2004).

4 F.R. Root, *Entry Strategies for International Markets* (Lexington, MA: Lexington Books, 1994).

5 This section draws on G. Albaum, J. Strandskov and E. Duerr, *International Marketing and Export Management* (London: FT-Prentice Hall, 2002).

6 Pontus Braunerhjelm, Lars Oxelheim and Per Thulin, 'The Relationship between Domestic and Outward Foreign Direct Investment: The Role of Industry-specific Effects' *International Business Review*, 2005, 14(6), 67–76.

7 U. Elg, P.N. Ghauri and V. Tarnovskaya, 'The Role of Networks and Matching in Market Entry to Emerging Retail Markets', *International Marketing Review*, 2008, 25(6), 674–99.

8 Preet Aulakh, Tamer Cavusgil and M.B. Sarkar, 'Compensation in International Licensing Agreements', *Journal of International Business Studies*, 1998, 29(2), 409–20.

9 This section draws on Peter Buckley and Pervez Ghauri (eds), *The Internationalization of the Firm: A Reader* (London: Thomson Learning, 2004).

10 Jan Johanson and Finn Wiethersheim-Paul, 'The Internationalization of the Firm: Four Swedish Cases', *Journal of Management Studies*, 1975 (October), pp 305–22.

11 J. Johanson and J.-E. Vahlne, 'The Uppsala Internationalization Model Re-visited: From Liability of Foreignness to Liability of Outsidership', *Journal of International Business Studies,* 2009, 40(9), 1411–31.

12 For further details on this topic, see Michael Row, *Countertrade* (London: Euromoney Books, 1989).

Chapter 11

International Segmentation and Positioning

Chapter Outline

Chapter Learning Objectives

What you should learn from Chapter 11

- Understand the major steps in segmentation targeting and positioning
- What the basic characteristics for international segments and the major considerations in creating effective segments are
- How to do international segmentation
- Understand the different international targeting strategies and when the different strategies are preferred.
- What positioning is and how perceptual maps can help with positioning
- How firms position their brand or products

Market segmentation, targeting and positioning

Firms' choices and strategies in marketing can be understood and evaluated by the segmentation targeting and positioning process (STP). This process provides a deeper understanding of the market and firms' competitive strategies. Competitive strategy perspectives in strategy literature hold that firms which are able to identify attractive consumer segments, accurately analyse the competitive factors within such markets and effectively position themselves can generate competitive advantages.[1] In parallel, strategic marketing focuses on the STP process which involves segmenting markets, identifying and targeting attractive segments and offering products suitable for such segments.

The purpose of market **segmentation** is to identify relatively homogeneous groups of consumers with similar consumption patterns. In market segmentation, a market is divided into subgroups of consumers which exhibit similar behaviour or have similar needs in order to create a marketing strategy which can effectively reach such groups.[2] After defining the market segments, firms choose the segments they want to target. **Targeting** is the process of evaluating segments and focusing marketing efforts on a country, region or groups of people that have a significant potential to respond to the firms' products.[3] Firms target segments by looking at the size and the potential of the segment, competitor intensity, resources necessary to meet the demands of the segments and the company's ability to meet such demands.

> **targeting**
> assessing market segments that the company wants to cover

Firms' positioning decisions are influenced by the characteristics of the targeted segment. Positioning decisions involve firms' choices in creating an image in the consumers' minds and their decisions regarding the product in relation to competitors.[4] Positioning is carried out by implementing the appropriate marketing strategy for the targeted segment, designed to create the planned image of the company's offering in the consumer's mind.

In a given market, the firm defines the product range which appeals to the consumers and differentiates the firm within the market. In international marketing, firms consider the attractiveness of the segment they can target and their competitive position within this segment which reveals the firm's ability to differentiate itself from the competitors.[5] Positioning is related to a firms' decisions to manage its product/brand by stressing the differentiating value according to the segment characteristics.[6]

Using the STP process using the international marketers aim to break down heterogeneous markets and find groups of consumers who can respond to a given product and marketing strategy in a consistent manner. In international marketing, the first step of this process involves identifying countries or consumer groups across countries or in a particular market which have similar characteristics and needs. The second step is distinguishing the segments to which the company can appeal, given consumer needs, preferences, company resources and the competitive landscape. The final stage is positioning the product in order to create or emphasise the product's unique benefits and differentiate the product.[7] Within this process marketers are faced with challenges due to increased heterogeneity among different markets stemming from factors such as cultural differences, country characteristics, environmental differences, legal and political considerations.[8] Exhibit 11.1 summarises the STP.

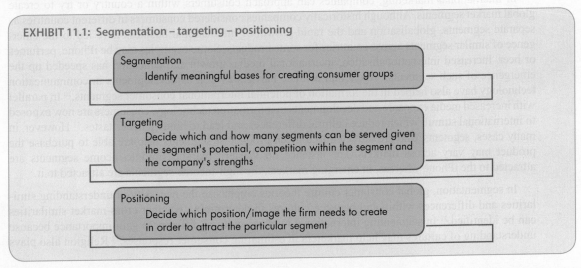

EXHIBIT 11.1: Segmentation – targeting – positioning

Segmentation
Identify meaningful bases for creating consumer groups

Targeting
Decide which and how many segments can be served given the segment's potential, competition within the segment and the company's strengths

Positioning
Decide which position/image the firm needs to create in order to attract the particular segment

International market segmentation

segmentation

identifying subsets of consumers with homogenous characteristics in a market

Segmentation is done by identifying common demographics, behaviour or characteristics among customers.[2] In parallel, segments are different groups within markets which are relatively more homogenous. A market segment has four components: (1) it must be identifiable; (2) it must be economically reachable; (3) it is more homogeneous in its characteristics than the market as a whole; and (4) it is large enough to be profitable. By segmenting markets, firms may be able to offer products which better meet the needs of the identified group, increase brand equity and loyalty and decrease marketing expenditure by creating segment-specific marketing plans.[9]

global market segmentation

defined as the process of identifying specific segments, with homogenous attributes who are likely to respond to a company's product/brand in a similar manner

Generally **global market segmentation** is defined as the process of identifying specific segments, whether they are country groups or across countries comprising potential customers with homogenous attributes who are likely to respond to a company's product/brand in a similar manner. In international marketing, firms are faced with multiple contexts and diverse consumer bases; groups which display similar behaviour or characteristics may be prevalent across multiple countries.[2] Fundamentally, international marketers look for an identifiable segment of consumers who have the same (or at least mostly similar) needs and wants across several country markets.

In international segmentation, *measurability*, *accessibility*, *substantiality* and *actionability* are major criteria in identifying effective segments. In this respect, measurability refers to the ability to find information regarding the segment, such as demographics or income level. If such information is unavailable or unobtainable, firms cannot determine basic segment characteristics such as its size or profitability.

Accessibility refers to the need to identify segments which can be accessed by the company. A company needs to be able to communicate with the consumers within the segment and access them through the relevant distribution channels.

Substantiality emphasises the need to find segments which can be sizeable and profitable for the company. In segmentation, firms customise their marketing to meet the needs of a specific segment. In this way, firms can generate economies of scale by accessing a particular segment in different markets. They can also compete successfully by meeting the needs or the wants of the segment more effectively than the competition. However, the size and the opportunities of the segment should be large enough to compensate for the cost of deploying marketing strategies geared for the segment.

Finally, actionability emphasises the necessity of identifying segments for which the company can design effective and attractive marketing programmes. The company needs to ensure that it has the capability and the resources to service the segments. Also, the segments need to possess specific characteristics which the company can effectively use in creating its marketing strategy.

In international marketing, companies can approach consumers within a country or try to create global market segments. Although historically companies considered consumers in different countries as separate segments, globalisation and the rapid growth of international business have led to the emergence of similar segments across countries for some products. Some examples may be iPhone, perfumes or beer. Increased internationalisation, international media, growth and education has speeded up the emergence of such segments.[5] Reduction of trade barriers as well as developments in communication technology have also helped in the formation of potential international consumer segments.[10] In parallel with increased media exposure and developments in information technology, consumers are now exposed to international stimuli which reduce cultural differences and lead to homogeneous tastes.[11] However, in many cases, segments who are attracted to a given product or segments who are able to purchase the product may vary across markets. For instance, in Western markets, middle-income segments are attracted to the iPhone whereas, in emerging markets, the high-income segments are attracted to it.

In segmentation, global consumer culture theories emphasise the necessity of understanding similarities and differences within and between cultures in determining whether cross-market similarities can be identified.[11] In segmenting international markets, cultural differences gain importance because understanding of cultures may help marketers in estimating consumer responses.[12] Religion also plays a major role in international segmentation. In many countries, firms cannot sell products that contain pork while in other countries firms cannot sell beef products. For instance, McDonald's in India sells lamb or vegetable burgers.

Often firms try to identify global market segments which are subgroups observed in many countries. In such a way the firm can create a unique positioning in the consumers' minds and emphasise their product's differences. With such a global positioning strategy, firms are able to reduce marketing costs and adaptation costs.[13] In parallel with globalisation, firms focus on generating efficiencies and synergies globally, regionally or across multiple markets. In developing products in this way firms can also benefit from knowledge obtained in different markets.[14] In this manner, firms are able to decrease marketing costs and increase their knowledge base by obtaining information from each market.[4] By segmentation, marketers can reap the benefits from standardisation if they find a global segment or may address the requirements of specific groups in a particular country to satisfy those needs if the segments are different in different countries. Economies of scale can be generated and customers across different countries can be effectively reached in this manner with relatively standardised or accurately adopted products and marketing strategies.[2]

Implementation of market segmentation poses issues arising from concerns related to difficulties in measuring proceeds, difficulties in identifying segments, concerns related to contraction in sales volume stemming from specialised focus on a segment, etc.[15] Moreover, markets are more dynamic in parallel, consumer needs and preferences continually change, which may cause inconsistencies in segmentation. A segment's structure and content is influenced by the changes in customer behaviour and needs, which may be instigated by changes in income levels, education or technological developments.[16]

International market segments

Scholars analysing international segmentation predominantly focus on economic, cultural, geographic and technological bases of different countries. More recently, behavioural and lifestyle factors are gaining importance.[6] In defining broad segments, country-based segmentation or consumer-based segmentation can be used. In country-based segmentation, geographic, economic or demographic variables can be used. For instance a clothing company may choose a segment consisting of countries within a particular region which share a similar climate. In consumer-based segmentation, cultural values, lifestyles or attitudes can be analysed. For instance, a company producing organic products may focus on consumers who value healthy lifestyles.

In looking at international segments, marketers can assume that consumers are heterogeneous among countries and homogenous within a given country and focus on the macro-level differences. Alternatively, international marketers can consider differences within a given country and the emergence of international homogenous segments. Country-based segmentation assumes that consumers within a country exhibit similar behaviour. As such the strategy fails to realise further gains which can be generated by expanding the operations to meet the needs of segments which exists in multiple markets.[3] Increasingly, behavioural and attitudinal segmentation is highlighted in discussing marketing strategies as opposed to economic factors. Behavioural segmentation is based on the consumer lifestyle or behaviour in different countries. Attitudinal segmentation is based on consumers' attitudes and acceptance of foreign products.[14] Exhibit 11.2 shows the factors that influence international segmentation.

Geographic segmentation

In looking at international segments on the basis of geographic characteristics, marketers consider factors such as countries, cities, neighbourhoods, regions, population density or climate. For instance, in countries such as India, Pakistan or China, there are two parallel markets: one in cities and urban areas and the other in villages or rural areas. Customers in the different areas have different buying behaviour and needs.

Geographic segmentation may allow companies to take advantage of cultural differences. Moreover, firms with limited resources may be able to operate efficiently in a defined geographic region. Within geographic segmentation, economic status, industrialisation level and stage of economic development can be considered. On the other hand, solely relying on geographic criteria may

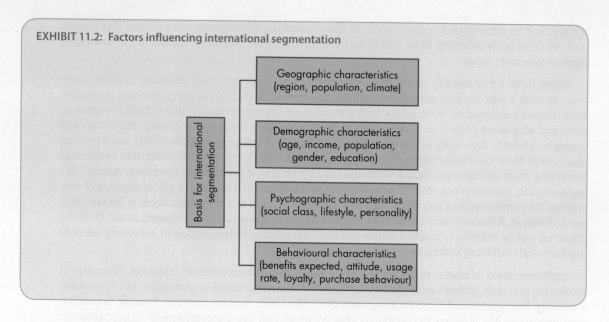

EXHIBIT 11.2: Factors influencing international segmentation

be misleading as consumers in a given area are often heterogeneous. Treating countries as homogenous may not be efficient.[6]

Demographic segmentation

Demographic segmentation is a popular basis for segmentation because such variables are relatively easy to measure. In demographic segmentation, variables such as income, age, gender, population and education level are often utilised. For instance, a company may segment on the basis of income and focus on the global elite, defining the target segment as affluent consumers who have the means to spend money on exclusive products. Some examples of this are Louis Vuitton bags, iPads and Porsche cars.

Going International 11.1

COMPANIES TARGET FEMALE CUSTOMERS

Never mind the fight to get people to open their wallets in the recession – some companies are taking a different tack, and trying to get customers to open their purses instead. In America, where female consumers make more than 80 per cent of discretionary purchases, companies have started tailoring their products and messages to appeal to women in an effort to boost their sales.

Gender-based segmentation can be observed in marketing strategies directed to women or men, such as Coke's focus on appealing to women in promoting Diet Coke and appealing to men in marketing Coke Zero.

Frito-Lay, a snack-food company owned by PepsiCo, has launched an advertising campaign called 'Only in a Woman's World' to convince women that crisps and popcorn are not just for male, beer-guzzling sport fans. OfficeMax, America's second-largest office-supplies company, has redesigned its notebooks and file-holders to appeal to women and has run advertisements that encourage women to make their work spaces more colourful. For the first time, McDonald's was a sponsor of New York Fashion Week, promoting a new line of hot drinks to trendsetting women.

Aside from their greater purchasing clout, women are valuable customers for three reasons. First, they are loyal, says Marti Barletta, author of *Marketing to Women*, and more likely to continue to buy a brand if they like

▶

◄

it. Second, women are more likely than men to spread information about products they like through word of mouth and social networking sites. Third, most of the lay-offs so far in America have been in male-dominated fields, like manufacturing and construction. This means women may bring home a greater share of household income in the months ahead and have even more buying power.

But marketing to women may not work for every company. In particular, for firms (such as some carmakers) with brands that are regarded as strongly male, 'gender bending', or trying to attract the opposite sex, could enhance short-term sales but cause a longer-term decline. Jill Avery of the Simmons School of Management in Boston researched this trend with cars. When Porsche released a sport-utility vehicle designed for women, sales temporarily increased, but men started to move away from the brand, on the basis that it had compromised its masculine image. In this recession, however, having a tarnished brand is better than having no brand at all.

- Do you think targeting female customers for such products will hurt the companies in the long run?

Source: compiled from several sources.

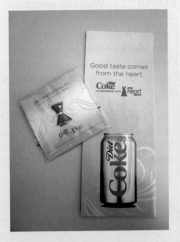

The Diet Coke Women's Heart Foundation marketing campaign is an example of how Coca-Cola has targeted Diet Coke at the female market.
'Heidi Klum Gave Me a Pin' © Kevin Trotman, The Rocketeer. CC BY 2.0 UK.

Similarly, different age groups may have similar needs or wants. Age-based segmentation can be observed in products focusing on children's formula products or on products highlighting their appeal to teens such as MTV or Diesel. Characteristics of global youth such as their music preferences, style or clothing can help companies in global segmentation.[17]

In demographic segmentation, marketers need to select the variables carefully. For instance, per capita income in a country does not always reflect the standard of living. In China, per capita income as a whole is low, but, the high-income segment is growing rapidly and is of considerable size because the total population is 1.4 billion people. Even if only 10 per cent of this population is considered as affluent, the potential market size is 14 million. In contrast, a market such as Norway with a high-income per capita is not necessarily associated with a large affluent segment.

Psychographic segmentation

In psychographic segmentation, marketers aim to identify segments with similar characteristics, psychology, values or lifestyle by considering consumer values and opinions. This approach provides a deeper understanding of the consumer and enables the company to create offers and marketing plans which are better suited to the identified segments. Marketers focus on consumer lifestyles in psychographic segmentation. For instance, outdoor enthusiasts, over-achievers and fun-loving youth can form different segments. On the other hand, psychographic segmentation is reliant on detailed data which is costly to obtain and is also open to interpretation. In psychographic segmentation, criteria based on social class, lifestyles or personality characteristics can be used in identifying these segments.

Segmentation based on social class takes into account the ordered nature of the classes in markets and the effect of such classes on the consumers' preferences. For instance social classes often influence people's selection of clothing, habits and activities. Lifestyle segmentation looks at the consumers' pattern of acting and view of the world. Examples of lifestyle segmentation can be observed in marketing which focuses on products that fit healthy lifestyles. Exhibit 11.3 presents a discussion of the VALS segmentation procedure often used in psychographic segmentation.

EXHIBIT 11.3: VALS segmentation

A major methodology used in psychographic segmentation is VALS, which stands for values, attitudes and lifestyles. VALS was developed by SRI International as a frame to segment consumers as a function of their motives and resources. VALS can provide a relatively detailed view of consumer profiles and help companies design and communicate their products and offers to selected segments.

Factors such as income, intelligence or education level help determine the resources available to a consumer. Motivation of the consumer is based on what drives them. Major motivations identified in VALS are ideals, achievement and self-expression. Consumer decisions are guided by knowledge and principles if they are motivated by ideals. Consumers motivated by achievement often base their decisions in relation to the expectations of groups which they value. Motives of self-expression lead to risk-taking decisions and search for variety.

High resources:

- innovators: sophisticated consumers with high self-esteem and income. Motivated by all three categories. Innovators are active consumers who are most receptive to new ideas
- thinkers: mature and comfortable consumers who seek information and are rational in making their decisions. Thinkers are motivated by ideals and principles
- achievers: goal-oriented consumers who prioritise career and family
- experiencers: experiences are younger and impulsive consumers often motivated by self-expression

Low resources:

- believers: believers are motivated by ideals and are often characterised as traditional and conservative consumers with predictable consumption choices. Believers are often reliant on other consumers in making decisions
- strivers: strivers are trendy consumers motivated by achievement. Such consumers often prioritise the opinion of others in consumption choices and favour stylish products
- makers: markers are primary motivated by self-expression. Practical consumers who prioritise functional attributes
- survivors: consumers with very limited resources who are cautious and concerned with security

Source: Strategic Business Insights webpage, http://www.strategicbusinessinsights.com/vals/ustypes.shtml.[18,19]

Behavioural segmentation

Behavioural segmentation focuses on identifying segments on the basis of the consumers' relation to a given product.[20] In this process research focuses on analysing factors such as which consumers buy the product, how much they need the product, how often they use it and which benefits they value. Within this context, the consumer's approach to different brands and their loyalty to the brands are also considered. Companies may observe that some consumer groups use their products frequently whereas others use the products rarely, or different consumers may place different emphasis on the importance of different attitudes.

Behavioural segmentation may focus on the occasions when the product is used. For instance, a firm producing breakfast items may try to focus on their products' advantages when consumed throughout the day. Marketers can also focus on consumer behaviour on different occasions, such as Christmas or Valentine's day. Marketing efforts of chocolate manufacturers such as Cadbury, Godiva or Hershey on such occasions exemplify behavioural segmentation. In behavioural segmentation, marketers may also create segments according to the benefits sought. For instance, toothpaste companies may consider consumers who prioritise health and protection or the consumers who prioritise cosmetic benefits such as whitening teeth or pleasant breath.

Marketers need to examine buyer readiness in behavioural segmentation. In doing so, they need to assess the consumer awareness of their product. If the consumers lack information related to the product, then the marketing needs to be geared towards providing the information and educating the consumers accordingly.

Market targeting

In **targeting**, firms evaluate market segments and choose the segments which are more suitable for the firm. In doing so, marketers look at segment size and growth, segment structure and the fit among the needs of the segment and the company resources.

In assessing market segments and choosing target markets, firms need to consider growth potential and stability as well as the present size of the segment/market.[20] In international targeting, marketers need to consider the possible existence of segments which may be small in individual markets but may constitute a sizeable opportunity when multiple markets are considered.

In international targeting, firms also need to take into account the cultural influences, institutional structures and regulations in different markets. In doing so, the marketers can determine the adaptations that may be necessary and whether such adaptations are justifiable and financially feasible.

Firms also need to analyse the structural attractiveness of the segment and in doing so they need to examine the industry conditions as well as the competitors within the segment. In this analysis, it is also important to consider the possible changes which may influence the competitive structure.

In looking at their compatibility with the segment, firms need to consider the resource availability and competition within the segment, their ability to provide superior value within the segment and their ability to undertake operations efficiently in servicing the segment.

International target market strategies

Most international marketers have traditionally viewed each country as a single market segment unique to that country. In international marketing, segmentation solely on the basis of countries may be inappropriate as markets within a given country are often not homogenous. In parallel, targeting the whole market within the country may also be problematic as consumer groups within a country are usually heterogeneous and dominant local firms have often built strategies which encapsulate a significant portion of the domestic market.[21]

When a company does business in more than one country there are three approaches to the market. Target markets can be identified as: (1) all consumers within the borders of a country; (2) different segments in each country market – in this strategy, companies find the group of customers who are most suitable for their product/brand and then adopt their strategies to that group's behaviour; and (3) global market segments – all consumers with the same needs and wants in groups of country markets.

After identifying the segments it wants to enter, the company chooses the appropriate targeting strategy. In targeting, firms can follow undifferentiated, differentiated or concentrated approaches. In undifferentiated approaches, firms focus on targeting a large consumer base without tailoring its efforts to a select group. In differentiated approaches, firms focus on selected segments and use marketing efforts to meet the needs of such segments. In concentrated approaches, firms choose a single segment to focus on. Exhibit 11.4 shows the targeting strategies in international marketing.

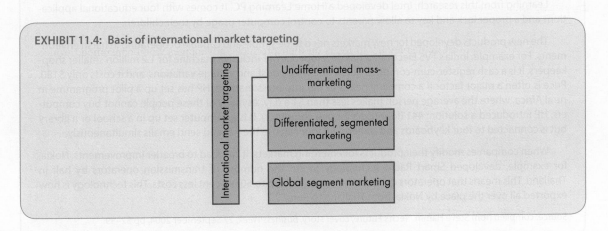

EXHIBIT 11.4: Basis of international market targeting

International market targeting
- Undifferentiated mass-marketing
- Differentiated, segmented marketing
- Global segment marketing

Undifferentiated targeting strategy

In following undifferentiated marketing strategies, firms approach all markets with the same marketing plan, ignoring differences among segments. Instead, firms often focus on features of the product which may appeal to most buyers. Companies can often economise in pursuing such strategies and offering a standardised product with a standardised marketing plan. However, this strategy assumes that all consumers are similar and have similar expectations and tastes.

Differentiated targeting strategy

In undertaking differentiated marketing strategies, firms develop separate marketing strategies for different segments. This strategy is especially beneficial for markets which consist of identifiable segments with different preferences. For instance, many airlines offer business- and economy-class tickets, with separate marketing strategies for each group.

Global targeting strategy

In pursuing concentrated targeted strategies, firms choose a specific segment among the consumers. In this way firms target a single segment with a specific marketing plan and aim to meet the expectations of the segment more fully when compared to competitors.

Going International 11.2

SUCCESS THROUGH CULTURAL CUSTOMISATION

Source: courtesy of Dell Inc.

The secret of success in emerging markets is to develop products that are especially designed to meet the needs of the customers in these markets. In 2000 Dell introduced a new consumer PC for the Chinese market called 'Smart PC', distinct from those it sells anywhere else. It was built by a Taiwanese company, which allowed Dell to sell it at a very low price. It helped Dell to become the number one foreign supplier in China. New markets need new strategies and new products. To develop new products to tap into these markets, companies are doing a lot of market research. Intel appointed 10 ethnographers to travel around the world to find out how to redesign its existing, or develop new, products to fit different cultures and segments in these markets. One of the ethnographers visited hundreds of families in China and reported that Chinese families were reluctant to buy PCs. Parents were concerned that their children would listen to pop music and surf the web, distracting them from their school work.

Learning from this research, Intel developed a 'Home Learning PC'. It comes with four educational applications and a proper lock and key to allow parents to control computer usage by their children.

The new products developed for new markets need to be simple and capable of operating in harsh environments. For example, India's TVS Electronics has developed an all-inclusive machine for 1.2 million smaller shopkeepers. It is a cash register-cum-computer, it tolerates heat, dust and voltage variations, and it costs only $180. Price is often a major factor if a company needs to tap into mass markets. HP has set up a pilot programme in rural Africa, where the average person makes less than $1 a day. As many of these people cannot buy computers, HP introduced a solution: 441 (four users for one computer). It is a computer set up in a school or a library but is connected to four keyboards and screens. All four can use the net and send emails simultaneously.

When companies modify their products for emerging markets, it can lead to broader improvements. Nokia, for example, developed Smart Radio Technology to cut the number of transmission operators by half in Thailand. This means that operators can build networks with up to 50 per cent less costs. This technology is now exported all over the place by Nokia, from Thailand to Peru.

Source: compiled from Steve Hamm, 'Tech's Future', cover story, *Business Week*, 27 September 2004, pp 52–59.

Marketers need to assess the company's resources and the resources needed to succeed in identified segments. For instance, if a company has limited resources, a global marketing strategy may be necessary to minimise product adaptation and marketing costs as it targets a specific segment across markets. However, a global marketing strategy might not be suitable for the particular market. Choice of targeting strategy is also influenced by the characteristics of a company's products. For instance, for products which are homogenous by nature such as commodity products, undifferentiated marketing strategies are more suitable. In contrast, for products where design quality and brand are important, differentiated marketing strategies are necessary.

In choosing target segments and markets, marketers should also have to examine the characteristics of the markets and consumer behaviour. For instance, if buyer tastes are uniform across markets, then global marketing can be preferable and enable the firm to generate cost efficiencies. In analysing the market structure, it is also important to determine where the company's product stands in terms of the market's lifecycle. As an example, if the market is mature and there are many alternatives to the company's products, focusing on differentiating the company's products is more important. In analysing the market, marketers also need to examine the competitive environment and make sure that they can compete successfully with the existing players. In international markets, it is especially important to identify the firm's competitors as well as the firm's customers. A company needs to know if it is entering a new market, from whom it has to win market share, or which competitors' products and offers it needs to beat in order to satisfy a particular segment and be successful.

Market positioning

In strategic management literature, decisions regarding where and how the firm competes determine its **positioning**.[22] Where the firm competes is based on decisions regarding target markets and how the firm competes involve a firm's competitive advantages and their deployment.[23] A firm's positioning is based on how consumers differentiate the firm's products from those of its competitors and how the consumers evaluate the firm's products in relation to its competitors.

> **positioning**
>
> firm's strategy in creating a unique perception of their product in the customers' minds

Positioning refers to a firm's strategy geared towards creating a unique perception of its product, brand or corporation in a given competitive landscape.[2] Positioning is closely related to how consumers define the important attributes of the product and how customers perceive the firm's products in relation to the competing products. By doing so, consumers create a certain image of the company/product in their minds with respect to price, quality, durability and credibility.

In order to be effective, a firm's positioning strategy must be meaningful to the consumers. The firm must also enforce its position over time, emphasising its main message. Moreover, firms need to be careful in communicating the position clearly; a mismatch between positioning and actual product or consumer perception can prove disastrous.

In order to make positioning decisions, firms identify the existing offerings to different segments within the market.[20] In parallel, they also distinguish their own competitive advantages which can enable them to create a position in the market. Afterwards, firm's activities are concentrated on communicating such advantages to strengthen their position. Product positioning is done by tailoring the marketing elements to meet the needs of the consumer segment that the company has decided to target.[24]

Resource positioning theories hold that generalist firms which concentrate on scale and scope meet the needs of the majority of the market and specialist firms meet the needs of unique consumer groups. In parallel, a firm's positioning and resource deployment are dependent on the firm's choice.[25] In markets with concentrated structures, firms are bound to choose specialist strategies. Firm positioning is also influenced by industry characteristics.[26] There are no widely accepted systematic models which explain the creation of competitive advantages as a result of the positioning strategy. Broadly, firms analyse internal environment and capabilities, the external environment and opportunities in identifying possible international market segments, decide to target a certain segment group and then design positioning strategies accordingly.[27] Exhibit 11.5 presents an example

EXHIBIT 11.5: Perceptual maps showing positioning for different cars

In making decisions on products' positioning, perceptual maps are often useful. Such maps are designed to display the consumer's opinions on the competing products in a market in selected dimensions. Such maps help the company to identify areas with less competition and highlight opportunities in a given market. Perceptual maps may also help the firm to identify the consumer criteria for decision making for given products. Marketers can then emphasise the attributes of the product which are valued by the consumers.

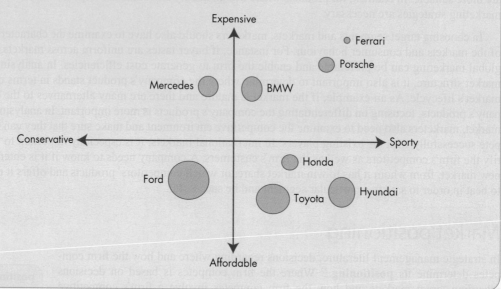

of positioning of different cars/brands in the consumer's mind according to the criteria they will use while evaluating different cars. The exhibit shows that customers may use different criteria to buy different products/services.

Approaches to positioning

Firms can differentiate their product in the consumer's mind by positioning.[2] Positioning strategies are implemented by exploiting certain product benefits or features, emphasising product quality for value, associating the brand with particular users' needs or highlighting the superior aspects of the product relative to competitors' products.[20]

Product characteristics or attributes

Firms whose approach to positioning is based on product characteristics focus on a particular feature of the product, such as its price, reliability, durability or benefits to the consumer. Marketing plans are then designed to emphasise the particular feature of the product. Some examples may be BMW's focus on performance, Visa's focus on reliability across the world or Ariel's emphasis on the ability to remove the toughest stains.

Price–quality

In this approach to positioning, firms focus on the relationship between the price and the quality of the product. For high-end products, firms can emphasise the exclusivity of the product and characteristics that make the product a premium one. Possible examples may be designer clothing or perfumes. For products with competitive prices, the firm can emphasise the low cost of the product with respect to its quality. Examples are Wal-Mart and easyJet.

Product users

This positioning approach centres on associating the product or the brand with a specific user or user group in order to correlate it with the user image or characteristics. Such positioning approaches can be observed in marketing which uses celebrities or professionals.

Going International 11.3

CARS FOR YOUNGSTERS

Renault has hired a product designer to woo younger consumers and a new Renault Twin'z was launched in April 2013 in Milan. Rose Lovegrove has earlier designed products such as Apple computers and bicycles and is recognised for his sharp designs. This is the first time he has been asked to design a car.

© Copyright Renault UK Limited

Renault's vice president explains that this car is launched not in a car exhibition but in a design exhibition in Milan to attract style conscious youngsters. The company wants to follow other design-focused products, such as Apple, which attract youngsters. The car is designed to look elegant and organic from wheels to roof. The wheels look like branches of alien trees and the tyres have been specially designed in two colours to meld seamlessly into the wheels. There are no door handles; instead a gold button opens the door. The back lights are most eye-catching, as they move and change colours when brakes are applied. The wheels and lights give the car a character that would appeal to younger consumers. But it will cost about the same as Renault's Twingo and will be launched later this year.

- Do you think a car specially designed for youngsters will be successful? Would you buy such a car?

Sources: based on Edwin Heathcote, *Financial Times*, 12 April 2013; and Leo Wilkinson, *The Telegraph*, 10 April 2013, http://www.telegraph.co.uk/motoring/car-manufacturers/renault/9982773/Renault-TwinZ-concept-car-previews-2014-Twingo.html.

Use or application

This positioning effort focuses on how the product is used and aims to associate the product with a specific application or use.

Competition

The product is implicitly or explicitly compared to that of the competitors in order to highlight the product's advantage over competitors' products or to alter the competitors' image in the consumers' minds. Possible examples are Body Shop's focus on natural ingredients or Burger King's emphasis on the flexibility of options.

Firms' strategic positioning decisions are also influenced by the industry and institutional framework in a given market.[25] For instance, consumer-product firms mostly focus on creating a unique perception of the product in the target market whereas industrial firms often focus on their ability to provide consistent quality and added value.[23]

Positioning in international marketing

Differences in factors such as culture, institutional framework, regulations and infrastructure in different countries influence many aspects of international marketing and also affect positioning strategies (see Exhibit 11.6). In international positioning decisions, firms need to examine whether the same

---

EXHIBIT 11.6: The importance of effective positioning

Positioning focuses on the perception of the firm in the consumer's mind with respect to the competitors. Hence in thinking about positioning strategies, firms need to be objective and determine their existing position given the market, and their position given the trends within the market.

If a firm is able to assess market positioning clearly then it can accurately examine the gaps in the market which it can fill or the value it can add. In the absence of this process, a firm may fail to create a distinct image of its product, choose a position which is too similar to that of existing players or form a position based on attributes which are not relevant to target consumers. In positioning, firms need to focus on understanding the competition in order to understand how they meet the needs of the consumers, their presence and dominance within the market as well as their resources.

A firm's positioning objectives and strategies influence most of its marketing plan, hence the firm needs to be very diligent in analysing its positioning within a market and selecting a target position. Moreover, a firm must also realise that inaccurate positioning would be a waste of resources.

Source: A. Ries, and J. Trout, *Positioning: The Battle for Your Mind* (New York: McGraw-Hill, 1986).

---

product attributes are valued across cultures, whether the product or the brand is perceived in the same manner and whether the competitive structure differs.[28]

Consideration should be given to factors such as technological level among countries, country of origin perceptions and regulations related to product packaging and standards. Moreover, adjustments may be necessary due to regulatory differences, infrastructure level and cultural perceptions. As the competitive landscape of each country varies, a firm's positioning choices vary.[29] In international positioning, a firm's focus is on differentiating its product, brand or the firm itself by focusing on specific features which make the firm unique when compared to competitors in that particular market.[7]

Marketers also need to focus on consistency across nations because developments in technology enable the marketing messages to be transmitted easily across different countries. In parallel, firms who develop positioning strategies which contradict each other in different markets may diminish their credibility. A major challenge in international market positioning is the need to maintain consistency in positioning strategies across different markets because information is easily permeated across markets. On the other hand, particular differences among different markets may require adjustments to the positioning strategies; hence the need to adopt the position while maintaining the identity.[30] A further issue arises where consumers have a pre-formed opinion of the capabilities or image of a country.

In-depth understanding of the target markets is, therefore, a precondition of successful positioning strategies.[12] In order to decide on positioning strategies, firms need to have an accurate picture of the market, and an understanding of how the forces within the market interact with each other[27] because differences in culture may cause differences in the perception of the customers.[12]

International positioning strategies

In international positioning, marketers need to decide whether they will use a uniform positioning strategy or to what extent they will modify the positioning strategy for different markets. If target segments exhibit similarities globally, such as similar buying patterns, attitudes, lifestyles or values, then the firm may be able to use the same positioning strategy across markets. In these cases the firm may create a consistent image.[26]

Some of the major topics in this area are: identification of determinants of competitive advantage; construction of generalisable and effective positioning strategies; and the influence of country and entry-mode selection on positioning decisions.[27] Positioning strategies may be categorised as: local consumer-culture positioning; foreign consumer-culture positioning; and, in line with new developments, global consumer-culture positioning. Global consumer-culture positioning emphasises a product's attractiveness to a given global culture. In contrast local culture positioning entails highlighting the local culture's values and meanings in marketing the product.[10] Global positioning strategies of a firm reflect its approach to differentiating itself from the global competitors. In individual markets, some adjustments are often necessary.[5]

Global consumer culture positioning

In line with rapid globalisation and increased interconnectedness across the world, global cultures have emerged. Relevance of the firm or its product to a global culture or a segment is emphasised for products which are influenced by globalisation. In practice such positioning may not always be effective, as different cultures are often associated with dissimilar lives, tastes and values, even if they seem to follow a global culture.[29]

Going International 11.4

SNICKERS – QUALITY THAT YOU CAN TASTE

In 1923, the Mars company introduced the nougat-laced Milky Way. It was an ingenious creation because it was both cheaper and bigger than a regular chocolate bar made by, say, Hershey's.

By 1933, Mars was taking in $25m annually. Forrest Sr. departed for Europe, with $50,000 and the Milky Way recipe from his father. He was a natural entrepreneur. After working in the Swiss chocolate factories of Henri Nestlé and Jean Tobler, Forrest Sr. developed the Mars bar – pretty much an even sweeter Milky Way – and in England he pioneered the notion of food for pets.

Then was born the idea for M&Ms. The 'Ms' were Forrest and R. Bruce Murrie, a son of the president of competitor Hershey's, which Mars asked to supply the chocolate because of limited cocoa availability during the Second World War. M&M 'plain chocolate candies,' in four colours, began selling in 1941, becoming the most popular candy in America. After his father's death at 50, Forrest Jr. eventually returned to the USA and in the 1960s merged both parts of the business.

As the Mars business burgeoned over the years, its culture was also taking hold. Forrest Sr. eliminated private offices and divisive trappings like the chauffeured $20,000 Duesenberg.

In 1973, with annual corporate revenue at about $1bn, Forrest Sr. turned control of the business over to his two sons, Forrest Jr. and John, who – like their father – were both Yale university graduates who went overseas to learn the ropes.

In 1982, Mars passed on the chance to have E.T. lured out of the forest by the M&Ms of a young boy named Elliott. Mars thought the creature too scary. The movie used Reese's Pieces instead and gave Hershey's a marketing coup. Forrest Sr. died in 1999, but not before inspiring in his hardworking sons their own peculiarities. Among the sons' strategic contributions was focusing on global expansion, eg into Russia. In 1979 they were also among the first to persuade shop-owners to put sweet displays near cash registers, the better to generate impulse purchases.

Today Mars has 11 billion-dollar brands. Snickers and M&Ms are the most popular sweets in the world and in the USA Mars' chocolate business is eclipsed only by Hershey's. Almost every dollar of profit gets reinvested in the company. Each Mars division functions with vast independence – subject to the core principles. When Chicago-based Wrigley was acquired by Mars in 2008, the storied 117-year-old chewing-gum manufacturer had to gut its interior offices to change to Mars' open-floor plan.

Forrest Jr. and John retired as Mars co-presidents in 1991 and 2001, respectively, setting the stage for different non-family members to run the company day-to-day. In 2004, Michaels became president. During Michaels' tenure as president, Mars revenue has doubled (in part because of the Wrigley purchase, which was partly funded by Warren Buffett's Berkshire Hathaway). *Adweek* credits him with driving Mars' 'creative renaissance' in advertising, an example of which is the commercial for Snickers Peanut Butter Squared featuring man-eating sharks.

- What do you think is the secret of Mars' success? What were its objectives when it launched M&Ms?

Source: compiled from several sources such as various issues of the *Economist* and *Financial Times*, 2012.

Often firms choose such positioning for technologically intensive products as such products are often associated with universal performance standards. For example, computers, tablets and other consumer electronic products are often in this category. Firms producing special-interest products may also choose such positioning strategies because consumers of such products often look for similar attributes. Examples are Canon cameras, Adidas sports gear and Rolex wrist watches.[20]

Local consumer culture positioning

In local consumer culture positioning, the product and the brand or the company itself are associated with local cultural values.

Foreign consumer culture positioning

The brand, product or the firm itself is associated with a foreign culture. National origin of the product is highlighted. Examples are Budweiser's use of small American towns in their marketing and perfume and cosmetics association with France.

Choice of the appropriate positioning strategy is influenced by multiple factors such as target markets, product category and characteristics, the positioning of the competitors or level of economic development within a market. For instance, if the target consumers share common characteristics, global culture positioning may be beneficial. On the other hand, if the competitors within the market are all using global culture positioning strategies, a firm may differentiate itself by using a local consumer culture positioning strategy.[26]

SUMMARY

The process of segmentation, targeting and positioning enables firms to create effective marketing strategies. In international markets firms are faced with multiple economic and demographic conditions, and cultures which may result in varying consumer behaviour. Hence in international segmentation they need to consider the influence of such variables when analysing potential markets.

In international market targeting, firms assess compatibility between suitable market segments and their ability to serve the needs of such segments. As part of this process, they also consider the most beneficial international targeting strategy for the firm, which determines whether it is advantageous to formulate a uniform marketing strategy for all targeted markets, develop different market strategies for each market or concentrate on a marketing strategy geared towards a particular segment present across multiple markets.

In international positioning, firms need to consider the characteristics of the firm, the target market and the perception of the firm or the competitors within the target markets. Analysing positioning in international markets necessitates an objective focus on the market structure, positions valued within such a structure and the potential opportunities which may prevail within the market. Always, firms need to consider their position in terms of the consumer's perception of their image, and of their product.

QUESTIONS

1   What are the bases for international positioning? Explain with examples.
2   What are the bases for international segmentation? Explain with examples.
3   Explain segmentation strategies of a multinational company, where it targets different segments in different markets for the same product.

4　How is international positioning related to international segmentation?

5　Is it important to know your target customers when entering a new market? Explain how it can help in entry strategy.

6　Take an advertisement from a magazine and identify its target customer. Justify your choice.

7　What are the international positioning strategies available to an international marketer? Explain each strategy and in what situation it should be used.

FURTHER READING

- D.W. Baack, E. Harris and D. Baack, *International Marketing* (London: Sage, 2012), Ch 5.
- A. Ries and J. Trout, *Positioning: The Battle for Your Mind* (New York: McGraw-Hill, 1986).
- J. Trout, S. Rivkin and A. Ries, *The New Positioning: The Latest on the World's# 1 Business Strategy* (New York: McGraw-Hill, 1996).

NOTES

1　J.J. Li, K.Z. Zhou and A.T. Shao, 'Competitive Position, Managerial Ties, and Profitability of Foreign Firms in China: An Interactive Perspective', *Journal of International Business Studies*, 2008, 40(2), pp 339–52.

2　E.K. Foedermayr and A. Diamantopoulos, 'Exploring the Construct of Segmentation Effectiveness: Insights from International Companies and Experts', *Journal of Strategic Marketing*, 2008, 16(2), pp 129–56.

3　M.K. Agarwal, 'Developing Global Segments and Forecasting Market Shares: A Simultaneous Approach Using Survey Data', *Journal of International Marketing*, 2003, 11(4), pp 56–80.

4　R.M. Papuc and O.S. Hudea, 'International Marketing Strategies in the Globalisation Era', *Lex et Scientia International Journal*, 2009, (XVI-2), pp 301.

5　H. Mühlbacher, H. Leihs and L. Dahringer, *International Marketing: A Global Perspective* (Melbourne: Thomson Learning, 2006).

6　S.S. Hassan and S.H. Craft, 'An Examination of Global Market Segmentation Bases and Strategic Positioning Decisions', *International Business & Economics Research Journal*, 2011, 3(9).

7　D.W. Baack, E. Harris and D. Baack, *International Marketing* (London: Sage, 2012).

8　M. Cleveland, N. Papadopoulos and M. Laroche, 'Identity, Demographics, and Consumer Behaviors: International Market Segmentation across Product Categories', *International Marketing Review*, 2011, 28(3), 244–66.

9　A. Weinstein, 'A Strategic Framework for Defining and Segmenting Markets', *Journal of Strategic Marketing*, 2006, 14(2), 115–27.

10　B.S. Gammoh, A.C. Koh and S.C. Okoroafo, 'Consumer Culture Brand Positioning Strategies: An Experimental Investigation', *Journal of Product & Brand Management*, 2011, 20(1), 48–57.

11　E. Ko *et al.*, 'Global Marketing Segmentation Usefulness in the Sportswear Industry', *Journal of Business Research*, 2012, 65(11), pp 1565–75.

12　A. Pankhania, N. Lee and G. Hooley, 'Within-country Ethnic Differences and Product Positioning: A Comparison of the Perceptions of Two British Sub-cultures,' *Journal of Strategic Marketing*, 2007, 15(2–3), 121–38.

13 S.T. Cavusgil, G. Knight and J.R. Riesenberger, *International Business: Strategy, Management, and the New Realities*, (Englewood Cliffs, NJ: Pearson Prentice Hall, 2008).

14 S.P. Douglas and C.S. Craig, 'Global Marketing Strategy: Past, Present, and Future', *Advances in International Management*, 2010, 23, 431–57.

15 J. Boejgaard and C. Ellegaard, 'Unfolding Implementation in Industrial Market Segmentation', *Industrial Marketing Management*, 2010, 39(8), 1291–9.

16 C.P. Blocker and D.J. Flint, 'Customer Segments as Moving Targets: Integrating Customer Value Dynamism into Segment Instability Logic', *Industrial Marketing Management*, 2007, 36(6), 810–22.

17 Dannie Kjeldgaard and Søren Askegaard, 'The Globalization of Youth Culture: The Global Youth Segment as Structures of Common Difference', *Journal of Consumer Research*, 2006, 33(2), 231–47.

18 N. Zonis, *Market Segmentation in European Markets* (Baston: GRIN Verlag, 2009).

19 O.C. Ferrell and M. Hartline, *Marketing Strategy* (Andover, MA: South-Western Publishing, 2010).

20 W.J. Keegan and M.C. Green, *Global Marketing* (Englewood Cliffs, NJ: Pearson Prentice Hall, 2008).

21 S. Onkvisit and J.J. Shaw, *International Marketing: Strategy and Theory* (London: Routledge, 2009).

22 G. Hooley *et al.*, 'Market-focused Resources, Competitive Positioning and Firm Performance', *Journal of Marketing Management*, 2001, 17(5–6), 503–20.

23 J. Juga, S. Pekkarinen and H. Kilpala, 'Strategic Positioning of Logistics Service Providers', *International Journal of Logistics Research and Applications*, 2008, 11(6), 443–55.

24 C. Blankson and S.P. Kalafatis, 'Positioning Strategies of International and Multicultural-oriented Service Brands', *Journal of Services Marketing*, 2007, 21(6), 435–50.

25 Y.H. Xie *et al.*, 'On the Determinants of Post-entry Strategic Positioning of Foreign Firms in a Host Market: A Strategy Tripod Perspective', *International Business Review*, 2011, 20(4), 477–90.

26 M. Kotabe and K. Helsen, *Global Marketing Management* (Hoboken, NJ: Wiley, 2004).

27 S.K. Sharma and R. Srinivasan, 'Modeling of International Positioning Process for New Trade Endeavours: A Radically Succinct Approach', *Journal of Academy of Business and Economics*, 2008, 8(1), 34–48.

28 J. Ganesh and G. Oakenfull, 'International Product Positioning', *Journal of Global Marketing*, 2000, 13(2), 85–111.

29 M.K. De Mooij and M. de Mooij, *Consumer Behavior and Culture: Consequences for Global Marketing and Advertising* (London: Sage, 2010).

30 A. Mishra, 'Strategic Brand Management of International Fashion Retailers', *Journal of Indian Management & Strategy, 8M*, 2010, 15(4), 26–34.

Chapter 12
International Branding Strategies

Chapter Outline

Chapter Learning Objectives

What you should learn from Chapter 12

- How branding has developed
- Why companies use brands
- The main functions of a brand and how they work
- How to develop brands and what process to follow
- The components of brand equity and how it is created.

Introduction to branding

Philip Kotler provides a definition that highlights the differentiation function of a brand:

> A name, term, sign, symbol, or design, or combination of them, intended to identify the goods or services of one seller or group of sellers and to differentiate them from those of competitors.[1]

Another definition that covers more functions of a brand is:

> A successful brand is an identifiable product, service, person or place, augmented in such a way that the buyer or user perceives relevant, unique added values which match their needs most closely. Furthermore, its success results from being able to sustain these added values in the face of competition.[2]

Companies use brands to be able to convey their marketing strategy and positioning to the markets. Brands are now the most valuable assets companies have. Nike, Coca-Cola, Adidas, Nokia, Philips and Sony are good examples. The best-managed brands increase in value with age and develop personalities of their own. Some even give birth to sub-brands or brand extensions and allow the company to exploit the brand in new areas. Coca-Cola's and Marlboro's clothing lines, different products of Sony and several models of BMW are good examples. Brand extension allows new products to be introduced with lower marketing expenditure. It also allows companies to utilise their existing customer base.

Brands have a profound impact on society, nation/country and customer emotions, thus awarding the brand owner a great responsibility. We have seen that during the wars in Vietnam and Iraq, consumers in many countries boycotted American brands. From a marketer's point of view, the most important impact of brands is that they lead to customer satisfaction and loyalty. A loyal customer base is the biggest asset of a company. The brands are thus the biggest value generators in many companies (see Exhibit 12.1).

brand loyalty

when a customer always buys the same brand

customer loyalty

when a customer always buys one company's products

branding

developing and building the reputation of a brand name

Brand loyalty leads to resistance to switching to another company's products. The more satisfied a customer is, the less inclined he or she will be to buy or even try a competing product. Sometimes switching cost is also an important factor (for example, for software users). However, by mismanaging their brands, many companies have lost their customers even in this product category. Products such as WordPerfect, Wordstar and Baan software are good examples.

Customer loyalty automatically creates barriers to entry for competitors. To snatch market shares from an established brand would require excessive resources. This is particularly important for companies trying to enter foreign (new) markets. The existence of established brands in the particular market, whether local or foreign, and loyalty of customers, will create entry barriers for newcomers. It will also increase the cost associated with the entrance and consequently the profits.

It is thus important for companies to establish brands. **Branding** means developing and building the reputation of a brand name. This is done by understanding the customer segments and creating a brand that can be perceived to satisfy these segments' needs/wants, and then conveying this through communication, advertising and other means. Branding decisions include deciding on the number of brands to be used and how many brands to be used in each market. For example, following the success of the EU, Unilever has decided to cut the number of its brands from 1,600 to 400. This will allow the company to achieve economies of scale as well as more focused recognition throughout Europe. This will also make distribution and promotion more efficient.

The development of branding

The roots of today's brands lie in classical Greek and Roman times. Ancient Greeks and Romans lived in cities, and tradesmen promoted their wares by means of written information so that the public would be aware that there were products and services available at a particular address.[3] In those days there were signs or route descriptions to 'shops' carved in stone, and there were even (brand) markings applied to pieces of silver. The signboards of shops often showed no more than pictures of the products sold there.

EXHIBIT 12.1: Top 25 global brands 2008 and 2012

Rank 2012	Rank 2008	Brand	Country	Sector	2012 brand value ($m)	Change in brand value
1	1	Coca-Cola	USA	Beverages	77,839.00	+8%
2	24	Apple	USA	Computer hardware	76,568.00	+129
3	2	IBM	USA	Computer services	75,532.00	+8
4	10	Google	USA	Internet services	69,726.00	+26
5	3	Microsoft	USA	Computer software	58,853.00	−2
6	4	General Electric	USA	Diversified	43,682.00	+2
7	8	McDonald's	USA	Restaurants	40,062.00	+13
8	7	Intel	USA	Computer hardware	39,385.00	+12
9	21	Samsung	Republic of Korea	Consumer electronics	32,893.00	+40
10	6	Toyota	Japan	Automotive	30,280.00	+9
11	11	Mercedes-Benz	Germany	Automotive	30,097.00	+10
12	13	BMW	Germany	Automotive	29,052.00	+18
13	9	Disney	USA	Media	27,438.00	−5
14	17	Cisco	USA	Computer services	27,197.00	+7
15	12	HP	USA	Computer hardware	26,087.00	−8
16	14	Gillette	USA	Personal care	24,898.00	+4
17	16	Louis Vuitton	France	Luxury	25,577.00	+2
18	23	Oracle	USA	Computer software	22,126.00	+28
19	5	Nokia	Finland	Consumer electronics	21,009.00	−16
20	New	Amazon	USA	Ecommerce services	18,625.00	+46
21	20	Honda	Japan	Automotive	17,280.00	−11
22	New	Pepsi	USA	Beverages	16,594.00	+14
23	22	H&M	Sweden	Apparel	16,571.00	+1
24	15	American Express	USA	Financial services	15,702.00	+8
25	New	SAP	USA	Computer software	15,641.00	+8

Source: http://www.interbrand.com/en/best-global-brands/2012/Best-Global-Brands-2012-Brand-View.aspx.

The English word 'brand' probably first appeared in the Middle Ages and comes from the old Norse word *brandr*, which refers to the branding of cattle to show property rights. The Vikings may have spread the word *brandr* in England, where it was eventually incorporated into daily language. In the Middle Ages there were several types of brand signs: craftsman, guild and city signs were used. The craftsman signs most resemble brand names; these signs showed who the maker of the product was but, just like the silver signs of the ancient Greeks and Romans, were no more than a method of identification.

The modern brand has its origin in the late nineteenth century with the introduction of factories and mass production, mass distribution and mass communication. In the beginning brands were created as a way to help the consumer distinguish one manufacturer's products from another. The idea was to create a bond with the consumer, hoping to win their loyalty.

Going International 12.1

AN INDUSTRY RIPE FOR A SHAKE-UP

The average Swiss watch costs $685. A Chinese one costs around $2 and tells the time just as well. So how on earth, a Martian might ask, can the Swiss watch industry survive? Yet it does. Exports of watches made in

▶

Switzerland have grown by 32 per cent in value over the past two years, to SFr21.4bn ($23.3bn). Demand in the biggest markets (China, America and Singapore) dipped recently, but some of the slack was picked up by watch-loving Arabs and Europeans.

No one buys a Swiss watch to find out what time it is. The allure is intangible: precise engineering, beautifully displayed. The art of fine watchmaking has all but died out elsewhere, but it thrives in Switzerland. 'Swiss-made' has become one of the world's most valuable brands.

In the popular imagination, Swiss watches are made by craftsmen at tiny firms nestled in Alpine villages. In fact, the industry is dominated by one big firm. The Swatch Group's stable of brands (Breguet, Blancpain, Omega and a dozen others) generated watch and jewellery sales of SFr7.3bn in 2012. That is up by 15.6 per cent over the previous year and accounts for one-third of all sales of Swiss watches. In January Swatch announced the purchase of Harry Winston, an American jeweller which also makes watches in Geneva.

Swatch's dominance goes even deeper than this. It is the biggest supplier of the bits that make Swiss watches tick. It owns ETA, which makes over 70 per cent of the movements (core mechanisms) put in watches by other Swiss watchmakers. Another subsidiary, Nivarox-FAR, supplies more than 90 per cent of the balance springs (which regulate watches).

Many big brands rely on Swatch. LVMH (owner of Bulgari, Hublot and TAG Heuer) and Richemont (owner of IWC, Piaget and Vacheron Constantin) use Swatch components. So do the British and German watchmakers that are trying to break into this lucrative market. Few, however, can match the precision of a Nivarox balance spring.

Swatch became the watchmaker to watch in the 1980s, when it merged two weak companies and launched Swatch watches as a relatively cheap brand (though not nearly as cheap as a typical Chinese timepiece). It remains dominant, in part, because other firms find it easier to let someone else go to all the trouble and expense of producing their watches' most fiddly and essential components.

But Swatch now finds this arrangement irksome. It supplies parts to rivals (Swiss and foreign) which then spend lavishly on advertising. Swatch would like to curb its sales of components, to 30 per cent of the Swiss total by 2018. The Swiss Competition Commission agreed to modest reductions in 2012. After lobbying by watchmakers, Swatch will make no more cuts this year, but next year it will probably try again.

Swatch may be doing the industry a favour. Its actions may prod other watchmakers to invest more in their own factories. Already, Richemont and LVMH are buying up smaller component-makers. 'Everyone could actually produce these components,' says a spokesman for the Competition Commission.

At present only a few high-end watchmakers can do without Swatch, for example Patek Philippe in Switzerland and Robert Loomes in Britain. But such Swatch-shunners typically make only a few (costly) watches each year. Firms that make larger batches of not-quite-so-pricey watches still need Swatch. So its retreat from the parts market will cause turmoil, and probably more consolidation.

Meanwhile the Swiss government seems about to tighten the definition of 'Swiss-made'. Currently, a watch may not claim to be Swiss unless 50 per cent of its components, by value, were crafted in the cantons. Swiss

◄

watchmakers are trying to get the threshold raised to 60 per cent. That will create demand for Swiss components even as Swatch curbs the supply. So watch out: prices will rise even higher.

● Can a brand be destroyed if it is overexposed? Discuss.

Sources: based on *The Economist*, 16 February 2013; and http://www.swatch.com/.

This strategy was very successful and some of the brands created during this time are still vital in today's marketplace. Many of the first brands had the same name as the manufacturer (Mr Gillette, Mr Kraft and Mr Lipton), but there were also other examples of brands (American Express, Coca-Cola and Kellogg's) that were invented.

In the beginning branded products were sold through 'rational' marketing campaigns. However, as the markets matured and the products became more similar, companies started to market their brands through image and lifestyle – creating different personalities around their brands.

The work of differentiating a brand became a central question for companies in the quest to become more competitive and to move towards building or producing a brand rather than a product.[4] This resulted in more and more companies considering their brand as one of their most valuable assets, which also increased the importance of marketing.

Brands are now recognised on balance sheets as assets in the same way as any other tangible. Rank Hovis McDougal valued their brands at £678m on their 1988 balance sheet, a move that has since been replicated by other companies.[5] Nestlé's purchase of Rowntree for €2.4bn was considerably above the market capitalisation of the company of around €1bn, emphasising the value of the brand.[6] Procter & Gamble paid $57bn to Gillette, while Tata paid around €1.5bn for both the Jaguar and Land Rover brands when they bought these from Ford.

A global brand generally means substantial cost savings and gives a company a uniform worldwide image that enhances efficiency and cost savings when introducing other products associated with the brand name. Not all companies, however, believe a global approach is best. Except for companies such as Philips, Kodak, Coca-Cola, Caterpillar, Sony and Levi's, which use the same brands worldwide, other multinationals such as Nestlé, Mars, Procter & Gamble, Unilever and Gillette have some brands that are promoted worldwide and others that are country specific. Unilever never uses the name 'Unilever' for any of its products. Among companies that have faced the question of whether or not to make all their brands global, not all have followed the same path.

Going International 12.2

THE CHINESE STORY IN THE MAKING

Haier, a home-grown electrical appliance company, began by making compact refrigerators for small homes in China, a market segment Western multinationals deemed unprofitable. Then, in the 1990s, Haier entered the US market, targeting a largely untapped group of consumers who would use its refrigerators in college dorms and hotel rooms. It has since captured almost half of that market segment. By 2009, Haier had surpassed Whirlpool as the world's top refrigerator producer by sales volume. Haier's current development path is similar to the early history of Toyota in the USA during the 1960s, when the company gained an initial foothold by targeting housewives and teenagers who needed a second and/or affordable vehicle to run around town.

Similarly, Chinese PC maker Lenovo was able to avoid the predicament of Taiwan's PC industry by focusing on the rural retail sector early on – again, a market segment that Western multinationals shunned. Starting in 1998, the company invested aggressively in infrastructure – including local offices, sales teams and supervisors – to directly

►

The Lenovo ThinkPad X200 Tablet.
© Istockphoto.com/PictureLake

manage a sprawling retail network that covered the most obscure cities and even villages in China. HP and Dell, by contrast, concentrated only on coastal cities where reputable, third-party distributors operated. As local demand soared, Lenovo achieved greater economies of scale, attained lower production costs, and generated healthy profits for reinvestment. In 2005, Lenovo acquired IBM's personal computing division, paving the way to enter more developed markets.

China's green energy sector faces a promising future for a similar reason. Domestic solar panel and wind turbine manufacturers have been focusing on serving rural areas of western China as they have better access than overseas competitors to remote areas. China's Suntech and Goldwind are now among the world's largest solar panel and wind turbine manufacturers. While it remains to be seen whether Chinese firms can beat GE and Siemens in leading the green energy revolution, the competitive landscape is tilted toward the East.

Such favourable conditions do not always coalesce, however. As the example of Taiwan's PC industry shows, the use of the acquired know-how of certain industries can sometimes be severely limited to the existing mainstream market. This also applies to some Chinese firms. For example, civil aircraft manufacturing is one of the industries where the requirements of all customers – existing and potential – are virtually the same. International and Chinese airlines require similar product performance and they must comply with universal safety standards. In such settings, the prospects of local firms in China become much less certain.

Mark Twain is supposed to have said that 'History does not repeat itself, but it rhymes.' An understanding of how companies in Japan, South Korea and Taiwan have evolved differently provides enormous insights into how Chinese companies across different industries might behave.

- Will China inevitably develop powerful global brands?

Source: adapted from http://www.imd.org/research/challenges/TC011-12.cfm.

---

country-specific brand

a brand that is sold in only one country

Companies that already have successful **country-specific brand** names must balance the benefits of a global brand against the risk of losing the benefits of an established brand. The cost of re-establishing the same level of brand preference and market share for the global brand that the local brand had must be offset against the long-term cost savings and benefits of having only one brand name worldwide.

A different strategy is followed by Nestlé, which has a stable of global and country-specific brands in its product line. The Nestlé name itself is promoted globally but its global brand expansion strategy is two-pronged. It acquires well-established local brands when it can and builds on their strengths; in other markets where there are no strong brands it can acquire, it uses global brand names. The company is described as preferring brands to be local, people regional and technology global. It does, however, own some of the world's largest global brands – Nescafé is but one.

Unilever is another company that follows a similar strategy of a mix of local and global brands. In Poland Unilever introduced its Omo brand detergent (sold in many other countries), but it also purchased a local brand, Paulina 2000. Despite the strong introduction of two competing brands, Omo by Unilever and Ariel by Procter & Gamble, a refurbished Paulina 2000 had the largest market share a year later. Unilever's explanation was that Eastern European consumers are wary of new brands; they want brands that are affordable and in keeping with their own tastes and values. Paulina 2000 is successful not just because it is cheaper but because it chimes with local values.[7] More recently, Unilever has decided to focus on fewer brands, and has cut the number of brands from 1,600 to 400 in its hygiene product group.

Country-of-origin effect and global brands

As discussed earlier, brands are used as external cues to taste, design, performance, quality, value, prestige and so forth. In other words, the consumer associates the value of the product with the brand. The brand can convey either a positive or a negative message about the product to the consumer and is affected by past advertising and promotion, product reputation and product evaluation and experience. In short, many factors affect brand image, and one factor that is of great concern to multinational companies that manufacture worldwide is the **country-of-origin effect (COE)** on the market's perception of the product.[8]

> **country-of-origin effect (COE)**
>
> influence of country of manufacture on a consumer's positive or negative perception of a product

COE can be defined as any influence that the country of manufacture has on a consumer's positive or negative perception of a product. Today a company competing in global markets will manufacture products worldwide and, when the customer is aware of the country of origin, there is the possibility that the place of manufacture will affect product/brand image.

The country, the type of product and the image of the company and its brands all influence whether or not the country of origin will engender a positive or negative reaction. There are a variety of generalisations that can be made about COEs on products and brands. Consumers tend to have stereotypes about products and countries that have been formed by experience, hearsay and myth. We will now look at some of the more frequently cited generalisations.

Consumers adhere to broad but somewhat vague stereotypes about specific countries and specific product categories that they judge 'best': English tea, French fashion garments and perfumes, Chinese silk, Italian leather, Japanese electronics, Jamaican rum, and so on. Stereotyping of this nature is typically product specific and may not extend to other categories of products from these countries.

Ethnocentrism can also have COEs. Feelings of national pride – the 'buy American' effect, for example – can influence attitudes towards foreign products. Honda, which manufactures one of its models almost entirely in the USA, recognises this phenomenon and points out how many component parts are made in America in some of its advertisements. On the other hand, others adhere to the stereotype of Japan as producing the 'best' cars. A recent study found that US car producers may suffer comparatively tarnished in-country images regardless of whether they actually produce superior products.[9]

Going International 12.3

NEW PRODUCTS CHALLENGING THE IMPERIALISTS

Boycotts are often used to demonstrate disapproval of policies at all levels. When France did not support the war in Iraq, the US administration and consumers openly boycotted French products. No official party was to serve French wine and French cheese. French fries were renamed freedom fries. After the war in Iraq, Muslim consumers in many countries also started boycotting American products. Some companies/entrepreneurs detected the opportunity and started providing alternatives. Mecca-Cola is perhaps the most famous example. Introduced by a French-Tunisian businessman in France, it targets consumers who do not want 'coca-colonisation' and those who want to boycott American products because of its foreign policy or for any other reason.

Mecca-Cola has been a big success; the launch in the British market was delayed twice as manufacturing capacity could not cope with excessive demand all over Europe.

The market for political food goes beyond fizzy drinks. Those moved by the plight of Palestinian farmers can now buy 'Zayton olive oil', harvested from the West Bank.

© P.N. Ghauri.

▶

◀

The demand, according to importers, has been enormous; the first two shipments were presold to distributors and shops.

● Do you think politics plays a role in brand selection? Discuss.

Source: compiled from 'Political Food: Mullah Moolah', *The Economist*, 30 October 2004, p 37.

Countries are also stereotyped on the basis of whether they are industrialised, emerging or less-developed economies. These stereotypes are less country-product specific; they are more a perception of the quality of goods in general produced within the country. Industrialised countries have the highest quality image, and there is generally a bias against products from developing countries. However, within countries grouped by economic development there are variations of image. For example, one study of COE between Mexico and Taiwan found that a microwave oven manufactured in Mexico was perceived as significantly more risky than an oven made in Taiwan. However, for jeans there was no difference in perception between the two countries.[10]

One might generalise that the more technical the product, the less positive is the perception of one manufactured in a less-developed country. There is also the tendency to favour **foreign-made products** over **domestic-made products** in less-developed countries. Not all foreign products fare equally well, because consumers in developing countries adhere to stereotypes about the quality of foreign-made products even from industrialised countries. A survey of consumers in the Czech Republic found that 72 per cent of Japanese products were considered to be of the highest quality, German goods followed with 51 per cent, Swiss goods with 48 per cent, Czech goods with 32 per cent and, last, the USA with 29 per cent.[11]

foreign-made products

those products made in a different country from the one they are being sold in

domestic-made products

those products sold in the country in which they were made

One final generalisation about COE involves fads that often surround products from particular countries or regions in the world. These fads are most often product specific and generally involve goods that are themselves faddish in nature. European consumers are apparently enamoured with a host of American-made products ranging from Jeep Cherokees to Bose sound systems.[12] In the 1970s and 1980s there was a backlash against anything American, but in the 1990s American was in. In China anything Western seems to be the fad. If it is Western, it is in demand, even at prices three or four times higher than domestic products.[13] In most cases, such fads wane after a few years as some new fad takes over.

Country stereotyping can be overcome with good marketing. The image of Korean electronics improved substantially in Western countries once the market gained positive experience with Korean brands. All of which stresses the importance of building strong global brands like Sony, General Electric, Samsung and Levi's. Brands effectively advertised and products properly positioned can help ameliorate a less-than-positive country stereotype. Consumers perceive **pioneering brands** more positively than **follower brands**, irrespective of COE. Apple's iPod is a good example.[14]

pioneering brands

brands that were first in the market

follower brands

brands that came later to the market

own brand

retailers' own brands (eg Tesco tea)

Own brands

Growing as challenges to manufacturers' brands, whether global or country-specific, are brands owned by retailers. In the food-retailing sector in Britain, the Netherlands and many European countries, manufacturers' brands are increasingly confronted by brands owned by national retailers. From blackberry jam, coffee, tea and vacuum-cleaner bags to smoked salmon and sun-dried tomatoes, **own brand** products dominate grocery stores in Britain and in many of the hypermarkets of Europe. It is estimated

EXHIBIT 12.2: Market share and growth rate for own brands

	Market share (%)	Growth rate (annual % 2003)
Global	15	4
Europe	22	6
North America	16	0
Asia Pacific	4	14
Emerging markets	4	48
Latin America	1	16

Source: compiled from Gary Silverman, 'Retailers Pack New Punch in Battle with Brands', *Financial Times*, 15 November 2004, p 20.

that own-brand products have captured nearly 30 per cent of the British and Swiss markets, and more than 20 per cent of the French and German markets. In some European markets, own-brand market share has doubled in just the past five years.

Sainsbury's, for example, one of Britain's largest grocery retailers with more than 450 stores, reserves the best shelf-space for its own brands. A typical Sainsbury's store has about 16,000 products, of which 8,000 are Sainsbury's own brands. The company avidly develops new products, launching 1,400 to 1,500 new own-brand items each year, and weeds out hundreds of others that are no longer popular. It launched its own Novonbrand laundry detergent and, in the first year, its sales climbed past Procter & Gamble's and Unilever's top brands to make it the top-selling detergent in Sainsbury's stores and the second-best seller nationally with a 30 per cent market share.[15] The 15 per cent margin on own-brand labels that chains such as Sainsbury boast about helps explain why their operating profit margins are as high as 8 per cent, or eight times the profit margins of their US counterparts.

Own-brand penetration has traditionally been high in Britain and, more recently, high in Europe as well. Own brands, with their high margins, will become even more important as the trend in consolidation of retailers continues and as discounters such as Ahold of the Netherlands, Aldi of Germany, Wal-Mart of the USA and Carrefour of France expand throughout Europe, putting greater pressure on prices.

As it stands now, own brands are formidable competitors. They provide the retailer with high margins, they receive preferential shelf-space and strong in-store promotion and, perhaps most important for consumer appeal, they are quality products at low prices. Contrast this with manufacturers' brands, which are traditionally premium priced and offer the retailer lower margins than they get from their own brands. Exhibit 12.2 shows the market share and growth rate for own brands.

To maintain market share, global brands will have to be priced competitively and provide real consumer value. Global marketers must examine the adequacy of their brand strategies in the light of such competition. This may make the cost and efficiency benefits of global brands even more appealing.

Brand elements

Ten main elements are identified on branding that represent the broad range of definitions and elements of a brand; such as: *legal instrument, logo, company, risk reducer, identity system, image in consumers' minds, value system, personality, relationship* and *adding value*.[16] The ten elements present a certain degree of overlapping among the tangible and intangible contents of the brand. Exhibit 12.3 shows these elements and lists their antecedents and consequences.

A brand's strength is based on the dimensions that customers find relevant and are different from other offers available in the market. The brand thus gives the consumer an added value, regardless of whether it is about taste or status. In other words, the truth is that brand functions can differ from situation to situation and customer to customer.

EXHIBIT 12.3: Elements of a brand and its functions

Brand elements	Contents	Functions
Legal instrument	– Mark of ownership – Name, logo, design – Trademark	– Prosecute infringers
Logo	– Name, term, symbol, design – Product characteristics	– Indentify and differentiate through visual identity and name – Quality assurance
Company	– Recognisable corporate name and image – Programmes of organisation define corporate personality	– Product lines benefit from corporate personality – Convey consistent message to stakeholders – Differentiation: establish relationship
Risk reducer	– Confidence that expectation being fulfilled	– Brand as a contract
Identity system	– More than just a name – Holistic structure including brand's personality	– Meaning – Strategic positioning – Communicate essence to stakeholders
Image	– Consumer centred – Image in consumers' minds is brand 'reality'	– Feedback of image to change identity – Market research – Manage brand concept over time
Value system	– Consumer relevant values imbue the brand	– Brand values match relevant consumer values
Personality	– Psychological values, communicated through advertising and packaging define brand's personality	– Differentiation from symbolism: human values projected – Stress added values beyond functional
Relationship	– Consumer has attitude to brand – Brand as person has attitude to consumer	– Recognition and respect for personality – Develop relationship
Adding value	– Non-functional extras – Value satisfier – Consumers imbue brand with subjective meaning they value enough to buy – Aesthetics	– Differentiate from competing products – Charge price premium – Consumer experience – Belief in performance

Source: adapted from Chernatony and Riley (1998), p 426.

Functions of brands

Brands satisfy and benefit both buyers and sellers. For buyers, brands reduce search costs by helping them identify specific products,[17] perceived risk by assuring a buyer of a level of quality,[18] and psychological risk by eliminating the negative social consequences of using the 'wrong' brand.[19] For sellers, brands 'facilitate' repeat purchases,[20] the introduction of new products,[21] promotional efforts,[22] premium pricing and enable marketers to communicate identical messages to target customers.[23]

Characteristics of brands

Brands include several levels of meaning that a brand is able to deliver, as shown in Exhibit 12.4:[24]

1 *Attributes*: ie product attributes such as the high level of safety features within a Volvo motor car.

2 *Benefits*: are what the customer is interested in, ie he or she feels more secure on overcrowded roads in his or her Volvo.

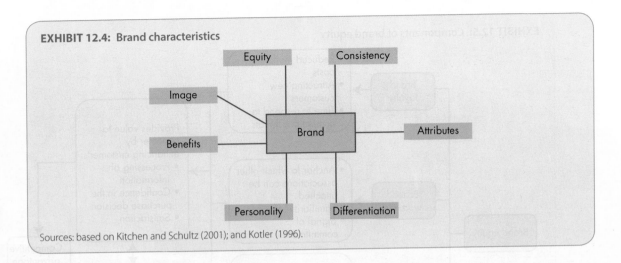

EXHIBIT 12.4: Brand characteristics

Sources: based on Kitchen and Schultz (2001); and Kotler (1996).

3 *Image*: the brand is in tune with the values of the consumer, ie the consumer feels that he or she is an individual and expresses this through his or her choice of car.

4 *Personality*: if the car were a person it would be professional, intelligent and solid.

5 *Consistency*: that the customer can be sure of the quality every time he or she buys the product or service.

6 *Differentiation*: convinces the customer that the offer is different to other offers.

7 *Equity*: the value it provides to the firm and its stakeholders.

There are three dimensions of *brand value*, namely *functional*, *expressive* and *central*. The functional values represent the performance of the product and reflect the rational reasons for purchase, ie a meal to satisfy hunger. Competitors can replicate functional elements. This then leads on to expressive values, which say more about the consumer and his or her self-image and how the brand fits in with his or her own image so that he or she can express it. Finally, the central value is the combination of the previous two; this combination plays the central role in the purchasing decisions of customers.[25]

Brand management

Brand equity

Brand equity refers to the incremental utility or value added to a product by its brand name, such as Nike, Nokia and Sony. Brand equity can be estimated by subtracting the utility of physical attributes of the product from the total utility of a brand. As a substantial asset to the company, brand equity increases cash flow to the business.[26] From a behavioural viewpoint, brand equity is critical to make points of differentiation that lead to competitive advantages based on non-price competition.[27]

Brand equity is based on the idea that a brand is an important (financial) asset and it can be calculated in financial terms.[28] Thus, the brand equity shows the part of a company's assets that can be derived from the brand, as it adds to (or subtracts from) the value provided by a product or service to a firm and/or that firm's customers.[29] Furthermore, the brand equity is composed of four substructures; *brand awareness*, *brand loyalty*, *perceived quality* and the *brand's associations*, as presented in Exhibit 12.5.[30]

Branding strategy

To create a strong international brand, a marketer needs to develop and implement a consistent and informed marketing strategy.[31] Such a strategy will help the firm to achieve the most benefits of developing brands. Brand development strategy should follow the following seven steps:

1 analyse the competition

2 identify your target customer

EXHIBIT 12.5: Components of brand equity

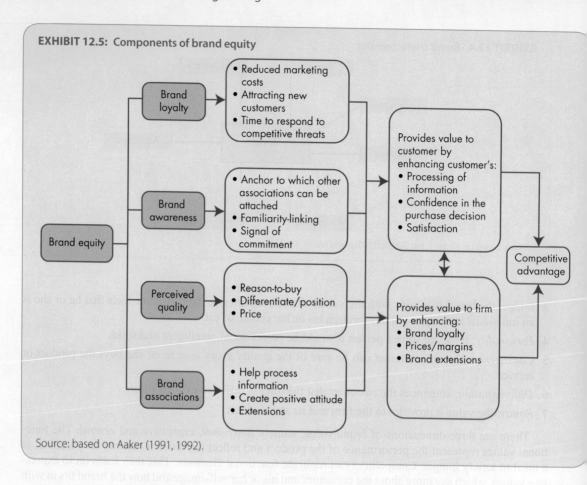

Source: based on Aaker (1991, 1992).

3 decide on the positioning in the particular market

4 develop a consistent marketing communication strategy

5 decide on global versus local content mix

6 create a balance between brand elements

7 establish an international brand equity measurement system.

This process is further illustrated by Exhibit 12.6.

An *analysis of the competing brands* in the particular market will enable the company to understand who it has to fight/race against. Coca-Cola entered the Indian market in the early 1990s without doing this analysis and struggled to beat the local brand (Thums Up) for several years. Finally, it acquired the local brand and kept selling it, as that is what the customers wanted.

Unless you know the exact *target customer segment*, it is impossible to develop a brand, as you do not know which characteristics to incorporate. Once you know the target customer, you can *position your brand* better, as you know what elements of the product/service the particular customers are looking for. For example, in the early years, when MTV went international, it broadcast the same contents as in the USA, considering that all customers liked Western music. However, very soon it realised that in most markets tastes for music were different. At present, MTV broadcasts mostly localised music. In India up to 80 per cent of the music comes from Bollywood movies.

Next, the firm has to decide on how much of its positioning and branding can be globalised and how much needs to be localised. Most markets differ in terms of tastes, rules, regulations and consumer behaviour. Many companies globalise the main message/contents of a brand, while adapting the contents and positioning. Examples include L'Oreal, with the 'you're worth it' slogan for the same brands, but still changing the elements of brands and communication in adapting to local markets.

EXHIBIT 12.6: The process of creating a brand

```
Analyse the competition
        ↓
Know your target customer
        ↓
Decide on the positioning in the
particular market
        ↓
Decide on global vs local content
and control mix
        ↓
Develop a consistent marketing
communication strategy
        ↓
Create a balance between brand
elements
        ↓
Establish an international brand
equity measurement system
```

Going International 12.4

DEVELOPING A NEW BRAND

The Baltimore headquarters of sports apparel maker Under Armour don't look much like the offices of a technology company.

Don't be fooled by the jock paraphernalia – or all the jocks working at the company: Under Armour is very much a high-tech place. The founder is an American football player who got really tired of being soaked when he exercised and found a special fabric made of lycra/polyester that didn't get completely wet. He started making underwear that didn't get wet. In just 12 years the company has sales of 725m per year.

It uses sophisticated design software, new manufacturing techniques, the latest in material engineering, and robust information technology systems to produce virtually everything it makes,

The sports apparel maker is sprinting into footwear – and trying to take on Nike – with the help of software and science.

from its original moisture-wicking T-shirts to kneepads and cleats. 'We try to be on the bleeding edge,' says CEO Kevin Plank, a former University of Maryland football player who founded the company in 1996. 'We're willing to look at wild, out-there ideas if they can make our products perform better.'

Executives at Under Armour, which had more than $700m in revenue last year, knew that making a run at $19bn-a-year Nike wouldn't be easy, so they set out to build state-of-the-art gear. A look at the process shows just how much innovation and technology companies have to pour into product development today – even for something as seemingly simple as a pair of athletic shoes.

Thinking in 3-D

Ask Under Armour management to talk about the technology in the new running shoes, and they'll tick off a list of advances in the composition of the foam in the sole or mention the moisture-resistant fabric used in the shoe's upper. But Under Armour wouldn't have been able to enter the running-shoe business if not for a game-changing upgrade in its enterprise software package implemented in 2006, not long after the company went public.

- Can Under Armour gain some market shares from Nike and/or Adidas? How?

Sources: Stephanie N. Mehta, *Fortune*, 2 February 2009, p 13; and other sources.

In the same manner, a firm has to decide how much of the *contents of the brand* should be globalised and how much localised. A firm may have to develop a totally new brand for a local market, as Unilever does with many markets. 'Paulina' detergent is only sold in Poland and 'Lifeboy' soap is only sold in some Asian markets.

Once the contents of the brand have been decided, you also need to know how these contents and other *elements of the brand should be combined*. The right mix is important, as it might differ from market to market. Now that Coca-Cola has abandoned its global branding strategy, it allows its subsidiaries to develop their own local brands of local drinks with different brand categories for different customer segments. This also has to do with the delivery/distribution of products, as different distribution channels create different brand images. For example, Coca-Cola provides refrigerators to its retailers and Unilever provides freezers to its retailers in emerging markets, to reassure the customer that they can always get a consistent product as promised.

Establishing an international brand equity measurement system is most crucial to controlling the branding and its consequences on a company's success or failure in a foreign market. What decisions should be made centrally at the head office and what decisions should be decentralised to country managers is a very difficult issue, particularly when companies want to maintain a consistent global brand image. For example, Colgate-Palmolive has created a 'bundle book' that contains how to market its brands to the smallest detail within each market. It provides formulas for pricing, ingredients, suppliers, brand attributes, graphics and advertising. Colgate can thus control its brand in all countries. Levi's also exercises an advanced brand-equity measurement system. It explains the differences between its brands and how consumer perceptions are monitored.[32]

Brand strategy
Brand portfolio strategy

Brand portfolio strategy is a field of growing importance, as most companies are including multiple brands in their brand portfolio. In a brand portfolio brands can differ from each other because they cater to different needs and wishes of consumers and because they can be characterised by different price indications. Moreover, companies use different brands in different countries, according to the differences in customer segments, and the pricing and values that customers are looking for. Exhibit 12.7 shows a brand portfolio for one of the multinational corporations.

EXHIBIT 12.7: Nestlé's branding strategy

Level 1	10 worldwide corporate brands	*For example*: Nestlé; Carnation; Buitoni; Maggi; Perrier
Level 2	45 worldwide strategic brands	*For example*: Kit-Kat; Polo; Cerelac; Baci; Mighty Dog; Smarties; After Eight; Coffee-Mate
Level 3	140 regional strategic brands	*For example*: Mackintosh; Vittel; Contadina; Stouffer's
Level 4	7,500 local brands	*For example*: Texicana; Brigadeiro; Rocky; Solis

Source: based on Andrew Parsons, 'Nestlé: The Visions of Local Managers', an Interview with Peter Brabeck-Letmathe, CEO Nestlé, *The McKinsey Quarterly*, 2 November 1996, pp 5–29.

There are several ways a firm can structure its brand portfolio. These structures can be *monolithic* (one name and visual identity, such as BMW), *endorsed* (corporate identity in association with subsidiary names, such as Marriott Hotel-Courtyard Hotel), and *branded* products (under totally different names and appearance, such as Unilever's brand portfolio).[33]

Another way to structure a brand portfolio is based on six levels.[34] These represent a certain role for the particular brand, its status and its relationship with the products which the brand encompasses:

1 *product brand*: is about one brand, one product, and one promise

2 *line brand*: builds on an extension of a specific concept over several product categories

3 *range brand*: similar to line brand but differs in that it holds a more long-term perspective of the extension strategy

4 *single brand name*: is promoted through a single promise over a range of products belonging to the same area of competence

5 *umbrella brand*: builds on an overarching, well-known master brand which supports own-product brands in its portfolio, such as Toyota and Honda

6 *endorsing brand*: builds on a strategy where the master brand only acts as a guarantor concerning a specific aspect, such as ISO 9000 or Rain Forest Alliance.

Brand architecture

This brand portfolio structure discusses the brand's strategic meaning, status, role and relationship and how that should be managed. The way this brand portfolio structure is managed is called the *brand architecture* and it helps companies to structure a brand portfolio that specifies the brand roles and the relationships among brands and different product/market contexts, defined by six dimensions (see Exhibit 12.8):[24]

1 *brand portfolio*: covers all brands and sub-brands which are included in the overall offering, including brands in associations with others (co-brands).

2 *portfolio roles*: emphasise that all brands in a portfolio must be seen in relation to each other rather than as silos, which often lead to misallocation of resources and synergy failures. The portfolio role also offers a tool for a broader view of a brand portfolio, including four brand roles which can be used simultaneously: *strategic brands* with good future prospects; *linchpin* brands with high customer loyalty; *silver-bullet brands* which have a positive impact on other brands' image; and *cash-cow brands* which generate margins to invest in the other three.

3 *product/market context roles*: define the different roles which brands can play in different products and markets, since there is often more than one brand exposed in an offering to the customer.

4 *brand portfolio structure*: concerns the internal structure of the portfolio and the relationship between the different brands to ensure that they are structured in a way which is clear to the customers and creates synergies.

5 *portfolio graphic*: regards the visual presentation of the brand to the customer such as the logo, design and advertising.

6 *brand scope*: refers to the product categories with which each brand in the portfolio is associated.

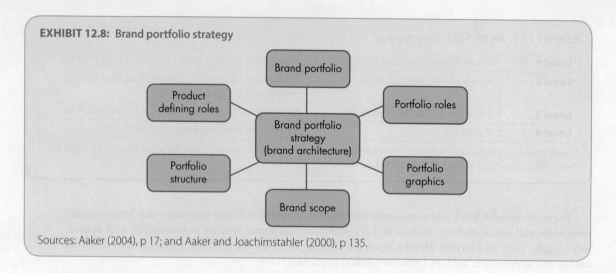

EXHIBIT 12.8: Brand portfolio strategy

Sources: Aaker (2004), p 17; and Aaker and Joachimstahler (2000), p 135.

Corporate branding

Branding versus advertising

Branding should not be confused with advertising. Advertising is one of many vehicles for building or maintaining a brand but it is not the only element necessary to build a brand. With the proliferation of products and services in today's society, consumers are increasingly turning to brands to simplify their purchase decision. As shown in Exhibit 12.9, customers go through a process on their way to adopting a brand and becoming loyal to it.[12, 35]

Here corporate branding, leading to customers' loyalty is critical. The aim of the corporate brand is, or should be, to supplement, underpin, and reinforce the various products and service marketing activities being used by the product brands. Thus, corporate communication should provide value to customers and other stakeholders.

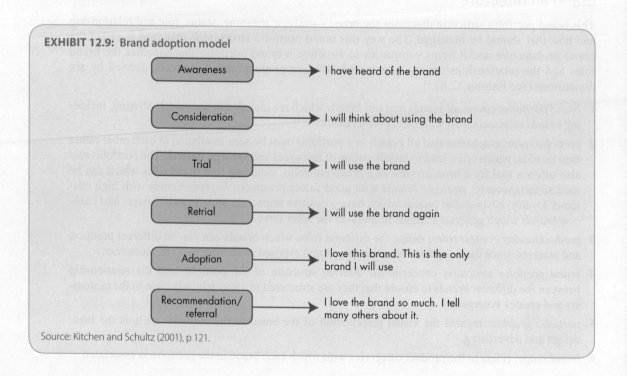

EXHIBIT 12.9: Brand adoption model

Source: Kitchen and Schultz (2001), p 121.

Corporate identity

A favourable corporate identity is considered one of an organisation's most important assets and therefore deserves management's constant attention. Changing or multiple corporate identities can create instability; this may adversely influence a company's internal processes and its corporate image, and thus endanger the realisation of strategic targets.

Going International 12.5

CHINESE SHOPPERS ARE FALLING OUT OF LOVE WITH FAKE BRANDS

Da Vinci, a retailer of expensive imported furniture, spared no expense when it opened its new showroom in Shanghai with over 10,000 square metres spread over four floors and filled with extravagant pieces from brands such as Armani Casa and Versace Home. The theme of the event was *zhen de jia bu liao*, which roughly translated means 'what is genuine cannot be counterfeited'. Counterfeiters are no longer popular amongst Chinese consumers as they were not long ago when fakers

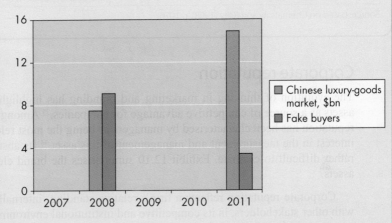

were applauded for saving them money. A study by the management consultancy firm McKinsey concludes that the proportion of consumers who said they were willing to buy fake jewellery dropped from 31 per cent in 2008 to 12 per cent in 2011. Bain, another consultancy, found that 'demand for counterfeit products is decreasing fast' for China's luxury market. Chinese who are over 30 and have a bit of money have become extremely brand-conscious and a 'comparison culture' is growing amongst consumers. People are ridiculed if spotted with a fake Gucci handbag.

Besides, Chinese firms now have intellectual property of their own to protect which puts extra pressure on fakers. The more Chinese innovators gripe about fakery, the more strictly the government enforces the law. Apart from tougher law enforcement, now foreign firms have learned how to cope with fakes. Some have set up their own branded retail outlets to control distribution. GlaxoSmithKline, a British drugs giant, has introduced fake-proof 'e-coding' of pills. Chinese consumers are learning that brands are not just about showing off but can also send useful signals about quality.

- What is the future for brands in emerging markets? Will branded products continue to be successful globally? Discuss.

Sources: based on Mckinsey and *The Economist*, January 2012, p 64.

The management of corporations' identities is being conducted in the context of empowered, socially engaged, culturally adept social actors who present organisations with a range of conflicting societal and economic expectations.[36] These social actors, referred to as societal constituents, claim moral legitimacy to influence the decisions and actions of corporations they feel have affected their personal and community space. Thus, there is a societal constituent perspective of corporate brand.

EXHIBIT 12.10: Brand value contents

Tangible and visual contents	Intangible contents
Symbol and slogans	Identity, corporate brand, integrated communications
Name, logo, colours, brand-mark, plus advertising slogan	Customer relationships
Name, trademark	Positioning, brand communications
Product delivery	User identification; opportunity to share a dream
Functional capabilities, name, legal protection	Symbolic value, service, sign of ownership
Functionality	Representationality
Physique	Personality, relationship, culture, reflection, self-image
Functional values	Social and personal values
Differentiation	Relevance, esteem and familiarity

Source: based on Chernatony and Riley (1998), p 1076.

Corporate reputation

The evolution of thinking in marketing and branding has highlighted the importance of intangible assets as a source of competitive advantage for companies.[37] Among these intangible assets, corporate reputation has been characterised by managers as being the most relevant, which has led to a growing interest in the measurement and management of this asset.[38] Its abstract nature, however, has made it rather difficult to evaluate. Exhibit 12.10 summarises the brand elements in tangible and intangible assets.

Corporate reputation reflects a firm's relative standing, internally with employees and externally with other stakeholders, in its competitive and institutional environment.[6]

Tangible assets, as well as some intangible assets (eg patents and trademarks), can be easily transferred, thereby allowing valuation through an arm's length transaction. Corporate reputation, an intangible asset that is not easily transferable to other parties, does not lend itself to easily determinable valuation. Reputations represent publics' cumulative judgements of the firm over time.

One of the best-known reputation-ranking systems is found in the annual *Fortune* survey of America's Most Admired Companies, which has been published by *Fortune* magazine since 1982 and includes the ingredients listed in Exhibit 12.11.

Corporate reputation has become one of the most important ingredients of corporate assets. Corporate reputation can make the difference in raising funds, recruiting the top graduates, keeping the best staff and persuading people to buy your products at a premium. It is common sense that, if the company is not favourably perceived, it is at a disadvantage.

EXHIBIT 12.11: Corporate reputation rankings in *Fortune* magazine

Fortune magazine ranking
1 Quality of management
2 Quality of products
3 Innovativeness
4 Long-term investment value
5 Financial soundness
6 Ability to attract, develop and keep people
7 Responsibility to the community and the environment
8 Wise use of corporate resources

Going International 12.6

THE OLYMPICS AND THE COUNTRY BRAND

In many ways, the Olympic Games are a marketer's dream. For the host city and host country, though, the marketing value is less clear. The Olympics are a monumentally costly undertaking, requiring massive investments of time, labour and funding to stage the two-week event. Those investments are made with the assumption that the host city will see a healthy return – and the city's own brand image will gain a spot in the international spotlight. But positive economic impacts are questionable at best, experts say; and when it comes to return on investment, image is everything.

The London 2012 Olympics signage.
© Istockphoto.com/Bikeworldtravel

Yet cities continue to give their all in the stiff competition to host the Olympic Games – those vying for the 2016 games are spending more than $170m combined on their Olympic bids – because many marketing experts argue that the games' exorbitant price tag is worth it.

According to Michael Payne, who served as the International Olympic Committee's (IOC) marketing director throughout the 1980s and 1990s, the Olympics' power to broadcast or reform a city's image is all the justification that a potential host should need. 'For any nation, the economics of staging the Olympic Games are best understood as a Herculean re-branding campaign,' Payne writes in his book, *Olympic Turnaround*. The games are the 'world's longest commercial,' he says, and are powerful enough to 'change certain perceptions of the country and dramatically enhance the country's global standing'.

The Olympics may earn big style points but they lack substance, economically speaking. Post-event studies are rarely conducted, because no city wants to prove how much money was wasted. And the post-event studies that do exist show that the massive financial outlay is rarely, if ever, recovered in tangible, long-term benefits for the host economy.

The Olympic Games are an expensive undertaking. The bidding process alone now requires a multi-million-dollar investment. For the 2016 Summer Games, Chicago's Organising Committee had to round up more than $49m to complete its bid campaign, according to the committee's bid plan. Tokyo dedicated $48m, Rio de Janeiro $42m and Madrid $40m.

The Games' actual costs usually greatly exceed their projected costs. The Beijing Games, for example, were initially projected to cost $1.6bn but many estimates say actual expenditure on the firework-bedazzled event hovered closer to $40bn. For the 2012 Summer Games, London originally projected costs totalling $8–9bn, but this projection was revised to more than $18bn.

- Do you think countries or cities can create brands? Is it worthwhile to use the Olympics to establish such brands?

Source: based on *Marketing News*, 11 January 2008, p 10.

SUMMARY

It is difficult to dispute the economic importance of brands. According to Interbrand, a brand consultancy, almost 70 per cent of the average FTSE (*Financial Times* Stock Exchange Index) company's value is based on 'intangibles'.

In the latest economic downturn, even very trusted brands like British Airways have lost their place on the FTSE 100 index. The value to businesses of owning strong brands is incontestable since brands that keep their promise attract loyal buyers who return to them at regular intervals, and the brand owner benefits from being able to forecast cash flows for developing the business with greater confidence. Thus brands, with their ability to secure profits, can be defined as productive, intangible and traditional assets in exactly the same way as any other business assets.

Following a systematic branding strategy is thus vital for achieving competitive advantage in international markets.

QUESTIONS

1   Pick up any brand and trace the country of origin and the level of adaptation that has been carried out between its marketing in the country of origin and your country. Explain why these adaptations have been done.

2   Is Coca-Cola a global brand? If it is adapted, why?

3   Explain the elements of a brand and its function. Pick up a branded product and explain what elements it includes and why.

4   What are the characteristics of a brand? Give examples.

5   Explain the process of brand-strategy development and how it is used in a high-value brand.

6   What are the factors that influence brand portfolio strategy? Explain three of these factors in detail, with examples.

7   What is brand equity? Which components of a brand create competitive advantage?

FURTHER READING

- J. Evans, K. Bridson and R. Rentschler, 'Drivers, Impediments and Manifestation of Brand Orientation: An International Museum Study, *European Journal of marketing*, (2012), 46(11–12), 1457–75.

- D.A. Aaker and R. Jacobson, 'The Value Relevance of Brand Attitude in High-technology Markets', *Journal of Marketing Research*, 2001, 38(4), 485–94.

- S. Samu, P. K. Lyndem and R.A. Litz, 'Impact of Brand Building Activities and Retailer-based Equity on Retailer Brand Communities', *European Journal of Marketing*, 2012, 46(11–12), 1581–1601.

NOTES

1   P. Kotler, *Marketing Management: Analysis, Planning, Implementation and Control* (Englewood Cliffs, NJ: Prentice-Hall, 1997).

2   L. Chernatony and M. McDonald, *Creating Powerful Brands – in Consumer Service and Industrial Markets*, 2nd edn (Oxford: Butterworth-Heinemann, 1998), p 20.

3   S. Hart and J. Murphy, *Brands: The New Wealth Creators* (London: Macmillan, 1998).

4   N. Klein, *No Logo* (Stockholm: Ordfront Förlang, 2000); and E. Delgado-Ballester and M. Hernandez-Espallardo, 'Building Online Brands through Brand Alliances on the Internet', *European Journal of Marketing*, 2008, 42(9–10), 954–76.

5   L. Chernatony and F.D.O. Riley, 'Defining A "Brand": Beyond The Literature With Experts' Interpretations', *Journal of Marketing Management*, 1998, 14(4/5), 417–43.

6   L. Chernatony and F.D.O. Riley, 'Modelling the Components of the Brand', *European Journal of Marketing*, 1998, 32(11/12), 1074–90.

7   'Unilever Chief: Refresh Brands', *Advertising Age*, 19 July 1994, pp 1–20.

8   For a comprehensive review of the literature on country-of-origin effects, see, eg Warren Bilky and Erik Nes, 'Country-of-origin Effects in Product Evaluations', *Journal of International Business Studies*, 1982, 13(1), 89–99; Aysegul Ozsomer and Tamer Cavusgil, 'Country-of-origin Effects on Product Evaluation: A Sequel to Bilky and Nes Review', in M.C. Gilly *et al.* (eds), *Proceedings of the American Marketing Association, Annual Conference, 1991*, pp 69–77; and Robert Peterson and Alain Jolibert, 'A Meta Analysis of Country-of-origin Effects', *Journal of International Business Studies*, 1996, 26(4), 883–900.

9   C.L. Wang, D. Li, B.R. Barnes and J. Ahn, 'Country Image, Product Image and Consumer Purchase Intention: Evidence from an Emerging Economy', *International Business Review*, 2012, 21(6), 1041–51.

10 M. Moeller, M. Harvey, D. Griffith and G. Richey, 'The Impact of Country of Origin on the Acceptance of Foreign Subsidiaries in Host Countries: An Examination of the Liability of Foreignness', 2013, 22(1), 89–99.

11 'Czech Republic: Consumers Think Foreign Goods are Overpriced', *Crossborder Monitor*, 3 August 1994, p 4.

12 P. Wang, X.-P. Zhang and M. Ouyang, 'Does Advertising Create Sustained Firm Value? The Capitalization of Brand Intangibles', *Journal of the Academy of Marketing Science*, 2009, 37(2), 130–43.

13 Sheila Tefft, 'China's Savvy Shoppers Load Carts with Expensive Imported Goods', *Advertising Age*, 20 June 1994, pp 1–21.

14 See Frank Alpert and Michael Kamins, 'An Empirical Investigation of Consumer Memory, Attitude, and Perceptions Towards Pioneer and Follower Brands', *Journal of Marketing*, 1995, 59(4), 34–45.

15 Eleena de Lisser and Kevin Helliker, 'Private Labels Reign in British Groceries', *Wall Street Journal*, 3 March 1994, p B1.

16 P. Håkansson, R. Wahlund *et al.*, *Varumarken-fran teori till praktik* (Stockholm: Stockholm School of Economics, 1996).

17 S. Moorthy and B.T. Ratchford, 'Consumer Information Search Revisited: Theory and Empirical Analysis', *Journal of Consumer Research*, 1997, 23(4), 263–78.

18 M.D. Smith, 'The Impact of Shopbots on Electronic Markets', *Journal of the Academy of Marketing Science*, 2002, 30(4), 446.

19 R.N. Stone and K. Gronhaug, 'Perceived Risk: Further Considerations for the Marketing Discipline', *European Journal of Marketing*, 1993, 27(3), 39.

20 D.A. Aaker and R. Jacobson, 'The Value Relevance of Brand Attitude in High-technology Markets', *Journal of Marketing Research*, 2001, 38(4), 485–94.

21 D.A. Aaker and K.L. Keller, 'Consumer Evaluations of Brand Extensions', *Journal of Marketing*, 1990, 54(Winter), 27–41.

22 R. Ahluwalia, H.R. Unnava *et al.*, 'The Moderating Role of Commitment on the Spillover Effect of Marketing Communications', *Journal of Marketing Research*, 2001, 38(4), 458–71.

23 T. Ambler, C.B. Bhattacharya *et al.*, 'Relating Brand and Customer Perspectives on Marketing Management', *Journal of Service Research*, 2002, 5(1), 13–26.

24 P. Kotler, 'Crisis in the Arts: The Marketing Response', *California Management Review*, 1996, 39(1), 28–52.

25 N. Kochan, *The World's Greatest Brands* (London: Macmillan, 1996).

26 C.J. Simon and M.W. Sullivan, 'The Measurement and Determinants of Brand Equity: A Financial Approach', *Marketing Science*, 1993, 12(Winter), 28–52.

27 D.A. Aaker, *Brand Portfolio Strategy: Creating Relevance, Differentiation, Energy, Leverage, and Clarity* (New York: Free Press, 2004).

28 P. Barwise, 'Brand Equity: Snark or Boojum?', *International Journal of Research in Marketing*, 1993, 10(1), 93–104.

29 S.C. Bahadir, S.G. Bharadwaj and R.K. Shivastava, 'Financial Value of Brands in Mergers and Acquisitions: Is Value in the Eye of the Beholder', *Journal of Marketing*, 2008, 72(6), 49–64.

30 D.A. Aaker, *Managing Brand Equity* (New York: Free Press, 1991); D.A. Aaker, 'Managing the Most Important Asset: Brand Equity', *Planning Review*, 1992, 20, 56–68.

31 K.L. Keller, *Strategic Brand Management: A European Perspective* (Harlow: Pearson Education, 2008).

32 D.A. Aaker and E. Joachimsthaler, 'The Brand Relationship Spectrum: The Key to the Brand Architecture Challenge', *California Management Review*, 2000, 42(4), 8–23.

33 W. Olins, *Corporate Identity* (London: Thames and Hudson, 1989).

34 K.L. Keller, *Strategic Brand Management: A European Perspective* (Harlow: Pearson Education, 2008); J.N. Kapferer, *Re-inventing the brand* (London: Kogan Page, 2001).

35 P.J. Kitchen and D.E. Schultz, 'Raising the Corporate Umbrella: Corporate Communication in the 21st Century', *Journal of Academy of Marketing Science*, 2001, 37(2), 121.

36 J.M. Handelman, 'Corporate Identity and the Societal Constituent', *Journal of the Academy of Marketing Science*, 2006, 34(2), 107–14.

37 H. Itami and T.W. Roehl, *Mobilizing Invisible Assets* (Cambridge, MA: Harvard University Press, 1987).

38 R. Hall, 'A Framework Linking Intangible Resources and Capabilities to Sustainable Competitive Advantage', *Strategic Management Journal*, 1993, 14, 607–18.

Chapter 13
Exporting and Logistics

Chapter Learning Objectives

What you should learn from Chapter 13

- How to manage the added steps necessary to move goods across country borders
- How various import restrictions influence exporting efforts
- The means of reducing import/export taxes to remain competitive
- How the mechanics of export documents work
- How to handle the logistics and problems inherent in the physical movement of goods
- Why exporting is an indispensable part of all international marketing, whether the company markets in one country or is a global marketer

Most countries control the movement of goods crossing their borders, whether leaving (exports) or entering (imports). Export and import documents, tariffs, quotas and other barriers to the free flow of goods between independent sovereignties are requirements that must be met by either the exporter, the importer, or both.

The mechanics of exporting add extra steps and costs to an international marketing sale that are not incurred when marketing domestically. In addition to selecting a target market, designing an appropriate product, establishing a price, planning a promotional programme and selecting a distribution channel, the international marketer must meet the legal requirements of moving goods from one country to another.

The exporting process (see Exhibit 13.1) includes the licences and documentation necessary to leave the country, an international carrier to transport the goods, and fulfilment of the requirements necessary to get the shipment into another country legally. These mechanics of exporting are sometimes considered the essence of foreign marketing. Although their importance cannot be minimised, they should not be seen as the primary task of international marketing.

The rules and regulations that cover the exportation and importation of goods, and the physical movement of those goods between countries are the special concerns of this chapter.

Regulations and restrictions on exporting and importing

export regulations

rules and regulations for export

import regulations

rules and regulations for import

There are many reasons why countries impose some form of regulation and restriction on the exporting and importing of goods. **Export regulations** can be designed to conserve scarce goods for home consumption or to control the flow of strategic goods to actual or potential enemies. **Import regulations** may be imposed to protect health, conserve foreign exchange, serve as economic reprisals, protect home industry or provide revenue in the form of tariffs. To comply with various regulations, the exporter may have to acquire licences or permits from the home country and ascertain that the potential customer has the necessary permits for importing goods.

Export controls

Delivering a product or service is a vital aspect of marketing, and product availability is an important part of customer satisfaction. In the case of EU cross-border restrictions, the Single Europe Act 1986 was quite clear: as from 31 December 1992 the EU is 'an area without internal frontiers, in which free movement of goods, persons, services and capital is ensured'.

In this respect real progress has been made. The Single Administrative Document was introduced in 1993 to replace a number of customs documents. There are no foreign exchange restrictions on transactions across Europe. There are standardised rules and regulations for transport methods and working

---

EXHIBIT 13.1: The exporting process

Leaving the exporting country	Physical distribution	Entering the importing country
Licences	*International shipping / air freight and logistics*	Tariffs, taxes
General	*Packing*	
Validated	*Insurance*	
Documentation		*Non-tariff barriers*
Export declaration		Standards
Commercial invoice		Inspection
Bill of lading		Documentation
Consular invoice		Quotas
Special certificates		Fees
Other documents		Licences
Other barriers		Special certificates
		Exchange permits

conditions. However, civil law codes vary across Europe and contract law is not the same in all EU countries. It is thus advised that each contract should specify which country's law is to apply.[1]

Import restrictions

When an exporter plans a sale to a foreign buyer, it is necessary to examine the export restrictions of the home country as well as the import restrictions and regulations of the importing country. Although the responsibility for import restrictions may rest with the importer, the exporter does not want to ship goods until it is certain that all import regulations have been met. Goods arriving without proper documentation can be denied entry.

There are many types of trade restriction besides import tariffs imposed by the foreign country. A few examples of the 30 basic **barriers to exporting** considered important by *Business International* include:

> **barriers to exporting**
> obstacles/hindrances to exporting into a country

1 import licences, quotas and other quantitative restrictions
2 currency restrictions and allocation of exchange at unfavourable rates on payments for imports
3 devaluation
4 prohibitive prior import deposits, prohibition of collection-basis sales and insistence on cash letters of credit
5 arbitrarily short periods in which to apply for import licences
6 delays resulting from pressure on overworked officials or from competitors' influence on susceptible officials.

The most frequently encountered trade restrictions, besides tariffs, are such non-tariff barriers as exchange permits, quotas, import licences, boycotts, standards and voluntary agreements.

The various market barriers that existed among members of the EU created a major impediment to trade. One study of 20,000 EU exporting firms indicated that the most troublesome barriers were administrative roadblocks, border-crossing delays and capital controls.[1]

As the EU becomes a single market, many of the barriers that existed among member countries have been erased. The single European market has no doubt made trade easier among its member countries but due to resistance by some member countries, such as the UK, Sweden and Denmark, a number of hidden barriers still exist. The success of the euro is in fact contributing positively towards a complete integration and elimination of barriers. There is, however, a rising concern that a fully integrated EU will become a market with strong protectionist barriers against non-member countries.[2]

Going International 13.1

FREE TRADE OR HYPOCRISY?

Much has been written about trade problems between the USA, Europe and other countries. The impression is that high tariffs, quotas and export trade subsidies are restrictions used by other countries – that the USA is a free, open market while the rest of the world's markets are riddled with trade restrictions.

Neither impression is completely true. The USA does engage in trade restrictions. One estimate is that over 25 per cent of manufactured goods sold in the USA are affected by trade barriers. The cost

© Istockphoto.com/MauritsVink

▶

◀

to US consumers is $50bn (€45bn) more annually than if there were no restrictions. Consider a sample of US trade hypocrisy.

Quotas: sugar quotas imposed by the USA result in a pound of sugar costing 10 cents in Canada versus 35 cents in the USA. US beef quotas cost consumers $873m (€788m) a year in higher prices.

Tariffs: tariffs average 26 per cent of the value of imported clothing, 40 per cent on orange juice, 40 per cent on peanuts, 115 per cent on low-priced watch parts imported from Taiwan and 40 per cent on leather imports from Japan.

Shipping: foreign ships are barred from carrying passengers or freight between any two US ports. Food donations to foreign countries cost an extra $100m (€90m) because they must be shipped on US carriers.

Subsidies: The USA provided export subsidies to US farmers of 111 per cent for poultry exports, 78 per cent for wheat and flour, and more than 100 per cent for rice. According to the EU, the US government is paying billions of dollars to Boeing as launching funds for its new 7E7 plane. The American government is in turn blaming the EU for subsidising Airbus' new jumbo A380. They are battling it out through the World Trade Organization (WTO).

Many of these restrictions will begin to disappear as the provisions of the WTO apply, but even then countries will operate tariffs, quotas and other barriers to trade.

● Has the WTO been successful in removing most export/import restrictions? If not, why not?

Sources: abstracted from 'Import Tariffs Imposed by a Protectionist US', *Fortune*, 12 December 1991, p 14; James Bovard, 'A US History of Trade Hypocrisy', *Wall Street Journal*, 8 March 1994, p 36; and M. Sanchanta, 'Long Relationship with Boeing Drags Japan's Aircraft Industry into Dispute', *Financial Times*, 11 October 2004, p 2.

Tariffs

Tariffs are the taxes or customs duties levied against goods imported from another country. All countries have tariffs for the purpose of raising revenue and protecting home industries from the competition of foreign-produced goods. Tariff rates are based on value or quantity, or a combination of both.

The EU is the largest member of the World Trade Organization (WTO) in terms of trade; including intra-EU trade, it accounts for almost 40 per cent of world merchandise trade. However, with increasing integration the EU's trade with third countries is decreasing. The Treaty of Rome required the EC to develop a **Common Commercial Policy (CCP)**, the aim of which is to liberalise world trade. The key element of CCP is the Common External Tariff (CET), which all member states must apply.

> **common commercial policy (CCP)**
>
> some rules for exports and imports whose aim is to liberalise world trade

The community has a number of preferential trade agreements, for example with the European Free Trade Association (EFTA) and Turkey. But at the same time, it has variable levies on imported food and quotas on imported textiles, as well as a number of other restrictions on imports that harm sensitive domestic industries such as agriculture and cars.

On the other hand, the American administration created a climate of uncertainty for a number of EU firms. The government proposed that no federal agencies should award contracts to companies from a number of EU states. The American government also proposed that all four-wheel-drive cars should be considered as trucks and thus attract a 25 per cent tariff instead of the 2.5 per cent for cars. Although the main purpose was to stop Japanese four-wheel-drive cars, EU manufacturers such as Land Rover, Mercedes-Benz and Volkswagen are also affected.

Exchange permits

Especially troublesome to exporters are **exchange restrictions** placed on the flow of currency by some foreign countries. To conserve scarce foreign exchange and alleviate balance-of-payment difficulties, many countries impose restrictions on the amount of their currency they will exchange for the currency of another country.

> **exchange restrictions**
> obstacles to the exchange of money

Exchange controls may be applied in general to all commodities, or a country may employ a system of multiple exchange rates based on the type of import. Essential products might have a very favourable exchange rate, while non-essentials or luxuries would have a less favourable rate of exchange. South Africa, for example, until recently had a two-tier system for foreign exchange: commercial rand and financial rand. At times, countries may not issue any exchange permits for certain classes of commodity.

Receiving an **import licence**, or even an exchange permit, however, is not a guarantee that a seller can exchange local currency for the currency of the seller. If local currency is in short supply (a common problem in some countries) other means of acquiring home-country currency are necessary. For example, in a transaction between the government of Colombia and a US truck manufacturer, there was a scarcity of US currency to exchange for the 1,000 vehicles Colombia wanted to purchase. The problem was solved through a series of exchanges. Colombia had a surplus of coffee that the truck manufacturer accepted and traded in Europe for sugar; the sugar was traded for pig iron; and finally the pig iron for US dollars.

> **import licence**
> permission to import into a country

Quotas

Countries may also impose limitations on the quantity of certain goods imported during a specific period. These quotas may be applied to imports from specific countries or from all foreign sources in general. Most EU countries, for example, have specific quotas for importing cotton, tobacco and cars; in the case of some of these items, there are also limitations on the amount imported from specific countries. Exhibit 13.2 shows the world's top 10 exporters and importers.

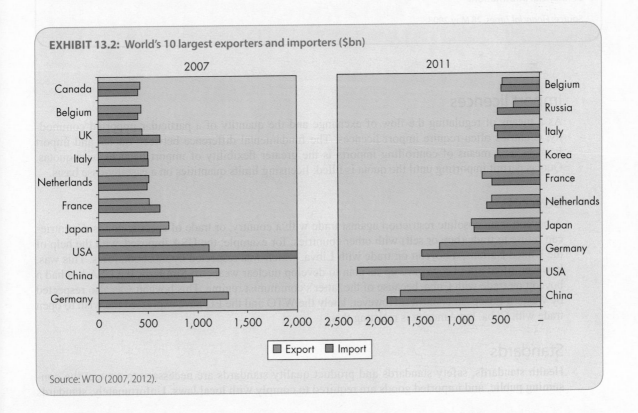

EXHIBIT 13.2: World's 10 largest exporters and importers ($bn)

Source: WTO (2007, 2012).

Going International 13.2

USA COULD CLASH WITH EU ON TECH TRADE TARIFFS

The USA was poised to launch a fresh trade dispute against the EU over tariffs on several technology products such as flat-screen monitors and printers. People familiar with the matter said the USA was preparing to file the case at the WTO barring an eleventh-hour change of heart.

The dispute centres on the EU's interpretation of the Information Technology Agreement (ITA), a decade-old, 70-nation pact, which prohibits countries from imposing tariffs on many high-tech products. Washington says the EU is violating the ITA by placing tariffs of 14 per cent on items such as large flat-screen monitors and cable television set-top boxes, and tariffs of 6 per cent on multi-function printers.

© Istockphoto.com/diego_cervo

As the prospects of a trade dispute with the EU over the ITA have grown, so has speculation that other leading technology producers, such as Japan, may flank the USA in its case. The Japanese embassy in Washington declined to comment.

If the USA were to file a WTO case against the EU over the ITA, it would start a 60-day consultation period, during which the sides would try to reach a settlement before the case moved to a dispute panel. In March, the USA and EU joined forces to file a WTO claim against China for what they saw as unfair restrictions on providers of financial information.

Source: *Financial Times*, 28 May 2008.

Import licences

As a means of regulating the flow of exchange and the quantity of a particular imported commodity, countries often require import licences. The fundamental difference between quotas and import licences as a means of controlling imports is the greater flexibility of import licences over quotas. Quotas permit importing until the quota is filled; licensing limits quantities on a case-by-case basis.

Boycotts

A boycott is an absolute restriction against trade with a country, or trade of specific goods. Countries can refuse to trade (buy or sell) with other countries; for example, the USA imposed, with the help of the United Nations, a boycott on trade with Libya, which was respected by most countries. This was, however, lifted after Libya gave up its plan to develop nuclear weapons. Similarly, the USA has had a boycott on trade with Cuba, because of the latter's communist regime. This boycott was also respected by Western European countries. However, lately the WTO and the EU have expressed the wish to open trade with Cuba, but America is resisting this.[3]

Standards

Health standards, safety standards and product quality standards are necessary to protect the consuming public, and imported goods are required to comply with local laws. Unfortunately, standards can also be used to slow down or restrict the procedures for importing to the point that the additional time and cost required to comply become, in effect, trade restrictions. Safety standards are a good example.

Most countries have safety standards for electrical appliances and require that imported electrical products meet local standards. However, the restrictiveness of safety standards can be escalated to the level of an absolute trade barrier by manipulating the procedures used to determine if products meet the standards. The simplest process for the importing nation is to accept the safety standard verification used by the exporting country. The EU has certain standards for electronic products and each company selling into the EU has to comply with these.

Going International 13.3

EXPORT RESTRICTIONS ON TECHNOLOGY

Most Western countries impose restrictions on the export of sensitive advanced technology to a number of countries. For example, while India and Pakistan were working to develop uranium enrichment capabilities, all export of technology related to uranium enrichment to these countries was banned. However, these restrictions have now been relaxed.

China successfully fired a new type of long-range, ground-to-ground missile and is running an extensive training programme for air-force officers. At the same time, tensions between China and Taiwan have intensified after Taiwan's president declared that relationships between Taipei and Beijing should be based on 'state-to-state' relationship principles.

© Roger Ressimeyer/CORBIS

The USA, being an ally of Taiwan, has restrictions on technology export to China, particularly technology that can be used in military applications. While most of the technology can be used for both civilian and military applications, it's the responsibility of the exporters to ensure that the technology exported is not used for military purposes.

- Is it justified to impose restrictions on technology exports to emerging markets? Discuss.

Source: compiled from various sources.

Voluntary agreements

Foreign restrictions of all kinds abound and the USA can be counted among those governments using restrictions. For decades, US government officials have been arranging 'voluntary' agreements with the Japanese steel and automotive industries to limit sales to the USA. Japan entered these voluntary agreements under the implied threat that if it did not voluntarily restrict the export of automobiles or steel to an agreed limit, the USA might impose even harsher restrictions including additional import duties. It is estimated that the cost of tariffs, quotas and voluntary agreements on all fibres is as much as €36bn ($44bn) at the retail level. This works out to be a hidden tax of almost €450 ($550) a year for every American family.[4]

Other restrictions

Restrictions may be imposed on imports of harmful products, drugs, medicines, and immoral products and literature. Products must also comply with government standards set for health, sanitation, packaging and labelling. For example, in the Netherlands all imported hen and duck eggs must be marked in indelible ink with the country of origin; in Spain, imported condensed milk must be labelled to show fat content if it is less than 8 per cent fat; and in EU countries, all animals imported from outside the EU must be accompanied by a sanitary certificate issued by an approved veterinary inspector – even then the animals have to spend a specified period in quarantine. Failure to comply with regulations can result in severe fines and penalties.

Going International 13.4

ASTRA-ZENECA FAILS TO GET FDA APPROVAL

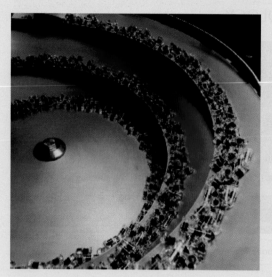

The Food and Drug Administration (FDA) in the USA approves all imports of food and drugs (pharmaceuticals) into the USA.

Astra-Zeneca, the UK–Swedish pharmaceutical company, is very upbeat about its new drug Exanta, which can prevent strokes and blood clots. Exanta is the first new type of oral anti-coagulant treatment in 50 years and is considered a good alternative to existing drugs that require extensive monitoring of patients. It has already been approved by 14 European countries.

The FDA has, however, refused to grant approval to Exanta. It says that Astra-Zeneca needs to monitor Exanta's side effects. According to FDA claims, evidence of its potential risks outweigh the benefits. The objection is related to potential liver toxicity, which the company has already disclosed. The FDA criticised the design of clinical trials to show the drug prevented strokes. It said that, although the statistical evidence supported the efficiency of Exanta, the criteria used to compare it with the existing treatment (warfarin) were too liberal.

This decision is considered a big blow to Astra-Zeneca. At the announcement of the decision, its shares fell by 4 per cent. Astra-Zeneca was hoping that Exanta would become one of its blockbuster drugs and fill the gap left by Prilosec, the ulcer medicine whose patent had expired. Prilosec's sales peaked at about €8bn and Exanta was expected to bring in a similar figure.

- Do you think the FDA is justified in refusing to grant approval to Exanta into be imported into the USA?

Source: abridged from C. Bowe, 'Astra-Zeneca Fails to Get the US Nod for Antistroke Drug', *Financial Times*, 9 September 2004, p M1.

---

content labelling

mention of the contents/ingredients of a product on the package

While sanitation certificates, **content labelling** and other such regulations serve a legitimate purpose, countries can effectively limit imports by using such restrictions as additional trade barriers. Most of the economically developed world encourages foreign trade and works through the WTO to reduce tariffs and non-tariff barriers to a reasonable rate. Yet, in times of economic recession, same countries revert to a protectionist philosophy and seek ways to restrict the importing of goods. Non-tariff barriers have become one of the most potent ways for a country to restrict trade. The elimination of non-tariff barriers has been a major concern of the WTO as well as tariffs and trade in services.[5]

Customs-privileged facilities

To facilitate export trade, countries designate areas within their borders as customs-privileged areas; that is, areas where goods can be imported for storage and/or processing with tariffs and quota limits postponed until the products leave the designated areas. Foreign-trade zones (also known as free-trade zones), free ports and in-bond arrangements are all types of customs-privileged facilities that countries use to promote foreign trade.

Going International 13.5

PRIVILEGED COMPANIES

Cartel arrangements, where competitors or would-be competitors join together, are often illegal in most countries but especially so in the USA and Europe. This position is enforced according to anti-trust regulations to restrict competitors' price fixing and other activities that may not be beneficial for the consumers or for free competition. However, many countries pass legislation to allow such collaborative ventures to strengthen domestic companies. For example in the USA, so-called 'Webb-Promerene Associations' (WPA) and 'Export Trading Companies' (ETC) formed under the Export Trading Company Act are exempt from anti-trust regulations if they meet certain conditions.

© Istockphoto.com/hbbolten

These arrangements are agreed by governments that want to promote exports from their country. Some governments also use 'tax incentives' by allowing certain types of organisational arrangement. The US government is doing this through fostering of Foreign Sales Corporations (FSCs). Here tax incentives/exemptions are given to companies that export to other countries.

Although a number of other countries are also using these methods to promote exports, many of these arrangements have been less successful than expected.

● Is it justifiable to allow cartels and export subsidies for some firms or industries? Discuss.

Source: based on G. Albaum, J. Strandkov and E. Derr, *International Marketing and Export Management* (Harlow: FT Prentice Hall, 2002) p 291.

Foreign-trade zones

> **foreign-trade zones (FTZs)**
>
> where products are produced mostly for exporting purposes

The number of countries with **foreign-trade zones (FTZs)** has increased as trade liberalisation has spread through Latin America, Eastern Europe and other parts of Europe and Asia. Most FTZs function in a similar manner regardless of the host country. The FTZs extend their services to thousands of firms engaged in a spectrum of international trade-related activities ranging from distribution to assembly and manufacturing.

In situations where goods are imported into a country to be combined with locally-made goods and re-exported, the importer or exporter can avoid payment of local import duties on the foreign portion and eliminate the complications of applying for a 'drawback'; that is, a request for a refund from the government of the duties paid on imports later re-exported. Other benefits for companies utilising foreign-trade zones include:

1 lower insurance costs due to the greater security required in FTZs

2 more working capital since duties are deferred until goods leave the zone

3 the opportunity to stockpile products when quotas are filled or while waiting for ideal market conditions

4 significant savings on goods or materials rejected, damaged or scrapped for which no duties are assessed

5 exemption from paying duties on labour and overhead costs incurred in an FTZ, which are excluded in determining the value of the goods.

The Special Economic Zone (SEZ) in Shenzhen, China, is an example of China's economic development programme that established SEZs as a means of attracting foreign capital and technology. In 10 years, Shenzhen's population grew from 30,000 to over 1 million. Hundreds of thousands of Chinese work in the SEZ. Hourly manufacturing labour costs in China are very low compared with the Western minimum wage. Many countries, including the USA, have such FTZs to encourage exports and to create jobs.[3]

Export documents

Each export shipment requires various documents to satisfy government regulations controlling exporting and to meet requirements for international commercial payment transactions. The most frequently required documents are export declarations, consular invoices or certificates of origin, bills of lading, commercial invoices and insurance certificates. In addition, documents such as import licences, export licences, packing lists and inspection certificates for agricultural products are often necessary.

The paperwork involved in successfully completing a transaction is considered by many to be the greatest of all non-tariff trade barriers. Generally, preparation of documents can be handled routinely, but their importance should not be under-estimated; incomplete or improperly prepared documents lead to delays in shipment. In some countries there are penalties, fines and even confiscation of goods as a result of errors in some of these documents. Export documents are the result of requirements imposed by the exporting government, of requirements set by commercial procedures established in foreign trade and, in some cases, of the supporting import documents required by the foreign government. Descriptions of the principal export documents follow.[6]

Export declaration To maintain a statistical measure of the quantity of goods shipped abroad and to provide a means of determining whether regulations are being met, most countries require shipments abroad to be accompanied by an export declaration. Usually such a declaration, presented at the port of exit, includes the names and addresses of the principals involved, the destination of the goods, a full description of the goods and their declared value.

Bill of lading The bill of lading is the most important document required to establish legal ownership and facilitate financial transactions. It serves the following purposes: (1) as a contract for shipment between the carrier and shipper; (2) as a receipt from the carrier for shipment; and (3) as a certificate of ownership or title to the goods.

Bills of lading are issued in the form of straight bills, which are non-negotiable and are delivered directly to a consignee, or order bills, which are negotiable instruments. Bills of lading are frequently referred to as being either clean or foul. A clean bill of lading means the items presented to the carrier for shipment were properly packaged and clear of apparent damage when received; a foul bill of lading means the shipment was received in damaged condition and the damage is noted on the bill of lading.

Commercial invoice Every international transaction requires a commercial invoice; that is, a bill or statement for the goods sold. This document often serves several purposes; some countries require a copy for customs clearance, and it is one of the financial documents required in international commercial payments.

Insurance policy or certificate The risks to shipment resulting from political or economic unrest in some countries, and the possibility of damage from sea and weather conditions, make it absolutely necessary to have adequate insurance covering loss due to damage, war or riots. Typically the method of payment or terms of sale require insurance on the goods, so few export shipments are uninsured. The insurance policy or certificate of insurance is considered a key document in export trade.

Licences Export or import licences are additional documents frequently required in export trade. In those cases where import licences are required by the country of entry, a copy of the licence or licence number is usually required to obtain a consular invoice. Whenever a commodity requires an export licence, it must be obtained before an export declaration can be properly certified.

Others Sanitary and health inspection certificates attesting to the absence of disease and pests may be required for certain agricultural products before a country allows goods to enter its borders. Packing lists with correct weights are also required in some cases.

Terms of sale

Terms of sale, or trade terms, differ somewhat in international marketing from country to country. In some countries it is customary to ship FOB (free on board, meaning that the price is established at the door of the factory), while in others CIF (cost, insurance and freight) is more common. International trade terms often sound similar to those used in domestic business but generally have different meanings. International terms indicate how buyer and seller divide risks and obligations and, therefore, the costs of specific kinds of international trade transaction. When quoting prices, it is important to make them meaningful. The most commonly used international trade terms include the following.

CIF (cost, insurance, freight) to a named overseas port of import. A CIF quote is more meaningful to the overseas buyer because it includes the costs of goods, insurance, and all transportation and miscellaneous charges to the named place of debarkation.

C&F (cost and freight) to named overseas port. The price includes the cost of the goods and transportation costs to the named place of debarkation. The cost of insurance is borne by the buyer.

FAS (free alongside) at a named port of export. The price includes cost of goods and charges for delivery of the goods alongside the shipping vessel. The buyer is responsible for the cost of loading on to the vessel, transportation and insurance.

FOB (free on board) at a named inland point of origin; at a named port of exportation; or a named vessel and port of export. The price includes the cost of the goods and delivery to the place named.

Going International 13.6

YOU DON'T LOOK LIKE A MEXICAN PEANUT TO ME!

The US government is serious about its import restrictions, especially on agricultural products. It doesn't look kindly, for example, on peanuts from China being shipped as Mexican peanuts. But how do you tell where peanuts, orange juice and other agricultural products come from? With an 'inductively coupled plasma mass spectrometer', that's how.

The US Customs Service uses such a machine to determine whether a peanut headed for Safeway matches a peanut grown in Mexico or Georgia. It's a little like DNA testing for plants. While the machine can't tell exactly whether the peanuts come from a specific country, it can

▶

◄

tell if the peanuts in a sample match a sample of peanuts known to come from a specific country. This process began about 10 years ago with the analysing of frozen orange juice. Since frozen orange juice from different countries has different tariff schedules, transshipment through a lower-tariff country can make a big difference in tariffs paid.

In a little over a year, with the help of the machine, US Customs was able to build a case of 'dumping' against Chinese garlic, an illegal transshipment case against Argentine peanuts, and a case against a California coffee distributor who was adulterating Hawaiian Kona coffee with cheaper Central American beans and selling the result as pure Kona.

● Is it justified to have different tariffs on the same product category, depending upon country of origin?

Sources: Guy Gugliotta, 'High-tech Trade Enforcement Tracks Peanuts across Borders', *Washington Post*, 4 December 1997, p A21; and Bob Dart, 'US Takes Aim at Peanut Traffickers: High-tech Equipment is Helping to Detect Illegal Over-the-border Shipments: Undercutting NAFTA', *Atlanta Journal and Constitution*, 9 December 1997, p A12.

EX (named port of origin). The price quoted covers costs only at the point of origin (for example, EX Factory). All other charges are the buyer's concern.

A complete list of terms and their definitions can be found in *Incoterms*, a booklet published by the International Chamber of Commerce. It is important for the exporter to understand exactly the meanings of terms used in quotations. A simple misunderstanding regarding delivery terms may prevent the exporter from meeting contractual obligations or make that person responsible for shipping costs he or she did not intend to incur. Exhibit 13.3 indicates who is responsible for a variety of costs under various terms.

EXHIBIT 13.3: Who is responsible for costs under various terms

Cost items/terms	FOB (free on board) inland carrier at factory	FOB (free on board) inland carrier at point of shipment	FAS (free alongside) vessel or plane at port of shipment	CIF (cost, insurance, freight) at port of destination
Export packing*	Buyer	Seller	Seller	Seller
Inland freight	Buyer	Seller	Seller	Seller
Port charges	Buyer	Buyer	Seller	Seller
Forwarder's fee	Buyer	Buyer	Buyer	Seller
Consular fee	Buyer	Buyer	Buyer	Buyer†
Loading on vessel or plane	Buyer	Buyer	Buyer	Seller
Ocean freight	Buyer	Buyer	Buyer	Seller
Cargo insurance	Buyer	Buyer	Buyer	Seller
Customs duties	Buyer	Buyer	Buyer	Buyer
Ownership of goods passes	When goods on board an inland carrier (truck, rail, etc) or in hands of inland carrier	When goods unloaded by inland carrier	When goods alongside carrier, in hands of air or ocean carrier	When goods on board air or ocean carrier at port of shipment

* Who absorbs export packing? This charge should be clearly agreed on. Charges are sometimes controversial.
† The seller has responsibility for arranging for consular invoices (and other documents requested by the buyer's government). According to official definitions, buyer pays fees, but sometimes, as a matter of practice, seller includes in quotations.

Letters of credit

These days most import and export is done through **letters of credit (LC)**. The letter of credit shifts the buyer's credit risk to the bank issuing the LC. When an LC is issued, the seller draws a draft against the bank issuing the credit and receives money by presenting shipping documents to show that he or she has already shipped the goods. The LC provides the greatest degree of protection to the seller – that he or she will receive his or her money once he or she has shipped the goods.

> **letters of credit (LC)**
>
> shifts the buyer's credit risk to bank issuing the LC

The procedure for LC starts at the signing of the contract, as it stipulates how the cash will be paid for goods (see Exhibit 13.4).[7] The buyer/importer goes to the local bank and arranges for the letter of credit, the buyer bank notifies its corresponding bank in the seller's country (seller's bank) of the conditions set forth in the LC. The seller can draw a draft against the LC for the payment of goods.

Packing and marking

Special packing and marking requirements must be considered for shipments destined to be transported over water, subject to excessive handling or destined for parts of the world with extreme climates or unprotected outdoor storage. Adequate packing for domestic shipments often falls short for goods subject to the conditions mentioned. Protection against rough handling, moisture, temperature extremes and pilferage may require heavy crating, which increases total packing costs as well as freight rates because of increased weight and size. Since some countries determine import duties on gross weight, packing can add a significant amount to import fees. To avoid the extremes of too much or too little packing, the marketer should consult export brokers, export freight forwarders or other specialists.

Export shipping

Whenever and however title to goods is transferred, those goods must be transported. Shipping goods to another country presents some important differences from shipping to a domestic site. The goods can be out of the shipper's control for longer periods of time than in domestic distribution, more shipping and collection documents are required, packing must be suitable and shipping insurance coverage is necessarily more extensive. The task is to match each order of goods to the shipping modes best suited for swift, safe and economical delivery. Ocean shipping, air freight, air express and parcel post are all possibilities. Ocean shipping is usually the least expensive and most frequently used method for heavy bulk shipment. For certain categories of goods, air freight can be the most economical and certainly the speediest.[8]

EXHIBIT 13.4: A letter-of-credit transaction

Here is what typically happens when payment is made by an irrevocable letter of credit confirmed by a bank:

1. Importer and exporter conclude a contract, payment by letter of credit.
2. Principal instructs his bank to open a letter of credit in favour of the beneficiary.
3. Importer's bank issues and presents the letter of credit to correspondent (exporter's) bank.
4. Exporter's bank advises the beneficiary about the opening of the credit.
5. Exporter checks the terms of the credit and makes goods ready for shipment.
6. Exporter collects documents stipulated in the documentary credit.
7. Exporter presents the documents to the nominated bank.
8. Advising bank makes payment; accept or negotiate after checking the documents.
9. Advising bank sends documents to opening bank.
10. Opening bank reimburse advising bank after examination of the documents.
11. Opening bank sends documents to importer.
12. Issuing bank obtains reimbursement from the importer in the pre-agreed manner.
13. Importer forwards documents to the carrier for delivery of the goods.

Source: adapted from TBC Bank, 2013, http://www.tbcbank.ge/en/corporate/finance_insurance_and_investment/international_trade_finance/documentary_credit_process

Going International 13.7

THE FIRST CONTAINER SHIP SETS SAIL, 26 APRIL 1956

On 26 April 1956 the *SS Ideal-X*, an ageing tanker, departed from the Port of Newark, and docked in the Port of Houston five days later.

What was unusual in this otherwise routine coastal trip was that part of the cargo consisted of 58 35ft-aluminium containers. The ship was owned by Malcom McLean of McLean Trucking, a man with little experience of shipping. What he did understand, however, was that if transportation could be integrated, the vast expense of shifting freight from land to sea, and back again, could be cut significantly.

McLean started buying ships. At first he tried transporting the loaded trailers by sea – after all, they could be wheeled on and off the boats. But this proved cumbersome and not particularly economic. The answer was to remove the trailers. Cranes would lift the boxed payloads from the trucks' trailers, stack them on and below deck, and reload the trucks with incoming, standard-sized boxes. Freight costs fell from up to 25 per cent of the price of a product to negligible levels.

Today, McLean's idea seems obvious, but it took years to convince the shipping industry. The Vietnam war provided a major boost, with container transport helping to keep American soldiers in a distant jungle fed, clothed and armed. The labour unions of the world's major ports fought bitterly throughout the 1960s and 1970s for their members' jobs, but it was a futile battle.

By the mid-1970s New York's docks were a memory, *On the Waterfront* a period piece and London's derelict Docklands the cut-rate location for car chases in *The Sweeney*. From the modest beginnings of the Ideal-X, with its 50-odd boxes, the *Emma Maersk*, launched in 2006, is 1,300 foot long and 180 foot wide (too wide for the Panama Canal). It can carry 13,500 containers – up to a total weight of 156,000 metric tonnes. Its crew, on the other hand, numbers 13.

- Are container ships here to stay or could these be taken over by air freight?

Source: *Financial Times*, 30 August 2008.

Shipping costs are an important factor in a product's price in export marketing; the transportation mode must be selected in terms of the total impact on cost. One estimate is that logistics account for between 19 and 23 per cent of the total cost of a finished product sold internationally. In ocean shipping, one of the important innovations in reducing or controlling the high cost of transportation is the use of containerisation. **Containerised shipments**, in place of the traditional bulk handling of full loads or break-bulk operations, have resulted in intermodal transport between inland points, reduced costs and simplified handling of international shipments.

containerised shipments

when products are packed into containers for transportation

With increased use of containerisation, rail container service has developed in many countries to provide the international shipper with door-to-door movement of goods under seal, originating and terminating inland. This eliminates several loadings, unloadings and changes of carriers and reduces costs substantially. Containerised cargo handling also reduces damage and pilferage in transit.

For many commodities of high unit value and low weight and volume, international air freight has become important. Air freight has shown the fastest growth rate for freight transportation even though it accounts for only a fraction of total international shipments.[4] While air freight can cost two to five times surface charges for general cargo, some cost reduction is realised through reduced packing requirements, paperwork, insurance and the cost of money tied up in inventory. Although usually not enough to offset the higher rates charged for air freight, if the commodity has high unit value or high inventory costs, or if there is concern with delivery time, air freight can be a justifiable alternative. Many products moving to foreign markets meet these criteria.

The selection of transportation mode has an important bearing on the cost of export shipping, but it is not the only cost involved in the physical movement of goods from point of origin to ultimate market. Indeed, the selection of mode, the location of inventory, warehouses and so forth, all figure in the cost of the physical movement of goods. A narrow solution to the physical movement of goods is the selection of transportation; a broader application is the concept of logistics management or physical distribution.

Logistics

When a company is primarily an exporter from a single country to a single market, the typical approach to the physical movement of goods is the selection of a dependable mode of transportation, which ensures safe arrival of the goods within a reasonable time for a reasonable carrier cost.

As a company becomes global, such a solution to the movement of products could prove costly and highly inefficient for seller and buyer. When a foreign marketer begins producing and selling in more than one country and becomes a global marketer, it is time to consider the concept of logistics management; that is, a total systems approach to management of the distribution process that includes all activities involved in physically moving raw material, in-process inventory and finished goods inventory from the point of origin to the point of use.[9]

The foreign-freight forwarder

The foreign-freight forwarder, licensed by the government, arranges for the shipment of goods as the agent for an exporter. The forwarder is an indispensable agent for an exporting firm that cannot afford an in-house specialist to handle paperwork and other export trade mechanics. Even in large companies with active export departments capable of handling documentation, a forwarder is useful as a shipment coordinator at the port of export or at the destination port. Besides arranging for complete shipping documentation, the full-service **foreign-freight forwarder** provides information and advice on routing and scheduling, rates and related charges, consular and licensing requirements, labelling requirements and export restrictions.

> **foreign-freight forwarder**
>
> a company that helps other companies in transportation and export/import matters

Further, the agent offers shipping insurance, warehouse storage, packing and containerisation, and ocean cargo or air freight space. Both large and small shippers find freight forwarders' wide range of services useful and well worth the fees normally charged. In fact, for many shipments, forwarders can save on freight charges because they can consolidate shipments into larger, more economical quantities. Experienced exporters regard the foreign-freight forwarder as an important addition to in-house specialists (see Exhibit 13.5).

EXHIBIT 13.5: Major services rendered by an international freight forwarder

- Develops most economic methods of shipment: figures costs, FOB, CIF, etc.
- Arranges export licences or import permits.
- Arranges transport from plant to port/airport and beyond.
- Prepares export declaration, bill of lading and other necessary documents.
- Arranges and executes formalities with authorities such as port and customs.
- Prepares or arranges documents in foreign language, if necessary.
- Assembles all documents necessary for export/import and presents them to relevant authorities when required.
- Prepares and presents documents to the bank for letter of credit or payment.

Source: based on Subhash Jain, *Export Strategy*, Westpol (Santa Barbara, CA: Praeger, 1989).

SUMMARY

An awareness of the mechanics of export trade is indispensable to the foreign marketer who engages in exporting goods from one country to another. Although most marketing techniques are open to interpretation and creative application, the mechanics of exporting are very exact; there is little room for interpretation or improvisation with the requirements of export licences, quotas, tariffs, export documents, packing, marketing and the various uses of commercial payments. The very nature of the regulations and restrictions surrounding importing and exporting can lead to frequent and rapid change. In handling the mechanics of export trade successfully, the manufacturer must keep abreast of all foreign and domestic changes in requirements and regulations pertaining to the product involved. For firms unable to maintain their own export staffs, foreign-freight forwarders can handle many details for a nominal fee.

With paperwork completed, the physical movement of goods must be considered. Transportation mode affects total product cost because of the varying requirements of packing, inventory levels, time requirements, perishability, unit cost, damage and pilfering losses, and customer service. Transportation for each product must be assessed in view of the interdependent nature of all these factors. To assure optimum distribution at minimal cost, a physical distribution system determines everything from plant location to final customer delivery in terms of the most efficient use of capital investment, resources, production, inventory, packing and transportation.

QUESTIONS

1 Explain the reasoning behind the various regulations and restrictions imposed on the exportation and importation of goods.

2 What is the purpose of an import licence? Discuss.

3 Explain foreign-trade zones and illustrate how they may be used by an exporter/by an importer. How do foreign-trade zones differ from bonded warehouses?

4 Explain each of the following export documents:

   a bill of lading

   b consular invoice or certificate of origin

   c commercial invoice

   d insurance certificate.

5 Why would an exporter use the services of a foreign-freight forwarder? Discuss.

6 Besides cost advantages, what are the other benefits of an effective physical distribution system?

FURTHER READING

- S. Estrin, K.E. Meyer, M. Wright and F. Foliano, 'Export Propensity and Intensity of Subsidiaries in Emerging Economies', *International Business Review*, 2008, 17(5), pp 574–86.

- J.H. Love and P. Ganotakis, 'Learning by Exporting: Lessons from High Technology SMEs', *International Business Review*, 2013, 22(1), 1–17.

- C.A. Solberg and E. Nes, 'Export Trust, Commitment and Marketing Control in Integrated and Independent Export Channels', *International Business Review*, 2002, 11(4), pp 385–405.

NOTES

1   S.T. Cavusgil, 'Guidelines for Export Market Research', *Business Horizon*, 1985, November/December, 283–95.

2   J.H. Love and P. Ganotakis, 'Learning by Exporting: Lessons from High Technology SMEs, *International Business Review,* 2013, 22(1), 1–17.

3   J. Yi and C. Wang, 'The Decision to Export: Firm Heterogeneity, Sunk Costs and Spatial Concentration,' *International Business Review*, 2012, 21(5), 766–81.

4   US COMMERCE, *Doing Business in China: Country Commercial Guide for US Companies,* (Washington, DC: US Commercial Services, 2011).

5   WTO, *Trade Policies* (Geneva: World Trade Organization, 2011).

6   S.T. Cavusgil, P.N. Ghauri and A. Akcal, *Doing Business in Emerging Markets*, 2nd edn (London: Sage, 2013).

7   http://www.tbcbank.ge/en/corporate/finance_insurance_and_investment/international_trade_finance/documentary_credit_process.

8   G. Albaum, J. Strandkov and E. Derr, *International Marketing and Export Management* (Harlow: FT Prentice Hall, 2002).

9   John Gorsuch, 'Air Cargo', *Trade and Culture*, 1995, March–April, 21–26.

Chapter 14

Ethics and Social Responsibility in International Marketing

Chapter Outline

Chapter Learning Objectives

What you should learn from Chapter 14

* The importance of ethics in international marketing
* How to evaluate the impact of ethical issues on marketing
* How to analyse factors that influence a responsible marketing strategy
* How to use social responsibility as a marketing tool

Ethical issues and social responsibility together comprise a difficult but important task for international marketers. Consumer awareness about ethics, particularly in the case of multinational companies (MNCs) and foreign firms has increased. In addition a number of organisations (such as Greenpeace), consumer associations and national health organisations have entered the debate and are questioning MNC strategies and operations in different countries. Although most of the criticism is directed towards the strategic level of the companies, it is normally the marketing department that has to convince the market that the company is socially responsible and follows ethical principles.

Ethical environment

Multinational companies (MNCs) operate in a number of countries, where legal and ethical standards may differ. There are huge differences as to right and wrong between the USA and Europe. Different countries in Europe also have different rules and regulations regarding Green marketing, marketing of cigarettes, alcoholic drinks and packaged food. Huge investments made by MNCs in emerging countries contribute towards their economic development but may have a huge impact on the environment (pollution) and other social issues. Some MNCs believe that, while in developing countries, they do not have to follow the same standards of social responsibility as in their home markets, which is in itself morally wrong. Depending on history, geography, religion and economic systems, countries such as the USA and Japan do have different attitudes towards work, leisure and pollution.

The existence of diverse nationalities within Europe means that attitudes are not quite homogeneous. In contrast to the Protestant values of hard work, self-control and saving for the future, four-week vacations, two-hour lunch breaks, 35-hour working weeks and excessive spending based on borrowing are quite common. This from an American or Japanese perspective can be considered lazy or perhaps even immoral. In Japan, for a senior executive to leave a company and join a competing firm is considered unethical.

Managers have also realised that instead of being defensive and reactive, they can use ethical issues proactively as marketing tools in many countries. Royal Shell, for example, has used this strategy for a number of years, where most of its advertising campaigns emphasise the role it is playing in the development of societies, particularly in developing countries. McDonald's has also changed its marketing strategies after being accused of selling 'junk food' to children. Not only did it change its product mix (eg adding fruit to its happy meals and salads to normal offerings), but it has also run an advertising campaign in recent years aiming to convince the market that it is a socially responsible company. One study asserts that two-thirds of consumers claim that their purchasing decision is influenced by ethical considerations.

Conversely, firms marketing products that are not considered high priority or that fall from favour often face unpredictable government restrictions. Continental Can Company's joint venture to manufacture cans for the Chinese market faced a barrage of restrictions when the Chinese economy weakened. China decreed that canned beverages were wasteful and must be banned from all state functions and banquets. Tariffs on aluminium and other materials imported for producing cans were doubled and a new tax was imposed on canned drink consumption. An investment that had the potential for profit after a few years was rendered profitless by a change in the attitude of the Chinese government and environmental awareness.

Going International 14.1

WHO IS RESPONSIBLE FOR SOCIAL RESPONSIBILITY?

Managers often complain of being held responsible for the well-being of society. They claim that, according to the free-market economic system (capitalism), by running a profitable company they are advancing the public good. They also claim that by having 'good management', ie dealing honestly with employees, customers and

▶

◀

Economist and philosopher Adam Smith.
© Bettmann.

suppliers, they are doing their job. They have responsibility towards their investors (owners) and if they reduce profits to raise social welfare then perhaps they are not being honest with their investors.

Rich multinationals operating in developing countries also claim that they in fact typically want to employ local people, and pay substantially higher wages and provide better benefits than the local norms. But how much more of this is required in order to be labelled a good corporate citizen? According to Joel Bakan, a professor at the University of Columbia:

Today, corporations govern our lives. They determine what we eat, what we watch, what we wear, where we work and what we do. We are inescapably surrounded by their culture, iconography and ideology. And, like the church and the monarchy in other times, they posture as infallible and omnipotent, glorifying themselves in imposing buildings and elaborate displays. Increasingly, corporations dictate the decisions of their supposed overseers in government and control domains of society once firmly embedded in the public sphere. Corporations now govern society, perhaps more than governments themselves do; yet ironically it is their very power, much of which they have gained through economic globalisation, that makes them vulnerable. As is true of any ruling institution, the corporation now attracts mistrust, fear and demands for accountability from an increasingly anxious public.

According to Adam Smith, the father of the free-market economic system:

Every individual necessarily labours to render the annual revenue of the society as great as he can. He generally, indeed, neither intends to promote the public interest, nor knows how much he is promoting it; he intends only his own gain, and he is in this, as in many other cases, led by an invisible hand to promote an end which was no part of his intention. Nor is it always the worse for the society that it was no part of it. By pursuing his own interest he frequently promotes that of the society more effectually than when he really intends to promote it. I have never known much good done by those who affected to trade for the public good.

It is not from the benevolence of the butcher, the brewer, or the baker, that we expect our dinner, but from their regard to their own interest. We address ourselves, not to their humanity but to their self-love, and never talk to them of our own necessities but of their advantages.

(According to Milton Friedman the only responsibility of business is to make profit and grow, as long as it stays within the rules and regulations.)

Although Adam Smith promotes selfishness, he admires benevolence. But his main thesis is that benevolence is not necessary to advance public interest, as long as people are free to engage with each other in voluntary economic interactions.

- Does Adam Smith's invisible hand, the private search for profit, advance public interest? Who, in your opinion, should be responsible for the well-being of society?

Source: *The Economist*, 'A Survey of Corporate Responsibility: The Good Company', 22 January 2005, pp 1–18.

Multinational corporations are facing a growing variety of legislation designed to address environmental issues. Global concern for the environment extends beyond industrial pollution, hazardous waste disposal and rampant deforestation to include issues that focus directly on consumer products. **Green marketing** laws focus on product packaging and its effect on solid waste management and environmentally friendly products.

> **green marketing**
>
> marketing decisions that take the environment into consideration

Germany has passed the most stringent Green marketing laws that regulate the management and recycling of packaging waste. The new packaging law was introduced in three phases. The first phase requires all transport packaging such as crates, drums, pallets and Styrofoam containers to be accepted back by the manufacturers and distributors for recycling.

The second phase requires manufacturers, distributors and retailers to accept all returned secondary packaging, including corrugated boxes, blister packs, all packaging designed to prevent theft, packaging for vending machine applications and packaging for promotional purposes. The third phase requires all retailers, distributors and manufacturers to accept returned sales packaging including cans, plastic containers for dairy products, foil wrapping, Styrofoam packages and folding cartons such as cereal boxes.[1]

The **green dot programme** mandates that the manufacturer must ensure a regular collection of used packaging materials directly from the consumer's home or from designated local collection points. A green dot on a package will identify those manufacturers participating in this programme. France, Belgium, Denmark and Austria have similar regulations to deal with solid waste disposal.[2]

> **green dot programme**
>
> a sign (logo) that shows that the product adheres to Green marketing
>
> **anti-trust laws**
>
> prevent businesses from creating unjust monopolies or competing unfairly in the marketplace
>
> **European Court of Justice**
>
> an institution of the EU

Anti-trust: an evolving issue

With the exception of the USA and some European countries, **anti-trust laws** were either non-existent or unenforced in most of the world's countries for the better part of the twentieth century. However, the EU has now begun actively to enforce its anti-trust laws. Anti-monopoly, price discrimination, supply restrictions and full-line forcing are areas in which the **European Court of Justice** has dealt severe penalties. For example, before Procter & Gamble was allowed to buy VP-Schickedanz AG, a German hygiene products company, it had to agree to sell off one of the German company's divisions that produced Camelia, a brand of sanitary towel. P&G already marketed a brand in Europe, and the Commission was concerned that allowing it to keep Camelia would give it a controlling 60 per cent of the German sanitary products market and 81 per cent of Spain's.[3] In another instance, Michelin was fined €630,000 ($700,000) for operating a system of discriminatory rebates to Dutch tyre dealers. Similar penalties have been assessed in relation to companies such as United Brands for price discrimination and F. Hoffmann-LaRoche for non-cost-justified fidelity discounts to its dealers.

What is social responsibility?

Ethics and social responsibility go hand in hand. If a company is misleading its consumers, not telling the truth about the serious negative impact of its products (eg in the case of pharmaceutical and food companies) or, once realising that its product has caused damage to consumer health or well-being, refusing to accept and take responsibility, then that company has not been socially responsible. The different views on these two concepts have been summarised by Fisher[4] as follows:

- Social responsibility is ethics in an organisational context.
- Social responsibility focuses on the impact that business activity has on society while ethics is concerned with the conduct of people within organisations.
- Social responsibility and ethics are unrelated concepts.
- Social responsibility has various dimensions, one of which is ethics.

One problem is understanding what social responsibility is, and that ideas about right and wrong and what is ethical and what is not may differ from country to country. For instance, even within Europe there are different opinions on under-age sex, bribes and lying to serve self-interest. These standards differ from Scandinavia in the north to Italy and Greece in the south. Some countries stress individual responsibility while others think it is society's responsibility to ensure that companies operate in a socially responsible manner.

> **social responsibility**
>
> when a company is concerned about the implications of its decisions on society in general

Social responsibility thus means that a company plays a role in society that is beyond its economic goals and that makes a constructive contribution towards society's well-being in the long term. A few decades ago, a number of authors stated that the main responsibility of a company is to maximise its profits within the rules of law.[5] Some even stated that if a company engages in activities other than profit maximisation, it is working against shareholder interests. They believe that society's well-being is the responsibility of the state.[6]

Going International 14.2

THE USA TAKES ON GLOBAL STANDARDS TO FIGHT OBESITY: 'PERSONAL RESPONSIBILITY'

How do you change the eating habits of several hundred million people? That's the daunting problem the World Health Organization (WHO) is trying to solve with a proposal for fighting obesity worldwide. It's a bold and necessary effort but, unfortunately, it may be undermined by the world's fattest nation: the USA.

The UN estimates that more than 300 million people worldwide are obese and a further 750 million are overweight, including more than 22 million children under five. Health experts around the world are unanimous in saying that something must be done. But that's where the unanimity ends. The WHO has spent the past year hammering out a series of non-binding actions that governments could undertake. The initiative is scheduled for adoption in May, but the USA, with backing from the powerful food lobby, is working furiously to water down the proposals. These include restrictions on advertising for some food items, changes in labelling, increased taxes on junk food and the elimination of sugar subsidies.

The playbook for the Administration's attack is much the same as the one it used to block international action on global warming. It is claiming that the WHO's conclusions are not supported by 'sufficient scientific evidence' that fats and sugars cause obesity. Technically, the USA has a point. William R. Steiger, the lead delegate to the WHO from the Health and Human Services Department (HHS), complained in a letter to the organisation that the evidence linking sugar and fats to obesity comes from epidemiological studies rather than stringently controlled clinical trials. 'In this country, you can't make a scientific claim unless you have the evidence to back it up,' argues an HHS spokesman.

Even the USA does not advocate doing nothing. The Center for Disease Control estimates that one in every three adults in the USA is obese, and 15 per cent of children are overweight – double the rate of 10 years ago. Poor self-control is only one aspect of the obesity problem, however.

▶

◀

The WHO, however, does recommend restrictions on advertisements that exhort us to eat more, particularly those aimed at children. 'Advertising junk food to children is unethical and immoral,' says Dr Walter C. Willett, head of the Department of Nutrition at Harvard University's School of Public Health.

- Do you think it is government's responsibility to control the food industry or is it our own personal responsibility to watch what we eat?

Source: 'Let Them Eat Cake – If They Want to', *Business Week*, 23 February 2004.

Later studies, however, stress that the role played by a company has to go beyond profit maximisation and self-interest. This view holds that the more a company behaves responsibly, the more it will create goodwill and its positive corporate image will enhance its positioning in customers' minds and thus its competitive advantage.[7]

As Friedman[7] comments, 'there is only one social responsibility of business, to use its resources and engage in activities designed to increase profits so long as it stays within the rules of the game, and engages in open and free competition without deception or fraud'.

From the marketer's point of view, we believe in the latter. It is important to realise that each company has its **stakeholders** who benefit or suffer or whose rights are violated or respected by its actions.[8] Just as owners have a right to demand that a company does not jeopardise their interests, so do other stakeholders have the right to demand the same. Even in the 'narrow definition', the stakeholders include owners, employees, management, suppliers, customers and the local community (see Exhibit 14.1).

stakeholders

parties that have an interest in the company's activities

Owners are the investors and they want some return on their investment. Sometimes pension funds or other organisational advisers also invest in corporations. This means that the future well-being of lots of people is dependent on how the company performs.

Employees have their own, and often their families', livelihoods to support and expect wages, security and other benefits. Employers have to follow management instructions and they represent the company with their behaviour inside and outside the firm.

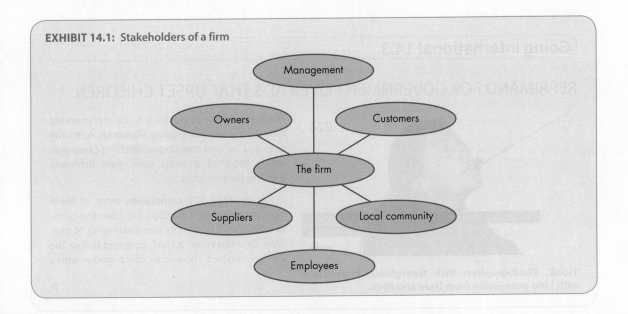

EXHIBIT 14.1: Stakeholders of a firm

Suppliers are important for firms and this relationship is in fact mutual and reciprocal. While suppliers' components and materials influence the quality and reputation of the firm, the firm's performance influences supplier success.

Customers are involved in the actual exchange with the firm as they pay to acquire its products. This payment is the lifeblood of the firm as it provides it with revenue. Understanding and satisfying customers' needs and wants are the main tasks of marketers. The better a firm can satisfy its customers, the more successful it will be and the better it can serve the interests of other stakeholders.

Local community benefits from the activities of the firm as it pays tax and provides job opportunities; it thus contributes towards the economic and social well-being of the local community. From a resident's perspective, the firm is expected to be a good citizen, just like all other citizens, individuals as well as organisations. It cannot endanger the community by its anti-social behaviour, such as causing pollution, dumping toxic waste or not paying taxes.

In case companies are not taking due care of their stakeholders or are violating the rules of good citizenship, the government intervenes and/or regulates company behaviour through industrial policy, penalities and taxation.

Analysing ethical issues and social responsibility

In international marketing, there is a tendency to find reasons to support company decision making. In the case of a company deciding to enter a particular market, its marketing research will show how lucrative the market is. It can make even small numbers look good. The dilemmas and temptations in market research to give in to unethical behaviour are well documented.[9]

Respecting the rights of respondents in marketing research is a matter of ethics. Collecting information on consumers without their consent (eg through observations) is considered unethical.

After a poisoning scandal in 1982, where several deaths were reported as a result of taking cyanide-laced, Tylenol-extra-strength pain reliever capsules, Johnson & Johnson learnt its lesson. The company convinced the market that the cyanide had been placed in the capsules by criminals. Johnson & Johnson was able to do this thanks to the trust it had developed with the market and local communities. As a result, it now openly states its code of conduct.

The company continued to market Tylenol-extra-strength, as it was a very successful brand with an annual market of $350m. However, after another tampering incident, where one person died, the company decided to terminate the marketing of this product and launched a new brand, Tylenol-caplets, in tablet form.[10]

Going International 14.3

REPRIMAND FOR GOVERNMENT OVER ADS THAT UPSET CHILDREN

'Hook', Photographer: Nick Georghiou. Reproduced with kind permission from Dare and NHS.

The Department of Health is to be reprimanded formally by the Advertising Standards Authority over its £7m anti-smoking advertising campaign, which depicted smokers with giant fishhooks piercing their mouths.

It attracted 771 complaints, most of them from parents who described the advertisements as offensive, frightening and distressing to children. One television advert, screened before the 9 pm watershed, showed an office worker with a

▶

◄

giant fishhook through his cheek being dragged from his desk to a smoking spot in a freezing car park. Another showed a hook pulling a mother away from her small daughter. A third depicted a man being dragged through traffic and into a newsagent's shop to buy cigarettes. The Advertising Standards Authority is to recommend that the adverts breached strict codes that are designed to protect children and that therefore the authority should uphold the complaints against the posters and television adverts and reprimand the Department of Health.

- Are such ads offensive or more effective?

Source: *The Times*, 7 April 2007.

Social responsibility refers to voluntary responsibilities that go beyond the purely economic and legal responsibilities of a firm. This means that the firm is willing to sacrifice part of its profit for the benefit of its stakeholders. It can thus be defined as corporate behaviour up to a level where it is congruent with the prevailing social norms, values and expectations of performance.[11]

These responsibilities can be presented at different levels (Exhibit 14.2). The inner circle in Exhibit 14.2 refers to the absolute minimum responsibility of a firm, where it has to perform efficiently economic functions such as products, job creation and growth. The second circle refers to the awareness of changing social values and priorities with regard to the environment, safety of employees and customers, and relationships with employees. The third circle refers to emerging priorities to which a firm should adhere. This includes improving the life of local communities and helping them solve problems such as poverty reduction and injustice. Companies can make a considerable contribution in this respect.

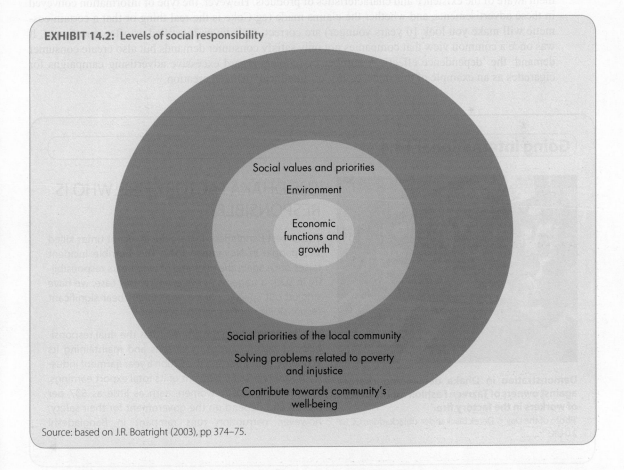

EXHIBIT 14.2: Levels of social responsibility

Social values and priorities

Environment

Economic functions and growth

Social priorities of the local community

Solving problems related to poverty and injustice

Contribute towards community's well-being

Source: based on J.R. Boatright (2003), pp 374–75.

Business ethics

In the real world of business, companies do generally behave.[12] With an increasing awareness of ethics among all the stakeholders, those companies that are more ethical are believed to perform better. Ethics refers to a standard of behaviour or code of conduct that is based on moral duties and obligations. These standards are based on values, beliefs, industry, society and government regulations.

There are two views on ethics: one is that you follow some absolute principles (eg based on religion); the other is that you follow a more consequential approach – you evaluate the consequences of your decisions and if they do not violate the ethical standards then they are fine. Many managers follow this approach as it fits into their normal decision-making models.[13] In reality, however, managers use a mixed approach.

Ethics have also become a matter of not violating basic human rights. The norms of morality are time and place bound. This means that they can change with time and increased awareness. For example, years ago it was considered alright for factories to throw their liquid waste into lakes and rivers, while at present it is considered totally wrong and unethical. In Europe, a couple of decades ago, all such factories were required to install anti-pollution systems to clean any such waste before dumping it into natural surroundings. No longer can ethics be confused with legality. Law and written codes of conduct are the minimum requirements; they provide only basic guidelines. All that is legal is not necessarily ethical. If a company is acquitted of any wrongdoing, this does not necessarily mean that it has been ethical.[14] An ethical company is not looking to meet minimum standards but instead is looking to do the maximum it can for the well-being of its stakeholders.

Ethics and international marketing

Consumers and societies have become increasingly wary (read sceptical) of the marketing activities of firms. The main purpose of marketing and advertising is to communicate with consumers and make them aware of the existence and characteristics of products. However, the type of information conveyed in these advertisements, and whether the claims made (eg Coke is the real thing or that a certain cosmetic will make you look 10 years younger) are correct, realistic and justified, is often questioned. It was once a common view that companies not only satisfy consumer demands but also create consumer demand: the 'dependence effect'. A number of scholars regard excessive advertising campaigns for cigarettes as an example of this unnecessary or 'unethical' demand creation.[15]

Going International 14.4

Demonstration in Dhaka demanding charges against owners of Tazreen Fashion for the deaths of workers in the factory fire.
'Photo of the Day' © Derek Blackadder, dblackadder, CC BY 2.0 UK.

THE DHAKA FACTORY FIRE: WHO IS RESPONSIBLE?

The largest Bangladesh factory fire in recent times killed 111 people in November 2012. This horrible incident raises once again the dilemma of who bears responsibility in such a tragedy. As we examine this case, we have singled out specific players who might bear significant responsibility for this particular event.

The Bangladeshi government has the dual responsibility of taking care of its citizens and maintaining its economy by supporting the $20bn a year garment industry that serves as 80 per cent of its total export earnings. The workers, mostly women, earn as little as $37 per month and depend on the government for their safety; however, corruption runs rampant in Bangladeshi

▶

◄

politics and the country is currently ranked 142nd out of 176 countries according to the Transparency International Corruption Perception Index. In this case, there are also implications of arson to further political interests of specific parties. Additionally, the owner of the factory constructed five more illegal floors beyond the original structure, and the factory location was in an area that large vehicles, specifically fire trucks, could not easily enter.

Major international retailers have often been criticised for not taking responsibility for their subcontractors; companies whose products were produced at this particular factory include major retailers such as Wal-Mart and Sears.

- Should multinationals be held responsible for their suppliers' negligence? Discuss.

Sources: http://www.scu.edu/ethics-center/ethicsblog/globaldialog.cfm?b=180&c=15006, 22 January, 2013; and http://www.usatoday.com/story/news/world/2012/12/07/bangladesh-factory-fire-clearance/1752883/.

In recent years, however, it has been widely accepted that marketing and advertising are essential parts of company activities and play important roles in modern society. Marketing should not, however, deceive, manipulate or exaggerate. Failure to tell the whole truth about a product, and misleading or unjustified pricing or packaging are considered unethical marketing practices. Product safety is a responsibility of the manufacturing company and, if there are any dangers, it is the company's responsibility to properly inform the customer. Moreover, despite being careful, if the company has not properly conveyed the dangers or possible risks of a product's usage, it will be held responsible for any hardship caused to anyone.[16] That is why car companies often call back a particular model to replace parts if they suspect they might malfunction and cause injury.

Going International 14.5

ATLANTIC TOYOTA BUYERS MAY SEE PRIUS LINEUP LEAD TOYOTA INTO THE FUTURE, REPLACING COROLLA AND CAMRY

Toyota Prius Timeline: First Launch to Present

The Prius came to the market more than 10 years ago, and over time has become a huge part of Toyota's lineup. Toyota customers should know the Prius may take the front line and lead Toyota into the future.

▶

◄

Toyota shoppers may have been following the Prius family as it has expanded quickly over the past few years, with new models and new additions added to the lineup. The economy and fuel efficiency that the Prius offers consumers is unmatched by most hybrid models in production today.

With the Prius being such an important part of the move to greener vehicles, Toyota Motor Corp may be seeing the Prius lineup moving into the forefront of the company. Where the Corolla and Camry were once the leaders for Toyota, the Prius and its expanding family seem to be the future leaders.

Toyota customers may have heard Toyota executives state, at a Prius event in Ypsilanti, Michigan, this week, that the company believes there will be a day that Prii models will outsell Camry as its top-selling vehicle. This seems very possible, especially with the strong growth and timeline of the Prius family as the Prius lineup will soon have four members.

Even with the success of the Prius models to this point, the Camry is still way ahead. The Camry was named the Best-Selling Car for 2010, with 327,804 units sold in the USA. In comparison, Prii sold 140,928 in the same year.

But analysts like IHS Automotive analyst Aaron Bragman have said that Toyota's view of the Prius taking the lead is very realistic because automakers have increased the number of fuel economy standards to adhere to by 2016.

Customers at Toyota should be excited to see so many choices of Prius models, especially with the mpg being between 50 mpg (Prius third generation) and 75 mpg (Prius Plug-in).

Source: *Fortune*, 6 March 2006, pp 65–68.

Green marketing

The twenty-first century has been dubbed 'the century of environmental awareness'. Consumers, business people and public administrators must now demonstrate a sense of 'Green' responsibility by integrating environmental habits into individual behaviour.

> **Green movement**
>
> political/consumer movement favouring environmentally-friendly approaches

Europe has been at the forefront of the **'Green movement'** (www.greendot.ie), with strong public opinion and specific legislation favouring environmentally-friendly marketing. Green marketing is a term used to identify concern with the environmental consequences of a variety of marketing activities. The EU, concerned that national restrictions on waste would create 15 different codes that could become clear barriers to trade, has passed legislation to control all kinds of packaging waste throughout its territory. Two critical issues that affect product development are the control of the packaging component of solid waste and consumer demand for environmentally-friendly products.[17]

Philips Lighting's first shot at marketing a standalone compact fluorescent light (CFL) bulb was Earth Light, at $15 each versus 75 cents for incandescent bulbs. The product had difficulty climbing out of its deep Green niche. The company re-launched the product as 'Marathon,' underscoring its new 'super long life' positioning and promise of saving $26 in energy costs over its five-year lifetime. Finally, with the US EPA's Energy Star label to add credibility as well as new sensitivity to rising utility costs and electricity shortages, sales climbed 12 per cent in an otherwise flat market.[18]

> **eco-labelling**
>
> a label or logo to show that a company is socially responsible

Germany has a strict **eco-labelling** programme to identify, for the concerned consumer, products that have a lesser impact on the environment than similar products. Under German regulation a manufacturer is permitted to display a logo, called the 'Blue Angel', on all products that comply with certain criteria that make them environmentally friendly. About 11,700 products and services in circa 120 product categories carry the Blue Angel eco-label. While it is difficult to judge the commercial value of a Blue Angel designation, manufacturers are seeking the eco-label for their products in

EXHIBIT 14.3: Examples of EC environmental symbols (eco-labels)

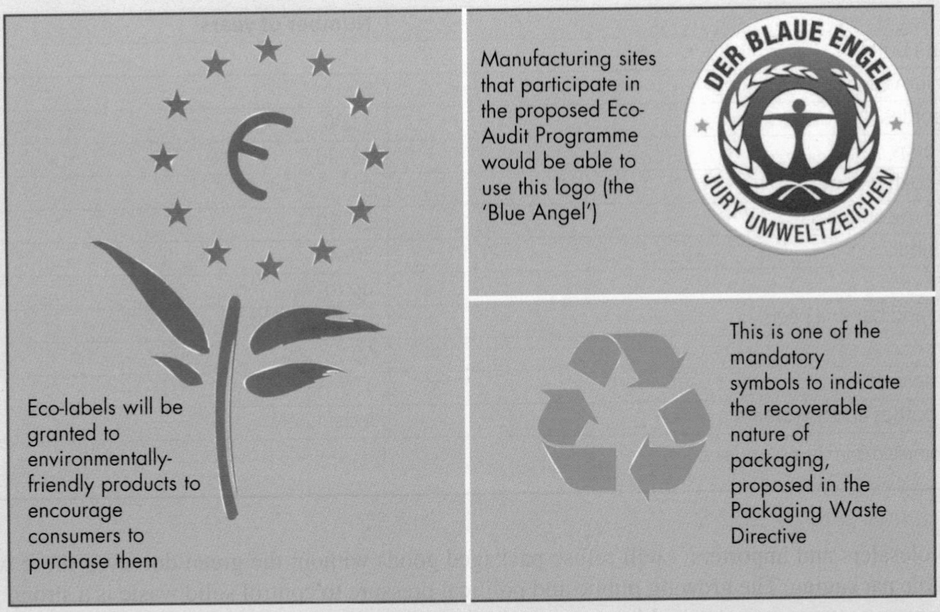

Manufacturing sites that participate in the proposed Eco-Audit Programme would be able to use this logo (the 'Blue Angel')

Eco-labels will be granted to environmentally-friendly products to encourage consumers to purchase them

This is one of the mandatory symbols to indicate the recoverable nature of packaging, proposed in the Packaging Waste Directive

response to growing consumer demand for environmentally-friendly products. Similar national labels exist in many countries of Asia, Australia, Europe, North America and South America.

Partly to offset an onrush of eco-labels from every European country, the European Commission issued guidelines for eco-labelling that became operational in October 1992. Under the EC directive, a product is evaluated on all significant environmental effects throughout its life cycle, from manufacturing to disposal: a cradle-to-grave approach.

Companies will be encouraged to continuously update their environmental technology, because eco-labels will be granted for a limited period only. As more environmentally-friendly products come onto the market, the standards will become tougher, and products that have not been improved will lose their eco-labels (see Exhibit 14.3).[19]

The Blue Angel and similar eco-labels are awarded on the basis of a product's environmental friendliness; that is, how 'friendly' it is when used and when its residue is released into the environment (see Exhibit 14.4). A detergent formulated to be biodegradable and not to pollute would be judged friendlier than a detergent whose formulation would be harmful when discharged. Aerosol propellants that do not deplete the ozone layer are another example of environmentally-friendly products. No country's laws yet require products to carry an eco-label for them to be sold. The designation that a product is 'environmentally friendly' is voluntary and its environmental success depends on the consumer selecting the eco-friendly product. However, laws that mandate systems to control solid waste, while voluntary in one sense, do carry penalties, albeit indirect ones.

Germany's law requires that packaging materials through all levels of distribution, from the manufacturer to the consumer, must be recycled or reused. To save retailers from having to shoulder the burden of the recovery of sales packaging alone, a parallel or dual waste collection system is part of German law. For the manufacturer's product to participate in direct collection and not have to be returned to the retailer for recycling, the manufacturer must guarantee financial support for kerbside or central collection of all materials. For participating manufacturers, a green dot can be displayed on the package, which signals to the consumer that a product is eligible for kerbside or central-location pick-up.

Goods sold without the green dot are not illegal; however, retailers will be reluctant to stock such products because they are responsible for their recycling. It is likely that the market – retailers,

EXHIBIT 14.4: How long will litter last?

	Number of years
Cigarette butts	1–5
Aluminium cans and tabs	500
Glass bottles	1,000
Plastic bags	10–20
Plastic-coated paper	5
Plastic film containers	20–30
Nylon fabric	30–40
Leather	up to 50
Orange and banana peels	up to 2
Tin cans	50
Plastic holders	100
Plastic bottles and Styrofoam	Indefinitely

Source: compiled from several sources.

wholesalers and importers – will refuse packaged goods without the green dot, even those with recyclable packaging. The growing public and political pressure to control solid waste is a strong incentive for manufacturers to comply. Many companies have thus detailed plans for recycling of their products (see Exhibit 14.5).

Packaging used by fast-food outlets is not covered by the German green-dot programme, and one German city, concerned about its waste disposal, imposed a tax on all fast-food containers. The local law requires fast-food restaurants to pay a tax equivalent to €0.27 for each paper plate, €0.22 for each can or non-returnable bottle, and €0.05 for each plastic spoon, fork or knife. The law was challenged by two McDonald's restaurants and two vending machine companies, but the German court upheld the tax. The impact has led some snack bars and fast-food outlets to adopt new packaging techniques. Cream is now served in reusable metal pitchers, and jam and yoghurt in glass jars. French fries are sold

EXHIBIT 14.5: The point of return

Here are recycling options from some major companies

Company	Shipping/recycling fees	In-store drop-off
Apple	Free with shipping form	Batteries and iPods accepted at Apple stores
HP	Free shipping via FedEx for HP and Compaq products with pre-printed voucher	Staples stores accept many HP and non-HP consumer products, except TVs
Dell	Free shipping or pickup of Dell products. Free pickup of non-Dell item with purchase of Dell product	Partnership with Goodwill for Dell Reconnect accepts any brand of electronics except mobile phones
Amazon	Free shipping for Kindles via UPS with pre-printed voucher	Not available
Samsung	Free mailback shipping for various Samsung products	Drop Samsung and non-Samsung products at over 1,000 third-party locations
Sony	Free shipping for Sony products weighing less than 25lb	Drop Sony products at about 850 third-party locations
Best Buy	Free appliance removal when purchasing new one. Or, $100 for home pickup of two items	Recycling kiosks for ink cartridges, rechargeable batteries, cord, cables, etc
Microsoft	Free shipping of Microsoft hardware, including Xbox	Cellphones, rechargeable phone batteries and computers accepted at Microsoft stores

Source: *Wall Street Journal*, May 2012.

on plates made of edible wafers, and soft drinks are offered in returnable bottles rather than in cans. The city is happy with the results.[20]

To stave off a multitude of individual country laws controlling solid-waste disposal, the European Commission has issued a global packaging directive. This law is considered weaker than the German law, but the limits of the law on total recovery of solid waste are seen as more workable than the German law, and collection of sales packaging materials by retailers is not mandated. The law leaves rules on collection up to individual member states, so the German green-dot programme is permissible.

Ethical behaviour in international marketing

Marketers need to adhere to their individual as well as collective responsibilities. They cannot just look at their own marketing campaign but have to put it in the context of all marketing campaigns targeting the same customer segment.[21] The marketers have responsibility for the entire market segment and not just those who are affected by their product. This is true for cigarette and liquor advertising and its impact on younger members of the market.

In salesperson/buyer relationships, bribery and other illegal/immoral payments are common issues. It is quite prevalent in many societies. In Hong Kong, it is said to be around 5 per cent, in Russia around 20 per cent and in Indonesia it can sometimes be as high as 30 per cent.[22] In many countries there is a formal way of doing business and there is also an informal way of doing business. The informal way often works faster, but might include bribes or 'commission' to be paid to 'experts'.[23]

A number of countries have signed a convention against bribery (see Exhibit 14.6) but, as it is an illegal activity, there is no guarantee that in these countries bribery does not take place.

China, India and Indonesia have passed anti-bribery laws (see Exhibit 14.7).

Product safety is a major issue in marketing ethics. Consumers have the right to be protected from harmful products. It is the responsibility of the marketer to ensure that the products meet these criteria. Consumers need to be informed sufficiently (eg on the package) to make a rational decision. The package must include crucial information about the product, eg the net quantity/weight and value comparison. Food articles should also include nutrition values and content. Exhibit 14.8 explains non-ethical behaviour in international marketing activities.

These days the use of universal price codes (UPCs) or barcodes does not always allow the customer to see and compare the price. It is the duty of the seller/retailer to provide information on price on each product. In case there is an operational cost (eg electric appliances, tyres, etc) the customer has to be informed about these 'hidden costs'.

EXHIBIT 14.6: OECD anti-bribery convention: signatory countries

Australia	Hungary	Poland
Austria	Iceland	Portugal
Belgium	Ireland	Slovak Republic
Canada	Israel	Slovenia
Chile	Italy	Spain
Czech Republic	Japan	Sweden
Denmark	Korea	Switzerland
Estonia	Luxembourg	Turkey
Finland	Mexico	UK
France	Netherlands	USA
Germany	New Zealand	
Greece	Norway	

Source: Report on Anti-Bribery Convention 2003. Cited in Blythe and Zimmerman (2005), p 361 (see Note 14) and http://www.oecd.org/general/listofoecdmembercountries-ratificationoftheconventionontheoecd.htm.

EXHIBIT 14.7: Bribes: payers and receivers rankings

Countries	BPI	CPI	Countries	BPI	CPI
Netherlands	8.80	8.90	Hong Kong	7.60	8.40
Switzerland	8.80	8.80	Italy	7.60	3.90
Belgium	8.70	7.50	Malaysia	7.60	4.30
Germany	8.60	8.00	South Africa	7.60	4.10
Japan	8.60	8.00	Taiwan	7.50	6.10
Australia	8.50	8.80	India	7.50	3.10
Canada	8.50	8.70	Turkey	7.50	4.20
Singapore	8.30	9.20	Saudi Arabia	7.40	4.40
UK	8.30	7.80	Argentina	7.30	3.00
USA	8.10	7.10	United Arab Emirates	7.30	6.80
France	8.00	7.00	Indonesia	7.10	3.00
Spain	8.00	6.20	Mexico	7.00	3.00
South Korea	7.90	5.40	China	6.50	3.60
Brazil	7.70	3.80	Russia	6.10	2.40

BPI = Bribe Payers Index   CPI = Corrupt Practices Index

EXHIBIT 14.8: Ethical issues in international marketing activities

Marketing activity	(Un)Ethical issues
Positioning	Positioning a low-quality product as a high-quality product Product positioned to perform a function that is not true, eg cholesterol-reducing food, anti-ageing cosmetics Blackmailing customers that if they do not use the product they will be harmed/disadvantaged in some way
Product	Product that can cause harm to customers/users, eg children's toys Products that pose a safety risk for the users, eg electric goods, automobiles Products that can cause health problems, eg side effects of medicines When customers are not fully informed about product content, eg in food articles – nuts, GM ingredients or sugar/salt level Use of environmentally-friendly packaging
Price	Price cartels, where two or more competitors fix a price that is higher than competitive pricing Charging discriminatory prices without any extra value provided Transfer pricing; over/underpricing internal invoices for taxation purposes Charging high monopolistic prices, eg medicines for epidemic diseases, such as AIDS in Africa Pay bribery/illegal payments or gifts to acquire sales
Promotion	Claiming inaccurate product benefits through advertising Not informing the customer fully through different means of communication Using inappropriate language in advertising Using discriminatory or degrading slogans Advertising directed towards younger children Paying illegal kickbacks to promote the product
Place/distribution	Discriminatory distribution, eg forcing wholesalers and retailers to discriminate among customers (to whom the product can be sold) Demanding unfair benefits/kickbacks/advances from retailers or suppliers Not taking responsibility for after-sales service, eg in electronic goods

Advertising is considered the most crucial aspect of marketing with regard to ethical issues. Quite often advertising is misleading or deceptive and customers are led to believe a false claim. Advertising is deceptive when it shows packaging that does not correspond with the price mentioned, eg the size and quantity versus price. A number of countries find slogans such as 'buy one, get one free' or '30 per cent free' manipulative and misleading.[24]

Moreover, it is unethical to market food knowing that it is unhealthy or harmful. It is not the customer's responsibility to check before buying.

In terms of guidelines for future managers, the ethical test, shown below, drawn up by the Institute of Business Ethics is useful because of its simplicity and clarity:

- Simple ethical test for a business decision:
  - *Transparency*
    Do I mind others knowing what I have done?

  - *Effect*
    Who does my decision affect or hurt?

  - *Fairness*
    Would my decision be considered fair by others?

  - *Check*
    Should I check the consequences of my decision for the public/customer?

Going International 14.6

SHOULD MULTINATIONALS BE HELD RESPONSIBLE?

The first Coca-Cola worker and trade unionist in Carepa to be assassinated was José Eleazar Manco, in April 1994. The second was killed days later on 20 April. He was Giraldo's brother, Enrique. In the mornings, Enrique travelled to work on the back of a friend's motorbike. Three men emerged from the side of the road and aimed guns at the bike, forcing it to stop. Enrique was dragged off into the bushes. Enrique's body was dumped at the side of the road.

When the surviving union leaders were threatened and intimidated, it became blindingly obvious that there was a campaign against the union at the Coca-Cola plant. These men were followed as they left work; cards were delivered to their homes saying, 'Go now or face death!'

The body of Isidro Gil lay inside the plant. The first bullet had hit him between the eyes. The remaining five shots were fired out of spite or bravado. Another Coca-Cola union leader had been disposed of.

The union in Carepa was smashed. The leadership was in hiding, exiled or dead. The members, cowed by guns, threats and intimidation, had signed away their rights. Meanwhile, the managers of the plant introduced a pay

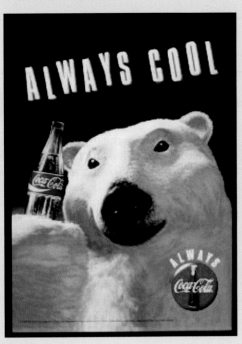

▶

◄

cut – according to Sinaltrainal, the wages for experienced workers dropped from between $380 and $450 a month to $130 a month: Colombia's minimum wage. When asked about this, Coca-Cola failed to respond. What was the Coca-Cola Company's response?

From the outset, the company's Atlanta headquarters denied 'any connection to any human-rights violations' and distanced itself from the bottlers, saying, 'The Coca-Cola Company does not own or operate any bottling plants in Colombia.' This is the standard use of the 'Coca-Cola system', operating as an entity but claiming no legal lines of accountability to the Coca-Cola Company. Coca-Cola does not own the bottling plants; the bottlers operate under a franchise. But the case here is similar to that of Gap and Nike in the 1990s. In these instances, the clothes giants had outsourced their production to factories in the developing world that operated sweatshop conditions. It was not Nike or Gap that forced the workers to do long hours for poor pay, it was the contractors. However, campaigners insisted the companies should have enforceable human rights standards applied throughout the supply chain, compelling the companies to take action. The argument was then, and is now, that no matter where the human rights abuse occurred, if it's your name on the label, then you're responsible for sorting it out.

In the Coca-Cola Company's case, the argument is made more compelling by the fact that, although it franchised Coke production to Bebidas y Alimentos and Panamerican Beverages (Panamco), Coca-Cola held 24 per cent of Panamco's shares – a controlling interest. Which gives it considerable clout in how the business is run.

Across the world, the Coca-Cola boycott had mixed results. In Dublin, Trinity College and University voted to 'Kick Coke off Campus' and refused to stock its products in student-run facilities, as did New York University and Michigan University in the USA. They were joined in the UK by Sussex, Manchester and Middlesex Universities, and London's School of Oriental and African Studies. Even though the contracts with US universities are usually worth millions, kicking Coca-Cola off campuses is unlikely to dent the balance sheet of a company that last year made $5.98bn profit. But the accompanying media attention, and headlines such as 'Has Coke become the new McDonald's' in the *Guardian*, and the *Nation* calling Coke 'the new Nike', must surely be part of the reason it has seen its 'brand value' drop. In 2007, Coca-Cola's brand value was estimated by *Business Week*/Interbrand at $65,324m – top of the league, but $2201m less than in 2005.

● Should Coca-Cola and Nike be held responsible? Discuss.

Source: *The Guardian Weekend*, 20 September 2008, pp 18–27.

SUMMARY

The classic view about the responsibilities of a firm believes that its main goals and obligations refer to economic behaviour. The firm has to be concerned about performance and growth, including innovations and technology. The modern view, however, states that a firm has to be responsible beyond its economic goals. It has to be responsible for the well-being and interest of its stakeholders: owners, employees, suppliers, customers, managers and local communities. Thus, it is a firm's responsibility to be fair and impartial towards its employees and to help society in eradicating poverty and injustice.

Ethics and social responsibility become particularly important for marketers as they are the ones who have to convey this to the market. Moreover, it is quite often the marketing function that has to take the major responsibility, at least towards the customers, and to ensure the positive performance of the company. Product safety, packaging and labelling have to be undertaken in a responsible way. The marketing message (advertising, etc) has to be honest and clean, and not manipulative or deceptive. The same is true for pricing – customers should be able to compare prices with competing products. Finally, the company has to participate in the community's social programmes such as education and equality.

QUESTIONS

1 Can a company behave legally and still be unethical? Give examples.

2 What is meant by Green marketing? How is it enforced?

3 What are the three levels of social responsibility? How can society evaluate whether a company is behaving in a responsible manner or not?

4 What are the implications of ethics and social responsibility for the marketing mix of a company? Discuss.

5 How can advertising be unethical? Give examples.

FURTHER READING

- D. Holtbrügge, N. Berg and J.F. Puck, 'To Bribe or to Convince? Political Stakeholders and Political Activities in German Multinational Corporations', *International Business Review*, 2007, 6(1), 47–67.
- M. Demirbag, J. Fredcknall-Hughes, K.W. Glaister and E. Tatoglu. ' Ethics and Taxation: A Cross-national Comparison of UK and Turkish Firms', *International Business Review*, 2013, 22(1), 100–111.
- J. Fisher, 'Social Responsibility and Ethics: Clarifying the Concepts', *Journal of Business Ethics*, 2004, 52, 391–400.

NOTES

1 Steve Zwick, 'A Better Package Deal? Germany's Green Dot – a Symbol of Success in Re-cycling Business', *Time International*, 21 May 2001, p 55.

2 Brandon Mitchener, 'Increasingly, Rules of Global Economy are set in Brussels', *Wall Street Journal*, 23 April 2002, p A1.

3 'P&G Will Drop Brand to Gain EU Takeover Clearance', Reuters News Service, 17 June 1994.

4 J. Fisher, 'Social Responsibility and Ethics: Clarifying the Concepts', *Journal of Business Ethics*, 2004, 52, 391–400.

5 B. Schlegelmich, *Marketing Ethics: An International Perspective* (London: Thomson, 1998).

6 C. Stone, 'Why Shouldn't Corporations Be Socially Responsible?', in W.M. Hoffman and J.M. Moore (eds), *Business Ethics: Readings and Cases in Corporate Morality* (New York: McGraw-Hill, 1990).

7 M. Friedman, 'The Social Responsibility of Business is to Increase its Profits', *New York Times*, 14 September 1970.

8 H. Mintzberg, 'The Case for Corporate Social Responsibility', *Journal of Business Strategy*, 1983, 4(2), 65–74.

9 J.M. Aurifielle and P.G. Quester, 'Predicting Business Ethical Tolerance in International Markets: A Concomitant Cluster-wise Regression Analysis', *International Business Review*, 2003, 12(2), 253–72.

10 J.R. Boatright, *Ethics and the Conduct of Business* (Hoboken, NJ: Pearson, 2003).

11 S.P. Sethi, 'Dimensions of Corporate Social Performance: An Analytical Framework for Measurement and Analysis', *California Management Review*, 17(Spring), 62–72.

12 This section draws on R.E. Freeman, 'A Stakeholder Theory of the Modern Corporation', in L.P. Hartman (ed), *Perspectives in Business Ethics*, 2nd edn (New York: McGraw-Hill, 2002), pp 177–204.

13   N. Bowie, 'It Seems Right in Theory but Does it Work in Practice?', in L.P. Harman (ed), *Perspectives in Business Ethics*, 2nd edn (New York: McGraw-Hill, 2002), pp 83–86.

14   J. Blythe and A. Zimmerman, *Business to Business Marketing Management: A Global Perspective* (London: Thomson, 2005).

15   M. Josephson, 'Ethics and Business Decision Making', in W. Hoffman, R. Fredrick and M. Schwartz (eds), *Business Ethics: Readings and Cases in Corporate Morality*, 4th edn (Boston, MA: McGraw-Hill, 2001), pp 87–116.

16   J.K. Galbraith, *The Affluent Society* (Boston: Houghton Mifflin, 1958).

17   Lynn S. Amine, 'The Need for Moral Champions in Global Marketing', *European Journal of Marketing*, 30(5), 1996, 81–94.

18   G. Fowler, 'Green Sales Pitch Isn't Moving Many Products', *Wall Street Journal*, 6 March 2002.

19   Kirsten Bergstrom, 'The Eco-label and Exporting to Europe', *Business America*, 29 November 1993, p 21.

20   Stephen Kinzer, 'Germany Upholds Tax on Fast-food Containers', *New York Times*, 22 August 1994, p C2.

21   G.G. Brenkest, 'Marketing to Inner-city Blacks: Power Master and Moral Responsibility', in W.M. Hoffman, R.E. Fredrick, and M.S. Schwartz (eds), *Business Ethics: Readings and Cases in Corporate Morality*, 4th edn (Boston, MA: McGraw-Hill, 2001), pp 394–403.

22   W.M. Hoffman, R.E. Fredrick and M.S. Schwartz (eds), *Business Ethics: Reading and Cases in Corporate Morality*, 4th edn (Boston, MA: McGraw-Hill, 2001), p 360.

23   V. Terpstra and K. David, *The Cultural Environment of International Business* (Cincinnati, OH: South Western Publishing, 1991).

24   Hoffman *et al.* (ibid), pp 277–82.

PART 5

Developing International Marketing Decisions

Chapter 15
Product Decisions for International Markets

Chapter Learning Objectives

What you should learn from Chapter 15

- The current dichotomy of standardised versus adapted products in international marketing
- How to manage the relationship between product acceptance and the market into which it is introduced
- How to identify physical, mandatory and cultural requirements for product evaluation
- How to identify and comply with physical, mandatory and cultural requirements for product adaptation
- The need to view all attributes of a product in order to overcome or modify resistance to its acceptance
- The impact of environmental awareness on product decisions

consumer goods

goods that consumers buy to consume

The opportunities for and challenges facing international marketers of **consumer goods** today have never been greater or more diverse. New consumers are springing forth in emerging markets in Eastern Europe, the Commonwealth of Independent States, China, India, other Asian countries and Latin America – in short, globally.[1] Emerging markets promise to be huge markets in the future.[2] In the more mature markets of the industrialised world, opportunity and challenge also abound as consumers' tastes become more sophisticated and complex, and as increases in purchasing power provide them with the means of satisfying new demands.

Never has the question 'Which products should we sell?' been more critical than it is today. For the company with a domestic market-extension orientation, the answer generally is, 'Whatever we are selling at home'. The company with a multidomestic-market orientation develops different products to fit the uniqueness of each country market; the global orientation seeks commonalities in needs among sets of country markets and responds with a somewhat global product.

All three strategies are appropriate somewhere but, because of the enormous diversity in international markets the appropriate strategy for a specific market is determined by the company's resources, the product and the target market. Consequently, each country market must be examined thoroughly, or a firm risks marketing poorly conceived products in incorrectly defined markets with an inappropriate marketing effort.[3]

The trend for larger firms is towards becoming global in orientation and strategy. However, product adaptation is as important a task in a smaller firm's marketing effort as it is for global companies. As competition for world markets intensifies and as market preferences become more global, selling what is produced for the domestic market in the same manner as it is sold at home proves to be increasingly less effective.

Most products cannot be sold at all in foreign markets without modification; others may be sold as is but their acceptance is greatly enhanced when tailored specifically to market needs. In a competitive struggle, quality products that meet the needs and wants of a market at an affordable price should be the goal of any marketing firm. For some product category groups and some country markets, this means **differentiated products** for each market. Other product groups and country market segments do well competitively with a global or standardised product but, for both, an effective marketing strategy is essential. Even standardised products may have to be sold by different and adapted marketing strategies.

differentiated products

products that are considered different from other similar products

International markets and product decisions

global products

standardised products that can be sold all over the world without adaptation

There is a recurring debate about product planning and development that focuses on the question of standardised or **global products** marketed worldwide versus differentiated products adapted, or even redesigned, for each culturally unique market. One extreme position is held by those with strong production and unit-cost orientation who advocate global standardisation, while at the other extreme are those, perhaps more culturally sensitive, who propose a different or adapted product for each market.[4]

Underlying the arguments offered by the proponents of standardised products is the premise that global communications and other worldwide socialising forces have fostered a homogenisation of tastes, needs and values in a significant sector of the population across all cultures.[5] This has resulted in a large global market with similar needs and wants that demands the same reasonably priced products offering good quality and reliability.

In support of this argument, a study found that products targeted for urban markets in emerging countries needed few changes from products sold to urban markets in developed countries: 'Modern products usually fit into lifestyles of urban consumers wherever they are.'[6] Other studies identify a commonality of preferences among population segments across countries. Families in New York need the same dishwashers as families in Paris, and families in Rome make similar demands on a washing

Going International 15.1

WII FIT PUTS THE FUN IN FITNESS

Nintendo's Wii strategy was conceived from the get-go to encourage a less sedentary form of gaming. Now the company is unveiling its calorie-burning coup, Wii Fit.

Wii Fit is Nintendo's second act to the wildly popular Wii console, which has sold nearly 10 million units in the USA since its launch in 2006. The $90 pressure-sensitive plastic slab, released on 19 May, comes packaged with sophisticated exercise and fitness-tracking software. It is yet another piece of hardware in the company's expanding ecosystem of unconventional gaming products related to the Wii, which also includes the Wii Wheel for racing and the Wii Zapper for shoot-'em-ups.

'Wii Launch Day In Japan' © Lonely Bob CC BY 2.0 UK.

The brainchild of Mario creator Shigeru Miyamoto, Wii Fit is a sturdy board slightly larger than a bathroom scale, about an inch high, that communicates with the Wii console wirelessly. Players step onto the board, which senses their movements, balance and centre of gravity. Included software features dozens of activities based on strength training, aerobics and yoga, as well as a calendar that tracks goals such as weight loss or improved flexibility. Players employ the board differently depending on the activity: standing on it to do a tree pose in yoga, for instance, or stepping on and off it for aerobics.

Some minor ego-bruising aside, Wii Fit accomplishes its mission. It may not replace your trainer, but it will allow beginners to start at their own pace and give fitness freaks yet another exercise outlet. Ultimately, Wii Fit shines because the bar to entry – and enjoyment – is extremely low: almost anybody can unpack and play. For the moment at least, Sony and Microsoft have nothing like it. But, more importantly, the product dovetails nicely with Wii's mission to improve general fitness.

- Could the Wii Fit replace a personal trainer?

Source: *Business Week*, 21 May 2008.

machine as do families in London. However, the sizes, colours, voltage requirements, switches and advertising may need to be adapted to each market.

Although recognising some cultural variations, advocates of **standardisation** believe that product standardisation leads to production economies and other savings that permit profits at prices that make a product attractive to the global market. Economies of production, better planning, more effective control and better use of creative managerial personnel are the advantages of standardisation. Such standardisation can result in significant cost savings but it makes sense only when there is adequate demand for the standardised product.

> **standardisation**
> when the same products are produced for many markets

Those who hold the opposing view stress that substantial cultural variation among countries dictates a need for differentiated products to accommodate the uniqueness of cultural norms and product use patterns. For example, Electrolux, the appliance manufacturer, finds the refrigerator market among European countries far from homogeneous. Northern Europeans want large refrigerators because they shop only once a week in supermarkets; Southern Europeans prefer small ones because they pick through open-air markets almost daily. Northerners like their freezers at the bottom, Southerners on top. And Britons, who devour huge quantities of frozen food, insist on units with 60 per cent freezer space.

Further, 100 appliance makers compete for that market. To be competitive, Electrolux alone produces more than 100 basic designs with 1,500 variations. Compare such differences to the relatively homogeneous US market where most refrigerators are standardised, have freezers on top, and come in only a few sizes, and where 80 per cent are sold by four firms.[7]

The issue between these two extremes cannot be resolved with a simple either/or decision since the prudent position probably lies somewhere in the middle. Most astute marketers concede that there are definable segments across country markets with some commonality of product preferences, and that substantial efficiencies can be attained by standardising. They also recognise, however, that there may be cultural differences that remain important. The key issue is not whether to adapt or standardise, but how much adaptation is necessary and to what point a product can be standardised.

Most products are adapted, at least to some degree, even those traditionally held up as examples of standardisation. Although the substantial portion of its product is standardised worldwide, in India McDonald's does not sell beefburgers but includes vegetarian and lamb-burgers in its stores, to accommodate dietary and religious restrictions, and in European stores it sells wine and beer. In Norway, it sells a salmon-burger that is not sold in other markets. In Indonesia and the Philippines it sells chicken and rice meals and in the Netherlands it sells Kroketburgers. Pepsi Cola reformulated its diet cola to be sweeter and more syrupy, and changed its name from Diet Pepsi to Pepsi Light and Pepsi Max to appeal to international markets where the idea of 'diet' is often shunned and a sweeter taste is preferred.[8]

If different products are necessary to satisfy local needs a fully standardised product may not be appropriate; however, some efficiencies may be achieved by standardising some aspects of the product. Whirlpool faced this problem when it acquired NV Philips, a division of Philips, the European appliance manufacturer, whose approach to the European market was to make a different product for each country market.

customised products

products that are modified for each customer

Whirlpool found that the Philips German plant produced feature-rich washing machines that sold at higher prices, while washers from the Italian plants ran at lower RPMs and were less costly. Each plant operated independently of the other and they produced **customised products** for their respective markets. The washing machines made in the Italian and German facilities differed so much that 'they did not have one screw in common', yet the reality was that the insides of the machines were very similar. Immediate steps were taken to standardise and simplify both the German and Italian machines by reducing the number of parts and using as many common parts as possible.

New products were developed to ensure that a wide variety of models could be built on a standardised platform. The same approach was taken for dryers and other product categories. Although complete standardisation could not be achieved, efficiencies were attained by standardising the platform (the core product) and customising other features to meet local preferences.[9]

As companies gain more experience of the idea of global markets, the approach is likely to be to standardise where possible and adapt where necessary. To benefit from standardisation as much as possible and still provide for local cultural differences, companies are using an approach to product development that allows for such flexibility. The idea is to develop a core platform containing the essential technology, and then base variations on this platform. Sony has used this approach for its Playstation. The basic Playstation platform gives it the flexibility rapidly to adjust production to shifts in market preference. The Apple iPad is a good example of a standardised product, but it uses different marketing channels and strategies in different countries. In the USA and Europe, it has its own outlets, while in many markets it sells via distributors and the customer segment is different in different markets.

To differentiate for the sake of differentiation is not a solution, nor is adaptation for the sake of adaptation or standardisation for the sake of standardisation. Realistic business practice requires that a company strives for uniformity in its marketing mix whenever and wherever possible, while recognising that cultural differences may demand some accommodation if the product is to be competitive.[10]

Going International 15.2

A NEW POP SENSATION

The latest hit from Japanese toymaker Bandai, the company that created the Tamagotchi digital pet, is: Mugen Puti Puti, which translates roughly as 'pop forever'. Bandai teamed up with packing-material maker Kawakami Sangyo to produce the gizmo. When pressed, it emits that satisfying sound of squeezing bubble wrap – from actual recordings of the packaging being popped. About as big as a pat of butter, the rubber-covered square, which contains a tiny speaker, is already a big success in Japan, where it has been on sale since September.

Consumers snapped up some 300,000 units in its first nine days in the stores. Bandai says it expects to sell more than 2 million by next March. The battery-powered device was the brainchild of 27-year-old Bandai toy designer Shimpei Takahashi. Venture partner Kawakami Sangyo, meanwhile, continues to operate its own frivolous packaging product line. The privately owned company sells Post-it note-size sheets of real bubble wrap (available in a gift box) and bubble-wrap calendars. No decision yet on whether Mugen Puti Puti will be offered in the USA or Europe.

Source: *Business Week*, 22 October 2007, p 24.

Products and brands

Hand in hand with global products are global brands. A **global brand** is defined as the worldwide use of a name, term, sign, symbol, design or combination thereof intended to identify goods or services of one seller and to differentiate them from those of competitors. Much like the experience with global products, there is no single answer to the question of whether or not to establish global brands. There is, however, little question of the importance of a brand name.

> **global brand**
> the worldwide use of a name, term, sign, symbol, design or combination thereof, to identify goods or services of one seller and differentiate them from those of competitors

A successful brand is the most valuable resource a company has. The brand name encompasses the years of advertising, goodwill, quality evaluation, product experience and the other beneficial attributes the market associates with the product. The value of Philips, Kodak, Sony, Coca-Cola, McDonald's, Nike, Adidas, Toyota and Shell is indisputable. One estimate of the value of 112-year-old Coca-Cola, the world's most valuable brand, places it at over $77.8bn and Microsoft at over $58.8bn and Nokia at over $21.0bn.[11]

Naturally, companies with such strong brands strive to use those brands globally. Even for products that must be adapted to local market conditions, a global brand can be used successfully. Philips produces several models of TVs and vacuum cleaners for different markets using the same brand name. Toyota markets several models in different countries using the same brand names. And Apple is, of course, a global brand.

Products and culture

To appreciate the complexity of standardised versus adapted products, one needs to understand how cultural influences are interwoven with the perceived value and importance a market places on a product. A product is more than a physical item; it is a bundle of satisfactions (or utilities) the buyer receives.

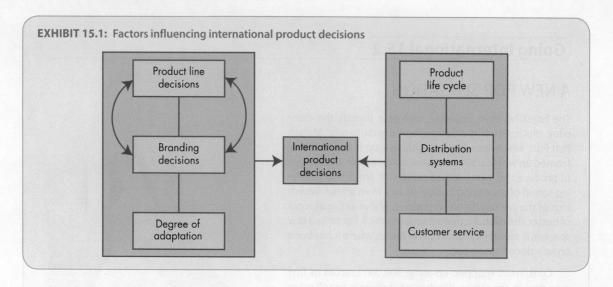

EXHIBIT 15.1: Factors influencing international product decisions

This includes its form, taste, colour, odour and texture, how it functions in use, the package, the label, the warranty, manufacturer's and retailer's servicing, the confidence or prestige enjoyed by the brand, the manufacturer's reputation, the country of origin and any other symbolic utility received from the possession or use of the goods. In short, the market relates to more than a product's physical form and primary function (see Exhibit 15.1).

physical attributes

physical characteristics of a product

Its **physical attributes** generally are required to create the primary function of the product. The primary function of a car, for example, is to move passengers from point A to point B. This ability requires an engine, transmission and other physical features to achieve its primary purpose. The physical features and primary function of a car are generally in demand in all cultures where there is a desire to move from one point to another, other than on foot or by animal power.

Few changes to the physical attributes of a product are required when moving from one culture to another. However, a car has a bundle of psychological features as important in providing consumer satisfaction as its physical features. Within a specific culture, other features (colour, size, design, brand name) have little to do with the car's primary function, the movement from point A to B, but do add value to the satisfaction received.

The meaning and value imputed to the psychological attributes of a product can vary among cultures and are perceived as negative or positive. To maximise the bundle of satisfactions received and to create positive product attributes rather than negative ones, adaptation of the **non-physical features** of a product may be necessary.

non-physical features

characteristics of a product that are not physical but perceptional

Coca-Cola, frequently touted as a global product, found it had to change Diet Coke to Coke Light when it was introduced in Japan and a number of European countries. Japanese women do not like to admit to dieting and, further, the idea of diet implies sickness or medicine. This also applies in some European countries. So, instead of emphasising weight loss, 'figure maintenance' is stressed.

The adoption of some products by consumers can be affected as much by how the product concept conflicts with norms, values and behaviour patterns as by its physical or mechanical attributes. As one authority states:

In short, it is not just lack of money, nor even differences in the natural environment, that constitutes major barriers to the acceptance of new products and new ways of behaving. A novelty always comes up against a closely integrated cultural pattern, and it is primarily this that determines whether, when, how and in what form it gets adopted. The Japanese have always found all body jewellery repugnant. The Scots have a decided resistance to pork and all its associated products, apparently from days long ago when such taboos were decided by strict interpretations of the Bible.

When analysing a product for a second market, the extent of adaptation required depends on cultural differences in product use and perception between the market the product was originally developed for and the new market. The greater these cultural differences between the two markets, the greater the extent of adaptation necessary.

An example of this involves an undisputed American leader in cake mixes, which tacitly admitted failure in the English market by closing down operations after five unsuccessful years. Taking its most successful mixes in the US market, the company introduced them into the British market. A considerable amount of time, money and effort was expended to introduce its variety of cake mixes to this new market.

Hindsight provides several probable causes for the company's failure. The British eat most of their cake with tea instead of dinner and have always preferred dry sponge cake, which is easy to handle; the fancy, iced cakes favoured in the USA were the type introduced. Fancy, iced cakes are accepted in Britain, but they are considered extra special and purchased from a bakery or made with much effort and care at home. Homemakers felt guilty about not even cracking an egg, and there was suspicion that dried eggs and milk were not as good as fresh products. Therefore, when the occasion called for a fancy cake, an easy cake-mix was simply not good enough.

When instant cake mixes were introduced in Japan, consumers' response was less than enthusiastic. Not only do Japanese reserve cakes for special occasions, they prefer them to be beautifully wrapped and purchased in pastry shops. The acceptance of instant cakes was further complicated by another cultural difference – most Japanese homes do not have ovens.

Going International 15.3

WHY COCA-COLA BECAME SO POPULAR

When Atlanta pharmacist John Pemberton invented Coca-Cola in 1886, he named it that for a reason. His 'brain tonic' included extracts of the kola nut, a high-caffeine stimulant thought to be an aphrodisiac, and coca leaf extract, containing a small amount of cocaine. It's been a hundred years since Coke included that particular ingredient.

Before Coca-Cola, Pemberton had created a version of coca wine, a popular cocaine-laced beverage endorsed by Queen Victoria and Pope Leo XIII. In his new cola beverage, he eliminated alcohol in a nod to the temperance movement but kept the coca extract. When pharmacies began mixing his syrup with carbonated water, sales bubbled up.

In the late nineteenth century cocaine was hailed as a pain-killing breakthrough and found in dozens of products, from throat lozenges to suppositories. But public concern began to grow about its safety, and by 1904 Coca-Cola was completely 'decocainised' (though coca extract, with all traces of the drug removed, remains an ingredient to this day).

Despite the omission, Coke's popularity continued to grow, owing in part to a successful promotion campaign. Growing suspicious of the drink's success, officials at the US Bureau of Chemistry (precursor to the Food and Drug Administration) had a shipment of Coke syrup seized in Chattanooga, Tennessee, in 1909. The product, they charged, violated the Pure Food and Drug Act of 1906, prohibiting sale of 'adulterated or misbranded' foods. The 'adulterating' chemical: caffeine. The government lost its case.

- Should companies be allowed to continue with established products and brands using suspicious ingredients, if proven harmless?

Source: M.G. Zackowitz, 'More Than Just a Sugar Buzz', *National Geographic*, October 2004, p 4.

Innovative products and adaptation

An important first step in adapting a product to a foreign market is to determine the degree of newness perceived by the intended market. How people react to newness and how new a product is to a market must be understood. In evaluating the newness of a product, the international marketer must be aware that many products successful in Western countries, having reached the maturity or even decline stage in their life cycles, may be perceived as new in another country or culture and, thus, must be treated as innovations. A new product would therefore demand a different type of marketing strategy than the one used at home for a rather mature product.

innovation

new product/ technology/method

Whether or not a group accepts an **innovation**, and the time it takes, depends on its characteristics. Products new to a social system are innovations, and knowledge about the diffusion (ie the process by which innovation spreads) of innovation is helpful in developing a successful product strategy.

Another US cake-mix company entered the British market but carefully eliminated most of the newness of the product. Instead of introducing the most popular American cake mixes, the company asked 500 British housewives to bake their favourite cake. Since the majority baked a simple, very popular dry sponge cake, the company brought to the market a similar easy mix. The sponge cake mix represented familiar tastes and habits that could be translated into a convenience item, and did not infringe on the emotional aspects of preparing a fancy product for special occasions. Consequently, after a short period of time, the second company's product gained 30 to 35 per cent of the British cake-mix market. Once the idea of a mix for sponge cake was acceptable, the introduction of other flavours became easier.

The goal of a foreign marketer is to gain product acceptance by the largest number of consumers in the market in the shortest time span. However, as many of the examples cited have illustrated, new products are not always readily accepted by a culture; indeed, they often meet resistance. Although they may ultimately be accepted, the time it takes for a culture to learn new ways, to learn to accept a new product, are of critical importance to the marketer since planning reflects a time frame for investment and profitability.

Diffusion of innovations

There is ample evidence of the fact that product innovations have a varying rate of acceptance. Some diffuse from introduction to widespread use in a few years, others take decades. Microwave ovens, introduced in the 1950s, reached widespread acceptance in the 1980s. The contraceptive pill was introduced during that same period and gained acceptance several years later. There is also a growing body of evidence that the understanding of diffusion theory may provide ways in which the process of diffusion can be accelerated. Knowledge of this process may provide the foreign marketer with the ability to assess the time it takes for a product to diffuse – before it is necessary to make a financial commitment.

Going International 15.4

NEW PRODUCTS FOR BETTER HYGIENE

Japanese companies are very active in developing new products: the Sony Walkman, PlayStation and Toyota Prius are not the only ones. In developing new types of toilet, they are competing with Dutch manufacturers.

Japan's abundance of water has allowed it to focus on cleanliness, frequent bathing and high-tech bathrooms. A Matsushita toilet reads your body temperature and blood pressure. It will soon be able to tell you about glucose and protein levels in your urine. The toilet also washes and dries your bottom.

The Dutch, on the other hand, are worried about using too much water, as most of their country is below sea level. They do not want to throw too much water into

© P.N. Ghauri.

▶

◄ the ground. Sphinx in Maastricht has developed a urinal for women that reduce the usage of water, and a fly embedded in the porcelain for its men's urinal. The latter reduces maintenance costs as the company's research has shown that most men will aim for the fly, which is strategically placed to minimise splash and enable quick cleaning. These Dutch innovations can be seen at Schiphol Airport in Amsterdam.

● Do you think a toilet that washes and dries your bottom has a market in Europe? Discuss.

Source: compiled from several sources.

At least three extraneous variables affect the **rate of diffusion** of an object: the degree of perceived newness, the perceived attributes of the innovation, and the method used to communicate the idea. Each variable has a bearing on consumer reaction to a new product and the time needed for acceptance. An understanding of these variables can produce better product strategies for the international marketer.

Degree of newness

As perceived by the market, varying degrees of newness categorise all new products. Within each category, myriad reactions affect the rate of diffusion. In giving a name to these categories, one might think of: (1) congruent innovations; (2) continuous innovations; (3) dynamically continuous innovations; and (4) discontinuous innovations.

1 A **congruent innovation** is actually not an innovation at all because it causes absolutely no disruption of established consumption patterns. The product concept is accepted by the culture and the innovativeness is typically one of introducing variety and quality or functional features, style or perhaps an exact duplicate of an already existing product – exact in the sense that the market perceives no newness, such as cane sugar versus beet sugar.

2 A **continuous innovation** has the least disruptive influence on established consumption patterns. Alteration of a product is almost always involved rather than the creation of a new product. Generally, the alterations result in better use patterns – perceived improvement in the satisfaction derived from its use. Examples include fluoride toothpaste, disposable razors and flavours in coffee. A continuous improvement in Gillette and Wilkinson Sword razors is another example.

3 A **dynamically continuous innovation** has more disruptive effects than a continuous innovation, although it generally does not involve new consumption patterns. It may mean the creation of a new product or considerable alteration of an existing one designed to fulfil new needs arising from changes in lifestyles or new expectations brought about by change. It is generally disruptive and therefore resisted because old patterns of behaviour must change if consumers are to accept and perceive the value of the dynamically continuous innovation. Examples include electric toothbrushes, electric hair-curlers, central air-conditioning and frozen dinners.

4 A **discontinuous innovation** involves the establishment of new consumption patterns and the creation of previously unknown products. It introduces an idea or behaviour pattern where there was none before. Examples include television, the computer, the fax machine, the electric car and microwave ovens.

The extent of a product's diffusion and its rate of diffusion are partly functions of the particular product's attributes. Each innovation has characteristics by which it can be described, and each person's perception of these characteristics can be utilised in explaining the differences in perceived newness of an innovation. These attributes can also be utilised in predicting the rate of adoption, and the adjustment of these attributes, or product adaptation can lead to changes in consumer perception and thus to altered rates of diffusion. Emphasis given to product adaptation for local cultural norms and the overall brand

rate of diffusion

speed at which a product spreads out in a specific area

congruent innovation

the innovativeness is typically one of introducing variety and quality, or functional features or style

continuous innovation

usually alteration of a product rather than creation of a new one

dynamically continuous innovation

this may mean the creation of a new product or considerable alteration of an existing one

discontinuous innovation

introduces an idea or behaviour that wasn't present before

image created are critical marketing decision areas. Thanks to these adaptation issues, more and more products/brands are being developed in emerging markets. These brands and innovations are more adapted to local needs and demands.

Physical or mandatory requirements and adaptation

> **mandatory requirements**
>
> requirements that a company must meet

A product may have to change in a number of ways to meet the physical or **mandatory requirements** of a new market; these can range from simple package changes to total redesign of the physical core product. Some changes are obvious with relatively little analysis; a cursory examination of a country will uncover the need to rewire electrical goods for a different voltage system, simplify a product when the local level of technology is not high, or print multilingual labels where required by law. Electrolux, for example, offers a cold-wash-only washing machine in Asian countries in which electric power is expensive or scarce.

Legal, economic, technological and climatic requirements of the local marketplace often dictate product adaptation. Specific package sizes and safety and quality standards are usually set by laws that vary among countries. To make a purchase more affordable in low-income countries, the number of units per package may have to be reduced from the typical quantities offered in high-income countries. Razor blades, cigarettes, chewing gum and other multiple-pack items are often sold singly or two to a pack instead of the more customary 10 or 20.

Changes may also have to be made to accommodate climatic differences. General Motors of Canada, for example, experienced major problems with several thousand Chevrolet cars shipped to a Middle Eastern country; it was quickly discovered they were unfit for the hot, dusty climate. Supplementary air filters and different clutches had to be added to adjust for the problem. Even peanuts and crackers have to be packaged differently (in tins) for humid areas.

The less economically developed a market, the greater degree of change a product may need for acceptance. One study found only 1 in 10 products could be marketed in developing countries without modification of some sort. Of the modifications made, nearly 25 per cent were mandatory; the other modifications were made to accommodate variations in culture and climate.

Going International 15.5

NEW PRODUCTS IN THE AUTO INDUSTRY

Toyota Prius - 2005 European Car of the Year
Issued 11/2004

Toyota launched its hybrid car, the Toyota Prius, in 2001 and sold 15,556 models in the first year. In 2005 it is expected to sell more than 100,000. The Prius cuts fuel consumption by combining an electric motor with a gas engine. It is not only cheaper to run but also environmentally friendly as compared to other cars.

Now Toyota is moving its hybrid technology to its main product lines. First it is being incorporated in Lexus models (RX SUVs); the Camry is next in line, which is America's best-selling car. Honda has also started using the technology in its Civic and Accord models.

▶

◀

The American auto industry is, however, far behind. In the age of high gas/oil prices, it is expected that hybrid autos will capture 20 per cent of the US car market. This will allow Toyota and Honda to achieve economies of scale, and means that customers will not have to pay any extra for the new technology. Both companies are focusing on power and luxury to attract more customers: the Toyota Highlander SUV features 270 horsepower and better economy than a normal compact sedan.

Ford is the only American auto-maker to launch a hybrid SUV, the Ford Escape; but, in applying the technology as a strategy, it is far behind. Land Rover, now a Ford brand, is next in line for the hybrid technology.

● Do you think these hybrids are the future of the car industry? Why/why not?

Source: *Business Week*, 'How Hybrids are Going Mainstream', 1 November 2004, p 37.

Product life cycle and adaptation

Even between markets with few cultural differences, substantial adaptation could be necessary if the product is in a different stage of its life cycle in each market. Product life cycle and the marketing mix are interrelated; a product in a mature stage of its life cycle in one market can have unwanted and/ or unknown attributes in a market where the product is perceived as new and thus in its introductory stage. Marketing history is replete with examples of mature products in one market being introduced in another and failing (see Exhibit 15.2).

Certainly an important approach in analysing products for foreign markets is determining the stage of the product's life cycle. All subsequent marketing plans must then include adaptations necessary to correspond to the stage of the product life cycle in the new market.

The success of these alternatives depends on the product and the fundamental need it fulfils, its characteristics, its perception within the culture and the associated costs of each programme. To know that foreign markets are different and that different product strategies may be needed is one thing; to know when adaptation of your product line and marketing programme is necessary is another and more complicated problem.

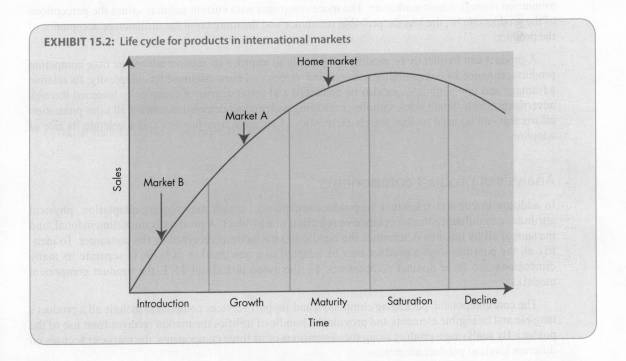

EXHIBIT 15.2: Life cycle for products in international markets

Screening products for adaptation

Evaluating a product for marketing in another country requires a systematic method of screening products to determine if there are cultural resistances to overcome and/or physical or mandatory changes necessary for product acceptance. Only when the psychological (or cultural) and physical dimensions of the product, as determined by the country market, are known can the decision for adaptation be made. Products can be screened on two different bases by using 'analysis of characteristics of innovations' to determine if there are cultural-perceptual reasons why a product will be better accepted if adapted, and/or 'analysis of product components' to determine if there are mandatory or physical reasons why a product must be adapted.

Analysis of characteristics of innovations

> **market resistance**
>
> when customers are reluctant to accept a new product/service

Attributes of a product that cause **market resistance** to its acceptance and affect the rate of acceptance can be determined if a product is analysed by the five characteristics of an innovation:

1 relative advantage – the perceived marginal value of the new product relative to the old

2 compatibility – its compatibility with acceptable behaviour, norms, values, and so forth

3 complexity – the degree of complexity associated with product use

4 trialability – the degree of economic and/or social risk associated with product use

5 observability – the ease with which the product benefits can be communicated.

In general, it can be postulated that the rate of diffusion is positively related to relative advantage, compatibility, trialability and observability, but negatively related to complexity.

The evaluator must remember it is the perception of product characteristics by the potential adopter, not the marketer, that is crucial to the evaluation. A market analyst's self-reference criterion may cause a perceptual bias when interpreting the characteristics of a product. Thus, instead of evaluating product characteristics from the foreign user's frame of reference, it is analysed from the marketer's frame of reference, leading to a misinterpretation of cultural importance.

Once the analysis has been made, some of the perceived newness or cause for resistance can be minimised through adroit marketing. The more congruent with current cultural values the perceptions of the product can be, the less the probable resistance and the more rapid the diffusion or acceptance of the product.

A product can frequently be modified physically to improve its relative advantage over competing products, enhance its compatibility with cultural values and even minimise its complexity. Its relative advantage and compatibility can also be enhanced and some degree of complexity lessened through advertising efforts. Small sizes, samples, packaging and product demonstrations are all sales promotion efforts that can be used to alter the characteristics of an innovative product and accelerate its rate of adoption.

Analysis of product components

In addition to cultural resistance to product acceptance, which may require adaptation, physical attributes can influence the acceptance or rejection of a product. A product is multidimensional, and the sum of all its features determines the bundle of satisfactions received by the consumer. To identify all the possible ways a product may be adapted to a new market, it helps to separate its many dimensions into three distinct components, as illustrated in Exhibit 15.3 (the product component model).

The core component, packaging component and support services component include all a product's tangible and intangible elements and provide the bundle of utilities the market receives from use of the product. By analysing a product along the dimensions of its three components, the marketer focuses on different levels of product adaptation.

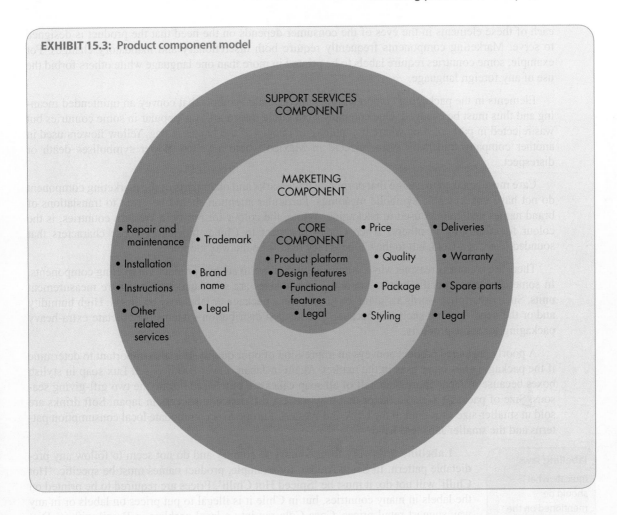

EXHIBIT 15.3: Product component model

SUPPORT SERVICES COMPONENT

MARKETING COMPONENT

CORE COMPONENT
- Product platform
- Design features
- Functional features
- Legal

- Price
- Quality
- Package
- Styling

- Trademark
- Brand name
- Legal

- Repair and maintenance
- Installation
- Instructions
- Other related services

- Deliveries
- Warranty
- Spare parts
- Legal

The core component

This component consists of the physical product – the platform that contains the essential technology – and all its design and functional features. It is on the product platform that product variations can be added or deleted to satisfy local differences. Major adjustments in the platform aspect of the core component may be costly because a change in the platform can affect product processes and thus require additional capital investment. However, alterations in design, functional features, flavours, colour and other aspects can be made to adapt the product to cultural variations.

In Japan, both Nestlé and Kellogg's sold the same kind of Corn Flakes and Sugar Pops that they sold in Western countries, but Japanese children ate them mostly as snacks instead of for breakfast. In order to move its product into the large breakfast market, Nestlé reformulated its cereals to fit Japanese tastes more closely. The Japanese traditionally eat fish and rice for breakfast, so Nestlé developed cereals with familiar tastes – seaweed, carrots and zucchini, and coconuts and papaya. The result was more than a 12 per cent share of a growing market.

Functional features can be added or eliminated depending on the market. In markets where hot water is not commonly available, washing machines have heaters as a functional feature. In other markets, automatic soap and bleach dispensers may be eliminated to cut costs and/or to minimise repair problems. Additional changes may be necessary to meet safety and electrical standards or other mandatory requirements. The physical product and all its functional features should be examined as potential candidates for adaptation.

The marketing component

The marketing component includes style features, packaging, labelling, trademarks, brand name, quality, price and all other aspects of a product's package. As with the core component, the importance of each of these elements in the eyes of the consumer depends on the need that the product is designed to serve. Marketing components frequently require both discretionary and mandatory changes. For example, some countries require labels to be printed in more than one language while others forbid the use of any foreign language.

Elements in the packaging component may incorporate symbols that convey an unintended meaning and thus must be changed. One company's red circle trademark was popular in some countries but was rejected in parts of Asia where it conjured up images of the Japanese flag. Yellow flowers used in another company trademark were rejected in Mexico where a yellow flower symbolises death or disrespect.

Care must be taken to ensure that corporate trademarks and other parts of the marketing component do not have unacceptable symbolic meanings. Particular attention should be given to translations of brand names and colours used in packaging. White, the colour for purity in Western countries, is the colour for mourning in others. When Coca-Cola went to China, translators chose characters that sounded like Coca-Cola, but to the Chinese they read 'bite the wax tadpole'.

There are countless reasons why a company might have to adapt a product's marketing components. In some countries, specific bottle, can and package sizes are stipulated by law, as are measurement units. Such descriptive words as 'giant' or 'jumbo' on a package or label may be illegal. High humidity and/or the need for long shelf-life because of extended distribution systems may dictate extra-heavy packaging for some products.

A poorly packaged product conveys an impression of poor quality. It is also important to determine if the packaging has other uses in the market. Again in Japan, Lever Brothers sell Lux soap in stylish boxes because in Japan more than half of all soap cakes are purchased during the two gift-giving seasons. Size of package is also a factor that may make a difference to success in Japan. Soft drinks are sold in smaller-size cans than in the USA and Western Europe to accommodate local consumption patterns and the smaller Japanese hand.

> **labelling laws**
>
> indicate what should be mentioned on the package

Labelling laws vary from country to country and do not seem to follow any predictable pattern. In Saudi Arabia, for example, product names must be specific. 'Hot Chilli' will not do, it must be 'Spiced Hot Chilli'. Prices are required to be printed on the labels in many countries, but in Chile it is illegal to put prices on labels or in any way suggest retail prices. Coca-Cola ran into a legal problem in Brazil with its Diet Coke. Brazilian law interprets diet to have medicinal qualities. Under the law, producers must give daily recommended consumption on the labels of all medicines. Coke had to get special approval to get around this restriction.

The support services component

This component includes repair and maintenance, instructions, installation, warranties, deliveries and the availability of spare parts. Many otherwise successful marketing programmes have ultimately failed because little attention was given to this product component. Repair and maintenance are especially difficult problems in developing countries.

In Europe and the USA, a consumer has the option of company service as well as a score of competitive service retailers ready to repair and maintain anything from cars to lawnmowers. Equally available are repair parts from company-owned or licensed outlets or the local hardware store. Consumers in a developing country and many developed countries may not have even one of the possibilities for repair and maintenance available in the West.

Literacy rates and educational levels of a country may require a firm to change a product's instructions. A simple term in one country may be incomprehensible in another. In rural Africa, for example, the consumer had trouble understanding that Vaseline Intensive Care lotion is absorbed into the skin. Absorbed was changed to soaks into, and the confusion was eliminated. The Brazilians have successfully overcome low literacy and technical skills of users of the sophisticated military tanks it sells to developing countries. They include DVD players and DVDs with detailed repair instructions as part of the standard instruction package. They also minimise spare parts problems by using standardised, off-the-shelf parts available throughout the world.

Quality products

The debate about product standardisation versus product adaptation is not just a textbook exercise. It can mean the difference between success and failure in today's markets. As discussed in an earlier chapter, a quality product is one that satisfies consumer needs, has minimum defects and is priced competitively. Gone are the days when the customer's knowledge was limited to one or at best just a few different products.

Today the customer knows what is best, cheapest and best quality. The power in the marketplace is shifting from a seller's market to the customers, who have more choices because there are more companies competing for their attention. It is the customer who defines quality in terms of his or her needs and resources. Quality is not just desirable, it is essential for success in today's competitive international market, and the decision to standardise or adapt a product is crucial in delivering quality.

SUMMARY

The growing globalisation of markets that gives rise to standardisation must be balanced with the continuing need to assess all markets for those differences that might require adaptation for successful acceptance. Each product must be viewed in light of how it is perceived by each culture with which it comes into contact. However, we should not mix brands with products. The bands can be global, but the product may still need some adaptations. What is acceptable and comfortable within one group may be radically new and resisted within others depending on the experiences and perceptions of each group. Understanding that an established product in one culture may be considered an innovation in another is critical in planning and developing consumer products for foreign markets. Analysing a product as an innovation and using the product component model may provide the marketer with important leads for adaptation.

In some cases, the marketer needs only to adapt the packaging, while in others product characteristics and features need to change to make it compatible with the foreign market. More and more consumers and societies/governments are becoming aware of environmental issues. Many countries/markets have put these responsibilities on the shoulders of companies that sell the products to ensure that their products and packaging are not causing environmental problems. The marketer thus has to check these rules and regulations when entering these markets.

QUESTIONS

1 Discuss the issue of global versus adapted products for the international marketer.

2 What is the difference between a product and a brand? Explain with examples.

3 Discuss how different stages in the life cycle of a product can influence the standardisation/adaptation decision. Give three examples.

4 Discuss the different promotional/product strategies available to an international marketer.

5 Assume you are deciding to 'go international'; outline the steps you would take to help you decide on a product line.

6 Products can be adapted physically and culturally for foreign markets. Discuss.

7 What are the three major components of a product? Discuss their importance to product adaptation.

8 How can knowledge of the diffusion of innovations help a product manager plan international investments?

9 Discuss the characteristics of an innovation that can account for differential diffusion rates.

10 Discuss 'environmentally friendly' products and product development.

FURTHER READING

- S. Schmid and T. Kotulla, '50 years of Research on International Standardization and Adaptation – From a Systematic Literature Analysis to a Theoretical Framework', *International Business Review*, 2011, 20(5), 491–508.

- P. Ghemawat, *Redefining Global Strategy: Crossing Borders in a World where Differences Still Matter* (Boston, MA: Harvard Business School Publishing, 2010).

- M.F. Svendsen, S.A. Haugland, K. Gronhaug and T. Hammervoll, 'Marketing Strategy and Customer Involvement in Product Development', *European Journal of Marketing*, 2011, 45(4), 513–30.

NOTES

1 Rahul Jacob, 'The Big Rise: Middle Classes Explode Around the Globe Bringing New Markets and New Prosperity', *Fortune*, 30 May 1994, pp 74–90; and 'Consumers Have Money to Burn', *Business Week*, 20 April 1998, pp 30–31.

2 S.T. Cavusgil, P.N. Ghauri and A. Akcal, *Doing Business in Emerging Markets,* 2nd edn (London: Sage, 2013).

3 For an empirical study of the debate, see David M. Szymanski, Sundar G. Bharadwaj and Rajan P. Varadarajan, 'Standardization versus Adaptation of International Marketing Strategy: An Empirical Investigation', *Journal of Marketing*, October 1993, pp 1–17.

4 For a balanced view, see S. Tamer Cavusgil, Shaoming Zou and G.M. Naidu, 'Product and Promotion Adaptation in Export Ventures: An Empirical Investigation', *Journal of International Business Studies*, Third Quarter 1993, pp 479–506.

5 P. Magnusson, D.W. Baack, S. Zdravkovic, K.M. Staub and L.S. Amine, 'Meta-analysis of Cultural Differences: Another Slice at the Apple', *International Business Review*, 2008, 17(5), 520–32.

6 P.G.P. Walters, P. Whitla and H. Davies, 'Global Strategy in the International Advertising Industry', *International Business Review*, 2008, 17(3), 235–49.

7 'Electrolux Targets Southeast Asia', *Dow Jones News Service*, 4 January 1995.

8 L. Alvarez, 'Consumers in Europe Resist Gene-altered Food', *New York Times*, 11 February 2003, p 43.

9 I. Chaney and J. Gamble, 'Retail Store Ownership Influences on Chinese Consumers', *International Business Review*, 2008, 17(2), 170–83.

10 For a good reference book on new product development, see E.M. Rogers, *Diffusion of Innovations*, 5th edn (New York: Free Press, 2003).

11 G.M. Eckhardt and M.J. Houston, 'Cultural Paradoxes Reflected in Brand Meaning: McDonald's in Shanghai, China', *Journal of International Marketing*, 2001, 9(2), 97–114.

Chapter 16

Marketing Industrial Products and Business Services

Chapter Learning Objectives

What you should learn from Chapter 16

- How demand is affected by technology in a particular market
- How characteristics of an industrial product influence international marketing activities
- What is meant by quality in industrial products and in an international context
- The importance of relationship marketing in industrial products
- The importance of trade shows in promoting industrial goods
- How the growth of business services and their fundamental characteristics are influencing international marketing
- How to market services internationally

The interest in industrial marketing, also referred to as business-to-business (B2B) marketing or inter-organisational buying and selling, gained real momentum in the 1970s. It is argued that marketing of **industrial products** is different from marketing of consumer products. In industrial markets buyers are well-informed, highly organised and sophisticated in their purchasing behaviour. Moreover, multiple influences participate actively in purchasing decisions.

> **industrial products**
>
> products developed for the industrial market (other firms/organisation), not the consumer market

By contrast, in consumer marketing buyers are often passive and the relationship between the buyers and sellers is indirect. In industrial marketing, the buyer most often is not the end user of the product and sells it to the next stage in the supply chain, as it is or as part of a package/product assembled or produced by him or her. In this type of market, interaction between the organisations and a network of relationships is considered more important than finding a marketing mix.[1]

Industrial products and services, from computers and photocopiers to machine tools and air freight or telecommunications, are different in nature. First, industrial goods are goods and services often used in the process of creating other goods and services. Consumer goods are in their final form and are consumed by individuals. Second, the motives are different: industrial buyers are seeking profits while final consumers are seeking satisfaction. Moreover, while in consumer markets the number of customers is huge, in industrial markets the number of buyers and sellers is small. These factors are manifest in specific buying patterns and demand characteristics, and in the special emphasis on relationship marketing as a tool.[2]

Industrial goods can be categorised in a variety of ways. A typical scheme involves construction material, heavy equipment, light equipment, components and sub-assemblies, raw materials, processed materials, maintenance materials and operating supplies.[3]

> **business services**
>
> services that are sold to other companies (eg advertising)

Along with industrial goods, **business services** are a highly competitive growth market seeking quality and value. Manufactured products generally come to mind when we think of international trade. Yet the most rapidly growing sector of international trade today consists of business and consumer services: accounting, advertising, banking, consulting, construction, hotels, insurance, law, transportation, travel, television programmes and films sold internationally. The intangibility of business services creates a set of unique problems to which the service provider must respond. A further complication is a lack of uniform laws that regulate market entry. Protectionism, while prevalent for industrial goods, can be much more pronounced for the business service provider, such as airlines and telecommunications.[4]

The industrial product market

Technology and market demand

Not only is technology the key to economic growth, for many products it is also the competitive edge in today's global markets. As precision robots, sophisticated computer programs and digital control systems take over the factory floor, manufacturing is becoming more science-oriented and access to inexpensive labour and raw materials is becoming less important. The ability to develop the latest technology and to benefit from its application is a critical factor in the international competitiveness of countries and companies.[5]

Three interrelated trends will spur demand for technologically advanced products:

1 expanding economic and industrial growth in emerging markets
2 the liberalisation of *most* markets
3 the privatisation of government-owned industries

Many countries have been in a state of rapid economic growth over the last 30 years. South Korea, Hong Kong, Singapore and Taiwan (the 'four tigers') have successfully moved from being cheap labour sources to industrialised nations. The emerging markets of China, India Brazil, Mexico, Malaysia, Russia and Indonesia are exporters of semi-manufactured and manufactured products to Europe and the USA.[6] Besides demand for goods to build new manufacturing plants, many of the emerging countries are making much-needed investments in infrastructure.[7]

As a market economy develops in the Newly Independent States (former republics of the USSR) and other Eastern European countries, new privately owned businesses are creating a demand for the latest technology to revitalise and expand manufacturing facilities. BRIC (Brazil, Russia, India and China) markets are demanding the latest technology to expand their industrial bases and build modern infrastructures.

Telmex, a €3.6bn ($4bn) joint venture between Southwestern Bell, France Telecom and Telefonos de Mexico, has invested hundreds of millions of dollars to bring the Mexican telephone system up to the most advanced standards. Telmex is only one of scores of new privatised companies from Poland to Patagonia that are creating a mass market for the most advanced technology.

The volatility of demand in industrial markets

In the consumer product market, firms are exposed to customers more directly and have better control over their strategies relating to consumer demand, product life cycle extension and demand fluctuations. For industrial product companies, however, the firms do not sell their products directly to consumers and therefore are not fully aware of the **volatility in demand**. Their customers (other industrial buyers) act according to the demand situation for their own products. The producer of industrial products thus faces a derived demand situation. For example, a semiconductor producer, whose main customers are computer and consumer electronics producers, is dependent on the general demand conditions in these two markets. The monitor demand for PCs or television sets would indirectly influence the demand for semiconductors. Simply speaking, derived demand can be defined as demand dependent on another product/industry.

> **volatility in demand**
>
> continuous changes in demand

Demand for aeroplanes, for instance the Airbus A380 or Boeing 787, depends on the demand for air travel and the potential/expected growth in that demand. Sometimes minor changes in consumer demands mean major changes in the related industrial demand. Exhibit 16.1 explains how suppliers of raw material and components do not have direct contact with customers and are dependent on the direct relationship they have with producers.

Attributes of product quality

As discussed earlier, the concept of quality encompasses many factors, and the perception of quality rests solely with the customer. The level of technology reflected in the product, compliance with standards that reflect customer needs, support services and follow-through, and the price relative to competitive products are all part of a customer's evaluation and perception of quality. As noted, these requirements are different for ultimate consumers and for industrial customers because of differing end uses. The factors themselves also differ among industrial goods customers because their needs are varied.

Industrial marketers frequently misinterpret the concept of quality. Good quality is not the same as *technically* good quality. For example, an African government had been buying hand-operated dusters to distribute pesticides in cotton fields; the dusters were loaned to individual farmers. The duster supplied was a finely machined device requiring regular oiling and good care. But the fact that this duster turned more easily than any other on the market was relatively unimportant to the farmers. Furthermore, the requirement for careful oiling and care simply meant that in a relatively short period of inadequate care the machines froze up and broke.

The result? The local government went back to an older type of French duster that was heavy, turned with difficulty and gave a poorer distribution of dust, but lasted longer because it required less care and lubrication. In this situation, the French machine possessed more relevant quality features and therefore, in marketing terms, possessed the higher quality for the particular customer.

It must be kept in mind that the concept of quality is not an absolute measure but one relative to use patterns and/or predetermined standards. Best quality is best because the product adheres exactly to

EXHIBIT 16.1: Customer contact

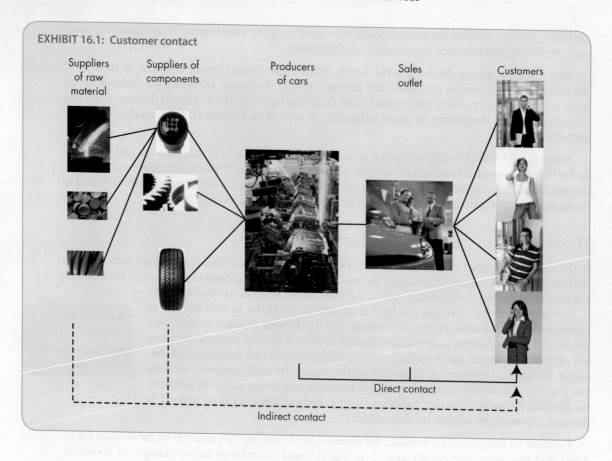

Suppliers of raw material   Suppliers of components   Producers of cars   Sales outlet   Customers

Direct contact

Indirect contact

specified standards that have been determined by expected use of the product. Since use patterns are frequently different from one buyer to another, standards vary so that superior quality for one customer falls short of superior quality as determined by the needs of another customer. One research report examining the purchase decision variables of import managers found that product quality, including dependability of suppliers and timely delivery, were the most important variables influencing purchase decisions.

Going International 16.1

FIVE COMMON B2B ADVERTISING MYTHS

Selling to a company is different from selling to a consumer. But there are some fundamental principles all ads should follow. We met with a business-to-business client that had hired us to help position its firm as a leader in a category it had recently entered. They presented a handful of concepts that were different, compelling, and that would stand out among all the bland ads in their targeted trade publications. Usually, when an ad agency is presenting new ideas, you can pretty much tell how the meeting is going by the looks on the clients' faces. This one wasn't going so well.

B2B is different: this is probably the most common misunderstanding – that somehow the rules of everyday marketing don't apply in a business-to-business context. Sure, selling to a company is different from selling to a consumer. But it's no more different than selling toothpaste is to selling paint, or even than selling wine is to selling beer. In each case you're trying to win over a unique group of people with an existing array of

▶

◀

preconceptions and a distinct set of needs. No two marketing assignments are alike, yet every marketing assignment is subject to the same fundamental and unchanging principles.

Anybody who has spent time working in business-to-business advertising will hear this: 'Make the product the hero', or 'Get right to the point', or 'Just make sure it has a strong call to action.' It's as if the people who read B2B ads don't buy Nike shoes, or attend Cirque du Soleil at the weekend.

In most advertising – consumer as well as B2B – it's the job of the ad to open the sale, not close it. And just because you want your prospects to know something doesn't mean they want to hear it. At least not at first. There's a saying that people don't care how much you know until they know how much you care, and there's truth to that even in advertising. First you must demonstrate that you understand the challenging world in which your prospects live, and then perhaps they will be willing to listen.

- Is it necessary to use advertising in B2B marketing? Discuss.

Source: based on *Business Week*, 11 April 2007.

An example of effective B2B advertising by Sungard. Reproduced with permission. © SunGard Availability Services, "How To Survive a Zombie Attack" campaign, 2012

Price–quality relationship

There is a price–quality relationship that exists in an industrial buyer's decision. One important dimension of quality is how well a product meets the specific needs of the buyer. When a product falls short of performance expectations, its poor quality is readily apparent. However, it is less apparent but nonetheless true that a product that exceeds performance expectations is also of poor quality.

A product whose design exceeds the wants of the buyer's intended use generally means a higher price that reflects the extra capacity. Quality for many goods is assessed in terms of fulfilling specific expectations, no more and no less. A product that produces 20,000 units per hour when the buyer needs one that produces only 5,000 units per hour is not a quality product in that the extra capacity of 15,000 units is unnecessary to meet the buyer's use expectations.

This does not mean quality is unimportant or that the latest technology is not sought by some buyers. Rather, it means that those buyers require products designed to meet their specific needs, not products designed for different uses and expectations, especially if the additional features result in higher prices.

This attitude was reflected in a study of the purchasing behaviour of Chinese import managers, who ranked product quality first, followed in importance by price. Timely delivery was third and product style/features ranked eleventh out of 17 variables studied.[8] Hence, a product whose design reflects the needs and expectations of the buyer – no more, no less – is a quality product.

Product design–quality relationship

Industrial marketers must keep in mind that buyers of industrial goods judge products by their contribution to profit or to the improvement of the buyer's own products and production processes. Consequently, products designed to meet the needs of individual industrial users are critical to competitive advantage.

Competitors from Japan, the USA and even the emerging countries stand ready to provide the customer with a product that fits its exact needs and is offered at a competitive price.

The design of a product must be viewed from all aspects of use. Extreme variations in climate create problems in designing equipment that is universally operable. Products that function effectively in Western Europe may require major design changes to operate as well in the hot, dry Sahara region or the humid tropical rainforests of Latin America. Trucks designed to travel the autobahns of Germany will almost certainly experience operational difficulties in the mountainous regions of Asia on roads that barely resemble jeep trails. Manufacturers must consider many variations in making products that will be functional in far-flung markets.

Service and replacement parts

Effective competition abroad not only requires proper product design but also effective service, prompt deliveries and the ability to furnish spare and replacement parts without delay.[9] In highly competitive markets such as Japan, for example, it is imperative to provide the same kind of service a domestic company or a Western company can give.

For many technical products, the willingness of the seller to provide installation and training may be the deciding factor for the buyers in accepting one company's product over another's. South Korean and other Asian business persons are frank in admitting they prefer to buy from Western firms, but the Japanese get the business because of service. Frequently heard tales of conflicts between Western and foreign firms over assistance expected from the seller are indicative of the problems of after-sales service and support. A South Korean businessman's experiences with a German engineer and some Japanese engineers typify the situation. The Korean electronics firm purchased semiconductor chip-making equipment for a plant expansion. The German engineer was slow in completing the installation; he stopped work at five o'clock and would not work at the weekends. The Japanese, installing other equipment, understood the urgency of getting the factory up and running; without being asked they worked day and night until the job was finished.

Unfortunately this is not an isolated case; Hyundai Motor Company bought two multi-million-euro presses to stamp body parts for cars. The 'presses arrived late, the engineers took much longer than promised to set up the machines, and Hyundai had to pay the Western workers extra to get the machines to work right'. The impact of such problems translate into lost business for Western firms. Samsung Electronics Company, Korea's largest chip maker, used Western equipment for 75 per cent of its first memory-chip plant. When it outfitted its most recent chip plant, it bought 75 per cent of the equipment from Japan.

Going International 16.2

NIKE'S FUTURE: DESIGN AND CUSTOMISATION

After the record revenues of $9.5bn in 1998, Nike's sales dropped to $8.8bn the next year. Finding growth since has not been easy, particularly in the domestic market. In 2002 this became the job of Mark Parker, one of the two co-presidents, who was put in charge of the entire global product and brand management and is also a footwear designer. Parker's appointment as president signified the growing importance played by design in Nike's fortunes. The challenge that is facing Nike now is to keep applying its skills of reinvention to the way the brand is perceived by its public, creating new connections and extending its reach. The future is not simply about selling more and better products – it's more dimensionalised.

One of the new dimensions is selling services. The company began to explore the viability of selling on-brand services in areas such as sports coaching or information. Such a move would give Nike access to top minds and methodologies in sport, which makes solid strategic sense for business. Second, Nike is planning to

▶

◄

extend its sponsorship of athletes into events sponsorship. And, third, the company is exploring the possibilities in personalisation and customisation of its products.

Nike's aim now is to devote time and resources to tomorrow's game plan. For this Mark Parker has set up a crack team called the 'explore group'. 'The explore group is way out there in what we call 'deep space'. It's a small group of Green Beret-Navy Seal-type operatives who are really big thinkers and are supported by a network of some of the most leading-edge technology specialists. We don't talk a lot about this, but it's really big,' Parker says. 'Together with the Massachusetts Institute of Technology (MIT), Nasa and digital companies like Philips, they are

© P.N. Ghauri.

exploring things like smart products that can feed into networks,' he continues. 'One of the biggest items on the agenda is customisation and personalisation.'

● What advice would you give on Nike's plan for the future?

Source: adapted from 'Design's Great Leap Forward', *Financial Times, Creative Business*, 3 December 2002, pp 2–3, www.nike.com.

Technical training is rapidly becoming a major **after-sales service** when selling technical products in countries that demand the latest technology but do not always have trained personnel. China demands the most advanced technical equipment but frequently has untrained people responsible for products they do not understand. Heavy emphasis on training programmes and self-teaching materials to help overcome the common lack of skills in operating technical equipment is a necessary part of the after-sales service package in much of the developing world.

> **after-sales service**
>
> service available after the product has been sold (eg repairs)

A recent study of international users of heavy construction equipment revealed that, next to the manufacturer's reputation, quick delivery of replacement parts was of major importance in purchasing construction equipment. Furthermore, 70 per cent of those questioned indicated they bought parts not made by the original manufacturer of the equipment because of the difficulty of getting original parts. Smaller importers complain of Western exporting firms not responding to orders or responding only after extensive delay. It appears that the importance of timely availability of spare parts to sustain a market is forgotten by some Western exporters. When companies are responsive, the rewards are significant.

Some international marketers also may be forgoing the opportunity of participating in a lucrative aftermarket. Certain kinds of machine tools use up to five times their original value in replacement parts during an average lifespan and thus represent an even greater market. One international machine tool company has capitalised on the need for direct service and available parts by changing its distribution system from the 'normal' to one of stressing rapid service and readily available parts.

Instead of selling through independent distributors, as do most machine tool manufacturers in foreign markets, this company has established a series of company stores and service centres similar to those found in the home market. This company can render service through its system of local stores, while most competitors despatch service people from their home-based factories. The service people are kept on tap for rapid service calls in each of its network of local stores, and each store keeps a large stock of standard parts available for immediate delivery. The net result of meeting industrial needs quickly is keeping the company among the top suppliers in foreign sales of machine tools.

Universal standards

A lack of universal standards is another problem in international sales of industrial products. The United Kingdom and the United States have two major areas of concern for the industrial goods exporter: one is a lack of common standards for manufacturing highly specialised equipment such as machine tools and computers, and the other is the use of the inch–pound or English system of measurement.[10]

Domestically, the use of the inch–pound and the lack of a universal manufacturing standard are minor problems, but they have serious consequences when affected products are scheduled for export. Conflicting standards are encountered in test methods for materials and equipment, quality control systems and machine specifications. In the telecommunications industry, the vast differences in standards among countries create enormous problems for expansion of that industry.

ISO 9000 certification: an international standard of quality

With quality becoming the cornerstone of global competition, companies are requiring assurance of standard conformance from suppliers just as their customers are requiring the same from them. **ISO 9000**, a series of five international industrial standards (ISO 9000–9004) originally designed to meet the need for product quality assurances in purchasing agreements, is becoming a quality assurance certification programme that has competitive and legal ramifications when doing business in the EU and elsewhere. [11]

> **ISO 9000**
>
> quality assurance certification of the production process

ISO 9000 refers to the registration and certification of a manufacturer's quality system. It is a certification of the existence of a quality control system a company has in place to ensure it can meet published quality standards. ISO 9000 standards do not apply to specific products. They relate to generic system standards that enable a company, through a mix of internal and external audits, to provide assurance that it has a quality control system. It is a certification of the production process only, and does not guarantee a manufacturer produces a 'quality' product. The series describes three quality system models, defines quality concepts and gives guidelines for using international standards in quality systems.[12]

A company requests a certifying body (a third party authorised to provide an ISO 9000 audit) to conduct a registration assessment; that is, an audit of the key business processes of a company. The assessor asks questions about everything from blueprints to sales calls to filing. 'Does the supplier meet promised delivery dates?' and 'Is there evidence of customer satisfaction?' are some of the questions asked and the issues explored.

The objective is to develop a comprehensive plan to ensure minute details are not overlooked. The assessor helps management create a quality manual, which will be made available to customers wishing to verify the organisation's reliability. When accreditation is granted, the company receives certification. A complete assessment for recertification is done every four years with intermediate evaluations during the four-year period.

Although ISO 9000 is voluntary, except for regulated products, the EU Product Liability Directive puts pressure on all companies to become certified. The Directive holds that a manufacturer, including an exporter, will be liable, regardless of fault or negligence, if a person is harmed by a product that fails because of a faulty component. Thus, customers in the EU need to be assured that the components of their products are free of defects or deficiencies. A manufacturer with a well-documented quality system will be better able to prove that its products are defect-free and thus minimise liability claims.

Outside regulated product areas, the importance of ISO 9000 registration as a competitive market tool in the EU varies from sector to sector. In some sectors, European companies may require suppliers to attest that they have an approved quality system in place as a condition for purchase. ISO 9000 may be used to serve as a means of differentiating different 'classes' of suppliers (particularly in high-tech areas) where high product reliability is crucial. In other words, if two suppliers are competing for the same contract, the one with ISO 9000 registration may have a competitive edge.

Relationship marketing

Relationship marketing has gained considerable attention in recent years. A number of studies on relational selling (key account management, database marketing, etc), customer and supplier retention (in industrial as well as consumer products), cooperative marketing arrangements (co-branding, just-in-time supplies, EDI, shared logistics, etc) and strategic partnerships (co-marketing, co-design, co-production, joint R&D, etc) have appeared in this area. Scholars from all parts of the world (Europe, America, Asia and Australia) are stressing relationship marketing.[13]

While traditional transactional marketing is believed to be based on competition and self-interest, relationship marketing is based more on mutual cooperation, trust and joint benefits.[14] The purpose of relationship marketing is considered to enhance marketing productivity by achieving efficiency and effectiveness.[15] Through interdependence and partnering, a lower cost and competitive advantages are achieved.

Relationship marketing is useful for both consumer products and industrial or business-to-business products. The relationship of consumers to business organisations is best described as that of membership.[16] The differences in the type of relationship and interdependence between the parties in business–consumer versus business-to-business relationships is explained in Exhibit 16.2. The table reveals that while business-to-consumer and business-to-business relationships have similarities, there are also major differences. It seems that the latter type of relationship is more long term and thus demands a higher level of relationship and commitment.

The importance of relationships in China, *guanxi* (connections), has been reported by a number of scholars, where a business relationship often started with a social relationship. The development of a good relationship 'with a friend' was usually considered a prerequisite for a business relationship. As a result of recent decentralisation of economic decision making in China, relationships have become even more important.[17]

The characteristics that define the uniqueness of industrial products discussed above lead naturally to relationship marketing.[18] The long-term relationship with customers, which is at the core of relationship marketing, fits the characteristics inherent in industrial products and is a viable strategy for industrial goods marketing. In order for an industrial marketer to fulfil the needs of its customers, the marketer must understand those needs as they exist today and how they will change as the buyer strives to compete in global markets that call for long-term relationships.[19]

Relationship marketing ranges all the way from gathering information on customer needs to designing products and services, channelling products to the customer in a timely and convenient manner, and following up to make sure the customer is satisfied. For example, SKF, the bearing manufacturer, seeks strong customer relations with after-sales follow-through.

The end of the transaction is not delivery; it continues as SKF makes sure the bearings are properly mounted and maintained. This helps customers reduce downtime, thus creating value in the relationship with SKF. SKF's marketing efforts encompass an array of activities to support long-term relationships that go beyond 'merely satisfying the next link in the distribution chain to meeting the more complex needs of the end user, whether those needs are technical, operational, or financial'.[20]

IBM of Brazil stresses stronger ties with its customers by offering planning seminars that address corporate strategies, competition, quality and how to identify marketing opportunities. One of these seminars showed a food import/export firm how it could increase efficiency by decentralising its computer facilities to serve its customers better. The company's computers were centralised at headquarters while branches took orders manually and mailed them to the home office for processing and invoicing. It took several days before the customer's order was entered and added several days to delivery time.

The seminar helped the company realise it could streamline its order processing by installing branch office terminals that were connected to computers at the food company's headquarters. A customer could then place an order and receive an invoice on the spot, shortening the delivery time by several days or weeks. Not all participants who attend the 30 different seminars offered annually become IBM customers,

EXHIBIT 16.2: Comparison of business-to-consumer and business-to-business relationships

	Characteristics	Business-to-consumer	Business-to-business
1	Relationship form	Membership	Working partnership, just-in-time exchange, co-marketing, alliance, strategic alliance, distribution channel relationship
2	Average sale size; potential lifetime value of the customer to the selling firm	Normally small sale size; relatively small and predictable lifetime value of the customer; limit on the amount of investment in relationship for any single customer	Normally large and consequential; allows for large and idiosyncratic investments in single relationship
3	Number of customers	Large number; requires large overall investments in relationship management, but low investment per customer	Relatively fewer customers over which to spread investments in relationships; investments often idiosyncratic
4	Seller's ability and cost to replace lost customer	Can normally be replaced quickly and at relatively low cost	Large customers can be difficult and time-consuming to replace
5	Seller's dependence on buyer	Low for any single customer	Varies based on customer size; can be devastating
6	Buyer's dependence on seller	Normally has viable alternatives, low switching costs and switch can be made quickly	Viable alternatives can take time to find, switching costs can be high and changes impact multiple people in the organisation
7	Purchasing time frame, process and buying centre complexity	Normally a short time frame, simple process, and simple buying centre, where one or two individuals fill most buying roles	Often a long time frame, complex process; may have multiple individuals for a single buying role; may be subject to organisation budget cycles
8	Personal knowledge of other party	Relatively few contact points with seller, even when loyal user; seller's knowledge of buyer often limited to database information	Multiple personal relationships; multiple inter-organisational linkages
9	Communication means to build and sustain relationships	Dependence on non-personal means of contact; knowledge generally limited to database information of customer	Emphasis on personal selling and personal contact; customer knowledge held in different forms and places
10	Relative size	Seller normally larger than buyer	Relative size may vary
11	Legal	Consumer protection laws unbalanced to favour consumer	Relationships governed by prevailing contract law as well as industry standard regulations and ethics

Source: based on Thomas Gruen, 'The Outcome of Relationship Marketing in Consumer Markets', *International Business Review*, 1995, 4(4), 447–69.

but it creates a continuing relationship among potential customers. 'So much so,' as one executive commented, 'that when a customer does need increased computer power, he will likely turn to us.'[21]

Promoting industrial products

The promotional problems encountered by foreign industrial marketers are little different from the problems faced by domestic marketers. Until recently there has been a paucity of specialised advertising media in many countries. In the last decade, however, specialised industrial media have been developed to provide the industrial marketer with a means of communicating with potential customers, especially in Western Europe and to some extent in Eastern Europe, the Commonwealth of Independent States (CIS) of the former USSR, and China.

In addition to advertising in print media and reaching industrial customers through catalogues and direct mail, the trade show has become the primary vehicle for doing business in many foreign countries.

Going International 16.3

HOW INTEL GOT INSIDE

In microprocessors Intel has the kind of monopoly that any company would be proud to control. More than 85 per cent of all personal computers (PCs) rely on Intel technology. Intel's current and very challenging goal is to maintain its PC monopoly while dominating the market for the new high-performance chips that promise to put PCs on a par with high-end workstations. Many computer analysts think that Intel could eventually control more than 90 per cent of the desktop market, including workstations.

By aggressively promoting the Pentium processor in the media, Intel bypassed its traditional customers (the computer manufacturers) and directly targeted PC users. This 'awareness campaign' for its processors has led the majority of PC buyers – especially business users – to specifi-

A future mobile Internet device enabled with platform power management.

cally demand an Intel processor in their computers. In turn this has created an additional barrier for Intel's competitors: they not only have to deliver processors that are faster and cheaper than Intel's but, more importantly, they also have to convince consumers that their products are fully compatible with Intel's. Andy Grove, Intel's chairman and until recently CEO, says, 'It was an attitude change, a change we actually stimulated, but one whose impact we did not fully comprehend.'

However, as Intel's business model is essentially based around selling a continuous stream of faster microprocessors, its investment in production, R&D and marketing has reflected this at every stage. But growth in high-powered (read high-margin) Pentium II chips has slowed down, mainly as consumers have flocked to sub-thousand-dollar PCs. In this price-sensitive segment, Pentium's premium image doesn't stand for much. Customers look at the best price-performance.

Source: *European Business Report*, Spring 1Q, 1998, p 31, http://www.intel.pk.

Industrial trade shows

One of the most powerful international promotional media is the trade show or **trade fair**. As part of their international promotion activities, the EU, Germany and the US Department of Commerce and many other countries sponsor trade fairs in many cities around the world. Additionally, there are annual trade shows sponsored by local governments in most countries. African countries, for example, host more than 70 industry-specific trade shows.

Trade shows serve as the most important vehicles for selling products, reaching prospective customers, contacting and evaluating potential agents and distributors, and marketing in most countries. They have been at the centre of commerce in Europe for

> **trade fair**
> exhibition where participants are able to show/sell their products and services. Also used to establish and maintain contacts

centuries and are where most prospects are found. European trade shows attract high-level decision-makers who are not attending just to see the latest products but are there to buy.[22]

The importance of trade shows to Europeans is reflected in the percentage of their media budget spent on participating in trade events. On average, Europeans spend 22 per cent of their total annual media budget on trade events, while American firms typically spend less than 5 per cent. The Hannover Industry Fair (Germany), the largest trade fair in the world, has nearly 6,000 exhibitors who show a wide range of industrial products to 600,000 visitors.

Going International 16.4

ADAPTATION IN INDUSTRIAL PRODUCTS

Many manufacturers participating in today's global business face the same issue: how to customise products to meet local preferences. Some companies' bottom lines and market shares suffer because of failure to customise. For example, Adidas-Salomon, the German sportswear maker, lost sales in the USA due to its inability to meet local consumers' tastes. Other companies, on the other hand, are succeeding.

Behr, a German company and a world leader in radiators and air-conditioning systems for cars, chooses to adapt its products to climatic conditions and consumer preferences in different countries. Its €3.8m laboratory in Stuttgart is capable of simulating wind speeds of up to 130kph and temperatures from −30°C to +50°C, which cover driving conditions in just about every part of the world.

Allowing for the driver's ability to 'tune' the conditions inside the vehicle to suit their individual tastes, the overall design of the company's units is influenced by national traits. 'German drivers like warm legs, the Japanese favour air being blown at their face to keep them cool, while Americans prefer an all-round effect in which air is directed over their entire bodies,' says Rudolf Riedel, manager of Behr's vehicle test operations. With the help of data from the laboratory, company engineers can work out how to alter key components inside standard air-conditioning systems so as to fit national preferences.

Bialetti is a much smaller company, but one of Europe's biggest makers of cooking utensils. About half of its production is exported. While Behr's focus is on its design laboratory, Bialetti has based its approach to variation on highly flexible production equipment. Across its range of aluminium pans, which account for about 70 per cent of sales, the company makes 2,500 variants, most of them based on standard designs, with changes to such details as the pan's dimensions and the type of handle.

'For Russia, we have to make very deep pans because of the interest in cooking casseroles on a stove; in Japan or China we have the wok variants, while among the types we sell in Italy is a special Grande Famiglia range for large households,' says Francesco Ranzoni, the company's chairman. To make such customisations possible, Bialetti invested heavily in automatic press machines. These make individual items in relatively short production runs, of perhaps 5,000 items per batch. The production equipment is sufficiently flexible to be switched to making a different kind of product, often within minutes.

- Do companies need to adapt their products in a B2B market? Discuss.

Sources: adapted from Uta Harnischfeger, 'Failure to Meet US Tastes Cuts Sales at Adidas', *Financial Times*, 7 August 2003, p 23, www.adidas.com/.

exhibitions

used to promote product range extensions and to launch activities in new markets

The number and variety of trade shows is such that almost any target market in any given country can be found through this medium. In the Commonwealth of Independent States (CIS), fairs and **exhibitions** offer companies the opportunity to meet new customers, including private traders, young entrepreneurs and representatives of non-state organisations. The exhibitions in the CIS offer a cost-effective way of reaching a large number of customers who might otherwise be difficult to target through individual sales calls. Specialised fairs in individual sectors such as computers, the automotive industry, fashion and home furnishings regularly take place. These days some trade shows are held online, providing excellent access with the minimum of expense.[23]

Marketing services globally

The service sectors in many industrial nations collectively account for up to 70 per cent of gross national product. This includes a broad range of industries as well as many government and non-profit activities. The changing patterns of government regulations, privatisation of public corporations and **non-profit organisations**, computerisation and technological innovations and the internationalisation of service businesses are some of the factors that are transforming service sectors in the EU, the USA, Japan and many emerging economies.

> **non-profit organisations**
>
> organisations whose purpose is not profit-oriented (eg Worldwide Fund for Nature, universities)

In many cases services are competing with products as they provide similar benefits. For example, buying a service may be an alternative to doing it yourself – jobs such as lawn care, equipment maintenance, etc. Using a rental service is an alternative to buying a product. Moreover, the service content of a number of products ranging from fast-food restaurants to automobile manufacture is increasing.[24]

Unlike merchandise trade, which requires a declaration of value when exported, most services do not have to have an export declaration; nor do they always pass through a tariff or customs barrier when entering a country. Consequently, an accurate tally of service trade exports is difficult to determine. Services not counted include advertising, accounting, management consulting, legal services and most insurance; ironically, these are among the fastest growing.[25]

Characteristics of services

In contrast to industrial and consumer goods, services are distinguished by unique characteristics and thus require special consideration. Products are classified as tangible or intangible. Cars, computers, furniture, and so on, are examples of *tangible products* that have a physical presence; they are a thing or object that can be stored and possessed, and whose intrinsic value is embedded within its physical presence. Insurance, dry cleaning, hotel accommodation and airline passage or freight service are *intangible products* whose intrinsic value is the result of a process, a performance or an occurrence that exists only while it is being created.

The intangibility of services results in characteristics unique to a service: it is *inseparable* in that its creation cannot be separated from its consumption; it is *heterogeneous* in that it is individually produced and is thus virtually unique; and it is *perishable* in that once created it cannot be stored but must be consumed simultaneously with its creation.

Contrast these characteristics with a tangible product that can be produced in one location and consumed elsewhere, that can be standardised, whose quality assurance can be determined and maintained over time, and that can be produced and stored in anticipation of fluctuations in demand.

Going International 16.5

KEYS TO SUCCESS IN THE EUROPEAN ENTERTAINMENT MARKET

Despite increased competition throughout the industry, Europe is still an attractive market for entertainment companies. This is partly due to more vacation days (the EU standard is at least 20 days), higher disposable incomes and leisure developments encouraged by city and county planning authorities.

▶

© AP/Wide World Photos.

Europe has a long and extensive history of theme parks and attractions, which historically were family-owned, small-scale operations. Although many of these parks and attractions have disappeared, Europe still boasts the oldest operating amusement park – in Bakken, Denmark.

Many family entertainment projects – such as Disneyland Paris, Port Aventura in Spain and LegoLand in Windsor, England – emerged within the last decade through various public and privately funded bodies.

Their success in Europe is often driven by weather considerations, the addition of rides and attractions, retail propositions linked to a park, and films or intellectual property that enhance the overall brand.

Based on our work with many US entertainment companies, we have developed the 'Top 10 Predictors of Success' for an entertainment venture in Europe:

10 Do your homework. Make sure you are aware of past case studies, regional and national consumer tastes, preferences and traditions:

9 Get your relationship right with HQ. Strike a balance between the amount of autonomy or control your headquarters and European teams are given, and develop a reporting structure that enables all involved to share best marketing practices with colleagues across geographic boundaries.

8 Manage expectations within your company about when your European activities will start showing a profit (or, at least, break even).

7 'Glocalise' your concepts, striking a balance between how much of your US ideas should be brought to Europe, while still making them appeal to 'local' European tastes.

6 Set realistic payback periods.

5 Understand that the different business customs across these 25 distinct markets mean that you have at least 25 different customer tastes, and therefore need to consider how 'entertainment' is defined by and made relevant to such a disparate population.

4 There is no such thing as the 'United States of Europe'. Because of differing consumer tastes, the implementation of your marketing plans within each of the EU countries will vary significantly.

3 Use local experts wherever possible, to ensure you've been given an accurate, current picture of your target market trends and concerns.

2 Test your concepts and ideas with your target guests to learn what they like, their propensity to pay various entry fees, promotional tie-ins and other marketing activities.

1 Plan, plan, plan!

Source: Allyson L. Stewart-Allen, 'Marketing Perspective', *Marketing News*, 17 August 1998, p 9.

Services can be classified as being either consumer or industrial in nature. Additionally, the same service can be marketed both as industrial and consumer, depending on the motive of, and use by, the purchaser. For example, travel agents and airlines sell industrial services to a business person and a consumer service to a tourist. Financial services, hotels, insurance, legal services and others all may be industrial or consumer services.

These fundamental characteristics explain why it is important that services be discussed separately from industrial and consumer goods and why their very nature affects the manner in which they are marketed internationally.

Entering international markets

Client followers and market seekers

Most Western service companies entered international markets to service their Western clients, business travellers and tourists. Banks, accounting and advertising firms were among the earlier companies to establish branches or acquire local affiliations abroad to serve their Western multinational clients. Hotels and car-rental agencies followed the business traveller and tourist to fill their needs. Their primary purpose for marketing their services internationally was to service home-country clients.

Once established, many of these **client followers**, as one researcher refers to them, expanded their client base to include local companies. As global markets grew, creating greater demand for business services, service companies became market seekers in that they actively sought customers for their services worldwide. One study of select types of service industries shows that the relative importance of client following or market seeking as a motive for entry into foreign markets varies by type of service.

> **client followers**
>
> companies that have followed their clients to other countries (become international) to service primary clients while they are abroad

The most important motive for engaging in international business for most business service firms is to seek new markets. The notable exceptions are accounting and advertising firms whose motives are about equally divided between being client followers and market seekers.

Entry modes

Because of the varied characteristics of business services, not all of the traditional methods of market entry discussed earlier are applicable to all types of services. Although most services have the inseparability of creation and consumption just discussed, there are those where these occurrences can be separated. Such services are those whose intrinsic value can be 'embodied in some tangible form (such as a blueprint or document) and thus can be produced in one country and exported to another'.

Data processing and data analysis services are other examples. The analysis or processing is completed on a computer located in a Western country and the output (the service) is transmitted via satellite to a distant customer. Some banking services could be exported from one country to another on a limited basis through the use of ATMs (automatic teller machines). Architecture and engineering consulting services are exportable when the consultant travels to the client's site and later returns home to write and submit a report or a blueprint. In addition to exporting as an entry mode, these services also use franchising, direct investment (joint ventures and wholly-owned subsidiaries) and licensing.

Most other services – car rentals, airline services, entertainment, hotels and tourism, to name a few – are inseparable and require production and consumption to occur almost simultaneously and, thus, exporting is not a viable entry method for them. The vast majority of services enter foreign markets by licensing, franchising and/or direct investment.

Market environment for business services

Service firms face most of the same environmental constraints and problems confronting merchandise traders. Protectionism, control of transborder data flows, competition and the protection of trademarks, processes and patents are possibly the most important problems confronting the MNC in today's international services market.

Going International 16.6

A TALE OF GLOBALISATION AND ITS MALCONTENTS

In Moscow on 21 May 2008, for the first time two English teams faced each other in the final of the Champions League, a football competition that pits 32 of the best teams across Europe against each other. Manchester United prevailed over Chelsea, as the rest of the continent looked on.

▶

This was no one-off fluke but the latest indicator of the growing dominance of England's Premier League, once a poor cousin of Spain's La Liga, Italy's Serie A and Germany's Bundesliga. Each of its big four clubs – Arsenal, Chelsea, Liverpool and Manchester United – has reached at least one Champions League final in the past four years.

This primacy owes little to home-grown talent. Twelve of the 22 players who started the game in Moscow were foreign. Roughly half of those fielded in an average Premier League weekend are neither British nor Irish. The most celebrated star (Manchester United's Cristiano

© Istockphoto.com/GordonBellPhotography

Ronaldo) is Portuguese. England's national team failed to qualify for the 2008 European championships.

Foreign investors have poured in (Liverpool and Manchester United are owned by Americans, Chelsea by a Russian). England's big four clubs are among the world's ten richest, according to Deloitte, an accounting firm. This allows the clubs to hire the best players, which in turn draws crowds and increases revenues.

In most industries such a virtuous circle would be a cause for celebration. But Sepp Blatter, the president of FIFA, football's governing body, cites English dominance of the Champions League as proof of the need to restrict how many foreigners a team may field. Michel Platini, the head of UEFA, the European wing of FIFA, concurs. Some old-style, hoof-it English managers claim that import restrictions would somehow help the coaching of young British talent.

- Should there be a restriction on how many foreign players can play in each team?

Source: *The Economist*, 22 May 2008, p 47.

Protectionism

protectionism

when governments do not allow freedom of activity for foreign companies, to protect their own companies

The most serious threat to the continued expansion of international services trade is **protectionism**. The growth of international services has been so rapid during the past decade that it has drawn the attention of domestic companies and governments. As a result, direct and indirect trade barriers have been imposed to restrict foreign companies' access to domestic markets. Every reason, from the protection of infant industries to national security, has been used to justify some of the restrictive practices.

Until the GATT and WTO agreements there were few international rules of fair play governing trade in services. Service companies faced a complex group of national regulations that impeded the movement of people and technology from country to country. The industrialised nations want their banks, insurance companies, construction firms and other service providers to be allowed to move people, capital and technology around the globe unimpeded.

The EU has made considerable progress towards establishing a single market for services. Legal services and the film industry seem to be two that are very difficult to negotiate. A directive regarding Transfrontier Television Broadcasting created a quota for European programmes requiring EU member states to ensure that at least 50 per cent of entertainment air time is devoted to 'European works'. The

EU argues that this set-aside for domestic programming is necessary to preserve Europe's cultural identity. The consequences for the US film industry are significant, because over 40 per cent of US film industry profits come from foreign revenues.

Transborder data flows

Restrictions on transborder data flows are potentially the most damaging to both the communications industry and other multinationals that rely on data transfers across borders to conduct business. Some countries impose tariffs on the transmission of data and many others are passing laws forcing companies to open their computer files to inspection by government agencies.

Most countries have a variety of laws to deal with the processing and electronic transmission of data across borders. There is intense concern about how to deal with this relatively new technology. In some cases, concern stems from not understanding how best to tax transborder data flows and, in other cases, there is concern over the protection of individual rights when personal data are involved.

The European Commission is concerned that data on individuals (such as income, spending preferences, debt repayment histories, medical records and employment data) are being collected, manipulated and transferred between companies with little regard for the privacy of the individuals about whom the data are collected. A proposed directive by the Commission would require the consent of the individual before data are collected or processed.

A wide range of foreign service companies would be affected by such a directive; insurance underwriters, banks, credit reporting firms, **direct marketing** companies and tour operators are a few examples. The directive would have a wide-ranging effect on data-processing and data-analysis firms because it would prevent a firm from transferring information electronically to other countries for computer processing if it concerns individual European consumers.

> **direct marketing**
> advertising sent directly to customers

Going International 16.7

IMPACT OF GLOBALISATION ON JOB SHIFT

As the wave of globalisation has swept the whole world and reshaped the global economy, it has also had great impact on what jobs are done where. Two decades ago the first wave started with an exodus of jobs making shoes, cheap electronics and toys, from the West to developing countries. Simple service work, such as processing credit-card receipts, and mind-numbing digital toil, such as writing software code, began fleeing high-cost countries too.

Now, the trend is characterised by all kinds of knowledge work that is done almost anywhere. Forrester Research Inc analyst John C. McCarthy predicts at least 3.3 million white-collar jobs and $136bn in wages will shift from the USA to low-

'Indian call centre' © barracuadz. CC BY 2.0 UK.

cost countries by 2015. It is the same story within Europe. Huge back offices for these developed countries have been established and continue to grow in emerging markets such as China, India, the Baltic nations and Eastern Europe.

▶

◀

It is digitalisation, the Internet and high-speed data networks that girdle the globe and drive the globalisation trends on job shifts. The basic business tenet is that things go to the areas where there is the best cost of production, not only in financial services such as banks and consulting but also in manufacturing. The job shift trend indicates that the rise of a globally integrated knowledge economy is a blessing for developing countries. When companies from Wall Street to Silicon Valley are downsizing at home, the unprecedented hiring binge in Asia, Eastern Europe and Latin America begins.

However, for security and practical reasons, corporations are likely to keep crucial R&D and the bulk of back-office operations close to home, so as to adjust the job distribution. Meanwhile, the benefits can be huge for the companies most adept at managing a global workforce, handling everything from product design and tech support to employee benefits.

On the other side of the coin there are issues of losing control of core business and the difficulty of coordinating manufacturing and design work overseas. Opposition to free trade could broaden if globalisation, having already made blue-collar workers in developed countries averse to some extent, continues to influence more politically powerful middle-class white-collar workers unfavourably.

In developing countries it might be different, especially for those loaded with college grads who speak Western languages. Outsourced white-collar work will likely contribute to the economic development even more than new factories making trainers or mobile phones. A tremendous pool of well-trained graduates such as those in India and China entice corporations to dip in, not only in IT but finances and architecture as well.

It is difficult to conclude whether this globalisation trend benefits more the employees in developing countries than it harms those in the West. What can be noted is that, with the rise of the global knowledge industry, the big beneficiaries will be those companies offering the speediest and cheapest telecom links, the most investor-friendly policies and ample college graduates.

● Do you think this job shift trend is good for developed countries? Do you think it is good for developing/emerging countries?

Source: 'The New Global Job Shift', *Business Week*, 3 February 2003.

Protection of intellectual property

An important form of competition difficult to combat is pirated trademarks, processes and patents. Computer design and software, trademarks, brand names and other forms of intellectual property are easy to duplicate and difficult to protect. The protection of intellectual property rights is a major problem in the services industries.

Countries seldom have adequate – or any – legislation; any laws they do have are extremely difficult to enforce. The Trade Related Intellectual Property Rights (TRIPS) part of the GATT/WTO agreement obligates all members to provide strong protection for copyright and related rights, patents, trademarks, trade secrets, industrial designs, geographic indications and layout designs for integrated circuits.

SUMMARY

Industrial goods marketing requires close attention to the exact needs of customers. Basic differences across various markets are fewer than for consumer goods but the motives behind purchases differ enough to require a special approach. Global competition has increased to the point that industrial goods marketers must pay close attention to the level of economic and technological development of each market to determine the buyer's assessment of quality. Companies that adapt their products to these needs are the ones that should be the most effective in the marketplace. Industrial markets are lucrative and continue to grow as more countries strive for at least a semblance of industrial self-sufficiency. The derived nature of demand for industrial products encourages these companies to have close relationships with their customers. Relationship marketing is therefore becoming important in this sector.

One of the fastest-growing areas of international trade is business services. This segment of marketing involves all countries at every level of development; even the least-developed countries are seeking computer technology and sophisticated data banks to aid them in advancing their economies. Their rapid growth and profit profile make them targets for protectionism and piracy. Increasing competition in the form of outsourcing of service jobs is resulting in some job losses in the service sector in developed countries. More qualified and sensitive jobs, such as R&D and design, are kept at home.

QUESTIONS

1   What are the differences between consumer and industrial goods, and what are the implications for international marketing? Discuss.

2   'The adequacy of a product must be considered in relation to the general environment within which it will be operated rather than solely on the basis of technical efficiency.' Discuss the implications of this statement.

3   What role do service, replacement parts and standards play in competition in foreign marketing? Illustrate.

4   Discuss the part industrial trade fairs play in international marketing of industrial goods.

5   Describe the reasons an MNC might seek ISO 9000 certification.

6   What ISO 9000 legal requirements are imposed on products sold in the EC? Discuss.

7   Discuss how the characteristics that define the uniqueness of industrial products lead naturally to relationship marketing. Give some examples.

8   Select several countries, each at a different stage of economic development, and illustrate how the stage affects the usage of relationship marketing.

FURTHER READING

- J. Sheth and A. Parvatiyar, 'The Evolution of Relationship Marketing', *International Business Review*, 1995, 4(4), 471–81.
- S. Yeniyurt, J.W. Henke Jr and E. Cavusgil, 'Integrating Global and Local Procurement for Superior Supplier Working Relations', *International Business Review*, 2013, 22(1), 351–62.
- J. Pla-Barber and P. N. Ghauri, 'Internationalization of Service Industry Firms: Understanding Distinctive Characteristics', Introduction to the special issue, *Service Industries Journal*, 2012, 32(7–8), 1007–10.

NOTES

1 For a discussion on networks in industrial marketing, see, eg, Pervez Ghauri (ed), *Advances in International Marketing: From Mass Marketing to Relationships and Networks* (Greenwich, NY: JAI Press, 1999).

2 U. Elg, S. Delgonul, W. Denis and P.N. Ghauri, 'Market-driving Strategy Implementation through Global Supplier Relationships', *Industrial Marketing Management,* 2012, 41, 919–28.

3 Frederick Webster, *Industrial Marketing Strategy*, 3rd edn (New York: Wiley, 1991).

4 Karin Venetis, 'Service Quality and Customer Loyalty in Professional Business Service', PhD thesis, Maastricht University, 1997.

5 John Naisbitt, *Mega Trends Asia* (New York: Simon & Schuster, 1996).

6 Philippe Lasserre and Helmut Schütte, *Strategies for Asia Pacific* (London: Macmillan, 1995).

7 X. Li and J. Roberts, 'A Stages Approach to Internationalization of Higher Education? The Entry of UK Universities into China', *Service Industries Journal*, 2012, 32(7–8), 1011–39.

8 Kyung-Il Ghymn, Paul Johnson and Weijiong Zhang, 'Chinese Import Managers' Purchasing Behaviour', *Journal of Asian Business*, 1993, 9(3), 35–45.

9 J. Carbone, 'Who Will Survive?' *Purchasing*, 15 May 2003, 33–42.

10 Tom Reilly, 'The Harmonization of Standards in the European Union and the Impact on US Business', *Business Horizons*, March–April 1995, pp 28–34.

11 Neil Morgan and Nigel Piercy, 'Interactions Between Marketing and Quality at the SBU Level: Influences and Outcomes', *Journal of the Academy of Marketing Science*, 1998, 26(3), 190–208.

12 Robert W. Peach (ed), *The ISO 9000 Handbook*, 2nd edn (Fairfax, VA: CEEM Information Services, 1994).

13 Jagdish Sheth and Atul Parvatiyar, 'The Evolution of Relationship Marketing', *International Business Review*, 1995, 4(4), 397–418.

14 R.M. Morgan and S.D. Hunt, 'The Commitment–trust Theory of Relationship Marketing', *Journal of Marketing*, 1994, 58, 20–38.

15 P.N. Ghauri, U. Elg and V. Tarnovskaya, 'Market Driving Supplier Strategy: A Study of IKEA's Global Sourcing Networks', *International Marketing Review*, 2008, 25(5), 504–19.

16 R. Salle, B. Cova and C. Pardo, 'Portfolio of Supplier–customer Relationships', in A.G. Woodside (ed), *Advances in Business Marketing and Purchasing*, vol 9 (Bingley: Emerald Publishing, 2000), pp 419–42.

17 See, eg, Ingemar Björkman and Sören Kock, 'Social Relationships and Business Networks: The Case of Western Companies in China', *International Business Review*, 1995, 4(4), 519–35.

18 Adrian Palmer, 'Relationship Marketing: Local Implementation of a Universal Concept', *International Business Review*, 1995, 4(4), 471–81.

19 For a comprehensive review of relationship literature, see Robert M. Morgan, and Shelby D. Hunt, 'The Commitment–trust Theory of Relationship Marketing', *Journal of Marketing*, July 1994, 20–38; and special issue of *International Business Review* on Relationship Marketing, 1995, 4(4).

20 K. Karjalainen and A. Salmi, 'Continental Differences in Purchasing Strategies and Tools', *International Business Review*, 2013, 22(1), 112–25.

21 S. Leek, P.W. Turnbull and P. Naude, 'How is Information Technology Affecting Business Relationships?', *Industrial Marketing Management*, 2003, 32(2), 119–26.

22 Marnik G. Dekimpe, Pierre François, Srinath Gopalakrishna, Gary L. Lilien and Christophe van den Bulte, 'Generalizing about Trade Show Effectiveness: A Cross-national Comparison', *Journal of Marketing*, 1997, 61(4), 55–64.

23 J. Saranow, 'The Show Goes On: Online Trade Shows Offer Low Cost, Flexible Alternatives for Organizers', *Wall Street Journal*, 13 June 2003, p B4.

24 Christopher Lovelock, *Service Marketing: Text, Cases and Readings*, 2nd edn (Englewood Cliffs, NJ: Prentice Hall, 1991).

25 'Service Exports', *Business America*, Annual Report to the US Congress, October 1994, p 87.

Chapter 17

International Distribution and Retailing

Chapter Learning Objectives

What you should learn from Chapter 17

- The variety in distribution channels and how they affect cost and efficiency in marketing
- The European distribution structure, and what it means to Western customers and to competing importers of goods
- How distribution patterns affect the various aspects of international marketing
- How the growing importance of e-commerce is influencing distribution channels internationally
- The functions, advantages and disadvantages of various middlemen
- The importance of selecting and maintaining relationships with middlemen

If expected marketing goals are to be achieved, a product must be made accessible to the target market in an efficient manner. In many markets, the biggest constraint to successful marketing is distribution.[1] Getting the product to the target market can be a costly process if inadequacies within the distribution structure cannot be overcome. Forging an efficient and reliable channel of distribution may be the most critical and challenging task facing the international marketer.

distribution network

how the product moves from the producer to the customer

Each market contains a **distribution network** with many channel choices whose structures are unique and, in the short run, fixed. In some markets, the distribution structure is multilayered, complex and difficult for new marketers to penetrate; in others, there are few specialised middlemen except in major urban areas; and in yet others, there is a dynamic mixture of traditional and new, evolving distribution institutions available. Regardless of the predominating distribution structure, competitive advantage will reside with the marketer best able to build the most efficient channel.

This chapter discusses the basic points involved in making channel decisions: (1) channel structures; (2) available alternative middlemen; (3) locating, selecting, motivating and terminating middlemen; and (4) controlling the channel process.

Structure of distribution channels

In every country and in every market, urban or rural, rich or poor, all consumer and industrial products eventually go through a distribution process. The process includes the physical handling and distribution of goods, the passage of ownership (title), and, most important from the standpoint of marketing strategy, the buying and selling negotiations between producers and middlemen and between middlemen and customers.[2]

A host of policy and strategy channel-selection issues confronts the international marketing manager. These issues are not in themselves very different from those encountered in domestic distribution, but the resolution of the issues differs because of different channel alternatives and market patterns.

Each country market has a channel structure through which goods pass from producer to user. Within this structure are a variety of middlemen whose customary functions, activities and services reflect existing competition, market characteristics, tradition and economic development. In short, the behaviour of channel members is the result of the interactions between the cultural environment and the marketing process. Channel structures range from those with little developed marketing infrastructure found in many emerging markets to the highly complex, multilayered system found in Western markets.[3]

Supplier-oriented distribution structure

Traditional channels in developing countries evolved from economies with a strong dependence on imported manufactured goods. Typically, an importer controls a fixed supply of goods and the marketing system develops around the philosophy of selling a limited supply of goods at high prices to a small number of affluent customers. In the resulting seller's market, market penetration and mass distribution are not necessary because demand exceeds supply and, in most cases, the customer seeks the supply. This produces a channel structure with a limited number of middlemen.

Contrast this with the mass-consumption distribution philosophy that prevails in Europe. In these markets, supply is not dominated by one supplier: it can be increased or decreased within a given range, and profit maximisation occurs at or near production capacity. Generally a buyer's market exists, and the producer strives to penetrate the market and push goods out to the consumer, resulting in a highly developed channel structure that includes a variety of intermediaries.

This supply-oriented philosophy permeates all aspects of market activities and behaviour. For example, a Brazilian bank had ordered piggy banks for a local promotion; because it went better than expected, the banker placed a reorder of three times the original. The local manufacturer immediately increased the price and, despite arguments pointing out reduced production costs and other supply-cost factors, could not be dissuaded from this action. True to a supply-oriented attitude, the notion of economies of scale and the use of price as a demand stimulus escaped the manufacturer who was going on the theory that, with demand up, the price also had to go up.

A one-deal mentality of pricing at retail and wholesale levels exists because in an import-oriented market, goods come in at a landed price and pricing is then simply an assessment of demand and diminishing supply. If the producer or importer has control of supply, then the price is whatever the market will bear.

Distribution systems are local rather than national in scope and the relationship between the supplier and any **middleman** in the marketplace is considerably different from that found in a mass-marketing system. The idea of a channel as a chain of intermediaries performing specific activities and each selling to a smaller unit beneath it until the chain reaches the ultimate consumer is not common in an import-oriented system.[4]

> **middleman**
> businessman, other than the producer and consumer, involved in exchange of goods

European distribution structure

The unified Europe has a larger population than the USA. However, this population is located in an area that is only 12 per cent of the land area of the USA. In spite of this concentration, transportation in the EU was overburdened with regulations and administrative routines. A truck from Glasgow to Athens was spending 30 per cent of its time on border crossings, waiting and filling out some 200 forms. These inefficiencies are now gone and only one piece of paper is required to move goods between EU member states. Transit documents have been simplified and custom formalities have been eliminated. As a result, companies are now working with centralised warehouses and distribution centres.

More and more companies are implementing **just-in-time (JIT)** production and purchasing methods. Pan-European franchising has increased following the removal of trade barriers. Retailers and supermarkets have undergone some restructuring, and companies like Hennes & Mauritz, Zara, Ahold, Aldi and Carrefour are now present in most major cities around Europe. As distribution becomes easier, concentration of production is becoming common. Nestlé, for example, is now producing confectionary in Berlin for distribution throughout Europe. The distributor's power is thus increasing.

> **just-in-time (JIT)**
> deliveries made at a time when the component is to be used and not before (often in manufacturing)

Distribution structure in the USA

In the USA the distribution system is most advanced and it is not difficult to reach all corners of the market. The huge size of the market has led to large-sized retailers who often buy direct from manufacturers. At the same time, many manufacturers have their own distribution channels or retail stores.

A comparison of the USA and Germany, the biggest market in Europe, is presented in Exhibit 17.1.

High density of middlemen

There is a density of middlemen, retailers and wholesalers in the Japanese market unparalleled in any Western industrialised country. The traditional structure serves consumers who make small, frequent purchases at small, conveniently located stores.

In Japan small stores (95.1 per cent of all retail food stores) account for 57.7 per cent of retail foods sales, whereas in the USA small stores (69.8 per cent of all retail food stores) generate 19.2 per cent of food sales. A disproportionate percentage of non-food sales are made in small stores in Japan as well. In the USA small stores (81.6 per cent of all stores) sell 32.9 per cent of non-food items; in Japan small stores (94.1 per cent of all stores) sell 50.4 per cent.[5]

Channel control

In Germany, manufacturers depend on wholesalers for a multitude of services to other members of the distribution network. Financing, physical distribution, warehousing, inventory, promotion and payment collection are provided to other channel members by wholesalers. The system works because wholesalers and all other middlemen downstream are tied to manufacturers by a set of practices and incentives

EXHIBIT 17.1: Number of retailers per sector in different countries

	Germany	USA	Spain	France	UK	Netherlands	Belgium	China	Japan
Fashion & clothing	114	149	147	131	107	96	123	78	46
Food	36	82	70	24	27	26	17	46	49
Consumer electronics	86	54	39	42	47	51	26	28	22
DIY & gardening	48	21	17	36	36	29	18	14	4
Furniture & decoration	38	69	30	27	23	22	29	22	5
Homeware	43	32	28	24	30	19	24	7	11
Footwear & leather	44	36	49	39	32	33	19	13	1
Personal care	31	36	36	25	30	28	27	9	6
Babyware	17	9	17	24	10	11	11	0	0
Sport & leisure	35	26	30	31	22	28	10	6	3
Toys & games	42	28	23	24	18	22	16	3	7
Books & magazines	27	18	19	18	15	24	11	3	4
Jewellery & watches	36	18	29	25	25	13	11	1	1
Optical	11	26	13	16	12	12	8	16	0
Pet care	50	7	6	15	19	17	4	0	0
Telecom	11	1	9	10	12	14	14	5	0
Petrol	32	4	14	20	17	16	7	0	0
Car parts & accessories	9	0	9	15	15	4	2	0	0
Gross total	**710**	**616**	**585**	**546**	**497**	**465**	**377**	**251**	**159**
Net total	**505**	**423**	**468**	**367**	**347**	**381**	**330**	**226**	**128**

Source: adapted from retail-index.com, http://www.retail-index.com/HomeSearch/CalculateNumberofRetailerspercountrysector.aspx.

designed to ensure strong marketing support for their products and to exclude rival competitors from the channel.[6]

Business philosophy

Coupled with the close economic ties and dependency created by trade customs and the long structure of German distribution channels is a unique business philosophy that emphasises loyalty, harmony and friendship. The value system supports long-term dealer/supplier relationships that are difficult to change provided each party perceives economic advantage. The traditional partner, the insider, generally has the advantage.

Trends: from traditional to modern channel structures

Today, few countries are so sufficiently isolated that they are unaffected by global economic and political changes. These currents of change are altering all levels of economic activity, including the distribution structure. Traditional channel structures are giving way to new forms, new alliances and new processes – some more slowly than others, but all changing. Pressures for change in a country come from within and without. Multinational marketers are seeking ways profitably to tap market segments that are served by costly, traditional distribution systems. Direct marketing, door-to-door selling, hypermarkets, discount houses, shopping malls, catalogue selling and selling through the Internet are being introduced in an attempt to provide efficient distribution channels.[7]

A single European market, national and international retailing networks are developing throughout Europe. An example is Sainsbury's, the UK supermarket giant, which has entered an alliance with Esselunga of Italy (supermarkets), Docks de France (hypermarkets, supermarkets and discount stores) and Belgium's Delhaize (supermarkets).

The alliance provides the opportunity for the four to pool their experience and buying power and prepare to expand into other European markets. Ahold (Albert Heijn) of the Netherlands is expanding globally from the USA to Asia. More than 60 per cent of its revenue is coming from abroad. While European retailers see a unified Europe as an opportunity for pan-European expansion, foreign retailers are attracted by the high margins and prices characterised as 'among the most expensive anywhere in the world'.

Costco, the US-based warehouse retailer, saw the high gross-margins British supermarkets command, 7 to 8 per cent compared with 2.5 to 3 per cent in the USA, as an opportunity. Costco prices are 10 to 20 per cent cheaper than rival local retailers. The impact of these and other trends is to change traditional distribution and marketing systems, leading to greater efficiency in distribution. Competition will translate those efficiencies into lower consumer prices. Exhibit 17.2 gives you an idea of the retail structures found in selected countries.

The Internet

The Internet is an important distribution method for multinational companies and a source of products for businesses and consumers. Computer hardware and software companies and book and music retailers were the early e-marketers using this method of distribution and marketing. More recently there was an expansion of other types of retailing and business-to-business (B2B) services into
e-commerce. Technically, e-commerce is a form of direct selling; however, because of its newness and the unique issues associated with this form of distribution, it is important to differentiate it from other types of direct marketing.

E-commerce is used to market business-to-business services, consumer services and consumer and industrial products via the World Wide Web. It involves the direct marketing from a manufacturer, retailer, service provider or some other intermediary to a final user. Some examples of e-marketers with an international presence are Dell Computer Corporation (www.dell.com), which generates nearly 50 per cent of its total sales, an average of about €84m a day, online, and Cisco Systems (www.cisco.com), which generates more than €1.2bn in sales annually. Cisco's website appears in 14 languages and has country-specific content for 49 nations. Gateway has global sites in Japan, France, the Netherlands, Germany, Sweden, Australia, the UK and the USA, to name a few (www.gateway.com).

> **e-commerce**
>
> buying and selling through the Internet or comparable systems

Besides consumer goods companies such as Levi's, Nike and others, many smaller and less well-known companies have established a presence on the Internet beyond their traditional markets. An Internet customer from the Netherlands can purchase a pair of brake levers for his mountain bike in California-based Price Point. He pays $159 (€130) in America instead of the $232 (€190) that the same items would cost in a local bike store.

For a Spanish shopper in Pamplona, buying sheet music used to mean a 400-km trip to Madrid. Now she crosses the Atlantic to shop – and the journey takes less time than a trip to the corner shop. Via the Internet she can buy directly from specialised stores and high-volume discounters in London or on Amazon.

EXHIBIT 17.2: Retail structure in selected countries

Country	All retailers (000)	People served per retailer	Internet users per 100 people (2011)
USA	702	395	78.2
Canada	112	276	82.7
Argentina	296	127	47.7
Germany	410	200	83.4
Poland	390	99	65.0
Israel	53	119	68.2
South Africa	93	482	20.9
China	21,188	61	38.4
Japan	1,202	106	78.9
Australia	93	208	78.7

Sources: *Euromonitor*; World Bank, 2003, 2011; and *World Fact Book*, 2009.

E-commerce is more developed in the USA than the rest of the world, partly because of the vast number of people who own personal computers and because of the much lower cost of access to the Internet than found elsewhere. However, according to some estimates, Europeans actually spent as much on e-commerce in 2008 as Americans, both at about €27bn ($35bn).[8]

Small and middle-sized firms are expected to generate substantial growth in international transactions, as well as to pool their purchases through various Internet exchanges for everything from telephone services and office furniture to electricity. Although each order is individually small, such purchases combined account for 30 to 60 per cent of firms' total non-labour costs and are usually bought inefficiently and expensively.

Overall costs are reduced by bulk buying through an online intermediary and the savings resulting from placing and processing orders online, which is much cheaper and faster than the traditional way. One study estimates that if all small and medium-sized firms in Britain used the Internet to buy indirect inputs, they could save more than €30bn ($36.7bn) a year.

Going International 17.1

TIME FOR E-COMMERCE 2.0

Every time I check my email, there's another one: 'ONE DAY ONLY!!! Save an EXTRA 50%', 'First time ever! TRIPLE INCIRCLE POINTS + Free gift wrap + Free online shipping at any price.' The all-caps and exclamation points make me wonder whether a teenage girl is writing the copy. How long before smiley faces? But as frenetic and frequent as the emails become, they're not getting me – or many other consumers – to do more online shopping.

More than a decade after the Internet revolutionised how we shop, innovation in e-commerce has hit a wall. Make no mistake: online shopping is still amazingly convenient and the best way to comparison shop. Who doesn't like buying gadgets in their underwear? Yet somewhere along the line the big players just stopped changing the online shopping game. Think about it: is your experience shopping online any different now than it was 10 years ago? Same old user interface, same promotions on the home page, same shopping cart, same too-long checkout process.

E-commerce is at a crossroads. The industry can delude itself that growth will pick up once the economy rebounds, or innovate its way to higher sales. Public companies aren't the best innovators, so I'm betting that it will be scrappy entrepreneurs who use the downturn to start a new e-commerce upheaval.

Amazon.com is among the few e-commerce companies that have been pushing the innovation envelope. E-commerce has a long way to go; it is one of those areas that's underpenetrated and needs to be reinvented. It is still way too hard to buy something online. On some sites, as many as 70 per cent of shoppers abandon carts midway through the checkout process, research shows. Even sites that wisely use email newsletters, microblogging tools or online advertising to lure you still make you whip out a credit card and spend 15 minutes to complete a transaction. By the fourth page of checkout, spontaneous shoppers start to wonder, 'Why did I need this new dress again?' Force me to sign up for a user name and password to check out and you better have one-of-a-kind inventory, because we're beyond password fatigue.

A few sites get the checkout religion. One is Amazon, with Amazon Prime, a loyalty program that offers free shipping and one-click purchasing. Sure, it requires a user name and password, but it also provides great benefit. With its purchase of PayPal, eBay has also taken a small step toward making checkout easier. As part of its attempt to make buying easier, Google created Google Checkout, which is easier to use than PayPal and has fewer fees. But few sites use it yet.

- Do you think e-commerce will take over traditional retailing? Discuss.

Source: *Business Week*, 11 December 2008.

EXHIBIT 17.3: Top 10 markets with most broadband penetration (subscriptions per 100 inhabitants, by technology)

Switzerland	41.6
Netherlands	39.4
Denmark	38.3
Korea	36.2
Norway	36.1
France	35.5
Iceland	34.3
Germany	33.8
UK	33.6
Belgium	32.7

Source: OECD Broadband Statistics, June 2012.

Services, the third engine for growth, are ideally suited for international sales via the Internet. All types of services – banking, education, consulting, retailing, gambling – can be marketed through a website that is globally accessible. As outsourcing of traditional inhouse tasks such as inventory management, quality control, accounting, secretarial, translation and legal services has become more popular among companies, the Internet providers of these services have grown internationally. The introduction of broadband has facilitated the usage of the Internet. Exhibit 17.3 shows broadband penetration in the top 10 countries.

E-commerce enables companies to cut costs in three ways. First, it reduces procurement costs, making it easier to find the cheapest supplier, and it cuts the cost of processing the transactions. Estimates are that a firm's possible savings from purchasing over the Internet vary from 2 per cent in the coal industry to up to 40 per cent in electronic components.

British Telecom claims that procuring goods and services online will reduce the average cost of processing a transaction by 90 per cent and reduce the direct costs of goods and services it purchases by 11 per cent. Second, it allows better supply-chain management. And, third, it makes possible tighter inventory control. With Wal-Mart's direct Internet links between its inventory control system and its suppliers, each sale automatically triggers a replenishment request. The results are fewer out-of-stock situations, the ability to make rapid inventory adjustments, and reduced ordering and processing costs.

Factors influencing marketing through the Internet

1 *Culture*: the website and the product must be culturally neutral or adapted to fit the uniqueness of a market, because culture does matter. In Japan, the pickiness of Japanese consumers about what they buy and their reluctance to deal with merchants at a distance must be addressed when marketing on the web. European sites are more consumer oriented. The different cultural reactions to colour can be a potential problem for websites designed for global markets. While red may be highly regarded in China or associated with love in the USA, in Spain it is associated with socialism. The point is that when designing a website, culture cannot be forgotten.

2 *Adaptation*: ideally, a website should be translated into the languages of the target markets. This may not be finally feasible for some companies, but at least the most important pages of the site should be translated. Simple translation of important pages is only a stop-gap, however. If companies are making a long-term commitment to sales in another country, web pages should be designed (in all senses of the term – colour, use of features, etc) for that market. As discussed earlier, culture does count, and as competition increases, a country-specific website may make the difference between success and failure.[9]

3 *Local contact*: companies fully committed to foreign markets are creating virtual offices abroad; they buy server space and create mirror sites, whereby a company has a voicemail or email contact point in key markets. Foreign customers are more likely to visit sites in their own country and in the local language. In countries, where consumers are particularly concerned about the ability to return goods easily, companies may have outlets where merchandise can be returned and picked up.

4 *Payment*: the consumer should be able to use a credit card number – by email (from a secure page on the website), online or over the phone.

5 *Delivery*: for companies operating in Europe, surface postal delivery of small parcels is most cost-effective but takes the longest time. For more rapid but more expensive deliveries, Federal Express, United Parcel Service and other private delivery services provide delivery worldwide.

Once sufficient volume in a country or region is attained, container shipments to free-trade zones or bonded warehouses can be used for distribution of individual orders via local delivery services within the region. These same locations can also be used for such after-sales services as spare parts, defective product returns and supplies.

6 *Promotion*: Although the web is a means of promotion, if you are engaging in e-commerce you also need to advertise your presence and the products or services offered. How do you attract visitors from other countries to your website? The same way you would at home – except in the local language. Search engine registration, press releases, local newsgroups and forums, mutual links and banner advertising are the traditional methods. A website should be seen as a retail store, with the only difference between it and a physical store being that the customer arrives over the Internet instead of on foot. These factors are shown in Exhibit 17.4.

Electronic advertising

Advertising and marketing, although not strictly in the category of electronic commerce, have also been profoundly affected by this development. Unlike traditional advertising, **Internet advertising** is interactive and can be customised for each viewer. Internet advertising cannot replace mass advertising in other media but is a good alternative to direct mail, which is normally quite expensive. The Internet makes it easier both to communicate with and target potential customers.[10]

> **Internet advertising**
>
> advertising on and through websites

Financial services and travel are two of the many sectors that have been using the Internet for marketing and customer services for some time. An Internet advertising banner provides a direct link to the advertiser's website for more information and alternatives. Compare it with television advertising where a customer sees the advertisement for a minute or less and may have to remember it for days until he or she next goes shopping. The Internet advertisement allows not only for more information, but also for an immediate response or purchase. The total Internet advertising revenues were \$31.74bn (€31.07bn) as compared to \$30bn (€19.91bn) for television advertising in America alone.

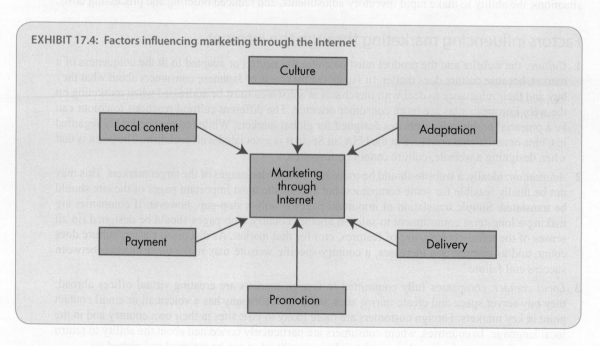

EXHIBIT 17.4: Factors influencing marketing through the Internet

It is not only retailers who believe that the traditional shop may soon become a rarity; manufacturers are equally worried. Procter & Gamble, one of the largest advertisers in the world, has revealed that it is considering moving 80 per cent of its $3bn (€2.7bn) advertising budget to the Internet. The Internet is considered the most important marketing media in history.

The quantity of goods and services sold through electronic commerce is growing at an amazing rate. In 1998 goods and services sold online in Europe and the USA exceeded $5bn (€4.5bn). In 2007 e-tail sales totalled just over $127.7bn (€98.5bn) in the USA. In the USA e-commerce sales grew from $72bn (€47.79bn) in 2002 to $256bn (€169.93bn) in 2011. EU online spending grew by 18 per cent to €202.86bn in 2011, exceeding US Internet sales.

Across Europe e-commerce has become a reliable alternative to traditional shopping. It has revived catalogue shopping, which was earlier considered a downmarket and lower-quality provider that would take weeks or months to arrive. With the help of the Internet, this method has become trendy for buying anything from a dress to computers. The Internet offering promises delivery within 24–48 hours.

Going International 17.2

BIG-BOX COOKIE-CUTTER STORES DON'T ALWAYS WORK

Wal-Mart, JCPenney and Office Depot are all going global with their successful US operating strategy. Friendly service, low prices, extensive variety and apples-to-appliance offerings – all hallmarks of such stores – make tradition-bound retail foreign markets look ripe for the picking with their poor service, high prices and limited products. Counting on their tremendous buying power and operating efficiency to enable them to lower prices, such large retailers went global. But not all is the same the world over.

Adaptation is still important, and many had to adapt their operating strategy to accommodate cultural and business differences. Growth strategies must be supported by three foundations: (1) the retailer must offer a competitively superior product as defined by local customers; (2) the retailer must be able to develop superior economies across the value chain that delivers the product to the local consumer; and (3) global retailers must be able to execute in the local environment.

'Walmart (South High) in Columbus' © Fan of Retail. CC BY 2.0 UK.

Consider, for example, some of the problems US retailers had when building their global strategies on these three pillars:

- In fashion and clothing markets, personal taste is critically important in the buying decision. Distinctions in culture, climate and even physiology demand that products be tailored to each market. Tight skirts, blouses and any other article that tightly hugs the female silhouette are sure sellers in southern Europe and sure losers in the north. Dutch women cycle to work, so tight skirts are out. Rayon and other artificial fabrics are impossible to sell in Germany, but next door in Holland artificial fabrics are popular because they are much cheaper.

▶

◀

- The best-selling children's lines in northern Europe don't have a significant following in France; the French dress their children as little adults, not as kids. One of the bestsellers is a downsized version of a women's clothing line for girls.

- Operational costs vary too. Costs in the USA, where the minimum wage is dramatically different to in Europe, including employer social charges. As a consequence, Toys 'Я' Us was forced to adapt its operating structure in France, where it uses one-third fewer employees per store than it does in the USA.

- Office Depot closed its US-style cookie-cutter stores in Japan and reopened stores one-third the size of the larger ones. Customers were put off by the warehouse-like atmosphere and confused by the English-language signs. The new stores have signs in Japanese and are stocked with office products more familiar to the Japanese.

- After initially doing well, Starbucks is no longer making a profit in Japan. It appears to be a matter of taste. One consumer reports, 'The coffee tastes artificial.'

- Why are American companies such as Wal-Mart and Starbucks having problems in foreign markets? How can they improve this situation?

Sources: Ernest Beck and Emily Nelson, 'As Wal-Mart Invades Europe, Rivals Rush to Match its Formula', *Wall Street Journal*, 6 October 1999; John C. Koopman, 'Successful Global Retailers: A Rare Breed', *Canadian Manager*, April 2000, p 22; Yumiko Ono, 'US Superstores Find Japanese Are a Hard Sell', *Wall Street Journal*, 14 February 2000, p C1; and Stanley Holmes, Irene M. Kunii, Jack Ewing and Kerry Capell, 'For Starbucks, There's No Place Like Home', *Business Week*, 9 June 2003, p 48.

Two years of research by the Consumer Direct Cooperative (CDC), a consortium of 31 organisations including Coca-Cola, Nabisco and Procter & Gamble, identified six major groups of potential online shoppers:

1 *Shopping avoiders*: customers who dislike the routine of regular grocery shopping.

2 *Necessity users*: people who are limited in their ability to go shopping, due to their working hours or having young children.

3 *New technologists*: younger customers who are eager to embrace and feel comfortable with new technologies.

4 *Time-starved*: people who do not worry much about the price and are willing to pay extra to save time.

5 *Responsibles*: customers who have a lot of free time and enjoy shopping.

6 *Traditional customers*: often older people who normally avoid new technologies and enjoy shopping in high-street shops.

According to this research, the first four groups are real online shoppers as they see a clear advantage in electronic commerce. The last two groups are initially reluctant, but real potential e-shoppers over time.

Distribution patterns

International marketers need a general awareness of the patterns of distribution that confront them in world marketplaces. Nearly every international trading firm is forced by the structure of the market to use at least some middlemen in the distribution arrangement. It is all too easy to conclude that, because the structural arrangements of foreign and domestic distribution seem alike, foreign channels are the same as or similar to domestic channels of the same name. This is misleading. Only when the varied intricacies of actual distribution patterns are understood can the complexity of the distribution task be appreciated.

General patterns

Generalising about the internal distribution channel patterns of various countries is almost as difficult as generalising about the behaviour patterns of people. Despite similarities, marketing channels are not the same throughout the world. Marketing methods taken for granted in most EU markets are rare in many countries. Even within Europe there are differences, but these rules are changing in many countries. A number of countries, such as France and the Netherlands, are changing these rules to protect small independent retailers from bigger chain stores.

Going International 17.3

WORLDWIDE WHOLESALERS

In some industries there are worldwide wholesalers who buy and distribute the products throughout the world. For example, in the flower industry the Netherlands has historically been the place for trading. Dutch traders brought tulips from the Ottoman Empire in 1593. They used to sell promissory notes to guarantee future delivery of tulips and bulbs. At today's present value, these promissory notes were priced around €1m for a single black tulip bulb – enough money to buy a five-storey house in central Amsterdam today.

Today at Amsterdam flower market you can buy a black tulip for about €1. From the wholesale warehouse at Aalsmeer 150 football fields of cut flowers worth more than €25m are auctioned every day. The bidders in four huge auction rooms pay attention to the 'clock' as high starting prices tick down. The wholesaler buyer that stops the clock pays the indicated price. Thus, at Aalsmeer the prices are set for flowers all over the world. The Dutch are the biggest exporter of flowers (60 per cent of the world total).

The late Pope John Paul II in St Peter's Square.
© Giansanti Gianni/CORBIS SYGMA).

Outside Aalsmeer auction house, trucks are constantly loaded for shipments by land across Europe and by air freight worldwide. The USA, China and Germany are the big buyers. Every Easter Sunday the Pope addresses the world from St Peter's Square in Rome, reciting 'Bedank voor bloemen.' Thus every Easter he thanks the Dutch nation for providing the flowers for this key Catholic ritual.

Breadth of middlemen services

Service attitudes of tradespeople vary sharply at both the retail and wholesale levels from country to country. In Egypt, for example, the primary purpose of the simple trading system is to handle the physical distribution of available goods. On the other hand, when margins are low and there is a continuing battle for customer preference, both wholesalers and retailers try to offer extra services to make their goods attractive to consumers. When middlemen aren't interested in promoting or selling individual items of merchandise, the manufacturer must provide adequate inducement to the middlemen, or undertake much of the promotion and selling effort.

Costs and margins

Cost levels and middleman margins vary widely from country to country, depending on the level of competition, services offered, efficiencies or inefficiencies of scale, and geographic and turnover factors related to market size, purchasing power, tradition and other basic determinants. In India competition in large cities is so intense that costs are low and margins thin; but in rural areas, the lack of capital has permitted the few traders with capital to gain monopolies, with consequent high prices and wide margins.

Channel length

In every country, channels are likely to be shorter for industrial goods and for high-priced consumer goods than for low-priced products. In general, there is an inverse relationship between channel length and the size of the purchase. Combination wholesaler–retailers or semi-wholesalers exist in many countries, adding one or two links to the length of the distribution chain. In China, for example, the traditional distribution system for over-the-counter drugs consists of large local wholesalers divided into three levels.

First-level wholesalers supply drugs to major cities such as Beijing and Shanghai. Second-level ones service medium-sized cities, while the third level distributes to counties and cities with 100,000 people or fewer. It can be profitable for a company to sell directly to the top two levels of wholesalers and leave them to sell to the third level, which is so small that it would be unprofitable for the company to handle.[11,12]

Non-existent channels

One of the things companies discover about international channel-of-distribution patterns is that, in many countries, adequate market coverage through a simple channel of distribution is nearly impossible. In many instances, appropriate channels do not exist; in others, parts of a channel system are available but other parts are not. Several distinct distribution channels are necessary to reach different segments of a market; channels suitable for distribution in urban areas seldom provide adequate rural coverage.

Eastern Europe presents a special problem. When Communism collapsed, so did the government-run distribution system. Local entrepreneurs are emerging to fill the gap but they lack facilities, training and product knowledge, and they are generally undercapitalised. Companies that have any hope of getting goods to customers profitably must be prepared to invest heavily in distribution.

Blocked channels

International marketers may be blocked from using the channel of their choice. Channel blockage can result from competitors' already-established lines in the various channels and trade associations or cartels having closed certain channels. Associations of middlemen sometimes restrict the number of distribution alternatives available to a producer. Drug manufacturers in many countries have inhibited distribution of a wide range of goods through any retail outlets except pharmacies. The pharmacies, in turn, have been supplied by a relatively small number of wholesalers who have long-established relationships with their suppliers. Thus, through a combination of competition and association, a producer may be kept out of the market completely.

Stocking

The high cost of credit, danger of loss through inflation, lack of capital and other concerns cause foreign middlemen in many countries to limit inventories. This often results in out-of-stock conditions and sales lost to competitors. Physical distribution lags intensify their problem so that, in many cases, the manufacturer must provide local warehousing or extend long credit to encourage middlemen to carry large inventories. Considerable ingenuity, assistance and, perhaps, pressure are required to induce middlemen in most countries to carry adequate or even minimal inventories.[13]

Power and competition

Distribution power tends to concentrate in countries where a few large wholesalers distribute to a mass of small middlemen. Large wholesalers generally finance middlemen downstream. The strong allegiance they command from their customers enables them to block existing channels successfully and force an outsider to rely on less effective and more costly distribution.

Retailing

Retailing shows even greater diversity in its structure than does wholesaling. In Italy and Morocco, retailing is largely composed of speciality houses that carry narrow lines, while in Finland most retailers carry a more general line of merchandise. Retail size is represented at one end by Japan's giant Mitsukoshi, which reportedly enjoys the patronage of more than 100,000 customers every day, and, at the other, by the market of Ibadan, Nigeria, where some 3,000 one- or two-person stalls serve not many more customers.

Size patterns

The extremes in size in retailing are similar to those that predominate in wholesaling. The retail structure and the problems it engenders cause real difficulties for the international marketing firm selling consumer goods. In Italy, official figures show there are 865,000 retail stores, or one store for every 66 Italians. Of the 340,000 food stores, fewer than 1,500 can be classified as large. Thus, middlemen are a critical factor in adequate distribution in Italy.

Emerging countries present similar problems. Among the large supermarket chains in South Africa there is considerable concentration. One thousand of the country's 31,000 stores control 60 per cent of all grocery sales, leaving the remaining 40 per cent of sales to be spread among 30,000 stores. It may be difficult to reach the 40 per cent of the market served by those 30,000 stores.

Direct marketing

Retailing around the world has been in a state of active ferment for several years. The rate of change appears to be directly related to the stage and speed of economic development, and even the least-developed countries are experiencing dramatic changes. Supermarkets of one variety or another are blossoming in developed and developing countries alike. Discount houses that sell everything from powdered milk and canned chilli to Korean TVs and VCRs are thriving and expanding worldwide.

Selling directly to the consumer through the mail, by telephone or door-to-door is becoming the distribution-marketing approach of choice in markets with insufficient and/or underdeveloped distribution systems. Avon has successfully expanded into Eastern Europe, Latin America and Asia with its method of direct marketing. Companies that enlist individuals to sell their products, such as Avon, are proving to be especially popular in Eastern Europe and other countries where many are looking for ways to become entrepreneurs.[14]

Going International 17.4

CHANGING THE NATURE OF RETAILING

A partnership between academic researchers and business called the Auto-ID Center, based in Cambridge, Massachusetts, and founded in 1999, has been developing a new 'smart tag' technology that is likely to replace the barcodes on consumer goods. The smart tags are a new, supercheap version of an old tracking technology called Radio Frequency Identification (RFID).

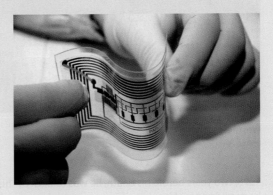

RFID systems are made up of readers and smart tags – or microchips attached to antennas. When the tag nears a reader, it broadcasts the information contained in its chip. From 1999 to 2003, the price of the cheapest tags plummeted from $2 to 20 cents. The technology is already widely used to track pets, livestock, parts in car factories and luggage at airports. Gillette announced that it had put in an order for half a billion smart tags, signalling the start of their adoption by the consumer-goods industry.

The smart tags can be combined with smart shelves, which are fitted with tag readers. Gillette says that retailers and consumer-goods firms in America lose around $30bn a year in sales because shop shelves run out of products and stand empty. With smart tags and readers, shop shelves will be able to keep count of the products and let the store staff know when the stock runs low.

Gillette is also piloting the use of smart tags to track products as they move from factory to supermarket, as using barcodes is an error-prone and labour-intensive task. That is expected to reduce shipment errors and cut

▶

◄

theft. Because manufacturers will be sure that they are shipping the right quantities of goods to the right place, they can also afford to shrink the inventories they maintain in case of error, thus increasing efficiencies in managing stocks.

The biggest worry is that consumers will reject the smart tags because of privacy concerns. If firms link products to consumers at the checkout, ordinary objects could become traceable after their purchase. To address this problem, the Auto-ID Center included a 'kill command' in its chip specifications that can permanently disable the tag at the checkout.

● Do you think RFID tags will infringe our right to privacy? Discuss.

Source: adapted from 'The IT Revolution: The Best Thing Since the Bar-code', *The Economist*, 8 February 2003, pp 71–72.

Going International 17.5

WHY THE WEST IS NO LONGER MALL CONTENT

Westfield, London
© P.N. Ghauri.

Victor Gruen would probably be chuckling at his enfant terrible's mid-life crisis. The Austrian-born father of the mall fled the Nazis to the USA in 1938 and, in the post-war years, noted that department stores moving to the suburbs were building adjacent strips of shops in an attempt to re-create urban shopping districts. In 1947, a shopping centre opened in Los Angeles featuring two department stores, a cluster of small shops and a large car park. It was, in effect, an outdoor mall.

In 1956 Gruen threw a roof over such a structure and installed air-conditioning. The mall was born. However, in

1978, two years before his death, he was to disavow his own creation and accused other mall developments of bastardising his idea.

However, forecasts of the ailing health of the mall fail to recognise the starkly different dynamics across world markets. The USA and the UK are, by global standards, hugely competitive retail environments where consumers are very well served by a wide variety of shopping environments. Store space per capita – the classic marker of whether a country is under- or over-shopped – is high. But this is not the case in a host of so-called 'emerging' markets rapidly opening up to consumerism. The Middle East, too, has seen staggering retail growth – almost exclusively focused on shopping centres.

Dubai Mall is the biggest yet: 350,000 square metres of shopping centre at the foot of the world's tallest tower – the Burj Dubai – will add not only hundreds of retail outlets but also one of the world's largest indoor aquariums and a massive gold and jewellery souk.

►

◄

However, for the emerging markets it is not all good news, as towns and cities become saturated with malls. In Romania, Razvan Gheorghe, managing director of agent Cushman & Wakefield ACTIV Consulting, says five major schemes are currently under development in Bucharest alone, backed by developers from around Europe.

In India, one of the most promising new retail centres, the vast majority of the 600 or so malls currently under construction have been designed locally and there is widespread industry concern that many will be poorly located, badly laid out and redundant before they even open. With property prices already crippling in India's main commercial cities, a lack of suitable retail sites may genuinely hamper its burgeoning consumer explosion.

The place	The time	The sell
Dubai Mall	2008, Dubai, UAE	Dubai does retail with French department store Galeries Lafayette as one anchor, a huge aquarium and much, much more
Forum Istanbul	2008, Istanbul, Turkey	This massive project is the latest to join the plethora of malls opening in the Turkish capital and will combine shopping with houses and offices
Liverpool One	2009, Liverpool, UK	Five-district open streets mixed-use development entwined within the existing city centre
Mall of Arabia	2010, Dubai, UAE	Part of the City of Arabia mega-tourism and leisure project, Mall of Arabia will have over 1,000 stores and is the grand-daddy of them all in the region
Milano Santa Giulia	2010, Milan, Italy	Massive mixed-use scheme with master plan by Foster Milan, Italy & Partners, with an upscale shopping district to rival nearby Milan at its heart, surrounded by housing and offices
Parklake Plaza	2011, Bucharest, Romania	Five-level mall close to the city centre – the biggest of the plethora of retail projects under construction in the Romanian capital
Puerto Venecia	2009, Zaragoza, Spain	Combining sports, leisure, big-box retail and a fashion mall around a 10,000 m² artificial lake, the scheme is designed as a major out-of-town destination
Somerset Central	2009, Singapore	An eight-storey fashion mall located at the gateway to Singapore's main shopping streets
Westfield London	2008, London, UK	Stunning mall in White City, just to the west of London's West End, featuring luxury zones, restaurants and over 270 stores
Meadowlands Xanadu	2009, New Jersey, USA	Complete with indoor ski slope. Original developer Mills went bust and the project is now run by Colony Capital
Westfield Stratford	2011, Stratford, UK	One of the largest urban shopping centres in Europe. Third-largest shopping centre in the UK by retail space, with 300 stores and 70 restaurants

Source: CNBC European Business, July/August 2008, pp 51–52.

Alternative middleman choices

A marketer's options range from assuming the entire distribution activity (by establishing its own subsidiaries and marketing directly to the end user) to depending on intermediaries for distribution of the product. Channel selection must be given considerable thought since, once initiated, it is difficult to change, and if it proves inappropriate, future growth of market share may be affected.

EXHIBIT 17.5: International channel-of-distribution alternatives

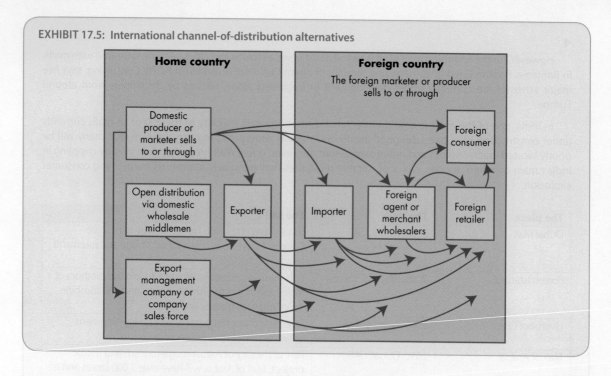

Exhibit 17.5 shows some of the possible channel-of-distribution alternatives. The arrows show those to whom the producer and each of the middlemen may sell. In the home country, the seller must have an organisation (generally the international marketing division of a company) to deal with channel members needed to move goods between countries. In the foreign market, the seller must supervise the channels that supply the product to the end user.

Once the marketer has clarified company objectives and policies, the next step is the selection of specific intermediaries needed to develop a channel. External middlemen are differentiated on whether or not they take title to the goods. Agent middlemen represent the principal rather than themselves, and merchant middlemen take title to the goods and buy and sell on their own account. The distinction between agent and merchant middlemen is important because a manufacturer's control of the distribution process is affected by who has title to the goods in the channel.

- *Agent middlemen*: work on commission and arrange for sales in the foreign country but do not take title to the merchandise. By using agents, the manufacturer assumes trading risk but maintains the right to establish policy guidelines and prices, and to require its agents to provide sales records and customer information.

- *Merchant middlemen*: actually take title to manufacturers' goods and assume the trading risks, so they tend to be less controllable than agent middlemen. Merchant middlemen provide a variety of import and export wholesaling functions involved in purchasing for their own account and selling in other countries. Because merchant middlemen are primarily concerned with sales and profit margins on their merchandise, they are frequently criticised for not representing the best interests of a manufacturer.

Middlemen are not clear-cut, precise, easily defined entities. It is exceptional to find a firm that represents one of the pure types identified here. What functions are performed by the British middleman called a *stockist*, or one called an *exporter* or *importer*? One company engages in both importing and exporting, acts as an agent and a merchant middleman, operates from offices in the USA, Germany and the UK, provides financial services and acts as a freight forwarder. It would be difficult to put this company into an appropriate pigeon-hole. Many firms work in a single capacity, but the conglomerate type of middleman described here is a major force in some international markets.

Only by analysing middlemen functions in skeletal simplicity can the nature of the channels be determined. Three alternatives are presented: first, middlemen physically located in the manufacturer's home country; next, middlemen located in foreign countries; and, finally, a company-owned system.

Going International 17.6

NIKE'S EUROPEAN DISTRIBUTION

Remember for a moment the scene in the Pixar movie *Monsters, Inc.* – millions of doors on conveyor belts. That scene is reminiscent of the inside of Nike's European distribution centre in Laakdal, Belgium. The shoes come from a variety of Asian low-cost manufacturers and arrive at the centre via Rotterdam and Antwerp and the adjacent canal.

Some 12,000 people work at the heavily automated facility where 8 million pairs of shoes are sorted and then shipped to customers all over the continent by truck. Even as sales grow the company will not need to expand the centre because the trend is for the factories to ship directly to the major European retailers, including Nike Sport in St Petersburg.

- Is there a place for middlemen in a modern distribution system? Discuss.

Source: adapted from http://en.convdocs.org/docs/index-28699.html?page=3.

Home-country middlemen

Home-country, or domestic, middlemen, located in the producing firm's country, provide marketing services from a domestic base. By selecting **domestic middlemen** as intermediaries in the distribution processes, companies delegate foreign-market distribution to others. Domestic middlemen offer many advantages for companies with a small international sales volume, those inexperienced with foreign markets, those not wanting to become immediately involved with the complexities of international marketing and those wanting to sell abroad with minimum financial and management commitment.

> **domestic middlemen**
>
> middlemen (eg wholesalers) in the home market of the company

A major trade-off for using domestic middlemen is limited control over the entire process. Domestic middlemen are most likely to be used when the marketer is uncertain and/or desires to minimise financial and managerial investment. A brief discussion of the more frequently used domestic middlemen follows.

Export management companies

The **export management company (EMC)** is an important middleman for firms with relatively small international volume or those unwilling to involve their own personnel in the international function. EMCs range in size from one person up to 100 and handle about 10 per cent of the manufactured goods exported. Whether handling five clients or 100, the EMC's stock-in-trade is personalised service. Typically, the EMC becomes an integral part of the marketing operations of the client companies. Working under the names of the manufacturers, the EMC functions as a low-cost, independent marketing department with direct responsibility to the parent firm. The working relationship is so close that customers are often unaware they are not dealing directly with the export department of the company (see Exhibit 17.6).

> **export management company (EMC)**
>
> important middleman for firms with relatively small international volume or those unwilling to involve their own personnel in the international function

Two of the chief advantages of EMCs are: (1) minimum investment on the part of the company to get into international markets; and (2) no company personnel or major

---

EXHIBIT 17.6: How does an EMC operate?

Most export management companies offer a wide range of services and assistance, including:
- researching foreign markets for a client's products
- travelling overseas to determine the best method of distributing the product
- appointing distributors or commission representatives as needed in individual foreign countries, frequently within an already existing overseas network created for similar goods
- exhibiting the client's products at international trade shows, such as US Department of Commerce-sponsored commercial exhibitions at trade fairs and US Export Development Offices around the world
- handling the routine details involved in getting the product to the foreign customer – export declarations, shipping and customs documentation, insurance, banking and instructions for special export packing and marking
- granting the customary finance terms to the trade abroad and assuring payment to the manufacturer of the product
- preparing advertising and sales literature in cooperation with the manufacturer and adapting it to overseas requirements for use in personal contacts with foreign buyers
- corresponding in the necessary foreign languages
- making sure that goods being shipped are suitable for local conditions, and meet overseas legal and trade norms, including labelling, packaging, purity and electrical characteristics
- advising on overseas patent and trademark protection requirements.

Source: 'The Export Management Company', US Department of Commerce, Washington, DC, 2009.

---

expenditure of managerial effort. The result, in effect, is an extension of the market for the firm with negligible financial or personnel commitments.

Trading companies

trading companies

accumulate, transport and distribute goods from many countries

sogo shosha

Japanese trading and investment organisations that also perform a unique and important role as risk takers

piggybacking

using another company's channels to export products

Trading companies have a long and honourable history as important intermediaries in the development of trade between nations. **Trading companies** accumulate, transport and distribute goods from many countries. In concept, the trading company has changed little in hundreds of years.

The British firm Gray MacKenzie & Company is typical of companies operating in the Middle East. It has some 70 sales people and handles consumer products ranging from toiletries to outboard motors and Scotch whisky. The key advantage to this type of trading company is that it covers the entire Middle East.

Large, established trading companies are generally located in developed countries; they sell manufactured goods to developing countries, and buy raw materials and unprocessed goods. Japanese trading companies (**sogo shosha**), dating back to the early 1700s, operate both as importers and exporters. Some 300 are engaged in foreign and domestic trade through 2000 branch offices outside Japan and handle over €0.9 trillion ($1 trillion) in trading volume annually.[15]

Complementary marketers

Companies with marketing facilities or contacts in different countries with excess marketing capacity or a desire for a broader product line sometimes take on additional lines for international distribution; although the generic name for such activities is complementary marketing, it is commonly called **piggybacking**.[16] General Electric has been distributing merchandise from other suppliers for many years. It accepts products that are non-competitive but complementary and that add to the basic distribution strength of the company itself.

Most piggyback arrangements are undertaken when a firm wants to fill out its product line or keep its seasonal distribution channels functioning throughout the year. Companies may work either on an agency or merchant basis, but the greatest volume of piggyback business is handled on an ownership (merchant) purchase–resale arrangement.

The selection process for new products for piggyback distribution determines whether: (1) the product relates to the product line and contributes to it; (2) the product fits the sales and distribution channel presently employed; (3) there is an adequate margin to make the undertaking worthwhile; and (4) the product will find market acceptance and profitable volume. If these requirements are met, piggybacking can be a logical way of increasing volume and profit for both the carrier and the piggybacker.

Manufacturer's export agent

The **manufacturer's export agent (MEA)** is an individual agent middleman or an agent middleman firm providing a selling service for manufacturers. Unlike the EMC, the MEA does not serve as the producer's export department but has a short-term relationship, covers only one or two markets, and operates on a straight commission basis. Another principal difference is that MEAs do business in their own names rather than in the name of the client.

> **manufacturer's export agent (MEA)**
> individual agent middleman or agent middleman firm providing a selling service for manufacturers
>
> **broker**
> catch-all for a variety of middlemen performing low-cost agent services

Home country brokers

The term **broker** is a catch-all for a variety of middlemen performing low-cost agent services. The term is typically applied to import–export brokers who provide the intermediary function of bringing buyers and sellers together and who do not have a continuing relationship with their clients. Most brokers specialise in one or more commodities for which they maintain contact with major producers and purchasers throughout the world.

Buying offices

A variety of agent middlemen may be classified simply as buyers or buyers for export. Their common denominator is a primary function of seeking and purchasing merchandise on request from principals; as such, they do not provide a selling service. In fact, their chief emphasis is on flexibility and the ability to locate merchandise from any source. They do not often become involved in continuing relationships with domestic suppliers and do not provide a continuing source of representation.

Export merchants

Export merchants are essentially domestic merchants operating in foreign markets. As such, they operate much like the domestic wholesaler. Specifically, they purchase goods from a large number of manufacturers, ship them to foreign countries and take full responsibility for their marketing. Sometimes they utilise their own organisations, but, more commonly, they sell through middlemen. They may carry competing lines, have full control over prices, and maintain little loyalty to suppliers, although they continue to handle products as long as they are profitable.

Going International 17.7

CORDIS DATABASE ACTS AS MATCHMAKER FOR EURO FIRMS

A company in Greece has invented an image-sensing quality control system for processing fruit and other difficult-to-handle consumer items.

A French firm has a simulator for trainees using a sheet-fed offset printer, which teaches good diagnostic practice and quality control.

A team in Italy has been working on a sampling device for pesticides in soil or water.

▶

◄

Cranfield Institute of Technology in the UK has developed a clever pocket-sized device that delivers the precision and accuracy of a laboratory analyser at a price of only €24.52 ($30).

All these advances were made possible with a share of the European Commission's €9.8bn ($12bn) grant budget for the fourth framework, which ran until 1999. European funding typically provides just 50 per cent of the costs of research and development.

Now these companies and many others are looking for corporate partners, further financing or marketing expertise, for example, which could provide small businesses with lucrative opportunities.

The European Commission is acting as a matchmaker in an attempt to put companies together through one of its huge databases. The community research and development information service (Cordis) contains information on tens of thousands of research projects that could point towards new products or processes for your company. While the Commission is not necessarily offering further funding, there are clear chances for commercial exploitation of existing programmes.

The service has nine databases, which range from news about research matters to a listing of acronyms to thousands of pages of Commission documentation. But it is the research and technical development projects database that is the starting point. Judith Sorensen, promotion coordinator of Cordis in Luxembourg, says the database is underused.

Companies do not realise the opportunities. Cordis offers a list of firms and their work, with a profile of what they do and their projects, results, potential partners and contact details.

- Are these type of efforts by the EU useful? Why/why not?

Source: abstracted from *The European*, 12–18 September 1996, p 39.

Export jobbers

Export jobbers deal mostly in commodities; they do not take physical possession of goods but assume responsibility for arranging transportation. Because they work on a job-lot basis, they do not provide a particularly attractive distribution alternative for most producers.

Exhibit 17.7 summarises information pertaining to the major kinds of domestic middlemen operating in foreign markets. No attempt is made to generalise about rates of commission, mark-up or pay because so many factors influence compensation.[17]

Foreign-country middlemen

The variety of agent and merchant middlemen in most countries is similar to those in Europe and the USA. An international marketer seeking greater control over the distribution process may elect to deal directly with middlemen in the foreign market. They gain the advantage of shorter channels and deal with middlemen in constant contact with the market. As with all middlemen, particularly those working at a distance, effectiveness is directly dependent on the selection of middlemen and on the degree of control the manufacturer can and/or will exert.

foreign-country middlemen

middlemen in foreign markets

Using **foreign-country middlemen** moves the manufacturer closer to the market and involves the company more closely with problems of language, physical distribution, communications and financing. Foreign middlemen may be agents or merchants; they may be associated with the parent company to varying degrees; or they may be temporarily hired for special purposes. Some of the more important foreign-country middlemen are manufacturers' representatives and foreign distributors.

Manufacturers' representatives

Manufacturers' representatives are agent middlemen who take responsibility for a producer's goods in a city, regional market area, entire country or several adjacent countries. When responsible for

Going International 17.8

CAPTIVE AND CONTENT

Does a traditional Japanese business model make sense in tough times?

Japanese trading companies have long been reviled by Western businessmen as inefficient middlemen and huge, monolithic entities that strangle the Japanese economy. However, as the credit crunch causes firms in America and Europe to flounder for lack of funds, throwing supply chains into disarray, Japan's trading-company model seems to have some merit.

© Istockphoto.com/AWSeebaran

This is because the *sogo shosha*, or trading houses, have always done far more than make a living from arbitrage and commissions: they also provide credit to the companies within their folds. Private firms in Japan receive more than ¥180 trillion (about $2 trillion) in trade credit and loans from outside the banking sector, with trading companies being most active. That is around two-thirds of the amount they receive from banks, notes Iichiro Uesugi, an economist at Hitotsubashi University.

The five big houses (Mitsubishi, Mitsui, Sumitomo, Itochu and Marubeni) tower over corporate Japan and worm their way into almost all business activity. Some date back to the seventeenth century. They came to the fore during Japan's rapid industrialisation in the late nineteenth century, procuring material from overseas for the resource-impoverished country and handling the export of finished goods. The *sogo shosha* attracted the brightest and most adventurous graduates. A retired Sumitomo man recalls an arduous elephant ride through the Burmese jungle in the 1950s to explore a mining site. The companies still sometimes act as diplomatic arms of the state.

The middleman model was abandoned in the 1990s. Now the firms use knowledge of one market to move into adjacent areas, take control of an entire supply chain and improve their pricing power. Mitsubishi, for example, imports food, processes it, distributes it and sells it via convenience stores in which it holds a stake, says Ichiro Mizuno, the firm's finance chief. The *sogo shosha* also anticipate future needs and invest accordingly, for example in rare minerals for electronic firms.

As ersatz investment banks, they make short- and long-term loans and take equity stakes. In their role as wholesalers, they provide trade credit to facilitate transactions. Together the trading houses represent 3 per cent of all trade credit in Japan, a huge figure (though down from a staggering 12 per cent in the 1970s). Critically, they provide market confidence that the debts of their subsidiaries will be honoured. This is often done implicitly, since no company wants to damage its reputation – the most important currency in corporate Japan.

Source: *The Economist*, 4 December 2008.

an entire country, the middleman is often called a 'sole agent'. The well-chosen, well-motivated, well-controlled manufacturers' representative can provide excellent market coverage for manufacturers in certain circumstances. The manufacturers' representative is widely used in distribution of industrial goods overseas and is an excellent representative for any type of manufactured consumer goods.

EXHIBIT 17.7: Characteristics of domestic middlemen serving overseas markets

Types of duty	Agent EMC	MEA	Broker	Buying offices	Selling groups	Export merchant	Merchant export jobber	Import and trading companies	Complementary marketers
Take title	No*	No	No	No	No	Yes	Yes	Yes	Yes
Take possession	Yes	Yes	No	Yes	Yes	Yes	No	Yes	Yes
Continuing relationship	Yes	Yes	No	Yes	Yes	No	Yes	Yes	Yes
Share of foreign output	All	All	Any	Small	All	Any	Small	Any	Most
Degree of control by principal	Fair	Fair	Nil	Nil	Good	None	None	Nil	Fair
Price authority	Advisory	Advisory	Yes (at market level)	Yes (to buy)	Advisory	Yes	Yes	No	Some
Represent buyer or seller	Seller	Seller	Either	Buyer	Seller	Self	Self	Self	Self
Number of principals	Few – many	Few – many	Many	Small	Few	Many sources	Many sources	Many sources	One per product
Arrange shipping	Yes	Yes	Not usually	Yes	Yes	Yes	Yes	Yes	Yes
Type of goods	Manu-factured goods and commodities	Staples and commodities	Staples and commodities	Staples and commodities	Comple-mentary to their own lines	Manufactured goods	Bulky and raw materials	Manu-factured goods	Comple-mentary to line
Breadth of line	Speciality – wide	All types of staples	All types of staples	Retail goods	Narrow	Broad	Broad	Broad	Narrow
Handle competitive lines	No	No	Yes	Yes – utilises many sources	No	Yes	Yes	Yes	No
Extent of promotion and selling effort	Good	Good	One shot	n.a.	Good	Nil	Nil	Good	Good
Extend credit to principal	Occasionally	Occasionally	Seldom	Seldom	Seldom	Occasionally	Seldom	Seldom	Seldom
Market information	Fair	Fair	Price and market conditions	For principal not for manufacturer	Good	Nil	Nil	Fair	Good

Note: n.a. = not available.

* The EMC may take title and thus become a merchant middleman.

manufacturers' representatives

represent the producing company in another country

Foreign **manufacturers' representatives** have a variety of titles including sales agent, resident sales agent, exclusive agent, commission agent and indent agent. They take no credit, exchange or market risk but deal strictly as field sales representatives. They do not arrange for shipping or for handling and usually do not take physical possession. Manufacturers who desire the type of control and intensive market coverage their own sales force would afford, but who cannot field one, may find the manufacturers' representative a satisfactory choice.

Distributors

A foreign distributor is a merchant middleman. This intermediary often has exclusive sales rights in a specific country and works in close cooperation with the manufacturer. The distributor has a relatively high degree of dependence on the supplier companies, and arrangements are likely to be on a long-term, continuous basis. Working through distributors permits the manufacturer a reasonable degree of control over prices, promotional effort, inventory, servicing and other distribution functions.

Foreign-country brokers

Like the export broker discussed earlier, brokers are agents who deal largely in commodities and food products. The **foreign brokers** are typically part of small brokerage firms operating in one country or in a few contiguous countries. Their strength is in having good continuing relationships with customers and providing speedy market coverage at low cost.

> **foreign brokers**
>
> agents who deal largely in commodities and food products, typically part of small firms operating in one or a few countries

Managing agents

A managing agent conducts business within a foreign nation under an exclusive contract arrangement with the parent company. The **managing agent** in some cases invests in the operation and in most instances operates under a contract with the parent company. Compensation is usually on the basis of cost plus a specified percentage of the profits of the managed company.

> **managing agent**
>
> conducts business within a foreign nation under exclusive contract to the parent company

Dealers

Generally speaking, anyone who has a continuing relationship with a supplier in buying and selling goods is considered a dealer. More specifically, dealers are middlemen selling industrial goods or durable consumer goods direct to customers; dealers are the last step in the channel of distribution. **Dealers** have continuing, close working relationships with their suppliers and exclusive selling rights for their producer's products within a given geographic area. Finally, they derive a large portion of their sales volume from the products of a single supplier firm. Usually a dealer is an independent merchant middleman, but sometimes the supplier company has an equity in its dealers.

> **dealer**
>
> anyone who has a continuing relationship with a supplier in buying and selling goods

Some of the best examples of dealer operations are found in the farm equipment, earthmoving and automotive industries. These categories include Massey Ferguson, with a vast, worldwide network of dealers; Caterpillar Tractor Company, with dealers in every major city of the world; and the various car companies.

Import jobbers, wholesalers and retailers

Import jobbers purchase goods directly from the manufacturer and sell to wholesalers and retailers and to industrial customers. Large and small **wholesalers and retailers** engage in direct importing for their own outlets and for redistribution to smaller middlemen. The combination retailer-wholesaler is more important in foreign countries than in Western countries. It is not uncommon to find large retailers wholesaling goods to local shops and dealers. Exhibit 17.8 summarises the characteristics of foreign-country middlemen.

> **wholesalers and retailers**
>
> facilitate the exchange of goods between manufacturer and consumer

Government-affiliated middlemen

Marketers must deal with governments in every country of the world. Products, services and commodities for the government's own use are always procured through government purchasing offices at federal, regional and local levels. As more and more social services are undertaken by governments, the level of government purchasing activity escalates.

In the Netherlands, the state's purchasing office deals with more than 10,000 suppliers in 20 countries. About one-third of the products purchased by that agency are produced outside the Netherlands;

EXHIBIT 17.8: Characteristics of foreign-country middlemen

Type of duty	Agent broker	Manufacturers' representative	Managing agent	Merchant distributor	Dealer	Import jobber	Wholesaler and retailer
Take title	No	No	No	Yes	Yes	Yes	Yes
Take possession	No	Seldom	Seldom	Yes	Yes	Yes	Yes
Continuing relationship	No	Often	With buyer, not seller	Yes	Yes	No	Usually not
Share of foreign output	Small	All or part for one area	n.a.	All, for certain countries	Assignment area	Small	Very small
Degree of control by principal	Low	Fair	None	High	High	Low	Nil
Price authority	Nil	Nil	Nil	Partial	Partial	Full	Full
Represent buyer or seller	Either	Seller	Buyer	Seller	Seller	Self	Self
Number of principals	Many	Few	Many	Small	Few major	Many	Many
Arrange shipping	No	No	No	No	No	No	No
Type of goods	Commodity and food	Manufactured goods	All types of manufactured goods	Manufactured goods	Manufactured goods	Manufactured goods	Manufactured consumer goods
Breadth of line	Broad	Allied lines	Broad	Narrow to broad	Narrow	Narrow to broad	Narrow to broad
Handle competitive lines	Yes	No	Yes	No	No	Yes	Yes
Extent of promotion and selling effort	Nil	Fair	Nil	Fair	Good	Nil	Nil usually
Extend credit to principal	No	No	No	Sometimes	No	No	No
Market information	Nil	Good	Nil	Fair	Good	Nil	Nil

Note: n.a. = not available.

90 per cent of foreign purchases are handled through Dutch representatives. The other 10 per cent are purchased directly from producing companies. In Sweden and Norway, the state has a monopoly on all alcoholic drinks and they can be bought only in state-monopoly stores.

Factors affecting choice of channel

The international marketer needs a clear understanding of market characteristics and must have established operating policies before beginning the selection of channel middlemen. The following points should be addressed prior to the selection process.

1 Identify specific target markets within and across countries.

2 Specify marketing goals in terms of volume, market share and profit margin requirements.

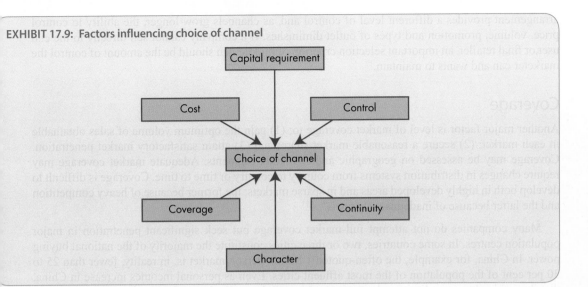

EXHIBIT 17.9: Factors influencing choice of channel

3 Specify financial and personnel commitments to the development of international distribution.

4 Identify control, length of channels, terms of sale and channel ownership.

Marketers must get their goods into the hands of consumers and must choose between handling all distribution or turning part or all of it over to various middlemen. Distribution channels vary depending on target market size, competition and available distribution intermediaries.

Although the overall marketing strategy of the firm must embody the company's profit goals in the short and long run, channel strategy itself is considered to have six influencing factors. These factors can be characterised as the 'six Cs' of channel strategy: cost, capital, control, coverage, character and continuity, as illustrated in Exhibit 17.9. In forging the overall channel-of-distribution strategy, each of the six Cs must be considered in building an economical, effective distribution organisation within the long-range channel policies of the company.

Cost

There are two kinds of channel cost: the capital or investment cost of developing the channel and the continuing cost of maintaining it. The latter can be in the form of direct expenditure for the maintenance of the company's selling force or in the form of margins, mark-up or commissions of various middlemen handling the goods. Marketing costs (a substantial part of which is channel cost) must be considered as the entire difference between the factory price of the goods and the price the customer ultimately pays for the merchandise. The costs of middlemen include transporting and storing the goods, breaking bulk, providing credit, and the cost of local advertising, sales representation and negotiations.

Capital requirement

The financial ramifications of a distribution policy are often overlooked. Critical elements are capital requirement and cash-flow patterns associated with using a particular type of middleman. Maximum investment is usually required when a company establishes its own internal channels: its own sales force. Use of distributors or dealers may lessen the cash investment, but manufacturers often provide initial inventories on consignment, loans, floor plans or other arrangements.

Control

The more involved a company is with the distribution, the more control it exerts. A company's own sales force affords the most control but often at a cost that is not practical. Each type of channel arrangement provides a different level of control and, as channels grow longer, the ability to control price, volume, promotion and types of outlet diminishes. If a company cannot sell directly to the end user or final retailer, an important selection criterion of middlemen should be the amount of control the marketer can and wants to maintain.[17]

Coverage

Another major factor is level of market coverage to: (1) gain the optimum volume of sales obtainable in each market; (2) secure a reasonable market share; and (3) attain satisfactory market penetration. Coverage may be assessed on geographic and/or market segments. Adequate market coverage may require changes in distribution systems from country to country or time to time. Coverage is difficult to develop both in highly developed areas and in sparse markets; the former because of heavy competition and the latter because of inadequate channels.

Many companies do not attempt full-market coverage but seek significant penetration in major population centres. In some countries, two or three cities constitute the majority of the national buying power. In China, for example, the often-quoted 1 billion-person market is, in reality, fewer than 25 to 30 per cent of the population of the most affluent cities. Even as personal incomes increase in China, distribution inadequacies limit marketers in reaching all those who have adequate incomes.

Character

The channel-of-distribution system selected must fit the character of the company and the markets in which it is doing business. Some obvious product requirements, often the first considered, relate to perishability or bulk of the product, complexity of sale, sales service required and value of the product.

Channel commanders must be aware that channel patterns change; they cannot assume that once a channel has been developed to fit the character of both company and market no more need be done. The UK, for example, has epitomised distribution through speciality-type middlemen, distributors, wholesalers and retailers; in fact, all middlemen have traditionally worked within narrow product speciality areas.

Continuity

Channels of distribution often pose longevity problems. Most agent middlemen firms tend to be small institutions. When one individual retires or moves out of a line of business, the company may find it has lost its distribution in that area. Wholesalers, and especially retailers, are not noted for their continuity in business either. Most middlemen have little loyalty to their vendors. They handle brands in good times when the line is making money, but quickly reject such products within a season or a year if they fail to produce during that period.

Locating, selecting and motivating channel members

Despite the chaotic condition of international distribution channels, international marketers can follow a logical procedure in developing channels. After general policy guides are established, marketers need to develop criteria for the selection of specific middlemen. Construction of the middleman network includes seeking out potential middlemen, selecting those who fit the company's requirements and establishing working relationships with them.

Locating middlemen

The search for prospective middlemen should begin with study of the market and determination of criteria for evaluating middlemen servicing that market. The company's broad policy guidelines should be followed, but expediency should be expected to override policy at times. The checklist of criteria differs according to the type of middlemen being used and the nature of their relationship with the company. Basically, such lists are built around four subject areas: (1) productivity or volume; (2) financial strength; (3) managerial stability and capability; and (4) the nature and reputation of the business. Emphasis is usually placed on either the actual or potential productivity of the middleman.

Screening

The screening and selection process itself should follow this sequence: (1) a letter including product information and distributor requirements in the native language to each prospective middleman; (2) a follow-up to the best respondents for more specific information concerning lines handled, territory covered, size of firm, number of sales people and other background information; (3) credit check and references from other clients and customers of the prospective middleman; and (4) if possible, a personal check of the most promising firms.

Selecting middlemen

Finding prospective middlemen is less of a problem than determining which of them can perform satisfactorily. Most prospects are hampered by low volume or low potential volume, many are underfinanced, and some simply cannot be trusted. In many cases, when a manufacturer is not well known abroad, the reputation of the middleman becomes the reputation of the manufacturer, so a poor choice at this point can be devastating.

The agreement

Once a potential middleman has been found and evaluated, there remains the task of detailing the arrangements with that middleman. So far the company has been in a buying position; now it must shift into a selling and negotiating position to convince the middleman to handle the goods and accept a distribution agreement that is workable for the company. Agreements must spell out the specific responsibilities of the manufacturer and the middleman, including an annual sales minimum. The sales minimum serves as a basis for evaluation of the distributor and failure to meet sales minimums may give the exporter the right of termination.

Motivating middlemen

Once middlemen are selected, a promotional programme must be started to maintain high-level interest in the manufacturer's products. A larger proportion of the advertising budget must be devoted to channel communications than in the head office because there are so many small middlemen to be contacted. Consumer advertising is of no avail unless the goods are actually available. On all levels, there is a clear correlation between the middleman's motivation and sales volume.

The hundreds of motivational techniques that can be employed to maintain middleman interest and support for the product may be grouped into five categories: financial rewards, psychological rewards, communications, company support and corporate rapport. Obviously, margins or commissions must be competitive and set to meet the needs of the middleman, and may vary according to the volume of sales and the level of services offered. Without a combination of adequate margin and adequate volume, a middleman cannot afford to give much attention to a product.

Being human, middlemen and their sales people respond to psychological rewards and recognition for the jobs they are doing. A trip to the parent company's home or regional office is a great honour. Publicity in company media and local newspapers also builds esteem and a sense of involvement among foreign middlemen.

Terminating middlemen

When middlemen do not perform up to standards or when market situations change, requiring a company to restructure its distribution, it may be necessary to terminate relationships with certain middlemen or certain types of middlemen. In Western markets, it is usually a simple action regardless of the type of middleman: agent or merchant, they are simply dismissed. However, in other parts of the world, the middleman typically has some legal protection that makes it difficult to terminate relationships. Some companies give all middlemen contracts for one year, or for another specified period, to avoid such problems. But as many experienced international marketers know, the best rule is to avoid the need to terminate distributors by screening all prospective middlemen carefully.

Controlling middlemen

The extreme length of channels typically used in international distribution makes control of middlemen particularly difficult. Some companies solve this problem by establishing their own distribution systems; others issue franchises or exclusive distributorships in an effort to maintain control through the first stages of the channels.

Some manufacturers have lost control through 'secondary wholesaling' – when rebuffed discounters have secured a product through an unauthorised outlet. A manufacturer may then face some of the toughest competition from its own products that have been diverted through other countries or manufactured by subsidiaries and exported or bootlegged into markets the parent would prefer to reserve. Such action can directly conflict with exclusive arrangements made with distributors in other countries and may undermine the entire distribution system by harming relationships between manufacturers and their channels.[18]

SUMMARY

From the foregoing discussion, it is evident that the international marketer has a broad range of alternatives for developing an economical, efficient, high-volume international distribution system. To the uninitiated, however, the variety may be overwhelming.

Careful analysis of the functions performed suggests more similarity than difference between international and domestic distribution systems; in both cases there are three primary alternatives of using agent middlemen, merchant middlemen or a company's own sales and distribution system. In many instances, all three types of middleman are employed on the international scene, and channel structure may vary from nation to nation or from continent to continent. The neophyte company in international marketing can gain strength from the knowledge that information and advice are available relative to the structuring of international distribution systems and that many well-developed and capable middleman firms exist for the international distribution of goods. Within the past decade, international middlemen have become more numerous, more reliable, more sophisticated and more readily available to marketers in all countries. Such growth and development offer an ever-wider range of possibilities for entering foreign markets, but the international business person should remember that it is just as easy for competitors.

QUESTIONS

1 Discuss the distinguishing features of the European distribution system.
2 Discuss how the globalisation of markets, especially in the EU, affects retail distribution.
3 In what ways and to what extent do the functions of domestic middlemen differ from those of their foreign counterparts?
4 Why is the EMC sometimes called an independent export department?
5 Discuss how physical distribution relates to channel policy and how they affect one another.
6 Explain how and why distribution channels are affected as they are when the stage of development of an economy improves.

7 In what circumstances is the use of an EMC logical?

8 In what circumstances are trading companies likely to be used?

9 How is distribution-channel structure affected by increasing emphasis on the government as a customer and by the existence of state trading agencies?

10 Review the key variable that affects the marketer's choice of distribution channels.

11 One of the first things companies discover about international channel-of-distribution patterns is that in most countries it is nearly impossible to gain adequate market coverage through a simple channel-of-distribution plan. Discuss.

12 Discuss the factors influencing marketing via the Internet.

FURTHER READING

- U. Elg, P.N. Ghauri and V. Tarnovskaya, 'The Role of Networks and Matching in Market Entry to Emerging Retail Markets', *International Marketing Review*, 2008, 25(6), 674–99.

- P.N. Ghauri, U. Elg and R.R. Sinkovics, 'Foreign Direct Investment – Location Attractiveness for Retailing Firms in the European Union', in Pervez N. Ghauri and Lars Oxelheim (eds), *European Union and the Race for Foreign Direct Investment in Europe*, (Oxford: Pergamon, 2004), pp 407–28.

- B. Hernandez, J. Jinenez and M.J. Martin, 'Adoption vs Acceptance of E-commerce: Two Different Decisions', *European Journal of Marketing*, 2009, 43(9–10), 1232–45.

NOTES

1 J. Evans, A. Treadgold and F.T. Movondo, 'Psychic Distance and the Performance of International Retailers: A Suggested Theoretical Framework', *International Marketing Review*, 2000, 17(4/5), 297–309.

2 D. Ford, 'Distribution, Internationalisation and Networks', *International Marketing Review*, 2002, 19(2/3), 225–35.

3 P. Ellis, 'Are International Trade Intermediaries Catalysts in Economic Development?', *Journal of International Marketing*, 2003, 112(12), 73–96.

4 For a report on research on a nation's level of economic development and marketing channels, see Janen E. Olsen and Kent L. Granzin, *Journal of Global Marketing*, 1994, 7(3), 7–39.

5 Arieh Goldman, 'Japan's Distribution System: Institutional Structure, Internal Political Economy, and Modernization', *Journal of Retailing*, Summer 1991, 156–61.

6 Gregory L. Miles, 'Unmasking Japan's Distributors', *International Business*, April 1994, 30–42.

7 T. Li, A.F.J. Nicholls and S. Roslow, 'Organisational Motivation and the Global Concurrent Launch in Markets with Accelerated Technology', *International Business Review*, 2003, 12(5), 523–42.

8 J.L. Nicolau, ' Direct vs Indirect Channels: Differentiated Loss Aversion in High-involvement Non-frequently Purchased Hedonic Products, *European Journal of Marketing*, 2013, 47(1/2), 260–78.

9 Mohammad Yamin and Rudolf R. Sinkovics, 'Online Internationalisation, Psychic Distance Reduction and the Virtuality Trap', *International Business Review*, 2006, 15(4), 339–60.

10 S. Dutta and B. Biren, 'Business Transformation on the Internet: Results from the 2000 Study', *European Management Journal*, 2001, 19(5), 449–62.

11 G. Bergendahl, 'Models for Investment in Electronic Commerce – Financial Perspectives with Empirical Evidence', *Omega*, 2005, p 33.

12 Maggie Chuoyan Dong, David K. Tse, S. Tamer Cavusgil, 'Efficiency of Governance Mechanisms in China's Distribution Channels', *International Business Review*, 2008, 17(5), 509–19.

13 Isabella Chaney and Jos Gamble, 'Retail Store Ownership Influences on Chinese Consumers', *International Business Review*, 2008, 17(2), 170–83.

14 M. Harvey and M. Novicevic, 'Seeking Marketing Managers to Effectively Control Global Channels of Distribution', *International Marketing Review*, 2002, 129(4), 525–44.

15 Yukio Onuma, 'Myths and Realities of the *Sogo-Shosha*', *Trade and Culture*, September–October 1994, 33–4.

16 G.I. Balabaris, 'Factors Affecting Export Intermediaries' Service Offerings: The British Example', *Journal of International Business Studies*, 2000, 31(1), 83–94.

17 C. Pahud de Mortanges and J. Vossen, 'Mechanisms to Control the Marketing Activities of Foreign Distributors', *International Business Review*, 1999, 8(1), 75–97.

18 J.M. Barutia and C. Echebarria, 'Networks: A Social Marketing Tool', *European Journal of Marketing*, 2013, 47(1/2), 324–43.

Chapter 18
Pricing for International Markets

Chapter Learning Objectives

What you should learn from Chapter 18

- How to use pricing as a competitive tool in international marketing
- How to identify the pricing pitfalls directly related to international marketing
- How to control pricing in parallel imports or grey markets in an international context
- How to identify and handle factors influencing international pricing strategy
- The reasons for price escalation and how to minimise its effect
- How firms are using transfer pricing for their benefit
- What is meant by countertrading and how it influences international pricing policies

Even when the international marketer produces the right product, promotes it correctly and initiates the proper channel of distribution, the effort fails if the product is not properly priced. Setting the right price for a product can be the key to success. While the quality of Western products is widely recognised in global markets, foreign buyers, like domestic buyers, balance quality and price in their purchase decisions. A product's price must reflect the quality/value the consumer perceives in the product. Of all the tasks facing the international marketer, determining what price to charge is one of the most difficult decisions. It is further complicated when the company sells its product to customers in different country markets.[1]

A unified Europe, economic reforms in Eastern Europe and economic growth in Asian and Latin American countries are creating new marketing opportunities with enhanced competition. As global companies vie for these markets, price becomes increasingly important as a competitive tool. Whether exporting or managing overseas operations, the international marketing manager is responsible for setting and controlling the actual price of goods as they are traded in different markets. The marketer is confronted with new sets of variables to consider with each new market: different tariffs, costs, attitudes, competition, currency fluctuations, methods of price quotation and the marketing strategy of the firm.

This chapter focuses on pricing considerations that are of particular concern in the international marketplace. Basic pricing policy questions that arise from the special cost, market and competitive factors in foreign markets are reviewed. A discussion of price escalation and its control and factors associated with price setting is followed by a review of the mechanics of international transfer pricing.

Pricing policy

Active marketing in several countries compounds the number of pricing problems and variables relating to price policy. Unless a firm has a clearly thought-out, explicitly defined price policy, prices are established by expediency rather than design. Pricing activity is affected by the country in which business is being conducted, the type of product, variations in competitive conditions and other strategic factors. Price and terms of sale cannot be based on domestic criteria alone.[2]

Parallel imports

The broader the product line and the larger the number of countries involved, the more complex the process of controlling prices to the end user. Besides having to meet price competition country by country and product by product, companies have to guard against competition from within the company and from their own customers.

If a large company does not have effective controls, it can find its products in competition with its own subsidiaries or branches. Because of different prices that can exist in different country markets, a product sold in one country may be exported to another and undercut the prices charged in that country. For example, to meet economic conditions and local competition, a British pharmaceutical company sells its drugs in a developing country at a lower price only to discover that these discounted drugs are exported to a third country where they are in direct competition with the same product sold for higher prices by the same firm.[3] These **parallel imports** (sometimes called the grey market) upset price levels and result from ineffective management of prices and lack of control.

> **parallel imports**
> when products are imported into a country without the consent of the brand owner

Parallel imports develop when importers buy products from distributors in one country and sell them in another to distributors who are not part of the manufacturer's regular distribution system. This practice is lucrative when wide margins exist between prices for the same products in different countries (see Exhibit 18.1). A variety of conditions can create the profitable opportunity for a parallel market.

Purposefully restricting the supply of a product in a market is another practice that causes abnormally high prices and thus makes a parallel market lucrative. Such was the case with the Mercedes-Benz cars whose supply was limited in the USA. The grey market that evolved in Mercedes cars was partially supplied by Americans returning to the USA with cars they could sell for double the price they had paid in Germany.

EXHIBIT 18.1: Showroom tactics: satellite navigation prices (€)

	Germany	Canada	France	Netherlands	UK
TomTom one V4	168	65	145	149	151
TomTom Go 930	328	162	340	298	352
TomTom XL	188	74	188	169	194
Navman S70	139	144	117	261	171
Garmin Nuvi 855	293	190	436	379	243
Garmin Nuvi 250	180	64	134	144	100
Navigon 7310	299	117	134	331	294
Navigon 3300	139	88	242	159	154

Source: compiled from several sources.

This situation persisted until the price differential that had been created by limited distribution evaporated. Restrictions brought about by import quotas and high tariffs can lead to parallel imports and make illegal imports attractive. India has a three-tier duty structure on computer parts ranging from 50 to 80 per cent on imports. As a result, estimates are that as much as 35 per cent of India's domestic computer hardware sales are accounted for by the grey market.[4]

Large **price differentials** between country markets is another condition conducive to the creation of parallel markets. Japanese merchants have long maintained very high prices for consumer products sold within the Japanese market. As a result, prices for Japanese products sold in other countries are often lower than they are in Japan. For example, the Japanese can buy Canon cameras from New York catalogue retailers and have them shipped to Japan for a price below that of the camera purchased in Japan.

> **price differentials**
> difference in price of a product

Going International 18.1

DRIVING A GOLF THROUGH THE GREY MARKET

Estimates of the grey market's current share of car sales range from 3 per cent to 10 per cent, depending on the country. Assuming a conservative 5 per cent, the total only in Europe could hit 600,000 vehicles' worth in just one year, which would total €10.8bn. The biggest source of grey market cars is Italy, where more than 10 per cent of the cars sold, roughly 185,000, end up in other countries. Re-importers also handle cars from the Netherlands and even from countries outside the EU, such as Canada. The major destination is Germany, where about 330,000 grey market cars are sold annually.

© Istockphoto.com/supergenijalac

The grey market has benefited consumers while giving fits to traditional dealers and car makers. Competition from the grey market is forcing dealers to negotiate lower prices, while producers have cancelled or delayed planned price increases. Because most of the re-importers are legitimate, the car manufacturers' only hope of stopping them is to block renegade dealers from selling to the grey market. In 1994, for example, Peugeot asked the European Commission to ban sales to re-importers, but was not successful.

▶

◄

Car makers can withdraw a dealer's franchise, as Peugeot did when it pulled its dealer in Italy. But it is almost impossible to spot and stop these side deals. Golf is a typical example: VW ships Golfs from its plant in Wolfsburg, Germany, to a VW distributor in Italy, pricing it low to compete locally. The distributor sells the car to a franchised VW dealer in, let's say, Florence. An independent re-importer buys the car from the Italian dealer and ships it back to Germany. A German consumer then buys the car from the re-importer for some €3,000–3,500 less than it would cost at a German VW dealer.

● How can VW handle this situation? Discuss.

Source: 'Carmakers Think Monetary Union is the Answer', *Business Week*, 20 November 1995, p 21.

The possibility of a parallel market occurs whenever price differences are greater than the cost of transportation between two markets. In Europe, because of different taxes and competitive price structures, prices for the same product vary between countries. When this occurs, it is not unusual for companies to find themselves competing in one country with their own product imported from another country at lower prices.

In the USA, wholesale prices for exclusive brands of fragrance are often 25 per cent more than wholesale prices in other countries. These are the ideal conditions for a lucrative grey market for unauthorised dealers in other countries who buy more than they need at wholesale prices lower than US wholesalers pay. They then sell the excess at a profit to unauthorised US retailers, but at a price lower than the retailer would have to pay to an authorised US distributor.

Going International 18.2

HOW DO LEVI'S 501s GET TO INTERNATIONAL MARKETS?

Levi Strauss sells in international markets – how else would 501 jeans get to market? The answer is via the grey market, or 'diverters'. Diverters are enterprising people who legally buy 501s at retail prices, usually during sales, and then resell them to foreign buyers. It is estimated that Levi Strauss sells millions of dollars of Levi's abroad at discount prices – all authorised sales.

Here is an example of what is repeated in city after city all over the USA. 'They come into a store in groups and buy every pair of Levi's 501 jeans they can,' says one store manager. He has seen two or three vans full of people come to the store when there is a sale and buy the six-pairs-a-day limit, returning day after day until the sale is over.

In another retail chain store, where a similar thing was happening, a month-long storewide sale was stopped, at the behest of Levi's, after only two weeks. The Levi's are then channelled to a diverter, who exports them to unauthorised buyers throughout the world. Many eventually end up in discount stores and are sold at discounted prices relative to those distributed through approved channels.

►

◀

These practices are feasible because the retail prices in the USA are often more competitive than in other countries where, historically, price competition is not as fierce. For example, Levi's 501s sell for $100 in Britain versus $70 in the USA. Some, but not all, of the price differences can be attributed to price escalation – that is, tariffs, shipping and other costs associated with exporting – but that portion of the difference attributable to higher margins creates an opportunity for profitable diverting.

In an attempt to stop discount stores not in the manufacturer's official distribution channel from selling 'unauthorised Levi's', Tesco, a UK supermarket chain, was sued by Levi Strauss & Company. After a four-year court battle, Levi's won when it was ruled that the supermarket had been selling Levi's illegally. However, Tesco, Costco, Wal-Mart and other mass retailers cater to a vast market interested in value-priced, quality products – a market Levi Strauss misses if its products are not sold there.

- How can Levi's handle this problem?

Sources: Jim Hill, 'Flight of the 501s', *Oregonian*, 27 June 1993, p G1; 'Diversion!', *Journal of Commerce*, 26 June 2000, p WP; Jean Eaglesham and Deborah Hargreaves, 'Court Left to Iron Out Brand Import Wrinkle: Levi's v Tesco', *National Post*, 24 January 2001, p C3; 'Levi's Win in Court', *Daily Record*, 1 August 2002; 'Levi Plans Tesco Line', *The Mirror*, 25 April 2003, p 4; and www.levistrauss.com/news, 2005.

Skimming versus penetration pricing

Firms must also decide when to follow a **skimming** or a **penetration-pricing** policy. Traditionally, the decision on which policy to follow depends on the level of competition, the innovativeness of the product, and market characteristics (see Exhibit 18.2).[5]

A company skims when the objective is to reach a segment of the market that is relatively price-insensitive and thus willing to pay a premium price for the value received. If limited supply exists, a company may follow a skimming approach in order to maximise revenue and to match demand to supply. When a company is the only seller of a new or innovative product, a skimming price may be used to maximise profits until competition forces a lower price.

Skimming is often used in those markets where there are only two income levels: the wealthy and the poor. Costs prohibit setting a price that will be attractive to the lower income market so the marketer charges a premium price and directs the product to the high-income, relatively price-inelastic segment. Today, such opportunities are fading away as the disparity in income levels is giving way to growing middle-income market segments.

A penetration-pricing policy is used to stimulate market growth and capture market share by deliberately offering products at low prices. Penetration pricing is most often used to acquire and hold share of a market as a competitive manoeuvre. However, in country markets experiencing rapid and sustained economic growth and where large parts of the population move into middle-income classes, penetration

skimming

charging a high price to maximise profit in the early stages of a product's introduction

penetration pricing

charging lower prices to gain market share in a new market

EXHIBIT 18.2: Skimming versus penetration strategies in marketing

	Promotion	
	high	low
Price high	Rapid-skimming strategy	Slow-skimming strategy
Price low	Rapid-penetration strategy	Slow-penetration strategy

pricing may be used to stimulate market growth even with minimum competition. Penetration pricing may be a more profitable strategy than skimming if it maximises revenues and builds market share as a base for the competition that is sure to come.

As many of the potential market growth trends that were set in place in the early 1990s begin to pay dividends with economic growth and a more equitable distribution of wealth within local economies, and as distinct market segments emerge within and across country markets, global companies will have to make more sophisticated pricing decisions than were made when companies directed their marketing efforts only towards single market segments.

Leasing in international markets

> **leasing**
>
> borrowing/renting or paying in instalments

An important selling technique to alleviate high prices and capital shortages for capital equipment is the leasing system. The concept of equipment **leasing** has become increasingly important as a means of selling capital equipment in overseas markets. In fact, it is estimated that €45bn ($50bn) worth (original cost) of foreign-made equipment is on lease in Western Europe.

The system of leasing used by industrial exporters is quite simple. Terms of the leases usually run from one to five years, with payments made monthly or annually; included in the rental fee are servicing, repairs and spare parts. Just as contracts for domestic and overseas leasing arrangements are similar, so are the basic motivations and the shortcomings. Here are some examples.

1 Leasing opens the door to a large segment of nominally financed foreign firms that can be sold on a lease option but might be unable to buy for cash.

2 Leasing can ease the problems of selling new, experimental equipment, because less risk is involved for the users.

3 Leasing helps guarantee better maintenance and service on overseas equipment.

4 Equipment leased and in use helps to sell to other companies in that country.

5 Lease revenue tends to be more stable over a period of time than direct sales would be.

The disadvantages or shortcomings take on an international flavour. Besides the inherent disadvantages of leasing, some problems are compounded by international relationships. In a country beset with inflation, lease contracts that include maintenance and supply parts, as most do, can lead to heavy losses towards the end of the contract period. The added problems of currency devaluation or other political risks are operative longer than if the sale of the same equipment is made outright. In the light of these perils, there is greater risk in leasing than in outright sale; however, there is a definite trend towards increased use of this method of selling internationally.[6]

Going International 18.3

BMW IN WARNING ON PRICING PRESSURES

BMW warned of increasing pricing pressure in the premium end of the auto market as the world's largest luxury car maker surprised the markets with a smaller than expected loss. Norbert Reithofer, BMW's chief executive, said rival premium car makers were offering heavy incentives to car buyers in an effort to rapidly reduce their large piles of unsold cars.

'Some rivals try to push their cars to the market with high incentives,' Mr Reithofer said, without naming the companies. 'This shows that the worldwide car market has not started to recover yet.' Analysts have said that a number of premium car makers were slow to put the brakes on production after global demand started to collapse late last year. They singled out BMW's rival Daimler in particular, which burned more than €1bn in

▶

◄

cash in the first quarter after its inventories weighed heavily on its financials.

Daimler said it had reduced its inventory of unsold cars by the end of March 2009 and it aimed to return to normal levels. But analysts suspected BMW was itself fuelling the price war with its leasing policy. 'Current leasing rates still suggest the company is selling at subsidised rates,' Arndt Ellinghorst, analyst at Credit Suisse, said.

Friedrich Eichiner, BMW's chief financial officer, conceded the group might have to join the incentive battle in the market, which had had an impact on its earnings in the first quarter. He said he expected the price pressure to abate during the year.

© P.N. Ghauri.

Analysts have pressed BMW and Daimler – which already collaborate on hybrid engine technologies and small purchasing projects – to work closer together. They have argued that both car makers lack the necessary scale to compete in a rapidly shrinking premium car market.

- Has the car industry recovered from the crisis? Discuss.

Source: *Financial Times*, 7 May 2009.

Factors influencing international pricing

People travelling abroad are often surprised to find goods that are relatively inexpensive in their home country priced outrageously higher in other countries. It is also possible that goods priced reasonably abroad may be priced enormously high in the home market. Beginning with the import tariff, each time a product changes hands an additional cost is incurred. First, the product passes through the hands of an importer, then to the company with primary responsibility for sales and service, then to a secondary or even a tertiary local distributor, and finally to the retailer and the consumer. The factors influencing pricing in international markets include the objective of the firm in a particular market, price escalation, competition, target customer segment and pricing control (see Exhibit 18.3).

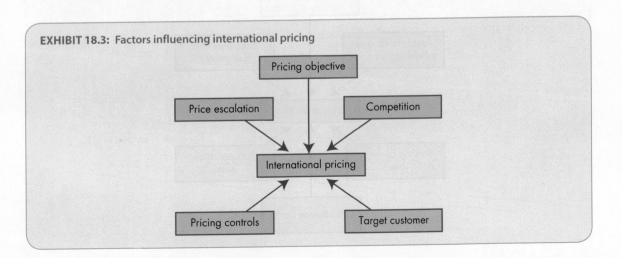

EXHIBIT 18.3: Factors influencing international pricing

Pricing objectives

In general, price decisions are viewed two ways: pricing as an active instrument of accomplishing marketing objectives or pricing as a static element in a business decision. If the former view is followed, the company uses price to achieve a specific objective, whether a targeted return on profits, a targeted market share or some other specific goal. The company that follows the second approach probably exports only excess inventory, places a low priority on foreign business and views its export sales as passive contributions to sales volume. Profit is by far the most important pricing objective. Pricing objectives should be consistent with the marketing objectives of the firm in a particular market as well as the overall strategy of the firm. Essentially, objectives are defined in terms of profit, market share or positioning.

The more control a company has over the final selling price of a product, the better it is able to achieve its marketing goals. However, it is not always possible to control end prices, and in this case, companies may resort to 'mill net pricing'; that is, the price received at the plant.

price escalation

an increase in price when products move from one country to another

Price escalation

Excess profits do exist in some international markets, but generally the cause of the disproportionate difference in price between the exporting country and the importing country, here termed **price escalation**, is the added costs incurred as a result of exporting products from one country to another. Specifically, the term relates to situations where ultimate prices are raised by shipping costs, insurance, packing, tariffs, longer channels of distribution, larger middlemen margins, special taxes, administrative costs and exchange-rate fluctuations (see Exhibit 18.4). The majority of these costs arise as a direct result of moving goods across borders from one country to another and combine to escalate the final price to a level considerably higher than in the domestic market.

Taxes, tariffs and administrative costs

'Nothing is surer than death and taxes' has a particularly familiar ring to the ears of the international trader because taxes include tariffs, and tariffs are one of the most pervasive features of international trading. Taxes and tariffs affect the ultimate consumer price for a product and, in most instances, the consumer bears the burden of both. Sometimes, however, the consumer benefits when manufacturers selling goods in foreign countries reduce their net return to gain access to a foreign market. Absorbed or passed on, taxes and tariffs must be considered by the international business person.

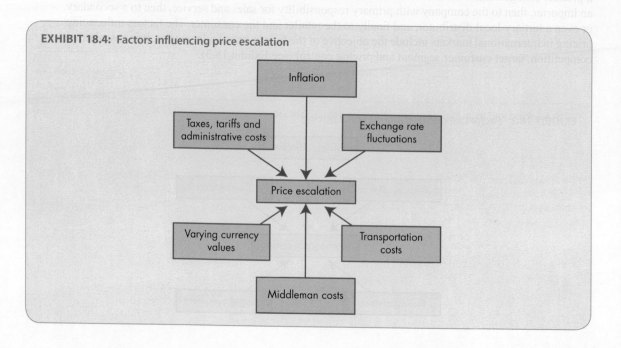

EXHIBIT 18.4: Factors influencing price escalation

A tariff, or duty, is a special form of taxation and, like other forms of taxes, may be levied for the purpose of protecting a market or for increasing government revenue. A tariff is a fee charged when goods are brought into a country from another country. The level of tariff is typically expressed as the rate of duty and may be levied as specific, *ad valorem*, or a combination. A *specific* duty is a flat charge per physical unit imported, such as 15 cents per bushel of rye. *Ad valorem* duties are levied as a percentage of the value of the goods imported, such as 20 per cent of the value of imported watches. *Combination* tariffs include both a specific and an *ad valorem* charge, such as €1 per camera plus 10 per cent of its value.

In addition to taxes and tariffs, there are a variety of administrative costs directly associated with exporting and importing a product. Acquiring export and import licences and other documents and the physical arrangements for getting the product from port of entry to the buyer's location mean additional costs. While such costs are relatively small, they add to the overall cost of exporting.

Inflation

The effect of inflation on cost must be taken into account. In countries with rapid inflation or **exchange variation**, the selling price must be related to the cost of goods sold and the cost of replacing the items. Goods are often sold below their cost of replacement plus overhead, and sometimes are sold below replacement cost. In these instances, the company would be better off not to sell the products at all. When payment is likely to be delayed for several months or is worked out on a long-term contract, inflationary factors must be figured into the price.

> **exchange variation**
> variation in the exchange rate of two currencies

Because inflation is beyond the control of companies, they use a variety of techniques to inflate the selling price to compensate for inflation pressure and price controls. They may charge for extra services, inflate costs in transfer pricing, break up products into components and price each component separately, or require the purchase of two or more products simultaneously and refuse to deliver one product unless the purchaser agrees to take another, more expensive, item as well. Exhibit 18.5 focuses on the different price strategies a company might employ under a weak or strong domestic currency.

Exchange-rate fluctuations

At one time, world trade contracts could be easily written and payment was specified in a relatively stable currency. The American dollar was the standard and all transactions could be related to it. Now

---

EXHIBIT 18.5: Pricing strategies under varying currency conditions

When domestic currency is WEAK...	When domestic currency is STRONG...
Stress price benefits	Engage in non-price competition by improving quality, delivery and after-sale service
Expand product line and add more costly features	Improve productivity and engage in vigorous cost reduction
Shift sourcing and manufacturing to domestic market	Shift sourcing and manufacturing overseas
Exploit export opportunities in all markets	Give priority to exports to relatively strong-currency countries
Conduct conventional cash-for-goods trade	Deal in countertrade with weak-currency countries
Use full-costing approach, but use marginal-cost pricing to penetrate new/competitive markets	Trim profit margins and use marginal-cost pricing
Speed repatriation of foreign-earned income and collections	Keep the foreign-earned income in host country, slow collections
Minimise expenditures in local, host-country currency	Maximise expenditures in local, host-country currency
Buy needed services (advertising, insurance, transportation, etc) in domestic market	Buy needed services abroad and pay for them in local currencies
Minimise local borrowing	Borrow money needed for expansion in local market
Bill foreign customers in domestic currency	Bill foreign customers in their own currency

that all major currencies are floating freely relative to one another, no one is quite sure of the value of any currency in the future. Increasingly, companies are insisting that transactions be written in terms of the vendor company's national currency, and forward **hedging** is becoming more common.

> **hedging**
>
> insuring against a negative currency rate

If exchange rates are not carefully considered in long-term contracts, companies find themselves unwittingly giving 15–20 per cent discounts. The added cost incurred as exchange rates fluctuate on a day-to-day basis must be taken into account, especially where there is a significant time lapse between signing the order and delivery of the goods. Exchange-rate differentials mount up. Due to exchange rate fluctuations in one year, Nestlé lost a million dollars in six months, while other companies have lost and gained even larger amounts.

Varying currency values

In addition to risks from exchange-rate variations, other risks result from the changing values of a country's currency relative to other currencies. Consider the situation in Germany for a purchaser of US-manufactured goods for the period 2001–2004. During this period, the value of the US dollar relative to the euro went from a very strong position ($0.80 to €1) in 2001 to a weaker position in late 2004 ($1.30 to €1). A strong dollar produces price resistance because it takes a larger quantity of local currency to buy a US dollar. Conversely, when the US dollar is weak, demand for US goods increases because fewer units of local currency are needed to buy a US dollar. The weaker US dollar, compared to most of the world's stronger currencies that existed during 2003 and 2004, helped the US economy to recover from the shocks of 9/11.[7]

When the value of the dollar is weak relative to the buyer's currency (ie it takes fewer units of the foreign currency to buy a dollar), companies generally employ cost-plus pricing. To remain price competitive when the dollar is strong (ie when it takes more units of the foreign currency to buy a dollar), companies must find ways to offset the higher price caused by currency values. By comparing the price of a relatively standardised product, it is possible to gain an insight into the under- or over-valuation of currencies (see Exhibit 18.6).

EXHIBIT 18.6: The hamburger standard (2011)

	Big Mac prices in dollars*	Implied PPP[†] of the dollar	Under(−)/over (+) valuation against the dollar, %
USA	4.33	1.00	0.00
Argentina	4.16	4.39	−3.85
Australia	4.68	1.05	8.15
Austria	3.87	0.74	−10.63
Belgium	4.61	0.88	6.46
Brazil	4.94	2.33	14.06
Britain	4.16	0.62	−3.82
Canada	5.02	1.18	16.06
Chile	4.16	473.71	−3.92
China	2.45	3.62	−43.39
Colombia	4.77	1987.29	10.13
Costa Rica	2.40	277.30	−44.65
Czech Republic	3.34	16.25	−22.79
Denmark	4.65	6.59	7.34
Egypt	2.64	3.70	−39.05
Estonia	2.47	0.47	−42.85
Euro area	4.34	0.83	0.39
Finland	4.55	0.87	5.06

▶

◀

EXHIBIT 18.6: The hamburger standard (2011)

	Big Mac prices in dollars*	Implied PPP† of the dollar	Under(−)/over (+) valuation against the dollar, %
France	4.36	0.83	0.85
Germany	4.41	0.84	1.97
Greece	3.25	0.62	−24.84
Hong Kong	2.13	3.81	−50.85
Hungary	3.48	191.80	−19.49
India	1.58	20.57	−63.38
Indonesia	2.55	5592.14	−41.03
Ireland	4.23	0.81	−2.23
Israel	2.92	2.75	−32.54
Italy	4.36	0.83	0.85
Japan	4.09	73.95	−5.46
Latvia	2.94	0.39	−32.01
Lithuania	2.74	1.80	−36.71
Malaysia	2.33	1.71	−46.12
Mexico	2.70	8.55	−37.53
Netherlands	4.10	0.78	−5.31
New Zealand	4.00	1.18	−7.46
Norway	7.06	9.94	63.11
Pakistan	3.01	65.86	−30.39
Philippines	2.80	27.27	−35.39
Poland	2.63	2.10	−39.23
Portugal	6.00	1.14	38.67
Russia	2.29	17.33	−47.11
Saudi Arabia	2.67	2.31	−38.38
Singapore	3.50	1.02	−19.21
South Africa	2.36	4.61	−45.56
South Korea	3.21	855.00	−25.72
Spain	4.24	0.81	−1.95
Sri Lanka	2.21	67.01	−48.84
Sweden	6.94	11.18	60.29
Switzerland	6.56	1.50	51.63
Taiwan	2.48	17.33	−42.60
Thailand	2.59	18.95	−40.23
Turkey	4.52	1.91	4.35
UAE	3.27	2.77	−24.50
Ukraine	1.86	3.47	−57.13
Uruguay	4.53	22.88	4.60
Venezuela	7.92	7.86	82.94

Sources: based on McDonald's; Thomson Reuters; IMF; and *The Economist,* July 2012.

Middleman

Channel length and marketing patterns vary widely. In some countries, channels are longer and middleman margins higher than is customary. The diversity of channels used to reach markets and the lack of standardised middleman mark-ups leave many producers unaware of the ultimate price of a product.

Besides channel diversity, the fully integrated marketer operating abroad faces various unanticipated costs because marketing and distribution channel infrastructures are underdeveloped in many countries. The marketer can also incur added expenses for warehousing and handling of small shipments, and may have to bear increased financing costs when dealing with underfinanced middlemen. Because no convenient source of data on middleman costs is available, the international marketer must rely on experience and marketing research to ascertain middleman costs.

Going International 18.4

PRICING AND SPECIAL OFFERS

© Tesco PLC http://www.tescoplc.com/
index.asp?pageid=69&mediastart=109

What a thrilling bargain. A Breville sandwich toaster in the Sainsbury's half-price sale, down from £19.99. Customers love it.

The toaster in question is on Breville's own website with a recommended retail price of £19.99. Curry's is selling it for £19.99, while at Pixmania it is £13.60.

As we all know, a manufacturer's RRP is the maximum you ever pay for an item, from which you usually obtain a discount. Sainsbury's, however, appears to have offered it at an extraordinarily high price, then cut it back to the standard price and told customers they were getting a 'half-price offer'.

A survey found that Asda was selling a Goodfella's Deep Pan Pepperoni Pizza at a standard price of about £1, but when it went on to a multibuy deal, the price jumped to £2.50 for one or £4.50 for two. Many multibuys actually left shoppers worse off.

Sainsbury's Breville deal was brought to our attention by a reader, David Godson. When asked, Sainsbury's replied: 'We aim to be fair and transparent about our pricing,' which is the sort of meaningless corporate speak PR people pump out all the time, though it went on to say, in this instance, 'we have not been as competitive as our customers would expect'.

When Godson originally wrote to Sainsbury's, it told him the toaster had been 'on sale in our stores on two separate occasions for a substantial period at £39.99 ... we benchmarked the price of this product against another leading electrical retailers (sic), this is standard industry practice'.

It says it will now mark the sandwich maker at £19.99 as full market price. But this is just one, small, example, spotted by a shopper who brought it to our attention. How many other promotions are not quite what they seem? We as consumers simply don't know.

- Do special offers give us better value for our money?

Source: based on *The Guardian*, 19 January 2013.

Transportation

Exporting also incurs increased transportation costs when moving goods from one country to another. If the goods go over water, there are additional costs for insurance, packing and handling not generally added to locally produced goods. Such costs add yet another burden because import tariffs in many

EXHIBIT 18.7: Sample causes and effects of price escalation (€)

	Domestic example	Foreign example 1: assuming the same channels with wholesaler importing directly	Foreign example 2: importer and same margins and channels	Foreign example 3: same as 2 but with 10% cumulative turnover tax
Manufacturing net	5.00	5.00	5.00	5.00
Transport cif	n.a.	6.10	6.10	6.10
Tariff (20% cif value)	n.a.	1.22	1.22	1.22
Importer pays	n.a.	n.a.	7.32	7.32
Importer margin when sold to wholesaler (25%) on cost	n.a.	n.a.	1.83	1.83
				+0.73 turnover tax
Wholesaler pays landed cost	5.00	7.32	9.15	9.88
Wholesaler margin (33.3% on cost)	1.67	2.44	3.05	3.29
				+0.99 turnover tax
Retailer pays	6.67	9.76	12.20	14.16
Retail margin (50% on cost)	3.34	4.88	6.10	7.08
				+1.42 turnover tax
Retail price	€10.01	€14.64	€18.30	€22.66

Notes: a All figures in euros; cif = cost, insurance and freight; n.a. = not applicable.
b The table assumes that all domestic transportation costs are absorbed by the middleman.
c Transportation, tariffs and middleman margins vary from country to country, but for purposes of comparison, only a few of the possible variations are shown.

countries are based on the landed cost that includes transportation, insurance and shipping charges. These costs add to the inflation of the final price. The next section details how a reasonable price in the home market may more than double in the foreign market.

Exhibit 18.7 illustrates some of the effects these factors may have on the end price of a consumer item. Because costs and tariffs vary so widely from country to country, a hypothetical but realistic example is used. It assumes: (1) that a constant net price is received by the manufacturer; (2) that all domestic transportation costs are absorbed by the various middlemen and reflected in their margins; and (3) that the foreign middlemen have the same margins as the domestic middlemen. In some instances, foreign middlemen margins are lower, but it is equally probable that these margins could be greater. In fact, in many instances, middlemen use higher wholesale and retail margins for foreign goods than for similar domestic goods.

Notice that the retail prices in Exhibit 18.7 range widely, illustrating the difficulty of **price control** by manufacturers in overseas retail markets. No matter how much the manufacturer may wish to market a product in a foreign country for a price equivalent to €10, there is little opportunity for such control. Even assuming the most optimistic conditions for foreign exchange, the producer would need to cut the net price by more than one-third to absorb freight and tariff costs if the goods are to be priced the same in both foreign and domestic markets.

> **price control**
> when prices are regulated/fixed by an authority

Unless price escalation can be reduced, marketers find that the only buyers left are the wealthier ones. If marketers are to compete successfully in the growth of markets around the world, cost containment must be among their highest priorities. If costs can be reduced anywhere along the chain from manufacturer's cost to **retailer mark-ups**, price escalation will be reduced. A discussion of some of the approaches to lessening price escalation follows.

> **retailer mark-ups**
> the profit margin of the retailer

Approaches to lessening price escalation

There are four efforts whereby costs may be reduced in attempting to lower price escalation: (1) lower the cost of goods; (2) lower the tariffs; (3) lower the distribution costs; and (4) use foreign-trade zones.

Lower the cost of goods

If the manufacturer's price can be lowered, the effect is felt throughout the chain. One of the important reasons for manufacturing in a third country is an attempt to reduce manufacturing costs and, thus, price escalation. The impact can be profound if you consider that the hourly cost of skilled labour in India is less than €1.8 ($2) an hour, including benefits, compared with more than €13 ($15) in Germany.

For the US General Electric company (GE), the costs of manufacturing a typical microwave oven are GE €197 ($218), compared to €140 ($155) for Samsung, a Korean manufacturer. A breakdown of costs reveals that assembly labour costs GE €7.2 ($8) per oven and the Korean firm only €0.57 ($0.63). Overhead labour for supervision, maintenance and set-up was €27 ($30) per GE oven and €0.66 ($0.73) for the Korean company. The largest area of difference was for line and central management; that came to €18 ($20) per oven for GE versus €0.02 ($0.02) for Samsung. Perhaps the most disturbing finding was that Korean labourers delivered more for less cost. GE produced four units per person whereas the Korean company produced nine.

Lowering manufacturing costs can often have a double benefit – the lower price to the buyer may also mean lower tariffs, since most tariffs are levied on an *ad valorem* basis.

Lower the tariffs

When tariffs account for a large part of price escalation, as they often do, companies seek ways to lower the rate. Some products can be reclassified into a different, and lower, customs classification. An American company selling data communications equipment in Australia faced a 25 per cent tariff, which affected the price competitiveness of its products. It persuaded the Australian government to change the classification for the types of product the company sells from 'computer equipment' (25 per cent tariff) to 'telecommunication equipment' (3 per cent tariff). Like many products, this company's products could be legally classified under either category.

There are often differential rates between fully assembled, ready-to-use products and those requiring some assembly, further processing, the addition of locally manufactured component parts or other processing that adds value to the product and can be performed within the foreign country. A ready-to-operate piece of machinery with a 20 per cent tariff may be subject to only a 12 per cent tariff when imported unassembled. An even lower tariff may apply when the product is assembled in the country and some local content is added.

Lower the distribution costs

Shorter channels can help keep prices under control. Designing a channel that has fewer middlemen may lower distribution costs by reducing or eliminating middleman mark-up. Besides eliminating mark-ups, fewer middlemen may mean lower overall taxes. Some countries levy a value-added tax on goods as they pass through various channels. Each time goods change hands, they are taxed. The tax may be cumulative or non-cumulative.

The cumulative value-added tax is based on total selling price and is assessed every time the goods change hands. Obviously, in countries where value-added tax is cumulative, tax alone provides a special incentive for developing short distribution channels. Where that is achieved, tax is paid only on the difference between the middleman's cost and the selling price.

Use foreign-trade zones

Some countries have established foreign- or free-trade zones (FTZs) or free ports to facilitate international trade. There are more than 300 of these facilities in operation throughout the world where imported goods can be stored or processed.

As free-trade policies in Asia, Eastern Europe and other developing regions expand, there has been an equally rapid expansion in the creation and use of FTZs. In a free port or FTZ, payment of import duties is postponed until the product leaves the FTZ area and enters the country. An FTZ is, in essence, a tax-free enclave and not considered part of the country as far as import regulations are concerned. When an item leaves an FTZ and is officially imported into the host country of the FTZ, all duties and regulations are imposed.[8]

By shipping unassembled goods to an FTZ in an importing country, a marketer can lower costs in a variety of ways.

1 Tariffs may be lower because duties are typically assessed at a lower rate for unassembled versus assembled goods.

2 If labour costs are lower in the importing country, substantial savings may be realised in the final product cost.

3 Ocean transportation rates are affected by weight and volume; thus, unassembled goods may qualify for lower freight rates.

4 If local content, such as packaging or component parts, can be used in the final assembly, there may be a further reduction of tariffs.

All in all, an FTZ is an important method for controlling price escalation. Incidentally, all the advantages offered by an FTZ for an exporter are also advantages for an importer. These zones are used in many countries in the West, as well as in the emerging markets. Over 100 FTZs in the USA are used by US importers to help lower their costs of imported goods.[9]

Competition

The nature of market structure in particular is an important determinant of price. It refers to the number of competing firms, their size and relative position. In the case of an oligopoly structure, the entering firm would have little freedom to choose a price. Depending on income levels, a certain market can take only a certain level of pricing. The prices have thus to be set at the level of the competing products.

A company can also use competitors' prices as a landmark for positioning its products as compared to those of competitors. For example, if it wants to position its product as being of higher quality than its competitors' products, it has to price it accordingly. On the other hand, if a company decides to compete with its competitors on price, it has to set a competitive price. When entering a market and using competitive pricing, a company needs also to check on the cost structure of its competitors. The price is just one of the elements of the marketing mix and has thus to be matched with other elements of it. When a higher price is charged, the company should be able to convince the market that it has a better product, thereby justifying its higher price.

Target customer

Marketers have to evaluate and understand a particular segment or target customer group in the market that they are entering. Knowledge of **demand elasticity** and price is essential, as is knowledge of how customers would react in the case of price change. Demand for a product is *elastic* if demand can be considerably increased by lowering the price. If a decrease in price would have little effect on demand, it will be considered *inelastic*.

> **demand elasticity**
>
> when demand for a product changes due to minor changes in the price

Other than buying behaviour, the ability of customers to buy, prices of substitute and competing products, and the nature of non-price competition are of the utmost importance. In the case of undifferentiated products, the competition is more focused on pricing, but with differentiated products, market share of a company can even be enhanced through higher prices. Brand names and an image of high quality are two of the factors that characterise differentiated products that can be sold at premium prices.

Going International 18.5

HOW ARE FOREIGN-TRADE ZONES USED?

There are more than 100 foreign-trade zones (FTZs) in the USA and FTZs exist in many other countries as well. Companies use them to postpone the payment of tariffs on products while they are in the FTZ. Here are some examples of how FTZs are used in the USA.

- A Japanese firm assembles motorcycles, jet skis and three-wheel all-terrain vehicles for import as well as for export to Canada, Latin America and Europe.

- A US manufacturer of window blinds and miniblinds imports and stores fabric from Holland in an FTZ, thereby postponing a 17 per cent tariff until the fabric leaves the FTZ.

- A manufacturer of hair-dryers stores its products in an FTZ, which it uses as its main distribution centre for products manufactured in Asia.

- A European-based medical supply company manufactures kidney dialysis machines and sterile tubing using raw materials from Germany and US labour. It then exports 30 per cent of its products to Scandinavian countries.

- A Canadian company assembles electronic teaching machines using cabinets from Italy, electronics from Taiwan, Korea and Japan, and labour from the USA, for export to Colombia and Peru.

In all these examples, tariffs are postponed until the products leave the FTZ and enter the USA. Further, in most situations the tariff is at the lower rate for component parts and raw materials versus the higher rate that would have been charged if imported directly as finished goods. If the finished products are not imported into the USA from the FTZ, but shipped to another country, no US tariffs apply.

Sources: Lewis E. Leibowitz, 'An Overview of Foreign Trade Zones', *Europe*, Winter–Spring 1987, p 12; and 'Cheap Imports', *International Business*, March 1993, pp 98–100.

Pricing controls

Companies doing business in foreign countries encounter a number of different types of government price setting. To control prices, governments may establish margins, set prices and floors or ceilings, restrict price changes, compete in the market, grant subsidies or act as a purchasing **monopsony** or selling monopoly. The government may also influence prices by permitting, or even encouraging, businesses to collude in setting manipulative prices.

monopsony

the buying-side of a selling-side monopoly

In most countries, governments regulate pricing. All these rules and regulations need to be considered while setting prices. A number of governments, although liberal on price setting, restrict price changes. A company entering a foreign market with a penetration strategy of a lower price, hoping to increase the price after achieving a certain market share, might not be able to change its price. In Europe, a number of rules and regulations are being changed and standardised.

Price controls are normally exercised for political and social reasons such as to control inflation, protect consumers from unjustified price increases and stimulate equal distribution of wealth. Price controls are not only limited to developing countries. In the 1980s countries such as France, Sweden and the USA enforced **price freezes** to control inflation and balance of payments. To cover against the impact of price freezes and controls, firms should regularly review prices in inflationary markets. Firms should watch out for such measures and pre-empt such controls. One way out of them is to keep introducing new products. Another way is to review payment terms and other conditions of sale such as discounts and credits.

price freezes

when the price of a product cannot be increased

Administered pricing

Administered pricing relates to attempts to establish prices for an entire market. Such prices may be arranged through the cooperation of competitors, through national, state or local governments or by international agreement. The legality of administered pricing arrangements of various kinds differs from country to country and from time to time. A country may condone price fixing for foreign markets but condemn it for the domestic market.

In general, the end goal of all administered pricing activities is to reduce the impact of price competition or eliminate it. Price fixing by business is not viewed as an acceptable practice but when governments enter the field of price administration, they presume to do it for the general good: to lessen the effects of 'destructive' competition.

> **administered pricing**
>
> relates to attempts to establish/fix prices for an entire market

Price setting by industry groups

The pervasiveness of **price fixing** attempts in business is reflected by the diversity of the language of administered prices: pricing arrangements are known as agreements, arrangements, combines, conspiracies, cartels, communities of profit, profit pools, licensing, trade associations, price leadership, customary pricing or informal interfirm agreements. The arrangements themselves vary from the completely informal, with no spoken or acknowledged agreement, to highly formalised and structured arrangements. Any type of price-fixing arrangement can be adapted to international business; but of all the forms mentioned, the three most directly associated with international marketing are licensing, cartels and trade associations.

> **price fixing**
>
> when competing companies agree to set a price for their products

---

Going International 18.6

BA, VIRGIN FINED IN PRICE-FIXING SCHEME

The airlines agreed to resolve a class action on fuel-surcharge price-fixing. Individual awards could be small, but the lawyers stand to make a bundle

© British Airways http://www.britishairways.com/travel/press-office-image-gallery/public/en_gb;
© Virgin Atlantic, Digital News Agency 2010, http://virginatlantic.digitalnewsagency.com/stories/5385/images

British Airways and Virgin Atlantic are to pay around £100m to passengers following a US lawsuit brought on behalf of UK and American travellers affected by fuel surcharge price-fixing. But while lawyers involved could end up many millions of pounds richer, passengers in the UK might get as little as £1 per ticket in compensation.

▶

◄

BA said that BA and Virgin had agreed in principle to resolve the class-action litigation pending in a California court. It is thought that the settlement, which still has to be finally approved, will cost BA about £70m and Virgin about £34m. The BA total includes about £45.5m for UK passengers affected.

BA said that about 11 million passengers – including 7 million in the UK – were affected by the settlement. It added that the settlement was worth between £1 and £11.50 per ticket purchased for the affected long-haul flights by UK passengers and between $1.50 (about 75p) and $20.50 (about £11.25) for US passengers.

BA was already fined £121.5m by the Office of Fair Trading (OFT) last year and a further $300m (about £150m) by the US Department of Justice after it was found guilty of conspiring to fix fuel surcharges.

Virgin escaped financial punishment last year after the group came forward to expose the collusion. BA chief executive Willie Walsh, said: 'As we have previously said, we absolutely condemn any anti-competitive activity by anybody.

'This settlement, which BA and Virgin Atlantic have jointly agreed with the lawyers for the plaintiffs, is fair and reasonable. BA can now move on and do what we do best – delivering excellent customer service.'

A spokesman for Virgin Atlantic said: 'We deeply regret our involvement in this matter and believe that the provisional settlement reached draws a line under this episode.' BA could be forced to set aside more cash on top of the £350m provision made last year as the group also faces possible further regulatory fines and class action suits across Europe.

BA and Virgin admitted colluding over fuel surcharges on long-haul flights between August 2004 and January 2006. The charges, which came in response to rising oil prices, increased from £5 to £60 per ticket for a typical BA or Virgin long-haul return flight over that period.

Sources: *The Independent*, 15 February 2008; 'Virgin', http://www.theasiasun.com/virgin-airlines-australia-and-singapore-airlines-announced-collaboration; and British Airways, www.planespotters.net/Aviation_Photos.

Licensing agreements

In industries where technological innovation is especially important, patent or process agreements are the most common type of international combination. In most countries, licensing agreements are legally acceptable because the owners of patents and other processes are granting an exclusive licence to someone in another country to produce a product.

By contractual definition, a patent holder can control territorial boundaries and, because of the monopoly, can control pricing. Often such arrangements go beyond a specific licensing agreement to include a gentlemen's agreement to give their foreign counterparts first rights on patents and new developments. Such arrangements can lead to national monopolies that significantly restrict competition and thereby raise product prices. Like so many other agreements related to restricting competition, the legality of licensing agreements is difficult to discuss outside the context of a specific situation.[10]

Cartels

cartels

exist when various companies producing similar products work together to control markets for the types of goods they produce

Generally, a **cartel** involves more than a patent licensing agreement and endows the participants with greater power. The cartel association may use formal agreements to set prices, establish levels of production and sales for the participating companies, allocate market territories and even redistribute profits. In some instances, the cartel organisation itself takes over the entire selling function, sells the goods of all the producers and distributes the profits.

The economic role of cartels is highly debatable, but their proponents argue that they eliminate cut-throat competition and 'rationalise' business, permitting greater technical progress and lower prices to consumers. However, in the view of most experts, it is doubtful that the consumer benefits very often from cartels.

The Organization of Petroleum Exporting Countries (OPEC) is probably the best-known international cartel. Its power in controlling the price of oil resulted from the percentage of oil production it controlled. In 2004, a sudden rise in price, as a result of the war in Iraq, from €15 ($18) a barrel to €45 ($18) or more a barrel, was one of the factors which threw the world into a major recession. Non-OPEC oil exporting countries benefited from the price increase while net importers of foreign oil suffered economic downturns. Among less-developed countries, those producing oil prospered while oil importers suffered economically as a result of the high prices.[10]

The legality of cartels is not clearly defined at present. Domestic cartelisation is illegal in most Western countries, and the EU has specific provisions for controlling cartels. The USA, however, does permit firms to take cartel-like actions in foreign markets. Increasingly, it has become apparent that many governments have concluded that they cannot ignore or destroy cartels completely, so they have chosen to establish ground rules and regulatory agencies to oversee the cartel-like activities of businesses within their jurisdiction.

Trade associations

The term **trade association** is so broad that it is almost meaningless. Trade associations may exist as hard, tight cartels or merely informal trade organisations having nothing to do with pricing, market share or levels of production. In many countries, trade associations gather information about prices and transactions within a given industry. Such associations have the general goal of protecting and maintaining the pricing structure most generally acceptable to industry members.

> **trade association**
> association of companies belonging to the same industry

Going International 18.7

DE BEERS: ONE OF THE RICHEST CARTELS

Other than OPEC, DeBeers, the diamond company, is one of the world's largest cartels. It practically controls most of the world's diamond trade and is thus able to maintain artificially high prices for diamonds. One of the ways in which it maintains control is illustrated by a recent agreement with Russia's diamond monopoly, where DeBeers will buy at least $550m in rough gem diamonds from Russia, which is half of the country's annual output. By controlling output from Russia, the second-biggest diamond producer in the world, the DeBeers cartel will continue to control the diamond trade and keep the prices at a very high level. Thus the South African cartel will control the diamond trade for a long time to come.

© Susan Van Etten/Photo Edit.

- Should cartels such as those of DeBeers and OPEC be allowed? Why/why not?

Source: compiled from various sources.

In most industrial nations manufacturers' associations frequently represent 90 to 100 per cent of an industry. The association is a club one must join for access to customers and suppliers. It often handles industry-wide labour negotiations and is capable of influencing government decisions relating to the industry.

International agreements

Governments of producing and consuming countries seem to play an ever-increasing role in the establishment of international prices for certain basic commodities. There is, for example, an international coffee agreement, an international cocoa agreement and an international sugar agreement. The world price of wheat has long been at least partially determined by negotiations between national governments.

Despite the pressures of business, government and international price agreements, most marketers still have wide latitude in their pricing decisions for most products and markets.

Transfer pricing

As companies increase the number of worldwide subsidiaries, joint ventures, company-owned distributing systems and other marketing arrangements, the price charged to different affiliates becomes a pre-eminent question. Prices of goods transferred from operations or sales units in one country to a company's units elsewhere may be adjusted to enhance the ultimate profit of the company as a whole. The benefits of **transfer pricing** are as follows:

> **transfer pricing**
>
> when a company uses selective prices for internal transactions (eg between two subsidiaries)

1 Lowering duty costs by shipping goods into high-tariff countries at minimal transfer prices so duty base and duty are low.

2 Reducing income taxes in high-tax countries by overpricing goods transferred to units in such countries; profits are eliminated and shifted to low-tax countries. Such profit shifting may also be used for 'dressing up' financial statements by increasing reported profits in countries where borrowing and other financing are undertaken.

3 Facilitating dividend repatriation; when dividend repatriation is curtailed by government policy, invisible income may be taken out in the form of high prices for products or components shipped to units in that country.

4 Showing more or less profit in crucial times; for example, in the case of new emissions, government rules, to please shareholders or to show the good performance of new/old management.

The tax and financial manipulation possibilities of transfer pricing have not been overlooked by government authorities. Transfer pricing can be used to hide subsidiary profits and to escape foreign market taxes. Transfer pricing is managed in such a way that profit is taken in the country with the lowest tax rate. For example, a foreign manufacturer makes a Blu-ray player for €45 ($50) and sells it to its European subsidiary for €135 ($150). The European subsidiary sells it to a retailer for €180 ($200), but it spends €45 ($50) on advertising and shipping so it shows no profit and pays no taxes. Meanwhile, the parent company makes a €90 ($100) gross margin on each unit and pays a lower tax rate in the home country. If the tax rate was lower in the country where the subsidiary resides, the profit would be taken there and no profit taken in the home country.[11]

The overall objectives of the transfer pricing system include: (1) maximising profits for the corporation as a whole; (2) facilitating parent-company control; and (3) offering management at all levels, both in the product divisions and in the international divisions, an adequate basis for maintaining, developing and receiving credit for their own profitability.

An intracorporate pricing system should employ sound accounting techniques and be defensible to the tax authorities of the countries involved. All of these factors argue against a single uniform price or even a uniform pricing system for all international operations.

Four arrangements for pricing goods for intracompany transfer are:

1 sales at the local manufacturing cost plus a standard mark-up

2 sales at the cost of the most efficient producer in the company plus a standard mark-up

3 sales at negotiated prices

4 arm's length sales using the same prices as quoted to independent customers.

Of the four, the arm's length transfer is most acceptable to tax authorities and most likely to be acceptable to foreign divisions, but the appropriate basis for intracompany transfers depends on the nature of the subsidiaries and market conditions.

Going International 18.8

PREDATORY PRICING

Predatory pricing is exercised when a stronger competitor sets its prices very low with the purpose of forcing out an equally efficient competitor who is unable to match these prices as it cannot incur losses for a longer period because of its weaker financial position. Sometimes, predatory pricing is also used to discourage a competitor from entering a foreign market. In this case, the local or existing competitor will set its prices so low that a new entrant will not find the market worth entering, as it will not be able to make any profits.

Often predatory pricing is set below the cost, manufacturing plus marketing, of the products so that other competitors cannot make a profit. In this case, the company that exercises this type of pricing is normally financially very strong or has other long-term objectives in relation to the market so that it is willing to face losses for some time. It is thus often used to keep or drive the smaller competitors out of the market.

Predatory pricing is also used to warn the competitors to not use price discounts as a competitive measure. Sometimes it is used to drive out smaller competitors in the decline stage of the product life cycle. The company exercising this strategy can often compensate for the losses in one market with profits in the other, or losses in one product with profits from other products in a multi-product company. Legal systems in most countries facilitate complaints from competing firms regarding predatory pricing.

Going International 18.9

IT IS HARD TO DISTINGUISH PREDATORY PRICING

Allegations of predatory pricing have a long history. The foundation of America's competition policy, the Sherman Antitrust Act of 1890, was partly a response to complaints by small firms that larger rivals wanted to drive them out of business. Low prices are one of the fruits of competition: penalising business giants for price cuts would not be good. But in rare circumstances, a big firm with cash in reserve may cut prices below costs and scarify the profit in the short term in order to move the competitors out of the way.

Uncovering that a firm is pricing below its costs is tricky in practice and, if rivals fail, that may be down to their own inefficiency or poor products. Predation is even trickier to prove when goods are sold together. A firm with a hefty profit on one

An example of a supermarket bundle deal.
'Irresistible Offer' © Jim Champion, treehouse1977.
CC BY 2.0 UK.

good may 'bundle' it with another on which margins are lower. If the discount on the bundle is big enough, other firms may struggle to offer as enticing a deal. In 2001 the EU blocked a proposed tie-up between GE and Honeywell for fear that the merged firm might use bundled discounts to squeeze rival suppliers. A few years ago the American government appointed a committee of antitrust experts who proposed a test for whether bundling is predatory. Assuming the discount applies to the low-margin good only, the proposition says that if each good sells for $10 separately and $16 as a bundle, then a $4 discount can be allocated to the more

▶

◄

competitive product. Then, a price–cost test can be applied: if the product costs over $6 to make, the bundle is predatory.

Offering rebates to customers that reach certain sales targets is another tactic. Bulk buyers generally pay lower unit prices to reflect suppliers' economies of scale. Rebates can also help align incentives. Suppliers want retailers to promote their products, offer in-store information and keep plentiful stocks. Rebates provide incentives for retailers to drive sales, as profits are bigger once the target is met.

● Should predatory pricing be involved? Why/why not?

Source: based on *The Economist*, August 2009, p 66.

Dumping

A logical outgrowth of a market policy in international business is goods priced competitively at widely differing prices in various markets. Marginal (variable) cost pricing, as discussed above, is one way prices can be reduced to stay within a competitive price range. The market for and economic logic of such pricing policies can hardly be disputed, but the practices are often classified as dumping and are subject to severe penalties and fines (see Exhibit 18.8). **Dumping** is defined differently by various economists. One approach classifies international shipments as dumped if the products are sold below their cost of production. The other approach characterises dumping as selling goods in a foreign market below the price of the same goods in the home market. Even rate cutting on cargo shipping has been called dumping.

> **dumping**
>
> when a product is sold for a lesser price than its actual cost

In the 1960s and 1970s dumping was hardly an issue because world markets were strong, but since the 1980s dumping has become a major issue for a large number of industries. Excess production capacity relative to home-country demand caused many companies to price their goods on a marginal-cost basis, figuring that any contribution above variable cost was beneficial to company profits. In a classic case of dumping, prices are maintained in the home-country market and reduced in foreign markets. For example, the EU recognised that differences in prices between Japan and EU countries ranged from 4.8 to 86 per cent. To correct for this dumping activity, a special import duty of 33.4 per cent was imposed on Japanese computer printers.

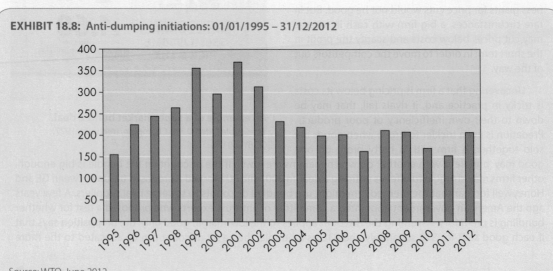

EXHIBIT 18.8: Anti-dumping initiations: 01/01/1995 – 31/12/2012

Source: WTO, June 2012.

Assembly in the importing country is one way in which companies attempt to lower prices and avoid dumping charges. However, these screwdriver plants, as they are often called, are subject to dumping charges if the price differentials reflect more than the cost savings that result from assembly in the importing country. The increased concern and enforcement in the EU reflects the changing attitudes among all countries towards dumping. The EU has had anti-dumping legislation from its inception and its Department of Trade has imposed duties on a variety of products.

Countertrade as a pricing tool

The challenges of **countertrade** must be viewed from the same perspective as all other variations in international trade. Marketers must be aware of which markets will be likely to require countertrades just as they must be aware of social customs and legal requirements. Assessing this factor along with all other market factors will enhance a marketer's competitive position.

> **countertrade**
> when products are exchanged for other products instead of cash

Ben and Jerry's, a well-known US ice-cream vendor, is manufacturing and selling ice cream in Russia. With the roubles it earns, it is buying Russian walnuts, honey and *matryoshky* (Russian nesting dolls) to sell in the USA. This was the only means of getting its profit out of Russia because there was a shortage of hard currency in Russia, making it difficult to convert roubles to dollars.

PepsiCo sold Pepsi to Russians in exchange for the exclusive rights to sell Stolichnaya vodka in the USA. In neither transaction did cash change hands; these were barter deals, a type of countertrade. Although cash may be the preferred method of payment, countertrades are becoming an important part of trade with Eastern Europe, China and, to a varying degree, some Latin American and African nations. Today, an international company must include in its market-pricing toolkit some understanding of countertrading.

Types of countertrade

Countertrade includes four distinct transactions: barter, compensation deals, counter-purchase and buy-back.[12]

Barter

One of the largest **barter** deals to date involved Occidental Petroleum corporation's agreement to ship superphosphoric acid to the former Soviet Union for ammonia urea and potash under a two-year, €18bn ($20bn) deal. No money changed hands, nor were any third parties involved.

> **barter**
> direct exchange of goods between two parties

Obviously, in a barter transaction, the seller (Occidental Petroleum) must be able to dispose of the goods at a net price equal to the expected selling price in a regular, for-cash transaction. Further, during the negotiation stage of a barter deal, the seller must know the market and the price for the items offered in trade.

In the Russian barter trade example, the price and a market for the ammonia urea and potash were established because Occidental could use the products in its operations. But bartered goods can range from hams to iron pellets, mineral water, furniture or olive oil – all somewhat more difficult to price and market when potential customers must be sought.

Compensation deals

A Western seller delivers lathes to a buyer in Pakistan and receives 70 per cent of the payment in convertible currency and 30 per cent in tanned hides and raw cotton. In an actual deal, General Motors sold €11.8m ($12m) worth of locomotives and diesel engines to the former Yugoslavia and took cash and €3.6m ($4m) in Yugoslavian cutting tools as payment.

> **compensation deals**
> involve payment in goods and in cash

An advantage of a compensation deal over barter is the immediate cash settlement of a portion of the bill; the remainder of the cash is generated after successful sale of the goods received. If the company has a use for the goods received, the process is relatively simple and uncomplicated. On the other hand, if the seller has to rely on a third party to find a buyer, the cost involved must be anticipated in the original compensation negotiation if the net proceeds to the seller are to be equal to the market price.

Counter-purchase

This is also known as offset-trade and is probably the most frequently used type of countertrade. For this trade, two contracts are negotiated. The seller agrees to sell a product at a set price to a buyer and receives payment in cash. However, the first contract is contingent on a second contract that is an agreement by the original seller to buy goods from the buyer for the total monetary amount involved in the first contract or for a set percentage of that amount.

This arrangement provides the seller with more flexibility than the compensation deal because there is generally a time period (6 to 12 months or longer) for completion of the second contract. During the time that markets are sought for the goods in the second contract, the seller has received full payment for the original sale. Further, the goods to be purchased in the second contract are generally of greater variety than those offered in a compensation deal.

The 'offset' trades, as they are sometimes called, are becoming more prevalent among economically weak countries. Several variations of a counter-purchase or offset have developed to make it more economical for the selling company.

Product buy-back

product buy-back

when a company promises to buy back some of the products produced in its subsidiaries

Product buy-back agreements are made when the sale involves goods or services that produce other goods and services; that is, production plant, production equipment or technology. The buy-back agreement usually involves one of two situations: the seller agrees to accept as partial payment a certain portion of the output; or the seller receives full price initially but agrees to buy back a certain portion of the output.

When Massey Ferguson, a British farm equipment manufacturer, sold a tractor plant to Poland it was paid part in hard currency and the balance in Polish-built tractors. In another situation, General Motors built a motor-vehicle manufacturing plant in Brazil and was paid under normal terms but agreed to the purchase of resulting output when the new facilities came on stream. Levi Strauss took Hungarian-made blue jeans, which it sells abroad, in exchange for setting up a jeans factory near Budapest.[13]

A major drawback to product buy-back agreements emerges when the seller finds that the products bought back are in competition with its own similarly produced goods. On the other hand, some have found that a product buy-back agreement provides them with a supplemental source in areas of the world where there is demand but they have no available supply.

Western firms and countertrade

Countertrade transactions are on the increase in world trade; some estimates of countertrade in international trade go as high as 30 per cent. More conservative estimates place the amount closer to 20 per cent. Regardless, a significant amount of all international trade now involves some type of countertrade transaction, and this percentage is predicted to increase substantially in the near future. Much of that increase will come in trading with emerging countries; in fact, some require countertrades of some sort with all foreign trade. Countertrade arrangements are involved in an estimated 50 per cent or more of all international trade with Eastern European and developing countries.[14]

The crucial problem confronting a seller in a countertrade negotiation is determining the value of and potential demand for the goods offered. Frequently there is inadequate time to conduct a market analysis; in fact, it is not unusual to have sales negotiations almost completed before countertrade is introduced as a requirement in the transaction.

Going International 18.10

WHY PURCHASERS IMPOSE COUNTERTRADE

To preserve hard currency. Countries with non-convertible currencies look to countertrade as a way of guaranteeing that hard currency expenditures (for foreign imports) are offset by hard currency (generated by the foreign party's obligation to purchase domestic goods).

To improve balance of trade. Nations whose exports have not kept pace with imports increasingly rely on countertrade as a means to balance bilateral trade ledgers.

To gain access to new markets. As a non-market or developing country increases its production of exportable goods, it often lacks a sophisticated marketing channel to sell the goods to the West for hard currency. By imposing countertrade demands, foreign trade organisations utilise the marketing organisations and expertise of Western companies to market their goods for them.

To upgrade manufacturing capabilities. By entering compensation arrangements under which foreign (usually Western) firms provide plant and equipment and buy back resultant products, the trade organisations of less-developed countries can enlist Western technical cooperation in upgrading industrial facilities.

To maintain prices of export goods. Countertrade can be used as a means to dispose of goods at prices that the market would not bear under cash-for-goods terms. Although the Western seller absorbs the added cost by inflating the price of the original sale, the nominal price of the counter-purchased goods is maintained, and the seller need not concede what the value of the goods would be in the world supply-and-demand market. Conversely, if the world price for a commodity is artificially high, such as the price for crude oil, a country can barter its oil for Western goods (eg weapons) so that the real 'price' the Western partner pays is below the world price.

To force reinvestment of proceeds from weapon deals. Many Arab countries require that a portion of proceeds from weapons purchases be reinvested in facilities designated by the buyer – anything from pipelines to hotels and sugar mills.

- Do you think these are good reasons to impose countertrade?

Source: compiled from several sources

Barter houses specialise in trading goods acquired through barter arrangements and are the primary outside source of aid for companies beset by the uncertainty of a countertrade. While barter houses, most of which are found in Europe and Asia, can find a market for bartered goods, it requires time, which puts a financial strain on a company because capital is tied up longer than in normal transactions. Seeking loans to tide it over until sales are completed usually solves this problem.

barter houses

international trading companies able to introduce merchandise to outlets and geographic areas previously untapped

There are many examples of companies losing sales to competitors who were willing to enter into countertrade agreements. A Western oilfield equipment manufacturer claims it submitted the lowest dollar bid in an Egyptian offer but lost the sale to a bidder who offered a counter-purchase arrangement.

Proactive countertrade strategy

Some authorities suggest that companies should have a defined countertrade strategy as part of their marketing strategy rather than be caught unprepared when confronted with a countertrade proposition. Currently most companies follow a reactive strategy; that is, they use countertrade when they believe it is the only way to make a sale. Even when these companies include countertrade as a permanent feature of their operations, they use it to react to a sales demand rather than using countertrade as an aggressive marketing tool for expansion.[15]

Successful countertrade transactions require that the marketer: (1) accurately establishes the market value of the goods being offered; and (2) disposes of the bartered goods once they are received. Most countertrades judged unsuccessful result from not properly resolving one or both of these factors.

In short, unsuccessful countertrades are generally the result of inadequate planning and preparation. One experienced countertrader suggests answering the following questions before entering into a countertrade agreement: (1) Is there a ready market for the goods bartered? (2) Is the quality of the goods offered consistent and acceptable? (3) Is an expert needed to handle the negotiations? (4) Is the contract price sufficient to cover the cost of barter and net the desired revenue?

SUMMARY

Pricing is one of the most complicated decision areas encountered by international marketers. Rather than deal with one set of market conditions, one group of competitors, one set of cost factors and one set of government regulations, international marketers must take all these factors into account, not only for each country in which they are operating, but often for each market within a country. The continuing growth of the less-developed country markets, coupled with their lack of investment capital, has increased the importance of countertrades for most marketers, making it an important tool to include in pricing policy.

Market prices at the consumer level are much more difficult to control in international than in domestic marketing, but the international marketer must still approach the pricing task on a basis of objectives and policy, leaving enough flexibility for tactical price movements. Pricing in the international marketplace requires a combination of intimate knowledge of market costs and regulations, an awareness of possible countertrade deals, infinite patience for detail and a shrewd sense of market strategy.

QUESTIONS

1 Discuss the causes of and solutions for parallel imports and their effect on price.

2 Why is it so difficult to control consumer prices when selling overseas?

3 What are the causes of price escalation? Do they differ for exports and goods produced and sold in a foreign country?

4 Define the following: parallel imports, skimming, price escalation, dumping, transfer pricing and cartel.

5 Price escalation is a major pricing problem for the international marketer. How can this problem be counteracted? Discuss.

6 'Price fixing by business is not generally viewed as an acceptable practice (at least in the domestic market); but when governments enter the field of price administration, they presume to do it for the general welfare, to lessen the effects of destructive competition.' Discuss.

7 Do value-added taxes discriminate against imported goods?

8 Explain specific tariffs, *ad valorem* tariffs and combination tariffs.

9 Suggest an approach a marketer may follow in adjusting prices to accommodate exchange-rate fluctuations.

10 Why has dumping become such an issue in recent years?

11 Discuss the various ways in which governments set prices. Why do they engage in such activities?

12 Discuss the alternative objectives possible in setting transfer prices.

13 Why do governments scrutinise transfer pricing arrangements so carefully?

14 Discuss why countertrading is on the increase.

15 Of the four types of countertrade discussed in the text, which is the most beneficial to the seller? Explain.

FURTHER READING

- S.T. Cavusgil, 'Unravelling the Mystique of Export Pricing', *Business Horizon*, 1988, 31(3), 54–63.
- R. Veale and P. Quester, 'Do Consumer Expectations Match Experience? Predicting the Influence of Price and Country of Origin on Perceptions of Product Quality', *International Business Review*, 2009, 18(2), 134–44.
- N. Tzokas, S. Hart, P. Argouslidis and M. Saren, 'Strategic Pricing in Export Markets: Empirical Evidence from the UK', *International Business Review*, 2000, 9(1), 95–117.

NOTES

1 For a comprehensive review of pricing and the integration of Europe, see Wolfgang Gaul and Ulrich Luz, 'Pricing in International Marketing and Western European Economic Integration', *Management International Review*, 1994, 34(2), 101–24.

2 S.T. Cavusgil, 'Unravelling the Mystiques of Export Pricing', in Sidney J. Levy *et al.* (eds), *Marketing Manager's Handbook* (New York: Dartnell, 1994), pp 1357–74; and 'The Debate on Export Subsidies', *European Business Report*, Spring IQ, 1998, p 58.

3 For a complete and thorough discussion of parallel markets, see Robert E. Weigand, 'Parallel Import Channels – Options for Preserving Territorial Integrity', *Columbia Journal of World Business*, Spring 1991, pp 53–60.

4 S.T. Cavusgil, K. Chan and C. Zhang, 'Strategic Orientations in Export Pricing: A Clustering Approach to Create Firm Taxonomies', *Journal of International Marketing*, 2003, 11(1), 47–72.

5 For a comprehensive review of pricing in foreign markets, see James K. Weekly, 'Pricing in Foreign Markets: Pitfalls and Opportunities', *Industrial Marketing Management*, May 1992, pp 173–9.

6 See, for example, Joseph Neu, 'Profiting from Leasing Abroad', *International Business*, April 1995, pp 56–8.

7 B. Seyoum 'Trade Liberalization and Patterns of Strategic Adjustment in the US Textiles and Clothing Industry, *International Business Review*, 2007, 16(1), 109–35.

8 'Special Section: FTZs', *Global Trade and Transportation*, September 1994, pp 24–27.

9 D. Scott Freeman, 'Foreign Trade Zones: An Underutilized US Asset', *Trade and Culture*, September–October 1994, pp 94–95.

10 P. Verburg, 'Diamond Cartels Are Forever', *Canadian Business*, 10 July 2000, p 135.

11 L.W. Siegel, 'Critics Believe DeBeers Manipulates the Market to Keep Diamonds High', *All Things Considered* (NPR), 11 November 2001.

12 Most countertrade is found in countries with shortages of foreign exchange, which is often given as the reason why countertrades are mandated by these countries. An interesting study, however, casts

some doubt on this thesis and suggests instead that countertrades may be a reasonable way for countries to minimise transaction costs. For an insightful report on this research, see Jean-Francois Hennart and Erin Anderson, 'Countertrade and the Minimization of Transaction Costs: An Empirical Examination', *Journal of Law, Economics, and Organization*, 1993, 9(2), 290–313.

13 N. Hanna and H.R. Dodge, *Pricing: Policies and Procedures* (London: Macmillan, 1995).

14 D. West, 'Countertrade', *Business Credit*, April 2002, p 48.

15 M.R. Snyder, 'Doing Business in Russia Again?', *Moscow Times*, 9 January 2002.

Chapter 19
International Promotion and Advertising

Chapter Outline

Chapter Learning Objectives

What you should learn from Chapter 19

- How to evaluate local market characteristics that affect the advertising and promotion of products
- Whether pan-European advertising is possible
- When global advertising is most effective and when modified advertising is necessary
- How to understand the effects of a single European market on advertising
- What the impact is of limited media, excessive media, and government regulations on advertising and promotion budgets
- How to understand and handle the creative challenges in international advertising
- How sales promotions can be used efficiently in foreign markets
- How to handle the communication process and avoid advertising misfires

Promotional mix

Advertising, sales promotion, personal selling and public relations, the mutually reinforcing elements of the promotional mix, have as their common objective successful sale of a product or service. Once a product is developed to meet target market needs and is properly distributed, intended customers must be informed of the product's value and availability. Advertising and promotion are basic ingredients in the marketing mix of an international company. Exhibit 19.1 presents Olympic broadcast right fees, which is becoming an increasingly important promotional activity, and Exhibit 19.2 shows global advertising spending.

Of all the elements of the marketing mix, decisions involving advertising are those most often affected by cultural differences among country markets. Consumers respond in terms of their culture, its style, feelings, value systems, attitudes, beliefs and perceptions.[1] Because advertising's function is to interpret or translate the need/want-satisfying qualities of products and services in terms of consumer needs, wants, desires and aspirations, the emotional appeals, symbols, persuasive approaches and other characteristics of an advertisement must coincide with cultural norms if it is to be effective. Because advertising is mainly based on language and images, it is influenced by culture.[2]

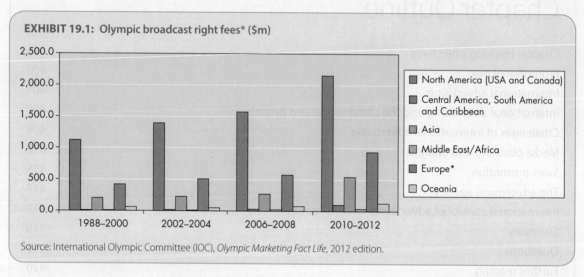

EXHIBIT 19.1: Olympic broadcast right fees* ($m)

Legend:
- North America (USA and Canada)
- Central America, South America and Caribbean
- Asia
- Middle East/Africa
- Europe*
- Oceania

Source: International Olympic Committee (IOC), *Olympic Marketing Fact Life*, 2012 edition.

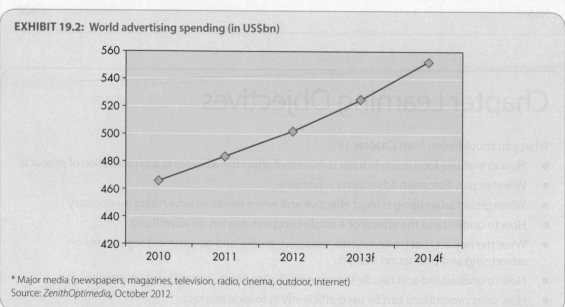

EXHIBIT 19.2: World advertising spending (in US$bn)

* Major media (newspapers, magazines, television, radio, cinema, outdoor, Internet)
Source: *ZenithOptimedia*, October 2012.

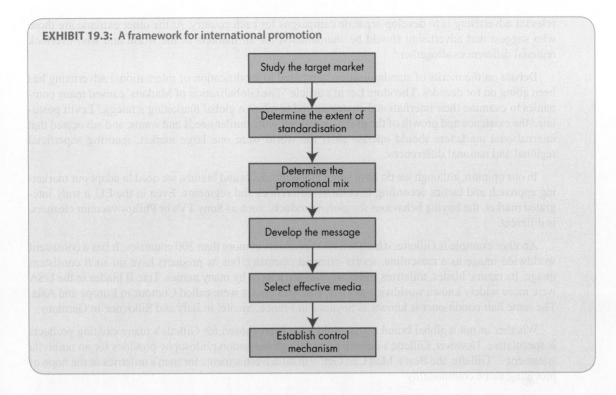

EXHIBIT 19.3: A framework for international promotion

- Study the target market
- Determine the extent of standardisation
- Determine the promotional mix
- Develop the message
- Select effective media
- Establish control mechanism

Reconciling an international advertising and sales promotion effort with the cultural uniqueness of markets is the challenge confronting the international marketer. The basic framework and concepts of international promotion are essentially the same wherever employed. Six steps are involved (see Exhibit 19.3).

To be able to design an effective promotion programme for a particular product/country, you need to first of all understand your target customer/segment. All the other steps are dependent on that understanding. Once you know your target group, you can easily decide whether and how much adaptation you need to make or not as compared to your domestic promotion mix and message. The selection of media will also depend upon the reach and habits of your target group. Each promotion plan/strategy must also have some control mechanism, so that you can evaluate your promotion mix and plan.

A review of some of the global trends that can impact international advertising is followed by a discussion of global versus modified advertising. A survey of problems and challenges confronting international advertisers – including basic creative strategy, media planning and selection, sales promotions and the communications process – concludes the chapter.

International advertising

Intense competition for world markets and the increasing sophistication of foreign consumers have led to a need for more sophisticated advertising strategies. Increased costs, problems of coordinating advertising programmes in multiple countries, and a desire for a common worldwide company or product image have caused companies to seek greater control and efficiency without sacrificing **local responsiveness**. In the quest for more effective and responsive promotion programmes, the policies covering centralised or decentralised authority, use of single or multiple foreign or domestic agencies, appropriation and allocation procedures, copy, media and research are being examined.

One of the most widely debated policy areas pertains to the degree of specialised advertising necessary from country to country.[3] One view sees advertising customised for each country or region because every country is seen as posing a special problem. Executives with this viewpoint argue that the only way to achieve adequate and

local responsiveness

when a company adapts its products and strategies according to local needs and requirements

relevant advertising is to develop separate campaigns for each country. At the other extreme are those who suggest that advertising should be standardised for all markets of the world and who overlook regional differences altogether.[4]

Debate on the merits of standardisation compared to modification of international advertising has been going on for decades. Theodore Levitt's article 'The Globalization of Markets' caused many companies to examine their international strategies and to adopt a global marketing strategy.[5] Levitt postulated the existence and growth of the global consumer with similar needs and wants, and advocated that international marketers should operate as if the world were one large market, ignoring superficial regional and national differences.

In our opinion, although we do have some global products and brands, we need to adapt our marketing approach and tactics according to cultural differences and segments. Even in the EU, a truly integrated market, the buying behaviour for global products, such as Sony TVs or Philips vacuum cleaners, is different.

Another example is Gillette, which sells 800 products in more than 200 countries. It has a consistent worldwide image as a masculine, sports-oriented company, but its products have no such consistent image. Its razors, blades, toiletries and cosmetics are known by many names. Trac II blades in the USA were more widely known worldwide as G-II, and Atra blades were called Contour in Europe and Asia. The same hair conditioner is known as Soyance in France, Sientel in Italy and Silkience in Germany.

Whether or not a global brand name could have been chosen for Gillette's many existing products is speculative. However, Gillette's current corporate globalisation philosophy provides for an umbrella statement – 'Gillette, the Best a Man Can Get' – in all advertisements for men's toiletries in the hope of providing some commonality.

It would be difficult for Procter & Gamble or Unilever to standardise their products and brand names across different markets, since each brand is established in its market. Yet, with such a diversity of brand names it is easy to imagine the problem of coordination and control, and the potential competitive disadvantage experienced by a company with global brand recognition.

As discussed earlier, there is a fundamental difference between a multidomestic marketing strategy and a global marketing strategy. One is based on the premise that all markets are culturally different and a company must adapt marketing programmes to accommodate the differences, whereas the other assumes similarities as well as differences, and standardises where there are similarities but adapts where culturally required. Further, it may be possible to standardise some parts of the marketing mix and not others. Also, the same standardised products may be marketed globally but, because of differences in cultures, target segments or stages in the product life cycle, have a different advertising appeal in different markets.

The Parker Pen Company sells the same pen in all markets, but advertising differs dramatically from country to country. Print ads in Germany simply show the Parker pen held in a hand that is writing a headline: 'This is how you write with precision'. In the UK, where it is the brand leader, the exotic processes used to make pens, such as gently polishing the gold nibs with walnut chips, is emphasised. In the USA, the ad campaign's theme is status and image. The headlines in the ads are: 'You walk into a boardroom and everyone's naked. Here's how to tell who's boss; and 'There are times when it has to be a Parker'. The company considers the different themes necessary because of the different product images and different customer motives in each market. On the other hand, its most expensive Duofold Centennial pen (about €180, or $200), created to coincide with the company's 100th anniversary and targeted for an upscale market in each country, is advertised the same way throughout the world. The advertising theme is designed to convey a statement about the company as well as the pricey new product. The importance of advertising is, however, different for different industries/product groups. Exhibit 19.4 shows global spending on advertisement based on four major media types.

The seasoned international marketer or advertiser realises the decision for standardisation or modification depends more on motives for buying than on geography. Advertising must relate to motives. If people in different markets buy similar products for significantly different reasons, advertising must focus on such differences. An advertising programme developed by Chanel, the perfume manufacturer,

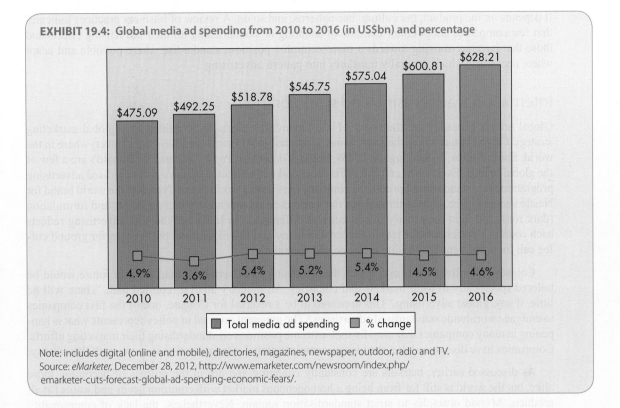

EXHIBIT 19.4: Global media ad spending from 2010 to 2016 (in US$bn) and percentage

$475.09	$492.25	$518.78	$545.75	$575.04	$600.81	$628.21
4.9%	3.6%	5.4%	5.2%	5.4%	4.5%	4.6%
2010	2011	2012	2013	2014	2015	2016

▨ Total media ad spending   ▨ % change

Note: includes digital (online and mobile), directories, magazines, newspaper, outdoor, radio and TV.
Source: *eMarketer*, December 28, 2012, http://www.emarketer.com/newsroom/index.php/
emarketer-cuts-forecast-global-ad-spending-economic-fears/.

failed in the USA although it was very popular in Europe. Admitting failure in its attempt to globalise the advertising, one fragrance analyst commented, 'There is a French–American problem. The French concept of prestige is not the same as America's.'

Pattern advertising: plan globally, act locally

As discussed in Chapter 12, a product is more than a physical item; it is a bundle of satisfactions the buyer receives. This package of satisfactions or utilities includes the primary function of the product along with many other benefits imputed by the values and customs of the culture. Different cultures often seek the same value or benefits from the primary function of a product; for example, the ability of a car to get from point A to point B, a camera to take a picture or a wristwatch to tell the time. But while agreeing on the benefit of the primary function of a product, other features and psychological attributes of the item can have significant differences.

Consider the different market-perceived needs for a camera. In the UK, excellent pictures with easy, foolproof operation are expected by most of the market; in most countries of Europe, the USA and Japan, a camera must take excellent pictures but the camera must also be state-of-the-art in design.

In Africa, where penetration of cameras is less than 30 per cent of households, the concept of picture-taking must be sold. In all three markets, excellent pictures are expected (ie the primary function of a camera is demanded) but the additional utility or satisfaction derived from a camera differs among cultures. There are many products that produce these different expectations beyond the common benefit sought by all.

Thus, many companies follow a strategy of **pattern advertising**, a global advertising strategy with a standardised basic message allowing some degree of modification to meet local situations. As the popular saying goes, 'Think globally, act locally'. In this way, some economies of standardisation can be realised while specific cultural differences are accommodated.

Evidence indicates that no generalised recommendation can be made about whether to adapt or standardise international advertising. The only answer is 'it depends'.

pattern advertising

global advertising strategy with a standardised basic message allowing some degree of modification to meet local situations

It depends on the product, the culture, use patterns, and so on. A review of business practices indicates that few companies adopt either extreme of adapting or standardising all their advertising efforts and those that have are moving towards a more centralist position: standardise where possible and adapt where necessary, which generally translates into pattern advertising.

International advertising and world brands

Global brands generally are the result of a company that elects to be guided by a global marketing strategy. Global brands carry the same name, same design and same creative strategy everywhere in the world; Sony, Philips, Nokia, Jaguar, BMW, Volvo, Coca-Cola, Pepsi Cola and McDonald's are a few of the global brands. Even when cultural differences make it ineffective to have a standardised advertising programme or a standardised product, a company may have a world brand. Nescafé, the world brand for Nestlé instant coffee, is used throughout the world even though advertising messages and formulation (dark roast and light roast) vary to suit cultural differences. In India and the UK, advertising reflects each country's preference for tea; in France, Germany and Brazil, cultural preferences for ground coffee call for a different advertising message and formulation.

Colgate-Palmolive announced it was decentralising its advertising; marketing in future would be tailored specifically to local markets and countries. An industry analyst reported that, 'There will be little, if any, global advertising.' This appeared to be a reversal for Colgate, one of the first companies to embrace worldwide standardised advertising.[6] The apparent reversal in policy represents what is happening in many companies that initially took extreme positions on standardising their marketing efforts. Companies have discovered that the idea of complete global standardisation is more myth than reality.

As discussed earlier, markets are constantly changing and are in the process of becoming more alike, but the world is still far from being a homogeneous market with common needs and wants for all products. Myriad obstacles to strict standardisation remain. Nevertheless, the lack of commonality among markets should not deter a marketer from being guided by a global strategy; that is, a marketing philosophy that directs products and advertising towards a worldwide rather than a local or regional market, seeking standardisation where possible and modifying where necessary. To achieve global advertising huge sums are being spent on a worldwide basis. Top companies spend billions on advertising.

Pan-European advertising

The attraction of a single European market has enticed many companies to standardise as much of their promotional effort as possible. As media coverage across Europe expands, it will become more common for markets to be exposed to multiple advertising messages and brand names for the same product. To avoid the confusion that results when a market is exposed to these, as well as for reasons of efficiency, companies will strive for harmony in brand names, advertising and promotions across Europe.

Mars, the confectionery company, traditionally used several brand names for the same product but recently has achieved uniformity by replacing them with a single name. A chocolate bar sold in some parts of Europe under the brand name Raider was changed to Twix, the name used in the USA and the UK.

Along with changes in behaviour patterns, legal restrictions are gradually being eliminated, and viable market segments across country markets are emerging. While Europe will never be a single homogeneous market for every product, it does not mean that companies should shun the idea of developing European-wide promotional programmes especially for global, European brands and for corporate image. A pan-European promotional strategy would mean identifying a market segment across all European countries and designing a promotional concept appealing to market-segment similarities.

promotional strategy

systematic planning to promote a product

International market segmentation and promotional strategy

Rather than approach a **promotional strategy** decision as having to be either standardised or adapted, a company should first identify market segments. Market segments can be defined within country boundaries or across countries. Global market segmentation involves identifying homogeneous market segments across groups of countries.

Procter & Gamble is an example of a company that identified mass-market segments across the world and designed brand and advertising concepts that apply to all. The company's shampoo positioning strategy, 'Pro-V vitamin formula strengthens the hair and makes it shine', was developed for the Taiwanese market, and then launched successfully in several other countries with only minor adaptation for hair types and languages. L'Oréal's 'I'm worth it' brand position also works well worldwide. Unilever's fabric softener's teddy bear brand concept has worked well across borders, even though the 'Snuggle' brand name changes in some countries; it is Kuschelweich in Germany, Coccolino in Italy and Mimosin in France.[7]

Other companies have identified niche segments too small for country-specific development but, when taken in aggregate, they have become profitable markets. The luxury-brand luggage Louis Vuitton is an example of a product designed for a niche segment. It is marketed as an exclusive, high-priced, glamorous product worldwide to relatively small segments in most countries.

While there are those who continue to argue the merits of standardisation versus adaptation, most will agree that identifiable market segments for specific products exist across country markets, especially in some types of product, and that companies should approach promotional planning from a global perspective, standardise where feasible and adapt where necessary.

Going International 19.1

SELLING LEVI'S AROUND THE WORLD

Levi's clothing is sold in more than 70 countries, with different cultural and political aspects affecting advertising appeals. Here are some of the appeals used.

In Indonesia, ads show Levi's-clad teenagers cruising around Dubuque, Iowa, in 1960s convertibles.

In the UK, ads emphasise that Levi's is an American brand and star an all-American hero, the cowboy, in fantasy Wild West settings.

In Japan, local jeans companies had already positioned themselves as American. To differentiate Levi's, the company positioned itself as legendary American jeans with commercials on the

© Istockphoto.com/winhorse

theme of 'Heroes Wear Levi's', featuring clips of cult figures such as James Dean. The Japanese responded: awareness of Levi's in Japan went from 35 per cent to 95 per cent as a result of this campaign.

In Brazil, the market is strongly influenced by fashion trends emanating from Europe rather than from America. Thus, the ads for Brazil are filmed in Paris, featuring young people, cool amid a wild Parisian traffic scene.

In Australia, commercials were designed to build brand awareness with product benefits. The lines 'fit looks tight, doesn't feel tight, can feel comfortable all night' and 'a legend doesn't come apart at the seams' highlighted Levi's quality image, and 'since 1850 Levi's jeans have handled everything from bucking broncos . . .' emphasised Levi's' unique positioning.

- Is Levi's still the number one brand in jeans? Why/why not?

Sources: compiled from several sources.

International advertising and the communication process

Promotional activities (advertising, personal selling, sales promotions and public relations) are basically a communications process. All the attendant problems of developing an effective promotional strategy in domestic marketing plus all the cultural problems discussed earlier must be overcome to create a successful international promotional programme.

A major consideration for foreign marketers is to ascertain that all constraints (cultural diversity, media limitations, legal problems, and so forth) are controlled so the right message is communicated to and received by prospective consumers. International communications may fail for a variety of reasons: a message may not get through because of media inadequacy; the message may be received by the intended audience but not be understood because of different cultural interpretations; or the message may reach the intended audience and be understood but have no effect because the marketer did not correctly assess the needs and wants of the target market.[8]

The effectiveness of promotional strategy can be jeopardised by so many factors that a marketer must be certain no influences are overlooked. Those international executives who understand the communications process are better equipped to manage the diversity they face in developing an international promotional programme.[9]

In the communications process, each of the seven identifiable segments can ultimately affect the accuracy of the process. As illustrated in Exhibit 19.5, the process consists of:

1 an information source – an international marketing executive with a product message to communicate

2 encoding – the message from the source converted into effective symbolism for transmission to a receiver

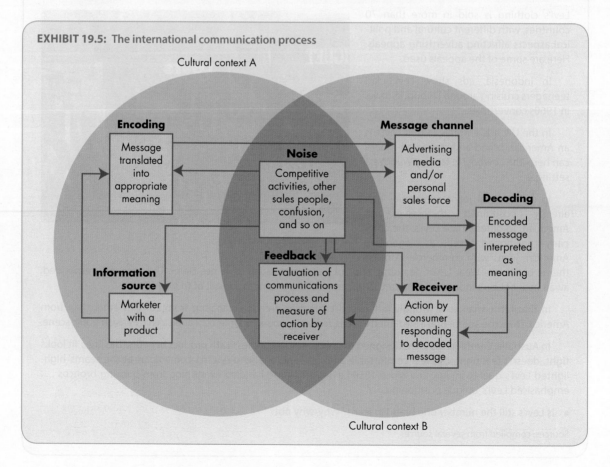

EXHIBIT 19.5: The international communication process

Cultural context A

Encoding
Message translated into appropriate meaning

Noise
Competitive activities, other sales people, confusion, and so on

Message channel
Advertising media and/or personal sales force

Decoding
Encoded message interpreted as meaning

Information source
Marketer with a product

Feedback
Evaluation of communications process and measure of action by receiver

Receiver
Action by consumer responding to decoded message

Cultural context B

3 a message channel – the sales force and/or advertising media that conveys the encoded message to the intended receiver

4 decoding – the interpretation by the receiver of the symbolism transmitted from the information source

5 receivers – consumer action by those who receive the message and are the target for the thought transmitted

6 feedback – information about the effectiveness of the message, which flows from the receiver (the intended target) back to the information source for evaluation of the effectiveness of the process, and to complete the process

7 noise – uncontrollable and unpredictable influences such as competitive activities and confusion detracting from the process and affecting any or all of the other six steps.

Unfortunately, the process is not as simple as just sending a message via a medium to a receiver and being certain that the intended message sent is the same one perceived by the receiver. In Exhibit 19.5, the communications-process steps are encased in cultural context A and cultural context B to illustrate the influences complicating the process when the message is encoded in one culture and decoded in another. If not properly considered, the different cultural contexts can increase the probability of misunderstandings.

According to one researcher, effective communication demands that there exists a psychological overlap between the sender and the receiver, otherwise a message falling outside the receiver's perceptual field may transmit an unintended meaning. It is in this area that even the most experienced companies make blunders.[10]

Most **promotional misfires**, or mistakes, in international marketing are attributable to one or several of these steps not properly reflecting cultural influences and/or a general lack of knowledge about the target market. A review of some of the points discussed in this chapter serves to illustrate this. The information source is a marketer with a product to sell to a specific target market.

> **promotional misfires**
>
> mistakes made in the advertising activities of a company

The product message to be conveyed should reflect the needs and wants of the target market; however, as many previous examples have illustrated, the marketer's perception of market needs and actual market needs do not always coincide. This is especially true when the marketer relies more on the self-reference criterion (SRC) than on effective research. It can never be assumed that, 'If it sells well in one country, it will sell in another.'

Bicycles designed and sold in the USA to fulfill recreational-exercise needs are not sold as effectively for the same reasons in a market where the primary use of the bicycle is transportation. From the onset of the communications process, if basic needs are incorrectly defined, communications fail because an incorrect or meaningless message is received even though the remaining steps in the process are executed properly.

The encoding step causes problems even with a proper message. At this step such factors as colour, values, beliefs and tastes can cause the international marketer to symbolise the message incorrectly. For example, the marketer wants the product to convey coolness, so the colour green is used; however, people in the tropics might decode green as dangerous or associate it with disease.

Message channels must be selected carefully if an encoded message is to reach the consumer. Media problems are generally thought of in terms of the difficulty in getting a message to the intended market. Problems of literacy, media availability and types of media create problems in the communications process at this step. Errors such as using television as a medium when only a small percentage of an intended market is exposed to TV, or using print media as a channel of communication when the majority of the intended users do not read newspapers, are examples of ineffective media channel selection in the communications process.

Decoding errors may also occur accidentally. In some cases, the intended symbolism has no meaning to the decoder. Errors at the receiver end of the process generally result from a combination of factors: an improper message resulting from incorrect knowledge of use patterns; poor encoding producing a meaningless message; poor media selection that does not get the message to the receiver; or inaccurate decoding by the receiver.

Finally, the feedback step of the communications process is important as a check on the effectiveness of the other steps. Companies that do not measure their communications efforts are apt to allow errors of source, encoding, media selection, decoding or receiver to continue longer than necessary. In fact, a proper feedback system allows a company to correct errors before substantial damage occurs.

In addition to the problems inherent in the steps outlined, the effectiveness of the communications process can be impaired by noise. Noise comprises all other external influences such as competitive advertising, other sales personnel and confusion at the receiving end that can detract from the ultimate effectiveness of the communications. In designing an international promotional strategy, the international marketer can effectively use this model as a guide to help ensure all potential constraints and problems are considered so that the final communication received and the action taken correspond with the intent of the source.

Going International 19.2

BUZZ MARKETING

With thanks to Red Bull.

For the past 10 years, the effectiveness of television advertising and other traditional techniques in reaching younger consumers in the developed world has been in decline. As a result, companies are turning to new approaches such as guerrilla marketing, also called 'buzz' marketing.

The traditional media have become less effective for several reasons. First is increasing fragmentation: as the number of television channels, radio stations and consumer publications proliferates, audiences split into smaller groups, making it more difficult and expensive to reach an audience of a given size. Second is competition from other media: computer games and the Internet draw people away from TV. Third, people have grown cynical towards brands and multinational companies.

Yet, while the younger generation is turned off by slick advertising and suspicious of corporate manipulation, it remains conscious of brands and image. Buzz marketing – also known as word-of-mouth or stealth marketing – has emerged as a way for companies to get on the right side of consumers in the battle for sales. Buzz marketing involves getting trendsetters in any community to carry the brand's message, creating interest with no overt promotion. The message can be transmitted physically (people seen with the brand), verbally (through conversation) or virtually (via the Internet).

Red Bull is a company at the forefront of buzz marketing. When the drink was originally formulated, bars refused to stock it, seeing it as a medicinal or health-related product rather than a mixer. But snowboarders and clubbers soon recognised the boost it gave them and began taking it to alcohol-free discos, and before long bars began stocking the drink.

Red Bull hired consumer education teams to drive cars that were painted blue and silver with logos on the side and a giant Red Bull can mounted on the back. The vehicles contained fridges stocked with cans of Red Bull, which the teams handed out for free to 'those in need of energy,' at truck stops, office buildings, gyms and construction sites. Red Bull also gave cans to DJs to drink while mixing in clubs. It also left empty cans on tables in trendy bars and pubs, as well as in rubbish bins outside select nightclubs.

Red Bull also hired student brand managers at university campuses, giving each a case of Red Bull and encouraging them to throw a party, as well as raise the profile of Red Bull in the university press.

Red Bull also sponsors a number of 'extreme' sports, backed by TV and press advertisements, and allies itself with those who push boundaries. Today, it has a 65 per cent share of the US energy drink market. The company keeps tight control on how it markets itself to clubs and bars.

▶

◄

Besides this it has also sponsored pop culture events, many of which were participatory. For example, the Red Bull Music Academy (RMBA) brought together aspiring musicians and DJs for two weeks to attend workshops and studio sessions, and listen to guest lecturers. The academy was held in different cities: Berlin in 1998, Dublin in 1999, New York in 2001, London in 2002, Capetown in 2003 and Rome in 2004.

Red Bull is not alone in using buzz marketing. Among others are the following.

- *Piaggio*: during its Vespa campaign, Piaggio had models drive around Los Angeles on Vespa scooters and chat up customers in cafés and bars. If asked about the Vespa, they would casually mention its various qualities and drop the names of celebrities who had recently purchased one. If anyone showed interest, the model would give them details of the nearest Vespa dealer.

- *Ford*: Ford identified 120 people in six core markets as trendsetters (for example, local DJs). Each was given a Focus to drive for six months as well as promotional material to distribute to anyone who expressed interest.

- Do you think buzz marketing is a successful way to market products like Red Bull or cars? Which products are most suitable for this type of marketing? Discuss.

Sources: adapted from Nirmalya Kumar and Sophie Linguri, 'Buzz, Chat and Branding Give Red Bull Wings', *Financial Times* Summer School, 8 August 2003, p 13; and 'The Anti-brand Brand – Red Bull', 1 July 2004, www.redbull.com.

Challenges of international advertising

The growing intensity of international competition, coupled with the complexity of marketing multinationally, demands that the international advertiser function at the highest creative level. Advertisers from around the world have developed their skills and abilities to the point that advertisements from different countries reveal basic similarities and a growing level of sophistication. To complicate matters further, boundaries are placed on creativity by legal, tax, language, cultural, media, production and cost limitations.

Legal and tax considerations

Laws that control **comparative advertising** vary from country to country in Europe. In Germany, it is illegal to use any comparative terminology; you can be sued by a competitor if you do. Belgium and Luxembourg explicitly ban comparative advertising, whereas it is clearly authorised in the UK, Sweden, Ireland, Spain and Portugal.

> **comparative advertising**
> directly compares you with your competitors

The European Commission is issuing several directives to harmonise the laws governing advertising. Many fear that, if the laws are not harmonised, member states may close their borders to advertising that does not respect their national rules. The directive covering comparative advertising will allow implicit comparisons that do not name competitors, but will ban explicit comparisons between named products. In Asia, an advertisement showing chimps choosing Pepsi over Coke was banned from most satellite television channels. The term 'the leading cola' was accepted only in the Philippines.[11]

Advertising on television is strictly controlled in many countries. In Kuwait, the government-controlled TV network allows only 32 minutes of advertising per day, in the evening. Commercials are controlled to exclude superlative descriptions, indecent words, fearful or shocking shots, indecent clothing or dancing, contests, hatred or revenge shots, and attacks on competition. It is also illegal to advertise cigarettes, lighters, pharmaceuticals, alcohol, airlines, and chocolates or other sweets. In the USA, advertising pharmaceuticals is allowed.

Some countries have special taxes that apply to advertising, which might restrict creative freedom in media selection. The tax structure in Austria best illustrates how advertising taxation can distort media choice by changing the cost ratios of various media. In federal states, with the exception of Bergenland and Tyrol, there is a 10 per cent tax on ad insertions; for posters, there is a 10–30 per cent tax according to state and municipality. Radio advertising carries a 10 per cent tax, except in Tyrol where it is 20 per cent. In Salzburg, Steiermark, Karnten and Voralbert there is no tax. There is a uniform tax of 10 per cent throughout the country on television ads. Cinema advertising has a 10 per cent tax in Vienna, 20 per cent in Bergenland and 30 per cent in Steiermark. There is no cinema tax in the other federal states.

Language limitations

Language is one of the major barriers to effective communication through advertising. The problem involves different languages of different countries, different languages or dialects within one country, and the subtler problems of linguistic nuance and vernacular.

Incautious handling of language has created problems in nearly every country. Some examples suffice. Chrysler Corporation was nearly laughed out of Spain when it translated the US slogan 'Dart Is Power'. To the Spanish, the phrase implied that buyers sought but lacked sexual vigour. Bacardi Limited concocted a fruity bitter with a made-up name, 'Pavane', suggestive of French *chic*. Bacardi wanted to sell the drink in Germany, but 'Pavane' is perilously close to 'pavian', which means 'baboon'.

A company marketing tomato paste in the Middle East found that in Arabic the phrase 'tomato paste' translates as 'tomato glue'. In Spanish-speaking countries you have to be careful of words that have different meanings in the different countries. The word 'ball' translates in Spanish as 'bola'. Bola means ball in one country, revolution in another, a lie or fabrication in another and in yet another it is an obscenity. Tropicana-brand orange juice was advertised as 'jugo de China' in Puerto Rico, but when transported to Miami's Cuban community it failed. To the Puerto Rican, 'China' translated into orange, but to the Cuban it was 'China' and the Cubans were not in the market for Chinese juice. One Middle Eastern advertisement features a car's new suspension system that, in translation, said the car was 'suspended from the ceiling'. Since there are at least 30 dialects among Arab countries, there is ample room for error. What may appear as the most obvious translation can come out wrong. 'A whole new range of products' in a German advertisement came out as 'a whole new stove of products'.

Low literacy in many countries seriously impedes communications and calls for greater creativity and use of verbal media. Multiple languages within a country or advertising area provide another problem for the advertiser. Even a small country such as Switzerland has four separate languages.

Cultural diversity

The problems of communicating to people in diverse cultures is one of the great creative challenges in advertising. Communication is more difficult because cultural factors largely determine the way various phenomena are perceived. If the perceptual framework is different, perception of the message itself differs.

Going International 19.3

SHARAPOVA SPARKS OUTRAGE IN LOS ANGELES

Los Angeles, the city of *Playboy* magazine and lap-dancing clubs, was mortified by an advertising campaign that featured a scantily clad Maria Sharapova simply sitting on a tennis court. Sharapova, the 2004 Wimbledon women's champion, was considered to be the perfect model to market the World Women's Tennis Association (WTA) tournament in Los Angeles, which she later won. She is attractive and talented and what tournament director would not use her image to promote the event?

The tournament took place at the Staple Center, the LA Lakers' (basketball team) home. The nearby Convention Center was to stage the USA's annual trade fair for adult entertainment soon after.

Previously it had been difficult to attract people to this tournament; spotting a full row at the 19,000-seat arena was a challenge. Yet the reactions to the advertising campaign have been appalling. A *Los Angeles Times'* sport columnist wrote, 'Take a look at this picture of Maria Sharapova. What do you think? Can you say it out loud?'

▶

◄

Even the number one female player, Lindsay Davenport, said, 'I would not do it, and I would not allow my daughter to do it either'. However, Serena Williams spoke out, 'It's a wonderful picture. But it's unfortunate that if you're a female actress or singer, it's the sexiest ones that sell more tickets. I hate it, but sex sells.'

The WTA chief executive replied, 'I don't think those advertisements are racy or inappropriate. I also find it a bit ironic that in LA, the home of the entertainment industry, somebody finds it out of line.' John Lloyd, former British tennis number one and a resident of LA, agreed: 'Anybody who finds the picture offensive must have a strange mind.'

Sharapova doesn't seem to be bothered. After the first week of the tournament she got another $6m (€5.2m) endorsement from Canon. Maria's trainer, however, revealed that she was furious that the writer in the newspaper thought they couldn't sell her as a winner but only as sexy.

● Do you think the picture sounds inappropriate? Do you think the WTA is trying to sell itself using sex?

Source: Barry Flatman, 'More Than Just a Pretty Face', *The Times*, 14 November 2004, p 218.

Maria Sharapova at a film premiere.
© Istockphoto.com/EdStock

International marketers are becoming accustomed to the problems of adapting from culture to culture. Knowledge of differing symbolisms of colours is a basic part of the international marketer's encyclopaedia. An astute marketer knows that, as we have already seen, white in Europe is associated with purity but in Asia it is commonly associated with death. The marketer must also be sophisticated enough to know that the presence of black in the West or white in Eastern countries does not automatically connote death. Colour is a small part of the communications package, but if the symbolism in each culture is understood, the marketer has an educated choice of using or not using various colours.

Knowledge of cultural diversity must encompass the total advertising project. Existing perceptions based on tradition and heritage are often hard to overcome. Marketing researchers in Hong Kong found that cheese is associated with *Yeung-Yen* (foreigners) and rejected by some Chinese. The concept of cooling and heating the body is important in Chinese thinking; malted milk is considered heating, while fresh milk is cooling; brandy is sustaining, whisky harmful.

A soap commercial featuring a man touching a woman's skin while she bathes, a theme used in some European countries and in the USA, would be rejected in countries where the idea of a man being in the same bathroom with a woman would be taboo.

As though it were not enough for advertisers to be concerned with differences among nations, they find subcultures within a country require attention as well. In India, there are several patterns of breakfast eating. The youth of a country almost always constitute a different consuming culture from the older people, and urban dwellers differ significantly from rural dwellers. Besides these differences, there is the problem of changing traditions. In all countries, people of all ages, urban or rural, cling to their heritage to a certain degree but are willing to change some areas of behaviour.

Production and cost limitations

Creativity is especially important when a budget is small or where there are severe production limitations, poor-quality printing and a lack of high-grade paper. For example, the poor quality of high-circulation glossy magazines and other quality publications has caused Colgate-Palmolive to depart from its customary heavy use of print media in the West for other media in Eastern Europe. The necessity for low-cost reproduction in small markets poses another problem in many countries.

For example, hand-painted **billboards** must be used instead of printed sheets because the limited number of billboards does not warrant the production of printed sheets. In

> **billboards**
> large stands that comprise advertising space, usually found at the sides of roads

Western societies, the increasing cost of advertising on television and the radio is forcing companies to look for alternative advertising methods. The increasing cost of advertising through sports events is illustrated by Olympic broadcast right fees over the years.

Media planning and analysis

Tactical considerations

Although nearly every sizeable nation essentially has the same kind of media, there are a number of specific considerations, problems and differences encountered from one nation to another. In international advertising, an advertiser must consider the availability, cost and coverage of the media. Local variations and lack of market data provide areas for additional attention.

Imagine the ingenuity required of advertisers confronted with the following situations:

1 TV commercials are sandwiched together in a string of 10–50 commercials within one station break in Brazil.

2 In many countries, national coverage means using as many as 40–50 different media.

3 Specialised media reach small segments of the market only. In some countries of Europe, there are socialist, neutral and other specialised broadcasting systems.

4 In Germany, TV scheduling for an entire year must be arranged by 30 August of the preceding year, and there is no guarantee that commercials intended for summer viewing will always be run in the specified period.

5 In Vietnam, advertising in newspapers and magazines will be limited to 10 per cent of space and to 5 per cent of time, or three minutes an hour, on radio and TV.

Availability

> **advertising media**
> different alternatives available to a company for its advertising (eg TV, magazine)

One of the features of international advertising is that some countries have too few advertising media and others have too many. In some countries, certain **advertising media** are forbidden by government edict to accept some advertising materials. Such restrictions are most prevalent in radio and television broadcasting.

In many countries, there are too few magazines and newspapers to run all the advertising offered to them. Conversely, some nations segment the market with so many newspapers that the advertiser cannot gain effective coverage at a reasonable cost. Gilberto Sozzani, head of an Italian advertising agency, comments about his country: 'One fundamental rule. You cannot buy what you want.'

Cost

Media prices are susceptible to negotiation in most countries. Agency space discounts are often split with the client to bring down the cost of media. The advertiser may find that the cost of reaching a prospect through advertising depends on the agent's bargaining ability. The per-contract cost varies widely from country to country. One study showed the cost of reaching 1,000 readers in 11 different European countries ranged from €1.43 ($1.75) in Belgium to €5.33 ($6.52) in Italy; in women's service magazines, the page cost per thousand circulation ranged from €2.27 ($2.78) in Denmark to €9.81 ($12.00) in Germany. In some markets, shortages of advertising time on commercial television have caused substantial price increases.

Coverage

Closely akin to the cost dilemma is the problem of coverage. Two points are particularly important: one relates to the difficulty of reaching certain sectors of the population with advertising and the other to the lack of information on coverage. In many world marketplaces, a wide variety of media must be used to reach the majority of the markets. In some countries, large numbers of separate media have divided markets into uneconomical advertising segments. With some exceptions, a majority of the native population of developing countries cannot be reached readily through the medium of advertising. In Brazil, an exception, television is an important medium with a huge audience. One network, in fact, can reach 90 per cent of Brazil's more than 17 million TV households.

In the Czech Republic, for example, TV advertising rates are high for prime-time spots, forcing companies to use billboard advertising. Outdoor advertising has become popular and in Prague alone billboards have increased from 50 in 1990 to over 10,000 in 2008.[12]

Going International 19.4

HOW DO WE MEASURE THE EFFECTIVENESS OF ADVERTISING?

A firm can spend millions of dollars on advertising, and it is only natural to want some feedback on the results of such an expenditure: to what extent did the advertising really pay?

Most of the methods for measuring effectiveness focus not on sales changes but on how well the communication is remembered, recognised or recalled. Most evaluative methods simply tell which ad is the best among those being appraised. But even though one ad may be found to be more memorable or to create more attention than another, that fact alone gives no assurance of relationship to sales success. A classic example of the dire consequences that can befall advertising people as a result of the inability to measure directly the impact of ads on sales is reflected in the following example.

A billboard advert for Nationwide Insurance's 'Life Comes at You Fast' campaign, using a fictional company, 'Coop's Paints'.
'Coop's Paints Mural' © tlarrow CC BY 2.0 UK.

The Doyle Dane Bernbach advertising agency created memorable TV commercials for Alka-Seltzer, such as the 'spicy meatball man' and the 'poached oyster bride'. These won professional awards as the best commercials of their year and received high marks for humour and audience recall. But the $22m (€20m) account was abruptly switched to another agency. The reason? Alka-Seltzer's sales had dropped somewhat. Of course, no one will ever know whether the drop might have been much worse without these notable commercials.

So, how do we measure the value of millions of dollars spent on advertising? Not well. Nor can we determine what is the right amount to spend on advertising (versus what is too much or too little).

- Can we measure the effectiveness of advertising? Can a business succeed without advertising? Why/why not?

Source: compiled from different sources.

Lack of market data

Verification of circulation or coverage figures is a difficult task. Even though many countries have organisations similar to the Audit Bureau of Circulation (ABC), accurate circulation and audience data are not assured. For example, the president of the Mexican National Advertisers Association stated that newspaper circulation figures are 'grossly exaggerated'. He suggested that, 'as a rule agencies divide these figures in two and take the result with a grain of salt'. The situation in China is no better: surveys of habits and penetration are available only for the bigger cities. Radio and television audiences are always difficult to measure, but at least in most countries geographic coverage is known.

Specific media information

An attempt to evaluate the specific characteristics of each medium is beyond the scope of this discussion. Furthermore, such information would quickly become outdated because of the rapid changes in the international advertising media field. It may be interesting, however, to examine some of the unique international characteristics of various advertising media. In most instances, the major implications of each variation may be discerned from the data presented.

Newspapers

The newspaper industry is suffering in some countries from lack of competition, and choking because of it in others. Most European cities have just one or two major daily newspapers but, in many countries, there are so many newspapers that an advertiser has trouble reaching even partial market coverage. Uruguay, population 3 million, has 21 daily newspapers with a combined circulation of 553,000.

Norway, on the other hand, with a population of more than 4 million, has only one national daily morning newspaper. Turkey has 380 newspapers, and an advertiser must consider the political position of each newspaper so the product's reputation is not harmed through affiliations with unpopular positions.

Japan has only five national daily newspapers, but the complications of producing a Japanese-language newspaper are such that they each contain just 16–20 pages. Connections are necessary to buy advertising space; *Asahi*, Japan's largest newspaper, has been known to turn down over a million dollars a month in advertising revenue.

Separation between editorial and advertising content in newspapers provides another basis for differences on the international scene. In some countries, it is possible to buy editorial space for advertising and promotional purposes. The news columns are for sale not only to the government but to anyone who has the money. Since there is no indication that the space is paid for, it is impossible to tell exactly how much advertising appears in a given newspaper.

Magazines

The use of foreign national consumer magazines by international advertisers has been notably low for many reasons. Few magazines have large circulations or provide dependable circulation figures. Technical magazines are used extensively to promote export goods; but, as in the case of newspapers, paper shortages cause placement problems.

Increasingly, Western publications are publishing overseas editions. *Reader's Digest International* has added a new Russian-language edition to its more than 20 languages. Other print media available in international editions range from *Playboy* to *The Economist*. Advertisers now have several new magazines to reach females in China: Hachette Filipacfchi Presse, the French publisher, now offers Chinese-language editions of *Elle*, a fashion magazine; *Woman's Day* is aimed at China's 'busy modern' woman; and *L'Événement Sportif* is a sports magazine.[13]

Radio and TV

Possibly because of their inherent entertainment value, radio and TV have become major communications media in most nations. In China, for example, virtually all homes in major cities have a TV, and most adults view television and listen to radio daily.[14] Radio has been relegated to a subordinate position in the media race in countries where TV facilities are well-developed.

Entrepreneurs in the radio/TV field have discovered that audiences in commercially restricted countries are hungry for commercial TV and radio, and that marketers are eager to bring their messages into these countries.

A major study in 22 countries revealed that the majority were in favour of advertising. Individuals in former communist countries were among the more enthusiastic supporters. In a 22-country survey, Egypt was the only one where the majority of responses were anti-advertising. Only 9 per cent of Egyptians surveyed agreed that many TV commercials are enjoyable, compared to 80 per cent or more in Italy, Uruguay and Bulgaria.[15] Italy, which had no private/local radio or TV until 1976, currently has some 300 privately owned stations.

Satellite and cable TV

Of increasing importance in TV advertising is the growth and development of satellite TV broadcasting. Sky, a UK-based commercial satellite TV station, beams its programmes and advertising into most of Europe via cable TV subscribers.

Parts of Asia and Latin America receive TV broadcasts from satellite television networks. Univision and Televisa are two Latin American satellite television networks broadcasting via a series of affiliate stations in each country to most of the Spanish-speaking world, including the USA. *Sabado Gigante*, a popular Spanish-language programme broadcast by Univision, is seen by tens of millions of viewers in 16 countries.

Star TV, a pan-Asian satellite television network, has a potential audience of 2.7 billion people living in 38 countries from Egypt through India to Japan, and from Russia to Indonesia. Star TV was the first to broadcast across Asia but was quickly joined by ESPN and CNN. The first Asian 24-hour all-sports channel was followed by MTV Asia and a Mandarin Chinese-language channel that delivers dramas, comedies, films and financial news aimed at the millions of overseas Chinese living throughout Asia.[16]

Direct mail

Direct mail is a viable medium in many countries. It is especially important when other media are not available. As is often the case in international marketing, even such a fundamental medium is subject to some odd and novel quirks. Despite some limitations with direct mail, many companies have found it a meaningful way to reach their markets. The Reader's Digest Association has used **direct-mail advertising** in many countries to market its magazines successfully.

In Southeast Asian markets where print media are scarce, direct mail is considered one of the most effective ways to reach those responsible for making industrial goods purchases, even though accurate mailing lists are a problem in Asia as well as in other parts of the world. **Industrial advertisers** are heavy mail users and rely on catalogues and sales sheets to generate large volumes of international business.

> **direct-mail advertising**
> advertising that comes through the post, directly addressed to the recipient
>
> **industrial advertisers**
> companies that advertise industrial products

Other media

Restrictions on traditional media or their availability cause advertisers to call on lesser media to solve particular local-country problems. The cinema is an important medium in many countries, as are billboards and other forms of outside advertising. Billboards are especially useful in countries with high illiteracy rates.

Sales promotion

Other than advertising, personal selling and publicity, all marketing activities that stimulate consumer purchases and improve retailer or middlemen effectiveness and cooperation are sales promotions. In-store demonstrations, samples, coupons, gifts, product tie-ins, contests, sweepstakes, sponsorship of special events, such as concerts and fairs, and point-of-purchase displays are types of sales promotion devices designed to supplement advertising and personal selling in the promotional mix. Multinational companies spend millions of dollars to get exposure through big events such as the football World Cup.

sales promotions
activities to attract consumers and promote products

Sales promotions are short-term efforts directed at the consumer and/or retailer to achieve such specific objectives as:

1 consumer product trial and/or immediate purchase

2 consumer introduction to the store

3 gaining retail point-of-purchase displays

4 encouraging stores to stock the product

5 supporting and augmenting advertising and personal sales efforts.

6 sales promotions activities to attract consumers and promote products

An especially effective promotional tool when the product concept is new or has a very small market share is product sampling. Nestlé Baby Foods faced such a problem in France in its attempt to gain share from Gerber, the leader. The company combined sampling with a novel sales promotion programme to gain brand recognition and to build goodwill.

Most French people take off for a long vacation in the summertime. They pile the whole family into the car and roam around France, or head for Spain or Italy, staying at well-maintained campsites found throughout the country. It is an inexpensive way to enjoy the month-long vacation. However, travelling with a baby still in nappies can be a chore. Nestlé came up with a way to improve dramatically the quality of life for any parent and baby on the road.

Going International 19.5

MOBILE BRAND AMBASSADORS (AT A DISCOUNT)

With thanks to Taxi Media and Clear Channel UK.

Advice on skin care or your next holiday destination is the last thing you would expect when you hop into a black cab. But at Taxi Media, which controls over 85 per cent of taxi ads in the UK, the cabbie is not just a taxi driver but a 'brand ambassador'. In the age of digital TV, where consumers can fast-forward during ads, and SMS, advertisers are looking for new ways to grab consumers' attention.

Bus and taxi ads fall within the outdoor advertising category. Brand owners can pay to have ads on the sides of vehicles or opt for a full deal, which includes ads right across the cab's exterior and on receipts and tip-up seats. And the idea is that drivers provide the added value, promoting the brand to the passenger. Knowledge of the brand comes courtesy of the advertisers. For example, drivers who carry ads for Clinique were given facials and seminars on the company's 'three-step skin care system'. Qantas, the airline, offered free air tickets to Australia for the 40 cabbies carrying its ads, and the South African Tourist Board organised a trip to South Africa. The apparently good-natured and chatty character of the drivers makes them perfect brand ambassadors if they are enthusiastic about the product or service advertised on their cab.

Taxi Media, which has about 10,000 drivers on its books, says the market, which is worth about £17m in the UK, was flat in 2002, and will grow slightly in 2003. Of the 16,000 licensed cabs in London, 10 per cent carry advertisements. Compared to other outdoor media, taxi ads can be relatively cheap: £3,000 to £5,000 for a full livery per taxi for 12 months, of which £1,000 will go to the driver. An outdoor poster in London can cost more than double that, depending on the location, for only a few weeks. Buses and taxis also cover areas often denied to other outdoor media. They are seen in every tourist spot as well as the royal parks, residential areas and the City of London.

● Is this an effective way to advertise? How do you react to this as a customer?

Source: adapted from Emiko Terazono. 'Do Ask Me, Guv', *Financial Times Creative Business*, 12 August 2003, p 6, http://www.clearchannel.co.uk/ and http://www.verifonemedia.co.uk/.

It provided rest-stop structures along the road where parents could feed and change their babies. Sparkling clean Le Relais Bébés were located along main travel routes. Sixty-four hostesses at these rest stops welcomed 120,000 baby visits and dispensed 600,000 samples of baby food each year. There were free disposable nappies, a changing table and highchairs for the babies to sit in during meals. A strong tie between Nestlé and French mothers developed as a result of Le Relais Bébé. A market research survey showed an approval rating of 94 per cent and Nestlé's share of the market climbed to more than 43 per cent – close to a 24 share-point rise.

As is true in advertising, the success of a promotion may depend on local adaptation. Major constraints are imposed by local laws, which may not permit premiums or free gifts to be given. Some countries' laws control the amount of discount given at retail, others require permits for all sales promotions. Effective sales promotions can enhance advertising and personal selling efforts and, in some instances, may be effective substitutes when environmental constraints prevent full utilisation of advertising.

The advertising agency

Just as manufacturing firms have become international, US and European advertising agencies are expanding internationally to provide sophisticated agency assistance worldwide. Local agencies have also expanded as the demand for advertising services by MNCs has developed. Thus, the international marketer has a variety of alternatives available. In most commercially significant countries, an advertiser has the opportunity to employ:

1 a local domestic agency
2 its company-owned agency
3 one of the multinational advertising agencies with local branches.

A local domestic agency may provide a company with the best cultural interpretation in situations where local modification is sought, but the level of sophistication can be weak. Another drawback of local agencies is the difficulty of coordinating a worldwide campaign. One drawback of the company-owned agency is the possible loss of local input when it is located outside the area and has little contact within the host country.

The best compromise is the multinational agency with local branches because it has the sophistication of a major agency with local representation. Further, the multinational agency with local branches is better able to provide a coordinated worldwide **advertising campaign**. This has become especially important for firms doing business in Europe. With the interest in global or standardised advertising, many agencies have expanded to provide worldwide representation. Many companies with a global orientation employ one or perhaps two agencies to represent them worldwide.

> **advertising campaign**
>
> designed and implemented for a particular product/ purpose over a fixed period

International control of advertising

EU officials are establishing directives to provide controls on advertising as cable and satellite broadcasting expands. Deception in advertising is a major issue because most member countries have different interpretations of what constitutes a **misleading advertisement**. Demands for regulation of advertising aimed at young consumers is a trend appearing in both industrialised and developing countries.

> **misleading advertisement**
>
> gives incorrect message/impression of a product/ company

Decency and the blatant use of sex in advertisements are also receiving public attention. One of the problems in controlling decency and sex in ads is the cultural variations around the world. An ad perfectly acceptable to a European may be very offensive to someone from the USA or, for that matter, a Spaniard. Standards for appropriate behaviour as depicted in advertisements vary from culture to culture.

The difficulty that business has with self-regulation and restrictive laws is that sex can be powerful in some types of advertisement. European advertisements for Häagen-Dazs, a premium ice cream, and LapPower, a Swedish laptop computer company both received criticism for their ads as being too sexy.

The Häagen-Dazs ad showed a couple, in various states of undress, in an embrace feeding ice cream to one another. Some British editorial writers and radio commentators were outraged. One commented that 'the ad was the most blatant and inappropriate use of sex as a sales aid'. The ad for LapPower personal computers that the Stockholm Business Council on Ethics condemned featured the co-owner of the company with an 'inviting smile and provocative demeanour displayed'. (She was bending over a LapPower computer in a low-cut dress.)

The bottom line for both these companies was increased sales. In the UK, sales soared after the 'Dedicated to Pleasure' ads appeared, and in Sweden the co-owner stated that, 'Sales are increasing daily.' Whether laws are passed or the industry polices itself, there is international concern about advertising and its effect on people's behaviour.

The advertising industry is sufficiently concerned with the negative attitudes of consumers and governments and with the poor practices of some advertisers that the International Advertising Association and other national and international industry groups have developed a variety of self-regulating codes. Sponsors of these codes feel that, unless the advertisers themselves come up with an effective framework for control, governments will intervene. This threat of government intervention has spurred interest groups in Europe to develop codes to ensure that the majority of ads conform to standards set for 'honesty, truth and decency'.

Going International 19.6

Product placement of Coca-Cola on the TV show 'American Idol'.
'Judges', © Rob Lee, robthecommguy. CC BY 2.0 UK.

A KILLER MOVIE PROMOTION WITH YOUR BRAND

Brand partnerships can be a super investment, if done correctly and not as a dog's breakfast. There are great examples of brands that have done it well. Brands have been doing film sponsorships for some time. For years, Volvo was the gold standard and probably cemented this practice as a viable marketing platform for brands. Back in the 1980s, you couldn't see a film without someone driving a Volvo in the story.

When it comes to product integration, Apple has been the darling of Hollywood. iOS devices last year appeared in 40 per cent of the top box office movies according to Brandchannel, which tracks product appearances. Intel Free Press writes that, unlike all other brands, Apple doesn't pay to play. For example, Apple's iPhone, iMac and iPad got eight minutes of screen time in the latest *Mission Impossible* film. Many filmmakers are fine with this policy (those behind *Mission Impossible: Ghost Protocol*, *Girl with the Dragon Tattoo* and *Chronicle*), but not everyone in Hollywood is willing to give Apple a free ride according to IFP.

Brands that invest in a movie promotion can expect to pay for the placement in the film, the production of the TV commercial, the music rights, and the talent. Plus the media costs to run the promotional TV commercial that you've made. But these costs may well be worth it depending on the project and its impact for the brand.

The challenge these days is how do you integrate a brand into a film and its promotion in a way that fits with the story and doesn't look awful. Many times it is like 'Shakespeare being paid to write with a biro rather than a quill', says the *Independent*. 'Product placement is a fact of life.'

Film integrated advertising has lost its subtlety. No longer is it merely embedded within cinema, gently filtering into our brains and only whispering at us to buy; now it shouts to us from inside Coca-Cola cans and slaps us in the face with an Omega watch-wearing wrist.

● Is product placement in films and TV dramas ethical? Is it effective?

Source: adapted from *Forbes*, 11 July 2012.

SUMMARY

Global advertisers face unique legal, language, media and production limitations in every market that must be considered when designing a promotional mix. As the world and its markets become more sophisticated, there is greater emphasis on international marketing strategy. The current debate among marketers is the effectiveness of standardised versus modified advertising for culturally varied markets. And, as competition increases and markets expand, greater emphasis is being placed on global brands and/or image recognition.

The most logical conclusion seems to be that, when buying motives and company objectives are the same for various countries, the advertising orientation can be the same. When they vary from nation to nation, the advertising effort will have to reflect these variations. In any case, variety in media availability, coverage and effectiveness will have to be taken into consideration in the advertiser's plans. If common appeals are used, they may have to be presented by a radio broadcast in one country, by cinema in another, and by television in a third.

A skilled advertising practitioner must be sensitive to the environment and alert to new facts about the market. It is also essential for success in international advertising endeavours to pay close attention to the communications process and the steps involved.

QUESTIONS

1   'Perhaps advertising is the side of international marketing with the greatest similarities from country to country throughout the world. Paradoxically, despite its many similarities, it may also be credited with the greatest number of unique problems in international marketing.' Discuss.

2   Discuss the difference between advertising strategy when a company follows a multidomestic strategy rather than a global market strategy.

3   With satellite TV able to reach many countries, discuss how a company can use it and deal effectively with different languages, different cultures and different legal systems.

4   Outline some of the major challenges confronting an international advertiser.

5   Defend either side of the proposition that advertising can be standardised for all countries.

6   How can advertisers overcome the problem of low literacy in their markets?

7   What special media problems confront the international advertiser?

8   Discuss the reason for pattern advertising.

9   Will the ability to broadcast advertisements over satellite TV increase or decrease the need for standardisation of advertisements? What are the problems associated with satellite broadcasting? Comment.

10 What is sales promotion and how is it used in international marketing?

11 Show how the communications process can help an international marketer avoid problems in international advertising.

12 Take each of the steps of the communications process and give an example of how cultural differences can affect the final message received.

FURTHER READING

- A.G. Parsons and C. Schumacher, 'Advertising Regulations and Market Drivers', *European Journal of Marketing*, 2012, 46(11–12), 1539–58.
- P. Walters, P. Whitla and H. Davies, 'Global Strategy in the International Advertising Industry', *International Business Review*, 2008, 17(3), 235–49.
- E.L. Olson and H.M. Thjomoe, 'The Relative Performance of TV Sponsorship versus Spot Advertising', *European Journal of Marketing*, 2012, 46 (11–12), 1727–42.

NOTES

1   Laurent Gallissor, 'The Cultural Significance of Advertising: A General Framework of the Cultural Analysis of the Advertising Industry in Europe', *International Sociology*, March 1994, pp 13–28.

2   Jean-Claude Usunier, *Marketing across Cultures* (Hemel Hempstead: Prentice Hall, 1996).

3   F.S.L. Cheung and W.-F. Leung, 'International Expansion of Transnational Advertising Agencies in China: An Assessment of the Stages Theory Approach', *International Business Review*, 2007, 16(2), 251–68.

4   Michel Laroche, V.H. Kirpalani, Frank Pons and Lianxi Zhou, 'A Model of Advertising Standardization in Multinational Corporations', *Journal of International Business Studies*, 2001, 32(2), 249–66.

5   Theodore Levitt, 'The Globalization of Markets', *Harvard Business Review*, May–June 1983, pp 92–102.

6   'How Colgate-Palmolive Crafts Ad Strategies in Eastern Europe', *Crossborder Monitor*, 2 March 1994, p 8.

7   Carl Arthur Solberg, 'The Perennial Issue of Adaptation or Standardization of International Marketing Communication: Organisational Contingencies and Performance', *Journal of International Marketing*, 2002, 10(3), 1–21.

8   A.S. Hoon, 'Advertising Strategy and Effective Advertising: Comparing the USA and Australia', *Journal of Marketing Communications*, 2002, 8(3), 179–88.

9   R.A. Kustin, 'Marketing Mix Standardization: A Cross-cultural Study of Four Countries', *International Business Review*, 2004, 13(5), 637–49.

10 Sudhir H. Kale, 'How National Culture, Organizational Culture and Personality Impact Buyer–seller Interactions', in Pervez Ghauri and Jean-Claude Usunier (eds), *International Business Negotiations* (Oxford: Pergamon, 1996).

11 'Pepsi Spots Banned in Asia', *Advertising Age International*, 21 March 1994, pp 1–2.

12 D.K. Boojihawon, P. Dimitratos and S. Young, 'Characteristics and Influences of Multinational Subsidiary Entrepreneurial Culture: The Case of the Advertising Sector', *International Business Review*, 2007, 16(5), 549–72.

13 N.S. Hong and C.Y. Poon, *Business Restructuring in Hong Kong* (Oxford: Oxford University Press, 2004).

14 L.S. Amine, 'Country-of-origin, Animosity and Consumer Response: Marketing Implications of Anti-Americanism and Francophobia', *International Business Review*, 2008, 17(4), 402–22.

15 Swee Hoon Ang, 'Advertising Strategy and Advertising: Comparing the USA and Australia', *Journal of Marketing Communications*, 2002, 8(3), 179–88.

16 S. Samee, I. Jeong, J.H. Pae and S. Tai, 'Advertising Standardization in Multinational Corporations: The Subsidiary Perspective', *Journal of Business Research*, 2003, 56(8), 613–26.

Chapter 20

Personal Selling and Negotiations

Chapter Learning Objectives

What you should learn from Chapter 20

- The importance of relationships in international selling
- The nuances of cross-cultural communication and its impact on sales negotiations
- The attributes of international sales personnel and how to manage a multicultural sales force
- How to handle the problems unique to selecting and training foreign sales staff
- The importance of skill in a foreign language while negotiating internationally
- How to identify the factors influencing cross-cultural negotiation
- How to handle international sales negotiations

There are four ways of achieving marketing communication: advertising, sales promotions, personal selling and public relations. Cultural differences as well as the type of product have a major impact on how an optimal mix is found among the above-mentioned four ways to achieve the objectives of a company. People who want to take into account cultural differences have to be **relationship-centred** rather than purely **deal-centred**.[1]

The sales person provides a company's most direct contact with the customer and, in the eyes of most customers, the sales person *is* the company. As the presenter of the company's offerings and gatherer of customer information, the sales person is the final link in the culmination of a company's marketing and sales effort.

The tasks of building, training, compensating and motivating an international marketing group generate unique problems at every stage of management and development. This chapter discusses the importance of communications and negotiations in building marketing relationships with international customers.

> **relationship-centred**
>
> when the sales person aims to build an ongoing relationship with the customer
>
> **deal-centred**
>
> when a sales person is solely concerned with completing the particular transaction

Selling in international markets

Increased global competition coupled with the dynamic and complex nature of international business increases the need for closer ties with both customers and suppliers. Selling in international marketing, built on effective communications between the seller and buyer, focuses on building long-term relationships rather than treating each sale as a onetime event.[2] This approach is becoming increasingly important for successful international marketers, especially in industrial buyer–seller interactions.[3] In **personal selling**, persuasive arguments are presented directly in a face-to-face relationship between sellers and potential buyers. To be effective, sales people must be certain that their communication and negotiation skills are properly adapted to a cross-cultural setting.

> **personal selling**
>
> when a product is sold through personal methods (eg sales people)

In many countries a low status is associated with selling. It is associated with the negative connotation of taking money from people rather than usefully bringing products and services to them. Seller status can also be associated with a particular group of people, eg Chinese, Dutch or Lebanese. In this perception, the seller's role is to convince and show the buyer the worth of the product on offer. In marketing, however, one of the seller's roles is to recognise the customer's needs and make them known to his or her company.

The style of selling is often related to national culture, but it also depends on the personality of the sales person and the type of industry. Selling styles can also depend on which types of result or achievement are sought – for example, whether it is to win a new customer or maintaining an old relationship.

EXHIBIT 20.1: Selling orientations

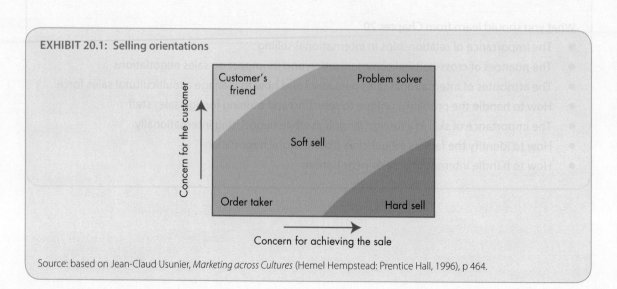

Source: based on Jean-Claud Usunier, *Marketing across Cultures* (Hemel Hempstead: Prentice Hall, 1996), p 464.

We believe that, when preparing arguments, a sales person has two main concerns: one is for the customers and their needs; the other is for achieving the sales.[4] This is illustrated in Exhibit 20.1.

If we separate the seller's role from that of the negotiator, the role of the sales person is mainly persuasion. There are, however, differences between persuasion and rather insistent and annoying behaviour. The main issue here is to understand what arguments will be best and quickest to persuade a particular customer.

In addition to the above factors, the two main components of personal selling are content and style. Content refers to the substantive aspects of the interaction for which the buyer and the seller come together. It includes suggesting, offering and negotiating. Style refers to the rituals, format, mannerisms and ground rules that the buyer and the seller follow in their encounter.

A satisfactory interaction between the buyer and the seller is contingent upon buyer–seller compatibility with respect to both the content and the style of communication. The level of this compatibility is determined by cultural and personality factors.[5] The effectiveness of personal selling in international marketing is influenced by a number of factors, such as the nature of the sales person–customer relationship, the behaviour of the sales person, the resources of the sales person and the nature of the customer's buying task, as illustrated by Exhibit 20.2.

The nature of the sales person–customer relationship

The sales person–customer relationship is very important in international marketing as keeping a sales force in a foreign market means that the company is concerned about continuity in the relationship with its customers and that it wants to meet people face to face rather than through printed material and advertising. Development of the relationship thus becomes very important. The sales person has to develop a relationship of trust and friendship with the company's customers. In most relationships one party is more dominant than the other; this is also true in the sales person–customer relationship.

Here, the sales person should seek to create a balance in this power/dependence situation. Depending on the above and the nature of the relationship, the parties perceive it as cooperative or conflicting. This issue is directly related to the bargaining power of the parties. The sales person's job is to drive the relationship towards being cooperative. The nature of this relationship and willingness to cooperate also depends on what the parties expect from each other in the future. The more they anticipate a future beneficial interaction, the more the relationship is improved.

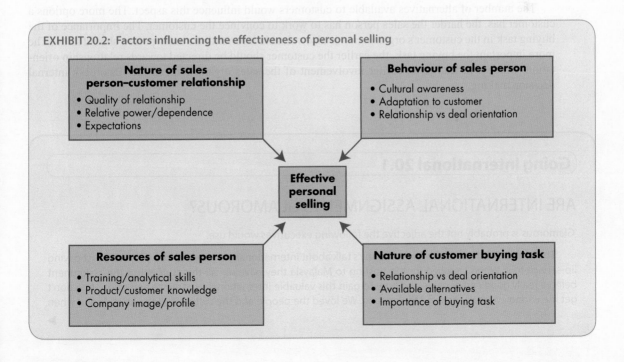

EXHIBIT 20.2: Factors influencing the effectiveness of personal selling

Nature of sales person–customer relationship
- Quality of relationship
- Relative power/dependence
- Expectations

Behaviour of sales person
- Cultural awareness
- Adaptation to customer
- Relationship vs deal orientation

Effective personal selling

Resources of sales person
- Training/analytical skills
- Product/customer knowledge
- Company image/profile

Nature of customer buying task
- Relationship vs deal orientation
- Available alternatives
- Importance of buying task

Behaviour of the sales person

The behaviour of the sales person in international marketing interaction is highly dependent on his or her awareness of the local culture, values and norms. For this reason, companies normally use a local sales force. Whether the sales person is an **expatriate** or a local, the sales message, approach and behaviour with the customer should be adapted in terms of language, level of argument and local norms.

> **expatriate**
>
> employee of the company/organisation sent to another country to work

A relationship orientation instead of a one-shot deal orientation is essential in interaction with customers. In fact, this is often the main reason behind having a sales force. Sales people should also use the influential techniques mentioned earlier and in the negotiation section of this chapter. One should be aware that these techniques can be different in different markets, depending on culture, type of product and company.

Resources of the sales person

The sales person to be used in international marketing needs to be trained not only for a particular market/culture but also for general skills such as analytical techniques and negotiation. These skills are essential for international marketing activities and for developing relationships with customers. The sales force should be fully aware of the company's products and customers' needs, and how these two could be matched.

A holistic view of the company's capabilities and resources is essential for representing the company fully and efficiently. The sales person should have full knowledge of the market and customer segmentation, not only of existing customers. Having a full picture of all available alternatives is a good resource that helps customer relationships. The image and positioning of a company in a particular market is of the utmost importance and is good baggage for the sales person. There should be some consistency in the company image and the message a sales person is taking to customers.

Nature of customer's buying task

Another important factor, external to the sales person, is the nature and characteristics of the customer's buying task. Although it is beyond the sales person's control, he or she can in fact influence it. One way is to make the customer believe that there is a perfect match between his or her needs and what the sales person is offering. The relationship orientation from both sides is thus crucial, as it can allow the sales person to get involved at an early stage of the customer's buying process.

The number of alternatives available to customers would influence this aspect. The more options a customer has, the harder the sales person has to work to convince the customer. The importance of the buying task in the customer's organisation is also valuable information a sales person should know. The more important the buying task, the earlier the customer should be directed towards relationship orientation, which will lead to an earlier involvement of the sales organisation in the customer's internal decision making.

Going International 20.1

ARE INTERNATIONAL ASSIGNMENTS GLAMOROUS?

'Glamorous' is probably not the adjective the following executives would use.

'The problem as I see it with the company's talk about international managers is that they were just paying lip-service to it. When I applied for the posting to Malaysia they gave me all this stuff about the assignment being a really good career move and how I'd gain this valuable international experience and so on. And don't get me wrong, we really enjoyed the posting. We loved the people and the culture and the lifestyle and when

▶

◀

it came to returning home, we weren't really all that keen. ... The problem was that while I had been away, the company had undergone a wholesale restructuring.... This meant that when I got back, my job had effectively been eliminated.'

'We have been in the United States for 11 months and I reckon it will be another six to 12 months before my wife and the kids are really settled here. I'm still learning new stuff every day at work and it has taken a long time to get used to the American way of doing things.'

And 'glamorous' would not be on the tip of these expatriate spouses' tongues either.

© Istockphoto.com/sjlocke.

'I found I haven't adapted to Spanish hours. I find it a continual problem because the 2–5 pm siesta closure is really awkward. I always find myself where I have to remind myself that from 2–5 I have a blank period in which I can't do anything. ... We started adjusting to the eating schedule. Whether we like it or not, we eat a lot later.'

'Well, we went down to Club Med for a vacation and the French were all topless and my eight-year-old son didn't say anything, but my ten-year-old daughter now refuses to wear a top. I will not let her get away with it back in the US.'

'We've been really fortunate we haven't had to use health care services here ... The thought of going to a doctor is scary because for me it would have to be someone English speaking or I wouldn't, you know, feel comfortable.'

- Given these kinds of problems, do you think that international sales positions are as attractive as they look? Will such a position help your career?

Sources: compiled from several sources.

The international selling sequence

Knowing the customer in international sales means more than understanding the customer's product needs. It includes knowing the customer's culture. A cosmopolitan sales person will become more adept at cross-cultural selling if given a thorough grounding in the sequence that should be followed. Exhibit 20.3 presents a flowchart of international selling transactions. This step-by-step approach can be utilised for sales force planning and training.[6]

The selling sequence starts with a self-appraisal, which is quite similar to the self-reference criteria (SRC) discussed in earlier chapters. The aim of self-appraisal is to develop a frame of reference whereby one's own communication preferences with regard to content and style can be understood. Dimensions of SRC (that is, an unconscious reference to one's own cultural values, experience and knowledge) serve as a basis for self-awareness (see Chapter 1).

Impression formation involves understanding the buyer's cultural position. Typically, national culture and **organisational culture** can be assessed even before the seller meets with the buyer. Hofstede provides scores and ranks for 50 countries on the basis of positions on the four dimensions of national culture.[7]

> **organisational culture**
>
> values and norms of working in an organisation

The organisational culture of most large and medium-sized companies can be gleaned from their press releases, annual reports and from popular literature. A trained sales person can assess a buyer's temperament with a fair degree of accuracy during a

EXHIBIT 20.3: The international selling sequence

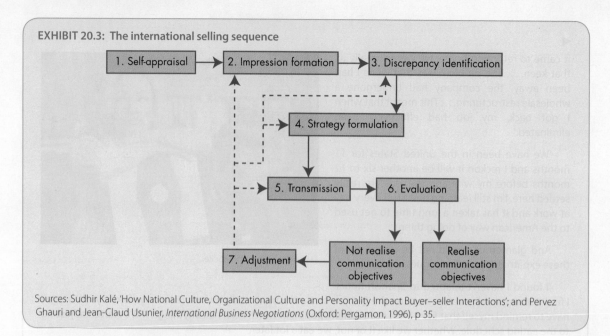

Sources: Sudhir Kalé, 'How National Culture, Organizational Culture and Personality Impact Buyer–seller Interactions'; and Pervez Ghauri and Jean-Claud Usunier, *International Business Negotiations* (Oxford: Pergamon, 1996), p 35.

relatively short period of interaction. An accurate impression of the buyer in terms of national culture, organisational culture and temperament lays the foundation for relationship building, which is so critical to successful selling.

In the third step, the seller goes through the mental exercise of 'discrepancy identification'. This involves comparing the buyer's estimated position on the various dimensions of culture with one's own. This alerts the seller to potential problem areas in communication arising out of differences in temperament and cultural conditioning.

Strategy formulation involves minimising the impact of problem areas identified in the earlier step. For instance, if the buyer is a feeler, and the seller is a thinker, the seller needs to modify his or her persuasion style. While his or her preferred persuasion style is logical and impersonal, this may not fit well with the buyer. The appropriate style in this instance would be to appeal to the buyer's feelings and emotions, and to point out the people-benefits behind the seller's offering. Similar adjustments need to be made on other dimensions as well where discrepancies exist between the seller and the buyer.

Transmission involves implementation of the communication/persuasion strategy. During the course of transmission, the seller should be sensitive to the verbal and nonverbal feedback received from the buyer. If the seller has correctly identified the seller's mindset based on temperament and culture, the strategy should be on target and the feedback received from the buyer will be encouraging.

Assessing the effect of the communication strategy constitutes the 'evaluation' phase. If the seller's communication objectives are realised, then the encounter has been successful. If not, the seller goes through the 'adjustment' process whereby buyer impressions, discrepancies and strategy are re-evaluated and the transmission is modified. At the evaluation and adjustment phase, the seller always has the choice of cutting short the encounter, and trying again at some time in the future. Regardless of the outcome, every encounter adds to the seller's repertoire of experiences, skills, strategies and alternative transmission approaches.

Understanding the nuances of cross-cultural communications

Communications and the art of persuasion, knowledge of the customer and product, the ability to close a sale and after-sale service are all necessary for successful selling. These are the attributes sought when hiring an experienced person and those taught to new employees. Since culture impacts on the international sales effort just as it does on international advertising and promotion, the marketer must be certain that all international sales personnel have an understanding of the influence of culture on communications. After all, selling is communication and, unless the sales person understands the overtones of cross-cultural communications, the sales process could be thwarted.

Effective communication requires an understanding of the nuances of the spoken language as well as the silent language.[8] Perhaps more important than language nuances are the meanings of different **silent languages** spoken by people from different cultures. They may think they are understanding one another when, in fact, they are misinterpreting one another. For example:

> A Briton visits a Saudi official to convince him to expedite permits for equipment being brought into the country. The Saudi offers the Briton coffee, which is politely refused (he had been drinking coffee all morning at the hotel while planning the visit). The latter sits down and crosses his legs, exposing the sole of his shoe. He passes the documents to the Saudi with his left hand, enquires after the Saudi's wife and emphasises the urgency of getting the needed permits.

> **silent languages**
> communication without the use of words

In less than three minutes, the Briton unwittingly offended the Saudi five times. He refused his host's hospitality, showed disrespect, used an 'unclean' hand, implied a familial familiarity and displayed impatience with his host. He had no intention of offending his host and probably was not aware of the rudeness of his behaviour. The Saudi might forgive his British guest for being ignorant of local custom, but the forgiven sales person is in a weakened position.

Knowing your customer in international sales means more than knowing your customer's product needs; it includes knowing your customer's culture. One international consultant suggests five rules of thumb for successful selling abroad:

1 **Be prepared** and do your homework. Learn about the host's culture, values, geography, religion and political structure. In short, do as complete a cultural analysis as possible to avoid cultural mistakes.

2 **Slow down**. Westerners are slaves to the clock. Time is money to a Westerner but, in many countries, emphasis on time implies unfriendliness, arrogance and untrustworthiness.

3 **Develop relationships** and trust before getting down to business. In many countries, business is not done until a feeling of trust has developed.

4 **Learn the language**, its nuances and the idiom, and/or get a good interpreter. There are just too many ways for miscommunication to occur.

5 **Respect the culture**. Manners are important. You are the guest, so respect what your host considers important.[9]

In international sales and purchase transactions, the responsibilities need to be clearly defined. For example, who is responsible for freight and insurance and from which point (ex-factory, on board, etc) are crucial issues and, if ignored, can lead to serious problems. What are the penalties for delays, and how is responsibility for delays to be determined, for example, in the case of strike, accident or fire? What if the goods do not correspond to the agreed sample or specifications? What if the payment is not made on time? Although a number of middlemen, such as clearing agents, are available to handle these issues, the sales person is solely responsible for negotiating these terms. The price or terms might be different with different responsibilities.

Recruitment of an international sales force

The number of marketing management personnel from the home country assigned to foreign countries varies according to the size of the operation and the availability of qualified locals. Increasingly, the number of home-country nationals (expatriates) assigned to foreign posts is smaller as the pool of trained, experienced locals grows.

The largest personnel requirement abroad for most companies is the sales force, drawn from three sources: expatriates, **local nationals** and **third-country nationals**. A company's staffing pattern may include all three types in any single foreign operation, depending on qualifications, availability and a company's needs.

> **local nationals**
> employees of a company who are local to the market
>
> **third-country nationals**
> expatriates from the business's own country working for a foreign company in a third country

Going International 20.2

CROSS-CULTURAL SELLING

Golf course negotiations are common in many business cultures.
© Macduff Everton/CORBIS.

Some stereotypes of selling styles are often associated with different markets. Here are some examples.

In Asian countries, where arrogance and displays of extreme confidence are not appreciated, sales people should make modest, rational, down-to-earth points. They should avoid trying to win arguments with the customers, who could suffer from a 'loss of face' and react negatively. In Japan, one is expected to play golf with one's customers.

In Italy, in contrast, lack of self-confidence would be perceived as a clear sign of lack of personal credibility and reliability; thus one needs to argue strongly in order to be taken seriously.

In Switzerland, you have to speak precisely and your words will be taken quite literally.

In the UK, it is advisable to use the *soft sell* approach. Do not be pushy; instead try to 'chat' and convince.

In Germany, you should use the *hard sell* approach by being persistent. Make visits, offer trials and be very visible.

Blending company sales objectives and the personal objectives of sales people is a task worthy of the most skilled manager. The Western manager must be constantly aware that many of the techniques used to motivate Western personnel and their responses to these techniques are based on Western cultural premises and may not work in other countries.

Expatriates

The number of companies relying on expatriate personnel is declining as the volume of world trade increases and as more companies use locals to fill marketing positions. However, when products are highly technical, or when selling requires an extensive background of information and applications, an expatriate sales force remains the best choice. The expatriate sales person may have the advantages of greater technical training, better knowledge of the company and its product line and proven dependability and effectiveness. And, because they are not locals, expatriates sometimes add to the prestige of the product line in the eyes of local customers.

Local nationals

At the sales level, the picture is clearly biased in favour of the locals because they transcend both cultural and legal barriers. More knowledgeable about a country's business structure than an expatriate would be, local sales people are better able to lead a company through the maze of unfamiliar distribution systems.

In Asia many locals will have earned Master's or MBA degrees in Europe or the USA; thus you get the cultural knowledge of the local meshed with an understanding of Western business management. Although expatriates' salaries may be no more than those of their national counterparts, the total cost of keeping comparable groups of expatriates in a country can be considerably higher because of special cost-of-living benefits, moving expenses, taxes and other costs associated with keeping an expatriate abroad.

Third-country nationals

The internationalisation of business has created a pool of third-country nationals (TCNs), expatriates from their own countries working for a foreign company in a third country. The TCNs are a group whose nationality has little to do with where they work or for whom. An example would be a German working in Malaysia for a US company. Historically, there have been a few expatriates or TCNs who have spent the majority of their careers abroad, but now a truly 'global executive' has begun to emerge.

At one time, Burroughs Corporation's Italian subsidiary was run by a Frenchman, the Swiss subsidiary by a Dane, the German subsidiary by an Englishman, the French subsidiary by a Swiss, the Venezuelan subsidiary by an Argentinean, and the Danish subsidiary by a Dutchman. The CEO of Up John-Pharmacia, an American-Swedish pharmaceutical multinational with its head office in Michigan, was a Pakistani.

TCNs are often sought because they speak several languages and know an industry or foreign country well. More and more companies are realising that talent flows to opportunity regardless of nationality.

Host country restrictions

The host governments' attitudes towards foreign workers complicate flexibility in selecting expatriate nationals or local nationals. Concern about foreign corporate domination, local unemployment and other issues cause some countries to restrict the number of non-nationals allowed to work within the country.

Selecting an international sales force

People operating in the home country need only the attributes of effective sales persons, whereas a transnational manager can require skills and attitudes that would challenge a diplomat. Personnel requirements for various positions vary considerably, but despite the range of differences, some basic requisites leading to effective performance should be considered because effective executives and sales people, regardless of the foreign country in which they are operating, share certain characteristics.

Maturity is a prime requisite for expatriate and third-country personnel. Sales personnel working abroad must typically work more independently than their domestic counterparts. The company must have confidence in their ability to make decisions and commitments without constant recourse to the home office, or they cannot be individually effective.

The marketer who expects to be effective in the international marketplace needs to have a positive outlook on an international assignment. People who do not like what they are doing and where they are doing it stand little chance of success. Failures are usually the result of overselling the assignment, showing the bright side of the picture, and not warning about the bleak side.

Successful adaptation in international affairs is based on a combination of attitude and effort. A careful study of the customs of the market country should be initiated before the marketer arrives, and should continue as long as there are facets of the culture that are not clear. One useful approach is to listen to the advice of national and foreign business people operating in that country. Cultural empathy is clearly a part of basic orientation because it is unlikely that anyone can be effective if antagonistic towards or confused about the environment.

The personal characteristics, skills and orientation that identify the potentially effective sales person have been labelled in many different ways. Each person studying the field has a preferred list of characteristics, yet rising above all the characteristics there is an intangible something that some have referred to as a 'sixth sense'. This implies that, regardless of individual attributes, there is a certain blend of personal characteristics, skills and orientation that is hard to pinpoint and that may differ from individual to individual, but that produces the most effective overseas personnel.

Going International 20.3

LIGHTSTREAM TECHNOLOGIES

© Istockphoto.com/africa924

When Vice Chairman Josh Lanier and his co-founders started LightStream in 1998, they knew that water purification was a $6bn business, largely dominated by the production and sale of chlorine. But dependence on chlorine is changing, Lanier insists, because of health and environmental problems associated with excessive chlorine use and security concerns about transporting the chemical.

Lanier and his colleagues needed a fast, reliable, cost-effective way of finding distributors in key markets. They assumed their technology would be in demand, especially in developing countries, where pollution management is a primary need.

It remained a challenge until Lanier met Sandra Collazo, a US Commercial Service trade specialist at the Northern Virginia Export Assistance Center. Collazo, whose specialities include environmental equipment, told Lanier about a Commercial Service trade mission to India. Numerous trade missions are organised each year, some of which are specific to a country, region or industry. Participants pay their own travel expenses, plus a fee that covers finding interested, qualified buyers.

Navigating the shoals of India's environmental sector can be tricky. Many firms are eager to partner with US companies, but finding the right one is crucial. Some appear established but are financially shaky. Others present long lists of contacts but lack the network to distribute products. Choosing the right partner can take months.

With help from the Commercial Service, Lanier whittled the list of candidates down to Subhash Projects and Marketing Ltd, a leading Indian engineering and construction firm. LightStream formed a strategic alliance with Subhash, and both companies expect sales of $15m in India over the next five years. The agreement calls for technology transfer and joint marketing throughout India. 'Subhash is a good group,' says Lanier. 'They're solid, they have growth potential, and they are publicly traded.'

Lanier accelerated his overseas business development and took advantage of more Commercial Service products. Under the Gold Key programme, US business people travel on their own to a market and meet potential buyers selected by Commercial Service officers. Lanier calculates that he has participated in dozens of Gold Keys around the world. Recently, he took a Gold Key trip to Europe. A cheap dollar makes LightStream's products a relative bargain in Europe right now. The Gold Key visit to Ireland concluded with a distribution agreement for the UK and South Africa, generating sales of $4.2m, with subsequent purchases of 40 systems worth even more.

- Is this the right way to help start-ups?

Source: adapted from http://export.gov/basicguide/eg_main_038339.asp.

Training and motivation

The nature of a training programme depends largely on whether expatriate or local personnel are being trained as sales people. Training for the expatriates focuses on the customs and the special foreign sales problems that will be encountered, whereas local personnel require greater emphasis on the company, its products, technical information and selling methods. In training either type of personnel, the sales training activity is burdened with problems stemming from long-established behaviour and attitudes.

Continual training is more important in foreign markets than in domestic ones because of the lack of routine contact with the parent company and its marketing personnel. One aspect of training is frequently overlooked: home-office personnel dealing with international marketing operations need training designed to make them responsive to the needs of the foreign markets. In most companies, the requisite sensitivities are expected to be developed by osmosis in the process of dealing with foreign affairs; a few companies send home-office personnel abroad periodically to increase their awareness of the problems of the foreign markets.[10]

A common complaint among international sales people is that their head office does not understand them. They often feel left alone or deserted. Their morale can be boosted through realistic sales targets, giving them full support and making them feel that head office is fully behind them. Their achievements should be properly rewarded in accordance with their career goals. Job stability is another issue: sales people often have an uneasy feeling that while they are on the road other people at the office are getting all the benefits with regard to promotions and job stability. They may also be afraid about what will happen if they do not meet their targets.

Going International 20.4

PERSONAL SELLING TIPS, FROM BRUSSELS TO BANGKOK

The best training programmes are much more than just a list of tips. But a quick read-through of such tips provides a glimpse of the cultural variation facing sales representatives around the globe.

Belgium: be able to identify the decision makers. In Flanders, the Dutch-speaking region, group decisions are common, but in Wallonia (the French-speaking region), the highest-level execs have the final say.

China: expect to continue negotiations after a deal is inked. To Chinese, signing a contract is just the beginning of the business relationship; therefore, they expect both sides to continue working together to fix problems that arise.

Colombia: business counterparts want to get to know you personally and form a strong friendship with you. Be sure not to change reps in midstream, because a switch often puts an end to negotiations.

© istock.

Germany: be prepared with data and empirical evidence that supports your sales proposition. German business people are unimpressed by flashy advertising and brochures, so keep them serious and detailed, with unexaggerated information.

India: make sure your schedule remains flexible. Indians are more casual about time and punctuality. Because of India's rigid hierarchy, decisions are made only by the highest-level boss.

▶

◀

Mexico: when planning a meeting, breakfast and lunch are preferable. Take your time and cultivate relationships with business contacts. Those relationships are generally considered more important than professional experience.

Peru: Peruvians relate to individuals and not corporate entities. Establish personal rapport and don't switch your representative in the middle of negotiations.

Russia: your first meeting will be just a formality. Your Russian counterparts will take this time to judge your credibility, so it's best to be warm and approachable.

Scotland: Scottish people tend to be softly-spoken and private. It takes time to build relationships, but business counterparts seem friendlier after bonds are established. (By the way, Scotch is a drink, not a nationality: the correct terminology is Scottish or Scots.)

South Korea: status is important. Make sure your business card clearly indicates your title. Don't send a rep to meet with a Korean executive of higher status – it could be viewed as disrespectful.

Thailand: the Thai culture emphasises non-conflict, so don't make assertive demands when making sales pitches.

Source: *Sales and Marketing Management* publishes these tips regularly in its magazine and on its website (www. salesandmarketing.com).

Cross-cultural negotiations

The keystone of effective marketing and buyer–seller interactions is effective negotiation. Poorly conducted negotiations can leave the seller and the buyer frustrated, and do more to destroy effective relationships than anything else. Negotiation should be handled in such a way that a long-term relationship between buyer and seller is ensured.[11]

The basic elements of business negotiations are the same in every country; they relate to the product, its price and terms, services associated with the product and, finally, friendship between vendors and customers. Selling is often thought of as a routine exchange with established prices and distribution networks from which there is little deviation. But, particularly in international sales, the selling transaction is almost always a negotiated exchange. Price, delivery dates, quality of goods or services, volume of goods sold, financing, exchange rate risk, shipping mode, insurance, and so on, are all set by bargaining or negotiations. Such negotiations should not be conducted in a typical 'win–lose' situation but as a shared benefit that will ensure a long-term relationship.[12]

Simply stated, to negotiate is to confer, bargain or discuss with a view to reaching an agreement. It is a sequential rather than simultaneous give-and-take discussion resulting in a mutually beneficial understanding. Most authorities on negotiating include three stages in the negotiating process: (1) pre-negotiation stage; (2) negotiation stage; and (3) post-negotiation stage. In the pre-negotiation stage, parties attempt to understand each other's needs and offers, which is done through informal meetings and arrangements. The negotiation stage refers to face-to-face negotiations, and the post-negotiation stage refers to the stage when parties have agreed on most of the issues and are to agree on contract language and format, the signing of the contract, and how it leads to more business and relationship development.

In addition to these stages, the process of international business negotiation has two more dimensions: (1) strategic factors; and (2) cultural factors (see Exhibit 20.4).

Cultural factors play an important role in each and every stage of the international negotiation process. Cultural factors include time, pattern of communication and emphasis on personal relationships. While 'time is money' in Western cultures, it has no such value attached to it in Asia, Latin America and Africa. Knowing whether the other party is looking for a collective solution or an individual benefit is very important. According to Hofstede's studies, we can place different countries on different scales of individual and collective behaviour.[13]

EXHIBIT 20.4: The process of international sales negotiations

Cultural factors	Negotiation process	Strategic factors
• Time orientation • Collective/individualist • Pattern of communication • Personal relationships	• Pre-negotiation • Face-to-face negotiation • Post-negotiation	• Strategy • Decision making • Need for an agent • Tactics

Different cultures have different patterns of communication as regards direct versus indirect and explicit versus implicit communication. Some languages are traditionally vague, others exaggerate, which makes communication difficult for those from outside who are not familiar with the language. Finally, different cultures attach different importance to personal relations in negotiations. In the West, the negotiators are more concerned with the issue at hand, irrespective of who is representing the other side.

Pre-negotiation stage

Before entering into an international negotiation process, the two parties should know which type of decision-making procedure is going to be followed by the other party and which type of strategy should be used to match it. How should a party present its offer and capabilities? The formal versus informal and argumentative versus informative presentation style is very distinct in many countries. If not prepared, negotiators can make serious blunders.

In negotiations people refer to different types of strategy, such as tough, soft or intermediate. In this respect too it is important to have information on the other party's strategy, so that you can match it. Furthermore, it is important to know who makes the decisions, and whether the negotiators taking part in the negotiation have decision-making powers.

Under strategic factors, it is also important to evaluate your position and realise whether there is a need for an agent or consultant for a particular negotiation process. It is a generally held opinion that the more unfamiliar or complex is the other party or market, the greater is the need for an agent or consultant.

Business people have to understand the cultural context of negotiations. An authoritative source on cross-cultural negotiating suggests that one of the major difficulties in any cross-cultural negotiation is that expectations about the normal process of negotiations differ among cultures. Two important areas where differences can arise in cross-cultural negotiating are rapport and the degree of emphasis placed on each of the stages in the negotiating process by those involved in a negotiation.[14]

In the pre-negotiation stage the parties gather as much relevant information as possible on each other. Some informal meetings are held to check each other's positions and capabilities. This stage is often more important than the formal negotiation stage, as buyers and sellers can develop social, informal relationships. Trust and confidence gained from these relationships increase the chances of an agreement.

The most important issue at this stage, however, is to do the preparation thoroughly. An insight into the buying behaviour of the customer and his or her priorities is crucial, as it is necessary to present the product/service in a manner consistent with those priorities and behaviour. For a new customer, the amount of homework to be done is quite heavy, but it will help in subsequent interactions. The idea is to read the map before getting lost. The necessary first step in getting started on an overseas venture is to 'study the map' and learn as much as possible about the target country, culture and individuals before leaving home. Preparation on some practical details such as availability of office equipment and computers in the new country or the necessity of having an agent, and so on, are also some of the essentials of this stage.

Going International 20.5

HOW TO INSULT A MEXICAN CUSTOMER

© Istockphoto.com/ayzek.

Señor José Garcia Lopez, a Mexican importer-distributor, had been negotiating with a Danish manufacturing company for several months when he decided to visit Copenhagen to finalise a distribution agreement and purchase contract. He insisted on coming over as soon as possible.

To accommodate his potential customer, Flemming, the 40-year-old export manager, welcomed Sr Garcia to Denmark for meetings on Thursday and Friday. Flemming warned Sr Garcia that he had a long-scheduled flight to Tokyo early Saturday, but the Mexican customer saw no problem at all since he was also booked to leave Denmark that Saturday morning.

The business meetings went very smoothly, so on Friday afternoon Sr Garcia confided that he looked forward to signing the contract after his return to Mexico City. That evening the Danes invited Sr Garcia out for an evening on the town. Flemming and his 21-year-old assistant Margrethe hosted an excellent dinner and then took their Mexican prospect on a tour of Copenhagen nightspots. Around midnight Flemming glanced at his watch. 'Sr Garcia, as you know, I have a very early flight tomorrow to Tokyo. I hope you'll forgive me if I leave you now. When you are ready, Margrethe will make sure you get back to your hotel all right. And then she will drive you to the airport tomorrow morning. Have a good flight!'

Next morning in the car on the way to the airport José Garcia was uncharacteristically silent. Then he turned to the young assistant: 'Margrethe, would you please tell your boss that I have decided not to sign that contract after all. It is not your fault of course. If you think about what happened last evening I believe you will understand why I no longer want to do business with your company.'

Source: © Copenhagen Business School Press, 2002. With thanks to the author, Richard R. Gesteland, Global Management LLC, 2002, and CBS Press (http://www.cbspress.dk/).

Face-to-face negotiation stage

In the formal face-to-face negotiation stage, parties evaluate alternatives. The differences in preferences and expectations are explored and possibilities of coming closer to each other are sought. Negotiators give and take and come to their final positions. In this stage, a balance between firmness and credibility is important, and parties give and receive signals for further movement in the process.

Time plays an important role in cross-cultural negotiation. In a culture where time is money, little importance is given to relationship building and small talk. In the West people are constantly on the move, while Asians believe that considerable time should be spent in building general understanding, trust and relationships. Selling in international markets takes much longer than in domestic transactions, not only because of the culture, but also because the tempo is generally slower.

In some countries there are long religious or national holidays. In Muslim countries Ramadan is not really appropriate for negotiations. In Europe the months of July and August are not suitable as most people are on holiday. In the USA the period between Thanksgiving and New Year is considered difficult. And so on. All these aspects need to be considered when planning for negotiations.

While negotiating in other countries a combination of solid know-how, experience and common sense is required to master the process. Now that an extensive literature on such negotiations exists, it is possible to acquire this know-how and learn from others' experience. Some of the literature that is available is general in nature, but there are also specialist books on regional negotiation styles.[14] When negotiating, it is important to remember the following points:

1 *Understand the value of the particular deal*: the first step in each negotiation process is to realise the implication of that deal in the short run as well as in the long run. Unless you have a clear picture of the deal you cannot formulate a true strategy regarding a transaction versus relational approach.

2 *Evaluate the competition*: if you know what range of alternatives the other party has, you can see more clearly how important the deal is for them. In this way, you can create arguments and alternatives that match or compete with the alternatives the other party has.

3 *Check your language and communication capabilities*: depending on the other party and the market/country involved, you have to decide how best you can manage the communication process. The messages should be adapted to the level and culture of the other party. Also consider non-verbal communication, especially those things you cannot/should not do.[15]

4 *Understand the decision-making process*: both your own and that of the other party. It is clear that you can make all decisions while you are out there. Do you know that the negotiators coming from the other side can make all decisions? Who in their team or head office is in fact the decision-maker?

5 *Remember that patience is an asset in international business negotiations*: in many cultures, Asian, Middle Eastern and even in Eastern Europe, things take their time. Negotiators from these cultures are not to be hurried; they really need to feel the negotiation process before they are ready to make a decision. In such cases it is not useful to push them to make a decision.

Going International 20.6

RUSSIA: OPPORTUNITIES AND RULES OF ENGAGEMENT

Russia is the world's biggest country: it crosses 11 time zones and has 150 million inhabitants. Although it remains difficult to crack, the Russian market holds attraction for foreign investors, not least because of its high potential and abundance of raw materials. At present, more than 1,000 North American and more than 900 German companies are registered in Moscow. As purchasing power is recovering from the 1998 crisis that wiped out people's savings, sales are rising for everything from beer to hair colouring. Sales of Carlsberg's popular Baltika beer soared 60 per cent and L'Oréal's sales jumped 52 per cent in recent years.

A Russian hypermarket.
'HPIM3155', © Petri Piirainen. CC BY 2.0 UK.

Hypermarkets are gaining a hold in the retailing arena as Russian consumers, who do not have mortgages and loans to pay off due to underdeveloped banking systems, spend most of their income on food and other household products. Economic growth fostered by FDI has created a new social class in Moscow and St Petersburg: *Novye Bysinessmeny* (the new business people).

On the downside, the cost of living has risen considerably in recent years, making Moscow the most expensive city in the world after Tokyo and London. Rising inflation has meant that ordinary people can afford less now than before. The chaos and corruption of Russia's labyrinthine bureaucracy has had a serious effect on business life, while crime has reached alarming proportions in some parts of the country. However, those who are prepared to brave the difficulties and take advantage of the opportunities that Russia offers may find the following advice useful:

● During business negotiations in Russia, the relaxed and humorous Western way of communicating is not really appropriate. Negotiations are a serious matter and should be treated accordingly. The first encounter

▶

◀

is usually calm and formal. However, subsequent meetings can be lively and spirited – occasional emotional outbursts are not uncommon.

- Personal relationships are very important, and in many cases the success of the venture depends on them rather than on official petitions or applications. Russian negotiators generally do not expect help from bureaucracy.

- Most Russians are suspicious of public authorities and red tape, and will be mistrustful of any changes to contracts. If you have to make changes to meet laws or regulations, you will have to offer a good explanation.

- The dress code in Russia is rather formal and conservative. When you are introduced to a business partner, use your family name and your title, not your first name. Later on, during the conversation, you can switch to the Russian style of combining your own and your father's first name, although the *Novye Bysinessmeny* usually address each other by their first names.

- It is a good idea to bring a supply of business cards showing your title and academic qualifications.

- Business meetings usually take place in restaurants. Invitations to private houses are rare, but if invited you should not refuse such an opportunity.

- Russians drink a lot of vodka. Be careful to take part in a toast, which is an important ritual. The host has the honour of performing the first toast. Think about an honest toast in reply and use it to create a positive feeling and move the business along.

- Russian business partners are rather slow, but once you have won their sympathy, you will have formed a long-lasting relationship.

- Negotiation can be difficult outside big cities because the use of foreign languages is not as widespread there. Do not expect your business partner to speak English. Interpreters play an important role when doing business in Russia; it is worth spending some time to find a good one.

- Negotiations can be protracted, starting up to an hour late. They are often interrupted and sometimes two or more talks are held at the same time, which can distract your business partner. However, your partner will take all the time they need to consider the information – Russians believe you can never gather enough information about a prospective deal.

- Enterprises operating in Russia commonly encounter fiscal obscurities, problematic legal issues and difficulties in dealing with public authorities. New laws and regulations have only added to the complications. Some licences (especially for export) are hard to obtain. Make sure you have trustworthy professionals such as lawyers and accountants on your side.

Sources: compiled from several issues of *Financial Times* and *Business Week*.

Post-negotiation stage

In the post-negotiation stage the contract is drawn up. Experience shows that writing the contract and its language and formulations can be a negotiation process in itself as meanings and values differ between the two parties. If not properly handled, this stage can lead to renewed face-to-face negotiations. The best way to avoid this is to make sure that both parties thoroughly understand what they have agreed on before leaving each negotiation session.

SUMMARY

An effective international sales force constitutes one of the international marketer's greatest concerns. The company sales force represents the major alternative method of organising a company for foreign distribution and, as such, is on the front line of a marketing organisation.

The role of marketers in both domestic and foreign markets is changing rapidly, along with the composition of international managerial teams and sales forces. These last two have many unique requirements that are being filled by expatriates, locals, third-country nationals, or a combination of the three. In recent years, the pattern of development has been to place more emphasis on local personnel operating in their own countries.

The importance of negotiations is more evident in international as compared to domestic marketing. The sales force needs to be trained in cross-cultural communication and negotiation for successful marketing performance. For successful negotiations in an international context, you have to understand the other party and its priorities. The impact of culture on the decision-making process of the parties involved is of utmost importance and should be fully understood in order to handle the negotiations efficiently. Moreover, you need to adapt your communication pattern to one that is easily understandable by the other party.

QUESTIONS

1 What are the factors that influence the effectiveness of personal selling in international marketing? Explain.

2 Define the following: expatriate, third-country national, non-verbal feedback, cultural empathy.

3 Why might it be difficult to adhere to set job criteria in selecting foreign personnel? What compensating actions might be necessary?

4 Under what circumstances should expatriate sales people be utilised?

5 Discuss the problems that might be encountered in having an expatriate sales person supervising foreign sales people.

6 'It is costly to maintain an international sales force.' Comment.

7 Adaptability and maturity are traits needed by all sales people. Why should they be singled out as especially important for international sales people?

8 Discuss the stages in cross-cultural negotiations. How can you effectively manage an international negotiation process? Discuss.

9 Why is sound negotiation the key to effective relationship marketing? Discuss.

FURTHER READING

- P.N. Ghauri and T. Fang, 'Negotiating with the Chinese: A Socio-cultural Analysis', *Journal of World Business*, 2001, 36(3), 303–25.

- P.N. Ghauri and J.-C. Usunier, *International Business Negotiations,* 2nd edn (Oxford: Elsevier, 2003).

- G.S. Insch and J.D. Daniel, 'Causes and Consequences of Declining Early Departure from Foreign Assignments', *Business Horizon*, 2003, 45(6), 39–48.

NOTES

1 L.S. Amine, 'Country-of-origin, Animosity and Consumer Response: Marketing Implications of Anti-Americanism and Francophobia', *International Business Review*, 2008, 17(4), 402–22.

2 R.B. Money, M.C. Gilly and J.L. Graham, 'National Culture and Referral Behaviour in the Purchase of Industrial Services in the United States and Japan', *Journal of Marketing*, 1998, 62(4), 76–87.

3 S. Kale, 'How National Culture, Organisational Culture and Personality Impact Buyer–seller Interaction', in P.N. Ghauri and J.-C. Usunier, *International Business Negotiations*, 2nd edn (Oxford: Elsevier, 2004).

4 Jean-Claude Usunier, *Marketing across Cultures* (Hemel Hempstead: Prentice Hall, 1996).

5 Jagdish Sheth, 'Cross-cultural Influences on the Buyer–seller Interaction/Negotiation Process', *Asia Pacific Journal of Management*, 1983, 1(1), 46–55.

6 This section is based on Sudhir Kalé, 'How National Culture, Organizational Culture and Personality Impact Buyer–seller Interactions', in Pervez Ghauri and Jean-Claude Usunier, *International Business Negotiations* (Oxford: Pergamon, 1996), pp 21–37.

7 Geert Hofstede, 'National Cultures in Four Dimensions: A Research-based Theory of Cultural Differences among Nations', *International Studies of Management and Organization*, 1983, xii(1–2), 46–74.

8 See, for example, 'Nonverbal Negotiation in China: Cycling in Beijing', *Negotiation Journal*, January 1995, pp 11–18.

9 This section draws on Lennie Copeland, 'The Art of International Selling', *Business America*, 25 June 1984, pp 2–7; and Roger E. Axtell, *The Do's and Taboos of International Trade* (New York: Wiley, 1994).

10 For a comprehensive review of the difference between human resource management in Europe and the USA, see Chris Brewster, 'Towards a "European Model of Human Resource Management"', *Journal of International Business Studies*, First Quarter 1995, pp 1–21.

11 This section draws on Pervez Ghauri and Jean-Claude Usunier (eds), *International Business Negotiations*, 2nd edn (Oxford: Elsevier, 2004).

12 S.C. Schneider and J.-L. Barsoux, *Managing across Cultures*, 2nd edn (Harlow: Pearson, 2003).

13 T. Cavusgil, P.N. Ghauri and A. Akcal, *Doing Business in Emerging Markets*, 2nd edn (London: Sage, 2013).

14 See, for example, Lennie Copeland and Lewis Griggs, *Going International* (New York: Plume, 1985); John L. Graham and Yoshihiro Sano, *Smart Bargaining: Doing Business with the Japanese*, rev edn (New York: Harper, 1990); and Pervez Ghauri and Jean-Claude Usunier, *International Business Negotiations* (Oxford: Elsevier, 2004).

15 T. Fang, V. Worm and R.L. Tung, 'Changing Success and Failure Factors in Business Negotiations with the PRC', *International Business Review*, 2008, 17(2), 159–69.

PART 6

Supplementary Resources

The Country Notebook: A Guide for Developing a Marketing Plan

The Country Notebook Outline

A number of books and articles have described strategic marketing planning at corporate or business unit level.[1] Here we are mainly concerned about a marketing plan for a foreign market or a marketing plan for a particular product in one particular market. The guidelines provided here can be used for different markets; however, depending on the market and the product, the emphasis on different parts of the framework may change.[2]

The first stage in the planning process is a preliminary country analysis. The marketer needs basic information to: (1) evaluate a country market's potential; (2) identify problems that would eliminate a country from further consideration; (3) identify aspects of the country's environment that need further study; (4) evaluate the components of the marketing mix for possible adaptation; and (5) develop a strategic marketing plan. One further use of the information collected in the preliminary analysis is as a basis for a country notebook.

Many companies, large and small, have a country notebook for each country in which they do business. The country notebook contains information a marketer should be aware of when making decisions involving a specific country market. As new information is collected, the country notebook is continually updated by the country or product manager. Whenever a marketing decision is made involving a country, the country notebook is the first database consulted. New product introductions, changes in advertising programmes, and other marketing programme decisions begin with the country notebook. It also serves as a quick introduction for new personnel assuming responsibility for a country market.[3]

This section presents four separate sets of guidelines for collection and analysis of market data and preparation of a country notebook: (1) guideline for cultural analysis; (2) guideline for economic analysis; (3) guideline for market audit and competitive analysis; (4) guideline for a preliminary marketing plan. These guidelines suggest the kinds of information a marketer can gather to enhance planning.

The points in each of the sets of guidelines are general. They are designed to provide direction to areas to explore for relevant data. In each set, specific points must be adapted to reflect a company's products. The decision as to the appropriateness of specific data and the depth of coverage depends on company objectives, product characteristics, and the country market. Some points in the guidelines are unimportant for some countries and/or some products and should be ignored. Preceding chapters of this book provide specific content suggestions for the topics in each guideline.

Cultural analysis

The data suggested in the cultural analysis include information that helps the marketer make market planning decisions. However, its application extends beyond product/market analysis to an important source of information for someone interested in understanding business customs and other important cultural features of the country.

The information in this analysis must be more than a collection of facts. Whoever is responsible for the preparation of this material should attempt to interpret the meaning of cultural information. That is, how does the information help in understanding the effect on the market? For example, the fact that almost all the populations of Italy and Ireland are Catholic is an interesting statistic but not nearly as useful as understanding the effect of Catholicism on values, beliefs and other aspects of market/consumer behaviour. Even though both countries are predominantly Catholic, the influence of their individual and unique interpretation and practise of Catholicism can result in important differences in market behaviour.

Guidelines

I Introduction.

Include short profiles of the company, the product to be exported, and the country with which you wish to trade.

II Brief discussion of the country's relevant history.

III Geographical setting.

    A Location.

    B Climate.

    C Topography.

IV Social institutions.

    A Family.

        1 The nuclear family.

        2 The extended family.

        3 Female/male roles (are they changing or static?).

    B Education.

        1 The role of education in society.

        2 Literacy rates.

    C Political system.

        1 Political structure.

        2 Stability of government.

        3 Special taxes.

        4 Role of local government.

    D Legal system.

        1 Organisation of the judiciary system.

        2 Code, common, socialist or Islamic law country?

        3 Participation in patents, trademarks and other conventions.

    E Social organisations.

        1 Group behaviour.

        2 Social classes.

        3 Race, ethnicity and subcultures.

    F Business customs and practices.

V Religion and aesthetics.

    A Religion and other belief systems.

        1 Which religions are prominent?

        2 Membership of each religion.

    B Aesthetics.

        1 Visual arts (fine arts, plastics, graphics, public colours, etc).

        2 Importance given to aesthetics.

VI Living conditions.

    A Diet and nutrition: typical meals.

    B Housing.

        1 Types of housing available.

        2 Do most people own or rent?

        3 Do most people live in one-family dwellings or with other families?

    C Clothing.

        1 National dress.

        2 Types of clothing worn at work.

    D Recreation, sports and other leisure activities.

    E Social security.

    F Health care.

VII Language.

    A Official language(s).

    B Spoken versus written language(s).

VIII Executive summary.

After completing all of the other sections, prepare a two-page (maximum length) summary of the major points and place it at the front of the report. The purpose of an executive summary is to give the reader a brief glimpse of the critical points of your report. Those aspects of the culture a reader should know in order to do business in the country but would not be expected to know or would find different based on his or her SRC should be included in this summary.

  IX Sources of information.

   X Appendices.

Economic analysis

The reader may find that the data collected for the economic analysis guidelines are more straightforward than for the cultural analysis guidelines. There are two broad categories of information in these guidelines: general economic data that serve as a basis for an evaluation of the economic soundness of a country and information on channels of distribution and media availability. As mentioned earlier, these guidelines focus only on broad categories of data and must be adapted to particular company/product needs.

Guidelines

I Introduction.

II Population.

 A Total and growth rates

 B Distribution of population.

  1 Age.

  2 Sex.

  3 Geographic areas (urban, suburban and rural density and concentration).

  4 Ethnic groups.

III Economic statistics and activity.

 A Gross national product (GNP or GDP).

  1 Total.

  2 Rate of growth (real GNP or GDP).

 B Personal income per capita.

 C Average family income.

 D Distribution of wealth.

  1 Income classes.

  2 Proportion of the population in each class.

  3 Is the distribution distorted?

 E Minerals and resources.

 F Surface transportation.

  1 Modes.

  2 Availability.

 G Communication systems.

  1 Types.

  2 Availability.

 H Working conditions.

  1 Employer–employee relations.

  2 Employee participation.

  3 Salaries and benefits.

 I Principal industries.

  1 What proportion of the GNP does each industry contribute?

  2 Ratio of private to publicly owned industries.

 J Foreign investment.

  1 Opportunities?

  2 Which industries?

 K International trade statistics.

  1 Major exports.

   a Dollar/euro value.

   b Trends.

  2 Major imports.

   a Dollar/euro value.

   b Trends.

  3 Balance-of-payments situation.

   a Surplus or deficit?

   b Recent trends.

  4 Exchange rates.

   a Single or multiple exchange rates?

   b Current rate of exchange.

 L Trade restrictions.

  1 Embargoes.

  2 Quotas.

  3 Import taxes.

  4 Tariffs.

  5 Licensing.

  6 Customs duties.

 M Extent of economic activity not included in cash income activities.

  1 Countertrades.

   a Products generally offered for countertrading.

   b Types of countertrades requested (ie barter, counterpurchase, etc).

  2 Foreign aid received (relevance for the product in question).

 N Labour force.

  1 Size.

  2 Unemployment rates.

 O Inflation rates.

IV Developments in science and technology.

 A Current technology available (computers, machinery, tools, etc).

 B Technological skills of the labour force and general population.

V Channels of distribution (macroanalysis).

This section reports data on all channel middlemen available within the market. Later, you will select a specific channel as part of your distribution strategy relevant to your product.

 A Middlemen.

  1 Retailers.

   a Number of retailers.

   b Typical size of retail outlets.

   c Customary mark-up for various classes of goods.

   d Methods of operation (cash/credit).

   e Scale of operation (large/small).

   f Role of chain stores, department stores and speciality shops.

  2 Wholesale middlemen.

a Number and size.
b Customary mark-up for various classes of goods.
c Method of operation (cash/credit).

3 Import/export agents.
4 Warehousing.
5 Penetration of urban and rural markets.

VI Media.

This section reports data on all media available within the country/market. Later, you will select specific media as part of the promotional mix/strategy relevant for your product.

A Availability of media.

B Costs.

1 Television.
2 Radio.
3 Print.
4 Other media (cinema, outdoor, etc).

C Agency assistance.

D Coverage of various media.

E Percentage of population reached by each of the media.

VII Executive summary.

After completing the research for this report, prepare a two-page (maximum) summary of the major economic points and place it at the front of the report.

VIII Sources of information.

IX Appendices.

Market audit and competitive market analysis

Of the guidelines presented, this set is mostly product brand-specific. Information in the other sets of guidelines is general in nature, focusing on product categories, whereas data in this set are brand- specific and are used to determine competitive market conditions and market potential.

Two different components of the planning process are reflected in these guidelines. Information in Parts I and II, 'Cultural analysis' and 'Economic analysis', serve as the basis for an evaluation of the product/brand in a specific country market. Information in these guidelines provides an estimate of market potential and an evaluation of the strengths and weaknesses of competitive marketing efforts. The data generated in this step are used to determine the extent of adaptation of the company's marketing mix necessary for successful market entry and to develop the final step: the action plan.

The detailed information needed to complete these guidelines is not necessarily available without conducting a thorough marketing research investigation.

Thus, another purpose of this part of the country notebook is to identify the correct questions to ask in a formal market study.

Guidelines

I Introduction.

II The product.

A Evaluate the product as an innovation as it is perceived by the intended market.

1 Relative advantage.
2 Compatibility.
3 Complexity.

B Major problems and resistance to product acceptance based on the preceding evaluation. (See Chapter 15 for a discussion of this topic.)

III The market.

A Describe the market(s) in which the product is to be sold.

1 Geographical region(s).
2 Forms of transportation and communication available in that/those region(s).
3 Consumer buying habits.

a Product-use patterns.
b Product feature preferences.
c Shopping habits.

4 Distribution of the product.

a Typical retail outlets.
b Product sales by other middlemen.

5 Advertising and promotion.

a Advertising media usually used to reach your target market(s).
b Sales promotions customarily used (sampling, coupons, etc).

6 Pricing strategy.

a Customary mark-ups.
b Types of discount available.

B Compare and contrast your product and the competition's product(s).

1 Competitors' product(s).

a Brand name.
b Features.
c Package.

2 Competitors' prices.
3 Competitors' promotion and advertising methods.
4 Competitors' distribution channels.

C Market size.

    1 Estimate industry sales for the planning year.

    2 Estimate sales for your company for the planning year.

D Government participation in the marketplace.

    1 Agencies that can help you.

    2 Regulations you must follow.

IV Executive summary.

Based on your analysis of the market, briefly summarise (two pages maximum) the major problems and opportunities requiring attention in your marketing mix and place the summary at the front of the report.

V Sources of information.

VI Appendices.

Preliminary marketing plan

Information gathered in the previous sets of guidelines serves as the basis for developing a marketing plan for your product/brand in a target market. How the problems and opportunities that surfaced in the preceding steps are overcome and/or exploited to produce maximum sales/profits are presented here. The action plan reflects, in your judgement, the most effective means of marketing your product in a country market. Budgets, expected profits and/or losses, and additional resources necessary to implement the proposed plan are also presented.

Guidelines

I The marketing plan.

  A Marketing objectives.

    1 Target market(s) (specific description of the market segment).

    2 Expected sales 20–.

    3 Profit expectations 20–.

    4 Market penetration and coverage.

  B Product adaptation, or modification – using the product component model as your guide, indicate how your product can be adapted for the market (see Chapter 15).

    1 Core component.

    2 Packaging component.

    3 Support services component.

  C Promotion mix.

    1 Advertising.

      a Objectives.

      b Media mix.

      c Message.

    2 Sales promotions.

      a Objectives.

      b Coupons.

      c Premiums.

    3 Personal selling.

    4 Other promotional methods.

  D Distribution: from origin to destination.

    1 Port selection.

      a Origin port.

      b Destination port.

    2 Mode selection: advantages/disadvantages of each mode.

      a Railroads.

      b Air carriers.

      c Ocean carriers.

      d Motor carriers.

    3 Packing.

      a Marking and labelling regulations.

      b Containerisation.

    4 Documentation required.

    5 Insurance claims.

    6 Freight forwarder.

If your company does not have a transportation or traffic management department, then consider using a freight forwarder. There are distinct advantages and disadvantages to hiring one.

  E Channels of distribution (micro-analysis).

This section presents details about the specific types of distribution in your marketing plan.

    1 Retailers.

      a Type and number of retail stores.

      b Retail mark-ups for products in each type of retail store.

      c Methods of operation for each type (cash/credit).

      d Scale of operation for each type (small/large).

    2 Wholesale middlemen.

      a Type and number of wholesale middlemen.

      b Mark-up for class of products by each type.

      c Methods of operation for each type (cash/credit).

      d Scale of operation (small/large).

    3 Import/export agents.

    4 Warehousing.

      a Type.

      b Location.

F Price determination.

    1 Cost of the shipment of goods.

    2 Transportation costs.

    3 Handling expenses.

    4 Insurance costs.

    5 Customs duties.

    6 Import taxes and value-added tax.

    7 Wholesale and retail mark-ups and discounts.

    8 Company's gross margins.

    9 Retail price.

G Terms of sale (ex-works, fob, fas, c&f, cif)

H Methods of payment.

    1 Cash in advance.

    2 Letters of credit.

II Pro forma financial statements and budgets.

A Marketing budget.

    1 Selling expense.

    2 Advertising/promotion expense.

    3 Distribution expense.

    4 Product cost.

    5 Other costs.

B Pro forma annual profit and loss statement (first year and fifth year).

III Resource requirements.

A Finances.

B Personnel.

C Production capacity.

IV Executive summary.

After completing the research for this report, prepare a summary (two pages maximum) of the major points of your successful marketing plan and place it at the front of the report.

V Sources of information.

VI Appendices.

The intricacies of international operations and the complexity of the environment within which the international marketer must operate create an extraordinary demand for information. When operating in foreign markets, the need for thorough information as a substitute for uninformed opinion is equally as important as it is in domestic marketing. This information should be systematically collected and analysed before it is presented as a base for decision making.[4]

SUMMARY

Market-oriented firms build strategic market plans around company objectives, markets and the competitive environment. Planning for marketing can be complicated even for one country, but when a company is doing business internationally the problems are multiplied. Company objectives may vary from market to market, from product to product and from time to time; the structure of international markets also changes periodically and from country to country, and the competitive, governmental and economic parameters affecting market planning are in a constant state of flux. These variations require international marketing executives to be especially flexible and creative in their approach to strategic marketing planning.

NOTES

1 See, for example, David Aaker, *Strategic Marketing Management*, 8th edn (New York: Wiley, 2007).

2 For going into a new market see, for example, Franklin Root, *Entry Strategies for International Markets* (Washington, DC: Heath and Company, 1994).

3 Tamer Cavusgil, Pervez Ghauri and Milind Aganwal, *Doing Business in Emerging Markets: Entry and Negotiation Strategies* (Thousand Oaks, CA: Sage, 2002).

4 Pervez Ghauri and Kjell Grønhaug, *Research Methods in Business Studies: A Practical Guide* (Hemel Hempstead: FT Prentice Hall, 2005).

Case Studies to Accompany Parts 1–5

PART 1

Case Studies to Accompany Parts 1–5

Cases Outline

Case 1.1

Strategy Formulation at Audi

Audi: the success of cars 'Made in Germany'

The German company Audi, part of the Volkswagen Group, is enjoying unprecedented levels of success, particularly in the international marketplace. In 2012, over 1.45 million Audi brand vehicles were delivered to customers worldwide. In the same year, the company's sales turnover stood at €48.8bn and its net profit was €4.4bn. The company has become one of the world leaders in the 'premium' car segment, where it competes against other German companies like BMW and Mercedes (Daimler Group). Audi has developed a differentiation strategy mainly based on the technology and quality of the services it offers. This strategic positioning is manifested by the slogan *'Vorsprung durch Technik'*,[1,2] which emphasises the country of origin of the company: 'Made in Germany'.[1,2] The slogan is used by the brand in its communication campaigns throughout the world.

Audi: a brand of the Volkswagen Group

Audi is part of the German Volkswagen Group, which is one of the world's leading automobile manufacturers and the largest carmaker in Europe. The group owns 12 brands: Audi, Bentley, Bugatti, Ducati, Lamborghini, MAN, Porsche, Scania, Seat, Skoda, Volkswagen Commercial Vehicles and Volkswagen Passenger Cars. Each brand targets a specific market segment and operates as an independent entity in the market. The product portfolio ranges from low-consumption small cars to luxury class vehicles.

Like the other brands, Audi can benefit from the financial expertise and resources of the Volkswagen Group, particularly when the company needs to make important investments. The size of the group means they can make substantial savings, especially with regard to supplies. For example, specialists estimate that, because it is part of the Volkswagen Group, Audi can save almost 10 per cent on supplies compared with its competitor, BMW. In fact, unlike BMW and Mercedes, Audi can make relatively high margins on smaller-sized models, eg the Audi A1 model,[3] as numerous parts and components can be bought via Volkswagen's central purchasing unit. In the same way, the costs associated with certain projects carried out by several brands can be shared, and synergies can be exploited. However, the Audi company enjoys strong autonomy in the purchase of certain higher quality materials for its 'premium' vehicles.

The development of a premium brand

Since the company's creation in 1909, Audi's models have met with great success, first in the field of motor sports, then with the general public. For a long time, Audi was perceived as a mid-range manufacturer, producing cars with a classic style offering safety and security to an essentially family target. The image projected was relatively close to that of the non-specialised car brands. At the end of the 1980s, the company made a significant strategic change of direction: Ferdinand Piëch became managing director and decided to reposition the brand in the 'premium' segment. The objective was to make a clearer distinction between the Audi brand and the other brands marketed by the Volkswagen Group and to differentiate Audi from its competitors, particularly BMW and Mercedes. In the absence of an image, the company decided to put the accent on its advanced technologies (for example, the 'quattro' system, permanent four-wheel drive, the TDI technology – a direct injection diesel engine and the use of aluminium). In the automotive sector, the 'premium' segment is between the general public segment (for example, Ford, Peugeot) and the luxury car segment (for example, Bentley, Jaguar). It has the following characteristics: high technology, high price, personalised customer service, exclusive distribution, customer experience enhancement and product with a strong image.

Since then, Audi has chosen to target a clientele which can be characterised by its high income level and strong geographic mobility. This is a relatively homogeneous target at the international level. Audi seeks to differentiate itself from its competitors through the technological superiority of the models it sells and by the quality of the service offered, which applies to all dealerships, everywhere in the world. As Patrice Franke, managing director of Audi France, stated: 'we believe that our technological competence and the quality of our service constitute significant competitive advantages in the international marketplace … we do our utmost to apply the same standards at the international level in order to build a uniform brand image and respond to the demands of a mobile clientele.'

The location of production activities

The head office of Audi is located in Ingolstadt (near Munich) in Germany. The company has chosen to manufacture a significant volume of its vehicles in Germany, even though labour costs are high there: Audi has two production facilities in the country, one at Ingolstadt in Bavaria, the other in Neckarsulm in Baden-Württemburg. The company also produces some of its models and components outside Germany. It has a production unit in Brussels (100 per cent-owned subsidiary) where it produces the Audi A1.[3] In 2011, the production of the Audi Q3 started at the Seat plant in Martorell, Spain. Since 1993, it has been manufacturing engines and some models in a factory at Győr, in Hungary (100 per cent-owned subsidiary). At this site, Audi produces 1.9 million engines per year, some of which are for other brands in the Volkswagen Group. The labour cost in Hungary is 80 per cent lower than in Germany. Since 2005, Audi has produce the Audi Q7 at the Volkswagen plant in Bratislava, in Slovakia. Audi has also set up a production facility in Changchun, in China (in the form of a joint venture signed between the Volkswagen Group and the Chinese manufacturer FAW (First Auto Works), where it produces vehicles for the local market. More recently, the company has set up an assembly unit at the Skoda plant in Aurangabad, in India where it plans to produce vehicles for the local market (see Exhibit 1).

It should be stressed that Audi was the first brand in the 'premium' segment to produce vehicles in

EXHIBIT 1: Geographic location of Audi's production facilities (2012)

Production site	Number of employees	Number of vehicles produced
Ingolstadt (Germany)	33,729	583,824
Neckarsulm (Germany)	14,247	265,622
Brussels (Belgium)	2,372	118,200
Martorell (Spain)	1,500	19,654
Győr (Hungary)	7,322	39,518
Bratislava (Slovakia)	2,200	53,707
Changchun (China, joint venture)	9,700	310,036
Aurangabad (India)	140	4,674

Source: http://www.audi.com.

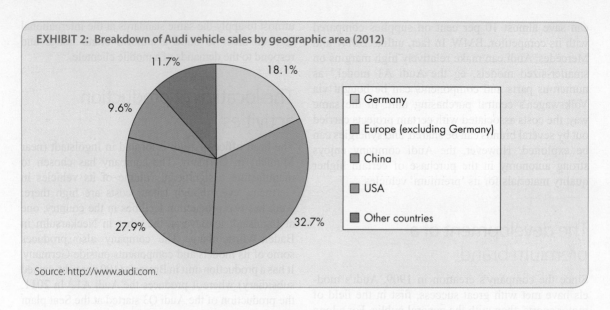

EXHIBIT 2: Breakdown of Audi vehicle sales by geographic area (2012)

- Germany
- Europe (excluding Germany)
- China
- USA
- Other countries

18.1%
11.7%
9.6%
27.9%
32.7%

Source: http://www.audi.com.

China. As far back as 1988, a licence agreement was signed with the Chinese manufacturer FAW for the manufacture of the Audi 100 model. In 1991, FAW and the Volkswagen Group decided to set up a joint venture under the name 'FAW-Volkswagen Automotive Company (FAW-VW)'. Today, the joint venture is owned by Volkswagen (20 per cent of the capital), Volkswagen China Invest (10 per cent of the capital), Audi AG (10 per cent of the capital since 1995) and FAW (60 per cent of the capital). The factory, which is Audi's main production facility outside Germany, manufactures vehicles for the Volkswagen Passenger Cars and Audi brands.

International sales of the Audi brand

Over the past decade, Audi has significantly reinforced its presence in the international marketplace. In 2012, Audi's foreign sales reached 1.19 million vehicles, or 81.9 per cent of the brand's sales. The company has succeeded in conquering the European market (not including Germany), where it makes 32.7 per cent of its sales. The main market outside Europe is China, where Audi has been present since 1988 (which has given it a leadership position compared to its competitors, BMW and Mercedes), and where it now makes 27.9 per cent of its sales. On the other hand, Audi's presence in the strategically important US market remains limited (9.6 per cent of its sales) (see Exhibit 2). The aim is to reach a volume of 200,000 vehicles in the American market in 2015. This seems a difficult challenge as the company is not recognised as a 'premium' brand on a level with Mercedes, BMW and Lexus. The same holds true for the Latin American and for other Asian countries.

Exhibit 3 shows the breakdown of vehicles sold by Audi in its main markets. It can be seen that four markets account for 64 per cent of total sales: China, Germany, the USA and the UK. It also shows that Audi sales are experiencing strong growth in several emerging markets (China: +29.6 per cent, Russia: +44.1 per cent), but also in the USA (+18.5 per cent) where the company has launched important communication campaigns. In Germany (+3.6 per cent), the UK (+7.2 per cent) and France (+0.3 per cent), growth rates are more moderate, and in Italy (−17 per cent) and Spain (−11.7 per cent), one can observe a significant drop in sales.

Currently, the global automotive industry is subject to several major trends: the stagnation, or even decline, in demand and production in the three 'traditional' automotive regions (Western Europe, North America and Japan), the growing importance of emerging markets as outlets but also as recipients

EXHIBIT 3: Breakdown of Audi vehicle sales by main market (2012)

Country	Number of vehicles sold in 2012	Variation compared with 2011 (in %)
China	405.838	+ 29.6
Germany	263.163	+ 3.6
USA	139.310	+ 18.5
UK	123.640	+ 7.2
France	62.202	+ 0.3
Italy	50.085	-17.0
Spain	36.139	-11.7
Russia	33.512	+ 44.1
TOTAL	1.455.100	+ 11.7

Source: http://www.audi.com.

of investments, the appearance of new competitors in emerging markets, particularly in Asian countries such as China (for example, Geely which recently bought Volvo), India (for example, the Tata group which acquired the Jaguar and Land Rover brands from the American manufacturer Ford) and South Korea. To meet these new challenges, the manufacturers of the three production regions are obliged to revise their development strategies, in particular by optimising the location of their activities.[4,5] This is the case for a number of non-specialist manufacturers, but also for manufacturers in niche markets. Audi has responded to these trends by assembling several car models abroad, even if its major production facilities continue to be located in Germany.

QUESTIONS

1 In order to develop its presence in new geographical markets, Audi has chosen to favour export activities and the creation of several 100 per cent-owned subsidiaries (with the exception of the joint venture set up in China). What are the main advantages and disadvantages for Audi associated with these two forms of international development?

2 If we look at the company's global value chain, it is clear that the majority of its activities are still located in Germany. The company has, in fact, decided to relocate only part of its production activities, particularly to China. What are the reasons behind these choices?

FURTHER READING

- Audi, *Annual Report* (2012).
- http://www.audi.com.
- http://www.volkswagenag.com.

NOTES

1   Ch. Barmeyer and S. Hertrich, 'Les Stratégies des Constructeurs Franco-Allemands', *Problèmes Économiques*, 2003, 2836, pp 1–6.

2   U. Mayrhofer, *Marketing International*, 2nd edn (Paris: Economica, 2012)

3   S. Hertrich and U. Mayrhofer, Audi A1: *Marketing a Premium City Car* (Paris: Centrale de Cas et de Médias Pédagogiques, 2011).

4   A. Colovic and U. Mayrhofer, 'Optimising the Location of R&D and Production Activities: Trends in the Automotive Industry', *European Planning Studies*, 2011, 19(8), 1481–98.

5   St. Schmid and Ph. Grosche, *Managing the International Value Chain in the Automotive Industry: Strategy, Structure, and Culture* (Gütersloh: Bertelsmann Stiftung, 2008).

This case was written by Sylvie Hertrich, Ecole de Management Strasbourg, University of Strasbourg, and Ulrike Mayrhofer, IAE Lyon, Jean Moulin Lyon 3 University.

Sylvie Hertrich and Ulrike Mayrhofer have developed a rich expertise in the field of marketing case studies: they have written more than 20 case studies in close collaboration with companies like Adidas, Audi (Volkswagen Group), Club Méditerranée, Hilton Group, Peugeot and W Hotels (Starwood Group). These case studies, available in English and French, are published at the Centrale de Cas et de Médias Pédagogiques, CCMP, Paris (http://www.ccmp.fr). The authors have received the Golden Pen of the Chamber of Commerce and Industry in Paris ten times. This prestigious award distinguishes authors whose case studies are extensively used by European business schools and universities.

Case 1.2

Starbucks: Going Global Fast

© P.N. Ghauri.

The Starbucks coffee shop on Sixth Avenue and Pine Street in downtown Seattle sits serenely and orderly, as unremarkable as any other in the chain bought 15 years ago by entrepreneur Howard Schultz. A little less than three years ago, however, the quiet store-front made front pages around the world. During the World Trade Organization talks in November 1999, protesters flooded Seattle's streets, and among their targets was Starbucks, a symbol, to them, of free-market capitalism run amok, another multinational out to blanket the earth. Amid the crowds of protesters and riot police were black-masked anarchists who trashed the store, leaving its windows smashed and its tasteful green-and-white decor smelling of tear gas instead of espresso. Says an angry Schultz: 'It's hurtful. I think people are ill-informed. It's very difficult to protest against a can of Coke, a bottle of Pepsi, or a can of Folgers. Starbucks is both this ubiquitous brand and a place where you can go and break a window. You can't break a can of Coke.'

The store was quickly repaired, and the protesters have scattered to other cities. Yet cup by cup, Starbucks really is caffeinating the world, its green-and-white emblem beckoning to consumers on three continents. In 1999 Starbucks Corp had 281 stores abroad. Today, it has about 1,200 – and it's still in the early stages of a plan to colonise the globe. If the protesters were wrong in their tactics, they weren't wrong about Starbucks' ambitions. They were just early.

The story of how Schultz & Co. transformed a pedestrian commodity into an upscale consumer

accessory has a fairytale quality. Starbucks has grown from 17 coffee shops in Seattle 15 years ago to 5,689 outlets in 28 countries. Sales have climbed an average of 20 per cent annually since the company went public 10 years ago, to $2.6bn in 2001, while profits bounded ahead an average of 30 per cent per year, hitting $181.2m last year. And the momentum continues. In the first three-quarters of this fiscal year, sales climbed 24 per cent, year to year, to $2.4bn, while profits, excluding one-time charges and capital gains, rose 25 per cent, to $159.5m.

Moreover, the Starbucks name and image connect with millions of consumers around the globe. It was one of the fastest-growing brands in a *Business Week* survey of the top 100 global brands published 5 August. At a time when one corporate star after another has crashed to earth, brought down by revelations of earnings misstatements, executive greed, or worse, Starbucks hasn't faltered. The company confidently predicts up to 25 per cent annual sales and earnings growth this year. On Wall Street, Starbucks is the last great growth story. Its stock, including four splits, has soared more than 2,200 per cent over the past decade, surpassing Wal-Mart, General Electric, PepsiCo, Coca-Cola, Microsoft and IBM in total return. Now at $21, it is hovering near its all-time high of $23 in July, before the overall market drop.

After a slowdown last fall and winter, when consumers seemed to draw inward after 11 September, Starbucks is rocketing ahead once again. Sales in stores open at least 13 months grew by 6 per cent in the 43 weeks through 28 July, and the company predicts monthly samestore sales gains as high as 7 per cent through the end of this fiscal year. That's below the 9 per cent growth rate in 2000, but investors seem encouraged. 'We're going to see a lot more growth,' says Jerome A. Castellini, president of Chicago-based CastleArk Management, which controls about 300,000 Starbucks shares. 'The stock is on a run.'

But how long can that run last? Already, Schultz's team is hard-pressed to grind out new profits in a home market that is quickly becoming saturated. Amazingly, with 4,247 stores scattered across the USA and Canada, there are still eight states in the USA with no Starbucks stores. Frappuccino-free cities include

Butte, Montana and Fargo, North Dakota. But big cities, affluent suburbs and shopping malls are full to the brim. In coffee-crazed Seattle, there is a Starbucks outlet for every 9,400 people, and the company considers that the upper limit of coffee-shop saturation. In Manhattan's 24 square miles, Starbucks has 124 cafés, with four more on the way this year. That's one for every 12,000 people – meaning that there could be room for even more stores. Given such concentration, it is likely to take annual same-store sales increases of 10 per cent or more if the company is going to match its historic overall sales growth. That, as they might say at Starbucks, is a tall order to fill.

Indeed, the crowding of so many stores so close together has become a national joke, eliciting quips such as this headline in *The Onion*, a satirical publication: 'A New Starbucks Opens in Restroom of Existing Starbucks'. And even the company admits that, while its practice of blanketing an area with stores helps achieve market dominance, it can cut sales at existing outlets. 'We probably self-cannibalise our stores at a rate of 30 per cent a year,' Schultz says. Adds Lehman Brothers, Inc analyst Mitchell Speiser: 'Starbucks is at a defining point in its growth. It's reaching a level that makes it harder and harder to grow, just due to the law of large numbers.'

To duplicate the staggering returns of its first decade, Starbucks has no choice but to export its concept aggressively. Indeed, some analysts give Starbucks only two years at most before it saturates the US market. The chain now operates 1,200 international outlets, from Beijing to Bristol. That leaves plenty of room to grow. Indeed, about 400 of its planned 1,200 new stores this year will be built overseas, representing a 35 per cent increase in its foreign base. Starbucks expects to double the number of its stores worldwide, to 10,000 in three years. During the past 12 months, the chain has opened stores in Vienna, Zurich, Madrid, Berlin, and even in far-off Jakarta. Athens comes next. And within the next year, Starbucks plans to move into Mexico and Puerto Rico. But global expansion poses huge risks for Starbucks. For one thing, it makes less money on each overseas store because most of them are operated with local partners. While that makes it easier to start up on foreign turf, it reduces the company's share of the profits to only 20–50 per cent.

Unpredictable market

Moreover, Starbucks must cope with some predictable challenges of becoming a mature company in the USA. After riding the wave of successful baby boomers through the 1990s, the company faces an ominously hostile reception from its future consumers, the twenty- or thirty-somethings of Generation X. Not only are the activists among them turned off by the power and image of the well-known brand, but many others say that Starbucks' latte-sipping sophisticates and piped-in Kenny G music are a real turn-off. They don't feel wanted in a place that sells designer coffee at $3 a cup.

Even the thirst of loyalists for high-price coffee can't be taken for granted. Starbucks' growth over the past decade coincided with a remarkable surge in the economy. Consumer spending has continued strong in the downturn, but if that changes, those $3 lattes might be an easy place for people on a budget to cut back. Starbucks executives insist that won't happen, pointing out that, even in the weeks following the terrorist attacks, same-store comparisons stayed positive while those of other retailers skidded.

Starbucks also faces slumping morale and employee burnout among its store managers and its once-cheery army of baristas. Stock options for part-timers in the restaurant business was a Starbucks innovation that once commanded awe and respect from its employees. But now, though employees are still paid better than comparable workers elsewhere (about $7 per hour), many regard the job as just another fast-food gig. Dissatisfaction over odd hours and low pay is affecting the quality of the normally sterling service and even the coffee itself, say some customers and employees. Frustrated store managers among the company's roughly 470 California stores sued Starbucks in 2001 for allegedly refusing to pay legally mandated overtime. Starbucks settled the suit for $18m this past April, shaving $0.03 per share off an otherwise strong second quarter. However, the heart of the complaint – feeling over-worked and under-appreciated – doesn't seem to be going away.

To be sure, Starbucks has a lot going for it as it confronts the challenge of maintaining its growth. Nearly free of debt, it fuels expansion with internal cash flow. And Starbucks can maintain a tight grip on its image because stores are company-owned: there are no franchisees to get sloppy about running things. By relying on mystique and word-of-mouth, whether here or overseas, the company saves a bundle on marketing costs. Starbucks spends just $30m annually on advertising, or roughly 1 per cent of revenues, usually just for new flavours of coffee drinks in the summer, and product launches, such as its new instore web service. Most consumer companies its size shell out upwards of $300m per year. Moreover, unlike a McDonald's or a Gap Inc, two other retailers that rapidly grew in the USA, Starbucks has no nationwide competitor.

Starbucks also has a well-seasoned management team. Schultz, 49, stepped down as chief executive in 2000 to become chairman and chief global strategist. Orin Smith, 60, the company's number-cruncher, is now CEO and in charge of day-to-day operations. The head of North American operations is Howard Behar, 57, a retailing expert who returned last September, two years after retiring. The management trio is known as H2O, for Howard, Howard, and Orin.

Schultz remains the heart and soul of the operation. Raised in a Brooklyn public housing project, he found his way to Starbucks, a tiny chain of Seattle coffee shops, as a marketing executive in the early 1980s. The name came about when the original owners looked to Seattle history for inspiration and chose the moniker of an old mining camp: Starbo. Further refinement led to Starbucks, after the first mate in the novel *Moby-Dick*, which they felt evoked the seafaring romance of the early coffee traders (hence the mermaid logo). Schultz got the idea for the modern Starbucks format while visiting a coffee bar in Milan. He bought out his bosses in 1987 and began expanding. Today, Schultz has a net worth of about $700m, including $400m of company stock.

Starbucks has travelled light-years from those humble beginnings, but Schultz and his team still think there's room to grow in the USA – even in communities where the chain already has dozens of stores. Clustering stores increases total revenue and market share, Smith argues, even when individual stores poach on each other's sales. The strategy works, he says, because of Starbucks' size. It is large enough to absorb losses at existing stores as new ones open up, and soon overall sales grow beyond what they would have with just one store. Meanwhile, it's cheaper to deliver to and manage stores located close together. And by clustering, Starbucks can quickly dominate a local market.

The company is still capable of designing and opening a store in 16 weeks or less and recouping the initial investment in three years. The stores may be oases of tranquillity, but management's expansion tactics are something else. Take what critics call its 'predatory real estate' strategy: paying more than market-rate rents to keep competitors out of a location. David C. Schomer, owner of Espresso Vivace in Seattle's hip Capitol Hill neighbourhood, says Starbucks approached his landlord and offered to pay nearly double the rate to put a coffee shop in the same building.

The landlord stuck with Schomer, who says: 'It's a little disconcerting to know that someone is willing to pay twice the going rate.' Another time, Starbucks and Tully's Coffee Corp, a Seattle-based coffee chain, were competing for a space in the city. Starbucks got the lease but vacated the premises before the term was up. Still, rather than let Tully's get the space, Starbucks decided to pay the rent on the empty store so its competitor could not move in. Schultz makes no apologies for the hardball tactics, 'The real estate business in America is a very, very tough game,' he says. 'It's not for the faint of heart.'

Still, the company's strategy could backfire. Not only will neighbourhood activists and local businesses increasingly resent the tactics, but customers could also grow annoyed over having fewer choices. Moreover, analysts contend that Starbucks can maintain about 15 per cent square-footage growth in the USA – equivalent to 550 new stores – for only about two more years. After that, it will have to depend on overseas growth to maintain annual 20 per cent revenue growth.

Beyond coffee

Starbucks was hoping to make up much of that growth with more sales of food and other non-coffee items, but has stumbled somewhat. In the late 1990s Schultz thought that offering $8 sandwiches, desserts and CDs in his stores, and selling packaged coffee in supermarkets would significantly boost sales. The speciality business now accounts for about 16 per cent of sales, but growth has been less than expected. A healthy 19 per cent this year, but it's still far below the 38 per cent growth rate of fiscal 2000. That suggests that, while coffee can command high prices in a slump, food (at least at Starbucks) cannot. One of Behar's most important goals is to improve that record. For instance, the company now has a test programme of serving hot breakfasts in 20 Seattle stores and may move to expand supermarket sales of whole beans.

What's more important for the bottom line, though, is that Starbucks has proven to be highly innovative in the way it sells its main course: coffee. In 800 locations it has installed automatic espresso machines to speed up service. And in November, it began offering prepaid Starbucks cards, priced from $5 to $500, which clerks swipe through a reader to deduct a sale. That, says the company, cuts transaction times in half. Starbucks has sold $70 million-worth of the cards.

In early August Starbucks launched Starbucks Express, its boldest experiment yet, which blends java, web technology and faster service. At about 60 stores in the Denver area, customers can pre-order and prepay for beverages and pastries via phone or on the Starbucks Express website. They just make the call or click the mouse before arriving at the store, and their beverage will be waiting – with their name printed on the cup. The company will decide in January on a national launch.

Starbucks is bent on even more fundamental store changes. On 21 August it announced expansion of a high-speed wireless Internet service to about 1,200 Starbucks locations in North America and Europe. Partners in the project – which Starbucks calls the world's largest Wi-Fi network – include Mobile International, a wireless subsidiary of Deutsche Telekom, and Hewlett-Packard. Customers sit in a store and check email, surf the web, or download multimedia presentations without looking for connections or tripping over cords. They start with 24 hours of free wireless broadband before choosing from a variety of monthly subscription plans.

Starbucks' executives hope such innovations will help surmount their toughest challenge in the home market: attracting the next generation of customers. Younger coffee drinkers already feel uncomfortable in the stores. The company knows that because it once had a group of twenty-somethings hypnotised for a market study. When their defences were down, out came the bad news: 'They either can't afford to buy coffee at Starbucks, or the only peers they see are those working behind the counter,' says Mark Barden, who conducted the research for the Hal Riney & Partners ad agency (now part of Publicis Worldwide) in San Francisco. One of the recurring themes the hypnosis brought out was a sense that 'people like me aren't welcome here except to serve the yuppies', he says. Then there are those who just find the whole Starbucks scene a bit pretentious. Katie Kelleher, 22, a Chicago para-legal, is put off by Starbucks' Italian terminology of *grande* and *venti* for coffee sizes. She goes to Dunkin' Donuts, saying: 'Small, medium and large is fine for me.'

Happy staff

As it expands, Starbucks faces another big risk: that of becoming a far less special place for its employees. For a company modelled around enthusiastic service, that could have dire consequences for both image and sales. During its growth spurt of the mid- to late 1990s, Starbucks had the lowest employee turnover rate of any restaurant or fast-food company, thanks largely to its then unheard-of policy of giving health insurance and modest stock options to part-timers making barely more than minimum wage.

Such perks are no longer enough to keep all the workers happy. Starbucks' pay doesn't come close to matching the workload it requires, complain some staff. Says Carrie Shay, a former store manager in West Hollywood, California: 'If I were making a decent living, I'd still be there.' Shay, one of the plaintiffs in the suit against the company, says she earned $32,000 a year to run a store with 10 to 15 part-time employees. She hired employees, managed their schedules, and monitored the store's weekly profit-and-loss statement. But she was also expected to put in significant time behind the counter and had to sign an affidavit pledging to work up to 20 hours of overtime a week without extra pay – a requirement the company has dropped since the settlement. Smith says that Starbucks offers better pay, benefits and training than comparable companies, while it encourages promotion from within.

For sure, employee discontent is far from the image Starbucks wants to project of relaxed workers cheerfully making cappuccinos. But perhaps it is inevitable. The business model calls for lots of low-wage workers. And the more people who are hired as Starbucks expands, the less they are apt to feel connected to the original mission of high service: bantering with customers and treating them like family. Robert J. Thompson, a professor of popular culture at Syracuse University, says of Starbucks: 'It's turning out to be one of the great twenty-first-century American success stories – complete with all the ambiguities.'

Overseas, though, the whole Starbucks package seems new and, to many young people, still very cool. In Vienna, where Starbucks had a gala opening for its first Austrian store last December, Helmut Spudich, a business editor for the paper *Der Standard*, predicted that Starbucks would attract a younger crowd than the established cafés. 'The coffeehouses in Vienna are nice, but they are old. Starbucks is considered hip,' he says.

But if Starbucks can count on its youth appeal to win a welcome in new markets, such enthusiasm cannot be relied upon indefinitely. In Japan, the company beat even its own bullish expectations, growing to 368 stores after opening its first in Tokyo in 1996. Affluent young Japanese women like Anna Kato, a 22-year-old Toyota Motor Corp. worker, loved the place. 'I don't care if it costs more, as long as it tastes sweet,' she says, sitting in the world's busiest Starbucks, in Tokyo's Shibuya district. Yet same-store sales growth has fallen in the past 10 months in Japan, Starbucks' top foreign market, as rivals offer similar fare. Add to that the depressed economy, and Starbucks Japan seems to be losing steam. Although it forecasts a 30 per cent gain in net profit, to $8m, for the year started in April, on record sales of $516m, same-store sales are down 14 per cent for the year ended in June. Meanwhile in

EXHIBIT 1: Starbucks Factfile

Since this case was written, Starbucks has further expanded its stores worldwide:

- **January 2004** – first store opened in Paris, France
- **August 2005** – first store opened in Dublin, Ireland
- **September 2005** – Starbucks Discoveries© launched its chilled cup coffee in Japan and Taiwan, the first ready-to-drink coffee beverage outside of North America developed specifically to appeal to Asian tastes and lifestyles
- **2006** – Starbucks opens its five-hundredth store in the UK, in St Martin's Lane, London
- **April 2007** – first store opened in Bucharest, Romania
- **September 2007** – first store opened store in Moscow, Russia
- **January 2008** – first store opened in Prague, Czech Republic
- **September 2008** – first store opened in Lisbon, Portugal
- **November 2008** – first store opened in Sofia, Bulgaria
- **April 2009** – first store opened in Warsaw, Poland
- As of the second half of **2009**, Starbucks had:
  - more than 1,550 stores in 29 countries throughout much of continental Europe, the UK, Ireland and the Middle East: Austria, Bahrain, Belgium, Bulgaria, Cyprus, the Czech Republic, Denmark, Egypt, France, Germany, Greece, Ireland, Jordan, Kuwait, Lebanon, the Netherlands, Oman, Poland, Portugal, Qatar, Republic of Ireland, Romania, Russia, Saudi Arabia, Spain, Switzerland, Turkey, the United Arab Emirates, and the UK;
  - 1,744 stores in 9 countries throughout the Asia Pacific region: Australia, Indonesia, Japan, Malaysia, New Zealand, Philippines, Singapore, South Korea and Thailand (nearly half of these in Japan);
  - 690 stores in Greater China, including the People's Republic of China, Hong Kong, Macau and Taiwan;
  - more than 1,350 in America and Canada

Source: http://news.starbucks.com/

England, Starbucks' second-biggest overseas market, with 310 stores, imitators are popping up left and right to steal market share.

Entering other big markets may be tougher yet. The French seem to be ready for Starbucks' sweeter taste, says Philippe Bloch, cofounder of Columbus Cafe, a Starbucks-like chain. But he wonders if the company can profitably cope with France's arcane regulations and generous labour benefits. And in Italy, the epicentre of European coffee culture, the notion that the locals will abandon their own 200,000 coffee bars *en masse* for Starbucks strikes many as ludicrous. For one, Italian coffee bars prosper by serving food as well as coffee, an area where Starbucks still struggles. Also, Italian coffee is cheaper than US java and, say Italian purists, much better. Americans pay about $1.50 for an espresso. In northern Italy, the price is 67 cents; in the south, just 55 cents. Schultz insists that Starbucks will eventually come to Italy. It'll have a lot to prove when it does. Carlo Petrini, founder of the anti-globalisation movement Slow Food, sniffs that Starbucks' 'substances served in Styrofoam' won't cut it. The cups are paper, of course. But the scepticism is real.

As Starbucks spreads out, Schultz will have to be increasingly sensitive to those cultural challenges. In December, for instance, he flew to Israel to meet with Foreign Secretary Shimon Peres and other Israeli officials to discuss the Middle East crisis. He won't divulge the nature of his discussions. But subsequently, at a Seattle synagogue, Schultz let the Palestinians have it. With Starbucks outlets already in Kuwait, Lebanon, Oman, Qatar and Saudi Arabia, he created a mild uproar among Palestinian supporters. Schultz quickly backpedalled, saying that his words were taken out of context and asserting that he is 'pro-peace' for both sides.

There are plenty more minefields ahead. So far, the Seattle coffee company has compiled an envious record of growth. But the giddy buzz of that initial expansion is wearing off. Now, Starbucks is waking up to the grand challenges faced by any corporation bent on becoming a global powerhouse.

Profit at Starbucks Coffee Japan fell 70 per cent in the first nine months of the year because of growing competition from rival coffee chains. Sales at stores open more than one year fell 16 per cent. The firm expects a loss for the full year.

QUESTIONS

1   Identify the controllable and uncontrollable elements that Starbucks has encountered in entering global markets.
2   What are the major sources of risk facing the company? Discuss potential solutions.
3   Critique Starbucks' overall corporate strategy.
4   How might Starbucks improve profitability in Japan?

Visit www.starbucks.com for more information.

Sources: Stanley Holmes, Drake Bennett, Kate Carlisle and Chester Dawson, 'Planet Starbucks: To Keep Up the Growth It Must Go Global Quickly', *Business Week*, 9 December 2002, pp 100–10. Reprinted by permission of *Business Week*; and Ken Belson, 'Japan: Starbucks Profit Falls', *New York Times*, 20 February 2003, p 1.

Case 1.3

Wal-Mart in Africa

'Africa is awakening. It's a huge market of almost a billion people with huge resources and a young population. People spend when they're young.'[1]

Christo Wiese, Chairman, Pepkor Ltd (Pepkor), in August, 2012

'Whenever Walmart enters a new market, it introduces its global operating belief that being a responsible global citizen begins with being a responsible local citizen.'[2]

Doug McMillon, Wal-Mart International CEO, in June, 2011

'Walmart, with sales of more than $405bn [£258bn – more than South Africa's GDP] in 2010, has massive power to dominate the world's global supply chains, and national retail sectors, and to dictate the conditions of trade to thousands of supply firms in other sectors.'[3]

A union spokesman, Cosatu, a South African Trades Union, in 2011

On 9 March 2012, the Competition Appeal Court of South Africa ruled that US-based Wal-Mart Stores, Inc, the world's biggest retailer, could go ahead with its US$ 2.4bn purchase of a stake in the South African retailer Massmart Holdings Limited.[4] By ruling in favour of the deal, the Competition Appeal Court upheld the 2011 ruling of South Africa's Competition Tribunal. Wal-Mart had started expanding into international markets in 1991. It experienced successes in international markets such as Mexico and bitter failure in markets such as Germany and South Korea. The financial crisis of 2008 resulted in Wal-Mart putting even more emphasis on the international markets to fuel its growth as there were limited growth opportunities in the domestic sector. Wal-Mart started to focus on Africa as other markets with good potential like India were still closed to foreign players. Africa remained the last major market yet to be explored by big MNCs like Wal-Mart. Despite political instability and poor economic conditions plaguing the continent, some countries in Africa offered good potential for growth due to their stable political environment and rising disposable incomes.

Wal-Mart decided to expand its presence in Africa in the inorganic way and made a preliminary offer to buy South African Retailer, Massmart. Massmart was the second-biggest retailer in South Africa and its operations were spread across many African countries. Wal-Mart's offer was accepted by Massmart's shareholders and South Africa's Competition Tribunal in June 2011.

The deal was cleared with some conditions. But Wal-Mart quickly ran into trouble as the deal was opposed by some trade unions and government departments of South Africa. The coalition which was opposing the deal alleged that Wal-Mart's entry would lead to huge job losses and adversely affect the domestic manufacturing sector of South Africa. Wal-Mart refuted the allegations and said that it was willing to create 15,000 new jobs within three years of the takeover. Wal-Mart's past record of being a low-wage, low-benefit employer which discouraged its employees from forming labour unions compounded the fears of the opposition coalition. While some analysts expressed optimism that Wal-Mart's low price model could prove successful in Africa due to its poverty and low income levels, others were sceptical. They said that much of the population in Africa lived below the poverty line and might not have good buying potential. Analysts also warned Wal-Mart of repeating the mistakes it had committed in Germany and South Korea like trying to use the same business model as it followed in the US market without understanding the needs of the local market.

Background note

Wal-Mart was founded in 1962 by Samuel Moore Walton in Rogers, Arkansas, USA. Walton worked at JC Penney Corporation, Inc.[5] before starting Wal-Mart. He also ran a franchise of Ben Franklin stores. When working with other retailers and later running a franchise, the conviction grew in Walton that the changing buyer behaviour in the USA made discount stores the future of retailing, especially in the smaller towns. He traveled across the USA before starting his own discount store and was convinced that Americans wanted a new type of discount store which would offer more discounts than the traditional discount stores. Wal-Mart was founded on the principle of passing on the discounts that retailers could manage from the wholesalers to the consumers and making money through the higher volumes achieved.[5] Walton's business clicked and Wal-Mart made better profits than many of its competing stores. By 1967, Wal-Mart had 24 stores with sales of US$12.6m. By 1968, it had expanded to Oklahoma and Missouri. Wal-Mart was incorporated as a company under the name Wal-Mart Stores, Inc in 1969.

Wal-Mart achieved significant growth during the 1970s. It opened its first distribution centre and Wal-Mart

Home Office in Bentonville in the first year of the decade. In 1977, Wal-Mart acquired 16 Mohr-Value stores based in Michigan and Illinois – its first acquisition. Wal-Mart expanded its business into other retail formats in 1978 and set up pharmacy, auto service centre, and jewellery divisions. In 1979, Wal-Mart's annual sales reached US$1bn and it became the first company to reach that goal within the quickest time. It had expanded its stores to 276 by 1980. In the years 1981 and 1982, Wal-Mart entered new states in the USA such as Georgia, South Carolina, Florida, and Nebraska and expanded its reach. It opened its first Sam's Club in Midwest City, Oklahoma, in the year 1983. Sam's Club, a chain of membership-only warehouse clubs, proved highly successful. It was later expanded across 47 states in the USA. Strong customer demand in small towns drove the rapid growth of Wal-Mart in the 1980s. In the 1980s, the number of Wal-Mart stores expanded to 640 with annual sales of US$4.5bn.

Walton appointed David Glass as the new CEO of Wal-Mart in 1988. Soon after taking over, Glass started a joint venture with Cullum Companies (a Dallas-based supermarket chain) called Hypermart USA. Wal-Mart bought out Cullum Companies' stake in the joint venture in 1989. Hypermart USA was a discount store/supermarket chain with an average space of over 200,000 square feet. It featured branch banks, fast food outlets, photo developers, and playrooms for shoppers' children. Hypermart USA stores were later renamed Wal-Mart's Super Centers. In 1990, Wal-Mart became the largest retailer in the USA

after it entered California, Nevada, North Dakota, Pennsylvania, South Dakota, and Utah.[6] In the same year, it acquired McLane Company (a grocer and retail distributor) and launched a new retail format: Bud's Discount City. Walton died in 1992 after a prolonged illness. But Wal-Mart continued its impressive growth under the leadership of Glass. After Walton's death, Sam Robson Walton, Walton's eldest son, was named the chairman of the company. In 1997, Wal-Mart's annual sales crossed the US$100bn mark. Even as Wal-Mart was enjoying successes, controversies regarding its business practices and labour issues began to surface. Wal-Mart faced several criticisms relating to its business practices.

Apart from following the strategy of selling products at a lower cost, Wal-Mart followed several practices unique in the USA to emerge as the leader. It developed a strategy where it did not allow retailers any control over its merchandise. It limited the percentage of merchandise that it sourced from a single supplier to have good bargaining power over them. Wal-Mart was one of the first retailers to use information technology to its advantage. In the early 1980s, it adopted the barcode technology to track sales of items in its stores on specific days and to manage its inventory better than any other business in the world. The adoption of barcode technology helped the company in the communication process with its suppliers. It saved a lot of money through inventory management practices. Wal-Mart also started using a new technology

EXHIBIT 1: Criticisms against Wal-Mart

Issues	Description of issues
Anti-unionist	Since the 1970s, Wal-Mart had been anti-unionist, taking the stand that it was adhering to an open-door employee policy
Employee discrimination	The company was charged with discrimination against women employees in 2003
Employee surveillance	A former employee of Wal-Mart contended that the retailer carried out a large surveillance operation involving employees, shareholders, critics, etc
Poor working conditions	Wal-Mart was accused of forcing its workers to work off-the-clock, denying over-time payments, child-labour law infringements, and of employing illegal immigrant workers
Low wages	The retail giant was charged with discouraging labour costs and of paying lower wages to its workforce
Health insurance	Critics alleged that employees were paid so little that they could not afford health insurance, and if they could afford it, they preferred the state's health insurance programme to Wal-Mart's
Overseas labour concerns	Critics accused Wal-Mart for its supervision of overseas operations, where issues like poor working conditions, employing prison labour, low wages, etc were allegedly prevalent
Predatory pricing and supplier issues	The company was also accused of intentionally selling the merchandise at low costs, driving competitors away from the market. It was also alleged that it used its scale to squeeze the margins of its suppliers

Source: adapted from various sources.

called Radio-Frequency Identification (RFID) to track its merchandise better. Over the years, it used technology to gain good control over its supply chain.

It hired some of the best people in the area of logistics and supply chain management. Wal-Mart developed the largest commercial satellite system in the world to collect and give information to its vendors. The vast amounts of data that Wal-Mart was able to gather gave it good control over its vendors. Through these practices, Wal-Mart could stock the latest merchandise in its stores and replenish it faster. The use of the latest technology also facilitated recruitment of employees who did not need to be trained heavily to handle store operations. This kept its employee recruitment and training costs under control. The savings which resulted from the use of technology, good logistics, supply chain management practices, and lower employee costs were passed on to the consumers in the form of lower prices. This helped Wal-Mart and cemented its leadership position in the US market.

The 1990s also saw Wal-Mart expanding into international markets. In 1991, the company opened its first overseas store, in Mexico City, Mexico. It entered Mexico through a joint venture with Mexican company Cifra and opened its first Sam's Club in the country. Wal-Mart's global expansion got a boost when an international division was created in 1993. Wal-Mart entered Canada in 1993 after acquiring 122 former Woolco stores from Woolworth in Canada. During the first five years of its global expansion (1991–95), Wal-Mart concentrated on markets like Mexico, Canada, Argentina, and Brazil, which were close to its home market. For the fiscal year 2002, Wal-Mart's revenue stood at US$218bn and it overtook ExxonMobil[7] as the biggest company in the world on the *Fortune* 500 list of 2002. By 2005, Wal-Mart had expanded to 10 countries across the world. It had 1,991 stores, which included 1,175 discount stores, 285 Super Centers, 91 Sam's Clubs, and 36 Neighborhood Markets. But global expansion showed mixed results. While it had good results in some countries, it faced many problems in some countries and even had to exit some. Wal-Mart exited South Korea and Germany in 2006. Cultural discrepancies and intense competition from local retailers were cited as the reasons for its failure in these markets. At the same time, Wal-Mart experienced tremendous success in some global markets. It emerged as the largest retailer in Mexico, Argentina, Canada, and Puerto Rico. By 2005, it had emerged as one of the top three retailers in the UK. By 2012, Wal-Mart had a presence in 27 countries across the world with 10,130 retail stores. Its revenues for the fiscal year 2012 were US$443.85bn.

EXHIBIT 2: Countries in which Wal-Mart operated in 2012

Country	Year of entry
Argentina	1995
Botswana	2011
Brazil	1995
Canada	1994
Chile	2009
China	1996
Costa Rica	2005
El Salvador	2005
Ghana	2011
Guatemala	2005
Honduras	2005
India	2007
Japan	2002
Lesotho	2011
Malawi	2011
Mexico	1991
Mozambique	2011
Namibia	2011
Nicaragua	2005
Nigeria	2011
South Africa	2011
Swaziland	2011
Tanzania	2011
Uganda	2011
UK	2000
Zambia	2011

Source: 'Saving People Money So They Can Live Better – Worldwide', http://www.walmartstores.com.

Wal-Mart's past experience in international markets

Wal-Mart had mixed results in its operations in foreign countries. It operated very successfully in rich markets like Mexico, Canada, and the UK. It operated in Mexico through its subsidiary called Wal-Mart de Mexico. Right from the time it first started its overseas operations in Mexico in 1991 through a joint venture with a local retailer called Cifra, it had grown in size to become the biggest retailing company in the whole of Latin America. In 1997, Wal-Mart increased its stake in the joint venture with Cifra and acquired 51 per cent in Cifra. After the acquisition of the majority stake in Cifra, Wal-Mart expanded its operations across Mexico under different brands like Walmart, Superama, Suburbia, VIPS, Sam's Club, and Bodega Aurrerá. By the end of 2011, it had a total of 2,037 outlets and restaurants in

EXHIBIT 3: Consolidated income statement of Wal-Mart for fiscal years 2010–2012 (in US$m)

	2012	2011	2010
Net sales	443,854	418,952	405,132
Membership and other income	3,096	2,897	2,953
Cost of sales	335,127	314,946	304,106
Operating, selling, general and administrative expenses	85,265	81,361	79,977
Operating income	26,558	25,542	24,002
Interest	2,160	2,004	1,884
Income from continuing operations before income taxes	24,398	23,538	22,118
Provision for income taxes	7,944	7,579	7,156
Consolidated net income	16,387	16,993	14,883

Source: Wal-Mart 2012 Annual Report.

EXHIBIT 4: Socio-economic data of key countries where Wal-Mart operated

Country	GDP (US$ trillion)	GDP per capita (US$)	GDP real growth rate (%)	GNI per capita (US$)	Population	Literacy rate (%)	Unemployment rate (%)
USA	15.04	48,100	1.5	47,310	313,847,465	99	9
Mexico	1.657	15,100	3.8	14,400	114,975,406	86.1	5.2
Canada	1.389	40,300	2.2	38,370	34,300,083	99	7.5
UK	2.25	35,900	1.1	35,840	63,047,162	99	8.1
Japan	4.389	34,300	− 0.5	34,610	127,368,088	99	4.6

Sources: https://www.cia.gov/library/publications/the-world-factbook; and http://data. worldbank. org/indicator/NY. GNP. PCAP. PP. CD/countries.

Mexico. It was also the biggest employer in Mexico by the end of 2011. Though highly successful in Mexico, Wal-Mart faced fierce competition from local competitors. Some of Mexico's local retailers formed a purchasing association in 2004 called Sinergia to face up to the tremendous purchasing ability of Wal-Mart.[8]

Wal-Mart had also been operating successfully in Canada since it entered the Canadian market in 1993. By the end of January 2012, it operated 333 discount stores and supercentres across Canada through its subsidiary, Walmart Canada Corp.[9] Wal-Mart employed 82,000 people in Canada and was one of its largest employers. It was expected to face severe competition in Canada with Target announcing its intentions to enter the Canadian market by the spring of 2013.[9]

Wal-Mart experienced similar success in the UK market after it entered there through the acquisition of the third-largest supermarket chain in the UK, Asda, in 1999. Even after the takeover, Wal-Mart continued its operations in the UK under the Asda brand. Very soon, it opened the American-style supercentres in the UK, which got a good response from customers.

Wal-Mart expanded its operations in the UK quickly and very soon emerged as the second-largest supermarket chain in the country. However, it experienced some problems in the UK related to labour issues as it was accused of following illegal practices. It was fined in 2006 for offering its staff a pay rise in return for their giving up a collective union agreement. But it quickly sorted out these issues before they escalated out of its control. Wal-Mart had 544 retail units including 32 supercentres in the UK as of 31 May 2012.[10]

On the other hand, Wal-Mart experienced its biggest fiasco in Germany. It entered Germany by acquiring the 21 hypermarket stores of Wertkauf in 1997.[11] It later acquired 74 hypermarket stores of another local retailer to increase its presence in Germany. But analysts pointed out that Wal-Mart had failed to understand the German market right from the beginning and had tried to implement the business model it followed in the USA unchanged. Though it offered lower prices to German customers just as it did in the USA, its local competitors could easily match its prices. Germany was the most price-sensitive market in Europe and Germans were accustomed to lower prices from domestic retailers. Wal-Mart also failed to build a good image for its stores in the German market. The stores which Wal-Mart acquired when entering Germany had a poor reputation, which compounded its problems. While not being able to differentiate itself on the price front, Wal-Mart also failed in offering any compelling value proposition to the German customers to visit its stores. Wal-Mart's vendors in Germany opposed the centralised distribution system followed by Wal-Mart globally. Another operational problem Wal-Mart faced in Germany was labour unrest. Wal-Mart paid lower wages and didn't encourage its employees to form unions.

Wal-Mart's employees organised a two-day strike in protest against employee lay-offs and store closures in 2002 which further tarnished its reputation in Germany. Wal-Mart also faced problems on the legal front and was accused of violating various German competition laws. In May 2000, Wal-Mart reportedly sold some goods in its stores at a price which was lower than the cost price at which it bought them. Apart from regulatory issues, Wal-Mart also faced problems in integrating its culture with the culture of the retail businesses it acquired in Germany. Wal-Mart strongly discouraged office romance between employees in its stores, which many employees found to be intrusive. Commenting on Wal-Mart's attitude when it entered the German retail market, Bryan Roberts, an analyst at Planet Retail said, 'Wal-Mart was not very humble when they went in. They wanted to impose their own culture.'[12] Analysts said that even by 2003, five years after it entered the German market, Wal-Mart was losing nearly US$200–300m per annum. It remained a secondary player in the German retail market and was never able to recover.[13] Unable to understand the German market, Wal-Mart exited the country in 2006.

Wal-Mart similarly exited from the South Korean retail market in 2006 and struggled to establish itself in the Japanese retail market. It entered the South Korean market in 1998 and implemented its US business model of low prices just as it did in Germany. But the South Korean customers did not like Wal-Mart's offerings. The South Korean retail market was highly sophisticated with lavish stores and the South Korean customers did not like the 'warehouse style' environment of Wal-Mart's stores. Housewives were not satisfied with the food and beverage offerings in Wal-Mart's stores.[14] As a result, sales did not pick up in Wal-Mart's South Korean stores and the retailer could not open new stores in the country. Limited operations prevented Wal-Mart from extracting better discounts from its suppliers.[15] Analysts said that Wal-Mart had failed to localise its operations to suit the needs of the South Korean market, unlike the other global retailing giant, Tesco. Homeplus, the South

Korean subsidiary of Tesco, emerged as the second-biggest retailer in South Korea by 2006 by localising its operations to suit the needs of South Korean customers. Wal-Mart Korea reported sales of just US$800m and a loss of US$10m in 2005.[14] Unable to sustain its operations in South Korea, Wal-Mart sold its 16 stores in the country for US$882m and exited the market in 2006.[16] Wal-Mart struggled to establish itself in Japan after it entered the Japanese retail market in 2002. But it later began adjusting its business model to suit the needs of the Japanese retail market. Japanese customers initially equated Wal-Mart's lower prices and unsophisticated stores with inferior products.[17] Wal-Mart rectified its problems in Japan through some measures like renovating its stores to look better and creating improved consumer awareness about the quality of its products. Later, Wal-Mart expanded its operations in Japan and acquired a 100 per cent stake in its Japanese subsidiary in 2008.

Wal-Mart embarks on an African safari

Wal-Mart started putting more emphasis on the international markets to drive its expansion after the financial crisis of 2008. The main reason for its enhanced international focus was the limited growth opportunities in its domestic (US) market since the financial crisis. Strong sales growth and a record number of new stores opened made its international segment grow faster. Wal-Mart's international segment grew by 15.2 per cent year on year for the fiscal year 2012.[18] Its operating income from international operations for the fiscal year ending 31 January 2012 was US$6,241m. According to an estimate by *Forbes* magazine, Wal-Mart's international segment was approximately contributing 40 per cent to its stock price in March 2012. This estimate highlighted the importance of international operations for Wal-Mart. It had been trying for a long time to enter the Indian retail market due to the tremendous growth opportunities for the retail sector there. The Indian retail sector was projected to grow from US$396bn in 2012 to US$785bn by 2015.[18] But the Indian retail market was still closed to foreign multi-brand retailers and Wal-Mart's operations were limited to some wholesale outlets there. That had left Wal-Mart to focus on Africa as another important growth opportunity.

With most of the developed Western markets reaching saturation levels and the Asian markets becoming highly competitive, many big multinational companies (MNCs) were turning their attention toward Africa. Africa was being considered the last major emerging market left to be captured by the

EXHIBIT 5: Operating income from international operations for fiscal years 2010–2012 (in US$m)

Fiscal year	Operating income from international operations	% of total operating income
2012	6,214	23.4
2011	5,606	21.99
2010	4,901	20.4

Source: Wal-Mart 2012 Annual Report.

EXHIBIT 6: Major retailers in South Africa

No	Company
1	Shoprite
2	Massmart
3	Pick n Pay
4	SPAR
5	Steinhoff International
6	Woolworths

Source: http://www.prnewswire.com/news-releases/south-africa-retail-direct-selling-b2c-e-commerce-report-2012-150747085.html.

MNCs. The unstable political environment in most African countries made it unviable for businesses to set up shop there. But some African countries like South Africa and Nigeria with elected governments and rule of law were seen as viable options for big MNCs to enter the African continent. Wal-Mart decided to gain a foothold in the African market in the inorganic way by acquiring an established retailing company. Since 2008, Wal-Mart had been on the lookout for an acquisition target in Africa. South Africa had some sophisticated retailers such as Shoprite Holdings (Shoprite), Massmart, Pick n Pay Stores Ltd (Pick n Pay), Spar, and Woolworths. In September 2010, Wal-Mart announced that it had made a preliminary offer to buy the South African retailer, Massmart.[19] Analysts felt that Wal-Mart had gone in for Massmart rather than Africa's biggest grocer, Shoprite, as Massmart had rapidly increased its presence in the food-retailing business and, by then, operated 40 grocery stores in South Africa.[20]

South Africa had a relatively mature organised retail market and some of South Africa's leading retailers like Pepkor were planning to expand their operations into other African markets like Nigeria.[1] Commenting on the preference given by Wal-Mart to South Africa, Andy Bond, Executive Vice President of Wal-Mart, said, 'South Africa presents a compelling

growth opportunity for Wal-Mart and offers a platform for growth and expansion in other African countries.'[9] The preliminary offer was non-binding to Wal-Mart and it could withdraw the offer any time after conducting due diligence.

Massmart was the second-biggest retailer in Africa and owned several established local retail brands like Game, Makro, Builders' Warehouse, and CBW.[21] Massmart was founded in 1990 and the group comprised nine wholesale and retail chains. The group functioned through four operating divisions: Massdiscounters, Masswarehouse, Massbuild, and Masscash. Even though most of Massmart's operations were concentrated in South Africa, Massmart had operations across many sub-Saharan countries. Wal-Mart hoped to gain an instant footprint across Africa through the acquisition of Massmart. Saying that 'Walmart likes emerging markets and South Africa in particular',[3] Bond added that Massmart hoped to open 40 new outlets a year in countries including South Africa, Nigeria, Malawi, and Zambia. It was also looking at opportunities in countries like Senegal, Cameroon, and Angola. The retailer said that its aim was not to change Massmart's strategy, but simply 'to put the foot on the accelerator'.[21]

However, the news of Wal-Mart's entry into South Africa led to huge protests from powerful trade unions and some government departments in South Africa who contended that Wal-Mart's entry would drive down wages and lead to unemployment. They threatened to respond with strike action, demonstrations, and boycotts. Faced with such opposition, Wal-Mart defended itself and also warned that it would walk away from the deal.[22]

EXHIBIT 7: List of countries in which Massmart operated in 2012

Country	No of stores
Botswana	9
Lesotho	2
Ghana	1
Malawi	2
Mauritius	1
Mozambique	1
Namibia	3
Nigeria	1
South Africa	188
Tanzania	1
Uganda	1
Zambia	1

Source: http://www.massmart.co.za/pdf/massmarts_operations_in_Africa_2011.pdf.

After the negotiations were completed in June 2010, Wal-Mart's offer was accepted by the shareholders of Massmart and South Africa's Competition Tribunal in May 2011.[23] According to the tribunal, 'The merging parties contend that the merger will indeed be good for competition by bringing lower prices and additional choice to South African consumers. We accept that this is a likely outcome of the merger based on Walmart's history in bringing about lower prices. However, the extent of this consumer benefit is by no means clear – Walmart itself has not been able to put a number to this claim, only that it is likely.'[22]

According to the figures of the United Nations Conference on Trade and Development, Wal-Mart's entry helped boost South Africa's foreign direct investment in 2011 to US$4.5bn.[24]

Initial hiccups

Wal-Mart's offer was to buy a controlling 51 per cent stake in the South African retailer. Its offer was accepted with some conditions. First of all, Wal-Mart would be restrained from cutting any jobs in Massmart for two years after the merger. Wal-Mart was also to give preference to the 503 Massmart employees who had been retrenched in June 2010 in its future recruitments. Wal-Mart agreed to honour labour bargaining rights for at least three years after the merger. In a move to develop the local manufacturing sector, Wal-Mart agreed to implement a programme to improve the competitiveness of local suppliers within three years of the merger approval date. It earmarked 100m rand (US$13.37m) for a supply-chain training programme.[24]

Wal-Mart hoped to create at least 15,000 new jobs within three years of the merger.[25] But it started to run into trouble from various quarters in Africa who were opposed to the deal. The opposition to the deal was similar to that faced in markets like India against foreign participation in the retail sector. The main opposition was from some trade unions and government departments who feared job losses in the retail sector. People who were opposed to the deal included the organised labour unions of South Africa such as the Congress of South African Trade Unions, the South African Commercial, and Catering and Allied Workers Union. Opposition to the deal also came from three government departments: Economic Development, Trade and Industry, and Agriculture, Forestry and Fisheries. In addition to the fear of job losses, the opposition was also opposed to some of the terms of the merger.

The coalition opposed to the deal claimed that there would be huge job losses due to the entry of Wal-Mart as it might import a large part of its merchandise from cheaper markets like China. They claimed that 4,000 jobs would be lost immediately even if Wal-Mart imported just 1 per cent of its merchandise. They also claimed that importing the merchandise from cheaper markets like China would hit the manufacturing sector in South Africa. The main reason for opposition to Wal-Mart's entry into South Africa stemmed from the high levels of unemployment prevailing in that country. The South African government was wary of Wal-Mart's entry leading to huge job losses.

The manufacturing and agriculture sectors in South Africa had been declining just before Wal-Mart decided upon entering South Africa. According to a report on the South African labour market published by the Development Policy Research Unit (DPRU), the employment rate in the South African agriculture, forestry, and fishing sector contracted by 13 per cent and the employment rate in the manufacturing sector contracted by 11 per cent between the second quarter of 2009 and the second quarter of 2010.[25] But Wal-Mart refuted the allegations made by the opposition coalition.

Many analysts too supported the deal, arguing that the fears expressed by the opposition coalition were ill-founded. Some said that the fears raised by the opposition were misguided as the retrenchment ban forming part of the terms of the deal made it difficult for Wal-Mart to cut any jobs for at least two years after the merger. Some industry observers said that the supplier development programme agreed upon by Wal-Mart at the time of the merger would help in improving the efficiency of South Africa's manufacturing sector.

Wal-Mart was also known for being a low-wage and low-benefit employer in the USA. Its founder Walton feared and hated worker unions and Wal-Mart's workers were often discouraged from forming themselves into any labour unions. The opposition coalition feared that Wal-Mart might bring the same work culture to South Africa and other African countries. African countries like South Africa, Kenya, and Nigeria traditionally had a culture of very strong labour unions.

The three government departments opposed to the deal criticised the South Africa's Competition Tribunal approval of the deal, saying that the commission had failed to consider some vital issues relating to public interest. Many labour unions in South Africa too voiced their opposition to the deal. Patrick Craven, spokesperson for the South African workers' union, Cosatu, said, 'Walmart, however, is more likely to destroy jobs, by using its competitive advantage to force its competitors out of business, and destroying South African manufacturing businesses, which will not be able to compete with a flood of cheap imports....'[2] The group opposed to the deal approached the Competition Appeal Court of South Africa for a review of the ruling by South Africa's Competition Tribunal. However, the Competition Appeal Court of South Africa ruled in favour of the deal on 9 March 2012, saying that the fears expressed over the deal were unfounded. The ruling by the appeals court finally paved the way for Wal-Mart to enter the South African retail market. Ruling in favour of the deal, the appeals court said, 'There was insufficient evidence to conclude that the detrimental effects of the merger would outweigh the clear benefits.'[4] As part of the ruling, the appeal court also ordered Wal-Mart to conduct a study to determine the best possible way to safeguard the interests of small producers who would not be able to compete against low cost foreign producers from whom Wal-Mart would be importing goods at cheaper rates.[4] Based on this study, the court would decide how Wal-Mart should use the 100m rand fund that it had earmarked for improving the competitiveness of local industry. The court also ordered the retailer to reinstate the 503 workers who had been fired just before the merger.[24]

Smooth ride?

As the court was deliberating on the appeal against the merger, Wal-Mart and Massmart were busy moving ahead with their integration, which included aligning product sourcing.[24] McMillon said, 'Massmart is currently located in 12 markets so that's our focus. Building our business in the markets that we are currently in is our primary focus.... We are excited about the region. We have a long-term view.'[26]

Analysts were divided in their opinion about Wal-Mart's prospects in Africa. Just before the Competition Appeal Court of South Africa ruled in favour of Wal-Mart's deal with Massmart, Massmart announced that it was going to expand and open 20 more stores in Nigeria. Nigeria was another major market for retailing business in Africa, with a population of 160m. Announcing the expansion plans in Nigeria, Grant Pattison, CEO of Massmart, said that Nigeria had the potential to be a bigger market than South Africa. He said, 'By all simple metrics, Nigeria has the potential to be larger than South Africa, but it has some way to go in terms of infrastructure and political stability.'[27] This showed Massmart's desire to expand in all the major markets across Africa, which could ultimately benefit Wal-Mart in its quest to gain a foothold across the African continent. Some analysts said that Wal-Mart's financial muscle could help Massmart to expand across the continent faster.

But some analysts expressed the view that Wal-Mart could face more problems in Africa than it had faced in countries like Germany. As the market potential of many individual African countries was limited, Wal-Mart would have to expand its operations to many countries across Africa to achieve good economies of scale and make its operations viable. Rampant poverty and low income levels would make

EXHIBIT 8: Socio-economic data of countries where Massmart operated

Country	GDP (US$bn)	GDP per capita (US$)	GDP real growth rate (%)	GNI per capita (US$)	Population	Literacy rate (%)	Unemployment rate (%)
Botswana	30.09	16,300	6.2	13,700	2,098,018	81.2	7.5
Lesotho	3.672	1,400	5.2	1,970	1,930,493	84.8	45
Ghana	74.77	3,100	13.5	1,620	25,241,998	57.9	11
Malawi	13.77	900	4.6	860	16,323,044	62.7	NA
Mauritius	19.28	15,000	4.2	13,980	1,313,095	84.4	7.8
Mozambique	23.87	1,100	7.2	930	23,515,934	47.8	21
Namibia	15.5	7,300	3.6	6,420	2,165,828	85	51.2
Nigeria	414.5	2,600	6.9	2,240	170,123,710	68	21
South Africa	554.6	11,000	3.4	10,360	48,810,427	86.4	24.9
Tanzania	63.44	1,500	6.1	1,440	43,601,796	69.4	NA
Uganda	45.9	1,300	6.4	1,250	35,873,253	66.8	NA
Zambia	21.93	1,600	6.7	1,380	14,309,466	80.6	14

Sources: https://www.cia.gov/library/publications/the-world-factbook; and http://data. worldbank. org/indicator/NY. GNP. PCAP. PP. CD/countries.

operations in some African countries simply unviable to Wal-Mart, they said.

Nearly 61 per cent of Nigeria's population lived on less than one US$1 per day, which could limit the country's potential.[27] Some other problems cited by critics to the deal were unstable political environment and poor infrastructure in many parts of Africa that might hit Wal-Mart's ambitions there. David Strasser, an analyst at Janney Montgomery Scott,[28] said, 'For this deal to drive returns, we believe it is essential to succeed by using this acquisition as a springboard. For every relatively stable country like Botswana, there is a Zimbabwe.'[19]

Some analysts were optimistic about the viability of Wal-Mart's US business model in Africa. They said that its business model of offering everyday low pricing for its customers would be very successful in a market like Africa where high poverty and very low income levels prevailed. Wal-Mart might not face the problem of being seen as a low quality retailer as it was seen in countries like Germany and South Korea. However, others warned Wal-Mart against repeating the mistakes it had made in countries like Germany and South Korea like failing to understand the needs of the local markets and trying to follow the same business model it followed in the USA.

NOTES

1 Sikonathi Mantshantsha, 'Billionaire Wiese Targets Nigeria as Wal-Mart Enters Africa', http://www. businessweek.com, 12 August 2011.

2 Max Clarke, 'Walmart Enters Africa Despite Union Opposition', http://www.freshbusinessthinking.com, 1 June 2011.

3 Richard Wachman, 'South Africa Resists March of Walmart', http://guardian.co.uk, 10 October 2011.

4 Donna Bryson, 'Wal-Mart Gets Go-ahead in South Africa', http://news.yahoo.com, 9 March 2012.

5 T.A. Frank, 'A Brief History of Wal-Mart', http://www.reclaimdemocracy.org.

6 'History Timeline', http://www.walmartstores.com.

7 'About Us', http://www.walmartstores.com/AboutUs/.

8 'Mexican Retailers Unite against Wal-Mart', http://www.expresstextile.com, 29 July 2004.

9 Allison Martell and Jessica Wohl, 'Target to Test Wal-Mart's Mettle in Canada', http://www.reuters.com, 11 April 2011.

10 www.walmartstores.com/AboutUs/275.aspx.

11 Christine Lepisto, 'Walmart Leaves Germany: Blame Smiles, Love or Plastic Bags', http://www. treehugger.com, 30 June 2006.

12 Kate Norton, 'Wal-Mart's German Retreat', http://www.businessweek.com, 28 July 2006.

13 'Wal-Mart: Struggling in Germany', http://www.businessweek.com, 11 April 2005.

14 Daniel Workman, 'Wal-Mart Finally Get It: Lessons from South Korea & Germany', http:// danielworkman. suite101.com, 31 July 2006.

15 Choe Sang-Hun, 'Wal-Mart Selling Stores and Leaving South Korea', http://www.nytimes.com, 23 May 2006.

16 Kelly Olsen, 'Wal-Mart Pulls Out of South Korea, Sells 16 Stores', http://www.usatoday.com, 22 May 2006.

17 Matthew Boyle, 'Wal-Mart's Painful Lessons', http://www.businessweek.com, 13 October 2009.

18 'Wal-Mart's Africa and India Plans Boost its International Outlook', http://www.forbes.com, 25 March 2012.

19 Stephanie Clifford, 'Wal-Mart Bids for Massmart to Expand into Africa', http://www.nytimes.com, 27 September 2010.

20 'Walmart in South Africa: The Beast in the Bush', www.economist.com, 17 February 2011.

21 Tiisetso Motsoeneng, 'Massmart Could Open up to 20 Stores in Nigeria', http://af.reuters.com, 22 February 2012.

22 David Smith, 'Walmart Gets First Foothold in Africa', http://guardian.co.uk, 31 May 2011.

23 Jennifer Booton, 'Wal-Mart Enters South Africa with Massmart Deal', http://www.foxbusiness.com, 20 June 2011.

24 Devon Maylie, 'Wal-Mart, Massmart Merger Approved in South Africa', http://online.wsj.com, 9 March 2012.

25 Olumide Taiwo and Jessica Smith, 'Big Box vs Spring Boks: Wal-Mart's Troubles Entering the South African Retail Market', www.brookings.edu, 1 November 2011.

26 'Wal-Mart Focused on Existing Africa Markets', www.reuters.com, 10 May 2012.

27 'Massmart Could Open up to 20 Stores in Nigeria', http://af.reuters.com, 22 February 2012.

This case was written by Adapa Srinivasa Rao, under the direction of Debapratim Purkayastha, IBS Hyderabad. It was compiled from published sources, and is intended to be used as a basis for class discussion rather than to illustrate either effective or ineffective handling of a management situation.

©2013, IBS Center for Management Research

PART 2

Case 2.1

Abercrombie & Fitch: Expanding into the European Market

The US retailing chain Abercrombie & Fitch has recently opened several stores in the European market: London in 2007, Milan in 2009, Copenhagen in 2010, Paris, Madrid, Düsseldorf and Brussels in 2011, and Hamburg, Munich, Dublin and Amsterdam in 2012. The opening of an Abercrombie & Fitch store is usually considered a major event by the young urban dwellers target. For example, on the opening day of the Paris store which is located on the Champs Elysées, nearly 500 people were waiting outside to be the first to discover the collections presented in the new flagship store.

The implementation of stores in the European market is consistent with the Abercrombie & Fitch Group's internationalisation strategy. The company which sells clothes and accessories for men, women and children has its head office located in New Albany, Ohio. It experienced rapid growth in the USA before expanding in international markets. In 2011, its turnover was US$4.158bn and its net income amounted to US$127.7m.

The brand portfolio of the Abercrombie & Fitch Group

The Abercrombie & Fitch Group owns four brands: (1) Abercrombie & Fitch (A&F); (2) abercrombie kids; (3) Hollister Co; and (4) Gilly Hicks.

Created in 1892 by David T. Abercrombie and Ezra H. Fitch, the Abercrombie & Fitch brand is positioned as a premium 'casual luxury' brand. It is associated with the traditions of the East coast of the USA, in particular New York City, and the Ivy League heritage (group of eight private universities in the northeastern USA which rank amongst the country's oldest and most prestigious universities: Brown, Columbia, Cornell, Dartmouth, Harvard, Pennsylvania, Princeton, Yale). The clothing brand epitomises the American lifestyle: young and preppy. The history of the brand is presented in Exhibit 1.

The abercrombie kids brand is associated with the prep schools of the East coast of the USA (schools

---

EXHIBIT 1: History of the Abercrombie & Fitch brand

1892	Creation of the first Abercrombie & Fitch store in Manhattan, New York (selling sport and hiking equipment, with a reputation for hunting rifles, fishing rods and tents)
1977	Closing of the store (company bankruptcy)
1979	Store name taken over by Oshman's Sporting Goods, a chain of stores based in Houston (mail order sales of hunting clothes and novelty items; opening of stores in Beverly Hills, Dallas and New York)
1988	Company's name and activities sold to The Limited, a clothing chain based in Columbus, Ohio
2005	Brand positioning as 'casual luxury' and opening of a flagship store on New York's Fifth Avenue

Source: http://www.abercrombie.com.

---

preparing 14–18 year-olds for higher education). It reflects the energetic attitude of young sportsmen adopting a casual, classic and preppy style. The target is 7–14 year olds.

The Hollister Co brand embodies the relaxed lifestyle of southern California, with its surfers and beautiful beaches. It is meant to be 'young and fun', with a touch of humour. It proposes cheaper items than Abercrombie & Fitch and targets teenagers. Hollister is very popular among teenagers and young adults. As pointed out by David (a young Brit aged 12, interviewed in December 2012):

'I love the Hollister brand. It's my favourite brand. It is really cool. My Mum used to pick my clothes for me, and I often wore Benetton clothes. Now I decide and I want to be hip like a teenager. … When I go to Bluewater shopping centre in Kent with my parents, I always ask them to go to Hollister. Then I pick clothes I like. The store is really cool.'

The Gilly Hicks brand is defined as the 'cheeky cousin' of Abercrombie & Fitch. It embodies the free spirit of Sydney, Australia. It offers underwear and nightwear for women over 18.

The expansion into foreign markets

After having established a large number of stores in the USA, the Abercrombie & Fitch Group decided to conquer international markets. The objective is to open flagship stores in large cities. The internationalisation of the Group's activities started in 2006, initially at a deliberately slow pace to set up sales outlets. In view of the high profitability of its stores located abroad (due to a differentiated pricing policy), the Group decided to accelerate the pace of its international development and multiply its sales outlets. In 2012, 15 new stores were inaugurated in Europe and Asia.

The Abercrombie & Fitch Group currently owns 1,073 stores in 16 countries. The breakdown of stores by brand is indicated in Exhibit 2. The stores established abroad are located in Canada (19), Europe and Asia (China: 3; Japan: 2; Hong Kong: 1; Singapore: 1).

The expansion into the European market

Exhibit 3 presents the geographical breakdown of the stores owned by the Group in Europe. The figures indicated in Exhibit 3 show that the UK ranks first, followed by Germany and Spain.

The Abercrombie & Fitch brand in Europe

The Abercrombie & Fitch chain owns 14 sales outlets abroad. To set up its stores, they favour the prestigious shopping districts of large cities. The A&F chain plays on the limited number of stores

---

EXHIBIT 2: Breakdown of Abercrombie & Fitch Group stores (as of 28 January 2012)

Brand	Abercrombie & Fitch	abercrombie kids	Hollister	Gilly Hicks	TOTAL
USA	280	154	494	18	946
International	14	5	77	3	99
TOTAL	294	159	571	21	1.045

Source: Abercrombie & Fitch (2011), *Annual Report*, p 3.

EXHIBIT 3: Geographical breakdown of the stores owned by the Abercrombie & Fitch Group in Europe (as of 28 January 2012)

Country	Number of stores owned
UK	29
Germany	15
Spain	9
Italy	7
France	5
Austria	3
Belgium	3
Sweden	2
Denmark	1
Ireland	1
TOTAL	73

Source: Abercrombie & Fitch (2011), *Annual Report*, p 26.

and therefore products (exclusive distribution) to attract a young target looking for brands that have not become too common. Before the first stores were opened abroad, only young people who travelled to the USA had 'access' to A&F products. The brand relies on the positive image associated with the USA in the casual wear domain (country of origin 'made-in' effect) and New York City (as a trendy, fashionable city).[1]

As explained by Melanie (a German teenager, aged 16, interviewed in December 2012):

'I went to New York with my aunt in 2010 and discovered the brand on Fifth Avenue. I was very curious when I saw the branded bags and the queue down the street. We waited 20 minutes outside the store before entering an extraordinary universe. During our stay, we returned to the store three times; I love the décor, the smell ... and of course the gorgeous models. When I returned to Düsseldorf, I was one of the first to wear Abercrombie & Fitch clothes. When I saw other young people wearing the brand, it reminded me of my trip to New York and I shared my American experience with them. ... One year later, I went to Copenhagen with my parents. I was keen to visit the Abercrombie & Fitch store to buy more clothes. ... With the opening of several stores in Europe, the brand is becoming more commonplace and I find it less attractive. A store opened in Düsseldorf recently and everybody can go. I visited the store a few times on the Königsallee [where the store is located] but I didn't buy anything.'

The experiential marketing policy of the A&F brand

The A&F chain has embarked on an experiential strategy, placing the emphasis on its sales outlets to showcase the brand values. The objective is to stand out from the competition by providing the consumer with a significant experience, or even by creating a brand community.[2] The annual report stresses the importance of the stores in the company's strategy: 'The Company considers the in-store experience to be its primary marketing vehicle.'[3] The company focuses on product staging, lighting, music, fragrances and its salespersons who strive to create a festive atmosphere in the store. The in-store staff are themselves part of the brand's campaigns, photographed by Bruce Weber, the emblematic photographer of other brands such as Ralph Lauren, Calvin Klein and Versace. The personification of the brand through the image of timeless youth is, however, anchored in time (since 1892) and space (East coast of the USA).

Flagship stores or concept stores are experiential contexts scripted around a brand, for which they are powerful relational vectors. The spectacular launches of A&F flagship stores (London, Milan, Copenhagen, Paris, etc) are non-media experiential contexts aimed at showcasing the brand's identity and providing the target group with brand experiences. A&F chooses to make stores more entertaining by implementing certain rituals (welcome at the entrance, dancing personnel in the aisles, snapshot taken with the bare-chested male model from the entrance at the end of the experience as a souvenir), and a tasteful décor highlighting a festive atmosphere in well planned obscurity. This can be referred to as shopping entertainment, where the purchase of clothes seems to be of secondary importance. The website seems designed to facilitate purchases in a more functional manner (focused on purchases, promotions, little room for developing the brand's story).

This type of approach corresponds in principle with what young Europeans expect of sales outlets. This target group is looking first and foremost for a frequently renewed and surprising range of exclusive products as well as gateways to other universes (music, art, etc).[4] Flagship stores are conducive to the development of the shopping experience. However, this experience is subjective and can be perceived in many different ways (see Exhibit 4).

Experiential strategies are designed to give a significant competitive advantage to the brands by differentiating them considerably from the competition.[6] However, these strategies are not without risk. Creating thematic sales outlets with a view to generating unforgettable consumer experiences requires a substantial effort in terms of design, with investment and operating costs increasing as the consumer gets used to an environment marked by increasingly thematic and dramatic places of consumption. The A&F brand therefore needs to elaborate carefully the marketing strategy and marketing-mix for the European market in order to continue its successful expansion.

EXHIBIT 4: Visitors' testimonies: A&F's shopping experience in Paris

'I came to the A&F store with my son. Honestly, I was amazed by the place, it's like a mansion house, there is a magnificent wrought iron gate, topiaries leading to the entrance ... in fact, it doesn't look like a store at all ... it's luxurious ... given the property prices on the Champs Elysées, I can't imagine how many tee-shirts they need to sell to break even ... especially with so many people on the payroll ... gorgeous young people (boys and girls) who welcome you ... salespersons, and oh yes this gorgeous hunk at the entrance with whom you can get your picture taken... OK, he was about my son's age so I thought it was a bit silly, if not unhealthy to get my picture taken with him, but a lot of young girls were delighted to be given the polaroid ...' *(Julie, 48, a shopkeeper from outside Paris, interviewed in July 2012)*

'I came into a very dark and noisy store, with a supercharged, almost futuristic atmosphere. I didn't buy anything because the atmosphere in the store did not stimulate my desire, my buying process was also hampered by the fact that the salespersons were unavailable and by the layout of the products; it was very difficult to find the product I was looking for (size, colour). I wanted a waistcoat that I had seen someone wear in the street. It seemed fairly thick and comfortable, ideal for the winter, grey with the logo in white and in capitals with a hood.' *(Arthur, 21, student, lives in Paris, interviewed in October 2012)*

'We used to bring A&F clothes back from the USA; it wasn't common for boys, now it's great, with the Paris store, you don't need to cross the Atlantic any more. Overall, I like it, they're well made, wash-resistant, good quality clothes.' *(Anne, 50, doctor, mother of three boys, interviewed in May 2012)*

QUESTIONS

1   What would be the most appropriate marketing strategy (segmentation, targeting, positioning) for the A&F brand in Europe?

2   Is it preferable to standardise or adapt the product policy to the European market?

3   The company has opted for a differentiated pricing policy between the USA and the European markets. What are the principal risks associated with this choice?

4   Should the A&F brand stick to its exclusive distribution policy or extend its distribution channels in European countries?

5   What elements must be taken into consideration when developing the communication policy designed for the European market?

FURTHER READING

- E.J. Arnould, L.L. Price and G. Zinham, *Consumers*, (New York: McGraw-Hill, 2002).
- U. Mayrhofer, and C. Roederer, *Abercrombie & Fitch: Experiential Marketing on International Markets* (Paris: Centrale de Cas et de Médias Pédagogiques, 2013).

- http://www.abercrombie.com.
- http://www.abercrombiemagasin.eu.

NOTES

1 U. Mayrhofer, *Marketing International*, 2nd edn (Paris: Economica, 2012).

2 C. Roederer, *Marketing et Consommation Expérientiels* (Cormelles-le-Royal: Management & Société Publishers, 2012).

3 Abercrombie & Fitch (2011), *Annual Report*, p 3.

4 IFM – Institut Français de la Mode, *Junior Génération, la Mode Des 15–25 Ans* (Paris, 2012).

5 J.B. Pine and J.H. Gilmore, *The Experience Economy: Work is Theatre and Every Business a Stage* (Boston, MA: Harvard Business School Press, 1999).

6 B.H. Schmitt, 'Experiential Marketing', *Journal of Marketing Management*, 1999, 15, 53–67.

This case was written by Ulrike Mayrhofer, IAE Lyon, Jean Moulin Lyon 3 University, and Claire Roederer, Ecole de Management Strasbourg, University of Strasbourg.

Case 2.2

Tellyo: A Start-up Company from Northern Europe and the Quest for Customers and Markets

Born global or incremental internationaliser?

Mr Kimmo Koivisto, a driven CEO of a young start-up company, Tellyo, is back from a business trip to Spain. He has had a successful meeting with a local media company, RTVE, that is interested in partnership with Tellyo. During the journey back to Helsinki, Mr Koivisto is pondering the best internationalisation strategy for Tellyo.

Tellyo (www.tellyo.com) is a start-up company originating from Helsinki, Finland. It was founded in 2012 and its main offering, a mobile application for 'sharing the moment' (see Exhibit 1), was piloted in May 2013. Tellyo could best be described as a 'born global' or 'international new venture' that aims for international markets from the inception rather than gradually increasing its internationalisation activities over time (also known as the Uppsala model).

Tellyo provides a 'share the moment' application which allows its users to grab video clips from TV and share them in social media with comments

EXHIBIT 1: Tellyo.com website

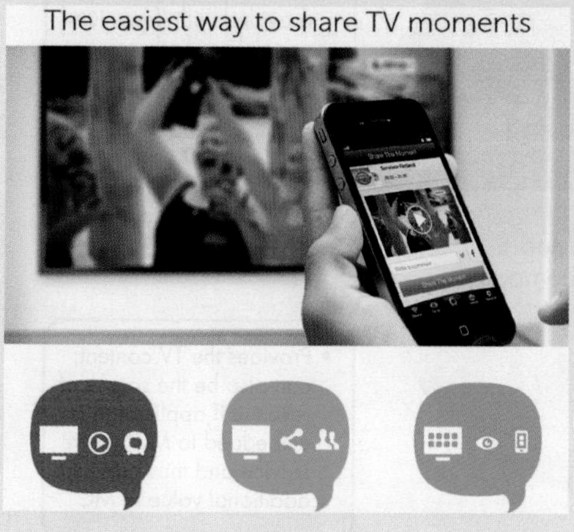

The easiest way to share TV moments

attached. After watching a moment worth sharing, the user opens the Tellyo application on a second screen (eg on their smart phone) and is offered a list of TV shows that are currently on air on every TV channel. After clicking a selected show, Tellyo automatically grabs the last 30 seconds of the selected show for the user to preview and add comments to. Following that, the clip is ready to be posted to Facebook or Twitter.

Currently the Tellyo application is available for mobile devices based on Android and iOS platforms. It can be downloaded for free from the respective app stores. The Tellyo application can also be embedded in other applications (for example, in a TV channel's application). This ability allows the potential extension of the service as a 'Tellyo button' in host applications.

Tellyo is a fully digital product geared towards the mobile industry and from its product characteristics as a digitised product enjoys some benefits that traditional manufacturers can only dream about. After establishing itself in a country, Tellyo's application can be marketed and distributed via online channels to an unlimited number of people. However, the company needs to tweak the application for every country in order to make it work as it is supposed to. From a strategic marketing perspective there is the question of whether to choose a 'sprinkler-or-waterfall approach'. In the sprinkler approach the company aims to enter several markets at the same time and in the waterfall approach it internationalises incrementally.

The day after returning from Spain, Mr Koivisto is having a meeting with Tellyo's board of directors. Enthusiastic CEO Mr Koivisto is ready to expand Tellyo's operations simultaneously to several lead markets (eg the UK, Germany, France, Italy and Spain) as he believes the company has what it takes to follow a born global approach. Chairman of the board Justyna Kowalska worries that the resources of the company do not allow such radical expansion and that they may not be able to attract enough external funding. Mr Koivisto reminds Ms Kowalska that Tellyo is operating in a mobile industry, where the products, distribution and marketing channels are digital and therefore allow faster expansion than in the more traditional industries. The board of directors starts discussing whether they should enter several countries simultaneously or concentrate on one market at a time.

Business model – where's the money?

A week after his business trip to Spain, the CEO Mr Koivisto is travelling again. This time he visits Lappeenranta University of Technology and meets a group of LUT international business students who have offered their help in figuring out options for Tellyo's business model. As Tellyo is still a young start-up in the middle of important negotiations that will decide the future course of the firm and the final business model, nothing is set in stone and the firm has many possibilities to explore.

Although the end users of the application are individual consumers, the current business model of the company indicates that the revenue comes from business customers, eg TV channels, advertisers or media companies only. As the application builds a bridge between TV and social media, it provides opportunities to complement TV advertising with advantages previously available in digital marketing only such as interaction, targeting and effectiveness of measurement. This makes Tellyo a good proposition for

advertisers that find calculating TV advertising return on investments cumbersome. Popular clips might reach a substantial amount of views, and advertisements added to these clips might reach millions of people.

Tellyo can use a number of different revenue models depending on the customer. For its advertiser customers it can use models such as 'cost-per-impression', often referred to as a cost for advertiser when the ad has been shown 1,000 times to the target audience, or 'cost-per-click' in which it is taken into account how many times the viewer actually clicks the advertisement shown. If a media company acts as an intermediate between Tellyo and the advertiser, part of the cost naturally ends up in the media company's pocket. For using Tellyo as an embedded application, a different revenue model may apply (see Exhibit 2 for the revenue model overview).

When Tellyo is thinking about its internationalisation and business model, there are sector-specific matters it has to consider. For a company providing an application in which customers interact with each other, it needs to gain a large customer base as quickly as possible. It needs to do the same for social TV that Dropbox did for storing one's data: Dropbox has managed to lock-in its customers so that they now would have difficulty in changing to another product, technology or supplier because everyone they know is using Dropbox to store and share data.

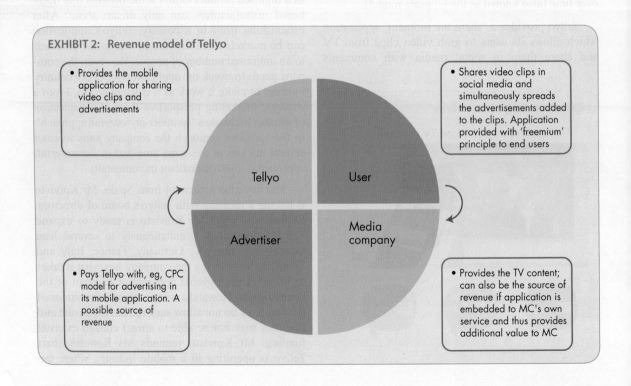

EXHIBIT 2: Revenue model of Tellyo

- Provides the mobile application for sharing video clips and advertisements

- Shares video clips in social media and simultaneously spreads the advertisements added to the clips. Application provided with 'freemium' principle to end users

Tellyo   User

Advertiser   Media company

- Pays Tellyo with, eg, CPC model for advertising in its mobile application. A possible source of revenue

- Provides the TV content; can also be the source of revenue if application is embedded to MC's own service and thus provides additional value to MC

Thus, in addition to an internationalisation model, Tellyo needs a business model that gives it the same advantage, ie will help it to gain a large customer base in a short time. A large customer base brings network effects: the value of the product increases as more people adapt to it. The classic example of this is the phone: if no-one else had a phone, the value of owning one would be non-existent. When trying to gain network effects, the producer may even give away products for free to increase the number of users. As Tellyo aims for a large customer base to attract advertisers, it gives the application for free to the end users. This model is often referred to as the 'freemium model'. The large customer base can also help with co-creation as the users start generating content for the company to use in advertising as the advertisements are added to the clips that users create. The 'need for speed' approach will also help Tellyo to get ahead of its competitors.

As a young start-up with limited resources, Tellyo needs to utilise its resource-base smartly. Although trade fairs would have been useful channels for meeting potential customers (eg media companies) and investors, Tellyo has saved the often excessive cost of trade fair spots and opted for participating in events specialising in start-ups. Tellyo has participated in Startup Sauna 2011, Pioneers Festival 2012 and Barca Starta 2013 events, for instance. These events are often filled with investors and other useful contacts. Also for Tellyo the events have been invaluable as the company has met potential leads such as Qbrick, an expert technology company from Sweden, which could be an ideal channel for Tellyo's service, and RTVE, a Spanish radio and television corporation that is now using the Tellyo button in its own applications. There are also possible partners in the Finnish market, such as one of the biggest television and radio corporations in Finland, MTV Oy. (See Exhibit 3 for more information on European media companies.)

For Tellyo, the number one aim at the moment is to secure the first big deals that would serve as references when entering new markets. And the company is in a hurry: in the business of delivering content produced by someone else, the matter of intellectual property rights cannot be overlooked. The one who gets the leading position in the market first might be able to reach the position as 'standard' custom or dominant design. And if only one player is chosen as the one who will be allowed to share this kind of copyright protected content, Tellyo needs to make sure that it will be in the right place at the right time.

However, IPR rights and the final business model are closely linked to each other: customers might be media companies who already have rights to the content and use Tellyo as an embedded solution. Business model also affects the need for Tellyo's presence in the chosen markets: if Tellyo wants to foster the community of fans sharing clips from TV, it needs to have a community manager for every market. The question of where Tellyo functionalities are available also affects the decision about who needs to do all the marketing activities. The possible embedding of the Tellyo application in the host application reduces the need for Tellyo's own marketing for the end customers and opens the door for co-marketing possibilities.

As Mr Koivisto meets the group of MSc business students, he asks their opinion on how Tellyo could best optimise the obtaining of a market share such that it could benefit from network effects and co-creation; in other words, how could it gain as large a customer base as possible in the shortest time possible with the resources of a small start-up? He instructs the students to take into account the digital nature of Tellyo's business as it affects the business model (as well as internationalisation). To help the students in planning their suggestion, he presents them with a tool (www.businessmodelgeneration.com/canvas) that Tellyo has been using before.

Time for the decisions: which markets to enter?

A month has passed by after the board meeting where Tellyo's internationalisation strategy was discussed. The CEO Mr Koivisto opens his email on Monday morning and finds out that two other media companies have agreed to meet him for a pitch of Tellyo's service offering. These companies are from the UK and Germany. Now, more than ever, Tellyo needs to decide if it wants to enter several countries simultaneously, pick for example two of the prospective countries, or concentrate on only one at a time. Mr Koivisto has already secured written orders from Spanish RTVE and Finnish MTV Oy but the leads from the UK and Germany are tempting.

Tellyo has previously used a simple method for selecting the markets it has entered: it has expanded its operations to countries where customers have exhibited interest in its service. They have not conducted any systematic market analysis by using a clearly-defined set of screening and selection criteria. They have used an approach that Mr Koivisto labels a 'shotgun approach'. Tellyo has followed possible leads gained from the start-up events, although naturally the experience within the team has played a role. However, as Tellyo originates from Finland and Poland, European markets are a natural choice when

EXHIBIT 3: The largest media companies in Europe by revenue 2011 (€m) (NORDICOM, 2011)

Company	Country	Media revenue[1] (€m)	Total revenue (€m)	Media share of total revenue (%)
1 Bertelsmann AG	Germany	15,253	15,253	100
2 Vivendi[2]	France	9,054	28,813	31
3 Lagardère	France	7,657	7,657	100
4 BSkyB[3]	UK	7,603	7,603	100
5 Pearson	UK	6,756	6,756	100
6 Reed Elsevier	The Netherlands/UK	6,521	6,521	100
7 ARD	Germany	6,221	6,221	100
8 BBC[4]	UK	5,862	5,862	100
9 Mediaset[5]	Italy	4,250	4,250	100
10 Virgin Media	UK/USA	3,871	4,601	84
11 Bonnier	Sweden	3,374	3,374	100
12 Wolters Kluwer	The Netherlands	3,354	3,354	100
13 Axel Springer	Germany	3,185	3,185	100
14 France Télévision[6]	France	3,140	3,140	100
15 RAI	Italy	3,012	3,012	100
16 ProSiebenSat.1	Germany	2,971	2,971	100
17 Hubert Burda Media	Germany	2,745	2,745	100
18 Grupo Prisa	Spain	2,734	2,734	100
19 TF-1 – Société Télévision Française	France	2,620	2,620	100
20 ITV Plc	UK	2,466	2,466	100
21 Sanoma	Finland	2,367	2,746	86
22 Verlagsgruppe Georg von Holtzbrink[6]	Germany	2,255	2,255	100
23 Daily Mail & General Trust	UK	2,141	2,293	93
24 RCS Media Group	Italy	2,075	2,075	100
25 Bauer Media Group	Germany	2,004	2,004	100

1 Media revenue refers to revenue from advertising, publishing, radio or television transmissions, TV and film production, music publishing, printing, distribution services, subscriptions, government support etc. Retail sales, theme parks, games etc are not included.
2 Telecom (SFR and Maroc Telecom), revenue €16,368m, and games, revenue €3,432m, not included in media revenue.
3 Fiscal year 2010 (07)–2011 (06).
4 Fiscal year 2011 (04)–2012 (03).
5 Revenue for the advertising agency Publitalia 80 unknown and therefore not excluded from media revenue.
6 Fiscal year 2010.

pondering where to enter next. Luckily for Tellyo, the mobile market in Europe has reached a tipping point: a majority of consumers (55 per cent) are now using smart phones in the top-five markets including the UK, France, Germany, Italy and Spain. The number of smart phone users has reached 131.5 million people and the proportion only continues to grow. Also Europe's share of the social TV market revenue is the largest at the moment.[1] According to Marketsandmarkets (2012), the region's share was $55.48bn in 2012 and is expected to grow to $77.74bn by 2017. The compound annual growth rate is 7 per cent,

which is slightly below the overall market growth rate. The worldwide figure for social TV market was $151.14bn in 2012 and is expected to reach $256.44bn by 2017.

Tellyo is one of the applications that belongs to a category also known as 'social TV'. The term 'social TV' refers to the use of social media platforms to enrich the experience of consuming a TV programme.[2] Social applications help consumers with connecting to their friends to express their views about what they are watching. Social TV is tied to the second screen phenomenon, but second-screen applications are not always in the social TV domain. One part of the the social TV phenomenon is the rise of video clip sharing. Today's consumers like watching and sharing video clips and they do it 200 billion times every month. Tellyo's user-generated TV clips stand a good chance of promoting both TV channels and shows, and video viewers are referred to TV networks and online services. Television as a medium passed through its biggest changes in the 1950s and 1960s. Since then, not much has changed in the ways that people enjoy their television watching moments. The recent emergence of smart phones and tablets has the potential to revolutionise that scene.

The target users of the Tellyo app are second-screen users, who use their tablets, smart phones and laptops while watching TV. According to Philpott,[3] 70 per cent of connected users use a second screen while watching TV, 50 per cent seek more information about what they see on TV and 40 per cent discuss TV shows using social media. Among 15–35 year olds the usage of the second screen is the highest. Also The Guardian's (2012) summary of the second-screen industry indicates that 75–85 per cent of TV viewers use other devices while watching. However, it is noted that some of these tasks are unrelated to the show they are watching, for example emailing. Show-related second-screen use is estimated to be between 37–52 per cent. The number of people browsing through products spotted in a show or ad is between 27–44 per cent. A fifth of TV viewers are chatting on Facebook or Twitter about the shows they are watching. Additional customer segmentation is driven by socio-demographic metrics, TV viewing habits, social networking usage and interest in value-added services like mobile betting and mobile commerce/coupons. Taking into consideration all the facts mentioned above, Tellyo targets people aged from 16 to 45 years.

More specifically, a study on British markets by Red Bee Media[4] reveals that, of second-screen application users, 55 per cent were interested in responding to polls about TV shows in the apps and 52 per cent would like the ability to influence a show. One-third of respondents using the second screen said they were more likely to watch a show live if there was lots of social buzz around it; 44 per cent of 'dual screeners' use the second screen to find out more about brands or ads, 56 per cent are open to receiving targeted ads through synchronous apps, and 40 per cent would be willing to receive offers and promotions on their devices based on products featured on the TV.

Competition in the application industry is fierce. App stores run by Apple and Google now offer more than 700,000 apps each.[5] Many developers try to fill the same niche. One of Tellyo's competitors offering a similar type of sharing tool is Yap.tv. Yap.tv, founded in 2010 and headquartered in Los Altos, CA, provides a content feed about all the user's favourite shows, including pictures, videos and other content. The only difference in sharing the videos is that, with Tellyo, one can select a part of the show to grab and share, while Yap.tv's videos are ready-made. Yap.tv has already spread further: the free iPhone and iPad application is available in 22 countries and seven languages. In addition to the USA, countries supported include the UK, Germany, France, Denmark, Spain, Finland, Ireland, Norway, the Netherlands, Poland, Canada, Mexico, Brazil, Argentina, Colombia, Chile, Nicaragua, El Salvador and Panama. Android and web versions are under development.[6] In the market for social TV applications, there is also an ever-increasing number of other players fighting for customers' attention and time, although not with exactly similar ideas. In addition to Tellyo, US-based GetGlue, IntoNow and PlayUp are trying to conquer European social TV markets and be the preferred application of choice for watching TV.

Tellyo is interested in the 'top-five markets' in Europe, namely the UK, France, Germany, Italy and Spain. As can be seen from the market data[7] in Exhibit 4, one of these countries could be a possible next step for Tellyo. The smartphone ownership ranges from 45 per cent of the population in France to 64 per cent in Spain and nearly one-quarter of the population in Italy and Spain owned a tablet in 2012. The number of citizens accessing the Internet via mobile varies from 30 per cent in France to 46 per cent in Spain. The percentage of mobile owners accessing social networking sites ranges from 26 per cent in Germany to 43 per cent in Spain. The advertising industry has also realised the importance of the phenomenon: between 2007 and 2012, the mobile Internet advertising spend has grown over 70 per cent in these five markets.

Tellyo currently employs eight people, four of them from the original founding team: co-founder and CEO Kimmo Koivisto, co-founder and CFO Jakub Majkowski, co-founder and Chief Architect Mariusz Ostoja-Swierczynski and co-founder and Chairman of the Board Justyna Kowalska, designer Shakti Dash, programmer Pawel Predki, programmer, Agnieszka Przekopowska and programmer Jan Wychowaniak (see more information on the personnel roles and background in Exhibit 5).

EXHIBIT 4: Market information from the UK, France, Germany, Italy and Spain (Ofcom, 2012)

	UK	France	Germany	Italy	Spain
TV revenue (£bn)	11,3	10,2	11,6	7,8	4,8
TV revenue per capita from advertising (£)	56	46	43	63	36
Smart phone ownership (%)	58	45	50	55	64
Tablet ownership (%)	19	15	10	23	24
Watch TV (%)	95	93	94	93	95
Use smart phone (%)	57	41	44	52	62
TV viewing (mins/day)	242	227	225	253	239
Accessing TV content over Internet (%, ever)	42	31	19	26	34
Cellular broadband connections per 100 population	8	5	7	10	7
Internet access via mobile phone (%)	38	30	31	37	46
Mobile Internet advertising expenditure growth 2007–2012 (%)	136	44	69	32	75
Internet access with tablet (%)	13	10		15	14
Mobile owners accessing social networking sites (%)	40	27	26	32	43

EXHIBIT 5: Tellyo personnel: roles, education and professional background

Person	Role	Education	Background
Kimmo Koivisto	CEO	MSc in Corporate Strategy and Industrial Engineering	Previously at Vectia Management Consulting and Nokia working on strategy development, customer engagement concepts and solution business for 6 years
Jakub Majkowski	CTO	PhD in Telecommunications	Previously at Nokia working on local and personal wireless area networks for 4 years
Mariusz Ostoja-Swierczynski	Chief Architect	MSc in Computer Science, SW Engineering and Network Systems	Previously at Cybercom and Kuehne + Nagel software development on enterprise, web and mobile for 7 years
Justyna Kowalska	Business development	MSc in Industrial Engineering and MSc in Finance and Banking	Previously at Nokia and MasterCard with 10 years of experience in business development, GTM and product planning
Pawel Predki	Developer: Android & iOS	PhD candidate in Electronics and Computer Science	Working at Cybercom mobile software development
Agnieszka Przekopowska	Developer: Android	MSc in Computer Science	Working at Mobica and previously at Teleca on mobile software development
Jan Wychowaniak	Developer: Backend	MSc in Computer Science	Working at Mobica and previously at Teleca on mobile software development
Shakti Dash	Designer	MA student in New Media, Aalto University School of Art and Design	Visual Communication Design, Srishti School of Art, Design and Technology

As the CEO, Mr Koivisto concentrates on the business side of operations, CTO Mr Majkowski on technology and Chief Architect Mr Ostoja-Swierczynski on product development. Tellyo's organisation is nearly a virtual one, as Mr Koivisto works from Finland, Mr Ostoja-Swierczynski from Poland and Mr Majkowski and Ms Kowalska from London, England. Officially, the company has offices in Helsinki, Finland and Lodz, Poland. In addition to the core team, the company has also used developers in Poland and Finland but as the resources are scarce for a small company, the developers have been used on an on-demand basis. Part of the team has also lived in Spain for many years, which has allowed them to gather information from Spanish markets. Hence, Tellyo is able to utilise hands-on market expertise from Finnish, Polish,

Spanish and UK markets. As the technical development team of Tellyo is located in Poland, substantial cost advantages are achieved. Because of the founders' background, Tellyo has excellent access to the best local talent.

Now Mr Koivisto is sitting at his desk and thinking what he should suggest to the board of directors. Should they concentrate on their home market in Finland or perhaps somewhere else? Should they in addition take full advantage of their written order from Spain? Or should Mr Koivisto also travel to the UK and Germany to pitch their service offering to reach even more markets? He needs to take into account the lure of the new markets but also consider the limited resources of a small company. The time has come to make the final decisions about Tellyo's future activities.

QUESTIONS

1 What are the characteristics of born global/international new ventures and how does Tellyo fit in?
2 Should Tellyo pursue a gradual expansion strategy?
3 How does Tellyo make money?
4 Which countries should Tellyo enter next and how?

FURTHER READING

- Marketsandmarkets, 'Social TV Market [Social EPG, Content Discovery, Social Analytics, Social Curation, AD Platforms]: Global Advancements, Ecosystem, Business Models, Technology Roadmap, Worldwide Market Forecasts & Analysis (2012–2017)', in N. Lomas, 'Report: Social TV Market To Be Worth $256.44BN by 2017; Europe Taking Largest Share Now', http://techcrunch.com/2012/10/12/report-social-tv-market-to-be-worth-256–44bn-by-2017-europe-taking-largest-share-now/, 2012.
- NORDICOM, 'The Largest Media Companies in EUROPE by Revenue 2011 (Euro Millions) and Their Main Media Activities', http://www.medienorge.uib.no/files/Eksterne_pub/Topmediacompanies_2011_PDF.pdf, 2012.
- 'Social TV and Second-screen Viewing: The Stats in 2012', http://www.guardian.co.uk/technology/appsblog/2012/oct/29/social-tv-second-screen-research, 2012.

NOTES

1   I. Lunden, 'ComScore: Smartphone Penetration In Europe's Big-5 Markets Now At 55 per cent, Samsung Is the One To Beat', http://techcrunch.com/2012/12/17/smartphone-penetration-in-europes-big-5-markets-now-at-55-apple-continues-to-feel-the-heat-from-fast-rising-samsung/, 2012.

2   Digital Marketing Glossary, 'What is Social TV Definition?', http://digitalmarketing-glossary.com/What-is-Social-TV-definition, 2013.

3   M. Philpott, 'Unlocking the Second Screen. Ovum View. Summary', http://ovum.com/2011/10/03/unlocking-the-second-screen/, 2012.

4   Red Bee Media, 'Broadcast Industry Not Capitalising on Rise of Second Screen', http://www.redbeemedia.com/sites/all/files/downloads/second_screen_research.pdf, 2012.

5   J.E. Lessin and E. Spencer Ante, 'Apps Rocket Toward $25 Billion in Sales', http://online.wsj.com/article/SB10001424127887323293704578334401534217878.html, 2013.

6   Yap.tv http://www.yap.tv/, 2012.

7   Ofcom, 'International Communications Market Report 2012', http://stakeholders.ofcom.org.uk/binaries/research/cmr/cmr12/icmr/ICMR-2012.pdf, 2012.

This case was prepared by Olli Kuivalainen, Lappeenranta University of Technology, Rudolf R. Sinkovics, University of Manchester, Manchester Business School, and Heini Vanninen, Lappeenranta University of Technology.

The authors are grateful to Kimmo Koivisto and his help and support in the preparation of this case study.

Case 2.3

Dating at IKEA China: An Unexpected Management Challenge

Jerome Deloix, the manager of IKEA's Xu Hui store in Shanghai, could not quite believe either the noise or the scene before his eyes. One of the store's security guards had summoned him urgently to the restaurant. It was 2.30 pm on a Tuesday and, ever since the store had opened at 9 am, a stream of middle-aged and older people had been filling up the restaurant. By this time, nearly 500 of them had gathered to socialise and spend the day drinking the free coffee to which they were entitled as IKEA Family Member cardholders. Not only were they drinking many cups of coffee and taking all the sugar, they were also eating food they had brought with them – instead of enjoying the tasty meals available for purchase from the counter – and were playing radios, calling out to each other and generally behaving as though they were in their own homes. They were also checking out members of the opposite sex. A seniors' dating club had adopted the IKEA Xu Hui restaurant as the location for its meetings.

Arguments sometimes broke out between dating club members, and one man had thrown hot coffee over the security guard who had tried to intervene. If they were asked not to eat food brought from home, club members just yelled and carried on as before. Ordinary IKEA customers were getting upset that every Tuesday and Thursday (the days that the club met) there was no space for them to relax and eat in the restaurant. IKEA co-workers[1] were unhappy at what was going on. The ambiance of the store was disrupted and sales suffered on the dating club days as none of the club members bought things from the store and each might spend only RMB10 on food. The problem had been growing over the last 18 months, as club meetings became more and more popular. At first, in 2009, when there were under 250 seniors participating, IKEA co-workers felt they could cope, but when numbers climbed in 2011 to around 700 the situation got beyond a joke.

Enough was enough. Something had to be done to stop this disruptive behaviour. 'We want to be nice, but there are limits!' remarked Deloix to his fellow managers. Ruefully he reflected: 'If you have a weakness, people will find it immediately.' But what measures could he take against the seniors' activities that

would be respectful of ordinary customers' needs while also remaining true to IKEA's deeply-held customer service concepts? Being a good member of the community was just as important to IKEA as its commitment to customers and co-workers. Was it fair that his co-workers – all Chinese – had to bear the brunt of dating club members' bad behaviour? How far did the store's concept of community engagement require it to go?

A very different culture: IKEA in China

As in every IKEA outlet worldwide, the Xu Hui store's restaurant lay at its centre, halfway along the path mapped out for visitors through the enormous display of furniture and home interior furnishings. The Xu Hui store stocked 8,500 different items in its 35,000 square metre floor space, so it was bigger than the typical 25,000–30,000 square metre IKEA outlets in Europe. Still, it was the smallest of IKEA's 11 stores in China, which averaged around 45,000 square metres in size. The Xu Hui store was also unusual in that it occupied a city-centre site and 60 per cent of its visitors arrived by public transport. With well over 5 million visitors per year, the store ranked in IKEA's top 10 worldwide revenue-generators although the average spend per customer was relatively low. An indication of its popularity was that 80,000 people visited on the opening day in 2003, even though it was the middle of the SARS epidemic. IKEA's Shanghai Beicai store was newer, its largest in Asia, and had plenty of car-parking space, so most people arrived with their own transport. An even bigger third store was scheduled to open in 2013. Compared with both of these stores, by mid-2012 the Xu Hui branch was beginning to look a little tired.

Part of the IKEA concept was to provide a spacious, clean location where customers could rest and eat Swedish-inspired meals and snacks, as a means of encouraging them to stay longer in the store. The restaurant did not operate as a profit centre but as a marketing tool, to support the customer service ethos. Because many women came to shop there, the Xu Hui store restaurant offered breakfast deals from 9 am for mothers who had dropped their children off at school, lunch sets that varied from day to day, 'happy hour' snacks during the afternoon, and other special offers right up until the store closed at 11 pm each evening. Customers who had IKEA Family Member cards (which they could get by simply filling in a form) were entitled to free coffee, as was the case in IKEA worldwide. People who did not have a Family Member card paid RMB5 for a cup of coffee – far cheaper than in coffee shop chains like Starbucks or Costa Coffee – and could have a free refill. In China, drinking coffee was still a rather exotic pastime even 30 years after the country began to embrace Western ideas. After the scandal over adulterated milk in 2008, good milk was expensive but was offered freely to IKEA coffee-drinkers.

While the IKEA vision was 'to create a better life for the many people'[2] – comprising customers, co-workers and the community – determining who the 'many people' were in China was very different than in Sweden which, after all, had only 9 million citizens. Shanghai's population alone was 23 million. During his 10 years with IKEA in China, Deloix had seen many things he had never experienced at IKEA France, his previous posting. At the store in Dalian, which he had opened and managed before coming to Shanghai, families had sat at tables in the dining room display area to eat food that they had brought with them and then walked away leaving a mess. He had seen ayis (nannies) put small children to sleep in cots in the roomsets during the morning, wake them for lunch in the restaurant, and put them down again for a nap in the afternoon. On hot days in Shanghai, the sofas and beds were attractive places to stretch out and sleep for a while.

Sometimes long-distance tour buses arrived too early for hotels to be ready, so the drivers would drop their passengers off to rest in the conveniently located Xu Hui store. IKEA co-workers did their best to respond sensitively to all this, for example waking people who were sleeping too long or had sprawled inappropriately, or explaining to nannies that other people wanted to look at the children's rooms.

Deloix admired some of the entrepreneurial spirit he encountered. One company organised tours of the Xu Hui store, complete with tour guide wearing a microphone – but very often participants bought something afterwards. He knew that people in distant parts of China, where IKEA was not present, commissioned contacts to buy items and despatch them for an extra fee. And after a special offer had ended, it was not uncommon to see those products offered for sale on the online retailing site TaoBao.com or in another province at the higher price. There was

nothing IKEA could do about that. On the other hand, informal taxi drivers hassling customers inside the store could be dealt with by the police.

'It's not so much a question of whether something is good or bad,' said Deloix, 'but whether we accept it. And if the answer is yes, then how?'

The Free Coffee Dating club (as IKEA co-workers dubbed it) was also making money for its organiser by charging membership fees of RMB10 per person when they signed up online. Dating clubs had become a big business in China, and huge 'marriage markets' occurred regularly in many cities where young people paid a fee and, often with their mothers, gathered to post their own mini-CV, scan other CVs for promising members of the opposite sex and – for the brave ones (or even their mothers!) – get up on a podium to 'sell' their virtues to the passing crowds. The differences in IKEA's case were the age group the Free Coffee Dating club catered to and the location it chose for its meetings.

Deloix tried but failed to identify the Free Coffee Dating club organiser. Concerned that the reputation of IKEA would be damaged by customers' negative comments on social networking sites, he took the unusual step of inviting journalists to come and see the problem for themselves. The story appeared in a variety of Chinese and English-language newspapers and on Chinese TV – which believed it was the government's duty to halt the group's activities because it was responsible for people's behaviour.

The store's co-workers debated what to do. Deloix proposed cancelling the free coffee for IKEA Family Members and instead giving them a free drink with a set meal, but the IKEA China head office told him, 'Don't touch the free coffee!' It was too important a part of IKEA's culture worldwide to abandon. Chinese co-workers were protective of the company and highly critical of the Free Coffee Daters. Some even said that the group demonstrated the attitude typical of the over-45 generation, which had no sense of civic behaviour – they only took and never gave. Deloix wanted to look through his customers' eyes and see what could be learned.

'It's nice that older people like to date.' IKEA believed in being socially responsible within its local community; it wanted to be close to people and part of their lives. Maybe it should go into the dating club business itself? Or should Deloix simply crack down and ban the group?

Eventually Deloix and his team defined a specific area in the restaurant where the group could meet and provided them with special green cups for their coffee. Extra security guards were posted to keep order and notices were posted at the entrance asking for good behaviour and banning shouting, radio-playing and knitting. Says Deloix: 'We can't solve this problem, so we have to manage it in the right way. It takes time to change people's habits.'

In early 2013 he was going to begin a phased renovation of the store. Maybe he should start with the restaurant? Perhaps, by the time the remodelled store fully re-opened in 2014, the senior dating club would have gone to look for romance elsewhere.

NOTES

1   All IKEA employees are called co-workers, no matter what their job was, reflecting the company's core values of openness and equality.

2   http://www.ikea.com/ms/en_CN/about_ikea/the_ikea_way/our_business_idea/index.html.

This case was prepared by Jocelyn Probert and Sumelika Bhattacharyya under the supervision of Professor Hellmut Schütte at CEIBS. It is intended to be used as a basis for class discussion rather than an illustration of an either effective or

ineffective handling of a management situation. The case was developed from field research and published sources.

© 2013 by CEIBS

PART 3

Case 3.1

To Be or Not to Be (a Main Supplier of Mercadona)? The MBF Case

Nearing the end of 2011, Alberto Garcia, Managing Director of MBF, SL (MyBaby-Food), a Spanish family-owned company dedicated to the food industry sub-sector of baby food, received a call in his office; it was one of the top managers of Mercadona, a leader in the field of food retail distribution in Spain.

'Alberto, our model consists of four very clear ideas, and our main suppliers must be 100 per cent aligned so that everything runs smoothly. If you want to continue being our main supplier, you must cease production for other food retailers ... at least in Spain.'

Mercadona's demands were clear; it wanted to be the sole customer of MBF in order to strengthen its strategic logic and 'minimise costs and pass on to the final consumer only the production costs'.

Alberto Garcia quickly summoned the members of the two families that owned the company for an emergency meeting. Among them was Martin Roth, a Dutchman living in Spain and current president of MBF, who had been instrumental in the management of the company from the very beginning. The new demands by Mercadona placed the management team of MBF between a rock and a hard place. On the one hand, if they accepted Mercadona's demands, they should forget about the rest of their customers in Spain, with whom they had always maintained an excellent relationship, and represented a significant part of their profits. However, Mercadona had provided them with a steady and solid growth, allowing them to maintain good results during the economic crisis in which Spain had been immersed since 2008.

On the other hand, if they were to rely on their own brands and develop the business through their remaining customers, abandoning the strategic alliance with Mercadona, they should disengage[1] within a period of three years and probably turn away from the industry leader in Spain, neglecting significant domestic and international growth prospects.

That was the dilemma facing the management team of MBF: to keep or to abandon the company's status as Mercadona main-supplier? It was not the first time that a company faced this situation. Another family-owned main supplier of Mercadona, the SIRO group (pasta and biscuits),[2] had publicly announced in 2009 the sale of its brands and the company's exclusive focus on accompanying Mercadona's growth.

Others, like Dailycer[3] (cereals) or Ubago[4,5] (frozen cod and canned food), were evaluating other options, such as disengaging from Mercadona or splitting their businesses, maintaining the relationship for some products and disengaging others. But the decision represented a wide range of consequences, which would certainly affect the future strategy of MBF and determine the success or failure of this family-owned company.

Mercadona: the leader of supermarkets in Spain

Mercadona SA is a retailer company that operates in the supermarket sector, whose capital is family owned and 100 per cent Spanish. Mercadona's beginnings date back to 1977, when the Roig Meat Group decided to create a company to expand the marketing of meat and spread out into the grocery business. In 1981 Mercadona had eight grocery stores in the city of Valencia and under the leadership of Juan Roig (son of the founders), the owners sought to transform the eight stores into a small supermarket chain.

During the 1980s and early 1990s, Mercadona began a period of inorganic expansion, making a series of acquisitions of supermarket chains[5] aimed at expanding to new geographical areas of Spain.

In those years, the food distribution sector grew considerably as a result of the social and economic changes taking place in the country, such as the concentration of the population in urban centres or the progressive incorporation of women into the labour market[6] (among other factors). The leading European retailers pursued aggressive growth based on low prices achieved through harsh conditions in their negotiations with suppliers. As the industry matured, it experienced a progressive concentration in the hands of European supply chains and a growing hardening of the intensity of competition. Mercadona responded to this pressure by increasing its spending on advertising and strong price adjustments, also achieved through tough negotiations with suppliers. Nevertheless, although the company was selling more and more, its benefits gradually decreased. At that time, the unwavering dream of Mercadona of becoming the largest supermarket chain in Spain led them to make key decisions aimed at achieving a sharp drop in prices, applying a model of total quality management and creating a culture based on work and daily effort, aspects which have prevailed in the company till this day. The result was fundamentally to create value for all the stakeholders involved in the business, from the suppliers to 'The Boss'.[7]

The new model aimed to develop a competitive response clearly different from the rest of its competitors. Mercadona removed its advertising costs and promotions based on special offers. It promised always to sell at the same price and always 'low prices'. In order to do this it developed a business model based on commitments to customers, employees, suppliers, society and the capital[8] itself.

The business model of Mercadona

The central axis of the model is customer satisfaction. Mercadona tries to satisfy the customer by offering a wide variety and complete range to the consumers. It does not offer a great variety of brands, but the formats and selection continued in the entire range of products, are sufficient to cover the whole spectrum of customer needs. In addition, Mercadona is also the food chain with the greatest ratio of proximity in urban neighbourhoods, with parking available in most of them, and on average between 1,500 and 1,800 square metres of surface. The said model also endeavours to make the shopping experience satisfactory and pleasant, giving the best service and a very functional store design organised into different zones. In its stores it is rare to see queues at the checkouts because the versatility and attention of the employees prevent the accumulation of several customers at the checkout. It also offers an Internet and telephone buying service, and the home delivery service is punctual and efficient. These features provide high levels of convenience in the purchasing process and considerably reduce the time necessary to make it.

In order to achieve customer satisfaction it is necessary to have also satisfied and engaged employees. If they feel cared for by the company, they will transmit this to the customer. For this reason they do not skimp on investments in training (in 2011 it represented a ratio of €450 per employee). In addition, 100 per cent of their employees have permanent contracts in the belief that job security stimulates greater involvement in the day-to-day work. The company's remuneration policy is also well above the industry average.

Another key element of the business model relies on the satisfaction of the suppliers with which the company works. Mercadona works basically with three types of suppliers:[8] (1) the standards, with whom it has conventional contractual relationships, and whose products (with their own brands) are demanded by customers as a result of investment in quality and marketing of such suppliers; (2) the main suppliers, who are those who accept and share with Mercadona its total quality model; and (3) suppliers 'al coll' (in dire straits) who are struggling companies from whom Mercadona buys in great quantities in very advantageous conditions, in turn aiding to the survival of the said companies.

In the case of main suppliers, long-term agreements are established which aim to develop a joint effort focused on the satisfaction of 'The Boss'. This commitment is built through stable and close relationships with suppliers, in many cases through indefinite agreements, which seek to create synergies that result in the benefit of the customers. Mercadona establishes an open book agreement, by which the company works closely with the supplier to improve processes and reduce all unnecessary costs that do not provide value to the end customer.

Both Mercadona and its suppliers know the processes and margins of the other party, sharing information and investment risks. Mercadona contributes with the knowledge of the threshold prices that customers are willing to pay, the potential volume of sales, the quality, the product range sought by the customers, etc. The main supplier contributes with expertise, product know-how and the pursuit of excellence in the production processes. Furthermore, Mercadona encourages and supports its suppliers in implementing R&D + I + i policies (Research, Development and Innovation backed by the investment lever), and rewards innovation among its suppliers. The long duration of the agreements allows the main supplier to make significant investment in R&D + I and in quality, reducing manufacturing and marketing costs and developing new products, due to the peace of mind and stability which Mercadona offers them. Mercadona's private label brands differ from the traditional white brands in so far as the end customer

recognises in them both Mercadona's brand and the manufacturer's, who are often well-known companies and even leaders in their respective sectors.

In order to enter the select group of main suppliers, Mercadona demands from its 'partners' compliance with a series of requirements[9] such as the following:

- owners must have 'passion' for what they do
- they must be leaders in their respective sectors
- they must be prepared to make continuous improvements in accordance with customer needs
- they must produce goods of the highest quality at the lowest price
- they must share with Mercadona the same model of total quality

The model is sealed with the satisfaction of society and shareholders. Mercadona holds the recognition of the Reputation Institute of New York, which has placed it among the best companies in the world in terms of corporate reputation,[6] and meets with the approval of shareholders through the achievement of sustained and satisfactory profits.

Model results

When this model was first adopted the first results were not at all promising: sales were increasing but profits were falling sharply. However, Mercadona maintained its determination and results slowly began to improve. From 1995 the company began a continuous growth cycle which has converted it into one of the largest supermarket chains (both in size and profitability) in the sector. Its rate of store openings (usually through organic growth and in the

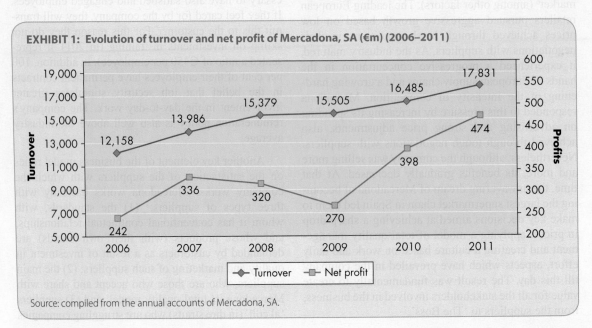

EXHIBIT 1: Evolution of turnover and net profit of Mercadona, SA (€m) (2006–2011)

Source: compiled from the annual accounts of Mercadona, SA.

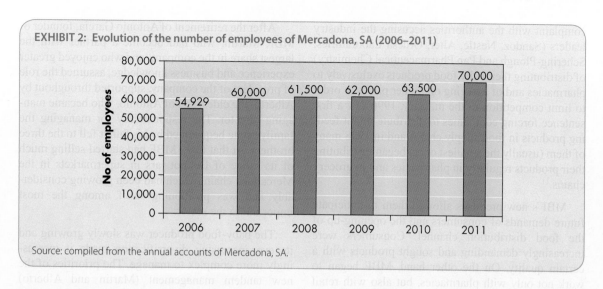

EXHIBIT 2: Evolution of the number of employees of Mercadona, SA (2006–2011)

Source: compiled from the annual accounts of Mercadona, SA.

form of 'oil slick') stands at around 100 new stores annually (see Exhibits 1 and 2). In 2011, Mercadona reached a total of 70,000 employees with permanent contracts,[10] creating 6,500 jobs just in 2011, with predominantly female employment (67 per cent of the total workforce).

The arrival of the economic crisis in late 2007 marked a turning point in the evolution of the company and in the steady improvement in its ability to empathise with customers in the following years. The effects of the crisis began to become evident in 2008, with a sharp reduction in household consumption. Mercadona got to work, holding meetings with all stakeholders, from suppliers (over 2,000) and main suppliers (over 100) to workers (over 61,000), in order to adapt to the new situation, eliminating anything that did not add value to the customer and whose removal allowed for price reduction without affecting product quality, to meet the changing needs of customers. As a result Mercadona's market share increased from 13 per cent in 2003 to 24 per cent in 2010.

MyBaby-Food SL: the leader in jarred baby food in Spain

MBF SL is a family-owned company, whose main business is the production of baby food (purees, soups, baby food and combined cereals). Its origins go back to 1969 when Antonio Garcia founded the company Cerenules, engaged in the manufacture and commercialisation of biscuits and cereal products. Within a few years the company began to be recognised for the quality of its products and their great taste. In the 1970s, Antonio decided to address the market for baby products (Babycer), because in Spain there was a significant 'baby boom' (considerable increase

in the birth rate), and also began to observe a growing concern of parents for the quality and nutritional characteristics of baby food. In 1984 the company adopted a new name in order to identify itself better with its new business: My Baby-Food (MBF).

During a holiday, Martin Roth, a young Dutch doctor specialising in child nutrition and a friend of the Garcia family, had the opportunity to visit the factory of MBF. Martin, driven by the attraction of living permanently on the Mediterranean coast and the friendship that had been forged with the Garcia family years earlier, arrived at an agreement with Antonio by which Martin and his wife Linda would become partners of MBF, with a 34 per cent stake, and Martin would become part of the senior management team to assist in providing business management experience in the sector.

Various market tests were conducted at the same time with a wide variety of products (mainly cereal-based baby food, both powdered and ready-to-eat), seeking business take-off in the newly chosen sector and developing highly recognised products, for example, in the case of baby food, jars of 'Delicious'. The argument that this baby food was made with natural ingredients and no artificial additives and the introduction of an original type of container which made handling easier, contributed to the successful introduction of MBF into the market for baby food, shelving the production of biscuits, which so far had produced high levels of income. With the cash flow generated by the sale of the biscuits division in 1990, and in view of the wide acceptance of its new products, in 1992 MBF built a plant to produce 'Delicious'.

In Spain in the 1980s and 1990s baby food products were sold only in pharmacies. However, in 1994 the Consumers Union of Spain filed an anti-trust complaint with the authorities accusing the industry leaders (Sandoz, Nestlé, Alter, Ordesa Laboratories, Schering-Plough and Pan Pharmaceutical Chemistry) of distributing their baby food products exclusively to pharmacies and of agreeing on higher prices in order to limit competition in the industry. 1996 saw a first sentence forcing companies to distribute infant feeding products in food supply chains and in 1998 many of them (usually the smallest ones) began distributing their products regularly in pharmacies and in grocery chains.[11]

MBF's new premises allowed them to anticipate future demands of consumers and the opening-up of the food distribution channel. Consumers were increasingly demanding and sought products with a certain quality. On the other hand, MBF began to work not only with pharmacies, but also with retail food distribution chains, which, in addition to requiring certified quality standards and a lot of innovation, were extremely tough in negotiating prices and created competition in the leveling of costs in order to maintain margins in the supply channel.

The company had developed a wide range of varieties, following the trends of the main competitors, maintaining a balance between healthy eating and a diversified offer, adapted to all needs and tastes. Its range of products included baby paps with different varieties of cereal (with honey, fruit and cocoa). In 1999 MBF made a major investment in setting up a new expansion of its production plant with a view to expanding its product range to include minced food with a meat and fish base (generally referred to as baby jars).

The road, however, was not without its challenges and difficulties. The baby food jars did not have the same acceptance in Spain as in other European countries such as Germany or France, where the product line was more successful than that of paps, and sometimes that of baby milk (infant formula). Spanish families still preferred to prepare purees and porridges, using the jars only on special occasions, such as short trips or one-day outings away from home. In addition, the sector was heavily concentrated in the hands of a few multinationals. Hero had 40 per cent of the total market, although its dominance in the supply channel (67 per cent of sales) was absolute. Nestlé, however, dominated the chemist's market (69 per cent of sales) but was content with 25 per cent of the category. The entry into the category of baby jars, sold mostly in the food channel, opened the door to that channel and posed a possible springboard for progressive change towards selling porridge in the channel, facilitating the foreseeable transfer from pharmacies to food supply chains.

After the retirement of Antonio Garcia, founder of MBF, Martin, who had become a partner with the largest share in the company, and who enjoyed greater experience and business knowledge, assumed the role of president of the company, supported throughout by Alberto, the eldest son of Antonio, who became managing director. The responsibility for managing the family estate bequeathed by his father fell to the three brothers. At that time, MBF had started selling much of its range of Delipot jars in supermarkets in the Mercadona chain, which had been growing considerably and was positioning itself among the most important in the sector.

The baby-food producer was slowly growing and its ever-increasing diversification made it increasingly more complex to manage. The priorities of the new tandem management (Martin and Alberto) focused on the following aspects:

- ensuring the food safety system and quality of production in order to satisfy the increasing demands of customers and prospects
- professionalising of the family company to create a large enterprise that could compete on equal terms with the big multinationals in the sector, and establishing the necessary formalised system of organisation.

However, the aggressive competition in the sector, accompanied by a declining birth rate, still more marked in Spain, represented a context in which it was difficult to grow and gain market share from the major multinationals of the industry. At this time, Martin Roth and Alberto Garcia held a series of talks with top managers of Mercadona. This chain had become a key player and began to have a significant regional presence. Its president dreamed and announced to the four winds that his company would stand at the head of the sector of the retail food distribution, for which purpose he was looking for partners who would forge strategic alliances by which they would treat him preferentially in service and commit to grow with Mercadona.

The strategic alliance

In 2004 the infant food industry reflected the relative stagnation of the infant population as well as the trend toward greater concern for the quality of food for children. Simultaneously a number of significant changes in lifestyles and consumption were occurring: increased frequency of meals outside the home and the increased presence of women in the labour market (among other factors) were creating shifts in the popularity of the different product families in the infant feeding category. The baby jars had overtaken paps in both volume and value, and, as had happened earlier with the jars, paps had gone from being sold mainly in pharmacies to being sold mostly in food chains.

The positioning in the food channel was increasingly important. However, the field of food retail distribution in Spain experienced simultaneously a moment of full bloom, full of acquisitions, mergers and alliances between companies, and a time of upheaval, with the entrance of new foreign operators, which by this time already controlled a significant market share. Competition from foreign companies, increased rivalry in the baby food industry as it matured, fierce competition and low margins (among other things) set up a highly volatile and turbulent environment.

Conscious of the need to be very competitive in order to survive in an increasingly hostile context, MBF decided to create a plant dedicated exclusively to manufacture and trade with the large distribution chains (Carrefour, Mercadona, Alcampo, etc), aiming to investigate and optimise the performance of their business with the big fish of retail distribution, who brought them about 60 per cent of their revenue. In this context, MBF continued its efforts to strengthen its competitive position within the industry, while supplying its products to various food retail distribution chains, among which was Mercadona, with whom it had enjoyed a long and good relationship, although the volume supplied to this supermarket chain was similar to that supplied to other large customers such as El Corte Ingles, Carrefour or Alcampo.

In December 2005 an agreement was signed by which MBF went from being a plain supplier, to occupying a privileged position within the Mercadona supply chain, being considered a main supplier. That kind of strategic alliance implicitly required a set of demands by both parties, which could be summarised in just over a single page. More than a contract, it was a long-term gentlemen's agreement.

After signing the agreement, they began manufacturing and including baby paps and jars for babies on the shelves of Mercadona supermarkets with the Hacendado[12] brand name. This commitment to the retailer's brand was very novel in the sector. So far, almost no distributor offered jars or baby food with a white label. As a notable exception, Carrefour had just announced the inclusion of jars of vegetables, with organic ingredients, with their brand name.[13] For MBF, the fact of joining the group of main suppliers of Mercadona was a way to strengthen trade ties with a customer who was growing at an increasing rate,[14] and thus have a greater presence on its shelves. The results of the agreement were immediately reflected in new investments in the production facilities and turnover increase for MBF (Exhibit 3).

The evolution of the agreement

The close relationship between MBF and Mercadona led to misunderstandings by other MBF customers who had heard rumours of the possibility of Mercadona having a stake in MBF. This caused the loss of some business relationships with some customers. It was in 2008, however, that one of the most difficult situations to manage in the alliance between the two companies occurred. Mercadona proposed that MBF manufacture a new type of fruit jar, a product family that was growing dramatically and had a place in the Hacendado brand. MBF pondered and evaluated the challenge: on the one hand, it called for an important financial investment at a time when the effects of the economic crisis were beginning to be

EXHIBIT 3: Highlights of the MBF company (2007–2011)

	2007	2008	2009	2010	2011
Production (thousands of tonnes)	71.828	76.662	81.000	85.954	95.836
– Delicious brand (%)	70	60	49	39	36
– Private labels (%)	30	40	51	61	64
– Mercadona (%)	25	30	35	49	46
– Other distributors (%)	75	70	65	51	54
Sales (€m)	139	156	174	184	204
Exports (%)	1	2	3	3	3
Investments (€m)	14	15	19	21	24
Employees	1.440	1.540	1.600	1.570	1.610

Source: Annual MBF Accounts.

felt; on the other hand, it was felt necessary to acquire the expertise necessary for the production (MBF had never worked with fruit products before).

MBF measured up the pros and cons of the project, and decided to take the step forward and tackle the project. The company went ahead with the acquisition of the machinery and facilities needed and started the development of the new product lines. However, after obtaining outstanding success in the first product tests, Mercadona suggested that the entire production should be for the Hacendado brand. Martin Roth did not like the idea of relying on one customer. The investment and the risk were very high, and with this new product MBF could also supply other customers who demanded the product. The company would offer this product on the shelves of Mercadona, but with an MBF own-brand label and not with the Hacendado brand label. This refusal produced a jolt in the relationship between the two companies, but the relationship as main supplier was maintained in consideration of the gentlemen's agreement and its long-term character. Martin was convinced that he had made the right decision, because with the launch of this product, not only did the business meet part of the needs of Mercadona, but it also attracted new customers, and some who had left them returned.

As of 2008, the financial crisis created a significant decline in the sales of baby food in the pharmacy channel, to the advantage of the food distribution channel (Exhibit 4), which led to an increase in the consumption of private label products such as Hacendado.

During these years, Mercadona held many meetings with all its main suppliers, demanding great dedication and effort to improve value for money. The high production volumes required by Mercadona in subsequent years forced MBF to focus on meeting the needs of Mercadona, a fact that led them to neglect further their trade policy with respect to other customers and market segments, and to bring to a standstill the projects focused on the development of foreign markets.

In July 2011 Mercadona worked with another of its main suppliers, a fourth scale producer of vegetables and salads, to initiate a series of tests through a subsidiary of the said main supplier called Alnut (Food and Family Nutrition) to develop a new line of fruit jars 100 per cent dedicated to the Hacendado brand.[15] Soon they had developed 11 varieties, different to those offered by MBF, but similar in terms of characteristics. MBF showed its annoyance with this agreement, but Mercadona responded that their business model demanded exclusivity and commitment. They had offered this possibility to MBF a couple of years earlier, but MBF had rejected it. In addition, the product was not the same, as Alnut exclusively specialised in fruit and vegetables, and did not produce jars of meat or fish. The moment was problematic, but MBF considered that the company, despite the difficulties, was doing splendidly. No one could have dreamed of a better situation under the circumstances, and saving the difference in any alliance, the relationship between MBF and Mercadona was good and favourable to both partners, reporting great benefits and with no hint that it might come to an end.

Nevertheless, on 3 December 2011, Alberto Garcia, CEO of MBF, picked up his phone and listened attentively to the demands of Mercadona: 'It's all or nothing; you decide.'

EXHIBIT 4: Sales (%) of baby food by distributor format type (2006–2011)

DISTRIBUTION FORMAT	SALES (%)					
	2006	2007	2008	2009	2010	2011
Bricks and mortar distribution	99,82	99,80	99,79	99,78	99,75	99,72
Food retailers	44,65	47,85	50,40	53,59	55,20	56,65
Supermarkets/hypermarkets	31,50	34,35	36,40	38,52	39,40	40,30
Discounts	10,25	10,40	10,85	12,22	13,20	13,90
Groceries	2,90	3,10	3,15	2,85	2,60	2,45
Non-food distribution	55,17	51,95	49,39	46,19	44,55	43,07
Pharmacy	53,55	48,85	46,65	43,60	42,40	41,60
Others	1,62	3,10	2,74	2,59	2,15	1,47
Internet distribution	0,18	0,20	0,21	0,22	0,25	0,28
TOTAL	100,00	100,00	100,00	100,00	100,00	100,00

Source: *Euromonitor International.*

QUESTIONS

1 What were the reasons which motivated MBF to become a main supplier for Mercadona in 2005?

2 Should MBF continue its strategic alliance with Mercadona, or should it break an alliance which has brought so many benefits thus far? What are the advantages and disadvantages of each option?

3 In the event that you decided to break the strategic alliance with Mercadona, what would be the first steps or measures you would take to replace the loss of a customer as important to you as Mercadona?

NOTES

1 The term 'disengagement' is used by Mercadona to refer to the period in which a main supplier gradually abandons its characteristic as a main supplier over a period of approximately three years.

2 'Siro Does Not Want Own Brands,' *El País*, 1 November 2009.

3 'The Former Number Two of Juan Roig Plans to Compete with Mercadona', *Expansion*, 23 November 2011.

4 'Ubago Splits into Two Companies and is no Longer a Main Supplier of Mercadona', www.diariodesevilla.es, 22 September 2011.

5 'La Historia de Mercadona', www.franquiciashoy.es, 9 February 2010.

6 Blanco y Gutiérre, 'El Empleo del Modelo de Gestión de la Calidad Total en el Sector de la Distribución Comercial en España: El Caso de Mercadona', *Universia Business Review*, first quarter, 2008.

7 'The Boss' is how the customers are referred to in the milieu of Mercadona.

8 www.noticiasmercadona.es/modelo-mercadona/, viewed on 6 August 2012.

9 O. Amat and J.F. Valls, 'Mercadona: Adaptando el Modelo de Negocio en Años de Recesión' *Revista de Contabilidad y Dirección*, 11, 2010.

10 'Spanish Aísles: Why a Low Price Retailer is Thriving', *The Economist*, 2 June 2011.

11 The Court Prohibits the Exclusive Sale of Baby Food in Pharmacies ', *El Pais*, 24 January 2003.

12 This is the term given to the white label or distributor label (MDD) of Mercadona, understood as that which is owned and controlled by a company whose main economic objective is the distribution in the stores of the chain.

13 'Carrefour Launches the First Distributor Label Baby Food,' *Alimarket, Dietary and Child Nutrition*, 7 November 2005.

14 See Exhibit 4.

15 www.expansion.com/2011/07/22/.

This case was written by Carlos del Val, Alejandro Escribá-Esteve and Francisco Puig (University of Valencia, Spain). The information about Mercadona has been obtained from secondary sources and information published by the company itself. MyBaby-Food is a fictitious company. The history and information about the company has been fabricated by the authors from multiple enterprise sources, and on the whole do not correspond to any actually existing company. The case does not pretend to be an example of either good or bad management practices, but has been developed only for class discussion. It is not the goal of the case to serve as endorsement, source of primary data or example of a good or efficient administration.

Case 3.2

El Dawar Foods (Egypt)

On 17 December 2012, Khaled Fawzy, the owner of El Dawar stores, had just finished analysing the company's performance for the year. El Dawar was an oriental Egyptian fast food chain, which offered a meal called *fiteer*. *Fiteer* was a unique type of food that could be described as a blend of pizza and pancakes. Khaled Fawzy's venture started off in 1989 with just one outlet, which served on-the-go food to all classes of society. This was primarily due to the affordable prices and distinctive taste of the food. After the initial success, Khaled Fawzy decided to expand locally and by the end of 2012, El Dawar could be found in several areas across Cairo, Egypt.

After becoming successful and reaching his initial goals, Khaled Fawzy was now considering international expansion. His recent visit to relatives in the USA presented him with an opportunity after the insights he obtained when witnessing the culture first-hand. Americans are risk-takers, open to different cultures and always willing to try new things. These factors, as well as a large Arab population in the country, were great advantages for such a project. In addition, after travelling to several other destinations, Hong Kong posed an interesting option. On one hand, it was booming with new and exotic offerings that indicated the potential for success for something like *fiteer*. On the other hand, culture-wise Hong Kong was extremely different, so would the product be accepted? After several deliberations and investigations, Khaled Fawzy was ready to take risk and work even harder to turn his dream to reality, but he couldn't be in two places at the same time. So the first decision he had to make was which country to explore first: the USA or Hong Kong.

There was a certain degree of urgency in this decision. Until now, Khaled Fawzy had a very local mindset and was buying new locations and expanding in various governorates in Egypt. Now, however, Fawzy had to decide on his future expansion strategy before the end of the year, because John Goodwin, a close friend of his, had agreed to hold premises in Los Angeles and not put them up for sale or seek potential buyers until Fawzy made his final decision.

Like all entrepreneurs, Fawzy was a risk-taker. But were these risks justifiable? Was it an appropriate time to introduce such a new product to a different culture? Was Fawzy too ambitious and unrealistic with these international expansion plans? After deciding on a country, which mode of entry and marketing strategy should he use? All these questions were running through his mind as he was pensively browsing through the photos he had taken in the USA and Hong Kong.

A macroeconomic overview of Egypt

Politics[1]

The history of modern Egypt starts in 1882 when the British occupied the region. Egypt achieved its independence in 1922; however, British troops remained in the country until 1956. In 1952, the political system of Egypt was transformed and Egypt was finally declared a republic. This dramatic change was the result of a group of 'free officers' led by Mohamed Naguib who wanted to make immediate reforms and who finally succeeded in defeating the system and expelling 'King Farouk,' declaring Egypt a republic on 18 June 1953. Later on, Gamal Abd el Nasser evolved into a charismatic leader, not only for Egypt but also the Arab world, promoting 'Arabic socialism'. During his era, he united Egypt and Syria to form a state called the United Arab Republic which pertained until 1971 when the constitution of the country was formed.

After Nasser's death, Anwar el Sadat was elected as president. He set up a new economic reform that ended the socialistic control of Nasser. He introduced the 'Open Door Policy', which encouraged many private investments and boosted the economy. Moreover, he tried to expand participation in the political system. He also forged many bonds and made international treaties, including Camp David Accords. He was assassinated by Islamic extremists and Hosni Mubarak was elected in 1981. Mubarak made many domestic economic programme reforms. The legal system during his regime was based on 'Islamic Shariaa'. The Egyptian legal system only recognises three religions: Islam, Christianity and Judaism. Members of other minority faiths cannot obtain an identity card. It was in Mubarak's era that a diplomatic relationship with Israel was formed which helped in resolving disputes between many Arab states. During this time Egypt also joined many international organisations such as the IMF, UNESCO and the WTO. On 25 January 2011, Mubarak was overthrown by a revolution and Mohamed Morsi was elected president on 24 May 2012. Just over one year later President Morsi was removed from power by the army, an interim government put in place, and new elections planned for 2014.

Economy[2]

Egypt's economy was based on agriculture, media, petroleum, exports, tourism and the traffic trade that goes through the Suez Canal. The Egyptian government made a great effort to prepare the economy for the new millennium through economic reform and the large investment in communication and physical infrastructure. The economic conditions started to improve after a period of stagnation due to the acceptance of more liberal economic policies as well as the increase in revenues that resulted from the boom in the stock exchange market.

In 2003 the government led a crucial reform and in 2005 implemented the new taxation law that decreased corporate taxes from 40 per cent to 20 per cent and resulted in a 100 per cent increase in tax revenue in 2006. Moreover, there was a dramatic increase in FDI, which exceeded $6bn in 2006 as a result of the economic linearisation method.

Because of the international economic downturn, GDP growth in Egypt decreased to 4.5 per cent in 2009. This downturn affected export-oriented sectors, including manufacture and tourism, and led to an increase in the unemployment rate from 8.7 per cent in 2008 to 9.7 per cent in 2009. Moreover, it affected the inflation rate, which was 9.5 per cent in 2007 and rose to 18.3 per cent in 2008. The government tried to improve economic conditions and implemented a $2.7bn stimulus package, benefiting infrastructure projects and export subsidies.

Egypt's main agricultural products were cotton, rice, corn, wheat, vegetables, sheep and goats. Egyptian industry was also strong in textiles, metal, hydro-carbonates, pharmaceuticals, construction and cement. Egypt exported crude oil, petroleum products, cotton, textiles and chemicals to many countries such as Italy, the USA, Japan, Syria, India and Saudi Arabia. On the other hand, it imported machinery, equipment, fuels and wood products from the USA, China, Germany and Saudi Arabia.

Society[2]

Egypt was considered the most populated country in the Middle East and the third most populous in the

African continent. As a result of medical advances and technology, there was a rapid increase in population size, which reached almost 80 million (in 2009). Food- or water-borne disease was prominent. Almost all the population was concentrated along the banks of the Nile in cities such as Cairo, Alexandria, in the Delta region and near the Suez Canal. The life expectancy at birth was 72.2 years. Infant mortality was 27.6 deaths/1,000 live births. The statistics show that the majority of Egyptians were Muslims (90 per cent) while the remaining 10 per cent was made up of Coptic (9 per cent) and other Christians (1 per cent). Arabic is the official language; English and French, however, are widely understood by the educated class.

Communication

There has been a dramatic change in Egypt's communication generally. Most people depend more on the mobile cellular network than the land lines which are few. There are three major mobile network operators with a total of more than 41 million subscribers, roughly one in two of the population. The number of Internet users in 2008 was 11.414 million and the Internet is crucial for many business, education and communication.

The food industry

The food industry was a complex, global collective of diverse businesses that supplied much of the food consumed by the world population. Processed food sales worldwide were approximately US$3.2 trillion in 2009.

Given its importance for human wellbeing and survival, the food industry was operating under myriad local, regional, national and international rules and regulations for food production and sale. These regulations covered food quality and safety, and often involved industry lobbying activities in such sectors as agriculture (both crops and livestock), seafood, food processing and manufacturing and marketing of generic products (the Milk Board is an example of this). For new products, the industry influenced public opinion through advertising, packaging and public relations and was involved in wholesale, distribution, transportation, logistics and retail – the chain finally ending with the consumer. The end users naturally had the highest influence on the food industry through their buying preferences.

Regarding the competitive environment, the food industry was among the most competitive and globally-linked of all business sectors.[3] As the demand for food was always high, the food industry became a battle-field for many companies, creating fierce competition. Customers had become more and more demanding, and companies unable to meet customer preferences could ultimately be avoided by the consumers. Therefore, the aim of the competing companies was to create a product of an acceptable quality at a reasonable price.

The food industry has been traditionally a very localised industry as food taste and preferences develop in early childhood as a result of family meals transferred from one generation to another. However, due to globalisation and increased international travel, people started to acquire new tastes and some national foods such as Chinese cuisine, Japanese sushi, French pancakes and Italian pizza and pasta spread widely around the world.

Egyptian *fiteer* was very similar to a pizza and a pancake. 'Would it be possible for it to achieve a similar global recognition?' Fawzy thought.

El Dawar Foods

El Dawar started out as a small business idea that seemed at the time unattainable. The relentless efforts of Khaled Fawzy and his sister Zeinab Fawzy made it an instant success. Another factor that contributed to the success of the venture was that both partners focused on making it about the customers and not about the profit or brand recognition. The first shop was established in 1989 in Mohandeseen, a new upscale district of Cairo at that time. El Dawar's signature dish was a local snack (*fiteer*) which was of high quality and sold at a reasonable price. The incredible success of the outlet could also be attributed to the involvement of the owners, who participated at every level, ensuring that all orders were fulfilled in a manner guaranteeing customer satisfaction and approval.

The company took pride in its Egyptian background and, as a result, the stores were decorated in a style reflecting the rural atmosphere of a farm and highlighting the agricultural aspect of the countryside where this unique type of food originated. All raw materials and labour used to run the store also were local. In 2012, El Dawar had five well-known and well-established outlets across Cairo. In order to keep up with the ever-changing tastes of consumers, El Dawar also offered pastas, made with Egyptian ingredients and recipes, which also gained remarkable feedback and support. Furthermore, to coincide with the new food offered in the store, El Dawar started to offer seating areas, where customers could enjoy a quick meal while watching football matches and Arabic movies on big-screen TVs. This echoes the appeal of the more popular Egyptian cafes where

EXHIBIT 1: EL Dawar income statement for year ended 31 December 2010

	EGP
Domestic sales	2,548,387
Less	
Cost of goods sold – domestic sales	804,050
Total profit	**1,744,337**
Less	
Employee and managerial expenses	340,037
Cost of operations	43,400
Gross profit	**1,360,900**
Net income	**1,360,900**

people gather to enjoy meals with friends and companions, more commonly known as *Ahwa*.

Financially, the company was doing well (see Exhibit 1).

The food industry in Egypt, the USA and Hong Kong

Egypt

The food industry was one of the most important sectors in Egypt. It had grown significantly after the launching of the 1,000 factories project in the industrial sector in 2007. Seventy-three of these 1,000 factories were in the food industry, creating LE3,438.2bn worth of investments and providing 14,500 job opportunities.[4] There were numerous multinational and homegrown food chains in Cairo, Alexandria and other urban centres. Due to fierce competition with the multinational brands, many local brands and chains decided to expand internationally to attain exposure to a wider target market. For instance, a popular Cilantro coffee shop had launched its operations in London and signed franchising contracts in Saudi Arabia, Kuwait and Qatar – a strategy that was mainly driven by the high level of competition it faced in Egypt from Starbucks, Costa Coffee and Coffee Bean & Tea Leaf.[5]

USA

The food service business was the third-largest industry in the USA. It accounted for over $1 trillion annually in sales, and independent restaurants accounted for 15 per cent of that total. An average American spent 15 per cent of his/her income on meals away from home. This percentage had been increasing for the past seven years. Between 2005 and 2010, the restaurant industry had out-performed national GNP by 40 per cent mainly due to lifestyle changes, economic climate, and an increase in product variety. The predicted growth was also positive both in the short and long term.[6]

Generally, the food service sector consists of food service outlets and restaurants (independent units and chains). Between 2009 and 2010, there was a decline in consumer traffic at the food service outlets. However, in 2011 consumer traffic stabilised, reaching 60.72 million visitors (Exhibit 2). In 2012, total retail sales were $366.223bn and were expected to increase by 4 per cent in 2013 (Exhibit 3).[7]

US restaurant industry visits decreased from 62.7 billion in 2008 to 60.67 billion in 2011. The decline was mainly due to traffic losses in independent

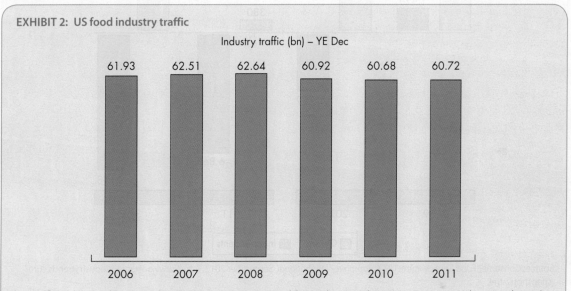

EXHIBIT 2: US food industry traffic

Industry traffic (bn) – YE Dec

2006	2007	2008	2009	2010	2011
61.93	62.51	62.64	60.92	60.68	60.72

Source: 'Consumer Food Service in the US', *Euromonitor International*, September 2012, http://www.restaurantindustrytrends.com/snapshots.html.

EXHIBIT 3: US food service industry forecast

Segment	2012 retail sales equivalent ($bn)	Nominal growth (%)	
		2012	2013(F)
Total restaurants and bars	366.223	4.5	4.0
Limited service	204.936	4.6	4.0
Full service	158.138	4.4	4.0
Bars and taverns	3.149	3.9	4.0
Total beyond restaurants and bars	196.988	3.6	3.7
Retail hosts	37.225	3.6	3.8
Travel and leisure	51.603	4.2	3.9
Business and industry	13.828	3.9	4.0
Education	32.667	3.3	3.4
Health care	23.288	4.4	4.5
All other	38.337	2.6	3.0
Total food service	563.211	4.2	3.9

Source: 'US Foodservice Industry Forecast', *Technomic*, January 2013, https://www.technomic.com/Resources/Industry_Facts/dynUS_Foodservice_Forcast.php.

restaurants, which accounted for a 2 billion loss (87 per cent). These independent restaurants mainly lost traffic to major restaurants chains and accordingly more than 7,000 independent restaurants were closed.

In November 2008, independent restaurants represented 28 per cent of industry traffic, in 2011 it represented 27 per cent of the industry's visits. Exhibits 4 and 5, on the other hand, show that restaurant chains

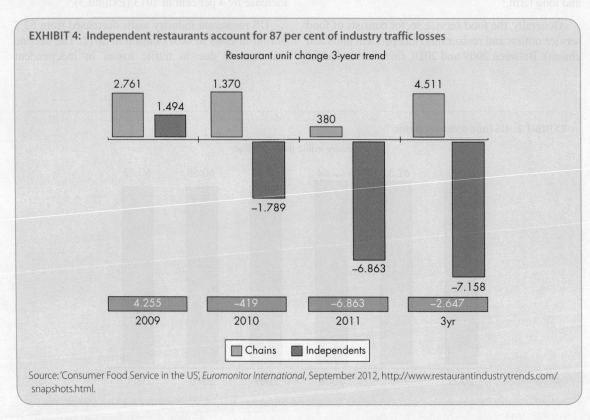

EXHIBIT 4: Independent restaurants account for 87 per cent of industry traffic losses

Restaurant unit change 3-year trend

Source: 'Consumer Food Service in the US', *Euromonitor International*, September 2012, http://www.restaurantindustrytrends.com/snapshots.html.

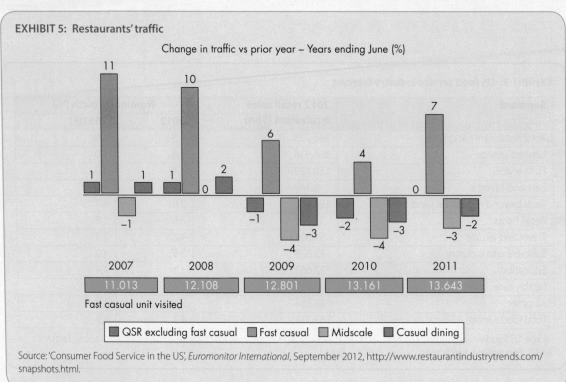

EXHIBIT 5: Restaurants' traffic

Change in traffic vs prior year – Years ending June (%)

Fast casual unit visited

Source: 'Consumer Food Service in the US', *Euromonitor International*, September 2012, http://www.restaurantindustrytrends.com/snapshots.html.

were holding a constant share in the market. In 2011 their market share reached 61 per cent compared to 60 per cent in 2011.[8]

Consumer buying behaviour[8]

Between 2009 and 2010, US consumers became more price conscious due to the financial crisis. In 2011, the frequency of food service purchase increased but the price-sensitivity still remained. Accordingly many restaurants adjusted their services to meet consumer demand by offering everyday value pricing and smaller, low-priced snacks to satisfy customers and keep prices low. Fast-food outlets and cafés/bars were able to offer high value to consumers and thus performed best during the recovery of the economy. In 2009, people who had an income between $40,00 and $50,000 spent $5,560 a year on food.[9]

Another change that occurred in US customer preferences was a growing concern for healthy food. Although consumers used to focus mostly on calories and other nutrition information, they became more concerned with freshness, responsible sourcing and high quality ingredients. These new trends increased consumer inquiries about the meat quality at fast-food restaurants and led to a controversial class-action lawsuit based on the quality of the beef served at Yum!, Brands Inc and Taco Bell.

Increasing competition in the food service industry in the USA changed the operations of many restaurants. Although in previous years major brands like Starbucks saw the bulk of their sales during breakfast hours, and many fast-food restaurants focused on lunch time, these trends changed. In 2011, many major brands promoted consumption during untraditional parts of the day, increasing the potential number of daily visits, and thus sales.

Competition

The top players in the US market in the limited service restaurants were McDonald's, Subway, Starbucks, Wendy's, Burger King, Taco Bell, Dunkin' Donuts, Pizza Hut, KFC, and Chick-Fil-A. McDonald's was the top brand, with $34.2bn in 2011 (5 per cent higher than 2010). The top 15 fast-food chains had combined sales of $115bn in 2010 and had 105,000 stores around the world.[10]

Regarding the non-US food outlets, there were 7 Eleven, Lawson, Habib's and Nandos. Some of these food outlets were targeting specific segments in the US market. For example, Habib's was a Brazilian outlet that offered traditional meals to Brazilian customers. Some outlets such as Nandos tried to compete with big fast-food chains through offering a differentiated

product. The spicy chicken they offered was different from that offered at KFC and accordingly was able to attract customers. Other brands such as Costa or Gloria Jean's were trying to compete with international brands by selling an 'experience'.

Marketing strategies

In order to increase sales and reach out to more customers, many food outlets started to turn to new formats to penetrate different locations. Moreover, the overcrowding of existing outlets forced many chain players, especially fast-food outlets, to partner with retail, leisure and travel locations. This partnership allowed them to enter locations such as amusement parks, gas stations, and convenience stores. Other brands introduced new outlet formats such as smaller eat-in areas to allow the brand to reach a larger market. In a different sector some chains of full-service restaurants offered fast, casual versions of existing brands or new concepts to exploit the growth in the fast-food market.[11]

Many food outlets were trying to move beyond price considerations by focusing on menu innovation and outlet remodelling. Some chains used menu innovation by offering premium menu items, such as burgers and salads, at single-digit prices. Other chains used large-scale remodelling projects that created more modern, efficient and comfortable outlets. Many fast-food outlets and all leading category players were using these strategies.[11]

Another marketing technique used by food outlets was the 'dining experience'. These outlets focused on the experience and culture that they were offering, rather than their dishes. For example, some Japanese sushi outlets offered people different varieties of sushi and enabled the customer to make their own selection. Benihana restaurant featured life cooking at the dining tables. Starbucks created a relaxing seating atmosphere with comfortable couches and dim lighting. Overall, these outlets offered consumers a different food consumption experience.[12]

Exhibit 6 reflects some demographic, economic and technological indicators for the USA.

Hong Kong

The food service industry in Hong Kong was flourishing. In 1993, individuals, on average, were spending more than half of their income on dining out. Although the food industry in Hong Kong was rapidly growing, it faced many challenges, such as fierce competition between international and local restaurants, as well as high inflation.[13]

EXHIBIT 6: Demographic, economic and technological factors in the USA and Hong Kong

	USA	Hong Kong
Demographics		
Total population	271,290,000	7,055,071
Population growth rate	0.98%	0.8%
Age structure	0–14 years: 20.2% 15–64 years: 67% 65 years and over: 12.8%	0–14 years: 12.2% 15–64 years: 74.6% 65 years and over: 13.1%
Middle class (as a percentage of population)	47%	29%
Economics		
GDP growth rate	– 2.4%	2.37%
GDP per capita	$46,400	US$34,587
Consumer inflation rate	– 0.7%	2.00%
Technological		
Fixed telephone market	54.1 (per 100)	4.108m
Wireless telephone market	84.7 (per 100)	5.5m
Internet users	231m	4,878,713

EXHIBIT 7: Restaurant revenues in Hong Kong

Year	Restaurant receipts (HK $m)	YOY growth (%)
2011	89, 321	6.4
2010	83, 969	5.1
2009	79, 863	0.6
2008	78, 984	13.1

Sources: Census and Statistics Department, *Report on Quarterly Survey of Restaurant Receipts and Purchases*; 'Food Service Company', *The Government of Hong Kong Special Administrative Region*, http://www.investhk.gov.hk/zh-hk/files/2012/07/2012.07-foodservice-en.pdf.

In 2011, restaurant receipts reached US$11.5bn, which was considered a 6.4 per cent increase over 2010 (Exhibit 7). The USA was considered the major food supplier to the Hong Kong market, and Hong Kong's food imports from that country reached US$3.3bn in 2011. Consumers in Hong Kong bought US ready-food products due to their competitive prices and consumer confidence in the quality and safety of US products.[14]

The food service industry in Hong Kong had been growing due to different factors. Tourism was considered the most important contributor; 42 million visitors came to Hong Kong in 2011. Restaurants catering to medium-scale travel groups enjoyed this boom. Moreover, the food service business was expected to increase.

Consumer buying behaviour

The food culture in Hong Kong had changed over time. In the past, people just filled their stomachs with simple local Chinese food from humble eateries or small restaurants. However, recently the situation had completely changed. Individuals shifted to gourmet enjoyment in splendid international restaurants. The evolution in the food culture in Hong Kong had helped in the development of individuals' social and economic lives over the past hundred years. Several traditional food industries declined over time due to the changes in consumer tastes. In order to leverage this trend, many producers tried to develop and integrate new tastes in the market to accommodate the new customers' needs.[13]

Similar to the USA, there was a growing trend in Hong Kong related to healthy eating. The Hong Kong culture was traditionally sensitive to freshness, and so customers were inherently health conscious. There were over 50 small to medium-sized health food stores in Hong Kong. There were also two leading supermarkets (Wellcome and ParknShop), and drug store chains (Manning's and Watson's) which sold natural and organic products.[14]

Competition

The food service industry in Hong Kong had around 13,910 restaurants that served a range of international cuisines. The restaurants were 37 per cent Chinese, 55 per cent non-Chinese and 8 per cent fast-food outlets. There were also over 1,000 bars, pubs and other eating and drinking establishments.[14]

The Chinese restaurants were appealing to both local citizens and tourists and were serving different regional cuisines such as Canton, Shanghai, Beijing, etc. The cost of a typical lunch in a Chinese restaurant was around HK$150–300 (US$19.23–38.46) per person. A dinner on the other hand would cost around HK$200–450 (US$25.64–57.69) per person.

Since many Hong Kong consumers and tourists enjoyed Western food, many non-Chinese (Western) restaurants were also visited. In addition, more Japanese restaurants, casual dining and coffee houses were being established. Lunch at a Western restaurant cost around HK$150–350 (US$19.23–44.87) per person, and a typical dinner cost around HK$250–500 (US$32.05–64.10) per person.[15]

Fast-food outlets were popular among Hong Kong customers. The main food outlets were McDonald's, KFC and Pizza Hut. There were also local fast-food chains such as Café De Coral, Maxim's and Fairwood that served both Chinese and Western food. The competition among fast-food chains was fierce as they were trying to make their prices competitive. The average cost was around HK$30 (US$3.85) for breakfast, HK$50 (US$6.41) for lunch, HK$25 (US$3.21) for afternoon tea and HK$70 (US$8.97) for dinner.

The coffee-shop market had also been growing in Hong Kong's commercial areas. The main outlets were Starbucks, which had 115 outlets, and Pacific Coffee, which had 110 outlets. These coffee shops also served basic food items including muffins, pastries, cakes and beverages.

Marketing strategies

Different types of marketing strategies were used in Hong Kong to attract the customers. The international restaurants offered a core product such as hamburgers, chicken or pizza and constructed their image using aggressive marketing and extensive advertising. On the other hand, local restaurants attracted customers by simply presenting local food. Since their strategy was mass-market oriented, they could compete with the international players by offering a wider variety of high quality food.

Since competition was so fierce in the food serving market, competitors sought distinctive marketing options to attract customers. Accordingly some fast-food outlets renovated their restaurants to make them look more modern, spacious and attractive. Other fast-food chains tried to meet the demand of the increasing number of health-conscious customers by introducing more healthy ingredients and developing healthy food options such as salads, fruit and fresh juices.[16]

There was also an increase in the use of different social media platforms among food service operators and customers. Social media acted as a tool for food service operators to advertise their products and interact with a larger customer base. On the other hand, customers were able to view and post comments about different restaurants. The increasing level of Internet penetration in Hong Kong allowed websites in the food service sector to develop. These websites such as 'tablemap.com' and 'diningcity.com' offered online booking facilities and reviews for various restaurants.[15]

Exhibit 6 above reflects some demographic, economic, and technological indicators for Hong Kong.

El Dawar expansion plans

As we said at the begining, Fawzy was encouraged by his success in the local market and decided to start expanding internationally, although he was not sure where to go first: the USA or Hong Kong. Such a decision might well be opposed by many people in his management team. However, in Fawzy's view, the time has come for such an expansion. Expanding in the USA would provide several advantages for El Dawar. For instance, the company could be exposed to a higher consumer demand due to the larger target market. The fact that the *fiteer* prices were generally low would appeal to the American individuals who were more price conscious. Furthermore, there was a large segment of Arabs living in the USA who would be delighted at the launch of this new Middle Eastern food chain.

Expanding to Hong Kong could also be beneficial. Relying on the information that customers in Hong Kong were open to different types of food, Fawzy thought that introducing the *fiteer* in this country would be profitable for El Dawar for several reasons. First, the *fiteer* prices were low in comparison with the other food products sold by the international fast-food chains. Moreover government restrictions in Hong Kong were relatively few for foreign companies because the government was encouraging foreign investments. Fawzy was also considering adding new ingredients to the *fiteer* to reflect Chinese or Asian culture, such as vegetables and Chinese spices. By doing this, the *fiteer* could attract customers even if they were not open to change and different types of food.

Marketing and sales strategy

In Egypt, El Dawar had no distinctive marketing strategy. Previously El Dawar showed no interest in expensive marketing and advertising campaigns and relied on customer loyalty and word of mouth. In order to achieve and maintain Fawzy's ambitions for his business, several factors had to be taken into account when expanding: societal factors, political factors and economic factors. With regard to the concept of standardisation versus adaptation of the product, El Dawar intended to consider local cultural needs and preferences without sacrificing the essence of the Egyptian El Dawar.

USA

The proposal to penetrate the US market was one with several advantages and arguments to support it. Love of food was an inherent part of US culture. They enjoyed good food and were always willing and eager to try new things. A significant percentage of American consumers were single and living alone, and so fast-food was a much easier and preferred alternative,[16] which itself could offer El Dawar certain advantages.

The USA is one of the largest and most culturally diverse countries in the world, where in the span of 10 years the Arab population has increased by more than 38 per cent (1990–2000).[17] The most populated Arab state is California; El Dawar's first target would therefore be this area. Fawzy thought that the Arabs would be a captive audience given their presumed knowledge of *fiteer*. After satisfying customers who were familiar with the product, Fawzy hoped that loyal customers would spread positive word of mouth to the Americans.

There would be a detailed plan with target dates for each stage of expansion, but taking it one step at a time was crucial in achieving overall success and profits. Furthermore, as we said earlier, a friend of Fawzy, John Goodwin, had secured a store in one of the most visited areas of the informal capital of California, Los Angeles. The location that had caught Fawzy's attention was in Westwood Los Angeles, next to UCLA. This was an extremely suitable location as it combined two of the most important factors: students living alone and an impressive Arab and Middle Eastern (Iranian) population. The area was already exposed to other Arabic and Middle Eastern food but nothing of the same kind, which provided El Dawar with a competition-free environment.

The sales strategy was simple. Sell, satisfy the customer and introduce foreigners to Egyptian food and culture. Fawzy envisaged El Dawar as an ambassador for Egypt and thus intended to present only the best they had to offer. He also had plans for home delivery that would facilitate the ordering process and increase appeal to the customers.

Hong Kong

Hong Kong was one of those risky projects where the market had great potential, yet contained factors, such as culture and geography, which posed equal threats. In the recent times, Hong Kong's food industry had been witnessing tremendous transformation. Citizens were eager to try different meals and new tastes. In addition, they were moving from elegant, seated restaurants and adopting the fast-food style of eating, where everything was faster paced and 'on the go'.

El Dawar's main marketing goal was to be situated in a central location to help gain recognition. Although El Dawar didn't carry out traditional marketing in Egypt, Fawzy decided that a different approach was needed in Hong Kong. Language was the biggest barrier to the company's success, and so Fawzy decided to prepare a marketing budget for Hong Kong which could enhance brand image, brand recognition and brand perception. Exhibits 8 and 9 indicate some costs that Fawzy should consider before deciding to expand to Hang Kong.

Fawzy decided to invest in advertising to popularise the brand and create a unique, distinctive image. He thought that this process would be easier, smoother and faster in Hong Kong because there was no obvious Middle Eastern competition there. However, El Dawar could face a problem of procuring raw materials, some of which were specific to Egypt. Given that not all ingredients were available in Hong Kong, should Fawzy ship the ingredients from nearby countries or should he just offer *fiteer* with ingredients attained in the country's home market?

Decision

Although Fawzy was an entrepreneur at heart, who was always quick at making decisions without much analysis, this time the situation was different. He felt like a fish in the water in his native Egypt, but venturing to such different and distant countries as the USA and Hong Kong required more preparation. Accustomed to being personally in charge, he had to choose only one country because he obviously couldn't be in both places at the same time. First, he had to evaluate country attractiveness, decide on the mode of entry and finally create a marketing plan and sales projections for the next three years. Without doing this work, even for a risk-taker like Fawzy, going abroad was not feasible.

However, the wish to promote his beloved *fiteer* in new locations and cultures stimulated Fawzy's imagination and he decided that no matter how boring it might seem, the proper analysis would need to be done (see Exhibits 8 and 9).

EXHIBIT 8: Office rental costs in Hong Kong

Approximate monthly office rental costs (HK$)

District	Shopping malls	Street-side premises
Central	$50–$200/sq. ft. or 10–13% of turnover	$60–$250/sq. ft.
Causeway Bay	$30–$150/sq. ft. or 10–13% of turnover	$100–$300/sq. ft.
Tsim Sha Tsui	$30–$200/sq. ft. or 10–13% of turnover	$80–$250/sq. ft.
Mong Kok	$30–$150/sq. ft. or 10–13% of turnover mover	$100–$300/sq. ft.

Sources: Jones Lang LaSalle, June 2012: 'Food Service Company'; *The Government of Hong Kong Special Administrative Region*, http://www.investhk.gov.hk/zh-hk/files/2012/07/2012.07-foodservice-en.pdf.

EXHIBIT 9: Monthly salaries for food service in Hong Kong

Average monthly salaries for food service staff (HK$)

Title	Chinese restaurants	Non-Chinese restaurants
Restaurant manager	$15,000–25,000	
Maitre D'	$14,056	$13,850
Chief cook	$20,535	$20,228
Captain	$12,503	$12,250
Cook	$14,604	$13,232
Junior cook	$11,762	$10,067
Bartender	–	$11,387
Waiter/waitress	$9.628	$9.920
Dishwasher	$8.954	$9.059

Sources: Classified Post, Salary Index Hong Kong 2011 and Census and Statistics Department, *Quarterly Report of Wage and Payroll Statistics*, March 2012; 'Food Service Company', *The Government of Hong Kong Special Administrative Region*, http://www.investhk.gov.hk/zh-hk/files/2012/07/2012.07-foodservice-en.pdf.

NOTES

1 'Background Notes: Egypt', Office of Public Communication Bureau of Public Affairs, http://dosfan.lib.uic.edu/ERC/bgnotes/nea/egypt9012.html.

2 'Egypt', *Answers*, http://www.answers.com/topic/egypt.

3 'Competition Number One Food Industry Concern', 14 January 2005, http://www.confectionerynews.com/Formulation/Competition-number-one-food-industry-concern.

4 'Industry in Egypt', *Industrial Development Authority*, 2006, http://www.ida.gov.eg/Industry_industry%20in%20Egypt.html.

5 O. Diab, 'From Egypt to the World: Bon Appétit', 2009, http://www.businesstodayegypt.com/article.aspx?ArticleID=8417.

6 'Restaurant Sample Business Plan Outline', 2010, http://www.virtualrestaurant.com/sample.htm.

7 'Restaurant Industry Trends', *NDP Group*, https://www.technomic.com/Resources/Industry_Facts/dynUS_Foodservice_Forcast.php.

8 'Consumer Food Service in the US', *Euromonitor International*, September 2012, http://www.restaurantindustrytrends.com/snapshots.html.

9 Bonnie Azab Powell, 'What US Citydwellers Really Spend on Food and Drink', http://grist.org/article/food-what-us-citydwellers-really-spend-on-food-and-drink/.

10   Alaina McConnell and Kim Bhasin, 'The Most Popular Fast Food Restaurants in America', *Business Insider*, 13 July 2012, http://finance.yahoo.com/news/the-most-popular-fast-food-restaurants-in-america.html.

11   'Consumer Food Service in the US', *Euromonitor International*, September 2012, http://www.euromonitor.com/consumer-foodservice-in-the-us/report.

12   'Global Players in Foodservice: Selling Experiences over Products', *Euromonitor International*, 30 August 2012, http://blog.euromonitor.com/2012/08/global-players-in-foodservice-selling-experiences-over-products-.html.

13   Randall J. van der Woning, 'Hong Kong's Food Culture', *BWG*, http://www.bigwhiteguy.com/baskets/food.php.

14   Chris Li, 'Food Service Hotel Restaurant Institutional', *HRI Food Service Sector*, 16 March 2012, http://www.usfoods-hongkong.net/res/mns/00164/HK1208a%20-%20Food%20Service%20-%20Hotel%20Restaurant%20Institutional.pdf.

15   'Hong Kong Foodservice: The Future of Foodservice in Hong Kong to 2016', *Market Watch*, 13 August 2013, http://www.marketwatch.com/story/hong-kong-foodservice-the-future-of-foodservice-in-hong-kong-to-2016–2012–08–13.

16   'Bureau of Labor Statistics', 6 October, 2008, http://www.bls.gov.

17   G. Patricia de la Cruz and Angela Brittingham, 'The Arab Population: 2000', *Census 2000 Brief*, 2003, http://www.census.gov/prod/2003pubs/c2kbr-23.pdf.

Case written by Dr Marina Apaydin, Hend Mostafa, Aisha Kandil, Farida Hossam, Mayamin El Saady and Salma Shafie (The American University in Cairo)

Case 3.3

Aldi and Lidl: International Expansion of Two German Grocery Discounters[1]

It's the best business model for retail in the world.

Philippe Suchet, food industry consultant, BNP Paribas

With a worldwide annual sales volume of €3.7 trillion in 2007 and an average annual sales growth of 2.7 per cent during the past ten years, the grocery retailing industry can be considered as one of the world's key economic sectors. Over the past decades, grocery discounters such as Aldi and Lidl have strengthened their position in the grocery retailing industry, especially in Germany and Europe. With their no-frills approach, they have led to significant changes in the industry and have challenged many companies which operate other store formats, such as supermarkets or hypermarkets. In this context, a *Financial Times* report on international retailing noted in 1995: 'The spread of the discount format has been particularly disruptive to Europe's grocery retail industry and has driven retailers to examine cross-border markets.' Exhibit 1 illustrates the leading grocery retailing companies in the world and on a European level.

The grocery discount format

The key terms describing a grocery discounter are 'minimalism' and 'efficiency', which are integrated into all business areas. In fact, grocery discounters' ambitions are to sell quality products at the lowest price possible. To realise profits in spite of the low prices, grocery discounters reduce their costs to a minimum and attempt to generate high volumes of sales through a limited product range of fast-moving items. The approach of cost reduction especially affects the spending for store design, customer service and

EXHIBIT 1: Leading grocery retailing companies in the world and in Europe

Worldwide top 10 grocery retailers 2007			European top 10 grocery retailers 2007				
Company	Home country	Worldwide sales volume in €bn	Company	Home country	European sales volume in €bn		
1	Wal-Mart	USA	287.6	1	Carrefour	France	83.4
2	Carrefour	France	103.2	2	Metro	Germany	67.4
3	Metro	Germany	74.8	3	Tesco	UK	66.1
4	Tesco	UK	73.3	4	Schwarz[1]	Germany	51.9
5	The Kroger	USA	53.8	5	REWE	Germany	48.4
6	Schwarz[1]	Germany	51.9	6	Auchan	France	39.3
7	Seven & I	Japan	51.1	7	Aldi	Germany	39.0
8	Costco	USA	50.9	8	Edeka	Germany	38.8
9	Target	USA	50.5	9	E. Leclerc	France	33.7
10	Aldi	Germany	47.1	10	ITM	France	31.0

[1]About 69% of Schwarz's sales can be assigned to Lidl (€35.9bn). Hence, on a worldwide basis Lidl would be ranked 19th and on a European basis Lidl would be ranked 9th.

advertising: grocery discounters try to save money by building up their stores in suburban areas and remote districts, where the rental fees or purchase prices for properties and buildings are low. Furthermore, all companies have a basic outlet format similar to that of a warehouse, with merchandise sold straight from cardboard boxes. In the stores, customers only have limited possibilities to contact service personnel in case of product-related questions since there is no dedicated customer service department. And with regard to advertising, grocery discounters usually do not launch costly TV ads or image campaigns – oftentimes they only use flyers and newspaper ads as promotion material.

With regard to the grocery discount concept, experts distinguish between so-called 'hard' and 'soft' discounters: today, the product range of a hard discounter covers some 800 items – and almost all of these are store brands. The product range of a soft discounter, however, covers a range of 2,500–3,000 goods and includes store brands as well as branded products.

Development of grocery discount in Germany

In the early 1960s Karl and Theo Albrecht opened the first Aldi (Aldi = Albrecht Discount) grocery discount stores in Germany. At that time, many industry experts questioned the potential success of the hard discounter's business model. However, within a few years, the two brothers built up several hundred stores

in Germany and started their international expansion in Europe. They confounded the experts and proved that their new store format was highly competitive and successful. Based on the national and international success of Aldi, the German grocery discount industry became an important segment within the worldwide grocery retailing industry. By 2007 Germany was the home base of six major grocery discounters with an annual sales volume of more than €50bn in Germany and more than €100bn on a worldwide level.

Today, however, success stories of the six major grocery discounters originating from Germany are being jeopardised: while the companies were able to expand their market share in Germany during the past years, they now increasingly face signs of market saturation and stagnating growth in their home market. The market share of grocery discounters in Germany is at a level of about 40 per cent and experts assume that this figure will remain unchanged in the coming years. Exhibit 2 provides a detailed illustration of sales volume distribution in the German retailing industry.

As a result, German grocery discounters have to adjust their strategies in order to fuel further growth. They face two key options for the future. They can:

- try to identify and target new customer segments within their home market Germany, and/or
- continue their growth through expansion in foreign markets.

The two leading grocery discounters in Germany (Aldi and Lidl) started their international expansion

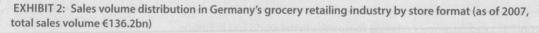

EXHIBIT 2: Sales volume distribution in Germany's grocery retailing industry by store format (as of 2007, total sales volume €136.2bn)

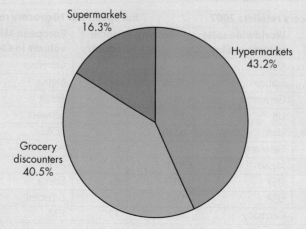

Supermarkets 16.3%

Hypermarkets 43.2%

Grocery discounters 40.5%

Supermarkets and other stores (such as grocery departments in gas stations, health food shops and kiosks) with a sales area <100 sq metres are not included in this overview.

well in advance of any other competitor. Today, both Aldi and Lidl generate more than 40 per cent of their revenues in foreign markets. Furthermore, the two belong to the top 10 companies of the pan-European and worldwide food retailing industry and are regarded as the world's largest food discounters by sales volume (see also Exhibit 1).

Aldi's history

Aldi was founded by the two Albrecht brothers in 1946, when Karl and Theo took over the grocery business from their parents. At that time, they faced a severe shortage of goods and groceries in post-war Germany. As a result, the two brothers were forced to narrow the product range in their stores. Even in the 1950s when the German economy again prospered, they did not decide to modify their product offerings. It was in the early 1960s when they realised that this limited product range was no disadvantage for them at all. Karl and Theo found out that their stores were highly profitable and they saw no need to implement the characteristic store concept of a supermarket, where shoppers could choose from a wide range of goods. Dieter Brandes, a former Aldi manager, states that the two brothers initially planned to convert their grocery stores into typical supermarkets before they noticed that their minimalistic business model was highly successful. Brandes describes the hands-on mentality at Aldi by claiming that the company did not set any financial targets: 'They have no budgets, no annual plans. Why on earth do they need them? Budgets are just toys for top managers. Budgets are one of the big money wasters.'

In 1961 the two brothers split up their company into two separate organisations. According to their agreement, Theo Albrecht was responsible for the northern part of Germany and founded the Aldi Nord GmbH & Co OHG based in Essen, Germany. Karl Albrecht took over the lead for the southern part of Germany and established the Aldi Süd GmbH & Co OHG based in Mülheim, Germany. Today, both companies operate independently, except on strategic decisions such as price promotions and purchasing conditions, where they consult each other.[2] During all market entries in foreign countries, the company followed the initial territorial agreement from 1961. So Theo Albrecht focused his expansion on the north eastern, western and southwestern countries in Europe. Karl Albrecht concentrated on the southern and south-eastern regions. Additionally, Karl was responsible for the market entries in the anglophone countries such as Australia, Ireland, the UK and the USA.

In 2007 Aldi operated more than 8,500 stores in 15 countries and generated sales revenues of about €47bn worldwide. Further statistics show that about 52 per cent of the worldwide sales can be assigned to Germany, 31 per cent were generated in other European markets and 17 per cent were achieved outside Europe.

Lidl's history

In 1973, 11 years after the Albrecht brothers opened their first Aldi stores, Dieter Schwarz established the grocery discount retailer Lidl in Ludwigshafen, Germany. Similarly to Karl and Theo Albrecht, Schwarz had worked in a small family-owned retail business before he launched his own discount retailer business. Today, the Lidl Stiftung GmbH & Co KG is part of the 'Unternehmens- gruppe Schwarz', a group of three independent companies: Lidl, Kaufland and Mega Cent.

At first sight, it seems that Dieter Schwarz has successfully copied Aldi's business model for his own grocery discount stores. However, a closer look reveals that Lidl follows a so-called 'soft' discount strategy where the product assortment in the stores is enlarged to almost 3,000 items and customers are offered branded products as well as store brands. Statistics show that Lidl's soft discount concept has been expanded successfully: in 2007 Lidl operated about 7,900 stores in 21 countries and generated sales of about €36bn on a worldwide level. Forty per cent of the sales were achieved in Germany and 60 per cent in European markets. Exhibit 3 presents a comparison of Aldi's and Lidl's key operating figures.

Nevertheless, today Lidl is still number two behind its rival Aldi with regard to sales volume and number of stores in Germany and on a worldwide level. However, on a European level, the company has already taken the lead with regard to the number of stores: Lidl operates about 7,900 stores whereas Aldi operates only 7,200 stores.

International expansion of Aldi and Lidl

Aldi realised early that international expansion could be a key lever in enhancing the company's growth. In 1967 the management decided to enter Austria by acquiring the local grocery retailer, Hofer. Then, from 1976 to 2006, Aldi entered another 13 foreign markets. However, the expansion plans were not limited to Europe only: ten years after the market entry in Austria, Aldi began to make gains in the US market and, in 2000, the grocery discounter extended its operations into Australia.

Unlike Aldi, Lidl limited its expansion plans to the German market first. Thereafter, in the period

EXHIBIT 3: Comparison of Aldi's and Lidl's key operating figures

	Aldi	Lidl
Founding year	1962	1,973
Business model	Hard discount	Soft discount
Sales volume (€bn) in 2007	47.1	35.9
– thereof Germany	24.3 (52%)	14.3 (40%)
– thereof European foreign markets	14.7 (31%)	21.6 (60%)
– thereof non-European foreign markets	8.1 (17%)	0.0 (0%)
Number of stores in 2007	8,541	7,879
– thereof Germany	4,228 (49%)	2,902 (37%)
– thereof European foreign markets	2,963 (35%)	4,977 (63%)
– thereof non-European foreign markets	1,350 (16%)	0 (0%)
Number of foreign markets in 2007	14	21
– thereof European foreign markets	12 (86%)	21 (100%)
– thereof non-European foreign markets	2 (14%)	0 (0%)

from 1989 to 2007, the company entered 21 foreign markets and impressed experts with its astonishing rate of internationalisation. Additionally, Lidl seized the opportunity to expand into a number of developing European markets and developed markets where no competitor had been present previously. While

Aldi – in most cases – preferred to wait for a retail sector to mature, Lidl has been far more adventurous and began its Eastern European expansion with the market entry into Poland in 2002. Exhibit 4 illustrates the international market presence of Aldi and Lidl as well as the number of stores in each country.

EXHIBIT 4: Aldi's and Lidl's market presence and number of stores in 2007

■ = number of Aldi stores
□ = number of Lidl stores

(1) In the USA 295 of 1,190 Aldi stores are operated by the grocery retailer 'Trader Joe's'.

(2) In Austria and Slovenia all 443 Aldi stores are labelled 'Hofer'.

Reference date for all data and information is end of 2007.

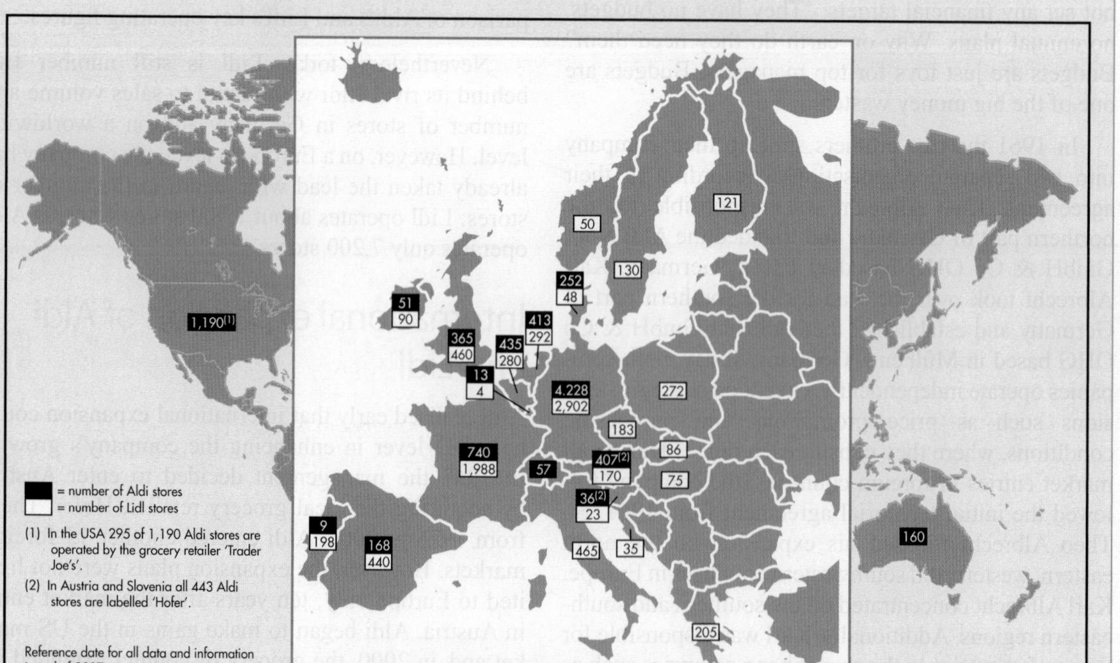

Supermarkets and other stores (such as grocery departments in gas stations, health food shops and kiosks) with a sales area <100 sq metres are not included in this overview.

Lidl's rapid expansion into Poland seems to have paid off: in 2007 the company achieved sales of about €759m and was ranked among the top three grocery discounters in the country. With this well-established position, Lidl has a clear advantage over its rival, Aldi, who entered the Polish market in 2008 and still has to build up consumer trust and market share.

Some of Aldi's and Lidl's market entries were a result of simple trial and error: often the grocery retailers declined support from market research companies or management consultants and judged the attractiveness of a foreign market on the basis of their own managers' gut feeling. In 2008 Lidl were forced to realise the defects of this strategy: after four years of unsatisfactory sales, the company retreated from the Norwegian market and sold its 50 stores to the local competitor, Rema. Norway's unique geographic structure and the distribution of its population were key factors that led to Lidl's failure. The thinly spread population density in Norway required Lidl to build up several central warehouses in order to ensure smooth supplies for each discount store in the country. Consequently, logistics became more expensive and the additional costs threatened the profitability of Lidl's stores. Werner Evertsen, head of Lidl Norway, explained that the stores were closed because they offered no further development potential, and he indicated that the store location was a key issue, which should have been checked more carefully: 'It can simply be a case of wrong location or too low population density. Of course, we want to be where the population is.' In addition to these mistakes, Lidl Norway had to cope with a high level of turnover among its top managers. One of the country managers left the company 20 months after he signed his employment contract. The frequent change in Lidl's top management and the resulting uncertainty among the employees also affected the long-term strategic planning of the company in a negative way.

Differences in the international timing strategies of Aldi and Lidl

Aldi's internationalisation pattern is characterised by phases of 'action' and 'recovery'. In the past the company entered one or more markets within a short period of time and then paused its market entry activities for about ten years. Since 2000 Aldi has accelerated the internationalisation process and has entered about one new market per year. Lidl, in contrast, acts much faster: although the company started its internationalisation quite late in 1989, it entered 20 foreign markets in the period between 1992 and 2007. On a country level, the two companies pursued different strategies as well: while Lidl opened up many stores in different regions at the same time, Aldi entered foreign markets more carefully and slowly: it began to build up stores by entering one region after another. In Switzerland, for example, the grocery discounter started its operations in the German-speaking regions first. Other districts followed successively.

Adaptation to local needs

Aldi and Lidl decided to implement their grocery discount strategies not only in their home country but in all their foreign markets. Nevertheless, both companies allow local managers to adapt the product range according to country-specific demands. In an attempt to increase consumer acceptance, Aldi, for example, re-labelled its German products in Switzerland so that former German-branded items became Swiss-branded goods. In the USA Aldi stores usually do not sell any German products at all. Only the famous German 'Christstollen' and almond paste are offered during the Christmas season. In the UK Lidl offers regional products as well: about 90 per cent of its meat and poultry is from the UK and Ireland and, when in season, lots of the fruit and vegetables are British. Lidl UK director Martin Bailie explains: 'It's not all pan-European buying; we have to look at what UK customers want.'

At first sight, this customer focus seems to conflict with the standardised grocery discount concept. However, Aldi and Lidl realised that this adaptation to local needs can help the grocery discounters successfully to develop a foreign market. In Switzerland and in the UK, where Aldi faced stiff competition from local retailers, the company departed from the rigorous hard discount concept and launched advertising campaigns in order to convince customers to shop at Aldi. An Aldi spokesperson explains the benefits of the advertising campaign: 'The activity has proved very successful and is an important part of our positioning as a quality mainstream supermarket with a discount proposition.' In addition to the advertising campaigns, stores in Switzerland and in the UK were stocked with a broader selection of meat and seafood products, more upscale frozen meals and a new 'food to go' counter. George Wallace, retail expert at Management Horizons Europe, explains why Aldi had to adjust the product assortment in the UK in order to overcome the reputation of an 'underclass-discounter': 'In Germany, cheap equates to value. You always hear the word "billig" (cheap) being used, and it means value. By contrast, in the UK low prices are not necessarily equated with value and are more often associated with poor quality.'

Further expansion of Aldi and Lidl

Aldi's and Lidl's success in their home market of Germany is beyond dispute. However, both companies realised that if they stuck to their original discount format, they might have limited growth prospects abroad. With their altered product and service strategies in the UK and in Switzerland, Lidl and Aldi are trying to meet the requirements of their demanding local customers. While Aldi managers retain their pricing strategy also in those countries where Aldi heads upmarket, Lidl has slightly increased the sales price for some of its products. It will be interesting to see whether the grocery

retailers will implement these strategies in other foreign markets as well. The next market entries could serve as an indicator for the strategic course of the two rivals: in 2008 Aldi opened its first stores in Poland, Hungary and Greece. In the following years the grocery discounter intends to expand its operations to Croatia, Romania and the Czech Republic. In the medium term, Aldi plans to enter Turkey, Russia, New Zealand and South Africa. It seems as if Lidl intends to continue its rapid internationalisation as well: in 2008 the company entered Malta and Cyprus. In spring 2009 the first stores in Switzerland were opened. In the medium term, Lidl plans to conquer Brazil, Mexico, Russia and the USA.

QUESTIONS

1 While Aldi and Lidl entered some foreign markets via acquisitions (see, for instance, the acquisition of Hofer by Aldi in Austria in 1967), they mostly opt for greenfield investments. Discuss the reasons why Aldi and Lidl are choosing greenfield investments as a primary market entry strategy.

2 In an attempt to change its image of an 'underclass-discounter' in the UK and in Switzerland, Aldi enlarged its product range and offered a higher level of service to the customers. What could be the rationales behind such a strategy in the UK and in Switzerland? Do you also see problems and risks associated with this approach?

3 In some trade journals experts characterise the internationalisation process of Lidl as 'fast' and 'pushing', whereas the internationalisation of Aldi is described as a 'slow' and 'well-considered' process. Do you agree with the experts? Identify reasons for the 'fast' and 'pushing' internationalisation of Lidl as well as for the 'slow' and 'well-considered' internationalisation of Aldi.

4 Until 2009 Lidl restricted its internationalisation to countries within Europe. Aldi, in contrast, decided to open stores in Europe, Australia and the USA. What are the advantages and disadvantages of Aldi's strategy? Which strategy would you recommend to Lidl in terms of its geographical presence until 2020?

FURTHER READING

- E. Colla, 'International Expansion and Strategies of Grocery Discount Retailers: The Winning Models', *International Journal of Retail & Distribution Management*, 2003, 31(1), 55–66.

- J. Dawson, 'Retailing at Century End: Some Challenges for Management and Research', *International Review of Retail, Distribution and Customer Research*, 2000, 10(2), 119–48.

- S. Schmid, T. Dauth and T. Kotulla, 'Die Internationalisierung von Aldi und Lidl – Möglichkeiten und Grenzen bei der Übertragung von im Inland Erfolgreichen Geschäftsmodellen auf das Ausland', Working Paper No 46, ESCP-EAP European School of Management, June 2009.

- M. Wortmann, 'Aldi and the German Model: Structural Change in German Grocery Retailing and the Success of Grocery Discounters', *Competition & Change*, 2004, 8(4), 425–41.

- 'World-class Retailer – Aldi Builds on Value Formula', *Retail Week*, 24 March 2000.
- 'Retailing in Germany – Discounters Dominate Germany', *Retail Week*, 30 June 2000.
- 'European Discount Retailing Uncovered', *European Retail Digest*, 22 June 2003.
- 'Inside Aldi', www.thegrocer.co.uk, 29 November 2003.
- 'Quality ads stay on', www.thegrocer.co.uk, 11 February 2006.
- 'Paul Foley: The Retail Boss Who Says He Can Save You £30 a Week', www.guardian.co.uk, 11 July 2008.
- 'The Germans are Coming', *The Economist*, 16 August 2008.
- 'All Smiles at Aldi', www.thegrocer.co.uk, 1 September 2008.
- 'A Lidl Goes a Long Way', *Retail Week*, 9 October 2008.
- 'Nielsen Universen 2008 – Handel und Verbraucher in Deutschland', www.nielsen.de, 14 October 2008.
- 'Aldi and Lidl Head Upmarket in Britain', *Business Week*, 21 October 2008.
- 'Aldi Group – Retailing – Germany', www.euromonitor.com, 17 March 2009.
- 'Lidl & Schwarz Group – Retailing – Germany', www.euromonitor.com, 17 March 2009.
- Aldi website: www.aldi.com.
- Lidl website: www.lidl.com.
- Planet Retail website: www.planetretail.net.

NOTES

1   A more comprehensive version of this case is available in German, published under the title 'Die Internationalisierung von Aldi und Lidl – Möglichkeiten und Grenzen bei der Übertragung von im Inland erfolgreichen Geschäftsmodellen auf das Ausland', Working Paper No 46, ESCP-EAP European School of Management, June 2009. This version contains an extensive list of references and further readings in English as well as in German.

2   In this case study, there will be no further distinction between Aldi Nord and Aldi Süd. Both entities are considered as one company.

This case was written by Stefan Schmid, Tobias Dauth and Thomas Kotulla, ESCP Europe, Campus Berlin, Heubnerweg 6, Berlin, 14059, Germany.

PART 4

Cases Outline

Case 4.1

For Fiat to Get Big in the USA, Did It Have to Start Small?

Founded in 1899 Fiat produced its first car in 1901. Since the very beginnings the company produced a large range of different products ranging from tractors to steel trucks, buses, trams, marine engines and railway products. During the following two world wars, Fiat mainly focused its production on military purposes and it was only after the Second World War that the company clearly emerged as the Italian leading producer of cars. Thanks to a significant growth of the domestic market (the so-called 'Italian economic miracle'), Fiat quickly grew and became the leader in the Italian car market but also one of the leading automotive producers in Europe. In order to meet a rising demand for economy cars, the company targeted consumers that were in large part *first-time buyers* specialising in small, stylish and affordable cars. Among the many successful cars of that period produced by Fiat surely the most appreciated vehicle

was the Fiat 500, which quickly became an iconic product summarising the best virtues of the Italian industry of that time: design, style and affordability. Born in 1957, this tiny car rapidly became a popular vehicle not only in Italy but throughout Europe. It was a definitive product that made history and it is no surprise that, when in 2006 Pixar decided to produce the animated movie *Cars*, the director John Alan Lasseter included in the film an enjoyable and funny character named 'Luigi' who is an almost human 1959-Fiat 500, and an extremely passionate lover of sport cars.

However, after the oil crisis in the 1970s and with the globalisation of markets what was once the strength of the company (ie its focus on small stylish cars) rapidly became a weakness. Since the 1980s the company did not manage successfully to upgrade its products or extend their range to embrace sedans on

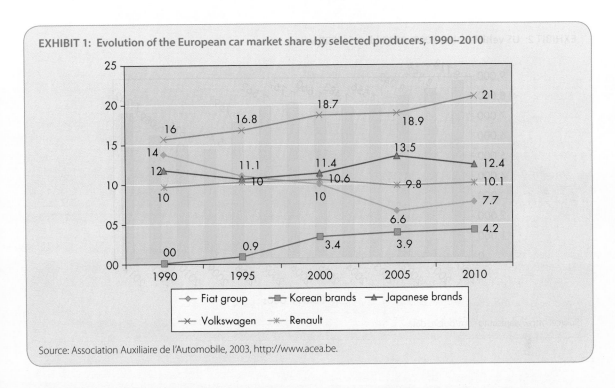

EXHIBIT 1: Evolution of the European car market share by selected producers, 1990–2010

Source: Association Auxiliaire de l'Automobile, 2003, http://www.acea.be.

the market (which generate larger profit margins). At the same time the lower end of the market was attacked by competitors coming from the emerging economies such as the Korean brands, Hyundai and Kia. Stuck in the middle, Fiat found its European market share constantly squeezed between high-end producer such as Volkswagen (which constantly upgrades its brands) and cheap economic competitors who carved out the traditional part of the market: typical Fiat territory.

Consequently Fiat market share in Europe declined consistently (see Exhibit 1) while at the global level the company remained focused in only a few markets outside Italy (namely, Poland and Brazil).

When in September 2008 the fall of Lehman Brothers signalled the beginning of one of the most severe and long-lasting economic crises in the Western world, severely affecting car sales on both sides of the Atlantic, Fiat's position, with a collapsing market share in Europe, no presence in the American market and a small market share in the emerging countries, looked extremely weak. In a sector where economies of scale for mass-market producers are vital to drive down average costs, the constant decline of Fiat's market share seemed the prelude to an imminent acquisition of Fiat by one of its larger competitors The Italian company, with a total production of around 2 million cars, seemed not suited to face the competition of world-class producers like Toyota or Volkswagen, with around 6 million units produced.

On the other side of the ocean, the sudden collapse of the US car market in terms of sales (see Exhibit 2) hit the three big American producers (GM, Ford and Chrysler) hard, but almost drove Chrysler, the smaller of the three in terms of volume and market share, to bankruptcy. With a shrinking market share due to Chrysler's difficulties in launching vehicles in accordance with customers' requirements, with few fuel-efficient vehicles, no successful small and mid-sized cars and a high concentration of sales in North America, Chrysler's fate also seemed sealed.

Paradoxically, the desperate situation of both companies generated a new unforeseen opportunity for both firms. The two companies mirrored each other perfectly: Chrysler's weakness was Fiat's strength: small and fuel-efficient cars with environmentally-friendly technologies. Also, the geographical distribution of sales of the two companies did not overlap: Chrysler sales were concentrated in North America and Fiat's in Europe and South America. In June 2009 Fiat acquired a Chrysler minority stake and, then, in the following year, became the majority shareholder.

With the help of Chrysler, Fiat finally entered the large American market and could offer strong brands such as Jeep in the largest sedan market in Europe, while Chrysler acquired much needed fuel-saving technology and could include small and mid-sized cars (which had been missing from their range) in

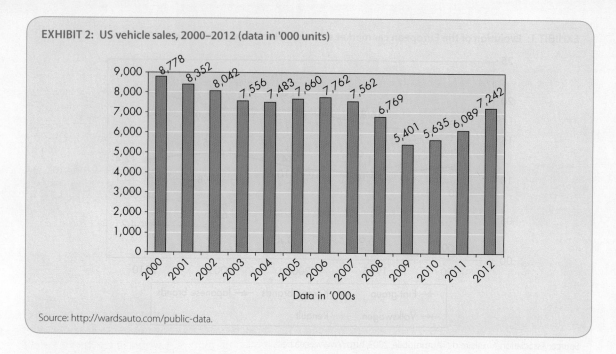

EXHIBIT 2: US vehicle sales, 2000–2012 (data in '000 units)

Data in '000s

Source: http://wardsauto.com/public-data.

their offering. Overall the new Fiat-Chrysler company reaches a production of around 4 million vehicles, getting close to the level of production attained by the largest rivals.

Not born in the USA: the launch in 2011

One of the first goals of the new management team was to launch Fiat products in the USA. In March 2011, the first new Fiat 500 rolled into dealerships. The new version of the iconic car had been launched in 2007 in Europe with huge success. In its first month, 70,000 Cinquecentos (500) were sold in Italy and the car since then has been enjoying much passion and enthusiasm all over Europe.

In November 2011, when Tim Kunikis replaced his predecessor Laura Soave to become head of the Fiat brand in North America, the new manager faced a tough new assignment: rescue the disappointing launch of the Fiat brand. Sales in the USA were around 20,000, well below the target of 50,000. The automaker said it had 130 'customer-ready' US dealerships selling the Fiat 500 as of October, but only 101 recorded sales.

He inherited a restless dealer network which had heavily invested in sales 'studios' for a single mid-sized Fiat model and was getting much less revenue than Chrysler-Fiat CEO Sergio Marchionne had

projected for the tiny Fiat 500. The 500's success was critical to Chrysler because it was at the core of the overall group strategy to bring small, fuel-efficient cars to the brand. The small subcompact was seen to set the stage for the entry of other Fiat products and, eventually, Alfa Romeos.

For some US consumers, the name Fiat evokes good memories of touring on thin European roads, swirling through green Tuscan hillsides or weaving through the small picturesque centres of ancient cities. For older US consumers who remember the brand from its previous US ventures 27 years ago, Fiat is the acronym for the mocking moniker 'Fix It Again, Tony'. However, for the large majority, according to Peter De Lorenzo, a Detroit-based auto analyst, the 'Fiat brand in the US is nonexistent' (*Washington Post*, 28 July 2011).

At the same time the Chrysler quality image was poor: noisy, unrefined power-trains, forgettable styling, mediocre ride and handling, and cheap-looking interiors had made their cars rank poorly in consumer surveys.

The new Fiat Cinquecento (500)

The small car came from Europe with an impressive number of awards (60), including the 'Car of the Year 2008' but Fiat managers knew the car had to be adapted to the palates of US consumers.

The suspension had been adapted for American roads to guarantee a softer ride, and the car was equipped with a more robust heating and air-conditioning system. The gas tank was enlarged because Americans generally drive longer distances and the car had a new, more fuel-saving and environmentally-friendly engine: the MultiAir engine. More insulation was also guaranteed to reduce noise in the cabin and a new automatic gear was included since most American drivers, and especially the young, are unused to manual gears. Much attention was also drawn to 'little touches': among others, the rear wiperblade was designed to emerge undamaged from car washes, cup-holders were redesigned for bigger drinks and pull-down armrests, to provide more comfort, were included.

Though surveys showed most consumers had little memory of the brand's last US foray, Fiat strengthened the warranty to allay potential quality and reliability concerns. The small car was equipped with a four-year or 50,000-mile bumper-to-bumper warranty and free three-year routine maintenance. 'We know all about customer care, being available 24-7,' said a dealer. 'If you had a problem, you wouldn't have to wait.' (*Automotive News*, 25 October 2010).

Colour selection is an important issue in the car world: in a recent PPG survey, 77 per cent of American car buyers said the exterior colour was a factor in their purchase and 31 per cent said they would be willing to pay more for a special colour that expressed their personality.

Accordingly, one feature, expected to win over buyers to the Fiat 500, was the opportunity to personalise their cars. They came in 14 bright exterior colours and 11 trendy interior hue and material combinations.

With the base models of the new Fiat 500 starting at about $20,000 and its fully equipped Cabriolet convertible at about $24,000, the first Fiat models were positioned to go head to head with upscale German brands such as the VW Beetle and the BMW Mini Cooper.

Slow store openings, even slower sales

After extensive market research, Chrysler decided it wanted Fiat dealerships in approximately 125 areas spread among 41 states. The locations selected had to show growth potential for small and fuel-efficient cars over the next five years.

'The Fiat dealer network will be appropriately sized to serve the market opportunity,' said Peter Grady, vice president of network and fleet, in a company press release. 'Our vision is to establish a dealer network that will reflect and enhance the brand's reputation for innovation and fun, and will offer a unique, personalized customer experience.'[1]

Dealerships had to prove to the automaker that they were capable and ready to sell the Italian vehicles. Instead of allowing existing Chrysler dealers to open Fiat sections in their showrooms, Fiat required the dealers to sign separate franchise agreements and open completely separate facilities, the so-called Fiat studios (which could cost as much as $3m) and provide a set of employees – Fiat specialists - devoted to the studio and service.

The move was targeted at the *Generation Y* buyers for whom the white and red Fiat studios should become the hippest news in a slowly recovering car market. To lure Millennials intimidated by car-buying, Fiat held training session for its dealers, helping them to guide prospective buyers as they customise the 500 with over 500,000 combinations. Fiat 'specialists' also serve non-traditional roles as they remain the customer's point of contact for future service.

On 12 March 2011, expectations were very high. The first day the Fiat store of Tom Miller had cars to display, about 100 people visited. The dealer said 'that's about three times the number of customers the Chrysler-Dodge-Jeep-Ram sees on a typical Saturday. Normally we sell 600 new and 500 used vehicles a year.' After one week Miller Fiat had sold five vehicles (*Sunday Times*, 21 March 2011).

Fiat largely underestimated the time it would take dealers to finish work on their Fiat studios. For most of 2011 it had 50–60 dealers as compared to the targeted fully-filled network of 200. Some dealers sold as few as four cars from March through to October, while others sold as many as 370, according to Fiat's Final Daily Sales Report for 1 November 2011.

Not enough and not the right communication?

Some dealers said that Fiat was slow to give them marketing support making customers aware of the car. During summer 2011, Fiat responded by increasing its advertising presence: the first national ad campaign came with the 1–4 July 2011 *USA Today* issues. The print ad showed a picture of the original 500 when it was launched on 4 July 1957 in Italy, with the slogan 'Over a half century ago it inspired a nation. And it's about to do it again.'[2]

As the brand aired the first nation-wide commercials on 1 August 2011, Fiat split with its agency, Impatto. The agency had been at the heart of Fiat's initial marketing plan to employ non-conventional

EXHIBIT 3: The 'Drive-in' and 'Simply More' campaign

Bigger isn't *better*.
It's just harder to park.

FIAT
500
Simply *more.*

The 2012 FIAT 500. Now available at a FIAT Studio.

Source: http://media.chrysler.com.

techniques, such as events and Internet marketing, with a limited budget to launch Fiat to target young, tech-savvy customers. The TV campaign featured two commercials. The first, called 'Drive-in', created by Impatto, showed a Fiat 500 entering a drive-in movie theatre with the tag line 'Simply more' (see Exhibit 3).

The second commercial, a music video featuring the Fiat 500 with Jennifer Lopez, was not created by Impatto, and was aired during the Super Bowl football games. Fiat also strengthened regional advertising support for dealers. The company provided print ads and radio and TV spots ready to be tailored to individual markets.

By the end of 2011 Fiat also had an active social media presence on Facebook, Twitter and YouTube, with close to 200,000 fans on Facebook and 13,000 followers on Twitter. The brand's website (www.FiatUSA.com) was designed to welcome consumers and create full brand experience for them while designing 'their personal car', locating a Fiat studio or browsing through a collection of merchandise and accessories.

The early 'Simply more' ad has been called 'simply less than expected', 'unsatisfying' and 'not memorable' referring to the tagline as banal and questionable for the target of the youthful consumer and the new and spry spirit of the car. Critics were even harder with the music video spot and J-Lo featuring in it. Peter De Lorenzo, strategic analyst and former auto-marketing executive, called it an out-of-the-box play and 'quite possibly the worst automotive spot of the last decade,

hands down' (www.thetruthaboutcars). The chief marketing officer and head of brand marketing communications for Fiat-Chrysler, Olivier Francois, defended the music video spot and the decision to air it during football games, even though the spot was geared toward women. 'America is aware that there is a car. We needed this kind of spark,' he said (*Automotive News*, 26 September 2011).

So far, the company's best advertising might have been the cool-looking car rolling around on the streets with the Fiat logo on it. Car journalists described the enthusiasm and emotions the small 500 evoked when they were testing the car: 'During my weeklong test, I was the recipient of dozens of "awwws" and thumbs-up wherever I drove and couldn't have done better than if I'd been walking around Times Square holding a baby in one hand and walking a puppy with the other...' (*New York Daily News*, 6 February 2012). 'The car attracted a lot of interest when it was parked and thumbs-up signals while we zipped along the highway. It seems this Cinquecento strikes the same emotional cord as the original. As one onlooker said, "It's so cute you just want to hug it"' (*The Gazette*, 14 February 2011).

In an attempt to get things moving...

At the end of 2011, Kuniskis based his action plan on the introduction of new models and started to overhaul the advertising and social media strategy.

Fiat unveiled three versions of the 500 Abarth at the Los Angeles Auto Show in November 2011 to debut in 2012. The highly anticipated Abarth sporty editions (the 500 Cabrio Italia and 695 Competizione) aimed at broadening the vehicle's appeal to men. Abarth has a stiffer suspension, wider tyres and performance-oriented exterior and interior design. The third model revealed was the 500C by Gucci, a cabriolet developed by Fiat's design studio and Gucci creative director, Frida Giannini. The convertible wears Gucci's green-red-green stripe lengthwise over the soft-top. Promoted with 'Couture you can buy' at the New York Fashion Week, the Gucci 500 aimed at building the car's image as a chic and stylish buy. An 'environmentally sexy' electric version was also announced, to be available in late 2012.

The sporty Abarth versions started promotion on YouTube with a short film called 'Seduction', which ranked nineteenth on *USA Today's* ad-meter rankings out of about 60 commercials. The film is available to watch at this url: www.youtube.com/watch?v=fMjavRu4v5c. Two months later, when the Abarth performance models began arriving in Fiat studios, it was found that the new 'risqué' promotion had helped raise awareness for the entire brand.

Fiat continued with sexy (and bawdy humour) commercials after 'Seduction', with 'House Arrest', featuring Hollywood bad boy Charlie Sheen, 'Baby' and 'Topless'. Social media campaigns were reinforced with a nationwide campaign offering a coupon for a $500 (of course) cash discount to potential buyers. Customers who went to see the 500 in the studios and presented their coupon to the dealers were eligible for a lottery of ten highly accessorised 500s.

The small car battleground

Almost all car makers are now betting on small cars, but selling small cars to American consumers has been described as being like convincing children to take cod liver oil (*The Globe and Mail*, 17 February 2011). For decades, US auto makers had ignored small cars, leaving the market to the big Japanese firms (Toyota, Honda and Nissan) and, to a lesser extent, the South Koreans. Honda, the market leader in the subcompact market, had made clear its intention to defend this position with new product launches and aggressive marketing.

Newcomer Ford also had announced that it was 'deadly serious about competing for the small group of customers at the very high end of the segment by offering them features and series that they have never seen from Ford' (*The Globe and Mail*, 18 March 2011). Also at the high end of the segment, Mini Cooper, the Beetle and the 500 accept the challenge of competing for and enlarging a still small segment of a huge car market.

Industry analysts see fuel prices as the main triggering factor for small-car sales. As gas prices go up, the market share of small vehicles goes up with them, and, interestingly, also the reverse applies: if gas prices go down, the market shares decrease accordingly.

A second trigger – one coming into play with the recent raft of new small cars – is the quality and design of the small cars themselves. Gas prices generate increased interest in small cars, but style can be an equally powerful driver. For small-car buyers interested in style and design, the USA has been mostly a desert. The Mini has been available and the Beetle was re-launched, but they all need intensive promotion to convince American consumers.

The Fiat 500 today

At the end of 2011, the 500 had managed to win 4 per cent of the subcompact segment, with around 20,000 units sold. To compare, BMW Mini with 90 dealers in place, sold roughly 24,000 in its first year with a non-conventional marketing campaign that had started about 11 months before they launched the car, a huge and well-crafted marketing blitz with the BMW halo effect above them.

All in all, Fiat managers consider the 500 to be a success. Fiat, in a recent press release states: 'The Fiat 500 has exceeded all its sales goals this year, breaking sales records for ten consecutive months. December sales figures for the Fiat 500 were 3,707, up 59 per cent over last year's December figures, bringing the total US sales of the 500 to 43,772 units.'

The numbers show that after a slow start the car is entering a new stage of growth (see Exhibit 4 and the 500 marketing milestones).

EXHIBIT 4: The launch of the 500 in the USA: main figures

	Dealers	Sales (cars)
2011	Yearly average 60	19,769
2012	170 in July	43,700
2013	Start with 200 dealers but still high potential areas unfilled	Average monthly sales 3,800

Product line-up

- March 2011: debut of the Fiat 500 in the market, base model.
- 2012: launch of 500 Cabriolet, two Abarth models and the 500 electric car.
- February 2013: launch of Abarth Cabriolet; in Q3-4 enlarged version of 500 branded 500 L expected.
- Expected 2014: crossover 500 X.

Communication

- No premarketing.
- 'Drive in' ads designed as trailers to be aired in cinemas and 'Simply more' campaigns begin six months after launch.
- Communication campaign switches in mid-course, moving from niche marketing to mass marketing.
- Jennifer Lopez commercial, aired at the Super Bowl.
- As from 2012 Fiat taps into 'sex tinged with bawdy humour'
  - a Short films for the Abarth tested on YouTube.
  - b 'Seduction' – aired at the Super Bowl.
  - c Followed by 'House arrest', 'Baby', 'Topless', etc.

QUESTIONS

1 Assess the Fiat 500 strategy in the USA using the adaptation/standardisation framework. Would you have adapted product, distribution and advertising to the local context?

2 The Fiat 500 aims to establish itself as a global brand. Why did Fiat decide to adapt the communication campaign locally and not go for a standardised global campaign?

3 Was it a wise move to enter the USA with the Fiat 500? Fiat could have entered with an Alfa Romeo, the iconic car driven by Dustin Hoffman in *The Graduate* as an alternative.

4 Do you consider the Fiat launch troubled, successful or a failure? If any, what have been the main mistakes made by the Fiat marketing managers? Consider Fiat objectives, marketing strategy and dimension of the segment/market.

5 Do you think the separation of Fiat and Chrysler brands was a sound decision in the US market? Discuss.

FURTHER READING

- Deloitte, *Automotive Bulletin, Report by Business Information Services*, August 2011.
- Various issues of *Automotive News*.
- Various issues of *Detroit News*.
- Various issues of *The Globe and Mail*.
- Various issues of *USA TODAY*.
- http://media.chrysler.com.
- http://wot.motortrend.com.

- http://www.fiatcom.usa.
- http://www.ppg.com/en/newsroom/news/Pages/20111005A.aspx.
- http://www.brettmalden.com/thoughts/fiats-simply-more-is-simply-less-than-expected.
- http://www.thetruthaboutcars.com/2011/11/ask-the-best-and-brightest-who-killed-the-fiat-500.
- *New York Daily News*, 6 February 2012.
- *The Gazette*, 14 February 2011.
- *The Sunday Times*, 21 March 2011.
- *The Washington Post*, 28 July 2011.
- YouTube

NOTES

1   Source: http://media.chrysler.com.
2   Fiat said the *USA Today* campaign increased traffic on fiatusa.com by 74 per cent.

Case 4.2

El-Sewedy Electrometers

On the bright, sunny morning of 19 February 2012, Ahmed Ashour, the Strategic Marketing Manager of El-Sewedy Electrometers (ESE), was drinking his usual morning cup of coffee in the company headquarters in Cairo, Egypt, while analysing the company sales. The major success that the company had been achieving locally made Ashour consider expanding internationally.

He decided to gather the company owners together to present them with his idea of opening a branch abroad. Ashour thought that international expansion could further increase company sales and help it to sustain its position in front of the fierce international competition. Since international expansion required significant investments, Ashour knew that the owners had to be convinced with concrete arguments backed by a solid analysis and so he started to consider his alternatives.

Ashour had a couple of countries in mind that, in his opinion, could have great potential. He vividly recalled the recent news about the Czech Republic, a new emerging country in Eastern Europe, where Tim Ash, the head of emerging market research at Royal Bank of Scotland Plc Fidesz, indicated that GDP was expected to increase. Ashour reasoned that an increased GDP would lead to an increased GDP per capita, the country's purchasing power and eventually demand. Tim Ash also mentioned that, 'Czech bonds were a "safe haven" as the country's borrowing level makes it less likely to face a Greek-style crisis.' Accordingly, if there were problems in obtaining loans from the bank, there would be other forms of safe investments that could provide ESE with cash. But the Czech Republic couldn't be the only option.

Ashour knew that the owners would ask him about his choices and the thought process behind them. So he decided to consider a totally different country on a different continent: Australia. He was intrigued to know more about the Australian market; a country where many of his friends had emigrated recently after the turbulent times in Egypt. He discovered great potential in Australia, as its economy had been consistently growing in the past 17 years at an impressive 3.5 per cent per annum and there was a high level of efficiency. Moreover, the government provided equal support to foreign investors as it did to domestic ones, which would help ESE grow quickly. In fact, Australia had a strong and flexible economy, which was the fourteenth largest in the world in 2008 and was recognised by the IMD World Competitiveness Yearbook as the third most resilient in the world in 2009, only behind Qatar and Norway. According to real estate researcher Investment Property Databank Ltd, Australian commercial properties would start to see capital growth in the next two quarters as the economy strengthened. However, this country was quite far away from Egypt. 'Would that be a major impediment?' Ashour thought.

Both countries had opportunities but Ashour knew he could afford to propose only one. Much research remained to be done an order to decide which one to choose, and to select the best mode of entry and assess the potential market. And so he started gathering initial data and developing a comparative analysis (see Exhibit 1).

Political and macroeconomic overview of Egypt

Political environment

The Arab Republic of Egypt introduced Parliamentary democracy in 1824 and issued the first constitution in 1882. After cancelling the British protectorate in 1922, Egypt issued the second constitution in 1923. The Constitution states that Arabic is the official language and principles of Islamic law (Shari'a) are the principal source of legislation.[1]

Egypt was a semi-presidential republic in which the president was both the head of state and government. The prime minister of the country was the leader of the Egyptian government. Executive power rested with the government while both the government and the parliament exercised the legislative power.[2] Egypt's parliament consisted of two chambers: the People's Assembly was the lower house and the principal legislative body; the Shura Council was the upper house with a limited legislative power.[2]

After the 2011 revolution, Egypt experienced a new phase of political development, aimed at deepening democratic practice, enhancing freedoms and

EXHIBIT 1: Demographic and economic indicators for Australia and the Czech Republic (2009)

	Australia	**Czech Republic**
Demographics		
Population	21,262,641	10,211,904
Population growth rate (%)	1.195	−0.094
0–14 years	18.1%	13.4%
15–24 years	13.4%	11.1%
25–54 years	42%	43.6%
55–64 years	11.8%	14.2%
65 years and over	14.7%	17.6%
Middle-class size	51.1%	70.9%
Economic		
GDP growth rate (%)	2.4	2.7
GDP – per capita ($)	38,500	25,100
Inflation rate (%)	1.9	1.1
Legal/government		
Currency convertibility	Highly convertible	Highly convertible
Economic freedom	82.6	69.8
Openness to FDI	$549bn	$125.2bn
Infrastructure		
Roads and highways (km)	922,234	128,512
Airports	462	122

Note: GDP = gross domestic product
Source: *CIA World Factbook* (2009), www.cia.gov.

laying down the state of law, institutions and respect for human rights. Mohamed Morsi became the first democratically elected Egyptian president on 24 May 2012. Just over one year later President Morsi was removed from power by the army, an interim government put in place, and new elections planned for 2014.

Economy

Egypt's economy depended mainly on agriculture, tourism and petroleum exports, with the second-biggest income source being the Suez Canal which brought in about US$2bn, contributing 5 per cent to GNP. Egypt's economy was considered the second-largest sound economy in the Arab world.[3]

Egypt's economy was highly centralised during the rule of President Gamal Abdel Nasser but has opened up greatly under later leadership. During the period from 2004 to 2008, Egypt assertively engaged in economic reforms to attract foreign investment and

improve GDP growth. The international economic downturn slowed Egypt's GDP growth from 7.2 per cent in 2008 to 4.5 per cent in 2009, influencing the export-oriented sectors, including manufacturing and tourism.[3]

In 2009 the government implemented a $2.7bn stimulus package favouring infrastructural projects and export subsidies, and was considering up to $3.3bn in additional stimulus spending in 2010 to lessen the slowdown in economic growth. The government started economic reforms to attract foreign investment, boost growth, and improve economic conditions for the broader population. Egypt still exhibited extreme differences between rich and poor, and was by any standard still to be considered an underdeveloped country. However, a growing number of the inhabitants could be considered as middle or upper class.[3]

Industry[4]

Egyptian efforts to industrialise the country began in the nineteenth century, under the rule of Muhammed Ali. Even though costly machines and technology were imported, local industries developed gradually. By the First World War, textile industries had gained a strong foothold. In the late 2000s, Egypt's industry included, in addition to the dominant textile industry, production of cement, iron and steel, chemicals, fertilisers, rubber products, refined sugar, tobacco, canned foods, cottonseed oil, small metal products, shoes and furniture.

Since the 1970s, billions of dollars in economic aid has poured into Egypt from the USA, Arab countries and the European nations. However, the country's inefficient state-run industries, its bloated public sector and its large military investments resulted in inflation, unemployment, a severe trade deficit and heavy public debt.[5]

Mining had become more important during the last 20 years. Products that were extracted included crude petroleum, salt, phosphate, iron and manganese. Energy did not represent a problem to Egypt. The country was self-sufficient with petroleum, and had smaller deposits of coal and natural gas. The Aswan Dam provided most of the electric power used. However, this source of income was slightly threatened, and could be reduced in the years to come.

Electrometer industry

Energy resources and especially electricity are important for all activities in the post-industrial age. Energy became a priority in all countries' agendas because of its high consumption levels in the face of the scarcity of natural resources. As a result, the role of electrometers became increasingly important.

An electrometer (or a 'meter') is a device that measures electric current, charge or voltage to determine electricity consumption. While individuals are not always directly aware of the importance of these devices, electrometers are required in all domains where electricity is used, such as lighting, television, microwave and other appliances requiring electricity. The government calculates a fee on electricity consumption by installing meters and requiring a monthly payment.

The consumption of electricity had become a norm a long time ago and people were not conscious that they required an electrometer to measure the level of their consumption. However, with the increased cost of electricity the role of electrometers became more apparent at the level of individual consumers.

On the national level, any economic development is accompanied by house building and creation of new neighbourhoods which, invariably, leads to an increased demand for electrometers. Therefore, short of a global economic crisis or a discovery of a new energy source, the electrometer industry has enormous demand and a prosperous future.

Types of electrometers

There were two types of electrometers, **mechanical** and **electrical**. The mechanical electrometer has been in use since the nineteenth century and was usually never replaced, while an electrical electrometer was more accurate, reliable in any condition, but had a short life-span. In the developed countries, mechanical electrometers were replaced with electrical ones.

Recently many developed countries were faced with high levels of electricity consumption due to excessive use of appliances such as air conditioners. Accordingly, there were different developments to improve the quality of electricity meters to provide more detailed information about consumption and price. There were two main types of electric meters: **accumulation** meters and **interval** meters. Accumulation meters recorded the total consumption of electricity at a connection point and customers were billed according to the volume of electricity consumed. The interval meters recorded consumption in defined time intervals, which allowed time-of-use billing.

The use of **smart meters**, a type of interval meter, had increased recently in developed countries. The main reason for using smart meters was to allow energy-users to self-manage their demand in response to price signals. As customers would reduce their use of electricity at peak times when prices were high this would ease congestion in network infrastructure. Smart meters also reduced carbon dioxide emission and thus supported environmentally-friendly projects. Many countries are therefore passing laws to force its citizens to transfer to smart meters.[6]

In 2008, there were 1,698 million electrometers installed in the world, with an annual demand of 132 million and an expected unit increase of 7.5 per cent in 2012. This forecast clearly indicated market opportunities for electrometer sales and guaranteed profit given an efficient market strategy. Although the financial crisis of late 2000 slowed down investment in buildings or homes, the recovery was expected to increase the investment rate again. However, to leverage this opportunity an appropriate market entry strategy was required and the optimal country for internationalisation should be selected based on specific numbers. According to forecasts, Europe and Asia had the highest growing demand for meters and electricity generation.

Main players in the international market

The global electrometer industry was dominated by five powerful and influential companies. Chinese companies had around 60–65 per cent of the market. The two main Chinese companies were Holley Meters and Ningbo Sanxing. Holley Meters manufactured and marketed various meters while Ningbo Sanxing manufactured electrical meters. The largest non-Chinese companies were ItronActaris and Landis + Gyr. ItronActaris was founded in the USA and optimised the delivery and use of energy and water. Landis + Gyr was a Swiss primitive metering distributer (Exhibit 2).[7]

Egyptian electrometer market

The Egyptian population was around 80 million and, given high birth rates and lack of birth control, was continuously increasing, thus requiring more cities and houses to be built. The retail sector in Egypt was also increasing. The electrometer market could sustain its growth as long as society was willing to invest and grow. Egypt's fast-growing domestic electricity demand was estimated to increase by around 7 per cent a year.[8] Egypt was classified as a developing nation, which meant that the market was still growing and would require spending on infrastructure. However, Egypt was divided between two extremes: the modernised cities and homes that use electrometers and the slums and poor areas that might not have access to electricity. This could obviously be a drawback for the electrometer market in Egypt.

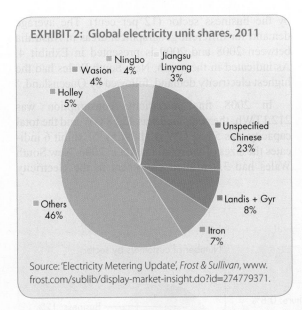

EXHIBIT 2: Global electricity unit shares, 2011

- Jiangsu Linyang 3%
- Ningbo 4%
- Wasion 4%
- Holley 5%
- Unspecified Chinese 23%
- Others 46%
- Landis + Gyr 8%
- Itron 7%

Source: 'Electricity Metering Update', *Frost & Sullivan*, www.frost.com/sublib/display-market-insight.do?id=274779371.

The meter market in Egypt was divided between three companies: El-Sewedy Electrometers, Global Tronics and a government-owned company. Almost 50 per cent of the market share was controlled by El-Sewedy. Their meters had a competitive advantage which included accurate measurement of electric current, reliable performance under working conditions and optimal operation throughout its life-span. However, consumers were not fully literate about the electrometer functions, operations and competitive advantages. They relied on brand familiarity and company reputation. The metering market was regulated by the Egyptian Electric Utility and Consumer Protection Regulatory Agency.

El-Sewedy Electrometers (ESE)

The El-Sewedy Group was a well-known electrical device company in Egypt and maintained a fair share of the electrical market. The company was founded more than 60 years ago and gained substantial electrical market experience. El-Sewedy became the largest industrial group in Africa and the Middle East, with 23 factories, 20 companies, 6,000 employees and more than US$500m in annual turnover.

The El-Sewedy journey began in the early 1930s as a supplier for electrical material in Egypt. In 1960, it was appointed by the Egyptian government to supply electrical materials for the High Dam project in Aswan. The company grew and expanded in Jeddah, developing a trustworthy name and reputation. In the 1980s El-Sewedy became the largest industrial group in the region, with 11 factories, involved in manufacturing electrical materials for electricity transmission

and distribution. After the turn of the century, El-Sewedy managed to further expand and create three more factories for Cable's Joint and Terminations, Transformers and Electricity Meters. On 6 October 2002, the group established El-Sewedy Electrometers (ESE) with its first factory in 6th of October city near Cairo, Egypt.

ESE managed to exploit market gaps around the world in the electrometer sector by expanding in Ghana, Mexico, Brazil, Zambia and Ethiopia. The company compiled many studies to expand its market further into Europe and Asia. ESE manufactured six types of meters within its factory, including electro-mechanical single-phased, multi-phased and digital electrometers.

Australia

Australia had a very strong economy that was based on its retail industry, including houses, department stores, schools, hospitals, etc. According to the Australian Bureau of Statistics, all industry groups increased their production in January 2010. The largest increase was in cafés, restaurants and takeaway food services (0.7 per cent) followed by department stores (0.4 per cent), clothing, footwear and personal accessory retailing (0.4 per cent), household goods retailing (0.3 per cent), food retailing (0.3 per cent) and other retailing (0.3 per cent). These trends indicated the possibility of high demand for electrometers because the economy was improving. After the financial crisis of the late 2000s, the government tightened its monetary policy, decreasing prices across the board. After the recovery prices should have increased, leading to increased profits. The other side of the coin is that the economy had a low inflation rate and a tight labour market.

Energy sector in Australia

The Australian Energy Market Operator (AEMO) required customers to install equipment to record their energy consumption. The AEMO registered, accredited and audited a range of metering services provided by local network service providers. These service providers were responsible for measuring the volume of electricity supplied, validating the data from the meters, and forwarding the information to AEMO.

Consumers had the right to choose their own supplier and accordingly AEMO was responsible for providing the system and processes to support competition and choice for all end users in the retail electricity market. In 2009, around 6.3 million customers transferred from one retailer to another. The competition between retailers helped in creating new and unique products.[9]

Market size and segments

Electricity consumption varied according to the business sector (Exhibit 3). The highest electricity consumption was in the residential sector (27.7 per cent), followed by the commercial sector (22.8 per cent). The Australian electricity market was dominated by individual domestic customers (88 per cent) followed by the business sector (12 per cent). The average demand for different geographical areas in Australia between 2008 and 2009 is presented in Exhibit 4. As indicated in the graph, New South Wales had the highest electricity demand, followed by Queensland. [9]

In 2008 final electricity consumption was 212.1TWh, the peak load was 42.58 GW and the total capacity was 55.51 GW (Exhibit 5).[10] Exhibit 6 indicates the sizes of the retail market in 2006. New South Wales had 3.9 million customers in the electricity

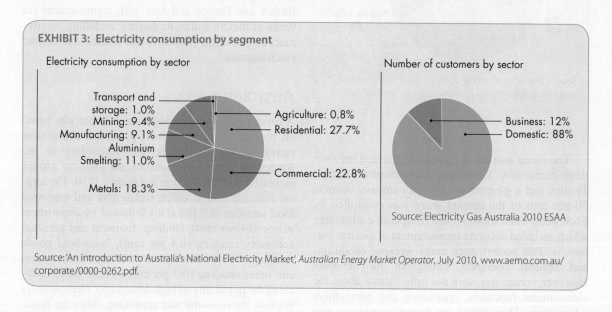

EXHIBIT 3: Electricity consumption by segment

Electricity consumption by sector

- Transport and storage: 1.0%
- Mining: 9.4%
- Manufacturing: 9.1%
- Aluminium Smelting: 11.0%
- Metals: 18.3%
- Agriculture: 0.8%
- Residential: 27.7%
- Commercial: 22.8%

Number of customers by sector

- Business: 12%
- Domestic: 88%

Source: Electricity Gas Australia 2010 ESAA

Source: 'An introduction to Australia's National Electricity Market', *Australian Energy Market Operator*, July 2010, www.aemo.com.au/corporate/0000-0262.pdf.

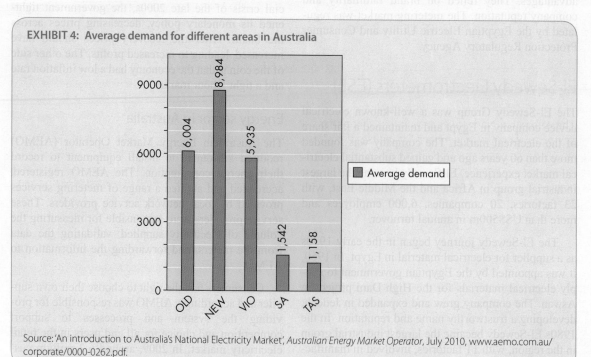

EXHIBIT 4: Average demand for different areas in Australia

Area	Average demand
QLD	6,004
NEW	8,984
VIC	5,935
SA	1,542
TAS	1,158

Source: 'An introduction to Australia's National Electricity Market', *Australian Energy Market Operator*, July 2010, www.aemo.com.au/corporate/0000-0262.pdf.

EXHIBIT 5: Market size for Australia and the Czech Republic

Country/*Region*	Full market opening	Market size in 2008		
		Final consumption (TWh)	*Peak load (GW)*	*Total/ capacity (GW)*
Australia – *NEM*	*2002*	212.1	42.58	55.51
Austria	*2001*	59.6	9.66	20.80
Belgium	*2007*	82.8	13.93	16.76
Czech Republic	*2006*	58.0	11.16	17.74
Denmark	*2003*	33.4	6.21	12.50
Finland	*1998*	82.6	13.29	16.65
France	*2007*	433.5	92.40	117.82
Germany	*1998*	525.5	77.80	139.28
Greece	*2007*	56.5	9.83	14.25
Hungary	*2000*	34.3	6.00	8.63
Ireland	*2000*	25.9	4.89	7.40
Italy	*2002*	309.3	51.87	98.63
Korea	*2001*	408.4	66.80	79.86
Netherlands	*2001*	109.1	16.96	24.88
New Zealand	*1994*	38.4	6.38	9.38
Norway	*1997*	111.5	23.99	30.79
Poland	*2007*	111.8	22.60	32.68
Portugal	*2006*	48.4	9.22	15.76
Spain	*2003*	265.1	44.44	93.53
Sweden	*1996*	128.6	24.90	33.94

Source: 'Empowering Customers' Choice in Electricity Markets', *International Energy Agency*, October 2011, http://www.iea.org/publications/freepublication/Empower.pdf.

retail market followed by 3.6 million in Victoria and 0.7 million customers in South Australia. Victoria's major electricity retailers and their market share in the domestic and business customers is reflected in Exhibit 7.[9]

Electricity pricing

The Australian National Electricity Market indicated that price elasticity was higher for industrial customers than for commercial residences. Industrial customers were more likely to gain from shifting loads, due to their large consumption volume, compared to residential customers. Accordingly, large users were more likely to have metering infrastructure and more flexible supply arrangements required to support a more flexible response as opposed to smaller commercial and residential users. Price elasticity differed by region (Exhibit 8).[11]

Electrometers industry in australia

The demand for electricity had increased tremendously in Australia due to the growing use of appliances such as air conditioners. Accordingly the

government was considering other options to reduce the overload of the power systems that were already struggling to cope. Moreover, customers needed to understand the changes in prices of electricity during peak and off-peak periods. Therefore efficient electricity metering could act as an integrated system that would help in the overall power supply and management during peak load conditions.[12]

Accordingly, the use of smart meters, a type of interval meter, had increased recently in Australia. As mentioned earlier, smart meters allowed energy-users to self-manage their demand in response to price signals. Moreover, smarts meters also reduced carbon-dioxide emission and thus supported the Australian government's environmentally-friendly projects.

In 2007, the Council of Australian Governments agreed on a 'national implement strategy' for the use of smart meters whenever a benefit was expected. The implementation was expected to take five years. In Victoria a programme was initiated in 2008 to install smart meters to all small customers over four to five years. In New South Wales, Energy Australia committed to a rollout of interval meters to customers

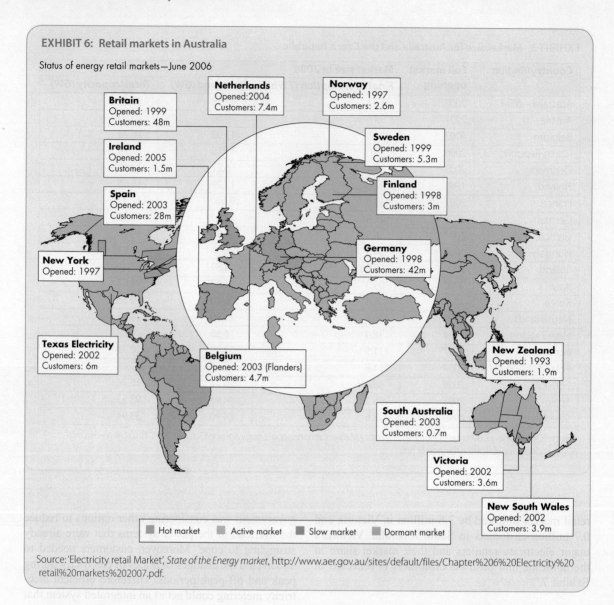

EXHIBIT 6: Retail markets in Australia

Status of energy retail markets—June 2006

Netherlands
Opened: 2004
Customers: 7.4m

Norway
Opened: 1997
Customers: 2.6m

Britain
Opened: 1999
Customers: 48m

Sweden
Opened: 1999
Customers: 5.3m

Ireland
Opened: 2005
Customers: 1.5m

Finland
Opened: 1998
Customers: 3m

Spain
Opened: 2003
Customers: 28m

Germany
Opened: 1998
Customers: 42m

New York
Opened: 1997

Texas Electricity
Opened: 2002
Customers: 6m

Belgium
Opened: 2003 (Flanders)
Customers: 4.7m

New Zealand
Opened: 1993
Customers: 1.9m

South Australia
Opened: 2003
Customers: 0.7m

Victoria
Opened: 2002
Customers: 3.6m

New South Wales
Opened: 2002
Customers: 3.9m

■ Hot market   ■ Active market   ■ Slow market   ■ Dormant market

Source: 'Electricity retail Market', *State of the Energy market*, http://www.aer.gov.au/sites/default/files/Chapter%206%20Electricity%20
retail%20markets%202007.pdf.

EXHIBIT 7: Electricity retail market shares – Victoria, 30 June 2006

Retailer	Domestic customers	Business customers	Total retail customers
AGL Energy	31%	24%	31%
Origin Energy	32%	38%	33%
TRUenergy	24%	23%	24%
Other	13%	15%	13%
Total customers	2,077,135	276,266	2,353,401

Sources: ESC, Energy Retail Business Compensative Performance Report for the 2005–06 Finished Year, November 2006, p 2; and
'Electricity Retail Market', *State of the Energy Market*, http://www.aer.gov.au/sites/default/files/Chapter%206%20Electricity%20
retail%20markets%202007.pdf.

EXHIBIT 8: Elasticity customer class and region – Australian National Electricity Market

		Elasticity (%)
Customer class	Residential	−0.25
	Commercial	−0.35
	Industrial	−0.38
NLM region	New South Wales	−0.16
	Victoria	−0.38
	Queensland	−0.29
	South Australia	−0.25
	Tasmania	−0.23

Source: AEMO, 2006 and 2010. 'Empowering Customers Choice in Electricity Markets', *International Energy Agency*, October 2011, http://www.iea.org/publications/freepublications/publication/Empower.pdf.

who consume more than 15 MWh of electricity a year, while Country Energy was installing interval meters on a new and replacement basis for all customers.[9]

Between 1995 and 2005, the Australian government owned key electricity industry stakeholders such as network service providers, electricity retailers, and the network regulatory body. However, each of these entities was now independent, increasing flexibility and thus competition.[13]

Competition

Competition in the metering service in Australia had been very limited, which resulted in increases in the prices of meters. Citizens in Victoria paid four times what their neighbouring country's citizens in New Zealand paid. This caused the metering services in Australia to become a 'nice little earner' for distribution companies. The cost of the metering service in Victoria was 40 per cent of the cost of the underlying electricity itself. In New Zealand, the meter could be owned by the power distributor, retailer, or someone else entirely. The house owner would pay a fee to use the meter of $NZ50 a year for old-style ones and $NZ75 a year for ones that can be read remotely. In Australia, however, the direct cost was $NZ220 per household for smart meters.[14]

Accordingly in 2012, there were moves to open the market for competition in order to achieve a better pricing structure and more market innovation. According to the Australian Energy Market Commission, 'Reforms to the present metering arrangements are necessary to promote investment in better metering technology and consumer choice.' The commission had 'put forward a

model where metering services are open to competition and can be provided to residential and small business consumers by any approved metering service provider'.[14]

Australia had several electrical companies (both private and public enterprises) that distributed electrometers. The Victorian Electricity Supply Industry comprised five distribution networks, namely CitiPower, Powercor, SP AusNet, Jemena and United Energy. Also, Switzerland's Landis + Gyr electrical company operated in Australia. The electrometer industry was competitive with various local and international companies.

Czech Republic

The Czech Republic's economy was transitioning from a centrally planned to a free-market economy to become more stable and prosperous. The transitional phase caused investments to increase and the country to flourish, therefore indirectly demanding electrometers. The Czech Republic was located in the middle of Europe, which could be advantageous in facilitating any movement within the European countries. Moreover, the country had low labour costs, making it attractive to foreign investment seeking resource efficiency.

Energy sector in the Czech Republic

OECD mentioned that the electricity share in the Czech Republic was 11.7 per cent in 1990 and grew to 17 per cent in 2003.[15] In 2006, the Czech electricity market was liberated and customers were allowed to choose between different suppliers. The transmission system operator was established as a separate state-owned company.[11]

The electricity market had revenues of $11.3bn in 2011, which was considered a 6.7 per cent increase from 2007. Between 2007 and 2011, the electricity consumption decreased by 1.3 per cent to reach a total of 58.6 TWh in 2011. It was forecasted that, in 2016, electricity market revenues would reach $13.1bn.[16]

The electricity market consisted of different segments such as industrial, commercial, households, transportation, and other end users such as agriculture.[16]

Electricity prices

Electricity prices for households had been increasing since 2000; however it was still 23 per cent below the average of other European countries. The prices for industrial users were also increasing but they were 3 per cent lower than the European averages.

Generally the industrial electricity prices were lower than the household prices.[11]

Electrometer industry in the Czech Republic

Being a member of the EU, the Czech Republic was obliged to follow EU regulations regarding the use of metering. The EU forced all member countries to deploy smart meters to 80 per cent of its customers by 2020 if it was economically feasible. Moreover the EU provided guidelines to help member countries in 'setting road maps, creating interoperability standards, ensuring data protection, and establishing costs and benefits for all stakeholders'.[17]

Most Central and Eastern European (CEE) countries found positive benefits in this requirement based on their cost–benefit analysis. Since electricity had the highest prices in the CEE countries compared to the rest of the world, many customers could benefit from controlling their electricity consumption. Moreover CEE countries were concerned with renewable sources of energy, so upgraded grids were required accordingly.

CEE was considered the most advanced region among emerging market countries for the deployment of smart grids and smart meters. Smart meter spending in the CEE region was expected to reach $10.3bn by 2023 (exchange rate $1 = 19.97 CZK).[12] The Czech Republic started deploying smart meters to customers; however the results were not satisfying. Although customers were equipped with smart meters, they were not interested in changing their consumption patterns despite having accurate consumption data and being offered financial incentives through reduced electricity tariffs.

Although the Czech Republic was obliged to follow EU regulations, it was still a struggle to sell the concept of smart meters to customers. Accordingly major players in the market, such as CEZ, decided to focus on ripple control, a successful mechanism used in the country and considered an alternative to smart meters. The ripple system allowed the utilities to switch on or off certain electrical appliances on consumers' premises. On the other hand, smart metering allowed customers to make better consumption decisions based on more reliable metering data.[13] Exhibit 9 shows a list of meter types and their prices (currency conversions are based on the current rate of 1 USD = 19.9699 CZK).[18]

Major competitors

The electricity industry was dominated by three major players in the market: CEZ, E.ON and PRE. These vertically integrated companies used to supply and distribute electricity. These three players had a

EXHIBIT 9: Types and prices of meters in the Czech Republic

Type of meter		Price/unit ($)
Meter low cost	EM101-1	8
Meter	EM 341-2	55
STS meter	Single phase	45

Source: 'XE-Universal Currency Converter', http://www.xe.com/ucc/.

market share of 95 per cent of final customers' total consumption (99 per cent share for small customers). There were 10 suppliers of electricity in the retail market. These suppliers offered electricity that was initially bought from small generators or imported from other countries. CEZ was controlling 73 per cent of the national production capacity of generators, and the rest of the market was held by small companies that had a 3 per cent share each.[11]

Reaching a decision

The Research and Development team of El-Sewedy Electrometers was composed of experts that studied and analysed any international expansion project. After assessing the country's attractiveness, the company assessed the feasibility of the project and investigated different options in order to determine which region was more qualified for international expansion.

Once the company had done the on-site visits and decided the place and mode of entry, ESE would start assessing its marketing and sales strategy. In fact, having a good marketing campaign was the priority for the project. Therefore, ESE started doing preliminary analysis of political, economic, societal and technological factors in Australia and the Czech Republic in order to evaluate overall country attractiveness and choose one of them. Once the preferred country was selected, they had to decide on an appropriate mode of entry and develop sales forecast and a marketing strategy. The main choices of entry mode usually were either a wholly-owned subsidiary (usually an acquired local company) or a joint venture. Another option might be direct export. These steps were fundamental in order to determine the optimum solution, which would include the types of equipment, the modes of meters' production and the team evaluation.[19]

The project team, on the other hand was responsible for following up the business development of the project abroad. The team was assigned to start installing the project equipment, to test it and to introduce technological enhancements or provide employees with training courses.

ESE was not aiming merely to sell electrometers, but to ensure their effective use by the customers. Thus, efficient customer support would be programmed in the chosen country to ensure that clients were able to use the meter software in such a way as to utilise all its beneficial features.

The after-sale service was also important in order to provide a high degree of reliability to the clients and the businesses. In fact, it had the facility to upgrade the meter's software through the Internet. Consequently, once the software was updated, it would be instantly distributed to the clients who would benefit from it immediately. ESE offered a two-year warranty and training for clients in order to provide them with the best maintenance possible. All ESE meters were made according to international standards to facilitate international implementation in any country. All software used the highest secure encryptions (DES).

The global demand for enhanced meters was expected to increase by 56 per cent in the next five years.[20] It was predicted that, with privatisation in Eastern Europe, the old mechanical electro meters would be replaced with the basic electric meters. The ESE team visited different factories in the Czech Republic which might be potential acquisitions.

When considering Australia, Ashour believed that its attraction lay in the high demand for meters and recent deregulation. The trends of opening the market for competition also represented a great opportunity for ESE. However the implementation cost was expected to be higher than in the Czech Republic, and accordingly additional research and assessment was necessary. Moreover, the feasibility projects should be done efficiently in order to help Ashour decide which country to choose.

QUESTIONS

1 What are the pros and cons of expanding into these two countries?
2 Which entry mode should the company use?
3 What marketing strategy should it pursue?

NOTES

1 'Egypt Political System', http://www.egypt-accounting.com/egypt-political-system.html.
2 'Egypt Economy and Politics', *Asiarooms.com*, http://www.asiarooms.com/travel-guide/egypt/egypt-overview/egypt-economy-and-politics.html.
3 'Egypt Economy 2010', *Countries of the World*, http://www.theodora.com/wfbcurrent/egypt/egypt_economy.html.
4 Tore, Kjeilen, 'Economy', *Looklex Encyclopedia*, http://lexicorient.com/e.o/egypt.economy.htm.
5 'Economy', *Infoplease*, http://www.infoplease.com/ce6/world/A0857909.html.
6 'Electricity Retail Market', *State of the Energy Market*, http://www.aer.gov.au/sites/default/files/Chapter%206%20Electricity%20retail%20markets%202007.pdf.
7 'Electricity Metering Update', *Frost & Sullivan*, www.frost.com/sublib/display-market-insight.do?id=274779371.
8 'Economic Performance: Alternative-energy Schemes Take Shape', *Economist Intelligence Unit,* http://www.eiu.com.lib.aucegypt.edu.
9 'An Introduction to Australia's National Electricity Market', *Australian Energy Market Operator*, July 2010, www.aemo.com.au/corporate/0000-0262.pdf.
10 'Empowering Customers' Choice in Electricity Markets', *International Energy Agency*, October 2011, http://www.iea.org/publications/freepublications/publication/Empower.pdf.
11 'Czech Republic', *Internal Market Factsheet*, January 2007, http://ec.europa.eu/energy/energy_policy/doc/factsheets/market/market_cz_en.pdf.

12 S. Bharath Srinivasan, 'The Future of Electricity Metering System Boosts Demand for Smart Meters in Australia', *Frost & Sullivan*, 3 November 2005, http://www.frost.com/sublib/display-market-insight.do?id=52388847.

13 Petr Stabrawa , 'Central Europe's Energy Giant Says No to Large-scale Smart-meter Deployment, Prefers Alternative Solution', *IDC Community Insights*, 23 May 2012, https://idc-insights-community.com/energy/smart-grid/central-europes-energy-giant-says-no-to-largescale~2.

14 Brian Robins, 'Call to Overhaul Electricity Meter Market', *The Sydney Morning Herald*, 6 September 2012, http://www.smh.com.au/business/call-to-overhaul-electricity-meter-market-20120906-25gmb.html.

15 OECD ilibrary, '*Energy Policies of IEA Countries*,' http://0-www.oecdilibrary.org.lib.aucegypt.edu.

16 'Czech Republic – Electricity', *MarketLine*, http://store.marketline.com/Product/czech_republic_electricity?productid=MLIP0773-0010.

17 'Central and Eastern Europe Smart Marketing Market to Reach $1003 billion by 2013', *Electric Light and Power*, http://www.elp.com/news/2013/04/10/central-eastern-europe-smart-metering-market-to-reach-10-3-billion-by-2023.html.

18 'XE-universal Currency Converter' , http://www.xe.com/ucc/.

19 'El-Sewedy ELECTROMETER', *El-Sewedy ELECTROMETER*, http://www.sewedy-eg.com/company.asp?id=5.

20 'Energy Research', *The World Electricity Meter Market Report and Database*, www.absenergyresearch.com/cmsfiles/reports/World-Electricity-Meters-2009.pdf.

This case was prepared by Dr Marina Apaydin, Hend Mostafa, Nadia Gamal El Din, Farida El Zomor, Dina El Alaily and Sherine Kabesh.

Case 4.3

IKEA: Entering Russia

'In Russia all possible things turn out to be impossible, and all impossible is possible.'

Lennart Dahlgren
Former IKEA Country Manager, Russia

When Swedish furniture retailer IKEA's country manager arrived in Russia to set up the first store, the country was in a state of deep shock. It was 17 August 1998, the day Russian monetary policy finally collapsed. Almost all foreign companies were leaving the country, but IKEA stayed and this may turn out to be a very favourable strategic move from a long-term perspective. The decision to remain in Russia in 1998 was, however, taken almost entirely by one man, IKEA's founder, Ingvar Kamprad. During one of his visits to Russia, he shared his vision of how IKEA Russia would develop in the coming years: 'IKEA becomes the main supplier of home furniture to the normal Russian families and our sales in Russia will exceed those in our old home country Sweden.' To realise this vision he stood in opposition to the entire management group when the decision was taken to enter the country.

The fact that IKEA's owner saw Russia as a long-term investment also enabled the management to apply a long-term perspective that may become a competitive advantage in the years to come. As a Russian manager commented: 'We have been on the market here for three and a half years now, and we can note the tendency, and if the tendency grows as quickly as it has done during this time, the market will be unlimited for a company like IKEA, and for most Western companies who are now interested to come here.'

Transferring the IKEA culture and values to Russia

IKEA is a leading home furnishing company with around 340 stores in 40 countries, selling a range of some 10,000 articles and having more than 150,000 employees. The company was founded in 1943 by Ingvar Kamprad in Småland, a province in Southern Sweden where people are renowned for working hard, being thrifty and innovative, and achieving big results with small means. Today, the IKEA group is controlled by a private foundation and the company is thus not on the stock market. Ingvar Kamprad's innovative idea was to offer home furnishing products of good function and design at prices much lower than competitors by using simple cost-cutting solutions that did not affect the quality of products. This is a prominent philosophy at IKEA, which is now realising its ambitious plans in Russia. IKEA has been operating in Russia since 1990 but opened its first store in Moscow, Khimki, only in March 2000, followed by one more in Moscow in 2001, one in St Petersburg in 2003, and one in Kazan in March 2004. In 2012 IKEA had 14 stores in Russia and some of them in distant places such as Novosibirsk (2007) and the newest ones in Ufa (2011) and Samara (2012). All Russian operations are controlled as fully owned ventures by the IKEA group.

IKEA is characterised by a strong brand based on its vision to create a better everyday life for many people. A set of explicit values is linked to the vision and plays a guiding principle in the strategy development. The values are the foundation of a culture called internally the 'IKEA Way', which is an expression of IKEA's history, the product range, the distribution system, the management style, the human resource ideas, etc. Brand and cultural values coincide and affect the strategy, organisational processes, product development and customer relationships. Thus the key value of cost-consciousness that lies at the heart of IKEA's flat-package concept dictates the necessity of global sourcing, defines the customer relationship where 'IKEA does a half and customers do a half' and guides the product design, choice of materials and logistics. The value of simplicity is reflected in the fast planning process, behaviours and routines governed by commonsense, straightforward relationships with suppliers and customers as well as in the product development process. By linking vision and values, IKEA thus creates a firm platform for entering a new market.

It was the overall company vision that guided the desire to establish business in Russia,; most particularly, the impression that few companies in Russia focused on solving the needs of the many people by offering attractive products at reasonable prices. However, knowledge of the Russian market when IKEA initially decided to open its first store in

Moscow was very scarce. No special market research was carried out before setting up the store. According to a company representative: 'If we had done such research, it should have shown that the consumption level is too low, the individual income level is too low, there are no traditions of retailing, which result in the fact that consumers generally don't go to the chains to shop.'

In each new market IKEA enters it must recreate its company culture from scratch. In Moscow that included the replication of the store design and layout in accordance with the latest version of the existing store and extensive cultural education that was implemented by the team of experienced IKEA people. It involved introducing the newly employed co-workers to IKEA routines and cultural traditions as well as helping them to develop the necessary competences (eg teamwork, leadership, skill diversity, etc) and the IKEA management style. It has its roots in Swedish leadership style and gives responsibility to each co-worker and emphasises 'learning by doing'. In the Russian case, the store played an additional role by becoming the training site for new employees who later got involved in new projects or formed teams for the newly opened stores – a sort of cultural incubator. The extensive in-store training produced some very positive results. According to a store manager, the second store in Moscow could operate well from the first minute it opened because the whole staff was trained in the first store in corresponding jobs: 'Here they just started and then they went on like this! No downturn, no nothing, no reaction, they just knew what to do!'

The role of IKEA's experienced management staff has also been indispensable in Russia. A major task is to train and prepare local people who will be ready to lead the expansion process further. As a manager commented about his management group: 'My main task is really to make this group more Russian and to export people for the upcoming expansion.' The demand for knowledgeable Russian staff is indeed very large, with a few new stores opening every year. The development of the experienced staff is impossible without extensive training.

As a whole, therefore, there is a strong emphasis on the vital role of training at IKEA Russia, both at an overall management level and the store level. The local staff on the store level with a primarily academic education and a prioritisation of abstract knowledge is faced with the necessity to translate this into concrete sales figures. This includes cultural training and education in IKEA values as well as different levels of professional on-the-job training.

Developing and positioning the retail proposition in Russia

As we have seen, market information was not regarded as necessary when selecting the Russian market. According to one manager, IKEA knew that a lot of people live in Moscow so that at least one store should succeed. A survey presenting this information was considered unnecessary. Furthermore it was considered less important to develop specific strategies for the market in advance. Instead entry was based on the view that there is a need to live and learn about the new market before setting the strategies. Within IKEA, setting up a new business was described as very little theory and very much practice. However, once the decision was made to enter the Russian market IKEA specialists were sent to Russia to investigate, but data about the Russian market was often uncertain and difficult to assess. For example, one initial conclusion was that the IKEA store should be situated near a Metro-station since there were hardly any cars in Moscow. Five years later, however, traffic jams were one of Moscow's biggest problems. The country manager argued that instead of information about the market it is better to acquire market knowledge and the best way to get that knowledge is to live and learn in the market.

IKEA introduces more or less the same product range in all new countries, irrespective of what is considered popular by local customers. In Russia IKEA's Scandinavian furniture design is in some contrast to the historically preferred dark wood, massive, lacquered, expensive furniture. In order to support this strategy, IKEA usually identifies the potential needs that are similar across markets: 'We have the IKEA range and we have the market knowledge and the people needs, which are pretty much the same needs in Moscow and in Malmö.' Another IKEA approach was to create the needs that the range could satisfy, and to inspire customers with numerous new solutions based on the existing range. The theme 'Living with small spaces' was one such solution used in Russia. The storage solutions are among those most popular in Russia, where average apartments are small and often house several families. Cheap and good-looking accessories for the home also became very popular with Russian customers and accounted for a large part of the stores' turnover.

IKEA's basic strategy to neither adjust the style of products to local needs nor follow the competitors' product development was central as the cornerstone in preserving the IKEA concept and image: 'The range is supposed to be IKEA-unique and typical IKEA.' All products are divided into four major categories or styles – Scandinavian, Country, Modern, and Young Swede – which are clearly distinguished in all business areas across the store. One of the reasons why IKEA was successful with its standard product ranges in Russia was the fact that several of these IKEA ranges emphasise the modern style, which is very different from the traditional Russian style but is attractive and fresh for the Russian customers because it symbolises change.

An important factor in the market approach was to identify needs that are not fully recognised and to teach customers what IKEA is about. IKEA's retail proposition is based to a large extent on its Swedish roots and history, which is, in turn, very different from Russian traditions. Therefore, learning as much as possible about the local culture and customer needs was considered essential. For example, IKEA made home visits to customers to talk to people, see how they lived and used their homes and to identify potential needs and wants not fully acknowledged by customers themselves. Understanding local family conditions and furnishing traditions then provided a basis for the effective introduction and marketing of the IKEA concept. As exemplified by a store manager, the main priority for Russians is normal living costs; then comes the car and TV; and afterwards maybe a trip abroad. The idea of changing people's priorities by explaining to them that a beautiful home does not have to cost a fortune, and they can afford both the wardrobe and a trip abroad, is an essential *leitmotif* of the marketing campaigns in Russia.

Since IKEA was totally new to many Russian customers, 'to bring people as much as possible in the store in order to learn about IKEA and get a positive attitude' was a main goal from the very beginning. IKEA put a strong emphasis on making Russian customers feel welcome and important in the store, which was very unusual for Russian stores at the time. The way the range was presented and the opportunity to touch and test everything in the store also made the products much more desirable to the Moscow customers. This was a new and unusual retail approach.

However, a great deal of IKEA's success with the product range can be attributed to its work in influencing the customer's decision making. One example of how IKEA has considered the local preferences is in creating the room settings to reflect local conditions in terms of apartment sizes and local furnishing traditions. As discussed earlier, it is vital to understand local customer needs and 'transfer the IKEA range into relevant solutions' for the families where three generations often live together in small apartments of 50–60 square metres. The range should also allow the possibility to 'mix and match' within the Russian home.

The importance of aligning the IKEA concept with the desired image was critical from the very beginning. The intention was to build an image with a low price brand that also guaranteed attractive and modern products of good quality. To achieve this, IKEA has faced many challenges such as: high customs fees; the requirement to purchase more from the local producers; difficulties in finding and developing suppliers in Russia; still low buying-power of Russian customers, etc. For IKEA, it was critical to associate the low price with the desired significance. For Russian customers low price was very strongly related to unattractive products of poor quality, and one challenge has been to overcome this and explain how it is possible to offer good product at low prices. Therefore, it has also been an ambition to provide the Russian market with the best and most attractive IKEA products.

Marketing communications became an important tool in creating the right image of IKEA in Russia. The ways to communicate the image were many: the outdoor product ads (prices), image ads in the glossy magazines, TV (though IKEA has used this very restrictively due to high costs), and articles in the newspapers (press coverage has become very broad and quite positive towards the IKEA culture and philosophy). Another very important communication means in Russia is the buzz network or word-of-mouth communication that works very effectively. In addition, IKEA had an open and friendly approach towards Russian journalists. This was in sharp contrast to most other large organisations. IKEA was completely open to the journalists and introduced them to the IKEA way and values by organising press trips to Älmhult in Sweden to learn how the range is created. The result was that the press coverage of IKEA in Russia became much more positive.

Government authorities and officials of different ranks were also critical stakeholder groups. Their goodwill and support was crucial for IKEA's expansion in Russia. What played a pivotal role in the present success of IKEA's operations in Russia was the fact that IKEA was the only company that stayed in Russia after the currency devaluation and subsequent economic collapse in August of 1998, when almost all foreign companies left the country. That created an immediate effect of trust and willingness to cooperate with IKEA on behalf of the major Russian politicians. In 2008 the firm was considered the most important foreign investor in Russia outside of the gas and oil industry. The positive image in Russia plays an increasingly important role in IKEA's further expansion, since it is crucial for creating new contacts with the local government and finding sites for the new stores in the distant regions.

Internal organisational processes also supported the positioning strategy. Common activities carried out on a regular basis were informal and formal discussions at the store level, where co-workers from one or several store departments participate. The discussions covered different customer issues and the best ways to present the range to the customers. Market data and experience were also transferred and shared within and between different departments and units at the company. The store managers and department heads meet regularly to share the sales information and the latest decisions regarding the room settings, etc. The data about local customer perceptions and opinions about IKEA's different product and service parameters collected by the store department heads was also quickly reported to the marketing and sales department at the service office in Moscow. This information in most cases is about product pricing, with the goal to lower the price for a specific product. These issues were discussed at the weekly, and even daily, store meetings since speed of reaction might be very crucial for store sales statistics. The topics included outgoing articles, a new range, and different solutions to present it, and take a form of an informal exchange of opinions. The inter-departmental and local corporate flows of information were prerequisites of the fast decision making at IKEA. For example, new product development supported the trading retailing organisations in Russia with ideas about new products and supplier capabilities.

In the spring of 2009 IKEA thus had 11 stores operating in Russia. Most of these locations were mega mall shopping complexes operated by IKEA. The shopping complex at the Tyoplyi Stan site in Moscow for example accommodates around 210,000 square metres of retail space and 240 retail outlets. The mega malls were treated as a separate business, and were an addition to IKEA's core concept. Normally, IKEA does not manage or develop shopping centres but this was considered necessary in Russia due to its lack of an existing structure of large branded stores and external as well as central shopping centres of a Western kind. Previously, many Russians have shopped for furniture as well as other products in outdoor markets or at smaller, local stores. From IKEA's perspective, developing a whole mega mall was part of attracting Russian customers to the stores.

Current developments and challenges

As a whole, IKEA has made substantial investments in Russia, and turnover is increasing rapidly. However, a major principle has been that monetary returns are needed to back up further expansion: 'As soon as we make a profit, I can see at least ten years ahead when we will need all the money that is generated in Russia in Russia. So, the day when we will start to take out profit from Russia and use it in other countries is perhaps 15 years away.'

In the near future IKEA hopes to open a number of new stores in Russia. A project team has been made responsible for the expansion: to look for new cities, acquire permissions, build a store and recruit and educate IKEA co-workers. As a whole, experiences and knowledge in general about the process of opening a new store, as well as specific market knowledge, is important in this expansion phase. One example is the knowledge about potential sites for the new stores. The choice of cities is to a large extent based on local attitude and IKEA's intention is to establish new stores only in cities where the authorities welcome the company. However, as a manager argued, the fact that authorities are hesitant about the establishment of a new large store in the area can be seen as an opportunity. If it is difficult to enter a new city or region other retailers will also face difficulties and may give up the attempt. IKEA can, on the other hand, take advantage of its previous experiences regarding this type of challenge and may eventually succeed in opening a new store in an area with little competition.

However, establishing new stores and shopping centres in remote and culturally different places involves risks and uncontrollable factors even for an experienced player like IKEA. In 2006, as a new mega mall was opened in Nizjnij Novgorod, an accident occurred. A woman lost control of her shopping cart and a five-year old boy was killed. The local court decided to close the whole establishment, possibly due to pressures from local business interests. It was re-opened after a week but the incident was considered to be very serious.

An even more problematic example was the new mega mall in Samara. It was completed in December 2008, with a skating rink, a number of restaurants, and about 200 shops, but the Russian administrative process delayed the opening. IKEA simply did not receive the necessary permissions to open from local authorities. The company argued that the local authorities continually set new, unreasonable, requirements. A major explanation was believed to be that another shopping centre owned by local interests was planned to open simultanueously. IKEA's manager for Russia and Eastern Europe declared that the outcome of this incident could seriously influence the firm's future plans for Russia. After being delayed another eight times, the complex was finally opened in 2012.

During the same time period IKEA also experienced another major incident in Russia. Two senior managers had to be dismissed after being accused of tolerating bribery. A Swedish newspaper published the story, and could present evidence based upon email conversations with details about how managers allowed bribes to be paid by a contractor in order to fix an electricity supply problem quickly at its store in St Petersburg.

At the moment, there seems to be renewed optimism when it comes to the Russian expansion. The realisation of these ambitious plans will also to a large extent depend on the progress in IKEA's local buying and production in Russia. An increased capacity and bigger volumes by the Russian suppliers will allow the company to cut costs and reduce prices in Russia as well as to export the Russian-made furniture to its other markets. As a matter of

fact, IKEA prices are still very high for many ordinary Russians. For example, even in St Petersburg, the second-largest city, shopping power is, according to different estimates, 30 to 50 per cent lower than in Moscow, where an average purchase value equals that in Stockholm.

As a whole, almost all IKEA managers have perceived the cultural differences between Sweden and Russia as very substantial. It is clear that the cultural aspect will continue to play a major role when considering that many of the regions and cities that IKEA plans to enter in the future are likely to be even more different from the West when compared to the major cities of Moscow and St Petersburg. As one manager commented: 'Everything we believed would have been a problem when we came to Russia has turned out to be no problem at all. Everything we believed would work nicely was and still is a problem.'

QUESTIONS

1   Can you see any alternative entry strategy that IKEA could have applied when entering the Russian market? What would have been the advantages and disadvantages of these alternative strategies?
2   To what extent do you think that IKEA's entry strategy for Russia is based on adaptation and on standardisation? How are those approaches balanced?
3   Would you consider IKEA to be a market-driving company?
4   In what respects do you think that IKEA's market behaviour in Russia has been different due to the fact that Russia is an emerging market?
5   IKEA has a vision of building up a global brand. Can IKEA be regarded as a global brand? How does IKEA's marketing strategy in Russia influence/contribute to the company's brand vision?
6   What do you think that the ownership form means for IKEA's entry strategy and its long-term activities in the Russian market.
7   Discuss IKEA's opportunities to achieve long-term success in the Russian market. What are the main challenges that IKEA faces? How can they be managed?

FURTHER READING

- www.IKEA.com.

Written by Ulf Elg, Anna Jonsson and Veronika Tarnovskaya at the School of Economics and Management, Lund University.

Case 4.4

Banco Mediano Español: Big Is Beautiful
Managing Growth and Shareholder Value during Recessions and Financially Constrained Markets

In April of 2010, José Ferret, President of Banco Mediano Español, had to present the bank's three-year strategic plan to the Board of Directors. Despite the positive financial results Banco Mediano Español achieved in 2009, the economic crisis continued to have a negative effect on the Spanish economy. The high levels of unemployment and company bankruptcies produced a constant deterioration of the bank's assets that could drive the Spanish regulator to restructure the national financial system. At the macroeconomic level the situation did not appear to be much better. On the one hand the central banks had to put a brake on the injection of liquidity into the market, and on the other hand new financial market regulations were expected to put pressure on banks' future profitability. Banco Mediano Español, the fourth-largest bank in the Spanish market, is one of the most capitalised and solvent in the country. However, its predominant focus on the Spanish economy, one of the economies most affected by the economic crisis, seriously jeopardises its future growth opportunities, its share value has dropped to the book value and the bank may be the target of a potential takeover bid.

Banco Mediano Español: history and evolution of the bank

Positioned as the fourth-largest Spanish banking group, Banco Mediano Español has constantly impressed analysts with superior profits. Benefitting from the highest coverage rate[1] in Europe, the bank has grown rapidly over the last decade since the appointment of Mr Ferret as the chairman of the Group in 1999.

Group Banco Mediano Español earned €522.5m in net profit in 2009. The Group classifies its service into four main business areas: (1) Commercial Banking; (2) Corporate Banking and Global Businesses; (3) Markets and Private Banking;[2] and (4) BME América (see Appendix 2). In addition, it has seven regional divisions with full responsibility for their geographic areas, and several business-focused support teams. Almost 90 per cent of the income comes from its Client Business, especially from the Corporate and Commercial banking business divisions.

Banco Mediano Español has taken a long road to become what it is today, making the jump from a regional bank to a major nation-wide player in recent decades. Founded in 1901, Banco Mediano Español was only a 'bank for businesses' until 1907. The experience that the bank gained during this period was critical in forming its current values, such as pragmatism and customer focus. Furthermore, Banco Mediano Español attached great importance to its objective 'of serving clients through exceptional financial advice and support'.

By 1964 Banco Mediano Español already owned more than 100 branches and had opened a representative office in London. In 1986, it opened additional offices in Paris, Milan and New York, with a total of 308 branches. In 1994, the bank expanded its commercial network to more than 400 branches, and opened additional branches in France, Mexico, Singapore, Beijing, Miami, Lisbon, London and New York. In 1999, Mr Ferret was appointed executive president of the Group. He initiated the new era of Banco Mediano Español's expansion in the twenty-first century.

At the beginning of the twenty-first century, Banco Mediano Español began a phase of major transformation by carrying out strategic alliances and acquisitions through the exchange of shares. One of the first strategic partners was Caja Portugués (CP), the first bank listed on the Portuguese exchange market. This was followed by the incorporation of Banco Hierro into the Banco Mediano Español Group. Banco Hierro had a prominent positioning in the Principado de Asturias and Castilla y León. Similar operations have been carried out with Banco Hispano del Este, Banco Comercial Asturiano, Banco de Crédito Regional, Banco Pacifico, Iberia Private Banking Group, and Bank of Miami (see Appendix 1). At the end of 2009, the Group was active in 18 countries covering four continents with different formats such as branch offices, representative offices, associates, and subsidiaries (see Appendix 3).

In a remarkably short time period, Banco Mediano Español has integrated several banks under one umbrella group with a flexible information technology system as the platform. The process of integrating these banks into the Group was carried out in less than half the time integrations usually take and therefore is considered an impressive achievement within the banking industry, both in Spain and in Europe. After the acquisition of Banco Pacifico in 2004, the Group achieved the fourth position in terms of assets in the Spanish banking industry[3] and was incorporated into the IBEX-35, the Spanish stock exchange.

In 2007 Banco Mediano Español's total assets reached €82.8bn. It was also one of Europe's most profitable banks, with a cost/income (or expense/income) ratio[4] of 43.05 per cent, among the lowest in Europe and one of the best in Spain. Currently it owns five separate brands (Banco Mediano Español, Banco Hierro, Banco Hipotecario Europeo, Banco de Crédito Regional, and Iberia Private Banking Group) in the Spanish market. Each of these brands offers a different aspect of banking to the markets in which they compete and provides financial services to different client segments (see Appendix 4).

The growth and consolidation business plan: 2002–2004

Banco Mediano Español's commitment to growth and profitability is formalised in the three-year strategic plans that the bank develops and implements. In 2002, it began implementing a business plan called 'Growth and Consolidation 2002–2004'. Through this plan the bank achieved a more competitive and balanced position in the national market in both business and geographical terms. During this time period, total assets grew from €27.2bn to €42.3bn, and market capitalisation increased from €2.8bn to €5.6bn. The bank organised itself in 2002 into three main divisions (Banco Mediano Español division, Banco Hierro division, and Private Banking services division). The first two divisions (Banco Mediano Español and Banco Herrero) had similar business structures, with their main focus on commercial banking (which includes retail and personal banking) and corporate banking.

Banco Mediano Español held a leadership position with 'SME'[5] customers and was also considered as a solid competitor with 'large mid-sized' companies as well as for 'large' corporations. In addition, Banco Mediano Español's business unit Banco Hipotecario Europeo had a leadership position in the non-resident[6] retail segment. The third division of the Group was composed of Private Banking services,

which provided important potential revenue synergies with the commercial and corporate divisions. The Group's private banking business operated under both the Banco Mediano Español brand and the Iberia Private Banking Group brand.

In addition to the three divisions, the Group had several business units, which could also be described as horizontal business lines, including such services as insurance or asset management, which enabled the Group to provide a full range of financial services to its customer base.

Regarding Banco Mediano Español's organisational strategy, the Group implemented a total quality management and ISO 9000[7] quality system certification programme. The Group also made large investments in information technology in order to integrate, support, and improve upon the execution of the bank's many activities.

To reinforce its presence in the Spanish market and to expand its range of services, in 2003 Banco Mediano Español acquired 100 per cent of Banco Pacifico, the eighth-largest bank in Spain at that time. The €1.5bn transaction included an estimated €766m of goodwill.[8] Banco Mediano Español estimated that, because of the synergy between the two banks, it could achieve annual savings of €115m (€41m in revenue synergies and €74m in cost/efficiency synergies), with total long-term synergies adding up to approximately €800m.

The acquisition of Banco Pacifico represented an important step for Banco Mediano Español to become a major national player, similar in size to Banco Popular and Banesto. Banco Pacifico had a business model and client base similar to that of Banco Mediano Español. In addition, the newly acquired bank provided an important geographical complement to Banco Mediano Español because of its presence in two key areas of Spain: Madrid and Andalucia.

Banco Mediano Español closed its three-year business plan 'Growth and Consolidation 2002–2004' with a number of important achievements. In the letter to the shareholders, Mr Ferret stated:

'The year 2004 saw the conclusion of the three-year action plan launched in 2002. The plan has focused on growing and consolidating our various business lines and has involved a major effort in investment and modernization by Banco Mediano Español. If we look at the growth achieved by our organization in the last three years, we find that the organization's total assets are 59% above what they were in 2002; lending in this same period has increased by 87%, and deposits and assets under management are up by 72%. Shareholders' equity stands at over 3 billion euros, a rise of 46.5%. On December 31, 2004 our market capitalization had increased by 87% to more than 5.2 billion euros. These figures show beyond a doubt that the aims and objectives of the three-year plan have been more than accomplished.'

Other results at the close of the three-year plan are also worth mentioning. For one, the bank's ROE improved from 9.59 per cent to 10.30 per cent. Its P/E ratio (considered as the market value growth expectation)[9] increased during this period from 14 to 16, with an increase of the EPS of 1 per cent to €1.07 per share (see Appendix 5). The number of branches (offices open to the public) increased by 20 per cent and the FTEs (full-time equivalent[10] or full-time employees) increased by 12.3 per cent.

The value and growth business plan: 2005–2007

Banco Mediano Español's next three-year business plan was named 'Value and Growth 2005–2007'. President Ferret described it in the following way:

'We are now at the start of a new phase in which profitability and shareholder value will be priority aims in our overall objective of increasing earnings per share. This is the main challenge that we have set ourselves as we start the 2005–2007 period, and it is on this that our efforts will be focused.'

The bank's main goals were to 'consolidate Banco Mediano Español as a domestic leader in corporate banking and (shareholder) value creation'. The bank aimed to increase the operating margin by €400m through a range of strategies that included: launching new products, increasing the number of transactions with the current customer base, gaining new clients, and increasing the bank's operating efficiency.

In 2006, through the acquisition of Iberia Private Banking Group, Banco Mediano Español increased its customer base in the commercial and corporate division and doubled its size in the 'on shore'[11] private banking business. The bank became the third-largest private banking institution in Spain behind Santander and BBVA, with a market share of almost 10 per cent. This acquisition increased Banco Mediano Español's customer base in the commercial and corporate division, and it doubled its size in the private banking business. The main source of

Banco Mediano Español's gross operating income remained commercial and corporate banking, but the private banking business gained relative importance.

In 2007 Banco Mediano Español took a very important step in its strategic growth: international diversification in the USA. Banco Mediano Español acquired a small but successful retail (commercial) bank called the 'Bank of Miami', based in Miami, Florida, USA, for $175m. Despite the relatively small size of the bank (a customer base of 13,000 clients) in comparison with Banco Mediano Español's latest acquisitions in Spain (Banco Pacifico and Iberia Private Banking Group), this acquisition provided the bank with attractive growth potential for several reasons: (1) the state of Florida represents the fourth-largest state in terms of US GDP contribution, with a yearly growth rate of 7.7 per cent; (2) Miami represents an optimal location to develop further its presence in the retail banking industry in the US market; (3) Florida is considered the financial centre for the entire Latin American market.

Banco Mediano Español closed the three-year business plan 'Value and Growth 2005–2007' with impressive results, as mentioned by Mr Ferret in his letter to the shareholders:

'Growth and value creation were, of course, the principal aims of the 2005–2007 master plan which came to an end on 31 December. It is clear from the final result that these aims were more than achieved and that the actions we took to bring this about were the right ones. Our consolidated balance sheet is now 68% above what it was when we launched the plan, and during this time lending has increased by 84% and customer funds under management by 90%. Our cost/income ratio has improved by 9% and our profitability as measured by ROE is 7 points higher, having risen to 20.4%.'

The bank's commitment to increasing efficiency yielded impressive results with an ROE increase of 97 per cent, but the P/E ratio decreased by 28 per cent to 11.59. The number of bank branches increased by 12 per cent, and the FTEs (full-time equivalent/employees) increased by 6 per cent (see Appendix 6).

The Optima 09 business plan: 2008–2009

At the end of 2007 the bank announced its next strategic plan, called 'Plan Optima 09'. The aims of this plan were directly influenced by the uncertainty and duration of the economic downturn. As President Ferret explained:

'The two-year plan is based on flexibility and prudence and has been designed for the environment of economic slowdown that we now face. Its aims are to boost operational efficiency and commercial productivity and thus increase business volumes by more than the average for the banking system as a whole, while keeping operating costs at a low level to ensure that it [the bank] remains one of the most efficient and profitable financial institutions in the Spanish market, consolidating its leadership and its unique positioning in corporate banking and retail banking.'

Regarding specific targets, the plan aimed to reach a cost/income ratio of 37.5 per cent and to maintain the ROE ratio at 20.5.

Despite the financial turmoil during this period, Banco Mediano Español reinforced its presence in the US market through two acquisitions. In April 2008, Banco Mediano Español purchased the BBVA Private Banking business in Miami, and in early 2010 it announced the acquisition of Miami-based Credit Bank of Florida (CBF), acquiring a total $1,675m in deposits and $875m in loans. With the acquisition of CBF, Sabadell Group now operates the sixth-largest local bank based in Miami in terms of deposits, managing a total of $6.4bn of business (investment and funds). BME United Bank will be the new brand of the bank in the US market.

'The successful completion of the Credit Bank of Florida transaction represents a major step in the growth of our US operations,' stated Fernando Uruita, Managing Director of Banco Mediano Español America. 'We are very pleased with this transaction and especially the quality of professionals that make up CBF, their loyalty to the bank, and its excellent relationship with their customers. We expect significant benefits for our customers and we are also pleased that our employees will enjoy new opportunities as part of a larger, international financial Group.'

On the business side, 2007–2009 were difficult years for the entire financial industry. Although Banco Mediano Español did beat analysts' expectations, its performance dropped during the 2007–2009 period: the balance sheet showed a decrease of almost 7 per cent, total deposits decreased by 2 per cent, shareholder equity dropped 16 per cent, and the Group's net profit decreased by 33 per cent.

In addition, the bank's ROE dropped to 11.36. The bank's capitalisation plunged by almost 50 per cent, with a P/E ratio of 8.74. The bank grew to 1,190 branches with 9,466 FTEs (see Appendix 7). The Optima 09 plan achieved its efficiency objectives, reducing its cost/income ratio by 8 per cent to 39.4.

Despite the challenging situation, Banco Mediano Español had one of the highest cover ratios in the banking sector, outperforming many Spanish and European banks (see Appendix 8). At the end of 2009, Banco Mediano Español earned €522m, mainly generated from its commercial and corporate divisions.

Despite the achievements of Banco Mediano Español during these challenging times, analyst opinions were not very favourable. Most of the analysts' recommendations were more oriented towards a 'maintain and underweight'[12] rather than 'buy and overweight' (see Appendix 9).

Given the low valuation of the share of Banco Mediano Español, the bank could be the target of a hostile takeover, especially by international banks aiming to expand business in Spain. But for the current situation a hostile takeover is just a remote possibility as Mr Suarez, Chief Executive of the Iberia Private Banking Group, explained clearly that: 'The best way to defend from a hostile takeover is to show to the market that nobody is capable of managing the bank better than you.' '[T]his does not guarantee you 100 per cent hostile takeover protection,' commented Mr Gutiérrez, Corporate Director of Operations of the Banco Mediano Español, however. Takeover bids for Spanish banks may come as soon as the economic outlook of the Spanish economy improves and if the Spanish banks' shares remain undervalued, and under these conditions 'there will come a moment when this will certainly happen … and we remain open,' comments Mr Gutiérrez.

The Spanish competitive landscape

The Spanish financial system is mainly composed of mainstream commercial banks, savings banks,[13] and credit cooperatives. Savings banks accounted for almost 50 per cent of Spain's outstanding loans in 2008 (up from 10 per cent in the 1960s), with commercial banks holding 40 per cent and credit cooperatives the remainder (see Appendix 10).

The national market was primarily served by Spanish commercial and savings banks. Only two foreign banks have commitments in the Spanish retail and commercial market: Barclays Bank and Deutsche Bank. In terms of size, the Spanish subsidiary of Barclays Bank has an estimated €43,000m in total assets and the Spanish subsidiary of the Deutsche Bank has an estimated €13,000m in total assets. Despite this relative small size in comparison to the market leader, Barclays Bank and Deutsche Bank were considered major global investment banks with a clear commitment to develop the retail business worldwide in order to diversify the risk of investment banking.

Savings banks have a different objective to commercial banks: they have to sustain the development of local communities and plough back a portion of their profit into the regional society as social contributions. By regulation they do not have shareholders but are controlled by a 'General Board' composed of local government, depositors, funding members and employees. Savings banks had 23,418 branch offices in 2008, compared to 15,096 owned by commercial banks. Spain's decade-long real estate bubble (during which prices rose 500 per cent) was an important source of growth for banks and especially savings banks. At the peak of Spain's property boom in 2008, 800,000 homes were built – more than in the UK, France and Germany combined.

That bubble has now burst. Having grown 3.7 per cent in 2007 and 0.9 per cent in 2008, Spain's economy is forecast to shrink 3.6 per cent in 2009 and 0.6 per cent in 2010. Unemployment currently stands at close to 20 per cent and is not expected to decrease until the beginning of 2010. The default rate[14] on mortgages[15] and loans has increased substantially and this is not expected to change in the foreseeable future. In addition, real estate assets held in the balance sheet of financial institutions have increased dramatically in the last two years. In January 2010 the Bank of Spain stepped in and imposed regulations on financial institutions by obligating them to increase their provisions (cover ratio) related to their mortgage loans (see Appendix 11).

The real estate bubble hit the 'savings banks' harder than it hit the traditional banks. In 2008 more than 70 per cent of savings banks' total loan portfolio was real estate and mortgage loans, compared to around 50 per cent for regular banks. The result has been to push up the ratio of non-performing loans (NPLs) among regional savings banks. Some analysts have suggested that the low credit quality of the Spanish savings banks' assets may require a recapitalisation[16] of €60bn to repair their balance sheet. According to the 2002 law on Spanish saving banks (LORCA), these financial institutions have the

possibility of issuing non-voting participatory rights called 'cuotas participativas' tradeable on the secondary market. This might allow the possibility of raising additional resources, but there are some limitations to this strategy: only up to 33 per cent of the institutions' total equity can be offered, for instance, which limits their contribution to recapitalisation. The non-voting nature of the instruments may not be tempting for investors, who may well shy away from buying the debts of the smallest and weakest institutions.

As a result of the financial crisis in Spain, the Spanish financial sector has moved into a consolidation phase in which a series of mergers and asset sell-offs will take place, especially within savings banks. It is quite possible that the Spanish regulator will soon give savings banks the option of being 'transformed' into banks in order to raise the required funds to cover their past credit excesses. This path will completely transform the competitive landscape with new national competitors (new Spanish national banks) of different sizes.[17] In addition, the economic situation will tighten the competitive environment between Spanish banks. For example, the Bank of Santander has taken aggressive action to attract new client deposits by offering a very high rate of 4 per cent interest. This competitive move was quickly answered by their main competitor, BBVA, as well as by other Spanish banks. This 'war on deposits' is essentially a price war that makes depositors happy, but reduces the profitability of the banks.

The European banking environment 'before' the 2007–2009 crisis

In the ten years leading up to the financial and economic downturn of 2007–2009, the international banking industry had been undergoing far-reaching structural changes. The processes of liberalisation, globalisation and integration have dramatically changed the banking landscape around the world.

Diversified banking models

In response to growing competition, banks have diversified into 'non-interest earning activities'[18] such as: insurance, mutual fund sales, and private banking and assets management. This diversified banking model has become the dominant business model in Europe. It is referred to as 'universal banking', in which the bank diversifies its activities with: (1) a branch network oriented to retail and wholesale businesses (ie private customers, SMEs, and corporate; and (2) complementary financial services, such as insurance, assets management, private banking and corporate and investment activities.

Financial mergers and acquisitions (M&As)

Initially the financial M&As took place at the national level, thus leading to the consolidation of countries' banking industries with fewer, larger banks. However, when M&A opportunities became scarce in the domestic markets, European banks increasingly looked across national borders for acquisition targets.

More incentives for consolidation

Additional factors were causing European banks to consolidate. One was technological progress, which resulted in high fixed cost investments in new technologies, and hence demanded a large volume of business to cover the initial investment.

International diversification

This strategy was considered an effective strategy for banks to increase financial stability and reduce risk. Consolidation in the banking sector accelerated in the early 1990s and peaked in 2000. It resulted in a reduction of the number of banks and an increase in the average bank size: between 1985 and 2004, the total number of banks operating in the 15 EU countries fell from 12,315 to 7,300.

The process of bank consolidation has resulted in a number of very large banks: Banco Santander and BBVA in Spain; Credit Agricole, Société Générale and BNP Parisbas in France; HSBC, Barclays, RBS in the UK; and Banca Intesa Sanpaolo and Unicredito in Italy.

The financial and economic crisis: 2007–2009

During the years 2007 to 2009 the European banking and financial industry was involved in what was considered the most devastating financial and economic downturn since the Great Depression of the 1930s. The financial system practically collapsed and the wave of European banking consolidation was greatly affected, especially due to the disappearance of some of its players like Lehman Brothers and Merrill Lynch.

At the beginning of 2006, the housing market boom ended and sales and prices dropped off sharply. Some industry analysts commented that, as a result of the devastation taking place, the financial industry would never be the same.

The European banking environment 'after' the 2007–2009 crisis

The financial crisis profoundly changed the competitive landscape within the banking industry. The banking sector went through important write-downs, many banks had to be bailed out by national governments, and others (ie ING and RBS) were forced to modify their business model or to reduce their size.

At the conclusion of 2009 and the first half of 2010, bank executives had several key strategic issues in mind. Many bank directors felt that these issues would have a big impact on their strategic decisions and ambitions, and that they would affect the progress of the consolidation of the European banking sector which had begun two years earlier. The key issues are described below.

Deterioration of asset quality or credit risk

The continuous deterioration of the quality of the banks' assets (ie real estate and consumer credit) represents a major issue for bank profitability and cash flow availability. The economic outlook still looks miserable, hence credit risk remains high and, because loan problems always lag behind economic recovery, the quality of banks' assets might continue to deteriorate.

Macroeconomic trends

Although some economies like the USA, Germany and France have shown signs of recovery, the economic outlook remains extremely uncertain for countries denominated as PIGS (Portugal, Ireland, Greece and Spain).

Regulation requirements

New regulation known as Basel III will be adopted worldwide by the end of 2012. This new regulation requires banks to strengthen capital bases, reduce the leverage and create buffers in 'good times' that can absorb shocks in periods of stress. Moreover, in order to make the Spanish financial system more robust, there are rumours that the Bank of Spain will require higher capital requirements than the one formalised by Basel III, especially for non-listed financial institutions (saving banks).

Tight capital requirements will certainly reduce the profitability and dividend payout for the coming years. Analysts forecast that the European banking industry needs to obtain €130m of fresh capital. The most affected would certainly be the French and the

British banks, while the Spanish banks are considered the least affected.

Capital availability

Shortage of capital for the banking industry was never a problem. Even during the crisis banks have been able to raise impressive amounts of new capital in order to clean their balance sheets and deleverage. But if difficult economic conditions persist, raising new capital could become a key issue. Higher capital requirements will mean higher costs for banks that would decrease their profitability (ROE). If shareholders pressure banks to increase their ROE, banks may feel obligated to begin taking unacceptable risks again.

Credit spread[19]

The sudden widening (increase) of credit spreads in mid-2007 was one of the causes of the crisis. Currently markets have reduced the credit spread to more relaxed levels. The concern today is whether the new spreads accurately reflect the level of risk in the system. If spreads are tightening (decreasing), once again, it may not reflect the correct balance that banks should maintain.

Big banks still in fashion

It is not clear what impact the new rules and competitive environment will have on the future profitability of financial institutions. What does seem clear is that the 'big bank' business model remains the most accepted model within the financial industry. In the USA, the strategy of the Federal Reserve to push solvent banks to merge with insolvent banks has once again accelerated the banking consolidation process. Emilio Botin, President of the Bank of Santander, stated, when presenting the bank's 2010 results, that: 'The crisis has shown the importance of diversification, which in our case is based on leadership positions in retail banking in 10 countries.'

Banco Mediano Español's strategic choices for the future

Over the past ten years, Banco Mediano Español has grown from a regional Spanish bank to a major competitor in the national financial market through a series of important acquisitions and an efficiency improvement programme. The bank managed to survive the financial crisis effectively, becoming one of the most capitalised and solvent banks within the Spanish financial system. Despite these important achievements, analysts' recommendations showed some doubts about the future growth opportunities of the bank.

Because Banco Mediano Español is primarily a domestic Spanish bank, some industry analysts were sceptical about the bank's opportunities for future growth and profitability due to the fact that Spain is one of the European countries that is suffering most from the economic crisis. Moreover, the new regulations being developed for the banking industry look as though they will become an impediment for banks to grow, and as a result could reduce banks' profitability.

As Mr Ferret prepared for the meeting with the bank's Board of Directors in April 2010, he reflected on the bank's evolution over the past ten years. He wondered about the effectiveness of the strategies that he and his team had formulated and implemented to achieve Banco Mediano Español's position today. He also realised that the financial and economic environment had changed around the world and that achieving continued success in this new environment was going to be a challenge. He opened up some strategic documents and reviewed the bank's past and current strategic objectives for growth and profitability.

Mr Ferret knew that in his presentation of Banco Mediano Español's 'three-year plan' to the Board of Directors he would need to focus on the following key strategic aspects for the bank:

1 An evaluation and analysis of its current strategic position indicating its strengths and weaknesses and the opportunities and threats it faces.

2 An identification of the key strategic alternatives the bank faces and the choice of the main strategic decisions to be implemented in the next strategic plan.

Appendices

Appendix 1 The banking profitability model based on bank size

A number of reasons have been identified that enable larger banks to earn higher profits. First, large banks, as a consequence of operating in concentrated markets (or, consolidated markets with fewer and larger banks as a result of M&As) are adopting collusive price-setting practices, resulting in higher rates being charged on loans, lower interest paid on deposits, higher fees and so on. Second, larger banks are able to reduce costs because of superior production and management techniques, and thus operate more efficiently than their smaller counterparts.

Third, market power, which is generally achieved by merging two competitors in the same market, can be used in two ways: the bank can manipulate prices on the assets side of its operation and, on the liabilities side of its business, a new bigger bank is likely to secure more favourable funding conditions than

Appendix 2 Group Structure of Banco Mediano Español

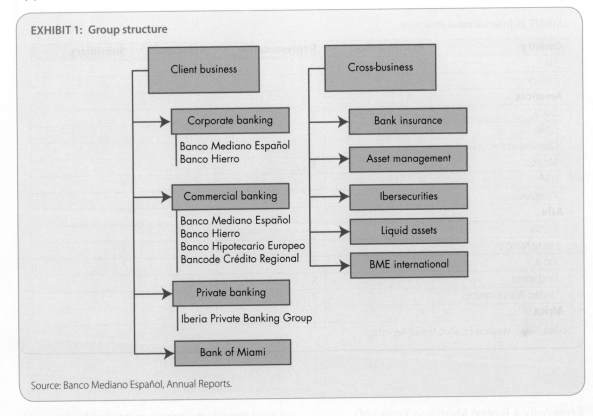

EXHIBIT 1: Group structure

Source: Banco Mediano Español, Annual Reports.

the individual banks because of its larger size (a larger bank is less vulnerable to economic shocks), enhanced reputation and the diversification effect.

Fourth, merging two banks with a similar line of activity can lead to economies of scale due to an increase in business volume and a simultaneous reduction of fixed costs, as well as a transfer of knowledge and managerial skill. Economies of scope are achieved by merging different support functions such as the information system, marketing, back office and personnel management, and by streamlining the branch network, often by merging two entities with complementary activities, for example a retail bank and an investment bank or a retail bank and an insurance company (ie Dresdner Bank and Allianz Insurance).

Managerial efficiency, which reflects the differences in managerial ability to control costs and/or maximise profits, is a capability that is clearly not equally distributed among European managers. In a merger and acquisition contest, the general idea is that one of the entities, generally the bidding bank, possesses superior management skills and practices, which are then applied in the newly merged/acquired bank and hence improves the managerial efficiency of this new bank.

As a result of banks' pursuit of higher profits, the most appropriate business model for maximising shareholder value appeared to follow the idea that 'big is beautiful'. This philosophy is combined with another common belief that large banks would become 'too big to fail' by reducing the systematic risk related to financial institutions.

Appendix 3 International structure of Banco Mediano Español

EXHIBIT 2: International structure

Country	Branch Office	Representative	Associate	Subsidiary
Europe				
France	X			
Portugal			X	

▶

EXHIBIT 2: International structure

Country	Branch Office	Representative	Associate	Subsidiary
UK	X			
Turkey	X			
Americas				
Brazil		X		
Chile		X		
Dominican Republic			X	
Mexico		X	X	
USA	X			X
Venezuela		X		
Asia				
China		X		
Hong Kong				X
India		X		
Singapore		X		
United Arab Emirates		X		
Africa	X	X		

Source: Banco Mediano Español, Annual Reports.

Appendix 4 Banco Mediano Español's brands

1 Banco Mediano Español
2 Banco Hierro
3 Banco Hipotecario Europeo
4 Banco de Crédito Regional
5 Iberia Private Banking Group

Banco Mediano Español

A reference brand in the Spanish market for business and private banking services that stands out, in the latter case, in personal banking. It is organised into two basic businesses, each with its own strategies and organisation: Corporate Banking (leader in the medium corporations segment and market reference for large companies) and Commercial Banking (leader in small companies and reference model in private and personal banking).

Banco Hierro

Sole brand of the bank operating in Asturias and León that implements a commercial banking model oriented towards the private sector and businesses. It is organised into two units: Corporate Banking and Commercial Banking.

Banco Hipotecario Europeo

This is the group brand specialised in the market composed of Europeans established in Spain, as well as enterprises revolving around the field of residential tourism.

Banco de Crédito Regional

Reference brand in the Spanish on-line banking market, with a competitive added-value proposal based on the quality of its products.

It complements the group offer and collaborates in the development of products and services in the on-line banking environment.

Iberia Private Banking Group

It is a specialised affiliate bank with a long tradition in rendering private banking services.

Appendix 5 Balance sheet, profit and loss and key performance indicators during the period 2002–2004

EXHIBIT 3: Balance sheet, 2002–2004

	2002	2003	2004
Balance sheet (€000)			
Total assets	27,224.2	30,511.6	42,294.0
Gross loans and advances to customers	20,727.3	23,757.4	32,308.0
On-balance sheet funds	21,382.7	24,935.8	35,316.1
Of which:	20,954.7	24,423.7	33,748.2
Customer deposits (ex-repos)	17,234.2	17,186.0	23,568.1
Mutual funds	4,569.6	5,166.2	7,780.1
Pension funds	1,522.8	1,697.1	2,220.5
Funds under management	27,439.3	31,184.3	44,201.3
Shareholders' equity	2,050.3	2,130.6	3,004.2
Profit and loss account (€000)			
Net interest income	714.4	759.9	972.7
Gross operating income	292.0	468.1	581.9
Net income before provisions	260.3	370.6	504.8
Attributable net profit	220.4	234.9	326.0
Ratios (%)			
ROA	0.86	0.84	0.78
ROE	10.02	11.65	10.30
Cost / income basic	66.75	55.38	57.56
Cost / income	66.18	52.93	54.85
Ratio BIS	11.85	10.85	12.49
Tier I	8.16	7.57	8.53
NPLs / Gross loans (%)	0.47	0.40	0.51
Coverage ratio (%)	351.07	475.01	419.64
Share data (period end)			
Number of shareholders	48,977	53,991	68,237
Number of shares	204.00	204.00	306.00
Share price (€)	13.80	17.01	17.20
Market capitalisation (€000)	2,815.2	3,470.1	5,263.3
Earnings per share (EPS) (€)	1.08	1.15	1.07
Price/earnings ratio (P/E) (times)	12.77 x	14.77 x	16.14 x
Book value per share (€)	10.11	10.47	9.82
Price/book value (times)	1.36 x	1.62 x	1.75 x
Dividend per share	0.50	0.50	0.50
Dividend yield	3.62%	2.94%	2.91%
Pay-out ratio	46.28%	43.42%	46.93%
Others			
Domestic branches	908	872	1,091
Employees	7,755	7,545	9,628

Source: Banco Mediano Español, Annual Reports.

Appendix 6 Balance sheet, profit and loss and key performance indicators (bank and divisions) during the period 2005 –2007

EXHIBIT 4: Balance sheet, 2005–2007

Balance sheet (€000)	2005	2006	2007
Total assets	52,320,395	72,779,833	76,776,002
Gross loans and advances to customers	41,642,703	55,632,966	63,219,330
Total deposits	41,717,235	59,304,579	65,620,880
Of which:			
Customer deposits	23,023,190	30,090,641	33,350,687
Customer deposits ex-repos	19,920,908	25,572,584	29,929,049
Mutual funds	10,648,615	16,482,067	15,548,492
Pension funds	2,655,895	3,317,514	3,502,159
Funds under management	56,049,715	80,247,702	86,578,086
Shareholders' equity	3,373,621	4,041,205	4,501,383
Profit and loss account (€000)			
Net interest income	976,603	1,097,871	1,317,237
Gross operating income	1,586,882	1,811,476	2,196,395
Net operating income	727,598	813,718	1,059,029
Profit before tax	593,161	629,781	989,840
Group net profit	453,128	908,398	782,335
Comparable group net profit			
Ratios (%)			
ROA	0.94	1.48	1.08
ROE	15.19	28.09	20.37
Comparable ROE		17.61	20.37
Cost/income (ex amortisation) (1)	53.53	52.96	50.08
Cost/income (ex amortisation) (2)	49.93	50.47	46.67
BIS ratio (%)	11.49	11.42	10.87
Tier I (%)	7.96	7.33	7.22
Asset quality			
Non-performing loans (€000)	235,937	250,610	331,673
Provisions for NPLs (€000)	903,804	1,169,254	1,307,765
NPLs/gross loans (%)	0.49	0.39	0.47
Coverage ratio (%)	383.07	466.56	394.29
Share data (period end)			
No. of shareholders	65,020	67,633	80,669
No. of shares	306,003,420	1,224,013,680	1,224,013,680
Share price (€)	22.16	8.48	7.41
Market capitalisation (€000)	6,781,036	10,376,576	9,069,941
Earnings per share annualised (EPS) (€)	1.48	0.74	0.64
Price/earnings ratio (P/E) (times)	14.96	11.42	11.59
Book value per share (€)	11.02	3.30	3.68
Price/book value (times)	2.01	2.57	2.01
Pay-out policy	0.4525	0.4461	0.4381
Other data			
Domestic branches	1,104	1,187	1,225
Employees	9,443	10,066	10,234

Source: Banco Mediano Español, Annual Reports.

EXHIBIT 5: Performance by division, 2005–2007

2005	Net operating income	Profit before tax	ROE (%)	Cost/ income ratio (%)	Employees	Domestic branches
Commercial banking	354,447	293,520	16.3	58.1	6,227	1,048
SME banking	340,389	269,005	10.4	27.9	1,102	49
Iberia Private Banking Group	6,081	3,680	11.3	55.6	76	7
Bancassurance	44,161	45,788	24.5	27.3	91	–
Asset management	16,538	16,538	96.2	32.1	96	–
2006						
Commercial banking	444,606	376,238	17.6	53.3	6,532	1,107
SME banking	441,710	289,846	11.0	23.9	1,237	63
Iberia Private Banking Group	13,384	10,522	17.9	40.2	267	17
Bancassurance	53,168	54,166	24.6	22.9	89	–
Asset management	26,615	26,615	145.5	25.4	144	–
2007						
Commercial banking	527,929	469,263	21.1	52.0	6,627	1,142
SME banking	525,093	407,026	11.5	21.2	1,156	66
Iberia Private Banking Group	31,719	29,844	20.8	49.9	267	17
Bancassurance	69,687	70,818	30.2	18.3	104	–
Asset management	37,226	37,226	135.4	30.0	155	–

Source: Banco Mediano Español, Annual Reports.

Appendix 7 Balance sheet, profit and loss and key performance indicators (bank and divisions) during the period 2008–2009

EXHIBIT 6: Balance sheet, 2008–2009

Balance sheet (€000)	2008	2009
Total assets	80,378,065	82,822,886
Gross loans and advances to customers	64,704,240	65,012,792
On-balance sheet funds	63,478,952	65,012,792
Of which:		
Customer deposits (ex-repos)	36,134,150	38,131,235
Mutual funds	9,436,042	9,150,665
Pension funds	2,440,533	8,168,367
Funds under management	80,414,900	82,247,095
Shareholders' equity	4,627,216	5,226,333
Profit and loss account (€000)		
Net interest income	1,452,844	1,600,647
Gross operating income	2,226,845	2,505,030
Net income before provisions	1,114,613	1,325,477
Attributable net profit	673,835	522,489
Ratios (%)		
ROA	0.85	0.64
ROE	16.16	11.36

▶

◄

EXHIBIT 6: Balance sheet, 2008–2009

Balance sheet (€000)	2008	2009
Cost/income (ex amortisation)	43.97	43.05
Core capital	6.67	7.66
Adjusted core capital	8.06	8.14
Tier I	7.28	9.10
Adjusted Tier I	8.68	9.58
BIS ratio	9.78	10.80
Risk management		
Non-performing loans (€000)	1,698,182	2,712,418
Provisions for NPLs (€'000)	1,815,843	1,872,443
NPLs / gross loans (%)	2.35	3.73
Coverage ratio (%)	106.93	69.03
Balance sheet provisions as % of gross loans	2.81	
Share data (period end)		
Number of shareholders	88,289	89,910
Number of shares	1,200,000,000	1,200,000,000
Share price (€)	4.85	3.875
Market capitalisation (€000)	5,820,000	4,650,000
Earnings per share (EPS) (€)	0.56	0.44
Price /earnings ratio (P/E) (times)	8.64	8.74
Book value per share (€)	3.86	4.36
Price /book value (times)	1.26	0.89
Pay-out policy	0.4986	0.5053
Other data		
Domestic branches	1,225	1,190
Employees	9,929	9,466

Source: Banco Mediano Español, Annual Reports.

EXHIBIT 7: Performance by division, 2008–2009

2008	Net operating income	Profit before tax (%)	ROE	Cost/income ratio	Employees
Commercial banking	861,617	18.2	41.0%	7,662	1,208
Corporate banking	91,126	10.9	10.1%	110	2
Iberia Private Banking	12,234	3.4	56.4%	275	15
Asset management	31,543	57.7	35.6%	148	–
2009	**Net operating income**	**Profit before tax**	**ROE**	**Cost/income ratio (%)**	**Employees**
Commercial banking	1,867,918	558,815	16.7%	43.9	6,583
Corporate banking	198,025	77,817	6.7%	12.8	95
Iberia Private Banking	50,589	13,340	5.6%	61.7	240
Asset management	35,101	17,728	34.3%	49.5	144

Source: Banco Mediano Español, Annual Reports.

Appendix 8 Average cover ratio within the Spanish banking sectors during the second quarter 2009

EXHIBIT 8: Average cover ratio

	Banco Santander	BBVA	Banco Popular	Banco Banesto	Bankinter	Banco Pastor	Banco Mediano Español
NPLs	21,7	11,5	4,7	2,1	0,9	1,3	2,2
Gross loans	709	336	96	79	40	23	64
NPL ratio (%)	3,03	3,42	4,90	2,66	2,55	5,65	3,44
Provisions	15,2	7,7	1,9	1,4	0,8	0,7	1,9
Coverage ratio (%)	70,70	66,96	40,43	66,67	88,89	53,85	86,36

Source: Banks' annual reports.

Appendix 9 Analysts' recommendations

EXHIBIT 9: Summary of analysts' recommendations

	Banco Mediano Español			
	Actual	1 week ago	1 month ago	2 months ago
Buy	1	1	2	1
Overponderate	2	2	3	3
Maintain	13	13	13	12
Underponderate	6	6	6	6
Sell				
Target price	3,82 (12/4/2010)			
PER 2009	11,95			
Average recommendation	**UNDERWEIGHT**			
	Banco Pastor			
	Actual	1 week ago	1 month ago	2 months ago
Buy	0	0	0	0
Overponderate	1	1	1	1
Maintain	6	6	6	6
Underponderate	10	10	10	10
Sell	0	0	0	0
Target price	4,28			
PER 2009	5,86			
Average recommendation	**SELL**			
	Banco Popular			
	Actual	1 week ago	1 month ago	2 months ago
Buy	3	3	3	3
Overponderate	12	13	13	13
Maintain	6	5	5	6
Underponderate	5	5	5	5
Sell	0	0	0	0
Target price	6,03			
PER 2009	6,29			
Average recommendation	**MAINTAIN**			

▶

EXHIBIT 9: Summary of analysts' recommendations

	Banco Bankinter			
	Actual	**1 week ago**	**1 month ago**	**2 months ago**
Buy	0	0	0	0
Overponderate	4	4	4	4
Maintain	12	12	12	10
Underponderate	8	8	8	8
Sell	0	0	0	0
Target price	6,23			
PER 2009	12,01			
Average recommendation	**UNDERWEIGHT**			

	Banco BBVA			
	Actual	**1 week ago**	**1 month ago**	**2 months ago**
Buy	6	7	6	9
Overponderate	11	9	9	9
Maintain	2	2	3	2
Underponderate	2	2	2	2
Sell	0	0	1	1
Target price	13,12			
PER 2009	9,19			
Average recommendation	**OVERWEIGHT**			

	Banco Santander			
	Actual	**1 week ago**	**1 month ago**	**2 months ago**
Buy	5	5	5	5
Overponderate	8	9	9	8
Maintain	3	2	2	1
Underponderate	1	1	1	1
Sell	0	0	0	0
Target price	12,17			
PER 2009	10,09			
Average recommendation	**OVERWEIGHT**			

Source: Cinco Dias.
Note: the table indicates the number of recommendations of the analysts ranging from the option to buy to the option to sell.

Appendix 10 Key figures of the major competitors in the Spanish market

EXHIBIT 10: Bank institutions in 2008 and 2009

	B. lPopular		B. lPastor		Bankinter	
	2008	**2009**	**2008**	**2009**	**2008**	**2009**
Total assets	110,376	129,290	27,121	32,325	53,469	54,467
Gross loans	93,274	97,362	20,787	20,385	40,427	39,883
Client deposits	51,658	59,557	14,221	14,588	22,914	21,782
Total equity	6,734	8,415	1,369	1,429	1,965	2,583
Total revenues	3,587	4,054	1,543	1,156	2,595	1,672
Net profit	1,052	766	164	101	252	254
Ratios						
Earnings per share (€/Sh)	0.87	0.61	0,63	0,39	0.63	0.57
ROE (%)	17.8	10.9	13,08	7,49	14.08	11.29

◀

EXHIBIT 10:   Bank institutions in 2008 and 2009

	B. lPopular		B. lPastor		Bankinter	
	2008	**2009**	**2008**	**2009**	**2008**	**2009**
ROA (%)	1.04	0.68	0,60	0,35	0.49	0.46
Cost to income ratio (%)	32	29.3	36,2	31,1	47.25	46.49
PER (%)		13.23	7.92	12.55		13.3
TIER 1 (%)	8.12	9.18	7,46	10.55	7.39	7.37
Core capital (%)	7.1	8.61	6.33	8.26	10.18	10.41
Ratings						
Fitch	AA–	AA–				
Moody's	Aa3	Aa3		A3		A
Standard & Poors	A	A				A1
Total assets	117,186	122,300	1,110,529	1,049,631	542,650	535,065
Gross loans	78,201	75,927	626,888	682,551	342,682	332,162
Client deposits	55,328	57,701	826,567	900,057	376,380	371,999
Total equity	5,069	5,299	63,768	70,000	26,586	29,362
Total revenues	1,578	1,730	20,945	26,299	11,686	13,882
Net profit	779	559	8,876	8,943	5,020	4,210
Ratios						
Earnings per share (€/Sh)	1.13	0.81	0.658	0.6	1.35	1.12
ROE (%)	16.56	10.54	18.6	14.15	21.5	16
ROA (%)	0.71	0.49	1.07	0.86	1.39	1
Cost to income ratio (%)			44.6	41.7	44.6	40.4
PER (%)	7.12	10.51	8.22	8.05		8.65
TIER 1 (%)	7.7	8.72	9.1	10.1	7.9	9.4
Core capital (%)		7.7	8.5	8.6	6.2	8
Ratings						
Fitch		AA		AA		AA–
Moody's		AA		Aa2		Aa2
Standard & Poors		Aa2		AA		Aa2

Source: banks' annual reports.

EXHIBIT 11:   Savings bank ranking by assets in 2009

Rank	Name	Assets in 2009 (€m)
1	La Caixa	271.873
2	Caja Madrid	189.515
3	Bancaja	89.605
4	CAM	71.441
5	Caixa Catalunya	61.883
6	Caixa Galicia	46.082
7	Ibercaja	42.351
8	Unicaja	32.845
9	Cajasol	29.920
10	BKK	28.920

Source: Confederación Española de Cajas de Ahorros (CECA).

In the bank ranking we include the **Banca March**, a medium-size private bank mainly in private investment banking (with total assets around €12bn) and **Banco Guipuzcoano**, a small to medium-sized regional bank (especially in the northwest of Spain) with core business in retail and corporate banking. The balance sheet of this bank was around €10bn in 2009.

Appendix 11: Default rate, unemployment rate and GDP rate of Spain, The USA and Europe

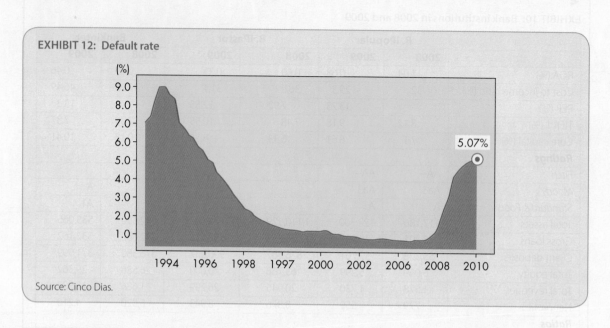

EXHIBIT 12: Default rate

Source: Cinco Dias.

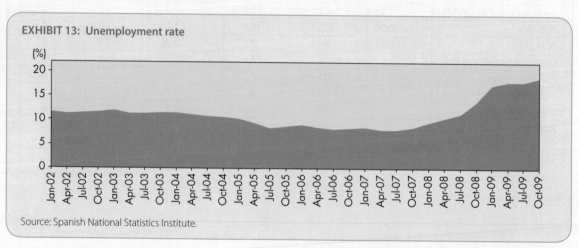

EXHIBIT 13: Unemployment rate

Source: Spanish National Statistics Institute.

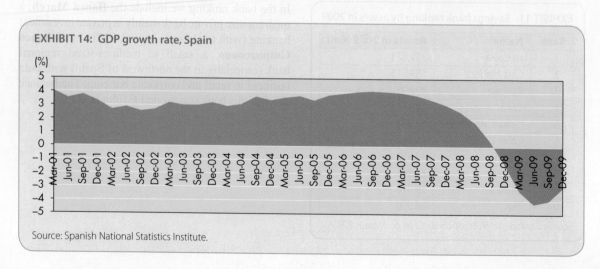

EXHIBIT 14: GDP growth rate, Spain

Source: Spanish National Statistics Institute.

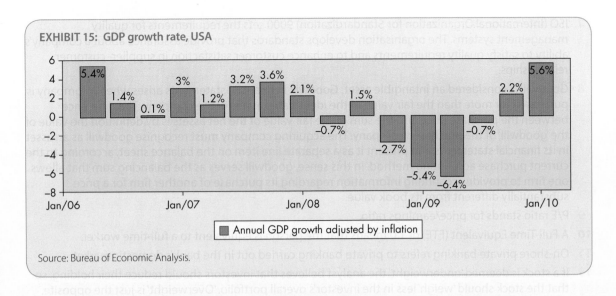

EXHIBIT 15: GDP growth rate, USA

Source: Bureau of Economic Analysis.

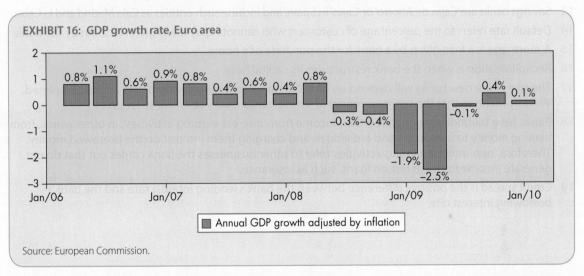

EXHIBIT 16: GDP growth rate, Euro area

Source: European Commission.

NOTES

1 A bank's coverage rate refers to the provisions, or capital, that the bank has on reserve to cover the non-performing loans (NPLs) (loans that are in default or close to being in default).

2 Private banking consists of managing the assets of high net-worth individuals and families.

3 Banco Mediano Español holds the fourth position behind national leaders Banco Santander, BBVA and Banco Popular.

4 The cost-to-income ratio is a key financial measure, particularly important in valuing banks. It shows a company's costs in relation to its income. To get the ratio, divide the operating costs (administrative and fixed costs, such as salaries and property expenses, but not bad debts that have been written off) by operating income. The ratio gives investors a clear view of how efficiently the firm is being run – the lower it is, the more profitable the bank will be. Changes in the ratio can also highlight potential problems: if the ratio rises from one period to the next, it means that costs are rising at a higher rate than income, which could suggest that the company has taken its eye off the ball in the drive to attract more business.

5 SME stands for small and medium-sized enterprises.

6 Non-resident retail banking is for customers from other countries who live in Spain part or all of the year. In Spain these non-residents are mainly northern Europeans.

7   ISO (International Organization for Standardization) 9000 sets the requirements for quality management systems. The organisation develops standards that provide assurance about a company's ability to satisfy quality requirements and to enhance customer satisfaction in supplier–customer relationships.

8   Goodwill is considered an intangible asset. Goodwill in financial statements arises when a company is purchased for more than the fair value of the identifiable assets of the company. The difference between the purchase price and the sum of the fair value of the net assets is by definition the value of the 'goodwill' of the purchased company. The acquiring company must recognise goodwill as an asset in its financial statements and present it as a separate line item on the balance sheet, according to the current purchase accounting method. In this sense, goodwill serves as the balancing sum that allows one firm to provide accounting information regarding its purchase of another firm for a price substantially different from its book value.

9   P/E ratio stands for price/earnings ratio.

10   A Full-Time Equivalent (FTE) of 1.0 means that the person is equivalent to a full-time worker.

11   On-shore private banking refers to private banking carried out in the bank's domestic market.

12   If a stock is deemed 'underweight' the analyst believes that investors should reduce their holding, so that the stock should 'weigh' less in the investor's overall portfolio. 'Overweight' is just the opposite.

13   Savings banks are 'Cajas de Ahorro' or 'Cajas' in Spain, and include such entities as Caja Madrid and la Caixa.

14   Default rate refers to the percentage of customers who cannot repay loans given to them by the bank.

15   A mortgage is a loan given by a bank for the purchase of a home.

16   Recapitalisation is when the bank restructures its capital base.

17   The size of the new banks will depend on how the mergers among saving banks will be completed. We only mention that the business model of saving banks is very sensitive to its size.

18   Banks have traditionally generated their income from 'interest-earning activities'; in other words, from loaning money to businesses and individuals and charging them interest on the borrowed money. Therefore, 'non-interest earning activities' refer to other businesses the bank carries out that do not generate income from interest on loans, such as insurance.

19   Credit spread is the positive difference between the bank's lending interest rate and the bank's borrowing interest rate.

Case written by Federico Marinelli and Joaquín López Pascual of the Colegio Universitario de Estudios Financieros (CUNEF).

This case discussion was made possible though the generous cooperation of Banco Mediano Español. We are grateful to the following people, without whom this case could not have been written: Alvaro Cuervo, Ying Ying Zhang, Fracisco Vallejo Vallejo, Simon James Adams, and all the students of CUNEF who participated in the 2010 Business Competition. The case is intended as a basis for class discussions rather than to illustrate either the effective or ineffective handling of management situations.

Important note to the case reader: this case aims to represent the situation of the Banco Mediano Español in April 2010 during which the national financial system was under full transformation especially for savings banks. In particular at that specific time, the new savings banks regulation had not yet been disclosed by the Spanish regulator. Hence, we only mention this issue and attempt to assess the possible scenarios and their potential impacts on the Banco Mediano Español.

Case 4.5

Luxottica: Excellence in Eyewear Distribution

Company profile

Luxottica is the undisputed world leader in the manufacturing and retail distribution of prescription eyewear and sunglasses. Founded in 1961 by the Italian entrepreneur Leonardo del Vecchio, counting about 65,600 employees worldwide, it is now listed on the New York and Milan stock exchanges. In 2012, revenues are estimated to total €3.9bn and net profit to stand at €279m. The firm owns iconic brands such as Ray-Ban (which was acquired in 1999), Oakley and Vogue, among others, but has also one of the industry's most prestigious portfolios of licensed brands (including brands such as Bulgari, Chanel, Polo Ralph Lauren, Prada, etc). This very well balanced brand portfolio of strong house brands and major luxury licences is one of the major strengths of Luxottica. Another strength is its vertically integrated business

model: Luxottica was born as a manufacturer of frame components but, as early as 1974, Del Vecchio moved his business into the wholesale business and in 1995 towards the retail business (see Exhibit 1).

In 2011 Luxottica managed a wholesale network which covered 130 countries and 40 direct operations through wholesale and retail chains in the world's largest eyewear markets.

The major world areas (USA, Europe, Asia Pacific and Emerging markets) accounted for 58 per cent, 20 per cent, 12 per cent and 10 per cent of its net sales, respectively. Its retail business, with more than 7,000 retail outlets, accounted for around 60 per cent of sales, while wholesale represented 40 per cent of revenues. In 2011 Luxottica distributed approximately 21.8 million prescription frames and approximately 43.7 million sunglasses in over 1,400 styles.

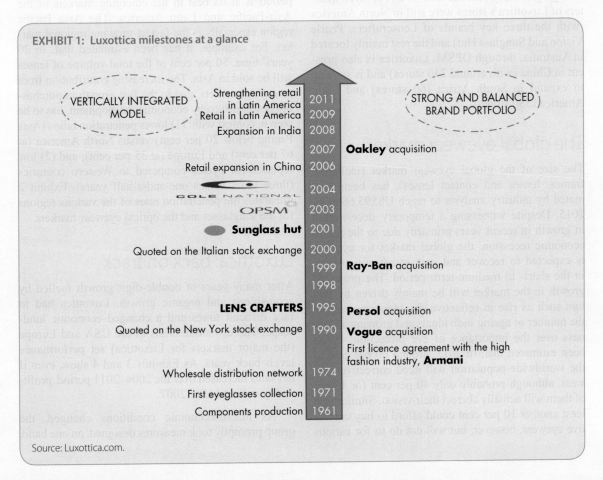

EXHIBIT 1: Luxottica milestones at a glance

VERTICALLY INTEGRATED MODEL		STRONG AND BALANCED BRAND PORTFOLIO
Strengthening retail in Latin America	2011	
Retail in Latin America	2009	
Expansion in India	2008	
	2007	**Oakley** acquisition
Retail expansion in China	2006	
COLE NATIONAL	2004	
OPSM	2003	
Sunglass hut	2001	
Quoted on the Italian stock exchange	2000	
	1999	**Ray-Ban** acquisition
	1998	
LENS CRAFTERS	1995	**Persol** acquisition
Quoted on the New York stock exchange	1990	**Vogue** acquisition
		First licence agreement with the high fashion industry, **Armani**
Wholesale distribution network	1974	
First eyeglasses collection	1971	
Components production	1961	

Source: Luxottica.com.

Luxottica: from Agorodo, a remote place in Italy, to the global stage

Over the years, Luxottica has gradually built up a very strong market position through a series of acquisitions that helped to diversify its business mix from pure manufacturing to a vertically integrated model.

A first-class brand portfolio and a vertically integrated business model

In the wholesale business, Luxottica holds licences for very popular luxury brands (such as Prada, Versace, Bulgari, Donna Karan, Chanel, Dolce & Gabbana, Polo Ralph Lauren, among others) and owns some very strong brands (Ray-Ban, Oakley, Vogue, Persol and Revo, among others).

The retail business has been a major source of growth for Luxottica. The expansion started in 1995 with the acquisition of Lenscrafters in the US market and continued with the takeovers of Sunglass Hut, OPSM and Cole National and is now gradually shifting to new areas, with a particular focus on emerging markets. At the end of 2011, three-quarters of Luxottica's stores were still in North America (with the three key brands of Lenscrafters, Pearle Vision and Sunglass Hut) and the rest mainly located in Australia, through OPSM. Luxottica is also present in China (with around 240 stores) and is starting to expand in South Africa (60 stores) and Latin America (580 stores).

The global eyewear market

The size of the global eyewear market (including frames, lenses and contact lenses), has been estimated by industry analysts to reach US\$95.66bn by 2015. Despite witnessing a temporary deceleration in growth in recent years primarily due to the recent economic recession, the global market for eyewear is expected to recover and gain steady momentum in the short- to medium-term period. The projected growth in the market will be mainly driven by factors such as rise in refractive disorders, increase in the number of ageing individuals and growing awareness over the importance of eye protection. It has been estimated that, in 2015, around 60 per cent of the worldwide population will need corrective eyewear, although probably only 40 per cent (or 1.6bn) of them will actually correct their vision. Similarly, at least another 10 per cent could afford to buy corrective eyewear, however, but will not do so for various

reasons (not aware of need for vision correction, not 'educated', children, etc).

Also, over the years, consumer behaviour and the perception of eye-care has changed. Eyeglasses have transformed their utilitarian image of being a vision correction contraption to being a fashion accessory. Innovative materials for lenses and frames and other technological advances have resulted in several new designs with improved aesthetics, style and quality and have contributed to the trend 'from eye-care to eyewear'.

Being the must-buy for individuals with poor eyesight, optical glasses have traditionally been more resilient to fluctuations in economic climate than sunglasses. Growth in the sunglasses segment is driven by increasing awareness of both the useful benefits (ie eye protection) and trendy appeal of these accessories. The latter also contributes to shorter replacement cycles (from three to five years to one-and-a-half years) as styles change frequently and people also buy sunglasses for different occasions.

Although developed markets such as the USA (45 per cent) and Europe (30 per cent) have been the traditional revenue contributors to the global eyeglasses market, growth in the short- to medium-term period is at its best in the emerging markets of the Asia-Pacific and Latin America. The Asia Pacific region especially is the fastest-growing regional market. For example, it has been estimated that, in 20 years' time, 50 per cent of the total volume of lenses will be sold in Asia. The increasing contribution from emerging markets, due to the fast growth in purchasing power driven by economic development, has to be seen in context with: (1) lower penetration ratios (Asia Pacific below 20 per cent) versus North America (at 67 per cent) and Europe (at 35 per cent); and (2) low replacement cycles compared to Western countries (three years versus one-and-a-half years). Exhibit 2 illustrates the penetration rates of the various regions for the sunglasses and the optical eyewear markets.

Luxottica: back on track

After many years of double-digit growth fuelled by acquisitions and organic growth, Luxottica had to face difficult times and a changed economic landscape. The economic crisis in the USA and Europe (the major markets for Luxottica) set performance levels back years. As Exhibits 3 and 4 show, even if net sales increased over the 2004–2011 period, profitability suffered after 2007.

As macro-economic conditions changed, the group promptly took measures designed, on one hand,

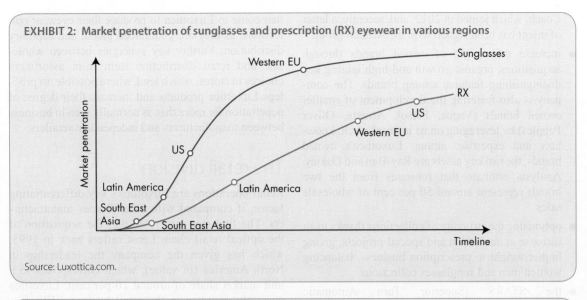

EXHIBIT 2: Market penetration of sunglasses and prescription (RX) eyewear in various regions

Source: Luxottica.com.

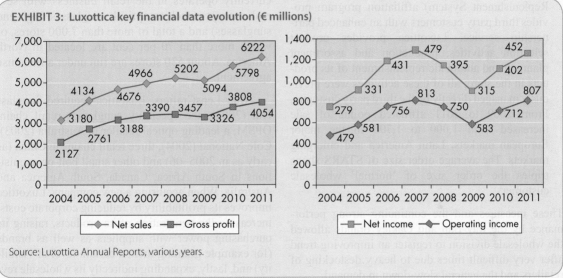

EXHIBIT 3: Luxottica key financial data evolution (€ millions)

Source: Luxottica Annual Reports, various years.

to boost sales and, on the other, to improve efficiency along its entire distribution network.

The wholesale division

Luxottica's wholesale distribution covers over 130 countries across five continents, with more than 40 directly controlled or majority-owned operations in major markets, and approximately 100 independent distributors in other markets. Each wholesale subsidiary operates its own network of sales representatives, normally retained on a commission basis. Customers of the wholesale business are mostly retailers of mid- to premium-priced eyewear, such as independent opticians, optical retail chains, speciality sunglasses retailers and duty-free shops. In North America and some other areas, the main customers also include independent optometrists, ophthalmologists and premium department stores.

Oakley, one of the two major house brands, is distributed also to sporting goods stores and speciality sports stores, including bike, surf, snow, skate, golf and motor sports stores.

In addition to making some of the best brands, with a broad array of models tailored to the needs of each market, Luxottica also seeks to provide its wholesale customers with pre- and post-sale services to enhance their business. These services are designed to deliver the best product and in a time frame and manner that best serve the customers' needs.

Over the past few years, Luxottica has been working to strengthen its brand portfolio through:

- optimisation of the licensed brand portfolio: non-strategic brands have been phased out, others have been added. The latest addition to its portfolio is

Coach, which joined in 2012, and, recently, a letter of intent has been signed with the Armani group

- increase the weight of owned brands through acquisitions, organic growth and highlighting key distinguishing features among brands. The company is also fostering the development of smaller owned brands (Vogue, Persol, Arnette, Oliver Peoples) by leveraging on its internal reach, know-how and expertise; among Luxottica's owned brands, the two key assets are Ray-Ban and Oakley. Analysts estimate that revenues from the two brands represent around 50 per cent of wholesale sales

- optimising the structure of collections thanks to an increase in innovation and special projects, giving higher weight to prescription business, balancing women/men and sunglasses collections

- the STARS (Superior Turn Automatic Replenishment System) affiliation program provides third party customers with an enhanced partnership service. Luxottica provides product selection activities, production and assortment planning and automatic replenishment of its products in the store; all of these activities were previously managed directly by the third party customer. From 2009 to 2011 affiliated points of sale increased from 1,000 to 1,700 in the major European markets, Latin America and emerging markets. The average order size of STARS shops triples the order size of 'normal' wholesale customers.

These measures and the continuing strong performance by the Ray-Ban and Oakley brands allowed the wholesale division to register an improving trend after very difficult times due to heavy destocking of retailers and the general slow-down in demand.

In 2011, the wholesale division represented around 39 per cent of net sales for Luxottica, realised by its portfolio of house and licensed brands. Europe is the main market for the company in the wholesale segment (46 per cent), followed by North America with 24 per cent, Latin America and Asia Pacific.

Luxottica distribution structure, unparalleled in the industry, complements its wholesale distribution with an extensive retail network. Direct distribution in the key markets gives the group a considerable competitive edge, making it possible to maintain close contact with customers and maximise the image and visibility of the group's brands. The group's experience in direct operation of stores in some of its most important countries has given it a unique understanding of the world's eyewear market, but it is also perceived as a strength by the stylists and fashion houses

that come to Luxottica to produce their eyewear collections, as they are guaranteed global and capillary distribution. Further key synergies between wholesale and retail distribution stem from assortment choices in stores, which tend, where possible, to privilege Luxottica products and increase their degree of penetration far more than is normally seen in business between manufacturers and independent retailers.

The retail division

Retail operations are Luxottica's key differentiating factor, if compared with other frames manufacturers. The first step into retail was the acquisition of the optical retail chain LensCrafters back in 1995, which has given the company the leadership in North America (in value), which corresponds to a unit market share of around 20 per cent. Luxottica currently operates in the retail business with several concepts (such as optical, sunglasses, high-end sunglasses) and a total of more than 7,000 stores, of which more than 70 per cent are located in North America. About 530 stores are run under a franchise agreement.

After LensCrafters, Luxottica acquired Sunglass Hut (2001), the speciality sunglasses retail chain, OPSM, a leading optical retailer in Australia (2003), Cole National (2004), three retail chains in China (as early as in 2005–06) and other small bolt-on acquisitions in South Africa, Canada, South America and Australia. When acquiring a new company, Luxottica improves its profitability by reducing corporate costs, increasing the penetration of its products, raising its purchasing power with suppliers as well as brands (for example granting them a certain level of visibility) and, lastly, expanding indirectly its wholesale revenues. Main brands in retail are LensCrafters, Sunglass Hut and OPSM in Australia.

LensCrafters: operates 1,204 optical stores, mainly in North America, but is also present in China and Hong Kong (221 shops). Most LensCrafters stores are located in malls, have an independent optometrist on site and offer the 'ready in one-hour service' on frames and lenses, having a laboratory within the stores.

Sunglass Hut: with 2,504 stores located worldwide, it is the leading destination for sunglasses. Its drivers are store openings (more than 270 stores in 2011, most of them opened through agreement with the department store, Macy's); strengthening presence in core markets (North America, Australia and the UK), emerging (South Africa, Middle East, India) and recently launched ones

EXHIBIT 4: Net sales and operating margin (%) by distribution (€m)

	2004	2005	2006	2007	2008	2009	2010	2011
Retail sales	2,271	3,062	3,294	3,234	3,109	3,139	3,561	3,766
Operating margin (%)	13,1	11,6	13,1	11,2	9,4	11,7	11,9	11,9
Retail sales % of total	67	70	66	62	60	62	61	61
Wholesale sales	1,095	1,310	1,715	1,993	2,092	1,955	2,236	2,456
Operating margin (%)	21,3	23,2	26	26,5	22,1	18,2	20,7	21,5
Wholesale sales % of total	33	30	34	38	40	38	39	39

Source: Luxottica Annual Reports, various years.

(Brazil and Mexico); shops in core markets are corporate shops whereas the latter ones are franchise locations (73 outlets).

Pearle Vision and Pearle franchising: it is one of the largest optical retail chains in North America with 662 stores, 352 of which are franchised. Although LensCrafters and Pearle Vision both address the mid/high-end customer segment, their positioning is complementary according to Luxottica. Pearle Vision focuses on customers' trust in the doctor's experience and the quality of service they receive.

OPSM: the largest of the three optical chains operated in Australia and New Zealand. It is a leading eyewear retail brand for luxury and fashion-minded customers. Luxottica carried out a store restyling and put a new management team in place following two years of sales decline in the region, which was only partially explained by a weakening consumer market. There are 400 stores.

GMO: recently, Luxottica purchased the GMO brand as part of its acquisition of Multiopticas Internacional (Opticas GMO, Econopticas and Sun Planet), a company that owned over 480 eyewear stores. It is present in Latin America as follows: 224 stores in Chile, 145 stores in Peru, 44 stores in Ecuador and 70 stores in Colombia.

Other store concepts: these include stores targeting high-end eyewear (Ilori and The Optical Shop of Aspen, a total of 48 stores in the USA), David Clulow (UK based with 75 stores) and 'O Stores' (around 150 stores) which are not optical stores but help to build the awareness of Oakley as a 'lifestyle brand'.

The sun shines for Luxottica

Hand-in-hand with the streamlining and strengthening of its wholesale and retail business, Luxottica entered and reinforced its presence in emerging markets: these

EXHIBIT 5: Luxottica position by major world area

Europe

20% of total sales
173 stores representing
3% of total retail
21 subsidiaries/46%
of total wholesale

North America

58% of total sales
4,946 stores representing
80% of total retail
6 subsidiaries/24%
total wholesale

Asia and Pacific

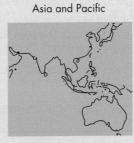

12% of total sales
952 stores representing
15% of total retail
9 subsidiaries/9%
of total wholesale

Rest of the world

10% of total sales
1,179 stores representing
2% of total retail
6 subsidiaries/21%
of total wholesale

Source: Luxottica Annual Report, 2011.

countries currently represent 20 per cent of wholesale revenues, up from 10 per cent in 2005, thanks to key emerging markets such as China, India, Brazil and Mexico. The development is driven by the launch of owned brands, namely Vogue and Oakley, and the enhancing of Ray-Ban. Eyewear penetration rates in these countries are still very low – in Brazil it stands at 22 per cent, in China and India at 7 per cent each – but

the investment in education, sales force and brand awareness is starting to bear fruit.

On the retail side, beside its recent acquisition of OGM in Latin America, Luxottica has started to expand the Sunglass Hut model globally. It aims to open more than 1,500 new locations, moving the American/Australian footprint to a global one.

QUESTIONS

1 Luxottica mainly internationalises through acquisition and subsequent extension of retail chains and direct wholesale operations.
  ● Do you think this will be an adequate strategy in the future?
  ● Which alternative distribution modes could be evaluated in order to accelerate international expansion and penetration of markets? Discuss pros and cons.
2 Would you recommend entering the European market through direct retail? Give reasons for your position.
3 Prepare a region/division roadmap and a related 'action plan'.

FURTHER READING

● www.borsaitaliana.com: industry analyses, various years, various companies.
● www.luxottica.com/en/.
● Luxottica, *Annual Report*, 2007, 2008, 2009, 2010, 2011.
● Luxottica, Press releases, various years.
● Lucia van der Post, 'How To Spend It: Eye-catching Shapes to Put You in the Shade – Expensive Sunglasses are No Longer just for Poseurs; They are becoming an Essential Fashion Accessory', *Financial Times*, 16 May 1992.
● Vanessa Friedman, 'How To Spend It: The Eyes Have It – Sunglasses are Now a Year-round Accessory', *Financial Times*, 3 June 2000.
● Goldman Sachs Global Investment Research, 'Europe: Branded Consumer Goods: Eyewear', 2010.
● www.companiesandmarkets.com.
● http://www.easevision.com/gia-announces-the-eyeglasses-market-outlook-by-2015.html.

This case was written by Birgit Hagen and Antonio Majocchi of the University of Pavia, Italy.

Case 4.6

FedEx versus UPS: Competing with Contrasting Strategies in China

I don't know that I agree that there's a sort of Chinese way and an American way. I think there is clearly more of an entrepreneurial and establishment way ... and China at the moment is a country that is very entrepreneurial in nature. We are more consonant with the new China.[1]

> Frederick W. Smith, Chairman and
> CEO, FedEx Corporation.

UPS expects continued strong and robust growth in China. We take a long-term approach to any expansion and believe the opportunity in China is great enough to overcome any business cycle.[2]

> Jim Kelly, Chairman and CEO, UPS.

Introduction

The US-based FedEx Corporation (FedEx),[3] one of the world's largest logistics solutions providers, announced a money-back guarantee scheme in September 2002 for its customers in China. Under the scheme, FedEx offered full refund of customers' money in case of late delivery of shipments. By introducing this scheme, FedEx became the first international logistics company to offer a money-back guarantee in China.

Analysts were quick to comment that this measure was taken by FedEx to counterattack the move announced by its global competitor, the US-based

United Parcel Service (UPS).[4] In early September 2002 UPS had opened two representative offices in the Chinese cities: Shenzhen and Qingdao. UPS had also announced its plans to open four more offices, in Xiamen, Dongguan, Hangzhou and Tianjin, by early 2003.

For a long time, FedEx and UPS had been arch-rivals in China, competing with each other for more market share in the Chinese logistics market (see Exhibit 1). According to the analysts, FedEx had adopted an aggressive approach to increase its market share in China. The company invested heavily in procuring air routes and in deploying its own aircraft within and outside China for shipping goods. FedEx had also developed a vast distribution network with pickup outlets across China. Until 2001 the company used global advertising campaigns to advertise in China.

By contrast, UPS had followed a more conservative and cautious approach while making inroads into the Chinese market. The company made efforts to position itself as a local company, rather than building an image of a global player. Instead of investing in building its own logistics infrastructure, the company decided to depend on leased facilities. Despite acquiring rights to fly its own plane in 2000, UPS was mostly dependent on its joint-venture relationships to ship goods within and outside China. Analysts felt that UPS' advertising was old-fashioned, even compared with the prevalent standards in China.

Until the late 1990s UPS followed a cautious approach, making limited investment in China compared to that of FedEx. However, with improving business prospects in China following its entry into the World Trade Organization (WTO) in 2001, the company started pursuing the Chinese market aggressively. This helped it in increasing its market presence in China.

Establishing presence in China

According to the Chinese legal regulations, foreign logistics management companies including FedEx and UPS could do business in China only through a

---

EXHIBIT 1: A snapshot of the logistics industry in China (2002)

There are about 1,500 licensed international freight-forwarding operators in China. Of these, 450 are Sino-foreign joint ventures, primarily involved in the management of international freight at the international level. Inland transportation is handled by Chinese freight forwarders – mainly single-truck operations subcontracted by international freight forwarders to move goods from warehouses to ports. Foreign logistics companies face a number of hurdles for conducting business in China. An overview of such hurdles and the future scenario is given below.

Entry barriers
Foreign logistics companies intending to do business in China can enter only through joint ventures with local Chinese companies.

Legal regulations
Foreign companies cannot:

- distribute products other than those they manufacture in China
- own and manage distribution networks, wholesale outlets or warehouses
- conduct customs brokerage and clearance, ground transportation, warehousing and related services outside a transport joint venture
- Hold a majority stake in a joint venture, with limitations on where and how fast joint ventures can expand.

Expected changes over the next decade
The Chinese government promised to make significant improvements to the regulations in the next decade, following the commitments made to the WTO. The promised improvements include the following:

- foreign companies will be allowed to distribute imported products, besides those made in China.
- China has agreed to phase out all restrictions on distribution services within three years. Restrictions on all services auxiliary to distribution will be phased out in three to four years. These include express delivery services, vehicle rental and leasing, freight forwarding, storage and warehousing. Foreigners engaged in these businesses will be able to set up their wholly-owned subsidiaries
- in the most sensitive and protected sectors – chemicals, oil and petroleum – China will provide distribution rights to foreigners within five years.

Source: adapted from David L. Cunningham, Jr, 'FedEx has Ideas for China,' *Nation* (Thailand), 15 October 2002.

---

partnership or joint venture with a local company (see Exhibit 1). Foreign companies were not allowed to run businesses independently in China. Further, they were required to handle only international express cargo business (they were not permitted to carry out cargo-handling business within Chinese cities).

FedEx – developing the services network

FedEx commenced its operations in April 1973 in Memphis, USA. In 1984 FedEx entered China after acquiring Gelco Express International, a UK-based courier company which had operations in Europe and Asia Pacific. During the first decade of its operations in China, FedEx focused on establishing the required infrastructure and distribution network to provide reliable express freight and documentation services.

Rather than targeting leading Chinese companies, FedEx focused on those multinational companies

which had Chinese operations and were already FedEx's customers in the USA or elsewhere. FedEx also targeted those Chinese entrepreneurs who were expanding their business and whom the company believed would readily adopt FedEx's fast and accurate delivery techniques.

To compete effectively with the established local competitors in China, FedEx in its initial years invested heavily in building its own distribution network. In 1989 FedEx invested $880m to acquire Flying Tiger Line Inc (Tiger).[5] The acquisition helped FedEx to get ready access to Tiger's Asian routes, including a high-traffic route between Japan and China.

By 1995 FedEx had started freight operations in China. The company appointed EAS International Transportation Limited (EAS) as a global service participant for China to ship the goods and packages within China. EAS acted as the carrier of the goods and packages of FedEx within China through its network spread across 34 major commercial cities covering nearly 50 per cent of the Chinese population. By mid-1995 FedEx had invested another $67.5m to acquire Evergreen International Airlines,[6] the only cargo carrier with flying rights into China. This allowed FedEx to get ready access to an all-cargo route to serve Chinese customers directly.

Following receipt of a permit from the Civil Aviation Administration of China (CAAC) in January 1996, FedEx earned the distinction of being the only US-based all-cargo carrier with aviation rights to China. Having secured the aviation rights in China and several other Asian countries, FedEx introduced the 'hub and spoke system'[7] in Asia. FedEx had already launched the Asia Pacific hub at Subic Bay, Philippines in September 1995 in order to expand its operations in other Asian countries. This enabled the company to launch an organised distribution system in Asia, called the FedEx AsiaOne network through which 13 major commercial and financial cities in Asia (spokes) were connected. This network enabled FedEx to provide overnight delivery of goods shipped within the Asian countries. The Asian shipments could be further routed to FedEx's global network through the Asia Pacific hub.

In March 1996 FedEx launched its first scheduled air service in China, using its own aircraft in and out of China with bi-weekly flights to Beijing and Shanghai. In September 1996 the two cities were integrated into the FedEx AsiaOne network. These enabled the customers in Shanghai and Beijing to ship and receive packages between China and the USA and the rest of Asia.

In April 1998 FedEx launched the Express Distribution Centers (EDCs) in Beijing and Hong Kong by entering into an agreement with U-Freight Holdings Limited.[8] The EDCs, which were connected to the AsiaOne network, enabled FedEx to ship the goods to the destination through the fastest possible route within 24 hours of the receipt of the order. The EDCs were capable of handling huge volumes of inventory and providing distribution services for fast-moving, high-turnover goods. The primary target customers for the EDCs were those customers who did not possess warehouses and required express transportation facilities to sell their products.

In 1999 FedEx launched the Chinese version of the 'FedEx Internet Ship' software. The software permitted shippers to prepare shipment documentation for consignments to more than 60 countries using their own Internet-linked computers and laser printers. It also allowed online tracking of shipment status through FedEx's website. In February 1999 the tracking application was enhanced to allow FedEx customers to query and receive package status information for up to 25 shipments simultaneously.

By the late 1990s FedEx had gained a strong position in the Chinese market. The company had developed a huge network of purple and orange trucks and express distribution centres. FedEx had built a customer-friendly image by providing its customers with quicker customs clearance and reliable pick-up and delivery services using its own aircraft linking China to extensive regional and global networks.

UPS – developing the services network

In 1907 Jim Casey (Jim), a 19-year-old messenger boy, started American Messenger Company (AMC) below a Seattle sidewalk in the USA, to offer a bicycle messenger service, with an initial investment of $100. His intention was to offer messenger service of the highest quality at the lowest price to customers. In 1913 Jim and Evert McCabe, who led the rival Motorcycle Delivery Company, agreed to merge with AMC and a new company was formed. It was named Merchants Parcel Delivery Company (MPDC). In the 1919 MPDC was renamed as United Parcel Service (UPS).

UPS commenced its operations in China in 1988 through an agent partnership[9] relationship with China's biggest freight forwarder (China National Foreign Trade Transportation Group), popularly known as Sinotrans. As its first move UPS started offering express delivery of small packages and documents. As per the agreement, UPS delivered the packages/documents to China while Sinotrans was responsible for delivering the packages in China.

Unlike FedEx, rather than using its own aircraft, UPS followed a low-investment strategy for almost a decade after its entry into China. During that period, the company entered into alliances with airline companies: Hong Kong Dragon Airlines Ltd[10] and China Eastern Airlines Corp,[11] who delivered the packages to China.

By 1995 UPS had sent its first flight to China from its two hubs located in Hong Kong and Singapore. By the end of 1995, the company had established its presence in 21 cities in China by leveraging on its partnership with Sinotrans. In 1996 UPS entered into a 50–50 joint venture with Sinotrans Beijing Airfreight Forwarding Company (Pekair) in China. Through the joint venture, UPS aimed at improving its market share in the growing air freight market in China. The venture had an initial fleet of 12 vehicles, employee strength of 65 and covered 74 Chinese cities. It planned to offer international shipping of documents and parcels and international cargo transport.

During the late 1990s UPS stepped up its investments in infrastructural facilities and acquisitions in order to expand its presence in China. In June 1998 UPS inaugurated a $2m air hub-facility at the express handling centre at Hong Kong airport. The facility enabled UPS to employ its own people and use its own infrastructure for loading and unloading of goods from its cargo carriers. Through this, the customers could be assured that their baggage was handled carefully, thus further enhancing the reliability of UPS services.

The launch of the hub facility enabled UPS to launch its international shipping processing system in China. The facility was equipped with an electronic data access system, which was interlinked to the Electronic Data Interface (EDI) of the Customs & Excise Department at the airport express centre. Through this, UPS could get its packages cleared by the customs authorities even before their arrival into the airport, thereby saving a lot of time.

In order to offer quicker delivery of the packages, in late 1998 UPS opened two spin-off centres in Hong Kong to sort and deliver packages. As a result, UPS could increase the productivity of its baggage handling by 100 per cent. Commenting on the launch of the facility, Perry Chao, UPS' Managing Director of Hong Kong, said, 'Our strategy is to build a flexible, high-tech, reliable and fully integrated operations network. As a result, our customers will continue to enjoy late cut-off time and speedy delivery even with the airport further away.'[12] UPS also launched a new web-based delivery service, UPS document exchange service, which permitted reliable delivery of documents online through its website (www.exchange. ups.com).

By 1999 UPS had spread its network across 108 cities in China, making it one of the largest networks operated by an international logistics company in China. In January 1999 UPS announced an agreement with Sinotrans to expand its operations to 22 more cities in China. Through this agreement, UPS expanded its network to 130 cities in China, competing directly with FedEx, which had operations in 144 cities at that time. UPS and Sinotrans also signed a memorandum of understanding (MOU) stating that UPS would make additional investments to improve its operations and train its own staff by getting the help of Sinotrans. The company also aimed at enhancing its brand identity in China. By signing the MOU, UPS intended to make its uniformed drivers and brown trucks a common site on the streets of major business centres in China.

In April 1999 UPS entered into a strategic alliance with 7-eleven, a leading convenience store in Hong Kong that operated round-the-clock. Through this agreement, UPS was able to expand its network by 350 locations in Hong Kong. At the stores, express envelopes were accepted, which were charged, depending upon the location to be shipped, irrespective of the weight of the package. In order to encourage the customers to try this service, UPS launched a limited-period promotional campaign in which customers who used the service were given a phone card showing three visuals of the Sydney Olympics.

In November 1999 UPS began a five-times-weekly scheduled express service to Shenzhen. By opening up an express-handling facility at Shenzhen airport, UPS became the first US carrier to be permitted to handle its own express traffic in Shenzhen. During the period 1996–99, according to reports, UPS had made investments of an estimated $400m in China.

The contrasting strategies

In the opinion of analysts, FedEx and UPS established themselves in China in the late 1990s following different corporate styles. The companies followed a significantly different approach, providing alternatives for companies planning to globalise. FedEx believed in tackling foreign competition head-on. UPS believed in partnerships with them. FedEx followed a high-risk approach, investing heavily to build its own manufacturing and distribution systems. UPS was happy to enter into lease agreements with companies already having a presence in China. FedEx's main thrust was on capturing the accounts of its multinational customers operating in China. UPS focused on local customers. To promote its services, FedEx adopted Western-style advertising. UPS tried to build an image of a local company.

Advertising and promotion

Until the mid-1990s the focus on advertising and promotion by both FedEx and UPS was relatively light. However, during the late 1990s, as the competition in the logistics business in China intensified, both FedEx and UPS changed the emphasis to promotion to attract the Chinese customers. However, up to the late 1990s there was a marked distinction in the approach of FedEx and UPS towards advertising and promotion of their services in China.

FedEx adopted an approach which put the emphasis on intensively publicising its service offerings in China. It launched intimidating ad campaigns to attract customers. For example, one of its advertisements in 1997 showed the tail of a FedEx plane parked in front of the Forbidden City saying 'Call FedEx. It's almost forbidden not to'. FedEx concentrated on promoting its service offerings and enhancing brand awareness among the customers in China. For this purpose, it hired a popular media company (OMD)[13] based in Hong Kong.

In contrast to FedEx's approach, UPS placed less emphasis on advertising. It preferred to project itself as a local Chinese company. In a six-week TV campaign in 1997, the company displayed a motorised three-wheeler, a larger van, a brown UPS truck and a Boeing 747 moving together in a line on a runway. This was to project a global image rather than showing itself as an American company. To target Chinese customers outside China, UPS sponsored Chinese New Year celebrations in Toronto and Vancouver, where many Chinese immigrants resided. UPS also sponsored the Olympic Games in China.

Targeting customers

While targeting customers in China, FedEx offered the same standardised logistics services it offered to customers in other foreign countries. However, FedEx seems to have annoyed a few companies in China who expected a personalised approach from the company. Li Ping, an executive at Chinatex Cotton Yarns & Fabrics Import & Export Corporation in Beijing, commented, 'I know they're [FedEx] one of the biggest companies in the US, but that doesn't matter here [in China]. The personal relationship matters most here. You have to talk to customers and make them feel good.... They haven't sent anyone here; so, we don't do business with them.'[14]

FedEx targeted those customers who valued a highly controlled distribution system and wanted constant information about the status of shipments. The company focused on providing solutions to all logistics-related problems of its customers. For instance, in the mid-1990s FedEx noticed that Chinese exporters who shipped goods to the USA faced problems due to their ignorance of the US customs-clearance procedures. This caused unnecessary cost and time overruns since their shipments were held up by the US customs department. FedEx realised that it could cash in on this opportunity to market its pre-clearance service[15] to Chinese exporters.

During July and August 1996 the company conducted seminars in two major Chinese cities (Shanghai and Hong Kong) explaining to customers the customs clearance procedures in the USA and how FedEx's service could solve their problems. This produced a tremendous response and resulted in an increase in shipments from China to the USA.

FedEx's main focus was on providing its customers with innovative and value-added services. For instance, in September 2000 FedEx pioneered the launch of two new services for Chinese customers: the AsiaOne and the North American Next Day Delivery. The new services enabled customers in Beijing, Shanghai, Guangzhou, Shenzhen and other neighbouring cities to deliver their packages to 15 Asian cities (through AsiaOne) and major US and Canadian cities (through North American Next Day Delivery) on the next working day. As a result, FedEx became the only company in China to offer such services. Commenting on FedEx's focus on providing best service to customers, Marco Lee, Managing Director (Regional Sales – China & Mid-Pacific) of FedEx said, 'FedEx always wants to add value to our customers' businesses. We are here not only to provide solutions to our customers; we are also committed to help them increase efficiency.'[16]

By contrast, UPS followed a personalised approach in targeting local Chinese customers. It attempted to adapt its services to the customs and traditions of Chinese customers. For instance, the company noticed that Chinese customers attached a great deal of importance to interpersonal relationships. Accordingly, UPS sales personnel first made a friendly approach to the customers, explaining to them how the services worked, and only then went on to strike deals. Even the courier personnel of UPS were recognised for their customer-friendly attitude. This approach enabled the company to develop a very good rapport with Chinese customers and encouraged those who patronised other companies to shift to UPS. For instance, an advertising executive from a Chinese company shifted his account from a government-owned mail service company to UPS when a UPS executive approached him and explained the utility (both in terms of convenience and cost) of using UPS's services for their business operations.

The investments made

Since its entry into China, FedEx had invested heavily in building its services network in China, adopting a long-term approach. Wilson Chung, general manager of FedEx China said, 'China is one of the most important markets for FedEx. We are dedicated to continually investing in this market.'[17] However, the company faced a major setback with the South East Asian currency crisis during 1997–98. Following significant currency devaluations in the South East Asian countries, FedEx reported its first quarterly loss (quarter ending February 1998) on international operations since 1996. This was largely attributable to the high investments made in its extensive air network in Asia, coupled with declining cargo volume and revenues from troubled Asian countries. Joseph M. Pyne (Vice-President – Marketing) of UPS, was quick to comment: 'Because of the investment [FedEx] made, they're almost stuck in that market. That's the plan they have to live with. We're looking at the market and moving with it in China.'[14]

In contrast to the FedEx approach, UPS decided to make investments according to the market conditions in China. Up until 1997 UPS had invested significantly less compared to FedEx in China. UPS had stepped up its operations as the demand increased, sacrificing some market share in its limited risk strategy. Lacking its own air service, UPS was unable to offer customers in China the range of logistical services that FedEx could offer. The management of UPS always felt that, if business prospects in China improved later, the company could fly its own aircraft in and out of China. The company's low investment strategy in China saved it from any major losses from the South East Asian currency crisis. As freight volumes reduced in China, UPS simply reduced the space it leased in other companies' planes.

FedEx felt that its high-investment strategy had helped in gaining more market share in China. According to Air Cargo Management Group, a Seattle-based consultancy, by mid-1998 FedEx had captured 13 per cent of the express market in China, excluding Hong Kong, while UPS had less than a 5 per cent share. Alan B. Graf, FedEx's chief financial officer commented: 'We knew it was risky when we built so much capacity, but we're staying. And that has just got to have a long-term payoff.'[14]

Logistics industry in China: improving prospects

China was viewed as the logistics industry's most important emerging market. According to an industry analyst at Merge Global Incorporated,[18] an Arlington, US-based research company, China's air-cargo market was the world's fifth largest and its emerging express market was valued at $400m in 1998. According to studies conducted during the late 1990s, China's demand for time-definite express freight was projected to grow by 20 per cent per year till 2002 – much faster compared to the global air-freight market.

By 2000 competition in the logistics industry in China had intensified. Both FedEx and UPS were facing competition from MNCs like DHL, and China's state-owned enterprises like China Post. Following the decision of the Chinese government to join the World Trade Organization in 2001, the competition in the industry intensified further. With the removal of a number of rules and regulations which had protected China's government-owned logistics companies, the business prospects for multinational logistics companies improved significantly.

With the improved business prospects, UPS decided to follow a more aggressive approach to expand its market presence in China. The company lobbied intensively in the USA to secure a right to operate its own flights directly into China. The company also decided to invest significantly in infrastructural facilities in the new millennium.

In November 2000 the US Department of Transportation (DOT) granted UPS air rights to operate direct flights from the USA to China. UPS was allowed six flights between the USA and China in a week. In December 2000, following DOT's decision to designate UPS as the fourth US air-carrier to service the China market, FedEx appealed to US DOT to allow it one more flight per week to China.

Rising competition

Analysts felt that granting of air rights to UPS would further intensify the competition in China and enable major US freight service carriers to access the Chinese market by offering low-cost and better service. Although FedEx had not questioned DOT's decision to permit six flights to UPS, the company objected to the awarding of three flights to United Airlines and Northwest Airlines, its other competitors in China. FedEx called DOT's decision 'fundamentally unfair' under the pretext that its contribution to export growth in the USA was significantly high when compared with that of Northwest Airlines or United Airlines.

In March 2001 UPS announced the launch of six weekly flights between China and the USA using Boeing 747 aircraft, directly servicing Beijing and Shanghai. Four weekly flights were to start from Ontario International airport, California and the other two at Newark, New Jersey. On 1 April 2001 the first flight landed in China. Commenting on the event, Jim Kelly, Chairman and CEO of UPS, said, 'This is the first time ever that a US cargo carrier will fly directly from the US to China. We believe this designation is a sign of the growing importance of global trade and UPS's place in the new global marketplace. With these new flights, UPS will offer the broadest portfolio of services to customers shipping to and from

China.'[16] The launch of the service turned out to be a successful move by UPS as its business in the US-China region grew by an estimated 40 per cent soon after the launch.

Reacting to this move by UPS, FedEx announced an additional aircraft to its existing fleet of 11 aircraft. In April 2001 FedEx also launched the Shanghai Express Freighter service. The newly launched flight service enabled FedEx to improve its services in the express segment between eastern China and the USA by reducing the shipment time by three to four hours. FedEx also stated its plans to inaugurate new infra-structure facilities in four Chinese states: Nanjing, Hangzhou, Dongguan and Ningbo.

UPS further intensified its promotional activities following the launch of its direct flight to China. In May 2001 UPS launched an advertising campaign developed by respected advertising agency, McCann-Erickson.[19] In the campaign titled 'Brown Survey,' a woman was asked to identify what immediately came into her mind when a series of colours were flashed at her. When the colour brown flashed up, she instantly related it to reliability, and then to UPS. The campaign focused on creating a unique brand identity for UPS, as UPS was traditionally recognised by its fleet of brown trucks, which offered reliable service to the customers, through its customer-friendly employees and couriers.

In an attempt to sell B2B e-commerce solutions to cost-conscious Chinese businesses, UPS launched the 'Customer Automation Program' in June 2001. Under this programme, UPS offered to computerise the business units of its customers by providing the required PCs and software and by linking them to the UPS shipping systems free of cost. The customers could print their own shipping labels. By doing this, UPS enabled its customers to understand the cost benefits of purchasing UPS B2B e-commerce solutions.

To further promote its business and compete effectively with UPS, FedEx implemented further innovative ideas. For instance in mid-2001, in association with OMD, FedEx began to sponsor popular TV shows in China. The first to be sponsored was a popular television game show, *Who Wants to be a Millionaire*,[20] aired on Asia Television (ATV). The purpose of choosing the game show for sponsorship was to associate FedEx with speed and accuracy – the two key ingredients emphasised in the game show. The effort paid off for FedEx, as within three months of sponsoring the show, its top-of-mind recall[21] increased by 42 per cent among viewers in China. Encouraged by this success, FedEx sponsored another game show on ATV, *The Vault*. This interactive game show was used to display the FedEx brand as a backdrop through an attractive FedEx motion TV billboard. This initiative was successful as FedEx's brand awareness increased and the company was able to position its services in terms of their speed and accuracy.

In October 2001 FedEx introduced a unique service in China. The company inaugurated a massive 6,080-square metre FedEx-DTW Express Center at Shanghai Pudong International Airport. The integrated warehouse management system[22] at the centre comprised a sorting and distribution system which employed state-of-the-art wireless technology to enhance productivity and provide accurate information. The system could handle 6,000–12,000 packages per hour. Analysts concluded that FedEx launched this system to cope with the increasing volume of goods and packages following China's entry into the WTO in 2001.

To counter FedEx's move, in December 2001 UPS launched two new services: UPS Signature Tracking TM and UPS Worldwide Express Plus TM. The signature tracking service provided proof of delivery of the package to the recipient (their signature) within minutes of its delivery.[23] This service was targeted primarily at business customers who needed to furnish proof of delivery to effect other business transactions. The UPS Worldwide Express Plus TM enabled shipping of packages or documents from China to any major US city next day by 8 am or to other non-metropolitan cities in the USA, 13 European countries and Canada by 8.30 am.

The rivalry intensifies

The rivalry between FedEx and UPS to grab more market share of the Chinese logistics market further intensified in 2002. In April 2002 UPS launched a new intra-Asia hub in the Philippines. The new hub along with two other UPS hubs located in Singapore, Hong Kong and Taipei comprised the worldwide network of UPS hubs. This move enabled UPS to enhance significantly its operational capacity in China, as well as to increase its ability to serve Chinese customers by offering quicker and more reliable service.

In May 2002, following the launch of an intra-Pacific air hub in the Philippines, which complemented the other hub facilities in Taiwan, Singapore and Hong Kong, UPS launched an advertising campaign titled 'Asia', showcasing UPS as an integrated logistics-solutions provider. This campaign, like the previous ad campaign, stressed the reliability of the UPS service. It also provided a glimpse at the advanced technology employed at UPS, including the WAP-enabled, package-tracking technology.

In September 2002 FedEx planned to further improve its services in Southern China and the Pearl River Delta region by upgrading the aircraft serving Shenzhen from a DC-10 to an MD-11. This move also increased the freight capacity by 30 tons.

In order to understand the needs of the Chinese customers in smaller cities better and to offer these customers express delivery service of higher quality, in September 2002 UPS opened two offices in Chinese cities: Shenzhen and Qingdao. UPS followed this by opening an office in the southern Chinese city of Xiamen in October 2002, in an effort to further penetrate the local Chinese market. Another significant factor of this launch was that all the employees of the office were hired locally.

Status in 2003

By 2003 the competition between FedEx and UPS was at its peak. Both the companies had been aggressively pursuing the Chinese market by regularly announcing new and better services, agreements and tie-ups. Both the companies continuously revised their strategies in answer to the moves announced by their competitor.

In January 2003 FedEx announced an agreement with Kodak to offer self-delivery services in 28 Kodak Express Shops in Shanghai. FedEx was the first company to offer express shipment delivery services in a retail context. The Kodak shops that were selected in Shanghai were mainly located in business centres and high-class residential areas, where there was greater demand for these services. FedEx's packaging and shipping documents service was available in-store so that consumers could handle the express shipment (below 2.5 kg) on their own with the assistance of the Kodak shop's trained staff.

In January 2003 UPS entered into an agreement with Yangtze River Express Airlines Company (Yangtze),[24] a Chinese cargo airline. According to the terms of the agreement, Yangtze would provide regular flights to link UPS hub in Shanghai with four major Chinese cities: Beijing, Qingdao, Xiamen and Guangzhou. The agreement required six Boeing 737 flights each week on a Shanghai–Xiamen–Guangzhou–Shanghai route. In March 2003 the route was changed to Shanghai–Beijing–Qingdao–Shanghai. This agreement enabled UPS to offer one-day faster service and more reliability for international shipments.

In June 2003 FedEx entered into agreements with two Chinese companies, Trade Port[25] and Sun Logistics,[26] in an attempt to improve its services. The agreement enabled FedEx to offer faster delivery of urgent packages by loading and unloading such goods at the 40,000-square-foot Trade Port facility located very close to the airport. This proximity to the airport saved cost and time for customers. In the same month FedEx announced plans to expand its business to 100 more cities in China by the end of 2003. The company expected to register revenue growth rates of 30 per cent in China over the following five years.

In June 2003 UPS signed an agreement with Lucent Technologies, a US company that designed and delivered networks for communication service providers, to undertake management of UPS logistics operations in the Asia Pacific region. In the same month UPS also announced plans to enhance its network from 21 to 40 cities in the Asia Pacific region by the end of 2003. The company also announced plans to open 20 more offices in 2003.

Thanks to better understanding of local conditions and its aggressive investment strategy during the past couple of years, UPS had been able to increase its market share among its existing customers and to attract new customers. The efforts made by UPS in China reaped positive rewards. The company's revenue increased by 56 per cent in 2001 (see Exhibit 2). For the fourth quarter, ending December 2002, UPS registered a significant growth of 60 per cent in revenue, with exports in China growing by 40 per cent. According to unconfirmed reports, the market share in 2003 of both FedEx and UPS had increased in China.

EXHIBIT 2: Revenues of top five logistics companies operating in China

Company/revenues	2000 (RMB-million)	2001 (RMB-million)	Growth (%)
China Couriers Service Company	1,562	1,600	2.4
DHL-Sinotrans	510	749	46.9
Federal Express Corporation	210	299.9	42.7
UPS	160	249.7	56.0
TNT Skypak-Sinotrans Ltd	110	149.9	36.3

Source: 'Couriers in China,' *Euromonitor*, August 2002; executive summary, www.euromonitor.com.

QUESTIONS

1 Considering the Chinese environment, analyse the UPS strategy in China in comparison with that of FedEx. Do you think it helped it to capture the local market?

2 Is China the right market for services firms to use a stepwise investment approach?

3 Which company do you think will take the lead in the Chinese market and why?

FURTHER READING

- 'Pass the Parcel', *Economist*, 18 March 1995.
- 'FedEx Gets Aviation Rights to China', *Asian Business Review*, October 1995.
- 'FedEx US Customs Brokerage Specialist Shared with Asian Shippers the Efficient Way of Sending Goods to the US', www.fedex.com, 9 August 1996.
- Michael White, 'Going UPS in China', *World Trade*, August 1996.
- Douglas A. Blackmon and Diane Brady, 'Orient Express: Just How Hard Should a US Company Woo Foreign Markets?' *Wall Street Journal*, 6 April 1998.
- 'UPS in China', pandaexpress.ups.com, 2 August 1999.
- 'FedEx JV Cements Expansion', *Export Today's Global Business*, January 2000.
- 'Choose Competition in China Trade', *Detroit News*, 1 May 2000.
- 'FedEx's Hub of Supply Chain Activity', www.ebnonline.com, 10 May 2000.
- 'UPS Appears Set to Win Battle for China Air Routes', *Wall Street Journal*, 22 September 2000.
- 'FedEx to Expand Service in China', *XINHUA*, 22 September 2000.
- Keith Wallis, 'Cargo "Capacity Crunch" Seen', *Hong Kong Imail*, 15 December 2000.
- Keith Wallis, 'FedEx Mulls Links to Mainland Carriers', *Hong Kong Imail*, 8 February 2001.
- 'UPS Begins Direct Service to China,' www.newswire.ca, 30 March 2001.
- Kristin S. Krause, 'Battle for China Begins', *Traffic World*, 2 April 2001.
- 'Foreign Express Companies Make the Cake Bigger', *China Franchise News*, www.chinalaw.cc, 18 April 2001.
- Jim Galligan, 'Express Giants UPS, FedEx Depend on Cargo to Set their Tables for a Chinese Feast', www.ttnews.com, 16 May 2001.
- Wang Yan, 'Foreign Businesses Eye China's Express Delivery Market', www.bizshanghai.com, 1 June 2001.
- Anne Chen, 'Scaling the Wall', www.eweek.com, 18 June 2001.
- P.T. Bangsberg, 'FedEx Planning Expansion in China,' *JoC Week*, 4 September 2001.
- 'FedEx Unveils Biggest Express Center in China', *People's Daily*, www.china.org.cn, 22 October 2001.
- 'FedEx Plans More Flights to Japan', *China Economic Review*, May 2002.
- 'FedEx to Cover 300 Chinese Cities in 5 yrs', www.chinafair.org.cn, 9 October 2002.
- David L. Cunningham, Jr., 'FedEx Has Ideas for China', *Nation* (Thailand), 15 October 2002.
- Keith Wallis, 'Express Cargo Teams Target Curbs', *Hong Kong Imail*, 30 October 2002.
- 'UPS Opens Representative Office in Xiamen', www.ups.com, 30 October 2002.

- Kristin S. Krause, 'Hong Kong Competition', *Traffic World*, 18 November 2002.
- Lara L. Sowinski, 'Good Things Come in Small Packages', www.worldtrademag.com, 1 December 2002.
- 'OMD's Chan drives FedEx Branding with Sponsorship', *Media Asia*, 13 December 2002.
- 'FedEx Offers Money-back Guarantee in China', www.dragonventure.com, 2002.
- 'FedEx Opens Express Center in Pudong', www.tdctrade.com, 2002.
- William Armbruster, 'Questions & Answers with David L. Cunningham Jr.', *Journal of Commerce*, 20 January, 2003.
- 'FedEx Rolls Out New Asia Shipping Service', www.ebnonline.com, 24 April 2003.
- 'Lucent Signs Five-year Pact with UPS Supply Chain Solutions', www.logisticsfocus.com, 9 June 2003.
- 'What Happens When One of the World's Largest Countries Meets the World's Largest Transportation Company?' www.chinaquest.ups.com.
- Press Releases, January 1996 to June 2003, www.fedex.com.
- Press Releases, January 1997 to June 2003, www.ups.com.

NOTES

1 As quoted in Douglas A. Blackmon and Diane Brady, 'Orient Express: Just How Hard Should a US Company Woo Foreign Markets', *Wall Street Journal*, 6 April 1998.

2 As quoted in 'UPS begins direct service to China', www.newswire.ca, 30 March 2001.

3 FedEx is one of the world's largest express transportation companies, providing information and logistics solutions services. For the financial year ending May 2003, the company generated revenues of $22.5bn and net income of $1.47bn.

4 UPS is one of the world's largest express carrier and package delivery companies. It is also a leading global provider of specialised transportation and logistics services. For the financial year ended December 2002, UPS generated revenues of $31.3bn and a net income of $3.18bn.

5 Founded in 1945 in the USA as a coast to coast freight carrier, Tiger was one of the largest air cargo airlines in the country. By the time of its acquisition by FedEx, it was known as an all-cargo airline with flying rights to 21 countries.

6 Headquartered at Oregon, USA, EIA owned one of the largest all-cargo fleets in the cargo business, with operations across the world.

7 According to the system, on a particular day, packages from various cities were sent to a central location, called a hub, where they would be sorted out and then sent across by plane to their ultimate destinations, called spokes, for delivery by early morning next day.

8 A global transportation service provider that provides customs clearance, warehousing, domestic distribution and other value-added services.

9 A relationship between two companies in which the agent company acts on behalf of the principal company, on the basis of mutually agreed terms.

10 Founded in 1985, Dragon Air served 27 passenger destinations across Asia with one of the most advanced aircraft fleets in the region.

11 China's second-largest air carrier, located in Shanghai.

12 As quoted in the press release, 'UPS Opens Hub Facility at Airport Express Centre: First Express Carrier Granted Self-Handling Right', www.ups.com, 30 June 1998.

13 Founded in 1996, OMD is the global media partner of the three leading advertising agencies in the world (BBDO, DDB and TBWA). It is a unit of Omnicom Group, the largest marketing and corporate communications company in the world.

14 As quoted in Douglas A. Blackmon and Diane Brady, 'Orient Express: Just How Hard Should a US Company Woo Foreign Markets,' *The Wall Street Journal*, 6 April 1998.

15 Through this service, the details regarding goods shipped into a country were intimated in advance to the customs authorities of that country prior to landing of the flight. This enabled faster customs clearance.

16 As quoted in the press release, 'FedEx US Customs Brokerage Specialist Shared with Asian Shippers the Efficient Way of Sending Goods to the US', in www.fedex.com, dated 6 August 1996.

17 As quoted in, 'FedEx to Expand Services in China', *Xinhua*, 22 September 2000.

18 A specialised strategy consulting firm, which focuses exclusively on developing competitive strategy for firms in the freight transportation and logistics industries. Its clients include many of the world's largest producers of transportation and logistics services.

19 Based in the USA, it is one of the world's leading integrated brands communications company with operations spread across the world.

20 The interactive game show comprised a series of rounds in which questions were shot at the participants, who were required to reply with the right answer as quickly as possible.

21 The immediate company or its brand which flashes to mind when confronted with an industry. For example, the brand which might immediately flash when one thinks of a cola drink might be Coke or Pepsi.

22 The automated system enables unloading and loading of goods, their sorting and their customs clearance with minimum physical effort.

23 Upon receiving the package, the recipient's signature was taken and converted into a digital format and displayed online. This served as the proof of delivery.

24 Yangtze River Express is 85 per cent controlled by a unit of Hainan Airlines Co. American Aviation fund, controlled by international financier George Soros, is Hainan Airlines' biggest shareholder, with a 14.8 per cent stake.

25 Trade Port Hong Kong is a logistics company, backed by an international conglomerate of prestigious companies, including Fraport AG (Frankfurt Airport Services Worldwide), Schiphol Group (Schiphol Amsterdam Airport), China National Aviation Corporation (CNAC), and Hongkong Land (a listed property developer and part of the Jardine Matheson Group), which possess good track records in specialised fields such as air logistics management, air transportation management, airline management, airport terminal management, and property development and management.

26 A logistics company, started on 28 August 2000, which offers a one-stop logistics service by consolidating logistics resources and expertise, infrastructure strengths and web-based technology.

Case 4.7
Tetra Pak's Packaging Innovations

The Tetra Pak package portfolio consists of 11 different packaging systems.

© Tetra Pak.

'At Tetra Pak, innovation is the result of the total process of developing an idea into a product or a new way of working which adds value to the business.'

www.tetrapak.com

'A good package should save more than it costs.'[1]

Dr Rubin Rausing, Founder, Tetra Pak

A company on an award-winning spree

On 2 April 2003, Tetra Pak Inc, the Sweden-based liquid food packaging company, received the 'EAFA[2] (European Aluminium Foil Association) Foil Pack of 2002 Award' in the EAFA packaging trophy award ceremony, for its product 'Tetra Recart'. This innovative product was the world's first fully retortable[3] carton system made for commercial use. EAFA's panel of judges regarded Tetra Recart as a 'significant advance in the packaging of retorted food products and one that could change the picture of this sector considerably'.[4]

Appreciating the innovative Tetra Recart, EAFA called it a 'groundbreaking and flexible' product since 'it saved significant space, weight and logistical costs throughout the whole packaging and retailing cycle'. Commenting on the benefits the new packaging system offered its customers, company officials said, 'Serving as an alternative to traditional metal, glass, and plastic-based packages, Tetra Recart offers a competitive advantage to manufacturers of solid foods and liquid foods with particulates such as fruits, vegetables, ready-to-eat foods, and pet food.'[4]

In the previous year (August 2002), Tetra Recart had received the 'DuPont Diamond Award', the highest packaging honour, for being the world's first retortable carton packaging system. This packaging honour was awarded to Tetra Pak after an international, independent judging panel evaluated various entries on criteria such as the degree of innovation and its potential impact on the food industry and consumers (refer to Exhibit 1 for the benefits Tetra Recart offered to consumers, retailers and manufacturers).

Compared to other packaging options (tin cans and paperboard packs) available till its introduction in Italy in 2001, Tetra Recart was much lighter. In addition its manufacturing cost was lower than that incurred for glass or tin containers because it used less costly material like paper pulp, plastic and aluminium. It had a laser perforated closure strip that could be torn away, providing an easy opening at the top. And its attractive look gave products a unique shelf presence. Analysts felt that the packet's rectangular shape provided ample space for brand managers to display high resolution graphics, which added to the product's appeal (refer to Exhibit 1 for a picture). The Tetra Recart was heat and moisture resistant and also environmentally friendly since cartons could be recycled.

Analysts observed that by making the retortable packaging option commercially viable, Tetra Recart had benefited the makers of many food products such as soups, ready meals and pet food. Commenting on this, Jan Juul Larsen, Managing Director, Tetra Recart

abroad, and this award is a wonderful entree into the US market.'[6] Analysts felt that the new packaging system would help the company grow further in terms of market share and also help it expand its business to providing packaging solutions to the food industry.

Though Tetra Pak was indeed happy with the above developments, such recognition and fame seemed to have become routine for the company. Its over-five-decade history was marked with many such

---

EXHIBIT 1: The Tetra Recart package

Source: www.tetrapak.com.

Tetra Recart – benefits derived by the consumers:

- Easy to open as the package does not require any tools to open and easy to use as the contents can be easily poured from the wide-mouthed opening.
- The package is easy to carry, is lightweight and has a convenient shape.
- Contents remain fresh for a long period without refrigeration.
- Easy to dispose off and can be recycled.

The manufacturers:

- Can be used for product differentiation and product revitalisation.
- Offers high print quality; the rectangular shape offers ample space for communication.
- Manufacturers can have a single supplier for packages for all product lines.

The retailers:

- The lightweight and rectangular shape makes it convenient for stacking and distribution.
- Has long shelf life without refrigeration.

Source: adapted from information available on www.tetrapak.com.

---

division of Tetra Pak, Sweden, said, 'We have discovered that there are many good ideas out there in the food industry, but so far the packaging options available are not really doing the job. We feel that this is the purpose of Tetra Recart – to help package good ideas.'[5]

Commenting on Tetra Recart's growing popularity, Steve Hellenschmidt, General Manager, Tetra Recart division of Tetra Pak, USA, said, 'Tetra Pak is constantly working to provide our customers with the best packaging solution in the marketplace. We already have seen great success with the Tetra Recart system

---

EXHIBIT 2: Tetra Pak fact sheet (2002)

Net sales in 2002 (m)	7,543
Number of Tetra Pak packages delivered in 2002 (m)	98,076*
Number of litres delivered in Tetra Pak packages in 2002 (m)	56,246*
Number of employees	20,900
Factories for packaging machine assembly	14
Production plants for packaging and packaging material	63
Number of countries covered	More than 165
Market companies (those focusing on marketing-related operations)	77
R&D centres	20
Service centres	59
Packaging machines in operation	8,440
Packaging machines delivered in 2002	739
Processing units in operation	18,100
Processing units delivered in 2002	22,49
Distribution equipment in operation	12,171
Distribution equipment delivered in 2002	12,80

* Plastic packages not included.
Source: www.tetrapak.com.

Tetra Pak – mission statement

- We work for and with our customers to provide preferred processing and packaging solutions for food.
- We apply our commitment to innovation, our understanding of consumer needs and our relationships with suppliers to deliver these solutions, wherever and whenever food is consumed.
- We believe in responsible industry leadership, creating profitable growth in harmony with environmental sustainability, and good corporate citizenship.

Source: www.tetrapak.com.

innovations that had radically transformed the packaging and processing solutions available for food product businesses across the world. For many decades, the company had enjoyed a monopoly in the carton packaging industry (it reportedly controlled more than half the European market in 2002). It was insulated against competition from other companies due to its ownership of numerous patents and a huge loyal customer base.

Due to the above factors, Tetra Pak had even become a generic brand for the food packaging industry. Not surprisingly, by 2002, Tetra Pak had emerged as a €7.54bn[7] enterprise with operations in over 165 countries and 20,900 employees (refer to Exhibit 2 for the company's mission statement and a few key facts).

The story of Tetra Pak: a 'classic' breakthrough

The roots of Tetra Pak can be traced back to Akerlund & Rausing (A&R), a packaging company established in 1920 in Sweden by Ruben Rausing and Erik Akerlund. Since its inception, A&R played an integral role in the way business was conducted in Sweden, thanks to its innovative packaging and distribution systems. In fact, the company is believed to be one of the catalysts for the modernisation of the country's distribution and retailing systems. A&R's contribution to introducing concepts like self-service, convenience shopping and supermarkets in Sweden was reported to be noteworthy by company watchers.

A&R primarily worked towards replacing the bulk selling of unpacked products with consumer-friendly packaging. Though the company packaged many products like sugar, flour and salt, two products that it gave a lot of attention to were milk and cream. Milk and cream, being perishable items, were traditionally sold in glass bottles or over the counter (in loose form). However, when manual services were replaced by self-service, following the emergence of supermarkets, there arose a need for more manageable and practical packaging for these products – a type of packaging that would be convenient for distribution (by manufacturers and retailers) and easy to carry for consumers. As consumer awareness regarding hygienic packaging increased, the demand for alternative packaging methods became stronger.

A&R planned to build a packet that was not only hygienic, but also cost effective (using minimum material). Since 1944 researchers at the company had been investigating the possibility of creating packaging in different geometrical forms to meet these twin objectives. Finally, A&R settled for a tetrahedron[8]

shape for the new packaging. Different factors such as how the packet would be formed, filled and sealed and the type of material to be used for fluid tight packing were identified. The company built a machine to manufacture these packages and also developed a six-sided distribution case (carton) that carried 18 tetrahedron packs.

After over a decade of research and collaboration with Swedish paper mills, a suitable material was finally decided upon to make the packs. A&R's specifications for this material were exhaustive: it had to be rigid but formable, have a uniform thickness and a flexible surface for lamination, it had to withstand dampness and moisture, provide protection against light and not give out any bad smell or taste. It also had to have an outer surface which was suitable for printing on and making colour impressions. Commenting on the tedious and long process of invention, Rausing said, 'Doing something that nobody else had done before is quite hard.'[9]

In 1951 A&R established Tetra Pak in association with Erik Wallenberg as a subsidiary company. In May 1951 the new tetrahedron packaging system was unveiled to the world as 'Tetra Classic'. The product was well received and generated a lot of interest in the media. By September 1952 a factory in the city of Lund began using Tetra Classic to package cream. Within a short period of time, many more dairy companies in Sweden began installing Tetra Pak machines and selling cream in the Tetra Classic cartons.

In 1954 the manufacture of half-litre tetrahedron milk cartons began at two factories (Mjlkcentralen and Stockholm) in Sweden. The breakthrough product gained popularity outside Sweden as well, and in 1954 Tetra Pak machines were exported to Germany. In June 1955 the first commercial production of tetrahedron milk packages (300ml) began at Helsingborg in Sweden. While Tetra Pak's packaging became popular in the corporate world because it was very cost effective and made optimal usage of material, it was liked by customers because it was hygienic and easy to handle.

In order to cater to the increasing demand, Tetra Pak soon moved into a huge factory in Lund, which went on to become the hub for many more innovations and inventions at the company in the future.

The story of Tetra Pak: the 'aseptic' advantage

In 1956, having tasted success with the milk and cream packaging initiatives, Tetra Pak began working towards creating packages for other liquid foods.

The company was aware of the fact that, while Tetra Classic was hygienic, it could not keep food fresh for long periods. Researchers at the company thus began working on 'Aseptic Packaging Technology'. They conceived the idea of sterilising the package itself before filling it with liquid food. This way liquid food could be preserved for a longer period of time without using preservatives or refrigeration.

Researchers at Tetra Pak identified three basic materials for making aseptic packs: paper, polyethylene and aluminium foil, each having its own benefits. While paper provided strength and stiffness to the package, polyethylene acted as a barrier to microorganisms and made the package tight, and aluminum foil prevented the food from deteriorating by keeping air, light and odour out. These materials were put together to manufacture a package that was safe, efficient and lightweight (refer to Exhibit 3 for the benefits of aseptic packaging).

Since aseptic packaging preserved liquid food for longer periods without refrigeration, it prevented food wastage. Reportedly, around 30 per cent of liquid food was wasted through improper packing and insufficient cooling during transportation. Since aseptic packaging preserved liquid food for longer periods without refrigerated distribution, food manufacturers could reduce costs incurred due to pilferage and wastage. Tetra Pak's research finally paid off in 1961, when the first aseptic filling machine was launched for commercial use (packaging bacteria-free milk) in Thun, Switzerland.

In 1959, even as research on the development of aseptic packages was under way, Tetra Pak began working on developing a new packaging design called 'Tetra Brik'. This task began when the company realised that it needed to design a rectangular shape for its packages in order to comply with international standards for pallet[10] loading and to make the distribution of food packed in its packages more convenient. In 1963 the company launched Tetra Brik in Motala and Stockholm in Sweden commercially.

Over the next few years it began exploring the idea of extending the aseptic technology to the Tetra Brik packaging system. Subsequently, in 1968, Tetra Pak tested the Tetra Brik aseptic system at a local dairy in Thun. Over the next five years the product became a commercial success in Sweden, America and Canada. It was being used by many dairy companies as well as beverage and juice manufacturing companies.

In 1969 the company launched Tetra Rex, a fibre package with a new design. The package featured a triangular top (gable) with the opening on one of the sloping sides. Unlike other paperboard-based packages, the design of Tetra Rex helped eliminate the product's contact with the paper edges when the pack was opened.

In 1989 Tetra Pak introduced the Tetra Top range of packaging. Unlike the company's previous packages Tetra Top was a square package with rounded corners (earlier packages had pointed corners) and an opening at the top of the package. The new design helped beverage manufacturers differentiate their products from those of others. In the same year Tetra Pak received the 'Innovation Award' for its aseptic technology by the Institute of Food Technologists, a US-based, world-renowned organisation carrying out research in the use of science and technology in food products. The Institute named the aseptic technology the 'most important food science innovation to have occurred in the past 50 years'. It judged the technology on parameters such as safety to consumers and the protection of the flavour and nutrients of the processed and packaged foods.

Innovations galore

During the 1990s Tetra Pak brought out many more innovative products that catered to the changing needs of customers, retailers and manufacturers. The company launched several new products and also spruced up its existing product lines. In 1997 the company introduced three packaging ranges: Tetra Prisma Aseptic, Tetra Wedge Aseptic and Tetra Fino Aseptic. Though aseptic technology was used in each of these products, they differed in shape and design.

The Tetra Prisma Aseptic package had an octagonal design with eight flat panels. The packaging was designed to suit products like iced tea, juice, wine, milk and iced coffee. The Wedge Aseptic package incorporated a new shape and packaging design. This helped food manufacturers using the package to make

EXHIBIT 4: Tetra Pak product profile

Product	Shape	Volume (ml)	Opening options	Benefits*
Tetra Brik	Rectangular brick	200, 250, 500, 1000	Flexicap, screw cap, perforation, straw hole	Economical, space saving and convenient to use
Tetra Brik Aseptic	Rectangular brick	125, 160, 180, 200, 236, 250, 300, 330, 355, 375, 400, 500, 750, 1000, 1500	Perforation, pull tab, recap, spin cap, straw hole, stream cap	Does not require refrigeration in distribution, safety, long shelf-life and cost efficient
Tetra Classic Aseptic	Tetrahedron	65, 150, 200	Pull tab, straw hole, straight	Low cost and high quality
Tetra Fino Aseptic	Pouch	200, 250, 500, 1000	Straw hole	Low-cost packaging for milk, hygienic and tamper evident
Tetra Prisma Aseptic	Octagonal	200, 250, 330, 1000, 2000	Pull tab, pull tab and straw, recap and ReCap3P	Has metallic finish on packaging material, attractive, different types of printing could be done on the package, easy to pour and drink
Tetra Wedge Aseptic	Wedge	200	Straw hole	Differentiating shape, long shelf-life
Tetra Rex	Gable top	200, 250, 300, 375, 500, 568, 600, 750, 1000, 1136	Fill cap barrier, twist cap barrier, twist cap standard	Flexible, convenient to use
Tetra Top	Box shape with injection moulded plastic top	Base family package, Midi family package and Mini family package	Big lid, dome S30, dome S38, flat off centre S30, flat off centre S38, grand tab, orinoco S38, ring pull, total lid	Reclosable, flexible, shelf appeal, consumer convenient, projects powerful product image, value added and enhanced design possibility
Tetra Recart	Rectangular	375	Perforation	Long shelf-life, lightweight, safe to use, easy distribution

* The names of packages and opening options are given as mentioned by the company website. The benefits listed are not exhaustive and may vary according to user perception.

Source: compiled from information available on www.tetrapak.com and other sources.

their products more visually appealing. At the same time, the Tetra Wedge Aseptic package consumed less material and kept costs low. The Tetra Fino Aseptic package catered specifically to the need for a low-cost carton, particularly for developing markets. The package was shaped as a pouch with no tucks or folds, thus using less material and incurring lower manufacturing costs. It was particularly suitable for manufacturers of UHT milk.[11]

By the late 1990s Tetra Pak had developed a wide range of packaging products to cater to the different needs of liquid food manufacturers and marketers. The company extended its product range to include plastic EBM (Extrusion Blow Moulded, a technique used to make hollow objects) bottles. In 1998 Tetra Pak manufactured the aseptic version of these bottles for packaging UHT milk.

Tetra Pak also introduced its existing packaging range in different sizes under four broad models (Baseline, Midline, Slimline and Squareline), with various simple as well as sophisticated opening options like Perforation, Straw Hole, Flexi Cap, Spin Cap, Recap, Pull Tab, Stream Cap and Twist Cap (see Exhibit 4 for details). Tetra Pak's wide range of packaging solutions helped many beverage manufacturers around the world effectively market their products (see Exhibit 5 for various Tetra Pak users around the world). The company undertook a host of marketing

EXHIBIT 5: Tetra Pak's customers around the world

Tetra Pak's packaging solutions have been used by a diverse group of food manufacturers (particularly liquid food) around the world. Some of the customers include companies like Coca-Cola, Tropicana Foods and Beverages, Britannia, Parle Agro Products, Parmalat (Italy) and Unilever. Following are some of the instances where Tetra Pak packaging systems were chosen by beverage manufacturers to differentiate their products and project them as contemporary products (lightweight, easy to use, hygienic, with longer shelf-life).

South Africa

Ceres Fruit Juices, Africa's leading fruit juice manufacturer, held a 55 per cent share of the domestic fruit juice (which have a longer shelf-life) market. The company's flagship brand 'Ceres', which was positioned as the best quality fruit juice available in the market, had won the Gold Award from the American Tasting Institute for its quality and taste in 1999, 2000 and 2001. It had also received ISO 9001 certification. Ceres was exclusively packed in Tetra Brik Aseptic (TBA) cartons, TBA 200 ml slim and TBA 1000 ml slim with ReCap. Other brands like Liqui-Fruit and Fruitee were also packaged in Tetra Brik Aseptic cartons.

USA

Imagine Foods Inc, California had manufactured and marketed its 'functional beverages'[12] product 'Power Dream', an energy drink that contained soya protein, since 1998. The company had reformulated the product with a new flavour. To market this, the company designed new graphics to print on the packaging. The graphics on the drink's Tetra Prisma Aseptic package included pictures of mountain-biking, running, skydiving and downhill skiing. After the reformulation and introduction of new packaging in 2002, the company's sales tripled.

Saudi Arabia

In 2002 Al Safi-Danone Co. Ltd, a leading beverage manufacturer in the country, launched a range of dairy products: full-cream milk, low-fat milk, full-cream Laban (a traditional drink made of cultured milk with a slightly salty taste) and low-fat Laban. These drinks were launched in Tetra Top Mini GrandTab 250ml cartons and Tetra Top packs to achieve market differentiation and project an on-the-go and 'fresh' image. The company claimed that the market response to the product was very positive.

Lebanon

Liban Lait, a dairy in Lebanon, sold the Aryan drink (a popular drink in the Middle East/Eastern Mediterranean made up of fermented milk, water and salt) under the Candia brand. The company packaged the drink in Tetra Prisma Aseptic cartons as it wanted the product to have a longer shelf-life than the traditional chilled Aryan. The company also chose Tetra Prisma Aseptic because it wanted to target the product at a younger and more modern consumer base.

Taiwan

Uni-President Enterprises Corporation, Taiwan's leading beverage manufacturer, launched two brands 'His Café' and 'Her Café' in 2002. The company wanted to introduce the brand in the premium segment with premium packaging. For this purpose, the company chose the Tetra Prisma Aseptic 250ml carton. 'His Café' packaging was given a gold metallic design and 'Her Café' packaging was given a silver metallic design. The cartons were fitted with a Pull Tab opening and a telescopic straw.

Poland

Spɫdzielnia Mleczarska Mlekovita, a Polish dairy, launched the 'Mlekovita' brand of feta cheese in 2002. The company used the Tetra Brik Aseptic 250ml and 200ml cartons to package the brand, which was targeted at young women with above average income and education.

Source: adapted from 'New Products from Tetra Pak Internationally' at www.tetrapak.com.

initiatives to promote itself to both corporate and retail customers (see Exhibit 6 for information on these initiatives).

In early 2000 Tetra Pak took a step further in the field of bottling technology by launching the Glaskin bottle. The inside of this unbreakable, re-sealable PET bottle was coated with a silicon film which prevented oxygen from entering and carbon dioxide from escaping. Thus, the bottle preserved the contents and the flavour for a long period of time, giving the product a longer shelf-life. Like most other Tetra Pak products, the Glaskin bottle was made of recyclable plastic to help reduce environmental pollution (see Exhibit 7 for

EXHIBIT 6: Tetra Pak's marketing initiatives

Part of Tetra Pak's success throughout the world can be attributed to its marketing efforts. Tetra Pak marketed itself through various modes such as corporate campaigns, product-level campaigns and business area-level campaigns. It also used campaigns that increased consumer awareness of the company's efforts to protect the environment. Since the company was present in many countries, it designed country-specific TV and print media campaigns. Tetra Pak advertisements emphasised various aspects of its packaging technology, like hygiene, safety, convenience and ease of use.

For over three decades Tetra Pak conveyed the benefits of its packaging technology for customers through the catch line 'More than the package'. When Tetra Pak acquired Alfa Laval, a US-based manufacturer of equipment for food provision, environmental care, pharmaceutical and light chemical industries (in the early 1990s), the company needed to communicate to the food industry that it had broadened its portfolio to include the full range of processing equipment for food. This requirement was well met by the old motto. However, in early 2003 Tetra Pak replaced the old catchline with a new one, 'Protects what's good'. The change was in tune with the company's global repositioning strategy for its packaging products. As part of this strategy, it wanted to communicate the benefits of its products not only to the food-processing companies but to all participants in the value chain (comprising suppliers, corporate customers and retail customers).

Source: compiled from www.tetrapak.com and other sources.

EXHIBIT 7: Tetra Pak's environmental conservation initiatives

One of Tetra Pak's key business objectives was to lead environmental protection initiatives related to the food processing and packaging industry. During the 1980s Tetra Pak began developing its environmental management system. The company's environmental managers working at production plants and market companies (those divisions of Tetra Pak which carried out only marketing activities) developed and implemented an environmental policy. Tetra Pak published its first environmental report in 2000. Some of the initiatives that the company took are described below:

- **Purchasing paperboard from well-managed forests**: Tetra Pak purchased paperboard from sustainable forests; that is, those forests that were managed according to recognised principles for maintaining a sustainable yield of timber and non-timber products, and ensuring biodiversity and a desirable socioeconomic impact.
- **Continuous improvements in manufacturing**: the company used only certified environmental management systems in its manufacturing operations. It also gave attention to energy reduction, waste management and hazardous substance reduction.
- **Tackling the environmental impact of transportation**: Tetra Pak developed a process for rating the performance of its transport suppliers on the basis of their compliance with the company's environmental management policy.
- **Employee awareness and commitment**: The company launched a programme called 'EcoDrive' (in September 2001) to raise the environmental awareness of consumers and the commitment of its employees to the conservation of the environment.
- **Recycling initiative**: Tetra Pak recycled its products. The company's recycled material was used as an energy source in paper mills, as raw material and an energy source in cement factories, and as raw material for different products like bags, pallets, etc.
- **Environment as part of customer services**: the company provided support to recycle the waste generated at the customer's own site. The company also provided information to customers about the environmental profile of its packages.
- **Supporting education programmes**: the company supported environmental education programmes for schoolchildren around the world. Through the 'Cultura Ambiental em Escolas' programme in Brazil, over 3 million schoolchildren were educated about the environment.

Source: adapted from 'Tetra Pak makes Promising Progress Towards Environmental Leadership', www.tetrapak.com.

information on how Tetra Pak worked towards conserving the environment).

Another advantage of the Glaskin bottle provided was its low weight. A 500ml returnable glass bottle weighed 354 grams whereas a 500ml Glaskin bottle weighed only 34 grams (including the weight of the label and the closure). As a result, the Glaskin bottle provided significant savings in terms of transportation costs. One of the first companies to use the Glaskin bottle was Sweden's leading brewer, Spenderups (February 2000). The next major customer was Bitburger, Germany's leading brewer (in March 2002).

Apart from designing innovative packages, Tetra Pak also developed a variety of drinking straws. The company designed, produced and marketed straws to suit different kinds of packages and products. In order to make the straws look appealing, Tetra Pak manufactured them in many designs: straight, u-shaped, twisted and striped. As in the case of packaging, Tetra Pak designed straws that were hygienic and that appealed to customers.

One such innovation was the development of telescopic straws in early 2000. Tetra Pak developed the telescopic straws in association with BioGaia, a Swedish biotech company. These type of straws had a small tube fitted inside them. This tube was filled with 'supplementary, health boosting ingredients' known as neutraceuticals. The neutraceuticals were placed in the straw to separate them from the liquid until consumption.

Telescopic straws were commercialised with the launch of the 'LifeTop' range of straws. LifeTop straws contained a blue inner straw filled with Lactobacillus Reuteri, a bacterium which released lactic acid. According to research conducted by the company, Reuteri helped reduce the risk of stomach disorders, improved nutrient absorption, and enhanced the body's immune and defence system. LifeTop straws released these probiotics[13] in the beverage when it was consumed through these straws.[14]

Commenting on the usefulness of the new product, Jacquelyn Paul, Global General Manager, COE, Nutritionals, Tetra Pak, said, 'Tetra Pak wants to provide innovative solutions to its clients. With a great product like LifeTop straw, Tetra Pak and BioGaia can drive both consumer satisfaction and a health conscious product at the same time.'[15]

The LifeTop straws were wrapped individually and attached to beverage cartons. Each straw was sealed in an aluminum sachet coated with polyethylene terepthlate and polyethylene, which acted as a barrier against moisture and prevented oxidation.

This extended the shelf-life of the bacteria from a few weeks to many months. The straw could be attached to all kinds of packages, thus allowing existing beverage packages to be used. The straw also allowed manufacturers to supply probiotics with any kind of beverage without having to compromise on its taste and ingredients. Moreover, the straw eliminated the concerns of food product manufacturers regarding providing a controlled dosage of probiotics, accurate blending and damage due to exposure to heat.

Commenting on the benefits of LifeTop to beverage manufacturers, Jonathan Middlemiss, Managing Director, Farm Produce Marketing Ltd (FPM, a UK-based dairy products manufacturer and marketer),[16] said, 'The great advantage of this is that it enables us to add an extra health dimension to our product without having to reformulate it. Like many really good ideas, this is really very simple, with a droplet of Reuteri attached to the inside of the telescopic straw that is only activated when used by the consumer.'[17]

In late 2001, Tetra Pak launched the 'EaZip' opening feature. In EaZip, the upper section of the straw cover could be torn along a tear point that was indicated by a red stripe. This EaZip mechanism was described as much more hygienic than the straws then available because it allowed the straw to be removed from its protective cover without requiring the customer to touch the end that came in contact with the product. Some of the first companies to use the EaZip straw system were Lego (for its soft drinks) and Coca-Cola (for its fruit drink 'Five Alive').

During the same period, to make the distribution and handling of the straws more efficient and cost-effective, the company introduced a new product called the Apogee box. The new distribution box was compact since its width was exactly the same as the length of the straw. This way the straws were tightly packed and protected from damage. In traditional packing methods, the straws were loosely packed with the product cartons and were therefore prone to damage during transportation. Due to the compactness of the Apogee box, many boxes could be stored on a pallet, leading to efficient handling and cost savings during transportation and storage in production plants.

Innovating into the future: exploring new areas

Having established its supremacy in packaging for milk, milk products and juices, Tetra Pak decided to venture into other food sectors like canned food (dry food like dehydrated potatoes and wet food like vegetables). In December 2002 the company began offering packaging solutions for dry fruits, cereal, sugar, confectionary and pet food. During the same year, the Siro Group, a Spanish biscuit and confectionary maker, launched chocolate-flavoured biscuits packaged in Tetra Rex packages.

Dori, a dry fruits company from Brazil, launched dry fruits (like cashew nuts and peanuts), sugar-coated candy, and fruit jellies (gumdrops) in 250ml Tetra Rex cartons. The company said that it chose Tetra Rex packaging because 'it looks novel, is easy to open, and is recyclable'. In early 2003, Bonduelle, a leading processed vegetables manufacturer (based in Europe), chose Tetra Pak's Tetra Recart for launching its premium range of vegetable products in Italy. Bonduelle was reportedly impressed by the fact that Tetra Pak's products could pack wet and shelf-stable foods of any size and offered a shelf-life of up to 24 months. Nestlé, the Swiss-based foods company, also reported that Tetra Recart packaging had played a major role in its Friskies range of pet food achieving a market share of 10 per cent in Italy in 2002.

In early 2003, Tetra Pak introduced another new straw concept into the market in the form of the 'Sensory' straw. The sensory straw was different from traditional straws as its opening end (top end) had four small holes punched on the sides with the top being closed. This mechanism enabled the liquid to flow into the mouth in four different directions at the same time. Research carried out by Tetra Pak on children aged between 7 and 12 (in Australia), revealed that the response to the new concept was very positive. Commenting on this, a Tetra Pak spokesperson said, 'Children and young teenagers in the age group 8 to 14 are particularly sensitive to this change and really appreciate this new way of drinking. In fact, during tests, as many as 72 per cent preferred the Sensory Straw compared to the traditional one.'[18]

Initially launched in the shape of a u-straw, sensory straws (which were packaged in a transparent cover) could be attached to any existing package. Tetra Pak stated that the new straws could be manufactured by the existing straw applicators without making any technical modifications to the machines. Analysts pointed out that for consumers (mainly kids) the straws provided 'excitement and interactivity' and for beverage marketers they created a point of differentiation at a very low cost. Aimed at juice, nectar and flavoured-milk drinkers, the sensory straw was first commercially launched in Australia through Paramalt, a beverage manufacturer. Tetra Pak reportedly planned to launch this straw in other markets once it was found to be commercially successful.

In 2003 Tetra Pak celebrated its 50 years in the packaging industry, providing innovative and revolutionary packaging solutions to food manufacturers and marketers. Analysts expected the company to remain the leading player in the liquid food packaging business in the future (see Exhibit 8 for a note on

---

EXHIBIT 8: Tetra Pak's competition profile

The global packaging industry has been termed a rather 'complex' industry due to the diverse nature of technologies and materials used for packaging, and the presence of a target market that spans the entire globe. The packaging industry can be divided into sectors such as liquid packaging, paper sacks, plastic packages, glass containers, etc. Most packaging companies concentrate on providing services to one established sector.

During the 1990s the packaging industry went through a phase of consolidation. The liquid packaging sector emerged as one of the most consolidated segments by the end of the century. Most of the leading companies consolidated, leaving room for new players to enter. The international market for liquid food packaging was dominated by Tetra Pak, SIG Combibloc (based in Germany) and Elopak (based in Norway), while many small and medium-sized packaging companies dominated local/regional markets across the world. Tetra Pak was the undisputed leader due to its innovative and useful products. The company advertised the benefits of its products directly to consumers and also initiated several recycling programmes to protect the environment. These two factors contributed greatly to its success.

SIG Combibolc was the second-largest liquid-food packaging company and the world's second-largest supplier of aseptic beverage cartons. The company had operations in Western Europe, Eastern Europe, North America, Latin America, Asia, China and Great Britain. In 2002 the company reported consolidated sales of €939m. Established in 1957 by Fred, one of the largest privately owned industrial groups in Norway, Elopak was the third-largest liquid packaging manufacturer in the world. The company had brands like Pure Lak, Pak Lok and D Pak. Elopak was present in over 100 markets in Europe, Africa Asia, Australia and the Pacific. In 2001 Elopak reported consolidated sales of 4.2bn NOK (Norwegnian Krone, Norway's currency).[19]

Source: compiled from various sources.

Tetra Pak's competitors). According to company sources, Tetra Pak would continue to strive to reshape the food industry by researching new technologies in functional food packaging and intelligent packaging (use of radiofrequency identification) (see Exhibit 9 for a look at different Tetra Pak offerings).

EXHIBIT 9: Tetra Pak's various packaging solutions

Talking of Tetra Pak's commitment to the development of innovative packaging solutions for its customers, Aaron L. Brody, President and CEO, Packaging, Brody Incorporation, a strategic integrated media and communications service provider based in the USA, said, 'Tetra Pak has thought outside the box for half a century. The food world stands to benefit from the company's continued commitment to delighting consumers through innovation in integrated packaging systems.'[20] Analysts observed that 'the surge of innovations in the opening systems, new packaging designs, ever-improving decorating techniques have ensured that they [Tetra Pak] will be around for another 50 years.'[21]

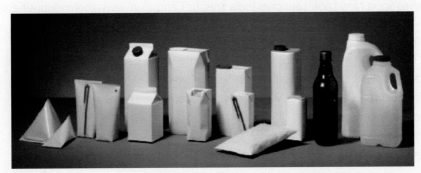

Source: www.tetrapak.com.

QUESTIONS

1   With specific reference to the invention of aseptic technology and the Tetra Recart system, explain the role played by packaging in the production, distribution and marketing of a product in general and beverages in particular.

2   Tetra Pak brought out many innovative products which catered to the needs of a variety of customers, retailers and manufacturers. Describe the major breakthrough products introduced by Tetra Pak and the way in which they helped manufacturers achieve differentiation and reduce costs.

3   'Packaging should save more than it costs.' Evaluate Tetra Pak's packaging products in light of this statement.

4   Examine Tetra Pak's decision to venture into new areas in the packaging industry. What knowledge do the innovations at the company provide for the packaging industry as a whole?

FURTHER READING

- 'Swedish Brewer Spendrups First to Launch Beer in Glaskin Bottles from TetraPak', www.tetra-plastics.com, January 2000.
- 'Swedish Brewer First to Use Glaskin', www.petpla.net, March 2000.
- 'Healthy Juice Dons Ergonomic Packaging', www.packagingdigest. com, May 2000.

- 'UK Introduces EaZip for TetraPak', www.indianpurchase. com, December 2001.
- 'Probiotic Straws', www.biotenz.org.nz, March 2002.
- 'BioGaia and Farm Produce Marketing Sign LifeTop Straw Agreement', www.biogaia.se, 23 May 2002.
- 'TetraPak Awarded Highest Packaging Honor at DuPont Awards for Innovation in Packaging', www.npicenter.com, 22 August 2002.
- 'Yogurt Drink Uses Culture Straw', www.dairyfoods.com, 2 September 2002.
- 'Sensory Straws Make Drinking Fun', www.beveragedaily. com, 1 January 2003.
- 'Tetra Recart Wins EAFA Award & Makes Inroads for Retort', http://pffc-online.com, 2 April 2003.
- 'Tetra Pak Gable Top Packaging System', www.beveragedaily. com, 28 April 2003.
- 'TetraPak to Sport New Look: Launches India Specific Campaign', www.thehindubusinessline.com, 26 May 2003.
- 'Tools for Innovation: Making Milk Interactive', www.dairyfoods. com, June 2003.
- Joanne Hunter, 'Cartons: The Shape of Things to Come', www. packagingmagazine.co.uk.
- Jann Koel, 'TetraPak Success Through Diversification', www. packaging-technology.com.
- 'Tetra Recart Enters Canned Food Market', www. foodoresound.com.
- www.bottledwaterweb.com.
- www.alufoil.org.
- www.tetrapak.com.

NOTES

1 'Tetra Pak: Packaging Itself for the Customer,' www.domain-b. com, 21 July 2001.

2 Founded in 1974, the EAFA represents manufacturers of aluminium foil containers and specialised packaging converters and foil rollers based in Europe. EAFA carries out market research, encourages information sharing and promotes the interests of its members. The EAFA Packaging Trophy Award honours companies that bring out interesting and novel packages by making use of aluminium foil.

3 Retorting is a packaging technology which uses pouches/packs made of several layers. Packets filled with food material are sealed in a sterilised environment using high temperature. Food packed in this manner has a long shelf-life and retains its natural flavours.

4 'Tetra Recart Wins EAFA Award & Makes Inroads for Retort,' http://pffc-online.com, 2 April 2003.

5 'Award Winning Tetra Recart: World's First Retortable Carton Package for Food,' www.tetrapak.com, 9 April 2003.

6 'Tetra Pak Awarded the Highest Packaging Honor at DuPont Awards for Innovation in Packaging,' www.npicenter.com, 22 August 2002.

7 €1= U$1.14770 as on 26 July 2003.

8 A four-sided three-dimensional figure in which all the sides are equilateral triangles.

9 'The History of an Idea', www.tetrapak.com.

10 A pallet is a portable platform used for moving or storing cargo/freight.

11 UHT milk is processed with a technology called Ultra High Temperature (UHT), which uses high temperatures for processing and packaging to ensure sterility and storage at room temperature.

12 Functional beverages are drinks enhanced with herbs and other ingredients which, when consumed, promise to improve the health of the person, eg protein and mineral-enriched drinks.

13 Live bacterial feed supplements.

14 Each LifeTop straw reportedly contained 99 million Reuteri bacteria.

15 'Probiotic Straws', www.biotenz.org.

16 Farm Produce Marketing (FPM) introduced the first probiotic drinkable yoghurt, Orchard Maid, in mid-2002, and earned a shelf space in two of the UK's largest supermarket chains (a task which FPM thought to be very difficult to achieve). The drink was positioned as a 'grab and go' beverage and was placed along with other chilled single serve beverages rather than in the dairy products section. The yoghurt was aseptically processed and packaged and had a shelf life of 12 months.

17 'Yogurt Drink Uses Culture Straw', www.dairyfoods.com.

18 'Sensory Straw Makes Drinking Fun', www.beveragedaily. com, 20 January 2003.

19 NOK 1 = US$0.139478 as on 26 July 2003.

20 'Thinking Outside The Box: Tetra Pak's Past and Future', www. tetrapak.com.

21 'Cartons: The Shape of Things to Come', www.packaginmaga-zine.co.uk.

PART 5

Case 5.1

Levi Strauss Signature®: A New Brand for Mass-channel Retail Stores

© P.N. Ghauri.

In 2003 the US company Levi Strauss decided to launch a new brand named 'Levi Strauss Signature®'. The main objective was 'to sell jeans where people shop'. After the conclusion of a first agreement with Wal-Mart for the US market, the company successfully introduced the Levi Strauss Signature® brand to Canada, Australia and Japan. In 2004 the group decided to expand the new brand into the European market. The success of the Levi Strauss Signature® brand largely depended upon the relationship established with the distributors.

Written in close collaboration with the marketing team of the European subsidiary of the Levi Strauss group, this case study presents the activities of the Levi Strauss group, its position in the European market, its brand portfolio and the European distribution system for jeans.

Presentation of the Levi Strauss group

Founded in 1853, the Levi Strauss group can be considered as one of the world's leading branded apparel companies, with sales in more than 110 countries. The company designs and markets jeans and jeans-related trousers, casual and dress trousers, tops, jackets and related accessories for men, women and children. It owns three brands: Levi's®, Dockers® and Levi Strauss Signature®.

EXHIBIT 1: The history of the Levi Strauss group

1873	Levi Strauss & Co created the world's first blue jeans
1890	The lot number '501' was assigned to Levi's® 'waist overalls' (blue jeans)
1935	Introduction of 'Lady Levi's®', the company's first jeans for women
1986	Launch of Dockers®, which became the fastest growing new brand in apparel history, bridging the gap between jeans and suits. The brand changed what office workers wear to work in the USA
2000	*Time* magazine's millennium issue named Levi's® 501 jeans the best fashion of the twentieth century, beating the miniskirt and the little black dress
2003	150th anniversary of the company; creation of the Levi Strauss Signature® brand

Source: Levi Strauss & Co (2003), *Annual Financial Report*.

EXHIBIT 2: Net sales of Levi Strauss group by geographic region (in 2003)

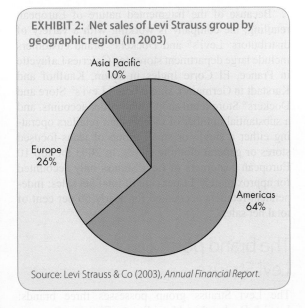

Source: Levi Strauss & Co (2003), *Annual Financial Report*.

The Levi Strauss group is named after its founder, Levi Strauss. In 1873 Levi Strauss and the tailor Jacob Davis received the US patent to make riveted denim clothing, thus creating the first blue jeans. Exhibit 1 presents the history of the company.

The headquarters of the Levi Strauss group are located in San Francisco. The stock is privately held, primarily by descendants of the family of Levi Strauss. The Levi Strauss group employs 12,300 people. In 2003 net sales were US$4.1bn and net income reached US$349m (losses).

The business is organised into three geographic regions: Americas (USA, Canada, Latin America), Europe (Europe, Middle East, Africa) and Asia Pacific. Exhibit 2 shows net sales achieved in each geographic region in 2003.

In order to maintain its leadership in the apparel market, the group has adopted the following business strategies:

- *Innovate and lead from the core*: creating innovative and consumer-relevant products, including updating of existing core products and introducing new products that can be quickly commercialised across different distribution channels.
- *Achieve operational excellence*: continually improving the go-to-market process to make it more responsive and faster, better linking supply to demand and reducing product costs in part by leveraging the global scale.

- *Revitalise retailer relationships and improve the company's presence at retail*: improving the collaborative planning, improving retailer margins and making products easier for consumers to find and to buy.
- *Sell where they shop*: making products accessible through multiple channels of distribution at price points that meet consumer expectations.

Levi Strauss in Europe

The European subsidiary of Levi Strauss is located in Brussels. Its president, Paul Mason, a British citizen, has acquired important experience in mass channel retail stores. In 2003 the European subsidiary (covering Europe, Middle East and Africa) reached net sales of US$1.1bn. Levi's® products represent 90 per cent and Dockers® products 10 per cent of total net sales.

The group has recently reorganised its activities in Europe: the objective is to decentralise and to return responsibility to individual countries rather than operating the region on a pan-European basis. Moreover, the company is attempting to return the Levi's® brand to its traditional premium position (in contrast to the US market where Levi's® jeans are positioned as 'ordinary jeans', thus being sold at a lower price than in Europe). A marketing campaign that highlights the fit benefits of 501 jeans intends to capture the attention of young consumers in order to increase sales trends across Europe. The region also takes substantial cost-reduction actions in order to improve margins.

Because of the fragmented nature of European retailing, the company is working with a variety of distributors: Levi's® and Dockers® brand customers include large department stores (eg Galeries Lafayette in France, El Corte Inglès in Spain, Kaufhof and Karstadt in Germany), single-brand Levi's® Store and Dockers® Store retail shops, mail-order accounts, and a substantial number of independent retailers operating either a single or small group of jeans-focused stores or general clothing stores. In 2003 the top 10 European customers of Levi Strauss only accounted for approximately 11 per cent of total net sales; independent retailers accounted for nearly 50 per cent of total net sales.

The brand portfolio of Levi Strauss

The Levi Strauss group possesses three brands: Levi's®, Dockers® and Levi Strauss Signature®.

Exhibit 3 indicates the net sales achieved by each brand in 2003.

The traditional Levi's® brand can be considered the main brand of the company. Created in 1873, Levi's® jeans have become one of the most widely recognised brands in the history of the apparel industry: the value of the brand is estimated at US$2.97bn (Interbrand, 2003). The Levi's® brand is the number one jeans brand in the USA in terms of unit sales: nearly 70 per cent of men in the USA, aged 15 to 49, own and wear Levi's® jeans. The original jeans have evolved to include a wide range of men's, women's and kids' products designed to

appeal to a variety of consumer segments who shop via a number of different retail channels. Levi's® brand products are sold in more than 110 countries around the world. In 2003 sales of Levi's® brand products reached US$2.9bn, representing approximately 70 per cent of the company's net sales.

The Dockers® brand covers casual clothing, primarily trousers and tops, sold in more than 57 countries. The brand played a major role in the resurgence of khaki trousers and the movement toward casual attire in the US workplace by helping create a standard for business casual clothing. The Dockers® brand is the number one men's trouser brand in the USA in terms of unit sales: nearly 75 per cent of men in the USA who wear casual trouser own and wear Dockers®. In 2003, sales of Dockers® brand products totalled US$1bn, which corresponds to 24 per cent of the company's net sales.

Levi's® and Dockers® products are mainly distributed through chain retailers and department stores in the USA. They are primarily sold through department stores and speciality retailers abroad. Levi's® and Dockers® products are also distributed through a small number of company-owned stores located in the USA, Europe and Asia and through approximately 950 independently owned franchised stores outside the USA.

In 2003 the Levi Strauss group introduced a new casual clothing brand named 'Levi Strauss Signature®'. The brand targets value-conscious consumers who shop in mass channel retail stores. The mass channel is considered as the largest retail channel in the USA, selling more than 29 per cent of all jeans sold in 2003. Levi Strauss Signature® brand products include a range of denim and non-denim trousers and shirts as well as denim jackets for men, women and kids with product styling, finish and design that is distinct from the traditional Levi's® brand.

The Levi Strauss Signature® brand was launched in July 2003: the products were initially sold by 3,000 Wal-Mart stores in the USA before being introduced at Target and Kmart Stores there. The company then expanded into Canada (where the brand is sold at Wal-Mart stores), Australia (where an agreement was signed with Lowes and Big W stores) and Japan (where the brand is sold at Justco and Saty). In 2003 sales of Levi Strauss Signature® brand products reached US$0.2bn, representing approximately 6 per cent of the company's net sales.

In 2004 the company introduced the Levi Strauss Signature® brand into the European market. The European subsidiary decided to enter three major markets: France, Germany and the UK. In these three countries, the mass channel plays a key role within

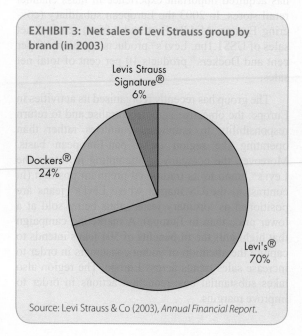

EXHIBIT 3: Net sales of Levi Strauss group by brand (in 2003)

Levis Strauss Signature®
6%

Dockers®
24%

Levi's®
70%

Source: Levi Strauss & Co (2003), *Annual Financial Report.*

EXHIBIT 4: Ranking of global retailers

Rank	Country of origin	Name of company	2002 group sales (US$m)	2002 retail sales (US$m)	2002 group income/(loss) (US$m)	5-year retail sales CAGR (%)	5-year net income CAGR (%)
1	USA	Wal-Mart	244,524	229,617	8,039	14.2	17.9
2	France	Carrefour	65,011	65,011	1,314	18.7	20.5
3	USA	Home Depot	58,247	58,247	3,664	19.2	25.9
4	USA	Kroger	51,760	51,760	1,205	14.3	23.9
5	Germany	Metro	48,738	48,349	475	12.4	NM
6	USA	Target	43,917	42,722	1,654	9.0	17.1
7	Netherlands	Ahold	59,292	40,755	(1143)	12.5	NM
8	UK	Tesco	40,394	40,071	1,451	9.7	13.4
9	USA	Costco	37,993	37,993	700	9.8	72.4
10	USA	Sears	41,366	35,698	1,376	−2.9	3.0

CAGR = Compound Annual Growth Rate

NM = Not Meaningful

Source: http://www.stores.org.

the national distribution system. In the UK and in Germany, Levi Strauss Signature® products are distributed by Wal-Mart, the US partner of Levi Strauss, which has established an important number of stores in both countries, thus allowing a satisfactory geographic coverage. In France, the company chose to cooperate with Carrefour, which is the most important hypermarket chain (the French distribution system is dominated by hypermarkets; Carrefour is the second-largest distributor in the world, behind Wal-Mart; see Exhibit 4).

The European distribution system for jeans

Jeans, a strong and indisputable symbol of the American way of life, represent a substantial market in Europe. Be it in a casual or sophisticated version, jeans are worn by both genders and all generations. In 2002 the European jeans market registered a growth of 7.4 per cent in volume compared to 2001. Jeans have been reinvented as a fashion item by designers' renewed vision. The fashion markets are known to be cyclical, and it takes the constant efforts of leading brands to come up with innovations to make the jeans market a dynamic one.

Jeans retailing in Europe is structured around four main channels:

1 'strongholds' encompassing department stores (eg Galeries Lafayette, Harrod's, El Corte Inglès), sports shops and jeans specialists (independent, multiple, single brand, eg US Forms)

2 'general clothing': designated multiple and independent general clothing stores (eg Cotton Street) and mail order (eg Les 3 Suisses)

3 'mass channels' are hypermarkets, supermarkets and discounters (eg Wal-Mart, Asda, Carrefour, Auchan)

4 'VISS' are vertically integrated specialised stores (eg Camaïeu, Zara, Benetton).

'General clothing' is by far the largest retailing channel, representing 50 per cent of total sales in volume. The three other channels share almost equally the other half of the market. Over the past three years, the market share of strongholds has decreased, while the market shares of the other channels have increased.

A recent survey revealed interesting data about customers of mass channels retail stores. The segment labelled 'mass loyalists' (14 per cent) designates customers already buying many clothes (including jeans) in mass channels. The 'mass pragmatists' are customers who 'are considering buying clothes in a hypermarket, and have already bought jeans there' or 'are considering buying clothes in a hypermarket, but have not yet bought jeans there'. According to the survey, the 'mass pragmatists' account for 54 per cent of the mass channel customers. The remaining 17 per cent would consider buying only basics in a hypermarket ('I just buy basic stuff there; if I am looking for fashionable clothes, I go somewhere else'), and the last 15 per cent have never and will never consider buying clothes in a hypermarket.

France represents the biggest mass channel in Europe. With a dominant hypermarket format, French retailers are key players in Southern and Eastern Europe (Carrefour, Auchan). The UK is the second-biggest mass channel in Europe; leading retailers for jeans are Wal-Mart and Matalan. In Germany, the mass channel is not as developed as it is in France and the UK.

A focus on the French market helps to understand an interesting aspect of mass channel performance, which is also true in the UK market. Mass channels are not as efficient at selling clothing in general and more specifically jeans, as they are at selling other types of goods. As a matter of fact, between 1999 and 2001, while mass channels were enjoying a total growth rate of 3 per cent, their clothing sales were decreasing by 0.4 per cent and their jeans sales by 6.3 per cent. At the same time, the total clothing market was slightly increasing (growth rate 1.2 per cent) and the total jeans market was enjoying an energising 5.8 per cent growth rate.

Why would mass channels want to sell more clothes? When posed to several leading retail managers, the question brings converging answers:

'We want to use clothing to fuel the growth of our stores. In order to do so, we want to bring strong brands in our department areas and prove we can market them without damaging their image.'

'We are really committed to turning around our clothing business. We have been working on shopping experience/comfort and we are now addressing logistic issues. But our offering is suffering from the lack of branded products.'

Brands with a rich heritage and know-how are able to provide, within a mass channel environment, a genuine brand experience for customers to enjoy. This brand experience, which is a subtle combination of the product's inner qualities, merchandising actions and adequate pricing, will make customers, who usually buy retailers' private brands or discount apparel, want to trade up to branded products. Moreover, clothing margins are on average higher than food margins, and strong brands build customer loyalty.

QUESTIONS

1 What are the main reasons that made Levi Strauss decide to launch Levi Strauss Signature® in Europe?
2 Should the company evolve towards using an intensive distribution policy?
3 Levi Strauss Europe has chosen the short distribution channel, avoiding the direct channel, eg stores run by the company or on the Internet. Would you recommend the use of the direct distribution channel to the company?
4 What kind of merchandising actions should the company take?
5 What are the main benefits of this new win–win relationship for Levi Strauss and the distributors?

FURTHER READING

- B. Berman and J.R. Evans, *Retail Management* (Upper Saddle River, NJ: Pearson Education, 2004).
- Levi Strauss & Co, *Annual Financial Report* (2003).
- Levi Strauss Europe, *Internal documents* (2006).
- U. Mayrhofer, *Marketing International* (Paris: Economica, 2004).
- U. Mayrhofer, *Marketing*, 2nd edn (Paris: Editions Bréal, Coll. Lexifac, 2006).
- U. Mayrhofer and C. Roederer, *Levi Strauss Signature: Sell Where People Shop* (Paris: Centrale de Cas et de Médias Pédagogiques, 2005).

- U. Mayrhofer and C. Roederer, '"Sell where they Shop", Levi Strauss Signature®: Une Nouvelle Marque Pour La Grande Distribution', *Gestion 2000*, 5, 2009.
- C. Roederer, 'Politique de Produit: Cas Levi's Eco', in S. Hertrich and U. Mayrhofer (eds), *Cas en marketing* (Cormelles-le-Royal: Editions Management & Société, Coll Etudes de cas, 2008), pp 77–93.
- http://www.levistrauss.com.
- http://www.levistrausssignature.com.
- http://www.stores.org.
- http://www.interbrand.com.

This case was written by Ulrike Mayrhofer, IAE de Lyon, Université Jean Moulin Lyon 3 and Groupe ESC Rouen, and Claire Roederer, Ecole de Management Strasbourg, Université de Strasbourg. The authors would like to thank Mr Bruno PFALZGRAF, Vice-President of Levi Strauss Signature®, for his valuable contribution to the project.

Case 5.2

Apple Inc.'s iPhone: Can iPhone Maintain Its Initial Momentum?

'When Apple's iPhone first went on sale in Europe six months ago, hopes were high that the device would be just as big a hit there as it had been in the US. But analysts are now raising concerns that the iPhone may not translate as well overseas, with sales sluggish in Europe because of the device's high price and strong competition from Nokia (NOK) and others.'[1]

Business Week, 2008

'When you consider that it launched part way through the year, with limited operator and country coverage, and essentially just one product, Apple has shown very clearly that it can make a difference and has sent a wakeup call to the market leaders.'[2]

Pete Cunningham, Senior Analyst,
Canalys,[3] 2008

Introduction

For the quarter ending June 2008, Apple Inc announced that it had posted revenues of US$7.46bn and a net profit of US$1.07bn. The company attributed these results primarily to the sales of Macintosh computers and iPhones. Apple sold 717,000 units of the iPhone in the third quarter of June 2008 compared to 270,000 units in the third quarter of June 2007. Commenting on the results, Steve Jobs, CEO, Apple, said, 'We're proud to report the best June quarter for both revenue and earnings in Apple's history.'[4]

Ever since Apple announced its plans to launch the iPhone in January 2007, it had created a buzz among consumers who sought to buy the product as soon as it was launched. The craze for the iPhone was evident from the fact that Apple's fans formed long queues outside Apple's stores to ensure that they got it immediately after the launch. iPhone was a revolutionary mobile phone, the first from Apple, and it featured some advanced features like a multi-touch screen and high memory capacity (refer to Exhibit 1 for the key features of the iPhone). Some analysts said that it was one of the best launches of a new product.

However, a controversy erupted when Jobs announced a steep price cut on the iPhone in September 2007, barely two months after the product was launched. The announcement left early adopters, who had purchased the iPhone at a premium, seething. While the company justified slashing the prices within 10 weeks of its launch, some analysts opined that the

---

EXHIBIT 1: The key features of iPhone

- Screen size – 3.5 inch (8.9 cm)
- Resolution – 320 × 480 pixels
- Memory – 4GB/8GB
- Wireless – Quad-band GSM-EDGE/Wi-Fi/ Bluetooth
- Camera – 2 megapixels
- Battery life – 5 hours talk/16 hours playback
- Size – 115 × 61 × 11.6 mm
- Weight – 135 grams
- Operating system – MAC OS X
- Input – Multi-touch screen
- CPU – 620 MHz ARM 1176

Source: compiled from various sources.

price cut was nothing short of a public relations (PR) fiasco for the company. Another growing concern for Apple was the discrepancy in the number of units sold by Apple and number of connections activated by telecom major, AT&T Wireless Services Inc.[5]

In addition to capturing a share in the US mobile phone market, Apple aimed to tap other markets for its iPhone. In November 2007 Apple launched the iPhone in three European markets: Germany, France and the UK. Though Apple initially received a good response in these markets, sales later slumped due to reasons such as high price, lack of 3G capability, and carrier exclusivity. In an attempt to control its declining sales, Apple reduced the price of the iPhone by £100 in April 2008.

Despite facing several challenges and analysts' predictions that Apple would face difficulties in cracking the mobile phone market as it was a late entrant, the company emerged as a successful player in the USA. Analysts opined that with its third-quarter results, Apple might not be too far from achieving its target of selling 1 million iPhones by 2008. On the other hand, a few industry observers opined that it remained to be seen whether Apple would be able to maintain its initial momentum in future since the mobile phone market was already dominated by established players. Analysts also raised doubts about whether iPhone would succeed in the intensely competitive Asian market, where Apple launched the product in the second half of 2008.

Background note

Apple was founded on 1 April 1976, by Jobs, Steve Wozniak, and Ronald Wayne in Jobs' garage. It was incorporated as Apple Computers Inc on 3 January 1977, and was headquartered in Cupertino, California, USA.

In 1980 Apple went public. In the same year, the company netted over US$100m and had 1,000 employees. [6] However, after its initial success, it faced some stiff competition from the market leader, International Business Machine Corporation (IBM),[7] when IBM introduced its own personal computers such as IBM PC (model 5150) on 12 August 1981, powered by MS-DOS (Microsoft disk operating system) along with the revolutionary spreadsheet application Lotus 1-2-3. As a result of this, Apple lost the business users who formed the most lucrative market segment for computers at that time.

In 1985 the last remaining founder in Apple, Jobs, was expelled from the company by the then - CEO John Schulley after a boardroom dispute. The reasons cited for Jobs' sacking were the low sales of Mac and bad leadership.

However, in 1996 Apple still remained a marginal player in the computer industry and was losing a lot of money. Many analysts believed that the company would be wound up or sold off. In late 1996 Apple's CEO Gil Amelio persuaded Jobs to work as an 'informal advisor' at Apple, with no contractual commitments. Apple also purchased NeXT for US$400m. In the space of a year, Apple posted profits in three consecutive quarters, starting from the last quarter of 1997. In 1998, Apple's board appointed Jobs as the 'interim CEO'.

The first step that Jobs took after re-joining Apple was to launch the new operating system Mac OSX based on the NeXT operating system. The next groundbreaking step was Apple's foray into the retail business with the establishment of Apple Retail Stores. Jobs cut many loss-making projects, which were in the implementation phase, and started efforts to make Apple profitable again. The company's emphasis on design received a further boost under him. In 1998 Apple introduced one of its most important products, the revolutionary iMac.

According to analysts, the defining moment in the company's transition came with the introduction of the portable digital music player, the iPod, in 2001. The second coming of Apple as a maker of consumer electronics goods was attributed to the charismatic leadership of Jobs. The iPod went on to become a hugely successful product.

On 28 April 2003 Apple started the iTunes Music Store (iTMS),[8] a paid online music service available only in the USA. However, it was later modified and made available to consumers in other countries too, including users of Microsoft Windows.

On 11 January 2005, Apple introduced the iPod Shuffle, a digital audio player, which used a flash memory. The iPod Shuffle became popular and captured 58 per cent of the flash player market in the USA by May 2005.[9]

On 9 January 2007, in a symbolic gesture, the company dropped the word 'Computer' from its name and became Apple Inc. On the same day, Jobs announced the introduction of another revolutionary product. This was the first mobile phone from the company, the 'iPhone'. This, coupled with the earlier launch of a set-top box called Apple TV (also called iTV) in September 2006, completed the company's transformation from being a computer manufacturer to a fully-fledged manufacturer of consumer electronic goods.

Launching the iPhone

On 29 January 2007 Jobs announced Apple's plans to launch the iPhone at Macworld Conference & Expo.[10]

Apple's entry into the mobile phone market with a revolutionary product called the 'iPhone' generated a lot of excitement among consumers. Apple created a buzz for its iPhone by slowly releasing details about the product. Much of the hype created was through word-of-mouth marketing. Analysts felt that, to succeed in the highly competitive mobile phone market, Apple had had to come out with something that was truly category-defying, and the company had managed to do just that. In addition to this, some analysts felt that a lot of credit for the success of the iPhone should go to Jobs, who, they believed, had mastered the art of generating tons of free publicity, thereby creating a buzz around Apple's product launches. Rob Enderle, principal analyst with the Enderle Group,[11] said, 'What Jobs does is he focuses like a laser on what makes the thing cool, they [Apple] keep the fervor up. They are very good at managing demand and keeping people excited.'[12]

Andy Neff, an analyst at Bear Stearns,[13] revealed Apple's marketing strategy for its iPhone during the Academy Awards[14] ceremony in February 2007. Apple launched a teaser campaign on television that had a 'hello' tagline (see Exhibit 2 for Apple's initial teaser campaign). The ad simply mentioned the word 'hello' and featured many eminent personalities from the film as well as television fraternity answering their calls. The commercial lasted for 30 seconds and ended with a brief glimpse of the iPhone, followed by the word 'Hello' and 'Coming in June'[15] followed by the company logo. The ad campaign was created by TBWA\Chiat\Day,[16] an Omnicom Group agency.[17]

According to estimates by analysts, the hype created by Apple for its iPhone would result in the company achieving sales in the range of 500,000 to 1 million units in the first two days of its launch.[19] Apple had set a sales target of 10 million iPhones by the end of 2008, thereby capturing 1 per cent of the global mobile phone industry.

For the US market, Apple had entered into a two-year network contract with AT&T whereby the iPhones could be used only with the AT&T network. Before the launch of the iPhone, Apple announced some service plans for people who opted for the iPhone (refer to Exhibit 3 for AT&T monthly plans for the iPhone). Jobs said, 'We want to make choosing a service plan simple and easy, so every plan includes unlimited data with direct Internet access, along with visual voicemail and a host of other goodies. We think these three plans give customers the flexibility to experience all of iPhone's revolutionary features at affordable and competitive prices.'[20]

Some analysts felt that the launch of the iPhone was probably the best ever launch of any product. Between 29 June 2007 and 29 September 2007 the company sold 1,389,000 units.[21] The buzz that surrounded the launch of the phone, which was referred to as the 'Jesus phone' by bloggers, was unprecedented as far as electronic products were concerned. One customer who bought the iPhone soon after it was launched remarked, 'I'm going to run home and ring people just to say "Guess what, I've got an iPhone, bye!"'[22] Such was the frenzy that surrounded the launch of this new mobile phone.

Industry observers appreciated the way the company had created a buzz around the product through its low key but highly effective marketing effort. They also felt that the product had lived up to the expectations

---

EXHIBIT 2: The iPhone teaser ad

Length: 30 seconds

The TV ad opens with the visual of an old-fashioned black phone ringing until it is answered by Lucille Ball, an actor of yesteryear. The ad goes on to show clips of various actors such as Will Ferrell, Audrey Tatou, Dustin Hoffman, Harrison Ford, Billy Crystal, Cameron Diaz, Sarah Jessica Parker, and Michael Douglas answering the phone. There is also a clip featuring the popular animated character Mr Incredible from Pixar Inc's[18] movie, *The Incredibles* (2004).

Then the visual of the iPhone is shown with the name and photograph of a John Appleseed showing in the caller ID. The ad ends with the words, 'Coming in June'.

Sources: adapted from Zaharov-Reutt, 'Apple iPhone Ad Says Hello to Oscars Women', www.itwire.com.au, 26 February 2007, and other sources.

EXHIBIT 3: Monthly rental plan for iPhone

AT&T monthly plans for iPhone		
Plans	Minutes	Night & weekend minutes
US$59.99	450	5000
US$79.99	900	Unlimited
US$99.99	1,350	Unlimited

* All these plans have additional features and services such as 200 SMS test messages, rollover minutes, unlimited data, unlimited mobile-to-mobile, and visual voicemail.

** In addition to these three monthly plans, customers could choose from any of AT&T's standard service plans.

Source: 'AT&T and Apple Announce Simple, Affordable Service Plans for iPhone', www.apple.com, 26 June 2007.

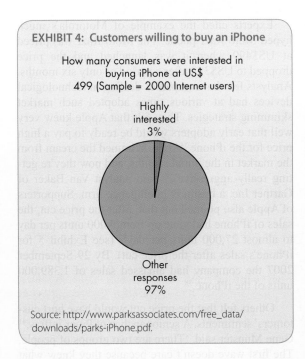

EXHIBIT 4: Customers willing to buy an iPhone

How many consumers were interested in buying iPhone at US$ 499 (Sample = 2000 Internet users)

Highly interested 3%

Other responses 97%

Source: http://www.parksassociates.com/free_data/downloads/parks-iPhone.pdf.

created. According to Al Ries, Chairman, Ries & Ries,[23] Apple's iPhone had generated more publicity than any other product. Commenting on the buzz created by Apple for its iPhone, Matt Williams, a partner at Martin Agency,[24] said, 'Apple is one of those rare brands that can create mystique around a product. They created a buzz that has taken on a life of its own.'[25]

However, some analysts felt that the iPhone had been over-hyped and could fall flat on its face after the initial euphoria died down. They were of the view that it was never good to hype a product so much as it could become difficult to match the hype with performance. Moreover, Apple was foraying into unknown terrain dominated by a number of competitors that had decades of experience in this sector behind them. Analysts felt that Apple had a long way to go to realise its target of conquering a 1 per cent market share in the mobile phone market. Some analysts also viewed its foray into this market as a defensive strategy necessitated by the introduction of music phones by some well-known mobile phone companies.

Pricing the iPhone

The iPhone was launched with such frenzy that even its premium price did not prove a deterrent to many consumers. Apple priced its 4GB version of iPhone at US$499 and its 8GB version at US$599, when it was launched in June 2007. The customers also had to enter into a two-year contract with AT&T. Along with the contract, the iPhone was considered the most expensive mobile handset in the world at the time of

its release. Moreover, there were hidden costs. For example, just as in the case of the iPod, customers would not be able to change the battery of the iPhone themselves. The phone had to be sent back to Apple for replacement for a fee (US$79, plus US$6.95 shipping). This was expected to pose a big challenge for Apple as some customers would not be willing to pay so much and also remain without a phone during the replacement period. The durability of the iPhone was also questioned by many critics as the front side of the phone was made of glass.

Some critics felt that the high price of the iPhone was not justified since it was double the cost incurred by the company for manufacturing the product. According to iSuppli, a research firm, Apple had a 50 per cent margin on its iPhone since the US$499 iPhone and the US$599 models cost Apple about US$246 and US$281 to manufacture, respectively.[26] In view of its high pricing, some analysts opined that Apple would face difficulties in penetrating the mobile phone market, which was so fragmented that there were hundreds of models catering to different types of users depending upon their affordability, needs and the features offered. Moreover, the market was dominated by established players like Nokia Corporation[27], Samsung Electronics[28], Sony Ericsson Mobile Communications AB[29], LG Electronics[30] and Motorola Inc[31], who provided various high-end products at affordable prices.

Though the early adopters bought the iPhone with much excitement, there were some incidents of customers accusing Apple and AT&T of issuing hefty bills. Some iPhone users were stunned when they started receiving bills running into hundreds of pages. Some of these customers got bills for US$3,000 or even more. One of the iPhone customers Justin, Ezarik, received a 300-page bill from AT&T in August 2007. Ezarik posted a video on YouTube[32] wherein he displayed the 300-page bill and said, 'I got my first AT&T bill, right here.'[33] Within no time, the video served as a catalyst and generated widespread media coverage. In response to the video, Mark Siegel, spokesperson, AT&T, said, 'It's no different than with any other bill for any other devices or any other service that we offer.'[34] However, AT&T decided to discontinue sending long bills to its customers.

The price-cut chaos

As we observed earlier, in September 2007, barely ten weeks after the launch of the iPhone, Jobs announced a steep price cut for the product. The 4GB version was made inoperable while the 8GB version was available at US$399 and a 16GB version was to be introduced at a price of US$499. The price cut, which was almost one-third of the original price of the product, took most by surprise. People couldn't believe their ears when they heard the new price of the handset. Not surprisingly, the news infuriated those who had bought the iPhone at the original price. Some of the customers who started protesting against the price cut were among the few early adopters who had waited in long queues to buy the handsets. A discontented and annoyed customer even went ahead and took legal action against Apple and AT&T. It was estimated that the company had sold 750,000 units of the iPhone at the US$599 price by September 2007.[35]

Many were upset at the company's decision and both Apple and Jobs came in for strong criticism. It had a negative effect on Apple's share prices as well. Though Apple denied having any hidden agenda behind the price cut other than making the phone more affordable to customers, industry watchers speculated that the company had resorted to this step to target shoppers in the impending festive season. According to analyst, Ezra Gottheil of Technology Business Research, Inc, the price cut was necessitated by the launch of the iPod Touch. 'Apple had to drop the price for the iPhone because it couldn't get away with selling the iPod Touch – something that was almost an iPhone – and charge substantially less for it,'[36] said Gottheil, adding that the company would benefit from cost savings as the two products shared parts. Some analysts also felt that the company had gone in for an early price cut because it had concerns regarding future revenues from the iPhone because other players had also entered the market with similar products.

The steep price cut led to Jobs being flooded with angry mails by customers. Initially, the company said that those who had bought the iPhone within 14 days prior to the price cut could apply for a refund under Apple's return policy, contingent on the product not being opened.[37] However, after critically analysing the entire situation, Jobs went ahead and posted a public apology on the company's official website. In addition to this, he offered a credit of US$100 to all the customers who had bought the handset at the introductory price to buy products at Apple Retail Stores. Justifying the price cut, Jobs said, 'I am sure that we are making the correct decision to lower the price of the 8GB iPhone from $599 to $399, and that now is the right time to do it. iPhone is a breakthrough product, and we have the chance to "go for it" this holiday season. iPhone is so far ahead of the competition, and now it will be affordable by even more customers. It benefits both Apple and every iPhone user to get as many new customers as possible in the iPhone "tent". We strongly believe the $399 price will help us do just that this holiday season.'[38]

Experts cited the example of Motorola's much hyped Moto Razr phone. The Moto Razr was priced at US$499 when it was launched and the price dropped to US$399 after a period of only six months. Analysts felt that companies dealing in technological devices had at various times adopted such market skimming strategies. They felt that Apple knew very well that early adopters would be ready to pay a high price for the iPhone. 'Apple skimmed the cream from the market in the initial months, and now they're getting really aggressive',[39] said analyst Van Baker of Gartner Inc, a business intelligence firm. Supporters of Apple also pointed out that, after the price cut, the sales of iPhone had gone up from 9,000 units per day to almost 27,000 units per day[40] (see Exhibit 5 for iPhone's sales after the price cut). By 29 September 2007 the company had amassed sales of 1,389,000 units of the iPhone.[38]

Others felt that the price cut would have hurt customers' sentiments. A senior analyst of Piper Jaffray,[41] Gene Munster said, 'There are two groups of people. The first wave doesn't care because they knew what they were getting into. The second wave is pretty upset, but with Apple everyone has an axe to grind. Whether it's a battery or a screen, it's always something.'[42] Though a majority felt that the sales of iPhones would increase due to the price cut, some felt that such a drastic price cut only a few weeks after the launch was bound to disappoint Apple's customers. 'They've [the early adopters] gone from being envied to being labelled as losers for having paid too much for their iPhones,'[35] explained JP Allen, a professor at the University of San Francisco. Some even suggested that the incident was a PR fiasco for Apple. They said that Apple's belated response of providing US$100 credit to the early purchasers after a section of its customers rose up in protest suggested that the company had failed to judge the impact of the price cut on its customer base.

iPhone goes to Europe

On 9 November 2007 Apple launched its iPhone in the European mobile phone market. The iPhone was initially launched in three markets, Germany, France and the UK. It was on sale from 29 November 2007 in these European markets. The initial response from customers in Germany was overwhelming. People waited in long queues just to get a glimpse of the iPhone. Reinhold Steinwasser, a customer in Germany, said, 'I just want to be the first to touch it, play with it, and try it.'[43] A similar response was cited in the French and UK markets.

The iPhone was available at a premium price of US$566 in the UK, US$587 in Germany and US$415

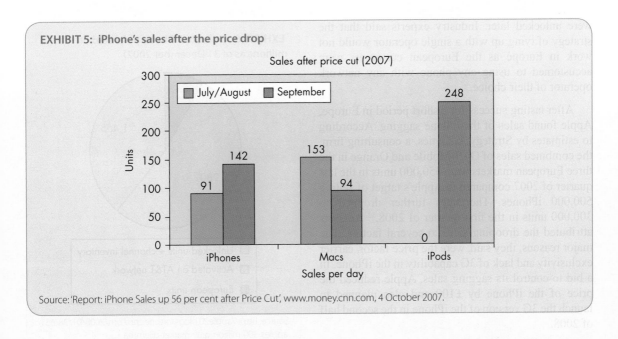

EXHIBIT 5: iPhone's sales after the price drop

Sales after price cut (2007)

Source: 'Report: iPhone Sales up 56 per cent after Price Cut', www.money.cnn.com, 4 October 2007.

in France. The price also included value-added tax (VAT).[44] However, the pricing did not dissuade customers from buying the iPhone.

Considering the buzz created by the iPhone and the response it received in the European markets, industry insiders said that iPhone's launch was as successful as it had been in the USA. Between November 2007 and December 2007 around 330,000 units of the iPhone were sold[45] in Europe.

Apple chose T-Mobile[46] in Germany, Orange[47] in France and Telefónica O₂ Europe Plc[48] (O₂) in the UK as its network partners, with 10 per cent revenue sharing on all calls and data transfers done through iPhones. Apple's revenue-sharing model faced protests initially from O₂ since sharing of revenues with handset manufacturers was non-existent in Europe. Though O₂ was not in sync with Apple's revenue sharing pattern, Peter Erskine, Chief Executive, O₂, said, 'If sharing revenue brings a bigger pie to the table, then we'll be happy to share that pie. The revenue-sharing model will play an increasingly important role in the future of converged communications.'[49]

However, Apple faced some stumbling blocks in Europe. The laws in Europe prevented companies tying up with partners in such a way that customers had to buy one product to get the other. This proved to be a major jolt to Apple's global strategy of tying up with network operators and to take a share of their profits in the European market. On the other hand, T-Mobile had announced its plans to offer the iPhone to customers without any contract. T-Mobile took the

decision in view of the injunction issued by a German court in reply to a lawsuit filed by another mobile operator in Germany, Vodafone Group Plc[50] protesting against the exclusive availability of the iPhone through T-Mobile's network. Later, T-Mobile gave customers the option of signing a two-year contract or buying the unlocked version of the iPhone by paying a prohibitive price (US$1,500).[51] However, T-Mobile argued that product bundling would actually help customers save money.

Analysts said that though Apple could prevent the customers from buying the unlocked iPhones by pricing them very high, it had to pay huge amounts of taxes on the profits it earned on the outright sale of the handsets at prohibitively expensive prices. Apple was also restricted from signing any such revenue-sharing agreements with operators in France.

Despite the initial hiccups and problems faced by Apple in Europe, the iPhone succeeded in some markets, such as England. Around 30,000 iPhones were reported to have been sold in the first week of its launch in England. And by the end of January 2008, 200,000 iPhones had been sold in the country.[52] Apple's partner O₂ said that iPhone was its best selling product. In France, the iPhone had seen moderate success by selling 70,000 units by the end of 2007. But the performance of the iPhone in Germany was dismal despite it being a bigger market than France or England. The post-sale revenues from iPhone were not rosy either for Apple as it was estimated that nearly one-third of the total handsets sold in Europe were unlocked later. Industry experts said that the strategy of tying up with a single operator would not work in Europe as the European customers were accustomed to using any phone with any network operator of their choice.

After tasting success for a short period in Europe, Apple found sales of the iPhone sagging. According to estimates by Strategy Analytics, a consulting firm, the combined sales of O_2, T-Mobile and Orange in the three European markets were 350,000 units in the last quarter of 2007 compared to Apple's target of selling 500,000 iPhones. The sales further dropped to 300,000 units in the first quarter of 2008.[53] Analysts attributed the drooping sales to several factors. The major reasons, they said, were the price factor, carrier exclusivity and lack of 3G capability in the iPhone. In a bid to control its sagging sales, Apple reduced the price of the iPhone by £100 and also planned to launch the 3G version of the iPhone in the second half of 2008.

Other challenges

A growing concern for Apple was the existence of a grey market in the mobile phone market. In February 2008 it was estimated that Apple sold around 3.7 million units of the iPhone while AT&T said that it had made only 2 million connections. The discrepancy of 1.7 million led to the conclusion that these iPhones were unlocked. Within the first week of iPhone's sales in 2007, there was a gap of 124,000 units in the sales figures released by both companies (refer to Exhibit 6 for the number of unlocked iPhones sold). Analysts predicted that several cases of unlocking of the phones had been reported during the festive season. According to Toni Sacconaghi, an analyst at Stanford C. Bernstein,[54] Apple had lost US$300 million to US$400m on its potential revenues and profits with every 1 million phones being unlocked. However, Apple announced its plans to launch a software that would disable unlocking of iPhones.

Another major challenge that Apple faced came in the form of allegations and accusations from environmental protection groups over the use of hazardous materials in the iPhone. In October 2007 Apple received a warning from the Center for Environmental Health (CEH) that it should discontinue the use of Polyvinyl Chloride (PVCs) and Brominated Flame Retardants (BFRs) in its iPhone. Though the CEH did not expect Apple to recall its products, it required Apple to put warning stickers on its iPhone, thereby alerting users of the potential risk involved with the the excessive usage of the product. Apple announced its plans to curb the usage of these materials by the end of 2008.

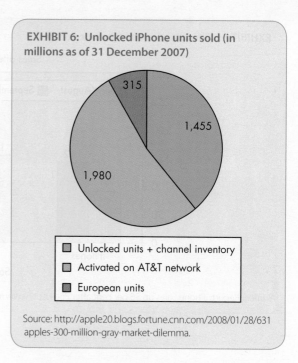

EXHIBIT 6: Unlocked iPhone units sold (in millions as of 31 December 2007)

- 315
- 1,455
- 1,980

☐ Unlocked units + channel inventory
☐ Activated on AT&T network
☐ European units

Source: http://apple20.blogs.fortune.cnn.com/2008/01/28/631 apples-300-million-gray-market-dilemma.

Outlook

Apple's move to go in for a steep price cut of iPhone in the USA attracted a high level of criticism directed at the company. According to some industry observers, it mainly hurt the sentiments of early adopters who had paid a premium to get hold of the product. Jobs also acknowledged that the steep price cut had abused the trust of customers. In a letter posted on Apple's site, Jobs said, 'Our early customers trusted us, and we must live up to that trust with our actions in moments like these.'[56] Subsequently, he announced a US$100 rebate to customers. However, analysts opined that Apple's strategy of reimbursing the money to pacify its angry customers would further dent its image. Rob Enderle, president of the Enderle Group, a technology advisory firm, said, 'A $100 credit could be perceived as adding insult to injury. It's a way to make you go buy something else, and gives the company a chance to make more money.'[55]

Some analysts described Apple's initial high pricing and sudden dropping of the price for its iPhone as a smart strategy since it helped it reap higher profits from its early adopters who had paid a premium. According to Dulaney, Vice President, Gartner Research, 'It's probably a formula taught in business school.'[55]

Brushing off speculations, Jobs said that the price cut was a move to increase the demand for the product and make it affordable for consumers during

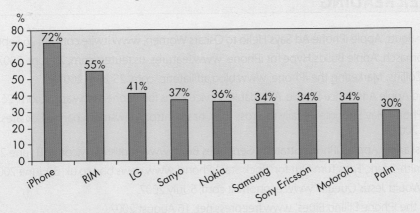

EXHIBIT 7: Customer satisfaction rating of different mobile phone manufacturers

%
- iPhone: 72%
- RIM: 55%
- LG: 41%
- Sanyo: 37%
- Nokia: 36%
- Samsung: 34%
- Sony Ericsson: 34%
- Motorola: 34%
- Palm: 30%

Source: 'iPhone is Top Choice for Next Cell Phone Purchase', www.ipodnn.com, 7 February 2008.

the approaching holiday season. On the other hand, analysts thought that Apple had cut the price since it had realised that it would be unable to achieve its 1 million mark by 2008. Charles Golvin, an analyst with Forrester Research, said, 'I don't think it's a stretch to deduce from this that maybe the rate of sales weren't meeting expectations, so they decided to drop the price. Bear in mind that Steve Jobs said at the last earnings call that they expected to sell a million devices in the following quarter. Maybe they recognized the trajectory wasn't going to get them there at that price.'[55]

Despite the glitches, the growth outlook for iPhone was expected to be positive since a survey by ChangeWave, a market research firm, in February 2008 revealed that around 72 per cent of the consumers were satisfied after buying an iPhone, while another 17 per cent who planned to buy a phone in the coming six months preferred to buy an iPhone[56] (refer to Exhibit 5 for customer satisfaction rating of different mobile phone manufacturers).

For its European market, Apple planned to launch a 3G iPhone in late 2008 since Europe mainly worked on 3G cell networks. Apple also planned to launch its iPhone in other European markets like Italy through Vodafone and Telecom Italia. By selling its iPhone through two mobile operators, Apple aimed to modify its strategy of carrier exclusivity. However, analysts remained sceptical about Apple's growth prospects in Europe considering its high pricing and iPhone's limitation of running slowly on GSM networks.

In August 2008, as part of its plan to foray into the Asian mobile phone market, Apple launched a 3G version of its iPhone in India. The iPhone was available with two operators, Vodafone and Bharti Airtel. According to Apple, the initial response was good since Airtel claimed that it had registered around 200,000 customers who were willing to buy an iPhone while Vodafone reported around 100,000 registered users.[57] However, industry experts said that iPhone's premium pricing coupled with a legally binding contract with Vodafone and Airtel would restrict iPhone from penetrating the intensely competitive mobile phone market dominated by established players like Nokia, Sony Ericsson, Samsung, Motorola, and LG. Apple planned to launch its iPhone in other Asian markets like Japan, South Korea and China by the end of 2008.

QUESTIONS

1   What do you think was the main reason for iPhone's success in America?

2   With tough competition from Nokia, HTC and BlackBerry, do you think the iPhone is as successful in Europe as in America? If not, why not?

3   Could you help Apple to formulate a strategy and a marketing plan for Europe?

4   Do you think Apple's pricing policy is helping it to achieve market share? Was dropping the price a good strategy?

FURTHER READING

- Zaharov-Reutt, 'Apple iPhone Ad Says Hello to Oscars Women', www.itwire.com.au, 26 February 2007.
- Paul Thomasch, 'Apple Builds Hype for iPhone', www.features. us.reuters.com, 20 June 2007.
- Shawn Collins, 'Marketing the iPhone', www.blog.affiliatetip. com, 25 June 2007.
- 'AT&T and Apple Announce Simple, Affordable Service Plans for iPhone', www.apple.com, 26 June 2007.
- 'Apple iPhone May Struggle Initially to Cross the Chasm', http://newsroom.parksassociates.com, 26 June 2007.
- Ville Heiskanen, 'Apple's IPhone Strategy Generates Buzz', www.turkishdaily.com, 30 June 2007.
- Laura Smith-Spark, 'Fans Turn Out for "Rock Star" iPhone', www.news.bbc.co.uk, 30 June 2007.
- 'Where Would Jesus Queue?' www.economist.com, 5 July 2007.
- 'Singing the iPhone Billing Blues', www.freepress.net, 16 August 2007.
- David Ho, 'Next Big Thing is the Size of the Bill', www. coxwashington.com, 16 August 2007.
- Jefferson Graham, 'Apple Dramatically Chops iPhone Cost', www.ustoday.com, 5 September 2007.
- May Wong and Rachel Konrad, 'Apple Cuts iPhone Price, Updates iPods', www.forbes.com, 5 September 2007.
- Patrick Seitz and Ken Spencer Brown, 'Apple Slashes iPhone Price and Dials up an iPhone-like iPod', www.yahoonews. com, 5 September 2007.
- Katie Hafner and Brad Stone, 'IPhone Owners Crying Foul over Price Cut', www.nytimes.com, 6 September 2007.
- '[First] Buyers Beware: Price Cut Coming', www.abcnews.go. com, 8 September 2007.
- Jim Dalrymple, 'Lessons Learnt from the iPhone Price Cuts', *Macworld*, www.pcworld.com, 11 September 2007.
- Mark Sutton, 'iPhone Sales Increase Three Fold after $200 Cut', www.pcretailmag.com, 13 September 2007.
- 'O$_2$ Defends iPhone Revenue-sharing', www.mobilemarketingnews.co.uk, 13 September 2007.
- 'Report: iPhone Sales up 56 per cent after Price Cut', www. money.cnn.com, 4 October 2007.
- Matt Moore, 'Hoping to Replicate US Success', http:abcnews. go.com, 9 November 2007.
- 'Apple iPhone Forced to Unlock in Europe – Crying to the Bank…', www.2aday.worldpress.com, 22 November 2007.
- 'iPhone Takes 28 per cent of the Smartphone Market', www. ipodnn.com, 5 February 2008.
- 'iPhone is Top Choice for Next Cell Phone Purchase', www. ipodnn.com, 7 February 2008.
- '72 per cent of iPhone Owners Satisfied; #1 in Planned Purchases', www.iphoneatlas.com, 7 February 2008.
- Cecilia Aronsson, 'The iPhone in Europe: A Patchy Success', www.venturebeat.com, 10 April 2008.
- Jennifer L. Schenker, 'The iPhone in Europe: Lost in Translation', www.businessweek.com, 16 April 2008.
- Charles Jade, 'Lackluster iPhone Sales in Europe', http://arstechnica.com, 18 April 2008.
- 'iPhone Prices Drop to US$ 154 in Europe', www.cellmad. com, 4 June 2008.
- 'Apple Reports Record Third Quarter Results', www. apple. com, 21 July 2008.
- 'iPhone Launched in India without Mass Hysteria', www. indianinfoline.com, 22 August 2008.
- 'Apple Inc: Competition from IBM', www.britannica.com.
- 'Apple Reports First Quarter Results', www.apple.com.
- http://apple20.blogs.fortune.cnn.com/2008/01/28/apples-300-million-gray- market-dilemma.

- http://www.macnn.com/articles/05/05/04/merill.on.aapl.
- http://www.parksassociates.com/free_data/downloads/parks-iPhone.pdf.
- www.apple.com.
- www.apple.com/hotnews/openiphoneletter.
- www.finance.google.com.
- www.media.corporate-ir.net/media_files/irol/10/107357/AAPL_10K_FY07.pdf.

NOTES

1 Jennifer L. Schenker, 'The iPhone in Europe: Lost in Translation', www.businessweek.com, 16 April 2008.

2 'iPhone Takes 28% of the Smartphone Market', www.ipodnn. com, 5 February 2008.

3 Canalys, headquartered in Grazeley, Reading, UK, is a leading consultancy and market research firm for technology companies.

4 'Apple Reports Record Third Quarter Results', www.apple. com, 21 July 2008.

5 AT&T Wireless Services Inc. (AT&T), headquartered in Redmond, Washington, USA, is one of the leading wireless carriers in the USA. In the USA, Apple entered into a two-year network contract with AT&T for the iPhone.

6 'Apple Inc: Competition from IBM', www.britannica.com.

7 International Business Machine Corporations, headquartered in Armonk, New York, USA, is one of the leading information technology companies.

8 iTMS allowed customers to pay and download music through Macs, and store it on their hard drives.

9 http://www.macnn.com/articles/05/05/04/merill.on.aapl.

10 Macworld Conference & Expo is an annual trade show held in the USA dedicated to the Apple Macintosh platform.

11 The Enderle Group is a provider of technology advisory services and consulting for technology companies.

12 Paul Thomasch, 'Apple Builds Hype for iPhone', www. features.us.reuters.com, 20 June 2007.

13 Bear Stearns, headquartered in New York, USA, is an investment bank and a brokerage firm that also deals in securities trading.

14 The Academy Awards (also known as the Oscars) are the annual awards presented in the USA in recognition of excellence in the film industry.

15 Paul Thomasch, 'Apple Builds Hype for iPhone with Less', www.reuters.com, 20 June 2007.

16 TBWA Worldwide, headquartered in New York, USA, is an ad agency that operates globally in several nations. However, the company operates as TBWA\Chiat\Day in the USA.

17 Omnicom is the world's biggest holding company of advertising agencies. The companies which form part of the group are BBDO, TBWA Worldwide and DDB Worldwide. It is the biggest ad agency in terms of revenue in the world.

18 Pixar Inc. is a well-known maker of animated movies. It was acquired by Jobs in 1986. In 2006 it was acquired by the leading entertainment company, The Walt Disney Company.

19 'Where would Jesus Queue?' www.economist.com, 5 July 2007.

20 'AT&T and Apple Announce Simple, Affordable Service Plans for iPhone', www.apple.com, 26 June 2007.

21 www.media.corporate-ir.net/media_files/irol/10/107357/ AAPL_10K_FY07.pdf.

22 Laura Smith-Spark, 'Fans Turn Out for "Rock Star" iPhone', www.news.bbc.co.uk, 30 June 2007.

23 Ries & Ries, based in Altanta, USA, is a marketing consulting company chaired by Al Ries.

24 Martin Agency was an advertising agency based in Virginia.

25 Ville Heiskanen, 'Apple's iPhone Strategy Generates Buzz', www.turkishdaily.com, 30 June 2007.

26 Shawn Collins, 'Marketing the iPhone', www.blog.affiliatetip. com, 25 June 2007.

27 Nokia Corporation, headquartered in Espoo, Finland, is the world's leading mobile phone company. Its revenues for the fiscal year 2006 were €4.306bn.

28 Samsung Electronics, headquartered in Suwon, South Korea, was the world's third-largest mobile phone company as of July 2007. Its revenues for the fiscal year 2005 were US$78 992.70m.

29 Sony Ericsson Mobile Communications AB, headquartered in Acton, London, UK, is a mobile phone company formed in 2001 as a joint venture between one of the leading consumer electronics companies, Sony Corporation of Japan, and a leading mobile phone company, Ericsson AB of Sweden. It was the world's fourth-largest mobile phone company as of July 2007. Its revenues for the fiscal year 2006 were €10,959m.

30 LG Electronics, headquartered in Seoul, South Korea, is the fifth-largest mobile phone company. Its revenues for the fiscal year 2006 were US$68.8bn.

31 Motorola Inc, headquartered in Schaumburg, Illionis, USA, was the world's second-largest mobile phone company as of July 2007. Its revenues for the year 2006 were US$ 41.2bn.

32 YouTube is the name of a popular website where users can upload, share and watch video clips.

33 'Singing the iPhone Billing Blues', www.freepress.net, 16 August 2007.

34 David Ho, 'Next Big Thing is the Size of the Bill', www. coxwashington.com, 16 August 2007.

35 '[First] Buyers Beware: Price Cut Coming', www.abcnews.go. com, 8 September 2007.

36 Patrick Seitz and Ken Spencer Brown, 'Apple Slashes iPhone Price and Dials up an iPhone-like iPod', www.yahoonews. com, 5 September 2007.

37 May Wong and Rachel Konrad, 'Apple Cuts iPhone Price, Updates iPods', www.forbes.com, 5 September 2007.

38 www.apple.com.

39 Jefferson Graham, 'Apple Dramatically Chops iPhone Cost', www.ustoday.com, 5 September 2007.

40 Mark Sutton, 'iPhone Sales Increase Three Fold after $200 Cut', www.pcretailmag.com, 13 September 2007.

41 Piper Jaffray is a leading investment banking firm.

42 Jim Dalrymple, 'Lessons Learnt from the iPhone Price Cuts', MacWorld, www.pcworld.com, 11 September 2007.

43 Matt Moore, 'Hoping to Replicate US Success', http:abc news. go.com, 9 November 2007.

44 VAT stands for Value Added Tax. It is an indirect tax charged on the sale of products and services. At present more than 135 countries around the world have adopted VAT.

45 'iPhone Prices Drop to US$ 154 in Europe', www.cellmad.com, 4 June 2008.

46 T-Mobile, headquartered in Bonn, Germany, was one of the leading mobile service providers across the globe. It is the subsidiary of Deutsche Telekom.

47 Orange is a brand owned by France Télécom, a leading telecommunication service provider in France.

48 Telefónica O$_2$ Europe Plc, headquartered in Slough, England, UK, was a leading telecommunication service operator in Europe. It is the subsidiary of Telefonica SA.

49 'O$_2$ Defends iPhone Revenue-sharing', www.mobilemarketing news.co.uk, 13 September 2007.

50 Vodafone Group Plc., headquartered in Newbury, England, UK, is one of the leading mobile operators in the world.

51 'Apple iPhone Forced to Unlock in Europe – Crying to the Bank . . .', www.2aday.worldpress.com, 22 November 2007.

52 Cecilia Aronsson, 'The iPhone in Europe: A Patchy Success', www.venturebeat.com, 10 April 2008.

53 Charles Jade, 'Lackluster iPhone Sales in Europe', http:// arstechnica.com, 18 April 2008.

54 Sanford C. Bernstein is a leading market research firm in the UK.

55 Katie Hafner and Brad Stone, 'IPhone Owners Crying Foul over Price Cut', www.nytimes.com, 6 September 2007.

56 '72 per cent of iPhone Owners Satisfied; #1 in Planned Purchases', www.iphoneatlas.com, 7 February 2008.

57 'iPhone Launched in India without Mass Hysteria', www. indianinfoline.com, 22 August 2008.

This case was written by Hadiya Faheem, under the direction of Debapratim Purkayastha, ICMR Center for Management Research. It was compiled from published sources, and is intended to be used as a basis for class discussion rather than to illustrate either effective or ineffective handling of a management situation.

Case 5.3

UGG Boots: Australian Generic Product to Global Luxury Brand

© P. Ghauri.

'We believe the strong demand for UGG products across a broad assortment of styles is an indication that UGG is becoming a strong brand versus a 'hot' trend in just one boot style.'[1]

Jeffrey Klinefelte, Research
Analyst at Piper Jaffray,[2] 2005

'We have been doing celebrity seeding. What happens is that when you have a good product and people start wearing it, it becomes word-of-mouth and it spreads. It was an undiscovered brand that was a surfer boot. Through a series of product placements, getting in magazines and being featured on shows such as Oprah it has been discovered.'[3]

Karen Bromley, owner of a New York
public relations company representing
UGG Australia, 2003

From fad to fashion

UGG boots,[4] which originated in Australia over 200 years ago, were considered to be a generic name for sheepskin boots in Australia. UGGs gained recognition in the USA in 1978 when the Californian surfing community began using them as it found them comfortable and warm. In 1995 Deckers acquired UGG Holdings Inc, a company that sold UGGs in the USA under the UGG Australia brand.

Though analysts opined that UGGs were a passing fad that would fizzle out after a few years, their popularity continued, and during the holiday season of 2007, they featured prominently among the 'season's must have items'. Even while most of the other fashion footwear brands were selling at heavily discounted prices during the season, UGGs continued to sell at full price. According to Jennifer Black, a retail analyst, 'There doesn't seem to be a fashion element that is working this year. The one exception is UGGs.'[5]

Background note

Deckers was founded by Doug Otto in 1973.[6] Initially, the company manufactured sandals under the Deckers brand name in a small factory in Carpentaria,[7] California. Later it acquired well-known footwear brands that proved to be profitable. In 1985, Deckers entered into a licensing agreement with Mark Thatcher, founder of sports sandal brand Teva.

In 1993 the company purchased a 50 per cent share of Simple Shoes, Inc from its founder Eric Myer. Simple Shoes produced sneakers, clogs and sandals mainly targeted at the teenage and men's and women's casuals markets. In 1994 the company acquired the remaining 50 per cent interest in Simple Shoes for US$1.5m.[8] Deckers experienced rapid growth during the 1990s and first appeared on the stock exchange in 1993 under the name DECK. As sales grew, Deckers set up independent manufacturing units in China, New Zealand and Australia to manufacture its footwear products.

Deckers acquired UGG Holdings Inc in 1995 from Brian Smith, an Australian surfer. Upon the purchase, Deckers acquired the UGG trademark in 25 countries. It positioned UGG as high end luxury footwear and popularised it in the USA and in some European countries (see Exhibit 1 for the history of UGG boots in Australia).

In 2001 the sales of Teva footwear accounted for about 67 per cent of Deckers' total sales. In November 2002 Deckers acquired Teva's trademarks and patents from Thatcher for approximately US$62m.[9]

By 2007 UGG boots had become very fashionable in America and were being sold in most major

EXHIBIT 1: History of UGG boots

The existence of sheepskin boots in Australia can be traced back over 200 years when European colonists first settled in Australia and used sheep hide to make clothes and footwear. Over the decades, the sheep industry grew extensively in Australia.

Workers in Australia and New Zealand who sheared sheep made boots from the sheepskin to keep their feet warm as the raw material was readily available to them. The boots they made were just two pieces of sheepskin attached in the front with a soft sole and they were called 'Ug' or 'Ugh' boots, short for 'ugly' because, though they were comfortable, they did not really appeal to the eye. There are different versions of the origin of the name 'UGG', as some think that the name came from the way the boot 'hugs' the wearer's feet and legs. As 'UGG' boots provided warmth and comfort, people started wearing them while carrying out outdoor activities like farming.

Later, during the First and Second World Wars and, pilots used these sheepskin boots. Because of their thermostatic property and their ability to keep feet warm,[10] the UGG boots became a rage among aviators who called them 'fug boots', meaning flying UGGs.

During the 1950s and 1960s the surfing communities at the beaches near Margaret River in Perth first adopted the UGGs while surfing. The boots resisted water, had no hard soles, and provided sock-like comfort while walking over slippery terrain. As UGGs made surfing comfortable, they were lapped up by the surfer communities and tourists in Australia.

By the mid-1960s the sheepskin boots had become very popular in Australia and were generically referred to as 'UGGs.' In 1981 UGG entered the Australian official dictionary, the *Macquarie* dictionary, as a generic description of sheepskin boots.

Shane Stedman, a surfing champion in Australia, registered the trademarks 'UGH-BOOTS' and 'UGH' in Australia in 1971 and 1982 respectively[11] and began selling the boots under these names. In 1978 Brian Smith, another Australian surfer, visited the USA and introduced the boots to the surfing enthusiasts in California. With their success in California, Smith decided to develop and market the sheepskin footwear in the USA. In 1986 Smith started a company called UGG Holdings to trade UGGs. In 1995 he sold all rights of UGG Holdings to Deckers.

Source: compiled from various sources.

department stores and footwear stores across the globe. In 2007 Deckers recorded net sales of US$448.9m, out of which US$291.9m was contributed by the UGG brand (see Exhibit 2 for Deckers' key financials 2003–2007).

In May 2008 Deckers acquired 100 per cent ownership of Tsubo LLC[12] for approximately US$6m in cash.[13] In the same year, it also entered into a joint venture with Stella International Holdings Ltd[14] to open retail stores and set up wholesale distribution in China for the UGG Australia brand. The joint venture was owned 51 per cent by Deckers and 49 per cent by Stella Holdings. The companies planned to invest about US$5m in total to open two stores in China in 2008.[15]

As of 2008 Deckers marketed its products under the brands Teva, Simple Shoes, UGG Australia, Tsubo, and Deckers Flip Flops (see Exhibit 3 for a brief overview of Deckers' brands). The company's brands were distinctive and Deckers used fine materials like leather, suede[16] and sheepskin to manufacture its footwear line. The company's goal was to establish its products as global lifestyle brands. With UGG Australia proving to be its most profitable brand, Deckers planned to open more UGG retail stores in the USA as well as in other international markets.

Marketing UGGs

The comfort, luxury and fashion element associated with the UGGs ensured that UGG Australia soon became a well-known brand. The UGGs were stylish and could be worn all through the year. And they were popular not only because of the fashion element associated with them but also because of their comfort factor. According to marketing analysts, Deckers adopted good promotion and distribution strategies to make the brand popular in the USA. The prices of UGG boots ranged from US$60 to US$350. No discounts were given by the company in any season.

Internationally, UGGs fastest-growing market was the UK. In other places like northern Europe and Canada there was considerable demand for UGG footwear. In 2007 a broad collection of UGG footwear was introduced in these countries to cater to the growing demand for UGGs. International sales for all three of Deckers' brands increased by 62.6 per cent to US$62.3m in 2007 compared to US$38.3m in 2006.[17] To improve UGG's international operations and sales and to position and promote the UGG brand, Deckers worked closely with its distributors, especially in the UK. As of 2007 the

EXHIBIT 2: Deckers outdoor corporation key financials 2003–2007 (in US$ thousands, except per share data)

Statement of operations data	2003*	2004*	2005*	2006*	2007*
Net sales:					
Teva wholesale	72 783	83 477	80446	75823	82003
UGG wholesale	34 561	101 806	150279	182369	291908
Simple wholesale	7210	9633	6980	10903	11163
eCommerce	6501	19 871	25912	28886	45473
Retail stores	–	–	1143	6982	18832
Net sales	121055	214 787	264760	304423	448 929
Cost of sales	69965	124 659	153598	163692	241 458
Gross profit	51090	90128	111162	140732	207 471
Selling, general and administrative expenses	32407	47971	59254	73989	101 918
Litigation income (1)	(500)	–	–	–	–
Impairment loss (2)	–	–	–	15300	–
Income from operations	19183	42157	51 908	51442	105 553
Other expense (income), net	4770	2517	374	(1910)	(4486)
Income before income taxes	14413	39640	51 534	53 352	110 039
Income taxes	5752	14713	20 387	22 743	43 602
Net income	8661	24927	31 147	30 609	66 437
Net income per share:					
Basic	0.86	2.27	2.52	2.45	5.18
Diluted	0.73	2.05	2.42	2.38	5.06
Weighted average common shares outstanding:					
Basic	9610	11005	12 349	12 519	12835
Diluted	11880	12142	12 866	12 882	13129

1 The litigation income in 2003 relates to a European anti-dumping duties matter that was ultimately resolved in Deckers' favour in 2003.

2 The impairment loss in 2006 relates to Teva trademarks. During annual assessment of goodwill and other intangible assets, it was concluded that fair value was lower than carrying amount and thus the trademarks were written down to their fair value.

*Years ending 31 December.

Source: Deckers Outdoor Corporation, *2007 Annual Report.*

UGG Australia boots were being sold in the USA, the UK, Australia, Japan, Switzerland, France, Germany and Italy.

UGGs had been in existence for several years, but their popularity grew after Deckers acquired UGG Australia. The UGG product line successfully evolved from being just sheepskin boots into a diverse collection of luxury and comfort styles, mainly due to some unique marketing strategies that Deckers adopted to popularise them. Initially, it was widely believed that the craze for UGGs would die down soon just like other fads, but it continued to remain popular and expanded into new categories likes sandals, clogs and crochet boots, with analysts saying that UGGs were in tune with the 'cultural zeitgeist'.

Luxury and comfort footwear

UGGs were made of high-quality sheepskin. Their soles were durable and the boots themselves were well-constructed. They were lightweight, giving the wearer a feeling of walking around in socks or slippers. Sheepskin's thermostatic property automatically regulates body temperature based on the temperature of the surroundings. The natural fibres of the sheepskin trap body heat in the boot when it is cold outside and release sweat and keep feet cool during the summer.

For many years the UGG Australia brand consisted of only footwear. In 1998 the UGG product line comprised two styles in boots, four in slippers, and a few casuals. In 2004 Deckers diversified its product range to introduce UGG handbags and outerwear. In 2005 it launched cold weather accessories in the USA. A year later, these accessories were introduced in other international markets.

With UGG boots becoming a fashion statement, Deckers decided to expand its market share in the countries where UGG boots were sold. To increase sales, it diversified into non-boot casuals and styles combining sheepskin with fine-grade suede and leather. Deckers diversified its product line to include coats, scarves, gloves, hats and sheepskin-lined handbags.

In 2006 Deckers expanded the UGG footwear collection to include additional styles and fabrications. In addition to autumn and winter collections, it also offered spring and summer collections. In its spring 2006 collection, Deckers introduced the UGG brand's first line of open-toe sandals and slides with a thin layer of sheepskin in a variety of styles and colours. In the autumn 2007 collection, Deckers added more styles to UGG brand's product line. From approximately 50 styles in 2002, the UGG

brand had about 125 styles in its footwear collections in 2007.[18] The expansion in product line and the continued addition of innovative product categories increased brand exposure and sustained consumer interest in the brand (see Exhibit 4 for the UGG Australia footwear line).

Deckers outsourced the production of UGGs to independent manufacturers in China, New Zealand and Australia. These manufacturers purchased high-quality sheepskin from tanneries in China that sourced sheep from Australia and New Zealand. To ensure that there would be no shortage of supply to meet any increase in demand, the company specified the production limit well in advance to its manufacturers. It had no long-term contracts with any of its manufacturers.

The designs for UGGs were conceptualised in the USA and communicated to the independent manufacturers. The company had set up on-site offices in Panyu City,[19] China, and Macau[20] and these served as local links to its independent manufacturers. The presence of supervisory offices in China helped the company keep an eye on the availability of raw

---

EXHIBIT 3: Deckers' brands

Name of the brand	Description
Teva	The Teva brand was founded in the early 1980s by a Colorado river guide to serve the footwear needs of professional river guides. Since then, the Teva sport sandal line has expanded to include casual open-toe footwear, adventure travel shoes, outdoor cross-training shoes, trail running shoes, and other rugged outdoor footwear styles. In 1985 Deckers entered into a licensing agreement with Mark Thatcher, founder of the Teva brand. From 1985 to November 2002, Deckers sold Teva products under a licence agreement. In 2001 the sales of Teva footwear accounted for about 67 per cent of Deckers' total sales. In November 2002, Deckers sold Teva products under a licensing agreement with Mark Thatcher, for approximately US$62m. Teva is one of the leading brands in the sport sandal market. It is marketed under the brand Go. Do. Be. The Go, the Do and the Be collections have their own unique properties.
UGG Australia	UGG Australia is Deckers' luxury sheepskin footwear brand. Deckers acquired the UGG brand in 1995 and repositioned it as a luxury brand sold through high-end retailers. Since the acquisition, UGG sales increased steadily and UGG Australia products were endorsed by leading international celebrities. In 2004 UGG Australia diversified to include handbags, cold-weather accessories, outer wear and headwear.
Simple	Deckers purchased a 50 per cent share of Simple Shoes Inc in 1993 from Eric Myer. Simple Shoes produced sneakers, clogs, sandals, and men's and women's casuals and were mainly targeted at teenagers. Early in 1994 the company acquired the remaining 50 per cent interest in Simple Shoes. Simple brand net sales for the second quarter ended June 2008 increased by 94.0 per cent to US$4.7m compared to US$2.4m for the same period last year.
Tsubo	In May 2008 Deckers acquired 100 per cent ownership of Tsubo LLC, a high-end casual footwear company based in California for approximately US$6m in cash. The Tsubo product line is a mix of ergonomics and style that includes sport and dress casuals, boots, sandals and heels. Tsubo is a worldwide brand being sold in the US, the UK, Canada, France, Belgium, Holland, Austria, Japan, Hong Kong and Korea.

Source: compiled from various sources.

EXHIBIT 4: UGG Australia footwear line

Classic Collection	The Classic Collection of sheepskin boots resembles the early UGG boots in appearance and includes styles for men, women and children in a wide array of colours.
Ultra Collection	The Ultra Collection is based on the classic collection with a three-part insole designed to provide comfort and support. This collection features styles for men, women and children.
Fashion Collection	The Fashion Collection offers fashionable and trendy footwear styles for women, men and children. The collection includes wedges and high heels for women, a European collection for men and fashionable styles for children.
Driving Collection	The collection features styles for men, women and children with suede and leather uppers lined with sheepskin. The men's collection includes boots with interchangeable leather insoles that can be worn with or without socks.
Surf Collection	The Surf Collection is based on the original surfing boots which were the first offering by the brand. The collection includes sandals, clogs and boots and is available for men, women and children.
Cold Weather Collection	This collection is designed for men, women and children. The line has outsoles from Vubram, a leading shoe-sole manufacturer, to help withstand the cold.
Slipper Collection	The Slipper Collection includes slippers for men, women and children in different colours and styles.

Source: adapted from Deckers Outdoor Corporation, *Annual Report 2006*.

materials and adherence to design specifications, to monitor the production process from the receipt of the design brief to production of final samples, and to oversee shipment of the finished product.

Distribution

Globally, UGG products were distributed through independent distributors and high-end retailers. Deckers distributed products through 30 independent retailers based in countries like Canada, China, France, Korea and those in Scandinavia. They were sold through retail concept stores, retail outlet stores, and also through its website. Deckers employed approximately 45 independent sales representatives throughout the USA to visit retail stores and communicate the features and styling of UGG boots.

The UGG boots business had spread all over the USA, particularly in the midwest and northeast regions. According to sources from the company, UGGs were sold in retail stores because the company wanted to be in direct contact with customers who sought fashion and functional elements in the UGG product line. In 2006 the first UGG flagship store was opened in New York City and the second UGG concept store in Chicago, Illinois, in 2007. Based on the success of the existing concept stores, Deckers planned to open more such stores in major metropolitan areas and malls in the USA by the end of 2008.

Promotion

According to company sources, Deckers spent nearly US$17m in 2007 to advertise, market and promote its brands. The promotional strategy aimed at positioning UGGs as premium luxury footwear. UGGs were extensively advertised via print media, product placement and celebrity endorsements, among others.

The UGG brand was advertised in the print media through high-end fashion magazines like *Teen Vogue*, *Glamour*, *Vanity Fair* and *O Magazine*, targeting mainly women. But with the introduction of innovative men's styles in 2005, the company began to advertise in men's magazines such as *Outside*, *Men's Vogue*, *GQ* and *Surfer* to attract customers to the brand. UGGs were also given editorial coverage in numerous articles that appeared in lifestyle and fashion magazines like *Glamour*, *InStyle*, *Cosmopolitan*, *Marie Claire*, *People*, *US Weekly*, *Maxim*, *Shape*, *Self*, *O Magazine* and *Real Simple*.

By the 2000s UGGs had become a fashion statement in New York, Milan, Tokyo, London, and Paris and were endorsed by international celebrities such as Pamela Anderson,[21] Kate Hudson[22] and Jessica Simpson.[23] These celebrities were often photographed wearing UGGs. David Wolfe, fashion consultant at Doneger,[24] said, 'No matter what the item is, if it has celebrity endorsement today, that's enough to move it.

But UGGs are more than a fad because they are practical, and they are warm, and they are so funky.'[25]

Analysts termed the product placement used for UGG Australia 'gratis product placement'.[26] Gary Mezzatesta, president and CEO of UPP Entertainment Marketing,[27] said, 'UGG is a great example of the power of how [gratis product placement] can work. It was an organic swelling of celebrities embracing the product, wearing it in public, and, because they are photographed often, it was a promotion that just happened as opposed to a paid situation. [UGG] might not have gotten where they are today without all that exposure in the lifestyle media, and they are still very successful – the short-term benefit has reaped long-term rewards.'[28]

UGG products were also featured at select events, which helped them gain popularity. They were featured in the Winter Olympic Games 2002 held in the USA, where the performers wore UGG boots. During the medal ceremonies, the Olympic staff who presented medals to the athletes also wore UGG boots. In 2006, a special range of UGGs with red-outsoles was launched for the Swiss Olympic team.

UGGs not only made strides in the fashion industry but were also involved in charitable events. In 2003, a fundraising event called 'Art and Sole'[29] was organised by Deckers and raised over US$33,000.[30] As a part of the event, some of Hollywood's and television's well-known names decorated UGG boots for an online auction. To support the online auction, the customised boots were displayed in Nordstrom stores across the country.

Another factor that helped UGGs make a mark was the number of awards it won. In 2003 UGG Australia was named 'Brand of the Year' by *Footwear News*.[31] In 2004, it was awarded 'Brand of the Year' by Footwear Plus. In the same year, it was also given the ACE Award[32] for the 'it' accessory of the year by the Accessories Council.[33]

The popularity of UGGs grew even further after they were featured on *The Oprah Winfrey Show*[34] as one of 'Oprah's Favorite Things' in 2005 and 2007. The UGG Uptown Boots which were featured on the show in 2005 were among the holiday best sellers that year. In 2007 Oprah featured UGG Classic Crochet Boots as a hot Christmas item. The endorsement by Oprah Winfrey sealed UGG's rise to fame because it led to them being adopted as street fashion in the USA and other European countries.

Results

The sales of UGGs rose from US$40m in 2003 to over US$116m in 2004.[35] According to the *Wall Street Journal*,[36] 'UGG Australia' brand products contributed to a 77 per cent jump in Deckers' overall sales in 2004, which were about US$215m.[35]

Many of the shoppers then resorted to buying UGGs online. The online demand for the boots reached its peak in 2003 when bidding on auction websites for the UGG Australia boots was as high as US$500,[37] for a single pair. To cash in on the popularity of the UGGs, Australian sheepskin boot manufacturers also began selling their UGGs in the USA through Internet auction sites such as eBay for a much lower price. Several consumers then started buying the UGGs from the Australian manufacturers through these auction websites. This irked Deckers, which was concerned about lost sales.

In 2003 Deckers issued legal notices to as many as 20 Australian sheepskin boot manufacturers and retailers who were using different versions of the word 'UGG'. Deckers demanded that they stop using the word 'UGG' while selling and marketing their products. The company felt that, as trademark owners, it had exclusive rights over the term 'UGG'. But Australian sheepskin boot manufacturers opposed the 'UGG' trademarked rights being granted to Deckers, pointing out that 'UGG' was a generic term that had been used to describe sheepskin boots in Australia for many years. In the legal battle that followed, the manufacturers and retailers of sheepskin shoes in Australia were allowed to call their products 'UGGs' by the Australian authorities (see Exhibit 5 for a brief overview of the UGG boot controversy).

In 2007 UGG boots were criticised by PETA[38] activist and celebrity Pamela Anderson, who stopped endorsing UGG boots after she learnt that the boots were made from shaved sheepskin. She even urged her fans to stop buying UGG boots. 'I'm getting rid of our UGGs – I feel so guilty for that craze being started around Baywatch days – I used to wear them with my red swim suit to keep warm – never realising that they were SKIN!'[39]

However, the controversies and criticisms did little to dent the popularity of UGGs or affect their sales. The UGG Australia brand experienced steady growth over the years as net wholesale sales of UGG products increased by 66.9 per cent between 2002 and 2006. In 2007 Deckers' net sales increased by 47.5 per cent to US$448.9m compared to the previous year's sales.[40] The increase was primarily due to increases in the sales of UGG Australia. Net sales for UGG Australia increased by 64.4 per cent to US$347.6m in 2007 compared to US$211.5m in 2006.[40] The sales included all categories of the UGG

EXHIBIT 5: The UGG boot controversy

In 2003 a controversy arose over the use of the name 'UGG'. For several years, Australian sheepskin boot manufacturers had been trading their products using 'UGG'. Though Deckers owned the UGG trademark in Australia, it did not raise the trademark issue for many years. It was only in 2003 when there was a rise in the popularity of and demand for UGG boots that it decided to take action against the manufacturers of UGGs in Australia, including those who were selling their products online.

Deckers claimed that its subsidiary UGG Holdings owned the trademark 'UGG', which had been trademarked in the USA, and also the 'UGH' and 'UGH-BOOTS', which it had acquired from Stedman. Deckers secured more than 45 registrations for the 'UGG' mark, covering 79 countries. According to it, the UGG trademarks were found to be suitable for registration and in the absence of any opposition during that time, they had been successfully registered. It claimed that unauthorised use of the brand was prohibited by the laws of the USA, Canada, Europe, Japan, Korea, China, and other countries where Deckers had established trademark rights. It wanted the Australian companies to refer to their products as 'sheepskin boots' instead of UGG boots.

The company issued legal letters to as many as 20 Australian sheepskin boot manufacturers and retailers that used different versions of the word 'UGG' telling them to stop using the word while selling and marketing their products. The firms were asked to withdraw catalogues, labels, signs, price lists, advertisements and business names that contained the words 'UGG', 'Ug' or 'Ugh'. The letter sought to prohibit the Australian companies from selling UGG boots to American consumers through auction sites in the USA. Deckers threatened them with legal action if they continued to use the term 'UGG'.

The Australian sheepskin boot manufacturers protested against Deckers' trademark rights on the grounds that 'UGG' was a generic term that had been used to describe sheepskin boots in Australia for many years. The Australian manufacturers alleged that Deckers was trying to bully smaller businesses. According to them, trademark laws in Australia offered no protection for generic words. Thus, a legal dispute started between Australian sheepskin boot manufacturers and UGG Holdings which claimed to own the UGG Australia brand.

In 2004 the manufacturers and retailers of UGG boots in Australia united to form an alliance known as the Australian Sheepskin Association. The aim of the association was to fight a legal battle against Deckers. Several small manufacturers of sheepskin boots lodged applications with IP Australia in 2003, seeking the removal of the UGG trademark in Australia.

On 16 January 2006 a decision related to the case ordered the removal of the trademark UGH-BOOTS from the trademark register as the evidence provided by Deckers was not sufficient to prove that the trademark had been used in Australia by Deckers within the relevant period.

Source: compiled from various sources.

Australia brand such as boots, slippers, sandals, casuals and cold-weather footwear.

For the second quarter ended June 2008, UGG Australia's net sales increased by 130.6 per cent to US$60.6m compared to US$26.3m for the same period the previous year, making UGG boots a leader in the fashion footwear industry.[41]

Looking ahead

Analysts felt that, though Deckers had efficiently positioned the UGG products in the market through extensive marketing, it had failed to maintain a balance between demand and supply and, consequently, was left unprepared when the demand for UGGs rose. This provided an opportunity for its competitors, who cashed in on the popularity of UGGs and raised their sales. Analysts were of the view that Deckers needed to be aware of cheap imitation UGG boots, as some online auction sites sold fake UGG boots in countries like the UK and New Zealand. Many high street stores were also taking advantage of the demand for UGG boots and were selling UGGs made from cow skin instead of sheepskin.

According to analysts, the main challenge for Deckers in the future would be to sustain the demand for UGG boots, which could diminish as trends in the fashion industry changed. With the fashion world ever ready to jump to the next footwear trend, the manufacturers needed to concentrate on their marketing strategy, and introduce innovative designs and fashionable styles in the UGG footwear line, they said.

UGG products constituted a significant portion of Deckers business and if its sales declined in the future, then the overall financial performance of the company itself would be adversely affected, analysts said. Deckers needed to diversify its UGG product line to non-footwear categories and increase its presence in retail stores across the USA and Europe.

Another concern for Deckers was the non-availability of high-grade sheepskin, which was used in making UGG footwear. The demand for this kind of sheepskin was high but its supply was limited. Flocks of sheep infected with foot-and-mouth disease had been exterminated and that had an adverse effect on the availability of top-grade sheepskin for UGG products. The drought conditions in Australia further affected the supply of sheepskin. The shortage led to a significant increase in the prices of top-grade sheepskin.

If the company failed to meet the production demands, it would lead to inventory shortages and result in lost sales. Analysts observed that the shortage in supply of UGGs would drive consumers to shop for UGG boots from other places, such as online shopping sites. They might go in for an alternative brand of UGGs, and this could result in decreased brand loyalty.

UGGs was an underdeveloped brand globally in terms of unit sales. It operated only in a handful of countries outside the USA, and the opportunities for it to grow were greater. In order to increase the sales volume internationally, Deckers planned to expand its footwear line with a broader assortment of footwear and greater floor space at retail stores by the end of 2008. As part of the spring 2008 collection, it planned to introduce a more evolved product line in its international markets with 25 additional styles including a large collection of espadrilles,[42] flats, luxury sandals and comfortable slippers.

The company planned to make the men's category a key focus in 2008, with the introduction of several new styles of footwear under the casual, comfort and rugged collections for everyday use. It expected the added collection to raise the level of excitement and help it capture market share in the men's footwear category. In 2008 Deckers also planned to update the UGG women's collection with new colours, unique materials and greater functionality.

QUESTIONS

1   Do you think UGG is an established brand or a 'passing fad'?
2   How do you think the UGG brand can remain sustainable?
3   Deckers wants to introduce UGG shoes for men. Do you think it is a good idea? Which segment should they focus on?

FURTHER READING

- 'Deckers Acquires Teva Trademarks and Patents For $62 Million', www.allbusiness.com, 15 October 2002.
- Lorrie Grant, 'UGG Boots a Fashion Kick', www.usatoday. com, 12 October 2003.
- Suzanne S. Brown, 'UGGs on the A-list', www.theage.com.au, 25 November 2003.
- 'Putting the Boot In', www.smh.com.au, 13 March 2004.
- Maya Roney, 'Deckers Outdoor Set for UGG Boots Boost', www.forbes.com, 12 July 2005.
- Vivian Manning Schaffel, 'Brand Gets Celebrity Exposure', www.brandchannel.com, 13 February 2006.
- 'Pamela Anderson Learns UGG Boots Made from Sheepskin, Speaks Out against Them', www.foxnews.com, 27 February 2007.
- 'Form 10-Q/A for Deckers Outdoor Corp', www.biz.yahoo. com, 11 October 2007.
- Barry Silverstein, 'UGG Australia – The Good, the Bad and the UGGly', www.brandchannel.com, 10 December 2007.
- Suzanne Kapner, 'UGGs Still Selling Comfortably', CNNMoney. com, 20 December 2007.
- 'USA: Plus Award Honors Deckers as Company of the Year', www.fibre2fashion.com, 6 February 2008.

- 'Deckers Outdoor Corporation Q4 2007 Earnings Call Transcript', www.seekingalpha.com, 28 February 2008.
- 'Deckers Outdoor Corporation Acquires TSUBO, LLC', www. reuters.com, 6 May 2008.
- 'Deckers Outdoor, Stella in Joint Venture to Open UGG Stores in China', www.forbes.com, 7 October 2008.
- 'Deckers Outdoor Corporation', www.answers.com.
- www.uggaustralia.com.
- www.deckers.com.

NOTES

1   Maya Roney, 'Deckers Outdoor Set for UGG Boots Boost', www.forbes.com, 12 July 2005.

2   Piper Jaffray is a US-based investment banking firm. It focuses on providing financial advice and investment products in the financial services marketplace.

3   Suzanne S. Brown, 'UGGs on the A-list', www.theage.com.au, 25 November 2003.

4   UGG is also known by its variants: UGG BOOTS, Ug Boots, UGH Boots, Ugh Boots, UGG Boots, Uggboots, UGGBOOTS, UGGs, UGG-BOOTS, etc.

5   Suzanne Kapner, 'UGGs Still Selling Comfortably', CNNMoney. com, 20 December 2007.

6   Doug Otto, after passing out from University of California, Santa Barbara (UCSB) along with two other students, found new ways to use advanced materials and designs to create durable, water-compatible sandals that could be used during rigorous outdoor activities. They manufactured Deckers brand sandals for over 20 years.

7   Carpentaria is a small city located by the ocean in the southeastern extremity of Santa Barbara County, California.

8   Deckers Outdoor Corporation, www.answers.com.

9   'Deckers Acquires Teva Trademarks and Patents for $62 Million', www.allbusiness.com, 15 October 2002.

10 Sheepskin boots have thick fleece fibres on the inner part of the boot which allow air to circulate during summer, absorb moisture, and keep the feet cool and dry. In cold weather, the soft wool fibres act as a natural insulator, keeping the feet warm and comfortable.

11 'Trade Mark Details', http://pericles.ipaustralia.gov.au/atmoss/Falcon.Result.

12 Tsubo LLC is a casual footwear company based in California.

13 'Deckers Outdoor Corporation Acquires TSUBO, LLC', www. reuters.com, 6 May 2008.

14 Stella International is a leading developer and manufacturer of quality footwear products in China.

15 'Deckers Outdoor, Stella in Joint Venture to Open UGG Stores in China', www.forbes.com, 7 October 2008.

16 Suede is leather with a napped surface (fuzzy or raised surface).

17 'Deckers Outdoor Corporation Q4 2007 Earnings Call Transcript', www.seekingalpha.com, 28 February 2008.

18 'Form 10-Q/A for Deckers Outdoor Corp', www.biz.yahoo. com, 11 October 2007.

19 Panyu city is located in Guangzhou Province of China.

20 Macau is one of the special administrative regions of the People's Republic of China located on the western side of the Pearl River delta.

21 Pamela Anderson is a Canada-born actress, model and TV personality. She wore UGG boots during the filming of the Australian version of the American television series *Baywatch*.

22 Kate Hudson is an American film actress. She wore UGG boots during the promotion of her film, *Raising Helen*.

23 Jessica Simpson is an American pop singer and actress. She sported pink UGG boots in an episode of reality television show *Newlyweds*.

24 The Doneger Group based in the USA provides information on global market trends and merchandising strategies to the retail and fashion industry.

25 Lorrie Grant, 'UGG Boots a Fashion Kick', www.usatoday. com, 12 October 2003.

26 In gratis product placement, the endorser of the brand gratuitously advertises the brand without being paid.

27 UPP Entertainment Marketing is a California-based marketing agency that offers innovative marketing solutions to its clients.

28 Vivian Manning Schaffel, 'Brand Gets Celebrity Exposure', www.brandchannel.com, 13 February 2006.

29 Celebrities such as Heather Locklear, Ted Danson, Alyssa Milano, Charlize Theron and Tracy Pollan were given a pair of UGGs, along with several colours of Mac nail polish, various gems and other decorative items to use along with their imagination to personalise the boots with a design of their own.

30 http://www.michaeljfox.org/newsEvents_mjffInTheNews_ events_article.cfm?ID=172.

31 *Footwear News* is a weekly news and fashion magazine that publishes the latest events related to the footwear industry.

32 The ACE Awards were started in 1996 to felicitate companies that contributed to increased accessories consumption in a particular year.

33 The Accessories Council established in 1994 is a not-for-profit, national trade association which aims to raise consumer awareness and demand for accessories.

34 The *Oprah Winfrey Show* is one of the highest rated television talk shows in the USA. The show is hosted and produced by Oprah Winfrey, who is a media mogul, book critic and philanthropist.

35 Barry Silverstein, 'UGG Australia – The Good, the Bad, and the UGGly', www.brandchannel.com, 10 December 2007.

36 The *Wall Street Journal* is an English-language daily newspaper published internationally by Dow Jones & Company in New York City. Stephanie Kang, 'UGGs Again? What Last Year's "It" Gift Does for an Encore', 9 December 2005.

37 'Putting the Boot In', www.smh.com.au, 13 March 2004.

38 People for the Ethical Treatment of Animals (PETA) is an animal rights organisation, based in the USA.

39 'Pamela Anderson Learns UGG Boots Made from Sheepskin, Speaks Out Against Them', www.foxnews. com, 27 February 2007.

40 'Deckers Outdoor Corporation Q4 2007 Earnings Call Transcript', www.seekingalpha.com, 28 February 2008.

41 'Deckers UGG Brand Sales Up', www.fibre2fashion.com, 8 August 2008.

42 Espadrilles are casual flat or high-heel fashion sandals with an upper canvas or cotton fabric and a sole made of natural or synthetic fibres moulded to look like a rope.

This case was written by Syeda Maseeha Qumer and Indu P., under the direction of Debapratim Purkayastha, ICMR Center for Management Research. It was compiled from published sources, and is intended to be used as a basis for class discussion rather than to illustrate either effective or ineffective handling of a management situation.

Case 5.4

L'Oréal – Building a Global Cosmetic Brand

'It is a strategy based on buying local cosmetics brands, giving them a facelift and exporting them around the world.'

'One Brand at a Time: The Secret of L'Oréal's Global Makeover', www.fortune.com
12 August 2002

L'Oréal makes waves

In November 2002 L'Oréal, the France-based leading global cosmetics company, received the 'Global Corporate Achievement Award 2002', for Europe by 'The Economist Group'.

In the same month L'Oréal's chairman and CEO, Lindsay Owen Jones was honoured with the 'Best Manager of the Last 20 Years' title by the French Minister of Finance and Economy, Francis Mer. This award, instituted by the leading French business publication, *Challenges*, was in recognition of Jones' outstanding achievements in transforming L'Oréal from a French company into a global powerhouse.

These honours were not just a 'cosmetic' eulogy; L'Oréal deserved them, for it was the only company in its industry to post a double-digit profit for 18 consecutive years (see Exhibit 1 for L'Oréal's key financials). L'Oréal, which had operations in 130 countries in the world, posted a turnover of €13.7bn[1] in 2001. The company recorded a 19.6 per cent and 26 per cent growth in profit in 2001 and 2002 (half-yearly results), respectively. Commenting on L'Oréal's performance, Jones said, 'At L'Oréal, we are 50,000 people who share the same desire; because it is not just about business but about a dream we have to realize, perfection.'

Known for its diverse mix of brands (from Europe, America and Asia), such as L'Oréal Paris, Maybelline, Garnier, Soft Sheen Carson, Matrix, Redken, L'Oréal Professionnel, Vichy, La Roche-Posay, Lancôme, Helena Rubinstein, Biotherm, Kiehl's, Shu Uemura, Armani, Cacharel and Ralph Lauren, L'Oréal was the only cosmetics company in the world to own more than one brand franchise and have a presence in all the distribution channels of the industry (see Exhibit 2 for a note on the global cosmetics industry).

Background note

In 1907 Eugene Schueller, a French chemist, developed an innovative hair-colour formula. The uniqueness of this formula, named Aureole, was that it did not damage hair while colouring it, unlike other hair-colour products that used relatively harsh chemicals. Schueller formulated and manufactured his products on his own and sold them to Parisian hairdressers. Two years later, in 1909, Schueller set up a company and named it 'Societé Francaise de Teintures inoffensives pour Cheveux'.

By 1920 the company was employing three in-house chemists and made brisk business selling hair colour in various countries like Holland, Austria and Italy. Schueller used advertising in a major way to market his products. He used promotional posters made by famous graphic artists like Paul Colin, Charles Loupot and Raymond Savignac to promote his company's products.

In 1933 Schueller, created and launched a beauty magazine for women named *Votre Beauté*. In 1937 he started the 'clean children' campaign and created a jingle 'Be nice and clean, smell good' for Dop shampoo, which went on to become one of the most famous jingles in France. In the early 1940s the company's name was changed to L'Oréal, which was an adaptation of one of the brands, 'L'Aureole' (the halo).

During the 1950s the company pioneered the concept of advertising products through film commercials screened at cinemas. The first movie advertisement was for L'Oréal's 'Amber Solaire' (suncare cream) with the tagline, 'Just as it was before the War, Amber Solaire is back.'[2]

In 1973 half of L'Oréal's stock was sold to Gesparal, a France-based manufacturer of personal care products, while the other half was publicly traded. Later, 49 per cent of Gesparal's stock was sold to Nestlé, the Swiss food products giant, while the remaining 51 per cent was held by Bettencourt (the founder's daughter).

In 1972 the company launched the legendary advertisement campaign 'Because I'm worth it' to promote the 'Preference' line of hair colour. The

EXHIBIT 1: L'Oréal – consolidated financial statements (1997–2002) (in €m)

	2002	2001	2000 (2)	1999 (1) (2)	1998 (1)	1998	1997
Results of operations							
Consolidated sales	14,288	13,740	12,671	10,751	9,588	11,498	10,537
Pre-tax profit of fully consolidated companies	1,698	1,502	1,322	1,125	979	1,339	1,183
As a % of consolidated sales	11.9	10.9	10.4	10.5	10.2	11.6	11.2
Corporate tax	580	536	488	429	375	488	422
Net profit before capital gains and losses and minority interests	1,464	1,236	1,033	833	722	807	722
As a % of consolidated sales	10.2	9	8.2	7.7	7.5	7	6.9
Net profit before capital gains and losses and after minority interests	1,456	1,229	1,028	827	719	719	641
Total dividend	433	365	297	230	191	191	165
Balance sheets							
Fixed assets	8,130	8,140	7,605	5,198	5,299	5,590	5,346
Current assets	6,843	6,724	6,256	5,139	4,229	4,937	4,512
Cash and short-term investments	2,216	1,954	1,588	1,080	762	903	825
Shareholders' equity (3)	7,434	7,210	6,179	5,470	5,123	5,428	5,015
Loans and debt	2,646	2,939	3,424	1,914	1,718	1,748	1,767
Per share data (Notes 4 to 7)							
Net profit before capital gains and losses and after minority interests per share (8) (9) (10)	2.15	1.82	1.52	1.22	1.06	1.06	0.95
Net dividend per share (11) (12)	0.64	0.54	0.44	0.34	0.28	0.28	0.24
Tax credit	0.32	0.27	0.22	0.17	0.14	0.14	0.12
Share price as of 31 December (11)	72.55	80.9	91.3	79.65	61.59	61.59	35.9
Weighted average number of shares outstanding	675,990,516	676,062,160	676 062 160	676,062,160	676062160	676,062,160	676,062,160

(1) For purposes of comparability, the figures include:
 – in 1998, the pro forma impact of the change in the consolidation method for Synthélabo, following its merger with Sanofi in May 1999;
 – the impact in 1998 and 1999 of the application of CRC Regulation no 99–02 from 1 January 2000 onwards. This involves the inclusion of all deferred tax liabilities, evaluated using the balance sheet approach and the extended concept, the activation of financial leasing contracts considered to be material, and the reclassification of profit sharing under 'Personal costs'.
(2) The figures for 1999 and 2000 also include the impact on the balance sheet of adopting the preferential method for the recording of employee retirement obligation and related benefits from 1 January 2001 onwards. However, the new method had no material impact on the profit and loss account of the years concerned.
(3) Plus minority interests.
(4) Including investment certificates issued in 1986 and bonus share issues. Public Exchange Offers were made for investment certificates and voting right certificates on the date of the Annual General Meeting on 25 May 1993. The certificates were reconstituted as shares following the Special General Meeting on 29 March 1999 and the Extraordinary General Meeting on 1 June 1999.
(5) Restated to reflect the ten-for-one share split decided at the Extraordinary General Meeting of 14 June 1990.
(6) Figures restated to reflect the one-for-ten bonus share allocation decided by the Board of Directors as of 23 May 1996.

(7) Ten-for-one share split (Annual General Meeting of 30 May 2000).

(8) Net earnings per share are based on the weighted average number of shares outstanding in accordance with the accounting standards.

(9) In order to provide data that are genuinely recurrent, L'Oréal calculates and publishes net earnings per share based on net profit before capital gains and losses and after minority interests, before allowing for the provision for depreciation of treasury shares, capital gains and losses on fixed assets, restructuring costs, and the amortisation of goodwill.

(10) No financial instruments have been issued which could result in the creation of new L'Oréal shares.

(11) The L'Oréal share has been listed in euros on the Paris Bourse since 4 January 1999, where it was listed in 1963. The share capital was fixed at €135,212,432 at the Annual General Meeting of 1 June 1999: the par value of one share is now €0.2.

(12) The dividend fixed in euros since the Annual General Meeting of 30 May 2000.

Source: www.loreal-finance.com.

EXHIBIT 2: A brief note on the global cosmetics industry

The term 'cosmetics industry' usually refers to the 'cosmetics, toiletry and perfumery' industry. Cosmetic products perform six functions: they clean, perfume, protect, change the appearance, correct body odours and keep the body in good condition. Cosmetics, toiletries and perfumes have become an important part of every individual's daily life and they have come to be regarded as equally important as health-related (pharmaceutical) products. On the basis of product usage, the cosmetics industry can be divided into four segments: luxury, consumer or mass-markets, professional and pharmaceuticals. Globally, the European cosmetics industry has maintained its position as the leader (since the 1980s) in the industry. In 2000 the European cosmetics industry generated almost €50bn in sales, which was twice the sales volume of the Japanese cosmetics industry and one-third more than that of the US cosmetics industry. L'Oréal has remained the global leader in the industry with a 16.8 per cent market share, followed by Estee Lauder with a 10.9 per cent market share, and Procter & Gamble with a 9.3 per cent market share.

Established in 1946 in New York, USA, Estée Lauder competed with L'Oréal in the luxury segment with brands like Estée Lauder, Aramis, Clinique, Prescriptives, Origins, M·A·C, Bobbi Brown Essentials, Tommy Hilfiger, Jane, Donna Karan, Aveda, La Mer, Stila, and Jo Malone. Procter & Gamble, the US-based FMCG manufacturer, competed with L'Oréal in the mass-market segment with skincare, haircare and bodycare products. Some of P&G's well-known brands include Biactol, Camay, Cover Girl, Ellen Betrix, Infasil, Max Factor (skincare), Herbal Essences, Loving Care, Natural Instincts, Nice n' Easy, Pantene Pro-V, Rejoice, Vidal Sassoon, Wash & Go (haircare), Laura Biagiotti, Hugo Boss and Helmut Lang (perfumes). The US-based Revlon Inc also competed with L'Oréal in the mass-market segment with brands like Charlie, Colorsilk, Colorstay, Fire&Ice and Skinlights. Other companies like Avon, Kose, Coty and Shiseido competed globally in the mass-market segment. L'Oréal remained the overall industry leader, as it was the only company that competed in all four segments (consumer, luxury, professional and pharmaceutical).

The cosmetics industry has always been characterised by extensive research and innovation by companies to introduce newer and better products. Since the 1990s the industry has witnessed many changes in terms of the manufacture of cosmetics owing to growing awareness among consumers about the harmful effects that harsh chemicals (generally used in cosmetics) may cause to their body (skin and hair). This was one of the reasons for the manufacture of products with natural or herbal ingredients by companies like L'Oréal and P&G. Due to the increased focus on 'wellness', the industry as a whole is now moving towards 'cosmeceuticals' and 'neutraceuticals; that is, products that combine the qualities of nutrients and beauty aids. Industry analysts speculate that the market for these products will rise sharply in the twenty-first century.

Source: compiled from various sources.

---

slogan summed up the company's philosophy of providing the most innovative, high-quality and advanced products at an affordable price. The campaign was considered brilliant by many marketing gurus. The slogan seemed to cleverly differentiate L'Oréal's products from others and proved to be a 'winning' factor.

In the cosmetics business, profit margins tend to be generally low as there is not much differentiation between the products offered by various companies. L'Oréal's decision to differentiate its products by attaching an emotional quality to its brands thus worked very well. The emotional pitch, 'Because I'm worth it', indirectly conveyed the message that 'I'm willing to pay more'. According to a www. republic. org article, it conveyed that, 'I will prove that I value myself by paying more than I have to.' This translated directly into profits for the company.

Over the next few years the company's business expanded considerably. It started distributing its products through agents and consignments to the USA, South America, Russia and the Far East. L'Oréal soon emerged as the only cosmetics brand in the world that had products in all segments of the industry; that is, consumer, luxury, professional and pharmaceutical. Although the company started as a hair-colour manufacturer, over the decades it had branched out into a wide range of beauty products (see Exhibit 3 for product launches up until the mid-1990s and Exhibit 4 for a segment-wise break-up of sales for the year 2002).

On the road to fame

During the late 1980s and early 1990s almost 75 per cent of the company's sales were in Europe, mainly in France. L'Oréal's image was so closely tied to Parisian

sophistication that it was difficult to market its brands internationally. Jones thus decided to take a series of concrete steps to make L'Oréal a globally recognised brand and the leading cosmetics company in the world. In what proved to be a major advantage later on, he decided to acquire brands of different origins.

In the cosmetics industry companies did not acquire diverse brands; they generally homogenised their brands to make them acceptable across different cultures. By choosing to work with brands from different cultures, Jones deliberately took L'Oréal down a different road. Commenting on his decision, Jones said, 'We have made a conscious effort to diversify the cultural origins of our brands.' The rationale for the above decision was to 'make the brands embody their country of origin'. The reason Jones had so much conviction in this philosophy was his own multicultural background (he was born in Wales, studied at Oxford and Paris, married an Italian, and has a French-born daughter). Many analysts were of the opinion that Jones had turned what many marketing gurus had considered a 'narrowing factor' into a 'marketing virtue'.

EXHIBIT 3: L'Oréal – product launches

Year	Product (segment)	Year	Product (segment)
1929	Immedia (Professional)	1977	Eau Jeune (Luxury)
1934	Dop (Consumer)	1978	Anais Anais (Luxury)
1936	Ambre Solaire (Consumer)	1982	Drakker Noire (Luxury)
1940	Oreol (Pharmaceuticals)	1983	Plentitude (Consumer)
1960	Elnett (Consumer)	1985	Studio Line (Professional)
1964	Dercos (Luxury)	1986	Nisome (Luxury)
1966	Maquimat, Recital (Consumer)	1990	Tresor (Luxury)
1967	Mini Vogue (Consumer)	1993	Capitol Soleil (Pharmaceutical)
1972	Elseve (Consumer)		

Source: www.loreal.com.

EXHIBIT 4: L'Oréal – segment-wise sales break-up (2002)

Division	Products	% of sales (2002)
Consumer products	Garnier, Le Club des Createurs de Beauté, L'Oréal Paris, Maybelline, Soft Sheen/Carson	56
Luxury	Biotherm, Cacharel, Giorgio Armani, Guy Laroche, Helena Rubinstein, Kiehl's, Lancome, Paloma Picasso, Ralph Lauren, Shu Uemura	24
Professional	Kerastase Paris, L'Oréal Professionnel, Matrix, Redken	14
Pharmaceuticals	La Roche-Posay, Vichy Laboratories	6

Source: adapted from 'L'Oréal's Global Makeover', www.fortune.com.

Maybe? No, it 'is' Maybelline

One of the first brands that L'Oréal bought in line with the above strategy was the Memphis (US)-based Maybelline.[3] The company acquired Maybelline in 1996 for $758m. Buying Maybelline was a risky decision because the brand was well known for bringing out ordinary, staid colour lipsticks and nail polishes. In 1996 Maybelline had a 3 per cent share in the US nail-enamel market. Maybelline was not a well-known brand outside the USA. In 1995–96, only 7 per cent of its revenue ($350m) came from outside the USA. L'Oréal decided to overcome this problem by giving Maybelline a complete makeover and turning it into a global mass-market brand while retaining its American image.

The first thing that L'Oréal did was to move Maybelline's headquarters to New York, a city known for its fast and sophisticated lifestyles. Commenting on this decision, Jones said, 'Memphis just did not quite fit the sort of profile for finding some of the key people we needed.' Then L'Oréal aggressively promoted the US origins of Maybelline by attaching the tagline 'Urban American Chic' to it. The company also attached 'New York' to the brand name in order to associate Maybelline with 'American street smart'.

This revamp was very successful: Maybelline's market share in the USA increased to 15 per cent in 1997 from just 3 per cent in 1996. In addition, Maybelline's sales rose steeply from just over $320m in 1996 to $600m in 1999. In 1999, buoyed by the success of Maybelline in the USA, L'Oréal acquired the Maybelline brand in Japan from Kose Corporation, the brand's Japanese distributor, thus gaining world rights to Maybelline.

L'Oréal introduced its new line of Maybelline lipsticks and nail polishes in the Japanese market. However, Maybelline's 'Moisture Whip' (a wet-look lipstick) did not do well in Japanese markets as it dried quickly after application. L'Oréal gave the lipstick a makeover by adding more moisturiser to it. The new Japanese version of 'Moisture Whip' was given a new name 'Water Shine Diamonds.' Water Shine Diamonds became a runaway success in Japan. Commenting on the success of the brand, Yoshitsugu Kaketa, L'Oréal's Consumer-Products General Manager (Japan), said, 'It was so successful in Japan that we started to sell Water Shine in Asia and then around the world.'

By the end of 1999 Maybelline was being sold in more than 70 countries around the world. While in 1999 50 per cent of the brand's total revenues came from outside the USA, by 2000 the figure increased to 56 per cent. Maybelline became the leading brand in the medium-priced make-up segment in Western Europe with a 20 per cent market share. Commenting on the company's superior brand management framework, an August 2000 www.industryweek.com article stated, 'L'Oréal achieved sales growth of nearly 20 per cent by developing new products, expanding into key international markets, and investing in new facilities, all the while concentrating on increasing the reach of the group's top 10 brands.'

Cashing in on the Maybelline formula

Maybelline's success proved Jones' philosophy of creating successful cosmetic brands by embracing two different yet prominent beauty cultures (French and American). Commenting on this, Guy Peyrelongue, head of Maybelline, Cosmair Inc,[4] US Division, said, 'It is a cross-fertilization.' L'Oréal followed this strategy for the other brands it acquired over the years, such as Redken (hair care), Ralph Lauren (fragrances), Caron (skin care and cosmetics), Soft Sheen (skin care and cosmetics), Helena Rubenstein (luxury cosmetics) and Kheil (skin care) (see Exhibit 5).

L'Oréal acquired the above relatively unknown brands listed on Exhibit 4, gave them a facelift, and repackaged and marketed them aggressively. The US-based hair-care firms Soft Sheen and Carson were acquired in 1998 and 2000, respectively. Both these brands catered to African-American women. Jones merged these two brands as Soft Sheen/Carson and used them as a launch pad to promote L'Oréal aggressively outside the USA – specifically Africa. As a result, the brand derived over 30 per cent of its $200m revenues in 2002 from outside the USA, most of it from South Africa.

Jones also encouraged competition between the different brands of the company. For instance, L'Oréal acquired Redken, a US-based hair-care brand in 1998, and introduced it in the French market, where it would

EXHIBIT 5: Origins of some L'Oréal brands	
Origin	**Brands**
European	L'Oréal Paris, Garnier, Vichy, La Roche-Posay, Lancome, Giorgio Armani, Cacharel, Biotherm, L'Oréal Professional Paris
US	Kiehl's, Ralph Lauren, Matrix, Redken, Soft Sheen-Carson, Maybelline, Helena Rubinstein
Asian	Shu Uemura

Source: www.loreal-finance.com.

have to compete with L'Oréal's Preference line of hair-care products. Analysts were sceptical of this move as they thought introducing new brands in the same category would cannibalise L'Oréal's own, established brands. However, Jones took a different point of view; he argued that the competition would inspire both the Redken and Preference marketing teams to work harder.

Since self-competition was encouraged at L'Oréal, teams had ample freedom to innovate and develop better products. This kind of competitive spirit from within allowed L'Oréal to beat competition from other players in the market. Commenting on this, Jones said, 'The only way to favor creativity in large corporations is to favor multiple brands in different places which compete with each other.'

To encourage competition and nurture creativity, L'Oréal operated two research centres: one in Paris and the other in New York. These centres helped Jones maintain L'Oréal's image as the 'scientific' beauty company. The company spent around 3 per cent of its revenues on research every year, which was more than the industry average of less than 2 per cent. L'Oréal employed 2,700 researchers from all over the world and had 493 patents registered in its name in 2001, the largest ever for any cosmetics company in one year.

L'Oréal made sure that each of its brands had its own image and took care that the image of one product did not overlap with the image of another product. A cosmetics industry analyst, Marlene Eskin, said, 'That is a big challenge for this company – to add brands, yet keep the differentiation.'

One of L'Oréal's most radical experiments was the makeover and re-launch of the Helena Rubinstein skin-care and cosmetics brand. Originally positioned in the luxury segment, Helena Rubinstein had the image of a product used by middle-aged women. In 1999 L'Oréal relaunched the brand and targeted it at a much younger and trendier audience than the brand's typical luxury customers (middle-aged women). Now, the target users were women aged between 20 and 30 years, living in urban centres like London, Paris, New York and Tokyo. The company also opened a Spa[5] in New York to promote the brand (the first instance of a company attempting to run a retail operation as part of a promotional package).

L'Oréal also made use of 'dramatic' advertisements to promote the brand. In one of its advertisements, the model sported a green lipstick and white eye-shadow. Many analysts even thought that such advertising for a traditional luxury brand was incoherent. However, Jones argued that industry observers who held this opinion had not taken into account how fast the market was changing. He said, 'Is it incoherent for younger people to buy luxury cosmetics? Why? Perhaps it was 10 years ago when luxury was equated to the middle-aged customer. But sorry, the biggest luxury consumers in all of Asia, which is one of the strongest luxury markets in the world, are between 20 and 25. This is why the Guccis and Pradas have taken the luxury-goods market by storm.'

L'Oréal attached a tinge of glamour to its brands to make them more appealing to customers. The company liberally used celebrities from various fields of life, from all parts of the world, for promoting its brands. Some of the well-known personalities featured in L'Oréal's promotional campaigns included Claudia Schiffer, Gong Li, Kate Moss, Jennifer Aniston, Heather Locklear, Vanessa Williams, Milla Jovovich, Diana Hayden, Dayle Haddon, Andie MacDowell, Laeticia Casta, Virginie Ledoyen, Catherine Deneuve, Noémie Lenoir, Jessica Alba, Beyoncé Knowles and Natalie Imbruglia.

L'Oréal's brand management strategists believed that good brand management was all about hitting the right audience with the right product. Commenting on the company's brand portfolio management strategies, Jones said, 'It is a very carefully crafted portfolio. Each brand is positioned on a very precise segment, which overlaps as little as possible with the others.'

Future prospects

L'Oréal's efforts paid off handsomely. The company posted a profit of €1,464m for the financial year 2002, as against €1,236m for the financial year 2001. Its overall sales grew by 10 per cent in 2002, and much of this increase was attributed to impressive growth rates achieved in emerging markets like Asia (of the 21 per cent increase in sales volume, China contributed 61 per cent), Latin America (sales grew by 22 per cent, with sales in Brazil increasing to 50 per cent) and Eastern Europe (sales grew by 30 per cent, with sales in Russia increasing by 61 per cent).

Industry observers noted that L'Oréal was much ahead of its competitors in terms of profitability and growth rate. L'Oréal's rival in the luxury segment, Estée Lauder, had reportedly posted a 22 per cent drop in profits in August 2002. The company had also announced a cost-cutting programme. Even Revlon, L'Oréal's competitor in the mass-market segment, had posted nine consecutive quarterly losses since late 2001.

Not all competitors were in such bad shape though; rival companies like Beiersdorf (a Germany-based company that owns the globally popular brand

Nivea), Avon and Procter & Gamble had been performing quite well. However, industry analysts agreed that no other cosmetics player matched L'Oréal's combination of 'strong brands, global reach, and narrow product focus'.

In March 2003 L'Oréal ventured into new businesses that were closely related to its core activities. One such initiative was Laboratoires Innéov, L'Oréal's joint venture with Nestlé. Through Inneov, L'Oréal entered the market of cosmetic nutritional supplements. Analysts observed that this would mark the beginning of 'neutraceutical'[6] development. A research analyst at Frost and Sullivan (US-based leading provider of strategic market and technical information), commented, 'The Inneov business will draw on both the growing demand for skin products designed to retain youthfulness and the growing market for dietary supplements.'

L'Oréal expected the cosmetics market to grow at 4–5 per cent per annum in the future. Looking at the future with optimism, Jones said, 'No other consumer products group has grown as quickly as we have. The prospects for the next three to four years seem promising to me. L'Oréal has the good fortune of being involved in a business that is a bit less sensitive than others to economic cycles. When the economic climate is bleak, you might put off buying a new car, but you will still buy a tube of lipstick that lets you "take a different sort of trip" for a much smaller price.'

In March 2003 the company entered the prestigious list of the world's 50 most admired companies compiled by leading business magazine, *Fortune*, for the first time. This was yet another indicator of the fact that L'Oréal seemed to be going from strength to strength each year. If the strategists at the helm of affairs continued focusing on enhancing stakeholder value year after year, the future would continue to be rosy for the company that sold millions of women the dream of living a 'beautiful' life.

QUESTIONS

1   Critically comment on L'Oréal's global brand-management strategies. Do you think L'Oréal's strategies were primarily responsible for its impressive financial performance? What other factors have helped the company remain profitable for over two decades?

2   With specific reference to Maybelline, critically comment on Jones' strategy of acquiring relatively unknown brands of different cultural origins, giving them a makeover and marketing them globally. What are the merits and demerits of acquiring an existing brand compared to creating a new brand?

3   L'Oréal maintained a large portfolio of brands and was present in all four segments of the cosmetics market. What positioning strategy did the company follow to ensure that the image of its brands did not overlap? How and why did L'Oréal encourage competition among its brands in a particular segment and at the same time prevent the brands from cannibalising each other?

FURTHER READING

- 'L'Oréal Reinforces its Presence in Eastern Europe', www. loreal.com, 13 October 1997.
- 'L'Oréal Acquires Maybelline in Japan', www.loreal.com, 30 March 1999.
- L'Oréal's Owen-Jones: 'I Strive for Something I Never Totally Achieve', www.businessweek.com, 28 June 1999.
- 'L'Oréal : The Beauty of Global Branding', www.businessweek. com, 28 June 1999.
- Tom Mudd, 'Global Movers and Shakers', www.industryweek. com, 21 August 2000.
- Milton Moskowitz and Robert Levering, '10 Great Companies in Europe: L'Oréal', www.fortune.com, 22 January 2002.

- 'The World-renowned Singer Natalie Imbruglia Joins L'Oréal Paris', www.newswire.com, 27 June 2002.
- 'One Brand at a Time: The Secret of L'Oréal's Global Makeover', www.fortune.com, 12 August 2002.
- Richard Tomlinson, 'L'Oréal's Global Makeover', www.fortune. com, 15 August 2002.
- 'Lindsay Owen-Jones Manager of the Year 2002', www.loreal. com, 20 November 2002.
- Lindsay Owen-Jones: '2003 Off to a Great Start', www.loreal. com, 28 February 2003.
- 'Cosmetic Food – The Next Nutraceuticals?' www.foodnavigator. com, 20 March 2003.
- www.scf-online.com.
- www.republic.org.
- www.maybelline.com.
- www.free-cliffnotes.com.
- www.indiainfoline.com.

NOTES

1   April 2003 exchange rate: $1.08569 = €1.

2   Initially launched in 1936, Amber Solaire was withdrawn from the market during the Second World War as a result of production hitches. It was re-launched in 1957.

3   Maybelline was established in 1915 in the USA by T.L. Williams. After beginning with the hugely successful mascara (a cosmetic to darken the eyelashes), Maybelline expanded its product portfolio to include other cosmetics and built up a sizeable brand equity. Until 1967 it was under the control of the Williams family. It was sold to Plough Inc (later Schering-Plough Corp) in 1971, to Wasserstein Perella & Co. in 1990, and finally to L'Oréal in 1996.

4   L'Oréal's wholly-owned US subsidiary.

5   The word 'spa' (taken from the original famous mineral springs in Spa, Belgium) refers to any place/ resort that has one or more of the following facilities: therapeutic baths, massages, mineral springs, health improvement, beauty treatment, exercise, relaxation and meditation (not an exhaustive list).

6   The term 'neutraceutical' is derived from combining the two words 'nutritional' and 'pharmaceutical' and refers to foods that act as medicines. Neutraceuticals act as a source of specific food that provides essential nutrients to users.

This case was written by V. Sarvani, under the direction of A. Mukund, ICMR Center for Management Research. It was compiled from published sources, and is intended to be used as a basis for class discussion rather than to illustrate either effective or ineffective handling of a management situation.

Glossary

act of God – An extraordinary natural event not reasonably anticipated by either party to a contract, ie earthquakes, floods, etc.

activist groups – People or organisations acting to bring about social, political, economic or environmental change. See *green activist*.

adaptation – Making changes to fit a particular culture/environment/conditions, eg when we produce special/modified products for different markets.

administered pricing Relates to attempts to establish prices for an entire market.

advertising campaign – Designing and implementing particular advertising for a particular product/purpose over a fixed period.

advertising media – Different alternatives available to a company for its advertising (eg TV, magazine).

after-sales service – Services that are available after the product has been sold (eg repairs).

analogy – Reasoning from parallel cases/examples.

anti-trust laws – Laws to prevent businesses from creating unjust monopolies or competing unfairly in the marketplace.

APEC – Asia Pacific cooperation among 21 member states. APEC promotes free trade and economic cooperation between members.

arbitration – Mediation done by a third party in case of a commercial dispute.

ASEAN – The fourth-biggest trade area of the world, comprising 10 Southeast Asian countries.

back translation – When a questionnaire/slogan/theme is translated into another language, then translated back to the original language by another party. Helps to pinpoint misinterpretation and misunderstandings.

balance of payments – System of accounts that records a nation's international financial transactions.

barriers to exporting – Obstacles/hindrances to export.

barter – Direct exchange of goods between two parties in a transaction.

barter house – International trading company that is able to introduce merchandise to outlets and geographic areas previously untapped.

billboards – Large stands that comprise advertising space, usually found on the sides of roads.

blocked currency – Blockage cuts off all importing or all importing above a certain level. Blockage is accomplished by refusing to allow importers to exchange national currency for the seller's currency.

Boston Consulting Group (BCG) – An international strategy and general management consulting firm; it uses specific models to tackle management problems.

boycott – A coordinated refusal to buy or use products or services of a certain company/country.

brand loyalty – When customers always buy the same brand.

branding – Developing and building a reputation for a brand name.

broker – A catch-all term for a variety of middlemen performing low-cost agent services.

business culture – Values and norms followed in business activities.

business services – Services that are sold to other companies (eg advertising).

capital account – A record of direct investment portfolio activities, and short-term capital movements to and from countries.

cartel – A cartel exists when various companies producing similar products work together to control markets for the types of goods they produce.

census data – A record of population and its breakdown.

centrally planned economic model – A model that is characterised by state monopoly of all means of production, lack of consumer orientation and lack of competition.

client followers – Companies that have followed their clients to other countries (ie become international) to service their primary clients while they are abroad.

collaborative relationships – Relationship between companies to cooperate with each other.

collective programming – When groups of people are taught about/indoctrinated with certain values.

committee decision making – Decision making by group or consensus.

Common Commercial Policy (CCP) – System of beliefs whose aim is to liberalise world trade.

common law – Tradition, past practices and legal precedents set by the courts through interpretations of statutes, legal legislation and past rulings.

common market – A free-trade area with a common external tariff, international labour mobility and common economic policies among member states.

compadre – Friendship according to Latin American culture.

comparability and equivalence – Information that is comparable and is understood in the same way.

comparative advertising – Advertising that directly compares you with your competitors.

compensation deals – Involve payment in goods and in cash.

competitive strength – Strength of a product/company as compared to competitors.

conciliation – A non-binding agreement between parties to resolve disputes by asking a third party to mediate the differences.

confiscation – Seizing a company's assets without payment.

congruent innovation – The innovativeness is typically one of introducing variety and quality or functional features, style or perhaps an exact duplicate of an already existing product – exact in the sense that the market perceives no newness, such as cane sugar versus beet sugar.

consumer goods – Goods purchased for personal use.

consumption patterns – How consumers buy a particular product.

containerised shipments – When products are packed into containers for transportation.

content labelling – Mention of the contents/ingredients of a product on the package.

continuous innovation – Alteration of a product is almost always involved rather than the creation of a new product. Generally, the alterations result in better use patterns: perceived improvement in the satisfaction derived from its use.

corporate strategy – Strategy of the company as a whole.

countertrade – When products are exchanged with other products instead of cash/money.

country-of-origin effect (COE) – Any influence that the country of manufacture has on a consumer's positive or negative perception of a product.

country-specific brand – A brand that is sold in only one country.

cultural adiaphora – Relates to areas of behaviour or to customs that cultural aliens may wish to conform to or participate in but that are not required.

cultural change – Change in cultural conditions, eg Americanisation.

cultural exclusives – Those customs or behaviour patterns reserved exclusively for the local people and from which the foreigner is excluded.

cultural imperative – Refers to the business customs and expectations that must be met and conformed to if relationships are to be successful.

cultural sensitivity – Being attuned to the nuances of culture so that a new culture can be viewed objectively, evaluated and appreciated.

culture – A set of values and norms followed by a group of people; human-made part of the human environment; the sum total of knowledge, beliefs, art, morals, laws, customs, and any other capabilities and habits acquired by humans as members of society.

current account – A record of all merchandise exports, imports and services plus unilateral transfers of funds.

customer loyalty – When the same customers always buy one company's products.

customised products – Products that are modified for each customer.

customs union – Creation of a common external tariff that applies for non-members, the establishment of a common trade policy and the elimination of rules.

database – A bank/storage of information on a particular issue.

deal-centred – When a sales person is solely concerned with closing the particular transaction.

dealer – Generally speaking, anyone who has a continuing relationship with a supplier in buying and selling goods is considered a dealer.

decentralised decision making – When every level of the organisation can make its own decisions.

decentring – A successive iteration process of translation and retranslation of a questionnaire, each time by a different translator.

demand elasticity – When demand for a product changes due to minor changes in the price.

demographic data – Information on the demographics of a country/city/area.

differential exchange rate – Mechanism requiring the importer to pay varying amounts of domestic currency for foreign exchange which is used to purchase products in different countries.

differentiated products – Products that are considered different from other similar products.

differentiation strategy – The marketer trying to convince the market/customers that his or her product is different to that of competitors.

direct-mail advertising – Advertising that is mailed through the post, directly addressed to you.

direct marketing – Advertisement sent directly to customers.

discontinuous innovation – This involves the establishment of new consumption patterns and the creation of previously unknown products. It introduces an idea or behaviour pattern where there was none before.

disposable income – That proportion of your income that is not already accounted for, for example on mortgages, loans, bills, etc.

distribution network – How the product moves from the producer to the customer.

domestic-made products – Those products sold in the country in which they were made.

domestic market extension concept – When foreign markets are treated as extensions of the domestic market and the domestic marketing mix is offered, as it is, to foreign markets.

domestic middlemen – Middlemen (eg wholesalers) in the home market of the company.

domestication – When host countries take steps to transfer foreign investments within national control and ownership through a series of government decrees.

dumping – When a product is sold for a lesser price than its actual cost.

dynamically continuous innovation – This may mean the creation of a new product or considerable alteration of an existing one, designed to fulfil new needs arising from changes in lifestyles or new expectations brought about by change. It is generally disruptive and therefore resisted because old patterns of behaviour must change if consumers are to accept and perceive the value of the dynamically continuous innovation.

eco-labelling – A label or logo to show that a company is ecologically responsible.

e-commerce – Buying and selling through the Internet or comparable systems.

economic change – Change in economic conditions, eg recession.

economic nationalism – The preservation of national economic autonomy where residents identify their interests with the preservation of the sovereignty of the state in which they reside.

economic needs – Things that are essential, such as minimal food, drink, shelter and clothing.

economic wants – Things that are desired but non-essential, and therefore limitless.

efficiency seeking – Firms want to enter countries/markets where they can achieve efficiency in different ways.

electronic commerce – Buying/selling a product via the Internet.

EPRG schema – A schema that classifies firms by their orientation: ethnocentric, polycentric, regiocentric or geocentric. The degree of commitment to internationalisation is what determines a firm's orientation.

establishment chain model – A stepwise internationalisation into foreign markets.

ethnocentric – Intense identification with the known and familiar within a particular culture, and a tendency to devalue the foreign and unknown of other cultures.

ethnocentrism – When we behave in an ethnocentric way; there is an exaggerated tendency to believe our own values/ norms/culture are superior to those of others.

European Court of Justice – An institution of the EU.

exchange controls – When rate of exchange (eg for money) is controlled or fixed by an authority.

exchange permits – Permission to exchange money.

exchange restrictions – Obstacles to exchanging money.

exchange variation – Variation in the exchange rate of the two currencies involved.

exhibitions – An organised display and presentation of products and services used to promote product range extensions and to launch activities in new markets.

expatriate – An employee of a company/organisation who is sent to another country to work.

export credit guarantee – A government/organisation commitment to give a loan to an exporter.

export management company (EMC) – An important middleman for firms with relatively small international volume or for those unwilling to involve their own personnel in international activities.

export regulations – Rules and regulations for export.

expropriation – Removing companies from the owners and into state ownership.

factual knowledge – Something that is usually obvious but that must be learnt.

focus groups – A group of people who are considered relevant for our product and can provide us with useful information about it.

focus strategy – A company's decision to focus on a particular market segment or part of the product line.

follower brands – Brands that come later to the market.

foreign brokers – Agents who deal largely in commodities and food products, typically part of small brokerage firms operating in one country or in a few countries.

foreign-country middlemen – Middlemen in foreign markets.

foreign-freight forwarder – A company that helps other companies in transportation and export/import matters.

foreign-made products – Those products made in a different country from the one they are being sold in.

foreign-trade zones (FTZs) – Where products are produced mostly for exporting purposes.

frame of reference – structure and concepts, views, customs, etc through which an individual interprets the world. *See self-reference criterion.*

free-trade area – Where products can move freely, without tariffs and restrictions.

generic strategy – The core strategy for the company as a whole.

geography – The study of the earth's surface, climate, continents, countries, peoples, industries and resources.

global brand – The worldwide use of a name, term, sign, symbol, design or combination thereof intended to identify goods or services of one seller and to differentiate them from those of competitors.

global market concept – The idea that the whole world is the market and, wherever cost- and culturally effective, an overall standardised marketing strategy is developed for entire groups of country markets.

global marketing – Using global market concepts in marketing decisions.

global products – Standardised products.

global sourcing – When you buy components and materials from all over the world.

GM foods – Genetically modified foods.

Green activists – Organisations or individuals who actively want to protect the environment.

green dot programme – A sign (logo) that shows a product adheres to *Green marketing* principles.

Green marketing – Marketing decisions that take the environment into consideration.

Green Movement – Political/consumer movement favouring environment-friendly approaches.

group decision-making – When a groups makes a decision together.

guan-xi – Relationship building/friendship in Chinese culture.

hedging – Insuring against a negative event. Companies use hedging techniques to reduce their exposure to exchange risks.

hedonistic – Carefree and pleasurable.

high-context culture – Cultures that demand implicit communication.

high-priority industries – When some industries are given extra benefits by authorities because they are considered important.

historical data – Information over a period of time.

idiomatic interpretation – Interpretations according to the characteristics of a particular language.

import licence – Permission to import.

import regulations – Rules and regulations for import.

import restrictions – When it is not permitted to import.

income elasticity – When higher or lower income would influence demand for a product.

individualism – When everybody is concerned only with their own well-being.

industrial advertisers – Companies that advertise *industrial products*.

industrial products – Products developed for the industrial market, not the consumer market.

innovation – New product/technology/method.

intellectual property – An immaterial asset that can be bought, sold, licensed, exchanged or gradually given away like any other form of property.

intellectual property rights – Laws governing *intellectual property*.

Inter-American Convention – Provides protection similar to that afforded by the *Paris Convention*.

International Monetary Fund (IMF) – Formed to overcome market barriers such as inadequate monetary reserves and unstable currency.

Internet advertising – Advertising on and through websites.

interpretive knowledge – The ability to understand and appreciate fully the nuances of different cultural traits and patterns.

interviews – Talking to people to elicit information on specific matters.

ISO 9000 – Quality assurance certification of the production process.

joint venture – When two companies together open/start a third company.

jurisdiction – Overall legal authority.

just-in-time (JIT) – When deliveries are made at a time when the component being delivered is to be used and not before (often in manufacturing).

Kyoto Agreement – Agreement signed by the EU, Russia and a number of other countries, determining the decrease required in pollution over the coming years.

labelling laws – Laws which indicate what should be mentioned on packaging.

leasing – Borrowing/renting.

letter of credit (LC) – Shifts the buyer's credit risk to the bank issuing the LC.

licensing – To let a local company use a firm's trademark/patent against a fee.

litigation – Taking the other party to court.

local content – Locally made parts.

local nationals – Employees of a company who are local to the market.

local responsiveness – When a company adapts its product and strategies according to local needs and requirements.

low-context culture – Cultures that demand explicit communication.

Madrid Arrangement – There are some 26 member countries in Europe that have agreed to automatic trademark protection for all members.

managing agent – Conducts business within a foreign nation under an exclusive contract arrangement with the parent company.

mañana – Spanish for 'tomorrow'.

mandatory requirements – Requirements that a company must meet.

manufacturer's export agent (MEA) – An individual agent middleman or an agent middleman firm providing a selling service for manufacturers.

manufacturers' representatives – Representative of the producing company in another country.

market barrier – A barrier to trade imposed by the government, against foreign business and imports, in an attempt to promote domestic industry; when market mechanisms work as obstacles to trade.

market-driven economies – Economies/countries that are following the free market economic system.

market planning – A systematic way of producing and selling a product.

market resistance – When customers are reluctant to accept a new product/service.

market seeking – Companies that venture into new countries/become international because they are looking for new markets.

marketing mix – An optimal combination of product, price, place (distribution) and promotion.

marketing research – The systematic gathering, recording and analysis of data to provide information useful in marketing decision making.

Marshall Plan – A plan designed to assist in the rebuilding of Europe after the Second World War.

Marxist-socialist approach – Where a communist or socialist economic system is followed.

merger – When two companies decide to join together.

methodology – Way of doing research.

middleman – Businessman, other than the producer and customer, involved in the exchange of goods.

misleading advertisement – Advertisement that gives incorrect message/impression of a product/company.

monetary barriers – Putting monetary restrictions on trade, eg availability of foreign exchange for imports.

monopsony – The buying-side monopoly.

M-time (monochronic) – Concentrating on one thing at a time. Time is divided up into small units and used in a linear way.

multicultural studies – Studies that are performed in different cultures.

multidomestic market concept – Each country is viewed as being culturally unique and an adapted marketing mix for each country market is developed.

multinational marketing information system (MMIS) – An interacting complex of people, machines and procedures designed to generate an orderly flow of relevant information and to bring all the flows of recorded information into a unified whole for decision making. An MMIS covers multiple countries and operates at each country level.

nationalism – An intense feeling of national pride and unity, an awakening of a nation's people's pride in their country.

newly industrialised countries (NICs) – Developing countries that have grown rapidly in the last few decades and do not fit the traditional pattern of economic development of other LDCs.

ningen kankei – Human relationships.

non-physical features – Characteristics of a product that are not physical but perceptional.

non-profit organisations – Organisations whose purpose is not profit oriented.

non-tariff barriers – Hurdles or restrictions on trade that are other than tariff rates, eg quotas.

organisational culture – Values and norms of working in an organisation.

outsourcing – When you let other companies take over part of your production process.

own brand – Retailers' own brands (eg Tesco tea).

parallel imports – When products are imported into a country without the consent of the brand owner.

parallel translation – When more than two translators are used for a *back translation*, and a comparison of the results is undertaken. (Overcomes problems with back translations.)

Paris Convention – A group of 100 nations that have agreed to recognise the rights of all members in the protection of trademarks, patents and other property rights.

patent – Any product or formula/technology registered with the relevant office that establishes who possesses the right of ownership.

patent rights – Only the owner of these rights is authorised/can use the particular product technology.

pattern advertising – A global advertising strategy with a standardised basic message allowing some degree of modification to meet local situations.

penetration pricing – To charge lower prices to gain some market share in a new market.

personal selling – When a product is sold through personal methods (eg sales people).

physical attributes – Physical characteristics of a product.

piggybacking – When a company does not export directly but uses another company's channels to export its products.

pioneering brands – Brands that were first in the market.

PLC stages – Stages in the *product life cycle*: introduction, growth, maturity and decline.

political climate – Political environment/conditions.

political risk assessment – An attempt to forecast political instability to help management identify and evaluate political events and their potential influence on current and future international business decisions.

positioning – Creating an image of your product and its quality in the customers' minds.

premium offers – Special offers or high-priced offers.

price control – When prices are regulated/fixed by an authority.

price differentials – Difference in price of a product.

price escalation – An increase in price.

price fixing – When competing companies agree to set a certain price for their products.

price freezes – When the price of a product cannot be increased.

primary data – Data that has been collected for the systematic research at hand.

privatisation – When a government company is sold to private investors.

proactive market selection – Actively and systematically selecting a market.

problem definition – Explaining the research problem.

product buy-back – When a company promises to buy back some of the products produced in its subsidiaries.

product life cycle (PLC) – Different stages (*PLC stages*) in a product's life; from introduction to decline.

promotional misfires – Mistakes made in the advertising activities of a company.

promotional strategy – Systematic planning to promote a product.

protectionism – When governments do not allow freedom of activity for foreign companies, to protect their own companies.

psychic distance – When a market is considered distant due to psychological barriers.

P-time (polychromic) – Characterised by the simultaneous occurrence of many things and by 'a great involvement with people'.

public-sector enterprises – Government-owned organisations.

qualitative research – Open-ended and in-depth, seeking unstructured responses. Expresses the respondents' thoughts and feelings.

quantitative research – Structured questioning, producing answers that can easily be converted to numerical data. Provides statistical information.

questionnaire design – Formulating exact questions to be asked, often in survey research.

quotas – Limitations on the quantity of certain goods imported during a specific period.

rate of diffusion – How quickly a product spreads out in a specific area.

reactive market selection – When selecting a market at random or without systematic analysis.

relationship-centred – When the sales person aims to build an ongoing relationship with the customer.

reliability – Whether information/the results of a study are trustworthy.

research design – Overall plan for relating a research problem to practical empirical research.

research hypothesis – A theory that can be proved or rejected via research.

resource seeking – Firms try to enter countries to get access to raw materials or other crucial inputs that can provide cost reduction and lower operational costs.

retailer mark-ups – The profit margin of the retailer.

riba – The unlawful advantage by way of excess of deferment; that is, excessive interest or usury.

sales promotions – Activities to attract consumers and promote products.

sampling – The selection of respondents.

secondary data – Information that somebody else has collected, but can be used for our own purposes.

segmentation – Part of the customer market that is our potential customers/market.

self-reference criterion (SRC) – Considering our own conditions, values and norms.

Shari'ah – Islamic Law.

silent language – Communication without the use of words.

skimming – To charge a high price to maximise profit in the early stages of a product's introduction.

social responsibility – When a company is concerned about the implications of its decisions for society in general.

socialist laws – Cluster around the core concept of economic, political and social policies of the state. Socialist countries are, or were, generally those that formerly had laws derived from the Roman or code-law system.

soga shosha – Japanese trading and investment organisations that also perform a unique and important role as risk-takers.

special drawing rights (SDRs) – Developed by the IMF to overcome universally floating exchange rates.

stakeholders – Parties that have an interest in the company's activities.

standardisation – Producing the same products for many markets.

state-owned enterprises (SOEs) – Companies owned by the government.

Statistical Yearbook – An annual publication of the United Nations, which provides comprehensive social and economic data for more than 250 countries around the world.

strategic alliance – When two companies cooperate for a certain purpose.

strategic planning – A systematised way of relating to the future.

surveys – When we collect information using a list of questions.

sustainable competitive advantage (SCA) – Advantages over other competitors that can be enjoyed over a long period of time in the future.

tactical planning – A systematic way of handling the issues and problems of today.

tariff – A tax imposed by a government on goods entering at its borders.

third-country nationals – Expatriates from the business's own country working for a foreign company in a third country.

total quality management (TQM) – A method by which management and employers are involved in the continuous improvement of the production of goods and services.

trade association – Association of companies belonging to the same industry.

trade fair – An exhibition where participants are able to show/sell their products and services to the visitors and general public. Also used to establish and maintain contacts.

trademark – Registered 'mark' or 'logo' for a company or business.

Trade-Related Aspects of Intellectual Property Rights (TRIPs) – The TRIPs agreement establishes substantially higher standards of protection for a full range of intellectual property rights (patents, copyrights, trademarks, trade secrets, industrial designs and semiconductor chip mask works).

Trade-Related Investment Measures (TRIMs) – Established the basic principle that investment restrictions can be major trade barriers and are therefore included, for the first time, under GATT procedures.

trade sanctions – A set of stringent penalties imposed on a country by means of import tariffs or other trade barriers.

trading companies – Such companies accumulate, transport and distribute goods from many countries and companies.

transfer pricing – When a company uses selective prices for internal transactions (eg between two subsidiaries).

Triad trade – The process of trade undertaken between the EU, North America and Canada, Japan and China.

unfamiliar environment – Environment with which a company is not familiar, especially when it is a foreign market.

urban growth – Growth of urban areas or cities.

validity – Whether the measures used are reasonable to measure what they are supposed to measure.

value systems – Values that are followed unconsciously.

VER – An agreement between the importing country and the exporting country for a restriction on the volume of exports.

volatility in demand – Changes in demand.

wholesalers and retailers – So-called middlemen who facilitate the exchange of goods between manufacturer and consumer.

Index